VOTING RIGHTS AND ELECTION LAW

VOTING RIGHTS AND ELECTION LAW

SECOND EDITION

Michael Dimino
Associate Professor of Law
Widener University School of Law

Bradley Smith
Josiah H. Blackmore II/Shirley M. Nault
Designated Professor of Law
Capital University Law School

Michael Solimine
Donald P. Klekamp Professor of Law
University of Cincinnati College of Law

ISBN: 978-1-6328-3384-6 (casebook)
ISBN: 978-1-6328-3385-3 (looseleaf)

Library of Congress Cataloging-in-Publication Data

Names: Dimino, Michael, author. | Smith, Bradley A., author. | Solimine, Michael E., 1956- author.
Title: Voting rights and election law / Michael Dimino, Associate Professor of Law, Widener University School of Law, Bradley Smith, Josiah H. Blackmore II/Shirley M. Nault Designated Professor of Law, Capital University Law School, Michael Solimine, Donald P. Klekamp Professor of Law, University of Cincinnati College of Law.
Description: Second edition. | New Providenc, NJ : LexisNexis, 2015. |
Includes index.
Identifiers: LCCN 2015038818 | ISBN 9781632833846 (hardbound)
Subjects: LCSH: Election law--United States.
Classification: LCC KF4886 .D56 2015 | DDC 342.73/07--dc23 LC record available at http://lccn.loc.gov/2015038818

NOTE TO USERS
To ensure that you are using the latest materials available in this area, please be sure to periodically check the LexisNexis Law School web site for downloadable updates and supplements at www.lexisnexis.com/lawschool.

Editorial Offices
630 Central Ave., New Providence, NJ 07974 (908) 464-6800
201 Mission St., San Francisco, CA 94105-1831 (415) 908-3200
www.lexisnexis.com

MATTHEW◆BENDER

(2015–Pub.3285)

Dedication

To Michael and Steven — with pride, affection, and love
M.R.D.

To Julie, Eleanor, and Emma
B.A.S.

To Pat, Jane, and Jimmy
M.E.S.

Preface

The law of politics is one of the most exciting, consequential, and fun subjects in the law-school curriculum. Disputes about political power involve much more than a single controversy; rather, they set the rules for the resolution of future disputes and go a long way toward determining who will resolve those disputes and how those disputes will be resolved. But courts don't (or aren't supposed to) make up these rules themselves; it is the political process itself that sets its own rules. Evaluating the judicial role in overseeing those rules and the process that creates them is a constant theme throughout this text. We hope the subject fascinates you as it fascinates us.

Readers should be aware of certain conventions we have used in editing cases. Footnotes, citations, and section headings have been deleted without indication. Our deletions of text are marked by asterisks. Footnotes appearing in the cases have retained their original numbers; our footnotes are indicated by letters. Paragraph breaks have occasionally been altered.

There are many persons with whom we have shared portions of this book, and whose suggestions have improved the final product. Among those persons, Heather Gerken and Allison Hayward deserve special mention. We are also indebted to others whose scholarship has created a field of election law, and whose work has enriched our understanding of the subject: Rick Hasen, Sam Issacharoff, Pam Karlan, Dan Lowenstein, Rick Pildes, and Dan Tokaji. In addition, we have benefited from several on-line resources, including Hasen's Election Law Blog and listserv, as well as Election Law @ Moritz and Ballot Access News.

We are thankful for the administrative support of Connie Miller, as well as the research assistance of Lisa Bemboom, Bill Cash, Alexander Czebiniak, Jacob Dean, Keely Espinar, Carol Herdman, Joe Holaska, Cecille Lucero, Clarke Madden, Julie Olivas, Justin Swartz, Jesse Unruh, and Shawn-Ryan White.

Dimino wishes to extend additional thanks to Professors Smith and Solimine. They have been delightful co-authors, and it has been a great pleasure to work with both. Their expertise, good humor, and cooperative attitudes have been essential in the more than two years it has taken to write this book, and I am indebted to them. Without their agreement to become part of this book it never would have been written, and without their insights it would not have been as good as it is.

Please contact us with ideas for improving the book in the next edition.

Michael Dimino
mrdimino@widener.edu
Bradley Smith
bsmith@law.capital.edu
Michael Solimine
michael.solimine@uc.edu

Table of Contents

Table of Contents

Table of Contents

Table of Contents

Chapter 6   **THE ROLES AND RIGHTS OF POLITICAL PARTIES**

Table of Contents

Chapter 7   TERM LIMITS

Chapter 8   POLITICAL SPEECH

Table of Contents

Table of Contents

Table of Contents

Table of Contents

Chapter 1

VOTING QUALIFICATIONS

A. INTRODUCTION

The constitutional law governing the political process involves conflicts among some of the values most important to a free society and an organized system of democratic self-governance. Liberty, speech, equality, and democracy collide when courts are called upon to police the methods by which the citizenry can influence government. Indeed, election law is so interesting and important not just because the questions presented are difficult and the facts are often dramatic, but because the stakes are so high. Rules affecting the distribution of political power favor certain interests at the expense of others,[a] affecting policy many years into the future. Accordingly, "it is as important to regulate in a republic, in what manner, by whom, to whom, and concerning what suffrages are to be given, as it is in a monarchy to know who is the prince, and after what manner he ought to govern." 2 CHARLES DE SECONDAT, BARON DE MONTESQUIEU, THE SPIRIT OF THE LAWS ch. 2, at 9 (Thomas Nugent trans. 1949) (1748); *see also* THE FEDERALIST No. 52, at 354 (James Madison) (Jacob E. Cooke ed. 1961) ("The definition of the right of suffrage is very justly regarded as a fundamental article of republican government.").

The "right to vote" itself does not appear explicitly in the Constitution. Despite the fact that the Constitution establishes a representative democracy for the nation as a whole, and despite the fact that Article IV, § 4 requires Congress to guarantee the states "a Republican Form of Government," the Constitution "does not confer the right of suffrage upon any one." *Minor v. Happersett*, 88 U.S. (21 Wall.) 162, 178 (1875). "Although the Constitution was promulgated in the name of 'We, the people of the United States,' the individual states retained the power to define just who 'the people' were." ALEXANDER KEYSSAR, THE RIGHT TO VOTE: THE CONTESTED HISTORY OF DEMOCRACY IN THE UNITED STATES 24 (2000).

The Constitution leaves questions about the scope of the franchise to states in the first instance,[b] subject to the prerogative of Congress under Article I, § 4 to "make

---

[a] All such decisions have the effect of favoring certain interests, whether or not the decisions are made with that purpose in mind. But in practice, of course, electoral rules are often constructed so as to achieve certain practical consequences — a practice political scientist William Riker labeled "heresthetics." WILLIAM H. RIKER, THE ART OF POLITICAL MANIPULATION ix (1986).

[b] *See* THE FEDERALIST No. 52, at 326 (James Madison) (Clinton Rossiter ed., 1961) ("To have reduced the different qualifications [for voting in elections for members of the House of Representatives] in the different States to one uniform rule would probably have been as dissatisfactory to some of the States as it would have been difficult to the convention. The provision made by the convention appears, therefore, to be the best that lay within their option. It must be satisfactory to every State, because it is conformable to the standard already established, or which may be established, by the State itself. It

or alter such Regulations" concerning the "Times, Places, and Manner of holding Elections for Senators and Representatives," and subject to the further limitation that persons able to vote for the most numerous branch of the state legislature must be able to vote for Senators and Representatives. Article I, § 2, cl. 1 (Representatives); Amendment XVII (Senators).

Since the Constitution's ratification, several amendments have broadened the scope of the franchise, but not by granting an affirmative right to vote. Instead, the Constitution continues to leave such questions to the states, but prohibits states from denying voting rights based on particular criteria: religion (Amendment I); "race, color, or previous condition of servitude" (Amendment XV; *see, e.g., Ex Parte Yarbrough,* 110 U.S. 651 (1884)); sex (Amendment XIX, *overturning Minor v. Happersett, supra*); failure to pay a poll tax (Amendment XXIV (which is applicable according to its terms only in federal elections)); and age for citizens eighteen or older (Amendment XXVI).

All these anti-discrimination provisions, however, fail to establish a right to vote that would bar states from limiting the franchise on the basis of any number of other characteristics, or even eliminating some elections entirely.[c] For example, there is nothing in the constitutional provisions cited above that prohibits the use of literacy tests, poll taxes in state elections, or property qualifications. One would be mistaken, however, to conclude that states are entirely free to enact such measures.

This Chapter will explore the ways in which statutes and court decisions have limited the ability of states to control access to the voting booth. One of the foundational cases establishing a constitutional right to vote[d] was the criminal case of *United States v. Classic,* 313 U.S. 299 (1941). The defendants were Louisiana election commissioners who committed election fraud in counting and certifying the votes in a Democratic primary election to nominate a candidate for Congress. They were indicted for violating two federal statutes that made it a crime to violate others' constitutional rights. Accordingly, it was necessary for the Court to determine whether the Federal Constitution protected the right to a fair count of one's vote in a primary election for the House of Representatives.

---

will be safe to the United States, because, being fixed by the State constitutions, it is not alterable by the State governments, and it cannot be feared that the people of the States will alter this part of their constitutions in such a manner as to abridge the rights secured to them by the federal Constitution.").

[c] *See San Antonio Independent School District v. Rodriguez,* 411 U.S. 1, 35 n.78 (1973) ("[T]he right to vote, *per se,* is not a constitutionally protected right * * *."); *Rodriguez v. Popular Democratic Party,* 457 U.S. 1 (1982) (upholding a law giving political parties the power to fill vacancies in the Puerto Rican legislature); *Valenti v. Rockefeller,* 393 U.S. 405 (1969) (*per curiam*), *summarily aff'g,* 292 F. Supp. 851 (W.D.N.Y. 1968) (upholding a law giving the governor power to fill vacancies in the U.S. Senate); *Fortson v. Morris,* 385 U.S. 231 (1966) (upholding a provision of the Georgia Constitution authorizing the state legislature to choose the governor from among the two candidates receiving the greatest number of popular votes if no candidate received a majority). *See generally* Richard H. Pildes, *The Future of Voting Rights Policy: From Anti-Discrimination to the Right to Vote,* 49 How. L.J. 741 (2006); Jamin Raskin, *A Right-to-Vote Amendment for the U.S. Constitution: Confronting America's Structural Democracy Deficit,* 3 ELECTION L.J. 559 (2004); Richard Briffault, *The Contested Right to Vote,* 100 MICH. L. REV. 1506 (2002) (book review).

[d] Or "manufactur[ing it] out of whole cloth." Nathaniel Persily, *Forty Years in the Political Thicket: Judicial Review of the Redistricting Process Since* Reynolds v. Sims, *in* PARTY LINES: COMPETITION, PARTISANSHIP, AND CONGRESSIONAL REDISTRICTING 67, 71 (Thomas E. Mann & Bruce E. Cain eds., 2005).

The Court concluded that it did, despite the fact that the Constitution did not guarantee any individual the right to vote in a general election, let alone in a primary. The Court reasoned that Article I, § 2 was designed "to secure to the people the right to choose representatives * * * by some form of election." 313 U.S. at 318. And because the primary occupied an important position in the electoral mechanism that culminated in the general election, the right to vote in the primary was included within Article I, § 2 as well: "Where the state law has made the primary an integral part of the procedure of choice [of representatives in Congress], or where in fact the primary effectively controls the choice, the right of the elector to have his ballot counted at the primary is likewise included in the right protected by Article I, § 2." 313 U.S. at 318. With *Classic* having tethered voting rights to the Constitution, the stage was set for the Court to reshape American election law by defining those rights.

Understanding court decisions expounding the rights to vote and participate in politics requires a familiarity with basic constitutional doctrine. The remainder of this section is presented as a refresher for students who need to be reminded of some concepts of constitutional law, and as a primer for students who have not yet studied equal protection and fundamental rights in constitutional law.[*]

Challenges to the constitutionality of restrictions on the right to vote may be based on either the Due Process Clauses of the Fifth and Fourteenth Amendments or the Equal Protection Clause of the Fourteenth Amendment. The Due Process Clause of the Fifth Amendment is applicable to the federal government, while the Due Process Clause of the Fourteenth Amendment is applicable to the states. There is only one Equal Protection Clause — applicable by its terms to the states — but the Supreme Court has long interpreted the Fifth Amendment Due Process Clause as binding the federal government to the same principles of equality contained in the Equal Protection Clause. *See Adarand Constructors, Inc. v. Peña*, 515 U.S. 200, 235–37 (1995); *Bolling v. Sharpe*, 347 U.S. 497 (1954).

Actions of private parties — as opposed to actions of government — do not violate the Due Process Clause or the Equal Protection Clause. Indeed, with the important exception of the Thirteenth Amendment, which prohibits slavery by both private individuals and the government, the entire Constitution restricts the power of government only. This "state-action" doctrine means that whether a constitutional violation occurs depends not only on what conduct occurs, but on *who* performs the conduct. For example, acts of violence designed to intimidate voters do not violate the Constitution if committed by private individuals, even though the acts may have the effect of preventing groups of people from exercising their constitutional rights. *See United States v. Cruikshank*, 92 U.S. 542, 554 (1875). Government may not avoid constitutional limits, however, by delegating all its power to seemingly private parties. Individuals who exercise "public functions" will be

---

[*] Students who need a more thorough treatment of these issues should consult one of the excellent secondary sources on constitutional law, including ERWIN CHEMERINSKY, CONSTITUTIONAL LAW: PRINCIPLES AND POLICIES (3d ed. 2006); JOHN E. NOWAK & RONALD D. ROTUNDA, PRINCIPLES OF CONSTITUTIONAL LAW (3d ed. 2007); NORMAN REDLICH, ET AL., UNDERSTANDING CONSTITUTIONAL LAW (3d ed. 2005); LOUIS MICHAEL SEIDMAN, CONSTITUTIONAL LAW: EQUAL PROTECTION OF THE LAWS (2003); and ENID TRUCIOS-HAYNES. MASTERING EQUAL PROTECTION (2010).

deemed to be state actors, even if they appear to be free from governmental control. The Supreme Court has held that conducting elections is one such public function, and has extended this reasoning to apply constitutional restrictions to political parties in nominating candidates. *See, e.g., Ray v. Blair*, 343 U.S. 214, 225–27 (1952); *Smith v. Allwright*, 321 U.S. 649 (1944) [p. 426]. We will consider state action more closely in Chapter 6, § B, when we confront the *"White Primary Cases."*

Most challenges to government action, under either due process or equal protection, proceed under the rational-basis test. Under that test, government action will be upheld unless the challenger proves that the action is not rationally related to a legitimate government interest. The rational-basis test is extraordinarily deferential to government, almost invariably resulting in the challenged law being upheld. It is possible to find some legitimate interest that is advanced by just about any statute, and there is no requirement that the state's actual purpose be to advance that interest, as long as a rational legislator *might* have thought the statute would do so.

Strict scrutiny occupies the opposite side of the spectrum from the rational-basis test. Strict scrutiny requires that the government prove that its regulation is narrowly tailored to advance a compelling interest. Narrow tailoring means that the regulation must accomplish its goal without harming the plaintiff any more than necessary to do so. This test is extraordinarily difficult to satisfy, both because few tasks performed by government are truly "compelling" and because virtually all government regulation achieves its goals imperfectly. Speed limits, for example, unnecessarily slow some safe drivers and fail to catch some drivers who are "unsafe at any speed." But the administrative costs of enforcing more narrowly tailored regulations are often prohibitive and it is often difficult to write narrowly tailored regulations without providing excessive discretion to law enforcement.

Historically, review under strict scrutiny has been " 'strict' in theory but fatal in fact," meaning that a law evaluated under that test is almost certain to be unconstitutional, while the rational-basis test has operated as a rubber stamp, validating all manner of government restrictions. Gerald Gunther, *The Supreme Court, 1971 Term — Foreword: In Search of Evolving Doctrine on a Changing Court: A Model for a Newer Equal Protection*, 86 HARV. L. REV. 1, 8 (1972). There are, however, a few counter-examples, where the Court has applied strict scrutiny and upheld a law, or struck down a law while applying only rational-basis scrutiny. *See McConnell v. Federal Election Commission*, 540 U.S. 93, 203–09 (2003) [p. 865]; *Burson v. Freeman*, 504 U.S. 191 (1992) [p. 1054] (plurality opinion); *Lawrence v. Texas*, 539 U.S. 558 (2003); *City of Cleburn v. Cleburn Living Center*, 473 U.S. 432 (1985).

Though the Due Process Clauses speak only of providing appropriate procedures before government deprives a person of life, liberty, or property, the Court has read the Clauses to provide *substantive* protection as well, meaning that certain "fundamental" liberties may not be abridged by government regardless of the procedures afforded. Exactly which rights are "fundamental," however, has always been a matter of considerable debate. The Court has reasoned that most rights contained in the first eight Amendments, such as the right to criminal juries, the freedoms of speech and religious exercise, and the freedom from unreasonable searches and seizures, are so important and historically recognized as to be fundamental. Accordingly, the Court has "incorporated" them through the Due Process Clause of the Fourteenth Amendment and applied them to the states, even though those rights were originally guaranteed as against only the federal government. *See Barron v. Mayor and City Council of Baltimore*, 32 U.S. (7 Pet.) 243 (1833). Not all fundamental rights, however, are listed in the Bill of Rights. The Court has also declared certain unenumerated rights to be fundamental, including the right to privacy, the right to direct the upbringing of one's children, and — most relevant here — the right to vote.

Once a right is determined to be fundamental, neither the state nor the federal government may infringe upon that right unless doing so is necessary to accomplish a compelling state interest, *i.e.*, unless the government satisfies strict scrutiny. If a claimed right is not fundamental, states may infringe it unless the law fails the rational-basis test.

Governments infringe rights when they prohibit persons from exercising them, but restrictions short of complete bans may constitute infringements as well. *See generally* ERWIN CHEMERINSKY, CONSTITUTIONAL LAW: PRINCIPLES AND POLICIES 796–97 (3d ed. 2006) (from which the material in this paragraph is drawn); Michael C. Dorf, *Incidental Burdens on Fundamental Rights*, 109 HARV. L. REV. 1175 (1996); Kathleen Sullivan, *Unconstitutional Conditions*, 102 HARV. L. REV. 1413 (1989). Thus, for example, the Supreme Court held that imposing a filing fee on indigent persons wishing to obtain a divorce was an unconstitutional infringement on the fundamental right to marry people other then their current spouses. *Boddie v. Connecticut*, 401 U.S. 371 (1971). Similarly, the right to marry was infringed by a state law prohibiting individuals from obtaining marriage licenses if they were behind in child-support payments. *Zablocki v. Redhail*, 434 U.S. 374 (1978). On the other hand, the Court did not apply strict scrutiny in upholding a law providing that disabled children would lose government benefits when they married. *Califano v. Jobst*, 434 U.S. 47 (1977). The standard applied by the Court to determine if a fundamental right has been infringed is to gauge the "directness and substantiality" of the interference." *Redhail*, 434 U.S. at 387 n.12.

In cases involving alleged infringements on the right to vote, strict scrutiny will obtain where the challenged law places a "severe" restriction on the right. Laws placing lesser burdens are subject to a balancing test that considers the extent of interference with fundamental rights, the state interests served by the laws, and the relationship between the laws and the state interests they serve. Such laws will be upheld if they are "reasonable" and "nondiscriminatory." *Clingman v. Beaver*, 544 U.S. 581, 586–87 (2005) [p. 470]; *Timmons v. Twin Cities Area New Party*, 520 U.S. 351, 358 (1997) [p. 534]; *Burdick v. Takushi*, 504 U.S. 428 (1992) [p. 525]; *Anderson v. Celebrezze*, 460 U.S. 780 (1983) [p. 517].

In contrast to a due-process claim, in which the challenger argues that the government may not interfere with certain of his or her individual rights regardless of the government's actions toward anyone else, an equal-protection claim argues that the statute in question unjustifiably treats the challenger worse than it treats others. For example, a statute that limits the right to vote to people who own land may be challenged under the Equal Protection Clause by a landless would-be voter.

When a law treats different groups of people unequally, the courts must assess whether such different treatment is constitutional; they do so by applying the rational-basis and strict-scrutiny tests discussed above.

Differential treatment on the ground of race or ethnicity triggers strict scrutiny, regardless of whether it is designed to benefit or burden minorities. *See, e.g., Rice v. Cayetano*, 528 U.S. 495 (2000) (invalidating a statute that limited the right to vote for trustees of a state agency that administered benefits programs for Hawaiian descendants to persons with ancestors living in Hawaii in 1778); *City of Richmond v. J.A. Croson Co.*, 488 U.S. 469 (1989) (invalidating a set-aside program designed to assist minorities in the awarding of public contracts). Whenever the law on its face makes a racial classification — providing one rule for a certain race and a different rule for another race — strict scrutiny is triggered and the classification will be sustained only if it is narrowly tailored to a compelling interest.

Laws may discriminate against a "suspect class," however, without expressly classifying people based on their membership in that class. For example, the Supreme Court held that a state statute establishing a literacy test for voting, but which grandfathered all lineal descendants of persons entitled to vote in 1865 or earlier, created a racial classification in violation of the Fifteenth Amendment. *Guinn v. United States*, 238 U.S. 347 (1915). *See also Rice*, 528 U.S. at 514–17 (treating the Hawaii statute's use of ancestry as a proxy for race); *Gomillion v. Lightfoot*, 364 U.S. 339, 341 (1960) [p. 115] (striking down a law re-drawing city boundaries in a manner that would have excluded "all save only four or five of its 400 Negro voters while not removing a single white voter or resident").

But not every law that has the effect of treating racial or ethnic groups differently is "discrimination on the ground of race or ethnicity." Rather, laws having different effects on different racial groups — but which do not make an express distinction between racial or ethnic groups — are subject to strict scrutiny only if they were enacted for the purpose of treating one racial group better than another. *See, e.g., Washington v. Davis*, 426 U.S. 229 (1976); *Jefferson v. Hackney*, 406 U.S. 535 (1972).

Discrimination on the ground of sex triggers intermediate scrutiny, which requires that the law be "substantially tailored to an important government interest." *Craig v. Boren*, 429 U.S. 190, 197 (1976). As with race discrimination, sex discrimination triggers heightened scrutiny when laws explicitly classify on the basis of sex or where a facially neutral classification is adopted for the purpose, and causes the effect, of creating disparate effects between the sexes. *See Personnel Administrator v. Feeney*, 442 U.S. 256 (1979). If a law has both a disparate effect on the sexes and a discriminatory purpose, intermediate scrutiny applies; if either or both is absent, then courts evaluate the constitutionality of the classification by applying the rational-basis test.

Discrimination on the ground of citizenship triggers only rational-basis scrutiny if the discriminatory law is federal, but strict scrutiny if the discrimination is contained in state law. *Compare Nyquist v. Mauclet*, 432 U.S. 1 (1977); *with Mathews v. Diaz*, 426 U.S. 67 (1976). The difference is due to Congress's "broad power over immigration and naturalization." *Mauclet*, 432 U.S. at 7 n.8. *See also* JOHN E. NOWAK & RONALD D. ROTUNDA, PRINCIPLES OF CONSTITUTIONAL LAW § 14.11 at

442 (3d ed. 2007) (citing "[t]he federal interest in international affairs, as well as the federal power over immigration and naturalization").

Discrimination on other grounds, such as education, wealth, disability, and hair color, ordinarily triggers rational-basis scrutiny. Occasionally, however, the Court will strike down distinctions even on grounds such as these, where the unequal treatment is motivated by "irrational prejudice" rather than a "legitimate government interest." *See, e.g., Cleburne Living Center, supra.*

Several post-Civil-War amendments, including the Thirteenth, Fourteenth, Fifteenth, Nineteenth, and Twenty-Sixth, not only prohibit certain governmental actions, but also give Congress the power to "enforce" the Amendments' substantive provisions "by appropriate legislation." The scope of Congress's authority under these "Enforcement Clauses," however, is controversial. Congress can certainly provide mechanisms for investigating and punishing constitutional violations. *See, e.g.,* 42 U.S.C. § 1983 (providing a private right of action against state actors who cause "the deprivation of any rights, privileges, or immunities secured by the Constitution and laws"); 28 U.S.C. § 1343(a)(3) (granting original jurisdiction in the district courts for actions to redress constitutional violations). What is unclear, however, is the extent to which Congress may use the Enforcement Clauses to punish conduct that is not itself a constitutional violation. May Congress, for example, "enforce" the right to vote by prohibiting literacy tests, even though the tests themselves do not violate the Constitution?

In *Katzenbach v. Morgan*, 384 U.S. 641, 650–51 (1966) [p. 22], the Court upheld the Voting Rights Act's literacy-test ban. In doing so, it interpreted the enforcement authority as granting Congress the power to pass legislation that, in the judgment of Congress, furthered the goals of the Amendments. *Cf. McCulloch v. Maryland,* 17 U.S. (4 Wheat.) 316, 421 (1819) (granting Congress similar authority under the Necessary and Proper Clause, Art. 1, § 8, cl. 18). Such an interpretation gave Congress broad discretion to determine for itself what the limits of its authority were, and the Supreme Court cut back on that discretion in *City of Boerne v. Flores,* 521 U.S. 507 (1997). Concerned that *Morgan*'s interpretation could undermine the Constitution's plan for limiting the federal government's powers, *Flores* held that Congress's authority under the Enforcement Clauses extended only to those statutes "congruent" with and "proportional" to the *courts'* understanding of the substantive meaning of the amendments. *Id.* at 534–35.

Voting rights present important questions under both equal protection and due process because, while few rights are as fundamental to a self-governing people as the right to vote, and while we are suspicious of measures to limit the voting power of certain groups, it may be equally fundamental to preserve the ability of states and communities to set standards for those who will determine the future policies of those areas. *See City of Rome v. United States*, 446 U.S. 156, 201 (1980) (Powell, J., dissenting) (noting that the Voting Rights Act imposes costs on "local control of the means of self-government, one of the central values of our polity"). As you read the remainder of this Chapter, as well as the rest of the book, ask yourself whether the court decisions balancing these interests are — or can be — neutral choices of constitutional principle, or whether the Justices are giving effect to their political philosophies.

B. DEFINING THE COMMUNITY AND EXCLUDING OUTSIDERS

1. *The Illiterate*

Beginning with Connecticut in 1855, many states adopted literacy tests as qualifications for voting, some of which remained in effect until outlawed by the Voting Rights Act (first in 1965 in "covered jurisdictions" mainly in the South, and then, in 1970, nationwide). There were three stated justifications for the tests: First, "illiterate men lacked the intelligence or knowledge necessary to be wise or even adequate voters." Second, "English-language literacy was essential for the foreign-born to become properly acquainted with American values and institutions." Third, "tying voting to literacy would encourage assimilation and education, which would benefit American society as well as immigrants themselves." ALEXANDER KEYSSAR, THE RIGHT TO VOTE: THE CONTESTED HISTORY OF DEMOCRACY IN THE UNITED STATES 143 (2000). Unstated, but powerful, was the further justification that literacy tests would reduce the voting power of immigrants and illiterate native-born Americans (who were almost exclusively Southern blacks). The effect was significant: "[A] minimum of several hundred thousand voters — and likely more than a million — were barred by these tests, *outside* of the South." *Id.* at 146 (emphasis added). The following case upheld the North Carolina literacy test against a constitutional challenge.

LASSITER v. NORTHAMPTON COUNTY BOARD OF ELECTIONS
Supreme Court of the United States
360 U.S. 45, 79 S. Ct. 985, 3 L. Ed. 2d 1072 (1959)

MR. JUSTICE DOUGLAS delivered the opinion of the Court [in which MR. CHIEF JUSTICE WARREN, MR. JUSTICE BLACK, MR. JUSTICE FRANKFURTER, MR. JUSTICE CLARK, MR. JUSTICE HARLAN, MR. JUSTICE BRENNAN, MR. JUSTICE WHITTAKER, and MR. JUSTICE STEWART join].

* * * Appellant, a Negro citizen of North Carolina, * * * applied for registration as a voter. Her registration was denied by the registrar because she refused to submit to a literacy test as required by [a] North Carolina statute.[1] * * *

The States have long been held to have broad powers to determine the conditions under which the right of suffrage may be exercised, absent of course the discrimination which the Constitution condemns. Article I, § 2 of the Constitution in its provision for the election of members of the House of Representatives and the Seventeenth Amendment in its provision for the election of Senators provide that officials will be chosen "by the People." Each provision goes on to state that "the Electors in each State shall have the Qualifications requisite for Electors of the most numerous Branch of the State Legislature." So while the right of suffrage is

---

[1] This Act, passed in 1957, provides * * * as follows: "Every person presenting himself for registration shall be able to read and write any section of the Constitution of North Carolina in the English language. * * *" * * *

established and guaranteed by the Constitution it is subject to the imposition of state standards which are not discriminatory and which do not contravene any restriction that Congress, acting pursuant to its constitutional powers, has imposed. While § 2 of the Fourteenth Amendment, which provides for apportionment of Representatives among the States according to their respective numbers counting the whole number of persons in each State (except Indians not taxed), speaks of "the right to vote," the right protected "refers to the right to vote as established by the laws and constitution of the state." *McPherson* v. *Blacker*, 146 U.S. 1, 39 [(1892)] [p. 1124].

We do not suggest that any standards which a State desires to adopt may be required of voters. But there is wide scope for exercise of its jurisdiction. Residence requirements, age, [and] previous criminal record are obvious examples indicating factors which a State may take into consideration in determining the qualifications of voters. The ability to read and write likewise has some relation to standards designed to promote intelligent use of the ballot. Literacy and illiteracy are neutral on race, creed, color, and sex, as reports around the world show. Literacy and intelligence are obviously not synonymous. Illiterate people may be intelligent voters. Yet in our society where newspapers, periodicals, books, and other printed matter canvass and debate campaign issues, a State might conclude that only those who are literate should exercise the franchise.[7] * * * We do not sit in judgment on the wisdom of that policy. We cannot say, however, that it is not an allowable one measured by constitutional standards.

Of course a literacy test, fair on its face, may be employed to perpetuate that discrimination which the Fifteenth Amendment was designed to uproot. No such influence is charged here. * * * The present requirement, applicable to members of all races, is that the prospective voter "be able to read and write any section of the Constitution of North Carolina in the English language." That seems to us to be one fair way of determining whether a person is literate, not a calculated scheme to lay springes for the citizen. Certainly we cannot condemn it on its face as a device unrelated to the desire of North Carolina to raise the standards for people of all races who cast the ballot.

Affirmed.

Notes and Questions

1.   Until they were banned by the Voting Rights Act, literacy tests of various strengths were imposed across states. Some, like those of North Carolina at issue in *Lassiter*, and of New York, reprinted on page 28 n.3, *infra*, were relatively mild. Others, however, required greater language ability and a greater knowledge of civics. Alabama, for example, employed a test that asked applicants to write certain sections of the Constitution dictated to them by registration officials, and in addition required them to answer a group of four questions "without assistance." There were

---

[7] Nineteen States, including North Carolina, have some sort of literacy requirement as a prerequisite to eligibility for voting. * * *

twelve different groupings of four questions each, and the groups would be rotated to make it more difficult to predict the questions that would be asked of any particular applicant. Here are the questions in the rotation, taken from the appendix to *United States v. Parker*, 236 F. Supp. 511, 519–29 (M.D. Ala. 1964):

What city is the capital of the United States?

How many states are there in the United States?

How many senators from each state are in the United States Senate?

The president of the United States is elected for a term of how many years?

What city is the capital of Alabama?

How old must a person be in order to be eligible to vote in Alabama?

What is the lawmaking body of the United States called?

The Constitution of the United States provides that Congress shall make no law respecting an establishment of religion, or prohibiting the free exercise thereof. (True or false)

In what town or city is the court-house located in this county?

How many stars are there in the United States Flag?

What is the lawmaking body of Alabama called?

Those who shall be convicted of any crime punishable by imprisonment in the state penitentiary shall be disqualified from voting in Alabama. (True or false)

What is the chief executive of the United States called?

Name the two major political parties in the United States.

Who coins money, the state or the United States?

If the president dies, who takes his place?

What is the chief executive of Alabama called?

Are post offices operated by the state or federal government?

What is the name of the president of the United States?

To what national lawmaking body does each state send senators and representatives?

What is the name of the governor of Alabama?

Of what political party is the president of the United States a member?

Name one of the United States senators from Alabama.

When residents of a city elect their officials, the voting is called a municipal election. (True or false)

2. It is important to keep in mind that while literacy tests were used as one of several techniques to prevent disfavored groups (mainly blacks in the South and

immigrants in the North) from voting, there was no allegation by Lassiter that North Carolina's literacy test was being applied discriminatorily. Indeed, Lassiter refused to submit to the test at all. As a result, the Court's holding was necessarily limited. It rejected Lassiter's facial challenge to the literacy test, but did not uphold the constitutionality of all literacy tests.

Three types of literacy tests would fail a constitutional challenge despite *Lassiter*. First, a test applied differently to applicants of different races (or other suspect classes) would violate the Equal Protection Clause, just as a neutrally written statute requiring a permit to operate a business would violate the Constitution if minorities' permit applications were uniformly denied. *See Yick Wo v. Hopkins*, 118 U.S. 356 (1886). For example, in *United States v. Louisiana*, 225 F. Supp. 353, 383–84 (E.D. La. 1963), *aff'd* 380 U.S. 145 (1965), the district court pointed to "unmistakable evidence" that white applicants had been given the answers (and one white applicant even signed the answer sheet by mistake), while black applicants received no such assistance.

In *Louisiana*, voting registrars discriminated against blacks both in the choice of constitutional provisions they were to interpret and in the grading of responses:

> [F]requently the choice of difficult sections has made it impossible for many Negro applicants to pass. White applicants were more often given easy sections, many of which could be answered by short, stock phrases such as "freedom of speech," "freedom of religion," "States' rights," and so on. Negro applicants, on the other hand, were given parts of the Louisiana Constitution [that were much harder to interpret]. * * *

> As in the selection process, gross abuses of discretion appear in the evaluation of the interpretations. One rejected Negro applicant stated that the registrar "said what I was saying was right, but it wasn't like she wanted me to say it." * * *

> Registrars were easily satisfied with answers from white voters. In one instance "FRDUM FOOF SPETGH" was an acceptable response to the request to interpret [the portion] of the Louisiana Constitution [protecting the freedom of speech].

> On the other hand, the record shows that Negroes whose application forms and answers indicate that they are highly qualified by literacy standards and have a high degree of intelligence have been turned down although they had given a reasonable interpretation of fairly technical clauses of the constitution.

Id. See also BRIAN K. LANDSBERG, FREE AT LAST TO VOTE: THE ALABAMA ORIGINS OF THE 1965 VOTING RIGHTS ACT 43–44, 121–22 (2007). As Landsberg summarizes some of the discrimination,

> Was a white applicant illiterate? A registrar would fill out the applicant's form. Did the white applicant know no one to serve as a supporting witness? A registrar would find a witness. But for African Americans, registration was a privilege, to be earned only by meeting some undefined and flexible

standard, depending on the registrars' and potential witnesses' exercise of a sort of lesè-majesté.

LANDSBERG, *supra*, at 68.

Second, a literacy test could violate the Constitution if its terms left too much discretion in the officials administering the test. Thus, a test that required an applicant not only to "read and write" a provision of the state constitution, but to "understand and explain" it was held unconstitutional in *Davis v. Schnell*, 81 F. Supp. 872 (S.D. Ala.), *aff'd*, 336 U.S. 933 (1949). *See also United States v. Louisiana*, *supra* (striking down Louisiana's test, which required potential voters to "interpret" part of the Louisiana Constitution and left "unlimited discretion" in the registrars). Are *Davis* and *Louisiana* consistent with the reasoning of *Lassiter*? *See Williams v. Mississippi*, 170 U.S. 213, 225 (1898) ("The[] [provisions of Mississippi law requiring voters to "read" or "understand" a provision of the Constitution] do not on their face discriminate between the races, and it has not been shown that their actual administration was evil; only that evil was possible under them."); *id.* at 222–23. Was the Alabama test reprinted above invalid under *Davis* and *Louisiana*?

Third, even neutrally *applied* literacy tests may have been established for the purpose of disqualifying disproportionate numbers of ethnic or racial minorities. Literacy tests having *both* the purpose and effect of discriminating on the ground of race or ethnicity would be examined under strict scrutiny and invalidated. The South, in particular, saw disproportionate effects from several types of voting restrictions that combined "to disfranchise nearly all blacks and many poor whites." KEYSSAR, *supra*, at 228. The situation was both predictable and intended: "[A]s Senator Theodore Bilbo observed in 1946, in Mississippi 'a man to register must be able to read and explain . . . a Constitution that damn few white men and no niggers at all can explain.' " *Id.* We will again confront the issue of discriminatorily motivated voting restrictions when we examine *Hunter v. Underwood*, 471 U.S. 222 (1985) [p. 57], later in this Chapter.

3.   Even with the qualifications noted above, literacy tests enabled a great deal of discrimination in practice. Should the Court have prevented the potentially discriminatory use of literacy tests by striking down even those literacy tests that were applied without regard to race (or where discrimination was not proven)?

4.   For what reasons other than discriminatory ones would a state adopt a literacy test? In other words, why does the Court say that literacy tests "ha[ve] some relation to standards designed to promote intelligent use of the ballot"? Could a state constitutionally require that voters attain a certain level of education, perhaps the successful completion of high school? Could a state accord different weight to people's votes depending on the levels of education the voters received? *See* John Stuart Mill, *Considerations on Representative Government*, *in* ON LIBERTY AND OTHER ESSAYS 334–37 (John Gray ed., Oxford University Press 1991).

5.   Could a state constitutionally employ a literacy test that would exclude all blind persons (or all persons blind at the time of their attempted registration) from the franchise? Would it make a difference if part of the reason for the literacy test were to limit the political influence of the disabled?

6. Between 1959, when *Lassiter* was decided, and the Court's decisions in *Harper v. Virginia State Board of Elections*, 383 U.S. 663 (1966) [p. 37]; *South Carolina v. Katzenbach*, 383 U.S. 301 (1966) [p. 14]; and *Katzenbach v. Morgan*, 384 U.S. 641 (1966) [p. 22], each of which appears as a principal case in this Chapter, the Court effected a revolution in the role of the federal judiciary in addressing the constitutionality of distributions of political power. *Colegrove v. Green*, 328 U.S. 549 (1946) [p. 109], had applied the political-question doctrine to hold that federal courts lacked jurisdiction to adjudicate constitutional challenges to malapportioned districts. *Baker v. Carr*, 369 U.S. 186 (1962) [p. 119], overruled *Colegrove* and concluded that courts could decide challenges under the Equal Protection Clause, but did not decide that unequally populated districts actually violated that Clause.

That conclusion would come two years later in *Reynolds v. Sims*, 377 U.S. 533 (1964) [p. 173]. *Reynolds* established the "one-person, one-vote" requirement in holding that each house of a state legislature must be elected from districts that are "substantially equal" in population. *See also Lucas v. Forty-Fourth General Assembly of Colorado*, 377 U.S. 713 (1964) (requiring both state house and senate districts to be apportioned by population); *Wesberry v. Sanders*, 376 U.S. 1 (1964) [p. 166] (applying the one-person, one-vote requirement to elections for the United States House of Representatives). The jurisdictional question is considered in depth in Chapter 2, and the one-person, one-vote doctrine is the subject of Chapter 3.

In another important election-law development, 1964 saw the ratification of the Twenty-Fourth Amendment, which prohibits poll taxes in federal elections. Further, the Civil Rights Act of 1964 and the Voting Rights Act of 1965 radically altered the degree of federal intervention in areas that theretofore had been left to the states. We will consider the Voting Rights Act extensively in later Chapters; you will receive an introduction to it in this Chapter with the next two principal cases, which upheld portions of the VRA against constitutional challenge.

Thus, by 1966, the law of elections had significantly changed from the way it was in 1959. Both the Court and Congress had committed themselves to greater involvement in protecting voting rights.[f] Of comparable importance, there had been significant changes in the Court's membership. In 1962, Eisenhower-appointee Charles Whittaker retired because of a mental disability and Roosevelt-appointee Felix Frankfurter retired because of the effect of two strokes. Frankfurter had written the plurality opinion in *Colegrove* and had been a vociferous critic of judicial involvement in the districting process. (Indeed, some, including apparently Frankfurter himself, have attributed the cause of the strokes to *Baker*.) His departure left Justice Harlan as the only Member of the Court who would reliably encourage the Court to exercise judicial restraint in reviewing election cases. President Kennedy

---

[f] In the early part of the twentieth century, the Court was reticent about enforcing voting rights against uncooperative states. In *Giles v. Harris*, 189 U.S. 475 (1903), for example, the Court refused to intervene to correct the allegedly unconstitutional voting registration system of Alabama, which required voters to pass tests but exempted those voters registered before the new requirements went into effect. The Court held that it could not decide the case, in part because it would be powerless to effect the equality to which the plaintiff was entitled: "Unless we are prepared to supervise the voting in that State by officers of the court, it seems to us that all that the plaintiff could get from equity would be an empty form." *Id.* at 488. The plaintiff's only recourse, according to the Court, was with Congress and the state itself. *See id.*

appointed Byron White and Arthur Goldberg to succeed Whittaker and Frankfurter, and when Goldberg resigned his seat to serve as Ambassador to the United Nations, President Johnson appointed Abe Fortas to take his place.

SOUTH CAROLINA v. KATZENBACH
Supreme Court of the United States
383 U.S. 301, 86 S. Ct. 803, 15 L. Ed. 2d 769 (1966)

MR. CHIEF JUSTICE WARREN delivered the opinion of the Court [in which MR. JUSTICE DOUGLAS, MR. JUSTICE CLARK, MR. JUSTICE HARLAN, MR. JUSTICE BRENNAN, MR. JUSTICE STEWART, MR. JUSTICE WHITE, and MR. JUSTICE FORTAS join].

By leave of the Court, South Carolina has filed a bill of complaint, seeking a declaration that selected provisions of the Voting Rights Act of 1965 violate the Federal Constitution, and asking for an injunction against enforcement of these provisions by the Attorney General. * * * We hold that the sections of the Act which are properly before us are an appropriate means for carrying out Congress' constitutional responsibilities and are consonant with all other provisions of the Constitution. * * *

I.

The constitutional propriety of the Voting Rights Act of 1965 must be judged with reference to the historical experience which it reflects. * * * Two points emerge vividly from the voluminous legislative history of the Act contained in the committee hearings and floor debates. First: Congress felt itself confronted by an insidious and pervasive evil which had been perpetuated in certain parts of our country through unremitting and ingenious defiance of the Constitution. Second: Congress concluded that the unsuccessful remedies which it had prescribed in the past would have to be replaced by sterner and more elaborate measures in order to satisfy the clear commands of the Fifteenth Amendment. * * *

The Fifteenth Amendment to the Constitution was ratified in 1870. Promptly thereafter Congress passed the Enforcement Act of 1870, which made it a crime for public officers and private persons to obstruct exercise of the right to vote. * * * As the years passed and fervor for racial equality waned, enforcement of the laws became spotty and ineffective, and most of their provisions were repealed in 1894. The remnants have had little significance in the recently renewed battle against voting discrimination.

Meanwhile, beginning in 1890, the States of Alabama, Georgia, Louisiana, Mississippi, North Carolina, South Carolina, and Virginia enacted tests still in use which were specifically designed to prevent Negroes from voting. Typically, they made the ability to read and write a registration qualification and also required completion of a registration form. These laws were based on the fact that as of 1890 in each of the named States, more than two-thirds of the adult Negroes were illiterate while less than one-quarter of the adult whites were unable to read or write. At the same time, alternate tests were prescribed in all of the named States to assure that white illiterates would not be deprived of the franchise. These included grandfather clauses, property qualifications, "good character" tests, and the requirement that registrants "understand" or "interpret" certain matter. * * *

* * * White applicants for registration have often been excused altogether from the literacy and understanding tests or have been given easy versions, have received extensive help from voting officials, and have been registered despite serious errors in their answers. Negroes, on the other hand, have typically been required to pass difficult versions of all the tests, without any outside assistance and without the slightest error. The good-morals requirement is so vague and subjective that it has constituted an open invitation to abuse at the hands of voting officials. Negroes obliged to obtain vouchers from registered voters have found it virtually impossible to comply in areas where almost no Negroes are on the rolls.

In recent years, Congress has repeatedly tried to cope with the problem by facilitating case-by-case litigation against voting discrimination. * * * [But this] previous legislation has proved ineffective for a number of reasons. Voting suits are unusually onerous to prepare, sometimes requiring as many as 6,000 man-hours spent combing through registration records in preparation for trial. Litigation has been exceedingly slow, in part because of the ample opportunities for delay afforded voting officials and others involved in the proceedings. Even when favorable decisions have finally been obtained, some of the States affected have merely switched to discriminatory devices not covered by the federal decrees or have enacted difficult new tests designed to prolong the existing disparity between white and Negro registration. Alternatively, certain local officials have defied and evaded court orders or have simply closed their registration offices to freeze the voting rolls. * * *

II.

The Voting Rights Act of 1965 reflects Congress' firm intention to rid the country of racial discrimination in voting. The heart of the Act is a complex scheme of stringent remedies aimed at areas where voting discrimination has been most flagrant. Section 4(a)–(d) lays down a formula defining the States and political subdivisions to which these new remedies apply. The first of the remedies, contained in § 4(a), is the suspension of literacy tests and similar voting qualifications for a period of five years from the last occurrence of substantial voting discrimination. Section 5 prescribes a second remedy, the suspension of all new voting regulations pending review by federal authorities to determine whether their use would perpetuate voting discrimination. The third remedy, covered in §§ 6(b), 7, 9, and 13(a), is the assignment of federal examiners on certification by the Attorney General to list qualified applicants who are thereafter entitled to vote in all elections. * * *

Coverage formula.

The remedial sections of the Act assailed by South Carolina automatically apply to any State, or to any separate political subdivision such as a county or parish, for which two findings have been made: (1) the Attorney General has determined that on November 1, 1964, it maintained a "test or device," and (2) the Director of the Census has determined that less than 50% of its voting-age residents were registered on November 1, 1964, or voted in the presidential election of November 1964. These findings are not reviewable in any court and are final upon publication in the Federal Register. § 4(b). As used throughout the Act, the phrase "test or device" means any requirement that a registrant or voter must "(1) demonstrate the ability to read, write, understand, or interpret any matter, (2) demonstrate any educational achievement or his knowledge of any particular subject, (3) possess good moral character, or (4) prove his qualifications by the voucher of registered voters or members of any other class." § 4(c).

Statutory coverage of a State or political subdivision under § 4(b) is terminated if the area obtains a declaratory judgment from the District Court for the District of Columbia, determining that tests and devices have not been used during the preceding five years to abridge the franchise on racial grounds. * * * For the purposes of this section, tests and devices are not deemed to have been used in a forbidden manner if the incidents of discrimination are few in number and have been promptly corrected, if their continuing effects have been abated, and if they are unlikely to recur in the future. § 4(d). * * *

South Carolina was brought within the coverage formula of the Act on August 7, 1965, pursuant to appropriate administrative determinations which have not been challenged in this proceeding. On the same day, coverage was also extended to Alabama, Alaska, Georgia, Louisiana, Mississippi, Virginia, 26 counties in North Carolina, and one county in Arizona. Two more counties in Arizona, one county in Hawaii, and one county in Idaho were added to the list on November 19, 1965. Thus far Alaska, the three Arizona counties, and the single county in Idaho have asked the District Court for the District of Columbia to grant a declaratory judgment terminating statutory coverage.

Suspension of tests.

In a State or political subdivision covered by § 4(b) of the Act, no person may be denied the right to vote in any election because of his failure to comply with a "test or device." § 4(a).

On account of this provision, South Carolina is temporarily barred from enforcing the portion of its voting laws which requires every applicant for registration to show that he: "Can both read and write any section of [the State] Constitution submitted to [him] by the registration officer or can show that he owns, and has paid all taxes collectible during the previous year on, property in this State assessed at three hundred dollars or more."

The Attorney General has determined that the property qualification is inseparable from the literacy test, and South Carolina makes no objection to this finding. Similar tests and devices have been temporarily suspended in the other sections of the country listed above.

Review of new rules.

In a State or political subdivision covered by § 4(b) of the Act, no person may be denied the right to vote in any election because of his failure to comply with a voting qualification or procedure different from those in force on November 1, 1964. This suspension of new rules is terminated, however, under either of the following circumstances: (1) if the area has submitted the rules to the Attorney General, and he has not interposed an objection within 60 days, or (2) if the area has obtained a declaratory judgment from the District Court for the District of Columbia, determining that the rules will not abridge the franchise on racial grounds. * * * § 5.

South Carolina altered its voting laws in 1965 to extend the closing hour at polling places from 6 p.m. to 7 p.m. The State has not sought judicial review of this change in the District Court for the District of Columbia, nor has it submitted the new rule to the Attorney General for this scrutiny, although at our hearing the Attorney General announced that he does not challenge the amendment. * * *

Federal examiners.

In any political subdivision covered by § 4(b) of the Act, the Civil Service Commission shall appoint voting examiners whenever the Attorney General certifies either of the following facts: (1) that he has received meritorious written complaints from at least 20 residents alleging that they have been disenfranchised under color of law because of their race, or (2) that the appointment of examiners is otherwise necessary to effectuate the guarantees of the Fifteenth Amendment. In making the latter determination, the Attorney General must consider, among other factors, whether the registration ratio of non-whites to whites seems reasonably attributable to racial discrimination, or whether there is substantial evidence of good-faith efforts to comply with the Fifteenth Amendment. § 6(b). These certifications are not reviewable in any court and are effective upon publication in the Federal Register. § 4(b).

The examiners who have been appointed are to test the voting qualifications of applicants * * *. §§ 7(a) and 9(b). Any person who meets the voting requirements of state law, insofar as these have not been suspended by the Act, must promptly be placed on a list of eligible voters. * * *

III.

These provisions of the Voting Rights Act of 1965 are challenged on the fundamental ground that they exceed the powers of Congress and encroach on an area reserved to the States by the Constitution. * * * The ground rules for resolving this question are clear. * * * As against the reserved powers of the States, Congress may use any rational means to effectuate the constitutional prohibition of racial discrimination in voting. We turn now to a more detailed description of the standards which govern our review of the Act.

Section 1 of the Fifteenth Amendment declares that "[t]he right of citizens of the United States to vote shall not be denied or abridged by the United States or by any State on account of race, color, or previous condition of servitude." * * *

South Carolina contends that [although the Amendment gives the *courts* authority to strike down statutes and procedures,] to allow an exercise of this authority by Congress would be to rob the courts of their rightful constitutional role. On the contrary, § 2 of the Fifteenth Amendment expressly declares that "Congress shall have power to enforce this article by appropriate legislation." By adding this authorization, the Framers indicated that Congress was to be chiefly responsible for implementing the rights created in § 1. "It is the power of Congress which has been enlarged. Congress is authorized to *enforce* the prohibitions by appropriate legislation. Some legislation is contemplated to make the [Civil War] amendments fully effective." *Ex parte Virginia*, 100 U.S. 339, 345 [(1880)]. Accordingly, in addition to the courts, Congress has full remedial powers to effectuate the constitutional prohibition against racial discrimination in voting. * * *

The basic test to be applied in a case involving § 2 of the Fifteenth Amendment is the same as in all cases concerning the express powers of Congress with relation to the reserved powers of the States. Chief Justice Marshall laid down the classic formulation, 50 years before the Fifteenth Amendment was ratified: "Let the end be legitimate, let it be within the scope of the constitution, and all means which are appropriate, which are plainly adapted to that end, which are not prohibited, but consist with the letter and spirit of the constitution, are constitutional." *McCulloch v. Maryland*, [17 U.S.] 4 Wheat. 316, 421 [(1819)].

The Court has subsequently echoed his language in describing each of the Civil War Amendments: "Whatever legislation is appropriate, that is, adapted to carry out the objects the amendments have in view, whatever tends to enforce submission to the prohibitions they contain, and to secure to all persons the enjoyment of perfect equality of civil rights and the equal protection of the laws against State denial or invasion, if not prohibited, is brought within the domain of congressional power." *Ex parte Virginia*, 100 U.S., at 345–346. [*Ex parte Virginia* upheld an act of Congress that made it a crime to disqualify jurors "on account of race, color, or previous condition of servitude." — Eds.] * * *

We therefore reject South Carolina's argument that Congress may appropriately do no more than to forbid violations of the Fifteenth Amendment in general terms — that the task of fashioning specific remedies or of applying them to particular localities must necessarily be left entirely to the courts. Congress is not circumscribed by any such artificial rules under § 2 of the Fifteenth Amendment. * * *

IV.

Congress exercised its authority under the Fifteenth Amendment in an inventive manner when it enacted the Voting Rights Act of 1965. First: The measure prescribes remedies for voting discrimination which go into effect without any need for prior adjudication. This was clearly a legitimate response to the problem, for which there is ample precedent under other constitutional provisions [citing Commerce Clause cases]. Congress had found that case-by-case litigation was inadequate to combat widespread and persistent discrimination in voting, because of the inordinate amount of time and energy required to overcome the obstructionist tactics invariably encountered in these lawsuits. After enduring nearly a century of systematic resistance to the Fifteenth Amendment, Congress might well decide to shift the advantage of time and inertia from the perpetrators of the evil to its victims. The question remains, of course, whether the specific remedies prescribed in the Act were an appropriate means of combatting the evil, and to this question we shall presently address ourselves.

Second: The Act intentionally confines these remedies to a small number of States and political subdivisions which in most instances were familiar to Congress by name. This, too, was a permissible method of dealing with the problem. Congress had learned that substantial voting discrimination presently occurs in certain sections of the country, and it knew no way of accurately forecasting whether the evil might spread elsewhere in the future. In acceptable legislative fashion, Congress chose to limit its attention to the geographic areas where immediate action seemed necessary. * * *

Coverage formula.

We now consider the related question of whether the specific States and political subdivisions within § 4(b) of the Act were an appropriate target for the new remedies. South Carolina contends that the coverage formula is awkwardly designed in a number of respects and that it disregards various local conditions which have nothing to do with racial discrimination. These arguments, however, are largely beside the point. Congress began work with reliable evidence of actual voting discrimination in a great majority of the States and political subdivisions affected by the new remedies of the Act. The formula eventually evolved to describe these areas was relevant to the problem of voting discrimination, and Congress was therefore entitled to infer a significant danger of the evil in the few remaining States and political subdivisions covered by § 4(b) of the Act. No more was required to justify the application to these areas of Congress' express powers under the Fifteenth Amendment. * * *

* * * Tests and devices are relevant to voting discrimination because of their long history as a tool for perpetrating the evil; a low voting rate is pertinent for the obvious reason that widespread disenfranchisement must inevitably affect the number of actual voters. Accordingly, the coverage formula is rational in both practice and theory. It was therefore permissible to impose the new remedies on the few remaining States and political subdivisions covered by the formula, at least in the absence of proof that they have been free of substantial voting discrimination in recent years. * * *

It is irrelevant that the coverage formula excludes certain localities which do not employ voting tests and devices but for which there is evidence of voting discrimination by other means. Congress had learned that widespread and persistent discrimination in voting during recent years has typically entailed the misuse of tests and devices, and this was the evil for which the new remedies were specifically designed. At the same time, * * * Congress strengthened existing remedies for voting discrimination in other areas of the country. Legislation need not deal with all phases of a problem in the same way, so long as the distinctions drawn have some basis in practical experience. See *Williamson* v. *Lee Optical Co.*, 348 U.S. 483, 488–489 [(1955)]; *Railway Express Agency* v. *New York*, 336 U.S. 106 [(1949)]. There are no States or political subdivisions exempted from coverage under § 4(b) in which the record reveals recent racial discrimination involving tests and devices. This fact confirms the rationality of the formula. * * *

Suspension of tests.

We now arrive at consideration of the specific remedies prescribed by the Act for areas included within the coverage formula. South Carolina assails the temporary suspension of existing voting qualifications, reciting the rule laid down by *Lassiter* v. *Northampton County Bd. of Elections*, 360 U.S. 45 [(1959)] [p. 8], that literacy tests and related devices are not in themselves contrary to the Fifteenth Amendment. In that very case, however, the Court went on to say, "Of course a literacy test, fair on its face, may be employed to perpetuate that discrimination which the Fifteenth Amendment was designed to uproot." *Id.*, at 53. The record shows that in most of the States covered by the Act, including South Carolina, various tests and devices have been instituted with the purpose of disenfranchising Negroes, have been framed in such a way as to facilitate this aim, and have been administered in a discriminatory fashion for many years. Under these circumstances, the Fifteenth Amendment has clearly been violated. See *Louisiana* v. *United States*, 380 U.S. 145 [(1965)]; *Alabama* v. *United States*, 371 U.S. 37 [(1962)]; *Schnell* v. *Davis*, 336 U.S. 933 [(1949)].

The Act suspends literacy tests and similar devices for a period of five years from the last occurrence of substantial voting discrimination. This was a legitimate response to the problem, for which there is ample precedent in Fifteenth Amendment cases. Underlying the response was the feeling that States and political subdivisions which had been allowing white illiterates to vote for years could not sincerely complain about "dilution" of their electorates through the registration of Negro illiterates. Congress knew that continuance of the tests and devices in use at the present time, no matter how fairly administered in the future, would freeze the effect of past discrimination in favor of unqualified white registrants. Congress permissibly rejected the alternative of requiring a complete re-registration of all voters, believing that this would be too harsh on many whites who had enjoyed the franchise for their entire adult lives.

Review of new rules.

The Act suspends new voting regulations pending scrutiny by federal authorities to determine whether their use would violate the Fifteenth Amendment. This may have been an uncommon exercise of congressional power, as South Carolina contends, but the Court has recognized that exceptional conditions can justify legislative measures not otherwise appropriate. Congress knew that some of the States covered by § 4(b) of the Act had resorted to the extraordinary stratagem of contriving new rules of various kinds for the sole purpose of perpetuating voting discrimination in the face of adverse federal court decrees. Congress had reason to suppose that these States might try similar maneuvers in the future in order to evade the remedies for voting discrimination contained in the Act itself. Under the compulsion of these unique circumstances, Congress responded in a permissibly decisive manner. * * *

Federal examiners.

The Act authorizes the appointment of federal examiners to list qualified applicants who are thereafter entitled to vote, subject to an expeditious challenge procedure. This was clearly an appropriate response to the problem, closely related to remedies authorized in prior cases. In many of the political subdivisions covered by § 4(b) of the Act, voting officials have persistently employed a variety of procedural tactics to deny Negroes the franchise, often in direct defiance or evasion of federal court decrees. Congress realized that merely to suspend voting rules which have been misused or are subject to misuse might leave this localized evil undisturbed. * * *

After enduring nearly a century of widespread resistance to the Fifteenth Amendment, Congress has marshalled an array of potent weapons against the evil, with authority in the Attorney General to employ them effectively. * * * We here hold that the portions of the Voting Rights Act properly before us are a valid means for carrying out the commands of the Fifteenth Amendment. * * *

The bill of complaint is

Dismissed.

MR. JUSTICE BLACK, concurring and dissenting.

I agree with substantially all of the Court's opinion sustaining the power of Congress under § 2 of the Fifteenth Amendment to suspend state literacy tests and similar voting qualifications and to authorize the Attorney General to secure the appointment of federal examiners to register qualified voters in various sections of the country. * * * In addition to th[e Amendment's] unequivocal command to the States and the Federal Government that no citizen shall have his right to vote denied or abridged because of race or color, § 2 of the Amendment unmistakably gives Congress specific power to go further and pass appropriate legislation to protect this right to vote against any method of abridgement no matter how subtle. I have no doubt whatever as to the power of Congress under § 2 to enact the provisions of the Voting Rights Act of 1965 dealing with the suspension of state voting tests that have been used as notorious means to deny and abridge voting rights on racial grounds. This same congressional power necessarily exists to authorize appointment of federal examiners. I also agree with the judgment of the Court upholding § 4(b) of the Act which sets out a formula for determining when and where the major remedial sections of the Act take effect. I reach this conclusion, however, for a somewhat different reason than that stated by the Court, which is that "the coverage formula is rational in both practice and theory." I do not base my conclusion on the fact that the formula is rational, for it is enough for me that Congress by creating this formula has merely exercised its hitherto unquestioned and undisputed power to decide when, where, and upon what conditions its laws shall go into effect. * * *

Though, as I have said, I agree with most of the Court's conclusions, I dissent from its holding that every part of § 5 of the Act is constitutional. * * *

* * * Section 5, by providing that some of the States cannot pass state laws or adopt state constitutional amendments without first being compelled to beg federal authorities to approve their policies, so distorts our constitutional structure of government as to render any distinction drawn in the Constitution between state and federal power almost meaningless. One of the most basic premises upon which our structure of government was founded was that the Federal Government was to have certain specific and limited powers and no others, and all other power was to be reserved either "to the States respectively, or to the people." Certainly if all the provisions of our Constitution which limit the power of the Federal Government and reserve other power to the States are to mean anything, they mean at least that the States have power to pass laws and amend their constitutions without first sending their officials hundreds of miles away to beg federal authorities to approve them. Moreover, it seems to me that § 5 which gives federal officials power to veto state laws they do not like is in direct conflict with the clear command of our Constitution that "The United States shall guarantee to every State in this Union a Republican Form of Government." I cannot help but believe that the inevitable effect of any such law which forces any one of the States to entreat federal authorities in far-away places for approval of local laws before they can become effective is to create the impression that the State or States treated in this way are little more than conquered provinces. And if one law concerning voting can make the States plead for this approval by a distant federal court or the United States Attorney General, other laws on different subjects can force the States to seek the advance approval not only of the Attorney General but of the President himself or any other chosen members of his staff. It is inconceivable to me that such a radical degradation of state power was intended in any of the provisions of our Constitution or its Amendments.

KATZENBACH v. MORGAN
Supreme Court of the United States
384 U.S. 641, 86 S. Ct. 1717, 16 L. Ed. 2d 828 (1966)

Mr. Justice Brennan delivered the opinion of the Court [in which Mr. Chief Justice Warren, Mr. Justice Black, Mr. Justice Clark, Mr. Justice White, and Mr. Justice Fortas join, and in which Mr. Justice Douglas joins in part].

These cases concern the constitutionality of § 4(e) of the Voting Rights Act of 1965. That law, in the respects pertinent in these cases, provides that no person who has successfully completed the sixth primary grade in a public school in, or a private school accredited by, the Commonwealth of Puerto Rico in which the language of instruction was other than English shall be denied the right to vote in any election because of his inability to read or write English. * * *[3] * * * We hold that * * * § 4(e) is a proper exercise of the powers granted to Congress by § 5 of the Fourteenth

---

[3] [A]side from the schools in the Commonwealth of Puerto Rico, there are no public or parochial schools in the territorial limits of the United States in which the predominant language of instruction is other than English and which would have generally been attended by persons who are otherwise qualified to vote save for their lack of literacy in English.

Amendment[5] and that by force of the Supremacy Clause, the New York English literacy requirement cannot be enforced to the extent that it is inconsistent with § 4(e). * * *

The Attorney General of the State of New York argues that an exercise of congressional power under § 5 of the Fourteenth Amendment that prohibits the enforcement of a state law can only be sustained if the judicial branch determines that the state law is prohibited by the provisions of the Amendment that Congress sought to enforce. More specifically, he urges that § 4(e) cannot be sustained as appropriate legislation to enforce the Equal Protection Clause unless the judiciary decides — even with the guidance of a congressional judgment — that the application of the English literacy requirement prohibited by § 4(e) is forbidden by the Equal Protection Clause itself. We disagree. Neither the language nor history of § 5 supports such a construction. * * * A construction of § 5 that would require a judicial determination that the enforcement of the state law precluded by Congress violated the Amendment, as a condition of sustaining the congressional enactment, would depreciate both congressional resourcefulness and congressional responsibility for implementing the Amendment. It would confine the legislative power in this context to the insignificant role of abrogating only those state laws that the judicial branch was prepared to adjudge unconstitutional, or of merely informing the judgment of the judiciary by particularizing the "majestic generalities" of § 1 of the Amendment.

Thus our task in this case is not to determine whether the New York English literacy requirement as applied to deny the right to vote to a person who successfully completed the sixth grade in a Puerto Rican school violates the Equal Protection Clause. Accordingly, our decision in *Lassiter* v. *Northampton Election Bd.*, 360 U.S. 45 (1959) [p. 8], sustaining the North Carolina English literacy requirement as not in all circumstances prohibited by the first sections of the Fourteenth and Fifteenth Amendments, is inapposite. *Lassiter* did not present the question before us here: Without regard to whether the judiciary would find that the Equal Protection Clause itself nullifies New York's English literacy requirement as so applied, could Congress prohibit the enforcement of the state law by legislating under § 5 of the Fourteenth Amendment? In answering this question, our task is limited to determining whether such legislation is, as required by § 5, appropriate legislation to enforce the Equal Protection Clause.

By including § 5 the draftsmen sought to grant to Congress, by a specific provision applicable to the Fourteenth Amendment, the same broad powers expressed in the Necessary and Proper Clause.[9] The classic formulation of the

---

[5] "Section 5. The Congress shall have power to enforce, by appropriate legislation, the provisions of this article."

It is therefore unnecessary for us to consider whether § 4(e) could be sustained as an exercise of power under the Territorial Clause, Art. IV, § 3 * * *. Nor need we consider whether § 4(e) could be sustained insofar as it relates to the election of federal officers as an exercise of congressional power under Art. I, § 4; nor whether § 4(e) could be sustained, insofar as it relates to the election of state officers, as an exercise of congressional power to enforce the clause guaranteeing to each State a republican form of government, Art. IV, § 4; Art. I, § 8, cl. 18.

[9] In fact, earlier drafts of the proposed Amendment employed the "necessary and proper"

reach of those powers was established by Chief Justice Marshall in *McCulloch* v. *Maryland*, 17 U.S. (4 Wheat.) 316, 421 (1819): "Let the end be legitimate, let it be within the scope of the constitution, and all means which are appropriate, which are plainly adapted to that end, which are not prohibited, but consist with the letter and spirit of the constitution, are constitutional."

Ex parte Virginia, 100 U.S. (10 Otto) 339, 345–346 (1880), decided 12 years after the adoption of the Fourteenth Amendment, held that congressional power under § 5 had this same broad scope:

> "Whatever legislation is appropriate, that is, adapted to carry out the objects the amendments have in view, whatever tends to enforce submission to the prohibitions they contain, and to secure to all persons the enjoyment of perfect equality of civil rights and the equal protection of the laws against State denial or invasion, if not prohibited, is brought within the domain of congressional power."

Section 2 of the Fifteenth Amendment grants Congress a similar power to enforce by "appropriate legislation" the provisions of that amendment; and we recently held in *South Carolina* v. *Katzenbach*, 383 U.S. 301, 326 (1966) [p. 14], that "[t]he basic test to be applied in a case involving § 2 of the Fifteenth Amendment is the same as in all cases concerning the express powers of Congress with relation to the reserved powers of the States." That test was identified as the one formulated in *McCulloch* v. *Maryland*. Thus the *McCulloch* v. *Maryland* standard is the measure of what constitutes "appropriate legislation" under § 5 of the Fourteenth Amendment. Correctly viewed, § 5 is a positive grant of legislative power authorizing Congress to exercise its discretion in determining whether and what legislation is needed to secure the guarantees of the Fourteenth Amendment.

We therefore proceed to the consideration whether § 4(e) is "appropriate legislation" to enforce the Equal Protection Clause, that is, under the *McCulloch* v. *Maryland* standard, whether § 4(e) may be regarded as an enactment to enforce the Equal Protection Clause, whether it is "plainly adapted to that end" and whether it is not prohibited by but is consistent with "the letter and spirit of the constitution."[10]

There can be no doubt that § 4(e) may be regarded as an enactment to enforce the Equal Protection Clause. Congress explicitly declared that it enacted § 4(e) "to secure the rights under the fourteenth amendment of persons educated in American-flag schools in which the predominant classroom language was other than English." The persons referred to include those who have migrated from the

---

terminology to describe the scope of congressional power under the Amendment. The substitution of the "appropriate legislation" formula was never thought to have the effect of diminishing the scope of this congressional power.

[10] Contrary to the suggestion of the dissent, § 5 does not grant Congress power to exercise discretion in the other direction and to enact "statutes so as in effect to dilute equal protection and due process decisions of this Court." We emphasize that Congress' power under § 5 is limited to adopting measures to enforce the guarantees of the Amendment; § 5 grants Congress no power to restrict, abrogate, or dilute these guarantees. Thus, for example, an enactment authorizing the States to establish racially segregated systems of education would not be — as required by § 5 — a measure "to enforce" the Equal Protection Clause since that clause of its own force prohibits such state laws.

Commonwealth of Puerto Rico to New York and who have been denied the right to vote because of their inability to read and write English, and the Fourteenth Amendment rights referred to include those emanating from the Equal Protection Clause. More specifically, § 4(e) may be viewed as a measure to secure for the Puerto Rican community residing in New York nondiscriminatory treatment by government — both in the imposition of voting qualifications and the provision or administration of governmental services, such as public schools, public housing and law enforcement.

Section 4(e) may be readily seen as "plainly adapted" to furthering these aims of the Equal Protection Clause. The practical effect of § 4(e) is to prohibit New York from denying the right to vote to large segments of its Puerto Rican community. Congress has thus prohibited the State from denying to that community the right that is "preservative of all rights." *Yick Wo v. Hopkins*, 118 U.S. 356, 370 (1886). This enhanced political power will be helpful in gaining nondiscriminatory treatment in public services for the entire Puerto Rican community. Section 4(e) thereby enables the Puerto Rican minority better to obtain "perfect equality of civil rights and the equal protection of the laws." It was well within congressional authority to say that this need of the Puerto Rican minority for the vote warranted federal intrusion upon any state interests served by the English literacy requirement. It was for Congress, as the branch that made this judgment, to assess and weigh the various conflicting considerations — the risk or pervasiveness of the discrimination in governmental services, the effectiveness of eliminating the state restriction on the right to vote as a means of dealing with the evil, the adequacy or availability of alternative remedies, and the nature and significance of the state interests that would be affected by the nullification of the English literacy requirement as applied to residents who have successfully completed the sixth grade in a Puerto Rican school. It is not for us to review the congressional resolution of these factors. It is enough that we be able to perceive a basis upon which the Congress might resolve the conflict as it did. There plainly was such a basis to support § 4(e) in the application in question in this case. Any contrary conclusion would require us to be blind to the realities familiar to the legislators.

The result is no different if we confine our inquiry to the question whether § 4(e) was merely legislation aimed at the elimination of an invidious discrimination in establishing voter qualifications. We are told that New York's English literacy requirement originated in the desire to provide an incentive for non-English speaking immigrants to learn the English language and in order to assure the intelligent exercise of the franchise. Yet Congress might well have questioned, in light of the many exemptions provided,[13] and some evidence suggesting that prejudice played a prominent role in the enactment of the requirement,[14] whether

---

[13] The principal exemption complained of is that for persons who had been eligible to vote before January 1, 1922.

[14] This evidence consists in part of statements made in the Constitutional Convention first considering the English literacy requirement, such as the following made by the sponsor of the measure: "More precious even than the forms of government are the mental qualities of our race. While those stand unimpaired, all is safe. They are exposed to a single danger, and that is that by constantly changing our voting citizenship through the wholesale, but valuable and necessary infusion of Southern and Eastern European races * * *. The danger has begun. * * * We should check it." * * * This evidence was

these were actually the interests being served. Congress might have also questioned whether denial of a right deemed so precious and fundamental in our society was a necessary or appropriate means of encouraging persons to learn English, or of furthering the goal of an intelligent exercise of the franchise. Finally, Congress might well have concluded that as a means of furthering the intelligent exercise of the franchise, an ability to read or understand Spanish is as effective as ability to read English for those to whom Spanish-language newspapers and Spanish-language radio and television programs are available to inform them of election issues and governmental affairs. Since Congress undertook to legislate so as to preclude the enforcement of the state law, and did so in the context of a general appraisal of literacy requirements for voting, to which it brought a specially informed legislative competence, it was Congress' prerogative to weigh these competing considerations. Here again, it is enough that we perceive a basis upon which Congress might predicate a judgment that the application of New York's English literacy requirement to deny the right to vote to a person with a sixth grade education in Puerto Rican schools in which the language of instruction was other than English constituted an invidious discrimination in violation of the Equal Protection Clause.

There remains the question whether the congressional remedies adopted in § 4(e) constitute means which are not prohibited by, but are consistent "with the letter and spirit of the constitution." The only respect in which appellees contend that § 4(e) fails in this regard is that the section itself works an invidious discrimination in violation of the Fifth Amendment by prohibiting the enforcement of the English literacy requirement only for those educated in American-flag schools (schools located within United States jurisdiction) in which the language of instruction was other than English, and not for those educated in schools beyond the territorial limits of the United States in which the language of instruction was also other than English. This is not a complaint that Congress, in enacting § 4(e), has unconstitutionally denied or diluted anyone's right to vote but rather that Congress violated the Constitution by not extending the relief effected in § 4(e) to those educated in non-American-flag schools. We need not pause to determine whether appellees have a sufficient personal interest to have § 4(e) invalidated on this ground, since the argument, in our view, falls on the merits.

* * * In deciding [whether Congress may limit § 4(e)'s protection to persons educated in American-flag schools], the principle that calls for the closest scrutiny of distinctions in laws denying fundamental rights is inapplicable; for the distinction challenged by appellees is presented only as a limitation on a reform measure aimed at eliminating an existing barrier to the exercise of the franchise. Rather, in deciding the constitutional propriety of the limitations in such a reform measure we are guided by the familiar principles that a "statute is not invalid under the Constitution because it might have gone farther than it did," that a legislature need not "strike at all evils at the same time," and that "reform may take one step at a time, addressing itself to the phase of the problem which seems most acute to the legislative mind," *Williamson* v. *Lee Optical Co.*, 348 U.S. 483, 489 (1955).

---

reinforced by an understanding of the cultural milieu at the time of proposal and enactment, spanning a period from 1915 to 1921 — not one of the enlightened eras of our history.

Guided by these principles, we are satisfied that appellees' challenge to this limitation in § 4(e) is without merit. In the context of the case before us, the congressional choice to limit the relief effected in § 4(e) may, for example, reflect Congress' greater familiarity with the quality of instruction in American-flag schools, a recognition of the unique historic relationship between the Congress and the Commonwealth of Puerto Rico, an awareness of the Federal Government's acceptance of the desirability of the use of Spanish as the language of instruction in Commonwealth schools, and the fact that Congress has fostered policies encouraging migration from the Commonwealth to the States. We have no occasion to determine in this case whether such factors would justify a similar distinction embodied in a voting-qualification law that denied the franchise to persons educated in non-American-flag schools. We hold only that the limitation on relief effected in § 4(e) does not constitute a forbidden discrimination since these factors might well have been the basis for the decision of Congress to go "no farther than it did."

We therefore conclude that § 4(e), in the application challenged in this case, is appropriate legislation to enforce the Equal Protection Clause and that the judgment of the District Court must be and hereby is reversed.

Reversed.

MR. JUSTICE DOUGLAS joins the Court's opinion except for the discussion of the question whether the congressional remedies adopted in § 4(e) constitute means which are not prohibited by, but are consistent with "the letter and spirit of the constitution." On that question, he reserves judgment until such time as it is presented by a member of the class against which that particular discrimination is directed.

MR. JUSTICE HARLAN, whom MR. JUSTICE STEWART joins, dissenting.

Worthy as its purposes may be thought by many, I do not see how § 4(e) of the Voting Rights Act of 1965 can be sustained except at the sacrifice of fundamentals in the American constitutional system — the separation between the legislative and judicial function and the boundaries between federal and state political authority. * * *

* * * The Court declares that since § 5 of the Fourteenth Amendment gives to the Congress power to "enforce" the prohibitions of the Amendment by "appropriate" legislation, the test for judicial review of any congressional determination in this area is simply one of rationality; that is, in effect, was Congress acting rationally in declaring that the New York statute is irrational? Although § 5 most certainly does give to the Congress wide powers in the field of devising remedial legislation to effectuate the Amendment's prohibition on arbitrary state action, I believe the Court has confused the issue of how much enforcement power Congress possesses under § 5 with the distinct issue of what questions are appropriate for congressional determination and what questions are essentially judicial in nature.

When recognized state violations of federal constitutional standards have occurred, Congress is of course empowered by § 5 to take appropriate remedial measures to redress and prevent the wrongs. But it is a judicial question whether the condition with which Congress has thus sought to deal is in truth an infringement of the Constitution, something that is the necessary prerequisite to bringing the § 5 power into play at all. * * *

* * * The question here is not whether the statute is appropriate remedial legislation to cure an established violation of a constitutional command, but whether there has in fact been an infringement of that constitutional command, that is, whether a particular state practice or, as here, a statute is so arbitrary or irrational as to offend the command of the Equal Protection Clause of the Fourteenth Amendment. That question is one for the judicial branch ultimately to determine. Were the rule otherwise, Congress would be able to qualify this Court's constitutional decisions under the Fourteenth and Fifteenth Amendments, let alone those under other provisions of the Constitution, by resorting to congressional power under the Necessary and Proper Clause. In view of this Court's holding in *Lassiter* that an English literacy test is a permissible exercise of state supervision over its franchise,[3] I do not think it is open to Congress to limit the effect of that decision as it has undertaken to do by § 4(e). In effect the Court reads § 5 of the Fourteenth Amendment as giving Congress the power to define the substantive scope of the Amendment. If that indeed be the true reach of § 5, then I do not see why Congress should not be able as well to exercise its § 5 "discretion" by enacting statutes so as in effect to dilute equal protection and due process decisions of this Court. In all such cases there is room for reasonable men to differ as to whether or not a denial of equal protection or due process has occurred, and the final decision is one of judgment. Until today this judgment has always been one for the judiciary to resolve.

---

[3] * * * The 1943 test, submitted by the Attorney General of New York as representative, is reproduced below: * * *

Read this and then write the answers to the questions

Read it as many times as you need to

The legislative branch of the National Government is called the Congress of the United States. Congress makes the laws of the Nation. Congress is composed of two houses. The upper house is called the Senate and its members are called Senators. There are 96 Senators in the upper house, two from each State. Each United States Senator is elected for a term of six years. The lower house of Congress is known as the House of Representatives. The number of Representatives from each state is determined by the population of that state. At present there are 435 members of the House of Representatives. Each Representative is elected for a term of two years. Congress meets in the Capital at Washington.

The answers to the following questions are to be taken from the above paragraph

1 How many houses are there in Congress?

2 What does Congress do?

3 What is the lower house of Congress called?

4 How many members are there in the lower house?

5 How long is the term of office of a United States Senator?

6 How many Senators are there from each state?

7 For how long a period are members of the House of Representatives elected?

8 In what city does Congress meet?

[Relocated. — Eds.]

I do not mean to suggest in what has been said that a legislative judgment of the type incorporated in § 4(e) is without any force whatsoever. Decisions on questions of equal protection and due process are based not on abstract logic, but on empirical foundations. To the extent "legislative facts" are relevant to a judicial determination, Congress is well equipped to investigate them, and such determinations are of course entitled to due respect. * * *

But no such factual data provide a legislative record supporting § 4(e) by way of showing that Spanish-speaking citizens are fully as capable of making informed decisions in a New York election as are English-speaking citizens. Nor was there any showing whatever to support the Court's alternative argument that § 4(e) should be viewed as but a remedial measure designed to cure or assure against unconstitutional discrimination of other varieties, *e.g.*, in "public schools, public housing and law enforcement," to which Puerto Rican minorities might be subject in such communities as New York. * * *

Thus, we have here not a matter of giving deference to a congressional estimate, based on its determination of legislative facts, bearing upon the validity *vel non* of a statute, but rather what can at most be called a legislative announcement that Congress believes a state law to entail an unconstitutional deprivation of equal protection. Although this kind of declaration is of course entitled to the most respectful consideration, coming as it does from a concurrent branch and one that is knowledgeable in matters of popular political participation, I do not believe it lessens our responsibility to decide the fundamental issue of whether in fact the state enactment violates federal constitutional rights. * * * At least in the area of primary state concern a state statute that passes constitutional muster under the judicial standard of rationality should not be permitted to be set at naught by a mere contrary congressional pronouncement unsupported by a legislative record justifying that conclusion. * * *

I would affirm * * *.

Notes and Questions

1.   The Court in *Morgan* proclaimed *Lassiter* "inapposite" because the question in *Morgan* was not whether New York's literacy test was constitutional, but instead whether Congress's ban on literacy tests was constitutional. The answer to that question depended on the extent of Congress's power to "enforce" the provisions of the Civil War Amendments. *Lassiter* and *Morgan* can coexist only if Congress has the power under the Enforcement Clauses to prohibit, by statute, at least *some* conduct that does not itself violate the Constitution. *Morgan* did not, however, settle the question of what limits, if any, the Constitution places on the enforcement power.

2.   *Katzenbach v. Morgan* can be read narrowly or broadly. The narrow reading focuses on the Court's discussion of the discrimination against minorities — "both in the imposition of voting qualifications and the provision or administration of governmental services, such as public schools, public housing and law enforcement" — that elimination of the literacy test could rectify. Under this narrow theory of *Morgan*, Congress is permitted to "enforce" the Civil War Amendments by adopting

remedial measures when Congress has made a rational judgment that actual violations of the Amendments are occurring but would be difficult to prove.

By contrast, the broad reading of *Morgan* permits Congress to expand the substance of the Amendment. This reading focuses on *Morgan*'s language providing Congress discretion to take actions " 'plainly adapted' to furthering the[] aims of the Equal Protection Clause," leaving it to Congress to determine whether national legislation is appropriate.

3. The Supreme Court has since rejected the broad theory of *Morgan*. In *City of Boerne v. Flores*, 521 U.S. 507 (1997), the Court explained that while Congress possesses broad discretion to determine the appropriate way to enforce the protections of the Amendments, such "remedial" power does not include the ability to redefine what the Amendments mean:

> * * * The design of the [Fourteenth] Amendment and the text of § 5 are inconsistent with the suggestion that Congress has the power to decree the substance of the Fourteenth Amendment's restrictions on the States. * * * Congress does not enforce a constitutional right by changing what the right is. It has been given the power "to enforce," not the power to determine what constitutes a constitutional violation. Were it not so, what Congress would be enforcing would no longer be, in any meaningful sense, the "provisions of [the Fourteenth Amendment]."

> While the line between measures that remedy or prevent unconstitutional actions and measures that make a substantive change in the governing law is not easy to discern, and Congress must have wide latitude in determining where it lies, the distinction exists and must be observed. There must be a congruence and proportionality between the injury to be prevented or remedied and the means adopted to that end. Lacking such a connection, legislation may become substantive in operation and effect. History and our case law support drawing the distinction, one apparent from the text of the Amendment.

Id. at 519–20. *Flores* interpreted *Morgan* as approving Congress's "reasonable attempt to combat" "unconstitutional discrimination by New York," rather than granting Congress the power to "interpret the Constitution." *Id.* at 528.

4. Recall that in *Morgan* the Court relied in part on an early draft of the Fourteenth Amendment for the proposition that Congress's enforcement power was to be coextensive with its power under the Necessary and Proper Clause to "carr[y] into Execution" the other powers of the national government. *See* footnote 9. *Flores* countered *Morgan*'s view of history, contending that the replacement of the language of the draft with the narrower "enforce" language established that Congress's power was to be more limited:

> In February [1866], Republican Representative John Bingham of Ohio reported the following draft Amendment to the House of Representatives on behalf of the Joint Committee:

> "The Congress shall have power to make all laws which shall be necessary and proper to secure to the citizens of each State all

privileges and immunities of citizens in the several States, and to all persons in the several States equal protection in the rights of life, liberty, and property." Cong. Globe, 39th Cong., 1st Sess., 1034 (1866).

The proposal encountered immediate opposition, which continued through three days of debate. Members of Congress from across the political spectrum criticized the Amendment, and the criticisms had a common theme: The proposed Amendment gave Congress too much legislative power at the expense of the existing constitutional structure. Democrats and conservative Republicans argued that the proposed Amendment would give Congress a power to intrude into traditional areas of state responsibility, a power inconsistent with the federal design central to the Constitution. * * *

As a result of these objections having been expressed from so many different quarters, the House voted to table the proposal until April. The congressional action was seen as marking the defeat of the proposal. * * * The Amendment in its early form was not again considered. Instead, the Joint Committee began drafting a new article of Amendment[.] * * *

Under the revised Amendment, Congress' power was no longer plenary but remedial. * * * The revised Amendment proposal did not raise the concerns expressed earlier regarding broad congressional power to prescribe uniform national laws with respect to life, liberty, and property. [T]he new measure passed both Houses and was ratified in July 1868 as the Fourteenth Amendment.

Flores, 521 U.S. at 520–23.

5.   As a result of *Flores*, the test when considering the constitutionality of an act of Congress ostensibly enacted to enforce the Civil War Amendments is whether the statute is "congruent" with and "proportional" to violations of constitutional rights, *as those rights are interpreted by the judiciary. See* 521 U.S. at 534–35. Thus, the prevailing test is not, as *Morgan* suggested, whether Congress could rationally have found that the statute advances the purpose of the Amendments, nor is the test whether the activity punished by the congressional statute itself violates the Constitution. Rather, after *Flores*, the Court will permit Congress to enact statutes that are somewhat over-inclusive relative to the constitutional violations they are designed to remedy, as long as the statutes are not *too* over-inclusive.

Such over-inclusive statutes are referred to as "prophylactic remedies" because they interpose a statutory prohibition against conduct that approaches (but does not violate) the prohibition established by the Constitution as a way of ensuring that the Constitution itself will not be violated. To give a practical example, a total nationwide ban on literacy tests (at issue in *Oregon v. Mitchell*, which is discussed in Note 6, *infra*) helps ensure that literacy tests will not be used to discriminate against potential voters on racial grounds. After all, if there can be no literacy tests, there certainly can be no discriminatory ones. Nevertheless, the effect of a nationwide ban is to prohibit the use of some literacy tests that could be administered constitutionally under *Lassiter*. Might *Flores*, as well as *Morgan*, give too much power to Congress by enabling the creation of these prophylactic remedies? Consider *Tennessee v. Lane*, 541 U.S. 509, 556, 558–60 (2004) (Scalia, J., dissenting):

> I joined the Court's opinion in *Boerne* with some misgiving. I have generally rejected tests based on such malleable standards as "proportionality," because they have a way of turning into vehicles for the implementation of individual judges' policy preferences. * * * I would replace "congruence and proportionality" with another test — one that provides a clear, enforceable limitation supported by the text of § 5. Section 5 grants Congress the power "to *enforce*, by appropriate legislation," the other provisions of the Fourteenth Amendment. *Morgan* notwithstanding, one does not, within any normal meaning of the term, "enforce" a prohibition by issuing a still broader prohibition directed to the same end. One does not, for example, "enforce" a 55-mile-per-hour speed limit by imposing a 45-mile-per-hour speed limit — even though that is indeed directed to the same end of automotive safety and will undoubtedly result in many fewer violations of the 55-mile-per-hour limit. * * * That is simply not what the power to enforce means — or ever meant. The 1860 edition of Noah Webster's American Dictionary of the English Language, current when the Fourteenth Amendment was adopted, defined "enforce" as: "To put in execution; to cause to take effect; as, to *enforce* the laws." Nothing in § 5 allows Congress to go *beyond* the provisions of the Fourteenth Amendment to proscribe, prevent, or "remedy" conduct that does not *itself* violate any provision of the Fourteenth Amendment. So-called "prophylactic legislation" is reinforcement rather than enforcement.
>
> *Morgan* asserted that this commonsense interpretation "would confine the legislative power . . . to the insignificant role of abrogating only those state laws that the judicial branch was prepared to adjudge unconstitutional, or of merely informing the judgment of the judiciary by particularizing the 'majestic generalities' of § 1 of the Amendment." That is not so. * * * Section 5 authorizes Congress to create a cause of action through which the citizen may vindicate his Fourteenth Amendment rights. * * * Section 5 would also authorize measures that do not restrict the States' substantive scope of action but impose requirements directly related to the *facilitation* of "enforcement" — for example, reporting requirements that would enable violations of the Fourteenth Amendment to be identified. But what § 5 does *not* authorize is so-called "prophylactic" measures, prohibiting primary conduct that is itself not forbidden by the Fourteenth Amendment.

See also The Civil Rights Cases, 109 U.S. 3, 11, 13 (1883) ("[T]he last section of the amendment invests congress with power to enforce it by appropriate legislation. To enforce what? To enforce the prohibition. * * * [Congressional legislation under § 5] should be adapted to the mischief and wrong which the amendment was intended to provide against; and that is, state laws or state action of some kind adverse to the rights of the citizen secured by the amendment.").

6. As originally enacted, the Voting Rights Act of 1965, in § 4(a), temporarily suspended literacy tests in southern states. The literacy-test ban was expanded in

1970 to apply nationwide. In *Oregon v. Mitchell*, 400 U.S. 112 (1970), the Court upheld the nationwide ban despite Arizona's complaint that it had not discriminated on the ground of race and therefore should not be forced to suffer a remedy for such discrimination. As Justices Brennan, White, and Marshall explained,

> Arizona argues that it is and has been providing education of equal quality for all its citizens; that its literacy test is both fair and fairly administered; and that there is no evidence in the legislative record upon which Congress could have relied to reach a contrary conclusion. It urges that to the extent that any citizens of Arizona have been denied the right to vote because of illiteracy resulting from discriminatory government practices, the unlawful discrimination has been by governments other than the State of Arizona or its political subdivisions. Arizona, it suggests, should not have its laws overridden to cure discrimination on the part of governmental bodies elsewhere in the country.

Id. at 233 (Brennan, White, and Marshall, JJ., concurring in the judgment in part and dissenting in part). Every Justice rejected Arizona's argument, though in several different opinions. Justices Brennan, White, and Marshall pointed to the unequal educational opportunities provided to different racial groups,[g] in Arizona and elsewhere, as well as the racially disparate impact of the literacy test. *See id.* at 234–35. Chief Justice Burger and Justices Black, Stewart, and Blackmun noted that discrimination in education affected more states than simply the ones where the discrimination was practiced. Further, race discrimination was a problem faced by the entire country, though in different particulars, and therefore those Justices found no problem with Congress's nationwide ban. *See id.* at 133–34 (opinion of Black, J.); 283–84 (Stewart, J., joined by Burger, C.J., and Blackmun, J., concurring in part and dissenting in part). Justice Douglas thought it sufficient to note that Congress was aware that literacy tests had been used to discriminate against minorities. *See id.* at 147 (Douglas, J., concurring in the judgment in part and dissenting in part). Finally, Justice Harlan thought "the issue [wa]s not free from difficulty," but believed the nationwide ban was constitutional because "Congress could have determined that racial prejudice is prevalent throughout the Nation, and that literacy tests unduly lend themselves to discriminatory application, either conscious or unconscious." *Id.* at 216 (Harlan, J., concurring in part and dissenting in part).

7. Justice Harlan concurred in the Court's opinion in *South Carolina v. Katzenbach*, dissented in *Katzenbach v. Morgan*, and concurred in that part of *Oregon v. Mitchell* that upheld the nationwide literacy-test ban. Can his positions be reconciled?

---

[g] On the importance of disparities in educational opportunities in establishing a basis for banning literacy tests, see *Gaston County, North Carolina v. United States*, 395 U.S. 285 (1969). The Voting Rights Act of 1965 had permitted states to reinstate literacy tests upon proving that they had not used such tests with the purpose or effect of racially discriminating for the preceding five years. The County claimed that its test was neutrally applied, but the Court found that insufficient. The County's literacy test carried a discriminatory effect, according to the Court, because minorities of voting age had been educated in inferior schools, relative to the schools reserved for whites. *See id.* at 291. The result was that the County had made it more difficult for minorities to pass a literacy test, and for that reason the County was not permitted to use one.

8. The literacy-test ban was made permanent in 1975. *See* 52 U.S.C. § 10303(e)(2), 89 Stat. 400 (1975). Can Congress constitutionally ban literacy tests across the country *today*? Is there any point at which the federal literacy-test ban will become unconstitutional? *Cf. Northwest Austin Municipal Utility District No. 1 v. Holder*, 557 U.S. 193, 201–06 (2009) (opining that improvements in voting rights since 1964 rendered Congress's 2006 re-extension of the Voting Rights Act's preclearance requirements problematic, but interpreting the statute to avoid the constitutional question).

De jure school segregation has been outlawed for more than half a century, but many school districts with large concentrations of minorities are poorly funded relative to wealthier, suburban, and largely white districts. Such disparities in funding, per se, do not violate the Constitution. *See San Antonio Independent School District v. Rodriguez*, 411 U.S. 1 (1973). May Congress nevertheless point to the disparity in prohibiting states from enacting literacy tests?

9. In *City of Mobile v. Bolden*, 446 U.S. 55 (1980) [p. 288], a plurality of the Court held that the Fifteenth Amendment itself prohibits only those facially neutral election laws that have both a discriminatory purpose and a disparate effect based on race or some other suspect classification. The VRA, however, requires the Attorney General to deny preclearance whenever the proposed change would have *either* a discriminatory purpose *or* a discriminatory effect. *South Carolina v. Katzenbach* had reasoned that the preclearance requirement was "appropriate" legislation to enforce the Fifteenth Amendment because it placed the burden on the state to prove its compliance with the Constitution rather than on individuals to demonstrate the unconstitutionality of a challenged law. But what if the state proves that it did *not* have a discriminatory purpose? If discriminatory effect alone is enough under the VRA to defeat preclearance, does the VRA "enforce" a constitutional provision that requires both discriminatory purpose and effect? The Supreme Court confronted that issue in *City of Rome v. United States*, 446 U.S. 156 (1980), decided the same day as *Bolden*. In upholding the VRA's preclearance requirement as applied to changes in voting practices that had only a discriminatory effect, the Court reasoned as follows:

> The Court's treatment in *South Carolina* v. *Katzenbach* of the Act's ban on literacy tests demonstrates that, under the Fifteenth Amendment, Congress may prohibit voting practices that have only a discriminatory effect. The Court had earlier held in *Lassiter* v. *Northampton County Board of Elections*, 360 U.S. 45 (1959) [p. 8], that the use of a literacy test that was fair on its face and was not employed in a discriminatory fashion did not violate § 1 of the Fifteenth Amendment. In upholding the Act's *per se* ban on such tests in *South Carolina* v. *Katzenbach*, the Court found no reason to overrule *Lassiter*. Instead, the Court recognized that the prohibition was an appropriate method of enforcing the Fifteenth Amendment because for many years most of the covered jurisdictions had imposed such tests to effect voting discrimination and the continued use of even nondiscriminatory, fairly administered literacy tests would "freeze the effect" of past discrimination by allowing white illiterates to remain on the voting rolls while excluding illiterate Negroes. This holding makes clear that Congress may, under the authority of § 2 of the Fifteenth Amendment,

prohibit state action that, though in itself not violative of § 1, perpetuates the effects of past discrimination. [The Court also discussed *Katzenbach* v. *Morgan* and *Oregon* v. *Mitchell*, concluding that they "recognize Congress' broad power to enforce the Civil War Amendments."] * * *

It is clear, then, that under § 2 of the Fifteenth Amendment Congress may prohibit practices that in and of themselves do not violate § 1 of the Amendment, so long as the prohibitions attacking racial discrimination in voting are "appropriate," as that term is defined in *McCulloch* v. *Maryland* and *Ex parte Virginia*. In the present case, we hold that the Act's ban on electoral changes that are discriminatory in effect is an appropriate method of promoting the purposes of the Fifteenth Amendment, even if it is assumed that § 1 of the Amendment prohibits only intentional discrimination in voting. Congress could rationally have concluded that, because electoral changes by jurisdictions with a demonstrable history of intentional racial discrimination in voting create the risk of purposeful discrimination, it was proper to prohibit changes that have a discriminatory impact. We find no reason, then, to disturb Congress' considered judgment that banning electoral changes that have a discriminatory impact is an effective method of preventing States from " '[undoing] or [defeating] the rights recently won' by Negroes."

446 U.S. at 175–78.

Then-Justice Rehnquist was not persuaded:

Neither reason nor precedent supports the conclusion that here it is "appropriate" for Congress to attempt to prevent purposeful discrimination by prohibiting conduct which a locality proves is *not* purposeful discrimination.

Congress had before it evidence that various governments were enacting electoral changes and annexing territory to prevent the participation of blacks in local government by measures other than outright denial of the franchise. Congress could of course remedy and prevent such purposeful discrimination on the part of local governments. And given the difficulties of proving that an electoral change or annexation has been undertaken for the purpose of discriminating against blacks, Congress could properly conclude that as a remedial matter it was necessary to place the burden of proving lack of discriminatory purpose on the localities. But all of this does not support the conclusion that Congress is acting remedially when it continues the presumption of purposeful discrimination even after the locality has disproved that presumption. Absent other circumstances, it would be a topsy-turvy judicial system which held that electoral changes which have been affirmatively proved to be permissible under the Constitution nonetheless violate the Constitution.

446 U.S. at 214–15 (Rehnquist, J., dissenting). Do you agree with then-Justice Rehnquist that *City of Rome* is incompatible with the remedial theory of Congress's § 5 powers? If so, did *Flores* overrule *City of Rome*?

10. Section 4(e) provided special rights to persons educated in Puerto Rican schools that were not afforded to persons who learned Spanish in foreign countries. Should that favoritism for "American-flag" schools violate equal protection? What is the Court's response? What is the Court's reason for applying rational-basis scrutiny?

11. Section 4(e) forbade states from enforcing English-literacy tests only against "person[s] who ha[d] successfully completed the sixth primary grade." Is it constitutional for Congress to limit the VRA's coverage in that manner? Recall Note 4 following *Lassiter*, which asked whether it would be constitutional for a state to restrict the franchise to persons attaining a certain level of education.

12. The Court decided the constitutionality of the preference for "American-flag" schools despite the fact that no party to the case was discriminated against because of the preference. Such an approach would not be followed today (unless the merits claim is frivolous or "insubstantial"). *See Steel Co. v. Citizens for a Better Environment*, 523 U.S. 83 (1998). Standing is considered a threshold question, and the power of the federal courts to reach the merits comes into being only upon the existence of an actual controversy. *See id.* at 101 ("Hypothetical jurisdiction produces nothing more than a hypothetical judgment — which comes to the same thing as an advisory opinion . . ."). *See also* Scott C. Idleman, *The Demise of Hypothetical Jurisdiction in the Federal Courts*, 52 VAND. L. REV. 235, 280–85 (1999).

13. The plaintiffs-appellees in *Katzenbach v. Morgan* were New York voters who claimed that the Voting Rights Act diluted their votes by permitting persons to vote who were ineligible to vote under New York law. Did the plaintiffs have standing? *Cf. United States v. Hays*, 515 U.S. 737 (1995); *Baker v. Carr*, 369 U.S. 186, 204–08 (1962); *United States v. Saylor*, 322 U.S. 385 (1944); Pamela S. Karlan, *Politics by Other Means*, 85 VA. L. REV. 1697, 1719 (1999).

14. The Court was careful to note that Congress possesses no "power to exercise discretion in the other direction and to enact" measures that *limit* constitutional rights as pronounced by the Court. *See* footnote 10. This conclusion has become known (rather redundantly) as the "one-way ratchet" theory because it permits Congress to expand upon, but not to contract, constitutional rights as interpreted by the courts. Is the Court correct that any enactment limiting the courts' reading of constitutional rights would be unconstitutional because it would not be "enforc[ing]" the Constitution, or is Justice Harlan correct that the theory underlying the majority opinion permits Congress to alter the meaning of the Constitution in any direction it chooses?

2. *The Poor*

HARPER v. VIRGINIA STATE BOARD OF ELECTIONS
Supreme Court of the United States
383 U.S. 663, 86 S. Ct. 1079, 16 L. Ed. 2d 169 (1966)

MR. JUSTICE DOUGLAS delivered the opinion of the Court [in which MR. CHIEF JUSTICE WARREN, MR. JUSTICE CLARK, MR. JUSTICE BRENNAN, MR. JUSTICE WHITE, and MR. JUSTICE FORTAS join].

These are suits by Virginia residents to have declared unconstitutional Virginia's poll tax.[1] * * *

While the right to vote in federal elections is conferred by Art. I, § 2, of the Constitution (*United States* v. *Classic*, 313 U.S. 299, 314–15 [(1941)]), the right to vote in state elections is nowhere expressly mentioned. It is argued that the right to vote in state elections is implicit, particularly by reason of the First Amendment and that it may not constitutionally be conditioned upon the payment of a tax or fee.[2] We do not stop to canvass the relation between voting and political expression. For it is enough to say that once the franchise is granted to the electorate, lines may not be drawn which are inconsistent with the Equal Protection Clause of the Fourteenth Amendment. That is to say, the right of suffrage "is subject to the imposition of state standards which are not discriminatory and which do not contravene any restriction that Congress, acting pursuant to its constitutional powers, has imposed." *Lassiter* v. *Northampton County Board of Elections*, 360 U.S. 45, 51 [(1959)] [p. 8]. We were speaking there of a state literacy test which we sustained, warning that the result would be different if a literacy test, fair on its face, were used to discriminate against a class. But the *Lassiter* case does not govern the result here, because, unlike a poll tax, the "ability to read and write * * * has some relation to standards designed to promote intelligent use of the ballot."

We conclude that a State violates the Equal Protection Clause of the Fourteenth Amendment whenever it makes the affluence of the voter or payment of any fee an electoral standard. Voter qualifications have no relation to wealth nor to paying or not paying this or any other tax.[4] Our cases demonstrate that the Equal Protection Clause of the Fourteenth Amendment restrains the States from fixing voter qualifications which invidiously discriminate. Thus without questioning the power of

---

[1] Section 173 of Virginia's Constitution directs the General Assembly to levy an annual poll tax not exceeding $1.50 [approximately $11 in today's dollars — Eds.] on every resident of the State 21 years of age and over (with exceptions not relevant here). * * * Section 18 of the Constitution includes payment of poll taxes as a precondition for voting. Section 20 provides that a person must "personally" pay all state poll taxes for the three years preceding the year in which he applies for registration. By § 21 the poll tax must be paid at least six months prior to the election in which the voter seeks to vote. * * *

[2] * * * "If the State of Texas placed a tax on the right to speak at the rate of one dollar and seventy-five cents per year, no court would hesitate to strike it down as a blatant infringement of the freedom of speech. Yet the poll tax as enforced in Texas is a tax on the equally important right to vote." *United States* v. *Texas*, 252 F. Supp. 234, 254 ([W.D. Tex.] 1966).

[4] Only a handful of States today condition the franchise on the payment of a poll tax. Alabama and Texas each impose a poll tax of $1.50. Mississippi has a poll tax of $2. Vermont has recently eliminated the requirement that poll taxes be paid in order to vote.

a State to impose reasonable residence restrictions on the availability of the ballot, we held in *Carrington* v. *Rash*, 380 U.S. 89 [(1965)] [p. 90], that a State may not deny the opportunity to vote to a bona fide resident merely because he is a member of the armed services. * * * Previously we had said that neither homesite nor occupation "affords a permissible basis for distinguishing between qualified voters within the State." *Gray* v. *Sanders*, 372 U.S. 368, 380 [(1963)] [p. 163]. We think the same must be true of requirements of wealth or affluence or payment of a fee.

Long ago in *Yick Wo* v. *Hopkins*, 118 U.S. 356, 370 [(1886)], the Court referred to "the political franchise of voting" as a "fundamental political right, because preservative of all rights." Recently in *Reynolds* v. *Sims*, 377 U.S. 533, 561–562 (1964) [p. 173], we said, "Undoubtedly, the right of suffrage is a fundamental matter in a free and democratic society. Especially since the right to exercise the franchise in a free and unimpaired manner is preservative of other basic civil and political rights, any alleged infringement of the right of citizens to vote must be carefully and meticulously scrutinized." * * *

We say the same whether the citizen, otherwise qualified to vote, has $1.50 in his pocket or nothing at all, pays the fee or fails to pay it. The principle that denies the State the right to dilute a citizen's vote on account of his economic status or other such factors by analogy bars a system which excludes those unable to pay a fee to vote or who fail to pay.

It is argued that a State may exact fees from citizens for many different kinds of licenses; that if it can demand from all an equal fee for a driver's license, it can demand from all an equal poll tax for voting. But we must remember that the interest of the State, when it comes to voting, is limited to the power to fix qualifications. Wealth, like race, creed, or color, is not germane to one's ability to participate intelligently in the electoral process. Lines drawn on the basis of wealth or property, like those of race, are traditionally disfavored. *See Edwards* v. *California*, 314 U.S. 160, 184–185 [(1941)] (Jackson, J., concurring); *Griffin* v. *Illinois*, 351 U.S. 12 [(1956)]; *Douglas* v. *California*, 372 U.S. 353 [(1963)].[h] To introduce wealth or payment of a fee as a measure of a voter's qualifications is to introduce a capricious or irrelevant factor. The degree of the discrimination is irrelevant. In this context — that is, as a condition of obtaining a ballot — the requirement of fee paying causes an "invidious" discrimination that runs afoul of the Equal Protection Clause. * * *

* * * In determining what lines are unconstitutionally discriminatory, we have never been confined to historic notions of equality, any more than we have restricted due process to a fixed catalogue of what was at a given time deemed to be the limits of fundamental rights. Notions of what constitutes equal treatment for purposes of the Equal Protection Clause *do* change. * * * When, in 1954 * * * we repudiated the "separate-but-equal" doctrine of *Plessy* [v. *Ferguson*, 163 U.S. 537 (1896)] as

---

[h] *Edwards* struck down, on Commerce Clause grounds, a California law prohibiting the importation of "indigent person[s]" into the state. Justice Jackson's concurrence argued that one's indigency should be "constitutionally an irrelevance, like race, creed, or color." *Griffin* required states to provide an indigent criminal defendant a transcript free of charge to enable him to file an appeal. *Douglas* required states to provide counsel for a criminal defendant during an initial appeal, where state law provided the defendant such an appeal as of right. [— Eds.]

respects public education we stated: "In approaching this problem, we cannot turn the clock back to 1868 when the Amendment was adopted, or even to 1896 when *Plessy* v. *Ferguson* was written." *Brown* v. *Board of Education*, 347 U.S. 483, 492 [(1954)].

* * * [W]e held [in *Reynolds* v. *Sims*, *supra*,] that "the opportunity for equal participation by all voters in the election of state legislators" is required. We decline to qualify that principle by sustaining this poll tax. Our conclusion, like that in *Reynolds* v. *Sims*, is founded not on what we think governmental policy should be, but on what the Equal Protection Clause requires.

We have long been mindful that where fundamental rights and liberties are asserted under the Equal Protection Clause, classifications which might invade or restrain them must be closely scrutinized and carefully confined.

Those principles apply here. For to repeat, wealth or fee paying has, in our view, no relation to voting qualifications; the right to vote is too precious, too fundamental to be so burdened or conditioned.

Reversed.

Mr. Justice Black, dissenting.

In *Breedlove* v. *Suttles*, 302 U.S. 277 [(1937)], * * * we unanimously upheld the right of the State of Georgia to make payment of its state poll tax a prerequisite to voting in state elections. We rejected at that time contentions that the state law violated the Equal Protection Clause of the Fourteenth Amendment because it put an unequal burden on different groups of people according to their age, sex, and ability to pay. * * *

* * * Later, * * * *Butler* v. *Thompson*, 341 U.S. 937 [(1951)], uph[eld], over the dissent of Mr. Justice Douglas, the Virginia state poll tax law challenged here against the same equal protection challenges. * * * I would adhere to the holding of those cases. * * *

It should be pointed out at once that the Court's decision is to no extent based on a finding that the Virginia law as written or as applied is being used as a device or mechanism to deny Negro citizens of Virginia the right to vote on account of their color. * * * What the Court does hold is that the Equal Protection Clause necessarily bars all States from making payment of a state tax, any tax, a prerequisite to voting.

I think the interpretation that this Court gave the Equal Protection Clause in *Breedlove* was correct. The mere fact that a law results in treating some groups differently from others does not, of course, automatically amount to a violation of the Equal Protection Clause. To bar a State from drawing any distinctions in the application of its laws would practically paralyze the regulatory power of legislative bodies. * * * Voting laws are no exception to this principle. All voting laws treat some persons differently from others in some respects. Some bar a person from voting who is under 21 years of age; others bar those under 18. Some bar convicted felons or the insane, and some have attached a freehold or other property qualification for voting. * * *

* * * State poll tax legislation can "reasonably," "rationally" and without an "invidious" or evil purpose to injure anyone be found to rest on a number of state policies including (1) the State's desire to collect its revenue, and (2) its belief that voters who pay a poll tax will be interested in furthering the State's welfare when they vote. Certainly it is rational to believe that people may be more likely to pay taxes if payment is a prerequisite to voting. And if history can be a factor in determining the "rationality" of discrimination in a state law * * *, then whatever may be our personal opinion, history is on the side of "rationality" of the State's poll tax policy. Property qualifications existed in the Colonies and were continued by many States after the Constitution was adopted. Although I join the Court in disliking the policy of the poll tax, this is not in my judgment a justifiable reason for holding this poll tax law unconstitutional. Such a holding on my part would, in my judgment, be an exercise of power which the Constitution does not confer upon me.[4]
* * *

The Court's justification for consulting its own notions rather than following the original meaning of the Constitution, as I would, apparently is based on the belief of the majority of the Court that for this Court to be bound by the original meaning of the Constitution is an intolerable and debilitating evil; that our Constitution should not be "shackled to the political theory of a particular era," and that to save the country from the original Constitution the Court must have constant power to renew it and keep it abreast of this Court's more enlightening theories of what is best for our society. It seems to me that this is an attack not only on the great value of our Constitution itself but also on the concept of a written constitution which is to survive through the years as originally written unless changed through the amendment process which the Framers wisely provided. Moreover, when a "political theory" embodied in our Constitution becomes outdated, it seems to me that a majority of the nine members of this Court are not only without constitutional power but are far less qualified to choose a new constitutional political theory than the people of this country proceeding in the manner provided by Article V. * * *

The people have not found it impossible to amend their Constitution to meet new conditions. The Equal Protection Clause itself is the product of the people's desire to use their constitutional power to amend the Constitution to meet new problems. Moreover, the people, in § 5 of the Fourteenth Amendment, designated the governmental tribunal they wanted to provide additional rules to enforce the

---

[4] The opinion of the Court, in footnote two, quotes language from a federal district court's opinion which implies that since a tax on speech would not be constitutionally allowed a tax which is a prerequisite to voting likewise cannot be allowed. But a tax or any other regulation which burdens and actually abridges the right to speak would, in my judgment, be a flagrant violation of the First Amendment's prohibition against abridgments of the freedom of speech which prohibition is made applicable to the States by the Fourteenth Amendment. There is no comparable specific constitutional provision absolutely barring the States from abridging the right to vote. Consequently States have from the beginning and do now qualify the right to vote because of age, prior felony convictions, illiteracy, and various other reasons. Of course the First and Fourteenth Amendments forbid any State from abridging a person's right to speak because he is under 21 years of age, has been convicted of a felony, or is illiterate.

guarantees of that Amendment. The branch of Government they chose was not the Judicial Branch but the Legislative. I have no doubt at all that Congress has the power under § 5 to pass legislation to abolish the poll tax in order to protect the citizens of this country if it believes that the poll tax is being used as a device to deny voters equal protection of the laws. But this legislative power which was granted to Congress by § 5 of the Fourteenth Amendment is limited to Congress. * * *

MR. JUSTICE HARLAN, whom MR. JUSTICE STEWART joins, dissenting.

The final demise of state poll taxes, already totally proscribed by the Twenty-Fourth Amendment with respect to federal elections and abolished by the States themselves in all but four States with respect to state elections, is perhaps in itself not of great moment. But the fact that the *coup de grace* has been administered by this Court instead of being left to the affected States or to the federal political process should be a matter of continuing concern to all interested in maintaining the proper role of this tribunal under our scheme of government. * * *

* * * In substance the Court's analysis of the equal protection issue goes no further than to say that the electoral franchise is "precious" and "fundamental," and to conclude that "[t]o introduce wealth or payment of a fee as a measure of a voter's qualifications is to introduce a capricious or irrelevant factor." These are of course captivating phrases, but they are wholly inadequate to satisfy the standard governing adjudication of the equal protection issue: Is there a rational basis for Virginia's poll tax as a voting qualification? I think the answer to that question is undoubtedly "yes."[5]

Property qualifications and poll taxes have been a traditional part of our political structure. In the Colonies the franchise was generally a restricted one. Over the years these and other restrictions were gradually lifted, primarily because popular theories of political representation had changed. Often restrictions were lifted only after wide public debate. * * *

[I]t is only by fiat that it can be said, especially in the context of American history, that there can be no rational debate as to [property qualifications'] advisability. Most of the early Colonies had them; many of the States have had them during much of their histories; and, whether one agrees or not, arguments have been and still can be made in favor of them. For example, it is certainly a rational argument that payment of some minimal poll tax promotes civic responsibility, weeding out those who do not care enough about public affairs to pay $1.50 or thereabouts a year for the exercise of the franchise. It is also arguable, indeed it was probably accepted as sound political theory by a large percentage of Americans through most of our history, that people with some property have a deeper stake in community affairs, and are consequently more responsible, more educated, more knowledgeable, more worthy of confidence, than those without means, and that the community and Nation would be better managed if the franchise were restricted to such citizens.

---

[5] I have no doubt that poll taxes that deny the right to vote on the basis of race or color violate the Fifteenth Amendment and can be struck down by this Court. * * * The Virginia poll tax is on its face applicable to all citizens, and there was no allegation that it was discriminatorily enforced. The District Court explicitly found "no racial discrimination * * * in its application as a condition to voting." * * *

Nondiscriminatory and fairly applied literacy tests, upheld by this Court in *Lassiter* v. *Northampton County Board of Elections*, find justification on very similar grounds.

These viewpoints, to be sure, ring hollow on most contemporary ears. Their lack of acceptance today is evidenced by the fact that nearly all of the States, left to their own devices, have eliminated property or poll-tax qualifications; by the cognate fact that Congress and three-quarters of the States quickly ratified the Twenty-Fourth Amendment; and by the fact that rules such as the "pauper exclusion" in Virginia law have never been enforced.

Property and poll-tax qualifications, very simply, are not in accord with current egalitarian notions of how a modern democracy should be organized. It is of course entirely fitting that legislatures should modify the law to reflect such changes in popular attitudes. However, it is all wrong, in my view, for the Court to adopt the political doctrines popularly accepted at a particular moment of our history and to declare all others to be irrational and invidious, barring them from the range of choice by reasonably minded people acting through the political process. It was not too long ago that Mr. Justice Holmes felt impelled to remind the Court that the Due Process Clause of the Fourteenth Amendment does not enact the *laissez-faire* theory of society, *Lochner* v. *New York*, 198 U.S. 45, 75–76 [(1905)]. The times have changed, and perhaps it is appropriate to observe that neither does the Equal Protection Clause of that Amendment rigidly impose upon America an ideology of unrestrained egalitarianism.

I would affirm the decision of the District Court.

Notes and Questions

1. *Harper* was one of a series of cases from the 1950s and 1960s calling into question the constitutionality of government distinctions based on wealth. By 1966, the Court had required states to provide counsel to criminal defendants on trial for felonies (*Gideon v. Wainwright*, 372 U.S. 335 (1963) (later extended to any crime punished by imprisonment, *Argersinger v. Hamlin*, 407 U.S. 25 (1972))) and during an appeal as of right, *i.e.*, which the appellate court must hear (*Douglas v. California*, 372 U.S. 353 (1963)). Further, the Court held that states must provide a transcript free of charge for an indigent defendant who needs the transcript to file an appeal (*Griffin v. Illinois*, 351 U.S. 12 (1956)). *Cf. Boddie v. Connecticut*, 401 U.S. 371 (1971) (invalidating a filing fee for divorce cases, as applied to persons unable to pay the fee); *Goldberg v. Kelly*, 397 U.S. 254 (1970) (holding that welfare recipients possessed a property right in anticipated government benefits, such that the benefits could not be terminated without a hearing); *Shapiro v. Thompson*, 394 U.S. 618 (1969) (invalidating laws that imposed a one-year residency requirement on the receipt of welfare benefits).

Note that the Court often used the Equal Protection Clause to prevent states from discriminating against certain classes of people, particularly with regard to important aspects of personal liberty. Even where the Court was unwilling to hold that a right was "fundamental" under the Due Process Clause, it was sometimes willing to apply strict scrutiny under the Equal Protection Clause, resulting in the invalidation of laws that in practice allowed only some people to exercise those important rights. *See Skinner v. Oklahoma ex rel. Williamson*, 316 U.S. 535 (1942) (Douglas, J.) (using the Equal Protection Clause to strike down a law providing for the sterilization of some (but not all) habitual criminals).

Soon after the appointment of Chief Justice Burger to replace Chief Justice Warren, the Court's jurisprudence began to shift away from a concern about the unequal distribution of property. The Court held that wealth was not a suspect classification and, applying the rational-basis test, upheld laws that limited a family's welfare benefits regardless of the number of children in the family (*Dandridge v. Williams*, 397 U.S. 471 (1970)); that funded local public schools by property taxes so that children in poorer school districts attended schools less funded than schools in wealthier areas (*San Antonio Independent School District v. Rodriguez*, 411 U.S. 1 (1973)); and that paid childbirth expenses for indigent women but did not pay for abortions (*Maher v. Roe*, 432 U.S. 464 (1977)).

The Court has not overruled the cases striking down wealth classifications, though. Instead, the Court has applied strict scrutiny only to those classifications that discriminate on the basis of wealth *as to the exercise of a fundamental right*. Voting is considered a fundamental right, so *Harper* continues to be good law. Similarly, because running for office is a fundamental right, states may not impose filing fees on candidates who are unable to afford them. *Lubin v. Panish*, 415 U.S. 709 (1974).

2.   *Harper* claimed that "[l]ines drawn on the basis of wealth or property, like those of race, are traditionally disfavored." Was the Court correct to treat the Virginia statute as such a "line," or was the $1.50 requirement a nondiscriminatory one, applicable to all voters regardless of their assets?

3.   Would the tax in *Harper* be constitutional if the poor — *i.e.*, those unable to pay the tax — were given an exemption?

4.   *Problem.* Suppose that instead of requiring all voters to pay a tax, Virginia had required potential voters either to pay the $1.50 poll tax or to watch a thirty-minute candidate debate or panel discussion of the issues involved in the election. The purpose of both would be to ensure that voters considered the election sufficiently important to justify the expenditure of time or money, and also to increase the likelihood that voters would be knowledgeable about the relevant issues. Would such a requirement be constitutional? If not, is there a constitutional problem with requiring voters to register prior to election day, on the belief that only people sufficiently motivated to register should be permitted to vote?

5.   The Court's discovery of a "tradition" against "[l]ines drawn on the basis of wealth or property" is curious given Anglo-American law's centuries-long explicit wealth discrimination. *See generally* CHILTON WILLIAMSON, AMERICAN SUFFRAGE: FROM PROPERTY TO DEMOCRACY, 1760–1860 (1960). "By the middle of the eighteenth century, all the American colonies save one had adopted property qualifications for the suffrage." Robert J. Steinfeld, *Property and Suffrage in the Early American Republic*, 41 STAN. L. REV. 335, 336 (1989). For a helpful catalogue of suffrage qualifications in the early years of the United States, see ALEXANDER KEYSSAR, THE RIGHT TO VOTE: THE CONTESTED HISTORY OF DEMOCRACY IN THE UNITED STATES 340–48

(2000); *see also Wesberry v. Sanders*, 376 U.S. 1, 25 n.7 (1964) [p. 166] (Harlan, J., dissenting). Even as property and taxpaying requirements were being eliminated in the nineteenth century, they were often replaced by "pauper exclusions" (to which Justice Harlan referred in his *Harper* dissent) that barred persons on public assistance from voting. *See* KEYSSAR, *supra*, at 61. By 1900, fourteen states had pauper exclusions. *See* Steinfeld, *supra*, at 335.

Professor Steinfeld has noted that debate over property qualifications and pauper exclusions presents a conflict between the traditional idea that only property ownership gave a voter true independence — a "will of his own" — and the notion that all men were "by nature equally free and independent." *Id.* at 338. As Blackstone stated the traditional view,

> If it were probable that every man would give his vote freely and without influence of any kind, then, upon the true theory and genuine principles of liberty, every member of the community, however poor, should have a vote in electing those delegates, to whose charge is committed the disposal of his property, his liberty, and his life. But, since that can hardly be expected in persons of indigent fortunes, or such as are under the immediate dominion of others, all popular states have been obliged to establish certain qualifications; whereby some, who are expected to have no will of their own, are excluded from voting, in order to set other individuals, whose wills may be supposed independent, more thoroughly upon a level with each other.

1 WILLIAM BLACKSTONE, COMMENTARIES ON THE LAWS OF ENGLAND *171 (1765). Professor Steinfeld has further stated that "[i]n the decades after the [American] Revolution, hardly anyone disputed the proposition that property ownership was necessary for personal independence." Steinfeld, *supra*, at 342. Was *Harper* right to regard such a view as "irrational"? Or is wealth in reality more than a "capricious or irrelevant factor" in determining one's qualifications to vote? In particular, is wealth less related to one's ability to cast a vote intelligently and virtuously than is one's ability to pass a literacy test, as in *Lassiter*?

6.   According to Professor Keyssar, the concern with the non-propertied class's lack of "independence" "coexisted with an altogether contradictory argument, often expressed by the same people: the poor, or the propertyless, should not vote because they would threaten the interests of property — that is, they would have too much will of their own." KEYSSAR, *supra*, at 10–11. Professor Keyssar went on to suggest that the Blackstonian invocation of concerns about independence "mask[ed]" the true class-based reasons for property qualifications, and "provid[ed] an ostensibly egalitarian defense of an overtly anti-egalitarian policy." *Id.* at 11.

7. On the propriety of property qualifications, consider the thoughts of Benjamin Franklin:

> Today a man owns a jackass worth fifty dollars and he is entitled to vote; but before the next election the jackass dies. The man in the mean time has become more experienced, his knowledge of the principles of government, and his acquaintance with mankind, are more extensive, and he is therefore better qualified to make a proper selection of rulers — but the jackass is

dead and the man cannot vote. Now gentlemen, pray inform me, in whom is the right of suffrage? In the man or in the jackass?

4 BENJAMIN FRANKLIN, THE CASKET, OR FLOWERS OF LITERATURE, WIT AND SENTIMENT 181 (1828).

8.   *Problem.* A state statute limits participation in city bond elections to those residents who have taxable property listed with the city tax assessor. Both real and personal property qualify, and listing any property, no matter how little the value, satisfies the statute. (Another statute requires city residents to list all their taxable property with the assessor yearly. There is no penalty for failing to do so, however.) The objective is to have such elections decided by the people who will have to pay the cost of any debt incurred by the city. Is the limitation constitutional? *See Hill v. Stone*, 421 U.S. 289 (1975).

3.   *The Law-Breaking*

RICHARDSON v. RAMIREZ
Supreme Court of the United States
418 U.S. 24, 94 S. Ct. 2655, 41 L. Ed. 2d 551 (1974)

MR. JUSTICE REHNQUIST delivered the opinion of the Court [in which MR. CHIEF JUSTICE BURGER, MR. JUSTICE STEWART, MR. JUSTICE WHITE, MR. JUSTICE BLACKMUN, and MR. JUSTICE POWELL join].

The three individual respondents in this case were convicted of felonies and have completed the service of their respective sentences and paroles. * * * They claimed, on behalf of themselves and others similarly situated, that application to them of the provisions of the California Constitution and implementing statutes which disenfranchised persons convicted of an "infamous crime" denied them the right to equal protection of the laws under the Federal Constitution. The Supreme Court of California [agreed]. * * *

Article XX, § 11, of the California Constitution has provided since its adoption in 1879 that "[l]aws shall be made" to exclude from voting persons convicted of bribery, perjury, forgery, malfeasance in office, "or other high crimes." At the time respondents were refused registration, former Art. II, § 1, of the California Constitution provided in part that "no alien ineligible to citizenship, no idiot, no insane person, no person convicted of any infamous crime, no person hereafter convicted of the embezzlement or misappropriation of public money, and no person who shall not be able to read the Constitution in the English language and write his or her name, shall ever exercise the privileges of an elector in this State." Sections 310 and 321 of the California Elections Code provide that an affidavit of registration shall show whether the affiant has been convicted of "a felony which disqualifies [him] from voting." * * *

Each of the individual respondents was convicted of one or more felonies, and served some time in jail or prison followed by a successfully terminated parole. * * *

All three respondents were refused registration because of their felony convictions.[9]
* * *

Unlike most claims under the Equal Protection Clause, for the decision of which we have only the language of the Clause itself as it is embodied in the Fourteenth Amendment, respondents' claim implicates not merely the language of the Equal Protection Clause of § 1 of the Fourteenth Amendment, but also the provisions of the less familiar § 2 of the Amendment:

> "Representatives shall be apportioned among the several States according to their respective numbers, counting the whole number of persons in each State, excluding Indians not taxed. But when the right to vote at any election for the choice of electors for President and Vice President of the United States, Representatives in Congress, the Executive and Judicial officers of a State, or the members of the Legislature thereof, is denied to any of the male inhabitants of such State, being twenty-one years of age, and citizens of the United States, or in any way abridged, *except for participation in rebellion, or other crime*, the basis of representation therein shall be reduced in the proportion which the number of such male citizens shall bear to the whole number of male citizens twenty-one years of age in such State." (Emphasis supplied.)

Petitioner contends that the italicized language of § 2 expressly exempts from the sanction of that section disenfranchisement grounded on prior conviction of a felony. She goes on to argue that those who framed and adopted the Fourteenth Amendment could not have intended to prohibit outright in § 1 of that Amendment that which was expressly exempted from the lesser sanction of reduced representation imposed by § 2 of the Amendment. This argument seems to us a persuasive one unless it can be shown that the language of § 2, "except for participation in rebellion, or other crime," was intended to have a different meaning than would appear from its face.

The problem of interpreting the "intention" of a constitutional provision is, as countless cases of this Court recognize, a difficult one. Not only are there deliberations of congressional committees and floor debates in the House and Senate, but an amendment must thereafter be ratified by the necessary number of States. The legislative history bearing on the meaning of the relevant language of § 2 is scant indeed; the framers of the Amendment were primarily concerned with the effect of reduced representation upon the States, rather than with the two forms of disenfranchisement which were exempted from that consequence by the language with which we are concerned here. Nonetheless, what legislative history there is indicates that this language was intended by Congress to mean what it says.

Throughout the floor debates in both the House and the Senate, in which

---

[9] Respondent Ramirez was convicted in Texas of the felony of "robbery by assault" in 1952. He served three months in jail and successfully terminated his parole in 1962. * * * Respondent Lee was convicted of the felony of heroin possession in California in 1955, served two years in prison, and successfully terminated his parole in 1959. * * * Respondent Gill was convicted in 1952 and 1967 of second-degree burglary in California, and in 1957 of forgery. He served some time in prison on each conviction, followed by a successful parole. * * *

numerous changes of language in § 2 were proposed, the language "except for participation in rebellion, or other crime" was never altered. The language of § 2 attracted a good deal of interest during the debates, but most of the discussion was devoted to its foreseeable consequences in both the Northern and Southern States, and to arguments as to its necessity or wisdom. What little comment there was on the phrase in question here supports a plain reading of it. * * *

Further light is shed on the understanding of those who framed and ratified the Fourteenth Amendment, and thus on the meaning of § 2, by the fact that at the time of the adoption of the Amendment, 29 States had provisions in their constitutions which prohibited, or authorized the legislature to prohibit, exercise of the franchise by persons convicted of felonies or infamous crimes.

More impressive than the mere existence of the state constitutional provisions disenfranchising felons at the time of the adoption of the Fourteenth Amendment is the congressional treatment of States readmitted to the Union following the Civil War. For every State thus readmitted, affirmative congressional action in the form of an enabling act was taken, and as a part of the readmission process the State seeking readmission was required to submit for the approval of the Congress its proposed state constitution. * * * The Act admitting Arkansas, the first State to be so admitted, attached a condition to its admission. That Act provided:

> "* * * [t]hat the constitution of Arkansas shall never be so amended or changed as to deprive any citizen or class of citizens of the United States of the right to vote who are entitled to vote by the constitution herein recognized, except as a punishment for such crimes as are now felonies at common law, whereof they shall have been duly convicted, under laws equally applicable to all the inhabitants of said State * * *."

* * * The same "fundamental condition" as was imposed by the act readmitting Arkansas was also, with only slight variations in language, imposed by the Act readmitting North Carolina, South Carolina, Louisiana, Georgia, Alabama, and Florida, enacted three days later. That condition was again imposed by the Acts readmitting Virginia, Mississippi, Texas, and Georgia early in 1870. * * *

Despite this settled historical and judicial understanding of the Fourteenth Amendment's effect on state laws disenfranchising convicted felons, respondents argue that our recent decisions invalidating other state-imposed restrictions on the franchise as violative of the Equal Protection Clause require us to invalidate the disenfranchisement of felons as well. * * *

As we have seen, however, the exclusion of felons from the vote has an affirmative sanction in § 2 of the Fourteenth Amendment, a sanction which was not present in the case of the other restrictions on the franchise which were invalidated in the cases on which respondents rely. We hold that the understanding of those who adopted the Fourteenth Amendment, as reflected in the express language of § 2 and in the historical and judicial interpretation of the Amendment's applicability to state laws disenfranchising felons, is of controlling significance in distinguishing such laws from those other state limitations on the franchise which have been held invalid under the Equal Protection Clause by this Court. We * * * may rest on the demonstrably sound proposition that § 1, in dealing with voting rights as it does, could not have been meant to bar outright a form of disenfranchisement which was expressly exempted from the less drastic sanction of reduced representation which § 2 imposed for other forms of disenfranchisement. * * *

We therefore hold that the Supreme Court of California erred in concluding that California may no longer, consistent with the Equal Protection Clause of the Fourteenth Amendment, exclude from the franchise convicted felons who have completed their sentences and paroles. * * * Accordingly, we reverse and remand for further proceedings not inconsistent with this opinion.

It is so ordered.

MR. JUSTICE MARSHALL, with whom MR. JUSTICE BRENNAN joins, dissenting.

The Court today holds that a State may strip ex-felons who have fully paid their debt to society of their fundamental right to vote without running afoul of the Fourteenth Amendment. This result is, in my view, based on an unsound historical analysis which already has been rejected by this Court. * * *

* * * The Court construes § 2 of the Fourteenth Amendment as an express authorization for the States to disenfranchise former felons. Section 2 does except disenfranchisement for "participation in rebellion, or other crime" from the operation of its penalty provision. As the Court notes, however, there is little independent legislative history as to the crucial words "or other crime"; the proposed § 2 went to a joint committee containing only the phrase "participation in rebellion" and emerged with "or other crime" inexplicably tacked on. * * *

The historical purpose for § 2 itself is, however, relatively clear and, in my view, dispositive of this case. The Republicans who controlled the 39th Congress were concerned that the additional congressional representation of the Southern States which would result from the abolition of slavery might weaken their own political dominance. There were two alternatives available — either to limit southern representation, which was unacceptable on a long-term basis, or to insure that southern Negroes, sympathetic to the Republican cause, would be enfranchised; but an explicit grant of suffrage to Negroes was thought politically unpalatable at the time. Section 2 of the Fourteenth Amendment was the resultant compromise. It put Southern States to a choice — enfranchise Negro voters or lose congressional representation. * * *

It is clear that § 2 was not intended and should not be construed to be a limitation on the other sections of the Fourteenth Amendment. Section 2 provides a special remedy — reduced representation — to cure a particular form of electoral abuse — the disenfranchisement of Negroes. There is no indication that the framers of the provisions intended that special penalty to be the exclusive remedy for all forms of electoral discrimination. This Court has repeatedly rejected that rationale. *See Reynolds* v. *Sims,* 377 U.S. 533 (1964) [p. 173]; *Carrington* v. *Rash,* 380 U.S. 89 (1965) [p. 90]. Rather, a discrimination to which the penalty provision of § 2 is inapplicable must still be judged against the Equal Protection Clause of § 1 to determine whether judicial or congressional remedies should be invoked. * * *

The Court's references to congressional enactments contemporaneous to the adoption of the Fourteenth Amendment * * * are inapposite. They do not explain the purpose for the adoption of § 2 of the Fourteenth Amendment. They merely indicate that disenfranchisement for participation in crime was not uncommon in the States at the time of the adoption of the Amendment. Hence, not surprisingly, that form of disenfranchisement was excepted from the application of the special penalty provision of § 2. But because Congress chose to exempt one form of electoral discrimination from the reduction-of-representation remedy provided by § 2 does not necessarily imply congressional approval of this disenfranchisement.[24] By providing a special remedy for disenfranchisement of a particular class of voters in § 2, Congress did not approve all election discriminations to which the § 2 remedy was inapplicable, and such discriminations thus are not forever immunized from evolving standards of equal protection scrutiny. There is no basis for concluding that Congress intended by § 2 to freeze the meaning of other clauses of the Fourteenth Amendment to the conception of voting rights prevalent at the time of the adoption of the Amendment. * * *

In my view, the disenfranchisement of ex-felons must be measured against the requirements of the Equal Protection Clause of § 1 of the Fourteenth Amendment. That analysis properly begins with the observation that because the right to vote "is of the essence of a democratic society, and any restrictions on that right strike at the heart of representative government," *Reynolds* v. *Sims*, 377 U.S., at 555, voting is a "fundamental" right. * * *

To determine that the compelling-state-interest test applies to the challenged classification is, however, to settle only a threshold question. * * * I think it clear that the State has not met its burden of justifying the blanket disenfranchisement of former felons presented by this case. There is certainly no basis for asserting that ex-felons have any less interest in the democratic process than any other citizen. Like everyone else, their daily lives are deeply affected and changed by the decisions of government. * * *

[One] asserted purpose [of disenfranchising ex-felons] is to keep former felons from voting because their likely voting pattern might be subversive of the interests of an orderly society. Support for the argument that electors can be kept from the ballot box for fear they might vote to repeal or emasculate provisions of the criminal code, is drawn primarily from this Court's decisions in *Murphy* v. *Ramsey*, 114 U.S. 15 (1885), and *Davis* v. *Beason*, 133 U.S. 333 (1890). In *Murphy*, the Court upheld the disenfranchisement of anyone who had ever entered into a bigamous or polygamous marriage and in *Davis*, the Court sanctioned, as a condition to the exercise of franchise, the requirement of an oath that the elector did not "teach, advise, counsel, or encourage any person to commit the crime of bigamy or polygamy." The Court's intent was clear — "to withdraw all political influence from

---

[24] To say that § 2 of the Fourteenth Amendment is a direct limitation on the protection afforded voting rights by § 1 leads to absurd results. If one accepts the premise that § 2 authorizes disenfranchisement for any crime, the challenged California provision could * * * require disenfranchisement for seduction under promise of marriage, or conspiracy to operate a motor vehicle without a muffler. Disenfranchisement extends to convictions for vagrancy in Alabama or breaking a water pipe in North Dakota, to note but two examples. Even a jaywalking or traffic conviction could conceivably lead to disenfranchisement, since § 2 does not differentiate between felonies and misdemeanors.

those who are practically hostile to" the goals of certain criminal laws. *Murphy*, 114 U.S. at 45; *Davis*, 133 U.S., at 334.

To the extent *Murphy* and *Davis* approve the doctrine that citizens can be barred from the ballot box because they would vote to change the existing criminal law, those decisions are surely of minimal continuing precedential value. We have since explicitly held that such "differences of opinion cannot justify for excluding [any] group from . . . 'the franchise,' " *Cipriano* v. *City of Houma*, 395 U.S. 701, 705–706 (1969). * * *

Although, in the last century, this Court may have justified the exclusion of voters from the electoral process for fear that they would vote to change laws considered important by a temporal majority, I have little doubt that we would not countenance such a purpose today. The process of democracy is one of change. Our laws are not frozen into immutable form, they are constantly in the process of revision in response to the needs of a changing society. The public interest, as conceived by a majority of the voting public, is constantly undergoing reexamination. This Court's holding in *Davis* and *Murphy*, that a State may disenfranchise a class of voters to "withdraw all political influence from those who are practically hostile" to the existing order, strikes at the very heart of the democratic process. A temporal majority could use such a power to preserve inviolate its view of the social order simply by disenfranchising those with different views. Voters who opposed the repeal of prohibition could have disenfranchised those who advocated repeal "to prevent persons from being enabled by their votes to defeat the criminal laws of the country." Today, presumably those who support the legalization of marihuana could be barred from the ballot box for much the same reason. The ballot is the democratic system's coin of the realm. To condition its exercise on support of the established order is to debase that currency beyond recognition. Rather than resurrect *Davis* and *Murphy*, I would expressly disavow any continued adherence to the dangerous notions therein expressed. * * *

I think it clear that measured against the standards of this Court's modern equal protection jurisprudence, the blanket disenfranchisement of ex-felons cannot stand.

I respectfully dissent.

Mr. Justice Douglas * * * dissents from a reversal of the judgment below as he cannot say that it does not rest on an independent state ground.

Notes and Questions

1. According to Professor Gabriel Chin, the Fifteenth Amendment's self-enforcing prohibition on racial discrimination in voting was inconsistent with (and provoked by the failure of) the more limited remedy specified in § 2 of the Fourteenth Amendment. As a result, the Fifteenth Amendment should be understood to have repealed § 2 of the Fourteenth Amendment, on which the Court relied in *Ramirez*. *See* Gabriel J. Chin, *Reconstruction, Felon Disenfranchisement, and the Right to Vote: Did the Fifteenth Amendment Repeal Section 2 of the Fourteenth Amendment?*, 92 Geo. L.J. 259 (2004). If the Supreme Court reconsiders the constitutionality of felon disenfranchisement without relying on § 2, as Chin proposes, might felon disenfranchisement still be constitutional?

2. In the years since *Ramirez*, more states have liberalized their laws and permitted (ex-)felons to vote. Maine and Vermont even permit felons to vote *during their periods of incarceration*. Recently, in 2007, Florida and Maryland changed their laws to permit most released felons to regain their voting rights. And in 2014, Virginia made two changes that make it easier for felons to become re-eligible to vote. Violent felons in that state used to have to wait five years before they could petition to be eligible to vote, but that period has been reduced to three years. And drug offenses have been reclassified as non-violent, so the waiting period does not apply at all and Virginia's drug felons can now petition for a restoration of their voting rights as soon as they complete their prison time and pay court costs. *See* Larry O'Dell, *Va. Gov. Changes Policy on Felons' Voting Rights*, WASH. TIMES (Apr. 18, 2014), *at* http://www.washingtontimes.com/news/2014/apr/18/mcauliffe-alters-felons-voting-rights-procedures/.

Some states, however, are moving in the opposite direction and making it more difficult for felons to vote. Massachusetts and Utah recently disenfranchised currently incarcerated felons. South Dakota has joined this counter-trend, extending its voting ban, which had prohibited imprisoned felons and parolees from voting, to probationers as well. Further, in 2011, both Florida and Iowa tightened their laws concerning the restoration of felons' voting rights. Whereas each had previously automatically restored the franchise to felons who had fulfilled all the requirements of their sentences, now felons are required to petition individually for the reestablishment of their voting rights.

Twelve states impose some form of voting restriction on felons even after they are no longer in prison, on parole, or on probation, though these states vary in the particulars of their schemes. One important difference is between the 37 states that automatically restore felons' rights after some period and the 11 that require felons to petition for the restoration of rights. There are other important differences as well. Arizona, for example, permanently disenfranchises persons who have committed two felonies. Iowa disenfranchises people who have committed "infamous" crimes, but it is not clear which crimes qualify. *See Chiodo v. Section 43.24 Panel*, 846 N.W.2d 845 (Iowa 2014). As an indication of how confusing the law can be in this area, consider the breakdown of the Iowa Supreme Court justices in *Chiodo*: The plurality opinion for three of the seven justices would hold that "infamous" crimes includes no misdemeanors (such as a second offense for operating a vehicle while impaired, the aggravated misdemeanor that was at issue in that case) and it includes only those felonies that suggest that the felons would "tend to undermine the process of democratic governance through elections." Two other justices believed that "infamous" crimes should mean all felonies and no misdemeanors. Another justice believed that the term included all felonies and some misdemeanors as well. And the seventh justice was recused.

Between those states permanently disenfranchising all felons and those for which criminal conviction does not affect voting rights at all, are the states that have adopted some temporary exclusion of felons. Such measures include suspension of voting rights while the offender is in prison, while the offender is in prison or on parole, and while the offender is in prison, on parole, or on probation. Nebraska restores voting rights two years after felons' release from prison, parole, or probation. California bans felons from voting during their imprisonment and parole, but it may be unclear whether certain offenders are "imprisoned." Recently plaintiffs filed a lawsuit challenging the secretary of state's interpretation that "imprisoned" applied to felons who are housed in county jails as well as those in state prisons. *See* Don Thompson, *Group Sues California, Wants Criminals to be Able to Vote*, THE REPORTER (Vacaville, Cal.) (Mar. 8, 2012), *at* http://www. sentencingproject.org/template/page.cfm?id=133. For summaries of states' laws, see Sentencing Project, *Felony Disenfranchisement*, *at* http://www. sentencingproject.org/template/page.cfm?id=133; Brennan Center for Justice, *Criminal Disenfranchisement Laws Across the United States*, *at* http://www. brennancenter.org/sites/default/files/legacy/d/download_file_48642.pdf.

In addition to laws that have actually been enacted, there is a bewildering variety of laws that are being considered by lawmakers in the several states. Consider this summary from 2012:

> "South Dakota lawmakers have sent the governor a bill to block voting by felons on probation or parole. However, legislators in New Jersey and New York are considering bills that would do the opposite by letting parolees and probationers vote. Legislation pending in Tennessee would stop requiring that convicts pay their restitution, court costs and child support before they can vote again. But Washington state legislators are considering a bill that would add the same repayment obligations that Tennessee may end. Some felons could vote absentee from their prison cells under bills introduced in Hawaii and Tennessee. A South Carolina bill would block registered sex offenders from voting at all. Lawmakers in New Jersey, New York and Pennsylvania could require state officials to help offenders register to vote as they complete their incarceration, probation or parole."

Thompson, *supra*.

3.   If Florida had permitted felons to vote in 2000, the result of the presidential election likely would have been different. Because felons are more likely than the general population to be poor, to be of a minority race, and to have relatively low levels of education — all of which are indications of Democratic sympathies — most analysts believe they would have preferred the Democrat Gore to the Republican Bush, and the differential would have been sufficient to overcome Bush's minuscule margin of victory.[i] If this analysis is accurate, does it indicate that the election of President Bush was illegitimate because it was predicated on the exclusion of potential voters, or that a Gore presidency predicated on the votes of convicted felons would have been the illegitimate outcome? In this light, consider that then-Democratic presidential candidate Barack Obama's campaign received briefings and advice concerning the registration of felons whose voting rights had recently been restored. The Obama campaign, however, was "reluctant to acknowledge any concerted effort" because of the potential negative reaction at being

---

[i] *See* JEFF MANZA & CHRISTOPHER UGGEN, LOCKED OUT: FELON DISENFRANCHISEMENT AND AMERICAN DEMOCRACY 191–93 (2006) (arguing that the 2000 election would have turned out differently had Florida not disenfranchised felons who completed their sentences, and further citing the 1960 and 1976 elections as ones that would have resulted in victories for the Republican candidates if those years had seen felon-disenfranchisement rates comparable to those in effect today). *But see id.* at 144–51 (arguing that disenfranchised felons' policy preferences are similar to those of people who are permitted to vote).

identified as the candidate of choice for felons. Solomon Moore, *States Restore Voting Rights for Ex-Convicts, but Issue Remains Politically Sensitive*, N.Y. TIMES Sept. 14, 2008, at A22. *See also* Traci Burch, *Did Disenfranchisement Laws Help Elect President Bush?: New Evidence on the Turnout Rates and Candidate Preferences of Florida's Ex-Felons*, 34 POLITICAL BEHAVIOR 1 (2012); Traci Burch, *Turnout and Party Registration Among Criminal Offenders in the 2008 General Election*, 45 LAW AND SOCIETY REV. 699 (2011); Alan Gerber et al., *Can Incarcerated Felons Be (Re)integrated into the Political System? Results from a Field Experiment* (working paper 2013), available at http://onlinelibrary.wiley.com/doi/10.1111/ajps.12166/abstract; Vesla Weaver & Amy E. Lerman, *Political Consequences of the Carceral State*, 104 AM. POL. SCI. REV. 817 (2010).

After assuming office, the Obama administration has continued its support for restoring felons' voting rights. In 2014, Attorney General Holder "call[ed] upon state leaders and other elected officials across the country to pass clear and consistent reforms to restore the voting rights of all who have served their terms in prison or jail, completed their parole or probation, and paid their fines." Nicole Flatow, *U.S. Attorney General: Time to Restore Voting Rights of Every Person Who Has Completed Their [sic] Criminal Sentence*, THINK PROGRESS (Feb. 11, 2014) *at* http://thinkprogress.org/justice/2014/02/11/3277531/attorney-general-time-restore-voting-rights-person-completed-criminal-sentence/.

4.   Justice Marshall argued that the Constitution did not permit states to limit felons' voting rights by pointing to the bad effects that would flow from having politicians appeal to the felon constituency. For a contrary view, consider *Green v. Board of Elections*, 380 F.2d 445, 451–52 (2d Cir. 1967) (Friendly, J.):

> The early exclusion of felons from the franchise by many states could well have rested on Locke's concept, so influential at the time, that by entering into society every man "authorizes the society, or which is all one, the legislature thereof, to make laws for him as the public good of the society shall require, to the execution whereof his own assistance (as to his own decrees) is due." [John Locke, *An Essay Concerning the True Original, Extent and End of Civil Government* 89 (1689).] A man who breaks the laws he has authorized his agent to make for his own governance could fairly have been thought to have abandoned the right to participate in further administering the compact. On a less theoretical plane, it can scarcely be deemed unreasonable for a state to decide that perpetrators of serious crimes shall not take part in electing the legislators who make the laws, the executives who enforce these, the prosecutors who must try them for further violations, or the judges who are to consider their cases. This is especially so when account is taken of the heavy incidence of recidivism and the prevalence of organized crime. A contention that the equal protection clause requires New York to allow convicted mafiosi to vote for district attorneys or judges would not only be without merit but as obviously so as anything can be.

Is there a difference between (a) allowing Mafiosi to vote for district attorneys, (b) allowing welfare recipients to vote for officials who will determine how much public assistance will be distributed, and (c) allowing billionaires to vote for officials who will determine the amount of the capital-gains tax?

5. The original justification for felon disenfranchisement — which dates from Ancient Greece and which came to the United States through Britain during the colonial period, *see* Alec C. Ewald, *"Civil Death": The Ideological Paradox of Criminal Disenfranchisement Law in the United States*, 2002 WIS. L. REV. 1045, 1059–61 (2002) — was not a fear that felons would vote for politicians who were soft on crime, but rather was the attitude that an infamous criminal was an outsider to the community, ineligible for all of the civil benefits that accompanied membership, including legal protection of his property.[j] Somewhat similarly, today we might defend felon disenfranchisement by arguing that people who have shown an unwillingness to abide by society's most important commands should not have a role in making the rules others are bound to follow. *See* Roger Clegg, et al., *The Case Against Felon Voting*, 2 U. ST. THOMAS J.L. & PUB. POL'Y 1 (2008). Is there anything unconstitutional about excluding felons from the political community and labeling them as outsiders?

6. Is it better for disenfranchisement of felons to take effect automatically upon conviction, or would it be better to incorporate disenfranchisement into the sentencing process, leaving it to the sentencing judge to determine whether disenfranchisement is appropriate, considering "the type of crime committed, the impact of that crime on the victim, and the individual's prior criminal record"? Susan E. Marquardt, Comment, *Deprivation of a Felon's Right to Vote: Constitutional Concerns, Policy Issues and Suggested Reform for Felony Disenfranchisement Law*, 82 U. DET. MERCY L. REV. 279, 297 (2005). Disenfranchisement might be particularly appropriate for election-related crimes or other crimes indicating a lack of trustworthiness. *See id.* at 297–98.

7. Are there any limits on the crimes for which a state may disenfranchise persons found guilty? May a state strip jaywalkers of their voting rights? Drunk drivers? *See* footnote 24 of Justice Marshall's *Ramirez* dissent.

8. Section 2 of the Voting Rights Act, 52 U.S.C. § 10301, as amended in 1982, 96 Stat. 134, prohibits voting qualifications that "result[] in" a class of citizens "hav[ing] less opportunity than other members of the electorate to participate in the political process and to elect representatives of their choice." Section 2 comprises an important part of election law and will be covered extensively in Chapter 5. For present purposes, consider whether § 2 outlaws felon-disenfranchisement laws where those laws have the effect of disenfranchising a disproportionate number of minorities. If § 2 does ban felon-disenfranchisement, does § 2 exceed Congress's power under the Fourteenth and Fifteenth Amendments? The Second, Sixth, and Eleventh Circuits have concluded that § 2 should be read not to outlaw felon-disenfranchisement, because a contrary holding would raise serious constitutional questions. *See Simmons v. Galvin*, 575 F.3d 24 (1st Cir. 2009); *Hayden v. Pataki*,

---

[j] *See* Howard Itzkowitz & Lauren Oldak, *Restoring the Ex-Offender's Right to Vote: Background and Developments*, 11 AM. CRIM. L. REV. 695 (1973). *See also* Gabriel J. Chin, *Felon Disenfranchisement and Democracy in the Late Jim Crow Era*, 5 OHIO ST. J. CRIM. L. 329, 337 (2007) (book review) ("When men wore powdered wigs and knee breeches, felon disenfranchisement was entirely consistent with an elite franchise, restricted as well by race, sex and wealth. Now, however, voting is thought of as a 'right' enjoyed by all adults.").

449 F.3d 305 (2d Cir. 2006) (*en banc*); *Johnson v. Governor*, 405 F.3d 1214 (11th Cir. 2005) (*en banc*); *Wesley v. Collins*, 791 F.2d 1255 (6th Cir. 1986). *See also Baker v. Pataki*, 85 F.3d 919 (2d Cir. 1996) (*en banc*) (dividing 5-5 on the question whether the VRA reaches felon-disenfranchisement). The Ninth Circuit, however, in *Farrakhan v. Gregoire*, 590 F.3d 989, *vacated, reh'g en banc granted*, 603 F.3d 1072 (9th Cir. 2010), held that Washington State's disenfranchisement of felons violated the Voting Rights Act. In the view of that court, "the discriminatory impact of Washington's felon disenfranchisement is attributable to racial discrimination in Washington's criminal justice system; thus, * * * Washington's felon disenfranchisement law violates § 2 of the VRA." *Id*. at 1016. *See also Farrakhan v. Washington*, 338 F.3d 1009 (9th Cir. 2003) (an earlier appeal in the *Farrakhan v. Gregoire* litigation) (concluding that the disproportionate racial backgrounds of persons convicted of felonies should be considered by courts assessing whether felon-disenfranchisement laws violate the Voting Rights Act).

9.   Some members of Congress have proposed legislation that would require states to re-enfranchise convicted felons. Most proposals have received support overwhelmingly from Democrats, but in 2014 Republican Rand Paul introduced a bill that would require states to restore the voting rights of "non-violent" felons (a category that would be clarified by the attorney general) one year after their release from prison or probation. Other proposals favored by supporters of expanded voting rights for criminals do not carve out violent felons and do not have the one-year delay. *See* Burgess Everett, *Rand Paul Seeks to Expand Voting Rights to Some Ex-Cons*, POLITICO (June 22, 2014), *at* http://www.politico.com/story/2014/06/rand-paul-voting-rights-ex-felons-108156.html. Would such measures be constitutional ways of enforcing the Fourteenth Amendment?

10.   *Problem*. New Vermont not only prohibits incarcerated felons from voting, but excludes from the franchise anyone who is confined, whether awaiting trial or as the result of a misdemeanor or felony conviction. Is the exclusion unconstitutional as to either pretrial detainees or convicted misdemeanants? *Cf. O'Brien v. Skinner*, 414 U.S. 524 (1974).

11.   *Problem*. Washington State allows felons to vote upon completion of all requirements of their sentences, including the payment of court costs, fees, and victim restitution. Is such a law constitutional under *Ramirez*, or does it violate the Equal Protection Clause under *Harper* to deny the right to vote to a felon who would be permitted to vote except for his inability (or unwillingness) to satisfy financial obligations? *See Madison v. State*, 163 P.3d 757 (Wash. 2007).

12.   The Court's opinions in *Richardson*, *Lassiter*, and *Harper* (as well as the *Harper* dissents) stressed that the regulations at issue in those cases were not put in place for the purpose of discriminating against disfavored racial groups, even though the regulations may have had the *effect* of disenfranchising proportionately more racial minorities than whites. But consider the situation where a plaintiff alleges that a restriction on voting *was* enacted for a discriminatory purpose. How is a court supposed to determine whether in fact the discriminatory purpose was present? And why should purpose matter at all?

In *Fletcher v. Peck*, 10 U.S. (6 Cranch) 87, 130 (1810), the Supreme Court confronted the question whether Georgia could rescind a land deal that had been entered into because the legislature had been bribed. Writing for the Court, Chief Justice Marshall discussed the problems with considering legislative purpose, and "doubted how far the validity of a law depends upon the motives of its framers":

> If the principle be conceded, that an act of the supreme sovereign power may be declared null by a court, in consequence of the means which procured it, still would there be much difficulty in saying to what extent those means must be applied to produce this effect. Must the vitiating cause operate on a majority, or on what number of its members? Would the act be null, whatever might be the wish of the nation, or would its obligation or nullity depend upon the public sentiment?

Similarly, in *Palmer v. Thompson*, 403 U.S. 217, 225 (1971), the Court refused to consider evidence of legislative purpose when the Jackson, Mississippi, city council closed all the public swimming pools after being faced with a judgment declaring segregation of the pools unconstitutional. As the Court stated,

> It is difficult or impossible for any court to determine the "sole" or "dominant" motivation behind the choices of a group of legislators. Furthermore, * * * [i]f the law is struck down [because of the bad motives of its supporters], * * * it would presumably be valid as soon as the legislature or relevant governing body repassed it for different reasons.

Even if it is agreed that legislative purpose is relevant, determining the legislature's purpose is difficult, and therefore conclusions about legislative purpose can be the subject of dispute. To nobody's surprise, legislators often say things that aren't exactly true. Relying on legislators' explanations for their votes, therefore, might allow legislators to conceal improper, or unconstitutional, motives. *See generally* McNollgast, *Positive Canons: The Role of Legislative Bargains in Statutory Interpretation*, 80 GEO. L.J. 705 (1992).

Further, legislators, like everyone else, take actions for several different reasons. If a legislator votes in favor of a bill partly out of racial prejudice, partly because doing so will get him votes, partly because doing so will get him more campaign contributions, and partly because he thinks the bill actually represents good policy, is his vote the product of a "discriminatory purpose"? Are courts supposed to assess whether he would have voted for the bill if he were not prejudiced? How might a court undertake such an inquiry?

The inquiry is complicated still more, as *Fletcher* recognized, when one attempts to assess the purposes of multiple legislators. Whose purpose matters if 40% of the legislature voted in favor of a statute for legitimate reasons, 15% voted in favor of the statute for unconstitutional reasons, and 45% voted against the statute? *See* WILLIAM N. ESKRIDGE, JR., ET AL., LEGISLATION AND STATUTORY INTERPRETATION 221–30 (2d ed. 2006); McNollgast, *supra*.

Despite the difficulty of articulating both why and how a court would look to legislative purpose in assessing constitutionality, it is settled that legislative purpose *does* matter in some instances. When a facially neutral statute produces a discriminatory effect against a "suspect class," courts will apply strict scrutiny to that statute if, but only if, the statute was enacted because of a discriminatory purpose. *See Hunter v. Underwood*, 471 U.S. 222 (1985), below; *see also Rogers v.*

Lodge, 458 U.S. 613 (1982) (declaring an at-large voting system unconstitutional because it had been maintained for a discriminatory purpose). If the statute was enacted for a different, legitimate purpose, rational-basis scrutiny applies. *See Village of Arlington Heights v. Metropolitan Housing Development Corp.*, 429 U.S. 252 (1977); *Washington v. Davis*, 426 U.S. 229 (1976). *See also Yick Wo v. Hopkins*, 118 U.S. 356 (1886). The Court, in *Arlington Heights*, specified that once the legislature's improper purpose is proven, the defendant bears "the burden of establishing that the same decision would have resulted even had the impermissible purpose not been considered." If the defendant meets that standard, then "the injury complained of [cannot be attributed] to improper consideration of a discriminatory purpose." 429 U.S. at 270.

Lastly, the Court has confronted the ambiguity of the term "purpose" in the context of legislative indifference to the disparate effects caused by statutes. Statutes may be enacted or maintained not out of hostility toward a disaffected group, but simply because the decision-maker does not care that the group is being harmed. Such a case was presented in *Personnel Administrator v. Feeney*, 442 U.S. 256 (1979), which involved a challenge to a veterans' preference for civil-service positions. The challengers argued that the preference advanced the job prospects of men much more than it advanced the prospects of women because the class of veterans was overwhelmingly male. The Court held, however, that rational-basis scrutiny was appropriate unless the challenged action was taken "at least in part 'because of,' not merely 'in spite of,' its adverse effects upon an identifiable group." *Id.* at 279. As a result, it did not matter whether the legislature would have reacted differently if men had been disadvantaged by the preference to the extent that women were.

HUNTER v. UNDERWOOD
Supreme Court of the United States
471 U.S. 222, 105 S. Ct. 1916, 85 L. Ed. 2d 222 (1985)

JUSTICE REHNQUIST delivered the opinion of the Court [in which CHIEF JUSTICE BURGER, JUSTICE BRENNAN, JUSTICE WHITE, JUSTICE MARSHALL, JUSTICE BLACKMUN, JUSTICE STEVENS, and JUSTICE O'CONNOR join].

We are required in this case to decide the constitutionality of Art. VIII, § 182, of the Alabama Constitution of 1901, which provides for the disenfranchisement of persons convicted of, among other offenses, "any crime . . . involving moral turpitude." Appellees Carmen Edwards, a black, and Victor Underwood, a white, have been blocked from the voter rolls pursuant to § 182 by the Boards of Registrars for Montgomery and Jefferson Counties, respectively, because they each have been convicted of presenting a worthless check. * * *

The predecessor to § 182 was Art. VIII, § 3, of the Alabama Constitution of 1875, which denied persons "convicted of treason, embezzlement of public funds, malfeasance in office, larceny, bribery, or other crime punishable by imprisonment in the penitentiary" the right to register, vote or hold public office. These offenses were largely, if not entirely, felonies. The drafters of § 182, which was adopted by the 1901 convention, expanded the list of enumerated crimes substantially to include the following:

"treason, murder, arson, embezzlement, malfeasance in office, larceny, receiving stolen property, obtaining property or money under false pretenses, perjury, subornation of perjury, robbery, assault with intent to rob, burglary, forgery, bribery, assault and battery on the wife, bigamy, living in adultery, sodomy, incest, rape, miscegenation, [and] crime against nature."

The drafters retained the general felony provision — "any crime punishable by imprisonment in the penitentiary" — but also added a new catchall provision covering "any . . . crime involving moral turpitude." This latter phrase is not defined, but it was subsequently interpreted by the Alabama Supreme Court to mean an act that is "immoral in itself, regardless of the fact whether it is punishable by law * * *."

The enumerated crimes contain within them many misdemeanors. If a specific crime does not fall within one of the enumerated offenses, the Alabama Boards of Registrars consult Alabama case law or, in absence of a court precedent, opinions of the Alabama Attorney General to determine whether it is covered by § 182. Various minor nonfelony offenses such as presenting a worthless check and petty larceny fall within the sweep of § 182, while more serious nonfelony offenses such as second-degree manslaughter, assault on a police officer, mailing pornography, and aiding the escape of a misdemeanant do not because they are neither enumerated in § 182 nor considered crimes involving moral turpitude. It is alleged, and the Court of Appeals found, that the crimes selected for inclusion in § 182 were believed by the delegates to be more frequently committed by blacks.

Section 182 on its face is racially neutral, applying equally to anyone convicted of one of the enumerated crimes or a crime falling within one of the catchall provisions. Appellee Edwards nonetheless claims that the provision has had a racially discriminatory impact. [T]he Court of Appeals implicitly found the evidence of discriminatory impact indisputable:

"The registrars' expert estimated that by January 1903 section 182 had disfranchised approximately ten times as many blacks as whites. This disparate effect persists today. In Jefferson and Montgomery Counties blacks are by even the most modest estimates at least 1.7 times as likely as whites to suffer disfranchisement under section 182 for the commission of nonprison offenses."

So far as we can tell the impact of the provision has not been contested, and we can find no evidence in the record below or in the briefs and oral argument in this Court that would undermine this finding by the Court of Appeals.

Presented with a neutral state law that produces disproportionate effects along racial lines, the Court of Appeals was correct in applying the approach of *Arlington Heights* [v. *Metropolitan Housing Development Corp.*, 429 U.S. 252, 264–65 (1977)] to determine whether the law violates the Equal Protection Clause of the Fourteenth Amendment:

"[O]fficial action will not be held unconstitutional solely because it results in a racially disproportionate impact. . . . Proof of racially discriminatory intent or purpose is required to show a violation of the Equal Protection Clause."

See Washington v. *Davis*, 426 U.S. 229, 239 (1976). Once racial discrimination is shown to have been a "substantial" or "motivating" factor behind enactment of the law, the burden shifts to the law's defenders to demonstrate that the law would have been enacted without this factor.

Proving the motivation behind official action is often a problematic undertaking. * * * With respect to Congress, the Court said in *United States* v. *O'Brien*, 391 U.S. 367, 383–384 (1968):

> "Inquiries into congressional motives or purposes are a hazardous matter. When the issue is simply the interpretation of legislation, the Court will look to statements by legislators for guidance as to the purpose of the legislature, because the benefit to sound decision-making in this circumstance is thought sufficient to risk the possibility of misreading Congress' purpose. It is entirely a different matter when we are asked to void a statute that is, under well-settled criteria, constitutional on its face, on the basis of what fewer than a handful of Congressmen said about it. What motivates one legislator to make a speech about a statute is not necessarily what motivates scores of others to enact it, and the stakes are sufficiently high for us to eschew guesswork."

But the sort of difficulties of which the Court spoke in *O'Brien* do not obtain in this case. Although understandably no "eyewitnesses" to the 1901 proceedings testified, testimony and opinions of historians were offered and received without objection. These showed that the Alabama Constitutional Convention of 1901 was part of a movement that swept the post-Reconstruction South to disenfranchise blacks. The delegates to the all-white convention were not secretive about their purpose. John B. Knox, president of the convention, stated in his opening address: "And what is it that we want to do? Why it is within the limits imposed by the Federal Constitution, to establish white supremacy in this State."

Indeed, neither the District Court nor appellants seriously dispute the claim that this zeal for white supremacy ran rampant at the convention.

* * * Having reviewed this evidence, we are persuaded that * * * § 182 was enacted with the intent of disenfranchising blacks. * * * At oral argument in this Court appellants' counsel essentially conceded this point, stating: "I would be very blind and naive [to] try to come up and stand before this Court and say that race was not a factor in the enactment of Section 182; that race did not play a part in the decisions of those people who were at the constitutional convention of 1901 and I won't do that."

In their brief to this Court, appellants maintain on the basis of their expert's testimony that the real purpose behind § 182 was to disenfranchise poor whites as well as blacks. * * * Even were we to accept this explanation as correct, it hardly saves § 182 from invalidity. The explanation concedes both that discrimination against blacks, as well as against poor whites, was a motivating factor for the provision and that § 182 certainly would not have been adopted by the convention or ratified by the electorate in the absence of the racially discriminatory motivation.

[A]ppellants make the further argument that the existence of a permissible motive for § 182, namely, the disenfranchisement of poor whites, trumps any proof of a parallel impermissible motive. Whether or not intentional disenfranchisement of poor whites would qualify as a "permissible motive," * * * an additional purpose to discriminate against poor whites would not render nugatory the purpose to discriminate against all blacks, and it is beyond peradventure that the latter was a "but-for" motivation for the enactment of § 182. * * *

At oral argument in this Court, the appellants' counsel suggested that, regardless of the original purpose of § 182, events occurring in the succeeding 80 years had legitimated the provision. Some of the more blatantly discriminatory selections, such as assault and battery on the wife and miscegenation, have been struck down by the courts, and appellants contend that the remaining crimes — felonies and moral turpitude misdemeanors — are acceptable bases for denying the franchise. Without deciding whether § 182 would be valid if enacted today without any impermissible motivation, we simply observe that its original enactment was motivated by a desire to discriminate against blacks on account of race and the section continues to this day to have that effect. As such, it violates equal protection under *Arlington Heights.*

* * * The single remaining question is whether § 182 is excepted from the operation of the Equal Protection Clause of § 1 of the Fourteenth Amendment by the "other crime" provision of § 2 of that Amendment. Without again considering the implicit authorization of § 2 to deny the vote to citizens "for participation in rebellion, or other crime," *see Richardson* v. *Ramirez,* 418 U.S. 24 (1974) [p. 45], we are confident that § 2 was not designed to permit the purposeful racial discrimination attending the enactment and operation of § 182 which otherwise violates § 1 of the Fourteenth Amendment. Nothing in our opinion in *Richardson* v. *Ramirez* suggests the contrary.

The judgment of the Court of Appeals is

Affirmed.

Justice Powell took no part in the consideration or decision of this case.

Notes and Questions

1.   Despite the Court's reliance on legislative history to understand the purpose behind the voting exclusion, the expert testimony in *Underwood* disclosed that the history may not accurately represent the motivations of the individuals who voted for the provision:

"A. * * * Repeatedly through the debates, the delegates say that they are interested in disfranchising blacks and not interested in disfranchising whites. And in fact, they go out of their way to make that point. . . . But the point that I am trying to make is that this is really speaking to the galleries, that it is attempting to say to the white electorate that must ratify this constitution what it is necessary for that white electorate to be convinced of in order to get them to vote for it, and not merely echoing what a great many delegates say. . . . [I]n general, the delegates aggressively say that they are not interested in disfranchising any whites. I think falsely, but that's what they say.

"Q. So they were simply trying to overplay the extent to which they wanted to disenfranchise blacks, but that they did desire to disenfranchise practically all of the blacks?

"A. Oh, absolutely, certainly."

Does this exchange indicate that legislative history is not to be trusted as a way of understanding legislative purpose, or, instead, that legislative history can be a powerful tool for understanding legislative purpose if placed in proper context?

2.   The opinion of the Court concludes "that § 182 certainly would not have been adopted by the convention *or ratified by the electorate* in the absence of the racially discriminatory motivation." 471 U.S. at 231 (emphasis added). Does the Court mean to imply that *voters*, acting out of racial prejudice, could render unconstitutional a facially neutral law? What if the provision were enacted as part of an initiative? Conversely, could a pure motive on the part of "the electorate" save a referendum that was presented to the voters by a biased legislature?

3.   If, one year after *Underwood* was decided, Alabama were to enact a law identical to the provision struck down in that case, would it violate the Equal Protection Clause? Would such a law be distinguishable from the one in *Richardson v. Ramirez*? *See Johnson v. Governor*, 405 F.3d 1214, 1223–24 (11th Cir. 2005) (holding that the 1968 re-enactment of Florida's 1868 disenfranchisement law "eliminated any taint from the allegedly discriminatory 1868 provision, particularly in light of the passage of time and the fact that, at the time of the 1968 enactment, no one had ever alleged that the 1868 provision was motivated by racial animus"); *Cotton v. Fordice*, 157 F.3d 388 (5th Cir. 1988) (holding that Mississippi's 1950 and 1968 revisions of a discriminatory 1890 disenfranchisement law, removing burglary and adding murder and rape as disenfranchising crimes, rendered the law constitutional). *Cf. McCreary County v. ACLU*, 545 U.S. 844, 870–74 (2005) (holding in an Establishment Clause case that previous religious displays could demonstrate the purpose behind a later display, but that "we do not decide that the Counties' past actions forever taint any effort on their part to" display the Ten Commandments as part of an educational message about the foundations of American law).

4.   If the hypothetical law discussed in Note 3 would be constitutional, was there any justification for the Court to strike down the actual provision? In other words, should a discriminatory purpose for a law passed generations ago nullify modern attempts to enforce it for legitimate reasons?

5.   If a felon-disenfranchisement provision were enacted for the sole purpose, and had the effect, of stripping the vote from poor persons of all races, would it be constitutional?

6.   Though the expansion of the franchise has proceeded unevenly, American democracy has seen several barriers to political participation fall, often through or enabled by the Supreme Court's interpretation of the Constitution. As this section has discussed, these barriers include qualifications based on property ownership,

wealth, payment of taxes, literacy, race, sex, and age (at least for those who have reached age eighteen), and the barrier to political participation by convicted felons has shown some signs of weakening despite *Ramirez*'s holding that it is constitutional. Does this history convince you that John Adams was correct in predicting that "[o]nce it was acknowledged that people had a *right* to vote, it would be difficult to deny the right to anyone: there would 'be no end of it' * * *"? ALEXANDER KEYSSAR, THE RIGHT TO VOTE: THE CONTESTED HISTORY OF DEMOCRACY IN THE UNITED STATES 13 (2000). Alexis de Tocqueville made a similar prediction in his classic *Democracy in America*:

> When a nation begins to modify the elective qualification, it may easily be foreseen that, sooner or later, that qualification will be entirely abolished. There is no more invariable rule in the history of society: the further electoral rights are extended, the greater is the need of extending them; for after each concession the strength of the democracy increases, and its demands increase with its strength. The ambition of those who are below the appointed rate is irritated in exact proportion to the great number of those who are above it. The exception at last becomes the rule; concession follows concession, and no stop can be made short of universal suffrage.

ALEXIS DE TOCQUEVILLE, DEMOCRACY IN AMERICA 57 (Richard D. Heffner trans., Mentor 1956) (1835).

4. *The Disinterested*

KRAMER v. UNION FREE SCHOOL DISTRICT NO. 15
Supreme Court of the United States
395 U.S. 621, 89 S. Ct. 1886, 23 L. Ed. 2d 583 (1969)

MR. CHIEF JUSTICE WARREN delivered the opinion of the Court [in which MR. JUSTICE DOUGLAS, MR. JUSTICE BRENNAN, MR. JUSTICE WHITE, and MR. JUSTICE MARSHALL join].[k]

In this case we are called on to determine whether § 2012 of the New York Education Law is constitutional. The legislation provides that in certain New York school districts residents who are otherwise eligible to vote in state and federal elections may vote in the school district election only if they (1) own (or lease) taxable real property within the district, or (2) are parents (or have custody of) children enrolled in the local public schools. Appellant, a bachelor who neither owns nor leases taxable real property, filed suit in federal court claiming that § 2012 denied him equal protection of the laws in violation of the Fourteenth Amendment. * * * Finding that § 2012 does violate the Equal Protection Clause of the Fourteenth Amendment, we reverse. * * *

Appellant is a 31-year-old college-educated stockbroker who lives in his parents' home in the Union Free School District No. 15, a district to which § 2012 applies. He is a citizen of the United States and has voted in federal and state elections since

---

[k] Justice Fortas resigned one month before this decision was released; only eight Justices participated in it. [— Eds.]

1959. However, since he has no children and neither owns nor leases taxable real property, appellant's attempts to register for and vote in the local school district elections have been unsuccessful. After the school district rejected his 1965 application, appellant instituted the present class action challenging the constitutionality of the voter eligibility requirements. * * *

At the outset, it is important to note what is not at issue in this case. The requirements of § 2012 that school district voters must (1) be citizens of the United States, (2) be bona fide residents of the school district, and (3) be at least 21 years of age are not challenged. Appellant agrees that the States have the power to impose reasonable citizenship, age, and residency requirements on the availability of the ballot. The sole issue in this case is whether the additional requirements of § 2012 — requirements which prohibit some district residents who are otherwise qualified by age and citizenship from participating in district meetings and school board elections — violate the Fourteenth Amendment's command that no State shall deny persons equal protection of the laws.

"In determining whether or not a state law violates the Equal Protection Clause, we must consider the facts and circumstances behind the law, the interests which the State claims to be protecting, and the interests of those who are disadvantaged by the classification." And, in this case, we must give the statute a close and exacting examination. "[S]ince the right to exercise the franchise in a free and unimpaired manner is preservative of other basic civil and political rights, any alleged infringement of the right of citizens to vote must be carefully and meticulously scrutinized." *Reynolds* v. *Sims*, 377 U.S. 533, 562 (1964) [p. 173]. This careful examination is necessary because statutes distributing the franchise constitute the foundation of our representative society. Any unjustified discrimination in determining who may participate in political affairs or in the selection of public officials undermines the legitimacy of representative government.

Thus, state apportionment statutes, which may dilute the effectiveness of some citizens' votes, receive close scrutiny from this Court. No less rigid an examination is applicable to statutes denying the franchise to citizens who are otherwise qualified by residence and age. Statutes granting the franchise to residents on a selective basis always pose the danger of denying some citizens any effective voice in the governmental affairs which substantially affect their lives. Therefore, if a challenged state statute grants the right to vote to some *bona fide* residents of requisite age and citizenship and denies the franchise to others, the Court must determine whether the exclusions are necessary to promote a compelling state interest.

And, for these reasons, the deference usually given to the judgment of legislators does not extend to decisions concerning which resident citizens may participate in the election of legislators and other public officials. Those decisions must be carefully scrutinized by the Court to determine whether each resident citizen has, as far as is possible, an equal voice in the selections. Accordingly, when we are reviewing statutes which deny some residents the right to vote, the general presumption of constitutionality afforded state statutes and the traditional approval given state classifications if the Court can conceive of a "rational basis" for the distinctions made are not applicable. The presumption of constitutionality and the approval given "rational" classifications in other types of enactments are based on an assumption that the institutions of state government are structured so as to represent fairly all the people. However, when the challenge to the statute is in effect a challenge of this basic assumption, the assumption can no longer serve as the basis for presuming constitutionality. And, the assumption is no less under attack because the legislature which decides who may participate at the various levels of political choice is fairly elected. Legislation which delegates decision making to bodies elected by only a portion of those eligible to vote for the legislature can cause unfair representation. Such legislation can exclude a minority of voters from any voice in the decisions just as effectively as if the decisions were made by legislators the minority had no voice in selecting.[10]

The need for exacting judicial scrutiny of statutes distributing the franchise is undiminished simply because, under a different statutory scheme, the offices subject to election might have been filled through appointment.[11] States do have latitude in determining whether certain public officials shall be selected by election or chosen by appointment and whether various questions shall be submitted to the voters. * * * However, "once the franchise is granted to the electorate, lines may not be drawn which are inconsistent with the Equal Protection Clause of the Fourteenth Amendment." *Harper* v. *Virginia Bd. of Elections*, 383 U.S. 663, 665 (1966) [p. 37]. * * *

Appellant asserts that excluding him from participation in the district elections denies him equal protection of the laws. He contends that he and others of his class are substantially interested in and significantly affected by the school meeting decisions. All members of the community have an interest in the quality and structure of public education, appellant says, and he urges that "the decisions taken by local boards * * * may have grave consequences to the entire population." Appellant also argues that the level of property taxation affects him, even though he does not own property, as property tax levels affect the price of goods and services in the community.

We turn therefore to question whether the exclusion is necessary to promote a compelling state interest. First appellees argue that the State has a legitimate interest in limiting the franchise in school district elections to "members of the community of interest" — those "primarily interested in such elections." Second, appellees urge that the State may reasonably and permissibly conclude that "property taxpayers" (including lessees of taxable property who share the tax burden through rent payments) and parents of the children enrolled in the district's schools are those "primarily interested" in school affairs.

We do not understand appellees to argue that the State is attempting to limit the franchise to those "subjectively concerned" about school matters. Rather, they appear to argue that the State's legitimate interest is in restricting a voice in school matters to those "directly affected" by such decisions. The State apparently reasons

---

[10] Thus, statutes structuring local government units receive no less exacting an examination merely because the state legislature is fairly elected. See *Avery* v. *Midland County*, 390 U.S. 474, 481, n.6 (1968).

[11] Similarly, no less a showing of a compelling justification for disenfranchising residents is required merely because the questions scheduled for the election need not have been submitted to the voters.

that since the schools are financed in part by local property taxes, persons whose out-of-pocket expenses are "directly" affected by property tax changes should be allowed to vote. Similarly, parents of children in school are thought to have a "direct" stake in school affairs and are given a vote.

Appellees argue that it is necessary to limit the franchise to those "primarily interested" in school affairs because "the ever increasing complexity of the many interacting phases of the school system and structure make it extremely difficult for the electorate fully to understand the whys and wherefores of the detailed operations of the school system." Appellees say that many communications of school boards and school administrations are sent home to the parents through the district pupils and are "not broadcast to the general public"; thus, nonparents will be less informed than parents. Further, appellees argue, those who are assessed for local property taxes (either directly or indirectly through rent) will have enough of an interest "through the burden on their pocketbooks, to acquire such information as they may need."

We need express no opinion as to whether the State in some circumstances might limit the exercise of the franchise to those "primarily interested" or "primarily affected." * * * For, assuming, *arguendo*, that New York legitimately might limit the franchise in these school district elections to those "primarily interested in school affairs," close scrutiny of the § 2012 classifications demonstrates that they do not accomplish this purpose with sufficient precision to justify denying appellant the franchise.

Whether classifications allegedly limiting the franchise to those resident citizens "primarily interested" deny those excluded equal protection of the laws depends, *inter alia*, on whether all those excluded are in fact substantially less interested or affected than those the statute includes. In other words, the classifications must be tailored so that the exclusion of appellant and members of his class is necessary to achieve the articulated state goal.[14] Section 2012 does not meet the exacting standard of precision we require of statutes which selectively distribute the franchise. The classifications in § 2012 permit inclusion of many persons who have, at best, a remote and indirect interest in school affairs and, on the other hand, exclude others who have a distinct and direct interest in the school meeting decisions.[15]

Nor do appellees offer any justification for the exclusion of seemingly interested and informed residents — other than to argue that the § 2012 classifications include those "whom the State could understandably deem to be the most intimately interested in actions taken by the school board," and urge that "the task of * * * balancing the interest of the community in the maintenance of orderly school district elections against the interest of any individual in voting in such elections

---

[14] Of course, if the exclusions are necessary to promote the articulated state interest, we must then determine whether the interest promoted by limiting the franchise constitutes a compelling state interest. We do not reach that issue in this case.

[15] For example, appellant resides with his parents in the school district, pays state and federal taxes and is interested in and affected by school board decisions; however, he has no vote. On the other hand, an uninterested unemployed young man who pays no state or federal taxes, but who rents an apartment in the district, can participate in the election.

should clearly remain with the Legislature." But the issue is not whether the legislative judgments are rational. A more exacting standard obtains. The issue is whether the § 2012 requirements do in fact sufficiently further a compelling state interest to justify denying the franchise to appellant and members of his class. The requirements of § 2012 are not sufficiently tailored to limiting the franchise to those "primarily interested" in school affairs to justify the denial of the franchise to appellant and members of his class.

The judgment of the United States District Court for the Eastern District of New York is therefore reversed. The case is remanded for further proceedings consistent with this opinion.

It is so ordered.

Mr. Justice Stewart, with whom Mr. Justice Black and Mr. Justice Harlan join, dissenting. * * *

Although at times variously phrased, the traditional test of a statute's validity under the Equal Protection Clause is a familiar one: a legislative classification is invalid only "if it rest[s] on grounds wholly irrelevant to achievement of the regulation's objectives." It was under just such a test that the literacy requirement involved in *Lassiter* [v. *Northampton County Board of Elections*, 360 U.S. 45 (1959)] [p. 8] was upheld. The premise of our decision in that case was that a State may constitutionally impose upon its citizens voting requirements reasonably "designed to promote intelligent use of the ballot." A similar premise underlies the proposition, consistently endorsed by this Court, that a State may exclude nonresidents from participation in its elections. Such residence requirements, designed to help ensure that voters have a substantial stake in the outcome of elections and an opportunity to become familiar with the candidates and issues voted upon, are entirely permissible exercises of state authority. Indeed, the appellant explicitly concedes, as he must, the validity of voting requirements relating to residence, literacy, and age. Yet he argues — and the Court accepts the argument — that the voting qualifications involved here somehow have a different constitutional status. I am unable to see the distinction.

Clearly a State may reasonably assume that its residents have a greater stake in the outcome of elections held within its boundaries than do other persons. Likewise, it is entirely rational for a state legislature to suppose that residents, being generally better informed regarding state affairs than are nonresidents, will be more likely than nonresidents to vote responsibly. And the same may be said of legislative assumptions regarding the electoral competence of adults and literate persons on the one hand, and of minors and illiterates on the other. It is clear, of course, that lines thus drawn can not infallibly perform their intended legislative function. Just as "[i]lliterate people may be intelligent voters," [*Lassiter*], nonresidents or minors might also in some instances be interested, informed, and intelligent participants in the electoral process. Persons who commute across a state line to work may well have a great stake in the affairs of the State in which they are employed; some college students under 21 may be both better informed and more passionately interested in political affairs than many adults. But such discrepancies are the inevitable concomitant of the line drawing that is essential to law making. So long as the classification is rationally related to a permissible legislative end, therefore — as are residence, literacy, and age requirements imposed with respect to voting — there is no denial of equal protection.

Thus judged, the statutory classification involved here seems to me clearly to be valid. New York has made the judgment that local educational policy is best left to those persons who have certain direct and definable interests in that policy: those who are either immediately involved as parents of school children or who, as owners or lessees of taxable property are burdened with the local cost of funding school district operations. True, persons outside those classes may be genuinely interested in the conduct of a school district's business — just as commuters from New Jersey may be genuinely interested in the outcome of a New York City election. But unless this Court is to claim a monopoly of wisdom regarding the sound operation of school systems in the 50 States, I see no way to justify the conclusion that the legislative classification involved here is not rationally related to a legitimate legislative purpose. * * *

With good reason, the Court does not really argue the contrary. Instead, it strikes down New York's statute by asserting that the traditional equal protection standard is inapt in this case, and that a considerably stricter standard — under which classifications relating to "the franchise" are to be subjected to "exacting judicial scrutiny" — should be applied. But the asserted justification for applying such a standard cannot withstand analysis.

The Court is quite explicit in explaining why it believes this statute should be given "close scrutiny":

> "The presumption of constitutionality and the approval given 'rational' classifications in other types of enactments are based on an assumption that the institutions of state government are structured so as to represent fairly all the people. However, when the challenge to the statute is in effect a challenge of this basic assumption, the assumption can no longer serve as the basis for presuming constitutionality."

I am at a loss to understand how such reasoning is at all relevant to the present case. The voting qualifications at issue have been promulgated, not by Union Free School District No. 15, but by the New York State Legislature, and the appellant is of course fully able to participate in the election of representatives in that body. There is simply no claim whatever here that the state government is not "structured so as to represent fairly all the people," including the appellant. * * *

In any event, it seems to me that under any equal protection standard, short of a doctrinaire insistence that universal suffrage is somehow mandated by the Constitution, the appellant's claim must be rejected. First of all, it must be emphasized — despite the Court's undifferentiated references to what it terms "the franchise" — that we are dealing here, not with a general election, but with a limited, special-purpose election.[9] The appellant is eligible to vote in all state, local,

---

[9] Special-purpose governmental authorities such as water, lighting, and sewer districts exist in various sections of the country, and participation in such districts is undoubtedly limited in many instances to those who partake of the agency's services and are assessed for its expenses. The

and federal elections in which general governmental policy is determined. He is fully able, therefore, to participate not only in the processes by which the requirements for school district voting may be changed, but also in those by which the levels of state and federal financial assistance to the District are determined. He clearly is not locked into any self-perpetuating status of exclusion from the electoral process.

Secondly, the * * * appellant's status is merely that of a citizen who says he is interested in the affairs of his local public schools. If the Constitution requires that he must be given a decision-making role in the governance of those affairs, then it seems to me that any individual who seeks such a role must be given it. * * *

Notes and Questions

1.   Note the slippery way in which Chief Justice Warren used the term "interested." New York sought to bar from voting people who lacked an "interest" in the outcome of school board elections, *i.e.*, those people who would not be "directly affected" thereby. In holding that the voting restriction was not narrowly tailored to accomplish that purpose, however, the Court (in footnote 15) pointed out that Kramer was "interested in and affected by school board decisions." The Court thus appeared to use "interest" in the sense of "subjectively concerned" — precisely the sense in which the state was *not* using the term.

2.   In what way was Kramer "affected by school board decisions"? Why should he have any say in the making of school policy?

3.   Dissenting from the three-judge district-court decision that was reversed by the opinion you have just read, Judge Weinstein pointed to other types of individuals who were denied the ability to vote under § 2012:

1. young adults such as plaintiff residing in family homes;

2. boarders and lodgers;

3. elder citizens and others living in the homes of their children or other relatives;

4. spouses of persons renting homes;

5. parents not owning or renting homes whose children attend private or parochial schools;

6. parents, not owning or renting homes, whose children attend special public schools outside the district;

7. parents, not owning or renting homes, whose children are too young or too old to attend public schools; and

8. clergy, military, and others living on tax exempt property.

---

constitutional validity of such a policy is, it seems to me, unquestionable. And while it is true, as the appellant argues, that a school system has a more pervasive influence in the community than do most other such special-purpose authorities, I cannot agree that that difference in degree presents anything approaching a distinction of constitutional dimension.

Kramer v. Union Free School District No. 15, 282 F. Supp. 70, 75 (E.D.N.Y. 1968) (Weinstein, J., dissenting), *rev'd*, 395 U.S. 621 (1969). Should states be able to exclude any of these groups from voting? All of them? Does *Kramer* permit the exclusion of any of these groups?

4.   Suppose New York had prohibited persons convicted of certain lewd acts involving minors from voting. Is such an exclusion narrowly tailored to a compelling interest? What if the exclusion extended to all sex-related crimes? Failure to pay child support?

5.   Was Kramer any more "affected" because he *resided* in the district? The Court was careful to note that the case did not present a challenge to the residency requirement for voting, and indeed residency requirements have been uniformly upheld. Nevertheless, one might question whether Kramer's interest was any more significant than, for example, that of a resident of a neighboring district who employs graduates of the school district in which he wishes to vote. Should states be required to permit such non-residents to vote in school-district elections?

6.   Or must states *prohibit* non-residents from voting, on the ground that if non-residents vote, they dilute the voting strength of residents? *Compare May v. Town of Mountain Village*, 132 F.3d 576 (10th Cir. 1997) (permitting voting by non-residents) *with Board of County Commissioners of Shelby County v. Burson*, 121 F.3d 244 (6th Cir. 1997) (striking down a scheme permitting Memphis city residents to vote for officials of both the Memphis City School District and the Shelby County School District, which was comprised of the areas of the county not including the city).

Should the Constitution recognize a difference between "dual residents," who maintain bona fide residences in multiple locales, and nonresident property owners? *See* Ashira Pelman Ostrow, Note, *Dual Resident Voting: Traditional Disenfranchisement and Prospects for Change*, 102 COLUM. L. REV. 1954 (2002). Professor Gerald Frug argues that extending the franchise to people who work, but do not live, in a locality could foster a sense of "regional citizenship." Gerald E. Frug, *Beyond Regional Government*, 115 HARV. L. REV. 1763, 1828–30 (2002). Should such a concept play a role in expounding the constitutional right to vote?

7.   Was the more important narrow-tailoring problem not that too few people (such as Kramer) were permitted to vote, but rather that *too many* people were permitted to vote? Could New York have complied with the Equal Protection Clause by excluding persons such as the Court's hypothetical "uninterested unemployed young man who pays no state or federal taxes, but who rents an apartment in the district"?

8.   If the "uninterested" — those who are subjectively unconcerned — are unlikely to vote when given the opportunity, why should the Equal Protection Clause be violated if a state permits them to vote? In other words, should New York be able to defend its decision to allow all leaseholders to vote by saying, "We want decisions in school-board elections to be made by interested voters, but only interested voters will in fact turn out to the polls"? In answering, be conscious of the ambiguity of the term "interested," as discussed in Note 1.

9.   Imagine that you are counsel to the New York Legislature, and are charged with drafting a replacement for § 2012. Can you construct voter qualifications that would limit the franchise to "interested" persons and pass the Court's narrow-tailoring analysis?

10.   *Problem.* Analyze the constitutionality of the restrictions on the franchise in these hypothetical school districts:

A. Chester A. Arthur School District permits all district residents who have reached age eighteen to vote. The statute is challenged by Alice, a seventeen-year-old, honor-roll high-school student, who alleges that excluding her from voting because of age violates the Equal Protection Clause.

B. James Buchanan School District permits all district residents who have reached age eighteen to vote, except that it prohibits current students in the district from voting. The rationale is that current students are too likely to vote out of short-term self-interest, and not to support policies that are designed to provide long-lasting educational benefits. Bianca, an eighteen-year-old high-school senior, challenges the restriction.

C. Grover Cleveland School District permits all district residents who have reached age eighteen to vote and, in addition, permits students currently enrolled at Calvin Coolidge High School, the only public high school in the district, to vote regardless of age. The scheme is challenged by Carter, a resident of the district and a sixteen-year-old junior at the Chesterfield Academy, a private high school located within the district.

11.   Remember that narrow tailoring is only part of the strict-scrutiny analysis. If strict scrutiny is applied to a classification, the classification is unconstitutional unless narrowly tailored *to a compelling government interest.* In *Kramer*, the Court struck down § 2012 because it was not sufficiently tailored to the government's cited interest in limiting the franchise to "interested" persons. Accordingly, the Court did not need to reach the question whether the interest was compelling. If § 2012 had been narrowly tailored, by permitting all persons — but only those persons — "interested" in school policy to vote, could the classification have survived the compelling-interest prong?

In this regard, consider Rex E. Lee, *Mr. Herbert Spencer and the Bachelor Stockbroker:* Kramer v. Union Free School District No. 15, 15 ARIZ. L. REV. 457, 464–65 (1973):

Clearly, there is no compelling reason why the State of New York should not allow Kramer and all other resident bachelors of voting age to vote in the school board elections for Union Free School District No. 15. For that matter, neither is there any compelling reason for denying the franchise to intelligent and well-informed 17 year olds, convicted felons, non-residents or non-citizens. * * * Indeed, there is no governmental regulation as to which some person cannot make a case for the proposition that it affects him unfairly vis-à-vis someone else. * * *

The net result [of requiring a compelling reason to deny an individual a right], nominally, is total and absolute equality where judicially declared "fundamental" interests are involved. Ironically, however, since application of the test will almost certainly result in constitutional invalidity, the real consequence of the Court's new equal protection test is a shift away from questions concerning equality and a new concentration on what is "fundamental."

12.   Before the Twenty-Sixth Amendment prohibited states and the national government from denying the right to vote to anyone eighteen or older on account of age, Congress attempted to accomplish the same result by statute. The 1970 amendments to the Voting Rights Act, 84 Stat. 314, purported to lower the voting age across the nation to eighteen. In *Oregon v. Mitchell*, 400 U.S. 112 (1970), the Supreme Court considered the constitutionality of that provision. Four Justices (Douglas, Brennan, White, and Marshall) thought the provision constitutional as a means of enforcing the Equal Protection Clause. Four Justices (Burger, Harlan, Stewart, and Blackmun) thought that Congress had no authority to alter the voting age. As Justice Harlan reasoned, "the suggestion that members of the age group between 18 and 21 are threatened with unconstitutional discrimination * * * is little short of fanciful. [A]ll the evidence indicates that Congress — led on by recent decisions of this Court — thought simply that 18-year-olds were fairly entitled to vote and that Congress could give it to them by legislation." *Id.* at 212–13 (Harlan, J., concurring in part and dissenting in part).

The controlling opinion of Justice Black held that Congress could lower the voting age in federal elections, but not in state ones. Justice Black reasoned that Congress's power to "make or alter" the "Manner" of congressional elections gave it the power to lower the qualifications for voters in such elections, and "[i]t cannot be seriously contended that Congress has less power over the conduct of presidential elections than it has over congressional elections." *Id.* at 124 (opinion of Black, J.). As to state elections, however, Justice Black held that the Constitution preserved the autonomous authority of states to set voting qualifications. Can the combination of these two halves of Justice Black's reasoning be squared with Art. I, § 2 of the Constitution and the Seventeenth Amendment, which provide that voters in congressional elections "shall have the Qualifications requisite for Electors of the most numerous Branch of the State Legislature"?

The Supreme Court appears to have rejected Justice Black's reasoning. In *Arizona v. Inter Tribal Council of Arizona, Inc.*, 133 S. Ct. 2247 (2013), the Court held that Arizona's requirement that persons registering to vote present proof of citizenship was preempted by a federal requirement in the National Voter Registration Act that states "accept and use" a federal form which demanded no proof of citizenship. 52 U.S.C. § 20505(a)(1). Arizona had insisted that if the federal form prevented it from requiring such proof, it would be an unconstitutional interference with the state power to determine voter qualifications. The Court suggested that Arizona may well have been correct (*see* 133 S. Ct. at 2258–59) ("Arizona is correct that it would raise serious constitutional doubts if a federal statute precluded a State from obtaining the information necessary to enforce its voter qualifications."), but that there was a way to avoid the conflict: Arizona could demand that the Election Assistance Commission to amend the form to add a state-specific instruction telling Arizona registrants of the need to present proof of citizenship.

For present purposes, the key question is the extent of Congress's power to regulate the registration process as part of its authority under the Elections Clause, U.S. Const. art. I, § 4, cl. 1, to "make or alter" * * * regulations concerning the "Times, Places and Manner of holding Elections for Senators and Representatives." *Inter Tribal Council* provided a bright-line rule: "[T]he Elections Clause empowers Congress to regulate *how* federal elections are held, but not *who* may vote in them." 133 S. Ct. at 2257.

This rule, although consistent with the Clause itself, is inconsistent with the outcome in *Oregon v. Mitchell*. *Inter Tribal Council* quoted approvingly from the dissent in *Mitchell*, which argued that "[i]t is difficult to see how words could be clearer in stating what Congress can control and what it cannot control. Surely nothing in these provisions lends itself to the view that voting qualifications in federal elections are to be set by Congress." 133 S. Ct. at 2258 (quoting *Mitchell*, 400 U.S. at 210 (Harlan, J., concurring in part and dissenting in part)). Although Justice Black's opinion in *Mitchell* did conclude that Congress could invoke the Elections Clause to require states to permit 18 year-olds to vote, *Inter Tribal Court* brushed it aside: "That result, which lacked a majority rationale, is of minimal precedential value here." *Inter Tribal Council*, 133 S. Ct. at 2258 n.8.

In *Kobach v. United States Election Assistance Commission*, 6 F. Supp. 3d 1252 (D. Kan. 2014), the district court followed the Supreme Court's suggestion and held that the EAC was required to include a proof-of-citizenship requirement among the state-specific instructions for Kansas and Arizona on the NVRA form. The Tenth Circuit reversed, however, holding that the EAC was "not compulsorily mandated to approve state-requested changes to the Federal Form." 772 F.3d 1183 (10th Cir. 2014).

13. States vary in their methods for selecting judges. Some states use the "Missouri Plan," or "merit selection," one element of which is the use of commissions to screen potential nominees. Details differ across states, but commonly the commission selects a certain number of candidates, and the governor must choose from among the candidates approved by the commission. The commission, therefore, has considerable power in the selection process.

The membership of the commissions is determined by a variety of methods in the states using forms of the Missouri Plan, but lawyers — and in particular the organized bar — are sometimes given disproportionate influence in the selection of commissioners. *See* Stephen J. Ware, *The Missouri Plan in National Perspective*, 74 Mo. L. Rev. 751 (2009). Some states' commissions, for example, have a certain number of members chosen by the organized bar; in Kansas, a majority of the nine-member commission is elected by the bar.[1]

Does such a system violate the Equal Protection Clause, as interpreted in *Kramer*? *See* Nelson Lund, *May Lawyers Be Given the Power to Elect Those Who Choose Our Judges? "Merit Selection" and Constitutional Law*, 34 Harv. J.L. & Pub. Pol'y 1043 (2011). *Cf. Hellebust v. Brownback*, 42 F.3d 1331 (10th Cir. 1994)

---

[1] The power granted to the bar may result in candidates approved by the commissions who are more ideologically attuned to the interests of the organized bar than would be the case if the bar lacked such influence. *See* Brian T. Fitzpatrick, *The Politics of Merit Selection*, 74 Mo. L. Rev. 675 (2009).

(striking down Kansas's procedure for selecting members of the state's Board of Agriculture because the procedure empowered delegates from private agricultural associations to select members of the board).

14.   Did it violate the Equal Protection Clause for states to restrict voting to twenty-one-year-olds, as forty-six of the states did at the time suit was filed in *Oregon v. Mitchell*? (Only two states, Georgia and Kentucky, permitted eighteen-year-olds to vote; Hawaii and Alaska set the voting age above eighteen but below twenty-one.) If not, how can Congress be held to be "enforc[ing]" the Equal Protection Clause by requiring states to grant the vote to eighteen-year-olds? *Compare Katzenbach v. Morgan*, 384 U.S. 641 (1966) [p. 22].

Did the Voting Rights Act itself violate the Constitution by setting the voting age at eighteen, rather than seventeen or a lower age? *See Oregon v. Mitchell*, 400 U.S. at 142 (Douglas, J., concurring in the judgment in part and dissenting in part) ("It is said, why draw the line at 18? Why not 17? Congress can draw lines and I see no reason why it cannot conclude that 18-year-olds have that degree of maturity which entitles them to the franchise.").

15.   In footnote 9 of his *Kramer* dissent, Justice Stewart argued that the school district should have been treated as a special-purpose district, exempt from the constitutional requirements applicable to governments exercising more general authority. The next case directly addressed the constitutional requirements governing elections for special-purpose districts.

SALYER LAND CO. v. TULARE LAKE BASIN WATER STORAGE DISTRICT
Supreme Court of the United States
410 U.S. 719, 93 S. Ct. 1224, 35 L. Ed. 2d 659 (1973)

MR. JUSTICE REHNQUIST delivered the opinion of the Court [in which MR. CHIEF JUSTICE BURGER, MR. JUSTICE STEWART, MR. JUSTICE WHITE, MR. JUSTICE BLACKMUN, and MR. JUSTICE POWELL join]. * * *

* * * Appellee district consists of 193,000 acres of intensively cultivated, highly fertile farm land located in the Tulare Lake Basin. Its population consists of 77 persons, including 18 children, most of whom are employees of one or another of the four corporations that farm 85% of the land in the district.

[Water storage] districts are authorized to plan projects and execute approved projects "for the acquisition, appropriation, diversion, storage, conservation, and distribution of water. . . ." Incidental to this general power, districts may "acquire, improve, and operate" any necessary works for the storage and distribution of water as well as any drainage or reclamation works connected therewith * * *. They may fix tolls and charges for the use of water and collect them from all persons receiving the benefit of the water or other services in proportion to the services rendered. The costs of the projects are assessed against district land in accordance with the benefits accruing to each tract held in separate ownership. And land that is not benefited may be withdrawn from the district on petition.

Governance of the districts is undertaken by a board of directors. Each director is elected from one of the divisions within the district * * *.

It is the voter qualification for such elections that appellants claim invidiously discriminates against them and persons similarly situated. Appellants are landowners, a landowner-lessee, and residents within the area included in the appellee's water storage district. * * * They allege that [California Water Code] §§ 41000[5] and 41001[6] unconstitutionally deny to them the equal protection of the laws guaranteed by the Fourteenth Amendment, in that only landowners are permitted to vote in water storage district general elections, and votes in those elections are apportioned according to the assessed valuation of the land. * * *

It is first argued that § 41000, limiting the vote to district landowners, is unconstitutional since nonlandowning residents have as much interest in the operations of a district as landowners who may or may not be residents. Particularly, it is pointed out that the homes of residents may be damaged by floods within the district's boundaries, and that floods may * * * cause them to lose their jobs. Support for this position is said to come from the recent decisions of this Court striking down various state laws that limited voting to landowners.

* * * *Kramer* [v. *Union Free School District*, 395 U.S. 621 (1969)] [p. 62] and *Hadley* v. *Junior College District* [397 U.S. 50 (1970)] extended the "one person, one vote" principle to school districts * * *.

But the Court was also careful to state [in *Hadley*] that:

> "It is of course possible that there might be some case in which a State elects certain functionaries whose duties are so far removed from normal governmental activities and so disproportionately affect different groups that a popular election in compliance with *Reynolds* might not be required, but certainly we see nothing in the present case that indicates that the activities of these trustees fit in that category. Education has traditionally been a vital governmental function and these trustees, whose election the State has opened to all qualified voters, are governmental officials in every relevant sense of that term."

We conclude that the appellee water storage district, by reason of its special limited purpose and of the disproportionate effect of its activities on landowners as a group, is the sort of exception to the rule laid down in *Reynolds* [v. *Sims*, 377 U.S. 533 (1964)] [p. 173], which the quoted language from *Hadley* * * * contemplated.

The appellee district in this case, although vested with some typical governmental powers,[7] has relatively limited authority. Its primary purpose, indeed the reason

---

[5] Calif. Water Code § 41000 provides: "Only the holders of title to land are entitled to vote at a general election."

[6] Calif. Water Code § 41001 provides: "Each voter may vote in each precinct in which any of the land owned by him is situated and may cast one vote for each one hundred dollars ($100), or fraction thereof, worth of his land, exclusive of improvements, minerals, and mineral rights therein, in the precinct."

[7] The board has the power to employ and discharge persons on a regular staff and to contract for the construction of district projects. It can condemn private property for use in such projects, and may cooperate (including contract) with other agencies, state and federal. Both general obligation bonds and interest-bearing warrants may be authorized.

for its existence, is to provide for the acquisition, storage, and distribution of water for farming in the Tulare Lake Basin.[8] It provides no other general public services such as schools, housing, transportation, utilities, roads, or anything else of the type ordinarily financed by a municipal body. * * *

Not only does the district not exercise what might be thought of as "normal governmental" authority, but its actions disproportionately affect landowners. All of the costs of district projects are assessed against land by assessors in proportion to the benefits received. Likewise, charges for services rendered are collectible from persons receiving their benefit in proportion to the services. When such persons are delinquent in payment, just as in the case of delinquency in payments of assessments, such charges become a lien on the land. In short, there is no way that the economic burdens of district operations can fall on residents *qua* residents, and the operations of the districts primarily affect the land within their boundaries.

Under these circumstances, it is quite understandable that the statutory framework for election of directors of the appellee focuses on the land benefited, rather than on people as such. * * *

* * * No doubt residents within the district may be affected by [the district's] activities. But this argument proves too much. Since assessments imposed by the district become a cost of doing business for those who farm within it, and that cost must ultimately be passed along to the consumers of the produce, food shoppers in far away metropolitan areas are to some extent likewise "affected" by the activities of the district. Constitutional adjudication cannot rest on any such "house that Jack built" foundation, however. The California Legislature could quite reasonably have concluded that the number of landowners and owners of sufficient amounts of acreage whose consent was necessary to organize the district would not have subjected their land to the lien of its possibly very substantial assessments unless they had a dominant voice in its control. Since the subjection of the owners' lands to such liens was the basis by which the district was to obtain financing, the proposed district had as a practical matter to attract landowner support. Nor, since assessments against landowners were to be the sole means by which the expenses of the district were to be paid, could it be said to be unfair or inequitable to repose the franchise in landowners but not residents. Landowners as a class were to bear the entire burden of the district's costs, and the State could rationally conclude that they, to the exclusion of residents, should be charged with responsibility for its operation. We conclude, therefore, that nothing in the Equal Protection Clause precluded California from limiting the voting for directors of appellee district by totally excluding those who merely reside within the district.

Appellants assert that even if residents may be excluded from the vote, lessees who farm the land have interests that are indistinguishable from those of the landowners. Like landowners, they take an interest in increasing the available water for farming and, because the costs of district projects may be passed on to them

---

[8] Appellants strongly urge that districts have the power to, and do, engage in flood control activities. The interest of such activities to residents is said to be obvious since houses may be destroyed and * * * jobs may disappear. But * * * any flood control activities are incident to the exercise of the district's primary functions of water storage and distribution.

either by express agreement or by increased rentals, they have an equal interest in the costs.

Lessees undoubtedly do have an interest in the activities of appellee district analogous to that of landowners in many respects. But in the type of special district we now have before us, the question for our determination is not whether or not we would have lumped them together had we been enacting the statute in question, but instead whether "if any state of facts reasonably may be conceived to justify" California's decision to deny the franchise to lessees while granting it to landowners.

* * * California may well have felt that landowners would be unwilling to join in the forming of a water storage district if short-term lessees whose fortunes were not in the long run tied to the land were to have a major vote in the affairs of the district.

The administration of a voting system which allowed short-term lessees to vote could also pose significant difficulties. Apparently, assessment rolls as well as state and federal land lists are used by election boards in determining the qualifications of the voters. Such lists, obviously, would not ordinarily disclose either long- or short-term leaseholds. While reference could be made to appropriate conveyancing records to determine the existence of leases which had been recorded, leases for terms less than one year need not be recorded under California law in order to preserve the right of the lessee. * * *

Under these circumstances, the exclusion of lessees from voting in general elections for the directors of the district does not violate the Equal Protection Clause.

The last claim by appellants is that § 41001, which weights the vote according to assessed valuation of the land, is unconstitutional. They point to the fact that several of the smaller landowners have only one vote per person whereas the J.G. Boswell Company has 37,825 votes, and they place reliance on the various decisions of this Court holding that wealth has no relation to resident-voter qualifications and that equality of voting power may not be evaded.

Appellants' argument ignores the realities of water storage district operation. * * * [A]s the District Court found, "the benefits and burdens to each landowner . . . are in proportion to the assessed value of the land." We cannot say that the California legislative decision to permit voting in the same proportion is not rationally based.

Accordingly, we * * * hold that the voter qualification statutes for California water storage district elections are rationally based, and therefore do not violate the Equal Protection Clause.

Affirmed.

MR. JUSTICE DOUGLAS, with whom MR. JUSTICE BRENNAN and MR. JUSTICE MARSHALL concur, dissenting. * * *

Provisions authorizing a selective franchise are disfavored, because they "always pose the danger of denying some citizens any effective voice in the governmental affairs which substantially affect their lives." *Kramer*, [395 U.S., at 627]. In order to overcome this strong presumption, it had to be shown up to now (1) that there is a compelling state interest for the exclusion, and (2) that the exclusions are necessary to promote the State's articulated goal. In my view, appellants in this case have made a sufficient showing to invoke the above principles, and the presumption thus established has not been overcome.

Assuming, *arguendo*, that a State may, in some circumstances, limit the franchise to that portion of the electorate "primarily affected" by the outcome of an election, the limitation may only be upheld if it is demonstrated that "all those excluded are in fact substantially less interested or affected than those the [franchise] includes." [*Id.* at 632.] The majority concludes that "there is no way that the economic burdens of district operations can fall on residents *qua* residents, and the operations of the districts primarily affect the land within their boundaries." * * * But irrigation, water storage, the building of levees, and flood control, implicate the entire community. All residents of the district must be granted the franchise. * * *

It is indeed grotesque to think of corporations voting within the framework of political representation of people. Corporations were held to be "persons" for purposes both of the Due Process Clause of the Fourteenth Amendment and of the Equal Protection Clause. Yet, it is unthinkable in terms of the American tradition that corporations should be admitted to the franchise. Could a State allot voting rights to its corporations, weighting each vote according to the wealth of the corporation? Or could it follow the rule of one corporation, one vote?

It would be a radical and revolutionary step to take, as it would change our whole concept of the franchise. California takes part of that step here by allowing corporations to vote in these water district matters that entail performance of vital governmental functions. One corporation can outvote 77 individuals in this district. Four corporations can exercise these governmental powers as they choose, leaving every individual inhabitant with a weak, ineffective voice. The result is a corporate political kingdom undreamed of by those who wrote our Constitution.

Notes and Questions

1. What justification does the Court provide for its application of the rational-basis test rather than strict scrutiny? What limitations are there on states' ability to designate "special-purpose" districts, free of the one-person, one-vote restraint?

2. Why is a school district, such as the one involved in *Kramer*, not a special-purpose district? In *Hadley v. Junior College District*, 397 U.S. 50, 54 (1970), quoted in *Salyer Land Co.*, the Court said that school districts' "powers are general enough and have sufficient impact throughout the district" to trigger the one-person, one-vote rule. Do you agree that school districts' powers are so different from those of water-storage districts or other special-purpose districts?

3. In *Ball v. James*, 451 U.S. 355 (1981), the Court, 5-4, applied *Salyer* to the Salt River Project, a district that stored and delivered water to almost half the population of Arizona, including much of Phoenix. The operating costs of the Project were raised through the sale of electric power, not by assessments according to land value, as was the case in *Salyer*. Bonds issued by the Project were, however, secured

by the landowners' property. The Court upheld the method of selecting Project directors, which was to apportion voting power by acreage owned, and to exclude non-landowners from the directorial elections entirely.

> The [Salt River] District * * * cannot impose ad valorem property taxes or sales taxes. It cannot enact any laws governing the conduct of citizens, nor does it administer such normal functions of government as the maintenance of streets, the operation of schools, or sanitation, health, or welfare services.

> * * * The District * * * do[es] not own, sell, or buy water, nor do[es it] control the use of any water [it] ha[s] delivered. * * * It is true * * * that as much as 40% of the water delivered by the District goes for nonagricultural purposes. But the distinction between agricultural and urban land is of no special constitutional significance in this context. The constitutionally relevant fact is that all water delivered by the Salt River District, like the water delivered by the Tulare Lake Basin Water Storage District, is distributed according to land ownership, and the District does not and cannot control the use to which the landowners who are entitled to the water choose to put it. * * *

> [N]either the existence nor size of the District's power business affects the legality of its property-based voting scheme. [T]he provision of electricity is not a traditional element of governmental sovereignty, and so is not in itself the sort of general or important governmental function that would make the government provider subject to [one-person, one-vote].

> [N]o matter how great the number of nonvoting residents buying electricity from the District, the relationship between them and the District's power operations is essentially that between consumers and a business enterprise from which they buy. * * *

> * * * [The District bears a disproportionate relationship] to the specific class of people whom the system makes eligible to vote. The voting landowners are the only residents of the District whose lands are subject to liens to secure District bonds. Only these landowners are subject to the acreage-based taxing power of the District, and voting landowners are the only residents who have ever committed capital to the District through stock assessments * * *. The *Salyer* opinion did not say that the selected class of voters for a special public entity must be the only parties at all affected by the operations of the entity, or that their entire economic well-being must depend on that entity. Rather, the question was whether the effect of the entity's operations on them was disproportionately greater than the effect on those seeking the vote.

Id. at 366–71.

The Court held that the voting scheme passed the rational-basis test. First, the vote could be restricted to landowners because the District might not have been created were landowners not assured a special voice in its operation. Second, "Arizona could rationally make the weight of [landowners'] vote[s] dependent upon the number of acres they own, since that number reasonably reflects the relative risks they incurred as landowners and the distribution of the benefits and burdens of the District's water operations." *Id.* at 371. Note that even though the Salt River Project did provide utility service — one of the services that *Salyer* suggested were "ordinarily financed by a municipal body" — *Ball* held that the Project was not subject to one person, one vote because "the provision of electricity is not a *traditional* element of governmental sovereignty" (emphasis added).

Justice Powell provided the fifth vote, and filed a concurrence in which he noted what was for him "decisive": "The Arizona Legislature recently has demonstrated its control over the electoral processes of the District [and has] increase[d] the political voice of the small householder at the expense of the large landowner." He argued that it was unnecessary to interfere with the District, as he expected that "the people will act through their elected legislature when further changes in the governance of the District are warranted." *Id.* at 374 (Powell, J., concurring). Justice White, joined by Justices Brennan, Marshall, and Blackmun, dissented, noting the importance of the Project's operations to thousands of non-voting residents.

4.   May a municipality provide that votes in fire-district elections should be weighted according to property ownership, on the theory that people with property have the most to lose by fire, and therefore are the ones "primarily interested" in the elections?

5.   *Problem.* The Grand Central Business Improvement District covers 337 properties with seventy-one million feet of commercial space, including Grand Central Terminal, and nine hundred thousand feet of residential space in seventy-five blocks of midtown Manhattan. The District is funded by assessments paid by property owners on a per-square-foot basis, but the taxes are laid and collected by New York City, and not by the District itself. The District exists to make capital improvements and provide services designed to promote business within the District. Outlays must be approved in advance by the City Council.

Capital improvements may "include the renovation of sidewalks and crosswalks; the planting of trees; the installation of new lighting, street signs, bus shelters, news kiosks, and trash receptacles; contributions to the renovation of Grand Central Terminal; and 'the creation of a restaurant facility' on 42nd Street." The services provided by the District "may include any services required for the enjoyment and protection of the public and the promotion and enhancement of the District," including security, sanitation, the provision of tourist information, and social services for the homeless.

The District employs sanitation workers and sixty-three security guards, and contributes to a twenty-four-hour facility for the homeless, which provides services such as job training. The security guards, however, do not have the power to arrest or detain suspects, and almost all of them are unarmed; their function is mainly to communicate with the New York City Police Department in the event of an incident requiring law-enforcement attention. The sanitation officials bag trash and remove graffiti, but do not enforce sanitation regulations or conduct inspections. In general, the District lacks the power to control the actions of persons within the District.

By contract with the City, the District is managed by a management company. The management company, the Grand Central District Management Association, is run by a board of fifty-three directors, five of whom are appointed by New York City officials. Of the remaining forty-eight, thirty-one are elected by property owners in the District, and seventeen are elected by tenants. The law authorizing the creation of the District provides that at no time may the owners' representatives constitute less than a majority of the board.

Is the representational scheme unconstitutional for failure to abide by one-person, one-vote? *See Kessler v. Grand Central District Management Association,* 158 F.3d 92 (2d Cir. 1998).

6.   *Problem.* The Southern California Rapid Transit District is charged with the construction, financing, and operation of a mass transit system for southern California, especially Los Angeles. To pay for such a system, the District is authorized to create "assessment districts" surrounding planned stations. The "assessment districts" would exercise no power, but rather would be a geographic zone within which an assessment (tax) would be imposed. Before such an assessment district is created, however, there must be a referendum taken of the property owners who would be subject to an assessment if the assessment district were to be created. Because residential property would be exempt from any assessment, residential property owners, along with non-property-owning residents of the District, are ineligible to vote in the referendum. Voting power in the referendum is distributed on the basis of the assessed value of property; owners receive one vote for every one thousand dollars of assessed valuation. Assessments, if they are imposed, however, would be calculated on the basis of square footage, not assessed valuation.

Is the voting scheme constitutional? Who would bear the burdens of the District's activities? Who would benefit? Should both burdens and benefits of a special-purpose district be relevant when analyzing the equal-protection implications of such districts? Should the relevant special-purpose district here be the SCRTD or the assessment district? *See Southern California Rapid Transit District v. Bolen,* 822 P.2d 875 (Cal. 1992).

7.   *Problem.* Dissatisfied with the performance of the city's public schools, the mayor of Los Angeles proposes that control of the schools be shifted from the Los Angeles Unified School District to a nonprofit. To be adopted in any individual school, the proposal must receive a majority vote of all teachers at that school and a majority of the votes cast by parents of students at the school. No one besides teachers and parents is permitted to vote. Further, parents' votes are not distributed on a one-parent, one-vote basis; rather, votes are accorded to parents based on the number of *children* they have in the school. *See* Howard Blume & Duke Helfand, *An Odd Civics Lesson for 7 L.A. Schools,* L.A. TIMES, Dec. 12, 2007, at 1. The nonprofit will seek to implement reforms that are "locally driven; increase autonomy and school site decision making; increase accountability; leverage city resources; and invest private and philanthropic resources." Each school will develop its own plan for achieving those goals, but the exact character of the reforms is vague. How would you defend the voting system against constitutional attack?

8.   According to the U.S. Census Bureau, there are more than 35,000 special-purpose districts in the United States. *See* 1 U.S. CENSUS BUREAU, 2002 CENSUS OF GOVERNMENTS: GOVERNMENT ORGANIZATION, GC02(1)-1 13 (2002), *available at* http://www.census.gov/prod/2003pubs/gc021x1.pdf. That number represents an increase of 47% over the number of special-purpose districts in existence in 1972, and an increase of 184% over the number of districts in 1952. *See id.* at 6. The districts fulfill myriad functions, including providing services relating to education, social services, transportation, environment and housing, and utilities. The largest single category is fire districts, of which there are 5,725, but all the categories under the heading of "environment and housing" — which includes such districts as sewer districts, flood-control districts, community-development districts, and soil- and water-conservation districts — contain 14,124 individual districts. *See id.* at 13.[1]

HOLT CIVIC CLUB v. CITY OF TUSCALOOSA
Supreme Court of the United States
439 U.S. 60, 99 S. Ct. 383, 58 L. Ed. 2d 292 (1978)

MR. JUSTICE REHNQUIST delivered the opinion of the Court [in which MR. CHIEF JUSTICE BURGER, MR. JUSTICE STEWART, MR. JUSTICE BLACKMUN, MR. JUSTICE POWELL, and MR. JUSTICE STEVENS join].

Holt is a small, largely rural, unincorporated community located on the northeastern outskirts of Tuscaloosa, the fifth largest city in Alabama. Because the community is within the three-mile police jurisdiction circumscribing Tuscaloosa's corporate limits, its residents are subject to the city's "police [and] sanitary regulations." Holt residents are also subject to the criminal jurisdiction of the city's court, and to the city's power to license businesses, trades, and professions. Tuscaloosa, however, may collect from businesses in the police jurisdiction only one-half of the license fee chargeable to similar businesses conducted within the corporate limits. * * *

In 1973 appellants, an unincorporated civic association and seven individual residents of Holt, brought this statewide class action * * * challenging the constitutionality of these Alabama statutes. They claimed that the city's extraterritorial exercise of police powers over Holt residents, without a concomitant extension of the franchise on an equal footing with those residing within the corporate limits, denies residents of the police jurisdiction rights secured by the Due Process and Equal Protection Clauses of the Fourteenth Amendment. * * *

[The Court summarized *Kramer* v. *Union Free School Dist.*, 395 U.S. 621 (1969) [p. 62], and *Cipriano* v. *City of Houma*, 395 U.S. 701 (1969), which held that states may not limit the franchise to property taxpayers in elections to approve the issuance of revenue bonds.] Appellants also place heavy reliance on *Evans* v. *Cornman*, 398 U.S. 419 (1970). In *Evans* the Permanent Board of Registry of Montgomery County, Md., ruled that persons living on the grounds of the National Institutes of Health (NIH), a federal enclave located within the geographical boundaries of the State, did not meet the residency requirement of the Maryland

---

[1] These figures do not include those districts with multiple functions, one of which is concerned, for example, with sewers or water conservation.

Constitution. Accordingly, NIH residents were denied the right to vote in Maryland elections. This Court rejected the notion that persons living on NIH grounds were not residents of Maryland: "Appellees clearly live within the geographical boundaries of the State of Maryland, and they are treated as state residents in the census and in determining congressional apportionment. * * *"

Thus, because inhabitants of the NIH enclave were residents of Maryland and were "just as interested in and connected with electoral decisions as they were prior to 1953 when the area came under federal jurisdiction and as their neighbors who live off the enclave," the State could not deny them the equal right to vote in Maryland elections.[7]

From these and our other voting qualifications cases a common characteristic emerges: The challenged statute in each case denied the franchise to individuals who were physically resident within the geographic boundaries of the governmental entity concerned. No decision of this Court has extended the "one man, one vote" principle to individuals residing beyond the geographic confines of the governmental entity concerned, be it the State or its political subdivisions. On the contrary, our cases have uniformly recognized that a government unit may legitimately restrict the right to participate in its political processes to those who reside within its borders. * * *

Appellants' argument that extraterritorial extension of municipal powers requires concomitant extraterritorial extension of the franchise proves too much. The imaginary line defining a city's corporate limits cannot corral the influence of municipal actions. A city's decisions inescapably affect individuals living immediately outside its borders. The granting of building permits for high rise apartments, industrial plants, and the like on the city's fringe unavoidably contributes to problems of traffic congestion, school districting, and law enforcement immediately outside the city. A rate change in the city's sales or ad valorem tax could well have a significant impact on retailers and property values in areas bordering the city. The condemnation of real property on the city's edge for construction of a municipal garbage dump or waste treatment plant would have obvious implications for neighboring nonresidents. Indeed, the indirect extraterritorial effects of many purely internal municipal actions could conceivably have a heavier impact on surrounding environs than the direct regulation contemplated by Alabama's police jurisdiction statutes. Yet no one would suggest that nonresidents likely to be affected by this sort of municipal action have a constitutional right to participate in the political processes bringing it about. * * *

The extraterritorial exercise of municipal powers is a governmental technique neither recent in origin nor unique to the State of Alabama. In this country 35 States authorize their municipal subdivisions to exercise governmental powers beyond their corporate limits. Although the extraterritorial municipal powers granted by these States vary widely, several States grant their cities more extensive

---

[7] In this case residents of the police jurisdiction are excluded only from participation in municipal elections since they reside outside of Tuscaloosa's corporate limits. * * * Treatment of the plaintiffs in *Evans* as nonresidents of Maryland had repercussions not merely with respect to their right to vote in city elections, but with respect to their right to vote in national, state, school board, and referendum elections. [Relocated.— Eds.]

or intrusive powers over bordering areas than those granted under the Alabama statutes.[8]

In support of their equal protection claim, appellants suggest a number of "constitutionally preferable" governmental alternatives to Alabama's system of municipal police jurisdictions. For example, exclusive management of the police jurisdiction by county officials, appellants maintain, would be more "practical." From a political science standpoint, appellants' suggestions may be sound, but this Court does not sit to determine whether Alabama has chosen the soundest or most practical form of internal government possible. Authority to make those judgments resides in the state legislature, and Alabama citizens are free to urge their proposals to that body. Our inquiry is limited to the question whether "any state of facts reasonably may be conceived to justify" Alabama's system of police jurisdictions, and in this case it takes but momentary reflection to arrive at an affirmative answer.

The Alabama Legislature could have decided that municipal corporations should have some measure of control over activities carried on just beyond their "city limit" signs, particularly since today's police jurisdiction may be tomorrow's annexation to the city proper. Nor need the city's interests have been the only concern of the legislature when it enacted the police jurisdiction statutes. Urbanization of any area brings with it a number of individuals who long both for the quiet of suburban or country living and for the career opportunities offered by the city's working environment. Unincorporated communities like Holt dot the rim of most major population centers in Alabama and elsewhere, and state legislatures have a legitimate interest in seeing that this substantial segment of the population does not go without basic municipal services such as police, fire, and health protection. Established cities are experienced in the delivery of such services, and the incremental cost of extending the city's responsibility in these areas to surrounding environs may be substantially less than the expense of establishing wholly new service organizations in each community.

Nor was it unreasonable for the Alabama Legislature to require police jurisdiction residents to contribute through license fees to the expense of services provided them by the city. The statutory limitation on license fees to half the amount exacted within the city assures that police jurisdiction residents will not be victimized by the city government. * * *

* * * Alabama's police jurisdiction statute, enacted in 1907, was a rational legislative response to the problems faced by the State's burgeoning cities. Alabama is apparently content with the results of its experiment, and nothing in the Equal Protection Clause of the Fourteenth Amendment requires that it try something new. * * *

---

[8] * * * We do not have before us, of course, a situation in which a city has annexed outlying territory in all but name, and is exercising precisely the same governmental powers over residents of surrounding unincorporated territory as it does over those residing within its corporate limits. * * * While the burden was on appellants to establish a difference in treatment violative of the Equal Protection Clause, we are bound to observe that among the powers *not* [exercised by the city within its police jurisdiction] are the vital and traditional authorities of cities and towns to levy ad valorem taxes, invoke the power of eminent domain, and zone property for various types of uses.

Affirmed.

MR. JUSTICE STEVENS, concurring.

The Court today holds that the Alabama statutes providing for the extraterritorial exercise of certain limited powers by municipalities are not unconstitutional. While I join the opinion of the Court, I write separately to emphasize that this holding does not make all exercises of extraterritorial authority by a municipality immune from attack under the Equal Protection Clause of the Fourteenth Amendment.

* * * Certainly there is nothing in the Federal Constitution to prevent a suburb from contracting with a nearby city to provide municipal services for its residents, even though those residents have no voice in the election of the city's officials or in the formulation of the city's rules. That is essentially what Alabama has accomplished here, through the elected representatives of all its citizens in the state legislature.[1] * * *

* * * The statutory scheme created by the Alabama Legislature is not unconstitutional by its terms, but it may well be, as the opinion of the Court recognizes, *ante*, n.8, that that scheme or another much like it might sometimes operate to deny the franchise to individuals who share the interests of their voting neighbors. * * *

MR. JUSTICE BRENNAN, with whom MR. JUSTICE WHITE and MR. JUSTICE MARSHALL join, dissenting. * * *

[Residency requirements "preserve the basic conception of a political community" and for that reason are exempt from strict scrutiny, provided they are "appropriately defined" to serve that purpose.] At the heart of our basic conception of a "political community," however, is the notion of a reciprocal relationship between the process of government and those who subject themselves to that process by choosing to live within the area of its authoritative application. Statutes such as those challenged in this case, which fracture this relationship by severing the connection between the process of government and those who are governed in the places of their residency, thus undermine the very purposes which have led this Court in the past to approve the application of bona fide residency requirements.

There is no question but that the residents of Tuscaloosa's police jurisdiction are governed by the city. * * * The Court seems to imply, however, that residents of the police jurisdiction are not governed enough to be included within the political community of Tuscaloosa, since they are not subject to Tuscaloosa's powers of eminent domain, zoning, or ad valorem taxation. But this position is sharply contrary to our previous holdings.

---

[1] I recognize that there is a difference between a suburb's decision to contract with a nearby city and a decision by the state legislature requiring all suburbs to do so. In some situations that difference might justify a holding that a particular extraterritorial delegation of power is unconstitutional. It does not, however, justify the view that all such delegations are invalid.

The residents of Tuscaloosa's police jurisdiction are vastly more affected by Tuscaloosa's decisionmaking processes than were the plaintiffs in either *Kramer* or *Cipriano* affected by the decisionmaking processes from which they had been unconstitutionally excluded. * * * A municipality, for example, may use its police powers to regulate, or even to ban, common professions and businesses. * * * The Court today does not explain why being subjected to the authority to exercise such extensive power does not suffice to bring the residents of Tuscaloosa's police jurisdiction within the political community of the city. Nor does the Court in fact provide any standards for determining when those subjected to extraterritorial municipal legislation will have been "governed enough" to trigger the protections of the Equal Protection Clause. * * *

The criterion of geographical residency is thus entirely arbitrary when applied to this case. It fails to explain why, consistently with the Equal Protection Clause, the "government unit" which may exclude from the franchise those who reside outside of its geographical boundaries should be composed of the city of Tuscaloosa rather than of the city together with its police jurisdiction. It irrationally distinguishes between two classes of citizens, each with equal claim to residency (insofar as that can be determined by domicile or intention or other similar criteria), and each governed by the city of Tuscaloosa in the place of their residency.

The Court argues, however, that if the franchise were extended to residents of the city's police jurisdiction, the franchise must similarly be extended to all those indirectly affected by the city's actions. This is a simple non sequitur. There is a crystal-clear distinction between those who reside in Tuscaloosa's police jurisdiction, and who are therefore subject to that city's police and sanitary ordinances, licensing fees, and the jurisdiction of its municipal court, and those who reside in neither the city nor its police jurisdiction, and who are thus merely affected by the indirect impact of the city's decisions. This distinction * * * is consistent with, if not mandated by, the very conception of a political community underlying constitutional recognition of bona fide residency requirements.

Appellants' equal protection claim can be simply expressed: The State cannot extend the franchise to some citizens who are governed by municipal government in the places of their residency, and withhold the franchise from others similarly situated, unless this distinction is necessary to promote a compelling state interest. No such interest has been articulated in this case. Neither Tuscaloosa's interest in regulating "activities carried on just beyond [its] 'city limit' signs," nor Alabama's interest in providing municipal services to the unincorporated communities surrounding its cities are in any way inconsistent with the extension of the franchise to residents of Tuscaloosa's police jurisdiction. Although a great many States may presently authorize the exercise of extraterritorial lawmaking powers by a municipality, and although the Alabama statutes involved in this case may be of venerable age, neither of these factors * * * can serve to justify practices otherwise impermissible under the Equal Protection Clause of the Fourteenth Amendment. * * *

Notes and Questions

1. Was Justice Brennan correct that there was a "crystal-clear" distinction between the residents of the police jurisdiction and outsiders? Or was the Court correct that the very principle Justice Brennan used to extend the franchise to residents of the police jurisdiction argues for extending it infinitely further?

2. Professor James Gardner has argued that the Court's opinion in *Holt*

> entirely missed the point of the plaintiffs' claim. The plaintiffs were not trying to minimize the fact that they lived in a different community — that was precisely their point. The problem, in their view, was that they were governed by a political community different from the one to which they belonged. * * * While the Court was correct that the actions of one jurisdiction inevitably have some kind of "spillover" effect on neighboring jurisdictions, there is a significant difference between living *with* neighbors and living *under* those neighbors — the difference between comity under independent self-government and outright political subjection.

James A. Gardner, *Liberty, Community and the Constitutional Structure of Political Influence: A Reconsideration of the Right to Vote*, 145 U. Pa. L. Rev. 893, 910–11 (1997). Do you agree?

3. If some line must be drawn based on residence, was Alabama's choice rational? Would it pass strict scrutiny? What is the justification for tying voting rights to geography in the first place? Not everyone agrees that residence should be so important:

> *The Miami Herald* won a Pulitzer Prize for an investigation proving that many of the ballots cast in the [1997] Miami city election were cast by people who did not, if you wanted to get picky about it, reside in Miami. The *Herald* contacted some of these people, who gave some truly wonderful, even heartwarming, explanations, including these, which I am not making up: * * *
>
> *A man who had moved to Hialeah, but continued to vote in Miami:* "I've always felt more in tune with things in Miami than anywhere else. Look, I'm an American citizen and I feel you don't violate the law when you vote. It's my right as an American citizen."
>
> Damn right! This is *America*, where a person has the fundamental right to vote in the municipality of his choosing, regardless of where he lives!

Dave Barry, Dave Barry Hits Below the Beltway 145–46 (2001).

4. Can *Holt* be squared with *Kramer*? As Professor Gardner notes, "[c]ompared to the plaintiffs in *Holt*, the plaintiff in *Kramer* had a far less plausible claim that his inability to vote impaired in any significant way his ability to protect his rights and liberties from government infringement." Gardner, *supra*, at 911–12. Perhaps, though, Kramer was harmed by "the *fact* of his exclusion, not the *result* of it," in that the exclusion from voting itself signaled that Kramer — despite residing within the school district — was "not a member of the community." *Id.* at 912.

5. *Problem. Holt* gave controlling significance to the geographical limits of municipalities, and treated only residents as possessing a fundamental right to vote in municipal elections. How far should this principle extend? A South Dakota statute provides:

> Every municipality shall have power to exercise jurisdiction for all authorized purposes over all territory within the corporate limits * * *, and in and over all places, except within the corporate limits of another municipality, within one mile of the corporate limits * * *, for the purpose of promoting the health, safety, morals, and general welfare of the community, and of enforcing its ordinances and resolutions relating thereto.

S.D. CODIFIED LAWS § 9-29-1. May South Dakota refuse to allow residents within one mile of municipalities to vote in municipal elections? Consider footnote 8 in *Holt.*

6. *Problem.* How are voting rights to be determined in instances where the whole point of voting is to establish municipal lines? Suppose a county is served by two school districts. Residents seek to form a third district out of land formerly controlled by each of the two existing districts. If the question of the creation of the third district is put to the voters in a ballot measure, is it constitutional to limit the franchise to residents of the area that would be within the new district? *See Herriman City v. Swensen*, 521 F. Supp. 2d 1233 (D. Utah 2007).

7. *Problem.* Counties in Ohio contain townships, which themselves may contain municipal corporations, such as villages. Freeholders in townships containing municipal corporations may petition for the creation of a new township, excluding the municipal corporation. If a majority of freehold electors in the township, but outside the municipal corporation, so petitions, the Board of County Commissioners shall establish the new township. Thus, the group permitted to petition for the creation of the new township is limited to (1) freeholders (2) who own land in the township but outside the municipal corporation. Does this scheme violate the Equal Protection Clause by discriminating against either non-freehold residents or residents of the municipal corporation who are also residents of the existing township? As to each of the two limitations, should a court apply strict or rational-basis scrutiny? *See Board of Lucas County Commissioners v. Waterville Township Board of Trustees*, 870 N.E.2d 791 (Ohio Ct. App. 2007).

8. States may prohibit resident aliens — even permanent resident aliens — from "basic governmental processes," such as voting, regardless of the aliens' interest in the outcome. As the Supreme Court has explained, "Self-government, whether direct or through representatives, begins by defining the scope of the community of the governed and thus of the governors as well: Aliens are by definition those outside of this community." *Cabell v. Chavez-Salido*, 454 U.S. 432, 439–40 (1982). *See Sugarman v. Dougall*, 413 U.S. 634, 649 (1975) ("[I]mplicit in many of this Court's voting rights decisions is the notion that citizenship is a permissible criterion for limiting such rights."); *Skafte v. Rorex*, 553 P.2d 830 (Colo. 1976). Of what relevance is § 2 of the Fourteenth Amendment, which reduces the representation of states that deny the vote to "any of the male inhabitants of such state, being twenty-one years of age, *and citizens of the United States* * * * except for participation in rebellion or other crime" (emphasis added)? *Cf. Richardson v. Ramirez*, 418 U.S. 24, 43 (1974) [p. 45] (upholding the disenfranchisement of felons);

Minor v. Happersett, 88 U.S. (21 Wall.) 162, 174–75 (1875) (upholding the disenfranchisement of women).

9. The United States Constitution, though leaving the question of voter qualifications largely to the states, does restrict the voter pool in a significant respect: Only "the People of the several States" may select Representatives and Senators,[m] and only the states (and the District of Columbia, by virtue of the Twenty-Third Amendment) have the privilege of appointing members of the electoral college. Accordingly, residents of U.S. territories, though they may be U.S. citizens, are not entitled to vote in presidential elections, or to select voting members of Congress. "That the franchise for choosing electors is confined to 'states' cannot be 'unconstitutional' because it is what the Constitution itself provides. Hence it does no good to stress how important is 'the right to vote' for President." *Igartúa-de la Rosa v. United States*, 417 F.3d 145, 148 (1st Cir. 2005).[n]

Might one argue that the Fifth Amendment, with its Due Process Clause and "equal protection component," was ratified after the original Constitution, and therefore it is improper to rely on the original Constitution to justify limiting the vote to state residents? Such an argument would presumably require the national government to provide the vote to "all persons" in territories and commonwealths subject to congressional control, rather than to U.S. citizens alone, because Fifth Amendment does not limit its protections to citizens. By the same reasoning, however, the Seventeenth Amendment's provision for the election of U.S. Senators from "each State" would appear to trump any equal-protection norm contained in the Fifth Amendment as to the composition of the Senate.

10. Is it constitutional for Congress to grant voting rights to *former* residents of states, who have taken up residence in a foreign country? *See* Uniformed and Overseas Citizens Absentee Voting Act, 52 U.S.C. § 20310(5)(c) (requiring states to count the absentee votes of "person[s] who reside[] outside the United States and (but for such residence) would be qualified to vote in the last place in which the person[s] [were] domiciled before leaving the United States").

---

[m] *See Alexander v. Mineta*, 531 U.S. 940 (2000), *summarily aff'g, Adams v. Clinton*, 90 F. Supp. 2d 35 (D.D.C. 2000) (holding that District of Columbia residents possess no constitutional right to elect congressional representatives). Territories and the District of Columbia do select *non-voting* delegates to Congress, however.

[n] *See also Attorney General of Territory of Guam v. United States*, 738 F.2d 1017 (9th Cir. 1984); Jamin B. Raskin, *Is This America? The District of Columbia and the Right to Vote*, 34 Harv. C.R.-C.L. L. Rev. 39 (1999); Amber L. Cottle, Comment, *Silent Citizens: United States Territorial Residents and the Right to Vote in Presidential Elections*, 1995 U. Chi. Legal F. 315 (1995). For a similarly frivolous argument concerning *candidates* rather than voters, see *Lindsay v. Bowen*, 750 F.3d 1061 (9th Cir. 2014) (rejecting the argument of a 27 year-old who claimed a constitutional right to be placed on the presidential ballot despite the Constitution's command that "[n]o Person except a natural born Citizen, or a Citizen of the United States, at the time of the Adoption of this Constitution, shall be eligible to the Office of President; neither shall any Person be eligible to that Office who shall not have attained to the Age of thirty five Years, and been fourteen Years a Resident within the United States"). U.S. Const. art II, § 1, cl. 5.

5. *The Newly Resident*

POPE v. WILLIAMS
Supreme Court of the United States
193 U.S. 621, 24 S. Ct. 573, 48 L. Ed. 817 (1904)

Statement by Mr. Justice Peckham: * * *

Plaintiff in error on September 29, 1903, presented his application to the board of registry of election district No. 7, Montgomery county, Maryland, * * * to be registered and entered as a qualified voter on the registry of voters of that election district, which application the board refused and declined to comply with, for the sole reason that he had not [registered with the clerk of the county's circuit court, as required by state law].† [Pope subsequently] alleged that he had, on June 7, 1902, with his wife and child, removed from the city of Washington, District of Columbia, into Montgomery county, in the state of Maryland, "having then had, and ever since and now having, the intention of making the state of Maryland the permanent domicil of himself and his family, and of becoming a citizen of said state[.]" * * *

[Pope argued that the statute violated the Constitution for three reasons: First, Pope alleged that the statute violated § 1 of the Fourteenth Amendment by failing to treat new residents as citizens of the state until the residents complied with the law. Second, he claimed that the statute violated the Equal Protection Clause. Third, he argued that the statute unreasonably burdened the ability to travel and migrate interstate.] * * *

Mr. Justice Peckham, after making the above statement of facts, delivered the opinion of the court [in which Mr. Chief Justice Fuller, Mr. Justice Harlan, Mr. Justice Brewer, Mr. Justice Brown, Mr. Justice White, Mr. Justice McKenna, Mr. Justice Holmes, and Mr. Justice Day join]: * * *

* * * The simple matter to be herein determined is whether, with reference to the exercise of the privilege of voting in Maryland, the legislature of that state had the legal right to provide that a person coming into the state to reside should make the declaration of intent a year before he should have the right to be registered as a voter of the state.

The privilege to vote in any state is not given by the Federal Constitution, or by any of its amendments. It is not a privilege springing from citizenship of the United States. It may not be refused on account of race, color, or previous condition of servitude, but it does not follow from mere citizenship of the United States. In other

---

† * * * "All persons who * * * shall remove into any county of this state or into the city of Baltimore from any other state, district, or territory, shall indicate their intent to become citizens and residents of this state by registering their names in a suitable record book, to be procured and kept for the purpose by the clerk of the circuit court for the several counties * * *; such record to contain their names, residence, age, and occupation * * *. And no person coming into this state from any other state, district, or territory shall be entitled to registration as a legal voter of this state until one year after his intent to become such legal voter shall be thus evidenced by such entry in such record book[.] * * *" [Relocated.— Eds.]

words, the privilege to vote in a state is within the jurisdiction of the state itself, to be exercised as the state may direct, and upon such terms as to it may seem proper, provided, of course, no discrimination is made between individuals, in violation of the Federal Constitution. The state might provide that persons of foreign birth could vote without being naturalized, and * * * such persons were allowed to vote in several of the states upon having declared their intentions to become citizens of the United States. Some states permit women to vote; others refuse them that privilege. A state, so far as the Federal Constitution is concerned, might provide by its own constitution and laws that none but native-born citizens should be permitted to vote, as the Federal Constitution does not confer the right of suffrage upon any one, and the conditions under which that right is to be exercised are matters for the states alone to prescribe, subject to the conditions of the Federal Constitution, already stated; although it may be observed that the right to vote for a member of Congress is not derived exclusively from the state law. *See* Fed. Const. art. 1, § 2. But the elector must be one entitled to vote under the state statute. In this case no question arises as to the right to vote for electors of President and Vice President, and no decision is made thereon. The question whether the conditions prescribed by the state might be regarded by others as reasonable or unreasonable is not a Federal one. We do not wish to be understood, however, as intimating that the condition in this statute is unreasonable or in any way improper.

We are unable to see any violation of the Federal Constitution in the provision of the state statute for the declaration of the intent of a person coming into the state before he can claim the right to be registered as a voter. The statute * * * is neither an unlawful discrimination against any one in the situation of the plaintiff in error nor does it deny to him the equal protection of the laws, nor is it repugnant to any fundamental or inalienable rights of citizens of the United States, nor a violation of any implied guaranties of the Federal Constitution. The right of a state to legislate upon the subject of the elective franchise as to it may seem good, subject to the conditions already stated, being, as we believe, unassailable, we think it plain that the statute in question violates no right protected by the Federal Constitution. * * *

[T]he judgment of the Court of Appeals of Maryland is, therefore,

Affirmed.

CARRINGTON v. RASH
Supreme Court of the United States
380 U.S. 89, 85 S. Ct. 775, 13 L. Ed. 2d 675 (1965)

MR. JUSTICE STEWART delivered the opinion of the Court [in which MR. JUSTICE BLACK, MR. JUSTICE DOUGLAS, MR. JUSTICE CLARK, MR. JUSTICE BRENNAN, MR. JUSTICE WHITE, and MR. JUSTICE GOLDBERG join].

A provision of the Texas Constitution prohibits "[a]ny member of the Armed Forces of the United States" who moves his home to Texas during the course of his military duty from ever voting in any election in that State "so long as he or she is a member of the Armed Forces." The question presented is whether this provision * * * deprives the petitioner of a right secured by the Equal Protection Clause of the Fourteenth Amendment. * * *

The petitioner, a sergeant in the United States Army, entered the service from Alabama in 1946 at the age of 18. The State concedes that he has been domiciled in Texas since 1962, and that he intends to make his home there permanently. He has purchased a house in El Paso where he lives with his wife and two children. He is also the proprietor of a small business there. The petitioner's post of military duty is not in Texas, but at White Sands, New Mexico. He regularly commutes from his home in El Paso to his Army job at White Sands. He pays property taxes in Texas and has his automobile registered there. But for his uniform, the State concedes that the petitioner would be eligible to vote in El Paso County, Texas.

Texas has unquestioned power to impose reasonable residence restrictions on the availability of the ballot. There can be no doubt either of the historic function of the States to establish, on a nondiscriminatory basis, and in accordance with the Constitution, other qualifications for the exercise of the franchise. * * *

This Texas constitutional provision, however, is unique.[3] Texas has said that no serviceman may ever acquire a voting residence in the State so long as he remains in service. It is true that the State has treated all members of the military with an equal hand. * * * But the fact that a State is dealing with a distinct class and treats the members of that class equally does not end the judicial inquiry. * * *

It is argued that this absolute denial of the vote to servicemen like the petitioner fulfills two purposes. First, the State says it has a legitimate interest in immunizing its elections from the concentrated balloting of military personnel, whose collective voice may overwhelm a small local civilian community. Secondly, the State says it has a valid interest in protecting the franchise from infiltration by transients, and it can reasonably assume that those servicemen who fall within the constitutional exclusion will be within the State for only a short period of time.

The theory underlying the State's first contention is that the Texas constitutional provision is necessary to prevent the danger of a "takeover" of the civilian community resulting from concentrated voting by large numbers of military personnel in bases placed near Texas towns and cities. A base commander, Texas suggests, who opposes local police administration or teaching policies in local schools, might influence his men to vote in conformity with his predilections. Local bond issues may fail, and property taxes stagnate at low levels because military personnel are unwilling to invest in the future of the area. We stress — and this a theme to be reiterated — that Texas has the right to require that all military personnel enrolled to vote be bona fide residents of the community. But if they are in fact residents, with the intention of making Texas their home indefinitely, they, as all other qualified residents, have a right to an equal opportunity for political representation. "Fencing out" from the franchise a sector of the population because of the way they may vote is constitutionally impermissible. "[T]he exercise of rights so vital to the maintenance of democratic institutions" cannot constitutionally be obliterated because of a fear of the political views of a particular group of bona fide

---

[3] While many States have rules which prescribe special tests for qualifying military personnel for the vote, none goes so far as completely to foreclose from the franchise all servicemen who were nonresidents before induction.

residents. Yet, that is what Texas claims to have done here.

The State's second argument is that its voting ban is justified because of the transient nature of service in the Armed Forces. * * * The Texas Constitution provides that a United States citizen can become a qualified elector if he has "resided in this State one (1) year next preceding an election and the last six (6) months within the district or county in which such person offers to vote." It is the integrity of this qualification of residence which Texas contends is protected by the voting ban on members of the Armed Forces.

But only where military personnel are involved has Texas been unwilling to develop more precise tests to determine the bona fides of an individual claiming to have actually made his home in the State long enough to vote. The State's law reports disclose that there have been many cases where the local election officials have determined the issue of bona fide residence. * * * By statute, Texas deals with particular categories of citizens who, like soldiers, present specialized problems in determining residence. Students at colleges and universities in Texas, patients in hospitals and other institutions within the State, and civilian employees of the United States Government may be as transient as military personnel. But all of them are given at least an opportunity to show the election officials that they are bona fide residents. * * *

We deal here with matters close to the core of our constitutional system. * * * States may not casually deprive a class of individuals of the vote because of some remote administrative benefit to the State. By forbidding a soldier ever to controvert the presumption of non-residence, the Texas Constitution imposes an invidious discrimination in violation of the Fourteenth Amendment. * * *

Reversed.

THE CHIEF JUSTICE [WARREN] took no part in the consideration or decision of this case.

MR. JUSTICE HARLAN, dissenting. * * *

I deplore the added impetus which this decision gives to the current tendency of judging constitutional questions on the basis of abstract "justice" unleashed from the limiting principles that go with our constitutional system. Constitutionally principled adjudication, high in the process of which is due recognition of the just demands of federalism, leaves ample room for the protection of individual rights. A constitutional democracy which in order to cope with seeming needs of the moment is willing to temporize with its basic distribution and limitation of governmental powers will sooner or later find itself in trouble. * * *

* * * The question here is simply whether the differentiation in voting eligibility requirements which Texas has made is founded on a rational classification. In judging this question I think that the dictates of history, even though the Court has seen fit to disregard them for the purpose of determining whether it should get into the matter at all, should cause the Court to take a hard look before striking down

a traditional state policy in this area as rationally indefensible.

Essentially the Texas statute establishes a rule that servicemen from other States stationed at Texas bases are to be treated as transients for voting purposes. No one disputes that in the vast majority of cases Texas' view of things accords with fact. Although it is doubtless true that this rule may operate in some instances contrary to the actual facts, I do not think that the Federal Constitution prevents the State from ignoring that possibility in the overall picture. In my opinion Texas could rationally conclude that such instances would likely be too minimal to justify the administrative expenditure involved in coping with the "special problems" entailed in winnowing out the bona fide permanent residents from among the transient servicemen living off base and sending their children to local schools.

Beyond this, I think a legitimate distinction may be drawn between those who come voluntarily into Texas in connection with private occupations and those ordered into Texas by military authority. Residences established by the latter are subject to the doubt, not present to the same degree with the former, that when the military compulsion ends, so also may the desire to remain in Texas.

And finally, I think that Texas, given the traditional American notion that control of the military should always be kept in civilian hands * * *, could rationally decide to protect state and local politics against the influences of military voting strength by, in effect, postponing the privilege of voting otherwise attaching to a service-acquired domicile until the serviceman becomes a civilian and by limiting Texas servicemen to voting in the counties of their original domicile. Such a policy on Texas' part may seem to many unduly provincial in light of modern conditions, but it cannot, in my view, be said to be unconstitutional. * * *

DUNN v. BLUMSTEIN
Supreme Court of the United States
405 U.S. 330, 92 S. Ct. 995, 31 L. Ed. 2d 274 (1972)

Mr. Justice Marshall delivered the opinion of the Court [in which Mr. Justice Douglas, Mr. Justice Brennan, Mr. Justice Stewart, and Mr. Justice White join].

* * * [Appellee James] Blumstein moved to Tennessee on June 12, 1970, to begin employment as an assistant professor of law at Vanderbilt University in Nashville. With an eye toward voting in the upcoming August and November elections, he attempted to register to vote on July 1, 1970. The county registrar refused to register him, on the ground that Tennessee law authorizes the registration of only those persons who, at the time of the next election, will have been residents of the State for a year and residents of the county for three months. * * *

I

* * * Appellee does not challenge Tennessee's power to restrict the vote to bona fide Tennessee residents. Nor has Tennessee ever disputed that appellee was a bona fide resident of the State and county when he attempted to register. But Tennessee insists that, in addition to *being* a resident, a would-be voter must *have been* a resident for a year in the State and three months in the county. It is this additional

durational residence requirement that appellee challenges.

Durational residence laws penalize those persons who have traveled from one place to another to establish a new residence during the qualifying period. Such laws divide residents into two classes, old residents and new residents, and discriminate against the latter to the extent of totally denying them the opportunity to vote. The constitutional question presented is whether the Equal Protection Clause of the Fourteenth Amendment permits a State to discriminate in this way among its citizens.

* * * In considering laws challenged under the Equal Protection Clause, this Court has evolved more than one test, depending upon the interest affected or the classification involved. First, then, we must determine what standard of review is appropriate. In the present case, whether we look to the benefit withheld by the classification (the opportunity to vote) or the basis for the classification (recent interstate travel) we conclude that * * * durational residence laws must be measured by a strict equal protection test: they are unconstitutional unless the State can demonstrate that such laws are *"necessary* to promote a *compelling* governmental interest." * * *

It is not sufficient for the State to show that durational residence requirements further a very substantial state interest. In pursuing that important interest, the State cannot choose means that unnecessarily burden or restrict constitutionally protected activity. Statutes affecting constitutional rights must be drawn with "precision," and must be "tailored" to serve their legitimate objectives. And if there are other, reasonable ways to achieve those goals with a lesser burden on constitutionally protected activity, a State may not choose the way of greater interference. If it acts at all, it must choose "less drastic means."

II

We turn, then, to the question of whether the State has shown that durational residence requirements are needed to further a sufficiently substantial state interest. We emphasize again the difference between bona fide residence requirements and durational residence requirements. We have in the past noted approvingly that the States have the power to require that voters be bona fide residents of the relevant political subdivision.[7] An appropriately defined and uniformly applied requirement of bona fide residence may be necessary to preserve the basic conception of a political community, and therefore could withstand close constitutional scrutiny. But *durational* residence requirements, representing a separate voting qualification imposed on bona fide residents, must be separately tested by the stringent standard. * * *

---

[7] Appellants * * * rely on *Pope* v. *Williams*, 193 U.S. 621 (1904) [p. 89]. Carefully read, that case simply *holds* that federal constitutional rights are not violated by a state provision requiring a person who enters the State to make a "declaration of his intention to become a citizen before he can have the right to be registered as a voter and to vote in the state." In other words, the case simply stands for the proposition that a State may require voters to be bona fide residents. To the extent that dicta in that opinion are inconsistent with the test we apply or the result we reach today, those dicta are rejected. [Relocated.— Eds.]

Tennessee tenders "two basic purposes" served by its durational residence requirements:

"(1) INSURE PURITY OF BALLOT BOX — Protection against fraud through colonization and inability to identify persons offering to vote, and

"(2) KNOWLEDGEABLE VOTER — Afford some surety that the voter has, in fact, become a member of the community and that as such, he has a common interest in all matters pertaining to its government and is, therefore, more likely to exercise his right more intelligently."

We consider each in turn.

A

Preservation of the "purity of the ballot box" is a formidable-sounding state interest. The impurities feared, variously called "dual voting" and "colonization," all involve voting by nonresidents, either singly or in groups. The main concern is that nonresidents will temporarily invade the State or county, falsely swear that they are residents to become eligible to vote, and, by voting, allow a candidate to win by fraud. Surely the prevention of such fraud is a legitimate and compelling government goal. But it is impossible to view durational residence requirements as necessary to achieve that state interest. * * *

Durational residence laws may once have been necessary to prevent a fraudulent evasion of state voter standards, but today in Tennessee, as in most other States, this purpose is served by a system of voter registration. Given this system, the record is totally devoid of any evidence that durational residence requirements are in fact necessary to identify bona fide residents. The qualifications of the would-be voter in Tennessee are determined when he registers to vote, which he may do until 30 days before the election. His qualifications — including bona fide residence — are established then by oath. There is no indication in the record that Tennessee routinely goes behind the would-be voter's oath to determine his qualifications. Since false swearing is no obstacle to one intent on fraud, the existence of burdensome voting qualifications like durational residence requirements cannot prevent corrupt nonresidents from fraudulently registering and voting. As long as the State relies on the oath-swearing system to establish qualifications, a durational residence requirement adds nothing to a simple residence requirement in the effort to stop fraud. The nonresident intent on committing election fraud will as quickly and effectively swear that he has been a resident for the requisite period of time as he would swear that he was simply a resident. Indeed, the durational residence requirement becomes an effective voting obstacle only to residents who tell the truth and have no fraudulent purposes.

Moreover, to the extent that the State makes an enforcement effort after the oath is sworn, it is not clear what role the durational residence requirement could play in protecting against fraud. * * * As long as the State permits registration up to 30 days before an election, a lengthy durational residence requirement does not increase the amount of time the State has in which to carry out an investigation into the sworn claim by the would-be voter that he is in fact a resident.

* * * Fixing a constitutionally acceptable period is surely a matter of degree. It is sufficient to note here that 30 days appears to be an ample period of time for the State to complete whatever administrative tasks are necessary to prevent fraud — and a year, or three months, too much. This was the judgment of Congress in the context of presidential elections.° And, on the basis of the statutory scheme before us, it is almost surely the judgment of the Tennessee lawmakers as well. * * *

B

The argument that durational residence requirements further the goal of having "knowledgeable voters" appears to involve three separate claims. The first is that such requirements "afford some surety that the voter has, in fact, become a member of the community." But here the State appears to confuse a bona fide residence requirement with a durational residence requirement. * * *

The second branch of the "knowledgeable voters" justification is that durational residence requirements assure that the voter "has a common interest in all matters pertaining to [the community's] government. . . ." By this, presumably, the State means that it may require a period of residence sufficiently lengthy to impress upon its voters the local viewpoint. This is precisely the sort of argument this Court has repeatedly rejected. In *Carrington* v. *Rash*, for example, the State argued that military men newly moved into Texas might not have local interests sufficiently in mind, and therefore could be excluded from voting in state elections. This Court replied:

> "But if they are in fact residents, . . . they, as all other qualified residents, have a right to an equal opportunity for political representation. . . . 'Fencing out' from the franchise a sector of the population because of the way they may vote is constitutionally impermissible." 380 U.S. [89], 94 [(1965)] [p. 90].

Similarly here, Tennessee's hopes for voters with a "common interest in all matters pertaining to [the community's] government" is impermissible.[27] To paraphrase what we said elsewhere, "All too often, lack of a ['common interest']

° In 1970, Congress amended the Voting Rights Act to prohibit durational residence requirements for presidential elections. *See* 52 U.S.C. § 10502(c). Further, the amendment required states to accept registrants until thirty days prior to an election. *See* 52 U.S.C. § 10502(d). Congress declared that durational residence requirements, as applied to presidential elections, "den[y] or abridge[] the inherent constitutional right of citizens to vote for their President and Vice President," "den[y] or abridge[] the inherent constitutional right of citizens to enjoy their free movement across State lines," violate the Privileges and Immunities Clause of Article IV, have "the effect" of denying rights protected by the Fourteenth Amendment, and "do[] not bear a reasonable relationship to any compelling State interest in the conduct of presidential elections." 52 U.S.C. § 10502(a). Congress also stated that a durational residence requirement in presidential elections "in some instances has the impermissible purpose or effect of denying citizens the right to vote for such officers because of the way they may vote," 52 U.S.C. § 10502(a)(4), though it is not clear what it means to create an "effect . . . because of the way [new residents] may vote" without having the "purpose" of so doing. [— Eds.]

[27] It has been noted elsewhere, and with specific reference to Tennessee law, that "[t]he historical purpose of [durational] residency requirements seems to have been to deny the vote to undesirables, immigrants and outsiders with different ideas." We do not rely on this alleged original purpose of durational residence requirements in striking them down today.

might mean no more than a different interest." "[D]ifferences of opinion" may not be the basis for excluding any group or person from the franchise. "[T]he fact that newly arrived [Tennesseeans] may have a more national outlook than longtime residents, or even may retain a viewpoint characteristic of the region from which they have come, is a constitutionally impermissible reason for depriving them of their chance to influence the electoral vote of their new home State."

Finally, * * * Tennessee argues that people who have been in the State less than a year and the county less than three months are likely to be unaware of the issues involved in the congressional, state, and local elections, and therefore can be barred from the franchise. We note that the criterion of "intelligent" voting is an elusive one, and susceptible of abuse. But without deciding as a general matter the extent to which a State can bar less knowledgeable or intelligent citizens from the franchise, we conclude that durational residence requirements cannot be justified on this basis. * * *

[T]he durational residence requirements in this case founder because of their crudeness as a device for achieving the articulated state goal of assuring the knowledgeable exercise of the franchise. The classifications created by durational residence requirements obviously permit any longtime resident to vote regardless of his knowledge of the issues — and obviously many longtime residents do not have any. On the other hand, the classifications bar from the franchise many other, admittedly new, residents who have become at least minimally, and often fully, informed about the issues. Indeed, recent migrants who take the time to register and vote shortly after moving are likely to be those citizens, such as appellee, who make it a point to be informed and knowledgeable about the issues. Given modern communications, and given the clear indication that campaign spending and voter education occur largely during the month before an election, the State cannot seriously maintain that it is "necessary" to reside for a year in the State and three months in the county in order to be knowledgeable about congressional, state, or even purely local elections. * * *

It is pertinent to note that Tennessee has never made an attempt to further its alleged interest in an informed electorate in a universally applicable way. Knowledge or competence has never been a criterion for participation in Tennessee's electoral process for longtime residents. * * * If the State seeks to assure intelligent use of the ballot, it may not try to serve this interest only with respect to new arrivals.

It may well be true that new residents as a group know less about state and local issues than older residents; and it is surely true that durational residence requirements will exclude some people from voting who are totally uninformed about election matters. But as devices to limit the franchise to knowledgeable residents, the conclusive presumptions of durational residence requirements are much too crude. They exclude too many people who should not, and need not, be excluded. * * * We are aware that classifications are always imprecise. By requiring classifications to be tailored to their purpose, we do not secretly require the impossible. Here, there is simply too attenuated a relationship between the state interest in an informed electorate and the fixed requirement that voters must have been residents in the State for a year and the county for three months. Given the exacting standard of precision we require of statutes affecting constitutional rights, we cannot say that durational residence requirements are necessary to further a compelling state interest. * * *

Affirmed.

Mr. Justice Powell and Mr. Justice Rehnquist took no part in the consideration or decision of this case.

Mr. Justice Blackmun, concurring in the result.

I cannot so blithely explain *Pope* v. *Williams* away, as does the Court, by asserting that if that opinion is "[c]arefully read," one sees that the case was concerned simply with a requirement that the new arrival declare his intention. The requirement was that he make the declaration *a year* before he registered to vote; time as well as intent was involved. For me, therefore, the Court today really overrules the holding in *Pope* v. *Williams* and does not restrict itself, as footnote 7 says, to rejecting what it says are mere dicta. * * *

The Tennessee plan, based both in statute and in the State's constitution, is not ideal. I am content that the one-year and three-month requirements be struck down for want of something more closely related to the State's interest. It is, of course, a matter of line drawing, as the Court concedes. But if 30 days pass constitutional muster, what of 35 or 45 or 75? The resolution of these longer measures, less than those today struck down, the Court leaves, I suspect, to the future.

Mr. Chief Justice Burger, dissenting.

The holding of the Court in *Pope* v. *Williams* is as valid today as it was at the turn of the century. It is no more a denial of equal protection for a State to require newcomers to be exposed to state and local problems for a reasonable period such as one year before voting, than it is to require children to wait 18 years before voting. In both cases some informed and responsible persons are denied the vote, while others less informed and less responsible are permitted to vote. Some lines must be drawn. To challenge such lines by the "compelling state interest" standard is to condemn them all. So far as I am aware, no state law has ever satisfied this seemingly insurmountable standard, and I doubt one ever will, for it demands nothing less than perfection.

The existence of a constitutional "right to travel" does not persuade me to the contrary. If the imposition of a durational residency requirement for voting abridges the right to travel, surely the imposition of an age qualification penalizes the young for being young, a status I assume the Constitution also protects.

Notes and Questions

1.   Recall the discussion, earlier in this Chapter, of felon disenfranchisement. Is there a constitutionally significant difference between the attempt to exclude outside influences in *Carrington* and *Blumstein*, on the one hand, and the attempt to limit the political influence of criminals, on the other?

2.   *Carrington* and *Blumstein* establish that states must allow bona-fide residents to vote, and cannot conclusively presume that certain categories of persons lack an intent to remain in the state permanently. Nevertheless, many college students and persons serving in the military intend to move elsewhere upon graduation or termination of their military service. How may a state identify which individuals within those classes intend to establish permanent residency? In *Symm v. United States*, 439 U.S. 1105 (1979), the Court summarily affirmed a lower-court judgment that held unconstitutional Waller County, Texas's, use of a residency questionnaire. The County, which is the home to Prairie View A&M University, a predominantly black institution, distributed the questionnaire to persons registering to vote. The questionnaire asked whether the applicant was a college student. Those applicants answering in the affirmative were then asked follow-up questions:

> [W]here do you attend school? How long have you been a student at such school? Where do you live while in college? How long have you lived in Texas? In Waller County? Do you intend to reside in Waller County indefinitely? How long have you considered yourself to be a bona fide resident of Waller County? What do you plan to do when you finish your college education? Do you have a job or position in Waller County? Own any home or other property in Waller County? Have an automobile registered in Waller County? Have a telephone listing in Waller County? Belong to a Church, Club or some Waller County Organization other than college related? If so, please name them[.] Where do you live when the college is not in session? What address is listed as your home address with the college? Give any other information which might be helpful:

United States v. Texas, 445 F. Supp. 1245, 1262 (S.D. Tex. 1978), *summarily aff'd*, 439 U.S. 1105 (1978). The official in charge of voter registration testified that he did not rely on any of these factors alone, but considered them together to determine residency. *Id.* at 1251. He further testified that "generally students are not regarded by him as residents unless they do something to qualify as permanent residents, such as marrying and living with their spouse or obtaining a promise of a job in Waller County when they complete school." *Id.* In what way(s) did Waller County's registration procedures violate the Constitution?

3.   Should college students be able to establish a domicile in the jurisdiction of their college even if they do not intend to stay after graduation? *See Hershkoff v. Board of Registrars of Voters of Worcester*, 321 N.E.2d 656 (Mass. 1974) (permitting students to establish a domicile in the place where they attend school). May a person establish a domicile in a place where he resides *involuntarily*, as by imprisonment or institutionalization? *See Dane v. Board of Registrars of Voters of Concord*, 371 N.E.2d 1358 (Mass. 1977) (permitting prisoners to establish a domicile in the place of incarceration, but establishing a rebuttable presumption that prisoners retain their former domicile).

4. *Problem.* You are counsel to the city council in Sleepyville, a quiet city with a population that is mostly elderly. The state has decided to create a large new state university, and locate it in Sleepyville. The residents are concerned that if resident university students vote in local elections, their strength will overcome the votes of the long-term residents, with the result that zoning regulations will be relaxed to permit more bars, nightclubs, tattoo parlors, and the like. City ordinances establish the qualifications for voting in city elections. What can you do to minimize the likelihood that the university students will elect councilors with views in line with those of the students?

5. *Carrington* and *Blumstein* may lead you to believe that all but the most minimal registration requirements for voting will be subjected to strict scrutiny and invalidated. Not so. *Rosario v. Rockefeller*, 410 U.S. 752 (1973), upheld a requirement that persons wishing to vote in a primary election join the party before the preceding general election, *i.e.*, eight to eleven months before the primary election. The following case, decided two days before *Rosario* and one year after *Blumstein* (but with the participation of Justices Powell and Rehnquist), upheld Arizona's fifty-day durational-residency requirement, despite *Blumstein*'s dictum that thirty days would be sufficient time to manage the voter rolls.

MARSTON v. LEWIS
Supreme Court of the United States
410 U.S. 679, 93 S. Ct. 1211, 35 L. Ed. 2d 627 (1973)

PER CURIAM. [MR. CHIEF JUSTICE BURGER, MR. JUSTICE STEWART, MR. JUSTICE WHITE, MR. JUSTICE BLACKMUN, MR. JUSTICE POWELL, and MR. JUSTICE REHNQUIST join in this opinion.]

Fourteen county recorders and other public officials of Arizona appeal from a judgment of a three-judge district court holding the State's 50-day durational voter residency requirement and its 50-day voter registration requirement unconstitutional under the decision in *Dunn* v. *Blumstein*, 405 U.S. 330 (1972) [p. 93]. * * * Appellants do not seek review of the District Court's judgment insofar as it enjoins application of the 50-day requirements in presidential elections. See 52 U.S.C. § 10502. Appellants assert, however, that the requirements, as applied to special, primary, or general elections involving state and local officials, are supported by sufficiently strong local interests to pass constitutional muster. We agree and reverse.

In *Dunn* v. *Blumstein*, we struck down Tennessee's durational voter residency requirement of one year in the State and three months in the county. We recognized that a person does not have a federal constitutional right to walk up to a voting place on election day and demand a ballot. States have valid and sufficient interests in providing for *some* period of time — prior to an election — in order to prepare adequate voter records and protect its electoral processes from possible fraud. A year, or even three months, was found too long, particularly in the context of "the judgment of the Tennessee lawmakers," who had set "the cutoff point for registration [at] 30 days before an election. . . ." 405 U.S., at 349. The Arizona scheme, however, stands in a different light. The durational residency requirement is only 50 days, not a year or even three months. Moreover, unlike Tennessee's, the Arizona requirement is tied to the closing of the State's registration process at 50 days prior to elections and reflects a state legislative judgment that the period is necessary to achieve the State's legitimate goals.

We accept that judgment, particularly in light of the realities of Arizona's registration and voting procedures. Those procedures, apparently first adopted during the Populist Era, rely on a "massive" volunteer deputy registrar system. According to appellants' testimony, although these volunteers make registration convenient for voters, they average 1.13 mistakes per voter registration and the county recorder must correct those mistakes before certifying to the "completeness and correctness" of each precinct register. The District Court itself noted that there were estimates that "in Maricopa County alone, some 4,400 registered voters might be denied the right to vote if the county voter list is in error by only one percent."

An additional complicating factor in Arizona registration procedures is the State's fall primary system. The uncontradicted testimony demonstrates that in the weeks preceding the deadline for registration in general elections — a period marked by a curve toward the "peak" in terms of the registration affidavits received — county recorders and their staffs are unable to process the incoming affidavits because of their work in the fall primaries. It is only after the primaries are over that the officials can return to the accumulated backlog of registration affidavits and undertake to process them in accordance with applicable statutory requirements.

On the basis of the evidence before the District Court, it is clear that the State has demonstrated that the 50-day voter registration cutoff (for election of state and local officials) is necessary to permit preparation of accurate voter lists. We said in *Dunn* v. *Blumstein* that "fixing a constitutionally acceptable period is surely a matter of degree. It is sufficient to note here that 30 days appears to be an ample period of time for the State to complete whatever administrative tasks are necessary to prevent fraud — and a year, or three months, too much." 405 U.S., at 348. In the present case, we are confronted with a recent and amply justifiable legislative judgment that 50 days rather than 30 is necessary to promote the State's important interest in accurate voter lists. The Constitution is not so rigid that that determination and others like it may not stand.

The judgment of the District Court, insofar as it has been appealed from, is

Reversed.

Mr. Justice Marshall, with whom Mr. Justice Douglas and Mr. Justice Brennan concur, dissenting.

In *Dunn* v. *Blumstein*, just last Term, we held that a 30-day residency requirement provided the State with "an ample period of time . . . to complete whatever administrative tasks are necessary to prevent fraud" in the process of voter registration. We made that judgment in light of the facts that Congress had made a similar judgment as to presidential and vice-presidential elections, that roughly half the States had periods of similar length, and that the evidence needed to determine residency was relatively easy to find. The District Court, after hearing evidence about the administrative burdens in Arizona, found that appellants needed no longer than 30 days to complete the same tasks. I find nothing in the record that leads me to conclude that this judgment was erroneous.

The Court relies on two factors to justify the longer period. First, Arizona's volunteer registrar system is said to result in so many errors that their correction requires 45 days. But these errors occur only because the deputy registrars are inadequately trained and the central supervision of the data-control process is not well organized. * * * Appellants presented no evidence that improvements in the administration of the deputy registrar system, including earlier recruitment and better training of deputy registrars and of data-processing personnel in the central offices, could not be adopted before the next election. If, as we held in *Dunn*, the State "cannot choose means which unnecessarily burden or restrict constitutionally protected activity," and if the State must carry "a heavy burden of justification," 405 U.S., at 343, surely it must show that it cannot, by better administration, eliminate the errors that justified a 50-day period in 1972. The District Court, in my view, correctly concluded that "the State has presented no facts demonstrating a compelling interest" in its 50-day requirement.

The second "complicating factor" is said to be the burden on county recorders caused by the need to interrupt the processing of affidavits filed by new registrants in order for them to work on the fall primaries. Here too the appellants showed no need to use small staffs. It is by no means obvious that the recorders' staffs could not be increased temporarily to deal with this "complication." Certainly that is a method of processing affidavits which less seriously burdens the right to vote. "And if there are other, reasonable ways to achieve those goals with a lesser burden on constitutionally protected activity, a State may not choose the way of greater interference." *Dunn* v. *Blumstein, supra*, at 343.

In addition, appellants have established a system to register voters for presidential and vice-presidential elections, in compliance with the requirement of 52 U.S.C. § 10502(d), that no State may impose a residency requirement of greater than 30 days for such elections. In Arizona, those voters who qualify for presidential and vice-presidential elections, but not for state elections, are given absentee ballots. This eliminates the necessity to prepare a separate list of registration lists. Any administrative problems caused by the inability to correct misspellings, to alphabetize the lists, and to determine in which precinct the voter lived — the only difficulties which appellants mentioned in their testimony — could be eliminated by similar treatment of late registrants for all elections. And if these voters did not have to appear at the polls, the fears of deterring other voters by delays at the polling places would disappear.

Even if the evidence below established that the administrative burdens of a 30-day limitation on general registration could not possibly be removed, that would not itself justify the same limitation on registration of newly arrived voters. General registration requirements affect every voter in the State. Durational residency requirements affect a much smaller class of potential voters, and the burdens of registering the members of that class will therefore be significantly smaller. Further, general registration requirements, with which any otherwise eligible voter may comply if he acts with sufficient diligence, might be thought to impair less substantially the right to vote than do durational residency requirements, which bar a newly arrived voter from any participation in the elections. Serious administrative problems might justify the less severe impairment, but a total bar to participation can be justified only by administrative problems of the highest order.

In short, the evidence produced below abundantly supports the District Court's conclusion that appellants had failed to carry the heavy burden of justifying the 50-day limitation period in light of reasonably available and less restrictive alternatives. If this Court has drawn a line beyond which reliance on administrative inconvenience is extremely questionable, as we did in *Dunn*, we can avoid an unprincipled numbers game only if we insist that any deviations from the line we have drawn, after mature consideration, be justified by far more substantial evidence than that produced in the District Court by appellants. I would therefore affirm the judgment of the District Court.

Notes and Questions

1.   Under what circumstances would a fifty-day requirement be unconstitutional, even after *Lewis*? What was different about this case that justified the fifty-day requirement here? What does *Lewis* tell us about how to evaluate the constitutionality of lengthier requirements — ones between the fifty-day requirement upheld in *Lewis* and the three-month requirement struck down in *Blumstein*?

2.   Under Justice Marshall's approach, would *any* durational-residency requirement be constitutional?

3.   Note that the materials in this portion of the Chapter involve durational-residency requirements for *voting*. Durational-residency requirements for *candidacy* for state office are subject to much less stringent constitutional review.[p] (Durational-residency requirements for federal office are unconstitutional because they add to the Constitution's exclusive list of qualifications for the House and Senate, which require only habitation in the state at the time of election. *See, e.g., Schaefer v. Townsend*, 215 F.3d 1031 (9th Cir. 2000); *cf. U.S. Term Limits, Inc. v. Thornton*, 514 U.S. 779 (1995) [p. 550].)

4.   After having explored the constitutional protection of political participation

---

[p] *See Sununu v. Stark*, 420 U.S. 958 (1975), *summarily aff'g*, 383 F. Supp. 1287 (D.N.H. 1974) (upholding a seven-year durational-residency requirement for state senators); *Chimento v. Stark*, 414 U.S. 802 (1973), *summarily aff'g*, 353 F. Supp. 1211 (D.N.H.) (upholding a seven-year durational-residency requirement for governor); *City of Akron v. Bell*, 660 F.2d 166 (6th Cir. 1981) (upholding a one-year durational-residency requirement for ward councilors); *Mobley v. Armstrong*, 978 S.W.2d 307 (Ky. 1998) (upholding a two-year durational-residency requirement for district judges); *Rivera v. Erie County Board of Elections*, 560 N.Y.S.2d 536 (App. Div. 1990) (upholding a one-year durational-residency requirement for members of the common council); *State ex rel. Brown v. Board of Elections*, 545 N.E.2d 1256 (Ohio 1989) (upholding two-year durational-residency requirement for city councilors); *White v. Manchin*, 318 S.E.2d 470 (W. Va. 1984) (upholding one-year durational-residency requirement for state senators). *But see Matthews v. City of Atlantic City*, 417 A.2d 1011 (N.J. 1980) (striking down a two-year durational-residency requirement for city commissioners in some New Jersey municipalities). *See also Schiavone v. Destefano*, 852 A.2d 862 (Conn. Super. Ct. 2001) (holding that a five-year residency requirement for mayor complied with the United States Constitution, but violated the Connecticut Constitution's Equal Protection Clause). *Compare Castner v. Homer*, 598 P.2d 953 (Alaska 1979) (upholding a durational-residency requirement of one year for city councilors), *with Peloza v. Freas*, 871 P.2d 687 (Alaska 1994) (striking down, under the state constitution, a different city's three-year durational residency requirement for city councilors).

in some depth through the materials in this Chapter, do you agree with Professor Gardner's assessment "that the right to vote has become so indeterminate that every observer may see in it whatever he or she wishes"? James A. Gardner, *Liberty, Community and the Constitutional Structure of Political Influence: A Reconsideration of the Right to Vote*, 145 U. PA. L. REV. 893, 896 (1997).

Chapter 2

POLITICAL QUESTIONS

A. INTRODUCTION

Under certain circumstances, federal and state courts will refuse to reach the merits of cases properly before them, on the basis that the case presents a "political question" more properly resolved in the other branches of government. Since the topics covered in this casebook all involve "political" issues to varying degrees, the political-question doctrine has the potential, depending how broadly and rigorously it is applied, to prevent many election law disputes from being resolved by the courts. Whether this result is a good or bad outcome depends on what one thinks about the appropriateness of courts deciding election issues.

The political-question doctrine in the federal courts has a venerable, if confusing and controversial, history. The doctrine can be traced back to no less than *Marbury v. Madison*, 5 U.S. (1 Cranch) 137, 170 (1803), in which Chief Justice John Marshall spoke of certain powers of the President lying in his sole discretion, beyond the control of courts. Challenges to the President's exercise of such discretionary authority presented "[q]uestions, in their nature political," unfit for judicial resolution. As the Court explained:

> Where the head of a department acts in a case, in which executive discretion is to be exercised; in which he is the mere organ of executive will; * * * any application to a court to control, in any respect, his conduct, would be rejected without hesitation.
>
> But where he is directed by law to do a certain act affecting the absolute rights of individuals, in the performance of which he is not placed under the particular direction of the President, and the performance of which, the President cannot lawfully forbid, and therefore is never presumed to have forbidden * * *, it is not perceived on what ground the courts of the country are further excused from the duty of giving judgment, that right be done to an injured individual, than if the same services were to be performed by a person not the head of a department.

Id. at 170–71.

The Supreme Court has since considered whether the political-question doctrine applies to issues besides the unique facts presented in *Marbury*. Some of these cases involved various aspects of election law, and the Court held that they did not present non-justiciable political questions. *See, e.g., Nixon v. Herndon*, 273 U.S. 536, 540 (1927) (holding racial discrimination in Texas Democratic primary unconstitutional, and remarking that to invoke the political-question doctrine because the political process was at issue was "little more than a play upon words"); *Baker v. Carr*, 369 U.S. 186 (1962) [p. 119] (holding that an equal-protection challenge to gerrymandering of state legislative districts did not present a political question, and distilling criteria to apply the doctrine, addressed below).

The doctrine has generated a large amount of scholarly commentary. Some writers defend the doctrine, arguing that federal judges should be able to exercise prudential judgment to defer reaching the merits of particularly difficult or contentious issues, which are better resolved by the other, more democratically accountable branches of government. *E.g.*, ALEXANDER BICKEL, THE LEAST DANGEROUS BRANCH (1962). In contrast, other writers argue that the doctrine is an inappropriate and unprincipled exercise of authority by judges, when they are presented with cases otherwise properly before them. On this account, the courts have a duty to reach the merits, particularly when constitutional rights are involved, and the doctrine itself is based on "political" considerations that judges should not take into account. *E.g.*, Martin H. Redish, *Judicial Review and the Political Question*, 79 Nw. U. L. REV. 1031 (1985). Scholarly discussion continues apace. *E.g.*, Rachel E. Barkow, *More Supreme than Court? The Fall of the Political Question Doctrine*, 102 COLUM. L. REV. 237 (2002); Jesse Choper, *The Political Question Doctrine: Suggested Criteria*, 54 DUKE L.J. 1457 (2005); Richard F. Fallon, Jr., *Judicially Manageable Standards and Constitutional Meaning*, 119 HARV. L. REV. 1275 (2006). As you read the cases in the remainder of this Chapter, consider whether the doctrine is more (or less) persuasively applied when the case involves the structure of governance, as election-law issues do, as opposed to some other aspect of the substantive authority of the other branches (*e.g.*, the foreign-affairs powers of the President).

The political-question doctrine has also been applied by state courts considering legal challenges to the actions of other branches of the state government. To the extent they apply the doctrine, some states borrow the criteria developed in federal courts. But on the whole, the doctrine has been applied less robustly by many state courts, in part because state constitutions are typically much longer and more detailed than the Federal Constitution, and seem to call for more judicial interpretation and application of those provisions. Since most state judges are subject to periodic elections to attain or retain office, some have argued that this greater democratic accountability makes the doctrine less appropriate at the state level. *Compare* Helen Hershkoff, *State Courts and the "Passive Virtues": Rethinking the Judicial Function*, 114 HARV. L. REV. 1833 (2001) (advancing such an argument), *with* Christine M. Durham, *The Judicial Branch in State Government: Parables of Law, Politics, and Power*, 76 N.Y.U. L. REV. 1601 (2001) (expressing skepticism of an activist role by state judiciaries). *See also* James A. Gardner, *A Post-*Vieth *Strategy for Litigating Partisan Gerrymandering Claims*, 3 ELECTION L.J. 643 (2004) (arguing that claims barred by the political-question doctrine in federal court can be pursued in state court).

B.   THE NON-JUSTICIABILITY OF THE GUARANTEE CLAUSE

Article IV, § 4 of the U.S. Constitution states that "[t]he United States shall guarantee to every State in this Union a Republican Form of Government." Beginning with the canonical decision in *Luther v. Borden*, 48 U.S. (7 How.) 1 (1849), the Supreme Court has held that federal courts cannot hear legal challenges to state governmental structures or processes on the ground that they violate the Guarantee Clause. *Luther* involved a series of changes to the state constitution of Rhode Island, which resulted in controversy and confusion about the proper governmental authority in that state. The case came before the Court due to a challenge to a search undertaken by a sheriff of the Rhode Island government. The challenger argued that the search was unlawful, since it was undertaken on behalf of a government that was not in a republican form. The Court held that the challenge was non-justiciable, since it was up to Congress to enforce the Guarantee Clause. Among other things, the Court observed that it was unclear how to determine whether or not a state had a republican form of government.

While *Luther* has long stood for the proposition that Guarantee Clause challenges in federal court are barred by the political-question doctrine, that understanding has not prevented litigants, and the Court, from revisiting the issue, as the following cases indicate.

PACIFIC STATES TELEPHONE & TELEGRAPH CO. v. OREGON
Supreme Court of the United States.
223 U.S. 118, 32 S. Ct. 224, 56 L. Ed. 377 (1912)

Mr. Chief Justice White delivered the opinion of the court [in which Mr. Justice McKenna, Mr. Justice Holmes, Mr. Justice Lurton, Mr. Justice Hughes, Mr. Justice Van Devanter, and Mr. Justice Lamar join].[a]

We premise by saying that while the controversy which this record presents is of much importance, it is not novel. It is important, since it calls upon us to decide whether it is the duty of the courts or the province of Congress to determine when a State has ceased to be republican in form, and to enforce the guaranty of the Constitution on that subject. It is not novel, as that question has long since been determined by this court conformably to the practise of the Government from the beginning to be political in character, and therefore not cognizable by the judicial power, but solely committed by the Constitution to the judgment of Congress.

The case is this: In 1902 Oregon amended its constitution. This amendment while retaining an existing clause vesting the exclusive legislative power in a General Assembly consisting of a senate and a house of representatives added to that provision the following: "But the people reserve to themselves power to propose laws and amendments to the Constitution, and to enact or reject the same at the

---

[a] The case was argued between Justice Harlan's death and Justice Pitney's investiture, and during the absence of Justice Day while he attended to his wife during her final illness. As a result, it was decided by a seven-Member Court. — Eds.

polls, independent of the legislative assembly, and also reserve power at their own option to approve or reject at the polls any act of the legislative assembly." Specific means for the exercise of the power thus reserved was contained in further clauses authorizing both the amendment of the constitution and the enactment of laws to be accomplished by the method known as the initiative and that commonly referred to as the referendum. As to the first, the initiative, it suffices to say that a stated number of voters were given the right at any time to secure a submission to popular vote for approval of any matter which it was desired to have enacted into law, and providing that the proposition thus submitted when approved by popular vote should become the law of the State. The second, the referendum, provided for a reference to a popular vote, for approval or disapproval, of any law passed by the legislature, such reference to take place either as the result of the action of the legislature itself, or of a petition filed for that purpose by a specified number of voters. * * *

By resort to the initiative in 1906 a law taxing certain classes of corporations was submitted, voted on and promulgated by the Governor in 1906 as having been duly adopted. By this law telephone and telegraph companies were taxed, by what was qualified as an annual license, two per centum upon their gross revenue derived from business done within the State. Penalties were provided for non-payment, and methods were created for enforcing payment in case of delinquency.

The Pacific States Telephone and Telegraph Company, an Oregon corporation engaged in business in that State, made a return of its gross receipts as required by the statute and was accordingly assessed 2 per cent. upon the amount of such return. The suit which is now before us was commenced by the State to enforce payment of this assessment and the statutory penalties for delinquency. * * *

[The company's legal challenges] are all based upon the single contention that the creation by a State of the power to legislate by the initiative and referendum causes the prior lawful state government to be bereft of its lawful character as the result of the provisions of § 4 of Art. IV of the Constitution, that "The United States shall guarantee to every State in this Union a Republican Form of Government, and shall protect each of them against Invasion; and on Application of the Legislature, or of the Executive (when the Legislature cannot be convened), against domestic Violence." This being the basis of all the contentions, the case comes to the single issue whether the enforcement of that provision, because of its political character, is exclusively committed to Congress, or is judicial in its character. * * *

"It was long ago settled that the enforcement of this guaranty belonged to the political department. *Luther* v. *Borden*, [48 U.S.] 7 How. 1 [(1849)]. In that case it was held that the question, which of the two opposing governments of Rhode Island, namely, the charter government or the government established by a voluntary convention, was the legitimate one, was a question for the determination of the political department; and when that department had decided, the courts were bound to take notice of the decision and follow it. . . ." [*Taylor* v. *Beckham, No. 1*, 178 U.S. 548 (1900).]

It is indeed a singular misconception of the nature and character of our constitutional system of government to suggest that the settled distinction which the doctrine just stated points out between judicial authority over justiciable controversies and legislative power as to purely political questions tends to destroy the duty of the judiciary in proper cases to enforce the Constitution. The suggestion but results from failing to distinguish between things which are widely different, that is, the legislative duty to determine the political questions involved in deciding whether a state government republican in form exists, and the judicial power and ever-present duty whenever it becomes necessary in a controversy properly submitted to enforce and uphold the applicable provisions of the Constitution as to each and every exercise of governmental power.

How better can the broad lines which distinguish these two subjects be pointed out than by considering the character of the defense in this very case? The defendant company does not contend here that it could not have been required to pay a license tax. It does not assert that it was denied an opportunity to be heard as to the amount for which it was taxed, or that there was anything inhering in the tax or involved intrinsically in the law which violated any of its constitutional rights. If such questions had been raised they would have been justiciable, and therefore would have required the calling into operation of judicial power. Instead, however, of doing any of these things, the attack on the statute here made is of a wholly different character. Its essentially political nature is at once made manifest by understanding that the assault which the contention here advanced makes it not on the tax as a tax, but on the State as a State. It is addressed to the framework and political character of the government by which the statute levying the tax was passed. It is the government, the political entity, which (reducing the case to its essence) is called to the bar of this court, not for the purpose of testing judicially some exercise of power assailed, on the ground that its exertion has injuriously affected the rights of an individual because of repugnancy to some constitutional limitation, but to demand of the State that it establish its right to exist as a State, republican in form.

As the issues presented, in their very essence, are, and have long since by this court been, definitely determined to be political and governmental, and embraced within the scope of the powers conferred upon Congress, and not therefore within the reach of judicial power, it follows that the case presented is not within our jurisdiction, and the writ of error must therefore be, and it is, dismissed for want of jurisdiction.

Dismissed for want of jurisdiction.

COLEGROVE v. GREEN
Supreme Court of the United States
328 U.S. 549, 66 S. Ct. 1198, 90 L. Ed. 1432 (1946)

MR. JUSTICE FRANKFURTER announced the judgment of the Court and an opinion in which MR. JUSTICE REED and MR. JUSTICE BURTON concur.

* * * [Appellants] are three qualified voters in Illinois districts which have much larger populations than other Illinois Congressional districts. They brought this suit against the Governor, the Secretary of State, and the Auditor of the State of Illinois, as members *ex officio* of the Illinois Primary Certifying Board, to restrain them, in

effect, from taking proceedings for an election in November 1946, under the provisions of Illinois law governing Congressional districts. * * *

We are of opinion that the petitioners ask of this Court what is beyond its competence to grant. This is one of those demands on judicial power which cannot be met by verbal fencing about "jurisdiction." It must be resolved by considerations on the basis of which this Court, from time to time, has refused to intervene in controversies. It has refused to do so because due regard for the effective working of our Government revealed this issue to be of a peculiarly political nature and therefore not meet for judicial determination.

This is not an action to recover for damage because of the discriminatory exclusion of a plaintiff from rights enjoyed by other citizens. The basis for the suit is not a private wrong, but a wrong suffered by Illinois as a polity. Compare *Nixon* v. *Herndon*, 273 U.S. 536 [(1927)] and *Lane* v. *Wilson*, 307 U.S. 268 [(1939)], with *Giles* v. *Harris*, 189 U.S. 475 [(1903)]. In effect this is an appeal to the federal courts to reconstruct the electoral process of Illinois in order that it may be adequately represented in the councils of the Nation. Because the Illinois legislature has failed to revise its Congressional Representative districts in order to reflect great changes, during more than a generation, in the distribution of its population, we are asked to do this, as it were, for Illinois.

Of course no court can affirmatively re-map the Illinois districts so as to bring them more in conformity with the standards of fairness for a representative system. At best we could only declare the existing electoral system invalid. The result would be to leave Illinois undistricted and to bring into operation, if the Illinois legislature chose not to act, the choice of members for the House of Representatives on a state-wide ticket. The last stage may be worse than the first. The upshot of judicial action may defeat the vital political principle which led Congress, more than a hundred years ago, to require districting. This requirement, in the language of Chancellor Kent, "was recommended by the wisdom and justice of giving, as far as possible, to the local subdivisions of the people of each state, a due influence in the choice of representatives, so as not to leave the aggregate minority of the people in a state, though approaching perhaps to a majority, to be wholly overpowered by the combined action of the numerical majority, without any voice whatever in the national councils." 1 Kent, *Commentaries* (12th ed., 1873) *230–31, n. (c). Assuming acquiescence on the part of the authorities of Illinois in the selection of its Representatives by a mode that defies the direction of Congress for selection by districts, the House of Representatives may not acquiesce. In the exercise of its power to judge the qualifications of its own members, the House may reject a delegation of Representatives-at-large. * * * Nothing is clearer than that this controversy concerns matters that bring courts into immediate and active relations with party contests. From the determination of such issues this Court has traditionally held aloof. It is hostile to a democratic system to involve the judiciary in the politics of the people. And it is not less pernicious if such judicial intervention in an essentially political contest be dressed up in the abstract phrases of the law.

The petitioners urge with great zeal that the conditions of which they complain are grave evils and offend public morality. The Constitution of the United States gives ample power to provide against these evils. But due regard for the Constitution as a viable system precludes judicial correction. Authority for dealing with such problems resides elsewhere. Article I, § 4 of the Constitution provides that "The Times, Places and Manner of holding Elections for . . . Representatives, shall be prescribed in each State by the Legislature thereof; but the Congress may at any time by Law make or alter such Regulations, . . ." The short of it is that the Constitution has conferred upon Congress exclusive authority to secure fair representation by the States in the popular House and left to that House determination whether States have fulfilled their responsibility. If Congress failed in exercising its powers, whereby standards of fairness are offended, the remedy ultimately lies with the people. Whether Congress faithfully discharges its duty or not, the subject has been committed to the exclusive control of Congress. An aspect of government from which the judiciary, in view of what is involved, has been excluded by the clear intention of the Constitution cannot be entered by the federal courts because Congress may have been in default in exacting from States obedience to its mandate.

The one stark fact that emerges from a study of the history of Congressional apportionment is its embroilment in politics, in the sense of party contests and party interests. The Constitution enjoins upon Congress the duty of apportioning Representatives "among the several States . . . according to their respective Numbers, . . ." Article I, § 2. Yet, Congress has at times been heedless of this command and not apportioned according to the requirements of the Census. It never occurred to anyone that this Court could issue mandamus to compel Congress to perform its mandatory duty to apportion. * * * Until 1842 there was the greatest diversity among the States in the manner of choosing Representatives because Congress had made no requirement for districting. 5 Stat. 491. Congress then provided for the election of Representatives by districts. Strangely enough the power to do so was seriously questioned; it was still doubted by a Committee of Congress as late as 1901. In 1850 Congress dropped the requirement. 9 Stat. 428, 432–33. The Reapportionment Act of 1862 required that the districts be of contiguous territory. 12 Stat. 572. In 1872 Congress added the requirement of substantial equality of inhabitants. 17 Stat. 28. This was reinforced in 1911. 37 Stat. 13, 14. But the 1929 Act * * * dropped these requirements. 46 Stat. 21. Throughout our history, whatever may have been the controlling Apportionment Act, the most glaring disparities have prevailed as to the contours and the population of districts. * * *

To sustain this action would cut very deep into the very being of Congress. Courts ought not to enter this political thicket. The remedy for unfairness in districting is to secure State legislatures that will apportion properly, or to invoke the ample powers of Congress. The Constitution has many commands that are not enforceable by courts because they clearly fall outside the conditions and purposes that circumscribe judicial action. Thus, "on Demand of the executive Authority," Art. IV, § 2, of a State it is the duty of a sister State to deliver up a fugitive from justice. But the fulfillment of this duty cannot be judicially enforced. *Kentucky* v. *Dennison*, [65 U.S.] 24 How. 66 [(1860)]. The duty to see to it that the laws are faithfully executed cannot be brought under legal compulsion. *Mississippi* v. *Johnson*, [71 U.S.] 4 Wall. 475 [(1866)]. Violation of the great guaranty of a republican form of government in States cannot be challenged in the courts. *Pacific States Telephone*

Co. v. *Oregon*, 223 U.S. 118 [(1912)] [p. 107]. The Constitution has left the performance of many duties in our governmental scheme to depend on the fidelity of the executive and legislative action and, ultimately, on the vigilance of the people in exercising their political rights.

Dismissal of the complaint is affirmed.

MR. JUSTICE JACKSON took no part in the consideration or decision of this case.

MR. JUSTICE RUTLEDGE. * * *

[T]his complaint should be dismissed for [want of equity]. Assuming that the controversy is justiciable, I think the cause is of so delicate a character * * * that the jurisdiction should be exercised only in the most compelling circumstances. * * *

If the constitutional provisions on which appellants rely give them the substantive rights they urge, other provisions qualify those rights in important ways by vesting large measures of control in the political subdivisions of the Government and the state. There is not, and could not be except abstractly, a right of absolute equality in voting. At best there could be only a rough approximation. And there is obviously considerable latitude for the bodies vested with those powers to exercise their judgment concerning how best to attain this, in full consistency with the Constitution.

The right here is not absolute. And the cure sought may be worse than the disease.

I think, therefore, the case is one in which the Court may properly, and should, decline to exercise its jurisdiction. Accordingly, the judgment should be affirmed and I join in that disposition of the cause.

MR. JUSTICE BLACK, dissenting.

The complaint alleges the following facts essential to the position I take: Petitioners, citizens and voters of Illinois, live in congressional election districts, the respective populations of which range from 612,000 to 914,000. Nineteen other congressional election districts have populations that range from 112,116 to 385,207. In seven of these districts the population is below 200,000. The Illinois Legislature established these districts in 1901 on the basis of the Census of 1900. The Federal Census of 1910, of 1920, of 1930, and of 1940, each showed a growth of population in Illinois and a substantial shift in the distribution of population among the districts established in 1901. But up to date, attempts to have the State Legislature reapportion congressional election districts so as more nearly to equalize their population have been unsuccessful. A contributing cause of this situation, according to petitioners, is the fact that the State Legislature is chosen on the basis of state election districts inequitably apportioned in a way similar to that of the 1901 congressional election districts. The implication is that the issues of state and congressional apportionment are thus so interdependent that it is to the interest of state legislators to perpetuate the inequitable apportionment of both state and congressional election districts. Prior to this proceeding a series of suits had been brought in the state courts challenging the State's local and federal apportionment system. In all these cases the Supreme Court of the State had denied effective relief.

In the present suit the complaint attacked the 1901 State Apportionment Act on the ground that it among other things violates Article I and the Fourteenth Amendment of the Constitution. Appellants claim that since they live in the heavily populated districts their vote is much less effective than the vote of those living in a district which under the 1901 Act is also allowed to choose one Congressman, though its population is sometimes only one-ninth that of the heavily populated districts. Appellants contend that this reduction of the effectiveness of their vote is the result of a wilful legislative discrimination against them and thus amounts to a denial of the equal protection of the laws guaranteed by the Fourteenth Amendment. They further assert that this reduction of the effectiveness of their vote also violates the privileges and immunities clause of the Fourteenth Amendment in abridging their privilege as citizens of the United States to vote for Congressmen, a privilege guaranteed by Article I of the Constitution. They further contend that the State Apportionment Act directly violates Article I which guarantees that each citizen eligible to vote has a right to vote for Congressmen and to have his vote counted. The assertion here is that the right to have their vote counted is abridged unless that vote is given approximately equal weight to that of other citizens. * * *

It is difficult for me to see why the 1901 State Apportionment Act does not deny petitioners equal protection of the laws. The failure of the Legislature to reapportion the congressional election districts for forty years, despite census figures indicating great changes in the distribution of the population, has resulted in election districts the populations of which range from 112,000 to 900,000. One of the petitioners lives in a district of more than 900,000 people. His vote is consequently much less effective than that of each of the citizens living in the district of 112,000. And such a gross inequality in the voting power of citizens irrefutably demonstrates a complete lack of effort to make an equitable apportionment. The 1901 State Apportionment Act if applied to the next election would thus result in a wholly indefensible discrimination against petitioners and all other voters in heavily populated districts. The equal protection clause of the Fourteenth Amendment forbids such discrimination. It does not permit the states to pick out certain qualified citizens or groups of citizens and deny them the right to vote at all. See *Nixon* v. *Herndon*, 273 U.S. [at] 541; *Nixon* v. *Condon*, 286 U.S. 73 [(1932)]. No one would deny that the equal protection clause would also prohibit a law that would expressly give certain citizens a half-vote and others a full vote. The probable effect of the 1901 State Apportionment Act in the coming election will be that certain citizens, and among them the appellants, will in some instances have votes only one-ninth as effective in choosing representatives to Congress as the votes of other citizens. Such discriminatory legislation seems to me exactly the kind that the equal protection clause was intended to prohibit.

The 1901 State Apportionment Act in reducing the effectiveness of appellants' votes abridges their privilege as citizens to vote for Congressmen and violates Article I of the Constitution. Article I provides that Congressmen "shall be . . . chosen . . . by the People of the several States." It thus gives those qualified a right to vote and a right to have their vote counted. *Ex parte Yarbrough*, 110 U.S. 651

[(1884)]; *United States* v. *Mosley*, 238 U.S. 383 [(1915)]. This Court in order to prevent "an interference with the effective choice of the voters" has held that this right extends to primaries. *United States* v. *Classic*, 313 U.S. 299, 314 [(1941)]. While the Constitution contains no express provision requiring that Congressional election districts established by the States must contain approximately equal populations, the constitutionally guaranteed right to vote and the right to have one's vote counted clearly imply the policy that state election systems, no matter what their form, should be designed to give approximately equal weight to each vote cast. To some extent this implication of Article I is expressly stated by § 2 of the Fourteenth Amendment which provides that "Representatives shall be apportioned among the several States according to their respective numbers . . ." The purpose of this requirement is obvious: It is to make the votes of the citizens of the several States equally effective in the selection of members of Congress. It was intended to make illegal a nation-wide "rotten borough" system as between the States. The policy behind it is broader than that. It prohibits as well Congressional "rotten boroughs" within the States, such as the ones here involved. The policy is that which is laid down by all the Constitutional provisions regulating the election of members of the House of Representatives, including Article I which guarantees the right to vote and to have that vote effectively counted: All groups, classes, and individuals shall to the extent that it is practically feasible be given equal representation in the House of Representatives, which, in conjunction with the Senate, writes the laws affecting the life, liberty, and property of all the people. * * *

Had Illinois passed an Act requiring that all of its twenty-six Congressmen be elected by the citizens of one county, it would clearly have amounted to a denial to the citizens of the other counties of their Constitutionally guaranteed right to vote. And I cannot imagine that an Act that would have apportioned twenty-five Congressmen to the State's smallest county and one Congressman to all the others, would have been sustained by any Court. Such an Act would clearly have violated the constitutional policy of equal representation. The 1901 Apportionment Act here involved violates that policy in the same way. The policy with respect to federal elections laid down by the Constitution, while it does not mean that the courts can or should prescribe the precise methods to be followed by state legislatures and the invalidation of all Acts that do not embody those precise methods, does mean that state legislatures must make real efforts to bring about approximately equal representation of citizens in Congress. Here the legislature of Illinois has not done so. Whether that was due to negligence or was a wilful effort to deprive some citizens of an effective vote, the admitted result is that the Constitutional policy of equality of representation has been defeated. Under these circumstances it is the Court's duty to invalidate the state law.

It is contended, however, that a court of equity does not have the power, or even if it has the power, that it should not exercise it in this case. To do so, it is argued, would mean that the Court is entering the area of "political questions." I cannot agree with that argument. * * *

It is true that voting is a part of elections and that elections are "political." But as this Court said in *Nixon* v. *Herndon, supra*, it is a mere "play on words" to refer to a controversy such as this as "political" in the sense that courts have nothing to do with protecting and vindicating the right of a voter to cast an effective ballot. * * *

Mr. Justice Douglas and Mr. Justice Murphy join in this dissent.

GOMILLION v. LIGHTFOOT
Supreme Court of the United States
364 U.S. 339, 81 S. Ct. 125, 5 L. Ed. 2d 110 (1960)

Mr. Justice Frankfurter delivered the opinion of the Court [in which Mr. Chief Justice Warren, Mr. Justice Black, Mr. Justice Douglas, Mr. Justice Clark, Mr. Justice Harlan, Mr. Justice Brennan, and Mr. Justice Stewart join].

This litigation challenges the validity, under the United States Constitution, of Local Act No. 140, passed by the Legislature of Alabama in 1957, redefining the boundaries of the City of Tuskegee. Petitioners, Negro citizens of Alabama who were, at the time of this redistricting measure, residents of the City of Tuskegee, brought an action in the United States District Court for the Middle District of Alabama for a declaratory judgment that Act 140 is unconstitutional, and for an injunction to restrain the Mayor and officers of Tuskegee and the officials of Macon County, Alabama, from enforcing the Act against them and other Negroes similarly situated. Petitioners' claim is that enforcement of the statute, which alters the shape of Tuskegee from a square to an uncouth twenty-eight-sided figure, will constitute a discrimination against them in violation of the Due Process and Equal Protection Clauses of the Fourteenth Amendment to the Constitution and will deny them the right to vote in defiance of the Fifteenth Amendment. * * *

* * * The complaint, charging that Act 140 is a device to disenfranchise Negro citizens, alleges the following facts: Prior to Act 140 the City of Tuskegee was square in shape; the Act transformed it into a strangely irregular twenty-eight-sided figure as indicated in the diagram appended to this opinion. The essential inevitable effect of this redefinition of Tuskegee's boundaries is to remove from the city all save four or five of its 400 Negro voters while not removing a single white voter or resident. The result of the Act is to deprive the Negro petitioners discriminatorily of the benefits of residence in Tuskegee, including, *inter alia*, the right to vote in municipal elections.

These allegations, if proven, would abundantly establish that Act 140 was not an ordinary geographic redistricting measure even within familiar abuses of gerrymandering. If these allegations upon a trial remained uncontradicted or unqualified, the conclusion would be irresistible, tantamount for all practical purposes to a mathematical demonstration, that the legislation is solely concerned with segregating white and colored voters by fencing Negro citizens out of town so as to deprive them of their pre-existing municipal vote.

It is difficult to appreciate what stands in the way of adjudging a statute having this inevitable effect invalid in light of the principles by which this Court must judge, and uniformly has judged, statutes that, howsoever speciously defined, obviously discriminate against colored citizens. "The [Fifteenth] Amendment nullifies sophisticated as well as simple-minded modes of discrimination." *Lane* v. *Wilson*, 307 U.S. 268, 275 [(1939)].

The complaint amply alleges a claim of racial discrimination. Against this claim the respondents have never suggested, either in their brief or in oral argument, any countervailing municipal function which Act 140 is designed to serve. The respondents invoke generalities expressing the State's unrestricted power — unlimited, that is, by the United States Constitution — to establish, destroy, or reorganize by contraction or expansion its political subdivisions, to wit, cities, counties, and other local units. We freely recognize the breadth and importance of this aspect of the State's political power. To exalt this power into an absolute is to misconceive the reach and rule of this Court's [prior] decisions[.] * * *

This line of authority conclusively shows that the Court has never acknowledged that the States have power to do as they will with municipal corporations regardless of consequences. Legislative control of municipalities, no less than other state power, lies within the scope of relevant limitations imposed by the United States Constitution. * * * The opposite conclusion, urged upon us by respondents, would sanction the achievement by a State of any impairment of voting rights whatever so long as it was cloaked in the garb of the realignment of political subdivisions. "It is inconceivable that guaranties embedded in the Constitution of the United States may thus be manipulated out of existence." *Frost & Frost Trucking Co.* v. *Railroad Commission of California*, 271 U.S. 583, 594 [(1926)].

The respondents find another barrier to the trial of this case in *Colegrove* v. *Green*, 328 U.S. 549 [(1946)] [p. 109]. * * * That case involved a complaint of discriminatory apportionment of congressional districts. The appellants in *Colegrove* complained only of a dilution of the strength of their votes as a result of legislative inaction over a course of many years. The petitioners here complain that affirmative legislative action deprives them of their votes and the consequent advantages that the ballot affords. When a legislature thus singles out a readily isolated segment of a racial minority for special discriminatory treatment, it violates the Fifteenth Amendment. In no case involving unequal weight in voting distribution that has come before the Court did the decision sanction a differentiation on racial lines whereby approval was given to unequivocal withdrawal of the vote solely from colored citizens. Apart from all else, these considerations lift this controversy out of the so-called "political" arena and into the conventional sphere of constitutional litigation.

In sum, as Mr. Justice Holmes remarked, when dealing with a related situation, in *Nixon* v. *Herndon*, 273 U.S. 536, 540 [(1927)], "Of course the petition concerns political action," but "The objection that the subject-matter of the suit is political is little more than a play upon words." A statute which is alleged to have worked unconstitutional deprivations of petitioners' rights is not immune to attack simply because the mechanism employed by the legislature is a redefinition of municipal boundaries. According to the allegations here made, the Alabama Legislature has not merely redrawn the Tuskegee city limits with incidental inconvenience to the petitioners; it is more accurate to say that it has deprived the petitioners of the municipal franchise and consequent rights and to that end it has incidentally changed the city's boundaries. While in form this is merely an act redefining metes and bounds, if the allegations are established, the inescapable human effect of this essay in geometry and geography is to despoil colored citizens, and only colored citizens, of their theretofore enjoyed voting rights. That was no *Colegrove* v. *Green*.

When a State exercises power wholly within the domain of state interest, it is insulated from federal judicial review. But such insulation is not carried over when state power is used as an instrument for circumventing a federally protected right. * * *

For these reasons, the principal conclusions of the District Court and the Court of Appeals are clearly erroneous and the decision below must be *Reversed*.

Mr. Justice Douglas, while joining the opinion of the Court, adheres to the dissents in *Colegrove* v. *Green* and *South* v. *Peters*, 339 U.S. 276 [(1950)].

APPENDIX TO OPINION OF THE COURT
Chart Showing Tuskegee, Alabama, Before and After Act 140

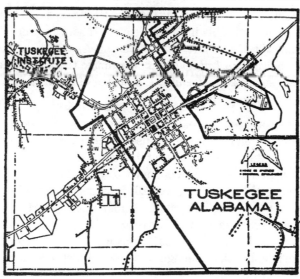

(The entire area of the square comprised the City prior to Act 140. The irregular black-bordered figure within the square represents the post-enactment city.)

Mr. Justice Whittaker, concurring.

I concur in the Court's judgment, but not in the whole of its opinion. It seems to me that the decision should be rested not on the Fifteenth Amendment, but rather on the Equal Protection Clause of the Fourteenth Amendment to the Constitution. I am doubtful that the averments of the complaint, taken for present purposes to be true, show a purpose by Act No. 140 to abridge petitioners' "right . . . to vote," in the Fifteenth Amendment sense. It seems to me that the "right . . . to vote" that is guaranteed by the Fifteenth Amendment is but the same right to vote as is enjoyed by all others within the same election precinct, ward or other political division. And, inasmuch as no one has the right to vote in a political division, or in a local election concerning only an area in which he does not reside, it would seem to follow that one's right to vote in Division A is not abridged by a redistricting that places his residence in Division B if he there enjoys the same voting privileges as all others in that Division, even though the redistricting was done by the State for the purpose of placing a racial group of citizens in Division B rather than A.

But it does seem clear to me that accomplishment of a State's purpose — to use the Court's phrase — of "fencing Negro citizens out of" Division A and into Division B is an unlawful segregation of races of citizens, in violation of the Equal Protection Clause of the Fourteenth Amendment, *Brown* v. *Board of Education*, 347 U.S. 483 [(1954)]; *Cooper* v. *Aaron*, 358 U.S. 1 [(1959)]; and, as stated, I would think the decision should be rested on that ground — which, incidentally, clearly would not involve, just as the cited cases did not involve, the *Colegrove* problem.

Notes and Questions

1.   Does or should *Luther v. Borden* stand for the proposition that all Guarantee Clause claims are non-justiciable in federal court? If so, why weren't *Pacific States* and *Colegrove* disposed of in short opinions citing *Luther*? Are the former cases more difficult to resolve than *Luther*? Is it relevant to the more recent cases if and how Congress (and perhaps other political actors) might consider and resolve issues related to Guarantee Clause claims?

2.   While most cases seem to read *Luther* and *Pacific States* for the proposition that all legal challenges on Guarantee Clause grounds are non-justiciable, that has not prevented commentators from arguing that some forms of direct democracy can violate the Clause. *See, e.g.*, Fred O. Smith, *Due Process, Republicanism, and Direct Democracy*, 89 N.Y.U. L. REV. 582 (2014) (arguing that initiative process can violate the Clause if it deprives individuals of liberty of property); Jacob M. Heller, Note, *Death by a Thousand Cuts: The Guarantee Clause Regulation of State Constitutions*, 62 STAN. L. REV. 1711 (2010) (arguing that frequent use of initiative in California to arguably micromanage legislative functions violates the Clause). Compare Robert G. Natelson, *A Republic, Not a Democracy? Initiative, Referendum, and the Constitution's Guarantee Clause*, 80 TEX. L. REV. 807 (2002) (originalist defense of direct democracy).

3.   Justice Frankfurter's opinion for a plurality in *Colegrove* is a classic exposition of the limits of federal judicial power. Did he adequately respond to Justice Black's dissent that the equal protection claims were being ignored? Conversely, did Justice Black fully appreciate the apparent dangers of courts entering the "political thicket," as described by Justice Frankfurter?

4.   In light of *Colegrove*, is the unanimous result in *Gomillion* — or the fact that the majority opinion was written by Justice Frankfurter — surprising? How did the Court distinguish *Colegrove*?

5.   In 1947, immediately after *Colegrove*, the governor of Illinois recommended a reapportionment. The state legislature not only reapportioned the electoral districts in that year, but did so again in 1951. Should that information be relevant to us in interpreting the political-question doctrine?

6. Justice Whittaker preferred to rest *Gomillion* on the Fourteenth Amendment rather than the Fifteenth. Was he right to do so? How were the plaintiffs denied the right to vote? How were they denied the equal protection of the laws? Should grounding such claims in the Fourteenth Amendment ameliorate "the *Colegrove* problem"? Consider your answer as you read the next section.

C. "WELL DEVELOPED AND FAMILIAR" STANDARDS OF EQUAL PROTECTION

The cases in the prior section illustrate that litigants and judges engaged in various efforts — some successful, some not — to circumvent the limits of *Luther* and other Guarantee Clause cases through explicit reliance on other constitutional provisions, particularly the Equal Protection Clause of the Fourteenth Amendment. But the jurisprudential shift to the Equal Protection Clause raised complications of its own, and did not automatically dispose of concerns raised by the political-question doctrine, as the following cases show.

BAKER v. CARR
Supreme Court of the United States
369 U.S. 186, 82 S. Ct. 691, 7 L. Ed. 2d 663 (1962)

MR. JUSTICE BRENNAN delivered the opinion of the Court [in which MR. CHIEF JUSTICE WARREN, MR. JUSTICE BLACK, MR. JUSTICE DOUGLAS, MR. JUSTICE CLARK, MR. JUSTICE STEWART and MR. JUSTICE GOLDBERG join]. * * *

[Plaintiffs, Tennessee voters, brought suit alleging that the apportionment of state legislative districts debased their votes in violation of the Equal Protection Clause.]

The General Assembly of Tennessee consists of the Senate with 33 members and the House of Representatives with 99 members. * * * [The Tennessee Constitution requires redistricting every ten years according to] the total number of qualified voters resident in the respective counties, subject to only minor qualifications. Decennial reapportionment in compliance with the constitutional scheme was effected by the General Assembly each decade from 1871 to 1901. * * * In the more than 60 years since [passage of the 1901 Apportionment Act, however], all proposals in both Houses of the General Assembly for reapportionment have failed to pass.

Between 1901 and 1961, Tennessee has experienced substantial growth and redistribution of her population. In 1901 the population was 2,020,616, of whom 487,380 were eligible to vote. The 1960 Federal Census reports the State's population at 3,567,089, of whom 2,092,891 are eligible to vote. The relative standings of the counties in terms of qualified voters have changed significantly. It is primarily the continued application of the 1901 Apportionment Act to this shifted and enlarged voting population which gives rise to the present controversy.

Indeed, the complaint alleges that the 1901 statute, even as of the time of its passage, "made no apportionment of Representatives and Senators in accordance with the constitutional formula . . . , but instead arbitrarily and capriciously apportioned representatives in the Senate and House without reference . . . to any logical or reasonable formula whatever." It is further alleged that "because of the population changes since 1900, and the failure of the Legislature to reapportion itself since 1901," the 1901 statute became "unconstitutional and obsolete." Appellants also argue that, because of the composition of the legislature effected by the 1901 Apportionment Act, redress in the form of a state constitutional amendment to change the entire mechanism for reapportioning, or any other change short of that, is difficult or impossible.[14] The complaint concludes that "these plaintiffs and others similarly situated, are denied the equal protection of the laws accorded them by the Fourteenth Amendment to the Constitution of the United States by virtue of the debasement of their votes." They seek a declaration that the 1901 statute is unconstitutional and an injunction restraining the appellees from acting to conduct any further elections under it. They also pray that unless and until the General Assembly enacts a valid reapportionment, the District Court should either decree a reapportionment by mathematical application of the Tennessee constitutional formulae to the most recent Federal Census figures, or direct the appellees to conduct legislative elections, primary and general, at large. * * *

In holding that the subject matter of this suit was not justiciable, the District Court relied on *Colegrove* v. *Green*, [328 U.S. 549 (1946)] [p. 109], and subsequent *per curiam* cases. * * * We understand the District Court to have read the cited cases as compelling the conclusion that since the appellants sought to have a legislative apportionment held unconstitutional, their suit presented a "political question" and was therefore nonjusticiable. We hold that this challenge to an apportionment presents no nonjusticiable "political question." The cited cases do not hold the contrary. * * *

We hold that the claim pleaded here neither rests upon nor implicates the Guaranty Clause and that its justiciability is therefore not foreclosed by our decisions of cases involving that clause. * * * [Our review of "political question" cases reveals that] it is the relationship between the judiciary and the coordinate branches of the Federal Government, and not the federal judiciary's relationship to the States, which gives rise to the "political question."

We have said that "In determining whether a question falls within [the political question] category, the appropriateness under our system of government of attributing finality to the action of the political departments and also the lack of satisfactory criteria for a judicial determination are dominant considerations." *Coleman* v. *Miller*, 307 U.S. 433, 454–455 [(1939)]. The nonjusticiability of a political

---

[14] The appellants claim that no General Assembly constituted according to the 1901 Act will submit reapportionment proposals either to the people or to a Constitutional Convention. There is no provision for popular initiative in Tennessee. Amendments proposed in the Senate or House must first be approved by a majority of all members of each House and again by two-thirds of the members in the General Assembly next chosen. The proposals are then submitted to the people at the next general election in which a Governor is to be chosen. Alternatively, the legislature may submit to the people at any general election the question of calling a convention to consider specified proposals. Such as are adopted at a convention do not, however, become effective unless approved by a majority of the qualified voters voting separately on each proposed change or amendment at an election fixed by the convention. Conventions shall not be held oftener than once in six years. [Legislation in 1951 and 1957] provided that delegates to the 1953 and 1959 conventions were to be chosen from the counties and floterial districts just as are members of the State House of Representatives. * * *

question is primarily a function of the separation of powers. Much confusion results from the capacity of the "political question" label to obscure the need for case-by-case inquiry. Deciding whether a matter has in any measure been committed by the Constitution to another branch of government, or whether the action of that branch exceeds whatever authority has been committed, is itself a delicate exercise in constitutional interpretation, and is a responsibility of this Court as ultimate interpreter of the Constitution. * * *

It is apparent that several formulations which vary slightly according to the settings in which the questions arise may describe a political question, although each has one or more elements which identify it as essentially a function of the separation of powers. Prominent on the surface of any case held to involve a political question is found a textually demonstrable constitutional commitment of the issue to a coordinate political department; or a lack of judicially discoverable and manageable standards for resolving it; or the impossibility of deciding without an initial policy determination of a kind clearly for nonjudicial discretion; or the impossibility of a court's undertaking independent resolution without expressing lack of the respect due coordinate branches of government; or an unusual need for unquestioning adherence to a political decision already made; or the potentiality of embarrassment from multifarious pronouncements by various departments on one question.

Unless one of these formulations is inextricable from the case at bar, there should be no dismissal for non-justiciability on the ground of a political question's presence. The doctrine of which we treat is one of "political questions," not one of "political cases." The courts cannot reject as "no law suit" a bona fide controversy as to whether some action denominated "political" exceeds constitutional authority. The cases we have reviewed show the necessity for discriminating inquiry into the precise facts and posture of the particular case, and the impossibility of resolution by any semantic cataloguing.

But it is argued that this case shares the characteristics of decisions that constitute a category not yet considered, cases concerning the Constitution's guaranty, in Art. IV, § 4, of a republican form of government. A conclusion as to whether the case at bar does present a political question cannot be confidently reached until we have considered those cases with special care. We shall discover that Guaranty Clause claims involve those elements which define a "political question," and for that reason and no other, they are nonjusticiable. In particular, we shall discover that the nonjusticiability of such claims has nothing to do with their touching upon matters of state governmental organization. * * *

[The Court discussed *Luther* v. *Borden*, *Pacific States*, and other cases.]

We come, finally, to the ultimate inquiry whether our precedents as to what constitutes a nonjusticiable "political question" bring the case before us under the umbrella of that doctrine. A natural beginning is to note whether any of the common characteristics which we have been able to identify and label descriptively are present. We find none: The question here is the consistency of state action with the Federal Constitution. We have no question decided, or to be decided, by a political branch of government coequal with this Court. Nor do we risk embarrassment of our government abroad, or grave disturbance at home if we take issue with

Tennessee as to the constitutionality of her action here challenged. Nor need the appellants, in order to succeed in this action, ask the Court to enter upon policy determinations for which judicially manageable standards are lacking. Judicial standards under the Equal Protection Clause are well developed and familiar, and it has been open to courts since the enactment of the Fourteenth Amendment to determine, if on the particular facts they must, that a discrimination reflects *no* policy, but simply arbitrary and capricious action.

This case does, in one sense, involve the allocation of political power within a State, and the appellants might conceivably have added a claim under the Guaranty Clause. Of course, as we have seen, any reliance on that clause would be futile. But because any reliance on the Guaranty Clause could not have succeeded it does not follow that appellants may not be heard on the equal protection claim which in fact they tender. True, it must be clear that the Fourteenth Amendment claim is not so enmeshed with those political question elements which render Guaranty Clause claims nonjusticiable as actually to present a political question itself. But we have found that not to be the case here. * * *

We conclude then that the nonjusticiability of claims resting on the Guaranty Clause which arises from their embodiment of questions that were thought "political," can have no bearing upon the justiciability of the equal protection claim presented in this case. Finally, we emphasize that it is the involvement in Guaranty Clause claims of the elements thought to define "political questions," and no other feature, which could render them nonjusticiable. Specifically, we have said that such claims are not held nonjusticiable because they touch matters of state governmental organization. * * *

When challenges to state action respecting matters of "the administration of the affairs of the State and the officers through whom they are conducted" have rested on claims of constitutional deprivation which are amenable to judicial correction, this Court has acted upon its view of the merits of the claim. For example, * * * only last Term, in *Gomillion* v. *Lightfoot*, 364 U.S. 339 [(1960)] [p. 115], we applied the Fifteenth Amendment to strike down a redrafting of municipal boundaries which effected a discriminatory impairment of voting rights, in the face of what a majority of the Court of Appeals thought to be a sweeping commitment to state legislatures of the power to draw and redraw such boundaries. * * *

We conclude that the complaint's allegations of a denial of equal protection present a justiciable constitutional cause of action upon which appellants are entitled to a trial and a decision. The right asserted is within the reach of judicial protection under the Fourteenth Amendment.

The judgment of the District Court is reversed and the cause is remanded for further proceedings consistent with this opinion.

Reversed and remanded.

MR. JUSTICE WHITTAKER did not participate in the decision of this case.

MR. JUSTICE DOUGLAS, concurring.

While I join the opinion of the Court and, like the Court, do not reach the merits, a word of explanation is necessary.[1] I put to one side the problems of "political" questions involving the distribution of power between this Court, the Congress, and the Chief Executive. We have here a phase of the recurring problem of the relation of the federal courts to state agencies. More particularly, the question is the extent to which a State may weight one person's vote more heavily than it does another's. * * *

With the exception of *Colegrove* v. *Green*; *MacDougall* v. *Green*, 335 U.S. 281 [(1948)]; *South* v. *Peters*, 339 U.S. 276 [(1950)], and the decisions they spawned, the Court has never thought that protection of voting rights was beyond judicial cognizance. Today's treatment of those cases removes the only impediment to judicial cognizance of the claims stated in the present complaint.

The justiciability of the present claims being established, any relief accorded can be fashioned in the light of well-known principles of equity.

MR. JUSTICE CLARK, concurring.

* * * I believe it can be shown that this case is distinguishable from earlier cases dealing with the distribution of political power by a State, that a patent violation of the Equal Protection Clause of the United States Constitution has been shown, and that an appropriate remedy may be formulated. * * *

The controlling facts cannot be disputed. It appears from the record that 37% of the voters of Tennessee elect 20 of the 33 Senators while 40% of the voters elect 60 of the 99 members of the House. But this might not on its face be an "invidious discrimination," *Williamson* v. *Lee Optical of Oklahoma*, 348 U.S. 483, 489 (1955), for a "statutory discrimination will not be set aside if any state of facts reasonably may be conceived to justify it."

It is true that the apportionment policy incorporated in Tennessee's Constitution, *i.e.*, state-wide numerical equality of representation with certain minor qualifications, is a rational one. On a county-by-county comparison a districting plan based thereon naturally will have disparities in representation due to the qualifications. But this to my mind does not raise constitutional problems, for the overall policy is reasonable. However, the root of the trouble is not in Tennessee's Constitution, for admittedly its policy has not been followed. The discrimination lies in the action of

---

[1] I feel strongly that many of the cases cited by the Court and involving so-called "political" questions were wrongly decided.

In joining the opinion, I do not approve those decisions but only construe the Court's opinion in this case as stating an accurate historical account of what the prior cases have held.

Tennessee's Assembly in allocating legislative seats to counties or districts created by it. Try as one may, Tennessee's apportionment just cannot be made to fit the pattern cut by its Constitution. * * * The frequency and magnitude of the inequalities in the present districting admit of no policy whatever. * * * [The] apportionment picture in Tennessee is a topsy-turvical of gigantic proportions. This is not to say that some of the disparity cannot be explained, but when the entire table is examined — comparing the voting strength of counties of like population as well as contrasting that of the smaller with the larger counties — it leaves but one conclusion, namely that Tennessee's apportionment is a crazy quilt without rational basis. * * *

The truth is that — although this case has been here for two years and has had over six hours' argument (three times the ordinary case) and has been most carefully considered over and over again by us in Conference and individually — no one, not even the State nor the dissenters, has come up with any rational basis for Tennessee's apportionment statute.

No one * * * contends that mathematical equality among voters is required by the Equal Protection Clause. But certainly there must be some rational design to a State's districting. The discrimination here does not fit any pattern — as I have said, it is but a crazy quilt. My Brother HARLAN contends that other proposed apportionment plans contain disparities. Instead of chasing those rabbits he should first pause long enough to meet appellants' proof of discrimination by showing that in fact the present plan follows a rational policy. Not being able to do this, he merely counters with such generalities as "classic legislative judgment," no "significant discrepancy," and "de minimis departures." I submit that even a casual glance at the present apportionment picture shows these conclusions to be entirely fanciful. If present representation has a policy at all, it is to maintain the *status quo* of invidious discrimination at any cost. * * *

Although I find the Tennessee apportionment statute offends the Equal Protection Clause, I would not consider intervention by this Court into so delicate a field if there were any other relief available to the people of Tennessee. But the majority of the people of Tennessee have no "practical opportunities for exerting their political weight at the polls" to correct the existing "invidious discrimination." Tennessee has no initiative and referendum. I have searched diligently for other "practical opportunities" present under the law. I find none other than through the federal courts. The majority of the voters have been caught up in a legislative strait jacket. Tennessee has an "informed, civically militant electorate" and "an aroused popular conscience," but it does not sear "the conscience of the people's representatives." This is because the legislative policy has riveted the present seats in the Assembly to their respective constituencies, and by the votes of their incumbents a reapportionment of any kind is prevented. The people have been rebuffed at the hands of the Assembly; they have tried the constitutional convention route, but since the call must originate in the Assembly it, too, has been fruitless. They have tried Tennessee courts with the same result,[9] and Governors have fought the tide only to flounder. It is said that there is recourse in Congress and perhaps that may be, but

---

[9] It is interesting to note that state judges often rest their decisions on the ground that this Court has precluded adjudication of the federal claim.

from a practical standpoint this is without substance. To date Congress has never undertaken such a task in any State. We therefore must conclude that the people of Tennessee are stymied and without judicial intervention will be saddled with the present discrimination in the affairs of their state government. * * *

MR. JUSTICE STEWART, concurring.

The separate writings of my dissenting and concurring Brothers stray so far from the subject of today's decision as to convey, I think, a distressingly inaccurate impression of what the Court decides. For that reason, I think it appropriate, in joining the opinion of the Court, to emphasize in a few words what the opinion does and does not say. * * *

The complaint in this case asserts that Tennessee's system of apportionment is utterly arbitrary — without any possible justification in rationality. The District Court did not reach the merits of that claim, and this Court quite properly expresses no view on the subject. Contrary to the suggestion of my Brother HARLAN, the Court does not say or imply that "state legislatures must be so structured as to reflect with approximate equality the voice of every voter." The Court does not say or imply that there is anything in the Federal Constitution "to prevent a State, acting not irrationally, from choosing any electoral legislative structure it thinks best suited to the interests, temper, and customs of its people." And contrary to the suggestion of my Brother DOUGLAS, the Court most assuredly does not decide the question, "may a State weight the vote of one county or one district more heavily than it weights the vote in another?" * * *

MR. JUSTICE FRANKFURTER, whom MR. JUSTICE HARLAN joins, dissenting.

The Court today reverses a uniform course of decision established by a dozen cases, including one by which the very claim now sustained was unanimously rejected only five years ago. The impressive body of rulings thus cast aside reflected the equally uniform course of our political history regarding the relationship between population and legislative representation — a wholly different matter from denial of the franchise to individuals because of race, color, religion or sex. Such a massive repudiation of the experience of our whole past in asserting destructively novel judicial power demands a detailed analysis of the role of this Court in our constitutional scheme. Disregard of inherent limits in the effective exercise of the Court's "judicial Power" not only presages the futility of judicial intervention in the essentially political conflict of forces by which the relation between population and representation has time out of mind been and now is determined. It may well impair the Court's position as the ultimate organ of "the supreme Law of the Land" in that vast range of legal problems, often strongly entangled in popular feeling, on which this Court must pronounce. The Court's authority — possessed of neither the purse nor the sword — ultimately rests on sustained public confidence in its moral sanction. Such feeling must be nourished by the Court's complete detachment, in fact and in appearance, from political entanglements and by abstention from injecting itself into the clash of political forces in political settlements.

A hypothetical claim resting on abstract assumptions is now for the first time made the basis for affording illusory relief for a particular evil even though it foreshadows deeper and more pervasive difficulties in consequence. The claim is hypothetical and the assumptions are abstract because the Court does not vouchsafe the lower courts — state and federal — guidelines for formulating specific, definite, wholly unprecedented remedies for the inevitable litigations that today's umbrageous disposition is bound to stimulate in connection with politically motivated reapportionments in so many States. In such a setting, to promulgate jurisdiction in the abstract is meaningless. It is as devoid of reality as "a brooding omnipresence in the sky," for it conveys no intimation what relief, if any, a District Court is capable of affording that would not invite legislatures to play ducks and drakes with the judiciary. For this Court to direct the District Court to enforce a claim to which the Court has over the years consistently found itself required to deny legal enforcement and at the same time to find it necessary to withhold any guidance to the lower court how to enforce this turnabout, new legal claim, manifests an odd — indeed an esoteric — conception of judicial propriety. * * * Even assuming the indispensable intellectual disinterestedness on the part of judges in such matters, they do not have accepted legal standards or criteria or even reliable analogies to draw upon for making judicial judgments. To charge courts with the task of accommodating the incommensurable factors of policy that underlie these mathematical puzzles is to attribute, however flatteringly, omnicompetence to judges. * * *

We were soothingly told at the bar of this Court that we need not worry about the kind of remedy a court could effectively fashion once the abstract constitutional right to have courts pass on a state-wide system of electoral districting is recognized as a matter of judicial rhetoric, because legislatures would heed the Court's admonition. This is not only a euphoric hope. It implies a sorry confession of judicial impotence in place of a frank acknowledgment that there is not under our Constitution a judicial remedy for every political mischief, for every undesirable exercise of legislative power. The Framers carefully and with deliberate fore-thought refused so to enthrone the judiciary. In this situation, as in others of like nature, appeal for relief does not belong here. Appeal must be to an informed, civically militant electorate. In a democratic society like ours, relief must come through an aroused popular conscience that sears the conscience of the people's representatives. In any event there is nothing judicially more unseemly nor more self-defeating than for this Court to make *in terrorem* pronouncements, to indulge in merely empty rhetoric, sounding a word of promise to the ear, sure to be disappointing to the hope. * * *

The *Colegrove* doctrine, in the form in which repeated decisions have settled it, was not an innovation. It represents long judicial thought and experience. From its earliest opinions this Court has consistently recognized a class of controversies which do not lend themselves to judicial standards and judicial remedies. To classify the various instances as "political questions" is rather a form of stating this conclusion than revealing of analysis.[10] * * *

The Court has been particularly unwilling to intervene in matters concerning the structure and organization of the political institutions of the States. The abstention

---

[10] See Bickel, *Foreword: The Passive Virtues*, 75 Harv. L. Rev. 40, 45 *et seq.* (1961).

from judicial entry into such areas has been greater even than that which marks the Court's ordinary approach to issues of state power challenged under broad federal guarantees. * * *

The cases involving Negro disfranchisement are no exception to the principle of avoiding federal judicial intervention into matters of state government in the absence of an explicit and clear constitutional imperative. For here the controlling command of Supreme Law is plain and unequivocal. An end of discrimination against the Negro was the compelling motive of the Civil War Amendments. The Fifteenth expresses this in terms, and it is no less true of the Equal Protection Clause of the Fourteenth. * * *

The influence of these converging considerations — the caution not to undertake decision where standards meet for judicial judgment are lacking, the reluctance to interfere with matters of state government in the absence of an unquestionable and effectively enforceable mandate, the unwillingness to make courts arbiters of the broad issues of political organization historically committed to other institutions and for whose adjustment the judicial process is ill-adapted — has been decisive of the settled line of cases, reaching back more than a century, which holds that Art. IV, § 4, of the Constitution, guaranteeing to the States "a Republican Form of Government," is not enforceable through the courts. * * * The subject was fully considered in *Pacific States Telephone & Telegraph Co.* v. *Oregon*, 223 U.S. 118 [(1912)] [p. 107], in which the Court dismissed for want of jurisdiction a writ of error attacking a state license tax statute enacted by the initiative, on the claim that this mode of legislation was inconsistent with a Republican Form of Government and violated the Equal Protection Clause and other federal guarantees. * * *

The present case involves all of the elements that have made the Guarantee Clause cases non-justiciable. It is, in effect, a Guarantee Clause claim masquerading under a different label. But it cannot make the case more fit for judicial action that appellants invoke the Fourteenth Amendment rather than Art. IV, § 4, where, in fact, the gist of their complaint is the same — unless it can be found that the Fourteenth Amendment speaks with greater particularity to their situation. * * * But where judicial competence is wanting, it cannot be created by invoking one clause of the Constitution rather than another. When what was essentially a Guarantee Clause claim was sought to be laid, as well, under the Equal Protection Clause in *Pacific States Telephone & Telegraph Co.* v. *Oregon*, the Court had no difficulty in "dispelling any mere confusion resulting from forms of expression, and considering the substance of things. . . ." * * *

What, then, is this question of legislative apportionment? Appellants invoke the right to vote and to have their votes counted. But they are permitted to vote and their votes are counted. They go to the polls, they cast their ballots, they send their representatives to the state councils. Their complaint is simply that the representatives are not sufficiently numerous or powerful — in short, that Tennessee has adopted a basis of representation with which they are dissatisfied. Talk of "debasement" or "dilution" is circular talk. One cannot speak of "debasement" or "dilution" of the value of a vote until there is first defined a standard of reference as to what a vote should be worth. What is actually asked of the Court in this case is to choose among competing bases of representation — ultimately, really, among competing theories of political philosophy — in order to establish an appropriate frame of government for the State of Tennessee and thereby for all the States of the Union.

In such a matter, abstract analogies which ignore the facts of history deal in unrealities; they betray reason. This is not a case in which a State has, through a device however oblique and sophisticated, denied Negroes or Jews or redheaded persons a vote, or given them only a third or a sixth of a vote. That was *Gomillion* v. *Lightfoot*. What Tennessee illustrates is an old and still widespread method of representation — representation by local geographical division, only in part respective of population — in preference to others, others, forsooth, more appealing. Appellants contest this choice and seek to make this Court the arbiter of the disagreement. They would make the Equal Protection Clause the charter of adjudication, asserting that the equality which it guarantees comports, if not the assurance of equal weight to every voter's vote, at least the basic conception that representation ought to be proportionate to population, a standard by reference to which the reasonableness of apportionment plans may be judged.

To find such a political conception legally enforceable in the broad and unspecific guarantee of equal protection is to rewrite the Constitution. See *Luther* v. *Borden*. Certainly, "equal protection" is no more secure a foundation for judicial judgment of the permissibility of varying forms of representative government than is "Republican Form." Indeed since "equal protection of the laws" can only mean an equality of persons standing in the same relation to whatever governmental action is challenged, the determination whether treatment is equal presupposes a determination concerning the nature of the relationship. This, with respect to apportionment, means an inquiry into the theoretic base of representation in an acceptably republican state. For a court could not determine the equal-protection issue without in fact first determining the Republican-Form issue, simply because what is reasonable for equal-protection purposes will depend upon what frame of government, basically, is allowed. To divorce "equal protection" from "Republican Form" is to talk about half a question.

The notion that representation proportioned to the geographic spread of population is so universally accepted as a necessary element of equality between man and man that it must be taken to be the standard of a political equality preserved by the Fourteenth Amendment — that it is, in appellants' words "the basic principle of representative government" — is, to put it bluntly, not true. However desirable and however desired by some among the great political thinkers and framers of our government, it has never been generally practiced, today or in the past. It was not the English system, it was not the colonial system, it was not the system chosen for the national government by the Constitution, it was not the system exclusively or even predominantly practiced by the States at the time of adoption of the Fourteenth Amendment, it is not predominantly practiced by the States today. Unless judges, the judges of this Court, are to make their private views of political wisdom the measure of the Constitution — views which in all honesty cannot but give the appearance, if not reflect the reality, of involvement with the business of partisan politics so inescapably a part of apportionment controversies — the Fourteenth Amendment, "itself a historical product," provides no guide for judicial oversight of the representation problem. * * *

[JUSTICE FRANKFURTER followed with a detailed historical review of legislative apportionment in Great Britain, in the 13 Colonies, and in the States demonstrating, as he saw it, the many different approaches to the issue.]

* * * Detailed recent studies are available to describe the present-day constitutional and statutory status of apportionment in the fifty States. They demonstrate a decided twentieth-century trend away from population as the exclusive base of representation. Today, only a dozen state constitutions provide for periodic legislative reapportionment of both houses by a substantially unqualified application of the population standard, and only about a dozen more prescribe such reapportionment for even a single chamber. * * * More than twenty States now guarantee each county at least one seat in one of their houses regardless of population, and in nine others county or town units are given equal representation in one legislative branch, whatever the number of each unit's inhabitants. Of course, numerically considered, "These provisions invariably result in over-representation of the least populated areas. . . ." And in an effort to curb and political dominance of metropolitan regions, at least ten States now limit the maximum entitlement of any single county (or, in some cases, city) in one legislative house — another source of substantial numerical disproportion. * * *

Manifestly, the Equal Protection Clause supplies no clearer guide for judicial examination of apportionment methods than would the Guarantee Clause itself. Apportionment, by its character, is a subject of extraordinary complexity, involving — even after the fundamental theoretical issues concerning what is to be represented in a representative legislature have been fought out or compromised — considerations of geography, demography, electoral convenience, economic and social cohesions or divergencies among particular local groups, communications, the practical effects of political institutions like the lobby and the city machine, ancient traditions and ties of settled usage, respect for proven incumbents of long experience and senior status, mathematical mechanics, censuses compiling relevant data, and a host of others. Legislative responses throughout the country to the reapportionment demands of the 1960 Census have glaringly confirmed that these are not factors that lend themselves to evaluations of a nature that are the staple of judicial determinations or for which judges are equipped to adjudicate by legal training or experience or native wit. And this is the more so true because in every strand of this complicated, intricate web of values meet the contending forces of partisan politics. The practical significance of apportionment is that the next election results may differ because of it. Apportionment battles are overwhelmingly party or intra-party contests. It will add a virulent source of friction and tension in federal-state relations to embroil the federal judiciary in them. * * *

Dissenting opinion of MR. JUSTICE HARLAN, whom MR. JUSTICE FRANKFURTER, joins. * * *

In the last analysis, what lies at the core of this controversy is a difference of opinion as to the function of representative government. It is surely beyond argument that those who have the responsibility for devising a system of representation may permissibly consider that factors other than bare numbers should be taken into account. The existence of the United States Senate is proof enough of that. To consider that we may ignore the Tennessee Legislature's judgment in this instance because that body was the product of an asymmetrical electoral apportionment would in effect be to assume the very conclusion here disputed. Hence we must accept the present form of the Tennessee Legislature as the embodiment of the State's choice, or, more realistically, its compromise, between competing political philosophies. The federal courts have not been empowered by the Equal Protection Clause to judge whether this resolution of the State's internal political conflict is desirable or undesirable, wise or unwise. * * *

The claim that Tennessee's system of apportionment is so unreasonable as to amount to a capricious classification of voting strength stands up no better under dispassionate analysis.

The Court has said time and again that the Equal Protection Clause does not demand of state enactments either mathematical identity or rigid equality. * * * It is not inequality alone that calls for a holding of unconstitutionality; only if the inequality is based on an impermissible standard may this Court condemn it.

What then is the basis for the claim made in this case that the distribution of state senators and representatives is the product of capriciousness or of some constitutionally prohibited policy? It is not that Tennessee has arranged its electoral districts with a deliberate purpose to dilute the voting strength of one race, cf. *Gomillion* v. *Lightfoot*, or that some religious group is intentionally underrepresented. Nor is it a charge that the legislature has indulged in sheer caprice by allotting representatives to each county on the basis of a throw of the dice, or of some other determinant bearing no rational relation to the question of apportionment. Rather, the claim is that the State Legislature has unreasonably retained substantially the same allocation of senators and representatives as was established by statute in 1901, refusing to recognize the great shift in the population balance between urban and rural communities that has occurred in the meantime. * * *

A Federal District Court is asked to say that the passage of time has rendered the 1901 apportionment obsolete to the point where its continuance becomes vulnerable under the Fourteenth Amendment. But is not this matter one that involves a classic legislative judgment? Surely it lies within the province of a state legislature to conclude that an existing allocation of senators and representatives constitutes a desirable balance of geographical and demographical representation, or that in the interest of stability of government it would be best to defer for some further time the redistribution of seats in the state legislature.

Indeed, I would hardly think it unconstitutional if a state legislature's expressed reason for establishing or maintaining an electoral imbalance between its rural and urban population were to protect the State's agricultural interests from the sheer weight of numbers of those residing in its cities. A State may, after all, take account of the interests of its rural population in the distribution of tax burdens, and recognition of the special problems of agricultural interests has repeatedly been reflected in federal legislation. Does the Fourteenth Amendment impose a stricter limitation upon a State's apportionment of political representatives to its central government? I think not. These are matters of local policy, on the wisdom of which the federal judiciary is neither permitted nor qualified to sit in judgment.

The suggestion of my Brother FRANKFURTER that courts lack standards by which to decide such cases as this, is relevant not only to the question of "justiciability," but also, and perhaps more fundamentally, to the determination whether any cognizable constitutional claim has been asserted in this case. Courts are unable to decide when it is that an apportionment originally valid becomes void because the factors entering into such a decision are basically matters appropriate only for legislative judgment. And so long as there exists a possible rational legislative policy for retaining an existing apportionment, such a legislative decision cannot be said to breach the bulwark against arbitrariness and caprice that the Fourteenth Amendment affords. * * *

In conclusion, it is appropriate to say that one need not agree, as a citizen, with what Tennessee has done or failed to do, in order to deprecate, as a judge, what the majority is doing today. Those observers of the Court who see it primarily as the last refuge for the correction of all inequality or injustice, no matter what its nature or source, will no doubt applaud this decision and its break with the past. Those who consider that continuing national respect for the Court's authority depends in large measure upon its wise exercise of self-restraint and discipline in constitutional adjudication, will view the decision with deep concern.

I would affirm.

VIETH v. JUBELIRER
Supreme Court of the United States
541 U.S. 267, 124 S. Ct. 1769, 158 L. Ed. 2d 546 (2004)

JUSTICE SCALIA announced the judgment of the Court and delivered an opinion, in which THE CHIEF JUSTICE [REHNQUIST], JUSTICE O'CONNOR, and JUSTICE THOMAS join.

Plaintiffs-appellants Richard Vieth, Norma Jean Vieth, and Susan Furey challenge a map drawn by the Pennsylvania General Assembly establishing districts for the election of congressional Representatives, on the ground that the districting constitutes an unconstitutional political gerrymander.[1] In *Davis* v. *Bandemer*, 478 U.S. 109 (1986), this Court held that political gerrymandering claims are justiciable, but could not agree upon a standard to adjudicate them. The present appeal presents the questions whether our decision in *Bandemer* was in error, and, if not, what the standard should be.

I

The facts, as alleged by the plaintiffs, are as follows. The population figures derived from the 2000 census showed that Pennsylvania was entitled to only 19 Representatives in Congress, a decrease in 2 from the Commonwealth's previous delegation. Pennsylvania's General Assembly took up the task of drawing a new districting map. At the time, the Republican Party controlled a majority of both state Houses and held the Governor's office. Prominent national figures in the Republican Party pressured the General Assembly to adopt a partisan redistricting

---

[1] The term "political gerrymander" has been defined as "[t]he practice of dividing a geographical area into electoral districts, often of highly irregular shape, to give one political party an unfair advantage by diluting the opposition's voting strength." Black's Law Dictionary 696 (7th ed. 1999).

plan as a punitive measure against Democrats for having enacted pro-Democrat redistricting plans elsewhere. The Republican members of Pennsylvania's House and Senate worked together on such a plan. On January 3, 2002, the General Assembly passed its plan, which was signed into law by Governor Schweiker as Act 1. * * *

II

Political gerrymanders are not new to the American scene. One scholar traces them back to the Colony of Pennsylvania at the beginning of the 18th century, where several counties conspired to minimize the political power of the city of Philadelphia by refusing to allow it to merge or expand into surrounding jurisdictions, and denying it additional representatives. See E. Griffith, The Rise and Development of the Gerrymander 26–28 (1974). * * * There were allegations that Patrick Henry attempted (unsuccessfully) to gerrymander James Madison out of the First Congress. And in 1812, of course, there occurred the notoriously outrageous political districting in Massachusetts that gave the gerrymander its name — an amalgam of the names of Massachusetts Governor Elbridge Gerry and the creature ("salamander") which the outline of an election district he was credited with forming was thought to resemble. "By 1840 the gerrymander was a recognized force in party politics and was generally attempted in all legislation enacted for the formation of election districts. It was generally conceded that each party would attempt to gain power which was not proportionate to its numerical strength." Griffith 123.

It is significant that the Framers provided a remedy for such practices in the Constitution. Article I, § 4, while leaving in state legislatures the initial power to draw districts for federal elections, permitted Congress to "make or alter" those districts if it wished. * * *

The power bestowed on Congress to regulate elections, and in particular to restrain the practice of political gerrymandering, has not lain dormant. In the Apportionment Act of 1842, 5 Stat. 491, Congress provided that Representatives must be elected from single-member districts "composed of contiguous territory." See Griffith 12 (noting that the law was "an attempt to forbid the practice of the gerrymander"). Congress again imposed these requirements in the Apportionment Act of 1862, 12 Stat. 572, and in 1872 further required that districts "contai[n] as nearly as practicable an equal number of inhabitants," 17 Stat. 28, § 2. In the Apportionment Act of 1901, Congress imposed a compactness requirement. 31 Stat. 733. The requirements of contiguity, compactness, and equality of population were repeated in the 1911 apportionment legislation, 37 Stat. 13, but were not thereafter continued. Today, only the single-member-district-requirement remains. See 2 U.S.C. § 2c. Recent history, however, attests to Congress's awareness of the sort of districting practices appellants protest, and of its power under Article I, § 4, to control them. Since 1980, no fewer than five bills have been introduced to regulate gerrymandering in congressional districting.[4]

Eighteen years ago, we held that the Equal Protection Clause grants judges the

---

[4] The States, of course, have taken their own steps to prevent abusive districting practices. A number

power — and duty — to control political gerrymandering, see *Davis* v. *Bandemer*. It is to consideration of this precedent that we now turn.

III

As Chief Justice Marshall proclaimed two centuries ago, "[i]t is emphatically the province and duty of the judicial department to say what the law is." *Marbury* v. *Madison*, 1 Cranch 137, 177 (1803). Sometimes, however, the law is that the judicial department has no business entertaining the claim of unlawfulness — because the question is entrusted to one of the political branches or involves no judicially enforceable rights. Such questions are said to be "nonjusticiable," or "political questions."

In *Baker* v. *Carr*, 369 U.S. 186 (1962) [p. 119], we set forth six independent tests for the existence of a political question: * * *

"[1] a textually demonstrable constitutional commitment of the issue to a coordinate political department; or [2] a lack of judicially discoverable and manageable standards for resolving it; or [3] the impossibility of deciding without an initial policy determination of a kind clearly for nonjudicial discretion; or [4] the impossibility of a court's undertaking independent resolution without expressing lack of the respect due coordinate branches of the government; or [5] an unusual need for unquestioning adherence to a political decision already made; or [6] the potentiality of embarrassment from multifarious pronouncements by various departments on one question." *Id.*, at 217.

These tests are probably listed in descending order of both importance and certainty. The second is at issue here, and there is no doubt of its validity. "The judicial Power" created by Article III, § 1, of the Constitution is not *whatever* judges choose to do, or even *whatever* Congress chooses to assign them. It is the power to act in the manner traditional for English and American courts. One of the most obvious limitations imposed by that requirement is that judicial action must be governed by *standard*, by *rule*. Laws promulgated by the Legislative Branch can be inconsistent, illogical, and ad hoc; law pronounced by the courts must be principled, rational, and based upon reasoned distinctions.

Over the dissent of three Justices, the Court held in *Davis* v. *Bandemer* that, since it was "not persuaded that there are no judicially discernible and manageable standards by which political gerrymander cases are to be decided," such cases *were* justiciable. The clumsy shifting of the burden of proof for the premise (the Court was "not persuaded" that standards do not exist, rather than "persuaded" that they do) was necessitated by the uncomfortable fact that the six-Justice majority could not discern what the judicially discernable standards might be. There was no majority on that point. Four of the Justices finding justiciability believed that the standard was one thing, see *id.*, at 127 (plurality opinion of WHITE, J., joined by Brennan, Marshall, and Blackmun, JJ.); two believed it was something else, see *id.*,

---

have adopted standards for redistricting, and measures designed to insulate the process from politics. * * *

at 161 (POWELL, J., joined by STEVENS, J., concurring in part and dissenting in part). The lower courts have lived with that assurance of a standard (or more precisely, lack of assurance that there is no standard), coupled with that inability to specify a standard, for the past 18 years. In that time, they have considered numerous political gerrymandering claims; this Court has never revisited the unanswered question of what standard governs.

Nor can it be said that the lower courts have, over 18 years, succeeded in shaping the standard that this Court was initially unable to enunciate. They have simply applied the standard set forth in *Bandemer*'s four-Justice plurality opinion. This might be thought to prove that the four-Justice plurality standard has met the test of time — but for the fact that its application has almost invariably produced the same result (except for the incurring of attorney's fees) as would have obtained if the question were nonjusticiable: Judicial intervention has been refused. * * * To think that this lower court jurisprudence has brought forth "judicially discernible and manageable standards" would be fantasy.

Eighteen years of judicial effort with virtually nothing to show for it justify us in revisiting the question whether the standard promised by *Bandemer* exists. As the following discussion reveals, no judicially discernible and manageable standards for adjudicating political gerrymandering claims have emerged. Lacking them, we must conclude that political gerrymandering claims are nonjusticiable and that *Bandemer* was wrongly decided.

A

We begin our review of possible standards with that proposed by Justice White's plurality opinion in *Bandemer* because, as the narrowest ground for our decision in that case, it has been the standard employed by the lower courts. The plurality concluded that a political gerrymandering claim could succeed only where plaintiffs showed "both intentional discrimination against an identifiable political group and an actual discriminatory effect on that group." 478 U.S., at 127. As to the intent element, the plurality acknowledged that "[a]s long as redistricting is done by a legislature, it should not be very difficult to prove that the likely political consequences of the reapportionment were intended." *Id.*, at 129. However, the effects prong was significantly harder to satisfy. Relief could not be based merely upon the fact that a group of persons banded together for political purposes had failed to achieve representation commensurate with its numbers, or that the apportionment scheme made its winning of elections more difficult. *Id.*, at 132. Rather, it would have to be shown that, taking into account a variety of historic factors and projected election results, the group had been "denied its chance to effectively influence the political process" as a whole, which could be achieved even without electing a candidate. *Id.*, at 132–133. * * * [I]n a challenge to an individual district the inquiry would focus "on the opportunity of members of the group to participate in party deliberations in the slating and nomination of candidates, their opportunity to register and vote, and hence their chance to directly influence the election returns and to secure the attention of the winning candidate." *Id.*, at 133. A statewide challenge, by contrast, would involve an analysis of "the voters' direct *or indirect* influence on the elections of the state legislature as a whole." *Ibid.*

(emphasis added). With what has proved to be a gross understatement, the plurality acknowledged this was "of necessity a difficult inquiry." *Id.*, at 143. * * *

In the lower courts, the legacy of the plurality's test is one long record of puzzlement and consternation. * * * Because this standard was misguided when proposed, has not been improved in subsequent application, and is not even defended before us today by the appellants, we decline to affirm it as a constitutional requirement.

B

Appellants take a run at enunciating their own workable standard based on Article I, § 2, and the Equal Protection Clause. We consider it at length not only because it reflects the litigant's view as to the best that can be derived from 18 years of experience, but also because it shares many features with other proposed standards, so that what is said of it may be said of them as well. Appellants' proposed standard retains the two-pronged framework of the *Bandemer* plurality — intent plus effect — but modifies the type of showing sufficient to satisfy each.

To satisfy appellants' intent standard, a plaintiff must "show that the mapmakers acted with a *predominant intent* to achieve partisan advantage," which can be shown "by direct evidence or by circumstantial evidence that other neutral and legitimate redistricting criteria were subordinated to the goal of achieving partisan advantage." As compared with the *Bandemer* plurality's test of mere intent to disadvantage the plaintiff's group, this proposal seemingly makes the standard more difficult to meet — but only at the expense of making the standard more indeterminate.

"Predominant intent" to disadvantage the plaintiff's political group refers to the relative importance of that goal as compared with all the other goals that the map seeks to pursue — contiguity of districts, compactness of districts, observance of the lines of political subdivision, protection of incumbents of all parties, cohesion of natural racial and ethnic neighborhoods, compliance with requirements of the Voting Rights Act of 1965 regarding racial distribution, etc. Appellants contend that their intent test *must* be discernible and manageable because it has been borrowed from our racial gerrymandering cases. See *Miller* v. *Johnson*, 515 U.S. 900 (1995) [p. 369]; *Shaw* v. *Reno*, 509 U.S. 630 (1993) [p. 354]. To begin with, in a very important respect that is not so. In the racial gerrymandering context, the predominant intent test has been applied to the challenged district in which the plaintiffs voted. See *Miller, supra*; *United States* v. *Hays*, 515 U.S. 737 (1995). Here, however, appellants do not assert that an apportionment fails their intent test if any single district does so. Since "it would be quixotic to attempt to bar state legislatures from considering politics as they redraw district lines," appellants propose a test that is satisfied only when "partisan advantage was the predominant motivation *behind the entire statewide plan*." ([E]mphasis added). Vague as the "predominant motivation" test might be when used to evaluate single districts, it all but evaporates when applied statewide. Does it mean, for instance, that partisan intent must outweigh all other goals — contiguity, compactness, preservation of neighborhoods, etc. — *statewide?* And how is the statewide "outweighing" to be determined? If three-fifths of the map's districts forgo the pursuit of partisan ends in favor of strictly observing political-subdivision lines, and only two-fifths ignore those lines to disadvantage the plaintiffs, is the observance of political subdivisions the "predominant" goal between those two? We are sure appellants do not think so.

Even within the narrower compass of challenges to a single district, applying a "predominant intent" test to *racial* gerrymandering is easier and less disruptive. The Constitution clearly contemplates districting by political entities, see Article I, § 4, and unsurprisingly that turns out to be root-and-branch a matter of politics. By contrast, the purpose of segregating voters on the basis of race is not a lawful one, and is much more rarely encountered. Determining whether the shape of a particular district is so substantially affected by the presence of a rare and constitutionally suspect motive as to invalidate it is quite different from determining whether it is so substantially affected by the excess of an ordinary and lawful motive as to invalidate it. Moreover, the fact that partisan districting is a lawful and common practice means that there is almost *always* room for an election-impeding lawsuit contending that partisan advantage was the predominant motivation; not so for claims of racial gerrymandering. Finally, courts might be justified in accepting a modest degree of unmanageability to enforce a constitutional command which (like the Fourteenth Amendment obligation to refrain from racial discrimination) is clear; whereas they are not justified in inferring a judicially enforceable constitutional obligation (the obligation not to apply *too much* partisanship in districting) which is both dubious and severely unmanageable. For these reasons, to the extent that our racial gerrymandering cases represent a model of discernible and manageable standards, they provide no comfort here.

The effects prong of appellants' proposal replaces the *Bandemer* plurality's vague test of "denied its chance to effectively influence the political process" with criteria that are seemingly more specific. The requisite effect is established when "(1) the plaintiffs show that the districts systematically 'pack' and 'crack' the rival party's voters,[7] *and* (2) the court's examination of the 'totality of circumstances' confirms that the map can thwart the plaintiffs' ability to translate a majority of votes into a majority of seats." This test is loosely based on our cases applying § 2 of the Voting Rights Act of 1965, 42 U.S.C. § 1973, to discrimination by race, see, *e.g.*, *Johnson* v. *De Grandy*, 512 U.S. 997 (1994) [p. 317]. But a person's politics is rarely as readily discernible — and *never* as permanently discernible — as a person's race. Political affiliation is not an immutable characteristic, but may shift from one election to the next; and even within a given election, not all voters follow the party line. We dare say (and hope) that the political party which puts forward an utterly incompetent candidate will lose even in its registration stronghold. These facts make it impossible to assess the effects of partisan gerrymandering, to fashion a standard for evaluating a violation, and finally to craft a remedy.

Assuming, however, that the effects of partisan gerrymandering can be determined, appellants' test would invalidate the districting only when it prevents a majority of the electorate from electing a majority of representatives. Before considering whether this particular standard is judicially manageable we question

---

[7] "Packing" refers to the practice of filling a district with a supermajority of a given group or party. "Cracking" involves the splitting of a group or party among several districts to deny that group or party a majority in any of those districts.

whether it is judicially discernible in the sense of being relevant to some constitutional violation. Deny it as appellants may (and do), this standard rests upon the principle that groups (or at least political-action groups) have a right to proportional representation. But the Constitution contains no such principle. It guarantees equal protection of the law to persons, not equal representation in government to equivalently sized groups. It nowhere says that farmers or urban dwellers, Christian fundamentalists or Jews, Republicans or Democrats, must be accorded political strength proportionate to their numbers.

Even if the standard were relevant, however, it is not judicially manageable. To begin with, how is a party's majority status to be established? Appellants propose using the results of statewide races as the benchmark of party support. But as their own complaint describes, in the 2000 Pennsylvania statewide elections some Republicans won and some Democrats won. * * * Moreover, to think that majority status in statewide races establishes majority status for district contests, one would have to believe that the only factor determining voting behavior at all levels is political affiliation. That is assuredly not true. As one law review comment has put it:

> "There is no statewide vote in this country for the House of Representatives or the state legislature. Rather, there are separate elections between separate candidates in separate districts, and that is all there is. If the districts change, the candidates change, their strengths and weaknesses change, their campaigns change, their ability to raise money changes, the issues change — everything changes. Political parties do not compete for the highest statewide vote totals or the highest mean district vote percentages: They compete for specific seats." Lowenstein & Steinberg, *The Quest for Legislative Districting in the Public Interest: Elusive or Illusory*, 33 UCLA L. Rev. 1, 59–60 (1985).

But if we could identify a majority party, we would find it impossible to ensure that that party wins a majority of seats — unless we radically revise the States' traditional structure for elections. In any winner-take-all district system, there can be no guarantee, no matter how the district lines are drawn, that a majority of party votes statewide will produce a majority of seats for that party. The point is proved by the 2000 congressional elections in Pennsylvania, which, according to appellants' own pleadings, were conducted under a judicially drawn district map "free from partisan gerrymandering." On this "neutral playing fiel[d]," the Democrats' statewide majority of the major-party vote (50.6%) translated into a minority of seats (10, versus 11 for the Republicans). Whether by reason of partisan districting or not, party constituents may always wind up "packed" in some districts and "cracked" throughout others. * * * Consider, for example, a legislature that draws district lines with no objectives in mind except compactness and respect for the lines of political subdivisions. Under that system, political groups that tend to cluster (as is the case with Democratic voters in cities) would be systematically affected by what might be called a "natural" packing effect.

Our one-person, one-vote cases, see *Reynolds* v. *Sims*, 377 U.S. 533 (1964) [p. 173]; *Wesberry* v. *Sanders*, 376 U.S. 1 (1964) [p. 166], have no bearing upon this question, neither in principle nor in practicality. Not in principle, because to say that each individual must have an equal say in the selection of representatives, and hence that a majority of individuals must have a majority say, is not at all to say that each discernible group, whether farmers or urban dwellers or political parties, must have representation equivalent to its numbers. And not in practicality, because the easily administrable standard of population equality adopted by *Wesberry* and *Reynolds* enables judges to decide whether a violation has occurred (and to remedy it) essentially on the basis of three readily determined factors — where the plaintiff lives, how many voters are in his district, and how many voters are in other districts; whereas requiring judges to decide whether a districting system will produce a statewide majority for a majority party casts them forth upon a sea of imponderables, and asks them to make determinations that not even election experts can agree upon.

For these reasons, we find appellants' proposed standards neither discernible nor manageable.

C

For many of the same reasons, we also reject the standard suggested by Justice Powell in *Bandemer.* He agreed with the plurality that a plaintiff should show intent and effect, but believed that the ultimate inquiry ought to focus on whether district boundaries had been drawn solely for partisan ends to the exclusion of "all other neutral factors relevant to the fairness of redistricting." * * *

While Justice Powell rightly criticized the *Bandemer* plurality for failing to suggest a constitutionally based, judicially manageable standard, the standard proposed in his opinion also falls short of the mark. It is essentially a totality-of-the-circumstances analysis, where all conceivable factors, none of which is dispositive, are weighed with an eye to ascertaining whether the particular gerrymander has gone too far — or, in Justice Powell's terminology, whether it is not "fair." "Fairness" does not seem to us a judicially manageable standard. Fairness is compatible with noncontiguous districts, it is compatible with districts that straddle political subdivisions, and it is compatible with a party's not winning the number of seats that mirrors the proportion of its vote. Some criterion more solid and more demonstrably met than that seems to us necessary to enable the state legislatures to discern the limits of their districting discretion, to meaningfully constrain the discretion of the courts, and to win public acceptance for the courts' intrusion into a process that is the very foundation of democratic decisionmaking.

IV

We turn next to consideration of the standards proposed by today's dissenters. We preface it with the observation that the mere fact that these four dissenters come up with three different standards — all of them different from the two proposed in *Bandemer* and the one proposed here by appellants — goes a long way to establishing that there is no constitutionally discernible standard.

A

JUSTICE STEVENS concurs in the judgment that we should not address plaintiffs' statewide political gerrymandering challenges. Though he reaches that result via standing analysis, while we reach it through political-question analysis, our conclusions are the same: these statewide claims are nonjusticiable.

JUSTICE STEVENS would, however, require courts to consider political gerrymandering challenges at the individual-district level. Much of his dissent is addressed to the incompatibility of severe partisan gerrymanders with democratic principles. We do not disagree with that judgment * * *. The issue we have discussed is not whether severe partisan gerrymanders violate the Constitution, but whether it is for the courts to say when a violation has occurred, and to design a remedy. On that point, JUSTICE STEVENS's dissent is less helpful, saying, essentially, that if we can do it in the racial gerrymandering context we can do it here.

We have examined, the many reasons why that is not so. Only a few of them are challenged by JUSTICE STEVENS. He says that we "mistakenly assum[e] that race cannot provide a legitimate basis for making political judgments." But we do not say that race-conscious decisionmaking is always unlawful. Race can be used, for example, as an indicator to achieve the purpose of neighborhood cohesiveness in districting. What we have said is impermissible is "the purpose of segregating voters on the basis of race" — that is to say, racial gerrymandering for race's sake, which would be the equivalent of political gerrymandering for politics' sake. JUSTICE STEVENS says we "er[r] in assuming that politics is 'an ordinary and lawful motive' " in districting — but all he brings forward to contest that is the argument that an *excessive* injection of politics is *un*lawful. So it is, and so does our opinion assume. That does not alter the reality that setting out to segregate voters by race is unlawful and hence rare, and setting out to segregate them by political affiliation is (so long as one doesn't go too far) lawful and hence ordinary.

JUSTICE STEVENS's confidence that what courts have done with racial gerrymandering can be done with political gerrymandering rests in part upon his belief that "the same standards should apply." But in fact the standards are quite different. A purpose to discriminate on the basis of race receives the strictest scrutiny under the Equal Protection Clause, while a similar purpose to discriminate on the basis of politics does not. * * *

Having failed to make the case for strict scrutiny of political gerrymandering, JUSTICE STEVENS falls back on the argument that scrutiny levels simply do not matter for purposes of justiciability. He asserts that a standard imposing a strong presumption of invalidity (strict scrutiny) is no more discernible and manageable than a standard requiring an evenhanded balancing of all considerations with no thumb on the scales (ordinary scrutiny). To state this is to refute it. As is well known, strict scrutiny readily, and almost always, results in invalidation. Moreover, the mere fact that there exist standards which this Court could apply — the proposition which much of JUSTICE STEVENS's opinion is devoted to establishing — does not mean that those standards are discernible in the Constitution. This Court may not willy-nilly apply standards — even manageable standards — having no relation to constitutional harms. * * *

B

JUSTICE SOUTER, like JUSTICE STEVENS, would restrict these plaintiffs, on the allegations before us, to district-specific political gerrymandering claims. Unlike JUSTICE STEVENS, however, JUSTICE SOUTER recognizes that there is no existing workable standard for adjudicating such claims. He proposes a "fresh start," a newly constructed standard loosely based in form on our Title VII cases, and complete with a five-step prima facie test sewn together from parts of, among other things, our Voting Rights Act jurisprudence, law review articles, and apportionment cases. Even if these self-styled "clues" to unconstitutionality could be manageably applied, which we doubt, there is no reason to think they would detect the constitutional crime which JUSTICE SOUTER is investigating — an "extremity of unfairness" in partisan competition.

Under JUSTICE SOUTER's proposed standard, in order to challenge a particular district, a plaintiff must show (1) that he is a member of a "cohesive political group"; (2) "that the district of his residence . . . paid little or no heed" to traditional districting principles; (3) that there were "specific correlations between the district's deviations from traditional districting principles and the distribution of the population of his group"; (4) that a hypothetical district exists which includes the plaintiff's residence, remedies the packing or cracking of the plaintiff's group, and deviates less from traditional districting principles; and (5) that "the defendants acted intentionally to manipulate the shape of the district in order to pack or crack his group." When those showings have been made, the burden would shift to the defendants to justify the district "by reference to objectives other than naked partisan advantage."

While this five-part test seems eminently scientific, upon analysis one finds that each of the last four steps requires a quantifying judgment that is unguided and ill suited to the development of judicial standards: *How much* disregard of traditional districting principles? *How many* correlations between deviations and distribution? *How much* remedying of packing or cracking by the hypothetical district? *How many legislators* must have had the intent to pack and crack — and *how efficacious* must that intent have been (must it have been, for example, a *sine qua non* cause of the districting, or a *predominant* cause)? At step two, for example, JUSTICE SOUTER would require lower courts to assess whether mapmakers paid "little or no heed to . . . traditional districting principles." What is a lower court to do when, as will often be the case, the district adheres to some traditional criteria but not others? JUSTICE SOUTER's only response to this question is to evade it: "It is not necessary now to say exactly how a district court would balance a good showing on one of these indices against a poor showing on another, for that sort of detail is best worked out case by case." But the devil lurks precisely in such detail. The central problem is determining when political gerrymandering has gone too far. It does not solve that problem to break down the original unanswerable question (How much political motivation and effect is too much?) into four more discrete but equally unanswerable questions.

JUSTICE SOUTER's proposal is doomed to failure for a more basic reason: No test — yea, not even a five-part test — can possibly be successful unless one knows what he is testing *for.* In the present context, the test ought to identify deprivation of that

minimal degree of representation or influence to which a political group is constitutionally entitled. As we have seen, the *Bandemer* test sought (unhelpfully, but at least gamely) to specify what that minimal degree was: "[a] chance to effectively influence the political process." So did the appellants' proposed test: "[the] ability to translate a majority of votes into a majority of seats." JUSTICE SOUTER avoids the difficulties of those formulations by never telling us what his test is looking for, other than the utterly unhelpful "extremity of unfairness." He vaguely describes the harm he is concerned with as vote dilution, a term which usually implies some actual effect on the weight of a vote. But no element of his test looks to the effect of the gerrymander on the electoral success, the electoral opportunity, or even the political influence, of the plaintiff's group. We do not know the precise constitutional deprivation his test is designed to identify and prevent.
* * *

Like us, JUSTICE SOUTER acknowledges and accepts that "some intent to gain political advantage is inescapable whenever political bodies devise a district plan, and some effect results from the intent." Thus, again like us, he recognizes that "the issue is one of how much is too much." And once those premises are conceded, the only line that can be drawn must be based, as JUSTICE SOUTER again candidly admits, upon a substantive "notio[n] of fairness." This is the same flabby goal that deprived Justice Powell's test of all determinacy. To be sure, JUSTICE SOUTER frames it somewhat differently: Courts must intervene, he says, when "partisan competition has reached an *extremity* of unfairness." We do not think the problem is solved by adding the modifier.

C

We agree with much of JUSTICE BREYER's dissenting opinion, which convincingly demonstrates that "political considerations will likely play an important, and proper, role in the drawing of district boundaries." This places JUSTICE BREYER, like the other dissenters, in the difficult position of drawing the line between good politics and bad politics. Unlike them, he would tackle this problem at the statewide level.

The criterion JUSTICE BREYER proposes is nothing more precise than "the *unjustified* use of political factors to entrench a minority in power." While he invokes in passing the Equal Protection Clause, it should be clear to any reader that what constitutes *unjustified* entrenchment depends on his own theory of "effective government." While one must agree with JUSTICE BREYER's incredibly abstract starting point that our Constitution sought to create a "basically democratic" form of government, that is a long and impassable distance away from the conclusion that the Judiciary may assess whether a group (somehow defined) has achieved a level of political power (somehow defined) commensurate with that to which they would be entitled absent *unjustified* political machinations (whatever that means).

JUSTICE BREYER provides no real guidance for the journey. [Like JUSTICE SOUTER], he never tells us what he is testing for, beyond the unhelpful "*unjustified* entrenchment." Instead, he "set[s] forth several sets of circumstances that lay out the indicia of abuse," "along a continuum," proceeding (presumably) from the most clearly unconstitutional to the possibly unconstitutional. With regard to the first "scenario," he is willing to assert that the indicia "would be sufficient to support a claim." This seems refreshingly categorical, until one realizes that the indicia consist not merely of the failure of the party receiving the majority of votes to acquire a majority of seats in two successive elections, *but also* of the fact that there is no "neutral" explanation for this phenomenon. But of course there *always is* a neutral explanation — if only the time-honored criterion of incumbent protection. The indicia set forth in JUSTICE BREYER's second scenario "*could* also add up to unconstitutional gerrymandering," and for those in the third "a court *may* conclude that the map crosses the constitutional line." We find none of this helpful. Each scenario suffers from at least one of the problems we have previously identified, most notably the difficulties of assessing partisan strength statewide and of ascertaining whether an entire statewide plan is motivated by political or neutral justifications. And even at that, the last two scenarios *do not even purport to provide an answer*, presumably leaving it to each district court to determine whether, under those circumstances, "*unjustified* entrenchment" has occurred. In sum, we neither know precisely what JUSTICE BREYER is testing for, nor precisely what fails the test.

But perhaps the most surprising omission from JUSTICE BREYER's dissent, given his views on other matters, is the absence of any cost-benefit analysis. JUSTICE BREYER acknowledges that "a majority normally can work its political will," and well describes the number of actors, from statewide executive officers, to redistricting commissions, to Congress, to the People in ballot initiatives and referenda, that stand ready to make that happen. He gives no instance (and we know none) of permanent frustration of majority will. But where the majority has failed to assert itself for some indeterminate period (two successive elections, if we are to believe his first scenario), JUSTICE BREYER simply assumes that "court action may prove necessary." Why so? In the real world, of course, court action that is available tends to be sought, not just where it is necessary, but where it is in the interest of the seeking party. And the vaguer the test for availability, the more frequently interest rather than necessity will produce litigation. Is the regular insertion of the judiciary into districting, with the delay and uncertainty that brings to the political process and the partisan enmity it brings upon the courts, worth the benefit to be achieved — an accelerated (by some unknown degree) effectuation of the majority will? We think not.

V

JUSTICE KENNEDY recognizes that we have "demonstrat[ed] the shortcomings of the other standards that have been considered to date," * * * [but] he concludes that courts should continue to adjudicate such claims because a standard *may* one day be discovered.

The first thing to be said about JUSTICE KENNEDY's disposition is that it is not legally available. The District Court in this case considered the plaintiffs' claims *justiciable* but dismissed them because the standard for unconstitutionality had not been met. It is logically impossible to affirm that dismissal without either (1) finding that the unconstitutional-districting standard applied by the District Court, or some other standard that it *should* have applied, has not been met, or (2) finding (as we have) that the claim is nonjusticiable. JUSTICE KENNEDY seeks to affirm "[b]ecause, in the case before us, we have no standard." But it is *our* job, not the plaintiffs', to explicate the standard that makes the facts alleged by the plaintiffs adequate or inadequate to state a claim. We cannot nonsuit *them* for our failure to do so.

JUSTICE KENNEDY asserts that to declare nonjusticiability would be incautious. Our rush to such a holding after a mere 18 years of fruitless litigation "contrasts starkly" he says, "with the more patient approach" that this Court has taken in the past. We think not. * * *

The only cases JUSTICE KENNEDY cites in defense of his never-say-never approach are *Baker* v. *Carr* and *Bandemer. Bandemer* provides no cover. There, all of the Justices who concluded that political gerrymandering claims are justiciable proceeded to describe what they regarded as the discernible and manageable standard that rendered it so. The lower courts were set wandering in the wilderness for 18 years not because the *Bandemer* majority thought it a good idea, but because five Justices could not agree upon a single standard, and because the standard the plurality proposed turned out not to work.

As for *Baker* v. *Carr*: It is true enough that, having had no experience *whatever* in apportionment matters of any sort, the Court there refrained from spelling out the equal protection standard. (It did so a mere two years later in *Reynolds* v. *Sims*.) But the judgment under review in *Baker*, unlike the one under review here, did not *demand* the determination of a standard. The lower court in *Baker* had held the apportionment claim of the plaintiffs *nonjusticiable*, and so it was logically possible to dispose of the appeal by simply disagreeing with the nonjusticiability determination. As we observed earlier, that is not possible here, where the lower court has held the claim *justiciable* but unsupported by the facts. We must either enunciate the standard that causes us to agree or disagree with that merits judgment, or else affirm that the claim is beyond our competence to adjudicate.

JUSTICE KENNEDY worries that "[a] determination by the Court to deny all hopes of intervention could erode confidence in the courts as much as would a premature decision to intervene." But it is the function of the courts to provide relief, not hope. What we think would erode confidence is the Court's refusal to do its job — announcing that there may well be a valid claim here, but we are not yet prepared to figure it out. Moreover, that course does more than erode confidence; by placing the district courts back in the business of pretending to afford help when they in fact can give none, it deters the political process from affording genuine relief. * * *

* * * Reduced to its essence, JUSTICE KENNEDY's opinion boils down to this: "As presently advised, I know of no discernible and manageable standard that can render this claim justiciable. I am unhappy about that, and hope that I will be able to change my opinion in the future." What are the lower courts to make of this pronouncement? We suggest that they must treat it as a reluctant fifth vote against justiciability at district and statewide levels — a vote that may change in some future case but that holds, for the time being, that this matter is nonjusticiable.

VI

We conclude that neither Article I, § 2, nor the Equal Protection Clause, nor (what appellants only fleetingly invoke) Article I, § 4, provides a judicially enforceable limit on the political considerations that the States and Congress may take into account when districting.

Considerations of *stare decisis* do not compel us to allow *Bandemer* to stand. That case involved an interpretation of the Constitution, and the claims of *stare decisis* are at their weakest in that field, where our mistakes cannot be corrected by Congress. They are doubly weak in *Bandemer* because the majority's inability to enunciate the judicially discernible and manageable standard that it thought existed (or did not think did not exist) presaged the need for reconsideration in light of subsequent experience. And they are triply weak because it is hard to imagine how any action taken in reliance upon *Bandemer* could conceivably be frustrated — except the bringing of lawsuits, which is not the sort of primary conduct that is relevant.

While we do not lightly overturn one of our own holdings, "when governing decisions are unworkable or are badly reasoned, 'this Court has never felt constrained to follow precedent.'" Eighteen years of essentially pointless litigation have persuaded us that *Bandemer* is incapable of principled application. We would therefore overrule that case, and decline to adjudicate these political gerrymandering claims.

The judgment of the District Court is affirmed.

It is so ordered.

JUSTICE KENNEDY, concurring in the judgment.

A decision ordering the correction of all election district lines drawn for partisan reasons would commit federal and state courts to unprecedented intervention in the American political process. The Court is correct to refrain from directing this substantial intrusion into the Nation's political life. While agreeing with the plurality that the complaint the appellants filed in the District Court must be dismissed, and while understanding that great caution is necessary when approaching this subject, I would not foreclose all possibility of judicial relief if some limited and precise rationale were found to correct an established violation of the Constitution in some redistricting cases.

When presented with a claim of injury from partisan gerrymandering, courts confront two obstacles. First is the lack of comprehensive and neutral principles for drawing electoral boundaries. No substantive definition of fairness in districting seems to command general assent. Second is the absence of rules to limit and confine judicial intervention. With uncertain limits, intervening courts — even when proceeding with best intentions — would risk assuming political, not legal, responsibility for a process that often produces ill will and distrust.

That courts can grant relief in districting cases where race is involved does not answer our need for fairness principles here. Those controversies implicate a different inquiry. They involve sorting permissible classifications in the redistricting context from impermissible ones. Race is an impermissible classification. Politics is quite a different matter.

A determination that a gerrymander violates the law must rest on something more than the conclusion that political classifications were applied. It must rest instead on a conclusion that the classifications, though generally permissible, were applied in an invidious manner or in a way unrelated to any legitimate legislative objective. * * *

* * * Because there are yet no agreed upon substantive principles of fairness in districting, we have no basis on which to define clear, manageable, and politically neutral standards for measuring the particular burden a given partisan classification imposes on representational rights. Suitable standards for measuring this burden, however, are critical to our intervention. Absent sure guidance, the results from one gerrymandering case to the next would likely be disparate and inconsistent. * * *

There are, then, weighty arguments for holding cases like these to be nonjusticiable; and those arguments may prevail in the long run. In my view, however, the arguments are not so compelling that they require us now to bar all future claims of injury from a partisan gerrymander. It is not in our tradition to foreclose the judicial process from the attempt to define standards and remedies where it is alleged that a constitutional right is burdened or denied. Nor is it alien to the Judiciary to draw or approve election district lines. Courts, after all, already do so in many instances. A determination by the Court to deny all hopes of intervention could erode confidence in the courts as much as would a premature decision to intervene.

Our willingness to enter the political thicket of the apportionment process with respect to one-person, one-vote claims makes it particularly difficult to justify a categorical refusal to entertain claims against this other type of gerrymandering. The plurality's conclusion that absent an "easily administrable standard," the appellants' claim must be nonjusticiable contrasts starkly with the more patient approach of *Baker* v. *Carr*, not to mention the controlling precedent on the question of justiciability of *Davis* v. *Bandemer*, the case the plurality would overrule. * * *

That no such standard has emerged in this case should not be taken to prove that none will emerge in the future. Where important rights are involved, the impossibility of full analytical satisfaction is reason to err on the side of caution. Allegations of unconstitutional bias in apportionment are most serious claims, for we have long believed that "the right to vote" is one of "those political processes ordinarily to be relied upon to protect minorities." *United States* v. *Carolene Products Co.*, 304 U.S. 144, 153, n.4 (1938). If a State passed an enactment that declared "All future apportionment shall be drawn so as most to burden Party X's rights to fair and effective representation, though still in accord with one-person, one-vote principles," we would surely conclude the Constitution had been violated. If that is so, we should admit the possibility remains that a legislature might attempt to reach the same result without that express directive. This possibility suggests that in another case a standard might emerge that suitably demonstrates how an apportionment's *de facto* incorporation of partisan classifications burdens rights of fair and effective representation (and so establishes the classification is unrelated to the aims of apportionment and thus is used in an impermissible fashion). * * *

If suitable standards with which to measure the burden a gerrymander imposes on representational rights did emerge, hindsight would show that the Court prematurely abandoned the field. That is a risk the Court should not take. Instead, we should adjudicate only what is in the papers before us. * * *

Because, in the case before us, we have no standard by which to measure the burden appellants claim has been imposed on their representational rights, appellants cannot establish that the alleged political classifications burden those same rights. Failing to show that the alleged classifications are unrelated to the aims of apportionment, appellants' evidence at best demonstrates only that the legislature adopted political classifications. That describes no constitutional flaw, at least under the governing Fourteenth Amendment standard.

The plurality thinks I resolve this case with reference to no standard, but that is wrong. The Fourteenth Amendment standard governs; and there is no doubt of that. My analysis only notes that if a subsidiary standard could show how an otherwise permissible classification, as applied, burdens representational rights, we could conclude that appellants' evidence states a provable claim under the Fourteenth Amendment standard.

Though in the briefs and at argument the appellants relied on the Equal Protection Clause as the source of their substantive right and as the basis for relief, I note that the complaint in this case also alleged a violation of First Amendment rights. The First Amendment may be the more relevant constitutional provision in future cases that allege unconstitutional partisan gerrymandering. After all, these allegations involve the First Amendment interest of not burdening or penalizing citizens because of their participation in the electoral process, their voting history, their association with a political party, or their expression of political views. See *Elrod* v. *Burns*, 427 U.S. 347 (1976) [p. 726] (plurality opinion). Under general First Amendment principles those burdens in other contexts are unconstitutional absent a compelling government interest. * * * First Amendment concerns arise where a State enacts a law that has the purpose and effect of subjecting a group of voters or their party to disfavored treatment by reason of their views. In the context of partisan gerrymandering, that means that First Amendment concerns arise where an apportionment has the purpose and effect of burdening a group of voters' representational rights. * * *

Where it is alleged that a gerrymander had the purpose and effect of imposing burdens on a disfavored party and its voters, the First Amendment may offer a sounder and more prudential basis for intervention than does the Equal Protection Clause. The equal protection analysis puts its emphasis on the permissibility of an enactment's classifications. This works where race is involved since classifying by race is almost never permissible. It presents a more complicated question when the inquiry is whether a generally permissible classification has been used for an impermissible purpose. That question can only be answered in the affirmative by the subsidiary showing that the classification as applied imposes unlawful burdens. The First Amendment analysis concentrates on whether the legislation burdens the representational rights of the complaining party's voters for reasons of ideology, beliefs, or political association. The analysis allows a pragmatic or functional assessment that accords some latitude to the States.

Finally, I do not understand the plurality to conclude that partisan gerrymandering that disfavors one party is permissible. Indeed, the plurality seems to acknowledge it is not. This is all the more reason to admit the possibility of later suits, while holding just that the parties have failed to prove, under our "well developed and familiar" standard, that these legislative classifications "reflec[t] *no* policy, but simply arbitrary and capricious action." *Baker*, 369 U.S., at 226. That said, courts must be cautious about adopting a standard that turns on whether the partisan interests in the redistricting process were excessive. Excessiveness is not easily determined. Consider these apportionment schemes: In one State, Party X controls the apportionment process and draws the lines so it captures every congressional seat. In three other States, Party Y controls the apportionment process. It is not so blatant or egregious, but proceeds by a more subtle effort, capturing less than all the seats in each State. Still, the total effect of Party Y's effort is to capture more new seats than Party X captured. Party X's gerrymander was more egregious. Party Y's gerrymander was more subtle. In my view, however, each is culpable. * * *

The ordered working of our Republic, and of the democratic process, depends on a sense of decorum and restraint in all branches of government, and in the citizenry itself. Here, one has the sense that legislative restraint was abandoned. That should not be thought to serve the interests of our political order. Nor should it be thought to serve our interest in demonstrating to the world how democracy works. * * *

Still, the Court's own responsibilities require that we refrain from intervention in this instance. The failings of the many proposed standards for measuring the burden a gerrymander imposes on representational rights make our intervention improper. If workable standards do emerge to measure these burdens, however, courts should be prepared to order relief. With these observations, I join the judgment of the Court.

JUSTICE STEVENS, dissenting.

The central question presented by this case is whether political gerrymandering claims are justiciable. Although our reasons for coming to this conclusion differ, five Members of the Court are convinced that the plurality's answer to that question is erroneous. Moreover, as is apparent from our separate writings today, we share the view that, even if these appellants are not entitled to prevail, it would be contrary to precedent and profoundly unwise to foreclose all judicial review of similar claims that might be advanced in the future. That we presently have somewhat differing views — concerning both the precedential value of some of our recent cases and the standard that should be applied in future cases — should not obscure the fact that the areas of agreement set forth in the separate opinions are of far greater significance.

The concept of equal justice under law requires the State to govern impartially. Today's plurality opinion would exempt governing officials from that duty in the context of legislative redistricting and would give license, for the first time, to partisan gerrymanders that are devoid of any rational justification. In my view, when partisanship is the legislature's sole motivation — when any pretense of neutrality is forsaken unabashedly and all traditional districting criteria are subverted for partisan advantage — the governing body cannot be said to have acted impartially. * * *

With purpose as the ultimate inquiry, other considerations have supplied ready standards for testing the lawfulness of a gerrymander. In his dissent in *Bandemer*, Justice Powell explained that "the merits of a gerrymandering claim must be determined by reference to the configurations of the districts, the observance of political subdivision lines, and other criteria that have independent relevance to the fairness of redistricting." 478 U.S., at 165. * * *

The Court has made use of all three parts of Justice Powell's standard in its recent racial gerrymandering jurisprudence. In those cases, the Court has examined claims that redistricting schemes violate the equal protection guarantee where they are "so highly irregular" on their face that they "rationally cannot be understood as anything other than an effort" to segregate voters by race," *Shaw* v. *Reno*, 509 U.S. [at] 646–647, or where "race for its own sake, and not other districting principles, was the legislature's dominant and controlling rationale in drawing its district lines," *Miller* v. *Johnson*, 515 U.S., at 913. * * *

Given this clear line of precedents, I should have thought the question of justiciability in cases such as this — where a set of plaintiffs argues that a single motivation resulted in a districting scheme with discriminatory effects — to be well settled. The plurality's contrary conclusion cannot be squared with our long history of voting rights decisions. Especially perplexing is the plurality's *ipse dixit* distinction of our racial gerrymandering cases. Notably, the plurality does not argue that the judicially manageable standards that have been used to adjudicate racial gerrymandering claims would not be equally manageable in political gerrymandering cases. Instead, its distinction of those cases rests on its view that race as a districting criterion is "much more rarely encountered" than partisanship, and that determining whether race — "a rare and constitutionally suspect motive" — dominated a districting decision "is quite different from determining whether [such a decision] is so substantially affected by the excess of an ordinary and lawful motive as to [be] invali[d]." But those considerations are wholly irrelevant to the issue of justiciability.

To begin with, the plurality errs in assuming that politics is "an ordinary and lawful motive." * * * On the contrary, "political belief and association constitute the core of those activities protected by the First Amendment," *Elrod* v. *Burns*, 427 U.S. [at] 356 (plurality opinion), and discriminatory governmental decisions that burden fundamental First Amendment interests are subject to strict scrutiny, *id.*, at 363. Thus, unless party affiliation is an appropriate requirement for the position in question, government officials may not base a decision to hire, promote, transfer, recall, discharge, or retaliate against an employee, or to terminate a contract, on the individual's partisan affiliation or speech. It follows that political affiliation is not an appropriate standard for excluding voters from a congressional district. * * *

State action that discriminates against a political minority for the sole and unadorned purpose of maximizing the power of the majority plainly violates the decisionmaker's duty to remain impartial. * * * Thus, the critical issue in both racial and political gerrymandering cases is the same: whether a single nonneutral criterion controlled the districting process to such an extent that the Constitution was offended. This Court has treated that precise question as justiciable in *Gomillion* and in the *Shaw* line of cases, and today's plurality has supplied no persuasive reason for distinguishing the justiciability of partisan gerrymanders. Those cases confirm and reinforce the holding that partisan gerrymandering claims are justiciable. * * *

"[L]egislatures," we have explained, "should be bodies which are collectively responsive to the popular will," *Reynolds*, 377 U.S., at 565, for "[l]egislators are elected by voters, not farms or cities or economic interests," *id.*, at 562. Gerrymanders subvert that representative norm because the winner of an election in a gerrymandered district inevitably will infer that her success is primarily attributable to the architect of the district rather than to a constituency defined by neutral principles. The *Shaw* cases hold that this disruption of the representative process imposes a cognizable "representational har[m]." Because that harm falls squarely on the voters in the district whose representative might or does misperceive the object of her fealty, the injury is cognizable only when stated by voters who reside in that particular district; otherwise the "plaintiff would be asserting only a generalized grievance against governmental conduct of which he or she does not approve." * * *

[District-specific challenges, however, allege] precisely the harm that the *Shaw* cases treat as cognizable in the context of racial gerrymandering. The same treatment is warranted in this case.

The risk of representational harms identified in the *Shaw* cases is equally great, if not greater, in the context of partisan gerrymanders. *Shaw I* was borne of the concern that an official elected from a racially gerrymandered district will feel beholden only to a portion of her constituents, and that those constituents will be defined by race. 509 U.S., at 648. The parallel danger of a partisan gerrymander is that the representative will perceive that the people who put her in power are those who drew the map rather than those who cast ballots, and she will feel beholden not to a subset of her constituency, but to no part of her constituency at all. The problem, simply put, is that the will of the cartographers rather than the will of the people will govern. * * *

[W]hile political considerations may properly influence the decisions of our elected officials, when such decisions disadvantage members of a minority group — whether the minority is defined by its members' race, religion, or political affiliation — they must rest on a neutral predicate. * * *

In evaluating a claim that a governmental decision violates the Equal Protection Clause, we have long required a showing of discriminatory purpose. See *Washington* v. *Davis*. That requirement applies with full force to districting decisions. The line that divides a racial or ethnic minority unevenly between school districts can be entirely legitimate if chosen on the basis of neutral factors — county lines, for example, or a natural boundary such as a river or major thoroughfare. But if the district lines were chosen for the purpose of limiting the number of minority students in the school, or the number of families holding unpopular religious or political views, that invidious purpose surely would invalidate the district.

Consistent with that principle, our recent racial gerrymandering cases have examined the shape of the district and the purpose of the districting body to determine whether race, above all other criteria, predominated in the line-drawing process. * * *

Just as irrational shape can serve as an objective indicator of an impermissible legislative purpose, other objective features of a districting map can save the plan from invalidation. We have explained that "traditional districting principles," which include "compactness, contiguity, and respect for political subdivisions," are "important not because they are constitutionally required . . . but because they are objective factors that may serve to defeat a claim that a district has been gerrymandered on racial lines." *Shaw I*, 509 U.S., at 647. * * *

In my view, the same standards should apply to claims of political gerrymandering, for the essence of a gerrymander is the same regardless of whether the group is identified as political or racial. Gerrymandering always involves the drawing of district boundaries to maximize the voting strength of the dominant political faction and to minimize the strength of one or more groups of opponents. In seeking the desired result, legislators necessarily make judgments about the probability that the members of identifiable groups — whether economic, religious, ethnic, or racial — will vote in a certain way. The overriding purpose of those predictions is political. It follows that the standards that enable courts to identify and redress a racial gerrymander could also perform the same function for other species of gerrymanders.

The racial gerrymandering cases therefore supply a judicially manageable standard for determining when partisanship, like race, has played too great of a role in the districting process. Just as race can be a factor in, but cannot dictate the outcome of, the districting process, so too can partisanship be a permissible consideration in drawing district lines, so long as it does not predominate. * * *

The plurality reasons that the standards for evaluating racial gerrymanders are not workable in cases such as this because partisan considerations, unlike racial ones, are perfectly legitimate. Until today, however, there has not been the slightest intimation in any opinion written by any Member of this Court that a naked purpose to disadvantage a political minority would provide a rational basis for drawing a district line. On the contrary, our opinions referring to political gerrymanders have consistently assumed that they were at least undesirable, and we always have indicated that political considerations are among those factors that may not dominate districting decisions. Purely partisan motives are "rational" in a literal sense, but there must be a limiting principle. * * * A legislature controlled by one party could not, for instance, impose special taxes on members of the minority party, or use tax revenues to pay the majority party's campaign expenses. The rational basis for government decisions must satisfy a standard of legitimacy and neutrality; an acceptable rational basis can be neither purely personal nor purely partisan. * * *

In sum, in evaluating a challenge to a specific district, I would apply the standard set forth in the *Shaw* cases and ask whether the legislature allowed partisan considerations to dominate and control the lines drawn, forsaking all neutral principles. Under my analysis, if no neutral criterion can be identified to justify the lines drawn, and if the only possible explanation for a district's bizarre shape is a naked desire to increase partisan strength, then no rational basis exists to save the district from an equal protection challenge. Such a narrow test would cover only a few meritorious claims, but it would preclude extreme abuses, * * * and it would perhaps shorten the time period in which the pernicious effects of such a gerrymander are felt. This test would mitigate the current trend under which partisan considerations are becoming the be-all and end-all in apportioning representatives. * * *

Accordingly, I respectfully dissent.

JUSTICE SOUTER, with whom JUSTICE GINSBURG joins, dissenting. * * *

* * * [S]ome intent to gain political advantage is inescapable whenever political bodies devise a district plan, and some effect results from the intent. Thus, the issue is one of how much is too much, and we can be no more exact in stating a verbal test for too much partisanship than we can be in defining too much race consciousness when some is inevitable and legitimate. Instead of coming up with a verbal formula for too much, then, the Court's job must be to identify clues, as objective as we can make them, indicating that partisan competition has reached an extremity of unfairness.

The plurality says, in effect, that courts have been trying to devise practical criteria for political gerrymandering for nearly 20 years, without being any closer to something workable than we were when *Davis* was decided. While this is true enough, I do not accept it as sound counsel of despair. For I take it that the principal reason we have not gone from theoretical justiciability to practical administrability in political gerrymandering cases is the *Davis* plurality's specification that any criterion of forbidden gerrymandering must require a showing that members of the plaintiff's group had "essentially been shut out of the political process," 478 U.S., at 139. * * *

Since this Court has created the problem no one else has been able to solve, it is up to us to make a fresh start. There are a good many voices saying it is high time that we did, for in the years since *Davis*, the increasing efficiency of partisan redistricting has damaged the democratic process to a degree that our predecessors only began to imagine. * * *

I would therefore preserve *Davis*'s holding that political gerrymandering is a justiciable issue, but otherwise start anew. I would adopt a political gerrymandering test analogous to the summary judgment standard crafted in *McDonnell Douglas Corp.* v. *Green*, 411 U.S. 792 (1973), calling for a plaintiff to satisfy elements of a prima facie cause of action, at which point the State would have the opportunity not only to rebut the evidence supporting the plaintiff's case, but to offer an affirmative justification for the districting choices, even assuming the proof of the plaintiff's allegations. My own judgment is that we would have better luck at devising a workable prima facie case if we concentrated as much as possible on suspect characteristics of individual districts instead of statewide patterns. It is not that a statewide view of districting is somehow less important; the usual point of gerrymandering, after all, is to control the greatest number of seats overall. But, as will be seen, we would be able to call more readily on some existing law when we defined what is suspect at the district level, and for now I would conceive of a statewide challenge as itself a function of claims that individual districts are illegitimately drawn. Finally, in the same interest of threshold simplicity, I would stick to problems of single-member districts; if we could not devise a workable scheme for dealing with claims about these, we would have to forget the complications posed by multimember districts.

For a claim based on a specific single-member district, I would require the plaintiff to make out a prima facie case with five elements. First, the resident plaintiff would identify a cohesive political group to which he belonged, which would normally be a major party, as in this case and in *Davis*. There is no reason in principle, however, to rule out a claimant from a minor political party (which might, if it showed strength, become the target of vigorous hostility from one or both major parties in a State) or from a different but politically coherent group whose members engaged in bloc voting, as a large labor union might do. The point is that it must make sense to speak of a candidate of the group's choice, easy to do in the case of a large or small political party, though more difficult when the organization is not defined by politics as such.

Second, a plaintiff would need to show that the district of his residence paid little or no heed to those traditional districting principles whose disregard can be shown straightforwardly: contiguity, compactness, respect for political subdivisions, and conformity with geographic features like rivers and mountains. Because such considerations are already relevant to justifying small deviations from absolute population equality, *Karcher* [v. *Daggett*], 462 U.S. [725], 740 [(1983)] and because compactness in particular is relevant to demonstrating possible majority-minority districts under the Voting Rights Act of 1965, *Johnson* v. *De Grandy*, 512 U.S. [at] 1008, there is no doubt that a test relying on these standards would fall within judicial competence.

Indeed, although compactness is at first blush the least likely of these principles to yield precision, it can be measured quantitatively in terms of dispersion, perimeter, and population ratios, and the development of standards would thus be possible. * * * It is not necessary now to say exactly how a district court would balance a good showing on one of these indices against a poor showing on another, for that sort of detail is best worked out case by case.

Third, the plaintiff would need to establish specific correlations between the district's deviations from traditional districting principles and the distribution of the population of his group. * * * That would begin, but not complete, the plaintiff's case that the defendant had chosen either to pack the group (drawn a district in order to include a uselessly high number of the group) or to crack it (drawn it so as to include fatally few), the ordinary methods of vote dilution in single-member district systems.

Fourth, a plaintiff would need to present the court with a hypothetical district including his residence, one in which the proportion of the plaintiff's group was lower (in a packing claim) or higher (in a cracking one) and which at the same time deviated less from traditional districting principles than the actual district. Cf. *Thornburg* v. *Gingles*, 478 U.S. 30, 50 (1986) [p. 301]. This hypothetical district would allow the plaintiff to claim credibly that the deviations from traditional districting principles were not only correlated with, but also caused by, the packing or cracking of his group. * * *

Fifth, and finally, the plaintiff would have to show that the defendants acted intentionally to manipulate the shape of the district in order to pack or crack his group. See *Washington* v. *Davis.* In substantiating claims of political gerrymandering under a plan devised by a single major party, proving intent should not be hard, once the third and fourth (correlation and cause) elements are established, politicians not being politically disinterested or characteristically naive. * * * I would, however, treat any showing of intent in a major-party case as too equivocal to count unless the entire legislature were controlled by the governor's party (or the dominant legislative party were vetoproof). * * *

A plaintiff who got this far would have shown that his State intentionally acted to dilute his vote, having ignored reasonable alternatives consistent with traditional districting principles. I would then shift the burden to the defendants to justify their decision by reference to objectives other than naked partisan advantage. They might show by rebuttal evidence that districting objectives could not be served by the plaintiff's hypothetical district better than by the district as drawn, or they might affirmatively establish legitimate objectives better served by the lines drawn than by the plaintiff's hypothetical.

The State might, for example, posit the need to avoid racial vote dilution. * * * It might plead one person, one vote, a standard compatible with gerrymandering but in some places perhaps unattainable without some lopsided proportions. The State might adopt the object of proportional representation among its political parties through its districting process. * * *

This is not, however, the time or place for a comprehensive list of legitimate objectives a State might present. The point here is simply that the Constitution should not petrify traditional districting objectives as exclusive, and it is enough to say that the State would be required to explain itself, to demonstrate that whatever reasons it gave were more than a mere pretext for an old-fashioned gerrymander.

As for a statewide claim, I would not attempt an ambitious definition without the benefit of experience with individual district claims, and for now I would limit consideration of a statewide claim to one built upon a number of district-specific ones. Each successful district-specific challenge would necessarily entail redrawing at least one contiguous district, and the more the successful claims, the more surrounding districts to be redefined. At a certain point, the ripples would reach the state boundary, and it would no longer make any sense for a district court to consider the problems piecemeal.

The plurality says that my proposed standard would not solve the essential problem of unworkability. * * * The enquiries I am proposing are not, to be sure, as hard edged as I wish they could be, but neither do they have a degree of subjectivity inconsistent with the judicial function.

* * * My test would no doubt leave substantial room for a party in power to seek advantage through its control of the districting process; the only way to prevent all opportunism would be to remove districting wholly from legislative control, which I am not prepared to say the Constitution requires. But that does not make it

impossible for courts to identify at least the worst cases of gerrymandering, and to provide a remedy. The most the plurality can show is that my approach would not catch them all. * * *

JUSTICE BREYER, dissenting. * * *

[A] single-member-district system helps to ensure certain democratic objectives better than many "more representative" (*i.e.*, proportional) electoral systems. Of course, single-member districts mean that only parties with candidates who finish "first past the post" will elect legislators. That fact means in turn that a party with a bare majority of votes or even a plurality of votes will often obtain a large legislative majority, perhaps freezing out smaller parties. But single-member districts thereby diminish the need for coalition governments. And that fact makes it easier for voters to identify which party is responsible for government decision-making (and which rascals to throw out), while simultaneously providing greater legislative stability. * * * This is not to say that single-member districts are preferable; it is simply to say that single-member-district systems and more-directly-representational systems reflect different conclusions about the proper balance of different elements of a workable democratic government.

If single-member districts are the norm, however, then political considerations will likely play an important, and proper, role in the drawing of district boundaries. In part, that is because politicians, unlike nonpartisan observers, normally under-stand how "the location and shape of districts" determine "the political complexion of the area." *Gaffney* v. *Cummings*, 412 U.S. 735, 753 (1973) [p. 206]. It is precisely *because* politicians are best able to predict the effects of boundary changes that the districts they design usually make some political sense. * * *

More important for present purposes, the role of political considerations reflects a surprising mathematical fact. Given a fairly large state population with a fairly large congressional delegation, districts assigned so as to be perfectly random in respect to politics would translate a small shift in political sentiment, say a shift from 51% Republican to 49% Republican, into a seismic shift in the makeup of the legislative delegation, say from 100% Republican to 100% Democrat. Any such exaggeration of tiny electoral changes — virtually wiping out legislative represen-tation of the minority party — would itself seem highly undemocratic.

Given the resulting need for single-member districts with nonrandom boundar-ies, it is not surprising that "traditional" districting principles have rarely, if ever, been politically neutral. Rather, because, in recent political memory, Democrats have often been concentrated in cities while Republicans have often been concen-trated in suburbs and sometimes rural areas, geographically drawn boundaries have tended to "pac[k]" the former. * * * Neighborhood or community-based boundaries, seeking to group Irish, Jewish, or African-American voters, often did the same. All this is well known to politicians, who use their knowledge about the effects of the "neutral" criteria to partisan advantage when drawing electoral maps. And were it not so, the iron laws of mathematics would have worked their extraordinary volatility-enhancing will.

This is to say that traditional or historically based boundaries are not, and should not be, "politics free." Rather, those boundaries represent a series of compromises of principle — among the virtues of, for example, close representation of voter views, ease of identifying "government" and "opposition" parties, and stability in government. They also represent an uneasy truce, sanctioned by tradition, among different parties seeking political advantage.

[R]eference back to these underlying considerations helps to explain why the legislature's use of political boundary-drawing considerations ordinarily does *not* violate the Constitution's Equal Protection Clause. The reason lies not simply in the difficulty of identifying abuse or finding an appropriate judicial remedy. The reason is more fundamental: Ordinarily, there simply is no abuse. The use of purely political boundary-drawing factors, even where harmful to the members of one party, will often nonetheless find justification in other desirable democratic ends, such as maintaining relatively stable legislatures in which a minority party retains significant representation.

At the same time, these considerations can help identify at least one circumstance where use of purely political boundary-drawing factors can amount to a serious, and remediable, abuse, namely, the *unjustified* use of political factors to entrench a minority in power. By entrenchment I mean a situation in which a party that enjoys only minority support among the populace has nonetheless contrived to take, and hold, legislative power. By *unjustified* entrenchment I mean that the minority's hold on power is purely the result of partisan manipulation and not other factors. These "other" factors that could lead to "justified" (albeit temporary) minority entrenchment include sheer happenstance, the existence of more than two major parties, the unique constitutional requirements of certain representational bodies such as the Senate, or reliance on traditional (geographic, communities of interest, etc.) districting criteria.

The democratic harm of unjustified entrenchment is obvious. * * *

The need for legislative stability cannot justify entrenchment, for stability is compatible with a system in which the loss of majority support implies a loss of power. The need to secure minority representation in the legislature cannot justify entrenchment, for minority party representation is also compatible with a system in which the loss of minority support implies a loss of representation. Constitutionally specified principles of representation, such as that of two Senators per State, cannot justify entrenchment where the House of Representatives or similar state legislative body is at issue. Unless some other justification can be found in particular circumstances, political gerrymandering that so entrenches a minority party in power violates basic democratic norms and lacks countervailing justification. For this reason, whether political gerrymandering does, or does not, violate the Constitution in other instances, gerrymandering that leads to entrenchment amounts to an abuse that violates the Constitution's Equal Protection Clause.

Courts need not intervene often to prevent the kind of abuse I have described, because those harmed constitute a political majority, and a majority normally can work its political will. Where a State has improperly gerrymandered legislative or congressional districts to the majority's disadvantage, the majority should be able to elect officials in statewide races — particularly the Governor — who may help to undo the harm that districting has caused the majority's party, in the next round of districting if not sooner. And where a State has improperly gerrymandered congressional districts, Congress retains the power to revise the State's districting determinations. See U.S. Const., Art. I, § 4.

Moreover, voters in some States, perhaps tiring of the political boundary-drawing rivalry, have found a procedural solution, confiding the task to a commission that is limited in the extent to which it may base districts on partisan concerns. According to the National Conference of State Legislatures, 12 States currently give "first and final authority for [state] legislative redistricting to a group other than the legislature." * * * A number of States use a commission for congressional redistricting[.] * * *

But we cannot always count on a severely gerrymandered legislature itself to find and implement a remedy. The party that controls the process has no incentive to change it. And the political advantages of a gerrymander may become ever greater in the future. The availability of enhanced computer technology allows the parties to redraw boundaries in ways that target individual neighborhoods and homes, carving out safe but slim victory margins in the maximum number of districts, with little risk of cutting their margins too thin. * * * By redrawing districts every 2 years, rather than every 10 years, a party might preserve its political advantages notwithstanding population shifts in the State. The combination of increasingly precise map-drawing technology and increasingly frequent map drawing means that a party may be able to bring about a gerrymander that is not only precise, but virtually impossible to dislodge. Thus, court action may prove necessary.

When it is necessary, a court should prove capable of finding an appropriate remedy. Courts have developed districting remedies in other cases. * * * Moreover, if the dangers of inadvertent political favoritism prove too great, a procedural solution, such as the use of a politically balanced boundary-drawing commission, may prove possible.

The bottom line is that courts should be able to identify the presence of one important gerrymandering evil, the unjustified entrenching in power of a political party that the voters have rejected. They should be able to separate the unjustified abuse of partisan boundary-drawing considerations to achieve that end from their more ordinary and justified use. And they should be able to design a remedy for extreme cases.

I do not claim that the problem of identification and separation is easily solved, even in extreme instances. But courts can identify a number of strong indicia of abuse. The presence of actual entrenchment, while not always unjustified (being perhaps a chance occurrence), is such a sign, particularly when accompanied by the use of partisan boundary-drawing criteria in the way that JUSTICE STEVENS describes, *i.e.*, a use that both departs from traditional criteria and cannot be explained other than by efforts to achieve partisan advantage. Below, I set forth several sets of circumstances that lay out the indicia of abuse I have in mind. The scenarios fall along a continuum: The more permanently entrenched the minority's hold on power becomes, the less evidence courts will need that the minority engaged in gerrymandering to achieve the desired result.

Consider, for example, the following sets of circumstances. First, suppose that the legislature has proceeded to redraw boundaries in what seem to be ordinary ways, but the entrenchment harm has become obvious. * * *

Second, suppose that plaintiffs could point to more serious departures from redistricting norms. * * *

Third, suppose that the legislature clearly departs from ordinary districting norms, but the entrenchment harm, while seriously threatened, has not yet occurred. * * *

The presence of these, or similar, circumstances — where the risk of entrenchment is demonstrated, where partisan considerations render the traditional district-drawing compromises irrelevant, where no justification other than party advantage can be found — seem to me extreme enough to set off a constitutional alarm. The risk of harm to basic democratic principle is serious; identification is possible; and remedies can be found. * * *

Notes and Questions

1.   *Baker v. Carr* is an influential political-question case, particularly given that, in synthesizing prior cases, the majority opinion summarizes the criteria for judges to consider in applying the doctrine. The most prominent of the criteria are whether there is a "textually demonstrable commitment of the issue to a coordinate branch of government," and whether there are "judicially manageable standards for resolving" the issue. *Baker* was mainly concerned with the latter criterion, and held that there were, or could be, such standards, and thus a dismissal of the claim on political-question doctrine grounds was inappropriate. From the discussion in the majority and concurring opinions, what were those standards? Did the majority and concurring opinions adequately respond to the arguments of the dissents that a judicially manageable standard was lacking? With regard to deciding the presence, or lack thereof, of a political question, to what extent was it relevant to the Justices that efforts to legislatively update the 1901 system of legislative apportionment in Tennessee had failed? To what extent *should* that fact have been relevant?

2.   Was it proper for Justice Kennedy to vote to dismiss *Vieth* while suggesting that perhaps at some point a judicially manageable standard would be developed? Is there any difference between his position and that of a Justice who votes with the plurality but who indicates a willingness to reconsider his views, and perhaps to overrule the case, in the future? Was it proper for *Baker* to decide the question of justiciability without first setting forth the standard for judging districts' compliance with the Equal Protection Clause?

3.   While *Baker* leaves the Guarantee Clause jurisprudentially far behind, is there an argument that the result in the case would have been better grounded in that Clause, as opposed to the Equal Protection Clause? For a trenchant presentation of that argument, see Michael W. McConnell, *The Redistricting Cases: Original Mistakes and Current Consequences*, 24 HARV. J.L. & PUB. POL'Y 103 (2000). McConnell contended that the serious political-process concerns raised in *Baker* — an entrenched rural minority maintaining control of governmental structures — could plausibly be said to implicate the Guarantee Clause. In contrast, he argued, the Equal Protection Clause is mainly concerned with individual rights,

not government political structure as such, and as of the date of *Baker*, the Clause had not been applied to districting, so a facile conclusion that there were, or would be, familiar and well developed standards to apply under that Clause was not convincing. He also contended that jurisprudence grounded in the Guarantee Clause might have led to more principled ways for courts to deal with racial and political gerrymandering of legislative districts. Thus, he suggested, a racial gerrymander, while perhaps objectionable to some as a matter of policy, does not offend the Constitution's guarantee of a republican form of government, while a political gerrymander arguably would. Consider these arguments in light of the opinions in *Vieth* comparing and contrasting *Baker* and its progeny, and the cases placing limits on racially gerrymandered districts.

4. Both Justice Frankfurter, dissenting in *Baker*, and Justice Scalia, writing for the plurality in *Vieth*, argued for applying the political-question doctrine because there were no judicially manageable standards to be found in the Constitution for resolving these kinds of districting disputes, and because the Court's reputation would suffer if it involved itself excessively in the political process. Should the second concern be of any relevance? That is, should the Court be able to evade constitutional decisions where it fears that such decisions will be unpopular? *Cf. Planned Parenthood v. Casey*, 505 U.S. 833, 998 (1992) (Scalia, J., dissenting) ("[W]hether it would 'subvert the Court's legitimacy' or not, the notion that we would decide a case differently from the way we otherwise would have in order to show that we can stand firm against public disapproval is frightening.").

5. For a vigorous argument that the opinions in *Vieth* and earlier cases reveal that partisan gerrymandering can have both positive and negative aspects, and one example of the former is that such gerrymandering can be a political safeguard of federalism, see Franita Tolson, *Partisan Gerrymandering as a Safeguard of Federalism*, 2010 UTAH L. REV. 859. The author argues that the power to gerrymander Congressional districts enables states to ensure that Congressional representatives are responsive to state interests.

6. Chapter 3 addresses in detail the considerable jurisprudential and policy aftermath of *Baker* and its progeny in the Supreme Court and the lower courts. Here, it is worth mentioning that the cases led to considerable reapportionment of state legislative districts, and the state drawing of districts for the U.S. House of Representatives. This redistricting now takes place every ten years, typically early in a decade, after the annual census is completed. For overviews of these developments, see STEPHEN ANSOLABEHERE & JAMES M. SNYDER, JR., THE END OF INEQUALITY: ONE PERSON, ONE VOTE AND THE TRANSFORMATION OF AMERICAN POLITICS (2008); GARY W. COX & JONATHAN N. KATZ, ELBRIDGE GERRY'S SALAMANDER: THE ELECTORAL CONSEQUENCES OF THE REAPPORTIONMENT REVOLUTION (2002); GERALD N. ROSENBERG, THE HOLLOW HOPE: CAN COURTS BRING ABOUT SOCIAL CHANGE? (2d ed. 2008).

7. The opinions in *Baker* and *Vieth* discuss how the other branches of government have dealt (or can deal) with the problem of various forms of gerrymandering. These include Congress itself directing the drawing of districts for the U.S. House of Representatives, or bipartisan or nonpartisan redistricting commissions in individual states. For an overview, see David Schultz, *Regulating the*

Political Thicket: Congress, the Courts, and State Reapportionment Commissions,
3 CHARLESTON L. REV. 107 (2008). Not surprisingly, the efforts to depoliticize the
drawing of legislative districts have not drawn universal support. The reaction of the
parties in states has often ranged from lukewarm to outright opposition, depending
on how favorable the status quo was to their interests. It appears that voters act in
a similar fashion, when asked to approve the creation of redistricting commissions
by initiative or referenda. Caroline J. Tolbert et al., *Strategic Voting and Legislative
Redistricting Reform,* 62 POL. RES. Q. 92 (2009). For discussions of attempts to
formulate non- or bipartisan redistricting processes, see Bruce E. Cain, *Redistricting Commissions: A Better Political Buffer?,* 121 YALE L.J. 1808 (2012).

8.   The opinions in *Vieth* sparred over the existence of judicially manageable
standards to police political gerrymandering. Who gets the better of the argument?
Does Justice Scalia adequately distinguish the cases (*e.g., Shaw v. Reno*) which
permit courts to regulate racially gerrymandered districts? The result in *Vieth* has
not deterred scholarly attempts to formulate standards to govern and potentially
limit partisan redistricting. *See, e.g.,* Laughlin McDonald, *The Looming 2010
Census: A Proposed Judicially Manageable Standard and other Reform Options
for Partisan Gerrymandering,* 46 HARV. J. ON LEGIS. 243 (2009) (proposing standard
that considers a predominately partisan purpose and disproportionate electoral
results); Douglass Calidas, Note, *Hindsight is 20/20: Revisiting the Reapportionment Cases to Gain Perspective on Partisan Gerrymanders,* 57 DUKE L.J. 1412
(2008) (arguing that just as *Baker*-type reapportionment cases came to enjoy
popular support, judicial regulation of partisan gerrymanders will also be
supported). Partisan gerrymandering is often said to be a cause of increased
political polarization in Congress and in state legislatures, since it is said to create
increasingly homogenous districts. For a study of congressional districting finding
little support for the posited linkage, see Nolan McCarty et al., *Does Gerrymandering Cause Polarization?,* 53 J. POL. 666 (2009).

9.   Following *Vieth,* lower courts have not found it easy to create or apply
judicially manageable standards to regulate gerrymandering in Congressional
districts, *e.g., Comm. For a Fair and Balanced Map v. Ill. St. Bd. of Elections,* 835
F. Supp. 2d 563 (N.D. Ill. 2011) (three-judge court) (rejecting as unmanageable
proposed standard focusing on both intent and effect to secure partisan advantage);
Perez v. Perry, 26 F. Supp. 3d 612 (W.D. Tex. 2014) (three-judge court), or state
legislative districts, *e.g., Radogno v. Ill. St. Bd. of Elections,* 2011 U.S. Dist. LEXIS
122053 (N.D. Ill. Oct. 21, 2011) (three-judge court) (proposed standard based on
First Amendment, as suggested by Justice Kennedy in *Vieth,* was unmanageable
since redistricting does not restrict political expression or association).

10.   Not specifically addressed in *Baker,* but raised in later cases, is the issue of
bipartisan gerrymanders, where both political parties collude to draw districts
favorable to their respective incumbents. The high reelection rate for incumbents
for both federal and state offices in recent decades, *see* Stephen Ansolabehere &
James M. Snyder, Jr., *The Incumbency Advantage in U.S. Elections: An Analysis
of State and Federal Offices, 1942-2000,* 1 ELECTION L.J. 315 (2002), is often
attributed to such collusion. But see John N. Friedman & Richard T. Holden, *The
Rising Incumbent Reelection Rate: What's Gerrymandering Got to Do With It?,* 71
J. POL. 593 (2009) (arguing that bipartisan gerrymandering has not been a

determinative factor). Does the lack of competitive districts raise legal and policy issues different from those concerning purely partisan gerrymanders, or call for a different judicial response? Compare Samuel Issacharoff, *Gerrymandering and Political Cartels*, 116 HARV. L. REV. 593 (2002), *with* Nathaniel Persily, *In Defense of Foxes Guarding Henhouses: The Case for Judicial Acquiescence in Incumbent-Protecting Gerrymanders*, 116 HARV. L. REV. 649 (2002) and Note, *Political Gerrymandering 2000-2008: "A Self-Limiting Enterprise"?*, 122 HARV. L. REV. 1467 (2009).

11.   In *LULAC v. Perry*, 548 U.S. 399, 419–20 (2006) [p. 385], plaintiffs argued that a mid-decade (re-)redistricting to benefit one party was unconstitutional. A plurality of the Court, in an opinion by Justice Kennedy, declined to address the claim, on the grounds that it was a political question. The plurality concluded that there were no judicially manageable standards to determine when such redistricting was unconstitutional. As in *Vieth*, however, a majority of the Justices appeared to leave open the possibility that suits against such redistricting might not always be considered a political question.

12.   In *Bush v. Gore*, 531 U.S. 98 (2000) (*per curiam*) [p. 1065], the Supreme Court, 5-4, reversed a decision of the Florida Supreme Court which had ordered a manual recount of certain ballots in the presidential election in Florida, effectively ensuring that George W. Bush would be elected President over Al Gore. The Court ruled that such a manual recount would lead to counting disparities that would violate the Due Process and Equal Protection Clauses. Some amicus curiae briefs argued that the case raised a political question and hence should not be decided by the Court. The argument was that the Twelfth Amendment reserves to Congress the right to determine if a state's presidential electors have been properly chosen. The plurality opinion in the case made no mention of the political-question doctrine, and it was only briefly mentioned in the concurring and dissenting opinions. For further discussion, see Rachel Barkow, *More Supreme Than Court? The Fall of the Political Question Doctrine and the Rise of Judicial Supremacy*, 102 COLUM. L. REV. 237, 273–300 (2002); Erwin Chemerinsky, Bush v. Gore *Was Not Justiciable*, 76 NOTRE DAME L. REV. 1093, 1105-09 (2001); Robert J. Pushaw, Jr., *The Presidential Election Dispute, the Political Question Doctrine, and the Fourteenth Amendment: A Reply to Professors Krent and Shane*, 29 FLA. ST. U. L. REV. 603 (2001).

13.   Professor Pildes has concluded that "there is less evidence than one might think to suggest that gerrymandered elections districts, which might still be pernicious for any number of other reasons, play a significant role in causing the rise of political polarization." Richard H. Pildes, *Why the Center Does Not Hold: The Causes of Hyperpolarized Democracy in America*, 99 CAL. L. REV. 273, 307–08 (2011). Among other things, Pildes observes that non-gerrymandered districts (such as for U.S. Senators) also have yielded less competitive elections, and that members of Congress have been voting in increasingly polarized ways, whether or not they come from competitive districts.

Chapter 3

ONE PERSON, ONE VOTE

A. INTRODUCTION

Once *Baker v. Carr*, 369 U.S. 186 (1962) [p. 119], held that challenges under the Equal Protection Clause could be adjudicated according to judicially manageable standards, the Court was forced to reach the merits of such challenges and determine what constraints, if any, the Constitution placed on electoral districting. It took little time for the Court to provide an answer: *Reynolds v. Sims*, 377 U.S. 533 (1964) [p. 173], established the famous one-person, one-vote rule. Under that rule, both houses of state legislatures must be apportioned on a population basis, and each district must be "as nearly of equal population as is practicable." *Id.* at 577.

Before the Court considered the mandate of the Equal Protection Clause in state-legislative districts in *Sims*, though, the Court was faced with two challenges to voting schemes in other contexts. In *Gray v. Sanders*, 372 U.S. 368 (1963) [p. 163], the Court held unconstitutional Georgia's scheme for selecting United States Senators and statewide officers. Georgia had used a unit system that operated much like the federal electoral college. Because the electoral power of each county was not based solely on population, the system did not give each voter equal influence in the election. The Court held the unit system unconstitutional, reasoning that the state could not treat its voters unequally by effectively weighting votes from less populous counties more heavily than the votes from other counties.

Wesberry v. Sanders, 376 U.S. 1 (1964) [p. 166], considered a constitutional challenge to population differentials in congressional districts. Rather than relying on the Equal Protection Clause, however, *Wesberry* held that Article I, § 2's requirement that members of the House of Representatives be elected "by the People of the several States" "means that as nearly as is practicable one man's vote in a congressional election is to be worth as much as another's." *Id.* at 7–8.

Article I, § 2 obviously had no applicability to state-legislative districts, so *Reynolds v. Sims* rested the one-person, one-vote rule for those districts on the Equal Protection Clause. Under *Sims*, districts were to be "substantially equal" in population. 377 U.S. at 568. Immediately after *Sims*, however, it was (and to some extent it still remains) unclear what level of population inequality would qualify as "substantial," and what reasons a state could offer to justify population differentials. According to *Sims*,

> So long as the divergences from a strict population standard are based on legitimate considerations incident to the effectuation of a rational state policy, some deviations from the equal-population principle are constitutionally permissible with respect to the apportionment of seats in either or

both of the two houses of a bicameral state legislature. But neither history alone, nor economic or other sorts of group interests, are permissible factors in attempting to justify disparities from population-based representation.

Id. at 579–80 (footnote omitted). *Sims* suggested that one justification in particular — allowing political subdivisions to have representation by drawing district lines along municipal boundaries — might permit states to enjoy "[s]omewhat more flexibility . . . with respect to state legislative apportionment than in congressional districting." *Id.* at 578.

As in *Gray v. Sanders, Sims* rejected a districting plan resembling the system established in the Constitution for the national government. *Gray* rejected a system resembling the Constitution's allocation of votes in selecting the President; *Sims* rejected a system resembling the Constitution's creation of different constituencies for the two houses of Congress. The United States Senate, of course, is not based on population, as each state is allocated two senators. *See* U.S. CONST. art. I, § 3, cl. 1. *Sims* held that Alabama could not similarly allocate one state senator to each county. In the Court's view, the United States Senate was a necessary compromise among formerly independent states, while Alabama's counties were merely convenient administrative units and did not need independent representation in the state legislature. *See Sims*, 377 U.S. at 571–77.

Mahan v. Howell, 410 U.S. 315 (1973) [p. 200], took up *Sims*'s suggestion that states may justify population disparities by citing a desire to allow political subdivisions some representation in state legislatures. *Howell* upheld Virginia's districting plan even though the districts varied in population by as much as 16.4%, reasoning that such a disparity was necessary for Virginia to allow its counties some influence in the state-legislative debates, especially regarding local legislation directed to particular political subdivisions.

By contrast, the Court has required states to justify even the smallest disparities in population between congressional districts. In *Kirkpatrick v. Preisler*, 394 U.S. 526 (1969) [p. 192], and *Karcher v. Daggett*, 462 U.S. 725 (1983), the Court struck down congressional districting plans where the population of the largest districts exceeded the population of the smallest by approximately 6% and 1%, respectively, but where the states failed to explain the need for even those differentials.

Similarly minuscule differences in state-legislative districts would not even make out a prima facie case of an equal-protection violation, and as a result the state need not justify such population disparities. *See Gaffney v. Cummings*, 412 U.S. 735 (1973) [p. 206]. A small difference in the populations of state-legislative districts does not completely insulate them from challenge, however; as the recent case of *Cox v. Larios*, 542 U.S. 947 (2004) [p. 212], shows, small disparities created to effectuate a partisan gerrymander will cause a plan to be struck down.

Lastly, even though super-majority requirements (that demand, for example, a 60% vote of the electorate before enacting certain types of legislation) allow electoral minorities to veto policy choices preferred by majorities of voters, those requirements do not violate the Equal Protection Clause unless used to disadvantage an identifiable class. *See Gordon v. Lance*, 403 U.S. 1, 7 (1971) [p. 216].

B.   THE CONSTITUTIONAL BASIS FOR ONE PERSON, ONE VOTE

Before 1963, the Constitution placed virtually no judicially enforceable constraints on the ability of states to allocate political power to different interests through legislative apportionment. *Gomillion v. Lightfoot*, 364 U.S. 339 (1960) [p. 115], ensured that states could not use the districting process to shut out racial minorities, but the "reapportionment revolution" begun with *Baker v. Carr*, 369 U.S. 186 (1962) [p. 119], and continued most prominently in *Reynolds v. Sims*, 377 U.S. 533 (1964) [p. 173], involved the federal judiciary in districting disputes to an extent unimaginable a short time earlier. This section traces the Court's discovery of the one-person, one-vote standard in both the Equal Protection Clause and the constitutional requirement that members of the Federal House of Representatives be elected "by the People of the several States." U.S. CONST. art. I, § 2, cl. 1.

GRAY v. SANDERS
Supreme Court of the United States
372 U.S. 368, 83 S. Ct. 801, 9 L. Ed. 2d 821 (1963)

MR. JUSTICE DOUGLAS delivered the opinion of the Court [in which MR. CHIEF JUSTICE WARREN, MR. JUSTICE BLACK, MR. JUSTICE CLARK, MR. JUSTICE BRENNAN, MR. JUSTICE STEWART, MR. JUSTICE WHITE, and MR. JUSTICE GOLDBERG join].

This suit was instituted by appellee, who is qualified to vote in primary and general elections in Fulton County, Georgia, to restrain appellants from using Georgia's county unit system as a basis for counting votes in a Democratic primary for the nomination of a United States Senator and statewide officers, and for declaratory relief. * * * Appellee alleges that the use of the county unit system in counting, tabulating, consolidating, and certifying votes cast in primary elections for statewide offices violates the Equal Protection Clause and the Due Process Clause of the Fourteenth Amendment and the Seventeenth Amendment. * * *

[Under the county unit system, candidates compete for the votes of each county, rather than for the votes of individuals. The winner is the candidate who wins the most unit (county) votes — not the one who wins the most individual votes. The candidate receiving the most votes in any particular county receives all the unit votes of that county, regardless of the closeness of the election in that county. Unit votes were apportioned in part by counties' populations, but with a significant weighting in favor of less-populous counties.]

This case * * * does not involve a question of the degree to which the Equal Protection Clause of the Fourteenth Amendment limits the authority of a State Legislature in designing the geographical districts from which representatives are chosen either for the State Legislature or for the Federal House of Representatives. * * * Nor does it present the question, inherent in the bicameral form of our Federal Government, whether a State may have one house chosen without regard to population. * * *

We think the analogies to the electoral college, to districting and redistricting, and to other phases of the problems of representation in state or federal legislatures or conventions are inapposite. The inclusion of the electoral college in the Constitution, as the result of specific historical concerns, validated the collegiate principle despite its inherent numerical inequality, but implied nothing about the use of an analogous system by a State in a statewide election.[8] No such specific accommodation of the latter was ever undertaken, and therefore no validation of its numerical inequality ensued. Nor does the question here have anything to do with the composition of the state or federal legislature. And we intimate no opinion on the constitutional phases of that problem beyond what we said in *Baker* v. *Carr*, [369 U.S. 186 (1962)] [p. 119]. The present case is only a voting case. Georgia gives every qualified voter one vote in a statewide election; but in counting those votes she employs the county unit system which in end result weights the rural vote more heavily than the urban vote and weights some small rural counties heavier than other larger rural counties. * * *

The Fifteenth Amendment prohibits a State from denying or abridging a Negro's right to vote. The Nineteenth Amendment does the same for women. If a State in a statewide election weighted the male vote more heavily than the female vote or the white vote more heavily than the Negro vote, none could successfully contend that that discrimination was allowable. How then can one person be given twice or 10 times the voting power of another person in a statewide election merely because he lives in a rural area or because he lives in the smallest rural county? Once the geographical unit for which a representative is to be chosen is designated, all who participate in the election are to have an equal vote — whatever their race, whatever their sex, whatever their occupation, whatever their income, and wherever their home may be in that geographical unit. This is required by the Equal Protection Clause of the Fourteenth Amendment. The concept of "we the people" under the Constitution visualizes no preferred class of voters but equality among those who meet the basic qualifications. * * *

The only weighting of votes sanctioned by the Constitution concerns matters of representation, such as the allocation of Senators irrespective of population and the use of the electoral college in the choice of a President. Yet when Senators are chosen, the Seventeenth Amendment states the choice must be made "by the people." Minors, felons, and other classes may be excluded. See *Lassiter* v. *Northampton County Election Board*, 360 U.S. [45,] 51 [(1959)] [p. 8]. But once the class of voters is chosen and their qualifications specified, we see no constitutional way by which equality of voting power may be evaded.[12] * * * The conception of political equality from the Declaration of Independence, to Lincoln's Gettysburg Address, to the Fifteenth, Seventeenth, and Nineteenth Amendments can mean only one thing — one person, one vote. * * *

---

[8] The electoral college was designed by men who did not want the election of the President to be left to the people. * * * Passage of the Fifteenth, Seventeenth, and Nineteenth Amendments shows that this conception of political equality belongs to a bygone day, and should not be considered in determining what the Equal Protection Clause of the Fourteenth Amendment requires in statewide elections. [Relocated. — Eds.]

[12] The county unit system * * * would allow the candidate winning the popular vote in the county to have the entire unit vote of that county. Hence the weighting of votes would continue, even if unit votes were allocated strictly in proportion to population. Thus if a candidate won 6,000 of 10,000 votes in a particular county, he would get the entire unit vote, the 4,000 other votes for a different candidate being worth nothing and being counted only for the purpose of being discarded. [Relocated — Eds.]

[Vacated and remanded.]

MR. JUSTICE STEWART, whom MR. JUSTICE CLARK joins, concurring.

In joining the opinion and judgment of the Court, I emphasize what — but for my Brother HARLAN's dissent — I should have thought would be apparent to all who read the Court's opinion. This case does not involve the validity of a State's apportionment of geographic constituencies from which representatives to the State's legislative assembly are chosen, nor any of the problems under the Equal Protection Clause which such litigation would present. * * * This case, on the contrary, involves statewide elections of a United States Senator and of state executive and judicial officers responsible to a statewide constituency. Within a given constituency, there can be room for but a single constitutional rule — one voter, one vote.

MR. JUSTICE HARLAN, dissenting. * * *

The Court's holding surely flies in the face of history. For, as impressively shown by the opinion of Frankfurter, J., in *Baker* v. *Carr*, "one person, one vote" has never been the universally accepted political philosophy in England, the American Colonies, or in the United States. The significance of this historical fact seems indeed to be recognized by the Court, for it implies that its newfound formula might not obtain in a case involving the apportionment of seats in the "State Legislature or for the Federal House of Representatives."

But * * * any such distinction finds persuasive refutation in the Federal Electoral College whereby the President of the United States is chosen on principles wholly opposed to those now held constitutionally required in the electoral process for statewide office. One need not close his eyes to the circumstance that the Electoral College was born in compromise, nor take sides in the various attempts that have been made to change the system, in order to agree with the court below that it "could hardly be said that such a system used in a state among its counties, assuming rationality and absence of arbitrariness in end result, could be termed invidious." * * *

* * * In my dissent in *Baker* v. *Carr*, I expressed the view that a State might rationally conclude that its general welfare was best served by apportioning more seats in the legislature to agricultural communities than to urban centers, lest the legitimate interests of the former be submerged in the stronger electoral voice of the latter. In my opinion, recognition of the same factor cannot be deemed irrational in the present situation[.] * * *

Notes and Questions

1.   The Court's footnote 8 argued that the Fifteenth, Seventeenth, and Nineteenth Amendments should have relevance to the interpretation of the *Fourteenth* Amendment. Certainly, constitutional amendments can change the meaning of earlier-enacted portions of the Constitution; for example, the Twenty-First Amendment repealed the Eighteenth, and the Eleventh Amendment altered the prior

understanding of the limits of the judicial power established in Article III. Indeed, changing the meaning of the existing Constitution is the entire point of proposing and ratifying an amendment. But the Court's argument here was different. The Court was stating that the democratic ideals in the background of the Fifteenth, Seventeenth, and Nineteenth Amendments change the meaning of the Fourteenth Amendment, *without there being any clear conflict*. Is it proper for the Court to use later amendments in this way?

2. If one accepts the Court's methodological approach and the substantive conclusion in *Gray*, is the Electoral College itself unconstitutional? *See New v. Pelosi*, 2008 U.S. Dist. LEXIS 87447 (S.D.N.Y. 2008); *New v. Ashcroft*, 293 F. Supp. 2d 256 (E.D.N.Y. 2003); *Williams v. Virginia State Board of Elections*, 288 F. Supp. 622 (E.D. Va. 1968), *aff'd* 393 U.S. 320 (1969). The Fifth Amendment contains an equal protection "component," *see Adarand Constructors, Inc. v. Peña*, 515 U.S. 200, 212–18 (1995); *Bolling v. Sharpe*, 347 U.S. 497, 499–500 (1954); why should that Amendment not be reinterpreted in light of the Fifteenth, Seventeenth, and Nineteenth Amendments?

3. *Problem*. Maine and Nebraska allocate their presidential electors in part by congressional district, and have done so since 1972 and 1996, respectively. Those states award two electors to the statewide plurality winner, and one elector for each congressional district won. (Maine has two congressional districts, and Nebraska has three.) Does such a system contravene *Gray*, especially footnote 12, even though the districts contain the same number of people? Does the answer to the constitutional question depend on the size of the state's congressional delegation?

4. The Court is surely correct that states may not give disproportionate weight to the votes of whites or males. Is there a reason for a different rule to obtain when the votes of rural-area residents are favored?

5. Did *Gray* effectively foreordain the extension of one-person, one-vote to congressional and state-legislative races, or were Justices Stewart and Clark correct that the issues are distinguishable?

WESBERRY v. SANDERS
Supreme Court of the United States
376 U.S. 1, 84 S. Ct. 526, 11 L. Ed. 2d 481 (1964)

Mr. Justice Black delivered the opinion of the Court [in which Mr. Chief Justice Warren, Mr. Justice Douglas, Mr. Justice Brennan, Mr. Justice White, and Mr. Justice Goldberg join].

Appellants are citizens and qualified voters of Fulton County, Georgia, and as such are entitled to vote in congressional elections in Georgia's Fifth Congressional District. That district, one of ten created by a 1931 Georgia statute, * * * has a population according to the 1960 census of 823,680. The average population of the ten districts is 394,312, less than half that of the Fifth. * * * Since there is only one Congressman for each district, this inequality of population means that the Fifth District's Congressman has to represent from two to three times as many people as do Congressmen from some of the other Georgia districts. * * *

We hold that, construed in its historical context, the command of Art. I, § 2, that Representatives be chosen "by the People of the several States" means that as nearly as is practicable one man's vote in a congressional election is to be worth as much as another's.[10] * * * It would be extraordinary to suggest that * * * the votes of inhabitants of some parts of a State * * * could be weighted at two or three times the value of the votes of people living in more populous parts of the State * * *. We do not believe that the Framers of the Constitution intended to permit the same vote-diluting discrimination to be accomplished through the device of districts containing widely varied numbers of inhabitants. To say that a vote is worth more in one district than in another would not only run counter to our fundamental ideas of democratic government, it would cast aside the principle of a House of Representatives elected "by the People," a principle tenaciously fought for and established at the Constitutional Convention. The history of the Constitution, particularly that part of it relating to the adoption of Art. I, § 2, reveals that those who framed the Constitution meant that, no matter what the mechanics of an election, whether statewide or by districts, it was population which was to be the basis of the House of Representatives. * * *

The debates at the [Constitutional] Convention make at least one fact abundantly clear: that when the delegates agreed that the House should represent "people" they intended that in allocating Congressmen the number assigned to each State should be determined solely by the number of the State's inhabitants. The Constitution embodied Edmund Randolph's proposal for a periodic census to ensure "fair representation of the people," an idea endorsed by [George] Mason as assuring that "numbers of inhabitants" should always be the measure of representation in the House of Representatives. The Convention also overwhelmingly agreed to a resolution offered by Randolph to base future apportionment squarely on numbers and to delete any reference to wealth. And the delegates defeated a motion made by Elbridge Gerry to limit the number of Representatives from newer Western States so that it would never exceed the number from the original States.

It would defeat the principle solemnly embodied in the Great Compromise — equal representation in the House for equal numbers of people — for us to hold that, within the States, legislatures may draw the lines of congressional districts in such a way as to give some voters a greater voice in choosing a Congressman than others. The House of Represenatives, the Convention agreed, was to represent the people as individuals, and on a basis of complete equality for each voter. The delegates were quite aware of what [James] Madison called the "vicious representation" in Great Britain whereby "rotten boroughs" with few inhabitants were represented in Parliament on or almost on a par with cities of greater population. * * * The delegates referred to rotten borough apportionments in some of the state legislatures as the kind of objectionable governmental action that the Constitution should not tolerate in the election of congressional representatives.

Madison in *The Federalist* described the system of division of States into congressional districts, the method which he and others assumed States probably would adopt: "The city of Philadelphia is supposed to contain between fifty and sixty

---

[10] We do not reach the arguments that the Georgia statute violates the Due Process, Equal Protection and Privileges and [*sic*] Immunities Clauses of the Fourteenth Amendment.

thousand souls. It will therefore form nearly two districts for the choice of Foderal Representatives." "[N]umbers," he said, * * * "are the only proper scale of representation." In the state conventions, speakers urging ratification of the Constitution emphasized the theme of equal representation in the House which had permeated the debates in Philadelphia. Charles Cotesworth Pinckney told the South Carolina Convention, "the House of Representatives will be elected immediately by the people, and represent them and their personal rights individually. . . ." Speakers at the ratifying conventions emphasized that the House of Representatives was meant to be free of the malapportionment then existing in some of the State legislatures * * * and argued that the power given Congress in Art. I, § 4,[43] was meant to be used to vindicate the people's right to equality of representation in the House. * * *

It is in the light of such history that we must construe Art. I, § 2, of the Constitution, which, carrying out the ideas of Madison and those of like views, provides that Representatives shall be chosen "by the People of the several States" and shall be "apportioned among the several States . . . according to their respective Numbers." It is not surprising that our Court has held that this Article gives persons qualified to vote a constitutional right to vote and to have their votes counted. *United States* v. *Mosley*, 238 U.S. 383 [(1915)]; *Ex parte Yarbrough*, 110 U.S. 651 [(1884)]. Not only can this right to vote not be denied outright, it cannot, consistently with Article I, be destroyed by alteration of ballots, see *United States* v. *Classic*, 313 U.S. 299 [(1941)], or diluted by stuffing of the ballot box, see *United States* v. *Saylor*, 322 U.S. 385 [(1944)]. No right is more precious in a free country than that of having a voice in the election of those who make the laws under which, as good citizens, we must live. Other rights, even the most basic, are illusory if the right to vote is undermined. * * *

While it may not be possible to draw congressional districts with mathematical precision, that is no excuse for ignoring our Constitution's plain objective of making equal representation for equal numbers of people the fundamental goal for the House of Representatives. That is the high standard of justice and common sense which the Founders set for us.

Reversed and remanded.

MR. JUSTICE CLARK, concurring in part and dissenting in part.

* * * [I]n my view, Brother HARLAN has clearly demonstrated that both the historical background and language preclude a finding that Art. I, § 2, lays down the *ipse dixit* "one person, one vote" in congressional elections.

On the other hand, I agree with the majority that congressional districting is subject to judicial scrutiny. * * * I therefore cannot agree with Brother HARLAN that

---

[43] "The Times, Places and Manner of holding Elections for Senators and Representatives, shall be prescribed in each State by the Legislature thereof; but the Congress may at any time by Law make or alter such Regulations, except as to the Places of chusing Senators. . . ."

the supervisory power granted to Congress under Art. I, § 4, is the exclusive remedy.

I would examine the Georgia congressional districts against the requirements of the Equal Protection Clause of the Fourteenth Amendment. * * * The trial court, however, did not pass upon the merits of the case * * *. In my view we should therefore vacate this judgment and remand the case for a hearing on the merits. * * *

Mr. Justice Harlan, dissenting.

I had not expected to witness the day when the Supreme Court of the United States would render a decision which casts grave doubt on the constitutionality of the composition of the House of Representatives. * * *

Disclaiming all reliance on other provisions of the Constitution, in particular those of the Fourteenth Amendment on which the appellants relied below and in this Court, the Court holds that the provision in Art. I, § 2, for election of Representatives "by the People" means that congressional districts are to be "as nearly as is practicable" equal in population.[4] Stripped of rhetoric and a "historical context" which bears little resemblance to the evidence found in the pages of history, the Court's opinion supports its holding only with the bland assertion that "the principle of a House of Representatives elected 'by the People' " would be "cast aside" if "a vote is worth more in one district than in another," *i.e.*, if congressional districts within a State, each electing a single Representative, are not equal in population. The fact is, however, that Georgia's 10 Representatives are elected "by the People" of Georgia, just as Representatives from other States are elected "by the People of the several States." This is all that the Constitution requires.

Although the Court finds necessity for its artificial construction of Article I in the undoubted importance of the right to vote, that right is not involved in this case. All of the appellants do vote. The Court's talk about "debasement" and "dilution" of the vote is a model of circular reasoning, in which the premises of the argument feed on the conclusion. Moreover, by focusing exclusively on numbers in disregard of the area and shape of a congressional district as well as party affiliations within the district, the Court deals in abstractions which will be recognized even by the politically unsophisticated to have little relevance to the realities of political life.

In any event, the very sentence of Art. I, § 2, on which the Court exclusively relies confers the right to vote for Representatives only on those whom *the State* has

---

[4] The Court's "as nearly as is practicable" formula sweeps a host of questions under the rug. How great a difference between the populations of various districts within a State is tolerable? Is the standard an absolute or relative one, and if the latter to what is the difference in population to be related? Does the number of districts within the State have any relevance? Is the number of voters or the number of inhabitants controlling? Is the relevant statistic the greatest disparity between any two districts in the State or the average departure from the average population per district, or a little of both? May the State consider factors such as area or natural boundaries (rivers, mountain ranges) which are plainly relevant to the practicability of effective representation? There is an obvious lack of criteria for answering questions such as these, which points up the impropriety of the Court's whole-hearted but heavy-footed entrance into the political arena. [Relocated. — Eds.]

found qualified to vote for members of "the most numerous Branch of the State Legislature." So far as Article I is concerned, it is within the State's power to confer that right only on persons of wealth or of a particular sex or, if the State chose, living in specified areas of the State. Were Georgia to find the residents of the Fifth District unqualified to vote for Representatives to the State House of Representatives, they could not vote for Representatives to Congress, according to the express words of Art. I, § 2. Other provisions of the Constitution would, of course, be relevant, *but, so far as Art. I, § 2, is concerned*, the disqualification would be within Georgia's power. How can it be, then, that this very same sentence prevents Georgia from apportioning its Representatives as it chooses? The truth is that it does not.

The Court purports to find support for its position in the third paragraph of Art. I, § 2, which provides for the apportionment of Representatives among the States. * * * Far from supporting the Court, the apportionment of Representatives among the States shows how blindly the Court has marched to its decision. Representatives were to be apportioned among the States on the basis of free population plus three-fifths of the slave population. Since no slave voted, the inclusion of three-fifths of their number in the basis of apportionment gave the favored States representation far in excess of their voting population. If, then, slaves were intended to be without representation, Article I did exactly what the Court now says it prohibited: it "weighted" the vote of voters in the slave States. * * *

There is a further basis for demonstrating the hollowness of the Court's assertion that Article I requires "one man's vote in a congressional election . . . to be worth as much as another's." Nothing that the Court does today will disturb the fact that although in 1960 the population of an average congressional district was 410,481, the States of Alaska, Nevada, and Wyoming each have a Representative in Congress, although their respective populations are 226,167, 285,278, and 330,066. In entire disregard of population, Art. I, § 2, guarantees each of these States and every other State "at Least one Representative." It is whimsical to assert in the face of this guarantee that an absolute principle of "equal representation in the House for equal numbers of people" is "solemnly embodied" in Article I. All that there is is a provision which bases representation in the House, generally but not entirely, on the population of the States. The provision for representation of *each State* in the House of Representatives is not a mere exception to the principle framed by the majority; it shows that no such principle is to be found.

Finally in this array of hurdles to its decision which the Court surmounts only by knocking them down is § 4 of Art. I which states simply:

> "The Times, Places and *Manner* of holding Elections for Senators and Representatives, shall be prescribed in each State by the Legislature thereof; but the Congress may at any time by Law make or alter such Regulations, except as to the Places of chusing Senators." (Emphasis added.)

* * * It cannot be supposed that delegates to the Convention would have labored to establish a principle of equal representation only to bury it, one would have thought beyond discovery, in § 2, and omit all mention of it from § 4, which deals explicitly with the conduct of elections. Section 4 states without qualification that the state legislatures shall prescribe regulations for the conduct of elections for

Representatives and, equally without qualification, that Congress may make or alter such regulations. There is nothing to indicate any limitation whatsoever on this grant of plenary initial and supervisory power. * * *

There is dubious propriety in turning to the "historical context" of constitutional provisions which speak so consistently and plainly. But, as one might expect when the Constitution itself is free from ambiguity, the surrounding history makes what is already clear even clearer.

* * * [T]he statements [at the Constitutional Convention] approving population-based representation were focused on the problem of how representation should be apportioned among the States in the House of Representatives. The Great Compromise concerned representation *of the States* in the Congress. In all of the discussion surrounding the basis of representation of the House and all of the discussion whether Representatives should be elected by the legislatures or the people of the States, there is nothing which suggests even remotely that the delegates had in mind the problem of districting within a State. * * *

[T]he language of Art. I, §§ 2 and 4, the surrounding text, and the relevant history are all in strong and consistent direct contradiction of the Court's holding. The constitutional scheme vests in the States plenary power to regulate the conduct of elections for Representatives, and, in order to protect the Federal Government, provides for congressional supervision of the States' exercise of their power. Within this scheme, the appellants do not have the right which they assert, in the absence of provision for equal districts by the Georgia Legislature or the Congress. The constitutional right which the Court creates is manufactured out of whole cloth. * * *

Congress exercised its power to regulate elections for the House of Representatives for the first time in 1842, when it provided that Representatives from States "entitled to more than one Representative" should be elected by districts of contiguous territory, "no one district electing more than one Representative." The requirement was later dropped, and reinstated. In 1872, Congress required that Representatives "be elected by districts composed of contiguous territory, and containing as nearly as practicable an equal number of inhabitants, . . . no one district electing more than one Representative." This provision for equal districts which the Court exactly duplicates in effect, was carried forward in each subsequent apportionment statute through 1911. There was no reapportionment following the 1920 census. The provision for equally populated districts was dropped in 1929, and has not been revived[.] * * *

Although there is little discussion of the reasons for omitting the requirement of equally populated districts, the fact that such a provision was included in the bill as it was presented to the House, and was deleted by the House after debate and notice of intention to do so, leaves no doubt that the omission was deliberate. [See *Wood* v. *Broom*, 287 U.S. 1, 7 (1932).] * * * Bills which would have imposed on the States a requirement of equally or nearly equally populated districts were regularly introduced in the House. None of them became law. * * *

Today's decision has portents for our society and the Court itself which should be recognized. This is not a case in which the Court vindicates the kind of individual rights that are assured by the Due Process Clause of the Fourteenth Amendment, whose "vague contours" of course leave much room for constitutional developments necessitated by changing conditions in a dynamic society. Nor is this a case in which an emergent set of facts requires the Court to frame new principles to protect recognized constitutional rights. The claim for judicial relief in this case strikes at one of the fundamental doctrines of our system of government, the separation of powers. In upholding that claim, the Court attempts to effect reforms in a field which the Constitution, as plainly as can be, has committed exclusively to the political process.

This Court, no less than all other branches of the Government, is bound by the Constitution. The Constitution does not confer on the Court blanket authority to step into every situation where the political branch may be thought to have fallen short. The stability of this institution ultimately depends not only upon its being alert to keep the other branches of government within constitutional bounds but equally upon recognition of the limitations on the Court's own functions in the constitutional system.

What is done today saps the political process. The promise of judicial intervention in matters of this sort cannot but encourage popular inertia in efforts for political reform through the political process, with the inevitable result that the process is itself weakened. By yielding to the demand for a judicial remedy in this instance, the Court in my view does a disservice both to itself and to the broader values of our system of government.

Believing that the complaint fails to disclose a constitutional claim, I would affirm the judgment below dismissing the complaint.

Mr. Justice Stewart.

I think it is established that "this Court has power to afford relief in a case of this type as against the objection that the issues are not justiciable," and I cannot subscribe to any possible implication to the contrary which may lurk in Mr. Justice Harlan's dissenting opinion. With this single qualification I join the dissent because I think Mr. Justice Harlan has unanswerably demonstrated that Art. I, § 2, of the Constitution gives no mandate to this Court or to any court to ordain that congressional districts within each State must be equal in population.

Notes and Questions

1.   What does Justice Harlan mean when he charges the majority with "circular reasoning" in its "talk about 'debasement' and 'dilution' of the vote"? *See also Baker v. Carr*, 369 U.S. 186, 300 (1962) (Frankfurter, J., dissenting) ("Talk of 'debasement' or 'dilution' is circular talk. One cannot speak of 'debasement' or 'dilution' of the value of a vote until there is first defined a standard of reference as to what a vote should be worth.").

2.   What does "as nearly as is practicable" mean? At the very end of its opinion, the Court states that precise equality "may not be possible." Should the standard require equality unless it is "[im]possible"? If a more lenient standard is to be

applied, what might be sufficient reasons for deviating from precise mathematical equality?

3.   Note Justice Harlan's attempt to distinguish the question in this case from issues involving the Due Process Clause. Is he convincing in arguing that the Due Process Clause, but not Article I, §§ 2 and 4, calls for "constitutional developments necessitated by changing conditions in a dynamic society"? (Note that three years earlier, in *Poe v. Ullman*, 367 U.S. 497 (1961) (dissenting opinion), Justice Harlan had famously called for an active judicial role in protecting the privacy of marital relationships through the Due Process Clause.) Should the Court's interpretation of the Equal Protection Clause take on a similarly dynamic character? *Wesberry v. Sanders* found it unnecessary to address the Equal Protection Clause, but that Clause is at the heart of the next case.

REYNOLDS v. SIMS
Supreme Court of the United States
377 U.S. 533, 84 S. Ct. 1362, 12 L. Ed. 2d 506 (1964)

MR. CHIEF JUSTICE WARREN delivered the opinion of the Court [in which MR. JUSTICE BLACK, MR. JUSTICE DOUGLAS, MR. JUSTICE BRENNAN, MR. JUSTICE WHITE, and MR. JUSTICE GOLDBERG join]. * * *

[Voters in Jefferson County, Alabama, challenged the apportionment of the State's legislature, which consisted of a 35-member Senate and a 106-member House of Representatives, as violating the Equal Protection Clause. Alabama's 1901 Constitution required the State to reapportion districts following each decennial census, but this had not been done. In the years since 1900, Alabama's proportion of city residents had greatly increased, causing the districts' population-variance ratios to be as high as 41-to-1 in the Senate and 16-to-1 in the House. The 1901 Constitution also required each county to have at least one representative and provided that no county could be divided between two Senate districts.

[During this litigation, the Alabama legislature passed a proposed constitutional amendment, which was to be submitted to the voters and would have created a 67-member Senate with 1 senator from each county, and would have given each county one representative in the 106-member House, with the remaining 39 representatives distributed according to population. The District Court held both the existing system and the proposed amendment unconstitutional.]

* * * The right to vote freely for the candidate of one's choice is of the essence of a democratic society, and any restrictions on that right strike at the heart of representative government. And the right of suffrage can be denied by a debasement or dilution of the weight of a citizen's vote just as effectively as by wholly prohibiting the free exercise of the franchise. * * *

Gray [v. *Sanders*, 372 U.S. 368 (1963)] [p. 163] and *Wesberry* [v. *Sanders*, 376 U.S. 1 (1964)] [p. 166] are of course not dispositive of or directly controlling on our decision in these cases involving state legislative apportionment controversies. * * * But neither are they wholly inapposite. *Gray*, though not determinative here since involving the weighting of votes in statewide elections, established the basic principle of equality among voters within a State, and held that voters cannot be classified, constitutionally, on the basis of where they live, at least with respect to voting in statewide elections. And our decision in *Wesberry* was of course grounded on that language of the Constitution which prescribes that members of the Federal House of Representatives are to be chosen "by the People," while attacks on state legislative apportionment schemes, such as that involved in the instant cases, are principally based on the Equal Protection Clause of the Fourteenth Amendment. Nevertheless, *Wesberry* clearly established that the fundamental principle of representative government in this country is one of equal representation for equal numbers of people, without regard to race, sex, economic status, or place of residence within a State. Our problem, then, is to ascertain, in the instant cases, whether there are any constitutionally cognizable principles which would justify departures from the basic standard of equality among voters in the apportionment of seats in state legislatures.

A predominant consideration in determining whether a State's legislative apportionment scheme constitutes an invidious discrimination violative of rights asserted under the Equal Protection Clause is that the rights allegedly impaired are individual and personal in nature. * * * While the result of a court decision in a state legislative apportionment controversy may be to require the restructuring of the geographical distribution of seats in a state legislature, the judicial focus must be concentrated upon ascertaining whether there has been any discrimination against certain of the State's citizens which constitutes an impermissible impairment of their constitutionally protected right to vote. Like *Skinner* v. *Oklahoma*, 316 U.S. 535 [(1942)], such a case " 'touches a sensitive and important area of human rights,' and 'involves one of the basic civil rights of man,' " presenting questions of alleged "invidious discriminations . . . against groups or types of individuals in violation of the constitutional guaranty of just and equal laws." Undoubtedly, the right of suffrage is a fundamental matter in a free and democratic society. Especially since the right to exercise the franchise in a free and unimpaired manner is preservative of other basic civil and political rights, any alleged infringement of the right of citizens to vote must be carefully and meticulously scrutinized. Almost a century ago, in *Yick Wo* v. *Hopkins*, 118 U.S. 356 [(1886)], the Court referred to "the political franchise of voting" as "a fundamental political right, because preservative of all rights."

Legislators represent people, not trees or acres. Legislators are elected by voters, not farms or cities or economic interests. As long as ours is a representative form of government, and our legislatures are those instruments of government elected directly by and directly representative of the people, the right to elect legislators in a free and unimpaired fashion is a bedrock of our political system. It could hardly be gainsaid that a constitutional claim had been asserted by an allegation that certain otherwise qualified voters had been entirely prohibited from voting for members of their state legislature. And, if a State should provide that the votes of citizens in one part of the State should be given two times, or five times, or 10 times the weight of votes of citizens in another part of the State, it could hardly be contended that the right to vote of those residing in the disfavored areas had not been effectively diluted. * * * And it is inconceivable that a state law to the effect that, in counting votes for legislators, the votes of citizens in one part of the State would be multiplied by two, five, or 10, while the votes of persons in another area would be counted only at face value, could be constitutionally sustainable. Of course, the effect of state legislative districting schemes which give the same number of representatives to unequal numbers of constituents is identical. * * * Weighting the votes of citizens differently, by any method or means, merely because of where they happen to reside, hardly seems justifiable. * * *

[R]epresentative government is in essence self-government through the medium of elected representatives of the people, and each and every citizen has an inalienable right to full and effective participation in the political processes of his State's legislative bodies. Most citizens can achieve this participation only as qualified voters through the election of legislators to represent them. Full and effective participation by all citizens in state government requires, therefore, that each citizen have an equally effective voice in the election of members of his state legislature. Modern and viable state government needs, and the Constitution demands, no less.

Logically, in a society ostensibly grounded on representative government, it would seem reasonable that a majority of the people of a State could elect a majority of that State's legislators. To conclude differently, and to sanction minority control of state legislative bodies, would appear to deny majority rights in a way that far surpasses any possible denial of minority rights that might otherwise be thought to result. Since legislatures are responsible for enacting laws by which all citizens are to be governed, they should be bodies which are collectively responsive to the popular will. And the concept of equal protection has been traditionally viewed as requiring the uniform treatment of persons standing in the same relation to the governmental action questioned or challenged. With respect to the allocation of legislative representation, all voters, as citizens of a State, stand in the same relation regardless of where they live. Any suggested criteria for the differentiation of citizens are insufficient to justify any discrimination, as to the weight of their votes, unless relevant to the permissible purposes of legislative apportionment. Since the achieving of fair and effective representation for all citizens is concededly the basic aim of legislative apportionment, we conclude that the Equal Protection Clause guarantees the opportunity for equal participation by all voters in the election of state legislators. Diluting the weight of votes because of place of residence impairs basic constitutional rights under the Fourteenth Amendment just as much as invidious discriminations based upon factors such as race or economic status. Our constitutional system amply provides for the protection of minorities by means other than giving them majority control of state legislatures. And the democratic ideals of equality and majority rule, which have served this Nation so well in the past, are hardly of any less significance for the present and the future.

We are told that the matter of apportioning representation in a state legislature is a complex and many-faceted one. We are advised that States can rationally consider factors other than population in apportioning legislative representation. We are admonished not to restrict the power of the States to impose differing views as to political philosophy on their citizens. We are cautioned about the dangers of entering into political thickets and mathematical quagmires. Our answer is this: a denial of constitutionally protected rights demands judicial protection; our oath and our office require no less of us. * * * To the extent that a citizen's right to vote is debased, he is that much less a citizen. The fact that an individual lives here or there is not a legitimate reason for overweighting or diluting the efficacy of his vote. The complexions of societies and civilizations change, often with amazing rapidity. A nation once primarily rural in character becomes predominantly urban. Representation schemes once fair and equitable become archaic and outdated. But the basic principle of representative government remains, and must remain, unchanged — the weight of a citizen's vote cannot be made to depend on where he lives. Population is, of necessity, the starting point for consideration and the controlling criterion for judgment in legislative apportionment controversies. A citizen, a qualified voter, is no more nor no less so because he lives in the city or on the farm. This is the clear and strong command of our Constitution's Equal Protection Clause. This is an essential part of the concept of a government of laws and not men. This is at the heart of Lincoln's vision of "government of the people, by the people, [and] for the people." The Equal Protection Clause demands no less than substantially equal state legislative representation for all citizens, of all places as well as of all races.

We hold that, as a basic constitutional standard, the Equal Protection Clause requires that the seats in both houses of a bicameral state legislature must be apportioned on a population basis. Simply stated, an individual's right to vote for state legislators is unconstitutionally impaired when its weight is in a substantial fashion diluted when compared with votes of citizens living in other parts of the State. * * *

Since neither of the houses of the Alabama Legislature * * * was apportioned on a population basis, we would be justified in proceeding no further. However, * * * the so-called 67-Senator Amendment, at least superficially resembles the scheme of legislative representation followed in the Federal Congress. Under this plan, each of Alabama's 67 counties is allotted one senator, and no counties are given more than one Senate seat. Arguably, this is analogous to the allocation of two Senate seats, in the Federal Congress, to each of the 50 States, regardless of population. Seats in the Alabama House, under the proposed constitutional amendment, are distributed by giving each of the 67 counties at least one, with the remaining 39 seats being allotted among the more populous counties on a population basis. This scheme, at least at first glance, appears to resemble that prescribed for the Federal House of Representatives, where the 435 seats are distributed among the States on a population basis, although each State, regardless of its population, is given at least one Congressman. Thus, although there are substantial differences in underlying rationale and result, the 67-Senator Amendment, as proposed by the Alabama Legislature, at least arguably presents for consideration a scheme analogous to that used for apportioning seats in Congress.

* * * We * * * find the federal analogy inapposite and irrelevant to state legislative districting schemes. * * *

The system of representation in the two Houses of the Federal Congress is one ingrained in our Constitution, as part of the law of the land. It is one conceived out of compromise and concession indispensable to the establishment of our federal republic. Arising from unique historical circumstances, it is based on the consideration that in establishing our type of federalism a group of formerly independent States bound themselves together under one national government. Admittedly, the original 13 States surrendered some of their sovereignty in agreeing to join together "to form a more perfect Union." But at the heart of our constitutional system remains the concept of separate and distinct governmental entities which have delegated some, but not all, of their formerly held powers to the single national government. The fact that almost three-fourths of our present States were never in fact independently sovereign does not detract from our view that the so-called federal analogy is inapplicable as a sustaining precedent for state legislative apportionments. The developing history and growth of our republic cannot cloud the fact that, at the time of the inception of the system of representation in the Federal Congress, a compromise between the larger and smaller States on this matter averted a deadlock in the Constitutional Convention which had threatened to abort the birth of our Nation. * * *

Political subdivisions of States — counties, cities, or whatever — never were and never have been considered as sovereign entities. Rather, they have been traditionally regarded as subordinate governmental instrumentalities created by the State to assist in the carrying out of state governmental functions. * * * The relationship of the States to the Federal Government could hardly be less analogous.

Thus, we conclude that the plan contained in the 67-Senator Amendment for apportioning seats in the Alabama Legislature cannot be sustained by recourse to the so-called federal analogy. Nor can any other inequitable state legislative apportionment scheme be justified on such an asserted basis. This does not necessarily mean that such a plan is irrational or involves something other than a "republican form of government." We conclude simply that such a plan is impermissible for the States under the Equal Protection Clause, since perforce resulting, in virtually every case, in submergence of the equal-population principle in at least one house of a state legislature.

Since we find the so-called federal analogy inapposite to a consideration of the constitutional validity of state legislative apportionment schemes, we necessarily hold that the Equal Protection Clause requires both houses of a state legislature to be apportioned on a population basis. The right of a citizen to equal representation and to have his vote weighted equally with those of all other citizens in the election of members of one house of a bicameral state legislature would amount to little if States could effectively submerge the equal-population principle in the apportionment of seats in the other house. If such a scheme were permissible, an individual citizen's ability to exercise an effective voice in the only instrument of state government directly representative of the people might be almost as effectively thwarted as if neither house were apportioned on a population basis. Deadlock between the two bodies might result in compromise and concession on some issues. But in all too many cases the more probable result would be frustration of the majority will through minority veto in the house not apportioned on a population basis, stemming directly from the failure to accord adequate overall legislative representation to all of the State's citizens on a nondiscriminatory basis. In summary, we can perceive no constitutional difference, with respect to the geographical distribution of state legislative representation, between the two houses of a bicameral state legislature.

We do not believe that the concept of bicameralism is rendered anachronistic and meaningless when the predominant basis of representation in the two state legislative bodies is required to be the same — population. A prime reason for bicameralism, modernly considered, is to insure mature and deliberate consideration of, and to prevent precipitate action on, proposed legislative measures. Simply because the controlling criterion for apportioning representation is required to be the same in both houses does not mean that there will be no differences in the composition and complexion of the two bodies. Different constituencies can be represented in the two houses. One body could be composed of single-member districts while the other could have at least some multimember districts. The length of terms of the legislators in the separate bodies could differ. The numerical size of the two bodies could be made to differ, even significantly, and the geographical size of districts from which legislators are elected could also be made to differ. And apportionment in one house could be arranged so as to balance off minor inequities in the representation of certain areas in the other house. In summary, these and other factors could be, and are presently in many States, utilized to engender differing complexions and collective attitudes in the two bodies of a state legislature, although both are apportioned substantially on a population basis.

By holding that as a federal constitutional requisite both houses of a state legislature must be apportioned on a population basis, we mean that the Equal Protection Clause requires that a State make an honest and good faith effort to construct districts, in both houses of its legislature, as nearly of equal population as is practicable. We realize that it is a practical impossibility to arrange legislative districts so that each one has an identical number of residents, or citizens, or voters. Mathematical exactness or precision is hardly a workable constitutional requirement.

In *Wesberry* v. *Sanders, supra*, the Court stated that congressional representation must be based on population as nearly as is practicable. In implementing the basic constitutional principle of representative government as enunciated by the Court in *Wesberry* — equality of population among districts — some distinctions may well be made between congressional and state legislative representation. Since, almost invariably, there is a significantly larger number of seats in state legislative bodies to be distributed within a State than congressional seats, it may be feasible to use political subdivision lines to a greater extent in establishing state legislative districts than in congressional districting while still affording adequate representation to all parts of the State. To do so would be constitutionally valid, so long as the resulting apportionment was one based substantially on population and the equal-population principle was not diluted in any significant way. Somewhat more flexibility may therefore be constitutionally permissible with respect to state legislative apportionment than in congressional districting. Lower courts can and assuredly will work out more concrete and specific standards for evaluating state legislative apportionment schemes in the context of actual litigation. For the present, we deem it expedient not to attempt to spell out any precise constitutional tests. What is marginally permissible in one State may be unsatisfactory in another, depending on the particular circumstances of the case. Developing a body of doctrine on a case-by-case basis appears to us to provide the most satisfactory means of arriving at detailed constitutional requirements in the area of state legislative apportionment. Thus, we proceed to state here only a few rather general considerations which appear to us to be relevant.

A State may legitimately desire to maintain the integrity of various political subdivisions, insofar as possible, and provide for compact districts of contiguous territory in designing a legislative apportionment scheme. Valid considerations may underlie such aims. Indiscriminate districting, without any regard for political subdivision or natural or historical boundary lines, may be little more than an open invitation to partisan gerrymandering. Single-member districts may be the rule in one State, while another State might desire to achieve some flexibility by creating multimember or floterial districts.[a] Whatever the means of accomplishment, the overriding objective must be substantial equality of population among the various districts, so that the vote of any citizen is approximately equal in weight to that of any other citizen in the State.

History indicates, however, that many States have deviated, to a greater or lesser degree, from the equal-population principle in the apportionment of seats in at least one house of their legislatures. So long as the divergences from a strict population standard are based on legitimate considerations incident to the effectuation of a rational state policy, some deviations from the equal-population principle are constitutionally permissible with respect to the apportionment of seats in either or both of the two houses of a bicameral state legislature. But neither history alone, nor economic or other sorts of group interests, are permissible factors in attempting to justify disparities from population-based representation. Citizens, not history or economic interests, cast votes. Considerations of area alone provide an insufficient justification for deviations from the equal-population principle. Again, people, not land or trees or pastures, vote. Modern developments and improvements in transportation and communications make rather hollow, in the mid-1960's, most claims that deviations from population-based representation can validly be based solely on geographical considerations. Arguments for allowing such deviations in order to insure effective representation for sparsely settled areas and to prevent legislative districts from becoming so large that the availability of access of citizens to their representatives is impaired are today, for the most part, unconvincing.

A consideration that appears to be of more substance in justifying some deviations from population-based representation in state legislatures is that of insuring some voice to political subdivisions, as political subdivisions. Several factors make more than insubstantial claims that a State can rationally consider according political subdivisions some independent representation in at least one body of the state legislature, as long as the basic standard of equality of population among districts is maintained. Local governmental entities are frequently charged with various responsibilities incident to the operation of state government. In many States much of the legislature's activity involves the enactment of so-called local legislation, directed only to the concerns of particular political subdivisions. And a

---

[a] A floterial district combines multiple single-member districts, where the conglomeration would be entitled to more representation than the total number of representatives allocated to each smaller district individually. For example, if the ideal district has 100,000 people, a state might create a floterial district out of four districts with populations of 125,000. Each of the four districts would be entitled to its one representative, and there would be an additional "floater" elected by the entire floterial district. [— Eds.]

State may legitimately desire to construct districts along political subdivision lines to deter the possibilities of gerrymandering. However, permitting deviations from population-based representation does not mean that each local governmental unit or political subdivision can be given separate representation, regardless of population. Carried too far, a scheme of giving at least one seat in one house to each political subdivision (for example, to each county) could easily result, in many States, in a total subversion of the equal-population principle in that legislative body. This would be especially true in a State where the number of counties is large and many of them are sparsely populated, and the number of seats in the legislative body being apportioned does not significantly exceed the number of counties. Such a result, we conclude, would be constitutionally impermissible. And careful judicial scrutiny must of course be given, in evaluating state apportionment schemes, to the character as well as the degree of deviations from a strict population basis. But if, even as a result of a clearly rational state policy of according some legislative representation to political subdivisions, population is submerged as the controlling consideration in the apportionment of seats in the particular legislative body, then the right of all of the State's citizens to cast an effective and adequately weighted vote would be unconstitutionally impaired.

One of the arguments frequently offered as a basis for upholding a State's legislative apportionment arrangement, despite substantial disparities from a population basis in either or both houses, is grounded on congressional approval, incident to admitting States into the Union, of state apportionment plans containing deviations from the equal-population principle. * * * Nevertheless, * * * Congress presumably does not assume, in admitting States into the Union, to pass on all constitutional questions relating to the character of state governmental organization. In any event, congressional approval, however well-considered, could hardly validate an unconstitutional state legislative apportionment. Congress simply lacks the constitutional power to insulate States from attack with respect to alleged deprivations of individual constitutional rights.

That the Equal Protection Clause requires that both houses of a state legislature be apportioned on a population basis does not mean that States cannot adopt some reasonable plan for periodic revision of their apportionment schemes. Decennial reapportionment appears to be a rational approach to readjustment of legislative representation in order to take into account population shifts and growth. * * * Limitations on the frequency of reapportionment are justified by the need for stability and continuity in the organization of the legislative system, although undoubtedly reapportioning no more frequently than every 10 years leads to some imbalance in the population of districts toward the end of the decennial period and also to the development of resistance to change on the part of some incumbent legislators. In substance, we do not regard the Equal Protection Clause as requiring daily, monthly, annual or biennial reapportionment, so long as a State has a reasonably conceived plan for periodic readjustment of legislative representation. While we do not intend to indicate that decennial reapportionment is a constitutional requisite, compliance with such an approach would clearly meet the minimal requirements for maintaining a reasonably current scheme of legislative representation. And we do not mean to intimate that more frequent reapportionment would not be constitutionally permissible or practicably desirable. But if reapportionment were accomplished with less frequency, it would assuredly be constitutionally suspect. * * *

* * * [W]e affirm the judgment below and remand the case for further proceedings consistent with the views stated in this opinion.

It is so ordered.

MR. JUSTICE CLARK, concurring in the affirmance. * * *

It seems to me that all that the Court need say in this case is that each plan considered by the trial court is "a crazy quilt," clearly revealing invidious discrimination in each house of the Legislature and therefore violative of the Equal Protection Clause. See my concurring opinion in *Baker* v. *Carr*, 369 U.S. 186, 253–258 (1962) [p. 119].

I, therefore, do not reach the question of the so-called "federal analogy." But in my view, if one house of the State Legislature meets the population standard, representation in the other house might include some departure from it so as to take into account, on a rational basis, other factors in order to afford some representation to the various elements of the State.

MR. JUSTICE STEWART.

All of the parties have agreed * * * that legislative inaction for some 60 years in the face of growth and shifts in population has converted Alabama's legislative apportionment plan enacted in 1901 into one completely lacking in rationality. Accordingly, for the reasons stated in my dissenting opinion in *Lucas* v. *Forty-Fourth General Assembly of Colorado*, [377 U.S. 713 (1964) (discussed in the Notes following this case)], I would affirm the judgment of the District Court holding that this apportionment violated the Equal Protection Clause. * * *

MR. JUSTICE HARLAN, dissenting. * * *

Today's holding is that the Equal Protection Clause of the Fourteenth Amendment requires every State to structure its legislature so that all the members of each house represent substantially the same number of people; other factors may be given play only to the extent that they do not significantly encroach on this basic "population" principle. Whatever may be thought of this holding as a piece of political ideology — and even on that score the political history and practices of this country from its earliest beginnings leave wide room for debate — I think it demonstrable that the Fourteenth Amendment does not impose this political tenet on the States or authorize this Court to do so.

* * * Stripped of aphorisms, the Court's argument boils down to the assertion that appellees' right to vote has been invidiously "debased" or "diluted" by systems of apportionment which entitle them to vote for fewer legislators than other voters, an assertion which is tied to the Equal Protection Clause only by the constitutionally frail tautology that "equal" means "equal." * * *

The Court relies exclusively on that portion of § 1 of the Fourteenth Amendment which provides that no State shall "deny to any person within its jurisdiction the equal protection of the laws," and disregards entirely the significance of § 2, which reads:

> "Representatives shall be apportioned among the several States according to their respective numbers, counting the whole number of persons in each State, excluding Indians not taxed. *But when the right to vote at any election for* the choice of electors for President and Vice President of the United States, Representatives in Congress, *the Executive and Judicial officers of a State, or the members of the Legislature thereof, is denied* to any of the male inhabitants of such State, being twenty-one years of age, and citizens of the United States, *or in any way abridged*, except for participation in rebellion, or other crime, the basis of representation therein shall be reduced in the proportion which the number of such male citizens shall bear to the whole number of male citizens twenty-one years of age in such State." (Emphasis added.)

* * * Whatever one might take to be the application to these cases of the Equal Protection Clause if it stood alone, I am unable to understand the Court's utter disregard of the second section which expressly recognizes the States' power to deny "or in any way" abridge the right of their inhabitants to vote for "the members of the [State] Legislature," and its express provision of a remedy for such denial or abridgment. * * * If indeed the words of the Fourteenth Amendment speak for themselves, as the majority's disregard of history seems to imply, they speak as clearly as may be against the construction which the majority puts on them. But we are not limited to the language of the Amendment itself.

The history of the adoption of the Fourteenth Amendment provides conclusive evidence that neither those who proposed nor those who ratified the Amendment believed that the Equal Protection Clause limited the power of the States to apportion their legislatures as they saw fit. Moreover, the history demonstrates that the intention to leave this power undisturbed was deliberate and was widely believed to be essential to the adoption of the Amendment. [MR. JUSTICE HARLAN discussed the legislative history surrounding the proposal of the Fourteenth Amendment, arguing that § 2 was seen as a politically acceptable alternative to requiring States to grant equal voting rights.]

* * * Of the 23 loyal States which ratified the Amendment before 1870, five had constitutional provisions for apportionment of at least one house of their respective legislatures which wholly disregarded the spread of population. Ten more had constitutional provisions which gave primary emphasis to population, but which applied also other principles, such as partial ratios and recognition of political subdivisions, which were intended to favor sparsely settled areas. Can it be seriously contended that the legislatures of these States, almost two-thirds of those concerned, would have ratified an amendment which might render their own States' constitutions unconstitutional? * * *

Each of the 10 "reconstructed" States was required to ratify the Fourteenth Amendment before it was readmitted to the Union. The Constitution of each was scrutinized in Congress. * * * The Constitutions of six of the 10 States contained provisions departing substantially from the method of apportionment now held to be required by the Amendment. * * *

It is incredible that Congress would have exacted ratification of the Fourteenth Amendment as the price of readmission, would have studied the State Constitutions for compliance with the Amendment, and would then have disregarded violations of it.

The facts recited above show beyond any possible doubt:

(1)   that Congress, with full awareness of and attention to the possibility that the States would not afford full equality in voting rights to all their citizens, nevertheless deliberately chose not to interfere with the States' plenary power in this regard when it proposed the Fourteenth Amendment;

(2)   that Congress did not include in the Fourteenth Amendment restrictions on the States' power to control voting rights because it believed that if such restrictions were included, the Amendment would not be adopted; and

(3)   that at least a substantial majority, if not all, of the States which ratified the Fourteenth Amendment did not consider that in so doing, they were accepting limitations on their freedom, never before questioned, to regulate voting rights as they chose. * * *

The years following 1868, far from indicating a developing awareness of the applicability of the Fourteenth Amendment to problems of apportionment, demonstrate precisely the reverse: that the States retained and exercised the power independently to apportion their legislatures. [MR. JUSTICE HARLAN noted the subordination of population equality in the constitutions of Alabama, Florida, Georgia, Louisiana, Mississippi, Missouri, Montana, New Hampshire, New York, North Carolina, Oklahoma, Pennsylvania, South Carolina, Utah, and Wyoming.]

Since the Court now invalidates the legislative apportionments in six States, and has so far upheld the apportionment in none, it is scarcely necessary to comment on the situation in the States today, which is, of course, as fully contrary to the Court's decision as is the record of every prior period in this Nation's history. As of 1961, the Constitutions of all but 11 States, roughly 20% of the total, recognized bases of apportionment other than geographic spread of population, and to some extent favored sparsely populated areas by a variety of devices[.] * * *

In this summary of what the majority ignores, note should be taken of the Fifteenth and Nineteenth Amendments. The former prohibited the States from denying or abridging the right to vote "on account of race, color, or previous condition of servitude." The latter, certified as part of the Constitution in 1920, added sex to the prohibited classifications. * * * If constitutional amendment was the only means by which all men and, later, women, could be guaranteed the right to vote at all, even for federal officers, how can it be that the far less obvious right to a particular kind of apportionment of state legislatures * * * can be conferred by judicial construction of the Fourteenth Amendment? * * *

It should by now be obvious that these cases do not mark the end of reapportionment problems in the courts. Predictions once made that the courts would never have to face the problem of actually working out an apportionment have proved false. This Court, however, continues to avoid the consequences of its decisions, simply assuring us that the lower courts "can and . . . will work out more concrete and specific standards." Deeming it "expedient" not to spell out "precise constitutional tests," the Court contents itself with stating "only a few rather general considerations."

Generalities cannot obscure the cold truth that cases of this type are not amenable to the development of judicial standards. No set of standards can guide a court which has to decide how many legislative districts a State shall have, or what the shape of the districts shall be, or where to draw a particular district line. No judicially manageable standard can determine whether a State should have single-member districts or multimember districts or some combination of both. No such standard can control the balance between keeping up with population shifts and having stable districts. In all these respects, the courts will be called upon to make particular decisions with respect to which a principle of equally populated districts will be of no assistance whatsoever. Quite obviously, there are limitless possibilities for districting consistent with such a principle. Nor can these problems be avoided by judicial reliance on legislative judgments so far as possible. Reshaping or combining one or two districts, or modifying just a few district lines, is no less a matter of choosing among many possible solutions, with varying political consequences, than reapportionment broadside. * * *

Although the Court — necessarily, as I believe — provides only generalities in elaboration of its main thesis, its opinion nevertheless fully demonstrates how far removed these problems are from fields of judicial competence. Recognizing that "indiscriminate districting" is an invitation to "partisan gerrymandering," the Court nevertheless excludes virtually every basis for the formation of electoral districts other than "indiscriminate districting." In one or another of today's opinions, the Court declares it unconstitutional for a State to give effective consideration to any of the following in establishing legislative districts:

(1) history;

(2) "economic or other sorts of group interests";

(3) area;

(4) geographical considerations;

(5) a desire "to insure effective representation for sparsely settled areas";

(6) "availability of access of citizens to their representatives";

(7) theories of bicameralism (except those approved by the Court);

(8) occupation;

(9) "an attempt to balance urban and rural power."

(10) the preference of a majority of voters in the State.

So far as presently appears, the *only* factor which a State may consider, apart from numbers, is political subdivisions. But even "a clearly rational state policy" recognizing this factor is unconstitutional if "population is submerged as the controlling consideration. . . ."

I know of no principle of logic or practical or theoretical politics, still less any constitutional principle, which establishes all or any of these exclusions. Certain it is that the Court's opinion does not establish them. So far as the Court says anything at all on this score, it says only that "legislators represent people, not trees or acres"; that "citizens, not history or economic interests, cast votes"; that "people, not land or trees or pastures, vote." All this may be conceded. But it is surely equally obvious, and, in the context of elections, more meaningful, to note that people are not ciphers and that legislators can represent their electors only by speaking for their interests — economic, social, political — many of which do reflect the place where the electors live. The Court does not establish, or indeed even attempt to make a case for the proposition that conflicting interests within a State can only be adjusted by disregarding them when voters are grouped for purposes of representation. * * *

Notes and Questions

1.   Is there an inconsistency between the Court's rejection of the "federal analogy" and its concession that some population disparity is acceptable to "insur[e] some voice to political subdivisions, as political subdivisions"?[b] Why should that interest trump absolute population equality? What "voice" do political subdivisions need if they are only "subordinate governmental instrumentalities created by the State to assist in the carrying out of state governmental functions"? Reconsider these questions after reading *Mahan v. Howell*, 410 U.S. 315 (1973) [p. 200], and *Gaffney v. Cummings*, 412 U.S. 735 (1973) [p. 206], later in this Chapter.

2.   Considering the matter from another perspective, why should population equality trump other goals states might try to achieve through their representational structures? Why can states not seek to apportion legislatures to balance the political power of economic, social, or political groups?

3.   Justices Clark and Stewart voted to strike down Alabama's districting because they viewed it as irrational. They understood the "well developed and familiar" standards of equal protection to embody the traditional rational-basis test applied to adjudicate equal-protection challenges to laws *not* implicating fundamental rights. (The Court rejected the rational-basis test in *Sims* by analogizing the right to an equally weighted vote to the fundamental right to procreate, at issue in *Skinner v. Oklahoma*, 316 U.S. 535 (1942), abridgments of which trigger strict scrutiny.) In *Lucas v. Forty-Fourth General Assembly of Colorado*, 377 U.S. 713 (1964), decided the same day as *Reynolds v. Sims*, Justice Stewart further explained how he would apply the rational-basis test to legislative apportionment.

Lucas involved a challenge to the apportionment of Colorado's state legislature, and the companion case of *WMCA, Inc. v. Lomenzo*, 377 U.S. 633 (1964), involved a challenge to the apportionment of New York's. The Court struck down each, but Justices Stewart and Clark dissented, finding the plans "rational":

---

[b] *See also Board of Estimate v. Morris*, 489 U.S. 688, 702–03 & 703 n.10 (1989) (holding unconstitutional New York City's method of selecting the Board, under which each borough president received a seat regardless of the borough's population, and rejecting the proposition that "exigencies of history or convenience" could justify such a departure from the one-person, one-vote rule).

Representative government is a process of accommodating group interests through democratic institutional arrangements. Its function is to channel the numerous opinions, interests, and abilities of the people of a State into the making of the State's public policy. Appropriate legislative apportionment, therefore, should ideally be designed to ensure effective representation in the State's legislature[.] * * *

[A] system of legislative apportionment which might be best for South Dakota, might be unwise for Hawaii with its many islands, or Michigan with its Northern Peninsula. * * * Montana with its vast distances is not Rhode Island with its heavy concentrations of people. [There are also] great variations among the several States in their historic manner of distributing legislative power [including powers of initiative and referendum, Governors' Councils, gubernatorial veto powers, and home-rule provisions for cities]. The Court today declines to give any recognition to these considerations and countless others, tangible and intangible, in holding unconstitutional the particular systems of legislative apportionment which these States have chosen. Instead, the Court says that the requirements of the Equal Protection Clause can be met in any State only by the uncritical, simplistic, and heavy-handed application of sixth-grade arithmetic.

But legislators do not represent faceless numbers. They represent people, or, more accurately, a majority of the voters in their districts — people with identifiable needs and interests which require legislative representation, and which can often be related to the geographical areas in which these people live. * * *

The fact is, of course, that population factors must often to some degree be subordinated in devising a legislative apportionment plan which is to achieve the important goal of ensuring a fair, effective, and balanced representation of the regional, social, and economic interests within a State. And the further fact is that throughout our history the apportionments of State Legislatures have reflected the strongly felt American tradition that the public interest is composed of many diverse interests, and that in the long run it can better be expressed by a medley of component voices than by the majority's monolithic command. What constitutes a rational plan reasonably designed to achieve this objective will vary from State to State, since each State is unique, in terms of topography, geography, demography, history, heterogeneity and concentration of population, variety of social and economic interests, and in the operation and interrelation of its political institutions. But so long as a State's apportionment plan reasonably achieves, in the light of the State's own characteristics, effective and balanced representation of all substantial interests, without sacrificing the principle of effective majority rule, that plan cannot be considered irrational. * * *

* * * I think that the Equal Protection Clause demands but two basic attributes of any plan of state legislative apportionment. First, it demands that, in the light of the state's own characteristics and needs, the plan must be a rational one. Secondly, it demands that the plan must be such as not

to permit the systematic frustration of the will of a majority of the electorate of the State. I think it is apparent that any plan of legislative apportionment which could be shown to reflect no policy, but simply arbitrary and capricious action or inaction, and that any plan which could be shown systematically to prevent ultimate effective majority rule, would be invalid under accepted Equal Protection Clause standards. But, beyond this, I think there is nothing in the Federal Constitution to prevent a State from choosing any electoral legislative structure it thinks best suited to the interests, temper, and customs of its people.

Lucas, 377 U.S. at 749–51, 753–54 (Stewart, J., joined by Clark, J., dissenting). Colorado's plan, Justice Stewart contended, was a rational means of representing the interests of the vastly different geographical areas of the state, while New York's was a rational way of ensuring that the population of New York City did not overwhelm the interests of the rest of the state. *See id.* at 754–65. *See also Wesberry v. Sanders*, 376 U.S. 1, 21 n.4 (1964) [p. 166] (Harlan, J., dissenting) (arguing that states should be able to take into account "the practicability of effective representation" in drawing district lines that conform to "natural boundaries (rivers, mountain ranges)"). The Court, however, held that neither concern was an adequate excuse for not apportioning districts on a population basis, partially because of "[m]odern developments and improvements in transportation and communications," which minimized the effect of those natural boundaries.

Is Justice Stewart's rationality standard capable of consistent application? Is ensuring that the population of New York City not overwhelm the rest of the state just a nicer way of characterizing "the systematic frustration of the will of a majority of the electorate"?

4.   Part of the attraction of the Court's one-person, one-vote rule is the capacity of other systems to "lock-up" the political process by permitting those with political power to determine the appropriate "balance" of political power for the future. *See generally* Richard L. Hasen, *The "Political Market" Metaphor and Election Law: A Comment on Issacharoff and Pildes*, 50 STANFORD L. REV. 719 (1998); Samuel Issacharoff & Richard H. Pildes, *Politics As Markets: Partisan Lockups of the Democratic Process*, 50 STANFORD L. REV. 643 (1998); Michael J. Klarman, *Majoritarian Judicial Review: The Entrenchment Problem*, 85 GEO. L.J. 491 (1997). Voters in cities, for example, may have no effective way of altering a representational structure giving rural interests disproportionate representation, if those rural interests will control any consideration of reapportionment. But what if a state's apportionment was a deliberate choice by the people, rather than a self-interested power-grab?

In *Lucas, supra*, Colorado's federal model of representation was passed by referendum. It received two-thirds of the statewide vote and majorities in every county. Nevertheless, the Court was not impressed. In a 6-3 decision, the Court, with Chief Justice Warren authoring the opinion, applied *Sims* to hold the plan invalid:

An individual's constitutionally protected right to cast an equally weighted vote cannot be denied even by a vote of a majority of a State's electorate, if the apportionment scheme adopted by the voters fails to measure up to the requirements of the Equal Protection Clause. Manifestly, the fact that an apportionment plan is adopted in a popular referendum is insufficient to sustain its constitutionality[.] * * * A citizen's constitutional rights can hardly be infringed simply because a majority of the people choose that it be. We hold that the fact that a challenged legislative apportionment plan was approved by the electorate is without federal constitutional significance, if the scheme adopted fails to satisfy the basic requirements of the Equal Protection Clause, as delineated in our opinion in *Reynolds* v. *Sims*.

377 U.S. at 736–37.

5.　What is the significance of Chief Justice Warren's insistence that the right to an equally weighted vote is an "individual," "personal" right? Does such a conclusion make sense? *See* Samuel Issacharoff, *Groups and the Right to Vote*, 44 EMORY L.J. 869 (1995). *Cf.* Heather K. Gerken, *Understanding the Right to an Undiluted Vote*, 114 HARV. L. REV. 1663, 1681–89 (2001).

6.　Should the Court have rested its holding on the Guarantee Clause rather than the Equal Protection Clause? *See* Michael W. McConnell, *The Redistricting Cases: Original Mistakes and Current Consequences*, 24 HARV. J.L. & PUB. POL'Y 103 (2000).

7.　*Problem.* The districts used to select Louisiana's seven supreme-court justices had not been reapportioned between 1921 and 1972, and as a result ranged in population from 369,485 to 682,072. Does the difference between the duties of judges and members of the "political" branches justify excusing judicial elections from the one-person, one-vote rule? *See Wells v. Edwards*, 347 F. Supp. 453 (M.D. La. 1972), *aff'd*, 409 U.S. 1095 (*per curiam*) (holding judicial elections immune from one-person, one-vote, because the doctrine is in place only "to preserve a truly representative form of government"). *But cf. Chisom v. Roemer*, 501 U.S. 380 (1991) (interpreting the Voting Rights Act, which requires states to provide members of racial groups an equal opportunity to elect "representatives" of their choice, to reach claims of minority vote dilution in judicial elections).

8.　*Which* populations must be equalized across state-legislative districts? Must a state equalize districts' total populations, or may a state equalize other populations, such as registered voters, eligible voters, voting-age population, or something else? May a districting plan that equalizes total population nonetheless violate the Constitution because of differences in *voting-age* population? *See Kalson v. Paterson*, 542 F.3d 281 (2d Cir. 2008) (holding that the right to an equally weighted vote does not require states to apportion congressional districts based on voting-age population); *Daly v. Hunt*, 93 F.3d 1212 (4th Cir. 1996) (holding that districts for the election of county commissioners may be based on total population rather than voting-age population). *Cf. Kirkpatrick v. Preisler*, 394 U.S. 526, 534 (1969) [p. 192] ("There may be a question whether distribution of congressional seats except according to total population can ever be permissible under Art. I, § 2."). Fifty years after first creating the one-person, one-vote doctrine, the Supreme Court has agreed to hear a case presenting that question. *Evenwel v. Perry*, 2014 U.S. Dist. LEXIS 156192 (W.D. Tex. 2014) (three-judge court), *prob. juris. noted sub nom. Evenwel v. Abbott*, 135 S. Ct. 2349 (2015). The district court in *Evenwel* upheld a

Texas districting plan that equalized districts' total populations, but contained variations in voting-age populations.

The determination of which populations must be equalized depends on which equality principle one gleans from *Reynolds v. Sims*:

> While apportionment by population and apportionment by number of eligible electors normally yield precisely the same result, they are based on radically different premises and serve materially different purposes. Apportionment by raw population embodies the principle of equal representation; it assures that all persons living within a district — whether eligible to vote or not — have roughly equal representation in the governing body. A principle of equal representation serves important purposes. It assures that constituents have more or less equal access to their elected officials, by assuring that no official has a disproportionately large number of constituents to satisfy. Also, assuming that elected officials are able to obtain benefits for their districts in proportion to their share of the total membership of the governing body, it assures that constituents are not afforded unequal government services depending on the size of the population in their districts.
>
> Apportionment by proportion of eligible voters serves the principle of electoral equality. This principle recognizes that electors — persons eligible to vote — are the ones who hold the ultimate political power in our democracy. * * * Apportionment by proportion of eligible voters assures that, regardless of the size of the whole body of constituents, political power, as defined by the number of those eligible to vote, is equalized as between districts holding the same number of representatives. It also assures that those eligible to vote do not suffer dilution of that important right by having their vote given less weight than that of electors in another location.

Garza v. County of Los Angeles, 918 F.2d 763, 781–82 (9th Cir. 1990) (Kozinski, J., concurring and dissenting in part). *See also* Ronald Keith Gaddie, et al., *Seats, Votes, Citizens, and the One Person, One Vote Problem*, 23 STAN. L. & POL'Y REV. 431 (2012).

Does it matter that the Fourteenth Amendment requires congressional districts to be apportioned among the states based on total population? *See* U.S. CONST. amend. XIV, § 2 ("Representatives shall be apportioned among the several States according to their respective numbers, counting the whole number of persons in each State, excluding Indians not taxed."); *Kalson, supra*, at 289 n.16 ("In light of the fact that Article I apportions seats between states based on total population and not on the basis of the number of voters, it would seem to follow that apportionment within a state must also be based on total population."). Might the Constitution require equality of different populations in congressional districts as opposed to state-legislative ones?

In *Burns v. Richardson*, 384 U.S. 73 (1966), the Supreme Court upheld the constitutionality of a plan based on the number of registered voters, rather than the number of citizens or total persons, in each of Hawaii's state-legislative districts.

Because many military personnel and tourists temporarily residing on the island of Oahu were counted in the census as part of Hawaii's total population but could not vote, the choice of relevant population affected the distribution of legislative seats. The Court held that the use of registered voters was permissible, but only because such use "produced a distribution of legislators not substantially different from that which would have resulted from the use of a permissible population basis" such as citizen population. *Id.* at 93. As the Court explained,

> [T]he Equal Protection Clause does not require the States to use total population figures derived from the federal census as the standard by which [] substantial population equivalency is to be measured. Although total population figures were in fact the basis of comparison in [*Reynolds* v. *Sims*] and most of the other[] [cases] decided that day, our discussion carefully left open the question what population was being referred to. At several points, we discussed substantial equivalence in terms of voter population or citizen population, making no distinction between the acceptability of such a test and a test based on total population.[20] Indeed, in *WMCA, Inc.* v. *Lomenzo*, 377 U.S. 633, decided the same day, we treated an apportionment based upon United States citizen population as presenting problems no different from apportionments using a total population measure. Neither in *Reynolds* v. *Sims* nor in any other decision has this Court suggested that the States are required to include aliens, transients, short-term or temporary residents, or persons denied the vote for conviction of crime, in the apportionment base by which their legislators are distributed and against which compliance with the Equal Protection Clause is to be measured. The decision to include or exclude any such group involves choices about the nature of representation with which we have been shown no constitutionally founded reason to interfere. Unless a choice is one the Constitution forbids, cf., *e.g.*, *Carrington* v. *Rash*, 380 U.S. 89 [(1965)] [p. 90], the resulting apportionment base offends no constitutional bar, and compliance with the rule established in *Reynolds* v. *Sims* is to be measured thereby.

Use of a registered voter or actual voter basis presents an additional problem. Such a basis depends not only upon criteria such as govern state citizenship, but also upon the extent of political activity of those eligible to register and vote. Each is thus susceptible to improper influences by which those in political power might be able to perpetuate underrepresentation of groups constitutionally entitled to participate in the electoral process, or perpetuate a "ghost of prior malapportionment." Moreover, "fluctuations in the number of registered voters in a given election may be sudden and substantial, caused by such fortuitous factors as a peculiarly controversial election issue, a particularly popular candidate, or even weather condi-

---

[20] Thus we spoke of "[t]he right of a citizen to equal representation and to have his vote weighted equally with those of all other citizens. . . ." *Reynolds* v. *Sims*, 377 U.S., at 576. We also said: "[I]t is a practical impossibility to arrange legislative districts so that each one has an identical number of residents, or citizens, or voters." *Id.*, at 577. "[T]he overriding objective must be substantial equality of population among the various districts, so that the vote of any citizen is approximately equal in weight to that of any other citizen in the State." *Id.*, at 579.

tions." Such effects must be particularly a matter of concern where, as in the case of Hawaii apportionment, registration figures derived from a single election are made controlling for as long as 10 years. In view of these considerations, we hold that the present apportionment satisfies the Equal Protection Clause only because on this record it was found to have produced a distribution of legislators not substantially different from that which would have resulted from the use of a permissible population basis.

384 U.S. at 91–93. Justice Harlan disagreed with the Court's limitation on states' ability to base apportionment calculations on the number of registered voters, arguing that *Reynolds v. Sims* required only that states use a rational system for ensuring that legislatures represent "'people,' not other interests." *Id.* at 99 (Harlan, J., concurring in the result).

9.   *Problem.* The County of Los Angeles, California, has a substantial noncitizen population that is ineligible to vote. Much of that population is Hispanic, and the Hispanic population tends to be concentrated in certain sections of the County. (In addition, the Hispanic sections also contain a greater proportion of voting-ineligible youth than do other areas of the County.) As a result, districts drawn according to total population will result in a 40% disparity in the population of eligible voters, and districts drawn according to voting-age citizen population will result in a similar disparity in total population.

California must re-draw its state-legislative districts, and you are asked how the state should account for the noncitizen population. Must the state draw districts according to total population? (In other words, would districts drawn according to another standard violate the equal-protection rights of the persons placed into districts with greater total populations?) Must the state draw districts according to voting-age citizen population? (In other words, would districts drawn according to total population violate the equal-protection rights of those whose votes are diluted by the presence of greater numbers of other voters?) Does the state have the option of apportioning districts on either basis? *See Garza, supra.*

10.   In distributing legislative seats, some states count prison populations as part of the districts in which the prisons are located, even though the prisoners are not permitted to vote. The effect is to give greater voting power to the others living in those districts, including prison guards' families, whose interests may not coincide with those of the inmates. By the same token, the areas in which the inmates used to live are not granted the influence they would possess if the prisoners were counted as residing in the last place they lived before imprisonment. Does this practice violate one person, one vote? Does it matter that minority races are disproportionately represented in prison populations and that prisons are often located in rural, mainly white, areas? *See* Dale Ho, *Captive Constituents: Prison-Based Gerrymandering and the Current Redistricting Cycle*, 22 Stan. L. & Pol'y Rev. 355 (2011).

In *Fletcher v. Lamone*, 133 S. Ct. 29 (2012), *summarily aff'g*, 831 F. Supp. 2d 887 (D. Md. 2011) (three-judge court), Maryland adopted a redistricting plan that counted prisoners as residing at their last addresses before incarceration. The plan was challenged as diluting minority communities' voting strength (even though Maryland's intent was to augment it). The district court turned away the challenge, holding that Maryland could constitutionally treat inmates as residing at their pre-prison addresses even if it did not accord similar treatment to members of the military and students (who, as the court pointed out, presented different situations from prisoners in that they could vote during their service and schooling). The Supreme Court unanimously summarily affirmed.

C. APPLYING THE CONSTITUTIONAL STANDARDS: HOW EQUAL IS EQUAL ENOUGH?

It is one thing to establish a constitutional standard of "substantially equal" district populations and to apply it where the population disparities are as broad as they were in *Baker v. Carr* and *Reynolds v. Sims*. It is quite another to apply that standard where the disparities are much narrower. Is the constitutional guarantee of equality offended if districts differ in their populations by as little as 1%?

As the following cases demonstrate, the Court has held congressional districts to a strict requirement of population equality, but has been more lenient with respect to state-legislative districts. In the latter context, the Court has permitted states to draw districts that correspond to boundaries of political subdivisions, even if doing so causes slight population variances across districts.

KIRKPATRICK v. PREISLER[c]
Supreme Court of the United States
394 U.S. 526, 89 S. Ct. 1225, 22 L. Ed. 2d 519 (1969)

Mr. Justice Brennan delivered the opinion of the Court [in which Mr. Chief Justice Warren, Mr. Justice Black, Mr. Justice Douglas, and Mr. Justice Marshall join].

In *Wesberry* v. *Sanders*, 376 U.S. 1 (1964) [p. 166], we held that "* * * Art. I, § 2, of the Constitution requires that "as nearly as is practicable one man's vote in a congressional election is to be worth as much as another's." *Id.*, at 7–8. We are required in these cases to elucidate the "as nearly as practicable" standard.

The Missouri congressional redistricting statute challenged in these cases [was enacted in 1967. At that time, the best population data available were the 1960 United States census figures, according to which] absolute population equality among Missouri's 10 congressional districts would mean a population of 431,981 in each district. The districts created by the 1967 Act, however, varied from this ideal within a range of 12,260 below it to 13,542 above it. The difference between the least and most populous districts was thus 25,802. In percentage terms, the most populous district was 3.13% above the mathematical ideal, and the least populous was 2.84% below.

---

[c] This case was argued with, and decided the same day as, *Wells v. Rockefeller*, 394 U.S. 542 (1969). *Wells* held unconstitutional New York's congressional districting plan, which divided the state into seven regions, and divided each of the regions into congressional districts. Although each district within a given region had the same population, the regions themselves varied in population. As a result, the population of the districts statewide varied by as much as 13%. The Court struck down the plan as indistinguishable from the plan in *Kirkpatrick v. Preisler*. The dissents of Justice Harlan and Justice White, reprinted here, appear in the U.S. Reports as part of *Wells*, though they apply to both cases. [— Eds.]

The District Court found that the General Assembly had not in fact relied on the census figures but instead had based its plan on less accurate data. In addition, the District Court found that the General Assembly had rejected a redistricting plan submitted to it which provided for districts with smaller population variances among them. Finally, the District Court found that the simple device of switching some counties from one district to another would have produced a plan with markedly reduced variances among districts. Based on these findings, the District Court, one judge dissenting, held that the 1967 Act did not meet the constitutional standard of equal representation for equal numbers of people "as nearly as practicable," and that the State had failed to make any acceptable justification for the variances. * * * We affirm. * * *

We reject Missouri's argument that there is a fixed numerical or percentage population variance small enough to be considered *de minimis* and to satisfy without question the "as nearly as practicable" standard. The whole thrust of the "as nearly as practicable" approach is inconsistent with adoption of fixed numerical standards which excuse population variances without regard to the circumstances of each particular case. The extent to which equality may practically be achieved may differ from State to State and from district to district. Since "equal representation for equal numbers of people [is] the fundamental goal for the House of Representatives," *Wesberry* v. *Sanders, supra,* at 18, the "as nearly as practicable" standard requires that the State make a good-faith effort to achieve precise mathematical equality. See *Reynolds* v. *Sims,* 377 U.S. 533, 577 (1964) [p. 173]. Unless population variances among congressional districts are shown to have resulted despite such effort, the State must justify each variance, no matter how small.

There are other reasons for rejecting the *de minimis* approach. We can see no nonarbitrary way to pick a cutoff point at which population variances suddenly become *de minimis.* Moreover, to consider a certain range of variances *de minimis* would encourage legislators to strive for the range rather than for equality as nearly as practicable. * * *

Equal representation for equal numbers of people is a principle designed to prevent debasement of voting power and diminution of access to elected representatives. Toleration of even small deviations detracts from these purposes. Therefore, the command of Art. I, § 2, that States create congressional districts which provide equal representation for equal numbers of people permits only the limited population variances which are unavoidable despite a good-faith effort to achieve absolute equality, or for which justification is shown.

Clearly, the population variances among the Missouri congressional districts were not unavoidable. Indeed, it is not seriously contended that the Missouri Legislature came as close to equality as it might have come. * * * Legislative proponents of the 1967 Act frankly conceded at the District Court hearing that resort to the simple device of transferring entire political subdivisions of known population between contiguous districts would have produced districts much closer to numerical equality. The District Court found, moreover, that the Missouri Legislature relied on inaccurate data in constructing the districts, and that it rejected without consideration a plan which would have markedly reduced population variances among the districts. Finally, it is simply inconceivable that population disparities of the magnitude found in the Missouri plan were unavoidable. * * *

We therefore turn to the question whether the record establishes any legally acceptable justification for the population variances. It was the burden of the State "to present . . . acceptable reasons for the variations among the populations of the various . . . districts. . . ." *Swann* v. *Adams*, [385 U.S. 440,] 443–444 [(1967)]. * * *

Missouri contends that variances were necessary to avoid fragmenting areas with distinct economic and social interests and thereby diluting the effective representation of those interests in Congress. But to accept population variances, large or small, in order to create districts with specific interest orientations is antithetical to the basic premise of the constitutional command to provide equal representation for equal numbers of people. "[N]either history alone, nor economic or other sorts of group interests, are permissible factors in attempting to justify disparities from population-based representation. Citizens, not history or economic interests, cast votes." *Reynolds* v. *Sims, supra*, at 579–580.

We also reject Missouri's argument that "[t]he reasonableness of the population differences in the congressional districts under review must . . . be viewed in the context of legislative interplay. The legislative leaders all testified that the act in question was in their opinion a reasonable legislative compromise. * * *" We agree with the District Court that "the rule is one of 'practicability' rather than political 'practicality.' " Problems created by partisan politics cannot justify an apportionment which does not otherwise pass constitutional muster.

Similarly, we do not find legally acceptable the argument that variances are justified if they necessarily result from a State's attempt to avoid fragmenting political subdivisions by drawing congressional district lines along existing county, municipal, or other political subdivision boundaries. The State's interest in constructing congressional districts in this manner, it is suggested, is to minimize the opportunities for partisan gerrymandering. But an argument that deviations from equality are justified in order to inhibit legislators from engaging in partisan gerrymandering[4] is no more than a variant of the argument, already rejected, that considerations of practical politics can justify population disparities.

Missouri further contends that certain population variances resulted from the legislature's taking account of the fact that the percentage of eligible voters among the total population differed significantly from district to district — some districts contained disproportionately large numbers of military personnel stationed at bases maintained by the Armed Forces and students in attendance at universities or colleges. There may be a question whether distribution of congressional seats except according to total population can ever be permissible under Art. I, § 2.[d] But assuming without deciding that apportionment may be based on eligible voter

---

[4] It is dubious in any event that the temptation to gerrymander would be much inhibited, since the legislature would still be free to choose which of several subdivisions, all with their own political complexion, to include in a particular congressional district. Besides, opportunities for gerrymandering are greatest when there is freedom to construct unequally populated districts. * * *

[d] Recall that *Burns v. Richardson*, 384 U.S. 73 (1966), discussed at page 190, which upheld an apportionment based on numbers of registered voters, concerned an equal-protection challenge to state-legislative districts. [— Eds.]

population rather than total population, the Missouri plan is still unacceptable. Missouri made no attempt to ascertain the number of eligible voters in each district and to apportion accordingly. At best it made haphazard adjustments to a scheme based on total population[.] * * *

Missouri also argues that population disparities between some of its congressional districts result from the legislature's attempt to take into account projected population shifts. We recognize that a congressional districting plan will usually be in effect for at least 10 years and five congressional elections. Situations may arise where substantial population shifts over such a period can be anticipated. Where these shifts can be predicted with a high degree of accuracy, States that are redistricting may properly consider them. By this we mean to open no avenue for subterfuge. Findings as to population trends must be thoroughly documented and applied throughout the State in a systematic, not an *ad hoc*, manner. Missouri's attempted justification * * * falls far short of this standard. * * *

Finally, Missouri claims that some of the deviations from equality were a consequence of the legislature's attempt to ensure that each congressional district would be geographically compact. However, in *Reynolds* v. *Sims*, *supra*, at 580, we said, "Modern developments and improvements in transportation and communications make rather hollow, in the mid-1960's, most claims that deviations from population-based representation can validly be based solely on geographical considerations. Arguments for allowing such deviations in order to insure effective representation for sparsely settled areas and to prevent legislative districts from becoming so large that the availability of access of citizens to their representatives is impaired are today, for the most part, unconvincing." In any event, Missouri's claim of compactness is based solely upon the unaesthetic appearance of the map of congressional boundaries that would result from an attempt to effect some of the changes in district lines which, according to the lower court, would achieve greater equality. A State's preference for pleasingly shaped districts can hardly justify population variances.

Affirmed.

MR. JUSTICE FORTAS, concurring [in the judgment]. * * *

In *Wesberry* v. *Sanders*, this Court recognized that "it may not be possible to draw congressional districts with mathematical precision," and it held that the Constitution requires that they be drawn so that, "as nearly as is practicable," each representative should cast a vote on behalf of the same number of people.

The Court now not only interprets "as nearly as practicable" to mean that the State is required to "make a good-faith effort to achieve precise mathematical equality," but it also requires that any remaining population disparities "no matter how small," be justified. It then proceeds to reject, *seriatim*, every type of justification that has been — possibly, every one that could be — advanced.

I agree that the state legislatures should be required to make "a good-faith effort to achieve" a result that allocates the population or the residents of the State in roughly equal numbers to each district, based upon some orderly and objective method. In my view, the State could properly arrive at figures for current population by taking the latest census returns and making modifications to allow for population movements since the last census (which the Court seems to find acceptable). It could also, in my opinion, discount the census figures to take account of the presence of significant transient or nonresident population in particular areas (an adjustment as to which the Court indicates doubt). If the State should proceed on some appropriate population basis such as I have suggested, producing approximately equal districts, trial courts, in my judgment, would be justified in declining to disapprove the result merely because of small disparities, in the absence of evidence of gerrymandering — the deliberate and arbitrary distortion of district boundaries and populations for partisan or personal political purposes.

In considering whether the State has "approximated" an equal division and allocation of the population, I sympathize with the majority's view that a *de minimis* rule of allowable disparities tends to demean in theory and in practice the constitutional objective because it suggests that it is not necessary even to aim at equality. On the other hand, to reject *de minimis* as a statement of the limits on the rule of equality should not lead us to toss aside the wise recognition of the inscrutability of fact and the imperfection of man which is implicit in the *Wesberry* standard: "as nearly as practicable." This phrase does not refer merely to arithmetical possibilities. Arithmetically, it is possible to achieve division of a State into districts of precisely equal size, as measured by the decennial census or any other population base. To carry out this theoretical possibility, however, a legislature might have to ignore the boundaries of common sense, running the congressional district line down the middle of the corridor of an apartment house or even dividing the residents of a single-family house between two districts. The majority opinion does not suggest so extreme a practical application of its teaching, and I mention it only because the example may dramatize the fallacy of inflexible insistence upon mathematical exactness, with no tolerance for reality.

Whatever might be the merits of insistence on absolute equality if it could be attained, the majority's pursuit of precision is a search for a will-o'-the-wisp. The fact is that any solution to the apportionment and districting problem is at best an approximation because it is based upon figures which are always to some degree obsolete. No purpose is served by an insistence on precision which is unattainable because of the inherent imprecisions in the population data on which districting must be based. * * *

Nothing that I have said should be taken as indicating that I do not believe that the *Wesberry* standard requires a high degree of correspondence between the demonstrated population or residence figures and the district divisions. Nor would I fix, at least at this relatively early stage of the reapportionment effort, a percentage figure for permissible variation.

In the present cases, however, I agree that the judgment of the District Court should be affirmed. The history of this reapportionment and of the legislature's failure to comply with the plain and patient directions of the three-judge District Court and the failure of the legislature to use either accurate 1960 census figures or other systematically obtained figures for all the districts — these factors strongly support the District Court's refusal to accept the Missouri plan. * * *

MR. JUSTICE HARLAN, with whom MR. JUSTICE STEWART joins, dissenting.

Whatever room remained under this Court's prior decisions for the free play of the political process in matters of reapportionment is now all but eliminated by today's Draconian judgments. Marching to the nonexistent "command of Art. I, § 2" of the Constitution, the Court now transforms a political slogan into a constitutional absolute. Straight indeed is the path of the righteous legislator. Slide rule in hand, he must avoid all thought of county lines, local traditions, politics, history, and economics, so as to achieve the magic formula: one man, one vote.

As my Brothers WHITE and FORTAS demonstrate, insistence on mathematical perfection does not make sense even on its own terms. Census figures themselves are inexact; our mobile population rapidly renders them obsolete; large groups of ineligible voters are unevenly distributed throughout the State. Nevertheless, the Court refuses to permit any room for legislative common sense to compensate for Census Bureau inadequacies. If no "scientific" data are available to justify a divergence from census figures, the Court holds that nothing can be done — "we mean to open no avenue for subterfuge."

This all-pervasive distrust of the legislative process is completely alien to established notions of judicial review. Nor does it have precedent in the prior reapportionment decisions themselves. * * * Even more important, the Court's exclusive concentration upon arithmetic blinds it to the realities of the political process. The fact of the matter is that the rule of absolute equality is perfectly compatible with "gerrymandering" of the worst sort. A computer may grind out district lines which can totally frustrate the popular will on an overwhelming number of critical issues. The legislature must do more than satisfy one man, one vote; it must create a structure which will in fact as well as theory be responsive to the sentiments of the community. * * *

* * * Of course, all districting decisions inevitably involve choices between different interest groups. But as *Reynolds* recognized, legislatures prefer to follow traditional county and regional lines so that the demands of blatant partisanship will be tempered by the constraints of history and tradition. If the Court believes it has struck a blow today for fully responsive representative democracy, it is sorely mistaken. Even more than in the past, district lines are likely to be drawn to maximize the political advantage of the party temporarily dominant in public affairs.

We do not deal here with the hopelessly malapportioned legislature unwilling to set its own house in order. Rather, the question before us is whether the Constitution requires that mathematics be a substitute for common sense in the art of statecraft. * * * I dissent. * * *

MR. JUSTICE WHITE, dissenting. * * *

* * * I would not quibble with the legislative judgment [concerning apportionment] if variations between districts were acceptably small. And I would be willing to establish a population variation figure which if not exceeded would normally not call for judicial intervention. As a rule of thumb, a variation between the largest and the smallest district of no more than 10% to 15% would satisfy me, absent quite

unusual circumstances not present in any of these cases. At the very least, at this trivial level, I would be willing to view state explanations of the variance with a more tolerant eye.

This would be far more reasonable than the Court's demand for an absolute but illusory equality or for an apportionment plan which approaches this goal so nearly that no other plan can be suggested which would come nearer. As MR. JUSTICE FORTAS demonstrates, the 1960 census figures were far from accurate when they were compiled by professional enumerators and statisticians bent on precision, in 1960. Massive growth and shifts in population since 1960 made the 1960 figures even more inaccurate by 1967. That is why a new census is taken every 10 years. When the Court finds a 3% variation from substantially inexact figures constitutionally impermissible it is losing perspective and sticking at a trifle. * * *

Today's decisions on the one hand require precise adherence to admittedly inexact census figures, and on the other downgrade a restraint on a far greater potential threat to equality of representation, the gerrymander. Legislatures intent on minimizing the representation of selected political or racial groups are invited to ignore political boundaries and compact districts so long as they adhere to population equality among districts using standards which we know and they know are sometimes quite incorrect. I see little merit in such a confusion of priorities.

Moreover, today's decisions will lead to an unnecessary intrusion of the judiciary into legislative business. It would be one thing if absolute equality were possible. But, admittedly, it is not. The Court may be groping for a clean-cut, *per se* rule which will minimize confrontations between courts and legislatures while also satisfying the Fourteenth Amendment. If so, the Court is wide of the mark. Today's results simply shift the area of dispute a few percentage points down the scale; the courts will now be engaged in quibbling disputes over such questions as whether a plan with a 1% variation is "better" than one with a larger variation, say 1.1% or even 2%. If county and municipal boundaries are to be ignored, a computer can produce countless plans for absolute population equality, one differing very little from another, but each having its own very different political ramifications. * * * Not only will the Court's new rule necessarily precipitate a new round of congressional and legislative districting, but also I fear that in the long run the courts, rather than the legislatures or nonpartisan commissions, will be making most of the districting decisions in the several States. Since even at best, with compact and equal districts, the final boundary lines unavoidably have significant political repercussions, the courts should not draw district lines themselves unnecessarily. I therefore dissent.

Notes and Questions

1. *Kirkpatrick v. Preisler* was reaffirmed and extended in *Karcher v. Daggett*, 462 U.S. 725 (1983). In that case, New Jersey's congressional districts varied in population by an average of 726 people (0.1384%), and the largest district exceeded the smallest by 3,674 people (0.6984% of the average district). Nevertheless, there were other proposed districting plans available with even smaller population differences.

The government argued that where the population difference between districts is less than the error rate of the census, the population difference should be constitutionally irrelevant. The Court rejected the argument, pointing out that

> the census data provide the only reliable — albeit less than perfect — indication of the districts' "real" relative population levels. Even if one cannot say with certainty that one district is larger than another merely because it has a higher census count, one *can* say with certainty that the district with a larger census count is more likely to be larger than the other district than it is to be smaller or the same size.

Id. at 738. Note, however, that in *Gaffney v. Cummings*, 412 U.S. 735 (1973) [p. 206], which appears as a principal case later in this Chapter, the Court did refer to the error rate of the census in holding that states need not justify minimal population differences between *state-legislative* districts. Not coincidentally, Justice White was among the dissenters in *Kirkpatrick* and *Daggett*, and authored the opinion of the Court in *Gaffney*.

2.   Is it reasonable to force states to justify population deviations of less than one percent? Is there *any* threshold under which states should not have to defend population differences between districts? Is one's right to an equally weighted vote or "fair and effective representation" abridged in any meaningful way if one's district is over-populated by a handful of people? *See generally* Heather K. Gerken, *The Costs and Causes of Minimalism in Voting Cases:* Baker v. Carr *and Its Progeny*, 80 N.C. L. Rev. 1411, 1437–41 (2002).

3.   *Kirkpatrick* required states to bear the burden of proof when justifying population disparities between districts. In *Daggett*, 462 U.S. at 730–31, the Court elaborated:

> [T]wo basic questions shape litigation apportioning congressional districts. First, the court must consider whether the population differences among districts could have been reduced or eliminated altogether by a good-faith effort to draw districts of equal population. Parties challenging apportionment legislation must bear the burden of proof on this issue, and if they fail to show that the differences could have been avoided the apportionment scheme must be upheld. If, however, the plaintiffs can establish that the population differences were not the result of a good-faith effort to achieve equality, the State must bear the burden of proving that each significant variance between districts was necessary to achieve some legitimate goal.

In *Tennant v. Jefferson County Commission*, 133 S. Ct. 3 (2012), the Supreme Court applied *Daggett* to uphold a West Virginia districting plan with a population variance of 0.79%. Alternative plans with smaller variations were considered, but none was effective at achieving three of the state's objectives: keeping counties intact, keeping incumbents in different districts, and limiting population shifts from the previous districts. The Court approved each of those objectives as "valid" and "neutral," and applied a balancing test to hold that they sufficed to justify the 0.79% population variance: "[G]iven the small 'size of the deviations,' as balanced against 'the importance of the State's interests, the consistency with which the plan as a whole reflects those interests,' and the lack of available 'alternatives that might substantially vindicate those interests yet approximate population equality more closely,' [the plan] is justified by the State's legitimate objectives." *Id.* at 8 (quoting *Daggett*, 462 U.S. at 741).

4. What is the effect of the one-person, one-vote requirement on partisan gerrymandering? Defenders of one-person, one-vote, such as Justice Brennan, argue that an equipopulation principle places limits on the ability of states to draw district lines for partisan purposes, and that at the very least the principle does no harm. *See Daggett*, 462 U.S. at 734 n.6. Without such a mandate, states would have one more tool available to effectuate a gerrymander. Critics respond that in the absence of a strict one-person, one-vote requirement states would face pressures to draw district lines that track political subdivisions and other established communities. While legally there might be no obligation to do so, legislators would be expected to draw lines in that fashion and gerrymanders would therefore attract considerable public attention. If, however, political subdivisions must be cut to equalize district populations, then a strict interpretation of one person, one vote, the argument goes, gives legislators cover to draw district lines for partisan purposes. You have seen this debate in *Reynolds* and *Kirkpatrick*; it continued in *Daggett*, with Justice Stevens, in concurrence, and Justices White and Powell, in dissent, particularly criticizing partisan gerrymanders as undercutting the right to an effective vote. *See id.* at 752–65 (Stevens, J., concurring); 775–78 (White, J., dissenting); 786–90 (Powell, J., dissenting).

MAHAN v. HOWELL
Supreme Court of the United States
410 U.S. 315, 93 S. Ct. 979, 35 L. Ed. 2d 320 (1973)

MR. JUSTICE REHNQUIST delivered the opinion of the Court [in which MR. CHIEF JUSTICE BURGER, MR. JUSTICE STEWART, MR. JUSTICE WHITE, and MR. JUSTICE BLACKMUN join]. * * *

[The issue in this case is the constitutionality of the Virginia General Assembly's 1971 apportionment of the State for the election of members of its House of Delegates.] The statute apportioning the House provided for a combination of 52 single-member, multimember, and floater delegate districts from which 100 delegates would be elected. As found by the lower court, the ideal district in Virginia consisted of 46,485 persons per delegate, and the maximum percentage variation from that ideal under the Act was 16.4% — the 12th district being overrepresented by 6.8% and the 16th district being underrepresented by 9.6%. The population ratio between these two districts was 1.18 to 1. The average percentage variance under the plan was 3.89%, and the minimum population percentage necessary to elect a majority of the House was 49.29%. Of the 52 districts, 35 were within 4% of perfection and nine exceeded a 6% variance from the ideal. With one exception, the delegate districts followed political jurisdictional lines of the counties and cities. That exception, Fairfax County, was allotted 10 delegates but was divided into two five-member districts.

Relying on *Kirkpatrick* v. *Preisler*, 394 U.S. 526 (1969) [p. 192], *Wells* v. *Rockefeller*, 394 U.S. 542 (1969), and *Reynolds* v. *Sims*, 377 U.S. 533 (1964) [p. 173], the District Court concluded that the 16.4% variation was sufficient to condemn the

House statute under the "one person, one vote" doctrine. While it noted that the variances were traceable to the desire of the General Assembly to maintain the integrity of traditional county and city boundaries, and that it was impossible to draft district lines to overcome unconstitutional disparities and still maintain such integrity, it held that the State proved no governmental necessity for strictly adhering to political subdivision lines. Accordingly, it undertook its own redistricting and devised a plan having a percentage variation of slightly over 10% from the ideal district[.] * * *

In *Kirkpatrick* v. *Preisler* and *Wells* v. *Rockefeller*, this Court invalidated state reapportionment statutes for federal congressional districts having maximum percentage deviations of 5.97% and 13.1% respectively. The express purpose of these cases was to elucidate the standard first announced in the holding of *Wesberry* v. *Sanders*, 376 U.S. 1, 7–8 (1964) [p. 166], that "the command of Art. I, § 2, that Representatives be chosen 'by the People of the several States' means that as nearly as is practicable one man's vote in a congressional election is to be worth as much as another's." And it was concluded that that command "permits only the limited population variances which are unavoidable despite a good-faith effort to achieve absolute equality, or for which justification is shown." *Kirkpatrick* v. *Preisler, supra,* at 531. The principal question thus presented for review is whether or not the Equal Protection Clause of the Fourteenth Amendment likewise permits only "the limited population variances which are unavoidable despite a good-faith effort to achieve absolute equality" in the context of state legislative reapportionment.

This Court first recognized that the Equal Protection Clause requires both houses of a bicameral state legislature to be apportioned substantially on a population basis in *Reynolds* v. *Sims*. In so doing, it suggested that in the implementation of the basic constitutional principle — equality of population among the districts — more flexibility was constitutionally permissible with respect to state legislative reapportionment than in congressional redistricting. 377 U.S., at 578. Consideration was given to the fact that, almost invariably, there is a significantly larger number of seats in state legislative bodies to be distributed within a State than congressional seats, and that therefore it may be feasible for a State to use political subdivision lines to a greater extent in establishing state legislative districts than congressional districts while still affording adequate statewide representation. *Ibid.* Another possible justification for deviation from population-based representation in state legislatures was stated to be:

> "[T]hat of insuring some voice to political subdivisions, as political subdivisions. Several factors make more than insubstantial claims that a State can rationally consider according political subdivisions some independent representation in at least one body of the state legislature, as long as the basic standard of equality of population among districts is maintained. Local governmental entities are frequently charged with various responsibilities incident to the operation of state government. In many States much of the legislature's activity involves the enactment of so-called local legislation, directed only to the concerns of particular political subdivisions. And a State may legitimately desire to construct districts along political subdivision lines to deter the possibilities of gerrymandering. . . ." *Id.,* at 580–581. * * *

We conclude, therefore, that the constitutionality of Virginia's legislative redistricting plan was not to be judged by the more stringent standards that *Kirkpatrick* and *Wells* make applicable to congressional reapportionment, but instead by the equal protection test enunciated in *Reynolds* v. *Sims*. We reaffirm its holding that "the Equal Protection Clause requires that a State make an honest and good faith effort to construct districts, in both houses of its legislature, as nearly of equal population as is practicable." 377 U.S., at 577. We likewise reaffirm its conclusion that "[s]o long as the divergences from a strict population standard are based on legitimate considerations incident to the effectuation of a rational state policy, some deviations from the equal-population principle are constitutionally permissible with respect to the apportionment of seats in either or both of the two houses of a bicameral state legislature." *Id.*, at 579. * * *

* * * The inquiry then becomes whether it can reasonably be said that the state policy urged by Virginia to justify the divergences in the legislative reapportionment plan of the House is, indeed, furthered by the plan adopted by the legislature, and whether, if so justified, the divergences are also within tolerable limits. For a State's policy urged in justification of disparity in district population, however rational, cannot constitutionally be permitted to emasculate the goal of substantial equality.

There was uncontradicted evidence offered in the District Court to the effect that the legislature's plan, subject to minor qualifications, "produces the minimum deviation above and below the norm, keeping intact political boundaries. . . ." That court itself recognized that equality was impossible if political boundaries were to be kept intact in the process of districting. But it went on to hold that since the State "proved no governmental necessity for strictly adhering to political subdivision lines," the legislative plan was constitutionally invalid. As we noted above, however, the proper equal protection test is not framed in terms of "governmental necessity," but instead in terms of a claim that a State may "rationally consider." *Reynolds* v. *Sims, supra*, at 580–581. * * *

We hold that the legislature's plan for apportionment of the House of Delegates may reasonably be said to advance the rational state policy of respecting the boundaries of political subdivisions. The remaining inquiry is whether the population disparities among the districts that have resulted from the pursuit of this plan exceed constitutional limits. We conclude that they do not. * * *

Neither courts nor legislatures are furnished any specialized calipers that enable them to extract from the general language of the Equal Protection Clause of the Fourteenth Amendment the mathematical formula that establishes what range of percentage deviations is permissible, and what is not. The 16-odd percent maximum deviation that the District Court found to exist in the legislative plan for the reapportionment of the House is substantially less than the percentage deviations that have been found invalid in the previous decisions of this Court [including *Reynolds* v. *Sims*, in which the largest district had a population more than forty times greater than that of the smallest]. While this percentage may well approach tolerable limits, we do not believe it exceeds them. Virginia has not sacrificed substantial equality to justifiable deviations.

The policy of maintaining the integrity of political subdivision lines in the process of reapportioning a state legislature, the policy consistently advanced by Virginia as a justification for disparities in population among districts that elect members to the House of Delegates, is a rational one. It can reasonably be said, upon examination of the legislative plan, that it does in fact advance that policy. The population disparities that are permitted thereunder result in a maximum percentage deviation that we hold to be within tolerable constitutional limits. We, therefore, hold the General Assembly's plan for the reapportionment of the House of Delegates constitutional and reverse the District Court's conclusion to the contrary. * * *

[R]eversed in [relevant] part.

Mr. Justice Powell took no part in the consideration or decision of th[is] cas[e].

Mr. Justice Brennan, with whom Mr. Justice Douglas and Mr. Justice Marshall join, * * * dissenting[.] * * *

* * * In my view, the problem in the case before us is in no sense one of first impression, but is squarely controlled by our prior decisions[, whose] * * * holdings * * * can be restated in two unequivocal propositions. First, the paramount goal of reapportionment must be the drawing of district lines so as to achieve precise equality in the population of each district. * * * The Constitution does not permit a State to relegate considerations of equality to secondary status and reserve as the primary goal of apportionment the service of some other state interest.

Second, it is open to the State, in the event that it should fail to achieve the goal of population equality, to attempt to justify its failure by demonstrating that precise equality could not be achieved without jeopardizing some critical governmental interest. The Equal Protection Clause does not exalt the principle of equal representation to the point of nullifying every competing interest of the State. But we have held firmly to the view that variations in weight accorded each vote can be approved only where the State meets its burden of presenting cogent reasons in explanation of the variations, and even then only where the variations are small.

The validity of these propositions and their applicability to the case before us are not at all diminished by the fact that *Kirkpatrick* v. *Preisler* and *Wells* v. *Rockefeller* — two of the many cases in which the propositions were refined and applied — concerned the division of States into federal congressional districts rather than legislative reapportionment. Prior to today's decision, we have never held that different constitutional *standards* are applicable to the two situations. True, there are significant differences between congressional districting and legislative apportionment, and we have repeatedly recognized those differences. In *Reynolds* v. *Sims*, for example, we termed "more than insubstantial" the argument that "a State can rationally consider according political subdivisions some independent representation in at least one body of the state legislature, as long as the basic standard of equality of population among districts is maintained." But the recognition of these differences is hardly tantamount to the establishment of two distinct controlling standards. What our decisions have made clear is that certain state interests that are pertinent to legislative reapportionment can have no possible relevance to congressional districting. Thus, the need to preserve the integrity of political subdivisions as political subdivisions may, in some instances, justify small variations in the population of districts from which state legislators are elected. But that interest can hardly be asserted in justification of malapportioned congressional districts. While the State may have a broader range of interests to which it can point in attempting to justify a failure to achieve precise equality in the context of legislative apportionment, it by no means follows that the State is subject to a lighter burden of proof or that the controlling constitutional standard is in any sense distinguishable. * * * On the contrary, the "as nearly as practicable" standard with which we were concerned [in *Kirkpatrick*] is identical to the standard that *Reynolds* v. *Sims* specifically made applicable to controversies over state legislative apportionment. * * *

[I]n asserting its interest in preserving the integrity of county boundaries, the Commonwealth offers nothing more than vague references to "local legislation," without describing such legislation with precision, without indicating whether such legislation amounts to a significant proportion of the legislature's business, and without demonstrating that the District Court's plan would materially affect the treatment of such legislation.

The Court assumes that county representation is an important goal of Virginia's reapportionment plan, and appellants suggest that the plan can be justified, at least in part, by the effort "to give an independent voice to the cities and counties [the legislature] daily governs." * * * That argument assumes that some significant number of issues will have an impact squarely on [a single c]ounty, while having no impact, or a differing impact, on the surrounding areas. For on issues affecting the entire region or the Commonwealth as a whole — presumably the vast majority of issues — the critical concern is not that each vote in [a c]ounty be cast in a single district, but that each vote cast be precisely equal in weight to votes in every other part of the Commonwealth. And the argument also assumes that the issues affecting only one county are of predominant concern to the voters. Under a representative form of government, the voters participate indirectly through the election of delegates. It should be obvious that as a voter's concern with regional or statewide issues increases relative to his interest in county issues, the significance of voting outside the county will correspondingly diminish.

But even if a substantial number of issues do have an impact primarily on a single county, and even if those issues are of deep concern to the voters, it still does not follow that the legislature's apportionment plan is a rational attempt to serve an important state interest. The plan would by no means provide, even in the legislature's own terms, effective representation for each county [because small counties are combined to form individual House districts]. * * *

In short, the best that can be said of appellants' efforts to secure county representation is that the plan can be effective only with respect to some unspecified but in all likelihood small number of issues that affect a single county and that are overwhelmingly important to the voters of that county; and even then it provides effective representation only where the affected county represents a large enough percentage of the voters in the district to have a significant impact on the election of the delegate. * * *

On this record — without any showing of the specific need for county representation or a showing of how such representation can be meaningfully provided to small counties whose votes would be submerged in a multi-county district — I see no basis whatsoever for upholding the Assembly's 1971 plan and the resulting substantial variations in district population. Accordingly, I would affirm the judgment of the District Court holding the plan invalid under the Equal Protection Clause of the Fourteenth Amendment.

Notes and Questions

1. What is the Court's rationale for subjecting state-legislative apportionment to a more lenient standard than the one applicable to congressional districting? Is the distinction convincing?

2. Does the Court or Justice Brennan have the better argument based on precedent?

3. If *Howell*'s standard of rationality were applied to *Reynolds v. Sims*, would that case have been decided differently? How can one tell when a given apportionment system is "irrational"?

4. Why does the Court say that the Virginia plan "may well approach tolerable limits"? What are those limits?

5. Practically speaking, would the dissent's application of the one-person, one-vote standard ever permit a state to deviate from precise mathematical equality?

6. *Problem.* Wyoming's Constitution provided since statehood in 1890 that each county shall be entitled to at least one member of the state Senate and one member of the state House of Representatives. The 1981 statute apportioning the legislature established a 64-member House. Dividing Wyoming's population by 64 yielded an ideal district size of 7,337 persons. Wyoming's smallest county, Niobrara County, however, had only 2,924 persons. Giving Niobrara County its own representative, therefore, yielded a total deviation of 89% of the ideal district. If each of the other districts was made equal in population, would the district for Niobrara County render the entire plan unconstitutional? *See Brown v. Thomson*, 462 U.S. 835 (1983); *see also Abate v. Mundt*, 403 U.S. 182 (1971).

7. Should states be permitted to vary from one-person, one-vote to keep *neighborhoods* together? Suppose that within the relatively well-to-do Town of Amherst, there is a neighborhood comprised of low-income housing, known derisively as Looney Acres. In drawing district lines for the town board or county legislature, may the government defend its overpopulation of the Looney Acres district on the ground that it wishes to preserve the representation of neighborhoods? What if Looney Acres were *under*-populated so as to increase the power of the low-income community?

GAFFNEY v. CUMMINGS
Supreme Court of the United States
412 U.S. 735, 93 S. Ct. 2321, 37 L. Ed. 2d 298 (1973)

MR. JUSTICE WHITE delivered the opinion of the Court [in which MR. CHIEF JUSTICE BURGER, MR. JUSTICE STEWART, MR. JUSTICE BLACKMUN, MR. JUSTICE POWELL, and MR. JUSTICE REHNQUIST join].

The questions in this case are whether the population variations among the election districts provided by a reapportionment plan for the Connecticut General Assembly, proposed in 1971, made out a prima facie case of invidious discrimination under the Equal Protection Clause and whether an otherwise acceptable reapportionment plan is constitutionally vulnerable where its purpose is to provide districts that would achieve "political fairness" between the political parties.

[After the 1970 census, the Connecticut General Assembly had the opportunity to reapportion the State's electoral districts, but] was unable to agree on a plan by the state constitutional deadline of April 1, 1971. The task was therefore transferred, as required by the [Connecticut] constitution, to an eight-member bipartisan commission. * * * The commission was given until July 1, 1971, to devise a reapportionment plan; but, although the commission approached agreement, it too was unable to adopt a plan within the deadline. Accordingly, as a final step in the constitutional process, a three-man bipartisan Board was constituted. The Speaker of the House of Representatives, a Democrat, and the Republican Minority Leader of the House each chose a judge of the State Superior Court to be a Board member, and the two judges in turn designated a third Board member, who was a justice of the State Supreme Court.

This Apportionment Board, using the census data available during the summer of 1971, and relying heavily on the legislative commission's tentative plans, filed a reapportionment plan on September 30, 1971, with one member dissenting.

According to the 1970 census data before the Board, the population of Connecticut is 3,032,217. The Board's reapportionment plan provides for a Senate consisting of 36 senators elected from single-member districts. The ideal senatorial district, in terms of population, would thus contain 84,228 people. The districts actually created deviate, on the average, by 0.45% from this ideal, the median deviation being 0.47%. The largest and smallest senatorial districts deviate by +0.88% and -0.93%, respectively, making the total maximum deviation 1.81%.

The reapportionment plan proposed a House of 151 single-member districts. The population of the ideal assembly district would be 20,081. The average deviation from perfect equality for all the plan's assembly districts is 1.9%, the median deviation, 1.8%. The maximum deviation from the ideal is +3.93% and -3.9%. The maximum deviation between any two districts thus totals 7.83%.

* * * [T]o reach what it thought to be substantial population equality, the Board cut the boundary lines of 47 of the State's 169 towns. The Board also consciously and overtly adopted and followed a policy of "political fairness," which aimed at a rough scheme of proportional representation of the two major political parties. Senate and House districts were structured so that the composition of both Houses would

reflect "as closely as possible . . . the actual [statewide] plurality of vote on the House or Senate lines in a given election." Rather than focusing on party membership in the respective districts, the Board took into account the party voting results in the preceding three statewide elections, and, on that basis, created what was thought to be a proportionate number of Republican and Democratic legislative seats.

In November 1971, * * * an action was brought in federal district court seeking declaratory and injunctive relief against implementation of the plan. * * * [T]he District Court * * * invalidat[ed] the Board plan and permanently enjoin[ed] its use in future elections. * * *

We think that appellees' showing of numerical deviations from population equality among the Senate and House districts in this case failed to make out a prima facie violation of the Equal Protection Clause of the Fourteenth Amendment, whether those deviations are considered alone or in combination with the additional fact that another plan could be conceived with lower deviations among the State's legislative districts. Put another way, the allegations and proof of population deviations among the districts fail in size and quality to amount to an invidious discrimination under the Fourteenth Amendment which would entitle appellees to relief, absent some countervailing showing by the State. * * *

We doubt that *Reynolds* [v. *Sims*, 377 U.S. 533 (1964)] [p. 173], would mandate any other result, if for no other reason than that the basic statistical materials which legislatures and courts usually have to work with are the results of the United States census taken at 10-year intervals and published as soon as possible after the beginning of each decade. [I]t makes little sense to conclude from relatively minor "census population" variations among legislative districts that any person's vote is being substantially diluted. The "population" of a legislative district is just not that knowable to be used for such refined judgments.

What is more, it must be recognized that total population, even if absolutely accurate as to each district when counted, is nevertheless not a talismanic measure of the weight of a person's vote under a later adopted reapportionment plan. The United States census is more of an event than a process. It measures population at only a single instant in time. District populations are constantly changing, often at different rates in either direction, up or down. Substantial differentials in population growth rates are striking and well-known phenomena. So, too, if it is the weight of a person's vote that matters, total population — even if stable and accurately taken — may not actually reflect that body of voters whose votes must be counted and weighed for the purposes of reapportionment, because "census persons" are not voters. [See *Burns* v. *Richardson*, 384 U.S. 73, 91–92 (1966).] The proportion of the census population too young to vote or disqualified by alienage or nonresidence varies substantially among the States and among localities within the States. The six congressional districts in Connecticut, for example, vary from one another by as much as 4% in their age-eligible voters, with the first district having 68% of its census population at voting age while the sixth district has 64% at 18 years or older. Other States have congressional districts that vary from one another by as much as 29% and as little as 1% with respect to their age-eligible voters. And these figures tell us nothing of the other ineligibles making up the substantially equal census populations among election districts: aliens, nonresident military personnel, non-resident students, for example. Nor do these figures tell anything at all about the proportion of all those otherwise eligible individuals whose vote cannot be counted or weighed because they either failed to register or failed to vote.

Reynolds v. *Sims*, of course, dealt with more than the statistical niceties involved in equalizing individual voting strength. It * * * recognized that "the achieving of fair and effective representation for all citizens is . . . the basic aim of legislative apportionment," [377 U.S.,] at 565–566, and it was for that reason that the decision insisted on substantial equality of populations among districts.

This is a vital and worthy goal, but surely its attainment does not in any commonsense way depend upon eliminating the insignificant population variations involved in this case. Fair and effective representation may be destroyed by gross population variations among districts, but it is apparent that such representation does not depend solely on mathematical equality among district populations. * * *

Nor is the goal of fair and effective representation furthered by making the standards of reapportionment so difficult to satisfy that the reapportionment task is recurringly removed from legislative hands and performed by federal courts which themselves must make the political decisions necessary to formulate a plan or accept those made by reapportionment plaintiffs who may have wholly different goals from those embodied in the official plan. * * * We doubt that the Fourteenth Amendment requires repeated displacement of otherwise appropriate state deci-sionmaking in the name of essentially minor deviations from perfect census-population equality that no one, with confidence, can say will deprive any person of fair and effective representation in his state legislature.

That the Court was not deterred by the hazards of the political thicket when it undertook to adjudicate the reapportionment cases does not mean that it should become bogged down in a vast, intractable apportionment slough, particularly when there is little, if anything, to be accomplished by doing so. * * *

* * * We have repeatedly recognized that state reapportionment is the task of local legislatures or of those organs of state government selected to perform it. Their work should not be invalidated under the Equal Protection Clause when only minor population variations among districts are proved. Here, the proof at trial demonstrated that the House districts under the State Apportionment Board's plan varied in population from one another by a maximum of only about 8% and that the average deviation from the ideal House district was only about 2%. The Senate districts had even less variations. On such a showing, we are quite sure that a prima facie case of invidious discrimination under the Fourteenth Amendment was not made out.

State legislative districts may be equal or substantially equal in population and still be vulnerable under the Fourteenth Amendment. A districting statute other-wise acceptable, may be invalid because it fences out a racial group so as to deprive them of their pre-existing municipal vote. *Gomillion* v. *Lightfoot*, 364 U.S. 339 (1960) [p. 115]. * * * We must, therefore, respond to appellees' claims in this case that even if acceptable populationwise, the Apportionment Board's plan was invidiously discriminatory because a "political fairness principle" was followed in making up the districts in both the House and Senate.

The record abounds with evidence, and it is frankly admitted by those who prepared the plan, that virtually every Senate and House district line was drawn with the conscious intent to create a districting plan that would achieve a rough approximation of the statewide political strengths of the Democratic and Republican Parties, the only two parties in the State large enough to elect legislators from discernible geographic areas. Appellant insists that the spirit of "political fairness" underlying this plan is not only permissible, but a desirable consideration in laying out districts that otherwise satisfy the population standard of the reapportionment cases. Appellees, on the other hand, label the plan as nothing less than a gigantic political gerrymander, invidiously discriminatory under the Fourteenth Amendment.[18]

We are quite unconvinced that the reapportionment plan offered by the three-member Board violated the Fourteenth Amendment because it attempted to reflect the relative strength of the parties in locating and defining election districts. It would be idle, we think, to contend that any political consideration taken into account in fashioning a reapportionment plan is sufficient to invalidate it. * * * The very essence of districting is to produce a different — a more "politically fair" — result than would be reached with elections at large, in which the winning party would take 100% of the legislative seats. Politics and political considerations are inseparable from districting and apportionment. The political profile of a State, its party registration, and voting records are available precinct by precinct, ward by ward. These subdivisions may not be identical with census tracts, but, when overlaid on a census map, it requires no special genius to recognize the political consequences of drawing a district line along one street rather than another. It is not only obvious, but absolutely unavoidable, that the location and shape of districts may well determine the political complexion of the area. District lines are rarely neutral phenomena. They can well determine what district will be predominantly Democratic or predominantly Republican, or make a close race likely. Redistricting may pit incumbents against one another or make very difficult the election of the most experienced legislator. The reality is that districting inevitably has and is intended to have substantial political consequences.

It may be suggested that those who redistrict and reapportion should work with census, not political, data and achieve population equality without regard for political impact. But this politically mindless approach may produce, whether intended or not, the most grossly gerrymandered results; and, in any event, it is most unlikely that the political impact of such a plan would remain undiscovered by the time it was proposed or adopted, in which event the results would be both known and, if not changed, intended.

It is much more plausible to assume that those who redistrict and reapportion work with both political and census data. Within the limits of the population equality standards of the Equal Protection Clause, they seek, through compromise or

---

[18] Appellees also maintain that the shapes of the districts would not have been so "indecent" had the Board not attempted to "wiggle and joggle" boundary lines to ferret out pockets of each party's strength. That may well be true * * *. But compactness or attractiveness has never been held to constitute an independent federal constitutional requirement for state legislative districts.

otherwise, to achieve the political or other ends of the State, its constituents, and its officeholders. * * * Even more plainly, judicial interest should be at its lowest ebb when a State purports fairly to allocate political power to the parties in accordance with their voting strength and, within quite tolerable limits, succeeds in doing so. There is no doubt that there may be other reapportionment plans for Connecticut that would have different political consequences and that would also be constitutional. Perhaps any of appellees' plans would have fallen into this category, as would the court's, had it propounded one. But neither we nor the district courts have a constitutional warrant to invalidate a state plan, otherwise within tolerable population limits, because it undertakes, not to minimize or eliminate the political strength of any group or party, but to recognize it and, through districting, provide a rough sort of proportional representation in the legislative halls of the State.

Reversed.

Mr. Justice Brennan, with whom Mr. Justice Douglas and Mr. Justice Marshall join, dissenting[.] * * *

Although not purporting to quarrel with the principle that precise mathematical equality is the constitutionally mandated goal of reapportionment, the Court today establishes a wide margin of tolerable error, and thereby undermines the effort to effectuate the principle. * * *

[I]t is important to understand that the demand for precise mathematical equality rests neither on a scholastic obsession with abstract numbers nor a rigid insensitivity to the political realities of the reapportionment process. Our paramount concern has remained an individual and personal right — the right to an equal vote. * * * We have demanded equality in district population precisely to insure that the weight of a person's vote will not depend on the district in which he lives. The conclusion that a State may, without any articulated justification, deliberately weight some persons' votes more heavily than others, seems to me fundamentally at odds with the purpose and rationale of our reapportionment decisions. * * *

Notes and Questions

1.   In *Gaffney* and other cases, the Court established that 10% was the figure that divided "minor deviations" from more significant ones, for which the state needed to provide a justification. *See Brown v. Thomson*, 462 U.S. 835, 842 (1983) ("Our decisions have established, as a general matter, that an apportionment plan with a maximum population deviation under 10% falls within this category of minor deviations."). *White v. Regester*, 412 U.S. 755 (1973), decided the same day as *Gaffney*, held that a Texas redistricting plan having a maximum deviation of 9.9% came within the *Gaffney* safe harbor. *Id.* at 764. In *Abate v. Mundt*, 403 U.S. 182 (1971), however, the Court held that a plan with a maximum deviation of 11.9% required a justification. Is there anything in the Constitution that can reasonably be interpreted as establishing a 10% safe harbor? If not, do you find acceptable the approach under *Kirkpatrick v. Preisler*, 394 U.S. 526 (1969) [p. 192], and *Karcher v. Daggett*, 462 U.S. 725 (1983), according to which virtually no population deviations

are constitutional? Is there a third possibility?

2.   In holding that a 16.4% population difference between state-legislative (but not congressional) districts could be justified, *Mahan v. Howell* reasoned that state legislatures are large enough to have representatives who can serve the interests of identifiable political subdivisions, and that state legislatures enact local legislation for which it would be useful to have legislators who can represent municipalities themselves. Thus, the differences between Congress and state legislatures mean that states will have a sufficient reason to draw district lines that track municipal boundaries.

Is there a comparable reason for *Gaffney* to distinguish *Kirkpatrick*? Why would states need to justify small deviations in the population of congressional districts, but not need to justify similar deviations in state-legislative districts?

3.   The one-person, one-vote rule applies to districts for the election of representatives to local governments as well as to Congress and state legislatures. *See Avery v. Midland County*, 390 U.S. 474 (1968). *Abate v. Mundt, supra*, elaborated on the permissible deviations from mathematical equality for local-government districts:

> [V]iable local governments may need considerable flexibility in municipal arrangements if they are to meet changing societal needs, and * * * a desire to preserve the integrity of political subdivisions may justify an apportionment plan which departs from numerical equality. These observations, along with the facts that local legislative bodies frequently have fewer representatives than do their state and national counterparts and that some local legislative districts may have a much smaller population than do congressional and state legislative districts, lend support to the argument that slightly greater percentage deviations may be tolerable for local government apportionment schemes.

Is this explanation consistent with the Court's explanation of its different tolerances for population variation in congressional and state-legislative districts? How much variation would qualify as a "slightly greater percentage deviation[]"? Nineteen percent? *See Blackmoon v. Charles Mix County*, 386 F. Supp. 2d 1108 (D.S.D. 2005).

COX v. LARIOS
Supreme Court of the United States
542 U.S. 947, 124 S. Ct. 2806, 159 L. Ed. 2d 831 (2004)

Affirmed on appeal from D.C. N.D. Ga. Reported below: 300 F. Supp. 2d 1320.

JUSTICE STEVENS, with whom JUSTICE BREYER joins, concurring.

Today we affirm the District Court's judgment that Georgia's legislative reapportionment plans for the State House of Representatives and Senate violate the one-person, one-vote principle of the Equal Protection Clause. [The maximum population variance was 9.8%.] The District Court's findings disclose two reasons for the unconstitutional population deviations in the state legislative reapportionment plans. The first was "a deliberate and systematic policy of favoring rural and inner-city interests at the expense of suburban areas north, east, and west of Atlanta." The second was "an intentional effort to allow incumbent Democrats to maintain or increase their delegation, primarily by systematically underpopulating the districts held by incumbent Democrats, by overpopulating those of Republicans, and by deliberately pairing numerous Republican incumbents against one another." * * * The District Court correctly held that the drafters' desire to give an electoral advantage to certain regions of the State and to certain incumbents (but not incumbents as such) did not justify the conceded deviations from the principle of one person, one vote.

In challenging the District Court's judgment, appellant invites us to weaken the one-person, one-vote standard by creating a safe harbor for population deviations of less than 10 percent, within which districting decisions could be made for any reason whatsoever. The Court properly rejects that invitation. After our recent decision in *Vieth* v. *Jubelirer*, 541 U.S. 267 (2004) [p. 131], the equal-population principle remains the only clear limitation on improper districting practices, and we must be careful not to dilute its strength. * * *

Drawing district lines that have no neutral justification in order to place two incumbents of the opposite party in the same district is probative of the same impermissible intent as the "uncouth twenty-eight-sided figure" that defined the boundary of Tuskegee, Alabama, in *Gomillion* v. *Lightfoot*, 364 U.S. 339, 340 (1960) [p. 115], or the "dragon descending on Philadelphia from the west" that defined Pennsylvania's District 6 in *Vieth*, 541 U.S., at 340 (STEVENS, J., dissenting). The record in this case, like the allegations in *Gomillion* and in *Vieth*, reinforce my conclusion that "the unavailability of judicially manageable standards" cannot justify a refusal "to condemn even the most blatant violations of a state legislature's fundamental duty to govern impartially." *Vieth*, 541 U.S., at 341. I remain convinced that in time the present "failure of judicial will" will be replaced by stern condemnation of partisan gerrymandering that does not even pretend to be justified by neutral principles.

JUSTICE SCALIA, dissenting.

When reviewing States' redistricting of their own legislative boundaries, we have been appropriately deferential. See *Mahan* v. *Howell*, 410 U.S. 315, 327 (1973) [p. 200]. A series of our cases established the principle that "minor deviations" among districts — deviations of less than 10% — are "insufficient to make out a prima facie case of invidious discrimination under the Fourteenth Amendment so as to require justification by the State." *Brown* v. *Thomson*, 462 U.S. 835, 842 (1983) (quoting *Gaffney* v. *Cummings*, 412 U.S. 735, 745 (1973)); see also *Voinovich* v. *Quilter*, 507 U.S. 146, 160–162 (1993). This case presents a question that *Brown*, *Gaffney*, and *Voinovich* did not squarely confront — whether a districting plan that *satisfies* this 10% criterion may nevertheless be invalidated on the basis of circumstantial evidence of partisan political motivation.

The state officials who drafted Georgia's redistricting plan believed the answer to that question was "no," reading our cases to establish a 10% "safe harbor" with which they meticulously complied. The court below disagreed. No party here contends that, beyond grand generalities in cases such as *Reynolds* v. *Sims*, 377

U.S. 533, 577 (1964) [p. 173], this Court has addressed the question. The opinion below is consistent with others to have addressed the issue; there is no obvious conflict among the lower courts. This is not a petition for certiorari, however, but an appeal, and we should not summarily affirm unless it is clear that the disposition of this case is correct.

In my view, that is not clear. A substantial case can be made that Georgia's redistricting plan *did* comply with the Constitution. Appellees do not contend that the population deviations — all less than 5% from the mean — were based on race or some other suspect classification. They claim only impermissible *political* bias — that state legislators tried to improve the electoral chances of Democrats over Republicans by underpopulating inner-city and rural districts and by selectively protecting incumbents, while ignoring "traditional" redistricting criteria. The District Court agreed.

The problem with this analysis is that it assumes "politics as usual" is not *itself* a "traditional" redistricting criterion. In the recent decision in *Vieth* v. *Jubelirer*, all but one of the Justices agreed that it *is* a traditional criterion, and a constitutional one, so long as it does not go too far. It is not obvious to me that a legislature goes too far when it stays within the 10% disparity in population our cases allow. To say that it does is to invite allegations of political motivation whenever there is population disparity, and thus to destroy the 10% safe harbor our cases provide. Ferreting out political motives in minute population deviations seems to me more likely to encourage politically motivated litigation than to vindicate political rights.

I would set the case for argument.

Notes and Questions

1. In reconciling *Larios* with *Vieth v. Jubelirer*, remember that *Larios* involved not just a partisan gerrymander, but a partisan gerrymander that achieved its results in part through deviations from one-person, one-vote. *Larios* thus stands for the proposition (questioned by Justice Scalia in dissent) that producing a partisan advantage does not excuse such deviations, even where those deviations are less than the 10% "safe harbor."

2. Does this case spell the end of the "safe harbor"? *See In re Municipal Reapportionment of Township of Haverford*, 873 A.2d 821, 834–36 (Pa. Commw. Ct. 2005). Under *Brown* and *Gaffney*, deviations of less than 10% were "insufficient to make out a prima facie case of invidious discrimination," and therefore required no justification from the state. *Larios* held that Georgia's justification for its less-than-10% deviations was insufficient, but such a conclusion is logically possible only if the state is obligated to provide some justification in the first place.

Consider one court's attempt to explain the proper approach to follow after *Cox v. Larios*:

> The formulaic [ten-percent] threshold is not an absolute determinant. Rather, it effectively allocates the burden of proof. Population deviation less than ten percent, for example, is not *per se* nondiscriminatory and is not an absolute bar to a claim of vote dilution. At the same time, a deviation in

population equality greater than ten percent establishes a *prima facie* case of discrimination and shifts the evidentiary burden to the state, requiring justification for the deviation. With a deviation less than ten percent, a plaintiff must prove that the redistricting process was tainted by arbitrariness or discrimination. That is, a deviation less than ten percent is not a safe harbor, barring any claim of discrimination[.] * * * [M]inor deviations do not amount to a *prima facie* case of discrimination under the Fourteenth Amendment, but they do not foreclose the possibility of success altogether; there may be other evidence.

Moore v. Itawamba County, 431 F.3d 257, 259–60 (5th Cir. 2005) (*per curiam*) (footnotes omitted). If *Moore* is correct, why aren't challenges such as *Larios* barred by *Vieth*? That is, once it is established that the population variance does not create a prima facie case of discrimination, the plaintiff is left to make essentially the same claim that *Vieth* refused to adjudicate.

Perhaps the result will be analogous to the doctrine that has developed concerning discriminatory peremptory challenges of jurors. Under *Batson v. Kentucky*, 476 U.S. 79 (1986), and its progeny, attorneys may not use their peremptory challenges to excuse jurors based on certain characteristics, including race and sex. But peremptory challenges — as distinguished from for-cause challenges — ordinarily do not require the challenging party to provide any reason whatever for exercising the challenges. The Supreme Court has resolved this conundrum by requiring the objecting party to make out a prima facie case of the other party's use of the characteristic through, for example, a pattern of striking jurors who are racial minorities. The challenging party will then have the opportunity to come forward with an explanation for the challenges that does not rely on the suspect characteristic. The judge then decides if the objecting party has demonstrated that the prohibited characteristic was used.

Such an approach in the districting context might require a party objecting to a districting plan to make a prima facie case that the population variance between districts was created for partisan reasons. The state would then be able to put forward a neutral explanation (*e.g.*, maintaining municipal boundaries). If the court were convinced, notwithstanding the explanation, that partisanship was the real motivation for the population variance, then the court would strike down the plan.

Thus, states would have to provide a justification for population variances under 10% only when a plaintiff could make a prima facie case that the variances were created to serve some illegitimate purpose. The easier it is to make such a prima facie case, the less significance there will be to the 10% threshold. Justice Scalia seemed to imply that after *Larios* it will be too easy for plaintiffs in "politically motivated litigation" to make a prima facie case. Was he correct?

3. If Georgia's plan had been designed to help all incumbent legislators, instead of just Democrats, should the result have been different?

4. Challenges to the apportionment of congressional districts or statewide legislative districts are heard in federal court not by a single district judge, as is the usual practice, but by a court of three judges, at least one of whom must be a circuit judge. 28 U.S.C. § 2284(b)(1). Appeals from such courts proceed directly to the

Supreme Court, and the Court must decide those appeals; they are not subject to the certiorari process that permits the Court to determine most of its own docket. *See* 28 U.S.C. § 1253. Thus, as Justice Scalia noted, the Court did not have the ability to deny certiorari in *Larios* and leave the issues presented for another day. *See generally* Michael E. Solimine, *The Three-Judge District Court in Voting Rights Litigation*, 30 U. MICH. J.L. REFORM 79 (1996). Not every case subject to the Supreme Court's "mandatory" jurisdiction is given full consideration, however. Sometimes, as in *Larios*, the Court decides such appeals summarily, without oral argument. It takes six Justices to invoke the summary process. Despite the cursory treatment the Court gives to such cases, however, they are entitled to precedential weight and must be treated as binding by lower courts. *See Hicks v. Miranda*, 422 U.S. 332 (1975).[e] The Supreme Court itself, however, will give summary dispositions less precedential weight than it gives to decisions reached after full consideration. *See, e.g., Edelman v. Jordan*, 415 U.S. 651, 671 (1974). *See generally* ROBERT L. STERN ET AL., SUPREME COURT PRACTICE § 4.28 (9th ed. 2007); Michael E. Solimine, *Institutional Process, Agenda Setting, and the Development of Election Law on the Supreme Court*, 68 OHIO ST. L.J. 767, 792–93 (2007).

D.   OTHER LIMITS ON MAJORITARIANISM: SUPER-MAJORITIES AND GEOGRAPHICAL DISTRIBUTION REQUIREMENTS

So far we have encountered several ways states may use electoral systems to allocate political power. For example, states may exclude groups of people from voting or draw district lines to affect the amount of political influence certain voters can exercise. Electoral systems can allocate power in other ways, too. Super-majority requirements prevent simple majorities from exercising political power, and allow a minority to maintain the status quo.[f] Accordingly, such requirements can be viewed as undermining the principle of majority rule underlying the one-person, one-vote standard. *See Reynolds v. Sims*, 377 U.S. 533, 565 (1964) ("Logically, in a society ostensibly grounded on representative government, it would seem reasonable that a majority of the people of a State could elect a majority of that State's legislators."); *id.* at 576 (condemning "frustration of the majority will through minority veto" if one house of a state legislature were permitted to be apportioned on a basis other than population). *See also Whitcomb v. Chavis*, 403

---

[e] Nevertheless, "[s]ummary actions * * * should not be understood as breaking new ground but as applying principles established by prior decisions to the particular facts involved." *Mandel v. Bradley*, 432 U.S. 173, 176 (1977).

[f] The Constitution itself, of course, employs this technique repeatedly. *See* U.S. CONST. art. I, § 5, cl. 2 (requiring a two-thirds vote of the Senate to convict an impeached official); *id.* (requiring a two-thirds vote of either the House or the Senate to expel a member); *id.* art. I, § 7, cls. 2, 3 (requiring a two-thirds vote of each House to override a presidential veto); *id.* art. II, § 2, cl. 2 (requiring a two-thirds vote of the Senate to ratify a treaty); *id.* art. V (establishing super-majority requirements for amending the Constitution); *id.* art. VII (requiring nine states to ratify the Constitution before the document would take effect). Additionally, the bicameralism requirements and even the substantive limits on legislation contained in such provisions as the Bill of Rights can be seen as supermajority requirements. *See generally* THE FEDERALIST No. 51 (James Madison); John O. McGinnis & Michael B. Rappaport, *Our Supermajoritarian Constitution*, 80 TEX. L. REV. 703 (2002).

U.S. 124, 166 (1971) [p. 268] (opinion of Harlan, J.) (suggesting that the one-person, one-vote "cases can best be understood * * * as reflections of deep *personal* commitments by some members of the Court to the principles of pure majoritarian democracy"). Likewise, states may seek to limit the ability of majorities to exert influence by requiring that a certain amount of support come from geographically disparate areas. As the following cases show, the Court has been kinder to super-majority requirements than an isolated reading of *Sims* might lead one to expect, while the Court has sent mixed signals regarding the constitutionality of geographical distribution requirements.

GORDON v. LANCE
Supreme Court of the United States
403 U.S. 1, 91 S. Ct. 1889, 29 L. Ed. 2d 273 (1971)

MR. CHIEF JUSTICE BURGER delivered the opinion of the Court [in which MR. JUSTICE BLACK, MR. JUSTICE DOUGLAS, MR. JUSTICE STEWART, MR. JUSTICE WHITE, and MR. JUSTICE BLACKMUN join]. * * *

The Constitution of West Virginia and certain West Virginia statutes provide that political subdivisions of the State may not incur bonded indebtedness or increase tax rates beyond those established by the Constitution without the approval of 60% of the voters in a referendum election.

On April 29, 1968, the Board of Education of Roane County, West Virginia, submitted to the voters of Roane County a proposal calling for the issuance of general obligation bonds in the amount of $1,830,000 for the purpose of constructing new school buildings and improving existing educational facilities. At the same election, by separate ballot, the voters were asked to authorize the Board of Education to levy additional taxes to support current expenditures and capital improvements. Of the total votes cast, 51.55% favored the bond issues and 51.51% favored the tax levy. Having failed to obtain the requisite 60% affirmative vote, the proposals were declared defeated.

Following the election, respondents appeared before the Board of Education on behalf of themselves and other persons who had voted in favor of the proposals and demanded that the Board authorize the bonds and the additional taxes. The Board refused.

Respondents then brought this action, seeking a declaratory judgment that the 60% requirements were unconstitutional as violative of the Fourteenth Amendment. * * * The West Virginia trial court dismissed the complaint. On appeal, the West Virginia Supreme Court of Appeals reversed, holding that the state constitutional and statutory 60% requirements violated the Equal Protection Clause of the Fourteenth Amendment. * * *

The court below relied heavily on two of our holdings dealing with limitations on the right to vote and dilution of voting power. The first was *Gray* v. *Sanders*, 372 U.S. 368 (1963) [p. 163], which held that Georgia's county-unit system violated the Equal Protection Clause, because the votes of primary electors in one county were accorded less weight than the votes of electors in other counties. The second was *Cipriano* v. *City of Houma*, 395 U.S. 701 (1969), in which we held impermissible the limitation to "property taxpayers" of the right to vote in a revenue bond referendum. From these cases the state court concluded that West Virginia's requirement was constitutionally defective, because the votes of these who favored the issuance of the bonds had a proportionately smaller impact on the outcome of the election than the votes of those who opposed issuance of the bonds.

We conclude that the West Virginia court's reliance on the *Gray* and *Cipriano* cases was misplaced. The defect this Court found in those cases lay in the denial or dilution of voting power because of group characteristics — geographic location and property ownership — that bore no valid relation to the interest of those groups in the subject matter of the election; moreover, the dilution or denial was imposed irrespective of how members of those groups actually voted.

Thus in *Gray*, we held that the county-unit system would have been defective even if unit votes were allocated strictly in proportion to population. We noted that if a candidate received 60% of the votes cast in a particular county he would receive that county's entire unit vote, the 40% cast for the other candidates being discarded. The defect, however, continued to be geographic discrimination. Votes for the losing candidates were discarded solely because of the county where the votes were cast. Indeed, votes for the winning candidate in a county were likewise devalued, because all marginal votes for him would be discarded and would have no impact on the statewide total.

Cipriano was no more than a reassertion of the principle, consistently recognized, that an individual may not be denied access to the ballot because of some extraneous condition, such as race, *e.g.*, *Gomillion* v. *Lightfoot*, 364 U.S. 339 (1960) [p. 115]; wealth, *e.g.*, *Harper* v. *Virginia State Board of Elections*, 383 U.S. 663 (1966) [p. 37]; tax status, *e.g.*, *Kramer* v. *Union Free School Dist.*, 395 U.S. 621 (1969) [p. 62]; or military status, *e.g.*, *Carrington* v. *Rash*, 380 U.S. 89 (1965) [p. 80].

Unlike the restrictions in our previous cases, the West Virginia Constitution singles out no "discrete and insular minority" for special treatment. The three-fifths requirement applied equally to all bond issues for any purpose, whether for schools, sewers, or highways. * * * [W]e can discern no independently identifiable group or category that favors bonded indebtedness over other forms of financing. Consequently no sector of the population may be said to be "fenced out" from the franchise because of the way they will vote.

Although West Virginia has not denied any group access to the ballot, it has indeed made it more difficult for some kinds of governmental actions to be taken. Certainly any departure from strict majority rule gives disproportionate power to the minority. But there is nothing in the language of the Constitution, our history, or our cases that requires that a majority always prevail on every issue. * * *

The Federal Constitution itself provides that a simple majority vote is insufficient on some issues; the provisions on impeachment and ratification of treaties are but two examples. Moreover, the Bill of Rights removes entire areas of legislation from the concept of majoritarian supremacy. The constitutions of many States prohibit or severely limit the power of the legislature to levy new taxes or to create or increase bonded indebtedness, thereby insulating entire areas from majority control. * * * It must be remembered that in voting to issue bonds voters are committing, in part, the credit of infants and of generations yet unborn, and some restriction on such commitment is not an unreasonable demand. That the bond issue may have the desirable objective of providing better education for future generations goes to the wisdom of an indebtedness limitation: it does not alter the basic fact that the balancing of interests is one for the State to resolve.

Wisely or not, the people of the State of West Virginia have long since resolved to remove from a simple majority vote the choice on certain decisions as to what indebtedness may be incurred and what taxes their children will bear.

We conclude that so long as such provisions do not discriminate against or authorize discrimination against any identifiable class they do not violate the Equal Protection Clause. We see no meaningful distinction between such absolute provisions on debt, changeable only by constitutional amendment, and provisions that legislative decisions on the same issues require more than a majority vote in the legislature. On the contrary, these latter provisions may, in practice, be less burdensome than the amendment process. Moreover, the same considerations apply when the ultimate power, rather than being delegated to the legislature, remains with the people, by way of a referendum. Indeed, we see no constitutional distinction between the 60% requirement in the present case and a state requirement that a given issue be approved by a majority of all registered voters.

That West Virginia has adopted a rule of decision, applicable to all bond referenda, by which the strong consensus of three-fifths is required before indebtedness is authorized, does not violate the Equal Protection Clause or any other provision of the Constitution.[6]

Reversed.

[Mr. Justice Harlan concurred in the result, arguing that the case represented a retreat from the majoritarianism exhibited in the one-person, one-vote cases, and hoping that "the day will come when the Court will frankly recognize the error of its ways in ever having undertaken to restructure state electoral processes." *Whitcomb* v. *Chavis*, 403 U.S. 124, 170 (1971) (separate opinion of Harlan, J.) [p. 268].]

Mr. Justice Brennan and Mr. Justice Marshall would affirm for the reasons expressed in the opinion of the West Virginia Supreme Court of Appeals, 170 S.E.2d 783 (W. Va. 1969).

Notes and Questions

1. Should the reasoning of *Gordon v. Lance* extend beyond bond measures to other types of legislation that does not commit "the credit of infants and of generations yet unborn"? Would it be constitutional for a minority of wealthy voters to block the majority from raising taxes? *See Brenner v. School District of Kansas*

---

[6] We intimate no view on the constitutionality of a provision requiring unanimity or giving a veto power to a very small group. Nor do we decide whether a State may, consistently with the Constitution, require extraordinary majorities for the election of public officers.

City, Missouri, 403 U.S. 913 (1971), *summarily aff'g* 315 F. Supp. 627 (W.D. Mo. 1970); *Santa Clara County Local Transportation Authority v. Guardino*, 902 P.2d 225 (Cal. 1995). Note that *Gordon* itself involved a super-majority requirement applicable both to bond indebtedness and taxation.

2.   Should it change the result if a super-majority was required to enact only a certain kind of bond, for example, bonds to finance road construction or schools, or bonds with interest rates exceeding a certain percentage? Would the answer depend on which kinds of bond were subject to the requirement? *See In re Contest of a Certain Special Election*, 659 P.2d 1294 (Ariz. Ct. App. 1982).

3.   Is there any constitutional limit to states' ability to insulate policy decisions from majority control? If a state prohibited amendments to its constitution, would it comport with the Equal Protection Clause?

4.   *Problem.* The West Dakota Constitution allows voters to recall officials elected statewide, but provides that such a recall will be successful only if it receives more affirmative than negative votes in a majority of the state's counties. Is the scheme constitutional? *Cf. Gray v. Sanders*, 372 U.S. 368 (1963) [p. 163].

MOORE v. OGILVIE
Supreme Court of the United States
394 U.S. 814, 89 S. Ct. 1493, 23 L. Ed. 2d 1 (1969)

Opinion of the Court by MR. JUSTICE DOUGLAS [in which MR. CHIEF JUSTICE WARREN, MR. JUSTICE BLACK, MR. JUSTICE BRENNAN, MR. JUSTICE WHITE, MR. JUSTICE FORTAS, and MR. JUSTICE MARSHALL join], announced by MR. JUSTICE BRENNAN.

[A]ppellants * * * are independent candidates for the offices of electors of President and Vice President of the United States from Illinois. * * * [They challenged the constitutionality of] a proviso added in 1935 to an Illinois statute requiring that at least 25,000 electors sign a petition to nominate such candidates. The proviso reads: "that included in the aggregate total of 25,000 signatures are the signatures of 200 qualified voters from each of at least 50 counties."

A three-judge District Court was convened, which, feeling bound by *MacDougall v. Green*, 335 U.S. 281 [(1948), which upheld this very statute against an equal-protection challenge], dismissed the complaint for failure to state a cause of action. * * *

MacDougall v. Green is indistinguishable from the present controversy. * * * Five members of the Court held in *MacDougall* that a State has "the power to assure a proper diffusion of political initiative as between its thinly populated counties and those having concentrated masses, in view of the fact that the latter have practical opportunities for exerting their political weight at the polls not available to the former." 335 U.S., at 284. * * *

When we struck down the Georgia county-unit system in statewide primary elections, we said:

"How then can one person be given twice or ten times the voting power of another person in a statewide election merely because he lives in a rural area or because he lives in the smallest rural county? Once the geographical unit for which a representative is to be chosen is designated, all who participate in the election are to have an equal vote — whatever their race, whatever their sex, whatever their occupation, whatever their income, and wherever their home may be in that geographical unit. This is required by the Equal Protection Clause of the Fourteenth Amendment." *Gray* v. *Sanders*, 372 U.S. 368, 379 [(1963)] [p. 163].

Reynolds v. *Sims*, 377 U.S. 533 [(1964)] [p. 173], held that a State in an apportionment of state representatives and senators among districts and counties could not deprive voters in the more populous counties of their proportionate share of representatives and senators. * * *

We have said enough to indicate why *MacDougall* v. *Green* is out of line with our recent apportionment cases. * * *

It is no answer to the argument under the Equal Protection Clause that this law was designed to require statewide support for launching a new political party rather than support from a few localities. This law applies a rigid, arbitrary formula to sparsely settled counties and populous counties alike, contrary to the constitutional theme of equality among citizens in the exercise of their political rights. The idea that one group can be granted greater voting strength than another is hostile to the one man, one vote basis of our representative government.

Under this Illinois law the electorate in 49 of the counties which contain 93.4% of the registered voters may not form a new political party and place its candidates on the ballot. Yet 25,000 of the remaining 6.6% of registered voters properly distributed among the 53 remaining counties may form a new party to elect candidates to office. This law thus discriminates against the residents of the populous counties of the State in favor of rural sections. It, therefore, lacks the equality to which the exercise of political rights is entitled under the Fourteenth Amendment.

MacDougall v. *Green* is overruled.

Reversed.

MR. JUSTICE STEWART, with whom MR. JUSTICE HARLAN joins, dissenting. * * *

* * * *Reynolds* v. *Sims* and its offspring at least involved situations in which the "debasement" or "dilution" of voting power found by the Court was the "certain" result of population variations among electoral districts. Under the Illinois statute now before us, however, no injury whatever is suffered by voters in heavily populated areas so long as their favored candidates are able to secure places on the ballot. And there is absolutely no indication in the record that the appellants could not, if they had made the effort, have easily satisfied Illinois' 50-county, 200-signature requirement. * * * The rationale of *Reynolds* v. *Sims* simply does not control this case. * * *

The Court held in *MacDougall* v. *Green*, in sustaining the very statutory requirement here at issue, that Illinois had pursued an "allowable State policy [of] requir[ing] that candidates for state-wide office should have support not limited to a concentrated locality." That conclusion seems to me to be no less sound today than it was at the time of the *MacDougall* decision. * * *

I respectfully dissent.

TOWN OF LOCKPORT v. CITIZENS FOR COMMUNITY ACTION AT THE LOCAL LEVEL, INC.
Supreme Court of the United States
430 U.S. 259, 97 S. Ct. 1047, 51 L. Ed. 2d 313 (1977)

MR. JUSTICE STEWART delivered the opinion of the Court [in which MR. JUSTICE BRENNAN, MR. JUSTICE WHITE, MR. JUSTICE MARSHALL, MR. JUSTICE BLACKMUN, MR. JUSTICE POWELL, MR. JUSTICE REHNQUIST, and MR. JUSTICE STEVENS join].

New York law provides that a new county charter will go into effect only if it is approved in a referendum election by separate majorities of the voters who live in the cities within the county, and of those who live outside the cities. A three-judge Federal District Court held that these requirements violate the Equal Protection Clause of the Fourteenth Amendment. * * *

In November 1972, a proposed charter for the county of Niagara was put to referendum. The charter created the new offices of County Executive and County Comptroller, and continued the county's existing power to establish tax rates, equalize assessments, issue bonds, maintain roads, and administer health and public welfare services. No explicit provision for redistribution of governmental powers from the cities or towns to the county government was made. The city voters approved the charter by a vote of 18,220 to 14,914. The noncity voters disapproved the charter by a vote of 11,594 to 10,665. A majority of those voting in the entire county thus favored the charter.

The appellees, a group of Niagara County voters, filed suit * * *, seeking a declaration that the New York constitutional and statutory provisions governing adoption of the charter form of county government are unconstitutional, and an order directing the appropriate New York officials to file the Niagara County charter as a duly enacted local law. A three-judge court was convened. Before its decision was announced, however, another new charter was put to referendum in Niagara County in November 1974. Again a majority of the city dwellers who voted approved the charter, a majority of the noncity voters disapproved it, and an aggregate majority of all those in the county who voted approved it. The District Court subsequently found the concurrent-majority requirements of the New York Constitution and the New York Municipal Home Rule Law violative of the Equal Protection Clause of the Fourteenth Amendment, and * * * decreed that the 1974 Charter "is in full force and effect as the instrument defining the form of local government for Niagara County." * * *

The equal protection principles applicable in gauging the fairness of an election involving the choice of legislative representatives are of limited relevance * * * in analyzing the propriety of recognizing distinctive voter interests in a "single-shot" referendum. In a referendum, the expression of voter will is direct, and there is no need to assure that the voters' views will be adequately represented through their representatives in the legislature. The policy impact of a referendum is also different in kind from the impact of choosing representatives — instead of sending legislators off to the state capitol to vote on a multitude of issues, the referendum puts one discrete issue to the voters. * * *

The argument that the provisions of New York law in question here are unconstitutional rests primarily on the premise that all voters in a New York county have identical interests in the adoption or rejection of a new charter, and that any distinction, therefore, between voters drawn on the basis of residence and working to the detriment of an identifiable class is an invidious discrimination. If the major premise were demonstrably correct — if it were clear that all voters in Niagara County have substantially identical interests in the adoption of a new county charter, regardless of where they reside within the county — the District Court's judgment would have to be affirmed under our prior cases. *Cipriano* v. *City of Houma*, [395 U.S. 701 (1969)]. That major premise, however, simply cannot be accepted. To the contrary, it appears that the challenged provisions of New York law rest on the State's identification of the distinctive interests of the residents of the cities and towns within a county rather than their interests as residents of the county as a homogeneous unit. This identification is based in the realities of the distribution of governmental powers in New York, and is consistent with our cases that recognize both the wide discretion the States have in forming and allocating governmental tasks to local subdivisions, and the discrete interests that such local governmental units may have *qua* units.

General-purpose local government in New York is entrusted to four different units: counties, cities, towns, and villages. The State is divided into 62 counties; each of the 57 counties outside of New York City is divided into towns, or towns and one or more cities. Villages, once formed, are still part of the towns in which they are located. The New York Legislature has conferred home rule and general governmental powers on all of these subdivisions, and their governmental activities may on occasion substantially overlap. * * *

The provisions of New York law here in question clearly contemplate that a new or amended county charter will frequently operate to transfer "functions or duties" from the towns or cities to the county, or even to "abolish one or more offices, departments, agencies or units of government." Although the 1974 Charter does not explicitly transfer governmental functions or duties from the towns to Niagara County, the executive-legislative form of government it provides would significantly enhance the county's organizational and service delivery capacity, for the purpose of "greater efficiency and responsibility in county government." The creation of the offices of County Executive and Commissioner of Finance clearly reflects this purpose. Such anticipated organizational changes, no less than explicit transfers of functions, could effectively shift any pre-existing balance of power between town and county governments toward county predominance. In terms of efficient delivery of government services, such a shift might be all to the good, but it may still be viewed as carrying a cost quite different for town voters and their existing town governments from that incurred by city voters and their existing city governments.

The ultimate question then is whether, given the differing interests of city and noncity voters in the adoption of a new county charter in New York, those differences are sufficient under the Equal Protection Clause to justify the classifications made by New York law. If that question were posed in the context of annexation proceedings, the fact that the residents of the annexing city and the residents of the area to be annexed formed sufficiently different constituencies with sufficiently different interests could be readily perceived. The fact of impending union alone would not so merge them into one community of interest as constitutionally to require that their votes be aggregated in any referendum to approve annexation. Similarly a proposal that several school districts join to form a consolidated unit could surely be subject to voter approval in each constituent school district.

Yet in terms of recognizing constituencies with separate and potentially opposing interests, the structural decision to annex or consolidate is similar in impact to the decision to restructure county government in New York. In each case, separate voter approval requirements are based on the perception that the real and long-term impact of a restructuring of local government is felt quite differently by the different county constituent units that in a sense compete to provide similar governmental services. Voters in these constituent units are directly and differentially affected by the restructuring of county government, which may make the provider of public services more remote and less subject to the voters' individual influence.

The provisions of New York law here in question no more than recognize the realities of these substantially differing electoral interests.[18] Granting to these provisions the presumption of constitutionality to which every duly enacted state and federal law is entitled, we are unable to conclude that they violate the Equal Protection Clause of the Fourteenth Amendment.

For the reasons stated in this opinion the judgment is reversed.

It is so ordered.

THE CHIEF JUSTICE [BURGER] concurs in the judgment [without opinion].

Notes and Questions

1. Is it appropriate to grant the New York laws at issue in *Citizens for Community Action* a "presumption of constitutionality"? *Compare Kramer v. Union Free School District No. 10*, 395 U.S. 621, 627–28 (1969) [p. 62].

2. Is it consistent with *Reynolds v. Sims* to structure the political process to allow for the representation of different interests? *Compare Citizens for Community Action* with Justice Stewart's dissenting opinion in *Lucas v. Forty-Fourth General Assembly of Colorado*, 377 U.S. 713 (1964), discussed and quoted at pages 186–188, *supra*.

---

[18] There is no indication that the classifications created by New York law work to favor city voter over town voter, or town voter over city voter. In some New York counties, city voters outnumber town voters; in other counties, the reverse is true. We are advised that of charters proposed in 14 counties, one failed to obtain majority approval of the city voters; two (including Niagara County) failed to obtain majority approval of noncity voters; eight failed to obtain a majority vote in either the towns or the cities; and three were approved by both city and town voters. * * *

3. Is *Citizens for Community Action* consistent with *Moore v. Ogilvie?*

4. *Problem.* For initiatives to appear on the ballot in Idaho, supporters must collect the signatures of six percent of the state's qualified voters, including six percent of the qualified voters in each of at least half of the state's forty-four counties. Are those requirements distinguishable from those in *Moore? See Idaho Coalition United for Bears v. Cenarrusa,* 342 F.3d 1073 (9th Cir. 2003). *See also Gallivan v. Walker,* 54 P.3d 1069 (Utah 2002).

Chapter 4

PRECLEARANCE UNDER SECTION 5 OF THE VOTING RIGHTS ACT

A. INTRODUCTION

Until 1964, Southern state officials bent on denying blacks political power could exact enormous costs on opposition forces simply by requiring plaintiffs to litigate. A plaintiff wishing to put a stop to unconstitutionally discriminatory limits on the right to vote, for example, would have to spend resources pursuing a court case. Even if successful in court, however, the state could simply replace the challenged law with another discriminatory one, and by staying one step ahead of plaintiffs, the state could significantly delay compliance.

In what was likely the most innovative aspect of the Voting Rights Act of 1965, Congress sought to correct this situation by "shift[ing] the advantage of time and inertia from the perpetrators of the evil to its victims." *South Carolina v. Katzenbach*, 383 U.S. 301, 328 (1966) [p. 14]. Instead of placing the burden on plaintiffs to demonstrate the unconstitutionality of election laws, § 5 of the VRA imposed upon certain governments the obligation to prove the laws' legality *before* those laws could go into effect. Under the preclearance provision, a state or political subdivision wishing to change its election laws must submit its proposed change to the Attorney General of the United States or obtain a declaratory judgment from the United States District Court for the District of Columbia. Under either route, preclearance will be granted and the proposed change will be permitted to take effect only if the change has neither the purpose nor the effect of "denying or abridging the right to vote on account of race or color." 52 U.S.C. § 10304. (The Act now applies as well to laws denying or abridging language minorities' right to vote. *See* 52 U.S.C. § 10303(f)(2).)

The preclearance provision does not apply to all changes to laws that conceivably may affect voting power. Rather, the preclearance obligation extends only to "voting qualification[s] or prerequisite[s] to voting, or standard[s], practice[s], or proce-dure[s] with respect to voting." 52 U.S.C. § 10304. Although the Supreme Court has recognized that this phrase implies some category of laws that need not be precleared, the Court has given it a broad interpretation, extending its coverage to such matters as the hours and locations of polling places, the drawing of district lines, whether certain government offices should be elective, and limitations on ballot access. *See Allen v. State Board of Elections*, 393 U.S. 544 (1969) [p. 226].

The preclearance provision is limited also in that it does not apply to the entire country. Its scope is restricted to "covered jurisdictions," which are identified in § 4(b) of the VRA, 52 U.S.C. § 10303(b), as those states or political subdivisions that used "tests or devices" in determining voter eligibility and in which fewer than 50% of the voting-age residents were registered or voted in the presidential elections of 1964, 1968, or 1972. The Act further defines a "test or device" as "any requirement that a person as a prerequisite for voting or registration for voting (1) demonstrate the ability to read, write, understand, or interpret any matter, (2) demonstrate any educational achievement or his knowledge of any particular subject, (3) possess good moral character, or (4) prove his qualifications by the voucher of registered voters or members of any other class." 52 U.S.C. § 10303(c).

As the Supreme Court has interpreted § 5, preclearance guards against "retrogression" — laws that reduce the political power of minority groups as compared to the power they held before the proposed change. *See Beer v. United States*, 425 U.S. 130 (1976) [p. 239]. Preclearance does not demand that states improve the lot of minorities, or even that minorities be given the power to which they are entitled by § 2 of the VRA, but simply that the proposed change not make the situation worse. If, however, the *purpose* of a proposed change (as distinguished from its effect) is to give minorities less political power than that to which they are entitled, preclearance should be denied. *See* 52 U.S.C. § 10304(c).

B. VOTING STANDARDS, PRACTICES, AND PROCEDURES

The preclearance procedure applies to only a subset of laws passed or administered by covered jurisdictions. Specifically, preclearance is required whenever a covered jurisdiction "shall enact or seek to administer any voting qualification or prerequisite to voting, or standard, practice, or procedure with respect to voting." 52 U.S.C. § 10304. There is little controversy as to the meaning of "voting qualification or prerequisite to voting," but the remaining statutory language has been the subject of important litigation.

Disputes concerning the meaning of "standard, practice, or procedure with respect to voting" confront two competing concerns. On the one hand, all manner of state and local laws can diminish the significance of the right to vote without directly stopping any person from casting a ballot. The Court has reasoned that the purposes of the Voting Rights Act would be undermined by an interpretation that permitted states to avoid its strictures through clever devices that formally did not involve voting. On the other hand, however, Congress did not intend to require *every* state and local law to be precleared. Requiring changes "with respect to voting," in other words, implied a desire to exempt some category of changes in laws not respecting voting. Exactly which laws comprise that category, however, has long been a matter of dispute, as the following cases attest.

ALLEN v. STATE BOARD OF ELECTIONS
Supreme Court of the United States
393 U.S. 544, 89 S. Ct. 817, 22 L. Ed. 2d 1 (1969)

MR. CHIEF JUSTICE WARREN delivered the opinion of the Court [in which MR. JUSTICE BRENNAN, MR. JUSTICE STEWART, MR. JUSTICE WHITE, and MR. JUSTICE FORTAS join, and in which MR. JUSTICE DOUGLAS and MR. JUSTICE MARSHALL join in relevant part]. * * *

Under § 5 [of the Voting Rights Act of 1965], if a State covered by the Act passes any "voting qualification or prerequisite to voting, or standard, practice, or procedure with respect to voting different from that in force or effect on November 1, 1964," no person can be deprived of his right to vote "for failure to comply with" the new enactment "unless and until" the State seeks and receives a declaratory judgment in the United States District Court for the District of Columbia that the new enactment "does not have the purpose and will not have the effect of denying or abridging the right to vote on account of race or color."

However, § 5 does not necessitate that a covered State obtain a declaratory judgment action before it can enforce any change in its election laws. It provides that a State may enforce a new enactment if the State submits the new provision to the Attorney General of the United States and, within 60 days of the submission, the Attorney General does not formally object to the new statute or regulation. The Attorney General does not act as a court in approving or disapproving the state legislation. If the Attorney General objects to the new enactment, the State may still enforce the legislation upon securing a declaratory judgment in the District Court for the District of Columbia. Also, the State is not required to first submit the new enactment to the Attorney General as it may go directly to the District Court for the District of Columbia. The provision for submission to the Attorney General merely gives the covered State a rapid method of rendering a new state election law enforceable. Once the State has successfully complied with the § 5 approval requirements, private parties may enjoin the enforcement of the new enactment only in traditional suits attacking its constitutionality; there is no further remedy provided by § 5.

In these four cases, the States have passed new laws or issued new regulations. The central issue is whether these provisions fall within the prohibition of § 5 that prevents the enforcement of "any voting qualification or prerequisite to voting, or standard, practice, or procedure with respect to voting" unless the State first complies with one of the section's approval procedures.

No. 25, *Fairley* v. *Patterson*, involves a 1966 amendment to § 2870 of the Mississippi Code of 1942. The amendment provides that the board of supervisors of each county may adopt an order providing that board members be elected at large by all qualified electors of the county. * * *

No. 26, *Bunton* v. *Patterson*, concerns a 1966 amendment to § 6271-08 of the Mississippi Code. The amendment provides that in 11 specified counties, the county superintendent of education shall be appointed by the board of education. Before the enactment of this amendment, all these counties had the option of electing or appointing the superintendent. * * *

No. 36, *Whitley* v. *Williams*, involves a 1966 amendment to § 3260 of the Mississippi Code, which changed the requirements for independent candidates running in general elections. The amendment makes four revisions: (1) it establishes a new rule that no person who has voted in a primary election may thereafter be placed on the ballot as an independent candidate in the general election; (2) the time for filing a petition as an independent candidate is changed to 60 days before the primary election from the previous 40 days before the general election; (3) the number of signatures of qualified electors needed for the independent qualifying petition is increased substantially; and (4) a new provision is added that each qualified elector who signs the independent qualifying petition must personally sign the petition and must include his polling precinct and county. * * *

In all three of these cases, the three-judge District Court ruled that the amendments to the Mississippi Code did not come within the purview of and are not covered by § 5, and dismissed the complaints. Appellants brought direct appeals to this Court.* * *

No. 3, *Allen* v. *State Board of Elections*, concerns a bulletin issued by the Virginia Board of Elections to all election judges. The bulletin was an attempt to modify the provisions of § 24-252 of the Code of Virginia of 1950 which provides, *inter alia*, that "any voter [may] place on the official ballot the name of any person *in his own handwriting. . . ."* The Virginia Code further provides that voters with a physical incapacity may be assisted in preparing their ballots. For example, one who is blind may be aided in the preparation of his ballot by a person of his choice. Those unable to mark their ballots due to any other physical disability may be assisted by one of the election judges. However, no statutory provision is made for assistance to those who wish to write in a name, but who are unable to do so because of illiteracy. When Virginia was brought under the coverage of the Voting Rights Act of 1965, Virginia election officials apparently thought that the provision in § 24-252, requiring a voter to cast a write-in vote in the voter's own handwriting was incompatible with the provisions of § 4(a) of the Act suspending the enforcement of any test or device as a prerequisite to voting. Therefore, the Board of Elections issued a bulletin to all election judges, instructing that the election judge could aid any qualified voter in the preparation of his ballot, if the voter so requests and if the voter is unable to mark his ballot due to illiteracy.

Appellants are functionally illiterate registered voters from the Fourth Congressional District of Virginia. They * * * clai[m] that [in requiring the voter's choice to be in his or her own handwriting] § 24-252 and the modifying bulletin violate the Equal Protection Clause of the Fourteenth Amendment and the Voting Rights Act of 1965. A three-judge court was convened and the complaint dismissed.* * *

These suits were instituted by private citizens; an initial question is whether private litigants may invoke the jurisdiction of the district courts to obtain the relief requested in these suits. * * *

The Voting Rights Act does not explicitly grant or deny private parties authorization to seek a declaratory judgment that a State has failed to comply with the provisions of the Act. However, § 5 does provide that "no person shall be denied the right to vote for failure to comply with [a new state enactment covered by, but not approved under, § 5]." Analysis of this language in light of the major purpose of the Act indicates that appellants may seek a declaratory judgment that a new state enactment is governed by § 5. Further, after proving that the State has failed to submit the covered enactment for § 5 approval, the private party has standing to obtain an injunction against further enforcement, pending the State's submission of the legislation pursuant to § 5.

The Act was drafted to make the guarantees of the Fifteenth Amendment finally a reality for all citizens. Congress realized that existing remedies were inadequate to accomplish this purpose and drafted an unusual, and in some aspects a severe, procedure for insuring that States would not discriminate on the basis of race in the enforcement of their voting laws.

The achievement of the Act's laudable goal could be severely hampered, however, if each citizen were required to depend solely on litigation instituted at the discretion of the Attorney General. For example, the provisions of the Act extend to States and the *subdivisions thereof.* The Attorney General has a limited staff and often might be unable to uncover quickly new regulations and enactments passed at the varying levels of state government. It is consistent with the broad purpose of the Act to allow the individual citizen standing to insure that his city or county government complies with the § 5 approval requirements. * * *

* * * The guarantee of § 5 that no person shall be denied the right to vote for failure to comply with an unapproved new enactment subject to § 5, might well prove an empty promise unless the private citizen were allowed to seek judicial enforcement of the prohibition. * * *

Finding that these cases are properly before us, we turn to a consideration of whether these state enactments are subject to the approval requirements of § 5. These requirements apply to "any voting qualification or prerequisite to voting, or standard, practice, or procedure with respect to voting. . . ." 42 U.S.C. § 1973c [now 52 U.S.C. § 10304 — Eds.]. The Act further provides that the term "voting" "shall include all action necessary to make a vote effective in any primary, special, or general election, including, but not limited to, registration, listing . . . or other action required by law prerequisite to voting, casting a ballot, and having such ballot counted properly and included in the appropriate totals of votes cast with respect to candidates for public or party office and propositions for which votes are received in an election." [52 U.S.C. § 10310(c)(1)]. Appellees in the Mississippi cases maintain that § 5 covers only those state enactments which prescribe who may register to vote. While accepting that the Act is broad enough to insure that the votes of all citizens should be cast, appellees urge that § 5 does not cover state rules relating to the qualification of candidates or to state decisions as to which offices shall be elective.

Appellees rely on the legislative history of the Act to support their view, citing the testimony of former Assistant Attorney General Burke Marshall before a subcommittee of the House Committee on the Judiciary:

> "Mr. CORMAN. We have not talked at all about whether we have to be concerned with not only who can vote, but who can run for public office and that has been an issue in some areas in the South in 1964. Have you given any consideration to whether or not this bill ought to address itself to the qualifications for running for public office as well as the problem of registration?

> "Mr. MARSHALL. The problem that the bill was aimed at was the problem of registration, Congressman. If there is a problem of another sort, I would like to see it corrected, but that is not what we were trying to deal with in the bill."

Appellees in No. 25 also argue that § 5 was not intended to apply to a change from district to at-large voting, because application of § 5 would cause a conflict in the administration of reapportionment legislation. They contend that under such a broad reading of § 5, enforcement of a reapportionment plan could be enjoined for failure to meet the § 5 approval requirements, even though the plan had been approved by a federal court. Appellees urge that Congress could not have intended to force the States to submit a reapportionment plan to two different courts.[29]

We must reject the narrow construction that appellees would give to § 5. The Voting Rights Act was aimed at the subtle, as well as the obvious, state regulations which have the effect of denying citizens their right to vote because of their race. * * * We are convinced that in passing the Voting Rights Act, Congress intended that state enactments such as those involved in the instant cases be subject to the § 5 approval requirements.

The legislative history on the whole supports the view that Congress intended to reach any state enactment which altered the election law of a covered State in even a minor way. For example, § 2 of the Act, as originally drafted, included a prohibition against any "qualification or procedure." During the Senate hearings on the bill, Senator Fong expressed concern that the word "procedure" was not broad enough to cover various practices that might effectively be employed to deny citizens their right to vote. In response, the Attorney General said he had no objection to expanding the language of the section, as the word "procedure" "was intended to be all-inclusive of any kind of practice." Indicative of an intention to give the Act the broadest possible scope, Congress expanded the language in the final version of § 2 to include any "voting qualifications or prerequisite to voting, or standard, practice, or procedure." [52 U.S.C. § 10301]. Similarly, in the House hearings, it was emphasized that § 5 was to have a broad scope[.] * * *

Also, the remarks of both opponents and proponents during the debate over passage of the Act demonstrate the Congress was well aware of another admonition of the Attorney General. He had stated in the House hearings that two or three types of changes in state election law (such as changing from paper ballots to voting machines) could be specifically excluded from § 5 without undermining the purpose of the section. He emphasized, however, that there were "precious few" changes that could be excluded "because there are an awful lot of things that could be started for purposes of evading the 15th amendment if there is the desire to do so." It is significant that Congress chose not to include even these minor exceptions in § 5, thus indicating an intention that all changes, no matter how small, be subjected to § 5 scrutiny.

In light of the mass of legislative history to the contrary, especially the Attorney General's clear indication that the section was to have a broad scope and Congress' refusal to engraft even minor exceptions, the single remark of Assistant Attorney

---

[29] Appellees in No. 3 also argue that § 5 does not apply to the regulation in their case, because that regulation was issued in an attempt to comply with the provisions of the Voting Rights Act. They argue that if § 5 applies to the Virginia regulation, covered States would be prohibited from quickly complying with the Act. We cannot accept this argument, however. A State is not exempted from the coverage of § 5 merely because its legislation is passed in an attempt to comply with the provisions of the Act. To hold otherwise would mean that legislation, allegedly passed to meet the requirements of the Act, would be exempted from § 5 coverage — even though it would have the effect of racial discrimination. It is precisely this situation Congress sought to avoid in passing § 5.

General Burke Marshall cannot be given determinative weight. Indeed, in any case where the legislative hearings and debate are so voluminous, no single statement or excerpt of testimony can be conclusive. * * *

The weight of the legislative history and an analysis of the basic purposes of the Act indicate that the enactment in each of these cases constitutes a "voting qualification or prerequisite to voting, or standard, practice, or procedure with respect to voting" within the meaning of § 5.

No. 25 involves a change from district to at-large voting for county supervisors. The right to vote can be affected by a dilution of voting power as well as by an absolute prohibition on casting a ballot. See *Reynolds* v. *Sims*, 377 U.S. 533, 555 (1964) [p. 173]. Voters who are members of a racial minority might well be in the majority in one district, but in a decided minority in the county as a whole. This type of change could therefore nullify their ability to elect the candidate of their choice just as would prohibiting some of them from voting.

In No. 26 an important county officer in certain counties was made appointive instead of elective. The power of a citizen's vote is affected by this amendment; after the change, he is prohibited from electing an officer formerly subject to the approval of the voters. Such a change could be made either with or without a discriminatory purpose or effect; however, the purpose of § 5 was to submit such changes to scrutiny.

The changes in No. 36 appear aimed at increasing the difficulty for an independent candidate to gain a position on the general election ballot. These changes might also undermine the effectiveness of voters who wish to elect independent candidates. One change involved in No. 36 deserves special note. The amendment provides that no person who has voted in a primary election may thereafter be placed on the ballot as an independent candidate in the general election. This is a "procedure with respect to voting" with substantial impact. One must forego his right to vote in his party primary if he thinks he might later wish to become an independent candidate.

The bulletin in No. 3 outlines new procedures for casting write-in votes. As in all these cases, we do not consider whether this change has a discriminatory purpose or effect. It is clear, however, that the new procedure with respect to voting is different from the procedure in effect when the State became subject to the Act; therefore, the enactment must meet the approval requirements of § 5 in order to be enforceable. * * *

In No. 3 the judgment of the District Court is vacated; in Nos. 25, 26, and 36 the judgments of the District Court are reversed. All four cases are remanded to the District Courts with instructions to issue injunctions restraining the further enforcement of the enactments until such time as the States adequately demonstrate compliance with § 5.

It is so ordered.

Mr. Justice Harlan, concurring in part and dissenting in part. * * *[1]

* * * It is best to begin by delineating the precise area of difference between the position the majority adopts and the one which I consider represents the better view of the statute. We are in agreement that in requiring federal review of changes in any "standard, practice, or procedure with respect to voting," Congress intended to include all state laws that changed the process by which voters were registered and had their ballots counted. The Court, however, goes further to hold that a State covered by the Act must submit for federal approval all those laws that could arguably have an impact on Negro voting power, even though the manner in which the election is conducted remains unchanged. I believe that this reading of the statute should be rejected on several grounds. It ignores the place of § 5 in the larger structure of the Act; it is untrue to the statute's language; and it is unsupported by the legislative history.

First, and most important, the Court's construction ignores the structure of the complex regulatory scheme created by the Voting Rights Act. The Court's opinion assumes that § 5 may be considered apart from the rest of the Act. In fact, however, the provision is clearly designed to march in lock-step with § 4 — the two sections cannot be understood apart from one another. Section 4 is one of the Act's central provisions, suspending the operation of all literacy tests and similar "devices" for at least five years in States whose low voter turnout indicated that these "tests" and "devices" had been used to exclude Negroes from the suffrage in the past. Section 5, moreover, reveals that it was not designed to implement new substantive policies but that it was structured to assure the effectiveness of the dramatic step that Congress had taken in § 4. The federal approval procedure found in § 5 only applies to those States whose literacy tests or similar "devices" have been suspended by § 4. As soon as a State regains the right to apply a literacy test or similar "device" under § 4, it also escapes the commands of § 5.

The statutory scheme contains even more striking characteristics which indicate that § 5's federal review procedure is ancillary to § 4's substantive commands. A State may escape § 5, *even though it has consistently violated this provision,* so long as it has complied with § 4, and has suspended the operation of literacy tests and other "devices" for five years. On the other hand, no matter how faithfully a State complies with § 5, it remains subject to its commands so long as it has not consistently obeyed § 4.

As soon as it is recognized that § 5 was designed solely to implement the policies of § 4, it becomes apparent that the Court's decision today permits the tail to wag the dog. * * * The fourth section of the Act had the profoundly important purpose of permitting the Negro people to gain access to the voting booths of the South once and for all. But the action taken by Congress in § 4 proceeded on the premise that once Negroes had gained free access to the ballot box, state governments would

---

[1] I concur in the Court's disposition of the complex jurisdictional issues these cases present. * * *

then be suitably responsive to their voice, and federal intervention would not be justified. * * *

The Court's construction of § 5 is even more surprising in light of the Act's regional application. For the statute, as the Court now construes it, deals with a problem that is national in scope. I find it especially difficult to believe that Congress would single out a handful of States as requiring stricter federal supervision concerning their treatment of a problem that may well be just as serious in parts of the North as it is in the South.[4]

The difficulties with the Court's construction increase even further when the language of the statute is considered closely.[7] When standing alone, the statutory formula requiring federal approval for changes in any "standard, practice, or procedure with respect to voting" can be read to support either the broad construction adopted by the majority or the one which I have advanced. But the critical formula does not stand alone. Immediately following the statute's description of the federal approval procedure, § 5 proceeds to describe the type of relief an aggrieved voter may obtain if a State enforces a new statute without obtaining the consent of the appropriate federal authorities: "no person shall be denied the right to vote *for failure to comply* with such qualification, prerequisite, standard, practice, or procedure." (Emphasis supplied.) This remedy serves to delimit the meaning of the formula in question. Congress was clearly concerned with changes in procedure with which voters could *comply*. But a law, like that in *Fairley* v. *Patterson*, No. 25, which permits all members of the County Board of Supervisors to run in the entire county and not in smaller districts, does not require a voter *to comply* with anything at all, and so does not come within the scope of the language used by Congress. * * *

The majority is left, then, relying on its understanding of the legislative history. With all deference, I find that the history the Court has garnered undermines its case, insofar as it is entitled to any weight at all. I refer not only to the unequivocal statement of Assistant Attorney General Burke Marshall, which the Court concedes to be diametrically opposed to the construction it adopts. For the lengthy testimony of Attorney General Katzenbach, upon which the Court seems to rely, actually provides little more support for its position. Mr. Katzenbach, unlike his principal

---

[4] Indeed, I would have very substantial constitutional difficulties with the statute if I were to accept such a construction.

[7] The Court seeks to strengthen its case by looking to the language of one of the definitional sections of the Act. Section 14(c)(1) defines the term "vote" or "voting" to "include all action necessary to make a vote *effective* in any primary, special, or general election, *including, but not limited to*, registration, listing pursuant to this Act, or other action required by law prerequisite to voting, casting a ballot, and having such ballot counted properly and included in the appropriate totals of votes cast with respect to candidates for public or party office and propositions for which votes are received in an election." (Emphasis supplied.) All of the aspects of voting that are enumerated in this definition concern the procedures by which voters are processed. When the statute cautions that its enumeration of stages in the election process is not exclusive, it merely indicates that the change of any other procedure that prevents the voter from having his ballot finally counted is also included within the range of the Act's concern. Surely the Court is entirely ignoring the textual context when it seeks to read the italicized phrases as embracing all electoral laws that affect the amount of political power Negroes will derive from the exercise of the franchise, even when the way in which voters are processed remains unchanged. [Relocated. — Eds.]

assistant, was never directly confronted with the question raised here, and we are left to guess as to his views. If guesses are to be made, however, surely it is important to note that though the Attorney General used many examples to illustrate the operation of § 5, each of them concerned statutes that had an immediate impact on voter qualifications or which altered the manner in which the election was conducted.[8] One would imagine that if the Attorney General believed that § 5 had the remarkable sweep the majority has now given it, one of his hypotheticals would have betrayed that fact.

Section 5, then, should properly be read to require federal approval only of those state laws that change either voter qualifications or the manner in which elections are conducted.

[Applying this standard, Mr. Justice Harlan concluded that preclearance was required in all of the cases under review except *Fairley* v. *Patterson*, No. 25, which involved a statute "giv[ing] each county the right to elect its Board of Supervisors on an at-large basis." In his view, the nomination process for independents was the "functional equivalent of the political primary," which was explicitly covered by the Act; making a formerly elective office appointive took away the right to vote for that office; and Virginia's regulations concerning illiterates' write-in votes "quite obviously altered the manner in which an election is conducted."]

[Mr. Justice Marshall, joined by Mr. Justice Douglas, concurred in most of the Court's opinion, but dissented as to an omitted portion giving only prospective relief in the Mississippi cases.]

Mr. Justice Black, dissenting.

Assuming the validity of the Voting Rights Act of 1965, as the Court does, I would agree with its careful interpretation of the Act, and would further agree with its holding as to jurisdiction and with its disposition of the four cases now before us. But I am still of the opinion that for reasons stated in my separate opinion in *South Carolina* v. *Katzenbach*, 383 U.S. 301, 355–362 (1966) [p. 14], a part of § 5 violates the United States Constitution. Section 5 * * * is reminiscent of old Reconstruction days * * *. The Southern States were at that time deprived of their right to pass laws on the premise that they were not then a part of the Union and therefore could be treated with all the harshness meted out to conquered provinces. The constitutionality of that doctrine was certainly not clear at that time. And whether the doctrine was constitutional or not, I had thought that the whole Nation had long since repented of the application of this "conquered province" concept, even as to the time immediately following the bitter Civil War. I doubt that any of the 13 Colonies would have agreed to our Constitution if they had dreamed that the time might come when they would have to go to a United States Attorney General or a District of Columbia court with hat in hand begging for permission to change their laws. Still less would any of these Colonies have been willing to agree to a Constitution that gave the Federal Government power to force one Colony to go

---

[8] The examples given by the Attorney General concerned changes in a State's voting age, residence, or property requirements; changes in the frequency that registrars' offices are open; and changes from paper ballots to machines or vice versa.

through such an onerous procedure while all the other former Colonies, now supposedly its sister States, were allowed to retain their full sovereignty. * * *

I would hold § 5 of the 1965 Voting Rights Act unconstitutional insofar as it commands certain selected States to leave their laws in any field unchanged until they get the consent of federal agencies to pass new ones.

Notes and Questions

1.   In what way can the regulations at issue in this case be characterized as "standard[s], practice[s], or procedure[s] with respect to voting"?

2.   It is important to understand that the issue in this case was only whether the regulations needed to go through the preclearance process. Changes in voting procedures in "covered jurisdictions" must be submitted for preclearance even if those regulations are not themselves discriminatory; indeed, the purpose of the preclearance process is to evaluate whether they are discriminatory before they take effect. Thus, in holding that preclearance was necessary for each of the regulations, the Court did *not* conclude that each of the regulations violated either the VRA or the Constitution.

3.   You know from reading Chapter 3 that states must redraw districts at least every 10 years to account for population shifts reported in the census. *Allen*, however, held that changes to voting procedures — including redrawn districts — may not go into effect until they have obtained preclearance. As a result, covered jurisdictions find themselves between a rock and a hard place, being constitutionally compelled to redraw districts but being unable to make such changes effective until the preclearance process is complete.

Perry v. Perez, 132 S. Ct. 934 (2012), presented such a dilemma. As a result of the 2010 census, Texas (a covered jurisdiction) received four additional congressional districts and was required to draw new district lines before the 2012 elections. The state passed a plan and submitted it to the D.C. District Court for preclearance, but there the process stalled. Not only was no timely decision on preclearance forthcoming, but the plan was challenged in a separate suit as violating the Constitution and § 2 of the Voting Rights Act for allegedly diluting the strength of minorities' votes. That suit likewise would not be resolved in time to make whatever adjustments would be required before the 2012 elections.

In reviewing the case, a nearly unanimous Supreme Court reaffirmed what it had earlier written in *Connor v. Finch*, 431 U.S. 407 (1977) — that where a state's existing districts have been rendered unconstitutional by a subsequent census, a federal district court must itself draw interim districts if the political process is unable to yield new districts on its own. Very well. But what standards should the district court use in crafting an interim plan? In particular, what consideration should be given to the plan that has been passed but that is awaiting preclearance?

The Court responded that even though such a plan may not have legal effect itself, it is an "important starting point" for the district court to use in devising an interim plan. "It provides important guidance that helps ensure that the district court appropriately confines itself to drawing interim maps that comply with the

Constitution and the Voting Rights Act, without displacing legitimate state policy judgments with the court's own preferences." *Perez*, 132 S. Ct. at 941.

Recall, however, that the state's new plan not only had not yet received preclearance; it had also been challenged as violating § 2 and the Equal Protection Clause. If the district court simply adopted the state's plan, it could be giving effect to an illegal or unconstitutional plan. If, on the other hand, the district court shied away from the state's plan, it would be preventing a state's policies from having effect simply because of an *allegation* of illegality — an action that would have federalism costs and would encourage the filing of meritless allegations in the future. Further, if the district court itself were to decide for itself whether the state's plan should be precleared, it would be usurping the role assigned by the VRA to the D.C. District Court and the Attorney General.

The Supreme Court's answer was that the district court should peek at the merits of the preclearance issue and any other challenges to the new districts, but should back away from actually deciding their legality. In the Court's words, "Where a State's plan faces challenges under the Constitution or § 2 of the Voting Rights Act, a district court should still be guided by that plan, except to the extent those legal challenges are shown to have a likelihood of success on the merits." *Id.* at 942. Similarly with regard to the preclearance issue, the state's plan should provide guidance to the district court except to the extent it contains elements "that stand a reasonable probability of failing to gain § 5 preclearance. And by 'reasonable probability' this Court means in this context that the § 5 challenge is not insubstantial." *Id.*

Eight members of the Court joined the *per curiam* opinion; Justice Thomas concurred in the judgment, arguing that § 5 was unconstitutional.

4.   Should at-large voting structures be considered diminutions of minority voting power? In an omitted portion of his opinion in *Allen*, Justice Harlan posited that "courts cannot intelligently compare" the benefits of an at-large system with those of one based on single-member districts: "Under one system, Negroes have *some* influence in the election of *all* officers; under the other, minority groups have *more* influence in the selection of *fewer* officers." 393 U.S. at 586 (Harlan, J., concurring in part and dissenting in part). Accordingly, he argued, the Supreme Court should have been reluctant to read the VRA as forcing courts to make such choices, as the D.C. District Court must do in deciding whether to grant preclearance to plans that switch from single-member to multi-member districts, or vice-versa.

5.   Are the relative benefits of at-large and single-member-district systems any harder to discern than are the relative benefits of elective and appointive offices? Recall that Justice Harlan was willing to require changes of the latter type to be precleared.

6.   Several states — including some covered jurisdictions — have recently passed laws requiring voters to show identification (often photo identification) at the polls. Critics charge that the laws disproportionately burden the elderly, the poor, and racial minorities. Nevertheless, the Supreme Court upheld one such law against a facial challenge, *see Crawford v. Marion County Election Bd.*, 553 U.S. 181 (2008)

[p. 1032]. The Bush Justice Department precleared Georgia's new photo-ID law in 2005, but the Obama Justice Department has denied preclearance to new laws in South Carolina and Texas, causing those states to seek preclearance in the D.C. District Court. Preclearance is pending for additional laws in Alabama, Mississippi, New Hampshire, and Virginia. According to the Justice Department in the Texas case, minorities are less likely than whites to possess IDs. Further, according to the Justice Department, obtaining an ID is likely to be more burdensome for minorities, who disproportionately lack access to cars — especially in counties not served by public transportation. Should such facts, if true, prevent those states from adopting such laws? *See* Daniel P. Tokaji, *If It's Broke, Fix It: Improving Voting Rights Act Preclearance*, 49 How. L.J. 785 (2006). If voter-ID laws do produce a discriminatory effect leading to denials of preclearance, does that affect the question of the VRA's constitutionality?

7.   Does the Court's construction of the Act raise questions about its constitutionality not resolved in *South Carolina v. Katzenbach*, 383 U.S. 301 (1966) [p. 14]? We will consider this question again later, in § D of this Chapter.

8.   *Problem.* Would the following actions require preclearance if passed in a covered jurisdiction?

   a.   A board of education passes a rule requiring its employees to take unpaid leaves of absence while they campaign for office. Would it matter in terms of the need for preclearance if the rule were passed one month after an employee — the first black person from the county to run for elective office in recent memory — declared his candidacy? What if the rule requires employees to take leaves of absence whenever they would be absent from their duties, rather than singling out absenteeism caused by an employee's campaign? *See Dougherty County Board of Education v. White*, 439 U.S. 32 (1978).

   b.   A county commission is restructured from a four-member body (with all four members being white) to a six-member body (including one black member). After the new commissioners take office, the commission reorganizes its members' responsibilities, reserving authority over the county's roads to the holdover white commissioners. What if a different county commission transfers authority over road construction from itself to a county engineer appointed by the commission? *See Presley v. Etowah County Commission*, 502 U.S. 491 (1992).

   c.   A county commission passes a resolution changing the commissioners' control over funds. Before the resolution, the county was divided into districts, with each commissioner having full control over the expenditure of money within his own district. Afterwards, the distribution of all money was to be controlled by the entire commission, meaning that expenditures would have to be approved by a majority of the commission and minority members could be outvoted. *See id.*

9.   The cases we have encountered thus far in this Chapter have involved the question whether certain types of laws required preclearance. They therefore focused on *what* the new law was. Later cases had to confront the *who* question. Specifically, covered jurisdictions must preclear voting changes, but not every

voting law *administered* by a covered jurisdiction is *enacted* by that jurisdiction. In *Lopez v. Monterey County*, 525 U.S. 266 (1999), the Supreme Court considered whether the County was required to preclear changes required by California state law. The County was a covered jurisdiction, but the state was not. The Court concluded that preclearance was required, even if the County did not exercise any discretion in implementing the state law. The Court relied on "the face of the [Voting Rights] Act itself" in holding that preclearance was required whenever a covered jurisdiction "seeks to administer" a voting change, whether or not that administration encompasses discretion. *Id.* at 278.

10.   But what if the covered jurisdiction "seeks to administer" a change that is required not by state law, but by a federal court? Again, the answer is complicated. Where the federal court is entirely responsible for the content of the change, the Court has created an exemption to the preclearance requirement. Because it would raise grave separation-of-powers concerns to require a federal court's decision to be precleared by the Attorney General or the D.C. District Court, *cf. Hayburn's Case*, 2 U.S. (2 Dall.) 409 (1792), the Court concluded that the federal court's plan need not be precleared. *See Connor v. Johnson*, 402 U.S. 690 (1971) (*per curiam*). *See also Lopez*, 525 U.S. at 286, 287 (describing *Connor* as exempting from preclearance those plans "crafted wholly by a federal district court in the first instance," and "wholly court-developed"). Where, however, the federal court orders a change that had been submitted to it by the covered jurisdiction, preclearance is necessary. *See McDaniel v. Sanchez*, 452 U.S. 130 (1981). Further, because *Connor*'s separation-of-powers concerns are absent when a voting change is ordered by a *state* court, such changes must be precleared. *See Branch v. Smith*, 538 U.S. 254, 262 (2003) (noting the lack of dispute on the point).

C.   RETROGRESSION

Once it is determined that a particular proposed change is "with respect to voting" and therefore requires preclearance, it becomes necessary to examine the standards by which the Attorney General or the D.C. District Court will decide to grant or deny preclearance. The VRA provides that preclearance should be granted only if the proposed change "does not have the purpose and will not have the effect of denying or abridging the right to vote on account of race or color." 52 U.S.C. § 10304. But what does it mean to "deny[]" or "abridg[e]" the right to vote? Specifically, what is the baseline against which to compare the proposed change? Should preclearance be denied only if the change makes the existing situation worse, *i.e.*, abridges voting power relative to the status quo? Or should preclearance be denied to any plan that fails to give racial groups the voting power to which they are entitled, even if the proposed change modestly improves the existing situation?

In *Beer v. United States*, 425 U.S. 130 (1976), which appears below, the Court interpreted "abridg[e]" to mean a reduction in voting power as compared to the status quo. Thus, a proposed change that had the effect of improving the political power of a racial group could not be said to have abridged it, even if neither the proposed plan nor the existing one gave the group the representation to which it was entitled.

Reno v. Bossier Parish School Board, 528 U.S. 320 (2000), applied *Beer* to hold that the "purpose" to discriminate proscribed by § 5 was a retrogressive purpose. Thus, after *Bossier Parish*, preclearance was to be denied only if a proposed change actually reduced a racial minority's voting power relative to the status quo, or was intended to do so.

Congress responded to overrule the Court's holding in *Bossier Parish*, but left the *Beer* holding intact. *See* 52 U.S.C. § 10304(c). As a result, the statute now provides that preclearance should be denied whenever a proposed change actually reduces a minority group's voting power relative to the status quo, or when it is intended to deprive a minority group of the voting power to which it is entitled. Thus, the "effect" inquiry uses the existing law as the baseline of comparison, while the "purpose" inquiry uses a hypothetical nondiscriminatory regime as its baseline.

BEER v. UNITED STATES
Supreme Court of the United States
425 U.S. 130, 96 S. Ct. 1357, 47 L. Ed. 2d 629 (1976)

Mr. Justice Stewart delivered the opinion of the Court [in which Mr. Chief Justice Burger, Mr. Justice Blackmun, Mr. Justice Powell, and Mr. Justice Rehnquist join].

Section 5 of the Voting Rights Act of 1965 prohibits a State or political subdivision subject to § 4 of the Act [including Louisiana and its political subdivisions] from enforcing "any voting qualification or prerequisite to voting, or standard, practice, or procedure with respect to voting different from that in force or effect on November 1, 1964," unless it has obtained a declaratory judgment from the District Court for the District of Columbia that such change "does not have the purpose and will not have the effect of denying or abridging the right to vote on account of race or color" or has submitted the proposed change to the Attorney General and the Attorney General has not objected to it. The constitutionality of this procedure was upheld in *South Carolina* v. *Katzenbach*, 383 U.S. 301 [(1964)] [p. 14], and it is now well established that § 5 is applicable when a State or political subdivision adopts a legislative reapportionment plan. *Allen* v. *State Board of Elections*, 393 U.S. 544 [(1968)] [p. 226]; *Georgia* v. *United States*, 411 U.S. 526 [(1973)].

The city of New Orleans brought this suit under § 5 seeking a judgment declaring that a reapportionment of New Orleans' councilmanic districts did not have the purpose or effect of denying or abridging the right to vote on account of race or color. The District Court entered a judgment of dismissal, holding that the new reapportionment plan would have the effect of abridging the voting rights of New Orleans' Negro citizens. The city appealed the judgment to this Court[.] * * *

New Orleans is a city of almost 600,000 people. Some 55% of that population is white and the remaining 45% is Negro. Some 65% of the registered voters are white, and the remaining 35% are Negro.[4] In 1954, New Orleans adopted a mayor-council form of government. Since that time the municipal charter has

---

[4] The difference in the two figures is due in part to the fact that proportionately more whites of voting age are registered to vote than are Negroes and in part to the fact that the age structures of the white and Negro populations of New Orleans differ significantly — 72.3% of the white population is of voting

provided that the city council is to consist of seven members, one to be elected from each of five councilmanic districts, and two to be elected by the voters of the city at large. The 1954 charter also requires an adjustment of the boundaries of the five single-member councilmanic districts following each decennial census to reflect population shifts among the districts.

In 1961, the city council redistricted the city based on the 1960 census figures. That reapportionment plan established four districts that stretched from the edge of Lake Pontchartrain on the north side of the city to the Mississippi River on the city's south side. The fifth district was wedge shaped and encompassed the city's downtown area. In one of these councilmanic districts, Negroes constituted a majority of the population, but only about half of the registered voters. In the other four districts white voters clearly outnumbered Negro voters. No Negro was elected to the New Orleans City Council during the decade from 1960 to 1970.

After receipt of the 1970 census figures the city council adopted a reapportionment plan (Plan I) that continued the basic north-to-south pattern of councilmanic districts combined with a wedge-shaped, downtown district. Under Plan I Negroes constituted a majority of the population in two districts, but they did not make up a majority of registered voters in any district. The largest percentage of Negro voters in a single district under Plan I was 45.2%. When the city submitted Plan I to the Attorney General pursuant to § 5, he objected to it, stating that it appeared to "dilute black voting strength by combining a number of black voters with a larger number of white voters in each of the five districts." * * *

Even before the Attorney General objected to Plan I, the city authorities had commenced work on a second plan — Plan II. That plan followed the general north-to-south districting pattern common to the 1961 apportionment and Plan I. It produced Negro population majorities in two districts and a Negro voter majority (52.6%) in one district. When Plan II was submitted to the Attorney General, he posed the same objections to it that he had raised to Plan I. In addition, he noted that "the predominantly black neighborhoods in the city are located generally in an east to west progression," and pointed out that the use of north-to-south districts in such a situation almost inevitably would have the effect of diluting the maximum potential impact of the Negro vote. Following the rejection by the Attorney General of Plan II, the city brought this declaratory judgment action in the United States District Court for the District of Columbia.

The District Court concluded that Plan II would have the effect of abridging the right to vote on account of race or color.[7] It calculated that if Negroes could elect city councilmen in proportion to their share of the city's registered voters, they would be able to choose 2.42 of the city's seven councilmen, and, if in proportion to their share of the city's population, to choose 3.15 councilmen.[8] But under Plan II

---

age, but only 57.1% of the Negro population is of voting age.

[7] The District Court did not address the question whether Plan II was adopted with such a "purpose."

[8] This Court has, of course, rejected the proposition that members of a minority group have a federal right to be represented in legislative bodies in proportion to their number in the general population. See *Whitcomb* v. *Chavis*, 403 U.S. 124, 149 [(1971)] [p. 268]. It is worth noting, however, that had the District Court applied its mathematical calculations to the five seats that were properly subject to its scrutiny, see *infra*, it would have concluded on the basis of registered voter figures that Negroes in New Orleans

the District Court concluded that, since New Orleans' elections had been marked by bloc voting along racial lines, Negroes would probably be able to elect only one councilman — the candidate from the one councilmanic district in which a majority of the voters were Negroes. * * *

As a separate and independent ground for rejecting Plan II, the District Court held that the failure of the plan to alter the city charter provision establishing two at-large seats had the effect in itself of "abridging the right to vote . . . on account of race or color." * * *

The appellants urge, and the United States * * * has conceded, that the District Court was mistaken in holding that Plan II could be rejected under § 5 solely because it did not eliminate the two at-large councilmanic seats that had existed since 1954. The appellants and the United States are correct in their interpretation of the statute in this regard.

The language of § 5 clearly provides that it applies only to proposed changes in voting procedures. "[D]iscriminatory practices . . . instituted prior to November 1964 . . . are not subject to the requirement of preclearance [under § 5]." The ordinance that adopted Plan II made no reference to the at-large councilmanic seats. * * * The at-large seats, having existed without change since 1954, were not subject to review in this proceeding under § 5.[10]

The principal argument made by the appellants in this Court is that the District Court erred in concluding that the makeup of the five geographic councilmanic districts under Plan II would have the effect of abridging voting rights on account of race or color. In evaluating this claim it is important to note at the outset that the question is not one of constitutional law, but of statutory construction. A determination of when a legislative reapportionment has "the effect of denying or abridging the right to vote on account of race or color," must depend, therefore, upon the intent of Congress in enacting the Voting Rights Act and specifically § 5.

The legislative history reveals that the basic purpose of Congress in enacting the Voting Rights Act was "to rid the country of racial discrimination in voting." *South Carolina* v. *Katzenbach*, 383 U.S., at 315. Section 5 was intended to play an important role in achieving that goal:

> "Section 5 was a response to a common practice in some jurisdictions of staying one step ahead of the federal courts by passing new discriminatory voting laws as soon as the old ones had been struck down. That practice had been possible because each new law remained in effect until the Justice Department or private plaintiffs were able to sustain the burden of proving that the new law, too, was discriminatory. . . . Congress therefore decided, as the Supreme Court held it could, 'to shift the advantage of time and inertia from the perpetrators of the evil to its victim,' by 'freezing

had a theoretical potential of electing 1.7 of the five councilmen. A realistic prediction would seem to be that under the actual operation of Plan II at least one and perhaps two Negro councilmen would in fact be elected.

[10] In reaching this conclusion, we do not decide the question reserved in *Georgia* v. *United States*, 411 U.S., [at] 535 n.7, whether a district in a proposed legislative reapportionment plan that is identical to a district in the previously existing apportionment may be subject to review under § 5. * * *

election procedures in the covered areas unless the changes can be shown to be nondiscriminatory.' " H.R. Rep. No. 94-196, pp. 57–58.

By prohibiting the enforcement of a voting-procedure change until it has been demonstrated to the United States Department of Justice or to a three-judge federal court that the change does not have a discriminatory effect, Congress desired to prevent States from "undo[ing] or defeat[ing] the rights recently won" by Negroes. H.R. Rep. No. 91-397, p.8. Section 5 was intended "to insure that [the gains thus far achieved in minority political participation] shall not be destroyed through new [discriminatory] procedures and techniques." S. Rep. No. 94-295, p. 19.

When it adopted a 7-year extension of the Voting Rights Act in 1975, Congress explicitly stated that "the standard [under § 5] can only be fully satisfied by determining on the basis of the facts found by the Attorney General [or the District Court] to be true whether the ability of minority groups to participate in the political process and to elect their choices to office is *augmented, diminished, or not affected* by the change affecting voting. . . ." In other words the purpose of § 5 has always been to insure that no voting-procedure changes would be made that would lead to a retrogression in the position of racial minorities with respect to their effective exercise of the electoral franchise.

It is thus apparent that a legislative reapportionment that enhances the position of racial minorities with respect to their effective exercise of the electoral franchise can hardly have the "effect" of diluting or abridging the right to vote on account of race within the meaning of § 5. We conclude, therefore, that such an ameliorative new legislative apportionment cannot violate § 5 unless the new apportionment itself so discriminates on the basis of race or color as to violate the Constitution.

The application of this standard to the facts of the present case is straightforward. Under the apportionment of 1961 none of the five councilmanic districts had a clear Negro majority of registered voters, and no Negro has been elected to the New Orleans City Council while that apportionment system has been in effect. Under Plan II, by contrast, Negroes will constitute a majority of the population in two of the five districts and a clear majority of the registered voters in one of them. Thus, there is every reason to predict, upon the District Court's hypothesis of bloc voting, that at least one and perhaps two Negroes may well be elected to the council under Plan II. It was therefore error for the District Court to conclude that Plan II "will . . . have the effect of denying or abridging the right to vote on account of race or color" within the meaning of § 5 of the Voting Rights Act.[14]

---

[14] It is possible that a legislative reapportionment could be a substantial improvement over its predecessor in terms of lessening racial discrimination, and yet nonetheless continue so to discriminate on the basis of race or color as to be unconstitutional. The United States has made no claim that Plan II suffers from any such disability, nor could it rationally do so.

There is no decision in this Court holding a legislative apportionment or reapportionment violative of the Fifteenth Amendment. The case closest to so holding is *Gomillion* v. *Lightfoot*, 364 U.S. 339 [(1960)] [p. 115][.] * * * But in at least four cases the Court has considered claims that legislative apportionments violated the Fourteenth Amendment rights of identifiable racial or ethnic minorities. *Fortson* v. *Dorsey*, 379 U.S. 433, 439 [(1965)]; *Burns* v. *Richardson*, 384 U.S. 73, 86–89 [(1966)]; *Whitcomb* v. *Chavis*, [*supra*], [at] 149; *White* v. *Regester*, 412 U.S. 755 [(1973)] [p. 274]. Plan II does not remotely approach a violation of the constitutional standards enunciated in those cases.

Accordingly, the judgment of the District Court is vacated, and the case is remanded to that court for further proceedings consistent with this opinion.

It is so ordered.

Mr. Justice Stevens took no part in the consideration or decision of this case.

Mr. Justice White, dissenting.

With Mr. Justice Marshall, I cannot agree that § 5 of the Voting Rights Act of 1965 reaches only those changes in election procedures that are more burdensome to the complaining minority than pre-existing procedures. As I understand § 5, the validity of *any* procedural change otherwise within the reach of the section must be determined under the statutory standard whether the proposed legislation has the purpose or effect of abridging or denying the right to vote based on race or color.

This statutory standard is to be applied here in light of the District Court's findings, which are supported by the evidence and are not now questioned by the Court. The findings were that the nominating process in New Orleans' councilmanic elections is subject to majority vote and "anti single-shot" rules and that there is a history of bloc racial voting in New Orleans, the predictable result being that no Negro candidate will win in any district in which his race is in the minority. In my view, where these facts exist, combined with a segregated residential pattern, § 5 is not satisfied unless, to the extent practicable, the new electoral districts afford the Negro minority the opportunity to achieve legislative representation roughly proportional to the Negro population in the community. Here, with a seven-member city council, the black minority constituting approximately 45% of the population of New Orleans would be entitled under § 5, as I construe it, to the opportunity of electing at least three city councilmen — more than provided by the plan at issue here. * * *

Applying § 5 in this way would at times require the drawing of district lines based on race; but Congress has this power where deliberate discrimination at the polls and the relevant electoral laws and customs have effectively foreclosed Negroes from enjoying a modicum of fair representation in the city council or other legislative body. * * *

Mr. Justice Marshall, with whom Mr. Justice Brennan joins, dissenting. * * *

Under the Court's reading of § 5, we cannot reach the abridgment question unless we have first determined that a proposed redistricting plan would "lead to a retrogression in the position of racial minorities" in comparison to their position under the existing plan. The Court's conclusion that § 5 demands this preliminary inquiry is simply wrong; it finds no support in the language of the statute and disserves the legislative purposes behind § 5. * * *

While the substantive reach of § 5 is somewhat broader than that of the Fifteenth Amendment in at least one regard — the burden of proof is shifted from discriminatee to discriminator — § 5 is undoubtedly tied to the standards of the

Constitution. Thus, it is questionable whether the "purpose and effect" language states anything more than the constitutional standard, and it is clear that the "denying or abridging" phrase does no more than directly adopt the language of the Fifteenth Amendment.

In justifying its convoluted construction of § 5, however, the Court never deals with the fact that, by its plain language, § 5 does no more than adopt, or arguably expand, the constitutional standard. Since it has never been held, or even suggested, that the constitutional standard requires an inquiry into whether a redistricting plan is "ameliorative" or "retrogressive," *a fortiori* there is no basis for so reading § 5. While the Court attempts to provide a basis by relying on the asserted purpose of § 5 to preserve present Negro voting strength[6] it is wholly unsuccessful. What superficial credibility the argument musters is achieved by ignoring not only the statutory language, but also at least three other purposes behind § 5.

Thus, the legislative history of the Voting Rights Act makes clear, and the Court assiduously ignores, that § 5 was designed to preclude new districting plans that "perpetuate discrimination," to prevent covered jurisdictions from "circumventing the guarantees of the 15th amendment" by switching to new, and discriminatory, districting plans the moment litigants appear on the verge of having an existing one declared unconstitutional, and promptly to end discrimination in voting by pressuring covered jurisdictions to remove all vestiges of discrimination from their enactments before submitting them for preclearance. None of these purposes is furthered by an inquiry into whether a proposed districting plan is "ameliorative" or "retrogressive."[12] Indeed, the statement of these purposes is alone sufficient to

---

[6] It may be that this single purpose looms so large to the Court because it thinks it would be counterproductive to bar enforcement of a proposed plan, even if discriminatory, that is at all less discriminatory than the pre-existing plan, which would otherwise remain frozen in effect. While this argument has superficial appeal, it is ultimately unrealistic because it will be a rare jurisdiction that can retain its pre-existing apportionment after the rejection of a modification by the Attorney General or District Court. Jurisdictions do not undertake redistricting without reason. In this case, for instance, the New Orleans City Charter requires redistricting every 10 years. If the plan before us now were disapproved, New Orleans would have to produce a new one or amend its charter. In other cases, redistricting will have been constitutionally compelled by our one-person, one-vote decisions. The virtual necessity of prompt redistricting argues strongly in favor of rejecting "ameliorative" but still discriminatory redistricting plans. The jurisdictions will eventually have to return with a nondiscriminatory plan.

[12] Today the Court finds it simple to conclude that Plan II is "ameliorative," but it will not always be so easy to determine whether a new plan increases or decreases Negro voting power relative to the prior plan. To the contrary, I believe the Court's test will prove unduly difficult of application and excessively demanding of judicial energies.

For instance, the Court today finds that an increase in the size of the Negro majority in one district, with a concomitant increased likelihood of electing a delegate, conclusively shows that Plan II is ameliorative. Will that always be so? Is it not as common for minorities to be gerrymandered into the same district as into separate ones? Is an increase in the size of an existing majority ameliorative or retrogressive? When the size of the majority increases in one district, Negro voting strength necessarily declines elsewhere. Is that decline retrogressive? [W]hen would an increase [in minority voting strength in a district] become retrogressive? As soon as the majority becomes "safe"? When the majority is achieved by dividing pre-existing concentrations of Negro voters?

* * * The Court's test will prove even more difficult of application outside the redistricting context. Some changes just do not lend themselves to comparison in positive or negative terms; others will always seem negative or positive no matter how good or bad the result. For instance, when a city goes from an

demonstrate the error of the Court's construction. * * *

Notes and Questions

1.   What is the basis for the Court's holding? Are you convinced?

2.   *Problem.* West Carolina, a covered jurisdiction, submits to the Attorney General a proposed change to its election laws that would keep the polls open an additional hour from 6:00 p.m. until 7:00 p.m. The purpose is to reduce lines at the polls and to make voting more convenient. Because a greater proportion of whites than blacks have jobs ending between 5:00 and 7:00, however, the effect of the change would be to dilute black voting strength by permitting a higher percentage of whites to vote than would be the case if polls closed at 6:00. Should the Attorney General grant preclearance?

3.   *Problem.* Georgia attempts to ensure against voter fraud by checking the accuracy of its lists of registered voters. The reports that alert the state to possible unregistered voters, however, generate thousands of false positives, requiring those persons to present proof of their eligibility to vote. A disproportionate number of those false positives affect minorities. The Supreme Court upheld the facial constitutionality of voter-ID requirements in *Crawford v. Marion County Election Board*, 553 U.S. 181 (2008), despite allegations that such requirements would disproportionately affect minorities. Should preclearance be granted?

4.   The Court in *Beer* held that because the districting plan was not retrogressive, it did not have the "effect of denying or abridging the right to vote." A nonretrogressive effect is not enough to satisfy § 5, though. The statute also demands that the change not have the "purpose . . . of denying or abridging the right to vote on account of race or color." 52 U.S.C. § 10304. Should this "purpose" requirement be interpreted to require a retrogressive purpose? The Court held so, in *Reno v. Bossier Parish School Board*, 528 U.S. 320 (2000), but Congress quickly overturned that interpretation.

In holding that the "purpose * * * of denying or abridging the right to vote" meant a retrogressive purpose, *Bossier Parish* not only followed *Beer*, but provided a rationale that might be better than the one in *Beer* itself: "The term 'abridge' * * * — whose core meaning is 'shorten' — necessarily entails a comparison. * * * In § 5 preclearance proceedings — which uniquely deal only and specifically with *changes* in voting procedures — the baseline is the status quo that is proposed to be changed." 528 U.S. at 333–34. Further, the Court provided a policy-based justification for its "retrogressive" interpretation: "To deny preclearance to a plan that is *not* retrogressive — *no matter how unconstitutional it may be* — would risk leaving in effect a status quo that is even worse." *Id.* at 336.

5.   Nevertheless, in 2006, Congress amended § 5 to overturn the *Bossier Parish*

---

appointed town manager to an elected council form of government, can the change ever be termed retrogressive, even if the new council is elected at large and Negroes are a minority? Or where a jurisdiction in which Negroes are a substantial minority switches from at-large to ward voting, can that change ever constitute a negative change, no matter how badly the wards are gerrymandered? * * * [Relocated. — Eds.]

holding. Title 52 U.S.C. § 10304(c) now provides that "purpose" in the preclearance provisions "shall include any discriminatory purpose." Thus, the VRA now provides that preclearance should be denied when a covered jurisdiction acts with a "discriminatory," albeit nonretrogressive, purpose, or with a retrogressive effect. Does the new provision render the preclearance requirement unconstitutional? *See* ABIGAIL THERNSTROM, VOTING RIGHTS — AND WRONGS: THE ELUSIVE QUEST FOR RACIALLY FAIR ELECTIONS 176–78 (2009); Nathaniel Persily, *The Promise and Pitfalls of the New Voting Rights Act*, 117 YALE L.J. 174, 217 n.165 (2007).

6. Retrogression is not always as simple as comparing the numbers of majority-minority districts in the challenged plan and the benchmark plan. The next case looks at Georgia's creation of "influence" districts and examines how they affect the retrogression analysis.

GEORGIA v. ASHCROFT
Supreme Court of the United States
539 U.S. 461, 123 S. Ct. 2498, 156 L. Ed. 2d 428 (2003)

JUSTICE O'CONNOR delivered the opinion of the Court [in which CHIEF JUSTICE REHNQUIST, JUSTICE SCALIA, JUSTICE KENNEDY, and JUSTICE THOMAS join].

In this case, we decide whether Georgia's [2001] State Senate redistricting plan should have been precleared under § 5 of the Voting Rights Act of 1965, 42 U.S.C. § 1973c [now 52 U.S.C. § 10304 — Eds.]. * * *

All parties here concede that the 1997 plan is the benchmark plan for this litigation because it was in effect at the time of the 2001 redistricting effort. The 1997 plan drew 56 districts, 11 of them with a total black population of over 50%, and 10 of them with a black voting age population of over 50%. The 2000 census revealed that these numbers had increased so that 13 districts had a black population of at least 50%, with the black voting age population exceeding 50% in 12 of those districts.

After the 2000 census, the Georgia General Assembly began the process of redistricting the Senate once again. No party contests that a substantial majority of black voters in Georgia vote Democratic, or that all elected black representatives in the General Assembly are Democrats. The goal of the Democratic leadership — black and white — was to maintain the number of majority-minority districts and also increase the number of Democratic Senate seats. * * * Part of the Democrats' strategy was not only to maintain the number of majority-minority districts, but to increase the number of so-called "influence" districts, where black voters would be able to exert a significant — if not decisive — force in the election process. * * *

The plan as designed by the Senate "unpacked" the most heavily concentrated majority-minority districts in the benchmark plan, and created a number of new influence districts. The new plan drew 13 districts with a majority-black voting age population, 13 additional districts with a black voting age population of between 30% and 50%, and 4 other districts with a black voting age population of between 25% and 30%. According to the 2000 census, as compared to the benchmark plan, the new plan reduced by five the number of districts with a black voting age population in excess of 60%. Yet it increased the number of majority-black voting age population districts by one, and it increased the number of districts with a black voting age population of between 25% and 50% by four. As compared to the benchmark plan enacted in 1997, the difference is even larger. Under the old census figures, Georgia had 10 Senate districts with a majority-black voting age population, and 8 Senate districts with a black voting age population of between 30% and 50%. The new plan thus increased the number of districts with a majority black voting age population by three, and increased the number of districts with a black voting age population of between 30% and 50% by another five.

The Senate adopted its new districting plan on August 10, 2001, by a vote of 29 to 26. Ten of the eleven black Senators voted for the plan. The Georgia House of Representatives passed the Senate plan by a vote of 101 to 71. Thirty-three of the thirty-four black Representatives voted for the plan. No Republican in either the House or the Senate voted for the plan, making the votes of the black legislators necessary for passage. The Governor signed the Senate plan into law on August 24, 2001, and Georgia subsequently sought to obtain preclearance [from the D.C. District Court]. * * * A three-judge panel of the District Court held that Georgia's State Senate apportionment violated § 5, and was therefore not entitled to preclearance. * * *

After the District Court refused to preclear the plan, Georgia enacted another plan, largely similar to the one at issue here, except that it added black voters to Districts 2, 12, and 26. The District Court precleared this plan. No party has contested the propriety of the District Court's preclearance of the Senate plan as amended. Georgia asserts that it will use the plan as originally enacted if it receives preclearance.

We noted probable jurisdiction to consider whether the District Court should have precleared the plan as originally enacted by Georgia in 2001, and now vacate the judgment below. * * *

Georgia argues that * * * its State Senate plan should be precleared because it does not lead to "a retrogression in the position of racial minorities with respect to their effective exercise of the electoral franchise." *Beer* v. *United States*, [425 U.S. 130,] 141 [(1976)] [p. 239].

While we have never determined the meaning of "effective exercise of the electoral franchise," this case requires us to do so in some detail. First, the United States and the District Court correctly acknowledge that in examining whether the new plan is retrogressive, the inquiry must encompass the entire statewide plan as a whole. Thus, while the diminution of a minority group's effective exercise of the electoral franchise in one or two districts may be sufficient to show a violation of § 5, it is only sufficient if the covered jurisdiction cannot show that the gains in the plan as a whole offset the loss in a particular district.

Second, any assessment of the retrogression of a minority group's effective exercise of the electoral franchise depends on an examination of all the relevant circumstances, such as the ability of minority voters to elect their candidate of choice, the extent of the minority group's opportunity to participate in the political process, and the feasibility of creating a nonretrogressive plan. See, *e.g.*, *Johnson* v. *De Grandy*, 512 U.S. 997, 1011–1012, 1020–1021 (1994) [p. 317]; *Thornburg* v.

Gingles, [478 U.S. 30,] 97–100 [(1986)] [p. 301] (O'CONNOR, J., concurring in judgment). "No single statistic provides courts with a shortcut to determine whether" a voting change retrogresses from the benchmark. *De Grandy*, *supra*, at 1020–1021.

In assessing the totality of the circumstances, a court should not focus solely on the comparative ability of a minority group to elect a candidate of its choice. While this factor is an important one in the § 5 retrogression inquiry, it cannot be dispositive or exclusive. The standard in § 5 is simple — whether the new plan "would lead to a retrogression in the position of racial minorities with respect to their effective exercise of the electoral franchise." *Beer*, 425 U.S., at 141.

The ability of minority voters to elect a candidate of their choice is important but often complex in practice to determine. In order to maximize the electoral success of a minority group, a State may choose to create a certain number of "safe" districts, in which it is highly likely that minority voters will be able to elect the candidate of their choice. Alternatively, a State may choose to create a greater number of districts in which it is likely — although perhaps not quite as likely as under the benchmark plan — that minority voters will be able to elect candidates of their choice.

Section 5 does not dictate that a State must pick one of these methods of redistricting over another. Either option "will present the minority group with its own array of electoral risks and benefits," and presents "hard choices about what would truly 'maximize' minority electoral success." On one hand, a smaller number of safe majority-minority districts may virtually guarantee the election of a minority group's preferred candidate in those districts. Yet even if this concentration of minority voters in a few districts does not constitute the unlawful packing of minority voters, such a plan risks isolating minority voters from the rest of the state, and risks narrowing political influence to only a fraction of political districts. And while such districts may result in more "descriptive representation" because the representatives of choice are more likely to mirror the race of the majority of voters in that district, the representation may be limited to fewer areas.

On the other hand, spreading out minority voters over a greater number of districts creates more districts in which minority voters may have the opportunity to elect a candidate of their choice. Such a strategy has the potential to increase "substantive representation" in more districts, by creating coalitions of voters who together will help to achieve the electoral aspirations of the minority group. It also, however, creates the risk that the minority group's preferred candidate may lose. * * * Section 5 gives States the flexibility to choose one theory of effective representation over the other.

In addition to the comparative ability of a minority group to elect a candidate of its choice, the other highly relevant factor in a retrogression inquiry is the extent to which a new plan changes the minority group's opportunity to participate in the political process. "The power to influence the political process is not limited to winning elections." *Thornburg* v. *Gingles*, *supra*, at 99 (O'CONNOR, J., concurring in judgment) (quoting *Davis* v. *Bandemer*, 478 U.S. 109, 132 (1986)); see also *White* v. *Regester*, 412 U.S. 755, 766–767 (1973) [p. 274]; *Whitcomb* v. *Chavis*, 403 U.S. 124, 149–160 (1971) [p. 368]; *Johnson* v. *De Grandy*, 512 U.S., at 1011–1012.

Thus, a court must examine whether a new plan adds or subtracts "influence districts" — where minority voters may not be able to elect a candidate of choice but can play a substantial, if not decisive, role in the electoral process. In assessing the comparative weight of these influence districts, it is important to consider "the likelihood that candidates elected without decisive minority support would be willing to take the minority's interests into account." *Id.*, at 100 (O'CONNOR, J., concurring in judgment). * * *

Section 5 leaves room for States to use * * * influence and coalitional districts. Indeed, the State's choice ultimately may rest on a political choice of whether substantive or descriptive representation is preferable. The State may choose, consistent with § 5, that it is better to risk having fewer minority representatives in order to achieve greater overall representation of a minority group by increasing the number of representatives sympathetic to the interests of minority voters. See [*id.*], at 87–89, 99.

In addition to influence districts, one other method of assessing the minority group's opportunity to participate in the political process is to examine the comparative position of legislative leadership, influence, and power for representatives of the benchmark majority-minority districts. * * * Indeed, in a representative democracy, the very purpose of voting is to delegate to chosen representatives the power to make and pass laws. The ability to exert more control over that process is at the core of exercising political power. A lawmaker with more legislative influence has more potential to set the agenda, to participate in closed-door meetings, to negotiate from a stronger position, and to shake hands on a deal. Maintaining or increasing legislative positions of power for minority voters' representatives of choice, while not dispositive by itself, can show the lack of retrogressive effect under § 5.

And it is also significant, though not dispositive, whether the representatives elected from the very districts created and protected by the Voting Rights Act support the new districting plan. * * * The representatives of districts created to ensure continued minority participation in the political process have some knowledge about how "voters will probably act" and whether the proposed change will decrease minority voters' effective exercise of the electoral franchise. * * *

Given the evidence submitted in this case, we find that Georgia likely met its burden of showing nonretrogression. * * * Section 5 gives States the flexibility to implement the type of plan that Georgia has submitted for preclearance — a plan that increases the number of districts with a majority-black voting age population, even if it means that in some of those districts, minority voters will face a somewhat reduced opportunity to elect a candidate of their choice. * * *

The purpose of the Voting Rights Act is to prevent discrimination in the exercise of the electoral franchise and to foster our transformation to a society that is no longer fixated on race. * * * While courts and the Department of Justice should be vigilant in ensuring that States neither reduce the effective exercise of the electoral franchise nor discriminate against minority voters, the Voting Rights Act, as properly interpreted, should encourage the transition to a society where race no longer matters: a society where integration and color-blindness are not just qualities to be proud of, but are simple facts of life.

The District Court is in a better position to reweigh all the facts in the record in the first instance in light of our explication of retrogression. The judgment of the District Court for the District of Columbia, accordingly, is vacated, and the case is remanded for further proceedings consistent with this opinion.

It is so ordered.

JUSTICE KENNEDY, concurring.

As is evident from the Court's accurate description of the facts in this case, race was a predominant factor in drawing the lines of Georgia's State Senate redistricting map. If the Court's statement of facts had been written as the preface to consideration of a challenge brought under the Equal Protection Clause or under § 2 of the Voting Rights Act of 1965, a reader of the opinion would have had sound reason to conclude that the challenge would succeed. Race cannot be the predominant factor in redistricting under our decision in *Miller* v. *Johnson*, 515 U.S. 900 (1995) [p. 369]. Yet considerations of race that would doom a redistricting plan under the Fourteenth Amendment or § 2 seem to be what save it under § 5.

I agree that our decisions controlling the § 5 analysis require the Court's ruling here. The discord and inconsistency between §§ 2 and 5 should be noted, however; and in a case where that issue is raised, it should be confronted. There is a fundamental flaw, I should think, in any scheme in which the Department of Justice is permitted or directed to encourage or ratify a course of unconstitutional conduct in order to find compliance with a statutory directive. This serious issue has not been raised here, and, as already observed, the Court is accurate both in its summary of the facts and its application of the controlling precedents. With these observations, I join the opinion of the Court.

JUSTICE THOMAS, concurring.

I continue to adhere to the views expressed in my opinion in *Holder* v. *Hall*, 512 U.S. 874, 891 (1994) [p. 335] (opinion concurring in judgment). I join the Court's opinion because it is fully consistent with our § 5 precedents.

JUSTICE SOUTER, with whom JUSTICE STEVENS, JUSTICE GINSBURG, and JUSTICE BREYER join, dissenting.

I agree with the Court that reducing the number of majority-minority districts within a State would not necessarily amount to retrogression barring preclearance under § 5 of the Voting Rights Act of 1965. The prudential objective of § 5 is hardly betrayed if a State can show that a new districting plan shifts from supermajority districts, in which minorities can elect their candidates of choice by their own voting power, to coalition districts, in which minorities are in fact shown to have a similar opportunity when joined by predictably supportive nonminority voters.

Before a State shifts from majority-minority to coalition districts, however, the State bears the burden of proving that nonminority voters will reliably vote along with the minority. It must show not merely that minority voters in new districts may have some influence, but that minority voters will have effective influence translatable into probable election results comparable to what they enjoyed under the existing district scheme. And to demonstrate this, a State must do more than produce reports of minority voting age percentages; it must show that the probable voting behavior of nonminority voters will make coalitions with minorities a real prospect. If the State's evidence fails to convince a factfinder that high racial polarization in voting is unlikely, or that high white crossover voting is likely, or that other political and demographic facts point to probable minority effectiveness, a reduction in supermajority districts must be treated as potentially and fatally retrogressive, the burden of persuasion always being on the State. * * *

The Court goes beyond recognizing the possibility of coalition districts as nonretrogressive alternatives to those with majorities of minority voters when it redefines effective voting power in § 5 analysis without the anchoring reference to electing a candidate of choice. It does this by alternatively suggesting that a potentially retrogressive redistricting plan could satisfy § 5 if a sufficient number of so-called "influence districts," in addition to "coalition districts" were created, or if the new plan provided minority groups with an opportunity to elect a particularly powerful candidate. On either alternative, the § 5 requirement that voting changes be nonretrogressive is substantially diminished and left practically unadministrable. * * *

The history of § 5 demonstrates that it addresses changes in state law intended to perpetuate the exclusion of minority voters from the exercise of political power. When this Court held that a State must show that any change in voting procedure is free of retrogression it meant that changes must not leave minority voters with less chance to be effective in electing preferred candidates than they were before the change. "The purpose of § 5 has always been to insure that no voting-procedure changes would be made that would lead to a retrogression in the position of racial minorities with respect to their effective exercise of the electoral franchise." *Beer* v. *United States*, 425 U.S., [at] 141. In addressing the burden to show no retrogression, therefore, "influence" must mean an opportunity to exercise power effectively.

The Court, however, says that influence may be adequate to avoid retrogression from majority-minority districts when it consists not of decisive minority voting power but of sentiment on the part of politicians: influence may be sufficient when it reflects a willingness on the part of politicians to consider the interests of minority voters, even when they do not need the minority votes to be elected. The Court holds, in other words, that there would be no retrogression when the power of a voting majority of minority voters is eliminated, so long as elected politicians can be expected to give some consideration to minority interests.

The power to elect a candidate of choice has been forgotten; voting power has been forgotten. It is very hard to see anything left of the standard of nonretrogression * * *.

Indeed, to see the trouble ahead, one need only ask how on the Court's new understanding, state legislators or federal preclearance reviewers under § 5 are supposed to identify or measure the degree of influence necessary to avoid the retrogression the Court nominally retains as the § 5 touchstone. Is the test purely *ad hominem*, looking merely to the apparent sentiments of incumbents who might run in the new districts? Would it be enough for a State to show that an incumbent had previously promised to consider minority interests before voting on legislative measures? Whatever one looks to, however, how does one put a value on influence that falls short of decisive influence through coalition? Nondecisive influence is worth less than majority-minority control, but how much less? Would two influence districts offset the loss of one majority-minority district? Would it take three? Or four? The Court gives no guidance for measuring influence that falls short of the voting strength of a coalition member, let alone a majority of minority voters. Nor do I see how the Court could possibly give any such guidance. The Court's "influence" is simply not functional in the political and judicial worlds.

Identical problems of comparability and administrability count at least as much against the Court's further gloss on nonretrogression, in its novel holding that a State may trade off minority voters' ability to elect a candidate of their choice against their ability to exert some undefined degree of influence over a candidate likely to occupy a position of official legislative power. The Court implies that one majority-minority district in which minority voters could elect a legislative leader could replace a larger number of majority-minority districts with ordinary candidates, without retrogression of overall minority voting strength. Under this approach to § 5, a State may value minority votes in a district in which a potential committee chairman might be elected differently from minority votes in a district with ordinary candidates.

It is impossible to believe that Congress could ever have imagined § 5 preclearance actually turning on any such distinctions. In any event, if the Court is going to allow a State to weigh minority votes by the ambitiousness of candidates the votes might be cast for, it is hard to see any stopping point. I suppose the Court would not go so far as to give extra points to an incumbent with the charisma to attract a legislative following, but would it value all committee chairmen equally? (The committee chairmen certainly would not.) And what about a legislator with a network of influence that has made him a proven dealmaker? Thus, again, the problem of measurement: is a shift from 10 majority-minority districts to 8 offset by a good chance that one of the 8 may elect a new Speaker of the House?

I do not fault the Court for having no answers to these questions, for there are no answers of any use under § 5. The fault is more fundamental, and the very fact that the Court's interpretation of nonretrogression under § 5 invites unanswerable questions points to the error of a § 5 preclearance regime that defies reviewable administration. We are left with little hope of determining practically whether a districting shift to one party's overall political advantage can be expected to offset a loss of majority-minority voting power in particular districts; there will simply be greater opportunity to reduce minority voting strength in the guise of obtaining party advantage.

One is left to ask who will suffer most from the Court's new and unquantifiable standard. If it should turn out that an actual, serious burden of persuasion remains on the States, States that rely on the new theory of influence should be guaranteed losers: nonretrogression cannot be demonstrated by districts with minority influence too amorphous for objective comparison. But that outcome is unlikely, and if in subsequent cases the Court allows the State's burden to be satisfied on the pretense that unquantifiable influence can be equated with majority-minority power, § 5 will simply drop out as a safeguard against the "unremitting and ingenious defiance of the Constitution" that required the procedure of preclearance in the first place.

Notes and Questions

1. In applying *Georgia v. Ashcroft*, how is one to know when a decrease in majority-minority districts has been offset by other increases in the political power of a minority group?

2. Did the 2001 Plan improve black voting strength over that experienced under the 1997 Plan? Is that a different question from asking whether the 2001 Plan improved *Democratic* voting strength?

3. Should this case have come out differently if the black legislative delegation were more evenly split on the wisdom of the 2001 Plan?

4. The 2006 amendments to the Voting Rights Act added a new provision, now codified at 52 U.S.C. § 10304(b), which provides, "Any voting qualification or prerequisite to voting, or standard, practice, or procedure with respect to voting that has the purpose of or will have the effect of diminishing the ability of any citizens of the United States on account of race or color, or [status as a language minority], to elect their preferred candidates of choice denies or abridges the right to vote within the meaning of" the statute, and should therefore result in a denial of preclearance. To what extent does the amendment overrule *Georgia v. Ashcroft*? *See* Abigail Thernstrom, Voting Rights — and Wrongs: The Elusive Quest for Racially Fair Elections 178–82 (2009); Nathaniel Persily, *The Promise and Pitfalls of the New Voting Rights Act*, 117 Yale L.J. 174, 216–51 (2007). Is it fair to characterize the amendment as placing covered jurisdictions in a "straitjacket" by requiring them to perform "a dual obligation: creating both majority-minority districts and maintaining those in which minority representation is increased by the potential for creating political coalitions in which black or Hispanic voters are a political force"? Thernstrom, *supra*, at 179.

5. Under the 2006 amendments, how is one to determine whether a change in an election law would have the effect of "diminishing [minorities' ability] to elect their preferred candidates of choice"? *Alabama Legislative Black Caucus v. Alabama*, 135 S. Ct. 1257 (2015), involved a redistricting plan put in place by the Alabama legislature. In an attempt to gain preclearance, the state attempted to ensure that the new plan not only preserved the number of majority-minority districts, but also minorities' voting strength within each majority-minority district. For example, if a district under the previous plan was 70% minority, the line-drawers attempted to ensure that the district would continue to be 70% minority. Otherwise, Alabama feared, the new plan would diminish minorities' voting strength. After all, as we have learned, because not all eligible voters turn out, and because of crossover votes, a slim population majority in a district hardly ensures that a group will be able to elect its candidates of choice. Thus, a reduction of minority population from 70% to, say, 55% in a district could diminish the minority's ability to elect its candidates of choice, even as the number of majority-minority districts was maintained.

The Supreme Court held that § 5 of the VRA was not so constraining. In the Court's view, the question of the diminishment of minority voting strength required a more "complex" analysis than simply a comparison of the percentage of minorities in a district before and after the district lines have been redrawn. *Id.* at 1273. Rather, it requires courts to "take account of all significant circumstances" bearing on minorities' voting power. *id.* Thus, while reducing the percentage of minorities in a district *might* decrease that group's ability to elect its preferred candidates, it might not.

In dissent, Justice Thomas criticized the Court's vague standard as "requir[ing] States to analyze race even *more* exhaustively, not less, by accounting for black voter registration and turnout statistics." *Id.* at 1288 (Thomas, J., dissenting). Is Justice Thomas correct that "States covered by § 5 have been whipsawed, first required to create 'safe' majority-black districts, then told not to 'diminis[h]' the ability to elect, and now told they have been too rigid in preventing and 'diminishing' of the ability to elect"? *Id.*

6.   In protesting the Court's entry into the "political thicket," Justices Frankfurter and Harlan argued that there are no judicially manageable standards for the allocation of political power. In particular, Justice Harlan's dissent in *Reynolds v. Sims*, 377 U.S. 533 (1964) [p. 173], which we encountered in Chapter 3, noted that

> cases of this type are not amenable to the development of judicial standards. No set of standards can guide a court which has to decide how many legislative districts a State shall have, or what the shape of the districts shall be, or where to draw a particular district line. No judicially manageable standard can determine whether a State should have single member districts or multi-member districts or some combination of both.

Id. at 621 (Harlan, J., dissenting). And in *Baker v. Carr*, 369 U.S. 186 (1962) [p. 119], which appears in Chapter 2, Justice Frankfurter argued that the Equal Protection Clause provided no judicially manageable standards against which to evaluate the constitutionality of apportionment decisions:

> Appellants invoke the right to vote and to have their votes counted. But they are permitted to vote, and their votes are counted. They go to the polls, they cast their ballots, they send their representatives to the state councils. Their complaint is simply that the representatives are not sufficiently numerous or powerful — in short, that Tennessee has adopted a basis of representation with which they are dissatisfied. Talk of "debasement" or "dilution" is circular talk. One cannot speak of "debasement" or "dilution" of the value of a vote until there is first defined a standard of reference as to what a vote should be worth. What is actually asked of the Court in this case is to choose among competing bases of representation — ultimately, really, among competing theories of political philosophy — in order to establish an appropriate frame of government for the State of Tennessee, and thereby for all the States of the Union.

Id. at 299–300 (Frankfurter, J., dissenting). Does the Court's difficulty in formulating a test for retrogression under § 5 prove that Justices Frankfurter and Harlan were correct?

D. THE CONSTITUTIONALITY OF SECTION 5 REVISITED

We saw in Chapter 1 that the Supreme Court upheld § 5 against a constitutional challenge shortly after the adoption of the Voting Rights Act. *South Carolina v. Katzenbach*, 383 U.S. 301 (1966) [p. 14]. The question of § 5's constitutionality would return to the Court more than 40 years later, after Congress in 2006 reauthorized the VRA for another 25 years but continued to use the same coverage formula that had been in place since 1975. Under that formula, a jurisdiction would be subject to preclearance if it had used voting tests and it had less than 50% voter registration or turnout in 1964, 1968, or 1972.

In *Northwest Austin Municipal Utility District No. One v. Holder*, 557 U.S. 193 (2009), the utility district, located in Texas, complained that Congress could not constitutionally require preclearance on the basis of an outdated coverage formula that rendered the state a covered jurisdiction. The Court dodged the constitutional issue, instead holding that the district was eligible to bail out of § 5's preclearance obligations if it could show that it met the requirements of 52 U.S.C. § 10303(a)(1): that within the preceding 10 years it has not used a voting test for the preceding 10 years, has not been denied preclearance, and has not been found guilty of other voting rights violations.

Even though the case thus turned on the statutory bailout question, the Court warned that Congress may have exceeded its constitutional power in passing the 2006 reauthorization:

> * * * Things have changed in the South. Voter turnout and registration rates now approach parity. Blatantly discriminatory evasions of federal decrees are rare. And minority candidates hold office at unprecedented levels.

> These improvements are no doubt due in significant part to the Voting Rights Act itself, and stand as a monument to its success. Past success alone, however, is not adequate justification to retain the preclearance requirements. It may be that these improvements are insufficient and that conditions continue to warrant preclearance under the Act. But the Act imposes current burdens and must be justified by current needs.

> The Act also differentiates between the States, despite our historic tradition that all the States enjoy "equal sovereignty." Distinctions can be justified in some cases. * * * But a departure from the fundamental principle of equal sovereignty requires a showing that a statute's disparate geographic coverage is sufficiently related to the problem that it targets.

557 U.S. at 202–03. In 2013, the Court faced another constitutional challenge to preclearance, this time by an Alabama county that was ineligible for bailout because it had been denied preclearance within the prior 10 years. The Court, therefore, was presented with the constitutional question that it had avoided in *Northwest Austin*.

SHELBY COUNTY, ALABAMA v. HOLDER
Supreme Court of the United States
570 U.S. __, 133 S. Ct. 2612 (2013)

CHIEF JUSTICE ROBERTS delivered the opinion of the Court [in which JUSTICE SCALIA, JUSTICE KENNEDY, JUSTICE THOMAS, and JUSTICE ALITO joined].

The Voting Rights Act of 1965 employed extraordinary measures to address an extraordinary problem. Section 5 of the Act required States to obtain federal permission before enacting any law relating to voting — a drastic departure from basic principles of federalism. And § 4 of the Act applied that requirement only to some States — an equally dramatic departure from the principle that all States enjoy equal sovereignty. This was strong medicine, but Congress determined it was needed to address entrenched racial discrimination in voting * * * . Reflecting the unprecedented nature of these measures, they were scheduled to expire after five years.

Nearly 50 years later, they are still in effect; indeed, they have been made more stringent, and are now scheduled to last until 2031. There is no denying, however, that the conditions that originally justified these measures no longer characterize voting in the covered jurisdictions. By 2009, "the racial gap in voter registration and turnout [was] lower in the States originally covered by § 5 than it [was] nationwide." *Northwest Austin Municipal Util. Dist. No. One v. Holder*, 557 U.S. 193, 203–04 (2009). Since that time, Census Bureau data indicate that African-American voter turnout has come to exceed white voter turnout in five of the six States originally covered by § 5, with a gap in the sixth State of less than one half of one percent.

At the same time, voting discrimination still exists; no one doubts that. The question is whether the Act's extraordinary measures, including its disparate treatment of the States, continue to satisfy constitutional requirements. As we put it a short time ago, "the Act imposes current burdens and must be justified by current needs." *Northwest Austin*, 557 U.S., at 203. * * *

In 1965, the States could be divided into two groups: those with a recent history of voting tests and low voter registration and turnout, and those without those characteristics. Congress based its coverage formula on that distinction. Today the Nation is no longer divided along those lines, yet the Voting Rights Act continues to treat it as if it were.

The Government's defense of the formula is limited. First, the Government contends that the formula is "reverse-engineered": Congress identified the jurisdictions to be covered and *then* came up with criteria to describe them. Under that reasoning, there need not be any logical relationship between the criteria in the formula and the reason for coverage; all that is necessary is that the formula happen to capture the jurisdictions Congress wanted to single out.

The Government suggests that [*South Carolina* v.] *Katzenbach* [383 U.S. 301 (1966)] [p. 14] sanctioned such an approach, but the analysis in *Katzenbach* was quite different. *Katzenbach* reasoned that the coverage formula was rational because the "formula . . . was relevant to the problem": "Tests and devices are relevant to voting discrimination because of their long history as a tool for perpetrating the evil; a low voting rate is pertinent for the obvious reason that widespread disenfranchisement must inevitably affect the number of actual voters." 383 U.S., at 329, 330.

Here, by contrast, the Government's reverse-engineering argument does not even attempt to demonstrate the continued relevance of the formula to the problem it targets. And in the context of a decision as significant as this one — subjecting a disfavored subset of States to "extraordinary legislation otherwise unfamiliar to our federal system," *Northwest Austin*, [557 U.S.,] at 211 — that failure to establish even relevance is fatal.

The Government falls back to the argument that because the formula was relevant in 1965, its continued use is permissible so long as any discrimination remains in the States Congress identified back then — regardless of how that discrimination compares to discrimination in States unburdened by coverage. This argument does not look to "current political conditions," *Northwest Austin*, *supra*, at 203, but instead relies on a comparison between the States in 1965. That comparison reflected the different histories of the North and South. It was in the South that slavery was upheld by law until uprooted by the Civil War, that the reign of Jim Crow denied African-Americans the most basic freedoms, and that state and local governments worked tirelessly to disenfranchise citizens on the basis of race. The Court invoked that history — rightly so — in sustaining the disparate coverage of the Voting Rights Act in 1966. See *Katzenbach*, *supra*, at 308 ("The constitutional propriety of the Voting Rights Act of 1965 must be judged with reference to the historical experience which it reflects.").

But history did not end in 1965. By the time the Act was reauthorized in 2006, * * * largely because of the Voting Rights Act, voting tests were abolished, disparities in voter registration and turnout due to race were erased, and African-Americans attained political office in record numbers. And yet the coverage formula that Congress reauthorized in 2006 ignores these developments, keeping the focus on decades-old data relevant to decades-old problems, rather than current data reflecting current needs.

The Fifteenth Amendment commands that the right to vote shall not be denied or abridged on account of race or color, and it gives Congress the power to enforce that command. The Amendment is not designed to punish for the past; its purpose is to ensure a better future. To serve that purpose, Congress — if it is to divide the States — must identify those jurisdictions to be singled out on a basis that makes sense in light of current conditions. It cannot rely simply on the past. We made that clear in *Northwest Austin*, and we make it clear again today. * * *

* * * The dissent [in attempting to justify the disparate coverage under § 4] relies on "second-generation barriers," which are not impediments to the casting of ballots, but rather electoral arrangements that affect the weight of minority votes. That does not cure the problem. Viewing the preclearance requirements as targeting such efforts simply highlights the irrationality of continued reliance on the § 4 coverage formula, which is based on voting tests and access to the ballot, not vote dilution. We cannot pretend that we are reviewing an updated statute, or try our hand at updating the statute ourselves, based on the new record compiled by

Congress. Contrary to the dissent's contention, we are not ignoring the record; we are simply recognizing that it played no role in shaping the statutory formula before us today. * * *

There is no valid reason to insulate the coverage formula from review merely because it was previously enacted 40 years ago. If Congress had started from scratch in 2006, it plainly could not have enacted the present coverage formula. It would have been irrational for Congress to distinguish between States in such a fundamental way based on 40-year-old data, when today's statistics tell an entirely different story. And it would have been irrational to base coverage on the use of voting tests 40 years ago, when such tests have been illegal since that time. But that is exactly what Congress has done. * * *

Our decision in no way affects the permanent, nationwide ban on racial discrimination in voting found in § 2. We issue no holding on § 5 itself, only on the coverage formula. Congress may draft another formula based on current conditions. Such a formula is an initial prerequisite to a determination that exceptional conditions still exist justifying such an "extraordinary departure from the traditional course of relations between the States and the Federal Government." Our country has changed, and while any racial discrimination in voting is too much, Congress must ensure that the legislation it passes to remedy that problem speaks to current conditions.

The judgment of the Court of Appeals is reversed.

It is so ordered.

JUSTICE THOMAS, concurring.

I join the Court's opinion in full but write separately to explain that I would find § 5 of the Voting Rights Act unconstitutional as well. * * *

While the Court claims to "issue no holding on § 5 itself," its own opinion compellingly demonstrates that Congress has failed to justify "current burdens" with a record demonstrating "current needs." By leaving the inevitable conclusion unstated, the Court needlessly prolongs the demise of that provision. For the reasons stated in the Court's opinion, I would find § 5 unconstitutional.

JUSTICE GINSBURG, with whom JUSTICE BREYER, JUSTICE SOTOMAYOR, and JUSTICE KAGAN join, dissenting.

In the Court's view, the very success of § 5 of the Voting Rights Act demands its dormancy. Congress was of another mind. Recognizing that large progress has been made, Congress determined, based on a voluminous record, that the scourge of discrimination was not yet extirpated. The question this case presents is who decides whether, as currently operative, § 5 remains justifiable, this Court, or a Congress charged with the obligation to enforce the post-Civil War Amendments "by appropriate legislation." With overwhelming support in both Houses, Congress concluded that, for two prime reasons, § 5 should continue in force, unabated. First, continuance would facilitate completion of the impressive gains thus far made; and second, continuance would guard against backsliding. Those assessments were well within Congress' province to make and should elicit this Court's unstinting approbation. * * *

Until today, in considering the constitutionality of the VRA, the Court has accorded Congress the full measure of respect its judgments in this domain should garner. *South Carolina v. Katzenbach* supplies the standard of review: "As against the reserved powers of the States, Congress may use any rational means to effectuate the constitutional prohibition of racial discrimination in voting." 383 U.S., at 324. Faced with subsequent reauthorizations of the VRA, the Court has reaffirmed this standard. *E.g.*, *City of Rome* [v. *United States*], 446 U.S. [156,] 178 [(1980)]. Today's Court does not purport to alter settled precedent establishing that the dispositive question is whether Congress has employed "rational means."

For three reasons, legislation reauthorizing an existing statute is especially likely to satisfy the minimal requirements of the rational-basis test. First, when reauthorization is at issue, Congress has already assembled a legislative record justifying the initial legislation. Congress is entitled to consider that preexisting record as well as the record before it at the time of the vote on reauthorization. This is especially true where, as here, the Court has repeatedly affirmed the statute's constitutionality and Congress has adhered to the very model the Court has upheld.

Second, the very fact that reauthorization is necessary arises because Congress has built a temporal limitation into the Act. It has pledged to review after a span of years (first 15, then 25) and in light of contemporary evidence, the continued need for the VRA.[1]

Third, a reviewing court should expect the record supporting reauthorization to be less stark than the record originally made. Demand for a record of violations equivalent to the one earlier made would expose Congress to a catch-22. If the statute was working, there would be less evidence of discrimination, so opponents might argue that Congress should not be allowed to renew the statute. In contrast, if the statute was not working, there would be plenty of evidence of discrimination, but scant reason to renew a failed regulatory regime.

This is not to suggest that congressional power in this area is limitless. It is this Court's responsibility to ensure that Congress has used appropriate means. The question meet for judicial review is whether the chosen means are "adapted to carry out the objects the amendments have in view." *Ex parte Virginia*, 100 U.S. 339, 346 (1880). The Court's role, then, is not to substitute its judgment for that of Congress, but to determine whether the legislative record sufficed to show that "Congress could rationally have determined that [its chosen] provisions were appropriate methods." *City of Rome*, 446 U.S., at 176–177. * * *

The 2006 reauthorization of the Voting Rights Act fully satisfies th[is] standard[.] * * *

I begin with the evidence on which Congress based its decision to continue the

---

[1] Although the preclearance provisions were reauthorized for twenty-five years, 52 U.S.C. § 10303(a)(7) provides that "[t]he Congress shall reconsider the provisions of this section at the end of the fifteen-year period following the effective date of the [2006] amendments * * * ." [— Eds.]

preclearance remedy. The surest way to evaluate whether that remedy remains in order is to see if preclearance is still effectively preventing discriminatory changes to voting laws. On that score, the record before Congress was huge. In fact, Congress found there were *more* DOJ objections between 1982 and 2004 (626) than there were between 1965 and the 1982 reauthorization (490).

All told, between 1982 and 2006, DOJ objections blocked over 700 voting changes based on a determination that the changes were discriminatory. Congress found that the majority of DOJ objections included findings of discriminatory intent and that the changes blocked by preclearance were "calculated decisions to keep minority voters from fully participating in the political process." On top of that, over the same time period the DOJ and private plaintiffs succeeded in more than 100 actions to enforce the § 5 preclearance requirements.

In addition to blocking proposed voting changes through preclearance, DOJ may request more information from a jurisdiction proposing a change. In turn, the jurisdiction may modify or withdraw the proposed change. The number of such modifications or withdrawals provides an indication of how many discriminatory proposals are deterred without need for formal objection. Congress received evidence that more than 800 proposed changes were altered or withdrawn since the last reauthorization in 1982. Congress also received empirical studies finding that DOJ's requests for more information had a significant effect on the degree to which covered jurisdictions "compl[ied] with their obligatio[n]" to protect minority voting rights.

Congress also received evidence that litigation under § 2 of the VRA was an inadequate substitute for preclearance in the covered jurisdictions. Litigation occurs only after the fact, when the illegal voting scheme has already been put in place and individuals have been elected pursuant to it, thereby gaining the advantages of incumbency. An illegal scheme might be in place for several election cycles before a § 2 plaintiff can gather sufficient evidence to challenge it. And litigation places a heavy financial burden on minority voters. Congress also received evidence that preclearance lessened the litigation burden on covered jurisdictions themselves, because the preclearance process is far less costly than defending against a § 2 claim, and clearance by DOJ substantially reduces the likelihood that a § 2 claim will be mounted. * * *

I turn next to the evidence on which Congress based its decision to reauthorize the coverage formula in § 4(b). Because Congress did not alter the coverage formula, the same jurisdictions previously subject to preclearance continue to be covered by this remedy. The evidence just described, of preclearance's continuing efficacy in blocking constitutional violations in the covered jurisdictions, itself grounded Congress' conclusion that the remedy should be retained for those jurisdictions. * * *

But, the Court insists, the coverage formula is no good; it is based on "decades-old data and eradicated practices." Even if the legislative record shows, as engaging with it would reveal, that the formula accurately identifies the jurisdictions with the worst conditions of voting discrimination, that is of no moment, as the Court sees it. Congress, the Court decrees, must "star[t] from scratch." I do not see why that should be so.[2]

Congress' chore was different in 1965 than it was in 2006. In 1965, there were a "small number of States . . . which in most instances were familiar to Congress by name," on which Congress fixed its attention. *Katzenbach*, 383 U.S., at 328. In drafting the coverage formula, "Congress began work with reliable evidence of actual voting discrimination in a great majority of the States" it sought to target. *Id.*, at 329. "The formula [Congress] eventually evolved to describe these areas" also captured a few States that had not been the subject of congressional factfinding. *Ibid.* Nevertheless, the Court upheld the formula in its entirety, finding it fair "to infer a significant danger of the evil" in all places the formula covered. *Ibid.*

The situation Congress faced in 2006, when it took up reauthorization of the coverage formula, was not the same. By then, the formula had been in effect for many years, and *all* of the jurisdictions covered by it were "familiar to Congress by name." *Id.*, at 328. The question before Congress: Was there still a sufficient basis to support continued application of the preclearance remedy in each of those already-identified places? There was at that point no chance that the formula might inadvertently sweep in new areas that were not the subject of congressional findings. And Congress could determine from the record whether the jurisdictions captured by the coverage formula still belonged under the preclearance regime. If they did, there was no need to alter the formula. * * *

[E]ven after 40 years and thousands of discriminatory changes blocked by preclearance, conditions in the covered jurisdictions demonstrated that the formula was still justified by "current needs." *Northwest Austin*, 557 U.S., at 203. * * * Although covered jurisdictions account for less than 25 percent of the country's population, * * * they accounted for 56 percent of successful § 2 litigation since 1982. Controlling for population, there were nearly *four* times as many successful § 2 cases in covered jurisdictions as there were in noncovered jurisdictions. [F]urther[,] § 2 lawsuits are more likely to succeed when they are filed in covered jurisdictions than in noncovered jurisdictions. From these findings — ignored by the Court — Congress reasonably concluded that the coverage formula continues to identify the jurisdictions of greatest concern. * * *

Congress was satisfied that the VRA's bailout mechanism provided an effective means of adjusting the VRA's coverage over time. Nearly 200 jurisdictions have successfully bailed out of the preclearance requirement, and DOJ has consented to every bailout application filed by an eligible jurisdiction since the current bailout procedure became effective in 1984. The bail-in mechanism has also worked. Several jurisdictions have been subject to federal preclearance by court orders, including the States of New Mexico and Arkansas.

This experience exposes the inaccuracy of the Court's portrayal of the Act as static, unchanged since 1965. Congress designed the VRA to be a dynamic statute, capable of adjusting to changing conditions. True, many covered jurisdictions have not been able to bail out due to recent acts of noncompliance with the VRA, but that truth reinforces the congressional judgment that these jurisdictions were rightfully subject to preclearance, and ought to remain under that regime. * * *

---

[2] This paragraph and the two that follow have been relocated. [— Eds.]

For the reasons stated, I would affirm the judgment of the Court of Appeals.

Notes and Questions

1.   The Court's holding striking down the coverage formula is grounded in "the principle that all States enjoy equal sovereignty" — a principle the Court deemed "highly pertinent in assessing * * * disparate treatment of States" by Congress. Using that principle, the Court held that the coverage formula could not stand unless the formula was at least a rational way of identifying states where voting discrimination was the most problematic. Is it appropriate to presume the unconstitutionality of laws that treat states differently? The dissent countered that it is common to treat states differently, and that the presumption should apply only in the context in which it was first developed — the entry of new states into the Union.

2.   The United States argued that the coverage formula resulted in identifying states with voting discrimination. The Court, however, held that it was not enough simply for the formula to result in outcomes that make some sense; rather, the formula itself must be "relevan[t] * * * to the problem it targets." That is, even if the covered jurisdictions happen to be the ones where voting discrimination is most prevalent currently, the voting data from 1964, 1968, and 1972 do not have anything to do with that fact.

Why should this make any difference? If a state has a vote-discrimination problem, why does it matter if Congress identified that state based on its history, the number of letters in the state's name, or the flip of a coin? Alternatively, would the constitutionality of § 5 be affected if Congress had specified the covered jurisdictions by name rather than relying on the coverage formula in § 4(b)? In other words, should it matter that the coverage formula relies on old data if those data still identify jurisdictions for which discrimination continues to be a problem?

3.   Is it appropriate for a court to defer to Congress's judgment that there have been few recent instances of overt discrimination in covered jurisdictions because § 5 has deterred potential violators? The Court rejected the deterrence argument because it would render § 5 "effectively immune from scrutiny; no matter how 'clean' the record of covered jurisdictions, the argument could always be made that it was deterrence that accounted for the good behavior." (slip op. at 17). The dissent argued that Congress's conclusions should be evaluated deferentially under the rational-basis test. Which side has the better of the argument? Would accepting deterrence allow Congress to escape limits on its power, or (as the dissent charged) would failing to accept a deterrence argument be "like throwing away your umbrella in a rainstorm because you are not getting wet" (slip op. at 33)?

4.   More generally, should Congress be able to assume that where there is smoke there is fire? That is, if Congress cannot point to many constitutional violations (because, for example, there is no showing of the jurisdiction's discriminatory intent), should it nonetheless be able to act on its belief that preclearance is necessary to prevent constitutional violations?

5.   As mentioned above in Note 3, the dissent argued that the 2006 reauthorization should be evaluated under the rational-basis test. The Court was not so clear

about whether the rationality standard or the congruence-and-proportionality standard from *City of Boerne v. Flores* was more appropriate. Rather, the Court held that the law failed to meet even the rationality standard, and so it was unnecessary to address whether a stricter standard might be more appropriate.

6. Would Congress have the power to apply the preclearance requirement throughout the entire country?

7. Perhaps the most striking aspect of *Shelby County* is the Court's refusal to engage in the debate about the proof of voting discrimination in the covered jurisdictions. Whereas the dissent at some length discusses Congress's evidence about "second-generation" barriers, DOJ objections, requests for more information, § 2 suits, and the like, the majority brushes off all those statistics by claiming that they do not relate to the coverage formula that Congress used in § 4. Is the Court correct to treat those data as beside the point? If Congress did update § 4 to rely on current conditions, and if it used § 2 suits as an indication of those current needs, would Congress be acting constitutionally or would Congress be exceeding its power because § 2 violations need not include discriminatory intent — a requirement for a violation of the Fourteenth and Fifteenth Amendments, which Congress would be attempting to enforce?

8. With the demise of the coverage formula in § 4 of the VRA, the bail-in provisions of § 3 have assumed greater prominence. According to § 3, "[i]f in any proceeding instituted by the Attorney General or an aggrieved person under any statute to enforce the voting guarantees of the Fourteenth or Fifteenth Amendment in any State or political subdivision the court finds that violations of the Fourteenth or Fifteenth Amendment justifying equitable relief have occurred within the territory of such State or political subdivision, the court, in addition to such relief as it may grant, shall retain jurisdiction for such period as it may deem appropriate and during such period" preclearance shall be required. 52 U.S.C. § 10302(c). *See generally* Travis Crum, Note, *The Voting Rights Act's Secret Weapon: Pocket Trigger Litigation and Dynamic Preclearance*, 119 YALE L.J. 1992 (2010).

Thus, § 3 permits a jurisdiction-by-jurisdiction identification of the places where preclearance is required, rather than the wholesale approach of § 4, which involved application of the formula struck down in *Shelby County*. Further, the decision whether to require preclearance under § 3 belongs with the courts. So far, most jurisdictions to have been bailed-in accepted that status through a consent decree. Only one jurisdiction — Arkansas — has been bailed-in without such an agreement. *See Jeffers v. Clinton*, 740 F. Supp. 585 (E.D. Ark. 1990).

Note that the bail-in procedure requires a finding of a constitutional violation — not simply a violation of the prophylactic guarantees of § 2, which protect minorities from laws that result in an abridgement of their ability to elect their candidates of choice. This standard will make it difficult for "aggrieved person[s]" to win a bail-in suit and requires the court to find intentional discrimination. But while it may be difficult to force a state or political subdivision to be bailed-in, perhaps it is not impossible.

Immediately after *Shelby County* was decided, intervenors in a case challenging redistricting in Texas moved to have that state bailed-in. *See* Defendant-

Intervenors' Motion for Leave to File Amended Answer and Counterclaim, *Texas v. United States*, No. 1:11-cv-1303 (D.D.C. July 3, 2013). The Department of Justice in a different case has joined in making the same argument. *See* Statement of Interest of the United States with Respect to Section 3(c) of the Voting Rights Act, *Perez v. Texas*, No. 5:11-cv-00360 (W.D. Tex. July 25, 2013); Charlie Savage & Adam Liptak, *Holder Wants Texas to Clear Voting Changes with the U.S.*, N.Y. Times (July 25, 2013), *available at* http://www.nytimes.com/2013/07/26/us/holder-wants-texas-to-clear-voting-changes-with-the-us.html?_r=0. The movants have argued that because Texas had earlier been found to have engaged in intentional discrimination in redistricting following the 2010 census, *Texas v. United States*, 887 F. Supp. 2d 133, 161, 166 (D.D.C. 2012), it is the paradigmatic example of the kind of jurisdiction that should be bailed-in. The cases are pending.

9.   In response to *Shelby County*, some members of Congress have introduced a bill that would amend the VRA's coverage formula and effect other changes. The bill is referred to as the Voting Rights Amendments Act of 2014, and both the bill and a summary are available at this link: https://beta.congress.gov/bill/113th-congress/house-bill/3899. The new coverage formula is based on a rolling 15-year calendar; states would be covered if they have committed five federal voting-rights violations within the preceding 15 years. Such a provision would cover only four states: Georgia, Louisiana, Mississippi, and Texas. (Political subdivisions would be covered if they have committed three federal statutory violations in the same 15-year period.) This rolling 15-year calendar was designed to address the *Shelby County* Court's insistence that Congress must be able to point to current evidence — and not just voting data from the 1964, 1968, and 1972 elections — to justify overriding the equal sovereignty of states.

The updated coverage formula might not solve the VRA's constitutional problems, however. In the first place, as stated above, preclearance under the amendment would be triggered by violations of federal statutory law, such as § 2 of the VRA — not merely violations of the federal constitution. Because those statutes sometimes prohibit laws that have a discriminatory effect and not just those laws that are motivated by a discriminatory purpose, states might be covered under the proposed VRA amendments without having committed constitutional violations. Similarly, the amendments would expand the bail-in provisions of § 3 to permit jurisdictions to be covered on the basis of statutory violations not necessarily indicative of discriminatory purpose.

Chapter 5

DISTRICTING BY RACE

A. INTRODUCTION

Preventing and remedying racial discrimination are the principal objectives of both the Voting Rights Act and the Civil War Amendments. As with race-conscious decisions concerning employment and school admissions, however, the use of race in electoral districting is controversial. Some argue that states (in drawing district lines) and Congress (in passing the VRA) should be able to protect minorities' interests by ensuring that they have an opportunity to influence the political process. Others, however, point to the use of race by government as constitutionally suspect, and argue that the goal of a color blind society is unlikely to be achieved if we promote racial and ethnic separatism by drawing district lines according to race and ethnicity.

In the next section of this Chapter, we examine the degree to which the Equal Protection Clause prevents states from minimizing the electoral influence of minorities. The one-person, one-vote doctrine and the constitutional protection of the right to vote ensure that members of minority groups have some access to the ballot. But granting an individual a vote does not ensure effective political power. Districts can be drawn to absorb minority voices within larger communities, resulting in those voices going unheard.

Constitutional challenges to the distribution of political power, however, contain an inherent difficulty: How much political power *should* any group possess? The Court has been consistent in holding that nothing in the Constitution entitles groups to representation proportional to their share of the population. Short of that standard, however, it is difficult or impossible to agree on another way to determine whether a given policy denies a group the power it is due. The Court has addressed this problem by holding that minorities may not prevail on a claim of vote dilution simply by showing a lack of success at the polls. Rather, a successful plaintiff must demonstrate that access to the political process more broadly has been hindered, or that minorities' electoral prospects have been minimized over a series of electoral cycles. Racial discrimination or burdensome registration requirements, for example, may comprise part of a state scheme that unconstitutionally dilutes minorities' political influence.

Such schemes are not unconstitutional, however, merely because they have the *effect* of diminishing minorities' political influence. Rather, as a plurality of the Court held in *City of Mobile v. Bolden*, 446 U.S. 55 (1980) [p. 288], the Fifteenth Amendment requires that plaintiffs prove both the disparate effect on minorities' political power and a discriminatory *purpose* on the part of the state.

Congress's reaction to *Bolden* forms the basis for the Section C of this Chapter. There we confront the 1982 amendments to § 2 of the Voting Rights Act, which replaced statutory language modeled on the Fifteenth Amendment (and therefore, *Bolden* held, required proof of both discriminatory purpose and effect) with a strictly effects-based test. The amended § 2 declares unlawful a state's voting practice or procedure "which results in a denial or abridgement of the right of any citizen of the United States to vote on account of race or color" or status as a member of a language minority. 52 U.S.C. § 10301(a). The statute further directs courts to find violations where, "based on the totality of circumstances, it is shown that the political processes leading to nomination or election in the State or political subdivision are not equally open to participation by members of a class of citizens protected by subsection (a) in that its members have less opportunity than other members of the electorate to participate in the political process and to elect representatives of their choice." 52 U.S.C. § 10301(b).

In *Thornburg v. Gingles*, 478 U.S. 30 (1986) [p. 301], the Court determined that plaintiffs in a § 2 suit must satisfy three "preconditions" before a court will proceed to the totality-of-the-circumstances test.

> First, the minority group must be able to demonstrate that it is sufficiently large and geographically compact to constitute a majority in a single-member district. * * * Second, the minority group must be able to show that it is politically cohesive. * * * Third, the minority must be able to demonstrate that the white majority votes sufficiently as a bloc to enable it * * * usually to defeat the minority's preferred candidate."

Id. at 50–51. The second and third requirements together are referred to as "racially polarized voting."

If a plaintiff can satisfy the three *Gingles* preconditions, the plaintiff still must demonstrate that, considering the totality of the circumstances, members of the plaintiff's minority group have an unequal opportunity "to participate in the political process and to elect representatives of their choice." 52 U.S.C. § 10301(b). In determining whether a minority group's opportunity is equal to that of other voters, courts will take into account whether the group controls a "roughly proportional" number of legislative seats compared to its population. *See Johnson v. De Grandy*, 512 U.S. 997, 1000 (1994) [p. 317]. As a result, § 2 will often require district line-drawers to ensure that minority groups comprise majorities in a sufficient number of districts.

Section D continues to examine § 2, concentrating on the section's scope. Section 2, like § 5, applies to "standard[s], practice[s], and procedure[s]," and in general the meaning of the § 2 phrase tracks the meaning of the corollary provision in § 5, which was covered in Chapter 4. Because the purposes of §§ 2 and 5 are different, however (§ 5 protects against retrogression, while § 2 protects minorities from laws that diminish their voting power relative to the strength they "should" possess), occasionally controversies arise, and we include two. In *Chisom v. Roemer*, 501 U.S. 380 (1991) [p. 325], the Court held that § 2's protection of the equal opportunity to elect "representatives" extended to vote-dilution claims as to judicial elections. The second controversy over the scope of § 2, *Holder v. Hall*, 512 U.S. 874 (1994) [p. 335], concerned the issue whether the size of a governmental body — concededly within the scope of § 5's preclearance requirement — could be the subject of a § 2 challenge. The Court held that it could not, though the five Justices agreeing on that conclusion were badly split as to rationale.

We return to the Equal Protection Clause in Section E. There, we consider the Court's racial-gerrymandering decisions that place limits on the power of states to allocate districts by race. *Shaw v. Reno*, 509 U.S. 630 (1993) [p. 354], established a constitutional cause of action for a gerrymander that segregates voters by race, and *Miller v. Johnson*, 515 U.S. 900 (1995) [p. 369], clarified that the constitutional violation occurs when the state disregards traditional districting criteria, such as the districts' compactness, in predominantly focusing on race.

The confluence of VRA § 2's command that states consider race in creating majority-minority districts and *Shaw*'s command that states not excessively consider race placed districters in a difficult position. Section E considers that quandary and additionally examines some recent cases in which minorities have exercised control or influence over an electoral district despite not amounting to a majority of the district's population. The Court has held, consistent with *Gingles*'s language, that § 2 provides no right to minorities unless they are large enough to comprise a majority in a single member district. *See Bartlett v. Strickland*, 556 U.S. 1 (2009). States may decide for themselves to create such "influence" or "coalition" districts, however. In "influence" districts, minorities do not have the ability to elect their preferred candidates, but can influence the choice of candidates. In "coalition" districts, minorities do elect their candidates of choice, but with the assistance of majority "crossover" voters who vote for the minority's preferred candidate. The power minorities exercise in such districts may be relevant to determining whether a state has violated § 2 or § 5 in depriving minority voters of the political power to which they are entitled. *See Georgia v. Ashcroft*, 539 U.S. 461 (2003) [p. 246].

B.   CONSTITUTIONAL CONSTRAINTS ON MINORITY VOTE DILUTION

We saw as early as Chapter 2, when we considered *Gomillion v. Lightfoot*, 364 U.S. 339 (1960) [p. 115], that the Constitution limits government's ability to draw electoral districts so as to minimize the political power of minorities. Because *Gomillion*'s rationale was difficult to determine, however, it remained unclear exactly what showing would be necessary to prove that a districting scheme abridged the constitutional right to vote. The fundamental problem in articulating such a standard is the same problem we saw in Chapter 2, namely, that it is necessary to establish a baseline representing the political power that a group should enjoy before it is possible to determine whether a law "dilutes" that amount.

In a series of cases in the 1970s, the Court attempted to clarify the constitutional protection against vote dilution. The Court was unwilling to accept one potential baseline — that the Constitution entitles groups to legislative representation commensurate with their share of the population. In the Court's view, all political groups should bear the risks that come with politics — that the popularity of candidates and parties varies from year to year, for example, and accordingly no group should be guaranteed a proportional share of representation when such a guarantee would free those groups from fielding popular candidates and appealing to voters. The Court also did not want to limit its consideration of political influence to a group's ability to elect its favored candidates. Political power, said the Court, was more nuanced than simple vote totals. Accordingly, in *White v. Regester*, 412 U.S. 755, 766 (1973) [p. 274], the Court held that a vote-dilution claim can succeed only when the plaintiffs demonstrate that they "had less opportunity than did other residents in the district to participate in the political process and to elect legislators of their choice."

In *City of Mobile v. Bolden*, 446 U.S. 55 (1980) [p. 288], a plurality of the Court held that plaintiffs must show not only that the challenged law had the effect of disproportionately reducing the political power of the disfavored group, but also that the law was motivated by a discriminatory purpose. Congress reacted to *Bolden* by amending § 2 of the Voting Rights Act to forbid states from taking actions that had the effect of diluting the political power of minorities, regardless of the purpose for taking those actions. That amendment is the subject of the next section.

WHITCOMB v. CHAVIS
Supreme Court of the United States
403 U.S. 124, 91 S. Ct. 1858, 29 L. Ed. 2d 363 (1971)

MR. JUSTICE WHITE delivered the opinion of the Court [in which MR. CHIEF JUSTICE BURGER, MR. JUSTICE BLACK, MR. JUSTICE STEWART, and MR. JUSTICE BLACKMUN join.] * * *

Indiana has a bicameral general assembly consisting of a house of representatives of 100 members and a senate of 50 members. Eight of the 31 senatorial districts and 25 of the 39 house districts are multi-member districts, that is, districts that are represented by two or more legislators elected at large by the voters of the district. Under the statutes here challenged, Marion County is a multi-member district electing eight senators and 15 members of the house. * * *

Plaintiffs level two quite distinct challenges to the Marion County district. The first charge is that any multi-member district bestows on its voters several unconstitutional advantages over voters in single-member districts or smaller multi-member districts. The other allegation is that the Marion County district, on the record of this case, illegally minimizes and cancels out the voting power of a cognizable racial minority in Marion County. The District Court sustained the latter claim and considered the former sufficiently persuasive to be a substantial factor in prescribing uniform, single-member districts as the basic scheme of the court's own plan.[a] * * *

The question of the constitutional validity of multi-member districts has been pressed in this Court since the first of the modern reapportionment cases. * * * [S]uch a district is not *per se* illegal under the Equal Protection Clause. *Fortson* v. *Dorsey*, 379 U.S. 433 (1965); *Burns* v. *Richardson*, 384 U.S. 73 (1966); *Kilgarlin* v. *Hill*, 386 U.S. 120 (1967). That voters in multi-member districts vote for and are represented by more legislators than voters in single-member districts has so far

---

[a] This paragraph has been relocated. [— Eds.]

not demonstrated an invidious discrimination against the latter. But we have deemed the validity of multi-member district systems justiciable, recognizing also that they may be subject to challenge where the circumstances of a particular case may "operate to minimize or cancel out the voting strength of racial or political elements of the voting population." *Fortson*, 379 U.S., at 439, and *Burns*, 384 U.S., at 88. Such a tendency, we have said, is enhanced when the district is large and elects a substantial proportion of the seats in either house of a bicameral legislature, if it is multi-member for both houses of the legislature or if it lacks provision for at-large candidates running from particular geographical subdistricts, as in *Fortson*. *Burns*, 384 U.S., at 88. But we have insisted that the challenger carry the burden of proving that multi-member districts unconstitutionally operate to dilute or cancel the voting strength of racial or political elements. We have not yet sustained such an attack. * * *

In asserting discrimination against voters outside Marion County, plaintiffs recognize that *Fortson, Burns,* and *Kilgarlin* proceeded on the assumption that the dilution of voting power suffered by a voter who is placed in a district 10 times the population of another is cured by allocating 10 legislators to the larger district instead of the one assigned to the smaller district. Plaintiffs challenge this assumption at both the voter and legislator level. They demonstrate mathematically that in theory voting power does not vary inversely with the size of the district and that to increase legislative seats in proportion to increased population gives undue voting power to the voter in the multimember district since he has more chances to determine election outcomes than does the voter in the single-member district. [The theory analyzes the chance of any particular voter in a district casting a tie-breaking or "critical" vote. Because voters in multi-member districts can determine the election of multiple representatives, their ability to cast a "critical" vote is enhanced.] This consequence obtains wholly aside from the quality or effectiveness of representation later furnished by the successful candidates. The District Court did not quarrel with plaintiffs' mathematics, nor do we. But like the District Court we note that the position remains a theoretical one and, as plaintiffs' witness conceded, knowingly avoids and does "not take into account any political or other factors which might affect the actual voting power of the residents, which might include party affiliation, race, previous voting characteristics or any other factors which go into the entire political voting situation." The real-life impact of multi-member districts on individual voting power has not been sufficiently demonstrated, at least on this record, to warrant departure from prior cases.

The District Court was more impressed with the other branch of the claim that multi-member districts inherently discriminate against other districts. This was the assertion that whatever the individual voting power of Marion County voters in choosing legislators may be, they nevertheless have more effective representation in the Indiana general assembly for two reasons. First, each voter is represented by more legislators and therefore, in theory at least, has more chances to influence critical legislative votes. Second, since multimember delegations are elected at large and represent the voters of the entire district, they tend to vote as a bloc, which is tantamount to the district having one representative with several votes. * * *

We are not ready, however, to agree that multi-member districts, wherever they exist, overrepresent their voters as compared with voters in single-member districts, even if the multi-member delegation tends to bloc voting. The theory that plural representation itself unduly enhances a district's power and the influence of its voters remains to be demonstrated in practice and in the day-to-day operation of the legislature. * * *

* * * Moreover, Marion County would have no less advantage, if advantage there is, if it elected from individual districts and the elected representatives demonstrated the same bloc-voting tendency, which may also develop among legislators representing singlemember districts widely scattered throughout the State. Of course it is advantageous to start with more than one vote for a bill. But nothing before us shows or suggests that any legislative skirmish affecting the State of Indiana or Marion County in particular would have come out differently had Marion County been subdistricted and its delegation elected from single-member districts.

Rather than squarely finding unacceptable discrimination against outstate voters in favor of Marion County voters, the trial court struck down Marion County's multi-member district because it found the scheme worked invidiously against a specific segment of the county's voters as compared with others. The court identified an area of the city as a ghetto, found it predominantly inhabited by poor Negroes with distinctive substantive-law interests and thought this group unconstitutionally underrepresented because the proportion of legislators with residences in the ghetto elected from 1960 to 1968 was less than the ghetto's proportion of the population, less than the proportion of legislators elected from Washington Township, a less populous district, and less than the ghetto would likely have elected had the county consisted of single-member districts. We find major deficiencies in this approach.

First, * * * there is no suggestion here that Marion County's multi-member district, or similar districts throughout the State, were conceived or operated as purposeful devices to further racial or economic discrimination. * * *

Nor does the fact that the number of ghetto residents who were legislators was not in proportion to ghetto population satisfactorily prove invidious discrimination absent evidence and findings that ghetto residents had less opportunity than did other Marion County residents to participate in the political processes and to elect legislators of their choice. We have discovered nothing in the record or in the court's findings indicating that poor Negroes were not allowed to register or vote, to choose the political party they desired to support, to participate in its affairs or to be equally represented on those occasions when legislative candidates were chosen. Nor did the evidence purport to show or the court find that inhabitants of the ghetto were regularly excluded from the slates of both major parties, thus denying them the chance of occupying legislative seats. It appears reasonably clear that the Republican Party won four of the five elections from 1960 to 1968, that Center Township ghetto voted heavily Democratic and that ghetto votes were critical to Democratic Party success. [Democrats appear to have slated candidates satisfactory to the ghetto throughout that period, but prevailed only in 1964.] * * * [I]t seems reasonable to infer that had the Democrats won all of the elections or even most of them, the ghetto would have had no justifiable complaints about representation. The fact is, however, that four of the five elections were won by Republicans, which was not the party of the ghetto and which would not always slate ghetto candidates — although in 1962 it nominated and elected one representative and in 1968 two representatives from that area. If this is the proper view of this case, the failure of the ghetto to have legislative seats in proportion to its population emerges more as a function of losing elections than of built-in bias against poor Negroes. The voting power of ghetto residents may have been "cancelled out" as the District Court held, but this seems a more euphemism for political defeat at the polls.

On the record before us plaintiffs' position comes to this: that although they have equal opportunity to participate in and influence the selection of candidates and legislators, and although the ghetto votes predominantly Democratic and that party slates candidates satisfactory to the ghetto, invidious discrimination nevertheless results when the ghetto, along with all other Democrats, suffers the disaster of losing too many elections. But typical American legislative elections are district-oriented, head-on races between candidates of two or more parties. As our system has it, one candidate wins, the others lose. Arguably the losing candidates' supporters are without representation since the men they voted for have been defeated; arguably they have been denied equal protection of the laws since they have no legislative voice of their own. This is true of both single-member *and* multi-member districts. But we have not yet deemed it a denial of equal protection to deny legislative seats to losing candidates, even in those so-called "safe" districts where the same party wins year after year.

* * * [T]he District Court thought the ghetto voters' claim to the partial allegiance of eight senators and 15 representatives was not equivalent to the undivided allegiance of one senator and two representatives; nor was the ghetto voters' chance of influencing the election of an entire slate as significant as the guarantee of one ghetto senator and two ghetto representatives. As the trial court saw it, ghetto voters could not be adequately and equally represented unless some of Marion County's general assembly seats were reserved for ghetto residents serving the interests of the ghetto majority. But are poor Negroes of the ghetto any more underrepresented than poor ghetto whites who also voted Democratic and lost, or any more discriminated against than other interest groups or voters in Marion County with allegiance to the Democratic Party, or, conversely, any less represented than Republican areas or voters in years of Republican defeat? We think not. The mere fact that one interest group or another concerned with the outcome of Marion County elections has found itself outvoted and without legislative seats of its own provides no basis for invoking constitutional remedies where, as here, there is no indication that this segment of the population is being denied access to the political system. * * *

The District Court's holding, although on the facts of this case limited to guaranteeing one racial group representation, is not easily contained. It is expressive of the more general proposition that any group with distinctive interests must be represented in legislative halls if it is numerous enough to command at least one seat and represents a majority living in an area sufficiently compact to constitute a single-member district. This approach would make it difficult to reject claims of Democrats, Republicans, or members of any political organization in Marion County who live in what would be safe districts in a single-member district system but who in one year or another, or year after year, are submerged in a one-sided multi-member district vote. There are also union oriented workers, the university community, religious or ethnic groups occupying identifiable areas of our heterogeneous cities and urban areas. Indeed, it would be difficult for a great many, if not most, multi-member districts to survive analysis under the District Court's view unless combined with some voting arrangement such as proportional representation or cumulative voting aimed at providing representation for minority parties or interests. At the very least, affirmance of the District Court would spawn endless litigation concerning the multi-member district systems now widely employed in this country.[37]

We are not insensitive to the objections long voiced to multi-member district plans. Although not as prevalent as they were in our early history, they have been with us since colonial times and were much in evidence both before and after the adoption of the Fourteenth Amendment.[39] Criticism is rooted in their winner-take-all aspects, their tendency to submerge minorities and to overrepresent the winning party as compared with the party's statewide electoral position, a general preference for legislatures reflecting community interests as closely as possible and disenchantment with political parties and elections as devices to settle policy differences between contending interests. The chance of winning or significantly influencing intraparty fights and issue-oriented elections has seemed to some inadequate protection to minorities, political, racial, or economic; rather, their voice, it is said, should also be heard in the legislative forum where public policy is finally fashioned. In our view, however, experience and insight have not yet demonstrated that multi-member districts are inherently invidious and violative of the Fourteenth Amendment. * * * Moreover, if the problems of multi-member districts are unbearable or even unconstitutional it is not at all clear that the remedy is a single-member district system with its lines carefully drawn to ensure representation to sizable racial, ethnic, economic, or religious groups and with its own capacity for overrepresenting and underrepresenting parties and interests and even for permitting a minority of the voters to control the legislature and government of a State. The short of it is that we are unprepared to hold that district-based elections decided by plurality vote are unconstitutional in either single- or multi-member districts simply because the supporters of losing candidates have no legislative seats assigned to them. As presently advised we hold that the District Court misconceived the Equal Protection Clause in applying it to invalidate the Marion County multi-member district. * * *

We therefore reverse the judgment of the District Court and remand the case to that court for further proceedings consistent with this opinion.

---

[37] As of November 1970, 46% of the upper houses and 62% of the lower houses in the States contained some multi-member districts. * * *

[39] In colonial days, "[m]ultiple districts were the rule, single ones the exception," and "[f]or nearly a century and a half after the Declaration of Independence the American states elected by far the greater part of their lawmakers in multiple constituencies." * * *

It is so ordered.

[MR. JUSTICE STEWART joins the portions of the Court's opinion reprinted here, but dissents from an excised portion concerning one-person, one-vote.]

Separate opinion of MR. JUSTICE HARLAN. * * *

[The Court neither suggests a manner of determining when voting power has been unconstitutionally distributed] nor considers the consequences of its inability to measure what it purports to be equalizing. Instead it becomes enmeshed in the haze of slogans and numerology which for 10 years has obscured its vision in this field, and finally remands the case "for further proceedings consistent with [its] opinion." This inexplicit mandate is at least subject to the interpretation that the court below is to inquire into such matters as "the actual influence of Marion County's delegation in the Indiana Legislature" and the possibility of "recurring poor performance by Marion County's delegation with respect to Center Township ghetto," with a view to determining whether "any legislative skirmish affecting the State of Indiana or Marion County in particular would have come out differently had Marion County been subdistricted and its delegation elected from single-member districts." If there are less appropriate subjects for federal judicial inquiry, they do not come readily to mind. The suggestion implicit in the Court's opinion that appellees may ultimately prevail if they can make their record in these and other like respects should be recognized for what it is: a manifestation of frustration by a Court that has become trapped in the "political thicket" and is looking for the way out.

* * * I hope the day will come when the Court will frankly recognize the error of its ways in ever having undertaken to restructure state electoral processes. * * *

MR. JUSTICE DOUGLAS, with whom MR. JUSTICE BRENNAN and MR. JUSTICE MARSHALL concur, dissenting in part and concurring in the result in part. * * *

The problem of the gerrymander is how to defeat or circumvent the sentiments of the community. The problem of the law is how to prevent it. * * *

It is said that if we prevent racial gerrymandering today, we must prevent gerrymandering of any special interest group tomorrow, whether it be social, economic, or ideological. I do not agree. Our Constitution has a special thrust when it come to voting; the Fifteenth Amendment says the right of citizens to vote shall not be "abridged" on account of "race, color, or previous condition of servitude."

Our cases since *Baker* v. *Carr* have never intimated that "one man, one vote" meant "one white man, one vote." Since "race" may not be gerrymandered, I think the Court emphasizes the irrelevant when it says that the effect on "the actual voting power" of the blacks should first be known. They may be all Democratic or all Republican; but once their identity is purposely washed out of the system, the system, as I see it, has a constitutional defect. It is asking the impossible for us to demand that the blacks first show that the effect of the scheme was to discourage or prevent poor blacks from voting or joining such party as they chose. On this record, the voting rights of the blacks have been "abridged," as I read the Constitution. * * *

I would affirm the judgment.

Notes and Questions

1. Why does the Court disregard the mathematical analysis of voting power offered by the plaintiffs? Do you agree with Justice Harlan's criticism (in an omitted portion of his separate opinion) that "[t]he only relevant difference between the elementary arithmetic on which the Court relies [in the 'one man, one vote' cases] and the elementary probability theory on which [plaintiffs] rel[y] is that calculations in the latter field cannot be done on one's fingers"? 403 U.S. at 168 n.2 (opinion of Harlan, J.).

2. What rule results from this case? What must plaintiffs show to demonstrate that electoral districts — though complying with the one-person, one-vote mandate — nevertheless allocate political power unconstitutionally? The next case may provide some insight . . . or further confusion.

WHITE v. REGESTER
Supreme Court of the United States
412 U.S. 755, 93 S. Ct. 2332, 37 L. Ed. 2d 314 (1973)

MR. JUSTICE WHITE delivered the opinion of the Court [in which MR. CHIEF JUSTICE BURGER, MR. JUSTICE DOUGLAS, MR. JUSTICE BRENNAN, MR. JUSTICE STEWART, MR. JUSTICE MARSHALL, MR. JUSTICE BLACKMUN, MR. JUSTICE POWELL, and MR. JUSTICE REHNQUIST join]. * * *

* * * [The 150-member Texas House of Representatives is selected from] 79 single-member and 11 multimember districts. [Plaintiffs sued, alleging that the] multimember districts for Bexar County and Dallas County operated to dilute the voting strength of racial and ethnic minorities. [The District Court held the multimember districts unconstitutional and ordered that they be redrawn into single-member districts. We affirm.] * * *

* * * Plainly, under our cases, multimember districts are not *per se* unconstitutional, nor are they necessarily unconstitutional when used in combination with single-member districts in other parts of the State. *Whitcomb* v. *Chavis*, 403 U.S. 124 (1971) [p. 268]. But we have entertained claims that multimember districts are being used invidiously to cancel out or minimize the voting strength of racial groups. To sustain such claims, it is not enough that the racial group allegedly discriminated against has not had legislative seats in proportion to its voting potential. The plaintiffs' burden is to produce evidence to support findings that the political processes leading to nomination and election were not equally open to participation by the group in question — that its members had less opportunity than did other residents in the district to participate in the political processes and to elect legislators of their choice. [*Id.*] at 149–150.

With due regard for these standards, the District Court first referred to the history of official racial discrimination in Texas, which at times touched the right of

Negroes to register and vote and to participate in the democratic processes. It referred also to the Texas rule requiring a majority vote as a prerequisite to nomination in a primary election and to the so-called "place" rule limiting candidacy for legislative office from a multimember district to a specified "place" on the ticket, with the result being the election of representatives from the Dallas multimember district reduced to a head-to-head contest for each position. These characteristics of the Texas electoral system, neither in themselves improper nor invidious, enhanced the opportunity for racial discrimination, the District Court thought.[10] More fundamentally, it found that since Reconstruction days, there have been only two Negroes in the Dallas County delegation to the Texas House of Representatives and that these two were the only two Negroes ever slated by the Dallas Committee for Responsible Government (DCRG), a white-dominated organization that is in effective control of Democratic Party candidate slating in Dallas County. That organization, the District Court found, did not need the support of the Negro community to win elections in the county, and it did not therefore exhibit good-faith concern for the political and other needs and aspirations of the Negro community. The court found that as recently as 1970 the DCRG was relying upon "racial campaign tactics in white precincts to defeat candidates who had the overwhelming support of the black community." Based on the evidence before it, the District Court concluded that "the black community has been effectively excluded from participation in the Democratic primary selection process," and was therefore generally not permitted to enter into the political process in a reliable and meaningful manner. These findings and conclusions are sufficient to sustain the District Court's judgment with respect to the Dallas multimember district and, on this record, we have no reason to disturb them.

The same is true of the order requiring disestablishment of the multimember district in Bexar County. * * * Surveying the historic and present condition of the Bexar County Mexican-American community, which is concentrated for the most part on the west side of the city of San Antonio, the court observed, based upon prior cases and the record before it, that the Bexar community, along with other Mexican-Americans in Texas, had long "suffered from, and continues to suffer from, the results and effects of invidious discrimination and treatment in the fields of education, employment, economics, health, politics and others." The bulk of the Mexican-American community in Bexar County occupied the Barrio, an area consisting of about 28 contiguous census tracts in the city of San Antonio. Over 78% of Barrio residents were Mexican-Americans, making up 29% of the county's total population. The Barrio is an area of poor housing; its residents have low income and a high rate of unemployment. The typical Mexican-American suffers a cultural and language barrier that makes his participation in community processes extremely difficult, particularly, the court thought, with respect to the political life of Bexar County. "[A] cultural incompatibility . . . conjoined with the poll tax and the most restrictive voter registration procedures in the nation have operated to effectively deny Mexican-Americans access to the political processes in Texas even longer than the Blacks were formally denied access by the white primary." The residual impact of this history reflected itself in the fact that Mexican-American voting registration

---

[10] There is no requirement that candidates reside in subdistricts of the multimember district. Thus, all candidates may be selected from outside the Negro residential area.

remained very poor in the county and that only five Mexican-Americans since 1880 have served in the Texas Legislature from Bexar County. Of these, only two were from the Barrio area. The District Court also concluded from the evidence that the Bexar County legislative delegation in the House was insufficiently responsive to Mexican-American interests.

Based on the totality of the circumstances, the District Court evolved its ultimate assessment of the multimember district, overlaid, as it was, on the cultural and economic realities of the Mexican-American community in Bexar County and its relationship with the rest of the county. Its judgment was that Bexar County Mexican-Americans "are effectively removed from the political processes of Bexar [County] in violation of all the *Whitcomb* standards, whatever their absolute numbers may total in that County." Single-member districts were thought required to remedy "the effects of past and present discrimination against Mexican-Americans," and to bring the community into the full stream of political life of the county and State by encouraging their further registration, voting, and other political activities.

The District Court apparently paid due heed to *Whitcomb* v. *Chavis*, did not hold that every racial or political group has a constitutional right to be represented in the state legislature, but did, from its own special vantage point, conclude that the multimember district, as designed and operated in Bexar County, invidiously excluded Mexican-Americans from effective participation in political life, specifically in the election of representatives to the Texas House of Representatives. On the record before us, we are not inclined to overturn these findings, representing as they do a blend of history and an intensely local appraisal of the design and impact of the Bexar County multimember district in the light of past and present reality, political and otherwise.

Affirmed in part, reversed in part, and remanded.

[MR. JUSTICE BRENNAN, with MR. JUSTICE DOUGLAS and MR. JUSTICE MARSHALL, joins the portion of the Court's opinion reprinted here, but dissents from the Court's acceptance, in this case and in *Gaffney* v. *Cummings*, 412 U.S. 735 (1973) [p. 206], of variations up to 9.9% in the populations of state legislative districts.]

Notes and Questions

1. What accounts for the different results in this case and in *Whitcomb v. Chavis*?

2. By the time *Regester* was argued and decided, Justices Black and Harlan had left the Court and had been replaced by Justices Powell and Rehnquist. If Justice Harlan were still on the Court, what would his reaction have been to the *Regester* opinion? Imagine that you are his law clerk, and draft a separate opinion that would reflect his thoughts.

UNITED JEWISH ORGANIZATIONS, INC. v. CAREY
Supreme Court of the United States
430 U.S. 144, 97 S. Ct. 996, 51 L. Ed. 2d 229 (1977)

MR. JUSTICE WHITE announced the judgment of the Court and filed an opinion in which MR. JUSTICE STEVENS joined; Parts I, II, and III of which are joined by MR. JUSTICE BRENNAN and MR. JUSTICE BLACKMUN; and Parts I and IV of which are joined by MR. JUSTICE REHNQUIST.

Section 5 of the Voting Rights Act of 1965 prohibits a State or political subdivision subject to § 4 of the Act from implementing a legislative reapportionment unless it has obtained a declaratory judgment from the District Court for the District of Columbia, or a ruling from the Attorney General of the United States, that the reapportionment "does not have the purpose and will not have the effect of denying or abridging the right to vote on account of race or color. . . ." The question presented is whether, in the circumstances of this case, the use of racial criteria by the State of New York in its attempt to comply with § 5 of the Voting Rights Act and to secure the approval of the Attorney General violated the Fourteenth or Fifteenth Amendment.

I

Kings County [Brooklyn], N.Y., together with New York (Manhattan) and Bronx Counties, became subject to §§ 4 and 5 of the Act, by virtue of a determination by the Attorney General that a literacy test was used in these three counties as of November 1, 1968, and a determination by the Director of the Census that fewer than 50% of the voting-age residents of these three counties voted in the Presidential election of 1968. * * * On January 31, 1974, the provisions of the [1972] statute districting these counties for congressional, state senate, and state assembly seats were submitted to the Attorney General. * * * On April 1, 1974, the Attorney General concluded that, as to certain districts in Kings County covering the Bedford-Stuyvesant area of Brooklyn, the State had not met the burden placed on it by § 5 and the regulations thereunder to demonstrate that the redistricting had neither the purpose nor the effect of abridging [blacks' and Puerto Ricans'] right to vote by reason of race or color.[5]

Under § 5, the State could have challenged the Attorney General's objections to the redistricting plan by filing a declaratory judgment action in a three-judge court in the District of Columbia. Instead, the State sought to meet what it understood to be the Attorney General's objections and to secure his approval in order that the 1974 primary and general elections could go forward under the 1972 statute. A revised plan, submitted to the Attorney General on May 31, 1974, in its essentials did not change the number of districts with nonwhite majorities, but did change the size of the nonwhite majorities in most of those districts. * * * The report of the legislative committee on reapportionment stated that these changes were made "to

---

[5] * * * The NAACP [which submitted a memorandum to the Attorney General opposing the 1972 plan], the Attorney General, and the court below classified Puerto Ricans in New York together with blacks as a minority group entitled to the protections of the Voting Rights Act. * * * [Relocated. — Eds.]

overcome Justice Department objections" by creating more "substantial nonwhite majorities" in two assembly districts and two senate districts. [The Attorney General precleared the 1974 plan.]

One of the communities affected by these revisions in the Kings County reapportionment plan was the Williamsburgh area, where about 30,000 Hasidic Jews live. Under the 1972 plan, the Hasidic community was located entirely in one assembly district (61% nonwhite) and one senate district (37% nonwhite); in order to create substantial nonwhite majorities in these districts, the 1974 revisions split the Hasidic community between two senate and two assembly districts. A staff member of the legislative reapportionment committee testified that in the course of meetings and telephone conversations with Justice Department officials, he "got the feeling . . . that 65 percent would be probably an approved figure" for the nonwhite population in the assembly district in which the Hasidic community was located, a district approximately 61% nonwhite under the 1972 plan. To attain the 65% figure, a portion of the white population, including part of the Hasidic community, was reassigned to an adjoining district.

Shortly after the State submitted this revised redistricting plan for Kings County to the Attorney General, petitioners sued on behalf of the Hasidic Jewish community of Williamsburgh, alleging that the 1974 plan "would dilute the value of each plaintiff's franchise by halving its effectiveness," solely for the purpose of achieving a racial quota and therefore in violation of the Fourteenth Amendment. Petitioners also alleged that they were assigned to electoral districts solely on the basis of race, and that this racial assignment diluted their voting power in violation of the Fifteenth Amendment. Petitioners sought an injunction restraining New York officials from enforcing the new redistricting plan and a declaratory judgment that the Attorney General of the United States had used unconstitutional and improper standards in objecting to the 1972 plan. [The District Court dismissed the complaint, and the Court of Appeals affirmed.] * * *

II

Petitioners argue that the New York Legislature, although seeking to comply with the Voting Rights Act as construed by the Attorney General, has violated the Fourteenth and Fifteenth Amendments by deliberately revising its reapportionment plan along racial lines. In rejecting petitioners' claim, we address four propositions: First, that whatever might be true in other contexts, the use of racial criteria in districting and apportionment is never permissible; second, that even if racial considerations may be used to redraw district lines in order to remedy the residual effects of past unconstitutional reapportionments, there are no findings here of prior discriminations that would require or justify as a remedy that white voters be reassigned in order to increase the size of black majorities in certain districts; third, that the use of a "racial quota" in redistricting is never acceptable; and fourth, that even if the foregoing general propositions are infirm, what New York actually did in this case was unconstitutional, particularly its use of a 65% nonwhite racial quota for certain districts. The first three arguments, as we now explain, are foreclosed by our cases construing and sustaining the constitutionality of the Voting Rights Act; the fourth we address in Parts III and IV. * * *

* * * Contrary to petitioners' first argument, neither the Fourteenth nor the Fifteenth Amendment mandates any *per se* rule against using racial factors in districting and apportionment. Nor is petitioners' second argument valid. The permissible use of racial criteria is not confined to eliminating the effects of past discriminatory districting or apportionment.[19]

Moreover, in the process of drawing black majority districts in order to comply with § 5, the State must decide how substantial those majorities must be in order to satisfy the Voting Rights Act. * * * At a minimum and by definition, a "black majority district" must be more than 50% black. But whatever the specific percentage, the State will inevitably arrive at it as a necessary means to ensure the opportunity for the election of a black representative and to obtain approval of its reapportionment plan. Unless we adopted an unconstitutional construction of § 5 in *Beer* and *City of Richmond*, a reapportionment cannot violate the Fourteenth or Fifteenth Amendment merely because a State uses specific numerical quotas in establishing a certain number of black majority districts. Our cases under § 5 stand for at least this much.

III

Having rejected these three broad objections to the use of racial criteria in redistricting under the Voting Rights Act, we turn to the fourth question, which is whether the racial criteria New York used in this case — the revision of the 1972 plan to create 65% nonwhite majorities in two additional senate and two additional assembly districts — were constitutionally infirm. We hold they are not, on two separate grounds. * * *

The first ground is that petitioners have not shown, or offered to prove, that New York did more than the Attorney General was authorized to require it to do under the non-retrogression principle of *Beer* [*v. United States*, 425 U.S. 130 (1976)] [p. 239], a principle that, as we have already indicated, this Court has accepted as constitutionally valid. [In *Beer*, the Court considered the question of what criteria a legislative reapportionment must satisfy under § 5 of the Voting Rights Act to demonstrate that it does not have the "effect" of denying or abridging the right to vote on account of race. *Beer* established that the Voting Rights Act does not permit the implementation of a reapportionment that "would lead to a retrogression in the position of racial minorities with respect to their effective exercise of the electoral franchise." 425 U.S., at 141.] Under *Beer*, the acceptability of New York's 1972 reapportionment for purposes of § 5 depends on the change in nonwhite voting strength in comparison with the previous apportionment, which occurred in 1966. Yet there is no evidence in the record to show whether the 1972 plan increased or decreased the number of senate or assembly districts with substantial nonwhite majorities of 65%. For all that petitioners have alleged or proved, the 1974 revisions may have accomplished nothing more than the restoration of nonwhite voting

---

[19] Petitioners also insist that, because the Attorney General concluded not that the 1972 plan would have a discriminatory effect but only that the State had failed to demonstrate that the plan would not have such an effect, there was insufficient justification for racial redistricting. This argument overlooks the central role of the shift in burden of proof in the congressional effort to combat discriminatory voting laws. Our cases have upheld this shift. * * *

strength to 1966 levels. To be successful in their constitutional challenge to the racial criteria used in New York's revised plan, petitioners must show at a minimum that minority voting strength was increased under the 1974 plan in comparison with the 1966 apportionment; otherwise the challenge amounts to a constitutional attack on compliance with the statutory rule of non-retrogression.

In the absence of any evidence regarding nonwhite voting strength under the 1966 apportionment, the creation of substantial nonwhite majorities in approximately 30% of the senate and assembly districts in Kings County was reasonably related to the constitutionally valid statutory mandate of maintaining nonwhite voting strength. The percentage of districts with nonwhite majorities was less than the percentage of nonwhites in the county as a whole (35%). The size of the nonwhite majorities in those districts reflected the need to take account of the substantial difference between the nonwhite percentage of the total population in a district and the nonwhite percentage of the voting-age population.[22] * * * We think it was reasonable for the Attorney General to conclude in this case that a *substantial* nonwhite population majority — in the vicinity of 65% — would be required to achieve a nonwhite majority of eligible voters.

Petitioners have not shown that New York did more than accede to a position taken by the Attorney General that was authorized by our constitutionally permissible construction of § 5. New York adopted the 1974 plan because it sought to comply with the Voting Rights Act. * * *

IV

[Additionally there is] a second, and independent, ground for sustaining the particulars of the 1974 plan for Kings County. Whether or not the plan was authorized by or was in compliance with § 5 of the Voting Rights Act, New York was free to do what it did as long as it did not violate the Constitution, particularly the Fourteenth and Fifteenth Amendments; and we are convinced that neither Amendment was infringed.

There is no doubt that in preparing the 1974 legislation the State deliberately used race in a purposeful manner. But its plan represented no racial slur or stigma with respect to whites or any other race, and we discern no discrimination violative of the Fourteenth Amendment nor any abridgment of the right to vote on account of race within the meaning of the Fifteenth Amendment.

It is true that New York deliberately increased the nonwhite majorities in certain districts in order to enhance the opportunity for election of nonwhite representatives from those districts. Nevertheless, there was no fencing out the white population from participation in the political processes of the county, and the plan did not minimize or unfairly cancel out white voting strength. Compare *White* v. *Regester*, 412 U.S. [755,] 765–767 [(1973)] [p. 274], and *Gomillion* v. *Lightfoot*, 364 U.S. 339 (1960) [p. 115], with *Gaffney* v. *Cummings*, 412 U.S. 735, 751–754 (1973) [p. 206]. Petitioners have not objected to the impact of the 1974 plan on the

---

[22] The NAACP, intervenor in this action, submitted census data to the Attorney General showing that roughly 75% of all whites in Kings County but only about 55% of all nonwhites were eligible to vote. * * *

representation of white voters in the county or in the State as a whole. [T]he plan left white majorities in approximately 70% of the assembly and senate districts in Kings County, which had a countywide population that was 65% white. Thus, even if voting in the county occurred strictly according to race, whites would not be underrepresented relative to their share of the population.

In individual districts where nonwhite majorities were increased to approximately 65%, it became more likely, given racial bloc voting, that black candidates would be elected instead of their white opponents, and it became less likely that white voters would be represented by a member of their own race; but as long as whites in Kings County, as a group, were provided with fair representation, we cannot conclude that there was a cognizable discrimination against whites or an abridgment of their right to vote on the grounds of race.[24] Furthermore, the individual voter in the district with a nonwhite majority has no constitutional complaint merely because his candidate has lost out at the polls and his district is represented by a person for whom he did not vote. Some candidate, along with his supporters, always loses. See *Whitcomb* v. *Chavis*, 403 U.S., at 153–160.

Where it occurs, voting for or against a candidate because of his race is an unfortunate practice. But it is not rare; and in any district where it regularly happens, it is unlikely that any candidate will be elected who is a member of the race that is in the minority in that district. However disagreeable this result may be, there is no authority for the proposition that the candidates who are found racially unacceptable by the majority, and the minority voters supporting those candidates, have had their Fourteenth or Fifteenth Amendment rights infringed by this process. Their position is similar to that of the Democratic or Republican minority that is submerged year after year by the adherents to the majority party who tend to vote a straight party line.

It does not follow, however, that the State is powerless to minimize the consequences of racial discrimination by voters when it is regularly practiced at the polls. In *Gaffney* v. *Cummings*, the Court upheld a districting plan "drawn with the conscious intent to . . . achieve a rough approximation of the statewide political strengths of the Democratic and Republican Parties." 412 U.S., at 752. We there recognized that districting plans would be vulnerable under our cases if "*racial or political groups* have been fenced out of the political process and their voting strength invidiously minimized," *id.*, at 754 (emphasis added); but that was not the case there, and no such purpose or effect may be ascribed to New York's 1974 plan. Rather, that plan can be viewed as seeking to alleviate the consequences of racial voting at the polls and to achieve a fair allocation of political power between white and nonwhite voters in Kings County.

In this respect New York's revision of certain district lines is little different in kind from the decision by a State in which a racial minority is unable to elect

---

[24] We also note that the white voter who as a result of the 1974 plan is in a district more likely to return a nonwhite representative will be represented, to the extent that voting continues to follow racial lines, by legislators elected from majority white districts. The effect of the reapportionment on whites in districts where nonwhite majorities have been increased is thus mitigated by the preservation of white majority districts in the rest of the county. Of course, if voting does not follow racial lines, the white voter has little reason to complain that the percentage of nonwhites in his district has been increased.

representatives from multimember districts to change to single-member districting for the purpose of increasing minority representation. This change might substantially increase minority representation at the expense of white voters, who previously elected all of the legislators but who with single-member districts could elect no more than their proportional share. If this intentional reduction of white voting power would be constitutionally permissible, as we think it would be, we think it also permissible for a State, employing sound districting principles such as compactness and population equality, to attempt to prevent racial minorities from being repeatedly outvoted by creating districts that will afford fair representation to the members of those racial groups who are sufficiently numerous and whose residential patterns afford the opportunity of creating districts in which they will be in the majority. * * *

The judgment is

Affirmed.

Mr. Justice Marshall took no part in the consideration or decision of this case.

Mr. Justice Brennan, concurring in part.

I join Parts I, II, and III of Mr. Justice White's opinion. * * * Yet, because this case carries us further down the road of race-centered remedial devices than we have heretofore traveled — with the serious questions of fairness that attend such matters — I offer this further explanation of my position. * * *

If we were presented here with a classification of voters motivated by racial animus, or with a classification that effectively downgraded minority participation in the franchise, we promptly would characterize the resort to race as "suspect" and prohibit its use. Under such circumstances, the tainted apportionment process would not necessarily be saved by its proportional outcome, for the segregation of voters into "separate but equal" blocs still might well have the intent or effect of diluting the voting power of minority voters. It follows, therefore, that if the racial redistricting involved here, imposed with the avowed intention of clustering together 10 viable nonwhite majorities at the expense of preexisting white groupings, is not similarly to be prohibited, the distinctiveness that avoids this prohibition must arise from either or both of two considerations: the permissibility of affording preferential treatment to disadvantaged nonwhites generally, or the particularized application of the Voting Rights Act in this instance.

The first and broader of the two plausible distinctions rests upon the general propriety of so-called benign discrimination: The challenged race assignment may be permissible because it is cast in a remedial context with respect to a disadvantaged class rather than in a setting that aims to demean or insult any racial group. Even in the absence of the Voting Rights Act, this preferential policy plausibly could find expression in a state decision to overcome nonwhite disadvantages in voter registration or turnout through redefinition of electoral districts — perhaps, as here, through the application of a numerical rule — in order to achieve a proportional distribution of voting power. Such a decision, in my view, raises particularly sensitive issues of doctrine and policy. Unlike Part IV of Mr. Justice

WHITE's opinion,[1] I am wholly content to leave this thorny question until another day, for I am convinced that the existence of the Voting Rights Act makes such a decision unnecessary and alone suffices to support an affirmance of the judgment before us.

I begin with the settled principle that not every remedial use of race is forbidden. For example, we have authorized and even required race-conscious remedies in a variety of corrective settings. See, *e.g.*, *Swann* v. *Charlotte-Mecklenburg Bd. of Education*, 402 U.S. 1, 25 (1971) [(permitting district courts to order busing to remedy school segregation)]. Once it is established that circumstances exist where race may be taken into account in fashioning affirmative policies, we must identify those circumstances, and further, determine how substantial a reliance may be placed upon race. If resort to the 65% rule involved here is not to be sanctioned, that must be because the benign use of such a binding numerical criterion (under the Voting Rights Act) generates problems of constitutional dimension that are not relevant to other, previously tolerated race-conscious remedies. As a focus for consideration of what these problems might or might not be, it is instructive to consider some of the objections frequently raised to the use of overt preferential race-assignment practices.

First, a purportedly preferential race assignment may in fact disguise a policy that perpetuates disadvantageous treatment of the plan's supposed beneficiaries. Accordingly, courts might face considerable difficulty in ascertaining whether a given race classification truly furthers benign rather than illicit objectives. An effort to achieve proportional representation, for example, might be aimed at aiding a group's participation in the political processes by guaranteeing safe political offices, or, on the other hand, might be a "contrivance to segregate" the group, thereby frustrating its potentially successful efforts at coalition building across racial lines. Indeed, even the present case is not entirely free of complaints that the remedial redistricting in Brooklyn is not truly benign. Puerto Rican groups, for example, who have been joined with black groups to establish the "nonwhite" category, protested to the Attorney General that their political strength under the 1974 reapportionment actually is weaker than under the invalidated 1972 districting. A black group similarly complained of the loss of a "safe" seat because of the inadequacy of the 65% target figure. These particular objections, as the Attorney General argued in his memorandum endorsing the 1974 reapportionment, may be ill-advised and

---

[1] Part IV limits its endorsement of proportional distribution of voting power to instances where the voters are polarized along racial lines and where the State intends "no racial slur or stigma with respect to" any race. I agree that, without such qualifications, the position taken in Part IV plainly would be intolerable. Yet, even as so limited, problems remain that, in my view, merit further consideration. For example, questions concerning the polarization of voters and the motives of the state policymakers may place formidable factfinding responsibilities on the courts. Such responsibilities, I believe, are greatly lessened when the Voting Rights Act is involved. Furthermore, I am not at rest with the notion that a "cognizable discrimination" cannot be found so long as whites "as a group [are] provided with fair representation. . . ." While voting may differ from other activities or entitlements in that one group of voters often derives benefits indirectly from a legislator serving a different constituency — and to that extent I agree that the adverse effects of a racial division are "mitigated" — I am not satisfied that this vicarious benefit fully answers the Hasidim's complaint of injustice. Finally, I have serious doubts that the Court's acceptance of political-party apportionment in *Gaffney* v. *Cummings* necessarily applies to apportionment by race. Political affiliation is the keystone of the political trade. Race, ideally, is not.

unpersuasive. Nevertheless, they illustrate the risk that what is presented as an instance of benign race assignment in fact may prove to be otherwise. This concern, of course, does not undercut the theoretical legitimacy or usefulness of preferential policies. At the minimum, however, it does suggest the need for careful consideration of the operation of any racial device, even one cloaked in preferential garb. And if judicial detection of truly benign policies proves impossible or excessively crude, that alone might warrant invalidating any race-drawn line.

Second, even in the pursuit of remedial objectives, an explicit policy of assignment by race may serve to stimulate our society's latent race consciousness, suggesting the utility and propriety of basing decisions on a factor that ideally bears no relationship to an individual's worth or needs. Furthermore, even preferential treatment may act to stigmatize its recipient groups, for although intended to correct systemic or institutional inequities, such policy may imply to some the recipients' inferiority and especial need for protection. Again, these matters would not necessarily speak against the wisdom or permissibility of selective, benign racial classifications. But they demonstrate that the considerations that historically led us to treat race as a constitutionally "suspect" method of classifying individuals are not entirely vitiated in a preferential context.

Third, especially when interpreting the broad principles embraced by the Equal Protection Clause, we cannot well ignore the social reality that even a benign policy of assignment by race is viewed as unjust by many in our society, especially by those individuals who are adversely affected by a given classification. This impression of injustice may be heightened by the natural consequence of our governing processes that the most "discrete and insular" of whites often will be called upon to bear the immediate, direct costs of benign discrimination. Perhaps not surprisingly, there are indications that this case affords an example of just such decisionmaking in operation. For example, the respondent-intervenors take pains to emphasize that the mandated 65% rule could have been attained through redistricting strategies that did not slice the Hasidic community in half. State authorities, however, chose to localize the burdens of race reassignment upon the petitioners rather than to redistribute a more varied and diffused range of whites into predominantly nonwhite districts. I am in no position to determine the accuracy of this appraisal, but the impression of unfairness is magnified when a coherent group like the Hasidim disproportionately bears the adverse consequences of a race-assignment policy.

In my view, if and when a decisionmaker embarks on a policy of benign racial sorting, he must weigh the concerns that I have discussed against the need for effective social policies promoting racial justice in a society beset by deep-rooted racial inequities. But I believe that Congress here adequately struck that balance in enacting the carefully conceived remedial scheme embodied in the Voting Rights Act. However the Court ultimately decides the constitutional legitimacy of "reverse discrimination" pure and simple, I am convinced that the application of the Voting Rights Act substantially minimizes the objections to preferential treatment, and legitimates the use of even overt, numerical racial devices in electoral redistricting.

The participation of the Attorney General, for example, largely relieves the judiciary of the need to grapple with the difficulties of distinguishing benign from malign discrimination. * * * [The preclearance requirement], coupled with the factfinding competence of the Justice Department, substantially reduces the likelihood that a complicated reapportionment plan that silently furthers malign racial policies would escape detection by appropriate officials. As a practical matter, therefore, I am prepared to accord considerable deference to the judgment of the Attorney General that a particular districting scheme complies with the remedial objectives furthered by the Voting Rights Act. * * *

This leaves, of course, the objection expressed by a variety of participants in this litigation: that this reapportionment worked the injustice of localizing the direct burdens of racial assignment upon a morally undifferentiated group of whites, and, indeed, a group that plausibly is peculiarly vulnerable to such injustice. This argument has both normative and emotional appeal, but for a variety of reasons I am convinced that the Voting Rights Act drains it of vitality.

First, it is important to recall that the Attorney General's oversight focuses upon jurisdictions whose prior practices exhibited the purpose or effect of infringing the right to vote on account of race, thereby triggering § 4 of the Act. This direct nexus to localities with a history of discriminatory practices or effects enhances the legitimacy of the Attorney General's remedial authority over individuals within those communities who benefited (as whites) from those earlier discriminatory voting patterns. Moreover, the obvious remedial nature of the Act and its enactment by an elected Congress that hardly can be viewed as dominated by nonwhite representatives belie the possibility that the decisionmaker intended a racial insult or injury to those whites who are adversely affected by the operation of the Act's provisions.[7] Finally, petitioners have not been deprived of their right to vote, a consideration that minimizes the detrimental impact of the remedial racial policies governing the § 5 reapportionment. True, petitioners are denied the opportunity to vote as a group in accordance with the earlier districting configuration, but they do not press any legal claim to a group voice as Hasidim. In terms of their voting interests, then, the burden that they claim to suffer must be attributable solely to their relegation to increased nonwhite-dominated districts. Yet, to the extent that white and nonwhite interests and sentiments are polarized in Brooklyn, the petitioners still are indirectly "protected" by the remaining white assembly and senate districts within the county, carefully preserved in accordance with the white proportion of the total county population. While these considerations obviously do not satisfy petitioners, I am persuaded that they reinforce the legitimacy of this remedy.

Since I find nothing in the first three parts of Mr. Justice White's opinion that is inconsistent with the views expressed herein, I join those parts.

Mr. Justice Stewart, with whom Mr. Justice Powell joins, concurring in the judgment.

The question presented for decision in this case is whether New York's use of

---

[7] In this regard, it is important that * * * petitioners themselves do not protest that their treatment under the 1974 plan was motivated by anti-Semitism. Indeed, it is undeniable that the Hasidic community is contiguous to several nonwhite neighborhoods, and, therefore, understandably is a candidate for redistricting given the goal of creating 10 viable nonwhite voting majorities.

racial criteria in redistricting Kings County violated the Fourteenth or Fifteenth Amendment. The petitioners' contention is essentially that racial awareness in legislative reapportionment is unconstitutional *per se*. Acceptance of their position would mark an egregious departure from the way this Court has in the past analyzed the constitutionality of claimed discrimination in dealing with the elective franchise on the basis of race.

The petitioners have made no showing that a racial criterion was used as a basis for denying them their right to vote, in contravention of the Fifteenth Amendment. * * *

Under the Fourteenth Amendment the question is whether the reapportionment plan represents purposeful discrimination against white voters. *Washington* v. *Davis*, 426 U.S. 229 [(1976)]. * * * The clear purpose with which the New York Legislature acted in response to the position of the United States Department of Justice under the Voting Rights Act forecloses any finding that it acted with the invidious purpose of discriminating against white voters.[*]

Having failed to show that the legislative reapportionment plan had either the purpose or the effect of discriminating against them on the basis of their race, the petitioners have offered no basis for affording them the constitutional relief they seek. Accordingly, I join the judgment of the Court.

MR. CHIEF JUSTICE BURGER, dissenting. * * *

* * * If *Gomillion* [v. *Lightfoot*, 364 U.S. 339 (1960)] [p. 115] teaches anything, I had thought it was that drawing of political boundary lines with the sole, explicit objective of reaching a predetermined racial result cannot ordinarily be squared with the Constitution. The record before us reveals and it is not disputed that this is precisely what took place here. In drawing up the 1974 reapportionment scheme, the New York Legislature did not consider racial composition as merely one of several political characteristics; on the contrary, race appears to have been the one and only criterion applied. * * *

Although reference to racial composition of a political unit may, under certain circumstances, serve as "a starting point in the process of shaping a remedy," rigid adherence to quotas, especially in a case like this, deprives citizens such as petitioners of the opportunity to have the legislature make a determination free from unnecessary bias for or against any racial, ethnic, or religious group. I do not quarrel with the proposition that the New York Legislature may choose to take ethnic or community union into consideration in drawing its district lines. * * * While petitioners certainly have no constitutional right to remain unified within a single political district, they do have, in my view, the constitutional right not to be

---

[*] It is unnecessary to consider whether the position of the Department of Justice in this case was required or even authorized by the Voting Rights Act. It is enough to note that the Voting Rights Act and the procedures used to implement it are constitutionally valid, and that the procedures followed in this case were consistent with the Act. Congress has established an exclusive forum — the District Court for the District of Columbia — and provided exclusive standing in the State or political subdivision to raise the issue of substantive compliance with the Act. That procedure was not invoked by New York here, and the issue of statutory compliance is consequently not properly before us.

carved up so as to create a voting bloc composed of some other ethnic or racial group through the kind of racial gerrymandering the Court condemned in *Gomillion* v. *Lightfoot.* * * *

The result reached by the Court today in the name of the Voting Rights Act is ironic. The use of a mathematical formula tends to sustain the existence of ghettos by promoting the notion that political clout is to be gained or maintained by marshaling particular racial, ethnic, or religious groups in enclaves. It suggests to the voter that only a candidate of the same race, religion, or ethnic origin can properly represent that voter's interests, and that such candidate can be elected only from a district with a sufficient minority concentration. The device employed by the State of New York, and endorsed by the Court today, moves us one step farther away from a truly homogeneous society. * * *

Notes and Questions

1.   How would you formulate the alleged "right" that formed the basis of the United Jewish Organizations' claim? Did the various opinions in *UJO* treat the right as one held by individuals or groups?

2.   The plurality characterized its holdings in Parts III and IV as "independent." As such, in the view of some Justices at least, an unconstitutional race-conscious districting plan might be authorized by the VRA and thereby legitimized. Should Congress be able to authorize states to engage in otherwise-unconstitutional conduct?

3.   The Court's usual practice is not to offer alternative holdings, especially in constitutional cases, because it prefers to decide questions of constitutional interpretation only when the proper case outcome depends on such a construction. Why might an exception have been made in this case?

4.   Justice White and Justice Brennan suggested that the interests of the white residents of majority-minority districts may benefit from the support of white legislators from other districts — a concept that has come to be called "virtual representation." Do you think the Hasidim could be virtually represented by white legislators from other districts? Do you believe that a violation of one group's rights of political access can be mitigated by the representation of that group's interests within a legislative body as a whole? Reconsider this last question after you read *LULAC v. Perry*, 548 U.S. 399 (2006) [p. 385], later in this Chapter.

5.   In Part II of its opinion, the plurality accepted as constitutional "specific numerical quotas" concerning the minimum number of minorities in majority-minority districts. Is such a permissive attitude toward racial quotas consistent with modern equal-protection law? *Cf. Grutter v. Bollinger*, 539 U.S. 306 (2003); *Gratz v. Bollinger*, 539 U.S. 244 (2003).

6.   In Part IV, the plurality held that states may use race-conscious means to provide minorities "fair representation," provided that they use "sound districting principles such as compactness and population equality." Even Chief Justice Burger, in dissent, accepted that states may take race into account in drawing district lines, though he believed the influence of race on the 1974 plan was

constitutionally excessive. Do you agree that states may use race to some extent without violating the Constitution? How crucial must racial considerations be before the constitutional threshold is crossed? Why might the constitutionality of a districting program turn on compactness? The Court, as we will see, has demonstrated a renewed interest in these questions with the line of cases beginning with *Shaw v. Reno*, 509 U.S. 630 (1993) [p. 354], which is discussed later in this Chapter.

7.   Was it proper to evaluate the Hasidim as part of the white "majority" in permitting New York to sacrifice their interests to those of the Puerto Rican and black communities? *Cf. Regents of the University of California v. Bakke*, 438 U.S. 265, 295 (1978) (opinion of Powell, J.) ("[T]he white 'majority' itself is composed of various minority groups, most of which can lay claim to a history of prior discrimination at the hands of the State and private individuals."). Or should the Court have treated the Hasidim themselves as a racial minority, permitting them to claim that the 1974 plan diluted their voting strength in violation of § 2 of the Voting Rights Act? How should the Constitution and the Voting Rights Act protect "minority" groups within the white "majority"?

8.   Should Puerto Ricans and blacks have been considered together as a racial group of "nonwhites"? Are "Hispanics" a racial group? What about "nonwhite Hispanics"? Latinos? As each of these questions illustrates, *UJO* forces us to ask what race means, and why we view racial identity as so central to American politics. As you read the remainder of this Chapter (and the remainder of this book), consider how answers to those questions may have changed since the middle of the twentieth century.

CITY OF MOBILE v. BOLDEN
Supreme Court of the United States
446 U.S. 55, 100 S. Ct. 1490, 64 L. Ed. 2d 47 (1980)

MR. JUSTICE STEWART announced the judgment of the Court and delivered an opinion, in which THE CHIEF JUSTICE [BURGER], MR. JUSTICE POWELL, and MR. JUSTICE REHNQUIST joined.

The city of Mobile, Ala., has since 1911 been governed by a City Commission consisting of three members elected by the voters of the city at large. The three Commissioners jointly exercise all legislative, executive and administrative power in the municipality. They are required after election to designate one of their number as Mayor, a largely ceremonial office, but no formal provision is made for allocating specific executive or administrative duties among the three. As required by the state law enacted in 1911, each candidate for the Mobile City Commission runs for election in the city at large for a term of four years in one of three numbered posts, and may be elected only by a majority of the total vote. This is the same basic electoral system that is followed by literally thousands of municipalities and other local governmental units throughout the Nation.[b]

The appellees brought this suit in the Federal District Court for the Southern District of Alabama as a class action on behalf of all Negro citizens of Mobile. * * *

---

[b] Most of this paragraph has been relocated. — Eds.

The complaint alleged that the practice of electing the City Commissioners at large unfairly diluted the voting strength of Negroes in violation of § 2 of the Voting Rights Act of 1965, of the Fourteenth Amendment, and of the Fifteenth Amendment. Following a bench trial, the District Court found that the constitutional rights of the appellees had been violated, entered a judgment in their favor, and ordered that the City Commission be disestablished and replaced by a municipal government consisting of a Mayor and a City Council with members elected from single-member districts. The Court of Appeals affirmed[.] * * *

[Appellees' complaint contains not only constitutional claims, but also a] statutory claim — that the Mobile electoral system violates § 2 of the Voting Rights Act of 1965. Even a cursory examination of that claim, however, clearly discloses that it adds nothing to the appellees' complaint.

Section 2 of the Voting Rights Act provides:

"No voting qualification or prerequisite to voting, or standard, practice, or procedure shall be imposed or applied by any State or political subdivision to deny or abridge the right of any citizen of the United States to vote on account of race or color." 42 U.S.C. § 1973 [now 52 U.S.C. § 10301 — Eds.].

[I]t is apparent that the language of § 2 no more than elaborates upon that of the Fifteenth Amendment, and the sparse legislative history of § 2 makes clear that it was intended to have an effect no different from that of the Fifteenth Amendment itself.

Section 2 was an uncontroversial provision in proposed legislation whose other provisions engendered protracted dispute. The House Report on the bill simply recited that § 2 "grants . . . a right to be free from enactment or enforcement of voting qualifications . . . or practices which deny or abridge the right to vote on account of race or color." The view that this section simply restated the prohibitions already contained in the Fifteenth Amendment was expressed without contradiction during the Senate hearings. Senator Dirksen indicated at one point that all States, whether or not covered by the preclearance provisions of § 5 of the proposed legislation, were prohibited from discriminating against Negro voters by § 2, which he termed "almost a rephrasing of the 15th [A]mendment." Attorney General Katzenbach agreed.

In view of the section's language and its sparse but clear legislative history, it is evident that this statutory provision adds nothing to the appellees' Fifteenth Amendment claim. * * *

Our decisions * * * have made clear that action by a State that is racially neutral on its face violates the Fifteenth Amendment only if motivated by a discriminatory purpose. In *Guinn* v. *United States*, 238 U.S. 347 [(1915)], this Court struck down a "grandfather" clause in a state constitution exempting from the requirement that voters be literate any person or the descendants of any person who had been entitled to vote before January 1, 1866 * * *, because it was not "possible to discover any basis in reason for the standard thus fixed other than the purpose" to circumvent the Fifteenth Amendment. *Id.*, at 365.

The Court's more recent decisions confirm the principle that racially discriminatory motivation is a necessary ingredient of a Fifteenth Amendment violation. In *Gomillion* v. *Lightfoot*, 364 U.S. 339 [(1960)] [p. 115], the Court held that allegations of a racially motivated gerrymander of municipal boundaries stated a claim under the Fifteenth Amendment. The constitutional infirmity of the state law in that case, according to the allegations of the complaint, was that in drawing the municipal boundaries the legislature was "solely concerned with segregating white and colored voters by fencing Negro citizens out of town so as to deprive them of their pre-existing municipal vote." *Id.*, at 341. The Court made clear that in the absence of such an invidious purpose, a State is constitutionally free to redraw political boundaries in any manner it chooses. *Id.*, at 347.

In *Wright* v. *Rockefeller*, 376 U.S. 52 [(1964)], the Court upheld by like reasoning a state congressional reapportionment statute against claims that district lines had been racially gerrymandered, because the plaintiffs failed to prove that the legislature "was either motivated by racial considerations or in fact drew the districts on racial lines"; or that the statute "was the product of a state contrivance to segregate on the basis of race or place of origin." *Id.*, at 56, 58. See also *Lassiter* v. *Northampton Election Bd.*, 360 U.S. 45 [(1959)] [p. 8]; *Lane* v. *Wilson*, 307 U.S. 268, 275–277 [(1939)]. * * *

The appellees have argued in this Court that *Smith* v. *Allwright* [321 U.S. 649 (1944)] [p. 426] and *Terry* v. *Adams* [345 U.S. 461 (1953)] [p. 431] support the conclusion that the at-large system of elections in Mobile is unconstitutional, reasoning that the effect of racially polarized voting in Mobile is the same as that of a racially exclusionary primary. The only characteristic, however, of the exclusionary primaries that offended the Fifteenth Amendment was that Negroes were not permitted to vote in them. The difficult question was whether the "State ha[d] had a hand in" the patent discrimination practiced by a nominally private organization.

The answer to the appellees' argument is that, as the District Court expressly found, their freedom to vote has not been denied or abridged by anyone. The Fifteenth Amendment does not entail the right to have Negro candidates elected, and neither *Smith* v. *Allwright* nor *Terry* v. *Adams* contains any implication to the contrary. That Amendment prohibits only purposefully discriminatory denial or abridgment by government of the freedom to vote "on account of race, color, or previous condition of servitude." Having found that Negroes in Mobile "register and vote without hindrance," the District Court and Court of Appeals were in error in believing that the appellants invaded the protection of that Amendment in the present case.

The Court of Appeals also agreed with the District Court that Mobile's at-large electoral system violates the Equal Protection Clause of the Fourteenth Amendment. There remains for consideration, therefore, the validity of its judgment on that score. * * *

Despite repeated constitutional attacks upon multimember legislative districts, the Court has consistently held that they are not unconstitutional *per se*, *e.g.*, *White* v. *Regester*, 412 U.S. 755 [(1973)] [p. 274]; *Whitcomb* v. *Chavis*, [403 U.S. 124 (1971)] [p. 268]; *Kilgarlin* v. *Hill*, 386 U.S. 120 [(1967)]; *Burns* v. *Richardson*, 384 U.S. 73 [(1966)]; *Fortson* v. *Dorsey*, 379 U.S. 433 [(1965)]. We have recognized, however, that such legislative apportionments could violate the Fourteenth Amendment if their purpose were invidiously to minimize or cancel out the voting potential of racial or ethnic minorities. To prove such a purpose it is not enough to show that the group allegedly discriminated against has not elected representatives in proportion to its numbers. A plaintiff must prove that the disputed plan was "conceived or operated as [a] purposeful devic[e] to further racial . . . discrimination," [*Chavis*, 403 U.S.], at 149.

This burden of proof is simply one aspect of the basic principle that only if there is purposeful discrimination can there be a violation of the Equal Protection Clause of the Fourteenth Amendment. See *Washington* v. *Davis*, 426 U.S. 229 [(1976)]; *Arlington Heights* v. *Metropolitan Housing Dev. Corp.*, 429 U.S. 252 [(1977)]; *Personnel Administrator of Mass.* v. *Feeney*, 442 U.S. 256 [(1979)]. The Court explicitly indicated in *Washington* v. *Davis* that this principle applies to claims of racial discrimination affecting voting just as it does to other claims of racial discrimination. [See *Davis*, 426 U.S., at 240.] * * *

In only one case has the Court sustained a claim that multimember legislative districts unconstitutionally diluted the voting strength of a discrete group. That case was *White* v. *Regester*. There the Court upheld a constitutional challenge by Negroes and Mexican-Americans to parts of a legislative reapportionment plan adopted by the State of Texas. The plaintiffs alleged that the multimember districts for the two counties in which they resided minimized the effect of their votes in violation of the Fourteenth Amendment, and the Court held that the plaintiffs had been able to "produce evidence to support findings that the political processes leading to nomination and election were not equally open to participation by the group[s] in question." 412 U.S., at 766, 767. In so holding, the Court relied upon evidence in the record that included a long history of official discrimination against minorities as well as indifference to their needs and interests on the part of white elected officials. The Court also found in each county additional factors that restricted the access of minority groups to the political process. In one county, Negroes effectively were excluded from the process of slating candidates for the Democratic Party, while the plaintiffs in the other county were Mexican-Americans who "suffer[ed] a cultural and language barrier" that made "participation in community processes extremely difficult, particularly . . . with respect to the political life" of the county. *Id.* at 768.

White v. *Regester* is thus consistent with "the basic equal protection principle that the invidious equality of a law claimed to be racially discriminatory must ultimately be traced to a racially discriminatory purpose," *Washington* v. *Davis*, 426 U.S., at 240. * * * Of course, "[t]he impact of the official action — whether it 'bears more heavily on one race than another' — may provide an important starting point." *Arlington Heights*, *supra*, at 266. But where the character of a law is readily explainable on grounds apart from race, as would nearly always be true where, as here, an entire system of local governance is brought into question, disproportionate impact alone cannot be decisive, and courts must look to other evidence to support a finding of discriminatory purpose. See *ibid.*; *Washington* v. *Davis*, *supra*, at 242.

* * * [I]t is clear that the evidence in the present case fell far short of showing

that the appellants "conceived or operated [a] purposeful devic[e] to further racial . . . discrimination." *Whitcomb* v. *Chavis*, 403 U.S., at 149. * * *

* * * The theory of [MR. JUSTICE MARSHALL'S] dissenting opinion * * * appears to be that every "political group," or at least every such group that is in the minority, has a federal constitutional right to elect candidates in proportion to its numbers.[22] * * *

Whatever appeal the dissenting opinion's view may have as a matter of political theory, it is not the law. The Equal Protection Clause of the Fourteenth Amendment does not require proportional representation as an imperative of political organization. The entitlement that the dissenting opinion assumes to exist simply is not to be found in the Constitution of the United States. * * *

The dissenting opinion erroneously discovers the asserted entitlement to group representation within the "one person-one vote" principle of *Reynolds* v. *Sims* [377 U.S. 533 (1964)] [p. 173] and its progeny.[25] * * * There can be, of course, no claim that the "one person, one vote" principle has been violated in this case, because the city of Mobile is a unitary electoral district and the Commission elections are conducted at large. It is therefore obvious that nobody's vote has been "diluted" in the sense in which that word was used in the *Reynolds* case.

The dissenting opinion places an extraordinary interpretation on these decisions, an interpretation not justified by *Reynolds* v. *Sims* itself or by any other decision of this Court. It is, of course, true that the right of a person to vote on an equal basis with other voters draws much of its significance from the political associations that its exercise reflects, but it is an altogether different matter to conclude that political groups themselves have an independent constitutional claim to representation.[26]

---

[22] The dissenting opinion seeks to disclaim this description of its theory by suggesting that a claim of vote dilution may require, in addition to proof of electoral defeat, some evidence of "historical and social factors" indicating that the group in question is without political influence. Putting to the side the evident fact that these gauzy sociological considerations have no constitutional basis, it remains far from certain that they could, in any principled manner, exclude the claims of any discrete political group that happens, for whatever reason, to elect fewer of its candidates than arithmetic indicates it might. Indeed, the putative limits are bound to prove illusory if the express purpose informing their application would be, as the dissent assumes, to redress the "inequitable distribution of political influence."

[25] The dissenting opinion also relies upon several decisions of this Court that have held constitutionally invalid various voter eligibility requirements * * *. But there is in this case no attack whatever upon any of the voter eligibility requirements in Mobile. * * * It is difficult to perceive any similarity between the excluded person's right to equal electoral participation in the cited cases, and the right asserted by the dissenting opinion in the present case, aside from the fact that they both in some way involve voting.

[26] It is difficult to perceive how the implications of the dissenting opinion's theory of group representation could rationally be cabined. Indeed, certain preliminary practical questions immediately come to mind: Can only members of a minority of the voting population in a particular municipality be members of a "political group"? How large must a "group" be to be a "political group"? Can any "group" call itself a "political group"? If not, who is to say which "groups" are "political groups"? Can a qualified voter belong to more than one "political group"? Can there be more than one "political group" among white voters (*e.g.*, Irish-American, Italian-American, Polish-American, Jews, Catholics, Protestants)? Can there be more than one "political group" among nonwhite voters? Do the answers to any of these questions depend upon the particular demographic composition of a given city? Upon the total size of its voting population? Upon the size of its governing body? Upon its form of government? Upon its history? Its geographic location? The fact that even these preliminary questions may be largely unanswerable

And the Court's decisions hold squarely that they do not. See *United Jewish Organizations* v. *Carey*, 430 U.S. 144, 166–167 [(1977)] [p. 277]; *id.*, at 179–180 (opinion concurring in judgment); *White* v. *Regester*, 412 U.S., at 765–766; *Whitcomb* v. *Chavis*, 403 U.S., at 149–150, 153–154, 156–157.

The fact is that the Court has sternly set its face against the claim, however phrased, that the Constitution somehow guarantees proportional representation. * * *

The judgment is reversed, and the case is remanded to the Court of Appeals for further proceedings.

It is so ordered.

Mr. Justice Blackmun, concurring in the result.

Assuming that proof of intent is a prerequisite to appellees' prevailing on their constitutional claim of vote dilution, I am inclined to agree with Mr. Justice White that, in this case, "the findings of the District Court amply support an inference of purposeful discrimination." I concur in the Court's judgment of reversal, however, because I believe that the relief afforded appellees by the District Court was not commensurate with the sound exercise of judicial discretion. * * *

Contrary to the District Court, I do not believe that, in order to remedy the unconstitutional vote dilution it found, it was necessary to convert Mobile's city government to a mayor-council system. In my view, the District Court at least should have considered alternative remedial orders that would have maintained some of the basic elements of the commission system Mobile long ago had selected — joint exercise of legislative and executive power, and citywide representation. In the first place, I see no reason for the court to have separated legislative and executive power in the city of Mobile by creating the office of mayor. In the second place, the court could have, and in my view should have, considered expanding the size of the Mobile City Commission and providing for the election of at least some commissioners at large. Alternative plans might have retained at-large elections for all commissioners while imposing district residency requirements that would have insured the election of a commission that was a cross section of all of Mobile's neighborhoods, or a plurality-win system that would have provided the potential for the effective use of single-shot voting by black voters. In failing to consider such alternative plans, it appears to me that the District Court was perhaps overly concerned with the elimination of at-large elections *per se*, rather than with structuring an electoral system that provided an opportunity for black voters in Mobile to participate in the city's government on an equal footing with whites. * * *

---

suggests some of the conceptual and practical fallacies in the constitutional theory espoused by the dissenting opinion, putting to one side the total absence of support for that theory in the Constitution itself.

Mr. Justice Stevens, concurring in the judgment. * * *

* * * In this case, if the commission form of government in Mobile were extraordinary, or if it were nothing more than a vestige of history, with no greater justification than the grotesque figure in *Gomillion*, it would surely violate the Constitution. That conclusion would follow simply from its adverse impact on black voters plus the absence of any legitimate justification for the system, without reference to the subjective intent of the political body that has refused to alter it.

Conversely, I am also persuaded that a political decision that affects group voting rights may be valid even if it can be proved that irrational or invidious factors have played some part in its enactment or retention. The standard for testing the acceptability of such a decision must take into account the fact that the responsibility for drawing political boundaries is generally committed to the legislative process and that the process inevitably involves a series of compromises among different group interests. If the process is to work it must reflect an awareness of group interests and it must tolerate some attempts to advantage or to disadvantage particular segments of the voting populace. * * * The standard cannot, therefore, be so strict that any evidence of a purpose to disadvantage a bloc of voters will justify a finding of "invidious discrimination"; otherwise, the facts of political life would deny legislatures the right to perform the districting function. Accordingly, a political decision that is supported by valid and articulable justifications cannot be invalid simply because some participants in the decisionmaking process were motivated by a purpose to disadvantage a minority group.

The decision to retain the commission form of government in Mobile, Ala., is such a decision. I am persuaded that some support for its retention comes, directly or indirectly, from members of the white majority who are motivated by a desire to make it more difficult for members of the black minority to serve in positions of responsibility in city government. I deplore that motivation and wish that neither it nor any other irrational prejudice played any part in our political processes. But I do not believe otherwise legitimate political choices can be invalidated simply because an irrational or invidious purpose played some part in the decisionmaking process. * * * A contrary view "would spawn endless litigation concerning the multi-member district systems now widely employed in this country," *id.*, at 157, and would entangle the judiciary in a voracious political thicket.

In sum, I believe we must accept the choice to retain Mobile's commission form of government as constitutionally permissible even though that choice may well be the product of mixed motivation, some of which is invidious. For these reasons I concur in the judgment of reversal.

Mr. Justice Brennan, dissenting.

I dissent because I agree with Mr. Justice Marshall that proof of discriminatory impact is sufficient * * *. I also dissent because, even accepting the plurality's premise that discriminatory purpose must be shown, I agree with Mr. Justice Marshall and Mr. Justice White that the appellees have clearly met that burden.

Mr. Justice White, dissenting.

* * * The Court's decision is flatly inconsistent with *White* v. *Regester* and it cannot be understood to flow from our recognition in *Washington* v. *Davis* that the Equal Protection Clause forbids only purposeful discrimination. Both the District Court and the Court of Appeals properly found that an invidious discriminatory purpose could be inferred from the totality of facts in this case. The Court's cryptic rejection of their conclusions ignores the principles that an invidious discriminatory purpose can be inferred from objective factors of the kind relied on in *White* v. *Regester* and that the trial courts are in a special position to make such intensely local appraisals. * * *

In the instant case the District Court and the Court of Appeals faithfully applied the principles of *White* v. *Regester* in assessing whether the maintenance of a system of at-large elections for the selection of Mobile City Commissioners denied Mobile Negroes their Fourteenth and Fifteenth Amendment rights. Scrupulously adhering to our admonition that "[t]he plaintiffs' burden is to produce evidence to support findings that the political processes leading to nomination and election were not equally open to participation by the group in question," *id.*, at 766, the District Court conducted a detailed factual inquiry into the openness of the candidate selection process to blacks. The court noted that "Mobile blacks were subjected to massive official and private racial discrimination until the Voting Rights Act of 1965" and that "[t]he pervasive effects of past discrimination still substantially affec[t] black political participation." Although the District Court noted that "[s]ince the Voting Rights Act of 1965, blacks register and vote without hindrance," the court found that "local political processes are not equally open" to blacks. Despite the fact that Negroes constitute more than 35% of the population of Mobile, no Negro has ever been elected to the Mobile City Commission. The plaintiffs introduced extensive evidence of severe racial polarization in voting patterns during the 1960's and 1970's with "white voting for white and black for black if a white is opposed to a black," resulting in the defeat of the black candidate or, if two whites are running, the defeat of the white candidate most identified with blacks. * * * After single-member districts were created in Mobile County for state legislative elections, "three blacks of the present fourteen member Mobile County delegation have been elected." Based on th[is] evidence, the District Court found "that the structure of the at-large election of city commissioners combined with strong racial polarization of Mobile's electorate continues to effectively discourage qualified black citizens from seeking office or being elected thereby denying blacks equal access to the slating or candidate selection process."

The District Court also reviewed extensive evidence that the City Commissioners elected under the at-large system have not been responsive to the needs of the Negro community. The court found that city officials have been unresponsive to the interests of Mobile Negroes in municipal employment, appointments to boards and committees, and the provision of municipal services in part because of "the political fear of a white backlash vote when black citizens' needs are at stake." The court also found that there is no clear-cut state policy preference for at-large elections and that past discrimination affecting the ability of Negroes to register and to vote "has helped preclude the effective participation of blacks in the election system today." The adverse impact of the at-large election system on minorities was found to be enhanced by the large size of the citywide election district, the majority vote requirement, the provision that candidates run for positions by place or number, and the lack of any provision for at-large candidates to run from particular geographical subdistricts.

After concluding its extensive findings of fact, the District Court addressed the question of the effect of *Washington* v. *Davis* on the *White* v. *Regester* standards. The court concluded that the requirement that a facially neutral statute involve purposeful discrimination before a violation of the Equal Protection Clause can be established was not inconsistent with *White* v. *Regester* in light of the recognition in *Washington* v. *Davis* that the discriminatory purpose may often be inferred from the totality of the relevant facts, including the discriminatory impact of the statute. After noting that "whenever a redistricting bill of any type is proposed by a county delegation member, a major concern has centered around how many, if any, blacks would be elected," the District Court concluded that there was "a present purpose to dilute the black vote . . . resulting from intentional state legislative *inaction*. . . ." Based on an "exhaustive analysis of the evidence in the record," the court held that "[t]he plaintiffs have met the burden cast in *White* and *Whitcomb*," and that "the multi-member at-large election of Mobile City Commissioners . . . results in an unconstitutional dilution of black voting strength." * * *

[T]he Court of Appeals reviewed the District Court's findings of fact, found them not to be clearly erroneous and held that they "compel the inference that [Mobile's at-large] system has been maintained with the purpose of diluting the black vote, thus supplying the element of intent necessary to establish a violation of the fourteenth amendment and the fifteenth amendment." The court observed that the District Court's "finding that the legislature was acutely conscious of the racial consequences of its districting policies," coupled with the attempt to assign different functions to each of the three City Commissioners "to lock in the at-large feature of the scheme," constituted "direct evidence of the intent behind the maintenance of the at-large plan." * * *

* * * Although the totality of the facts relied upon by the District Court to support its inference of purposeful discrimination is even more compelling than that present in *White* v. *Regester*, the plurality today rejects the inference of purposeful discrimination apparently because each of the factors relied upon by the courts below is alone insufficient to support the inference. The plurality states that the "fact [that Negro candidates have been defeated] alone does not work a constitutional deprivation," that evidence of the unresponsiveness of elected officials "is relevant only as the most tenuous and circumstantial evidence," that "the substantial history of official racial discrimination . . . [is] of limited help," and that the features of the electoral system that enhance the disadvantages faced by a voting minority "are far from proof that the at-large electoral scheme represents purposeful discrimination." By viewing each of the factors relied upon below in isolation, and ignoring the fact that racial bloc voting at the polls makes it impossible to elect a black commissioner under the at-large system, the plurality rejects the "totality of the circumstances" approach we endorsed in *White* v. *Regester*, *Washington* v. *Davis*, and *Arlington Heights* v. *Metropolitan Housing Dev. Corp.*, and leaves the courts below adrift on uncharted seas with respect to how to proceed on remand.

Because I believe that the findings of the District Court amply support an inference of purposeful discrimination in violation of the Fourteenth and Fifteenth Amendments, I respectfully dissent.

Mr. Justice Marshall, dissenting. * * *

In my view, our vote dilution decisions require only a showing of discriminatory impact to justify the invalidation of a multimember districting scheme, and, because they are premised on the fundamental interest in voting protected by the Fourteenth Amendment, the discriminatory impact standard adopted by them is unaffected by *Washington* v. *Davis* and its progeny. Furthermore, an intent requirement is inconsistent with the protection against denial or abridgment of the vote on account of race embodied in the Fifteenth Amendment and in § 2 of the Voting Rights Act of 1965. * * *

The Court does not dispute the proposition that multimember districting can have the effect of submerging electoral minorities and over-representing electoral majorities.[3] * * * Although we have held that multimember districts are not unconstitutional *per se*, there is simply no basis for the plurality's conclusion that, under our prior cases, proof of discriminatory intent is a necessary condition for the invalidation of multimember districting.

In *Fortson* v. *Dorsey*, 379 U.S. 433 (1965), the first vote-dilution case to reach this Court, we stated explicitly that such a claim could rest on either discriminatory purpose or effect:

> "It might well be that, *designedly or otherwise*, a multimember constituency apportionment scheme, under the circumstances of a particular case, would *operate* to minimize or cancel out the voting strength of racial or political elements of the voting population." *Id.* at 439 (emphasis added).

We reiterated these words in *Burns* v. *Richardson*, 384 U.S. 73 (1966), interpreted them as the correct test to apply to vote-dilution claims, and described the standard as one involving "invidious effect," *id.* at 88. * * * It could not be plainer that the Court in *Burns* considered discriminatory effect a sufficient condition for invalidating a multimember districting plan.

In *Whitcomb* v. *Chavis*, 403 U.S. 124 (1971) [p. 268], we again repeated and applied the *Fortson* standard, but determined that the Negro community's lack of

---

[3] * * * The electoral schemes in these cases involve majority-vote, numbered-post, and staggered-term requirements. These electoral rules exacerbate the vote-dilutive effects of multimember districting. A requirement that a candidate must win by a majority of the vote forces a minority candidate who wins a plurality of votes in the general election to engage in a runoff election with his nearest competitor. If the competitor is a member of the dominant political faction, the minority candidate stands little chance of winning in the second election. A requirement that each candidate must run for a particular "place" or "post" creates head-to-head contests that minority candidates cannot survive. When a number of positions on a governmental body are to be chosen in the same election, members of a minority will increase the likelihood of election of a favorite candidate by voting only for him. If the remainder of the electorate splits its votes among the other candidates, the minority's candidate might well be elected by the minority's "single-shot voting." If the terms of the officeholders are staggered, the opportunity for single-shot voting is decreased.

success at the polls was the result of partisan politics, not racial vote dilution. The Court stressed that both the Democratic and Republican Parties had nominated Negroes, and several had been elected. Negro candidates lost only when their entire party slate went down to defeat. * * *

More recently, in *White* v. *Regester*, 412 U.S. 755 (1973) [p. 274], we invalidated the challenged multimember districting plans because their characteristics, when combined with historical and social factors, had the discriminatory effect of denying the plaintiff Negroes and Mexican-Americans equal access to the political process. * * *

It is apparent that a showing of discriminatory intent in the creation or maintenance of multimember districts is as unnecessary after *White* as it was under our earlier vote-dilution decisions. Under this line of cases, an electoral districting plan is invalid if it has the effect of affording an electoral minority "less opportunity than . . . other residents in the district to participate in the political processes and to elect legislators of their choice," *id.* at 766. It is also apparent that the Court in *White* considered equal access to the political process as meaning more than merely allowing the minority the opportunity to vote. *White* stands for the proposition that an electoral system may not relegate an electoral minority to political impotence by diminishing the importance of its vote. The plurality's approach requiring proof of discriminatory purpose in the present cases is, then, squarely contrary to *White* and its predecessors.

The plurality fails to apply the discriminatory-effect standard of *White* v. *Regester* because that approach conflicts with what the plurality takes to be an elementary principle of law. "[O]nly if there is purposeful discrimination," announces the plurality, "can there be a violation of the Equal Protection Clause of the Fourteenth Amendment." That proposition is plainly overbroad. It fails to distinguish between two distinct lines of equal protection decisions: those involving suspect classifications, and those involving fundamental rights. * * *

Reynolds v. *Sims* and its progeny focused solely on the discriminatory *effects* of malapportionment. They recognize that, when population figures for the representational districts of a legislature are not similar, the votes of citizens in larger districts do not carry as much weight in the legislature as do votes cast by citizens in smaller districts. The equal protection problem attacked by the "one person, one vote" principle is, then, one of vote dilution: under *Reynolds*, each citizen must have an "equally effective voice" in the election of representatives. In the present cases, the alleged vote dilution, though caused by the combined effects of the electoral structure and social and historical factors, rather than by unequal population distribution, is analytically the same concept: the unjustified abridgment of a fundamental right. It follows, then, that a showing of discriminatory intent is just as unnecessary under the vote-dilution approach adopted in *Fortson* v. *Dorsey*, and applied in *White* v. *Regester*, as it is under our reapportionment cases. * * *

Our vote-dilution decisions, then, involve the fundamental interest branch, rather than the antidiscrimination branch, of our jurisprudence under the Equal Protection Clause. They recognize a substantive constitutional right to participate on an equal basis in the electoral process that cannot be denied or diminished for any reason, racial or otherwise, lacking quite substantial justification. They are premised on a rationale wholly apart from that underlying *Washington* v. *Davis*. That decision involved application of a different equal protection principle, the prohibition on racial discrimination in the governmental distribution of interests to which citizens have no constitutional entitlement. Whatever may be the merits of applying motivational analysis to the allocation of constitutionally gratuitous benefits, that approach is completely misplaced where, as here, it is applied to the distribution of a constitutionally protected interest.

Washington v. *Davis*, then, in no way alters the discriminatory impact test developed in *Fortson* v. *Dorsey*, and applied in *White* v. *Regester*, to evaluate claims of dilution of the fundamental right to vote. In my view, that test is now, and always has been, the proper method of safeguarding against inequitable distribution of political influence.

The plurality's response is that my approach amounts to nothing less than a constitutional requirement of proportional representation for groups. That assertion amounts to nothing more than a red herring: I explicitly reject the notion that the Constitution contains any such requirement. The constitutional protection against vote dilution found in our prior cases does not extend to those situations in which a group has merely failed to elect representatives in proportion to its share of the population. To prove unconstitutional vote dilution, the group is also required to carry the far more onerous burden of demonstrating that it has been effectively fenced out of the political process. * * *

[I]t is beyond dispute that a standard based solely upon the motives of official decisionmakers creates significant problems of proof for plaintiffs and forces the inquiring court to undertake an unguided, tortuous look into the minds of officials in the hope of guessing why certain policies were adopted and others rejected. An approach based on motivation creates the risk that officials will be able to adopt policies that are the products of discriminatory intent so long as they sufficiently mask their motives through the use of subtlety and illusion. * * *

* * * If this Court refuses to honor our long-recognized principle that the Constitution "nullifies sophisticated as well as simple-minded modes of discrimination," it cannot expect the victims of discrimination to respect political channels of seeking redress. I dissent.

Notes and Questions

1.   It is important to recognize that *Bolden* involved two separate holdings, both of which are significant. First, interpreting § 2 of the Voting Rights Act, the plurality held that the statutory language prohibited only the same "abridge[ments]" of the right to vote already prohibited by the Fifteenth Amendment. Thus, for the plaintiffs to succeed, they had to show that the City's districting violated their constitutional rights.

Second, interpreting the Fifteenth Amendment itself, the plurality held that the constitutional prohibition extended to vote dilution only where there was both the purpose and effect of diminishing the political power of minorities. Because, in the view of the plurality, the plaintiffs could not prove discriminatory intent, they could not succeed on either the constitutional or the statutory claim.

2. Justice Marshall, in dissent, pointed to *Reynolds v. Sims* and the Court's other one-person, one-vote cases in arguing that the Constitution provided a right against measures that diluted the voting strength of groups, regardless of the government's intent. Was the plurality right to dismiss these cases as inapposite?

3. Did *White v. Regester* require plaintiffs to prove discriminatory intent?

4. *Bolden*'s intent requirement for proving violations of the Fifteenth Amendment mirrors the intent requirement in Fourteenth Amendment jurisprudence. Plaintiffs must demonstrate that the challenged action was instituted or maintained "at least in part 'because of,' not merely 'in spite of,' its adverse effects upon an identifiable group." *Personnel Administrator v. Feeney*, 442 U.S. 256, 279 (1979). Is that definition of "purpose" appropriate, or should plaintiffs be able to succeed merely by proving that the government did not care about the effect of a law on the political power of minorities?

5. Should the purpose requirement be satisfied by a showing that an at-large district was *maintained* (but not instituted) for a discriminatory purpose? *See Rogers v. Lodge*, 458 U.S. 613, 622, 626 (1982).

C. SECTION 2'S POST-1982 RESULTS TEST

The plurality's constitutional holding in *City of Mobile v. Bolden* remains good law. Outright prohibitions on voting or registering violate the Fifteenth Amendment whether or not they were enacted for a discriminatory purpose. Measures that make a group's votes less *effective* than votes of other groups, however, are unconstitutional only if plaintiffs can show a discriminatory purpose in addition to the dilutive effect.

Bolden's statutory holding, on the other hand, had a very short life indeed. Congress reacted to *Bolden* by amending § 2 in 1982. The amendment attempted to overrule *Bolden* by making clear that a § 2 violation could be shown by pointing to a state "standard, practice, or procedure" that "*results* in a denial or abridgement" of citizens' votes on account of race, color, or membership in a language minority. 52 U.S.C. § 10301, 96 Stat. 134 (1982) (emphasis added). Thus, *Bolden*'s focus on discriminatory intent was replaced by amended § 2's "results test." This amendment made clear that § 2 was intended to have a broader scope than the Fifteenth Amendment, and accordingly most litigation under § 2 focuses on the application of the results test.[c] *Thornburg v. Gingles*, which appears immediately below, was the Court's first attempt to interpret the language of amended § 2. The three "preconditions" established by *Gingles* have proven central to later cases interpreting § 2.

---

[c] For an extensive and balanced discussion of the legislative history of the 1982 amendments, see Thomas M. Boyd & Stephen J. Markman, *The 1982 Amendments to the Voting Rights Act: A Legislative History*, 40 WASH. & LEE L. REV. 1347 (1983).

THORNBURG v. GINGLES
Supreme Court of the United States
478 U.S. 30, 106 S. Ct. 2752, 92 L. Ed. 2d 25 (1986)

JUSTICE BRENNAN announced the judgment of the Court and delivered the opinion of the Court with respect to Parts I, II, III-A, III-B, IV-A, and V [in which JUSTICE WHITE, JUSTICE MARSHALL, JUSTICE BLACKMUN, and JUSTICE STEVENS join], an opinion with respect to Part III-C, in which JUSTICE MARSHALL, JUSTICE BLACKMUN, and JUSTICE STEVENS join, and an opinion with respect to Part IV-B, in which JUSTICE WHITE joins. * * *

I

In April 1982, the North Carolina General Assembly enacted a legislative redistricting plan for the State's Senate and House of Representatives. Appellees, black citizens of North Carolina who are registered to vote, challenged seven districts, one single-member and six multimember districts, alleging that the redistricting scheme impaired black citizens' ability to elect representatives of their choice in violation of the Fourteenth and Fifteenth Amendments to the United States Constitution and of § 2 of the Voting Rights Act.

After appellees brought suit, but before trial, Congress amended § 2. The amendment was largely a response to this Court's plurality opinion in *Mobile* v. *Bolden*, 446 U.S. 55 (1980) [p. 288], which had declared that, in order to establish a violation either of § 2 or of the Fourteenth or Fifteenth Amendments, minority voters must prove that a contested electoral mechanism was intentionally adopted or maintained by state officials for a discriminatory purpose. Congress substantially revised § 2 to make clear that a violation could be proved by showing discriminatory effect alone and to establish as the relevant legal standard the "results test," applied by this Court in *White* v. *Regester*, 412 U.S. 755 (1973) [p. 274], and by other federal courts before *Bolden*. S. Rep. No. 97–417, p.28 (1982) (hereinafter S. Rep.).

Section 2, as amended, 96 Stat. 134, reads as follows:

> "(a) No voting qualification or prerequisite to voting or standard, practice, or procedure shall be imposed or applied by any State or political subdivision in a manner which results in a denial or abridgement of the right of any citizen of the United States to vote on account of race or color, or in contravention of the guarantees set forth in section 4(f)(2), as provided in subsection (b).

> "(b) A violation of subsection (a) is established if, based on the totality of circumstances, it is shown that the political processes leading to nomination or election in the State or political subdivision are not equally open to participation by members of a class of citizens protected by subsection (a) in that its members have less opportunity than other members of the electorate to participate in the political process and to elect representatives of their choice. The extent to which members of a protected class have been elected to office in the State or political subdivision is one circumstance which may be considered: *Provided*, That nothing in this section establishes

a right to have members of a protected class elected in numbers equal to their proportion in the population." Codified at 42 U.S.C. § 1973 [now 52 U.S.C. § 10301 — Eds.].

The Senate Judiciary Committee majority Report accompanying the bill that amended § 2 elaborates on the circumstances that might be probative of a § 2 violation, noting the following "typical factors":[4]

"1. the extent of any history of official discrimination in the state or political subdivision that touched the right of the members of the minority group to register, to vote, or otherwise to participate in the democratic process;

"2. the extent to which voting in the elections of the state or political subdivision is racially polarized;

"3. the extent to which the state or political subdivision has used unusually large election districts, majority vote requirements, anti-single shot provisions, or other voting practices or procedures that may enhance the opportunity for discrimination against the minority group;

"4. if there is a candidate slating process, whether the members of the minority group have been denied access to that process;

"5. the extent to which members of the minority group in the state or political subdivision bear the effects of discrimination in such areas as education, employment and health, which hinder their ability to participate effectively in the political process;

"6. whether political campaigns have been characterized by overt or subtle racial appeals;

"7. the extent to which members of the minority group have been elected to public office in the jurisdiction.

"Additional factors that in some cases have had probative value as part of plaintiffs' evidence to establish a violation are:

"whether there is a significant lack of responsiveness on the part of elected officials to the particularized needs of the members of the minority group.

"whether the policy underlying the state or political subdivision's use of such voting qualification, prerequisite to voting, or standard, practice or procedure is tenuous." S. Rep., at 28–29.

The District Court applied the "totality of the circumstances" test set forth in § 2(b) to appellees' statutory claim, and, relying principally on the factors outlined in the Senate Report, held that the redistricting scheme violated § 2 because it resulted in the dilution of black citizens' votes in all seven disputed districts. In light of this conclusion, the court did not reach appellees' constitutional claims. * * *

---

[4] These factors were derived from the analytical framework of *White* v. *Regester*, as refined and developed by the lower courts, in particular by the Fifth Circuit in *Zimmer* v. *McKeithen*, 485 F.2d 1297 (1973) (en banc), aff'd *sub nom. East Carroll Parish School Board* v. *Marshall*, 424 U.S. 636 (1976) *(per curiam)*. S. Rep., at 28, n.113. [Accordingly, they have become known as the *"Zimmer* factors." — Eds.]

II * * *

Appellees contend that the legislative decision to employ multimember, rather than single-member, districts in the contested jurisdictions dilutes their votes by submerging them in a white majority, thus impairing their ability to elect representatives of their choice.[12]

The essence of a § 2 claim is that a certain electoral law, practice, or structure interacts with social and historical conditions to cause an inequality in the opportunities enjoyed by black and white voters to elect their preferred representatives. * * * The theoretical basis for this type of impairment is that where minority and majority voters consistently prefer different candidates, the majority, by virtue of its numerical superiority, will regularly defeat the choices of minority voters. Multimember districts and at-large election schemes, however, are not *per se* violative of minority voters' rights. S. Rep., at 16. Minority voters who contend that the multimember form of districting violates § 2 must prove that the use of a multimember electoral structure operates to minimize or cancel out their ability to elect their preferred candidates.

While many or all of the factors listed in the Senate Report may be relevant to a claim of vote dilution through submergence in multimember districts, unless there is a conjunction of the following circumstances, the use of multimember districts generally will not impede the ability of minority voters to elect representatives of their choice.[15] Stated succinctly, a bloc voting majority must *usually* be able to defeat candidates supported by a politically cohesive, geographically insular

---

[12] The claim we address in this opinion is one in which the plaintiffs alleged and attempted to prove that their ability *to elect* the representatives of their choice was impaired by the selection of a multimember electoral structure. We have no occasion to consider whether § 2 permits, and if it does, what standards should pertain to, a claim brought by a minority group, that is not sufficiently large and compact to constitute a majority in a single-member district, alleging that the use of a multimember district impairs its ability *to influence* elections.

We note also that we have no occasion to consider whether the standards we apply to respondents' claim that multimember districts operate to dilute the vote of geographically cohesive minority groups that are large enough to constitute majorities in single-member districts and that are contained within the boundaries of the challenged multimember districts, are fully pertinent to other sorts of vote dilution claims, such as a claim alleging that the splitting of a large and geographically cohesive minority between two or more multimember or single-member districts resulted in the dilution of the minority vote.

[15] Under a "functional" view of the political process mandated by § 2, S. Rep., at 30, n.120, the most important Senate Report factors bearing on § 2 challenges to multimember districts are the "extent to which minority group members have been elected to public office in the jurisdiction" and the "extent to which voting in the elections of the state or political subdivision is racially polarized." If present, the other factors, such as the lingering effects of past discrimination, the use of appeals to racial bias in election campaigns, and the use of electoral devices which enhance the dilutive effects of multimember districts when substantial white bloc voting exists — for example antibullet voting laws and majority vote requirements, are supportive of, but *not essential to*, a minority voter's claim.

* * * It is obvious that unless minority group members experience substantial difficulty electing representatives of their choice, they cannot prove that a challenged electoral mechanism impairs their ability "to elect." And, where the contested electoral structure is a multimember district, * * * in the absence of significant white bloc voting it cannot be said that the ability of minority voters to elect their chosen representatives is inferior to that of white voters. Consequently, if difficulty in electing and white bloc voting are not proved, minority voters have not established that the multimember structure interferes with their ability to elect their preferred candidates. * * *

minority group. These circumstances are necessary preconditions for multimember districts to operate to impair minority voters' ability to elect representatives of their choice for the following reasons. First, the minority group must be able to demonstrate that it is sufficiently large and geographically compact to constitute a majority in a single-member district. If it is not, as would be the case in a substantially integrated district, the *multimember form* of the district cannot be responsible for minority voters' inability to elect its candidates.[17] Second, the minority group must be able to show that it is politically cohesive. If the minority group is not politically cohesive, it cannot be said that the selection of a multimember electoral structure thwarts distinctive minority group interests. Third, the minority must be able to demonstrate that the white majority votes sufficiently as a bloc to enable it — in the absence of special circumstances, such as the minority candidate running unopposed — usually to defeat the minority's preferred candidate. In establishing this last circumstance, the minority group demonstrates that submergence in a white multimember district impedes its ability to elect its chosen representatives.

Finally, we observe that the usual predictability of the majority's success distinguishes structural dilution from the mere loss of an occasional election.

III * * *

A * * *

* * * The District Court found that blacks and whites generally preferred different candidates and, on that basis, found voting in the districts to be racially correlated [to a statistically significant extent]. * * * [T]he court [further] found that in all but 2 of the 53 elections the degree of racial bloc voting was "so marked as to be substantively significant, in the sense that the results of the individual election would have been different depending upon whether it had been held among only the white voters or only the black voters."

The court also reported its findings * * * that a high percentage of black voters regularly supported black candidates and that most white voters were extremely reluctant to vote for black candidates. The court then considered the relevance to the existence of legally significant white bloc voting of the fact that black candidates have won some elections. It determined that in most instances, special circumstances, such as incumbency and lack of opposition, rather than a diminution in

---

[17] The reason that a minority group making such a challenge must show, as a threshold matter, that it is sufficiently large and geographically compact to constitute a majority in a single-member district is this: Unless minority voters possess the *potential* to elect representatives in the absence of the challenged structure or practice, they cannot claim to have been injured by that structure or practice. The single-member district is generally the appropriate standard against which to measure minority group potential to elect because it is the smallest political unit from which representatives are elected. Thus, if the minority group is spread evenly throughout a multimember district, or if, although geographically compact, the minority group is so small in relation to the surrounding white population that it could not constitute a majority in a single-member district, these minority voters cannot maintain that they would have been able to elect representatives of their choice in the absence of the multimember electoral structure.

usually severe white bloc voting, accounted for these candidates' success. The court also suggested that black voters' reliance on bullet voting [in which voters can allocate multiple votes to a single candidate] was a significant factor in their successful efforts to elect candidates of their choice. Based on all of the evidence before it, the trial court concluded that each of the districts experienced racially polarized voting "in a persistent and severe degree."

B * * *

The Senate Report states that the "extent to which voting in the elections of the state or political subdivision is racially polarized" is relevant to a vote dilution claim. * * *

The purpose of inquiring into the existence of racially polarized voting is twofold: to ascertain whether minority group members constitute a politically cohesive unit and to determine whether whites vote sufficiently as a bloc usually to defeat the minority's preferred candidates. Thus, the question whether a given district experiences legally significant racially polarized voting requires discrete inquiries into minority and white voting practices. A showing that a significant number of minority group members usually vote for the same candidates is one way of proving the political cohesiveness necessary to a vote dilution claim and, consequently, establishes minority bloc voting within the context of § 2. And, in general, a white bloc vote that normally will defeat the combined strength of minority support plus white "crossover" votes rises to the level of legally significant white bloc voting. The amount of white bloc voting that can generally "minimize or cancel" black voters' ability to elect representatives of their choice, however, will vary from district to district according to a number of factors, including the nature of the allegedly dilutive electoral mechanism; the presence or absence of other potentially dilutive electoral devices, such as majority vote requirements, designated posts, and prohibitions against bullet voting; the percentage of registered voters in the district who are members of the minority group; the size of the district; and, in multimember districts, the number of seats open and the number of candidates in the field.

Because loss of political power through vote dilution is distinct from the mere inability to win a particular election, a pattern of racial bloc voting that extends over a period of time is more probative of a claim that a district experiences legally significant polarization than are the results of a single election. Also for this reason, in a district where elections are shown usually to be polarized, the fact that racially polarized voting is not present in one or a few individual elections does not necessarily negate the conclusion that the district experiences legally significant bloc voting. Furthermore, the success of a minority candidate in a particular election does not necessarily prove that the district did not experience polarized voting in that election; special circumstances, such as the absence of an opponent, incumbency, or the utilization of bullet voting, may explain minority electoral success in a polarized contest.

As must be apparent, the degree of racial bloc voting that is cognizable as an element of a § 2 vote dilution claim will vary according to a variety of factual circumstances. Consequently, there is no simple doctrinal test for the existence of legally significant racial bloc voting. However, the foregoing general principles should provide courts with substantial guidance in determining whether evidence that black and white voters generally prefer different candidates rises to the level of legal significance under § 2. * * *

C

North Carolina and the United States * * * argue that the term "racially polarized voting" must, as a matter of law, refer to voting patterns for which the *principal cause* is race. * * *

Whether appellants and the United States believe that it is the voter's race or the candidate's race that must be the primary determinant of the voter's choice is unclear[.] * * * In either case, we disagree: For purposes of § 2, the legal concept of racially polarized voting incorporates neither causation nor intent. It means simply that the race of voters correlates with the selection of a certain candidate or candidates; that is, it refers to the situation where different races (or minority language groups) vote in blocs for different candidates. * * *

The first reason we reject appellants' argument that racially polarized voting refers to voting patterns that are in some way *caused by race*, rather than to voting patterns that are merely *correlated with the race of the voter*, is that the reasons black and white voters vote differently have no relevance to the central inquiry of § 2. By contrast, the correlation between race of voter and the selection of certain candidates is crucial to that inquiry.

Both § 2 itself and the Senate Report make clear that the critical question in a § 2 claim is whether the use of a contested electoral practice or structure results in members of a protected group having less opportunity than other members of the electorate to participate in the political process and to elect representatives of their choice. As we explained, multimember districts may impair the ability of blacks to elect representatives of their choice where blacks vote sufficiently as a bloc as to be able to elect their preferred candidates in a black majority, single-member district and where a white majority votes sufficiently as a bloc usually to defeat the candidates chosen by blacks. It is the *difference* between the choices made by blacks and whites — not the reasons for that difference — that results in blacks having less opportunity than whites to elect their preferred representatives. Consequently, we conclude that under the "results test" of § 2, only the correlation between race of voter and selection of certain candidates, not the causes of the correlation, matters. * * *

[Additionally, reading "racially polarized voting" to refer only] to voting patterns that are *determined primarily by the voter's race*, rather than by the voter's other socioeconomic characteristics * * * ignores the fact that members of geographically insular racial and ethnic groups frequently share socioeconomic characteristics, such as income level, employment status, amount of education, housing and other living conditions, religion, language, and so forth. Where such characteristics are shared, race or ethnic group not only denotes color or place of origin, it also functions as a shorthand notation for common social and economic characteristics. Appellants' definition of racially polarized voting is even more pernicious where shared characteristics are causally related to race or ethnicity. The opportunity to achieve high employment status and income, for example, is often influenced by the presence or absence of racial or ethnic discrimination. A definition of racially polarized voting which holds that black bloc voting does not exist when black voters' choice of certain candidates is most strongly influenced by the fact that the voters have low incomes and menial jobs — when the reason most of those voters have menial jobs and low incomes is attributable to past or present racial discrimination — runs counter to the Senate Report's instruction to conduct a searching and practical evaluation of past and present reality, S. Rep., at 30, and interferes with the purpose of the Voting Rights Act to eliminate the negative effects of past discrimination on the electoral opportunities of minorities.

Furthermore, under appellants' theory of racially polarized voting, even uncontrovertible evidence that candidates strongly preferred by black voters are *always* defeated by a bloc voting white majority would be dismissed for failure to prove racial polarization whenever the black and white populations could be described in terms of other socioeconomic characteristics. * * *

North Carolina's and the United States' suggestion that racially polarized voting means that voters select or reject candidates *principally* on the basis of the *candidate's race* is also misplaced.

First, both the language of § 2 and a functional understanding of the phenomenon of vote dilution mandate the conclusion that the race of the candidate *per se* is irrelevant to racial bloc voting analysis. Section 2(b) states that a violation is established if it can be shown that members of a protected minority group "have less opportunity than other members of the electorate to . . . elect representatives *of their choice*." (Emphasis added.) Because both minority and majority voters often select members of their own race as their preferred representatives, it will frequently be the case that a black candidate is the choice of blacks, while a white candidate is the choice of whites. Indeed, the facts of this case illustrate that tendency — blacks preferred black candidates, whites preferred white candidates. Thus, as a matter of convenience, we and the District Court may refer to the preferred representative of black voters as the "black candidate" and to the preferred representative of white voters as the "white candidate." Nonetheless, the fact that race of voter and race of candidate is often correlated is not directly pertinent to a § 2 inquiry. Under § 2, it is the *status* of the candidate as the *chosen representative of a particular racial group*, not the race of the candidate, that is important. * * *

Second, appellants' suggestion that racially polarized voting refers to voting patterns where whites vote for white candidates because they prefer members of their own race or are hostile to blacks, as opposed to voting patterns where whites vote for white candidates because the white candidates spent more on their campaigns, utilized more media coverage, and thus enjoyed greater name recognition than the black candidates, fails for another, independent reason. This argument, like the argument that the race of the voter must be the primary determinant of the voter's ballot, is inconsistent with the purposes of § 2 and would render meaningless the Senate Report factor that addresses the impact of low socioeconomic status on a minority group's level of political participation.

* * * If, because of inferior education and poor employment opportunities, blacks

earn less than whites, they will not be able to provide the candidates of their choice with the same level of financial support that whites can provide theirs. Thus, electoral losses by candidates preferred by the black community may well be attributable in part to the fact that their white opponents outspent them. But, the fact is that, in this instance, the economic effects of prior discrimination have combined with the multimember electoral structure to afford blacks less opportunity than whites to participate in the political process and to elect representatives of their choice. It would be both anomalous and inconsistent with congressional intent to hold that, on the one hand, the effects of past discrimination which hinder blacks' ability to participate in the political process tend to prove a § 2 violation, while holding on the other hand that, where these same effects of past discrimination deter whites from voting for blacks, blacks cannot make out a crucial element of a vote dilution claim.

Finally, we reject the suggestion that racially polarized voting refers only to white bloc voting which is caused by white voters' *racial hostility* toward black candidates. To accept this theory would frustrate the goals Congress sought to achieve by repudiating the intent test of *Mobile* v. *Bolden* and would prevent minority voters who have clearly been denied an opportunity to elect representatives of their choice from establishing a critical element of a vote dilution claim. * * *

The grave threat to racial progress and harmony which Congress perceived from requiring proof that racism caused the adoption or maintenance of a challenged electoral mechanism is present to a much greater degree in the proposed requirement that plaintiffs demonstrate that racial animosity determined white voting patterns. Under the old intent test, plaintiffs might succeed by proving only that a limited number of elected officials were racist; under the new intent test plaintiffs would be required to prove that most of the white community is racist in order to obtain judicial relief. It is difficult to imagine a more racially divisive requirement.

A second reason Congress rejected the old intent test was that in most cases it placed an "inordinately difficult burden" on § 2 plaintiffs. The new intent test would be equally, if not more, burdensome. In order to prove that a *specific factor* — racial hostility — *determined* white voters' ballots, it would be necessary to demonstrate that other potentially relevant *causal factors*, such as socioeconomic characteristics and candidate expenditures, do not correlate better than racial animosity with white voting behavior. * * *

[Finally, f]ocusing on the discriminatory intent of the voters, rather than the behavior of the voters, also asks the wrong question. All that matters under § 2 and under a functional theory of vote dilution is voter behavior, not its explanations. * * *

In sum, we would hold that the legal concept of racially polarized voting, as it relates to claims of vote dilution, refers only to the existence of a correlation between the race of voters and the selection of certain candidates. Plaintiffs need not prove causation or intent in order to prove a prima facie case of racial bloc voting and defendants may not rebut that case with evidence of causation or intent.

IV

A

North Carolina and the United States maintain that the District Court failed to accord the proper weight to the success of some black candidates in the challenged districts. Black residents of these districts, they point out, achieved improved representation in the 1982 General Assembly election. * * * Essentially, appellants and the United States contend that if a racial minority gains proportional or nearly proportional representation in a single election, that fact alone precludes, as a matter of law, finding a § 2 violation.

Section 2(b) provides that "[the] extent to which members of a protected class have been elected to office . . . is one circumstance which may be considered." The Senate Committee Report also identifies the extent to which minority candidates have succeeded as a pertinent factor. However, the Senate Report expressly states that "the election of a few minority candidates does not 'necessarily foreclose the possibility of dilution of the black vote[.]' " * * * The Senate Report also emphasizes that the question whether "the political processes are 'equally open' depends upon a searching practical evaluation of the 'past and present reality.' " *Id.*, at 30. Thus, the language of § 2 and its legislative history plainly demonstrate that proof that some minority candidates have been elected does not foreclose a § 2 claim. * * *

Nothing in the statute or its legislative history prohibited the court from viewing with some caution black candidates' success in the 1982 election, and from deciding on the basis of all the relevant circumstances to accord greater weight to blacks' relative lack of success over the course of several recent elections. Consequently, we hold that the District Court did not err, as a matter of law, in refusing to treat the fact that some black candidates have succeeded as dispositive of appellees' § 2 claim. Where multimember districting generally works to dilute the minority vote, it cannot be defended on the ground that it sporadically and serendipitously benefits minority voters.

B

The District Court did err, however, in ignoring the significance of the *sustained* success black voters have experienced in House District 23. In that district, the last six elections have resulted in proportional representation for black residents. This persistent proportional representation is inconsistent with appellees' allegation that the ability of black voters in District 23 to elect representatives of their choice is not equal to that enjoyed by the white majority.

In some situations, it may be possible for § 2 plaintiffs to demonstrate that such sustained success does not accurately reflect the minority group's ability to elect its preferred representatives,[38] but appellees have not done so here. Appellees presented evidence relating to black electoral success in the last three elections;

---

[38] We have no occasion in this case to decide what types of special circumstances could satisfactorily demonstrate that sustained success does not accurately reflect the minority's ability to elect its preferred representatives.

they failed utterly, though, to offer any explanation for the success of black candidates in the previous three elections. Consequently, we believe that the District Court erred, as a matter of law, in ignoring the sustained success black voters have enjoyed in House District 23, and would reverse with respect to that District.

V * * *

The District Court in this case carefully considered the totality of the circumstances and found that in each district racially polarized voting; the legacy of official discrimination in voting matters, education, housing, employment, and health services; and the persistence of campaign appeals to racial prejudice acted in concert with the multimember districting scheme to impair the ability of geographically insular and politically cohesive groups of black voters to participate equally in the political process and to elect candidates of their choice. It found that the success a few black candidates have enjoyed in these districts is too recent, too limited, and, with regard to the 1982 elections, perhaps too aberrational, to disprove its conclusion. Excepting House District 23, with respect to which the District Court committed legal error, we affirm the District Court's judgment. We cannot say that the District Court, composed of local judges who are well acquainted with the political realities of the State, clearly erred in concluding that use of a multimember electoral structure has caused black voters in the districts other than House District 23 to have less opportunity than white voters to elect representatives of their choice.

The judgment of the District Court is

Affirmed in part and reversed in part.

JUSTICE WHITE, concurring.

I join Parts I, II, III-A, III-B, IV-A, and V of the Court's opinion and agree with JUSTICE BRENNAN's opinion as to Part IV-B. I disagree with Part III-C of JUSTICE BRENNAN's opinion.

JUSTICE BRENNAN states in Part III-C that the crucial factor in identifying polarized voting is the race of the voter and that the race of the candidate is irrelevant. Under this test, there is polarized voting if the majority of white voters vote for different candidates than the majority of the blacks, regardless of the race of the candidates. I do not agree. Suppose an eight-member multimember district that is 60% white and 40% black, the blacks being geographically located so that two safe black single-member districts could be drawn. Suppose further that there are six white and two black Democrats running against six white and two black Republicans. Under JUSTICE BRENNAN's test, there would be polarized voting and a likely § 2 violation if all the Republicans, including the two blacks, are elected, and 80% of the blacks in the predominantly black areas vote Democratic. I take it that there would also be a violation in a single-member district that is 60% black, but enough of the blacks vote with the whites to elect a black candidate who is not the choice of the majority of black voters. This is interest-group politics rather than a rule hedging against racial discrimination. I doubt that this is what Congress had in mind in amending § 2 as it did, and it seems quite at odds with the discussion in *Whitcomb* v. *Chavis*, 403 U.S. 124, 149–160 (1971) [p. 268]. Furthermore, on the facts of this case, there is no need to draw the voter/candidate distinction. The District Court did not and reached the correct result except, in my view, with respect to District 23.

JUSTICE O'CONNOR, with whom THE CHIEF JUSTICE [BURGER], JUSTICE POWELL, and JUSTICE REHNQUIST join, concurring in the judgment.

In this case, we are called upon to construe § 2 of the Voting Rights Act of 1965, as amended June 29, 1982. Amended § 2 is intended to codify the "results" test employed in *Whitcomb* v. *Chavis* and *White* v. *Regester*, and to reject the "intent" test propounded in the plurality opinion in *Mobile* v. *Bolden*. S. Rep. [at] 27–28. * * * At the same time, however, § 2 unequivocally disclaims the creation of a right to proportional representation. This disclaimer was essential to the compromise that resulted in passage of the amendment. See *id.*, at 193–194 (additional views of Sen. Dole).

In construing this compromise legislation, we must make every effort to be faithful to the balance Congress struck. This is not an easy task. We know that Congress intended to allow vote dilution claims to be brought under § 2, but we also know that Congress did not intend to create a right to proportional representation for minority voters. There is an inherent tension between what Congress wished to do and what it wished to avoid, because any theory of vote dilution must necessarily rely to some extent on a measure of minority voting strength that makes some reference to the proportion between the minority group and the electorate at large. * * *

Although § 2 does not speak in terms of "vote dilution," I agree with the Court that proof of vote dilution can establish a violation of § 2 as amended. The phrase "vote dilution," in the legal sense, simply refers to the impermissible discriminatory effect that a multimember or other districting plan has when it operates "to cancel out or minimize the voting strength of racial groups." *White*, 412 U.S., at 765.* * *

In order to evaluate a claim that a particular multimember district or single-member district has diluted the minority group's voting strength to a degree that violates § 2, however, it is also necessary to construct a measure of "undiluted" minority voting strength. * * * Put simply, in order to decide whether an electoral system has made it harder for minority voters to elect the candidates they prefer, a court must have an idea in mind of how hard it "should" be for minority voters to elect their preferred candidates under an acceptable system. * * *

The Court's definition of the elements of a vote dilution claim is simple and invariable: a court should calculate minority voting strength by assuming that the minority group is concentrated in a single-member district in which it constitutes a voting majority. Where the minority group is not large enough, geographically concentrated enough, or politically cohesive enough for this to be possible, the minority group's claim fails. Where the minority group meets these requirements, the representatives that it could elect in the hypothetical district or districts in which it constitutes a majority will serve as the measure of its undiluted voting strength. Whatever plan the State actually adopts must be assessed in terms of the effect it has on this undiluted voting strength. * * *

* * * The Court requires the minority group that satisfies the threshold requirements of size and cohesiveness to prove that it will *usually* be unable to elect as many representatives of its choice under the challenged districting scheme as its undiluted voting strength would permit. This requirement, then, constitutes the true test of vote dilution. * * *

This measure of vote dilution, taken in conjunction with the Court's standard for measuring undiluted minority voting strength, creates what amounts to a right to *usual, roughly* proportional representation on the part of sizable, compact, cohesive minority groups. If, under a particular multimember or single-member district plan, qualified minority groups usually cannot elect the representatives they would be likely to elect under the most favorable single-member districting plan, then § 2 is violated. Unless minority success under the challenged electoral system regularly approximates this rough version of proportional representation, that system dilutes minority voting strength and violates § 2. * * *

To be sure, the Court also requires that plaintiffs prove that racial bloc voting by the white majority interacts with the challenged districting plan so as usually to defeat the minority's preferred candidate. In fact, however, this requirement adds little that is not already contained in the Court's requirements that the minority group be politically cohesive and that its preferred candidates usually lose. * * * If the minority can prove that it could constitute a majority in a single-member district, that it supported certain candidates, and that those candidates have not usually been elected, then a finding that there is "legally significant white bloc voting" will necessarily follow. Otherwise, by definition, those candidates would usually have won rather than lost.

As shaped by the Court today, then, the basic contours of a vote dilution claim require no reference to most of the *"Zimmer* factors" that were developed by the Fifth Circuit to implement *White*'s results test and which were highlighted in the Senate Report. If a minority group is politically and geographically cohesive and large enough to constitute a voting majority in one or more single-member districts, then unless white voters usually support the minority's preferred candidates in sufficient numbers to enable the minority group to elect as many of those candidates as it could elect in such hypothetical districts, it will routinely follow that a vote dilution claim can be made out, and the multimember district will be invalidated. * * *

In enacting § 2, Congress codified the "results" test this Court had employed, as an interpretation of the Fourteenth Amendment, in *White* and *Whitcomb*. The factors developed by the Fifth Circuit and relied on by the Senate Report simply fill in the contours of the "results" test as described in those decisions, and do not purport to redefine or alter the ultimate showing of discriminatory effect required by *Whitcomb* and *White*. In my view, therefore, it is to *Whitcomb* and *White* that we should look in the first instance in determining how great an impairment of minority voting strength is required to establish vote dilution in violation of § 2.

The "results" test as reflected in *Whitcomb* and *White* requires an inquiry into the extent of the minority group's opportunities to participate in the political processes. See *White*, 412 U.S., at 766. While electoral success is a central part of the vote dilution inquiry, *White* held that to prove vote dilution, "it is not enough that the racial group allegedly discriminated against has not had legislative seats in proportion to its voting potential," *id.*, at 765–766, and *Whitcomb* flatly rejected the proposition that "any group with distinctive interests must be represented in legislative halls if it is numerous enough to command at least one seat and represents a majority living in an area sufficiently compact to constitute a single member district." 403 U.S., at 156. To the contrary, the results test as described in *White* requires plaintiffs to establish "that the political processes leading to nomination and election were not equally open to participation by the group in question — that its members had less opportunity than did other residents in the district to participate in the political processes and to elect legislators of their choice." 412 U.S., at 766. By showing both "a history of disproportionate results" and "strong indicia of lack of political power and the denial of fair representation," the plaintiffs in *White* met this standard, which, as emphasized just today, requires "a substantially greater showing of adverse effects than a mere lack of proportional representation to support a finding of unconstitutional vote dilution." *Davis* v. *Bandemer* [478 U.S. 109, 131 (1986)] (plurality opinion).

When Congress amended § 2 it intended to adopt this "results" test, while abandoning the additional showing of discriminatory intent required by *Bolden*. The vote dilution analysis adopted by the Court today clearly bears little resemblance to the "results" test that emerged in *Whitcomb* and *White*. The Court's test for vote dilution, combined with its standard for evaluating "voting potential," means that any racial minority with distinctive interests must *usually* "be represented in legislative halls if it is numerous enough to command at least one seat and represents a minority living in an area sufficiently compact to constitute" a voting majority in "a single member district." *Whitcomb*, 403 U.S., at 156. Nothing in *Whitcomb*, *White*, or the language and legislative history of § 2 supports the Court's creation of this right to usual, roughly proportional representation on the part of every geographically compact, politically cohesive minority group that is large enough to form a majority in one or more single-member districts.

I would adhere to the approach outlined in *Whitcomb* and *White* and followed, with some elaboration, in *Zimmer* and other cases in the Courts of Appeals prior to *Bolden*. Under that approach, a court should consider all relevant factors bearing on whether the minority group has "less opportunity than other members of the electorate to participate in the political process *and* to elect representatives of their choice." [52 U.S.C. § 10301] (emphasis added). The court should not focus solely on the minority group's ability to elect representatives of its choice. Whatever measure of undiluted minority voting strength the court employs in connection with evaluating the presence or absence of minority electoral success, it should also bear in mind that "the power to influence the political process is not limited to winning elections." *Davis* v. *Bandemer, supra,* at 132. Of course, the relative lack of minority electoral success under a challenged plan, when compared with the success that would be predicted under the measure of undiluted minority voting strength the court is employing, can constitute powerful evidence of vote dilution. Moreover, the minority group may in fact lack access to or influence upon representatives it did not support as candidates. Nonetheless, a reviewing court should be required to find more than simply that the minority group does not usually attain an undiluted measure of electoral success. The court must find that even substantial minority success will be highly infrequent under the challenged plan before it may conclude, on this basis alone, that the plan operates "to cancel out or minimize the voting strength of [the] racial [group]." *White, supra*, at 765.

Only three Justices of the Court join Part III-C of Justice Brennan's opinion, which addresses the validity of the statistical evidence on which the District Court relied in finding racially polarized voting in each of the challenged districts. Insofar as statistical evidence of divergent racial voting patterns is admitted solely to establish that the minority group is politically cohesive and to assess its prospects for electoral success, I agree that defendants cannot rebut this showing by offering evidence that the divergent racial voting patterns may be explained in part by causes other than race, such as an underlying divergence in the interests of minority and white voters. I do not agree, however, that such evidence can never affect the overall vote dilution inquiry. Evidence that a candidate preferred by the minority group in a particular election was rejected by white voters for reasons other than those which made that candidate the preferred choice of the minority group would seem clearly relevant in answering the question whether bloc voting by white voters will consistently defeat minority candidates. Such evidence would suggest that another candidate, equally preferred by the minority group, might be able to attract greater white support in future elections.

I believe Congress also intended that explanations of the reasons why white voters rejected minority candidates would be probative of the likelihood that candidates elected without decisive minority support would be willing to take the minority's interests into account. In a community that is polarized along racial lines, racial hostility may bar these and other indirect avenues of political influence to a much greater extent than in a community where racial animosity is absent although the interests of racial groups diverge. * * * Similarly, I agree with Justice White that Justice Brennan's conclusion that the race of the candidate is always irrelevant in identifying racially polarized voting conflicts with *Whitcomb* and is not necessary to the disposition of this case. * * *

* * * I agree with Justice Brennan that consistent and sustained success by candidates preferred by minority voters is presumptively inconsistent with the existence of a § 2 violation. Moreover, I agree that this case presents no occasion for determining what would constitute proof that such success did not accurately reflect the minority group's actual voting strength in a challenged district or districts. * * *

I do not propose that consistent and virtually proportional minority electoral success should always, as a matter of law, bar finding a § 2 violation. But, as a general rule, such success is entitled to great weight in evaluating whether a challenged electoral mechanism has, on the totality of the circumstances, operated to deny black voters an equal opportunity to participate in the political process and to elect representatives of their choice. With respect to House District 23, the District Court's failure to accord black electoral success such weight was clearly erroneous, and the District Court identified no reason for not giving this degree of success preclusive effect. Accordingly, I agree with Justice Brennan that appellees failed to establish a violation of § 2 in District 23. * * *

Compromise is essential to much if not most major federal legislation, and confidence that the federal courts will enforce such compromises is indispensable to their creation. I believe that the Court today strikes a different balance than Congress intended to when it codified the results test and disclaimed any right to proportional representation under § 2. For that reason, I join the Court's judgment but not its opinion.

JUSTICE STEVENS, with whom JUSTICE MARSHALL and JUSTICE BLACKMUN join, concurring in part and dissenting in part.

In my opinion, the findings of the District Court * * * adequately support [its] judgment concerning House District 23 as well as the balance of that judgment.

I, of course, agree that the election of one black candidate in each election since 1972 provides significant support for the State's position. The notion that this evidence creates some sort of a conclusive, legal presumption is not, however, supported by the language of the statute or by its legislative history. I therefore cannot agree with the Court's view that the District Court committed error by failing to apply a rule of law that emerges today without statutory support. The evidence of candidate success in District 23 is merely one part of an extremely large record which the District Court carefully considered before making its ultimate findings of fact, all of which should be upheld under a normal application of the "clearly erroneous" standard that the Court traditionally applies.

The Court identifies the reason why the success of one black candidate in the elections in 1978, 1980, and 1982 is not inconsistent with the District Court's ultimate finding concerning House District 23. The fact that one black candidate was also elected in the 1972, 1974, and 1976 elections is not sufficient, in my opinion, to overcome the additional findings that apply to House District 23, as well as to other districts in the State for each of those years. [Here JUSTICE STEVENS quoted the Court's reference, in Part V of its opinion, to racially polarized voting, a history of discrimination, and campaign appeals to racial prejudice.] * * * Accordingly, I concur in the Court's opinion except Part IV-B and except insofar as it explains why it reverses the judgment respecting House District 23.

Notes and Questions

1.   What justification does the Court give for pegging the dilution inquiry to a minority group's potential electoral strength *in single-member districts*? Is the Court simply incorporating its own political theory into § 2 by preferring single-member to multimember districts?

2.   As interpreted by the Court, did the amendment to § 2 simply replace the test applied by the plurality in *City of Mobile v. Bolden* with the one that had been applied in *Whitcomb v. Chavis* and *White v. Regester*? Is that what Congress intended to do?

3.   Justice Brennan, writing for four Justices in Part III.C, concluded that § 2's inquiry into racially polarized voting is concerned only with the question whether voting patterns correlate with race, rather than with the question whether groups

vote as they do *because of* race. Is such an interpretation consistent with the text of § 2, which provides a right to be free from abridgment of the right to vote "on account of race or color"? What did the other five Justices conclude about the question Justice Brennan addressed in Part III.C?

4.   Is there racially polarized voting in a jurisdiction where whites and minorities vote for different candidates, but where partisan affiliation and not race best explains those voting patterns? *Compare League of United Latin American Citizens v. Clements*, 999 F.2d 831 (5th Cir. 1994) (*en banc*), *with Goosby v. Town of Hempstead*, 180 F.3d 476 (2d Cir. 1999).

5.   Is it appropriate to characterize a district as "racially polarized" if the majority prefers Candidate A to Candidate B by a 51%-49% margin, while the minority prefers Candidate B to Candidate A by the same margin? Would it be better to require, for example, 60% of the majority and the minority to support different candidates? *See United States v. City of Euclid*, 580 F. Supp. 2d 584, 603 (N.D. Ohio 2008).

6.   One consequence of *Gingles*'s focus on *voter* preference and polarized voting, rather than on the races of *candidates* is that it may be more difficult for a minority group to make out a claim under § 2 if the group itself is politically divided. Is such a result desirable? On the one hand, districting plans do not interfere with minority voters' political choices if the minority voters do not, as a group, prefer particular candidates. On the other hand, however, a district controlled by a minority group may provide an increased opportunity to elect a member of that minority group, and therefore a coalition district may enhance that group's opportunity for *descriptive* representation even if the minority group is divided in terms of political ideology.

7.   Did the Court (and Justice Brennan in those portions of his opinion that did not command a majority) appropriately make use of the legislative history surrounding the 1982 amendment to § 2, or did reliance on the Senate Report risk undermining the compromise that underlay the amendment? *See Holder v. Hall*, 512 U.S. 874, 931–36 (1994) [p. 335] (Thomas, J., concurring in the judgment) (criticizing *Gingles*'s reliance on legislative history).

8.   From an ideological perspective, Justice Brennan's decision to overturn the district court's judgment with respect to District 23 is puzzling. Justice Brennan was one of the Court's leading liberals, and it may be surprising that he held the evidence of blacks' unequal electoral opportunity to be insufficient to make out a § 2 claim. What other reason might account for Justice Brennan's position?

9.   *Gingles* was principally concerned with the dilutive effect of multimember districts on minority voting strength. *See* footnote 12. States can accomplish the same result, however, without resorting to multimember districts. If a districting plan "cracks" a minority community into many districts, it can split the votes of that minority community, so that those votes are ineffective. And if a plan "packs" a minority community into a small number of districts, the minority group may lose its opportunity to exert influence over a greater number of legislators. Accordingly, as demonstrated in *Johnson v. De Grandy*, which follows these Notes, the Court has applied *Gingles* to claims that gerrymandering has diluted the effectiveness of minorities' votes even within a system of single-member districts. *See also*

Voinovich v. Quilter, 507 U.S. 146, 153–54 (1993); *Growe v. Emison*, 507 U.S. 25, 37–42 (1993). As you read *De Grandy*, consider the ways in which application of *Gingles* should be modified in a challenge to the drawing of single-member districts.

10.   Justice O'Connor charged that the Court's vote-dilution standard essentially created a right to proportional representation, in contravention of § 2's proviso. Reread the proviso. Is a standard of proportionality inconsistent with the language of the statute? The proportionality baseline is at the forefront of the next case.

JOHNSON v. De GRANDY
Supreme Court of the United States
512 U.S. 997, 114 S. Ct. 2647, 129 L. Ed. 2d 775 (1994)

JUSTICE SOUTER delivered the opinion of the Court [in which CHIEF JUSTICE REHNQUIST, JUSTICE BLACKMUN, JUSTICE STEVENS, JUSTICE O'CONNOR, and JUSTICE GINSBURG join, and in all but Parts III-B-2, III-B-4, and IV of which JUSTICE KENNEDY joins].

These consolidated cases are about the meaning of vote dilution and the facts required to show it, when § 2 of the Voting Rights Act of 1965 is applied to challenges to single-member legislative districts. We hold that no violation of § 2 can be found here, where, in spite of continuing discrimination and racial bloc voting, minority voters form effective voting majorities in a number of districts roughly proportional to the minority voters' respective shares in the voting-age population. While such proportionality is not dispositive in a challenge to single-member districting, it is a relevant fact in the totality of circumstances to be analyzed when determining whether members of a minority group have "less opportunity than other members of the electorate to participate in the political process and to elect representatives of their choice."

I * * *

[O]n April 10, 1992, the [Florida] legislature adopted Senate Joint Resolution 2-G (SJR 2-G), [which] called for dividing Florida into 40 single-member Senate, and 120 single-member House, districts based on population data from the 1990 census. * * *

[Plaintiffs, a group of Hispanic voters, sued,] claim[ing] that SJR 2-G "unlawfully fragments cohesive minority communities and otherwise impermissibly submerges their right to vote and to participate in the electoral process" [in violation of § 2,] and they pointed to areas around the State where black or Hispanic populations could have formed a voting majority in a politically cohesive, reasonably compact district (or in more than one), if SJR 2-G had not fragmented each group among several districts or packed it into just a few. * * *

[T]he [District C]ourt reviewed the totality of circumstances as required by § 2 and *Thornburg v. Gingles*, 478 U.S. 30 (1986) [p. 301]. In explaining Dade County's "tripartite politics," in which "ethnic factors . . . predominate over all others," the court found political cohesion within each of the Hispanic and black populations but none between the two, and a tendency of non-Hispanic whites to vote as a bloc to bar minority groups from electing their chosen candidates except in a district where a given minority makes up a voting majority. The court further found that the nearly one million Hispanics in the Dade County area could be combined into 4 Senate and 11 House districts, each one relatively compact and with a functional majority of Hispanic voters, whereas SJR 2-G created fewer majority-Hispanic districts; and that one more Senate district with a black voting majority could have been drawn. Noting that Florida's minorities bore the social, economic, and political effects of past discrimination, the court concluded that SJR 2-G impermissibly diluted the voting strength of Hispanics in its House districts and of both Hispanics and blacks in its Senate districts. The findings of vote dilution in the senatorial districts had no practical effect, however, because the court held that remedies for the blacks and the Hispanics were mutually exclusive; it consequently deferred to the state legislature's work as the "fairest" accommodation of all the ethnic communities in south Florida. * * *

III * * *
B

* * * The District Court found that the three *Gingles* preconditions were satisfied, and that Hispanics had suffered historically from official discrimination, the social, economic, and political effects of which they generally continued to feel. Without more, and on the apparent assumption that what could have been done to create additional Hispanic supermajority districts should have been done, the District Court found a violation of § 2. But the assumption was erroneous, and more is required, as a review of *Gingles* will show.

1 * * *

Gingles provided some structure to the statute's "totality of circumstances" test in a case challenging multimember legislative districts. The Court * * * summarized the three now-familiar *Gingles* factors (compactness/numerousness, minority cohesion or bloc voting, and majority bloc voting) as "necessary preconditions," 478 U.S., at 50, for establishing vote dilution by use of a multimember district.

But if *Gingles* so clearly identified the three as generally necessary to prove a § 2 claim, it just as clearly declined to hold them sufficient in combination, either in the sense that a court's examination of relevant circumstances was complete once the three factors were found to exist, or in the sense that the three in combination necessarily and in all circumstances demonstrated dilution. This was true not only because bloc voting was a matter of degree, with a variable legal significance depending on other facts, but also because the ultimate conclusions about equality or inequality of opportunity were intended by Congress to be judgments resting on comprehensive, not limited, canvassing of relevant facts. Lack of electoral success is evidence of vote dilution, but courts must also examine other evidence in the totality of circumstances, including the extent of the opportunities minority voters enjoy to participate in the political processes. 478 U.S., at 46, 79–80; 478 U.S., at 98–99 (O'CONNOR, J., concurring in judgment). To be sure, some § 2 plaintiffs may have easy cases, but although lack of equal electoral opportunity may be readily imagined and unsurprising when demonstrated under circumstances that include the three essential *Gingles* factors, that conclusion must still be addressed explicitly, and without isolating any other arguably relevant facts from the act of judgment.

2

If the three *Gingles* factors may not be isolated as sufficient, standing alone, to prove dilution in every multimember district challenge, *a fortiori* they must not be when the challenge goes to a series of single-member districts, where dilution may be more difficult to grasp. Plaintiffs challenging single-member districts may claim, not total submergence, but partial submergence; not the chance for some electoral success in place of none, but the chance for more success in place of some. When the question thus comes down to the reasonableness of drawing a series of district lines in one combination of places rather than another, judgments about inequality may become closer calls. As facts beyond the ambit of the three *Gingles* factors loom correspondingly larger, factfinders cannot rest uncritically on assumptions about the force of the *Gingles* factors in pointing to dilution.

The cases now before us, of course, fall on this more complex side of the divide, requiring a court to determine whether provision for somewhat fewer majority-minority districts than the number sought by the plaintiffs was dilution of the minority votes. The District Court was accordingly required to assess the probative significance of the *Gingles* factors critically after considering the further circumstances with arguable bearing on the issue of equal political opportunity. We think that in finding dilution here the District Court misjudged the relative importance of the *Gingles* factors and of historical discrimination, measured against evidence tending to show that in spite of these facts, SJR 2-G would provide minority voters with an equal measure of political and electoral opportunity.

The District Court did not, to be sure, commit the error of treating the three *Gingles* conditions as exhausting the enquiry required by § 2. Consistently with *Gingles*, the court received evidence of racial relations outside the immediate confines of voting behavior and found a history of discrimination against Hispanic voters continuing in society generally to the present day. But the District Court was not critical enough in asking whether a history of persistent discrimination reflected in the larger society and its bloc-voting behavior portended any dilutive effect from a newly proposed districting scheme, whose pertinent features were majority-minority districts in substantial proportion to the minority's share of voting-age population. The court failed to ask whether the totality of facts, including those pointing to proportionality,[11] showed that the new scheme would deny minority

---

[11] "Proportionality" as the term is used here links the number of majority-minority voting districts to minority members' share of the relevant population. The concept is distinct from the subject of the proportional representation clause of § 2, which provides that "nothing in this section establishes a right to have members of a protected class elected in numbers equal to their proportion in the population." [52 U.S.C. § 10301(b)]. This proviso speaks to the success of minority candidates, as distinct from the political or electoral power of minority voters. And the proviso also confirms what is otherwise clear from the text of the statute, namely, that the ultimate right of § 2 is equality of opportunity, not a guarantee of electoral success for minority-preferred candidates of whatever race.

voters equal political opportunity.

Treating equal political opportunity as the focus of the enquiry, we do not see how these district lines, apparently providing political effectiveness in proportion to voting-age numbers, deny equal political opportunity. The record establishes that Hispanics constitute 50 percent of the voting-age population in Dade County and under SJR 2-G would make up supermajorities in 9 of the 18 House districts located primarily within the county. Likewise, if one considers the 20 House districts located at least in part within Dade County, the record indicates that Hispanics would be an effective voting majority in 45 percent of them (*i.e.*, nine), and would constitute 47 percent of the voting-age population in the area. In other words, under SJR 2-G Hispanics in the Dade County area would enjoy substantial proportionality. On this evidence, we think the State's scheme would thwart the historical tendency to exclude Hispanics, not encourage or perpetuate it. Thus in spite of that history and its legacy, including the racial cleavages that characterize Dade County politics today, we see no grounds for holding in these cases that SJR 2-G's district lines diluted the votes cast by Hispanic voters.

[P]laintiffs urge us to put more weight on the District Court's findings of packing and fragmentation, allegedly accomplished by the way the State drew certain specific lines * * *. We would agree that where a State has split (or lumped) minority neighborhoods that would have been grouped into a single district (or spread among several) if the State had employed the same line-drawing standards in minority neighborhoods as it used elsewhere in the jurisdiction, the inconsistent treatment might be significant evidence of a § 2 violation, even in the face of proportionality. The District Court, however, made no such finding. * * * [S]ome dividing by district lines and combining within them is virtually inevitable and befalls any population group of substantial size. Attaching the labels "packing" and "fragmenting" to these phenomena, without more, does not make the result vote dilution when the minority group enjoys substantial proportionality.

3

It may be that the significance of the facts under § 2 was obscured by the rule of thumb apparently adopted by the District Court, that anything short of the maximum number of majority-minority districts consistent with the *Gingles* conditions would violate § 2, at least where societal discrimination against the minority had occurred and continued to occur. But reading the first *Gingles* condition in effect to define dilution as a failure to maximize in the face of bloc voting (plus some other incidents of societal bias to be expected where bloc voting occurs) causes its own dangers, and they are not to be courted.

Assume a hypothetical jurisdiction of 1,000 voters divided into 10 districts of 100 each, where members of a minority group make up 40 percent of the voting population and voting is totally polarized along racial lines. With the right geographic dispersion to satisfy the compactness requirement, and with careful manipulation of district lines, the minority voters might be placed in control of as many as 7 of the 10 districts. Each such district could be drawn with at least 51 members of the minority group, and whether the remaining minority voters were added to the groupings of 51 for safety or scattered in the other three districts, minority voters would be able to elect candidates of their choice in all seven districts. The point of the hypothetical is not, of course, that any given district is likely to be open to such extreme manipulation, or that bare majorities are likely to vote in full force and strictly along racial lines, but that reading § 2 to define dilution as any failure to maximize tends to obscure the very object of the statute and to run counter to its textually stated purpose. One may suspect vote dilution from political famine, but one is not entitled to suspect (much less infer) dilution from mere failure to guarantee a political feast. However prejudiced a society might be, it would be absurd to suggest that the failure of a districting scheme to provide a minority group with effective political power 75 percent above its numerical strength indicates a denial of equal participation in the political process. Failure to maximize cannot be the measure of § 2.

4

While, for obvious reasons, the State agrees that a failure to leverage minority political strength to the maximum possible point of power is not definitive of dilution in bloc-voting societies, it seeks to impart a measure of determinacy by applying a definitive rule of its own: that as a matter of law no dilution occurs whenever the percentage of single-member districts in which minority voters form an effective majority mirrors the minority voters' percentage of the relevant population. Proportionality so defined would thus be a safe harbor for any districting scheme.

The safety would be in derogation of the statutory text and its considered purpose, however, and of the ideal that the Voting Rights Act of 1965 attempts to foster. An inflexible rule would run counter to the textual command of § 2, that the presence or absence of a violation be assessed "based on the totality of circumstances." [52 U.S.C. § 10301(b)]. * * * In modifying § 2, Congress thus endorsed our view in *White* v. *Regester*, 412 U.S. 755 (1973) [p. 274], that "whether the political processes are 'equally open' depends upon a searching practical evaluation of the 'past and present reality,'" Senate Report 30 (quoting 412 U.S., at 766, 770). In a substantial number of voting jurisdictions, that past reality has included such reprehensible practices as ballot box stuffing, outright violence, discretionary registration, property requirements, the poll tax, and the white primary; and other practices censurable when the object of their use is discriminatory, such as at-large elections, runoff requirements, anti-single-shot devices, gerrymandering, the impeachment of officeholders, the annexation or deannexation of territory, and the creation or elimination of elective offices. Some of those expedients could occur even in a jurisdiction with numerically demonstrable proportionality; the harbor safe for States would thus not be safe for voters. It is, in short, for good reason that we have been, and remain, chary of entertaining a simplification of the sort the State now urges upon us.

Even if the State's safe harbor were open only in cases of alleged dilution by the manipulation of district lines, however, it would rest on an unexplored premise of highly suspect validity: that in any given voting jurisdiction (or portion of that jurisdiction under consideration), the rights of some minority voters under § 2 may be traded off against the rights of other members of the same minority class. Under the State's view, the most blatant racial gerrymandering in half of a county's single-member districts would be irrelevant under § 2 if offset by political gerry-mandering in the other half, so long as proportionality was the bottom line.

Finally, we reject the safe harbor rule because of a tendency the State would itself certainly condemn, a tendency to promote and perpetuate efforts to devise majority-minority districts even in circumstances where they may not be necessary to achieve equal political and electoral opportunity. Because in its simplest form the State's rule would shield from § 2 challenge a districting scheme in which the number of majority-minority districts reflected the minority's share of the relevant population, the conclusiveness of the rule might be an irresistible inducement to create such districts. It bears recalling, however, that for all the virtues of majority-minority districts as remedial devices, they rely on a quintessentially race-conscious calculus aptly described as the "politics of second best." If the lesson of *Gingles* is that society's racial and ethnic cleavages sometimes necessitate majority-minority districts to ensure equal political and electoral opportunity, that should not obscure the fact that there are communities in which minority citizens are able to form coalitions with voters from other racial and ethnic groups, having no need to be a majority within a single district in order to elect candidates of their choice. Those candidates may not represent perfection to every minority voter, but minority voters are not immune from the obligation to pull, haul, and trade to find common political ground, the virtue of which is not to be slighted in applying a statute meant to hasten the waning of racism in American politics.

It is enough to say that, while proportionality in the sense used here is obviously an indication that minority voters have an equal opportunity, in spite of racial polarization, "to participate in the political process and to elect representatives of their choice," the degree of probative value assigned to proportionality may vary with other facts.[17] No single statistic provides courts with a shortcut to determine whether a set of single-member districts unlawfully dilutes minority voting strength. * * *

6

In sum, the District Court's finding of dilution did not address the statutory standard of unequal political and electoral opportunity, and reflected instead a misconstruction of § 2 that equated dilution with failure to maximize the number of reasonably compact majority-minority districts. Because the ultimate finding of dilution in districting for the Florida House was based on a misreading of the governing law, we hold it to be clearly erroneous.

IV

Having found insufficient evidence of vote dilution in the drawing of House districts in the Dade County area, we look now to the comparable districts for the state Senate. As in the case of House districts, we understand the District Court to have misapprehended the legal test for vote dilution when it found a violation of § 2

---

[17] So, too, the degree of probative value assigned to disproportionality, in a case where it is shown, will vary not only with the degree of disproportionality but with other factors as well. * * *

in the location of the Senate district lines. Because the court did not modify the State's plan, however, we hold the ultimate result correct in this instance. * * *

[*Affirmed in part and reversed in part.*]

JUSTICE O'CONNOR, concurring.

The critical issue in these cases is whether § 2 of the Voting Rights Act of 1965 requires courts to "maximize" the number of districts in which minority voters may elect their candidates of choice. * * * The Court today makes clear that * * * the Voting Rights Act does not require maximization.

But today's opinion does more than reject the maximization principle. The opinion's central teaching is that proportionality — defined as the relationship between the number of majority-minority voting districts and the minority group's share of the relevant population — is *always* relevant evidence in determining vote dilution, but is *never* itself dispositive. * * *

* * * Lack of proportionality can never by itself prove dilution, for courts must always carefully and searchingly review the totality of the circumstances, including the extent to which minority groups have access to the political process. Nor does the presence of proportionality prove the absence of dilution. Proportionality is not a safe harbor for States; it does not immunize their election schemes from § 2 challenge.

In sum, the Court's carefully crafted approach treats proportionality as relevant evidence, but does not make it the only relevant evidence. * * * With this understanding, I join the opinion of the Court.

JUSTICE KENNEDY, concurring in part and concurring in the judgment.

* * * I agree with the Court that the District Court's maximization theory was an erroneous application of § 2 [and that proportionality is relevant to the § 2 inquiry]. * * *

It is important to emphasize that [our precedents and] today's decision[] only construe the statute, and do not purport to assess its constitutional implications. Operating under the constraints of a statutory regime in which proportionality has some relevance, States might consider it lawful and proper to act with the explicit goal of creating a proportional number of majority-minority districts in an effort to avoid § 2 litigation. Likewise, a court finding a § 2 violation might believe that the only appropriate remedy is to order the offending State to engage in race-based redistricting and create a minimum number of districts in which minorities constitute a voting majority. The Department of Justice might require (in effect) the same as a condition of granting preclearance, under § 5 of the Act, 42 U.S.C. § 1973c [now 52 U.S.C. § 10304 — Eds.], to a State's proposed legislative redistricting. Those governmental actions, in my view, tend to entrench the very practices and stereotypes the Equal Protection Clause is set against. As a general matter, the sorting of persons with an intent to divide by reason of race raises the most serious constitutional questions. * * *

* * * But no constitutional claims were brought here, and the Court's opinion does not address any constitutional issues.

With these observations, I concur in all but Parts III-B-2, III-B-4, and IV of the Court's opinion and in its judgment.

JUSTICE THOMAS, with whom JUSTICE SCALIA joins, dissenting.

* * * In accordance with the views I express in *Holder* [v. *Hall*, 512 U.S. 891 (1994)] [p. 335], I would hold that an apportionment plan is not a "standard, practice, or procedure" that may be challenged under § 2. I therefore respectfully dissent.

Notes and Questions

1.   Do you agree with the Court that a minority group may enjoy proportional representation and still make out a claim under § 2 that its members lack an equal opportunity "to participate in the political process and to elect representatives of their choice"? What would the plaintiffs in *De Grandy* have needed to show to succeed on such a claim?

2.   The Court expressed doubt that a state could make up for racial gerrymandering in part of the state by political gerrymandering elsewhere, even if the result would be proportional representation of the minority group. Why should it matter *where* the districts are that result in minorities having the opportunity to elect candidates of their choice?

3.   Did the Court adequately distinguish its proportionality inquiry from the proviso in the amended § 2? Justice Thomas thought not:

> It should be clear that a system that gives a minority group proportional control effectively provides the "right" to elect a proportionate number of minority candidates that the Act disclaims. Whether that right is utilized by minority voters to elect minority candidates is a matter of the voters' choice. The *De Grandy* Court's position seems to be that the proviso is directed, not at a system intended to guarantee the *ability* to elect minority candidates in proportion to the minority's numbers, but only at a system that will *invariably guarantee* the election of a proportionate number of minority candidates. Only one system would fit that description: a system based on a racial register in which a quota of seats are [*sic*] set aside for members of a minority group. I think it would be preposterous to suggest that the disclaimer in § 2(b) was intended solely to prohibit the use of such a system. * * * Moreover, to the extent that the decisions in *White* and *Whitcomb* can inform our understanding of § 2(b), they suggest that in expressing a concern that "proportionality" not be used as the measure of a voting rights violation, Congress was concerned with proportional electoral power, not merely proportional election of minority candidates. The proviso has been understood in the past simply as a disclaimer of a right to proportional representation, see, *e.g.*, *Gingles*, 478 U.S., at 84–86,

94 (O'Connor, J., concurring in judgment), and I think that understanding is correct.

Holder v. Hall, 512 U.S. 874, 928–29 n.26 (1994) [p. 335]. Should it matter that the legislative history relied upon in *Thornburg v. Gingles* stated that § 2(b) "does not establish a right to proportional representation"? S. Rep. No. 97-417, p.2 (1982), *quoted in Chisom v. Roemer*, 501 U.S. 380, 394 n.20 (1991) [p. 325]).

4.   In any democratic system of government, there must be some mechanism for resolving policy disagreement. If every group is represented in the legislature, then the legislature itself serves as the locus of democratic compromise — the place where different factions resolve their differences and where policy is determined. Where representation is less proportional, elections themselves serve as the locus of compromise; voters settle on representatives, with the policy more or less determined by the results of the elections. Section 2's goal of increasing minority voting power advances the first vision of democracy by increasing the opportunity for minority groups to access — and influence — legislative deliberations. Is that the best — or a realistic — way of conceptualizing democracy? Consider The Federalist No. 35, at 220 (Alexander Hamilton) (Jacob E. Cooke ed., 1961) ("It is said to be necessary that all classes of citizens should have some of their own number in the representative body, in order that their feelings and interests may be the better understood and attended to. But * * * this will never happen under any arrangement that leaves the votes of the people free."). Is it better to control the negative effects of faction by allowing each faction to be represented in the legislature, or by making districts more uniform (and heterogeneous) so as to minimize the representation of minority factions? *See id.* No. 10, at 64 (James Madison) ("Extend the sphere [of a republic], and you take in a greater variety of parties and interests; you make it less probable that a majority of the whole will have a common motive to invade the rights of other citizens * * *.").

D.   "STANDARD, PRACTICE, OR PROCEDURE" IN SECTION 2

In Chapter 4, we examined the scope of § 5 of the Voting Rights Act, which requires covered jurisdictions to obtain preclearance of "any voting qualification or prerequisite to voting, or standard, practice, or procedure with respect to voting." 52 U.S.C. § 10304. Section 2 of the Act similarly applies to "standard[s], practice[s], [and] procedure[s]," 52 U.S.C. § 10301; accordingly, one might think that §§ 2 and 5 apply to the same laws. That intuition is generally correct, but the complete answer is more complicated. Consider the next two cases.

CHISOM v. ROEMER
Supreme Court of the United States
501 U.S. 380, 111 S. Ct. 2354, 115 L. Ed. 2d 348 (1991)

Justice Stevens delivered the opinion of the Court [in which Justice White, Justice Marshall, Justice Blackmun, Justice O'Connor, and Justice Souter join]. * * *

The Louisiana Supreme Court consists of seven justices, five of whom are elected from five single-member Supreme Court Districts, and two of whom are elected from one multimember Supreme Court District. Each of the seven members of the court must be a resident of the district from which he or she is elected and must have resided there for at least two years prior to election. Each of the justices on the Louisiana Supreme Court serves a term of 10 years. The one multimember district, the First Supreme Court District, consists of the parishes of Orleans, St. Bernard, Plaquemines, and Jefferson. Orleans Parish contains about half of the population of the First Supreme Court District and about half of the registered voters in that district. More than one-half of the registered voters of Orleans Parish are black, whereas more than three-fourths of the registered voters in the other three parishes are white.

Petitioners allege that "the present method of electing two Justices to the Louisiana Supreme Court at-large from the New Orleans area impermissibly dilutes minority voting strength" in violation of § 2 of the Voting Rights Act. * * * Petitioners seek a remedy that would divide the First District into two districts, one for Orleans Parish and the second for the other three parishes. If this remedy were adopted, the seven members of the Louisiana Supreme Court would each represent a separate single-member judicial district, and each of the two new districts would have approximately the same population. According to petitioners, the new Orleans Parish district would also have a majority black population and majority black voter registration. * * *

[The lower courts held for the defendants, reasoning that § 2 protected the right of minorities to elect "representatives" — a term which did not, in the courts' view, include elected judges.]

The text of § 2 of the Voting Rights Act as originally enacted read as follows:

> "No voting qualification or prerequisite to voting, or standard, practice, or procedure shall be imposed or applied by any State or political subdivision to deny or abridge the right of any citizen of the United States to vote on account of race or color."

The terms "vote" and "voting" were defined elsewhere in the Act to include "all action necessary to make a vote effective *in any primary, special, or general election.*" § 14(c)(1) of the Act (emphasis added). The statute further defined vote and voting as "votes cast with respect to candidates for public or party office and propositions for which votes are received in an election." * * *

Under the amended statute, proof of intent is no longer required to prove a § 2 violation. Now plaintiffs can prevail under § 2 by demonstrating that a challenged election practice has resulted in the denial or abridgment of the right to vote based on color or race. Congress not only incorporated the results test in the paragraph that formerly constituted the entire § 2, but also designated that paragraph as subsection (a) and added a new subsection (b) to make clear that an application of the results test requires an inquiry into "the totality of the circumstances." The full text of § 2 as amended in 1982 reads as follows:

> "(a) No voting qualification or prerequisite to voting or standard, practice, or procedure shall be imposed or applied by any State or political subdivision in a manner which results in a denial or abridgement of the right of any citizen of the United States to vote on account of race or color,

or in contravention of the guarantees set forth in section 4(f)(2), as provided in subsection (b).

"(b) A violation of subsection (a) is established if, based on the totality of circumstances, it is shown that the political processes leading to nomination or election in the State or political subdivision are not equally open to participation by members of a class of citizens protected by subsection (a) in that its members have less opportunity than other members of the electorate to participate in the political process and to elect representatives of their choice. The extent to which members of a protected class have been elected to office in the State or political subdivision is one circumstance which may be considered: *Provided*, That nothing in this section establishes a right to have members of a protected class elected in numbers equal to their proportion in the population." * * *

Respondents contend * * * that Congress' choice of the word "representatives" in the phrase "have less opportunity than other members of the electorate to participate in the political process and to elect representatives of their choice" in subsection (b) is evidence of congressional intent to exclude vote dilution claims involving judicial elections from the coverage of § 2. We reject that construction because we are convinced that if Congress had such an intent, Congress would have made it explicit in the statute, or at least some of the Members would have identified or mentioned it at some point in the unusually extensive legislative history of the 1982 amendment.[23] * * *

The [Court of Appeals] assumed that § 2 provides two distinct types of protection for minority voters — it protects their opportunity "to participate in the political process" and their opportunity "to elect representatives of their choice." Although the majority interpreted "representatives" as a word of limitation, it assumed that the word eliminated judicial elections only from the latter protection, without affecting the former. In other words, a standard, practice, or procedure in a judicial election, such as a limit on the times that polls are open, which has a disparate impact on black voters' opportunity to cast their ballots under § 2, may be challenged even if a different practice that merely affects their opportunity to elect representatives of their choice to a judicial office may not. This reading of § 2, however, is foreclosed by the statutory text and by our prior cases.

Any abridgment of the opportunity of members of a protected class to participate in the political process inevitably impairs their ability to influence the outcome of an election. As the statute is written, however, the inability to elect representatives of their choice is not sufficient to establish a violation unless, under the totality of the circumstances, it can also be said that the members of the protected class have less opportunity to participate in the political process. The statute does not create two separate and distinct rights. Subsection (a) covers every application of a qualification, standard, practice, or procedure that results in a denial or abridgment of "*the right*" to vote. The singular form is also used in subsection (b) when referring to an injury to members of the protected class who have less "opportunity" than others

---

[23] Congress' silence in this regard can be likened to the dog that did not bark. See A. Doyle, *Silver Blaze*, in The Complete Sherlock Holmes 335 (1927). * * *

"to participate in the political process *and* to elect representatives of their choice." 42 U.S.C. § 1973 [now 52 U.S.C. § 10301 — Eds.] (emphasis added). It would distort the plain meaning of the sentence to substitute the word "or" for the word "and." Such radical surgery would be required to separate the opportunity to participate from the opportunity to elect.[24]

The statutory language is patterned after the language used by JUSTICE WHITE in his opinions for the Court in *White* v. *Regester*, 412 U.S. 755 (1973) [p. 274], and *Whitcomb* v. *Chavis*, 403 U.S. 124 (1971) [p. 268]. In both opinions, the Court identified the opportunity to participate and the opportunity to elect as inextricably linked. In *White* v. *Regester*, the Court described the connection as follows: "The plaintiffs' burden is to produce evidence . . . that its members had less opportunity than did other residents in the district to participate in the political processes *and* to elect legislators of their choice." 412 U.S., at 766 (emphasis added). And earlier, in *Whitcomb* v. *Chavis*, the Court described the plaintiffs' burden as entailing a showing that they "had less opportunity than did other . . . residents to participate in the political processes *and* to elect legislators of their choice." 403 U.S., at 149 (emphasis added).

The results test mandated by the 1982 amendment is applicable to all claims arising under § 2. If the word "representatives" did place a limit on the coverage of the Act for judicial elections, it would exclude all claims involving such elections from the protection of § 2. For all such claims must allege an abridgment of the opportunity to participate in the political process *and* to elect representatives of one's choice. Even if [it would be wise] to preserve claims based on an interference with the right to vote in judicial elections while eschewing claims based on the opportunity to elect judges, we have no authority to divide a unitary claim created by Congress.

[R]espondents * * * place their principal reliance on Congress' use of the word "representatives" instead of "legislators" in the phrase "to participate in the political process and to elect representatives of their choice." [52 U.S.C. § 10301]. When Congress borrowed the phrase from *White* v. *Regester*, it replaced "legislators" with "representatives." This substitution indicates, at the very least, that Congress intended the amendment to cover more than legislative elections. Respondents argue * * * that the term "representatives" was used to extend § 2 coverage to executive officials, but not to judges. We think, however, that the better reading of the word "representatives" describes the winners of representative, popular elections. If executive officers, such as prosecutors, sheriffs, state attorneys general, and state treasurers, can be considered "representatives" simply because they are chosen by popular election, then the same reasoning should apply to elected judges.[27]

Respondents suggest that if Congress had intended to have the statute's

---

[24] JUSTICE SCALIA argues that our literal reading of the word "and" leads to the conclusion that a small minority has no protection against infringements of its right "to participate in the political process" because it will always lack the numbers necessary "to elect its candidate." This argument, however, rests on the erroneous assumption that a small group of voters can never influence the outcome of an election.

[27] Moreover, this Court has recently recognized that judges do engage in policymaking at some level. See *Gregory* v. *Ashcroft*, [501 U.S. 452, 466–467 (1991)]. * * *

prohibition against vote dilution apply to the election of judges, it would have used the word "candidates" instead of "representatives." But that confuses the ordinary meaning of the words. The word "representative" refers to someone who has prevailed in a popular election, whereas the word "candidate" refers to someone who is seeking an office. Thus, a candidate is nominated, not elected. When Congress used "candidate" in other parts of the statute, it did so precisely because it was referring to people who were aspirants for an office.

[O]f course, * * * "judges need not be elected at all," and * * * ideally public opinion should be irrelevant to the judge's role because the judge is often called upon to disregard, or even to defy, popular sentiment. * * * [But t]he fundamental tension between the ideal character of the judicial office and the real world of electoral politics cannot be resolved by crediting judges with total indifference to the popular will while simultaneously requiring them to run for elected office. When each of several members of a court must be a resident of a separate district, and must be elected by the voters of that district, it seems both reasonable and realistic to characterize the winners as representatives of that district. * * * Louisiana could, of course, exclude its judiciary from the coverage of the Voting Rights Act by changing to a system in which judges are appointed, and, in that way, it could enable its judges to be indifferent to popular opinion. The reasons why Louisiana has chosen otherwise are precisely the reasons why it is appropriate for § 2, as well as § 5, of the Voting Rights Act to continue to apply to its judicial elections.

The close connection between §§ 2 and 5 further undermines respondents' view that judicial elections should not be covered under § 2. * * * Section 5 uses language similar to that of § 2 in defining prohibited practices: "any voting qualification or prerequisite to voting, or standard, practice, or procedure with respect to voting." [52 U.S.C. § 10304]. This Court has already held that § 5 applies to judicial elections. *Clark* v. *Roemer*, 500 U.S. 646 (1991). If § 2 did not apply to judicial elections, a State covered by § 5 would be precluded from implementing a new voting procedure having discriminatory effects with respect to judicial elections, whereas a similarly discriminatory system already in place could not be challenged under § 2. It is unlikely that Congress intended such an anomalous result.

Finally, * * * respondents * * * suggest that no judicially manageable standards for deciding vote dilution claims can be fashioned unless the standard is based on the one-person, one-vote principle. They reason that because we have held the one-person, one-vote rule inapplicable to judicial elections, see *Wells* v. *Edwards*, 409 U.S. 1095 (1973), aff'g 347 F. Supp., at 454, it follows that judicial elections are entirely immune from vote dilution claims. The conclusion, however, does not follow from the premise.

The holding in *Wells* rejected a constitutional challenge based on the Equal Protection Clause of the Fourteenth Amendment. It has no more relevance to a correct interpretation of this statute than does our decision in *Mobile* v. *Bolden*, which also rejected a constitutional claim. The statute was enacted to protect voting rights that are not adequately protected by the Constitution itself. Cf. *City of Rome* v. *United States*, 446 U.S. 156, 172–183 (1980). The standard that should be applied in litigation under § 2 is not at issue here. Even if serious problems lie ahead in applying the "totality of circumstances" standard described in § 2(b), that task, difficult as it may prove to be, cannot justify a judicially created limitation on the coverage of the broadly worded statute, as enacted and amended by Congress.

* * * Congress amended the Act in 1982 in order to relieve plaintiffs of the burden of proving discriminatory intent, after a plurality of this Court had concluded that the original Act, like the Fifteenth Amendment, contained such a requirement. Thus, Congress made clear that a violation of § 2 could be established by proof of discriminatory results alone. It is difficult to believe that Congress, in an express effort to broaden the protection afforded by the Voting Rights Act, withdrew, without comment, an important category of elections from that protection. Today we reject such an anomalous view and hold that state judicial elections are included within the ambit of § 2 as amended.

The judgment of the Court of Appeals is reversed, and the cases are remanded for further proceedings consistent with this opinion.

It is so ordered.

JUSTICE SCALIA, with whom THE CHIEF JUSTICE [REHNQUIST] and JUSTICE KENNEDY join, dissenting. * * *

* * * I agree with the Court that th[e] original [§ 2], directed toward intentional discrimination, applied to all elections, for it clearly said so. * * * The 1982 amendments, however, radically transformed the Act. As currently written, the statute proscribes intentional discrimination only if it has a discriminatory effect, but proscribes practices with discriminatory effect whether or not intentional. * * * The question we confront here is how broadly the new remedy applies. The foundation of the Court's analysis, the itinerary for its journey in the wrong direction, is the following statement: "It is difficult to believe that Congress, in an express effort to broaden the protection afforded by the Voting Rights Act, withdrew, without comment, an important category of elections from that protection." There are two things wrong with this. First is the notion that Congress cannot be credited with having achieved anything of major importance by simply saying it, in ordinary language, in the text of a statute, "without comment" in the legislative history. As the Court colorfully puts it, if the dog of legislative history has not barked nothing of great significance can have transpired. * * * We are here to apply the statute, not legislative history, and certainly not the absence of legislative history. Statutes are the law though sleeping dogs lie.

The more important error in the Court's starting point, however, is the assumption that the effect of excluding judges from the revised § 2 would be to "withdraw . . . an important category of elections from [the] protection [of the Voting Rights Act]." There is absolutely no question here of *withdrawing* protection. Since the pre-1982 content of § 2 was coextensive with the Fifteenth Amendment, the entirety of that protection subsisted in the Constitution, and could be enforced through the other provisions of the Voting Rights Act. Nothing was lost from the prior coverage; *all* of the new "results" protection was an add-on. The issue is not, therefore, as the Court would have it, whether Congress has cut back on the coverage of the Voting Rights Act; the issue is how far it has extended it. Thus, even if a court's expectations were a proper basis for interpreting the text of a statute, while there would be reason to expect that Congress was not "withdrawing" protection, there is no particular reason to expect that the supplemental protection it provided was any more extensive than the text of the statute said.

What it said, with respect to establishing a violation of the amended § 2, is the following:

> ". . . A violation . . . is established if . . . it is shown that the political processes leading to nomination or election . . . are not equally open to participation by members of a [protected] class . . . in that its members have less opportunity than other members of the electorate *to participate in the political process* and *to elect representatives of their choice*." [52 U.S.C. § 10303] (emphasis added). * * *

The Court * * * asserts that before a violation of § 2 can be made out, *both* conditions of § 2(b) must be met. * * * This is unquestionably wrong. If both conditions must be violated before there is any § 2 violation, then minorities who form such a small part of the electorate in a particular jurisdiction that they could on no conceivable basis "elect representatives of their choice" would be entirely without § 2 protection. * * * The Court feels compelled to reach this implausible conclusion of a "singular right" because the "to participate" clause and the "to elect" clause are joined by the conjunction "and." It is unclear to me why the rules of English usage require that conclusion here, any more than they do in the case of the First Amendment — which reads "Congress shall make no law . . . abridging . . . the right of the people peaceably to assemble, and to petition the Government for a redress of grievances." This has not generally been thought to protect the right peaceably to assemble only when the purpose of the assembly is to petition the Government for a redress of grievances. So also here, one is deprived of an equal "opportunity . . . to participate . . . and to elect" if *either* the opportunity to participate *or* the opportunity to elect is unequal. * * *[2]

The Court, petitioners, and petitioners' *amici* have labored mightily to establish that there is *a* meaning of "representatives" that would include judges, and no doubt there is. But our job is not to scavenge the world of English usage to discover whether there is any possible meaning of "representatives" which suits our preconception that the statute includes judges; our job is to determine whether the *ordinary* meaning includes them, and if it does not, to ask whether there is any solid indication in the text or structure of the statute that something other than ordinary meaning was intended.

There is little doubt that the ordinary meaning of "representatives" does not include judges. The Court's feeble argument to the contrary is that "representatives" means those who "are chosen by popular election." On that hypothesis, the

---

[2] The Court denies that this conclusion follows, because, as it claims, it "rests on the erroneous assumption that a small group of voters can never influence the outcome of an election." I make no such assumption. I only assume that by "to elect" the statute does not mean "to influence," just as I assume that by "representatives" the statute does not mean "judges." We do not reject Conan Doyle's method of statutory interpretation only to embrace Lewis Carroll's. [See *Through the Looking Glass*, in The Complete Works of Lewis Carroll 196 (1939) (" 'When *I* use a word,' Humpty Dumpty said, in rather a scornful tone, 'it means just what *I* choose it to mean — neither more nor less.' ") — Eds.]

fan-elected members of the baseball all-star teams are "representatives" — hardly a common, if even a permissible, usage. Surely the word "representative" connotes one who is not only *elected by* the people, but who also, at a minimum, *acts on behalf of* the people. Judges do that in a sense — but not in the ordinary sense. As the captions of the pleadings in some States still display, it is the prosecutor who represents "the People"; the judge represents the Law — which often requires him to rule against the People. It is precisely because we do not *ordinarily* conceive of judges as representatives that we held judges not within the Fourteenth Amendment's requirement of "one person, one vote." *Wells* v. *Edwards*. The point is not that a State could not make judges in some senses representative, or that all judges must be conceived of in the Article III mold, but rather, that giving "representatives" its ordinary meaning, the ordinary speaker in 1982 would not have applied the word to judges. It remains only to ask whether there is good indication that ordinary meaning does not apply. * * *

* * * [T]he ordinary meaning of "representatives" gives clear purpose to congressional action that otherwise would seem pointless. As an initial matter, it is evident that Congress paid particular attention to the scope of elections covered by the "to elect" language. As the Court suggests, that language for the most part tracked this Court's opinions in *White* v. *Regester* and *Whitcomb* v. *Chavis*, but the word "legislators" was not copied. Significantly, it was replaced not with the more general term "candidates" used repeatedly elsewhere in the Act, but with the term "representatives," which appears nowhere else in the Act (except as a proper noun referring to Members of the federal lower House, or designees of the Attorney General). The normal meaning of this term is broader than "legislators" (it includes, for example, school boards and city councils as well as senators and representatives) but narrower than "candidates."

The Court says that the seemingly significant refusal to use the term "candidate" and selection of the distinctive term "representative" are really inconsequential, because "candidate" could not have been used. According to the Court, since "candidate" refers to one who has been nominated but *not yet* elected, the phrase "to elect candidates" would be a contradiction in terms. The only flaw in this argument is that it is not true, as repeated usage of the formulation "to elect candidates" by this Court itself amply demonstrates. * * * In other words, far from being an impermissible choice, "candidates" would have been the natural choice, even if it had not been used repeatedly elsewhere in the statute. It is quite absurd to think that Congress went out of its way to replace that term with "representatives," in order to convey what "candidates" naturally suggests (viz., coverage of *all* elections) and what "representatives" naturally does not.

A second consideration confirms that "representatives" in § 2 was meant in its ordinary sense. When given its ordinary meaning, it causes the statute to reproduce an established, eminently logical, and perhaps practically indispensable limitation upon the availability of vote dilution claims. Whatever other requirements may be applicable to elections for "representatives" (in the sense of those who are not only elected by but act on behalf of the electorate), those elections, unlike elections for *all* officeholders, must be conducted in accordance with the equal protection principle of "one person, one vote." And it so happens — more than coincidentally, I think — that in every case in which, prior to the amendment of § 2, we recognized the possibility of a vote dilution claim, the principle of "one person, one vote" was applicable. Indeed, it is the principle of "one person, one vote" that gives meaning to the concept of "dilution." One's vote is diluted if it is not, *as it should be*, of the same practical effect as everyone else's. Of course the mere fact that an election practice satisfies the constitutional requirement of "one person, one vote" does not establish that there has been no vote dilution for Voting Rights Act purposes, since that looks not merely to equality of individual votes but also to equality of minority blocs of votes. (*White* itself, which dealt with a multimember district, demonstrates this point.) But "one person, one vote" has been the premise and the necessary condition of a vote dilution claim, since it establishes the baseline for computing the voting strength that the minority bloc *ought to have*. As we have suggested, the first question in a dilution case is whether the "one-person, one-vote" standard is met, and if it is, the second is whether voting structures nonetheless operate to "minimize or cancel out the voting strength of racial or political elements of the voting population."

Well before Congress amended § 2, we had held that the principle of "one person, one vote" does not apply to the election of judges, *Wells* v. *Edwards*. If Congress was (through use of the extremely inapt word "representatives") making vote dilution claims available with respect to the election of judges, it was, for the first time, extending that remedy to a context in which "one person, one vote" did not apply. *That* would have been a significant change in the law, and given the need to identify some other baseline for computing "dilution," *that* is a matter which those who believe in barking dogs should be astounded to find unmentioned in the legislative history. If "representatives" is given its normal meaning, on the other hand, there is no change in the law (except elimination of the intent requirement) and the silence is entirely understandable.

I frankly find it very difficult to conceive how it is to be determined whether "dilution" has occurred, once one has eliminated *both* the requirement of actual intent to disfavor minorities, *and* the principle that 10,000 minority votes throughout the State should have as much practical "electability" effect as 10,000 nonminority votes. How does one begin to decide, in such a system, how much elective strength a minority bloc *ought* to have? I do not assert that it is utterly impossible to impose "vote dilution" restrictions upon an electoral regime that is not based on the "one-person, one-vote" principle. Congress can define "vote dilution" to be whatever it will, within constitutional bounds. But my point is that "one person, one vote" is inherent in the normal concept of "vote dilution," and was an essential element of the pre-existing, judicially crafted definition under § 2; that Congress did *not* adopt any new definition; that creating a new definition is a seemingly standardless task; and that the word Congress selected ("representative") seems specifically designed to avoid these problems. * * * The Court attributes to Congress not only the intent to mean something other than what it said, but also the intent to let district courts invent (for there is no precedent where "one person, one vote" did not apply that Congress could have been consulting) what in the world constitutes dilution of a vote that does not have to be equal.

Finally, the Court suggests that there is something "anomalous" about extending coverage under § 5 of the Voting Rights Act to the election of judges, while not extending coverage under § 2 to the same elections. This simply misconceives the different roles of § 2 and § 5. The latter requires certain jurisdictions to preclear changes in election methods before those changes are implemented; it is a means of assuring in advance the absence of all electoral illegality, not only that which violates the Voting Rights Act but that which violates the Constitution as well. In my view, judges *are* within the scope of § 2 for nondilution claims, and thus for those claims, § 5 preclearance would enforce the Voting Rights Act with respect to judges. Moreover, intentional discrimination in the election of judges, whatever its form, is constitutionally prohibited, and the preclearance provision of § 5 gives the Government a method by which to prevent that. The scheme makes entire sense without the need to bring judges within the "to elect" provision.

All this is enough to convince me that there is sense to the ordinary meaning of "representative" in § 2(b) — that there is reason to Congress' choice — and since there is, then, under our normal presumption, that ordinary meaning prevails. I would read § 2 as extending vote dilution claims to elections for "representatives," but not to elections for judges. For other claims under § 2, however — those resting on the "to participate in the political process" provision rather than the "to elect" provision — no similar restriction would apply. Since the claims here are exclusively claims of dilution, I would affirm the judgment of the Fifth Circuit. * * *

JUSTICE KENNEDY, dissenting.

I join JUSTICE SCALIA's dissent in full. I write to add only that the issue before the Court is one of statutory construction, not constitutional validity. Nothing in today's decision addresses the question whether § 2 of the Voting Rights Act of 1965, as interpreted in *Thornburg* v. *Gingles*, is consistent with the requirements of the United States Constitution.

Notes and Questions

1.   Do you believe § 2 should be interpreted to require plaintiffs to demonstrate both a diminished opportunity to participate in the political process and a diminished opportunity to elect candidates? Of what relevance is the majority's reminder in footnote 24 that minorities can influence election outcomes?

2.   How can a vote-dilution claim be evaluated if one person need not have one vote? If the Court were presented with the question, not of the scope of § 2 (which is what was at issue in *Chisom*), but of the elements necessary to prove a violation of § 2 with respect to judicial elections, do you think the Court would overrule *Wells v. Edwards*, which held one-person, one-vote inapplicable to judicial elections?

3.   Does the "ordinary" meaning of "representatives" include executive officials? If not, how should that affect Justice Scalia's interpretation of § 2?

4.   Do you think Congress gave any thought to judicial elections in amending § 2?

5.   Justice Scalia and the Court disagreed about whether including judicial elections within the scope of § 2 represented an expansion of the Act's coverage, because they began from different baselines. What is the baseline each used? Which is the appropriate one to use? Should it matter?

HOLDER v. HALL

Supreme Court of the United States

512 U.S. 874, 114 S. Ct. 2581, 129 L. Ed. 2d 687 (1994)

JUSTICE KENNEDY announced the judgment of the Court and delivered an opinion, in which THE CHIEF JUSTICE [REHNQUIST] joined, and in all but Part II-B of which JUSTICE O'CONNOR joined.

This case presents the question whether the size of a governing authority is subject to a vote dilution challenge under § 2 of the Voting Rights Act of 1965, 42 U.S.C. § 1973 [now 52 U.S.C. § 10301 — Eds.].

I

The State of Georgia has 159 counties, one of which is Bleckley County, a rural county in central Georgia. Black persons make up nearly 20% of the eligible voting population in Bleckley County. Since its creation in 1912, the county has had a single-commissioner form of government for the exercise of "county governing authority." Under this system, the Bleckley County Commissioner performs all of the executive and legislative functions of the county government, including the levying of general and special taxes, the directing and controlling of all county property, and the settling of all claims. In addition to Bleckley County, about 10 other Georgia counties use the single-commissioner system; the rest have multi-member commissions.

In 1985, the Georgia Legislature authorized Bleckley County to adopt a multimember commission consisting of five commissioners elected from single-member districts and a single chairman elected at large. In a referendum held in 1986, however, the electorate did not adopt the change to a multimember commission. (In a similar referendum four years earlier, county voters had approved a five-member district plan for the election of the county school board.)

In 1985, respondents (six black registered voters from Bleckley County and the Cochran/Bleckley County Chapter of the National Association for the Advancement of Colored People) challenged the single-commissioner system [as violating § 2]. * * * Under the statute, the suit contended, Bleckley County must have a county commission of sufficient size that, with single-member election districts, the county's black citizens would constitute a majority in one of the single-member districts. Applying the § 2 framework established in *Thornburg* v. *Gingles*, 478 U.S. 30 (1986) [p. 301], the District Court found that respondents satisfied the first of the three *Gingles* preconditions because black voters were sufficiently numerous and compact that they could have constituted a majority in one district of a multimember commission. In particular, the District Court found that "[i]f the county commission were increased in number to six commissioners to be elected from five single member districts and if the districts were the same as the present school board election districts, a black majority 'safe' district . . . would result." The court found, however, that respondents failed to satisfy the second and third *Gingles* preconditions — that whites vote as a bloc in a manner sufficient to defeat the black-preferred candidate and that blacks were politically cohesive.

* * * The Court of Appeals * * * found that the District Court had erred in concluding that the second and third *Gingles* preconditions were not met. Turning to the totality of the circumstances, the court found that those circumstances supported a finding of liability under § 2. The court therefore concluded that respondents had proved a violation of § 2, and it remanded for formulation of a remedy, which, it suggested, "could well be modeled" after the system used to elect the Bleckley County school board. * * *

II

A

Section 2 of the Voting Rights Act of 1965 provides that "[n]o voting qualification or prerequisite to voting, or standard, practice, or procedure shall be imposed or applied by any State or political subdivision in a manner which results in a denial or abridgement of the right of any citizen of the United States to vote on account of race or color." [52 U.S.C. § 10301(a)]. In a § 2 vote dilution suit, along with determining whether the *Gingles* preconditions are met and whether the totality of the circumstances supports a finding of liability, a court must find a reasonable alternative practice as a benchmark against which to measure the existing voting practice. As JUSTICE O'CONNOR explained in *Gingles:* "The phrase vote dilution itself suggests a norm with respect to which the fact of dilution may be ascertained. . . . [I]n order to decide whether an electoral system has made it harder for minority voters to elect the candidates they prefer, a court must have an idea in mind of how hard it should be for minority voters to elect their preferred candidates under an acceptable system." 478 U.S., at 88 (opinion concurring in judgment).

In certain cases, the benchmark for comparison in a § 2 dilution suit is obvious. The effect of an anti-single-shot voting rule, for instance, can be evaluated by comparing the system with that rule to the system without that rule. But where there is no objective and workable standard for choosing a reasonable benchmark by which to evaluate a challenged voting practice, it follows that the voting practice cannot be challenged as dilutive under § 2.

As the facts of this case well illustrate, the search for a benchmark is quite problematic when a § 2 dilution challenge is brought to the size of a government body. There is no principled reason why one size should be picked over another as the benchmark for comparison. Respondents here argue that we should compare Bleckley County's sole commissioner system to a hypothetical five-member commission in order to determine whether the current system is dilutive. Respondents and the United States as *amicus curiae* give three reasons why the single-commissioner structure should be compared to a five-member commission (instead of, say, a 3-, 10-, or 15-member body): (1) because the five-member commission is a common form of governing authority in the State; (2) because the state legislature had authorized Bleckley County to adopt a five-member commission if it so chose (it did not); and (3) because the county had moved from a single superintendent of education to a school board with five members elected from single-member districts.

These referents do not bear upon dilution. It does not matter, for instance, how popular the single-member commission system is in Georgia in determining whether it dilutes the vote of a minority racial group in Bleckley County. That the single-member commission is uncommon in the State of Georgia, or that a five-member commission is quite common, tells us nothing about its effects on a minority group's voting strength. The sole commissioner system has the same impact regardless of whether it is shared by none, or by all, of the other counties in Georgia. It makes little sense to say (as do respondents and the United States) that the sole commissioner system should be subject to a dilution challenge if it is rare — but immune if it is common.

That Bleckley County was authorized by the State to expand its commission, and that it adopted a five-member school board, are likewise irrelevant considerations in the dilution inquiry. At most, those facts indicate that Bleckley County could change the size of its commission with minimal disruption. But the county's failure to do so says nothing about the effects the sole commissioner system has on the voting power of Bleckley County's citizens. Surely a minority group's voting strength would be no more or less diluted had the State not authorized the county to alter the size of its commission, or had the county not enlarged its school board. One gets the sense that respondents and the United States have chosen a benchmark for the sake of having a benchmark. But it is one thing to say that a benchmark can be found, quite another to give a convincing reason for finding it in the first place.

B

To bolster their argument, respondents point out that our § 5 cases may be interpreted to indicate that covered jurisdictions may not change the size of their government bodies without obtaining preclearance from the Attorney General or the federal courts. [S]ee *Presley* v. *Etowah County Comm'n*, 502 U.S. 491, 501–503 (1992); *City of Lockhart* v. *United States*, 460 U.S. 125, 131–132 (1983); *City of Rome* v. *United States*, 446 U.S. 156, 161 (1980). Respondents contend that these § 5 cases, together with the similarity in language between §§ 2 and 5 of the Act, compel the conclusion that the size of a government body must be subject to a dilution challenge under § 2. It is true that in *Chisom* v. *Roemer*, 501 U.S. 380, 401–402 (1991) [p. 325], we said that the coverage of §§ 2 and 5 is presumed to be the same (at least if differential coverage would be anomalous). We did not adopt a conclusive rule to that effect, however, and we do not think that the fact that a change in a voting practice must be precleared under § 5 necessarily means that the voting practice is subject to challenge in a dilution suit under § 2.

To be sure, if the structure and purpose of § 2 mirrored that of § 5, then the case for interpreting §§ 2 and 5 to have the same application in all cases would be convincing. But the two sections differ in structure, purpose, and application. Section 5 applies only in certain jurisdictions specified by Congress and "only to proposed changes in voting procedures." *Beer* v. *United States*, 425 U.S. 130, 138 (1976) [p. 239]. In those covered jurisdictions, a proposed change in a voting practice must be approved in advance by the Attorney General or the federal courts. § 1973c. The purpose of this requirement "has always been to insure that no voting-procedure changes would be made that would lead to a retrogression in the position of racial minorities with respect to their effective exercise of the electoral franchise." 425 U.S., at 141. Under § 5, then, the proposed voting practice is measured against the existing voting practice to determine whether retrogression would result from the proposed change. See *id.* The baseline for comparison is present by definition; it is the existing status. While there may be difficulty in determining whether a proposed change would cause retrogression, there is little difficulty in discerning the two voting practices to compare to determine whether retrogression would occur.

Retrogression is not the inquiry in § 2 dilution cases. Unlike in § 5 cases, therefore, a benchmark does not exist by definition in § 2 dilution cases. And as explained above, with some voting practices, there in fact may be no appropriate benchmark to determine if an existing voting practice is dilutive under § 2. For that reason, a voting practice that is subject to the preclearance requirements of § 5 is not necessarily subject to a dilution challenge under § 2.

This conclusion is quite unremarkable. For example, in *Perkins* v. *Matthews*, 400 U.S. 379, 388 (1971), we held that a town's annexation of land was covered under § 5. Notwithstanding that holding, we think it quite improbable to suggest that a § 2 dilution challenge could be brought to a town's existing political boundaries (in an attempt to force it to annex surrounding land) by arguing that the current boundaries dilute a racial group's voting strength in comparison to the proposed new boundaries. Likewise, in *McCain* v. *Lybrand*, 465 U.S. 236 (1984), we indicated that a change from an appointive to an elected office was covered under § 5. Here, again, we doubt Congress contemplated that a racial group could bring a § 2 dilution challenge to an appointive office (in an attempt to force a change to an elective office) by arguing that the appointive office diluted its voting strength in comparison to the proposed elective office. We think these examples serve to show that a voting practice is not necessarily subject to a dilution challenge under § 2 even when a change in that voting practice would be subject to the preclearance requirements of § 5.

III

With respect to challenges to the size of a governing authority, respondents fail to explain where the search for reasonable alternative benchmarks should begin and end, and they provide no acceptable principles for deciding future cases. The wide range of possibilities makes the choice "inherently standardless," and we therefore conclude that a plaintiff cannot maintain a § 2 challenge to the size of a government body, such as the Bleckley County Commission. The judgment of the Court of Appeals is reversed, and the case is remanded * * *.

It is so ordered.

JUSTICE O'CONNOR, concurring in part and concurring in the judgment.

I agree with JUSTICES KENNEDY and THOMAS that a plaintiff cannot maintain a § 2 vote dilution challenge to the size of a governing authority, though I reach that conclusion by a somewhat different rationale. JUSTICE THOMAS rejects the notion that

§ 2 covers *any* dilution challenges, and would hold that § 2 is limited to "state enactments that regulate citizens' access to the ballot or the processes for counting a ballot." As JUSTICE STEVENS points out, however, *stare decisis* concerns weigh heavily here. These concerns require me to reject JUSTICE THOMAS' suggestion that we overhaul our established reading of § 2.

I also agree with JUSTICE BLACKMUN that our precedents compel the conclusion that the size of the Bleckley County Commission is both a "standard, practice, or procedure" under § 2 and a "standard, practice, or procedure with respect to voting" under § 5.

As JUSTICES KENNEDY and BLACKMUN both recognize, in these cases we have consistently said that a change in size is a "standard, practice, or procedure with respect to voting" that is subject to § 5 preclearance. And though our cases involving size have concerned § 5, I do not think it possible to read the terms of § 2 more narrowly than the terms of § 5. Section 2 covers any "standard, practice, or procedure," while § 5 covers any "standard, practice, or procedure with respect to voting." As a textual matter, I cannot see how a practice can be a "standard, practice, or procedure with respect to voting," yet not be a "standard, practice, or procedure." Indeed, the similarity in language led to our conclusion in *Chisom* v. *Roemer*, 501 U.S., [at] 401–402, that, at least for determining threshold coverage, §§ 2 and 5 have parallel scope.

But determining the threshold scope of coverage does not end the inquiry, at least so far as § 2 dilution challenges are concerned. * * * Section 2 vote dilution plaintiffs must establish that the challenged practice is dilutive. In order for an electoral system to dilute a minority group's voting power, there must be an alternative system that would provide greater electoral opportunity to minority voters. * * *

Accordingly, to determine whether voters possess the potential to elect representatives of choice in the absence of the challenged structure, courts must choose an objectively reasonable alternative practice as a benchmark for the dilution comparison. * * * We require preclearance of changes in size under § 5, because in a § 5 case the question of an alternative benchmark never arises — the benchmark is simply the former practice employed by the jurisdiction seeking approval of a change.

But § 2 dilution challenges raise more difficult questions. This case presents the question whether, in a § 2 dilution challenge to size, there can ever be an objective alternative benchmark for comparison. And I agree with JUSTICE KENNEDY that there cannot be. * * * In a dilution challenge to the size of a governing authority, choosing the alternative for comparison — a hypothetical larger (or smaller) governing authority — is extremely problematic. The wide range of possibilities makes the choice inherently standardless. Here, for example, respondents argued that the single-member commission structure was dilutive in comparison to a five-member structure, in which African-Americans would probably have been able to elect one representative of their choice. Some groups, however, will not be able to constitute a majority in one of five districts. Once a court accepts respondents' reasoning, it will have to allow a plaintiff group insufficiently large or geographically compact to form a majority in one of five districts to argue that the jurisdiction's failure to establish a 10-, 15-, or 25-commissioner structure is dilutive.

Respondents argue that this concern with arbitrary and standardless intrusions into the size of local governing authority is overstated. Respondents' principal support for this conclusion is that a five-member commission is the *most* common size for Georgia. But a five-member commission is not the *only* common size in Georgia: 22 Georgia counties have three-member commissions (and one county has an 11-member commission). Moreover, there is no good reason why the search for benchmarks should be limited to Georgia. Expanding the search nationwide produces many 20-person county commissions in Tennessee, and 40-member commissions in Wisconsin. In sum, respondents do not explain how common an alternative practice must be before it can be a reliable alternative benchmark for the dilution comparison, nor do they explain where the search for alternative benchmarks should begin and end.

Respondents' failure to provide any meaningful principles for deciding future cases demonstrates the difficulty with allowing dilution challenges to the size of a governing authority. Under respondents' open-ended test, a wide range of state governmental bodies may be subject to a dilution challenge. Within each State there are many forms of government, including county commissions that range dramatically in size. * * * Nor are deviations from the norm limited to counties. Statewide governing authorities also range dramatically in size, and often do not correlate to the size of the State. * * *

The discrepancies in size among state and local governing authorities reinforce my concern that the limiting principle offered by respondents will in practice limit very little. * * *

For these reasons, I concur in the conclusion that respondents' dilution challenge to the size of the Bleckley County Commission cannot be maintained under § 2 of the Voting Rights Act, and I join Parts I, II-A, and III of JUSTICE KENNEDY's opinion. * * *

JUSTICE THOMAS, with whom JUSTICE SCALIA joins, concurring in the judgment.

We are asked in this case to determine whether the size of a local governing body is subject to challenge under § 2 of the Voting Rights Act of 1965 as a "dilutive" practice. While I agree with JUSTICES KENNEDY and O'CONNOR that the size of a governing body cannot be attacked under § 2, I do not share their reasons for reaching that conclusion. * * * I would hold that the size of a government body is not a "standard, practice, or procedure" because, properly understood, those terms reach only state enactments that limit citizens' access to the ballot. * * *

As it was enforced in the years immediately following its enactment, the Voting Rights Act of 1965 was perceived primarily as legislation directed at eliminating literacy tests and similar devices that had been used to prevent black voter registration in the segregated South. * * *

The Act was immediately and notably successful in removing barriers to registration and ensuring access to the ballot. * * * By the end of 1967, black voter registration had reached at least 50% in every covered State.

The Court's decision in *Allen* v. *State Bd. of Elections*, 393 U.S. 544 (1969) [p. 226], however, marked a fundamental shift in the focal point of the Act. In an opinion dealing with four companion cases, the *Allen* Court determined that the Act should be given "the broadest possible scope." *Id.*, at 567. Thus, in *Fairley* v. *Patterson*, the Court decided that a covered jurisdiction's switch from a districting system to an at-large system for election of county supervisors was a "standard, practice, or procedure with respect to voting," subject to preclearance under § 5. *Id.*, at 569. Stating that the Act "was aimed at the subtle, as well as the obvious, state regulations which have the effect of denying citizens their right to vote because of their race," *id.*, at 565, the Court reasoned that § 5's preclearance provisions should apply, not only to changes in electoral laws that pertain to registration and access to the ballot, but to provisions that might "dilute" the force of minority votes that were duly cast and counted. See *id.*, at 569. The decision in *Allen* thus ensured that the terms "standard, practice, or procedure" would extend to encompass a wide array of electoral practices or voting systems that might be challenged for reducing the potential impact of minority votes.

As a consequence, *Allen* also ensured that courts would be required to confront a number of complex and essentially political questions in assessing claims of vote dilution under the Voting Rights Act. The central difficulty in any vote dilution case, of course, is determining a point of comparison against which dilution can be measured. As Justice Frankfurter observed several years before *Allen*, "[t]alk of 'debasement' or 'dilution' is circular talk. One cannot speak of 'debasement' or 'dilution' of the value of a vote until there is first defined a standard of reference as to what a vote should be worth." *Baker* v. *Carr*, 369 U.S. 186, 300 (1962) [p. 119] (dissenting opinion). See also *Thornburg* v. *Gingles*, 478 U.S., [at] 88 (O'CONNOR, J., concurring in judgment) ("[I]n order to decide whether an electoral system has made it harder for minority voters to elect the candidates they prefer, a court must have an idea in mind of how hard it 'should' be for minority voters to elect their preferred candidates under an acceptable system"). But in setting the benchmark of what "undiluted" or fully "effective" voting strength should be, a court must necessarily make some judgments based purely on an assessment of principles of political theory. As Justice Harlan pointed out in his dissent in *Allen*, the Voting Rights Act supplies no rule for a court to rely upon in deciding, for example, whether a multimember at-large system of election is to be preferred to a single-member district system; that is, whether one provides a more "effective" vote than another. * * * The choice is inherently a political one, and depends upon the selection of a theory for defining the fully "effective" vote — at bottom, a theory for defining effective participation in representative government. In short, what a court is actually asked to do in a vote dilution case is "to choose among competing bases of representation — ultimately, really, among competing theories of political philosophy." *Baker*, 369 U.S., at 300 (Frankfurter, J., dissenting).

Perhaps the most prominent feature of the philosophy that has emerged in vote dilution decisions since *Allen* has been the Court's preference for single-member districting schemes, both as a benchmark for measuring undiluted minority voting strength and as a remedial mechanism for guaranteeing minorities undiluted voting power.

It should be apparent, however, that there is no principle inherent in our constitutional system, or even in the history of the Nation's electoral practices, that makes single-member districts the "proper" mechanism for electing representatives to governmental bodies or for giving "undiluted" effect to the votes of a numerical minority. * * *

The obvious advantage the Court has perceived in single-member districts, of course, is their tendency to enhance the ability of any numerical minority in the electorate to gain control of seats in a representative body. But in choosing single-member districting as a benchmark electoral plan on that basis the Court has made a political decision and, indeed, a decision that itself depends on a prior political choice made in answer to Justice Harlan's question in *Allen*. Justice Harlan asked whether a group's votes should be considered more "effective" when they provide *influence* over a greater number of seats, or *control* over a lesser number of seats. In answering that query, the Court has determined that the purpose of the vote — or of the fully "effective" vote — is controlling seats. * * *

In fact, it should be clear that the assumptions that have guided the Court reflect only one possible understanding of effective exercise of the franchise, an understanding based on the view that voters are "represented" only when they choose a delegate who will mirror their views in the legislative halls. But it is certainly possible to construct a theory of effective political participation that would accord greater importance to voters' ability to influence, rather than control, elections. And especially in a two-party system such as ours, the influence of a potential "swing" group of voters composing 10% to 20% of the electorate in a given district can be considerable. Even such a focus on practical influence, however, is not a necessary component of the definition of the "effective" vote. Some conceptions of representative government may primarily emphasize the formal value of the vote as a mechanism for participation in the electoral process, whether it results in control of a seat or not. * * *

In short, there are undoubtedly an infinite number of theories of effective suffrage, representation, and the proper apportionment of political power in a representative democracy that could be drawn upon to answer the questions posed in *Allen*. I do not pretend to have provided the most sophisticated account of the various possibilities; but such matters of political theory are beyond the ordinary sphere of federal judges. And that is precisely the point. The matters the Court has set out to resolve in vote dilution cases are questions of political philosophy, not questions of law. As such, they are not readily subjected to any judicially manageable standards that can guide courts in attempting to select between competing theories.

But the political choices the Court has had to make do not end with the determination that the primary purpose of the "effective" vote is controlling seats or with the selection of single-member districting as the mechanism for providing that control. * * * Single-member districting tells a court "how" members of a minority are to control seats, but not "how many" seats they should be allowed to control.

But "how many" is the critical issue. Once one accepts the proposition that the effectiveness of votes is measured in terms of the control of seats, the core of any vote dilution claim is an assertion that the group in question is unable to control the "proper" number of seats — that is, the number of seats that the minority's percentage of the population would enable it to control in the benchmark "fair" system. The claim is inherently based on ratios between the numbers of the minority in the population and the numbers of seats controlled. * * * And once again, in selecting the proportion that will be used to define the undiluted strength of a minority — the ratio that will provide the principle for decision in a vote dilution case — a court must make a political choice. The ratio for which this Court has opted, and thus the mathematical principle driving the results in our cases, is undoubtedly direct proportionality. * * * While in itself that choice may strike us intuitively as the fairest or most just rule to apply, opting for proportionality is still a political choice, not a result required by any principle of law.

The dabbling in political theory that dilution cases have prompted, however, is hardly the worst aspect of our vote dilution jurisprudence. Far more pernicious has been the Court's willingness to accept the one underlying premise that must inform every minority vote dilution claim: the assumption that the group asserting dilution is not merely a racial or ethnic group, but a group having distinct political interests as well. Of necessity, in resolving vote dilution actions we have given credence to the view that race defines political interest. We have acted on the implicit assumption that members of racial and ethnic groups must all think alike on important matters of public policy and must have their own "minority preferred" representatives holding seats in elected bodies if they are to be considered represented at all.

It is true that in *Gingles* we stated that whether a racial group is "politically cohesive" may not be assumed, but rather must be proved in each case. See 478 U.S., at 51, 56. But the standards we have employed for determining political cohesion have proved so insubstantial that this "precondition" does not present much of a barrier to the assertion of vote dilution claims on behalf of any racial group. Moreover, it provides no test — indeed, it is not designed to provide a test — of whether race itself determines a distinctive political community of interest. According to the rule adopted in *Gingles*, plaintiffs must show simply that members of a racial group tend to prefer the same candidates. See 478 U.S., at 61–67 (opinion of Brennan, J.). There is no set standard defining how strong the correlation must be, and an inquiry into the cause for the correlation (to determine, for example, whether it might be the product of similar socioeconomic interests rather than some other factor related to race) is unnecessary. *Ibid.* See also *id.*, at 100 (O'CONNOR, J., concurring in judgment). Thus, whenever similarities in political preferences along racial lines exist, we proclaim that the cause of the correlation is irrelevant, but we effectively rely on the fact of the correlation to assume that racial groups have unique political interests. * * *

The assumptions upon which our vote dilution decisions have been based should be repugnant to any nation that strives for the ideal of a color-blind Constitution. * * * [O]ur voting rights decisions are rapidly progressing toward a system that is indistinguishable in principle from a scheme under which members of different racial groups are divided into separate electoral registers and allocated a proportion of political power on the basis of race. Under our jurisprudence, rather than requiring registration on racial rolls and dividing power purely on a population basis, we have simply resorted to the somewhat less precise expedient of drawing geographic district lines to capture minority populations and to ensure the existence of the "appropriate" number of "safe minority seats." * * * [F]ew devices could be better designed to exacerbate racial tensions than the consciously segregated districting system currently being constructed in the name of the Voting Rights Act.

As a practical political matter, our drive to segregate political districts by race can only serve to deepen racial divisions by destroying any need for voters or candidates to build bridges between racial groups or to form voting coalitions. "Black-preferred" candidates are assured election in "safe black districts"; white-preferred candidates are assured election in "safe white districts." Neither group needs to draw on support from the other's constituency to win on election day. * * *

While the results we have already achieved under the Voting Rights Act might seem bad enough, we should recognize that our approach to splintering the electorate into racially designated single-member districts does not by any means mark a limit on the authority federal judges may wield to rework electoral systems under our Voting Rights Act jurisprudence. On the contrary, in relying on single-member districting schemes as a touchstone, our cases so far have been somewhat arbitrarily limited to addressing the interests of minority voters who are sufficiently geographically compact to form a majority in a single-member district. See *Gingles*, 478 U.S., at 49–50. There is no reason *a priori*, however, that our focus should be so constrained. The decision to rely on single-member geographic districts as a mechanism for conducting elections is merely a political choice — and one that we might reconsider in the future. * * * Already, some advocates have criticized the current strategy of creating majority-minority districts and have urged the adoption of other voting mechanisms — for example, cumulative voting[15] or a system using transferable votes[16] — that can produce proportional results without requiring division of the electorate into racially segregated districts. * * *

* * * Once we candidly recognize that geographic districting and other aspects of electoral systems that we have so far placed beyond question are merely political choices, those practices, too, may fall under suspicion of having a dilutive effect on minority voting strength. And when the time comes to put the question to the test, it may be difficult indeed for a Court that, under *Gingles*, has been bent on creating roughly proportional representation for geographically compact minorities to find a principled reason for holding that a geographically dispersed minority cannot challenge districting itself as a dilutive electoral practice. In principle, cumulative voting and other non-district-based methods of effecting proportional representa-

---

[15] Under a cumulative voting scheme, * * * each voter has as many votes as there are posts to be filled, and the voter may cast as many of his votes as he wishes for a single candidate. The system thus allows a numerical minority to concentrate its voting power behind a given candidate without requiring that the minority voters themselves be concentrated into a single district.

[16] * * * Under such a system, each voter rank orders his choices of candidates. To win, a candidate must receive a fixed quota of votes, which may be set by any of several methods. Ballots listing a given candidate as the voter's first choice are counted for that candidate until the candidate has secured the quota of votes necessary for election. Remaining first-choice ballots for that candidate are then transferred to another candidate, usually the one listed as the second choice on the ballot. Like cumulative voting, the system allows a minority group to concentrate its voting power without requiring districting, and it has the additional advantage of ensuring that "surplus" votes are transferred to support the election of the minority voters' next preference.

tion are simply more efficient and straightforward mechanisms for achieving what has already become our tacit objective: roughly proportional allocation of political power according to race. * * *

* * * [U]nder our constitutional system, this Court is not a centralized politburo appointed for life to dictate to the provinces the "correct" theories of democratic representation, the "best" electoral systems for securing truly "representative" government, the "fairest" proportions of minority political influence, or, as respondents would have us hold today, the "proper" sizes for local governing bodies. We should be cautious in interpreting any Act of Congress to grant us power to make such determinations. * * *

* * * Properly understood, the terms "standard, practice, or procedure" in § 2(a) refer only to practices that affect minority citizens' access to the ballot. Districting systems and electoral mechanisms that may affect the "weight" given to a ballot duly cast and counted are simply beyond the purview of the Act.

* * * Under the plain terms of the Act, § 2(a) covers only a defined category of state actions. Only "voting qualification[s]," "prerequisite[s] to voting," or "standard[s], practice[s], or procedure[s]" are subject to challenge under the Act. The first two items in this list clearly refer to conditions or tests applied to regulate citizens' access to the ballot. They would cover, for example, any form of test or requirement imposed as a condition on registration or on the process of voting on election day. * * *

* * * The general terms in the section are most naturally understood, therefore, to refer to any methods for conducting a part of the voting process that might similarly be used to interfere with a citizen's ability to cast his vote, and they are undoubtedly intended to ensure that the entire voting process — a process that begins with registration and includes the casting of a ballot and having the ballot counted — is covered by the Act. Simply by including general terms in § 2(a) to ensure the efficacy of the restriction imposed, Congress should not be understood to have expanded the scope of the restriction beyond the logical limits implied in the specific terms of the statute.

Moreover, it is not only in the terms describing the practices regulated under the Act that § 2(a) focuses on the individual voter. The section also speaks only in the singular of the right of "any citizen" to vote. Giving the terms "standard, practice, or procedure" an expansive interpretation to reach potentially dilutive practices, however, would distort that focus on the individual, for a vote dilution claim necessarily depends on the assertion of a group right. At the heart of the claim is the contention that the members of a group collectively have been unable to exert the influence that their numbers suggest they might under an alternative system. Such a group right, however, finds no grounding in the terms of § 2(a). * * *

It is true that § 14(c)(1) also states that the term "voting" "include[s] all action necessary to make a vote *effective*," and the Court has seized on this language as an indication that Congress intended the Act to reach claims of vote dilution. See *Allen*, 393 U.S., at 566. But if the word "effective" is not plucked out of context, the rest of § 14(c)(1) makes clear that the actions Congress deemed necessary to make a vote "effective" were precisely the actions listed above: registering, satisfying other voting prerequisites, casting a ballot, and having it included in the final tally of votes cast. * * *

Reading the Act's prohibition of practices that may result in a "denial or abridgement of the right . . . to vote" as protecting only access to the ballot also yields an interpretation that is consistent with the Court's construction of virtually identical language in the Fifteenth Amendment. The use of language taken from the Amendment suggests that the section was intended to protect a "right to vote" with the same scope as the right secured by the Amendment itself; certainly, no reason appears from the text of the Act for giving the language a broader construction in the statute than we have given it in the Constitution. The Court has never decided, however, whether the Fifteenth Amendment should be understood to protect against vote "dilution."[20]

While the terms of § 2(a) thus indicate that the section focuses only on securing access to the ballot, it might be argued that reenactment of § 2 in 1982 should be understood as an endorsement of the interpretation contained in cases such as *Allen* that the terms "standard, practice, or procedure" were meant to reach potentially dilutive practices. It is true that we generally will assume that reenactment of specific statutory language is intended to include a "settled judicial interpretation" of that language. * * * But it was hardly well settled in 1982 that *Allen*'s broad reading of the terms "standard, practice, or procedure" in § 5 would set the scope of § 2 as a provision reaching claims of vote dilution.

On the contrary, in 1980 in *Mobile* v. *Bolden*, 446 U.S. 55 [p. 288], a plurality of the Court construed § 2 in a manner flatly inconsistent with the understanding that those terms were meant to reach dilutive practices. Emphasizing that the section tracked the language of the Fifteenth Amendment by prohibiting the use of practices that might "deny or abridge the right . . . to vote," the *Bolden* plurality determined that § 2 was "intended to have an effect no different from that of the Fifteenth Amendment itself." *Id.*, at 61. In the plurality's view, however, the Fifteenth Amendment did not extend to reach dilution claims; its protections were satisfied as long as members of racial minorities could "register and vote without hindrance." *Id.*, at 65. *Bolden* remained the last word from this Court interpreting § 2 at the time the section was amended in 1982. Thus, the reenactment in the amended section of the same language covering any "standard, practice, or procedure" and the retention of virtually identical language protecting against the "denial or abridgement of the right . . . to vote" can hardly be understood as an endorsement of a broad reading of the section as a provision reaching claims of vote dilution.[22] * * *

---

[20] * * * *Gomillion* v. *Lightfoot*, 364 U.S. 339 (1960) [p. 113], does not indicate that the Fifteenth Amendment, in protecting the right to vote, incorporates a concern for anything beyond securing access to the ballot. The *Gomillion* plaintiffs' claims centered precisely on access: Their complaint was not that the weight of their votes had been diminished in some way, but that the boundaries of a city had been drawn to prevent blacks from voting in municipal elections altogether. *Gomillion* thus "maintains the distinction between an attempt to exclude Negroes totally from the relevant constituency, and a statute that permits Negroes to vote but which uses the gerrymander to contain the impact of Negro suffrage." *Allen*, 393 U.S., [at] 589 (Harlan, J., concurring in part and dissenting in part).

[22] If anything, * * * by reenacting virtually the same language derived from the Fifteenth Amendment to define the basic interest protected by the Act, Congress [might have] intended to

As the Court concluded in *Gingles*, the 1982 amendments incorporated into the Act, and specifically into § 2(b), a "results" test for measuring violations of § 2(a). That test was intended to replace, for § 2 purposes, the "intent" test the Court had announced in *Bolden* for voting rights claims under § 2 of the Voting Rights Act and under the Fourteenth and Fifteenth Amendments. Section 2(a) thus prohibits certain state actions that may "resul[t] in a denial or abridgement" of the right to vote, and § 2(b) incorporates virtually the exact language of the "results test" employed by the Court in *White* v. *Regester*, 412 U.S. 755 (1973) [p. 274], and applied in constitutional voting rights cases before our decision in *Bolden*. The section directs courts to consider whether "based on the totality of circumstances," a state practice results in members of a minority group "hav[ing] less opportunity than other members of the electorate to participate in the political process and to elect representatives of their choice." [52 U.S.C. § 10301(b)].

But the mere adoption of a "results" test, rather than an "intent" test, says nothing about the *type* of state laws that may be challenged using that test. * * * Thus, as an initial matter, there is no reason to think that § 2(b) could serve to expand the scope of the prohibition in § 2(a), which, as I described above, does not extend by its terms to electoral mechanisms that might have a dilutive effect on group voting power.

Even putting that concern aside for the moment, it should be apparent that the incorporation of a results test into the amended section does not necessarily suggest that Congress intended to allow claims of vote dilution under § 2. A results test is useful to plaintiffs whether they are challenging laws that restrict access to the ballot or laws that accomplish some diminution in the "proper weight" of a group's vote. Nothing about the test itself suggests that it is inherently tied to vote dilution claims. A law, for example, limiting the times and places at which registration can occur might be adopted with the purpose of limiting black voter registration, but it could be extremely difficult to prove the discriminatory intent behind such a facially neutral law. The results test would allow plaintiffs to mount a successful challenge to the law under § 2 without such proof.

Moreover, nothing in the language § 2(b) uses to describe the results test particularly indicates that the test was intended to be used under the Act for assessing claims of dilution. * * * The section speaks in terms of an opportunity — a chance — to participate and to elect, not an assured ability to attain any particular result. And since the ballot provides the formal mechanism for obtaining access to the political process and for electing representatives, it would seem that one who has had the same chance as others to register and to cast his ballot has had an equal opportunity to participate and to elect, whether or not any of the candidates he chooses is ultimately successful. * * *

It is true that the terms "standard, practice, or procedure" in § 5 of the Act have been construed to reach districting systems and other potentially dilutive electoral mechanisms, see, *e.g.*, *Allen*, 393 U.S., at 569, and Congress has reenacted § 5 subsequent to our decisions adopting that expansive interpretation. Nevertheless,

---

preserve the limitation that the *Bolden* plurality found implicit in that language. It is clear from the terms of the amendments passed in 1982 that where Congress sought to alter the understanding of the Act announced in *Bolden*, it did so explicitly in the text of the statute. * * *

the text of the section suggests precisely the same focus on measures that relate to access to the ballot that appears in § 2. * * *

In my view, the tension between the terms of the Act and the construction we have placed on § 5 at the very least suggests that our interpretation of § 5 should not be adopted wholesale to supply the meaning of the terms "standard, practice, or procedure" under § 2. * * * Where a careful reading of the language of § 2 dictates a narrow interpretation of the section, there is no reason for transplanting our interpretation of the terms of § 5 — an interpretation that I believe is in tension with the text of § 5 itself — to another section of the Act.[27] * * *

"*Stare decisis* is not an inexorable command," *Payne* v. *Tennessee*, 501 U.S. 808, 828 (1991). Indeed, "when governing decisions are unworkable or are badly reasoned, this Court has never felt constrained to follow precedent." *Id.*, at 827. [O]ur decision in *Gingles* interpreting the scope of § 2 was badly reasoned; it wholly substituted reliance on legislative history for analysis of statutory text. In doing so, it produced a far more expansive interpretation of § 2 than a careful reading of the language of the statute would allow.

Our interpretation of § 2 has also proved unworkable. As I outlined above, it has mired the federal courts in an inherently political task — one that requires answers to questions that are ill-suited to principled judicial resolution. Under § 2, we have assigned the federal judiciary a project that involves, not the application of legal standards to the facts of various cases or even the elaboration of legal principles on a case-by-case basis, but rather the creation of standards from an abstract evaluation of political philosophy.

Worse, our interpretation of § 2 has required us to distort our decisions to obscure the fact that the political choice at the heart of our cases rests on precisely the principle the Act condemns: proportional allocation of political power according to race. Continued adherence to a line of decisions that necessitates such dissembling cannot possibly promote what we have perceived to be one of the central values of the policy of *stare decisis:* the preservation of "the actual and perceived integrity of the judicial process." * * *

For the foregoing reasons, I agree with the Court's conclusion that the size of a governing body is not subject to challenge under § 2 of the Voting Rights Act. I therefore concur in the Court's judgment * * *.

---

[27] I need not decide in this case whether I would overrule our decisions construing the terms "standard, practice, or procedure" in § 5; the challenge here involves only § 2. Although in my view our construction of § 5 may well be incorrect as a matter of first impression, *stare decisis* would suggest that such an error in prior decisions may not in itself justify overruling settled precedent. Determining whether to abandon prior decisions requires weighing a multitude of factors, one of the most important of which is the extent to which the decisions in question have proved unworkable. In that regard, while the practical differences in the application of §§ 2 and 5 that Justice Kennedy points out would not, in my view, suggest as an original matter that the same terms in the two sections should be read to have different meanings, Justice Kennedy's observations might suggest that different considerations would have a bearing on the question whether our past interpretations should be abandoned in the § 5 and § 2 contexts. Indeed, in the § 5 context they might suggest a contrary conclusion to the result I reach under § 2. That, however, is a question for another day.

JUSTICE BLACKMUN, with whom JUSTICE STEVENS, JUSTICE SOUTER, and JUSTICE GINSBURG join, dissenting. * * *

Consistent with the Act's remedial purposes, this Court has held that a wide variety of election- and voting-related practices fit within the term "standard, practice, or procedure." Among the covered practices are the annexation of land to enlarge city boundaries; a rule requiring employees to take leaves of absence while they campaign for elective office; candidate filing dates and other procedural requirements; and candidate residency requirements.

Specifically, this Court long has treated a change in the size of a governing authority as a change in a "standard, practice, or procedure" with respect to voting. In *City of Rome*, 446 U.S., at 161, it noted that it "is not disputed" that an expansion in the size of a board of education was "within the purview of the Act" and subject to preclearance under § 5. In *City of Lockhart* v. *United States*, it stated that a change from a three-member commission to a five-member commission was subject to § 5 preclearance. And, most recently, it said that the term "standard, practice, or procedure with respect to voting" included a change in the size of a governing authority or an increase or decrease in the number of elected offices. *Presley* v. *Etowah County Comm'n*, 502 U.S., [at] 500.

This conclusion flowed naturally from the holding in *Bunton* v. *Patterson* that a change from an elected to an appointed office was a "standard, practice, or procedure with respect to voting." In *Bunton*, the Court reasoned that the power of a citizen's vote is affected by the change because the citizen has been "prohibited from electing an officer formerly subject to the approval of the voters." [393 U.S.], at 570. The reverse is also true: A change from an appointed to an elected office affects a citizen's voting power by increasing the number of officials for whom he may vote. See *McCain* v. *Lybrand*. And, as the Court recognized in *Presley*, a change in the size of a governing authority is a "standard, practice, or procedure with respect to voting" because the change "increase[s] or diminish[es] the number of officials for whom the electorate may vote," 502 U.S., at 503 * * *.

To date, our precedent has dealt with § 5 challenges to a change in the size of a governing authority, rather than § 2 challenges to the existing size of a governing body. I agree with JUSTICE O'CONNOR that, as a textual matter, "standard, practice, or procedure" under § 2 is at least as broad as "standard, practice, or procedure with respect to voting" under § 5. In fact, because of the "close connection" between §§ 2 and 5, we interpret them similarly. See *Chisom* v. *Roemer*, 501 U.S., at 402. And in the context of § 2, the Court stated: "Section 2 protected the right to vote, and it did so without making any distinctions or imposing any limitations as to which elections would fall within its purview." *Id.*, at 392.

Congress repeatedly has endorsed the broad construction this Court has given the Act in general and § 5 in particular. Significantly, when Congress considered the 1982 amendments to the Voting Rights Act, it made no effort to curtail the application of § 5 to changes in size, in the face of the longstanding practice of submitting such changes for preclearance, and on the heels of this Court's recognition just two years earlier that it was "not disputed" that a change in the size of a governing body was covered under § 5. Similarly, the Attorney General, whose construction of the Act "is entitled to considerable deference," for years has required § 5 preclearance of the expansion or reduction of a governing body. It is not surprising that no party to this case argued that the size of a governing authority is not a "standard, practice, or procedure."

In light of this consistent and expansive interpretation of the Act by this Court, Congress, and the Attorney General, the Act's "all-inclusive" definition of "standard, practice, or procedure" cannot be read to exclude threshold coverage of challenges to the size of a governing authority. As five Members of the Court today agree, the size of a governing authority is a "standard, practice, or procedure" with respect to voting for purposes of § 2 as well as § 5 of the Voting Rights Act.

Although five Justices agree that the size of a governing body is a "standard, practice, or procedure" under § 2, a like number of Justices conclude [*sic*], under varying rationales, that Voting Rights plaintiffs nonetheless cannot bring size challenges under § 2. This conclusion is inconsistent with our precedent giving the Act " 'the broadest possible scope' in combating racial discrimination," *Chisom*, 501 U.S., at 403, quoting *Allen*, 393 U.S., at 567, and with the vote-dilution analysis prescribed in *Thornburg* v. *Gingles*.

To prevail in a vote-dilution challenge, minority voters must show that they "possess the *potential* to elect representatives *in the absence of the challenged structure* or practice." [*Gingles*, 478 U.S.], at 50 n.17 (second emphasis supplied). [M]inority voters' potential "in the absence of" the allegedly dilutive mechanism must be measured against the benchmark of an alternative structure or practice that is reasonable and workable under the facts of the specific case.

By all objective measures, the proposed five-member Bleckley County Commission presents a reasonable, workable benchmark against which to measure the practice of electing a sole commissioner. First, the Georgia Legislature specifically authorized a five-member commission for Bleckley County. Moreover, a five-member commission is the most common form of governing authority in Georgia. Bleckley County, as one of a small and dwindling number of counties in Georgia still employing a sole commissioner, markedly departs from practices elsewhere in Georgia. * * * Finally, the county itself has moved from a single superintendent of education to a school board with five members elected from single-member districts, providing a workable and readily available model for commission districts. Thus, the proposed five-member baseline is reasonable and workable.

In this case, identifying an appropriate baseline against which to measure dilution is not difficult. In other cases, it may be harder. But the need to make difficult judgments does not "justify a judicially created limitation on the coverage of the broadly worded statute, as enacted and amended by Congress." *Chisom*, 501 U.S., at 403. Vote dilution is inherently a relative concept, requiring a highly "flexible, fact-intensive" inquiry, *Gingles*, 478 U.S., at 46, and calling for an exercise of the "court's overall judgment, based on the totality of circumstances and guided by those relevant factors in the particular case," as mandated by Congress. Certainly judges who engage in the complex task of evaluating reapportionment plans and examining district lines will be able to determine whether a proposed baseline is an appropriate one against which to measure a claim of vote dilution based on the size of a county commission.

There are, to be sure, significant constraints on size challenges. Minority plaintiffs, who bear the burden of demonstrating dilution, also bear the burden of demonstrating that their proposed benchmark is reasonable and workable. One indication of a benchmark's reasonableness is its grounding in history, custom, or practice. This consideration will discourage size challenges to traditional single-member executive offices, such as governors and mayors, or even sheriffs or clerks of court. By tradition and practice, these executive positions are occupied by one person, so plaintiffs could rarely point to an objectively reasonable alternative size that has any foundation in the past or present. The sole commissioner, by contrast, holds plenary legislative, as well as executive, power. A one-member legislature, far from being the norm, is an anomaly. * * *

Additionally, every successful vote-dilution challenge will be based on the "totality of the circumstances," often including the lingering effects of past discrimination. Not every racial or language minority that constitutes 5% of the population has a claim to have a governing authority expanded to 20 members in order to give them an opportunity to elect a representative. Instead, the voters would have to prove that a 20-member governing authority was a reasonable benchmark — which, of course, respondents could not do here — and that their claim satisfied the three *Gingles* preconditions and was warranted under the totality of the circumstances.

* * * These limitations protect against a proliferation of vote-dilution challenges premised on eccentric or impracticable alternative methods of redistricting.

* * * We have recognized over the years that seemingly innocuous and even well-intentioned election practices may impede minority voters' ability not only to vote, but to have their votes count. It is clear that the practice of electing a single-member county commission can be one such dilutive practice. It is equally clear that a five-member commission is an appropriate benchmark against which to measure the alleged dilutive effects of Bleckley County's practice of electing a sole commissioner. I respectfully dissent.

JUSTICE GINSBURG, dissenting. * * *

Section 2 of the Voting Rights Act of 1965 calls for an inquiry into "[t]he extent to which members of a protected class have been elected to office," but simultaneously disclaims any "right to have members of a protected class elected in numbers equal to their proportion in the population." [52 U.S.C. § 10301(b)]. "There is an inherent tension between what Congress wished to do and what it wished to avoid" — between Congress' "inten[t] to allow vote dilution claims to be brought under § 2" and its intent to avoid "creat[ing] a right to proportional representation for minority voters." *Gingles*, 478 U.S., [at] 84 (O'CONNOR, J., concurring in judgment). Tension of this kind is hardly unique to the Voting Rights Act, for when Congress acts on issues on which its constituents are divided, sometimes bitterly, the give-and-take of legislative compromise can yield statutory language that fails to reconcile conflicting goals and purposes. * * *

When courts are confronted with congressionally crafted compromises of this kind, it is "not an easy task" to remain "faithful to the balance Congress struck."

[*Ibid.*] * * * However difficult this task may prove to be, it is one that courts must undertake because it is their mission to effectuate Congress' multiple purposes as best they can. See *Chisom* v. *Roemer*, 501 U.S., [at] 403 (1991) ("Even if serious problems lie ahead in applying the 'totality of the circumstances' [inquiry under § 2(b) of the Voting Rights Act], that task, difficult as it may prove to be, cannot justify a judicially created limitation on the coverage of the broadly worded statute[.]").

Separate opinion of JUSTICE STEVENS, in which JUSTICE BLACKMUN, JUSTICE SOUTER, and JUSTICE GINSBURG join.

JUSTICE THOMAS has written a separate opinion proposing that the terms "standard, practice, or procedure" as used in the Voting Rights Act of 1965 should henceforth be construed to refer only to practices that affect minority citizens' access to the ballot. Specifically, JUSTICE THOMAS would no longer interpret the Act to forbid practices that dilute minority voting strength. * * * [I]t is appropriate to supplement JUSTICE THOMAS' writing with a few words of history. * * *

* * * What JUSTICE THOMAS describes as "a fundamental shift in the focal point of the Act" occurred in 1969 when the Court unequivocally rejected the narrow reading, relying heavily on a broad definition of the term "voting" as including "all action necessary to make a vote effective." *Allen* v. *State Bd. of Elections*, 393 U.S., [at] 565–566.

Despite *Allen*'s purported deviation from the Act's true meaning, Congress one year later reenacted § 5 without in any way changing the operative words. During the next five years, the Court consistently adhered to *Allen*, and in 1975, Congress again reenacted § 5 without change. * * *

If the 1970 and 1975 reenactments had left any doubt as to congressional intent, that doubt would be set aside by the 1982 amendments to § 2[, which] * * * substituted a "results" test for an intent requirement. It is crystal clear that Congress intended the 1982 amendment to cover [more claims than just those alleging a lack of access to the ballot]. * * *

Throughout his opinion, JUSTICE THOMAS argues that this case is an exception to *stare decisis*, because *Allen* and its progeny have "immersed the federal courts in a hopeless project of weighing questions of political theory." There is no question that the Voting Rights Act has required the courts to resolve difficult questions, but that is no reason to deviate from an interpretation that Congress has thrice approved. Statutes frequently require courts to make policy judgments. The Sherman Act, for example, requires courts to delve deeply into the theory of economic organization. Similarly, Title VII of the Civil Rights Act has required the courts to formulate a theory of equal opportunity. Our work would certainly be much easier if every case could be resolved by consulting a dictionary, but when Congress has legislated in general terms, judges may not invoke judicial modesty to avoid difficult questions. * * *

Notes and Questions

1.   As the opinions in *Holder v. Hall* made clear, §§ 2 and 5 use virtually identical language concerning the scope of their coverage ("standard, practice, or procedure" in § 2, and "standard, practice, or procedure with respect to voting" in § 5). Is it appropriate to interpret the language in the two sections in a different manner, as Justice Kennedy and perhaps Justice Thomas would? Compare Justice Scalia's opinion for the Court in *Reno v. Bossier Parish School Board*, 528 U.S. 320 (2000). If §§ 2 and 5 should be interpreted together, does the lack of a baseline for § 2 claims suggest that *Allen v. State Board of Elections* was wrong to give § 5 such a broad reading?

2.   Did Justice Thomas provide adequate reasons for departing from precedent?

3.   In footnote 20 of his opinion, Justice Thomas characterized *Gomillion* not as a vote-dilution case, but rather as protecting blacks' ability to vote in municipal elections. Justice Stevens, in an omitted portion of his opinion, took issue with that characterization and argued that it undermined Justice Thomas's critique of *Allen*: "Under [Justice Thomas's] reasoning the substitution of an appointive office for an elective office, see *Bunton* v. *Patterson*, decided with *Allen*, 393 U.S., [at] 550–551, or a change in district boundaries that prevented voters from casting ballots for the reelection of their incumbent congressional Representatives, would also be covered practices." 512 U.S. at 959 n.1 (opinion of Stevens, J.). Must one accept *Allen*'s broad interpretation of "standard, practice, or procedure with respect to voting" if one accepts *Gomillion*?

4.   Justices Kennedy and O'Connor appeared concerned that there was no logical stopping point to the plaintiffs' dilution theory. Future plaintiffs, they worried, might demand greater increases in the size of legislatures so as to provide representation to smaller and smaller minority groups. Did Justice Blackmun provide an adequate response to that criticism?

5.   Justice O'Connor concluded that the size of a government body was a "standard, practice, or procedure," but that no benchmark existed against which to measure its dilutive effect. Is it reasonable to believe that Congress would include the size of government bodies within the scope of § 2 while making it impossible to succeed on claims alleging that the size of a government body has diluted the effectiveness of minority votes?

6.   Justice Thomas criticized *Allen* for reading the Voting Rights Act to authorize the Court to choose a theory of "effective" representation. Does his approach solve the problem he identified, or did he merely replace *Allen*'s political theory with one of his own?

7.   Justice Thomas alleged that one especially negative effect of the Court's § 2 jurisprudence was the racial segregation of voters into electoral districts. The next section examines the limitations that the Equal Protection Clause places on such race-conscious districting.

E. CONSTITUTIONAL CONSTRAINTS ON MAJORITY-MINORITY DISTRICTING

The last two sections explored how § 2 of the Voting Rights Act can require states to draw districts to ensure that members of minority groups have equal access to the political process and an equal opportunity to elect representatives of their choice, compared to other citizens. The Supreme Court has interpreted the Equal Protection Clause, however, to limit states' ability to take race into account in constructing electoral districts. In the Court's view, a districting scheme that subordinates traditional districting principles to considerations of race creates a racial classification and must pass strict scrutiny to be constitutional. This section examines the doctrine governing this type of racial gerrymandering, and the next section further examines the conflict that doctrine creates between the Equal Protection Clause and § 2 of the Voting Rights Act.

SHAW v. RENO

Supreme Court of the United States

509 U.S. 630, 113 S. Ct. 2816, 125 L. Ed. 2d 511 (1993)

JUSTICE O'CONNOR delivered the opinion of the Court [in which CHIEF JUSTICE REHNQUIST, JUSTICE SCALIA, JUSTICE KENNEDY, and JUSTICE THOMAS join].

This case involves two of the most complex and sensitive issues this Court has faced in recent years: the meaning of the constitutional "right" to vote, and the propriety of race-based state legislation designed to benefit members of historically disadvantaged racial minority groups. As a result of the 1990 census, North Carolina became entitled to a 12th seat in the United States House of Representatives. The General Assembly enacted a reapportionment plan that included one majority-black congressional district. After the Attorney General of the United States objected to the plan pursuant to § 5 of the Voting Rights Act of 1965, the General Assembly passed new legislation creating a second majority-black district. Appellants allege that the revised plan, which contains district boundary lines of dramatically irregular shape, constitutes an unconstitutional racial gerrymander. The question before us is whether appellants have stated a cognizable claim.

The voting age population of North Carolina is approximately 78% white, 20% black, and 1% Native American; the remaining 1% is predominantly Asian. The black population is relatively dispersed; blacks constitute a majority of the general population in only 5 of the State's 100 counties. Geographically, the State divides into three regions: the eastern Coastal Plain, the central Piedmont Plateau, and the western mountains. The largest concentrations of black citizens live in the Coastal Plain, primarily in the northern part. The General Assembly's first redistricting plan contained one majority-black district centered in that area of the State. * * *

The Attorney General, acting through the Assistant Attorney General for the Civil Rights Division, interposed a formal objection to the General Assembly's plan. The Attorney General specifically objected to the configuration of boundary lines drawn in the south-central to southeastern region of the State. In the Attorney General's view, the General Assembly could have created a second majority-minority district "to give effect to black and Native American voting strength in this area" by using boundary lines "no more irregular than [those] found elsewhere in the proposed plan," but failed to do so for "pretextual reasons."

Under § 5, the State remained free to seek a declaratory judgment from the District Court for the District of Columbia notwithstanding the Attorney General's objection. It did not do so. Instead, the General Assembly enacted a revised redistricting plan that included a second majority-black district. The General Assembly located the second district not in the south-central to southeastern part of the State, but in the north-central region along Interstate 85.

The first of the two majority-black districts contained in the revised plan, District 1, is somewhat hook shaped. Centered in the northeast portion of the State, it moves southward until it tapers to a narrow band; then, with finger-like extensions, it reaches far into the southernmost part of the State near the South Carolina border. District 1 has been compared to a "Rorschach ink-blot test" and a "bug splattered on a windshield."

The second majority-black district, District 12, is even more unusually shaped. It is approximately 160 miles long and, for much of its length, no wider than the I-85 corridor. It winds in snakelike fashion through tobacco country, financial centers, and manufacturing areas "until it gobbles in enough enclaves of black neighborhoods." Northbound and southbound drivers on I-85 sometimes find themselves in separate districts in one county, only to "trade" districts when they enter the next county. Of the 10 counties through which District 12 passes, 5 are cut into 3 different districts; even towns are divided. At one point the district remains contiguous only because it intersects at a single point with two other districts before crossing over them. One state legislator has remarked that "if you drove down the interstate with both car doors open, you'd kill most of the people in the district." The district even has inspired poetry: "Ask not for whom the line is drawn; it is drawn to avoid thee."
* * *

* * * Appellants are five residents of Durham County, North Carolina, all registered to vote in that county. Under the General Assembly's plan, two will vote for congressional representatives in District 12 and three will vote in neighboring District 2. * * * In their complaint, appellants did not claim that the General Assembly's reapportionment plan unconstitutionally "diluted" white voting strength. They did not even claim to be white. Rather, appellants' complaint alleged that the deliberate segregation of voters into separate districts on the basis of race violated their constitutional right to participate in a "color-blind" electoral process. Despite their invocation of the ideal of a "color-blind" Constitution, appellants appear to concede that race-conscious redistricting is not always unconstitutional. That concession is wise: This Court never has held that race-conscious state decision-making is impermissible in *all* circumstances. What appellants object to is redistricting legislation that is so extremely irregular on its face that it rationally can be viewed only as an effort to segregate the races for purposes of voting, without regard for traditional districting principles and without sufficiently compelling justification. For the reasons that follow, we conclude that appellants have stated a claim upon which relief can be granted under the Equal Protection Clause.
* * *

Appellants contend that redistricting legislation that is so bizarre on its face that it is "unexplainable on grounds other than race" demands the same close scrutiny that we give other state laws that classify citizens by race. Our voting rights precedents support that conclusion.

In *Guinn* v. *United States*, 238 U.S. 347 (1915), the Court invalidated under the Fifteenth Amendment a statute that imposed a literacy requirement on voters but contained a "grandfather clause" applicable to individuals and their lineal descendants entitled to vote "on [or prior to] January 1, 1866." The determinative consideration for the Court was that the law, though ostensibly race neutral, on its face "embodied no exercise of judgment and rested upon no discernible reason" other than to circumvent the prohibitions of the Fifteenth Amendment. *Id.*, at 363. In other words, the statute was invalid because, on its face, it could not be explained on grounds other than race.

The Court applied the same reasoning to the "uncouth twenty-eight-sided" municipal boundary line at issue in *Gomillion* [v. *Lightfoot*, 364 U.S. 339 (1960)] [p. 115]. Although the statute that redrew the city limits of Tuskegee was race neutral on its face, plaintiffs alleged that its effect was impermissibly to remove from the city virtually all black voters and no white voters. * * *

The majority resolved the case under the Fifteenth Amendment. * * * This Court's subsequent reliance on *Gomillion* in other Fourteenth Amendment cases [however] * * * supports appellants' contention that district lines obviously drawn for the purpose of separating voters by race require careful scrutiny under the Equal Protection Clause regardless of the motivations underlying their adoption.

The Court extended the reasoning of *Gomillion* to congressional districting in *Wright* v. *Rockefeller*, 376 U.S. 52 (1964). At issue in *Wright* were four districts contained in a New York apportionment statute. The plaintiffs alleged that the statute excluded nonwhites from one district and concentrated them in the other three. Every Member of the Court assumed that the plaintiffs' allegation that the statute "segregated eligible voters by race and place of origin" stated a constitutional claim. The Justices disagreed only as to whether the plaintiffs had carried their burden of proof at trial. The dissenters thought the unusual shape of the district lines could "be explained only in racial terms." The majority, however, accepted the District Court's finding that the plaintiffs had failed to establish that the districts were in fact drawn on racial lines. * * *

Wright illustrates the difficulty of determining from the face of a single-member districting plan that it purposefully distinguishes between voters on the basis of race. A reapportionment statute typically does not classify persons at all; it classifies tracts of land, or addresses. Moreover, redistricting differs from other kinds of state decisionmaking in that the legislature always is *aware* of race when it draws district lines, just as it is aware of age, economic status, religious and political persuasion, and a variety of other demographic factors. That sort of race consciousness does not lead inevitably to impermissible race discrimination. As *Wright* demonstrates, when members of a racial group live together in one community, a reapportionment plan that concentrates members of the group in one district and excludes them from others may reflect wholly legitimate purposes. The district lines may be drawn, for example, to provide for compact districts of contiguous territory, or to maintain the integrity of political subdivisions.

The difficulty of proof, of course, does not mean that a racial gerrymander, once established, should receive less scrutiny under the Equal Protection Clause than other state legislation classifying citizens by race. Moreover, it seems clear to us that proof sometimes will not be difficult at all. In some exceptional cases, a reapportionment plan may be so highly irregular that, on its face, it rationally cannot be understood as anything other than an effort to "segregate . . . voters" on the basis of race. *Gomillion*, in which a tortured municipal boundary line was drawn to exclude black voters, was such a case. So, too, would be a case in which a State concentrated a dispersed minority population in a single district by disregarding traditional districting principles such as compactness, contiguity, and respect for political subdivisions. We emphasize that these criteria are important not because they are constitutionally required — they are not — but because they are objective factors that may serve to defeat a claim that a district has been gerrymandered on racial lines.

Put differently, we believe that reapportionment is one area in which appearances do matter. A reapportionment plan that includes in one district individuals who belong to the same race, but who are otherwise widely separated by geographical and political boundaries, and who may have little in common with one another but the color of their skin, bears an uncomfortable resemblance to political apartheid. It reinforces the perception that members of the same racial group — regardless of their age, education, economic status, or the community in which they live — think alike, share the same political interests, and will prefer the same candidates at the polls. * * * By perpetuating such notions, a racial gerrymander may exacerbate the very patterns of racial bloc voting that majority-minority districting is sometimes said to counteract.

The message that such districting sends to elected representatives is equally pernicious. When a district obviously is created solely to effectuate the perceived common interests of one racial group, elected officials are more likely to believe that their primary obligation is to represent only the members of that group, rather than their constituency as a whole. This is altogether antithetical to our system of representative democracy. * * *

For these reasons, we conclude that a plaintiff challenging a reapportionment statute under the Equal Protection Clause may state a claim by alleging that the legislation, though race neutral on its face, rationally cannot be understood as anything other than an effort to separate voters into different districts on the basis of race, and that the separation lacks sufficient justification. It is unnecessary for us to decide whether or how a reapportionment plan that, on its face, can be explained in nonracial terms successfully could be challenged. Thus, we express no view as to whether "the intentional creation of majority-minority districts, without more," always gives rise to an equal protection claim. We hold only that, on the facts of this case, appellants have stated a claim sufficient to defeat the state appellees' motion to dismiss. * * *

The dissenters * * * suggest that a racial gerrymander of the sort alleged here is functionally equivalent to gerrymanders for nonracial purposes, such as political gerrymanders. * * * But nothing in our case law compels the conclusion that racial and political gerrymanders are subject to precisely the same constitutional scrutiny.

In fact, our country's long and persistent history of racial discrimination in voting — as well as our Fourteenth Amendment jurisprudence, which always has reserved the strictest scrutiny for discrimination on the basis of race — would seem to compel the opposite conclusion.

* * * JUSTICE STEVENS argues that racial gerrymandering poses no constitutional difficulties when district lines are drawn to favor the minority, rather than the majority. We have made clear, however, that equal protection analysis "is not dependent on the race of those burdened or benefited by a particular classification." Indeed, racial classifications receive close scrutiny even when they may be said to burden or benefit the races equally.

Finally, nothing in the Court's highly fractured decision in [*United Jewish Organizations of Williamsburgh, Inc.* v. *Carey*, 430 U.S. 144 (1977)] [p. 277] * * * forecloses the claim we recognize today. *UJO* concerned New York's revision of a reapportionment plan to include additional majority-minority districts in response to the Attorney General's denial of administrative preclearance under § 5. In that regard, it closely resembles the present case. But the cases are critically different in another way. The plaintiffs in *UJO* — members of a Hasidic community split between two districts under New York's revised redistricting plan — did not allege that the plan, on its face, was so highly irregular that it rationally could be understood only as an effort to segregate voters by race. Indeed, the facts of the case would not have supported such a claim. Three Justices approved the New York statute, in part, precisely because it adhered to traditional districting principles:

> "We think it . . . permissible for a State, *employing sound districting principles such as compactness and population equality*, to attempt to prevent racial minorities from being repeatedly outvoted by creating districts that will afford fair representation to the members of those racial groups who are sufficiently numerous *and whose residential patterns afford the opportunity* of creating districts in which they will be in the majority." 430 U.S., at 168 (opinion of WHITE, J., joined by STEVENS and REHNQUIST, JJ.) (emphasis added). * * *

* * * *UJO*'s framework simply does not apply where, as here, a reapportionment plan is alleged to be so irrational on its face that it immediately offends principles of racial equality. *UJO* set forth a standard under which white voters can establish unconstitutional vote dilution. But it did not purport to overrule *Gomillion* or *Wright*. Nothing in the decision precludes white voters (or voters of any other race) from bringing the analytically distinct claim that a reapportionment plan rationally cannot be understood as anything other than an effort to segregate citizens into separate voting districts on the basis of race without sufficient justification. Because appellants here stated such a claim, the District Court erred in dismissing their complaint. * * *

The state appellees suggest that a covered jurisdiction may have a compelling interest in creating majority-minority districts in order to comply with the Voting Rights Act. The States certainly have a very strong interest in complying with federal antidiscrimination laws that are constitutionally valid as interpreted and as applied. But in the context of a Fourteenth Amendment challenge, courts must bear in mind the difference between what the law permits and what the law requires.

For example, on remand North Carolina might claim that it adopted the revised plan in order to comply with the § 5 "nonretrogression" principle. * * * [But] the Voting Rights Act and our case law make clear that a reapportionment plan that satisfies § 5 still may be enjoined as unconstitutional. See [52 U.S.C. § 10304] (neither a declaratory judgment by the District Court for the District of Columbia nor preclearance by the Attorney General "shall bar a subsequent action to enjoin enforcement" of new voting practice); *Allen* [v. *State Bd. of Elections*], 393 U.S. [544,] 549–550 [(1969)] [p. 226] (after preclearance, "private parties may enjoin the enforcement of the new enactment . . . in traditional suits attacking its constitutionality"). Thus, * * * covered jurisdictions [do not have] *carte blanche* to engage in racial gerrymandering in the name of nonretrogression. A reapportionment plan would not be narrowly tailored to the goal of avoiding retrogression if the State went beyond what was reasonably necessary to avoid retrogression. * * *

Before us, the state appellees contend that the General Assembly's revised plan was necessary not to prevent retrogression, but to avoid dilution of black voting strength in violation of § 2[.] * * * Appellants maintain [however] * * * that the State's black population is too dispersed to support two geographically compact majority-black districts, as the bizarre shape of District 12 demonstrates, and that there is no evidence of black political cohesion. They also contend that recent black electoral successes demonstrate the willingness of white voters in North Carolina to vote for black candidates. * * * Appellants further argue that if § 2 did require adoption of North Carolina's revised plan, § 2 is to that extent unconstitutional. These arguments were not developed below, and the issues remain open for consideration on remand.

The state appellees alternatively argue that the General Assembly's plan advanced a compelling interest entirely distinct from the Voting Rights Act. We previously have recognized a significant state interest in eradicating the effects of past racial discrimination. But the State must have a "strong basis in evidence for [concluding] that remedial action [is] necessary."

* * * The state appellees assert that the deliberate creation of majority-minority districts is the most precise way — indeed the only effective way — to overcome the effects of racially polarized voting. This question also need not be decided at this stage of the litigation. We note, however, that only three Justices in *UJO* were prepared to say that States have a significant interest in minimizing the consequences of racial bloc voting apart from the requirements of the Voting Rights Act. And those three Justices specifically concluded that race-based districting, as a response to racially polarized voting, is constitutionally permissible only when the State "employ[s] sound districting principles," and only when the affected racial group's "residential patterns afford the opportunity of creating districts in which they will be in the majority." 430 U.S., at 167–168 (opinion of WHITE, J., joined by STEVENS and REHNQUIST, JJ.).

Racial classifications of any sort pose the risk of lasting harm to our society. They reinforce the belief, held by too many for too much of our history, that individuals should be judged by the color of their skin. Racial classifications with respect to voting carry particular dangers. Racial gerrymandering, even for remedial purposes, may balkanize us into competing racial factions; it threatens to carry us further from the goal of a political system in which race no longer matters — a goal that the Fourteenth and Fifteenth Amendments embody, and to which the Nation continues to aspire. It is for these reasons that race-based districting by our state legislatures demands close judicial scrutiny.

In this case, the Attorney General suggested that North Carolina could have created a reasonably compact second majority-minority district in the south-central to southeastern part of the State. We express no view as to whether appellants successfully could have challenged such a district under the Fourteenth Amendment. We also do not decide whether appellants' complaint stated a claim under constitutional provisions other than the Fourteenth Amendment. Today we hold only that appellants have stated a claim under the Equal Protection Clause by alleging that the North Carolina General Assembly adopted a reapportionment scheme so irrational on its face that it can be understood only as an effort to segregate voters into separate voting districts because of their race, and that the separation lacks sufficient justification. If the allegation of racial gerrymandering remains uncontradicted, the District Court further must determine whether the North Carolina plan is narrowly tailored to further a compelling governmental interest. Accordingly, we reverse the judgment of the District Court and remand the case for further proceedings consistent with this opinion.

It is so ordered.

JUSTICE WHITE, with whom JUSTICE BLACKMUN and JUSTICE STEVENS join, dissenting. * * *

The grounds for my disagreement with the majority are simply stated: Appellants have not presented a cognizable claim, because they have not alleged a cognizable injury. * * * As the majority recognizes, "redistricting differs from other kinds of state decisionmaking in that the legislature always is *aware* of race when it draws district lines, just as it is aware of age, economic status, religious and political persuasion, and a variety of other demographic factors." "Being aware," in this context, is shorthand for "taking into account," and it hardly can be doubted that legislators routinely engage in the business of making electoral predictions based on group characteristics — racial, ethnic, and the like. * * * Because extirpating such considerations from the redistricting process is unrealistic, the Court has not invalidated all plans that consciously use race, but rather has looked at their impact.

Redistricting plans also reflect group interests and inevitably are conceived with partisan aims in mind. To allow judicial interference whenever this occurs would be to invite constant and unmanageable intrusion. Moreover, a group's power to affect the political process does not automatically dissipate by virtue of an electoral loss. Accordingly, we have asked that an identifiable group demonstrate more than mere lack of success at the polls to make out a successful gerrymandering claim. See, *e.g.*, *White* v. *Regester*, 412 U.S. 755, 765–766 (1973) [p. 274]; *Whitcomb* v. *Chavis*, 403 U.S. 124, 153–155 (1971) [p. 268]. * * *

* * * Because districting inevitably is the expression of interest group politics, and because "the power to influence the political process is not limited to winning

elections," the question in gerrymandering cases is "whether a particular group has been unconstitutionally denied its chance to effectively influence the political process," [*Davis* v. *Bandemer*, 478 U.S. 109], 132–133 [(1986)]. * * * In short, even assuming that racial (or political) factors were considered in the drawing of district boundaries, a showing of discriminatory effects is a "threshold requirement" in the absence of which there is no equal protection violation, *id.*, at 143, and no need to "reach the question of the state interests . . . served by the particular districts," *id.*, at 142.

To distinguish a claim that alleges that the redistricting scheme has discriminatory intent and effect from one that does not has nothing to do with dividing racial classifications between the "benign" and the malicious — an enterprise which, as the majority notes, the Court has treated with skepticism. Rather, the issue is whether the classification based on race discriminatos [*sic*] against *anyone* by denying equal access to the political process. * * *

[I]t strains credulity to suggest that North Carolina's purpose in creating a second majority-minority district was to discriminate against members of the majority group by "impairing or burden[ing their] opportunity . . . to participate in the political process." The State has made no mystery of its intent, which was to respond to the Attorney General's objections by improving the minority group's prospects of electing a candidate of its choice. I doubt that this constitutes a discriminatory purpose as defined in the Court's equal protection cases — *i.e.*, an intent to aggravate "the unequal distribution of electoral power." But even assuming that it does, there is no question that appellants have not alleged the requisite discriminatory effects. Whites constitute roughly 76% of the total population and 79% of the voting age population in North Carolina. Yet, under the State's plan, they still constitute a voting majority in 10 (or 83%) of the 12 congressional districts. Though they might be dissatisfied at the prospect of casting a vote for a losing candidate — a lot shared by many, including a disproportionate number of minority voters — surely they cannot complain of discriminatory treatment.[6]

The majority attempts to distinguish *UJO* by imagining a heretofore unknown type of constitutional claim. * * * The logic of its theory appears to be that race-conscious redistricting that "segregates" by drawing odd-shaped lines is qualitatively different from race-conscious redistricting that affects groups in some other way.[7] The distinction is without foundation. * * * The consideration of race in "segregation" cases is no different than in other race-conscious districting; from the standpoint of the affected groups, moreover, the line-drawings all act in similar fashion. A plan that "segregates" being functionally indistinguishable from any of

---

[6] This is not to say that a group that has been afforded roughly proportional representation *never* can make out a claim of unconstitutional discrimination. Such districting might have both the intent and effect of "packing" members of the group so as to deprive them of any influence in other districts. Again, however, the equal protection inquiry should look at the group's overall influence over, and treatment by, elected representatives and the political process as a whole.

[7] I borrow the term "segregate" from the majority, but, given its historical connotation, believe that its use is ill advised. Nor is it a particularly accurate description of what has occurred. The majority-minority district that is at the center of the controversy is, according to the State, 54.71% African-American. Even if racial distribution was a factor, no racial group can be said to have been "segregated" — *i.e.*, "set apart" or "isolated." [Relocated. — Eds.]

the other varieties of gerrymandering, we should be consistent in what we require from a claimant: proof of discriminatory purpose and effect.

The other part of the majority's explanation of its holding is related to its simultaneous discomfort and fascination with irregularly shaped districts. Lack of compactness or contiguity, like uncouth district lines, certainly is a helpful indicator that some form of gerrymandering (racial or other) might have taken place * * *. Disregard for geographic divisions and compactness often goes hand in hand with partisan gerrymandering.

But while district irregularities may provide strong indicia of a potential gerrymander, they do no more than that. In particular, they have no bearing on whether the plan ultimately is found to violate the Constitution. Given two districts drawn on similar, race-based grounds, the one does not become more injurious than the other simply by virtue of being snakelike, at least so far as the Constitution is concerned and absent any evidence of differential racial impact. The majority's contrary view is perplexing in light of its concession that "compactness or attractiveness has never been held to constitute an independent federal constitutional requirement for state legislative districts." It is shortsighted as well, for a regularly shaped district can just as effectively effectuate racially discriminatory gerrymandering as an odd-shaped one. By focusing on looks rather than impact, the majority "immediately casts attention in the wrong direction — toward superficialities of shape and size, rather than toward the political realities of district composition."

Limited by its own terms to cases involving unusually shaped districts, the Court's approach nonetheless will unnecessarily hinder to some extent a State's voluntary effort to ensure a modicum of minority representation. This will be true in areas where the minority population is geographically dispersed. It also will be true where the minority population is not scattered but, for reasons unrelated to race — for example incumbency protection — the State would rather not create the majority-minority district in its most "obvious" location. When, as is the case here, the creation of a majority-minority district does not unfairly minimize the voting power of any other group, the Constitution does not justify, much less mandate, such obstruction. * * *

Although I disagree with the holding that appellants' claim is cognizable, the Court's discussion of the level of scrutiny it requires warrants a few comments. I have no doubt that a State's compliance with the Voting Rights Act clearly constitutes a compelling interest. Here, the Attorney General objected to the State's plan on the ground that it failed to draw a second majority-minority district for what appeared to be pretextual reasons. Rather than challenge this conclusion, North Carolina chose to draw the second district. As *UJO* held, a State is entitled to take such action.

The Court, while seemingly agreeing with this position, warns that the State's redistricting effort must be "narrowly tailored" to further its interest in complying with the law. It is evident to me, however, that what North Carolina did was precisely tailored to meet the objection of the Attorney General to its prior plan. Hence, I see no need for a remand at all, even accepting the majority's basic approach to this case.

Furthermore, how it intends to manage this standard, I do not know. Is it more "narrowly tailored" to create an irregular majority-minority district as opposed to one that is compact but harms other state interests such as incumbency protection or the representation of rural interests? Of the following two options — creation of two minority influence districts or of a single majority-minority district — is one "narrowly tailored" and the other not? Once the Attorney General has found that a proposed redistricting change violates § 5's nonretrogression principle in that it will abridge a racial minority's right to vote, does "narrow tailoring" mean that the most the State can do is preserve the status quo? Or can it maintain that change, while attempting to enhance minority voting power in some other manner? This small sample only begins to scratch the surface of the problems raised by the majority's test. But it suffices to illustrate the unworkability of a standard that is divorced from any measure of constitutional harm. In that, state efforts to remedy minority vote dilution are wholly unlike what typically has been labeled "affirmative action." To the extent that no other racial group is injured, remedying a Voting Rights Act violation does not involve preferential treatment. It involves, instead, an attempt to *equalize* treatment, and to provide minority voters with an effective voice in the political process. The Equal Protection Clause of the Constitution, surely, does not stand in the way. * * *

JUSTICE BLACKMUN, dissenting.

I join JUSTICE WHITE's dissenting opinion. * * * [T]he conscious use of race in redistricting does not violate the Equal Protection Clause unless the effect of the redistricting plan is to deny a particular group equal access to the political process or to minimize its voting strength unduly. It is particularly ironic that the case in which today's majority chooses to abandon settled law and to recognize for the first time this "analytically distinct" constitutional claim is a challenge by white voters to the plan under which North Carolina has sent black representatives to Congress for the first time since Reconstruction. I dissent.

JUSTICE STEVENS, dissenting.

For the reasons stated by JUSTICE WHITE, the decision of the District Court should be affirmed. I add these comments to emphasize that the two critical facts in this case are undisputed: First, the shape of District 12 is so bizarre that it must have been drawn for the purpose of either advantaging or disadvantaging a cognizable group of voters; and, second, regardless of that shape, it *was* drawn for the purpose of facilitating the election of a second black representative from North Carolina.

These unarguable facts, which the Court devotes most of its opinion to proving, give rise to three constitutional questions: Does the Constitution impose a requirement of contiguity or compactness on how the States may draw their electoral districts? Does the Equal Protection Clause prevent a State from drawing district boundaries for the purpose of facilitating the election of a member of an identifiable group of voters? And, finally, if the answer to the second question is generally "No," should it be different when the favored group is defined by race? * * *

The first question is easy. There is no independent constitutional requirement of compactness or contiguity, and the Court's opinion (despite its many references to the shape of District 12) does not suggest otherwise. The existence of bizarre and uncouth district boundaries is powerful evidence of an ulterior purpose behind the shaping of those boundaries — usually a purpose to advantage the political party in control of the districting process. Such evidence will always be useful in cases that lack other evidence of invidious intent. In this case, however, we know what the legislators' purpose was: The North Carolina Legislature drew District 12 to include a majority of African-American voters. Evidence of the district's shape is therefore convincing, but it is also cumulative, and, for our purposes, irrelevant.

As for the second question, I believe that the Equal Protection Clause is violated * * * when a group with power over the electoral process defines electoral boundaries solely to enhance its own political strength at the expense of any weaker group. That duty, however, is not violated when the majority acts to facilitate the election of a member of a group that lacks such power because it remains under-represented in the state legislature — whether that group is defined by political affiliation, by common economic interests, or by religious, ethnic, or racial characteristics. The difference between constitutional and unconstitutional gerry-manders has nothing to do with whether they are based on assumptions about the groups they affect, but whether their purpose is to enhance the power of the group in control of the districting process at the expense of any minority group, and thereby to strengthen the unequal distribution of electoral power. When an assumption that people in a particular minority group (whether they are defined by the political party, religion, ethnic group, or race to which they belong) will vote in a particular way is used to *benefit* that group, no constitutional violation occurs. Politicians have always relied on assumptions that people in particular groups are likely to vote in a particular way when they draw new district lines, and I cannot believe that anything in today's opinion will stop them from doing so in the future.[3]

Finally, we must ask whether otherwise permissible redistricting to benefit an underrepresented minority group becomes impermissible when the minority group is defined by its race. The Court today answers this question in the affirmative, and its answer is wrong. If it is permissible to draw boundaries to provide adequate representation for rural voters, for union members, for Hasidic Jews, for Polish Americans, or for Republicans, it necessarily follows that it is permissible to do the same thing for members of the very minority group whose history in the United States gave birth to the Equal Protection Clause. A contrary conclusion could only be described as perverse.

Accordingly, I respectfully dissent.

---

[3] The majority does not acknowledge that we *require* such a showing from plaintiffs who bring a vote dilution claim under § 2 of the Voting Rights Act. Under the three-part test established by *Thornburg* v. *Gingles*, a minority group must show that it could constitute the majority in a single-member district, "that it is politically cohesive," and "that the white majority votes sufficiently as a bloc to enable it . . . usually to defeat the minority's preferred candidate." At least the latter two of these three conditions depend on proving that what the Court today brands as "impermissible racial stereotypes" are true. * * *

JUSTICE SOUTER, dissenting. * * *

* * * Unlike other contexts in which we have addressed the State's conscious use of race, see, *e.g.*, *Richmond* v. *J.A. Croson Co.*, 488 U.S. 469 (1989) (city contracting); *Wygant* v. *Jackson Bd. of Ed.*, 476 U.S. 267 (1986) (teacher layoffs), electoral districting calls for decisions that nearly always require some consideration of race for legitimate reasons where there is a racially mixed population. As long as members of racial groups have the commonality of interest implicit in our ability to talk about concepts like "minority voting strength," and "dilution of minority votes," cf. *Thornburg* v. *Gingles*, and as long as racial bloc voting takes place, legislators will have to take race into account in order to avoid dilution of minority voting strength in the districting plans they adopt. One need look no further than the Voting Rights Act to understand that this may be required, and we have held that race may constitutionally be taken into account in order to comply with that Act. [*UJO*], 430 U.S., [at] 161–162 (plurality opinion of WHITE, J., joined by Brennan, BLACKMUN, and STEVENS, JJ.); *id.*, at 180 and n. (Stewart, J., joined by Powell, J., concurring in judgment).

A second distinction between districting and most other governmental decisions in which race has figured is that those other decisions using racial criteria characteristically occur in circumstances in which the use of race to the advantage of one person is necessarily at the obvious expense of a member of a different race. * * *

In districting, by contrast, the mere placement of an individual in one district instead of another denies no one a right or benefit provided to others. All citizens may register, vote, and be represented. * * * It is true, of course, that one's vote may be more or less effective depending on the interests of the other individuals who are in one's district, and our cases recognize the reality that members of the same race often have shared interests. "Dilution" thus refers to the effects of districting decisions not on an individual's political power viewed in isolation, but on the political power of a group. This is the reason that the placement of given voters in a given district, even on the basis of race, does not, without more, diminish the effectiveness of the individual as a voter.

* * * Presumably because the legitimate consideration of race in a districting decision is usually inevitable under the Voting Rights Act when communities are racially mixed * * * and because, without more, it does not result in diminished political effectiveness for anyone, we have not taken the approach of applying the usual standard of such heightened "scrutiny" to race-based districting decisions. * * *

* * * If a cognizable harm like dilution or the abridgment of the right to participate in the electoral process is shown, the districting plan violates the Fourteenth Amendment. If not, it does not. Under this approach, in the absence of an allegation of such cognizable harm, there is no need for further scrutiny because a gerrymandering claim cannot be proven without the element of harm. Nor if dilution is proven is there any need for further constitutional scrutiny; there has never been a suggestion that such use of race could be justified under any type of scrutiny, since the dilution of the right to vote can not be said to serve any legitimate governmental purpose.

There is thus no theoretical inconsistency in having two distinct approaches to equal protection analysis, one for cases of electoral districting and one for most other types of state governmental decisions. Nor, because of the distinctions between the two categories, is there any risk that Fourteenth Amendment districting law as such will be taken to imply anything for purposes of general Fourteenth Amendment scrutiny about "benign" racial discrimination, or about group entitlement as distinct from individual protection, or about the appropriateness of strict or other heightened scrutiny. * * *

* * * I would not respond to the seeming egregiousness of the redistricting now before us by untethering the concept of racial gerrymander in such a case from the concept of harm exemplified by dilution. In the absence of an allegation of such harm, I would affirm the judgment of the District Court. I respectfully dissent.

Notes and Questions

1.   What is the constitutional right that *Shaw* recognized? In other words, how would you complete this sentence: "*Shaw* held that voters' constitutional rights are violated when . . ."? Now the hard part: *Why* is such a harm a constitutional violation?

2.   Note that the Court did not declare that the use of race *per se* was unconstitutional. Rather, the Court focused on the question whether the *appearance* of a district was such that the districting plan could not "be understood as anything other than an effort to separate voters into different districts on the basis of race."

Should appearances matter? That is, is there a constitutional distinction between a districting plan that takes race into account and produces compact, pleasantly shaped districts, and a plan that takes race into account and produces sprawling districts such as North Carolina's District 12? If there is such a difference, what does it say about the character of the right that *Shaw* recognized?

3.   Related to the meaning of the right established in *Shaw* is the question of standing: *Who* is permitted to sue to vindicate the right? In *United States v. Hays*, 515 U.S. 737 (1995), the Court held that only residents of gerrymandered districts — not neighboring districts or others in the state — have endured the particularized injury that permits them standing to sue. Here is the Court's explanation:

> We noted [in *Shaw*] that, in general, "[racial classifications] threaten to stigmatize individuals by reason of their membership in a racial group and to incite racial hostility." 509 U.S., at 643. We also noted "representational harms" the particular type of racial classification at issue in *Shaw* may cause: "When a district obviously is created solely to effectuate the perceived common interests of one racial group, elected officials are more likely to believe that their primary obligation is to represent only the members of that group, rather than their constituency as a whole." *Id.*, at 648. Accordingly, we held that "redistricting legislation that is so bizarre on its face that it is 'unexplainable on grounds other than race' demands the same close scrutiny that we give other state laws that classify citizens by race." *Id.*, at 644. Any citizen able to demonstrate that he or she, personally,

has been injured by that kind of racial classification has standing to challenge the classification in federal court.

Demonstrating the individualized harm our standing doctrine requires may not be easy in the racial gerrymandering context, as it will frequently be difficult to discern why a particular citizen was put in one district or another. Where a plaintiff resides in a racially gerrymandered district, however, the plaintiff has been denied equal treatment because of the legislature's reliance on racial criteria, and therefore has standing to challenge the legislature's action. Voters in such districts may suffer the special representational harms racial classifications can cause in the voting context. On the other hand, where a plaintiff does not live in such a district, he or she does not suffer those special harms, and any inference that the plaintiff has personally been subjected to a racial classification would not be justified absent specific evidence tending to support that inference. Unless such evidence is present, that plaintiff would be asserting only a generalized grievance against governmental conduct of which he or she does not approve. * * *

Appellees insist that they challenged Act 1 [Louisiana's congressional redistricting plan] in its entirety, not District 4 in isolation. That is true. It is also irrelevant. The fact that Act 1 *affects* all Louisiana voters by classifying each of them as a member of a particular congressional district does not mean — even if Act 1 inflicts race-based injury on *some* Louisiana voters — that *every* Louisiana voter has standing to challenge Act 1 as a racial classification. Only those citizens able to allege injury "as a direct result of having *personally* been denied equal treatment" may bring such a challenge, and citizens who do so carry the burden of proving their standing, as well as their case on the merits.

515 U.S. at 744–46. *See also Sinkfield v. Kelley*, 531 U.S. 28 (2000) (*per curiam*). Are you convinced that the "representational harm[s]" of race-conscious districting "personally" affect those within the gerrymandered district, and that they do not "personally" affect those outside the district? Does it make sense to speak of "the" gerrymandered district, given that changes in district lines inevitably affect surrounding districts? For further discussion of the standing issue, see John Hart Ely, *Standing to Challenge Pro-Minority Gerrymanders*, 111 HARV. L. REV. 576 (1997); Samuel Issacharoff & Pamela S. Karlan, *Standing and Misunderstanding in Voting Rights Law*, 111 HARV. L. REV. 2276 (1998).

4.   As shown in the previous Note, standing turns on whether the plaintiff resides in the gerrymandered district. The plaintiff's race is not relevant to the question of standing. Should this be the law? Imagine four residents — one white and one black in each of two neighboring districts, one of which is majority-minority. Is the black person in the majority-minority district subject to any "representational harms"? Is the black person in the other district injured by the districting scheme? In what ways are the injuries of the white voters different depending on whether they reside in the challenged district?

5.   As *Hays* implied, racial-gerrymandering claims under *Shaw* focus on particular districts; it is not sufficient to claim that a state's redistricting plan *as a*

whole was infected with racial considerations. *Alabama Legislative Black Caucus v. Alabama*, 135 S. Ct. 1257, 1265 (2015).

6. The Court typically justifies its districting decisions — including its one-person, one-vote decisions as well as the racial-districting ones — as protecting the rights of individual voters. But, as voices on and off the Court have pointed out, individual voters do not elect candidates. Thus, constitutional and statutory protections of voters' ability to elect candidates are difficult to conceive of as part of an individual-rights regime.

Rather, it may be more appropriate to imagine rights such as those contained in § 2 of the Voting Rights Act and in *Shaw* as group rights. Section 2, in other words, may be thought of as protecting a minority *group's* ability to elect its candidates of choice, rather than the negligible ability of any particular minority voter to elect his or her preferred candidate. Likewise, *Shaw* does not provide much protection against an individual voter's being placed in a district because of race, but provides some protection against the excessive consideration of race in drawing district lines.

But if the right belongs to the group rather than an individual, the injury to the group is an inability to elect enough of its chosen representatives. The group right has nothing to do with the "representational harms" cited by the *Shaw* and *Hays* Courts. Accordingly, the injury is felt equally by all members of that group throughout the jurisdiction, and one's residence in a gerrymandered district should have no effect on one's standing.

Do you think potential plaintiffs challenging districting decisions are more likely to be upset by "representational harms" or by the overall distribution of legislative seats that results from the districting plan?

7. Do you view the use of race by the North Carolina legislature as "political apartheid"? Or is the use of race to create a district of diverse races laudable? Do you view North Carolina's adoption of majority-minority districts as segregating voters by race, or as its opposite — achieving diversity?

8. In this vein, *Shaw* should be considered with the Court's evolving attitude toward race-conscious measures to promote racial integration. In *Swann v. Charlotte-Meckenburg Board of Education*, 402 U.S. 1 (1971), the Court unanimously approved a busing plan ordered by a district court to remedy the effects of state-imposed school segregation. *Swann* was limited by *Milliken v. Bradley*, 418 U.S. 717 (1974), however, which held that district courts could not order busing across school-district lines to remedy segregation by only one of the districts. In subsequent decades, as the effects of *de jure* segregation have waned, courts have withdrawn their control over schools' decisions. *See Freeman v. Pitts*, 503 U.S. 467 (1992).

States' *voluntary* decisions to pursue racial integration by race-conscious means have produced hard-to-reconcile constitutional rulings. The Court has invalidated set-asides for minority workers and students, *Adarand Constructors, Inc. v. Peña*, 515 U.S. 200 (1995); *City of Richmond v. J.A. Croson Co.*, 488 U.S. 469 (1989); *Regents of the University of California v. Bakke*, 438 U.S. 265 (1978), as well as policies that give a quantifiable benefit to minorities, *Gratz v. Bollinger*, 539 U.S. 244 (2003); *Wygant v. Jackson Board of Education*, 476 U.S. 267 (1986). On the other hand, the Court held in *Grutter v. Bollinger*, 539 U.S. 306 (2003), that a state law school could adopt racial preferences for students, provided that the preferences were simply one part of an assessment of how the students would improve the diversity and educational environment of the school.

Most recently, in *Parents Involved in Community Schools v. Seattle School District No. 1*, 551 U.S. 701 (2007), the Court held unconstitutional two school districts' attempts to take race into account in assigning students to schools so as to achieve a more equal racial distribution. The controlling opinion of Justice Kennedy held that the particular methods employed in the assignment system did not adequately serve the interests in educational diversity accepted in *Grutter*. The other four Justices in the majority — Chief Justice Roberts, and Justices Scalia, Thomas, and Alito — expressed greater skepticism concerning the use of race in school assignments, suggesting that "[t]he way to stop discrimination on the basis of race is to stop discriminating on the basis of race." *Id.* at 748 (plurality opinion).

9.   Should *UJO* have controlled the outcome of this case? How does the Court distinguish *UJO*?

10.   Should legislators be less free to consider race in drawing district lines than they are to consider other types of group membership? Should consideration of race be any less "legitimate" than consideration of districts' compactness?

MILLER v. JOHNSON
Supreme Court of the United States
515 U.S. 900, 115 S. Ct. 2475, 132 L. Ed. 2d 762 (1995)

JUSTICE KENNEDY delivered the opinion of the Court [in which CHIEF JUSTICE REHNQUIST, JUSTICE O'CONNOR, JUSTICE SCALIA, and JUSTICE THOMAS join]. * * *

Between 1980 and 1990, one of Georgia's 10 congressional districts was a majority-black district, that is, a majority of the district's voters were black. The 1990 Decennial Census indicated that Georgia's population of 6,478,216 persons, 27% of whom are black, entitled it to an additional eleventh congressional seat, prompting Georgia's General Assembly to redraw the State's congressional districts. Both the House and the Senate adopted redistricting guidelines which, among other things, required single-member districts of equal population, contiguous geography, nondilution of minority voting strength, fidelity to precinct lines where possible, and compliance with §§ 2 and 5 of the [Voting Rights] Act. Only after these requirements were met did the guidelines permit drafters to consider other ends, such as maintaining the integrity of political subdivisions, preserving the core of existing districts, and avoiding contests between incumbents.

[T]he General Assembly submitted a congressional redistricting plan to the Attorney General for preclearance on October 1, 1991. The legislature's plan contained two majority-minority districts, the Fifth and Eleventh, and an additional district, the Second, in which blacks comprised just over 35% of the voting age population. Despite the plan's increase in the number of majority-black districts from one to two and the absence of any evidence of an intent to discriminate against minority voters, the Department of Justice refused preclearance on January 21, 1992. The Department's objection letter noted a concern that Georgia had created only two majority-minority districts, and that the proposed plan did not "recognize" certain minority populations by placing them in a majority-black district.

The General Assembly returned to the drawing board. A new plan was enacted and submitted for preclearance. This second attempt assigned the black population in Central Georgia's Baldwin County to the Eleventh District and increased the black populations in the Eleventh, Fifth, and Second Districts. The Justice Department refused preclearance again, relying on alternative plans proposing three majority-minority districts. * * * The State did not seek a declaratory judgment from the District Court for the District of Columbia.

Twice spurned, the General Assembly set out to create three majority-minority districts to gain preclearance. [T]he General Assembly enacted a plan that "bore all the signs of [the Justice Department's] involvement * * * split[ting] 26 counties, 23 more than the existing congressional districts." * * * The Eleventh District lost the black population of Macon, but picked up Savannah, thereby connecting the black neighborhoods of metropolitan Atlanta and the poor black populace of coastal Chatham County, though 260 miles apart in distance and worlds apart in culture. In short, the social, political and economic makeup of the Eleventh District tells a tale of disparity, not community. * * *

Elections were held under the new congressional redistricting plan on November 4, 1992, and black candidates were elected to Congress from all three majority-black districts. On January 13, 1994, appellees, five white voters from the Eleventh District, filed this action * * * alleg[ing] that Georgia's Eleventh District was a racial gerrymander and so a violation of the Equal Protection Clause as interpreted in *Shaw* v. *Reno* [509 U.S. 630 (1993)] [p. 354]. * * *

A majority of the [three-judge] District Court panel agreed that the Eleventh District was invalid under *Shaw*, with one judge dissenting. * * *

Finding that the "evidence of the General Assembly's intent to racially gerrymander the Eleventh District is overwhelming, and practically stipulated by the parties involved," the District Court held that race was the predominant, overriding factor in drawing the Eleventh District. Appellants do not take issue with the court's factual finding of this racial motivation. Rather, they contend that evidence of a legislature's deliberate classification of voters on the basis of race cannot alone suffice to state a claim under *Shaw*. They argue that, regardless of the legislature's purposes, a plaintiff must demonstrate that a district's shape is so bizarre that it is unexplainable other than on the basis of race, and that appellees failed to make that showing here. Appellants' conception of the constitutional violation misapprehends our holding in *Shaw* and the Equal Protection precedent upon which *Shaw* relied.

Shaw recognized a claim "analytically distinct" from a vote dilution claim. 509 U.S., at 652; see *id.*, at 649–650. Whereas a vote dilution claim alleges that the State has enacted a particular voting scheme as a purposeful device "to minimize or cancel out the voting potential of racial or ethnic minorities," *Mobile* v. *Bolden*, 446 U.S. 55, 66 (1980) [p. 288], an action disadvantaging voters of a particular race, the essence of the equal protection claim recognized in *Shaw* is that the State has used race as a basis for separating voters into districts. Just as the State may not, absent extraordinary justification, segregate citizens on the basis of race in its public parks, buses, golf courses, beaches, and schools, so did we recognize in *Shaw* that it may not separate its citizens into different voting districts on the basis of race. The idea is a simple one: "At the heart of the Constitution's guarantee of equal protection lies the simple command that the Government must treat citizens 'as individuals, not "as simply components of a racial, religious, sexual or national class.' " "" When the State assigns voters on the basis of race, it engages in the offensive and demeaning assumption that voters of a particular race, because of their race, "think alike, share the same political interests, and will prefer the same candidates at the polls." *Shaw*, *supra*, at 647. Race-based assignments "embody stereotypes that treat individuals as the product of their race, evaluating their thoughts and efforts — their very worth as citizens — according to a criterion barred to the Government by history and the Constitution." They also cause society serious harm. As we concluded in *Shaw*:

> "Racial classifications with respect to voting carry particular dangers. Racial gerrymandering, even for remedial purposes, may balkanize us into competing racial factions; it threatens to carry us further from the goal of a political system in which race no longer matters — a goal that the Fourteenth and Fifteenth Amendments embody, and to which the Nation continues to aspire. It is for these reasons that race-based districting by our state legislatures demands close judicial scrutiny." *Shaw*, *supra*, at 657.

Our observation in *Shaw* of the consequences of racial stereotyping was not meant to suggest that a district must be bizarre on its face before there is a constitutional violation. Nor was our conclusion in *Shaw* that in certain instances a district's appearance (or, to be more precise, its appearance in combination with certain demographic evidence) can give rise to an equal protection claim a holding that bizarreness was a threshold showing, as appellants believe it to be. Our circumspect approach and narrow holding in *Shaw* did not erect an artificial rule barring accepted equal protection analysis in other redistricting cases. Shape is relevant not because bizarreness is a necessary element of the constitutional wrong or a threshold requirement of proof, but because it may be persuasive circumstantial evidence that race for its own sake, and not other districting principles, was the legislature's dominant and controlling rationale in drawing its district lines. The logical implication * * * is that parties may rely on evidence other than bizarreness to establish race-based districting. * * *

Appellants and some of their *amici* argue that the Equal Protection Clause's general proscription on race-based decisionmaking does not obtain in the districting context because redistricting by definition involves racial considerations. Underlying their argument are the very stereotypical assumptions the Equal Protection Clause forbids. It is true that redistricting in most cases will implicate a political calculus in which various interests compete for recognition, but it does not follow from this that individuals of the same race share a single political interest. The view that they do is "based on the demeaning notion that members of the defined racial groups ascribe to certain 'minority views' that must be different from those of other citizens," the precise use of race as a proxy the Constitution prohibits. Nor can the argument that districting cases are excepted from standard equal protection precepts be resuscitated by *United Jewish Organizations of Williamsburgh, Inc.* v. *Carey*, 430 U.S. 144 (1977) [p. 277], where the Court addressed a claim that New

York violated the Constitution by splitting a Hasidic Jewish community in order to include additional majority-minority districts. As we explained in *Shaw*, a majority of the Justices in *UJO* construed the complaint as stating a vote dilution claim, so their analysis does not apply to a claim that the State has separated voters on the basis of race. 509 U.S., at 652. To the extent any of the opinions in that "highly fractured decision," can be interpreted as suggesting that a State's assignment of voters on the basis of race would be subject to anything but our strictest scrutiny, those views ought not be deemed controlling.

In sum, we make clear that parties alleging that a State has assigned voters on the basis of race are neither confined in their proof to evidence regarding the district's geometry and makeup nor required to make a threshold showing of bizarreness. Today's case requires us further to consider the requirements of the proof necessary to sustain this equal protection challenge.

* * * Although race-based decisionmaking is inherently suspect, until a claimant makes a showing sufficient to support that allegation the good faith of a state legislature must be presumed. The courts, in assessing the sufficiency of a challenge to a districting plan, must be sensitive to the complex interplay of forces that enter a legislature's redistricting calculus. Redistricting legislatures will, for example, almost always be aware of racial demographics; but it does not follow that race predominates in the redistricting process. *Shaw, supra*, at 646. The distinction between being aware of racial considerations and being motivated by them may be difficult to make. This evidentiary difficulty, together with the sensitive nature of redistricting and the presumption of good faith that must be accorded legislative enactments, requires courts to exercise extraordinary caution in adjudicating claims that a state has drawn district lines on the basis of race. The plaintiff's burden is to show, either through circumstantial evidence of a district's shape and demographics or more direct evidence going to legislative purpose, that race was the predominant factor motivating the legislature's decision to place a significant number of voters within or without a particular district. To make this showing, a plaintiff must prove that the legislature subordinated traditional race-neutral districting principles, including but not limited to compactness, contiguity, and respect for political subdivisions or communities defined by actual shared interests, to racial considerations. Where these or other race-neutral considerations are the basis for redistricting legislation, and are not subordinated to race, a State can "defeat a claim that a district has been gerrymandered on racial lines." *Shaw, supra*, at 647. * * *

In our view, the District Court applied the correct analysis, and its finding that race was the predominant factor motivating the drawing of the Eleventh District was not clearly erroneous. The court found it was "exceedingly obvious" from the shape of the Eleventh District, together with the relevant racial demographics, that the drawing of narrow land bridges to incorporate within the District outlying appendages containing nearly 80% of the district's total black population was a deliberate attempt to bring black populations into the district. * * * Although this evidence is quite compelling, we need not determine whether it was, standing alone, sufficient to establish a *Shaw* claim that the Eleventh District is unexplainable other than by race. The District Court had before it considerable additional evidence showing that the General Assembly was motivated by a predominant, overriding desire to assign black populations to the Eleventh District and thereby permit the creation of a third majority-black district in the Second.

The court found that "it became obvious," both from the Justice Department's objection letters and the three preclearance rounds in general, "that [the Justice Department] would accept nothing less than abject surrender to its maximization agenda." It further found that the General Assembly acquiesced and as a consequence was driven by its overriding desire to comply with the Department's maximization demands. * * * On this record, we fail to see how the District Court could have reached any conclusion other than that race was the predominant factor in drawing Georgia's Eleventh District; and in any event we conclude the court's finding is not clearly erroneous. * * *

* * * The evidence was compelling "that there are no tangible 'communities of interest' spanning the hundreds of miles of the Eleventh District." * * * It is apparent that it was not alleged shared interests but rather the object of maximizing the District's black population and obtaining Justice Department approval that in fact explained the General Assembly's actions. A State is free to recognize communities that have a particular racial makeup, provided its action is directed toward some common thread of relevant interests. "[W]hen members of a racial group live together in one community, a reapportionment plan that concentrates members of the group in one district and excludes them from others may reflect wholly legitimate purposes." *Shaw,* 509 U.S., at 646. But where the State assumes from a group of voters' race that they "think alike, share the same political interests, and will prefer the same candidates at the polls," it engages in racial stereotyping at odds with equal protection mandates. *Id.,* at 647.

Race was, as the District Court found, the predominant, overriding factor explaining the General Assembly's decision to attach to the Eleventh District various appendages containing dense majority-black populations. As a result, Georgia's congressional redistricting plan cannot be upheld unless it satisfies strict scrutiny, our most rigorous and exacting standard of constitutional review.

To satisfy strict scrutiny, the State must demonstrate that its districting legislation is narrowly tailored to achieve a compelling interest. There is a "significant state interest in eradicating the effects of past racial discrimination." *Shaw, supra,* at 656. The State does not argue, however, that it created the Eleventh District to remedy past discrimination, and with good reason: There is little doubt that the State's true interest in designing the Eleventh District was creating a third majority-black district to satisfy the Justice Department's preclearance demands. Whether or not in some cases compliance with the Voting Rights Act, standing alone, can provide a compelling interest independent of any interest in remedying past discrimination, it cannot do so here. As we suggested in *Shaw,* compliance with federal antidiscrimination laws cannot justify race-based districting where the challenged district was not reasonably necessary under a constitutional reading and application of those laws. See 509 U.S., at 653–655. * * *

Georgia's drawing of the Eleventh District was not required under the Act because there was no reasonable basis to believe that Georgia's earlier enacted plans violated § 5. Wherever a plan is "ameliorative," a term we have used to describe plans increasing the number of majority-minority districts, it "cannot violate § 5 unless the new apportionment itself so discriminates on the basis of race or color as to violate the Constitution." *Beer*, 425 U.S., at 141. Georgia's first and second proposed plans increased the number of majority-black districts from 1 out of 10 (10%) to 2 out of 11 (18.18%). These plans were "ameliorative" and could not have violated § 5's non-retrogression principle. * * *

The Voting Rights Act, and its grant of authority to the federal courts to uncover official efforts to abridge minorities' right to vote, has been of vital importance in eradicating invidious discrimination from the electoral process and enhancing the legitimacy of our political institutions. * * * Th[is] end is neither assured nor well served, however, by carving electorates into racial blocs. * * * It takes a shortsighted and unauthorized view of the Voting Rights Act to invoke that statute, which has played a decisive role in redressing some of our worst forms of discrimination, to demand the very racial stereotyping the Fourteenth Amendment forbids.

The judgment of the District Court is affirmed, and the cases are remanded for further proceedings consistent with this decision.

It is so ordered.

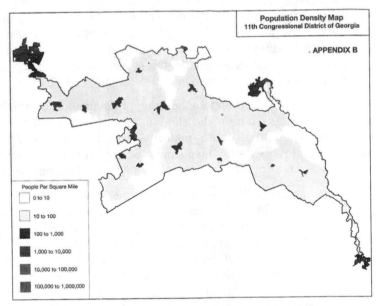

JUSTICE O'CONNOR, concurring.

I understand the threshold standard the Court adopts — "that the legislature subordinated traditional race-neutral districting principles . . . to racial considerations" — to be a demanding one. To invoke strict scrutiny, a plaintiff must show that the State has relied on race in substantial disregard of customary and traditional districting practices. Those practices provide a crucial frame of reference and therefore constitute a significant governing principle in cases of this kind.

The standard would be no different if a legislature had drawn the boundaries to favor some other ethnic group; certainly the standard does not treat efforts to create majority-minority districts *less* favorably than similar efforts on behalf of other groups. Indeed, the driving force behind the adoption of the Fourteenth Amendment was the desire to end legal discrimination against blacks.

Application of the Court's standard does not throw into doubt the vast majority of the Nation's 435 congressional districts, where presumably the States have drawn the boundaries in accordance with their customary districting principles. That is so even though race may well have been considered in the redistricting process. See *Shaw* v. *Reno*, 509 U.S., [at] 646. But application of the Court's standard helps achieve *Shaw*'s basic objective of making extreme instances of gerrymandering subject to meaningful judicial review. I therefore join the Court's opinion.

JUSTICE STEVENS, dissenting. * * *

Even assuming the validity of *Shaw*, I cannot see how respondents in these cases could [have standing to] assert the injury the Court attributes to them. Respondents, plaintiffs below, are white voters in Georgia's Eleventh Congressional District. The Court's conclusion that they have standing to maintain a *Shaw* claim appears to rest on a theory that their placement in the Eleventh District caused them "representational harms." The *Shaw* Court explained the concept of "representational harms" as follows: "When a district obviously is created solely to effectuate the perceived common interests of one racial group, elected officials are more likely to believe that their primary obligation is to represent only the members of that group, rather than their constituency as a whole." *Shaw*, 509 U.S., at 648. Although the *Shaw* Court attributed representational harms solely to a message sent by the legislature's action, those harms can only come about if the message is received — that is, first, if all or most black voters support the same candidate, and, second, if the successful candidate ignores the interests of her white constituents. Respondents' standing, in other words, ultimately depends on the very premise the Court purports to abhor: that voters of a particular race "think alike, share the same political interests, and will prefer the same candidates at the polls." This generalization, as the Court recognizes, is "offensive and demeaning."

* * * [A vote dilution] claim allows voters to allege that gerrymandered district lines have impaired their ability to elect a candidate of their own race. The Court emphasizes, however, that a so-called *Shaw* claim is " 'analytically distinct' from a vote dilution claim." [Nowhere] has the Court answered the question its analytic distinction raises: If the *Shaw* injury does not flow from an increased probability that white candidates will lose, then how can the increased probability that black candidates will win cause white voters, such as respondents, cognizable harm?

The Court attempts an explanation in these cases by equating the injury it imagines respondents have suffered with the injuries African Americans suffered under segregation. * * * This equation, however, fails to elucidate the elusive *Shaw* injury. Our desegregation cases redressed the *exclusion* of black citizens from public facilities reserved for whites. In this case, in contrast, any voter, black or white, may live in the Eleventh District. What respondents contest is the *inclusion* of too many black voters in the District as drawn. In my view, if respondents allege no vote dilution, that inclusion can cause them no conceivable injury. * * *

Equally distressing is the Court's equation of traditional gerrymanders, designed to maintain or enhance a dominant group's power, with a dominant group's decision to share its power with a previously underrepresented group. * * * I do not see how a districting plan that favors a politically weak group can violate equal protection. The Constitution does not mandate any form of proportional representation, but it certainly permits a State to adopt a policy that promotes fair representation of different groups. * * *

The Court's refusal to distinguish an enactment that helps a minority group from enactments that cause it harm is especially unfortunate at the intersection of race and voting, given that African Americans and other disadvantaged groups have struggled so long and so hard for inclusion in that most central exercise of our democracy. I have long believed that treating racial groups differently from other identifiable groups of voters, as the Court does today, is itself an invidious racial classification. Racial minorities should receive neither more nor less protection than other groups against gerrymanders. *A fortiori*, racial minorities should not be less eligible than other groups to benefit from districting plans the majority designs to aid them.

I respectfully dissent.

JUSTICE GINSBURG, with whom JUSTICE STEVENS and JUSTICE BREYER join, and with whom JUSTICE SOUTER joins except as to Part III-B, dissenting. * * *

In *Shaw*, the Court * * * wrote cautiously, emphasizing that judicial intervention is exceptional: "Strict [judicial] scrutiny" is in order, the Court declared, if a district is "so extremely irregular on its face that it rationally can be viewed only as an effort to segregate the races for purposes of voting." 509 U.S., at 642. * * * The problem in *Shaw* was not the plan architects' consideration of race as relevant in redistricting. Rather, in the Court's estimation, it was the virtual exclusion of other factors from the calculus. Traditional districting practices were cast aside, the Court concluded, with race alone steering placement of district lines.

The record before us does not show that race similarly overwhelmed traditional districting practices in Georgia. Although the Georgia General Assembly prominently considered race in shaping the Eleventh District, race did not crowd out all other factors, as the Court found it did in North Carolina's delineation of the *Shaw* district.

In contrast to the snake-like North Carolina district inspected in *Shaw*, Georgia's Eleventh District is hardly "bizarre," "extremely irregular," or "irrational on its face." Instead, the Eleventh District's design reflects significant consideration of "traditional districting factors (such as keeping political subdivisions intact) and the usual political process of compromise and trades for a variety of nonracial reasons." The District covers a core area in central and eastern Georgia, and its total land area of 6,780 square miles is about average for the State. The border of the Eleventh District runs 1,184 miles, in line with Georgia's Second District, which has a

1,243-mile border, and the State's Eighth District, with a border running 1,155 miles.

Nor does the Eleventh District disrespect the boundaries of political subdivisions. Of the 22 counties in the District, 14 are intact and 8 are divided. That puts the Eleventh District at about the state average in divided counties. * * * Seventy-one percent of the Eleventh District's boundaries track the borders of political subdivisions. Of the State's 11 districts, 5 score worse than the Eleventh District on this criterion, and 5 score better. Eighty-three percent of the Eleventh District's geographic area is composed of intact counties, above average for the State's congressional districts. And notably, the Eleventh District's boundaries largely follow precinct lines. * * * Georgia's Eleventh District, in sum, is not an outlier district shaped without reference to familiar districting techniques. * * *

The Court suggests that it was not Georgia's legislature, but the U.S. Department of Justice, that effectively drew the lines, and that Department officers did so with nothing but race in mind. Yet * * * Georgia could have demanded relief from the Department's objections by instituting a civil action in the United States District Court for the District of Columbia, with ultimate review in this Court. Instead of pursuing that avenue, the State chose to adopt the plan here in controversy   a plan the State forcefully defends before us. We should respect Georgia's choice by taking its position on brief as genuine.

Along with attention to size, shape, and political subdivisions, the Court recognizes as an appropriate districting principle, "respect for . . . communities defined by actual shared interests." The Court finds no community here, however, because a report in the record showed "fractured political, social, and economic interests within the Eleventh District's black population."

But ethnicity itself can tie people together, as volumes of social science literature have documented — even people with divergent economic interests. For this reason, ethnicity is a significant force in political life. * * * To accommodate the reality of ethnic bonds, legislatures have long drawn voting districts along ethnic lines. Our Nation's cities are full of districts identified by their ethnic character — Chinese, Irish, Italian, Jewish, Polish, Russian, for example. The creation of ethnic districts reflecting felt identity is not ordinarily viewed as offensive or demeaning to those included in the delineation.

III

To separate permissible and impermissible use of race in legislative apportionment, the Court orders strict scrutiny for districting plans "predominantly motivated" by race. No longer can a State avoid judicial oversight by giving — as in this case — genuine and measurable consideration to traditional districting practices. Instead, a federal case can be mounted whenever plaintiffs plausibly allege that other factors carried less weight than race. This invitation to litigate against the State seems to me neither necessary nor proper.

A

The Court derives its test from diverse opinions on the relevance of race in contexts distinctly unlike apportionment.[11] The controlling idea, the Court says, is "the simple command [at the heart of the Constitution's guarantee of equal protection] that the Government must treat citizens as individuals, not as simply components of a racial, religious, sexual or national class."

In adopting districting plans, however, States do not treat people as individuals. Apportionment schemes, by their very nature, assemble people in groups. States do not assign voters to districts based on merit or achievement, standards States might use in hiring employees or engaging contractors. Rather, legislators classify voters in groups — by economic, geographical, political, or social characteristics — and then "reconcile the competing claims of [these] groups."

That ethnicity defines some of these groups is a political reality. Until now, no constitutional infirmity has been seen in districting Irish or Italian voters together, for example, so long as the delineation does not abandon familiar apportionment practices. If Chinese-Americans and Russian-Americans may seek and secure group recognition in the delineation of voting districts, then African-Americans should not be dissimilarly treated. Otherwise, in the name of equal protection, we would shut out "the very minority group whose history in the United States gave birth to the Equal Protection Clause." See *Shaw*, 509 U.S., at 679 (STEVENS, J., dissenting).

B

Under the Court's approach, judicial review of the same intensity, *i.e.*, strict scrutiny, is in order once it is determined that an apportionment is predominantly motivated by race. It matters not at all, in this new regime, whether the apportionment dilutes or enhances minority voting strength. As very recently observed, however, "there is no moral or constitutional equivalence between a policy

---

[11] I would follow precedent directly on point. In [*UJO*], even though the State "deliberately used race in a purposeful manner" to create majority-minority districts, [430 U.S.], at 165 (opinion of White, J., joined by REHNQUIST and STEVENS, JJ.), seven of eight Justices participating voted to uphold the State's plan without subjecting it to strict scrutiny. Five Justices specifically agreed that the intentional creation of majority-minority districts does not give rise to an equal protection claim, absent proof that the districting diluted the majority's voting strength. See *ibid.* (opinion of White, J., joined by REHNQUIST and STEVENS, JJ.); *id.*, at 179–180 (Stewart, J., concurring in judgment, joined by Powell, J.).

Nor is *UJO* best understood as a vote dilution case. Petitioners' claim in *UJO* was that the State had "violated the Fourteenth and Fifteenth Amendments by *deliberately revising its reapportionment plan along racial lines.*" *Id.*, at 155 (opinion of White, J., joined by Brennan, Blackmun, and STEVENS, JJ.) (emphasis added). Petitioners themselves stated: "Our argument is . . . that the history of the area demonstrates that there could be — and in fact was — *no reason other than race* to divide the community at this time." *Id.*, at 154, n.14.

Though much like the claim in *Shaw*, the *UJO* claim failed because the *UJO* district adhered to traditional districting practices. See 430 U.S., at 168 (opinion of White, J., joined by REHNQUIST and STEVENS, JJ.) ("We think it . . . permissible for a State, *employing sound districting principles such as compactness and population equality*, . . . [to] create districts that will afford fair representation to the members of those racial groups who are sufficiently numerous *and whose residential patterns afford the opportunity of creating districts* in which they will be in the majority.") (emphasis added).

that is designed to perpetuate a caste system and one that seeks to eradicate racial subordination." *Adarand Constructors, Inc.* v. *Peña*, [515 U.S. 200], 243 [(1995)] (STEVENS, J., dissenting).

Special circumstances justify vigilant judicial inspection to protect minority voters — circumstances that do not apply to majority voters. A history of exclusion from state politics left racial minorities without clout to extract provisions for fair representation in the lawmaking forum. The equal protection rights of minority voters thus could have remained unrealized absent the Judiciary's close surveillance. The majority, by definition, encounters no such blockage. White voters in Georgia do not lack means to exert strong pressure on their state legislators. The force of their numbers is itself a powerful determiner of what the legislature will do that does not coincide with perceived majority interests. * * *

C

The Court's disposition renders redistricting perilous work for state legislatures. Statutory mandates and political realities may require States to consider race when drawing district lines. But today's decision is a counter force; it opens the way for federal litigation if "traditional . . . districting principles" arguably were accorded less weight than race. Genuine attention to traditional districting practices and avoidance of bizarre configurations seemed, under *Shaw*, to provide a safe harbor. See 509 U.S., at 647 ("Traditional districting principles such as compactness, contiguity, and respect for political subdivisions . . . are objective factors that may serve to defeat a claim that a district has been gerrymandered on racial lines."). In view of today's decision, that is no longer the case.

Only after litigation — under either the Voting Rights Act, the Court's new *Miller* standard, or both — will States now be assured that plans conscious of race are safe. Federal judges in large numbers may be drawn into the fray. This enlargement of the judicial role is unwarranted. The reapportionment plan that resulted from Georgia's political process merited this Court's approbation, not its condemnation. Accordingly, I dissent.

Notes and Questions

1.   The Court held in *Miller* that the shape of the district was *evidence* of an improper use of race, but that a district's irregular shape was not necessary to prove a constitutional violation. Rather, the trigger for strict scrutiny is the use of race as the "predominant factor" in drawing district lines. Is that consistent with *Shaw v. Reno*?

2.   Does the predominant-factor test make sense? Should the Constitution be interpreted to allow *some* consideration of race as long as other factors are more important? Or should the Court have to choose between forbidding all uses of race in redistricting and permitting states to consider race as they wish?

3.   Districting plans are facially race-neutral; they divide people not by race *per se*, but by geography. As the cases in this Chapter illustrate, however, those plans can have a racially disparate effect because of racially identifiable residency

patterns. Accordingly, one might think that the constitutionality of such districting plans would be evaluated according to the test established in *Washington v. Davis*, 426 U.S. 229 (1976), and *Village of Arlington Heights v. Metropolitan Housing Development Corp.*, 429 U.S. 252 (1977), under which strict scrutiny applies whenever race is "a motivating factor" in creating facially race-neutral laws. Consider the explanation provided in *Arlington Heights*:

> *Davis* does not require a plaintiff to prove that the challenged action rested solely on racially discriminatory purposes. Rarely can it be said that a legislature or administrative body operating under a broad mandate made a decision motivated solely by a single concern, or even that a particular purpose was the "dominant" or "primary" one. In fact, it is because legislators and administrators are properly concerned with balancing numerous competing considerations that courts refrain from reviewing the merits of their decisions, absent a showing of arbitrariness or irrationality. But racial discrimination is not just another competing consideration. When there is a proof that a discriminatory purpose has been a motivating factor in the decision, this judicial deference is no longer justified.

429 U.S. at 265–66 (footnote omitted). Why would *Davis* and *Arlington Heights* apply strict scrutiny whenever race is "a motivating factor" but *Miller v. Johnson* reserve strict scrutiny for instances where race "predominates" in the formation of a districting plan?

4. Under *Miller v. Johnson*, race cannot be the "predominant factor" in drawing district lines. But "predominant" relative to what other factors? Suppose that a state redraws its districts and considers race, but the one consideration that is given the most consideration is the need to place equal numbers of voters in the districts. In such a situation, would equality of population be the factor that "predominates"? No. The Court held in *Alabama Legislative Black Caucus v. Alabama*, 135 S. Ct. 1257, 1270 (2015), that "an equal population goal is not one factor among others to be weighed against the use of race to determine whether race 'predominates'" — even though, "in light of the Constitution's demands, th[e] role [of population equality] may often prove 'predominant' in the ordinary sense of that word." "Rather, it [population equality] is part of the redistricting background, taken as a given, when determining whether race, or other factors, predominate in a legislator's determination as to *how* equal population objectives will be met."

If population equality is not one of the considerations to be weighed against race to see which "predominated" in a legislature's redistricting decision, what considerations do qualify? *Alabama Legislative Black Caucus* listed several: "'compactness, contiguity, respect for political subdivisions or communities defined by actual shared interests,' incumbency protection, and political affiliation." *Id.* at 1270 (quoting *Miller v. Johnson*, 515 U.S. at 916 and citing *Bush v. Vera*, 517 U.S. 952, 964, 968 (principal opinion by O'Connor, J.)). The difference with equality of population, according to *Alabama Legislative Black Caucus*, is that the question under *Shaw* is which factor or factors predominate "in determining *which* persons were placed *in appropriately apportioned districts*." 135 S. Ct. at 1271 (quoting Brief of the United States as *amicus curiae* at 19) (some emphasis added by the Court).

5. After *Miller* established that strict scrutiny applied whenever race was the predominant factor in drawing district lines, two questions naturally presented themselves. First, how should a court determine when race predominates over politics in a legislature's districting decisions, especially when race correlates with political ideology? Second, what showing is necessary for a state to satisfy strict scrutiny? Both questions were at issue in *Bush v. Vera*, 517 U.S. 952 (1996).

As to the first issue, *Vera* held that the fact that a districting dispute involves concentrations of black voters

> would not, in and of itself, convert a political gerrymander into a racial gerrymander, no matter how conscious redistricters were of the correlation between race and party affiliation. If district lines merely correlate with race because they are drawn on the basis of political affiliation, which correlates with race, there is no racial classification to justify[.] * * *
>
> If the State's goal is otherwise constitutional political gerrymandering, it is free * * * to achieve that goal regardless of its awareness of its racial implications and regardless of the fact that it does so in the context of a majority-minority district. * * * But to the extent that race is used as a proxy for political characteristics, a racial stereotype requiring strict scrutiny is in operation.

Id. at 968 (plurality opinion). *See also id.* at 1001 (Thomas, J., concurring in the judgment) ("We have said that impermissible racial classifications do not follow inevitably from a legislature's mere awareness of racial demographics.").

Should strict scrutiny apply whenever a state consciously makes use of race for the purpose of creating a majority-minority district? This question divided the five Justices comprising the *Shaw* majority, with Justice O'Connor, Chief Justice Rehnquist, and Justice Kennedy concluding that strict scrutiny should not "apply to all cases of intentional creation of majority-minority districts." *Id.* at 958 (plurality opinion). Rather, a state can create a majority-minority district intentionally without triggering strict scrutiny, as long as other traditional districting criteria were not subordinated to the consideration of race.[d] Justices Thomas and Scalia, however, would have held that race necessarily predominates in a purposeful decision to create a majority-minority district. *See id.* at 1001 (Thomas, J., concurring in the judgment).

6. As to the second issue in *Vera* (the application of strict scrutiny), both the plurality and the Justices concurring in the judgment assumed that compliance with §§ 2 and 5 of the Voting Rights Act would qualify as a compelling governmental interest, but held that the districting scheme was not narrowly tailored to that interest. There was no need to comply with § 2 because the state could not create

---

[d] In *Shaw v. Hunt*, 517 U.S. 899 (1996) (*Shaw II*), the Court concluded that North Carolina did predominantly consider race, subordinating other concerns: "That the legislature addressed [nonracial] interests does not in any way refute the fact that race was the legislature's predominant consideration. Race was the criterion that, in the State's view, could not be compromised; respecting communities of interest and protecting Democratic incumbents came into play only after the race-based decision had been made." *Id.* at 907. Is this analysis consistent with the *Vera* plurality's view that race does not necessarily predominate in the intentional creation of majority-minority districts?

another *compact* majority-minority district, and § 2, as interpreted in *Gingles*, does not obligate states to create noncompact majority-minority districts. Accordingly, the state's creation of a noncompact majority-minority district was not necessary to remedy a § 2 violation. *See* 517 U.S. at 976–81 (plurality opinion); *id.* at 1003 (Thomas, J., concurring in the judgment). *See also Shaw v. Hunt*, 517 U.S. 899, 914–18 (1996) (*Shaw II*).

Nor did § 5 demand the drawing of the district lines at issue in *Vera*. The state contended that its decision to include more blacks in one district was necessary to satisfy § 5, but the new district did not simply maintain the minority voting strength in the district in question; rather, it augmented it. Accordingly, as in *Miller v. Johnson*, the use of race was not necessary to avoid § 5's prohibition on retrogression. *See id.* at 982–83 (plurality opinion). *See also Shaw II*, 517 U.S. at 911–13.

7. It follows from *Bush v. Vera* that a plaintiff may not prevail based simply on demonstrating the irregularity of district lines, coupled with information about the demographic characteristics of the districts. In *Hunt v. Cromartie*, 526 U.S. 541 (1999), the Court held that summary judgment was inappropriate in such a case, where the state claimed that its districts were drawn for predominantly political — not racial — reasons. Citing *Vera*, among other cases, the Court noted that "a jurisdiction may engage in constitutional political gerrymandering, even if it so happens that the most loyal Democrats happen to be black Democrats and even if the State were *conscious* of that fact." 526 U.S. at 551. Accordingly, "[e]vidence that blacks constitute even a supermajority in one congressional district while amounting to less than a plurality in a neighboring district will not, by itself, suffice to prove that a jurisdiction was motivated by race in drawing its district lines when the evidence also shows a high correlation between race and party preference." *Id.* at 551–52.

8. Does a district in which residents are connected only by a common ethnicity insult those residents by assuming that they "think alike, share the same political interests, and will prefer the same candidates at the polls," as the *Shaw* and *Miller* Courts alleged, or does such a district simply "accommodate the reality of ethnic bonds," as Justice Ginsburg argued? Is there a difference between the racial balancing underlying the intentional creation of majority-minority districts, and reliance on offensive stereotypes?

The television comedy *All in the Family* famously explored the role of race and ethnicity in American society, including in elections. In the following scene, the main character, Archie Bunker, tries to explain to his son-in-law, Michael "Meathead" Stivic, his view that a candidate's ethnicity should be an important consideration for voters. Are his opinions more offensive than the assumption that minority voters should be grouped together in districts because they have the same political preferences? Why?

Archie: I call this representative government. "Salvatore, Feldman, O'Reilly, Nelson." That's an Italian, a Jew, an Irishman, and a regular American there. What I call a "balanced ticket."

Michael: Why do you always have to label people by nationality?

Archie: 'Cause how else are you going to get the right man for the right job? Take Feldman, there. He's up for treasurer. Well, that's perfect. Them people know how to handle money. Know what I mean?

Michael: No, I don't.

Archie: Well, then you got Salvatore running for D.A. He can keep an eye on Feldman. You know, I want to tell you something about the Italians. When you do get an honest one, you really got something there.

Michael: Aw, come on, Arch.

Archie: Well, here you got O'Reilly, the Mick. He can see that the graft is equally spread around. You got Nelson, the American guy. He's good for TV appearances — make the rest of them look respectable.

All in the Family: The Election Story (CBS television broadcast, Oct. 30, 1971).

9.   Reconsider the justiciability questions discussed in Chapter 2. Are the standards for adjudicating racial-gerrymandering claims under *Miller* and *Shaw* any more judicially manageable than those for partisan-gerrymandering claims considered in *Vieth v. Jubelirer*, 541 U.S. 267 (2004) [p. 131], and *Davis v. Bandemer*, 478 U.S. 109 (1986)?

10.   In *Easley v. Cromartie*, 532 U.S. 234 (2001), the Court yet again confronted the constitutionality of North Carolina's District 12 — the same district at issue in *Shaw I* and *Shaw II*, as well as in *Hunt v. Cromartie*. The district court in *Easley* held that race predominated in the North Carolina Legislature's drawing of the district lines, but the Supreme Court reversed in an opinion authored by Justice Breyer and joined by the rest of the Justices (Stevens, Souter, and Ginsburg) who had consistently dissented in the *Shaw* cases, as well as by Justice O'Connor. The district court's finding was "clearly erroneous," in the Supreme Court's view, because the plaintiffs' evidence was insufficient to rebut the state's claim that it was motivated more by politics than by race.

The district court held that District 12 was drawn to include areas with high concentrations of blacks, passing over areas with higher concentrations of Democrats, even though the inclusion of the more highly Democratic precincts would have resulted in District 12 being far more compact. The district court reasoned that this evidence indicated that the state was attempting "to collect precincts with high racial identification rather than political identification." Nevertheless, the Supreme Court was not convinced:

> The problem with this evidence is that it focuses upon party registration, not upon voting behavior. [R]egistration figures do not accurately predict preference at the polls. In part this is because white voters registered as Democrats "cross-over" to vote for a Republican candidate more often than do African-Americans, who register and vote Democratic between 95% and 97% of the time. A legislature trying to secure a safe Democratic seat is interested in Democratic voting behavior. Hence, a legislature may, by placing reliable Democratic precincts within a district without regard to race, end up with a district containing more heavily African-American precincts, but the reasons would be political rather than racial.

Id. at 244–45. Is this rationale consistent with *Bush v. Vera* and *Hunt v. Cromartie*?

The district court in *Easley v. Cromartie* also had before it two pieces of direct evidence demonstrating the motives of some of the participants in the line-drawing. In the first, a state senator and "legislative redistricting leader" praised the districting plan as "provid[ing] for a fair, geographic, racial and partisan balance throughout the State of North Carolina." In the Supreme Court's view, the statement "shows that the legislature considered race, along with other partisan and geographic considerations; * * * it says little or nothing about whether race played a *predominant* role comparatively speaking." 532 U.S. at 253.

Similarly, the Court was not moved by an e-mail sent to two senators from a legislative staffer working on the redistricting. The e-mail stated that the staffer "moved Greensboro Black community into the 12th, and now need to take [about] 60,000 out of the 12th. I await your direction on this." The Court held that the e-mail was insufficient to support the district court's holding, in part because it did not explain "the point of the reference" to race — why the black voters were moved to the 12th District, or what would have been the "political consequences of failing to do so." *Id.* at 254.

Are you convinced that the North Carolina Legislature was predominantly motivated by politics? Was the district court's contrary finding "clearly erroneous"? Do you agree with the Court that a political motivation could cause the legislature to rely on race as the legislature did in drawing District 12? Justice Thomas, joined by Chief Justice Rehnquist and Justices Scalia and Kennedy, protested in dissent that the appropriate question in racial-gerrymandering cases is "*whether*, not *why*, race predominated. * * * It is not a defense that the legislature merely may have drawn the district based on the stereotype that blacks are reliable Democratic voters." *Id.* at 266–67 (Thomas, J., dissenting).

Note the conflict between the Court's approach in *Easley v. Cromartie* and the plurality's treatment of § 2 of the Voting Rights Act in *Thornburg v. Gingles*, 478 U.S. 30 (1986) [p. 301]. In *Easley v. Cromartie*, the Court found it crucial that politics, not race, was the most important factor in the drawing of district lines. In *Gingles*, however, the plurality disclaimed any interest in discerning whether race was the cause of polarized voting. Rather, the plurality focused on *whether*, not *why*, different races preferred different candidates. What explains the differing approaches?

11.   There has been a vigorous debate on whether majority-minority legislative districts, like those at issue in the *Shaw* litigation and its progeny, help or hurt the representation of African Americans and their interests, and whether they help or hurt the interests of the Republican or Democratic Parties. While these districts may increase the chance of electing black legislators, do they ultimately dilute the ability of black voters to influence non-African-American legislators? Do the districts lead to an increase in the number of conservative (often Republican) legislators in surrounding districts because majority-minority districts pull some reliable Democrats out of the neighboring districts and thereby limit their influence? As a matter of law or policy, is it, or should it be, possible to speak of one set of interests for all black (or other minority) voters that can be represented only

by a member of that minority?[e]

Likewise, there is ongoing discussion on the impact of the *Shaw* litigation itself. *See* ABIGAIL THERNSTROM, VOTING RIGHTS — AND WRONGS: THE ELUSIVE QUEST FOR RACIALLY FAIR ELECTIONS 155 (2009) (arguing that the *Shaw*-type litigation had little effect on the election of African-American representatives); Richard H. Pildes, *The Supreme Court, 2003 Term — Foreword: The Constitutionalization of Democratic Politics*, 118 HARV. L. REV. 28, 67–68 (2004) (noting that there has been relatively little litigation raising *Shaw*-type issues, and attributing this to the drawing of districts by state legislators who have "internalized the vague constraints of *Shaw* in ways that generated a stable equilibrium").

12.   For more information and background on the cases from *Shaw v. Reno* to *Easley v. Cromartie*, see TINSLEY E. YARBROUGH, RACE AND REDISTRICTING: THE *SHAW-CROMARTIE* CASES (2002); Melissa L. Saunders, *A Cautionary Tale:* Hunt v. Cromartie *and the Next Generation of* Shaw *Litigation*, 1 ELECTION L.J. 173 (2002).

F. RESOLVING THE *SHAW*/VRA CONFLICT

The Court's interpretation of the Equal Protection Clause in the racial-gerrymandering cases placed states in a difficult position. If they paid insufficient attention to race and failed to create enough districts in which minorities had the opportunity to elect their preferred representatives, they were vulnerable under § 2 or § 5 of the Voting Rights Act. If they took account of race, however, and drew district lines with the predominant purpose of conforming district lines to race, then they were vulnerable to a suit under the Constitution. The cases in this section try to draw a balance between those potentially (inevitably?) conflicting obligations.

LEAGUE OF UNITED LATIN AMERICAN CITIZENS v. PERRY

Supreme Court of the United States
548 U.S. 399, 126 S. Ct. 2594, 165 L. Ed. 2d 609 (2006)

JUSTICE KENNEDY announced the judgment of the Court and delivered the opinion of the Court with respect to Parts II-A and III [in which JUSTICE STEVENS, JUSTICE SOUTER, JUSTICE GINSBURG, and JUSTICE BREYER join], an opinion with respect to Parts I and IV, in which THE CHIEF JUSTICE [ROBERTS] and JUSTICE ALITO join, an opinion with respect to Parts II-B and II-C [in which no other Justice joins], and an

---

[e] For a sampling of the extensive scholarly literature offering differing perspectives on these questions, see Charles Cameron et al., *Do Majority-Minority Districts Maximize Substantive Black Representation in Congress?*, 90 AM. POL. SCI. REV. 794 (1996); Bernard Grofman et al., *Drawing Effective Minority Districts: A Conceptual Framework and Some Empirical Evidence*, 79 N.C. L. REV. 1383 (2001); David Lublin, *The Election of African Americans and Latinos to the U.S. House of Representatives, 1972–1994*, 25 AM. POL. Q. 269 (1997); Christine Leveaux Sharpe & James C. Garland, *Race, Roll Calls, and Redistricting: The Impact of Race-Based Redistricting on Congressional Roll-Call*, 54 POL. RES. Q. 31 (2001); Kenneth W. Shotts, *Does Racial Redistricting Cause Conservative Policy Outcomes? Policy Preferences and Southern Representatives in the 1980s and 1990s*, 65 J. POL. 216 (2003).

opinion with respect to Part II-D, in which JUSTICE SOUTER and JUSTICE GINSBURG join. * * *

Appellants contend [that Texas's 2003 congressional redistricting] plan is an unconstitutional partisan gerrymander and that the redistricting statewide violates § 2 of the Voting Rights Act of 1965, 42 U.S.C. § 1973 [now 52 U.S.C. § 10301 — Eds.]. Appellants also contend that the use of race and politics in drawing lines of specific districts violates the First Amendment and the Equal Protection Clause of the Fourteenth Amendment. * * *

I * * *

The 1990 census resulted in a 30-seat congressional delegation for Texas, an increase of 3 seats over the 27 representatives allotted to the State in the decade before. In 1991 the Texas Legislature drew new district lines. At the time, the Democratic Party controlled both houses in the state legislature, the governorship, and 19 of the State's 27 seats in Congress. Yet change appeared to be on the horizon. In the previous 30 years the Democratic Party's post-Reconstruction dominance over the Republican Party had eroded, and by 1990 the Republicans received 47% of the statewide vote, while the Democrats received 51%.

Faced with a Republican opposition that could be moving toward majority status, the state legislature drew a congressional redistricting plan designed to favor Democratic candidates. Using then-emerging computer technology to draw district lines with artful precision, the legislature enacted a plan later described as the "shrewdest gerrymander of the 1990s." * * *

Voters who considered this unfair and unlawful treatment sought to invalidate the 1991 plan as an unconstitutional partisan gerrymander, but to no avail. The 1991 plan realized the hopes of Democrats and the fears of Republicans with respect to the composition of the Texas congressional delegation. The 1990's were years of continued growth for the Texas Republican Party, and by the end of the decade it was sweeping elections for statewide office. Nevertheless, despite carrying 59% of the vote in statewide elections in 2000, the Republicans only won 13 congressional seats to the Democrats' 17.

These events likely were not forgotten by either party when it came time to draw congressional districts in conformance with the 2000 census and to incorporate two additional seats for the Texas delegation. The Republican Party controlled the governorship and the State Senate; it did not yet control the State House of Representatives, however. As so constituted, the legislature was unable to pass a redistricting scheme, resulting in litigation and the necessity of a court-ordered plan to comply with the Constitution's one-person, one-vote requirement. See *Balderas* v. *Texas*, [2001 U.S. Dist. LEXIS 25740] (E.D. Tex.) *(per curiam)*, summarily aff'd, 536 U.S. 919 (2002). The congressional districting map resulting from the *Balderas* litigation is known as Plan 1151C.

[T]wo members of the three-judge court that drew Plan 1151C later served on the three-judge court that issued the judgment now under review. Thus we have the benefit of their candid comments concerning the redistricting approach taken in the *Balderas* litigation. Conscious that the primary responsibility for drawing congressional districts is given to political branches of government, and hesitant to "und[o] the work of one political party for the benefit of another," the three-judge *Balderas* court sought to apply "only 'neutral' redistricting standards" when drawing Plan 1151C. Once the District Court applied these principles — such as placing the two new seats in high-growth areas, following county and voting precinct lines, and avoiding the pairing of incumbents — "the drawing ceased, leaving the map free of further change except to conform it to one-person, one-vote." Under Plan 1151C, the 2002 congressional elections resulted in a 17-to-15 Democratic majority in the Texas delegation, compared to a 59% to 40% Republican majority in votes for statewide office in 2000. * * *

The continuing influence of a court-drawn map that "perpetuated much of [the 1991] gerrymander" was not lost on Texas Republicans when, in 2003, they gained control of the State House of Representatives and, thus, both houses of the legislature. * * * After a protracted partisan struggle, during which Democratic legislators left the State for a time to frustrate quorum requirements, the legislature enacted a new congressional districting map in October 2003. It is called Plan 1374C. The 2004 congressional elections did not disappoint the plan's drafters. Republicans won 21 seats to the Democrats' 11, while also obtaining 58% of the vote in statewide races against the Democrats' 41%.

Soon after Texas enacted Plan 1374C, appellants challenged it in court, alleging a host of constitutional and statutory violations. [T]he District Court entered judgment against appellants on all their claims. * * *

II
A

Based on two similar theories that address the mid-decade character of the 2003 redistricting, appellants now argue that Plan 1374C should be invalidated as an unconstitutional partisan gerrymander. In *Davis* v. *Bandemer*, 478 U.S. 109 (1986), the Court held that an equal protection challenge to a political gerrymander presents a justiciable case or controversy, *id.*, at 118–127, but there was disagreement over what substantive standard to apply. That disagreement persists. A plurality of the Court in *Vieth* v. *Jubelirer* [541 U.S. 267 (2004)] [p. 131] would have held such challenges to be nonjusticiable political questions, but a majority declined to do so. We do not revisit the justiciability holding but do proceed to examine whether appellants' claims offer the Court a manageable, reliable measure of fairness for determining whether a partisan gerrymander violates the Constitution.

B

* * * Article I of the Constitution * * *, we have explained, "leaves with the States primary responsibility for apportionment of their federal congressional . . . districts." *Growe* v. *Emison*, 507 U.S. 25, 34 (1993). * * * That the federal courts sometimes are required to order legislative redistricting * * * does not shift the primary locus of responsibility.

"Legislative bodies should not leave their reapportionment tasks to the federal courts; but when those with legislative responsibilities do not respond, or the imminence of a state election makes it impractical for them to do so, it becomes the 'unwelcome obligation' of the federal court to devise and impose a reapportionment plan pending later legislative action." *Wise* v. *Lipscomb*, 437 U.S. 535, 540 (1978) (principal opinion)).

Quite apart from the risk of acting without a legislature's expertise, and quite apart from the difficulties a court faces in drawing a map that is fair and rational, the obligation placed upon the Federal Judiciary is unwelcome because drawing lines for congressional districts is one of the most significant acts a State can perform to ensure citizen participation in republican self-governance. That Congress is the federal body explicitly given constitutional power over elections is also a noteworthy statement of preference for the democratic process. As the Constitution vests redistricting responsibilities foremost in the legislatures of the States and in Congress, a lawful, legislatively enacted plan should be preferable to one drawn by the courts.

It should follow, too, that if a legislature acts to replace a court-drawn plan with one of its own design, no presumption of impropriety should attach to the legislative decision to act. * * * Judicial respect for legislative plans, however, cannot justify legislative reliance on improper criteria for districting determinations. With these considerations in mind, I now turn to consider appellants' challenges to the new redistricting plan.

C

Appellants claim that Plan 1374C, enacted by the Texas Legislature in 2003, is an unconstitutional political gerrymander. A decision, they claim, to effect mid-decennial redistricting, when solely motivated by partisan objectives, violates equal protection and the First Amendment because it serves no legitimate public purpose and burdens one group because of its political opinions and affiliation. The mid-decennial nature of the redistricting, appellants say, reveals the legislature's sole motivation. * * *

A rule, or perhaps a presumption, of invalidity when a mid-decade redistricting plan is adopted solely for partisan motivations is a salutary one, in appellants' view, for then courts need not inquire about, nor parties prove, the discriminatory effects of partisan gerrymandering — a matter that has proved elusive since *Bandemer*. Adding to the test's simplicity is that it does not quibble with the drawing of individual district lines but challenges the decision to redistrict at all.

For a number of reasons, appellants' case for adopting their test is not convincing. To begin with, the state appellees dispute the assertion that partisan gain was the "sole" motivation for the decision to replace Plan 1151C. There is some merit to that criticism, for the pejorative label overlooks indications that partisan motives did not dictate the plan in its entirety. The legislature does seem to have decided to redistrict with the sole purpose of achieving a Republican congressional majority, but partisan aims did not guide every line it drew. * * *

Evaluating the legality of acts arising out of mixed motives can be complex, and affixing a single label to those acts can be hazardous, even when the actor is an individual performing a discrete act. When the actor is a legislature and the act is a composite of manifold choices, the task can be even more daunting. Appellants' attempt to separate the legislature's sole motive for discarding Plan 1151C from the complex of choices it made while drawing the lines of Plan 1374C seeks to avoid that difficulty. We should be skeptical, however, of a claim that seeks to invalidate a statute based on a legislature's unlawful motive but does so without reference to the content of the legislation enacted.

Even setting this skepticism aside, a successful claim attempting to identify unconstitutional acts of partisan gerrymandering must do what appellants' sole-motivation theory explicitly disavows: show a burden, as measured by a reliable standard, on the complainants' representational rights. For this reason, a majority of the Court rejected a test proposed in *Vieth* that is markedly similar to the one appellants present today.

The sole-intent standard offered here is no more compelling when it is linked to the circumstance that Plan 1374C is mid-decennial legislation. The text and structure of the Constitution and our case law indicate there is nothing inherently suspect about a legislature's decision to replace mid-decade a court-ordered plan with one of its own. And even if there were, the fact of mid-decade redistricting alone is no sure indication of unlawful political gerrymanders. Under appellants' theory, a highly effective partisan gerrymander that coincided with decennial redistricting would receive less scrutiny than a bumbling, yet solely partisan, mid-decade redistricting. More concretely, the test would leave untouched the 1991 Texas redistricting, which entrenched a party on the verge of minority status, while striking down the 2003 redistricting plan, which resulted in the majority Republican Party capturing a larger share of the seats. A test that treats these two similarly effective power plays in such different ways does not have the reliability appellants ascribe to it. * * *

In the absence of any other workable test for judging partisan gerrymanders, one effect of appellants' focus on mid-decade redistricting could be to encourage partisan excess at the outset of the decade, when a legislature redistricts pursuant to its decennial constitutional duty and is then immune from the charge of sole motivation. If mid-decade redistricting were barred or at least subject to close judicial oversight, opposition legislators would also have every incentive to prevent passage of a legislative plan and try their luck with a court that might give them a better deal than negotiation with their political rivals.

D

Appellants' second political gerrymandering theory is that mid-decade redistricting for exclusively partisan purposes violates the one-person, one-vote requirement. * * * [A]ppellants contend that, because the population of Texas has shifted since the 2000 census, the 2003 redistricting, which relied on that census, created unlawful interdistrict population variances.

To distinguish the variances in Plan 1374C from those of ordinary, 3-year-old districting plans or belatedly drawn court-ordered plans, appellants again rely on the voluntary, mid-decade nature of the redistricting and its partisan motivation. Appellants * * * concede that States operate under the legal fiction that their plans are constitutionally apportioned throughout the decade, a presumption that is necessary to avoid constant redistricting, with accompanying costs and instability. * * *

In appellants' view, however, this fiction should not provide a safe harbor for a legislature that enacts a voluntary, mid-decade plan overriding a legal court-drawn plan, thus "unnecessarily" creating population variance "when there was no legal compulsion" to do so. * * *

[Appellants'] test * * * turns not on whether a redistricting furthers equal-population principles but rather on the justification for redrawing a plan in the first place. In that respect appellants' approach merely restates the question whether it was permissible for the Texas Legislature to redraw the districting map. Appellants' answer, which mirrors their attack on mid-decennial redistricting solely motivated by partisan considerations, is unsatisfactory for reasons we have already discussed. * * *

In sum, we disagree with appellants' view that a legislature's decision to override a valid, court-drawn plan mid-decade is sufficiently suspect to give shape to a reliable standard for identifying unconstitutional political gerrymanders. We conclude that appellants have established no legally impermissible use of political classifications. For this reason, they state no claim on which relief may be granted for their statewide challenge.

III

Plan 1374C made changes to district lines in south and west Texas that appellants challenge as violations of § 2 of the Voting Rights Act and the Equal Protection Clause of the Fourteenth Amendment. The most significant changes occurred to District 23, which — both before and after the redistricting — covers a large land area in west Texas, and to District 25, which earlier included Houston but now includes a different area, a north-south strip from Austin to the Rio Grande Valley.

After the 2002 election, it became apparent that District 23 as then drawn had an increasingly powerful Latino population that threatened to oust the incumbent Republican, Henry Bonilla. Before the 2003 redistricting, the Latino share of the citizen voting-age population was 57.5%, and Bonilla's support among Latinos had dropped with each successive election since 1996. In 2002, Bonilla captured only 8% of the Latino vote and 51.5% of the overall vote. Faced with this loss of voter support, the legislature acted to protect Bonilla's incumbency by changing the lines — and hence the population mix — of the district. * * * In the newly drawn district, the Latino share of the citizen voting-age population dropped to 46%, though the Latino share of the total voting-age population remained just over 50%.

These changes required adjustments elsewhere, of course, so the State inserted a third district between the two districts to the east of District 23, and extended all three of them farther north. New District 25 is a long, narrow strip that winds its way from McAllen and the Mexican-border towns in the south to Austin, in the center of the State and 300 miles away. * * * The Latino communities at the opposite ends of District 25 have divergent "needs and interests," owing to "differences in socio-economic status, education, employment, health, and other characteristics."

The District Court summed up the purposes underlying the redistricting in south and west Texas: "The change to Congressional District 23 served the dual goal of increasing Republican seats in general and protecting Bonilla's incumbency in particular, with the additional political nuance that Bonilla would be reelected in a district that had a majority of Latino voting age population — although clearly not a majority of citizen voting age population and certainly not an effective voting majority." The goal in creating District 25 was just as clear: "[t]o avoid retrogression under § 5" of the Voting Rights Act given the reduced Latino voting strength in District 23. * * *

Appellants argue that the changes to District 23 diluted the voting rights of Latinos who remain in the district. Specifically, the redrawing of lines in District 23 caused the Latino share of the citizen voting-age population to drop from 57.5% to 46%. The District Court recognized that "Latino voting strength in Congressional District 23 is, unquestionably, weakened under Plan 1374C." The question is whether this weakening amounts to vote dilution.

To begin the *Gingles* analysis [see *Thornburg* v. *Gingles*, 478 U.S. 30 (1986)] [p. 301], it is evident that the second and third *Gingles* preconditions — cohesion among the minority group and bloc voting among the majority population — are present in District 23. The District Court found "racially polarized voting" in south and west Texas, and indeed "throughout the State." The polarization in District 23 was especially severe: 92% of Latinos voted against Bonilla in 2002, while 88% of non-Latinos voted for him. Furthermore, the projected results in new District 23 show that the Anglo citizen voting-age majority will often, if not always, prevent Latinos from electing the candidate of their choice in the district. For all these reasons, appellants demonstrated sufficient minority cohesion and majority bloc voting to meet the second and third *Gingles* requirements.

The first *Gingles* factor requires that a group be "sufficiently large and geographically compact to constitute a majority in a single-member district." 478 U.S., at 50. Latinos in District 23 could have constituted a majority of the citizen voting-age population in the district, and in fact did so under Plan 1151C. Though it may be possible for a citizen voting-age majority to lack real electoral opportunity, the Latino majority in old District 23 did possess electoral opportunity protected by § 2.

While the District Court stated that District 23 had not been an effective opportunity district under Plan 1151C, it recognized the district was "moving in that direction." Indeed, by 2002 the Latino candidate of choice in District 23 won the majority of the district's votes in 13 out of 15 elections for statewide officeholders. And in the congressional race, Bonilla could not have prevailed without some Latino support, limited though it was. State legislators changed District 23 specifically because they worried that Latinos would vote Bonilla out of office. * * * Since the redistricting prevented the immediate success of the emergent Latino majority in District 23, there was a denial of opportunity in the real sense of that term.

Plan 1374C's version of District 23, by contrast, "is unquestionably not a Latino opportunity district." Latinos, to be sure, are a bare majority of the voting-age population in new District 23, but only in a hollow sense, for the parties agree that the relevant numbers must include citizenship. This approach fits the language of § 2 because only eligible voters affect a group's opportunity to elect candidates. In sum, appellants have established that Latinos could have had an opportunity district in District 23 had its lines not been altered and that they do not have one now.

Considering the district in isolation, the three *Gingles* requirements are satisfied. The State argues, nonetheless, that it met its § 2 obligations by creating new District 25 as an offsetting opportunity district. It is true, of course, that "States retain broad discretion in drawing districts to comply with the mandate of § 2." *Shaw* v. *Hunt*, 517 U.S. 899, 917 n.9 (1996) *(Shaw II)*. This principle has limits, though. The Court has rejected the premise that a State can always make up for the less-than-equal opportunity of some individuals by providing greater opportunity to others. See *id.*, at 917 ("The vote-dilution injuries suffered by these persons are not remedied by creating a safe majority-black district somewhere else in the State"). As set out below, these conflicting concerns are resolved by allowing the State to use one majority-minority district to compensate for the absence of another only when the racial group in each area had a § 2 right and both could not be accommodated.

As to the first *Gingles* requirement, it is not enough that appellants show the possibility of creating a majority-minority district that would include the Latinos in District 23. If the inclusion of the plaintiffs would necessitate the exclusion of others, then the State cannot be faulted for its choice. That is why, in the context of a challenge to the drawing of district lines, "the first *Gingles* condition requires the possibility of creating more than the existing number of reasonably compact districts with a sufficiently large minority population to elect candidates of its choice." [*Johnson* v.] *De Grandy*, [512 U.S. 997], 1008 [(1994)] [p. 317].

The District Court found that the current plan contains six Latino opportunity districts and that seven reasonably compact districts could not be drawn. * * * [T]he court's [finding] was not clearly erroneous.

A problem remains, though, for the District Court failed to perform a comparable compactness inquiry for Plan 1374C as drawn. *De Grandy* requires a comparison between a challenger's proposal and the "existing number of reasonably compact districts." 512 U.S., at 1008. To be sure, § 2 does not forbid the creation of a noncompact majority-minority district. The noncompact district cannot, however, remedy a violation elsewhere in the State. Simply put, the State's creation of an opportunity district for those without a § 2 right offers no excuse for its failure to provide an opportunity district for those with a § 2 right. And since there is no § 2 right to a district that is not reasonably compact, the creation of a noncompact district does not compensate for the dismantling of a compact opportunity district.

THE CHIEF JUSTICE claims compactness should be only a factor in the analysis, but his approach comports neither with our precedents nor with the nature of the right established by § 2. *De Grandy* expressly stated that the first *Gingles* prong looks only to the number of "reasonably compact districts." 512 U.S., at 1008. *Shaw II*, moreover, refused to consider a noncompact district as a possible remedy for a § 2 violation. 517 U.S., at 916. It is true *Shaw II* applied this analysis in the context of a State's using compliance with § 2 as a defense to an equal protection challenge, but the holding was clear: A State cannot remedy a § 2 violation through the creation of a noncompact district. *Shaw II* also cannot be distinguished based on the relative location of the remedial district as compared to the district of the alleged violation. The remedial district in *Shaw II* had a 20% overlap with the district the plaintiffs sought, but the Court stated "[w]e do not think this degree of incorporation could mean [the remedial district] substantially addresses the § 2 violation." *Id.*, at 918. The overlap here is not substantially different, as the majority of Latinos who were in the old District 23 are still in the new District 23, but no longer have the opportunity to elect their candidate of choice.

Apart from its conflict with *De Grandy* and *Shaw II*, THE CHIEF JUSTICE's approach has the deficiency of creating a one-way rule whereby plaintiffs must show compactness but States need not (except, it seems, when using § 2 as a defense to an equal protection challenge). THE CHIEF JUSTICE appears to accept that a plaintiff, to make out a § 2 violation, must show he or she is part of a racial group that could form a majority in a reasonably compact district. If, however, a noncompact district cannot make up for the lack of a compact district, then this is equally true whether the plaintiff or the State proposes the noncompact district.

The District Court stated that Plan 1374C created "six *Gingles* Latino" districts, but it failed to decide whether District 25 was reasonably compact for § 2 purposes. * * *

While no precise rule has emerged governing § 2 compactness, the "inquiry should take into account 'traditional districting principles such as maintaining communities of interest and traditional boundaries.'" The recognition of nonracial communities of interest reflects the principle that a State may not "assum[e] from a group of voters' race that they 'think alike, share the same political interests, and will prefer the same candidates at the polls.'" *Miller* [v. *Johnson*, 515 U.S. 900], 920 [(1995)] [p. 369] (quoting *Shaw* v. *Reno*, 509 U.S. 630, 647 (1993) [p. 354]). In the absence of this prohibited assumption, there is no basis to believe a district that combines two far-flung segments of a racial group with disparate interests provides the opportunity that § 2 requires or that the first *Gingles* condition contemplates. * * *

* * * [T]he District Court's findings regarding the different characteristics, needs, and interests of the Latino community near the Mexican border and the one in and around Austin are well supported and uncontested. Legitimate yet differing communities of interest should not be disregarded in the interest of race. The practical consequence of drawing a district to cover two distant, disparate communities is that one or both groups will be unable to achieve their political goals. * * * We do not question the District Court's finding that the groups' combined voting strength would enable them to elect a candidate each prefers to the Anglos' candidate of choice. We also accept that in some cases members of a racial group in different areas — for example, rural and urban communities — could share similar interests and therefore form a compact district if the areas are in reasonably close proximity. When, however, the only common index is race and the result will be to cause internal friction, the State cannot make this a remedy for a § 2 violation elsewhere. We emphasize it is the enormous geographical distance separating the Austin and Mexican-border communities, coupled with the disparate needs and

interests of these populations — not either factor alone — that renders District 25 noncompact for § 2 purposes. The mathematical possibility of a racial bloc does not make a district compact.

Since District 25 is not reasonably compact, Plan 1374C contains only five reasonably compact Latino opportunity districts. Plan 1151C, by contrast, created six such districts. * * *

Appellants have thus satisfied all three *Gingles* requirements as to District 23, and the creation of new District 25 does not remedy the problem.

We proceed now to the totality of the circumstances, and first to the proportionality inquiry, comparing the percentage of total districts that are Latino opportunity districts with the Latino share of the citizen voting-age population. As explained in *De Grandy*, proportionality is "a relevant fact in the totality of circumstances." 512 U.S., at 1000. It does not, however, act as a "safe harbor" for States in complying with § 2. *Id.*, at 1017–1018. * * *

The State contends that proportionality should be decided on a regional basis, while appellants say their claim requires the Court to conduct a statewide analysis. * * * We conclude the answer in these cases is to look at proportionality statewide. * * * Appellants have alleged statewide vote dilution based on a statewide plan, so the electoral opportunities of Latinos across the State can bear on whether the lack of electoral opportunity for Latinos in District 23 is a consequence of Plan 1374C's redrawing of lines or simply a consequence of the inevitable "win some, lose some" in a State with racial bloc voting. Indeed, several of the other factors in the totality of circumstances have been characterized with reference to the State as a whole. *Gingles, supra*, at 44–45 (listing Senate Report factors). Particularly given the presence of racially polarized voting — and the possible submergence of minority votes — throughout Texas, it makes sense to use the entire State in assessing proportionality.

Looking statewide, there are 32 congressional districts. The five reasonably compact Latino opportunity districts amount to roughly 16% of the total, while Latinos make up 22% of Texas' citizen voting-age population. * * * Latinos are, therefore, two districts shy of proportional representation. There is, of course, no "magic parameter," *De Grandy*, 512 U.S., at 1017, n.14, and "rough proportionality," *id.*, at 1023, must allow for some deviations. We need not decide whether the two-district deficit in these cases weighs in favor of a § 2 violation. Even if Plan 1374C's disproportionality were deemed insubstantial, that consideration would not overcome the other evidence of vote dilution for Latinos in District 23. "[T]he degree of probative value assigned to proportionality may vary with other facts," *id.*, at 1020, and the other facts in these cases convince us that there is a § 2 violation.

District 23's Latino voters were poised to elect their candidate of choice. They were becoming more politically active, with a marked and continuous rise in Spanish-surnamed voter registration. In successive elections Latinos were voting against Bonilla in greater numbers, and in 2002 they almost ousted him. * * * In response to the growing participation that threatened Bonilla's incumbency, the State divided the cohesive Latino community in Webb County, moving about 100,000 Latinos to District 28, which was already a Latino opportunity district, and leaving the rest in a district where they now have little hope of electing their candidate of choice.

The changes to District 23 undermined the progress of a racial group that has been subject to significant voting-related discrimination and that was becoming increasingly politically active and cohesive. * * *

Against this background, the Latinos' diminishing electoral support for Bonilla indicates their belief he was "unresponsive to the particularized needs of the members of the minority group." In essence the State took away the Latinos' opportunity because Latinos were about to exercise it. This bears the mark of intentional discrimination that could give rise to an equal protection violation. Even if we accept the District Court's finding that the State's action was taken primarily for political, not racial, reasons, the redrawing of the district lines was damaging to the Latinos in District 23. The State not only made fruitless the Latinos' mobilization efforts but also acted against those Latinos who were becoming most politically active * * *.

Furthermore, the reason for taking Latinos out of District 23, according to the District Court, was to protect Congressman Bonilla from a constituency that was increasingly voting against him. The Court has noted that incumbency protection can be a legitimate factor in districting, see *Karcher* v. *Daggett*, 462 U.S. [725], 740 [(1983)], but experience teaches that incumbency protection can take various forms, not all of them in the interests of the constituents. If the justification for incumbency protection is to keep the constituency intact so the officeholder is accountable for promises made or broken, then the protection seems to accord with concern for the voters. If, on the other hand, incumbency protection means excluding some voters from the district simply because they are likely to vote against the officeholder, the change is to benefit the officeholder, not the voters. By purposely redrawing lines around those who opposed Bonilla, the state legislature took the latter course. This policy, whatever its validity in the realm of politics, cannot justify the effect on Latino voters. The policy becomes even more suspect when considered in light of evidence suggesting that the State intentionally drew District 23 to have a nominal Latino voting-age majority (without a citizen voting-age majority) for political reasons. This use of race to create the façade of a Latino district also weighs in favor of appellants' claim. * * *

Based on the foregoing, the totality of the circumstances demonstrates a § 2 violation. Even assuming Plan 1374C provides something close to proportional representation for Latinos, its troubling blend of politics and race — and the resulting vote dilution of a group that was beginning to achieve § 2's goal of overcoming prior electoral discrimination — cannot be sustained.

Because we hold Plan 1374C violates § 2 in its redrawing of District 23, we do not address appellants' claims that the use of race and politics in drawing that district violates the First Amendment and equal protection. We also need not confront appellants' claim of an equal protection violation in the drawing of District 25. The districts in south and west Texas will have to be redrawn to remedy the violation in District 23, and we have no cause to pass on the legitimacy of a district that must be changed. District 25, in particular, was formed to compensate for the loss of District 23 as a Latino opportunity district, and there is no reason to believe District

25 will remain in its current form once District 23 is brought into compliance with § 2. We therefore vacate the District Court's judgment as to these claims.

IV

Appellants also challenge the changes to district lines in the Dallas area, alleging they dilute African-American voting strength in violation of § 2 of the Voting Rights Act. Specifically, appellants contend that an African-American minority effectively controlled District 24 under Plan 1151C, and that § 2 entitles them to this district.

Before Plan 1374C was enacted, District 24 had elected Anglo Democrat Martin Frost to Congress in every election since 1978. Anglos were the largest racial group in the district, with 49.8% of the citizen voting-age population, and third largest were Latinos, with 20.8%. African-Americans were the second-largest group, with 25.7% of the citizen voting-age population, and they voted consistently for Frost. The new plan broke apart this racially diverse district, assigning its pieces into several other districts.

Accepting that African-Americans would not be a majority of the single-member district they seek, and that African-Americans do not vote cohesively with Hispanics, appellants nonetheless contend African-Americans had effective control of District 24. As the Court has done several times before, we assume for purposes of this litigation that it is possible to state a § 2 claim for a racial group that makes up less than 50% of the population. See *De Grandy*, 512 U.S., at 1009; *Voinovich* v. *Quilter*, 507 U.S. 146, 154 (1993); *Gingles*, 478 U.S., at 46–47 n.12. Even on the assumption that the first *Gingles* prong can accommodate this claim, however, appellants must show they constitute "a sufficiently large minority to elect their candidate of choice with the assistance of cross-over votes." *Voinovich*, *supra*, at 158.

The relatively small African-American population can meet this standard, according to appellants, because they constituted 64% of the voters in the Democratic primary. Since a significant number of Anglos and Latinos voted for the Democrat in the general election, the argument goes, African-American control of the primary translated into effective control of the entire election.

The District Court found, however, that African-Americans could not elect their candidate of choice in the primary. In support of this finding, it relied on testimony that the district was drawn for an Anglo Democrat, the fact that Frost had no opposition in any of his primary elections since his incumbency began, and District 24's demographic similarity to another district where an African-American candidate failed when he ran against an Anglo. "In short, that Anglo Democrats control this district is," according to the District Court, "the most rational conclusion."

Appellants fail to demonstrate clear error in this finding. In the absence of any contested Democratic primary in District 24 over the last 20 years, no obvious benchmark exists for deciding whether African-Americans could elect their candidate of choice. The fact that African-Americans voted for Frost — in the primary and general elections — could signify he is their candidate of choice. Without a contested primary, however, it could also be interpreted to show (assuming racial bloc voting) that Anglos and Latinos would vote in the Democratic primary in greater numbers if an African-American candidate of choice were to run, especially given Texas' open primary system. The District Court heard trial testimony that would support both explanations, and we cannot say that it erred in crediting the testimony that endorsed the latter interpretation. * * *

That African-Americans had influence in the district does not suffice to state a § 2 claim in these cases. The opportunity "to elect representatives of their choice" requires more than the ability to influence the outcome between some candidates, none of whom is their candidate of choice. There is no doubt African-Americans preferred Martin Frost to the Republicans who opposed him. The fact that African-Americans preferred Frost to some others does not, however, make him their candidate of choice. Accordingly, the ability to aid in Frost's election does not make the old District 24 an African-American opportunity district for purposes of § 2. If § 2 were interpreted to protect this kind of influence, it would unnecessarily infuse race into virtually every redistricting, raising serious constitutional questions.

Appellants respond by pointing to *Georgia* v. *Ashcroft* [539 U.S. 461 (2003)] [p. 246], where the Court held that the presence of influence districts is a relevant consideration under § 5 of the Voting Rights Act. The inquiry under § 2, however, concerns the opportunity "to elect representatives of their choice," [52 U.S.C. § 10301(b)], not whether a change has the purpose or effect of "denying or abridging the right to vote," § [10304]. *Ashcroft* recognized the differences between these tests, 539 U.S., at 478, and concluded that the ability of racial groups to elect candidates of their choice is only one factor under § 5, *id.*, at 480. So while the presence of districts "where minority voters may not be able to elect a candidate of choice but can play a substantial, if not decisive, role in the electoral process" is relevant to the § 5 analysis, *id.*, at 482, the lack of such districts cannot establish a § 2 violation. The failure to create an influence district in these cases thus does not run afoul of § 2 of the Voting Rights Act. * * *

*   *   *

We reject the statewide challenge to Texas' redistricting as an unconstitutional political gerrymander and the challenge to the redistricting in the Dallas area as a violation of § 2 of the Voting Rights Act. We do hold that the redrawing of lines in District 23 violates § 2 of the Voting Rights Act. The judgment of the District Court is affirmed in part, reversed in part, and vacated in part, and the cases are remanded for further proceedings.

It is so ordered.

JUSTICE STEVENS, with whom JUSTICE BREYER joins * * *, concurring in part and dissenting in part. * * *

* * * [A]ny decision to redraw district boundaries — like any other state action that affects the electoral process — must, at the very least, serve some legitimate governmental purpose. A purely partisan desire "to minimize or cancel out the voting strength of racial or political elements of the voting population," *Fortson* v. *Dorsey*, 379 U.S. 433, 439 (1965), is not such a purpose. Because a desire to minimize

the strength of Texas Democrats was the sole motivation for the adoption of Plan 1374C, the plan cannot withstand constitutional scrutiny. * * *

* * * If, after finally achieving political strength in Texas, the Republicans had adopted a new plan in order to remove the excessively partisan Democratic gerrymander of the 1990's, the decision to do so would unquestionably have been supported by a neutral justification. But that is not what happened. Instead, * * * Texas Republicans abandoned a neutral apportionment map [drawn by the *Balderas* court] for the sole purpose of manipulating district boundaries to maximize their electoral advantage and thus create their own impermissible stranglehold on political power. * * *

The unique question of law that is raised in this appeal is one that the Court has not previously addressed. That narrow question is whether it was unconstitutional for Texas to replace a lawful districting plan "in the middle of a decade, for the sole purpose of maximizing partisan advantage." * * * It is undeniable that identifying the motive for making that basic decision is a readily manageable judicial task. Indeed, although the Constitution places no *per se* ban on midcycle redistricting, a legislature's decision to redistrict in the middle of the census cycle, when the legislature is under no legal obligation to do so, makes the judicial task of identifying the legislature's motive simpler than it would otherwise be. * * * In my judgment, there is not even a colorable basis for contending that the relevant intent — in this case a purely partisan intent[3] — cannot be identified on the basis of admissible evidence in the record.[4] * * *

The requirements of the Federal Constitution that limit the State's power to rely exclusively on partisan preferences in drawing district lines are the Fourteenth Amendment's prohibition against invidious discrimination, and the First Amendment's protection of citizens from official retaliation based on their political affiliation. The equal protection component of the Fourteenth Amendment requires actions taken by the sovereign to be supported by some legitimate interest, and further establishes that a bare desire to harm a politically disfavored group is not a legitimate interest. Similarly, the freedom of political belief and association guaranteed by the First Amendment prevents the State, absent a compelling interest, from "penalizing citizens because of their participation in the electoral process, . . . their association with a political party, or their expression of political views." *Vieth*, 541 U.S., at 314 (KENNEDY, J., concurring in judgment) (citing *Elrod* v. *Burns*, 427 U.S. 347 (1976) [p. 726] (plurality opinion)). These protections

---

[3] The State suggests that in the process of drawing districts the architects of Plan 1374C frequently followed county lines, made an effort to keep certain entire communities within a given district, and otherwise followed certain neutral principles. But these facts are not relevant to the narrow question presented by these cases: Neutral motivations in the implementation of particular features of the redistricting do not qualify the solely partisan motivation behind the basic decision to adopt an entirely unnecessary plan in the first place.

[4] [R]ather than identifying any arguably neutral reasons for adopting Plan 1374C, the record establishes a purely partisan single-minded motivation with unmistakable clarity. Therefore, there is no need at this point to discuss standards that would guide judges in enforcing a rule allowing legislatures to be motivated in part by partisan considerations, but which would impose an "obligation not to apply *too much* partisanship in districting." *Vieth*, 541 U.S., [at] 286 (plurality opinion). Deciding that 100% is "too much" is not only a manageable decision, but * * * it is also an obviously correct one. * * *

embodied in the First and Fourteenth Amendments reflect the fundamental duty of the sovereign to govern impartially.

The legislature's decision to redistrict at issue in this litigation was entirely inconsistent with these principles. By taking an action for the sole purpose of advantaging Republicans and disadvantaging Democrats, the State of Texas violated its constitutional obligation to govern impartially. * * *

[JUSTICE SOUTER, in a partial concurrence and partial dissent joined by JUSTICE GINSBURG, discussed the first *Gingles* precondition for § 2 vote-dilution claims, which requires that a minority group demonstrate "that it is sufficiently large and geographically compact to constitute a majority in a single-member district." 478 U.S., at 50. He argued that a minority group should be able to satisfy that precondition if it would be able to elect its candidate of choice in a coalition district, even if the members of the minority group could not constitute an absolute majority of the population in the district. The Court confronted that issue directly in *Bartlett* v. *Strickland*, 556 U.S. __ (2009) [p. 404], which follows this case.]

JUSTICE BREYER, concurring in part and dissenting in part. * * *

[Plan 1374C's] effort "to maximize partisan advantage" encompasses an effort not only to exaggerate the favored party's electoral majority but also to produce a majority of congressional representatives even if the favored party receives only a *minority* of popular votes.

[B]ecause the plan entrenches the Republican Party, the State cannot successfully defend it as an effort simply to *neutralize* the Democratic Party's previous political gerrymander. Nor has the State tried to justify the plan on nonpartisan grounds, either as an effort to achieve legislative stability by avoiding legislative exaggeration of small shifts in party preferences or in any other way.

In sum, "the risk of entrenchment is demonstrated," "partisan considerations [have] render[ed] the traditional district-drawing compromises irrelevant," and "no justification other than party advantage can be found." The record reveals a plan that overwhelmingly relies upon the unjustified use of purely partisan line-drawing considerations and which will likely have seriously harmful electoral consequences. For these reasons, I believe the plan in its entirety violates the Equal Protection Clause.

CHIEF JUSTICE ROBERTS, with whom JUSTICE ALITO joins, concurring in part, concurring in the judgment in part, and dissenting in part.

I join Parts I and IV of the plurality opinion. With regard to Part II, I agree with the determination that appellants have not provided "a reliable standard for identifying unconstitutional political gerrymanders." The question whether any such standard exists — that is, whether a challenge to a political gerrymander presents a justiciable case or controversy — has not been argued in these cases. I therefore take no position on that question, which has divided the Court, see *Vieth* v. *Jubelirer*, and I join the Court's disposition in Part II without specifying whether appellants have failed to state a claim on which relief can be granted, or have failed to present a justiciable controversy.

I must, however, dissent from Part III of the Court's opinion. According to the District Court's factual findings, the State's drawing of district lines in south and west Texas caused the area to move from five out of seven effective Latino opportunity congressional districts, with an additional district "moving" in that direction, to *six* out of seven effective Latino opportunity districts. The end result is that while Latinos make up 58% of the citizen voting-age population in the area, they control 85% (six of seven) of the districts under the State's plan.

In the face of these findings, the majority nonetheless concludes that the State's plan somehow dilutes the voting strength of Latinos in violation of § 2 of the Voting Rights Act of 1965. The majority reaches its surprising result because it finds that Latino voters in one of the State's Latino opportunity districts — District 25 — are insufficiently compact, in that they consist of two different groups, one from around the Rio Grande and another from around Austin. According to the majority, this may make it more difficult for certain Latino-preferred candidates to be elected from that district — *even though Latino voters make up 55% of the citizen voting-age population in the district and vote as a bloc.* The majority prefers old District 23, despite the District Court determination that new District 25 is "a more effective Latino opportunity district than Congressional District 23 had been." * * *

Unable to escape the District Court's factfinding, the majority is left in the awkward position of maintaining that its *theory* about compactness is more important under § 2 than the actual prospects of electoral success for Latino-preferred candidates under a State's apportionment plan. And that theory is a novel one to boot. Never before has this or any other court struck down a State's redistricting plan under § 2, on the ground that the plan achieves the maximum number of possible majority-minority districts, but loses on style points, in that the minority voters in one of those districts are not as "compact" as the minority voters would be in another district were the lines drawn differently. Such a basis for liability pushes voting rights litigation into a whole new area — an area far removed from the concern of the Voting Rights Act to ensure minority voters an equal opportunity "to elect representatives of their choice." [52 U.S.C. § 10301(b)]. * * *

The majority's only answer is to shift the focus to statewide proportionality. * * * [But t]he plaintiffs' § 2 claims concern "the impact of the legislative plan on Latino voting strength *in South and West Texas*," and that is the only area of the State in which they can satisfy the *Gingles* factors. That is accordingly the proper frame of reference in analyzing proportionality.

In any event, at a statewide level, 6 Latino opportunity districts out of 32, or 19% of the seats, would certainly seem to be "roughly proportional" to the Latino 22% share of the population. The District Court accordingly determined that proportionality suggested the lack of vote dilution, even considered on a statewide basis. The majority avoids that suggestion by disregarding the District Court's factual finding that District 25 is an effective Latino opportunity district. That is not only improper, for the reasons given, but the majority's rejection of District 25 as a Latino opportunity district is also flatly inconsistent with its statewide approach to analyzing proportionality. Under the majority's view, the Latino voters in the northern end of District 25 cannot "count" along with the Latino voters at the southern end to form an effective majority, because they belong to different communities. But Latino voters from everywhere around the State of Texas — even those from areas where the *Gingles* factors are not satisfied — can "count" for purposes of calculating the proportion against which effective Latino electoral power should be measured. Heads the plaintiffs win; tails the State loses. * * *

Whatever the majority believes it is fighting with its holding, it is not vote dilution on the basis of race or ethnicity. I do not believe it is our role to make judgments about which *mixes* of minority voters should count for purposes of forming a majority in an electoral district, in the face of factual findings that the district is an effective majority-minority district. It is a sordid business, this divvying us up by race. When a State's plan already provides the maximum possible number of majority-minority effective opportunity districts, and the minority enjoys effective political power in the area well in *excess* of its proportion of the population, I would conclude that the courts have no further role to play in rejiggering the district lines under § 2.

JUSTICE SCALIA, with whom JUSTICE THOMAS joins, and with whom THE CHIEF JUSTICE and JUSTICE ALITO join as to Part III, concurring in the judgment in part and dissenting in part.

I

* * * JUSTICE KENNEDY's discussion of appellants' political-gerrymandering claims ably demonstrates that, yet again, no party or judge has put forth a judicially discernible standard by which to evaluate them. Unfortunately, the opinion then concludes that appellants have failed to state a claim as to political gerrymandering, without ever articulating what the elements of such a claim consist of. That is not an available disposition of this appeal. We must either conclude that the claim is nonjusticiable and dismiss it, or else set forth a standard and measure appellants' claim against it. *Vieth*, [541 U.S.], at 301. Instead, we again dispose of this claim in a way that provides no guidance to lower court judges and perpetuates a cause of action with no discernible content. We should simply dismiss appellants' claims as nonjusticiable.

II

I would dismiss appellants' vote-dilution claims premised on § 2 of the Voting Rights Act of 1965 for failure to state a claim, for the reasons set forth in JUSTICE THOMAS's opinion, which I joined, in *Holder* v. *Hall*, 512 U.S. 874, 891–946 (1994) [p. 335] (opinion concurring in judgment). * * *

III

Because I find no merit in either of the claims addressed by the Court, I must consider appellants' race-based equal protection claims. * * * [The District Court found that the Texas Legislature removed 100,000 mostly Latino residents from District 23 not for racial reasons, but for political ones — specifically, ensuring Congressman Bonilla's continued reelection. That finding] dooms appellants' intentional-vote-dilution claim. * * *

* * * [In evaluating whether District 25 was an impermissible racial gerrymander,] the District Court applied the approach set forth in *Easley* [v. *Cromartie*, 532 U.S. 234, 241 (2001)], in which the Court held that race may be a motivation in redistricting as long as it is not the predominant one. See also *Bush* [v. *Vera*], 517 U.S. [952], 993 [(1996)] (O'Connor, J., concurring) ("[S]o long as they do not subordinate traditional districting criteria to the use of race for its own sake or as a proxy, States may intentionally create majority-minority districts, and may otherwise take race into consideration, without coming under strict scrutiny"). In my view, however, when a legislature intentionally creates a majority-minority district, race is necessarily its predominant motivation and strict scrutiny is therefore triggered. * * *

Texas must therefore show that its use of race was narrowly tailored to further a compelling state interest. Texas asserts that it created District 25 to comply with its obligations under § 5 of the Voting Rights Act. * * * Since its changes to District 23 had reduced Latino voting power in that district, Texas asserts that it needed to create District 25 as a Latino-opportunity district in order to avoid § 5 liability.

We have in the past left undecided whether compliance with federal antidiscrimination laws can be a compelling state interest. I would hold that compliance with § 5 of the Voting Rights Act can be such an interest. We long ago upheld the constitutionality of § 5 as a proper exercise of Congress's authority under § 2 of the Fifteenth Amendment to enforce that Amendment's prohibition on the denial or abridgment of the right to vote. See *South Carolina* v. *Katzenbach*, 383 U.S. 301 (1966) [p. 14]. If compliance with § 5 were not a compelling state interest, then a State could be placed in the impossible position of having to choose between compliance with § 5 and compliance with the Equal Protection Clause. Moreover, the compelling nature of the State's interest in § 5 compliance is supported by our recognition in previous cases that race may be used where necessary to remedy identified past discrimination. See, *e.g., Shaw II*, at 909 (citing *Richmond* v. *J.A. Croson Co.*, 488 U.S. 469, 498–506 (1989)). Congress enacted § 5 for just that purpose, and that provision applies only to jurisdictions with a history of official discrimination. In the proper case, therefore, a covered jurisdiction may have a compelling interest in complying with § 5.

To support its use of § 5 compliance as a compelling interest with respect to a particular redistricting decision, the State must demonstrate that such compliance was its "actual purpose" and that it had " 'a strong basis in evidence' for believing," *Shaw II, supra*, at 908–909 n.4, that the redistricting decision at issue was "reasonably necessary under a constitutional reading and application of" the Act, *Miller* [v. *Johnson*], 515 U.S. [900], 921 [(1995)] [p. 369]. Moreover, in order to tailor the use of race narrowly to its purpose of complying with the Act, a State cannot use racial considerations to achieve results beyond those that are required to comply with the statute. See *id.*, at 926 (rejecting the Department of Justice's policy that maximization of minority districts was required by § 5 and thus that this policy could serve as a compelling state interest). Section 5 forbids a State to take action that would worsen minorities' electoral opportunities; it does not require action that would improve them. * * *

In light of these many factors bearing upon the question whether the State had a strong evidentiary basis for believing that the creation of District 25 was reasonably necessary to comply with § 5, I would normally remand for the District Court to undertake that "fact-intensive" inquiry. Appellants concede, however, that the changes made to District 23 "necessitated creating an additional effective Latino district elsewhere, in an attempt to avoid Voting Rights Act liability." This is, of course, precisely the State's position. Nor do appellants charge that in creating District 25 the State did more than what was required by § 5. In light of these concessions, I do not believe a remand is necessary, and I would affirm the judgment of the District Court.

Notes and Questions

1. Why was District 25 not a sufficient remedy for the reduction of Latino voting strength in District 23? The Court's conclusion appears to rest on a conclusion that the right protected by § 2 is individual and personal; just as a state cannot deny person A the right to vote and instead give two votes to person B, a state cannot deny the voters in District 23 the right to equal electoral opportunity and instead grant special political opportunity to voters elsewhere. *See Shaw v. Hunt*, 517 U.S. 899, 917 (1996) (*Shaw II*) ("To accept that the [opportunity] district may be placed anywhere implies that the claim, and hence the coordinate right to an undiluted vote (to cast a ballot equal among voters), belongs to the minority as a group and not to its individual members. It does not. See [52 U.S.C. § 10301] ('the right of any citizen').").

But the analogy may be flawed. The right protected by § 2 is not a conventional individual right, because the opportunity to elect representatives is possessed by groups of like-minded voters; an individual voter cannot elect representatives.[f] Likewise, an individual voter does not have the right to be placed into any particular district. Even if § 2 demands that a district be drawn to give members of a minority group an opportunity to elect a representative of their choice, the state need not place every member of that group in the opportunity district. *See Shaw II*, 517 U.S. at 917 n.9.[g] If § 2 protects a group right, however, should it matter whether Latinos

---

[f] *See Bush v. Vera*, 517 U.S. 952, 1049 n.3 (1996) (Souter, J., dissenting) (arguing that "any sophisticated right to genuinely meaningful electoral participation must be evaluated and measured as a group right") (quoting Samuel Issacharoff, *Groups and the Right to Vote*, 44 Emory L.J. 869, 883 (1995)); T. Alexander Aleinikoff & Samuel Issacharoff, *Race and Redistricting: Drawing Constitutional Lines After* Shaw v. Reno, 92 Mich. L. Rev. 588 (1993) (group right); Lani Guinier, *[E]racing Democracy: The Voting Rights Cases*, 108 Harv. L. Rev. 109 (1994) (group right); Katherine Inglis Butler, *Affirmative Racial Gerrymandering: Rhetoric and Reality*, 26 Cumb. L. Rev. 313 (1996) (individual right). *See also* Heather K. Gerken, *Understanding the Right to an Undiluted Vote*, 114 Harv. L. Rev. 1663, 1684 (2001) ("[E]xamining the treatment of an individual voter * * * will reveal only whether that person had an equal opportunity to *cast* a vote. It will not tell us whether she had an equal opportunity to *aggregate* her vote.").

[g] Likewise, viewing § 2 as conveying an individual right presents a problem when considering the rights of the voters selected to fill up a majority-minority district — the so-called "filler people." T. Alexander Aleinikoff & Samuel Issacharoff, 92 Mich. L. Rev. 588, 601 (1993). *See Gonzalez v. City of Aurora*, 535 F.3d 594, 598 (7th Cir. 2008) ("There is a serious problem with any proposal to employ black or Asian or white citizens of some other ethnic background as 'fill' in districts carefully drawn to ensure three 70%-Latino wards — wards in which the remaining 30% are (by design) never going to be able to elect a candidate of *their* choice."). If, however, the "filler people" can be "virtually represented" by

are given the opportunity to elect a candidate in one part of the state rather than in another?

2.   Was it appropriate for the Court to punt on the justiciability question and proceed to consider whether the plaintiffs offered a judicially manageable standard for adjudicating the partisan-gerrymandering claim?

3.   In terms of establishing a judicially manageable standard for adjudicating partisan-gerrymandering cases, should the Court distinguish between cases where the legislature has a partisan motive in drawing district lines in particular places and cases where the legislature has a partisan motive in re-drawing district lines in the first place?

4.   Should the Constitution be interpreted to bar mid-decade (re-)redistricting completely?

5.   Concerning District 24, the plurality accepted the district court's determination that blacks would not be able to elect their candidates of choice, even in the Democratic primary. If an alternative districting plan would have given blacks the ability to elect their preferred candidates in the primary, and if the Democratic nominee would be expected to win the general election, should a districting plan that deprived them of that power be a violation of § 2? In such a scenario, would an open primary system, which would allow (mostly white) Republicans to vote in the Democratic primary, dilute black votes? *See Osburn v. Cox*, 369 F.3d 1283 (11th Cir. 2004).

6.   *LULAC v. Perry* mentioned, but did not decide, the question whether a plaintiff could succeed on a claim under § 2 of the Voting Rights Act if he or she was a member of a minority group that could exercise controlling influence in a differently drawn district, despite constituting less than a majority of the district's population. The next case decided that question.

BARTLETT v. STRICKLAND
Supreme Court of the United States
556 U.S. 1, 129 S. Ct. 1231, 173 L. Ed. 2d 173 (2009)

JUSTICE KENNEDY announced the judgment of the Court and delivered an opinion, in which THE CHIEF JUSTICE [ROBERTS] and JUSTICE ALITO join.

This case requires us to interpret § 2 of the Voting Rights Act of 1965, as amended, 42 U.S.C. § 1973 [now 52 U.S.C. § 10301 — Eds.]. The question is whether the statute can be invoked to require state officials to draw election-district lines to allow a racial minority to join with other voters to elect the minority's candidate of choice, even where the racial minority is less than 50 percent of the voting-age population in the district to be drawn. To use election-law terminology: In a district that is not a majority-minority district, if a racial minority could elect its candidate of choice with support from crossover majority voters, can § 2 require the district to be drawn to accommodate this potential? * * *

---

legislators chosen in other districts — if § 2 is satisfied by the representation of the filler people's racial group in the legislature as a whole — then § 2's right appears to rest with the group and not the individual.

* * * The North Carolina House of Representatives is the larger of the two chambers in the State's General Assembly. District 18 of that body lies in the southeastern part of North Carolina. Starting in 1991, the General Assembly drew District 18 to include portions of four counties, including Pender County, in order to create a district with a majority African-American voting-age population and to satisfy the Voting Rights Act. Following the 2000 census, the North Carolina Supreme Court, to comply with the Whole County Provision [of the North Carolina Constitution, which prohibits splitting counties in creating state-legislative districts], rejected the General Assembly's first two statewide redistricting plans.

District 18 in its present form emerged from the General Assembly's third redistricting attempt, in 2003. By that time the African-American voting-age population had fallen below 50 percent in the district as then drawn, and the General Assembly no longer could draw a geographically compact majority-minority district. Rather than draw District 18 to keep Pender County whole, however, the General Assembly drew it by splitting portions of Pender and New Hanover counties. District 18 has an African-American voting-age population of 39.36 percent. Had it left Pender County whole, the General Assembly could have drawn District 18 with an African-American voting-age population of 35.33 percent. The General Assembly's reason for splitting Pender County was to give African-American voters the potential to join with majority voters to elect the minority group's candidate of its choice. Failure to do so, state officials now submit, would have diluted the minority group's voting strength in violation of § 2.

In May 2004, Pender County and the five members of its Board of Commissioners filed the instant suit in North Carolina state court * * *. The plaintiffs alleged that the 2003 plan violated the Whole County Provision by splitting Pender County into two House districts. The state-official defendants answered that dividing Pender County was required by § 2. As the trial court recognized, the procedural posture of this case differs from most § 2 cases. Here the defendants raise § 2 as a defense. As a result, the trial court stated, they are "in the unusual position" of bearing the burden of proving that a § 2 violation would have occurred absent splitting Pender County to draw District 18.

The trial court first considered whether the defendant state officials had established the three threshold requirements for § 2 liability under *Thornburg* v. *Gingles*, 478 U.S. 30, 50–51 (1986) [p. 301] — namely, (1) that the minority group "is sufficiently large and geographically compact to constitute a majority in a single-member district," (2) that the minority group is "politically cohesive," and (3) "that the white majority votes sufficiently as a bloc to enable it . . . usually to defeat the minority's preferred candidate."

As to the first *Gingles* requirement, the trial court concluded that, although African-Americans were not a majority of the voting-age population in District 18, the district was a "de facto" majority-minority district because African-Americans could get enough support from crossover majority voters to elect the African-Americans' preferred candidate. The court ruled that African-Americans in District 18 were politically cohesive, thus satisfying the second requirement. And later, the plaintiffs stipulated that the third *Gingles* requirement was met. The court then determined, based on the totality of the circumstances, that § 2 required the

General Assembly to split Pender County. The court sustained the lines for District 18 on that rationale.

* * * The Supreme Court of North Carolina reversed. It held that a "minority group must constitute a numerical majority of the voting population in the area under consideration before Section 2 . . . requires the creation of a legislative district to prevent dilution of the votes of that minority group." * * * We granted certiorari, and now affirm. * * *

This case turns on whether the first *Gingles* requirement can be satisfied when the minority group makes up less than 50 percent of the voting-age population in the potential election district. The parties agree on all other parts of the *Gingles* analysis, so the dispositive question is: What size minority group is sufficient to satisfy the first *Gingles* requirement?

At the outset the answer might not appear difficult to reach, for the *Gingles* Court said the minority group must "demonstrate that it is sufficiently large and geographically compact to constitute a majority in a single-member district." 478 U.S., at 50. This would seem to end the matter, as it indicates the minority group must demonstrate it can constitute "a majority." But in *Gingles* and again in *Growe* [v. *Emison*, 507 U.S. 25 (1993)] the Court reserved what it considered to be a separate question — whether, "when a plaintiff alleges that a voting practice or procedure impairs a minority's ability to influence, rather than alter, election results, a showing of geographical compactness of a minority group not sufficiently large to constitute a majority will suffice." *Growe*, *supra*, at 41, n.5; see also *Gingles*, *supra*, at 46–47, n.12. The Court has since applied the *Gingles* requirements in § 2 cases but has declined to decide the minimum size minority group necessary to satisfy the first requirement.

It is appropriate to review the terminology often used to describe various features of election districts in relation to the requirements of the Voting Rights Act. In majority-minority districts, a minority group composes a numerical, working majority of the voting-age population. Under present doctrine, § 2 can require the creation of these districts. See, *e.g.*, *Voinovich* [v. *Quilter*, 507 U.S. 146], 154 [(1993)] ("Placing black voters in a district in which they constitute a sizeable and therefore 'safe' majority ensures that they are able to elect their candidate of choice"). At the other end of the spectrum are influence districts, in which a minority group can influence the outcome of an election even if its preferred candidate cannot be elected. This Court has held that § 2 does not require the creation of influence districts. [*League of United Latin American Citizens* v. *Perry*, 548 U.S. 399, 445 (2006) (opinion of KENNEDY, J.) (*LULAC*)] [p. 385].

The present case involves an intermediate type of district — a so-called crossover district. Like an influence district, a crossover district is one in which minority voters make up less than a majority of the voting-age population. But in a crossover district, the minority population, at least potentially, is large enough to elect the candidate of its choice with help from voters who are members of the majority and who cross over to support the minority's preferred candidate. * * *

Petitioners argue that although crossover districts do not include a numerical majority of minority voters, they still satisfy the first *Gingles* requirement because they are "effective minority districts." Under petitioners' theory keeping Pender County whole would have violated § 2 by cracking the potential crossover district that they drew as District 18. So, petitioners contend, § 2 required them to override state law and split Pender County, drawing District 18 with an African-American voting-age population of 39.36 percent rather than keeping Pender County whole and leaving District 18 with an African-American voting-age population of 35.33 percent. We reject that claim.

First, we conclude, the petitioners' theory is contrary to the mandate of § 2. The statute requires a showing that minorities "have less opportunity than other members of the electorate to . . . elect representatives of their choice." [52 U.S.C. § 10301(b)]. But because they form only 39 percent of the voting-age population in District 18, African-Americans standing alone have no better or worse opportunity to elect a candidate than does any other group of voters with the same relative voting strength. That is, African-Americans in District 18 have the opportunity to join other voters — including other racial minorities, or whites, or both — to reach a majority and elect their preferred candidate. They cannot, however, elect that candidate based on their own votes and without assistance from others. * * * Nothing in § 2 grants special protection to a minority group's right to form political coalitions. * * *

Although the Court has reserved the question we confront today and has cautioned that the *Gingles* requirements "cannot be applied mechanically," *Voino-vich, supra*, at 158, the reasoning of our cases does not support petitioners' claims. Section 2 does not impose on those who draw election districts a duty to give minority voters the most potential, or the best potential, to elect a candidate by attracting crossover voters. In setting out the first requirement for § 2 claims, the *Gingles* Court explained that "[u]nless minority voters possess the *potential* to elect representatives in the absence of the challenged structure or practice, they cannot claim to have been injured by that structure or practice." 478 U.S., at 50, n.17. The *Growe* Court stated that the first *Gingles* requirement is "needed to establish that the minority has the potential to elect a representative of its own choice in some single-member district." 507 U.S., at 40. Without such a showing, "there neither has been a wrong nor can be a remedy." *Id.*, at 41. * * *

Allowing crossover-district claims would require us to revise and reformulate the *Gingles* threshold inquiry that has been the baseline of our § 2 jurisprudence. Mandatory recognition of claims in which success for a minority depends upon crossover majority voters would create serious tension with the third *Gingles* requirement that the majority votes as a bloc to defeat minority-preferred candidates. It is difficult to see how the majority-bloc-voting requirement could be met in a district where, by definition, white voters join in sufficient numbers with minority voters to elect the minority's preferred candidate. (We are skeptical that the bloc-voting test could be satisfied here, for example, where minority voters in District 18 cannot elect their candidate of choice without support from almost 20 percent of white voters. We do not confront that issue, however, because for some reason respondents conceded the third *Gingles* requirement in state court.) * * *

We find support for the majority-minority requirement in the need for workable standards and sound judicial and legislative administration. The rule draws clear lines for courts and legislatures alike. The same cannot be said of a less exacting standard that would mandate crossover districts under § 2. Determining whether a § 2 claim would lie — *i.e.*, determining whether potential districts could function as crossover districts — would place courts in the untenable position of predicting many political variables and tying them to race-based assumptions. The judiciary would be directed to make predictions or adopt premises that even experienced polling analysts and political experts could not assess with certainty, particularly over the long term. For example, courts would be required to pursue these inquiries: What percentage of white voters supported minority-preferred candidates in the past? How reliable would the crossover votes be in future elections? What types of candidates have white and minority voters supported together in the past and will those trends continue? Were past crossover votes based on incumbency and did that depend on race? What are the historical turnout rates among white and minority voters and will they stay the same? Those questions are speculative, and the answers (if they could be supposed) would prove elusive. A requirement to draw election districts on answers to these and like inquiries ought not to be inferred from the text or purpose of § 2. Though courts are capable of making refined and exacting factual inquiries, they "are inherently ill-equipped" to "make decisions based on highly political judgments" of the sort that crossover-district claims would require. There is an underlying principle of fundamental importance: We must be most cautious before interpreting a statute to require courts to make inquiries based on racial classifications and race-based predictions. The statutory mandate petitioners urge us to find in § 2 raises serious constitutional questions.

Heightening these concerns even further is the fact that § 2 applies nationwide to every jurisdiction that must draw lines for election districts required by state or local law. Crossover-district claims would require courts to make predictive political judgments not only about familiar, two-party contests in large districts but also about regional and local jurisdictions that often feature more than two parties or candidates. Under petitioners' view courts would face the difficult task of discerning crossover patterns in nonpartisan contests for a city commission, a school board, or a local water authority. The political data necessary to make such determinations are nonexistent for elections in most of those jurisdictions. And predictions would be speculative at best given that, especially in the context of local elections, voters' personal affiliations with candidates and views on particular issues can play a large role.

Unlike any of the standards proposed to allow crossover-district claims, the majority-minority rule relies on an objective, numerical test: Do minorities make up more than 50 percent of the voting-age population in the relevant geographic area? That rule provides straightforward guidance to courts and to those officials charged with drawing district lines to comply with § 2. * * *

In arguing for a less restrictive interpretation of the first *Gingles* requirement petitioners point to the text of § 2 and its guarantee that political processes be "equally open to participation" to protect minority voters' "opportunity . . . to elect representatives of their choice." [52 U.S.C. § 10301(b)]. An "opportunity," petitioners argue, occurs in crossover districts as well as majority-minority districts; and these extended opportunities, they say, require § 2 protection.

But petitioners put emphasis on the word "opportunity" at the expense of the word "equally." The statute does not protect any possible opportunity or mechanism through which minority voters could work with other constituencies to elect their candidate of choice. Section 2 does not guarantee minority voters an electoral advantage. Minority groups in crossover districts cannot form a voting majority without crossover voters. In those districts minority voters have the same opportunity to elect their candidate as any other political group with the same relative voting strength. * * *

To the extent there is any doubt whether § 2 calls for the majority-minority rule, we resolve that doubt by avoiding serious constitutional concerns under the Equal Protection Clause. * * * If § 2 were interpreted to require crossover districts throughout the Nation, "it would unnecessarily infuse race into virtually every redistricting, raising serious constitutional questions." *LULAC*, 548 U.S., at 446 (opinion of KENNEDY, J.). That interpretation would result in a substantial increase in the number of mandatory districts drawn with race as "the predominant factor motivating the legislature's decision." *Miller* v. *Johnson*, 515 U.S. 900, 916 (1995) [p. 369]. * * *

* * * Much like § 5, § 2 allows States to choose their own method of complying with the Voting Rights Act, and we have said that may include drawing crossover districts. See [*Georgia* v. *Ashcroft*, 539 U.S. 461,] 480–483 [(2003)] [p. 246]. When we address the mandate of § 2, however, we must note it is not concerned with maximizing minority voting strength, [*Johnson* v.] *De Grandy*, 512 U.S. [997,] 1022 [(1994)] [p. 317]; and, as a statutory matter, § 2 does not mandate creating or preserving crossover districts.

Our holding also should not be interpreted to entrench majority-minority districts by statutory command, for that, too, could pose constitutional concerns. See *Miller* v. *Johnson, supra*; *Shaw* v. *Reno*, [509 U.S. 630 (1993)] [p. 354]. States that wish to draw crossover districts are free to do so where no other prohibition exists. Majority-minority districts are only required if all three *Gingles* factors are met and if § 2 applies based on a totality of the circumstances. In areas with substantial crossover voting it is unlikely that the plaintiffs would be able to establish the third *Gingles* precondition — bloc voting by majority voters. In those areas majority-minority districts would not be required in the first place; and in the exercise of lawful discretion States could draw crossover districts as they deemed appropriate. * * * Our holding recognizes only that there is no support for the claim that § 2 can require the creation of crossover districts in the first instance. * * *

The judgment of the Supreme Court of North Carolina is affirmed.

It is so ordered.

JUSTICE THOMAS, with whom JUSTICE SCALIA joins, concurring in the judgment.

I continue to adhere to the views expressed in my opinion in *Holder* v. *Hall*, 512 U.S. 874, 891 (1994) [p. 335] (opinion concurring in judgment). The text of § 2 of the Voting Rights Act of 1965 does not authorize any vote dilution claim, regardless of the size of the minority population in a given district. See [*id.*], at 893 (stating that the [statutory] terms "standard, practice, or procedure" "reach only state enactments that limit citizens' access to the ballot"). I continue to disagree, therefore, with the framework set forth in *Thornburg* v. *Gingles* for analyzing vote dilution claims because it has no basis in the text of § 2. I would not evaluate any Voting Rights Act claim under a test that "has produced such a disastrous misadventure in judicial policymaking." *Holder, supra,* at 893. For these reasons, I concur only in the judgment.

JUSTICE SOUTER, with whom JUSTICE STEVENS, JUSTICE GINSBURG, and JUSTICE BREYER join, dissenting. * * *

Though this case arose under the Constitution of North Carolina, the dispositive issue is one of federal statutory law: whether a district with a minority population under 50%, but large enough to elect its chosen candidate with the help of majority voters disposed to support the minority favorite, can ever count as a district where minority voters have the opportunity "to elect representatives of their choice" for purposes of § 2. I think it clear from the nature of a vote-dilution claim and the text of § 2 that the answer must be yes. There is nothing in the statutory text to suggest that Congress meant to protect minority opportunity to elect solely by the creation of majority-minority districts. On the contrary, § 2 "focuses exclusively on the consequences of apportionment," as Congress made clear when it explicitly prescribed the ultimate functional approach: a totality of the circumstances test. See [52 U.S.C. § 10301(b)] ("A violation . . . is established if, based on the totality of circumstances, it is shown . . ."). And a functional analysis leaves no doubt that crossover districts vindicate the interest expressly protected by § 2: the opportunity to elect a desired representative. * * *

[W]hether a district with a minority population under 50% of CVAP may redress a violation of § 2 is a question of fact with an obvious answer: of course minority voters constituting less than 50% of the voting population can have an opportunity to elect the candidates of their choice, as amply shown by empirical studies confirming that such minority groups regularly elect their preferred candidates with the help of modest crossover by members of the majority. The North Carolina Supreme Court for example, determined [in this case] that voting districts with a black voting age population of as little as 38.37% have an opportunity to elect black candidates, a factual finding that has gone unchallenged and is well supported by electoral results in North Carolina. Of the nine House districts in which blacks make up more than 50% of the voting age population (VAP), all but two elected a black representative in the 2004 election. Of the 12 additional House districts in which blacks are over 39% of the VAP, all but one elected a black representative in the 2004 election. It would surely surprise legislators in North Carolina to suggest that black voters in these 12 districts cannot possibly have an opportunity to "elect [the] representatives of their choice."

It is of course true that the threshold population sufficient to provide minority voters with an opportunity to elect their candidates of choice is elastic, and the proportions will likely shift in the future, as they have in the past. That is, racial polarization has declined, and if it continues downward the first *Gingles* condition will get easier to satisfy.

But this is no reason to create an arbitrary threshold; the functional approach will continue to allow dismissal of claims for districts with minority populations too small to demonstrate an ability to elect, and with "crossovers" too numerous to allow an inference of vote dilution in the first place. No one, for example, would argue based on the record of experience in this case that a district with a 25% black population would meet the first *Gingles* condition. And the third *Gingles* requirement, majority-bloc voting, may well provide an analytical limit to claims based on crossover districts. But whatever this limit may be, we have no need to set it here, since the respondent state officials have stipulated to majority-bloc voting. In sum, § 2 addresses voting realities, and for practical purposes a 39%-minority district in which we know minorities have the potential to elect their preferred candidate is every bit as good as a 50%-minority district.

In fact, a crossover district is better. Recognizing crossover districts has the value of giving States greater flexibility to draw districting plans with a fair number of minority-opportunity districts, and this in turn allows for a beneficent reduction in the number of majority-minority districts with their "quintessentially race-conscious calculus," *De Grandy*, 512 U.S., at 1020, thereby moderating reliance on race as an exclusive determinant in districting decisions. A crossover is thus superior to a majority-minority district precisely because it requires polarized factions to break out of the mold and form the coalitions that discourage racial divisions. * * *

The [plurality's] claim that another political group in a particular district might have the same relative voting strength as the minority if it had the same share of the population takes the form of a tautology: the plurality simply looks to one district and says that a 39% group of blacks is no worse off than a 39% group of whites would be. This statement might be true, or it might not be, and standing alone it demonstrates nothing.

Even if the two 39% groups were assumed to be comparable in fact because they will attract sufficient crossover (and so should be credited with satisfying the first *Gingles* condition), neither of them could prove a § 2 violation without looking beyond the 39% district and showing a disproportionately small potential for success in the State's overall configuration of districts. As this Court has explained before, the ultimate question in a § 2 case (that is, whether the minority group in question is being denied an equal opportunity to participate and elect) can be answered only by examining the broader pattern of districts to see whether the minority is being denied a roughly proportionate opportunity. See *LULAC*, 548 U.S., at 436–437. Hence, saying one group's 39% equals another's, even if true in particular districts where facts are known, does not mean that either, both, or neither group could show a § 2 violation. The plurality simply fails to grasp that an alleged § 2 violation can only be proved or disproved by looking statewide. * * *

In fact, the plurality's distinction is artificial on its own terms. In the past, when black voter registration and black voter turnout were relatively low, even black voters with 55% of a district's CVAP would have had to rely on crossover voters to elect their candidate of choice. But no one on this Court (and, so far as I am aware, any other court addressing it) ever suggested that reliance on crossover voting in such a district rendered minority success any less significant under § 2, or meant that the district failed to satisfy the first *Gingles* factor. Nor would it be any answer to say that black voters in such a district, assuming unrealistic voter turnout, theoretically had the "potential" to elect their candidate without crossover support; that would be about as relevant as arguing in the abstract that a black CVAP of 45% is potentially successful, on the assumption that black voters could turn out en masse to elect the candidate of their choice without reliance on crossovers if enough majority voters stay home.

The plurality is also concerned that recognizing the "potential" of anything under 50% would entail an exponential expansion of special minority districting; the plurality goes so far as to suggest that recognizing crossover districts as possible minority-opportunity districts would inherently "entitl[e] minority groups to the maximum possible voting strength." But this conclusion again reflects a confusion of the gatekeeping function of the *Gingles* conditions with the ultimate test for relief under § 2.

As already explained, the mere fact that all threshold *Gingles* conditions could be met and a district could be drawn with a minority population sufficiently large to elect the candidate of its choice does not require drawing such a district. This case simply is about the first *Gingles* condition, not about the number of minority-opportunity districts needed under § 2, and accepting Bartlett's position would in no way imply an obligation to maximize districts with minority voter potential. Under any interpretation of the first *Gingles* factor, the State must draw districts in a way that provides minority voters with a fair number of districts in which they have an opportunity to elect candidates of their choice; the only question here is which districts will count toward that total. * * *

The plurality argues that qualifying crossover districts as minority-opportunity districts would be less administrable than demanding 50%, forcing courts to engage with the various factual and predictive questions that would come up in determining what percentage of majority voters would provide the voting minority with a chance at electoral success. But claims based on a State's failure to draw majority-minority districts raise the same issues of judicial judgment; even when the 50% threshold is satisfied, a court will still have to engage in factually messy enquiries about the "potential" such a district may afford, the degree of minority cohesion and majority-bloc voting, and the existence of vote-dilution under a totality of the circumstances. The plurality's rule, therefore, conserves an uncertain amount of judicial resources, and only at the expense of ignoring a class of § 2 claims that this Court has no authority to strike from the statute's coverage.

The plurality again misunderstands the nature of § 2 in suggesting that its rule does not conflict with what the Court said in *Georgia* v. *Ashcroft*, 539 U.S., [at] 480–482: that crossover districts count as minority-opportunity districts for the purpose of assessing whether minorities have the opportunity "to elect their preferred candidates of choice" under § 5 of the VRA. While the plurality is, of course, correct that there are differences between the enquiries under § 2 and § 5, those differences do not save today's decision from inconsistency with the prior pronouncement. A districting plan violates § 5 if it diminishes the ability of minority voters to "elect their preferred candidates of choice," § 1973c(b), as measured against the minority's previous electoral opportunity, *Ashcroft, supra*, at 477. A districting plan violates § 2 if it diminishes the ability of minority voters to "elect representatives of their choice," [52 U.S.C. § 10301(b)], as measured under a totality of the circumstances against a baseline of rough proportionality. It makes no sense to say that a crossover district counts as a minority-opportunity district when comparing the past and the present under § 5, but not when comparing the present and the possible under § 2.

Finally, the plurality tries to support its insistence on a 50% threshold by invoking the policy of constitutional avoidance, which calls for construing a statute so as to avoid a possibly unconstitutional result. The plurality suggests that allowing a lower threshold would "require crossover districts throughout the Nation," thereby implicating the principle of *Shaw* v. *Reno* that districting with an excessive reliance on race is unconstitutional ("excessive" now being equated by the plurality with the frequency of creating opportunity districts). But the plurality has it precisely backwards. A State will inevitably draw some crossover districts as the natural byproduct of districting based on traditional factors. If these crossover districts count as minority-opportunity districts, the State will be much closer to meeting its § 2 obligation without any reference to race, and fewer minority-opportunity districts will, therefore, need to be created purposefully. But if, as a matter of law, only majority-minority districts provide a minority seeking equality with the opportunity to elect its preferred candidates, the State will have much further to go to create a sufficient number of minority-opportunity districts, will be required to bridge this gap by creating exclusively majority-minority districts, and will inevitably produce a districting plan that reflects a greater focus on race. The plurality, however, seems to believe that any reference to race in districting poses a constitutional concern, even a State's decision to reduce racial blocs in favor of crossover districts. A judicial position with these consequences is not constitutional avoidance.

More serious than the plurality opinion's inconsistency with prior cases construing § 2 is the perversity of the results it portends. Consider the effect of the plurality's rule on North Carolina's districting scheme. Black voters make up approximately 20% of North Carolina's VAP and are distributed throughout 120 State House districts. [B]lack voters constitute more than 50% of the VAP in 9 of these districts and over 39% of the VAP in an additional 12. Under a functional approach to § 2, black voters in North Carolina have an opportunity to elect (and regularly do elect) the representative of their choice in as many as 21 House districts, or 17.5% of North Carolina's total districts. North Carolina's districting plan is therefore close to providing black voters with proportionate electoral opportunity. According to the plurality, however, the remedy of a crossover district cannot provide opportunity to minority voters who lack it, and the requisite opportunity must therefore be lacking for minority voters already living in districts where they must rely on crossover. By the plurality's reckoning, then, black voters have an opportunity to elect representatives of their choice in, at most, nine North Carolina House districts. In the plurality's view, North Carolina must have a long way to go before it satisfies the § 2 requirement of equal electoral opportunity.[5]

---

[5] * * * The untenable implications of the plurality's rule do not end there. * * * [T]he logic of the plurality's position compels the absurd conclusion that the invidious and intentional fracturing of crossover districts in order to harm minority voters would not state a claim under § 2. After all, if the

A State like North Carolina faced with the plurality's opinion, whether it wants to comply with § 2 or simply to avoid litigation, will, therefore, have no reason to create crossover districts. Section 2 recognizes no need for such districts, from which it follows that they can neither be required nor be created to help the State meet its obligation of equal electoral opportunity under § 2. And if a legislature were induced to draw a crossover district by the plurality's encouragement to create them voluntarily, it would open itself to attack by the plurality based on the pointed suggestion that a policy favoring crossover districts runs counter to *Shaw*. The plurality has thus boiled § 2 down to one option: the best way to avoid suit under § 2, and the only way to comply with § 2, is by drawing district lines in a way that packs minority voters into majority-minority districts, probably eradicating crossover districts in the process.

Perhaps the plurality recognizes this aberrant implication, for it eventually attempts to disavow it. It asserts that "§ 2 allows States to choose their own method of complying with the Voting Rights Act, and we have said that may include drawing crossover districts. . . . [But] § 2 does not mandate creating or preserving crossover districts." But this is judicial fiat, not legal reasoning; the plurality does not even attempt to explain how a crossover district can be a minority-opportunity district when assessing the compliance of a districting plan with § 2, but cannot be one when sought as a remedy to a § 2 violation. The plurality cannot have it both ways. If voluntarily drawing a crossover district brings a State into compliance with § 2, then requiring creation of a crossover district must be a way to remedy a violation of § 2, and eliminating a crossover district must in some cases take a State out of compliance with the statute. And when the elimination of a crossover district does cause a violation of § 2, I cannot fathom why a voter in that district should not be able to bring a claim to remedy it.

In short, to the extent the plurality's holding is taken to control future results, the plurality has eliminated the protection of § 2 for the districts that best vindicate the goals of the statute, and has done all it can to force the States to perpetuate racially concentrated districts, the quintessential manifestations of race consciousness in American politics.

I respectfully dissent.

JUSTICE GINSBURG, dissenting.

I join JUSTICE SOUTER's powerfully persuasive dissenting opinion, and would make concrete what is implicit in his exposition. The plurality's interpretation of § 2 of the Voting Rights Act of 1965 is difficult to fathom and severely undermines the statute's estimable aim. Today's decision returns the ball to Congress' court. The Legislature has just cause to clarify beyond debate the appropriate reading of § 2.

---

elimination of a crossover district can never deprive minority voters in the district of the opportunity "to elect representatives of their choice," minorities in an invidiously eliminated district simply cannot show an injury under § 2.

JUSTICE BREYER, dissenting.

I join JUSTICE SOUTER's opinion in full. I write separately in light of the plurality's claim that a bright-line 50% rule (used as a *Gingles* gateway) serves administrative objectives. In the plurality's view, that rule amounts to a relatively simple administrative device that will help separate at the outset those cases that are more likely meritorious from those that are not. Even were that objective as critically important as the plurality believes, however, it is not difficult to find other numerical gateway rules that would work better.

Assume that a basic purpose of a gateway number is to separate (1) districts where a minority group can "elect representatives of their choice," from (2) districts where the minority, because of the need to obtain majority crossover votes, can only "elect representatives" that are consensus candidates. At first blush, one might think that a 50% rule will work in this respect. After all, if a 50% minority population votes as a bloc, can it not always elect the candidate of its choice? And if a minority population constitutes less than 50% of a district, is not any candidate elected from that district always a consensus choice of minority and majority voters? The realities of voting behavior, however, make clear that the answer to both these questions is "no."

No voting group is 100% cohesive. Except in districts with overwhelming minority populations, some crossover votes are often necessary. The question is how likely it is that the need for crossover votes will force a minority to reject its "preferred choice" in favor of a "consensus candidate." A 50% number does not even try to answer that question. To the contrary, it includes, say 51% minority districts, where imperfect cohesion may, in context, prevent election of the "minority-preferred" candidate, while it excludes, say, 45% districts where a smaller but more cohesive minority can, with the help of a small and reliable majority crossover vote, elect its preferred candidate.

Why not use a numerical gateway rule that looks more directly at the relevant question: Is the minority bloc large enough, is it cohesive enough, is the necessary majority crossover vote small enough, so that the minority (tending to vote cohesively) can likely vote its preferred candidate (rather than a consensus candidate) into office? We can likely find a reasonably administrable mathematical formula more directly tied to the factors in question.

To take a possible example: Suppose we pick a numerical ratio that requires the minority voting age population to be twice as large as the percentage of majority crossover votes needed to elect the minority's preferred candidate. We would calculate the latter (the percentage of majority crossover votes the minority voters need) to take account of both the percentage of minority voting age population in the district and the cohesiveness with which they vote. Thus, if minority voters account for 45% of the voters in a district and 89% of those voters tend to vote cohesively as a group, then the minority needs a crossover vote of about 20% of the majority voters to elect its preferred candidate. (Such a district with 100 voters would have 45 minority voters and 55 majority voters; 40 minority voters would vote for the minority group's preferred candidate at election time; the minority voters would need 11 more votes to elect their preferred candidate; and 11 is about 20% of the majority's 55.) The larger the minority population, the greater its cohesiveness, and thus the smaller the crossover vote needed to assure success, the greater the likelihood that the minority can elect its preferred candidate and the smaller the likelihood that the cohesive minority, in order to find the needed majority crossover vote, must support a consensus, rather than its preferred, candidate. * * *

I do not claim that the 2-to-1 ratio is a perfect rule; I claim only that it is better than the plurality's 50% rule. After all, unlike 50%, a 2-to-1 ratio (of voting age minority population to necessary non-minority crossover votes) focuses directly upon the problem at hand, better reflects voting realities, and consequently far better separates at the gateway likely sheep from likely goats. In most cases, the 50% rule and the 2-to-1 rule would have roughly similar effects. Most districts where the minority voting age population is greater than 50% will almost always satisfy the 2-to-1 rule; and most districts where the minority population is below 40% will almost never satisfy the 2-to-1 rule. But in districts with minority voting age populations that range from 40% to 50%, the divergent approaches of the two standards can make a critical difference — as well they should.

In a word, JUSTICE SOUTER well explains why the majority's test is ill suited to the statute's objectives. I add that the test the majority adopts is ill suited to its own administrative ends. Better gateway tests, if needed, can be found.

With respect, I dissent.

Notes and Questions

1. The plurality held that a minority group does not possess the opportunity to elect representatives of its choice unless it comprises more than 50% of the voting-age population in a district. Is that the appropriate denominator? Suppose, for example, that members of a particular minority group are registered to vote at a disproportionately low rate, either because of disqualifying felony convictions or simply because they have not completed the required paperwork. In such a situation, even if the minority group makes up a majority of a district's population, it may not be able to elect its chosen representative because comparatively fewer of its members will actually be able to vote. Should courts instead ask whether a minority group is numerous enough as a percentage of registered voters? Total population? *Citizen* voting-age population? *See Reyes v. City of Farmers Branch, Tex.*, 586 F.3d 1019, 1023–25 (5th Cir. 2009).

2. *Bartlett v. Strickland* dealt with a minority group that was not sufficiently numerous to constitute a majority in a district. The plurality held that such a group could not satisfy the first prong of *Gingles*, even if it could be expected to receive crossover votes from other racial groups. What about the converse situation, where a minority group is sufficiently large to constitute a bare majority of a district's voting-age population, but where some members of that group would be expected to support an opposing candidate? In such a situation, would the minority group be sufficiently numerous to satisfy *Gingles*? *See Thompson v. Glades County Board of County Commissioners*, 2004 U.S. Dist. LEXIS 30989 (M.D. Fla. Aug. 27, 2004), *rev'd* 493 F.3d 1253, 1262–65, *vacated en banc* 508 F.3d 975 (2007), *district-court decision aff'd by an equally divided en banc court* 532 F.3d 1179 (11th Cir. 2008), *cert. denied* 129 S. Ct. 1611 (2009).

3.   How does the plurality define bloc voting? Is its definition consistent with the definitions used in prior cases? Could there ever be racially polarized voting in a coalition district?

4.   What does it mean for a group to have a "candidate of choice"? Is a party's nominee the "candidate of choice" of that party? Or is he or she only the candidate of choice of those who supported him or her in the primary?

5.   Apart from the question of the requirements of the VRA, *should* states create coalition districts? Many identifiable minority groups are not sufficiently numerous to amount to a majority in a single-member district, but a coalition district may provide such a group with an opportunity for political influence that would otherwise be lost. *See* Keith Aoki, *A Tale of Three Cities: Thoughts on Asian American Electoral and Political Power After 2000*, 8 UCLA Asian Pac. Am. L.J. 1 (2002).

Chapter 6

THE ROLES AND RIGHTS OF POLITICAL PARTIES

A. INTRODUCTION

Political parties occupy an ambiguous position in the constitutional structure. On the one hand, the structure of government was believed to limit the influence of parties, and indeed parties were seen at the time of the framing as obstacles to the pursuit of the public good. *See, e.g.*, RICHARD HOFSTADTER, THE IDEA OF A PARTY SYSTEM: THE RISE OF LEGITIMATE OPPOSITION IN THE UNITED STATES, 1780–1840 (1969). On the other hand, the First Amendment's protections of "speech," "assembly," and "petition" seem to extend constitutional protection to associations, such as parties, that are vehicles for exercising all three of those rights. To complicate matters further, parties — and particularly the two major parties, which have been dominant in American politics for well over a century and whose members are the office-holders who create the statutes governing parties' place in government — are essential to the electoral machinery. For example, states depend on parties to winnow potential candidates to a small number whom the voters consider in the general election. If the parties did not perform that winnowing function, the state would have to do so, and our electoral structure would look very different from the way it does now.

The intertwinement between the two major parties and the state government has led to controversy concerning the degree to which the parties should be considered part of the state, and thus bound to abide by the constitutional limits on government action, and the degree to which parties should be considered private associations, whose autonomy from state control is constitutionally protected. This Chapter examines those issues.

In § B, we consider whether parties should be considered "state actors," such that they would be prohibited from discriminating on the ground of race against potential voters in primary elections. In a series of cases from *Nixon v. Herndon*, 273 U.S. 536 (1927), through *Terry v. Adams*, 345 U.S. 461 (1953) [p. 431], collectively referred to as the White Primary Cases, the Court held that neither states, nor the parties themselves, nor certain influential groups within the parties could exclude blacks from voting in primaries. As the fractured decision in *Terry* illustrates, however, it is unclear what principles motivated some of those conclusions. Accordingly, it is difficult to assess the extent to which those holdings extend to other sub-groups of parties, or whether parties should be considered state actors when engaged in activities other than primaries, such as advocating the election of particular candidates or for establishing rules for participating in party conventions.

Section C considers whether the First Amendment guarantees parties the freedom to determine their membership, their nominees, and their policies separate from the influence of the state. The Court has granted parties considerable autonomy to determine, for example, rules governing internal party operations. Further, parties enjoy some ability to determine qualifications for participating in primaries and for seeking nominations, though parties' decisions in this regard are subject to some restrictions. As the White Primary Cases demonstrate, some of these restrictions are grounded in the Constitution; others, however, are imposed by state law. This section principally focuses on the question which state-law restrictions are permissible and which abridge parties' First Amendment rights.

In § D, we turn to regulations that have a particular effect on third or minor parties and on independents. The Supreme Court has interpreted the Equal Protection Clause and the First Amendment as limiting states' ability to use ballot-access laws and other regulations to shut out third parties and independents. Accordingly, laws that leave them virtually no chance of appearing on the ballot are unconstitutional. On the other hand, the Court has also perceived a state interest in the orderly management of elections and has upheld certain regulations that have the effect of hindering third parties. Thus, minor parties and independent candidates may be required to demonstrate some showing of support, such as by collecting signatures on a petition, before being granted a spot on a ballot. If the requirement is too onerous, however, it will be held unconstitutional. Determining how onerous a requirement is too onerous has proven to be a major difficulty, as we shall see.

Finally, in § E, we consider parties' roles in substituting candidates on the ballot when the initial nominees withdraw. Though the rights of parties in such a circumstance are governed largely by state law, the interpretations of those laws reflect conceptions of the right to vote and the place of political parties that fit well with the themes of this Chapter.

B. STATE ACTION

With the exception of the Thirteenth Amendment, which prohibits slavery, the Constitution regulates the conduct of only government and government officials — not private parties. For example, the First Amendment prohibits "Congress" from making laws abridging certain liberties, and the Fourteenth Amendment provides that "[n]o State" shall deprive persons of the equal protection of the laws.[a] If a private employer discriminates against job applicants who are racial minorities, such discrimination may well violate state and/or federal statutes, but it does not violate the Constitution.

---

[a] As you learned in Constitutional Law, the Supreme Court has held that the Fourteenth Amendment's Due Process Clause "incorporates" many of the provisions of the Bill of Rights against state infringement, even though those provisions by themselves apply only to the United States government. Thus today, for example, states, as well as the United States, are prohibited from abridging the freedom of speech. Whether a right has been incorporated or not, however, the Constitution protects that right only against government action.

Establishing that rule is easy enough in clear cases, but distinguishing between government action and the actions of private parties becomes difficult when government and the rest of society occupy less distinct spheres. Political parties, as we see in this section, occupy an indeterminate position between state actors and private organizations. On the one hand, the very purpose of a party may be to change the approach of government, and therefore it may be anomalous to consider the party as part of the government whose policies the party opposes. Likewise, if all political parties are state actors, then the government will be considered to be acting in opposition to itself when those different parties criticize and campaign against each other.

On the other hand, treating parties as strictly private entities would permit the parties to eviscerate constitutional protections. If primary elections, for example, were strictly private matters, then parties could effectively exclude racial minorities from the political process. Minorities could, of course, participate in the general election, but by that time their chance to influence politics might have passed. Moreover, the government is hardly a bystander concerning parties' affairs. Governmental regulation pervades the parties' business, and parties (especially major parties) benefit from special treatment granted by the government, such as the automatic placement of the parties' nominees on the general-election ballot. One might argue that it is wrong for parties to take these advantages while maintaining that they need not follow constitutional norms.

The following "White Primary Cases" examine the Supreme Court's attempt to reconcile the role of political parties with the state-action doctrine. The cases involve the Texas Democratic Party's attempt to exclude blacks during a period when the Party was by far the dominant political force in the state. Our first principal case is *Grovey v. Townsend*, but two cases decided before *Grovey* deserve mention here. In *Nixon v. Herndon*, 273 U.S. 536 (1927), the Court held that a state statute prohibiting blacks from participating in the Democratic primary election was a "direct and obvious violation of the Fourteenth [Amendment]." *Id.* at 541.

Texas legislators responded to *Nixon* by passing a new statute. The new statute did not *require* parties to exclude blacks or anyone else, but *permitted* them to do so: "every political party in this State through its State Executive Committee shall have the power to prescribe the qualifications of its own members and shall in its own way determine who shall be qualified to vote or otherwise participate in such political party." The Democratic State Executive Committee adopted a resolution excluding blacks from participation in primaries. This exclusion was challenged (by the same black man who had been excluded from voting in *Nixon v. Herndon*), and the Court struck it down in *Nixon v. Condon*, 286 U.S. 73 (1932) (*Nixon II*), by a vote of 5-4. Despite finding the exclusion unconstitutional, the Court in *Nixon II* did not hold that the party's discrimination could be attributed to the state simply because parties were state actors. Rather, the Court held that the state statute took power away from the party *convention* and placed it in the *executive committee*:

> Whatever our conclusion might be if the statute had remitted to the party the untrammeled power to prescribe the qualifications of its members, nothing of the kind was done. Instead, the statute lodged the power in a committee, which excluded the petitioner and others of his race, not by

virtue of any authority delegated by the party, but by virtue of an authority originating or supposed to originate in the mandate of the law.

Id. at 84. Because the executive committee's power was granted by statute, the Court concluded that the actions of that committee could be attributed to the state.

As *Nixon II* noted, however, a different case would be presented if the limits on membership were decreed not by the executive committee, but by the convention, in which "resides" the power to "formulat[e] the party faith" as well as "[w]hatever inherent power a State political party has to determine the content of its membership." *Id.* at 84–85. It did not take long for that different case to make its way to the Court.

GROVEY v. TOWNSEND
Supreme Court of the United States
295 U.S. 45, 55 S. Ct. 622, 79 L. Ed. 1292 (1935)

MR. JUSTICE ROBERTS delivered the opinion of the Court [in which MR. CHIEF JUSTICE HUGHES, MR. JUSTICE VAN DEVANTER, MR. JUSTICE MCREYNOLDS, MR. JUSTICE BRANDEIS, MR. JUSTICE SUTHERLAND, MR. JUSTICE BUTLER, MR. JUSTICE STONE, and MR. JUSTICE CARDOZO join].

The petitioner, by complaint filed in the justice court of Harris county, Texas, alleged that, although he is a citizen of the United States and of the State and County, and a member of and believer in the tenets of the Democratic party, the respondent, the county clerk, a state officer, having as such only public functions to perform, refused him a ballot for a Democratic party primary election because he is of the negro race. * * * Referring to statutes which regulate absentee voting at primary elections, the complaint states the petitioner expected to be absent from the county on the date of the primary election, and demanded of the respondent an absentee ballot, which was refused him in virtue of a resolution of the state Democratic convention of Texas, adopted May 24, 1932, which is:

> "Be it resolved that all white citizens of the State of Texas who are qualified to vote under the Constitution and laws of the state shall be eligible to membership in the Democratic party and as such entitled to participate in its deliberations."

The complaint charges that the respondent acted without legal excuse, and his wrongful and unlawful acts constituted a violation of the Fourteenth and Fifteenth Amendments of the Federal Constitution. [The lower court held against the would-be voter.] * * *

The charge is that respondent, a state officer, in refusing to furnish petitioner a ballot, obeyed the law of Texas, and the consequent denial of petitioner's right to vote in the primary election because of his race and color was state action forbidden by the Federal Constitution, and it is claimed that [*Nixon* v. *Herndon*, 273 U.S. 536 (1927), and *Nixon* v. *Condon*, 286 U.S. 73 (1932),] require us so to hold. The cited cases are, however, not in point. * * * Here, the qualifications of citizens to participate in party counsels and to vote at party primaries have been declared by the representatives of the party in convention assembled, and this action upon its face is not state action. The question whether, under the constitution and laws of Texas, such a declaration as to party membership amounts to state action was expressly reserved in *Nixon* v. *Condon, supra,* pp. 84–85. Petitioner insists that, for various reasons, the resolution of the state convention limiting membership in the Democratic party in Texas to white voters does not relieve the exclusion of negroes from participation in Democratic primary elections of its true nature as the act of the state.

[Petitioner argues] that the primary election was held under statutory compulsion; is wholly statutory in origin and incidents; those charged with its management have been deprived by statute and judicial decision of all power to establish qualifications for participation therein inconsistent with those laid down by the laws of the state, save only that the managers of such elections have been given the power to deny negroes the vote. It is further urged that, while the election is designated that of the Democratic party, the statutes not only require this method of selecting party nominees, but define the powers and duties of the party's representatives and of those who are to conduct the election so completely, and make them so thoroughly officers of the state that any action taken by them in connection with the qualifications of members of the party is in fact state action, and not party action.

In support of this view, petitioner refers to Title 50 of the Revised Civil Statutes of Texas of 1925, which requires that any party whose members cast more than 100,000 ballots at the previous election shall nominate candidates through primaries, and fixes the date at which they are to be held; requires primary election officials to be qualified voters; declares the same qualifications for voting in such an election as in the general elections; permits absentee voting as in a general election; requires that only an official ballot shall be used, as in a general election; specifies the form of ballot and how it shall be marked, as other sections do for general elections; fixes the number of ballots to be provided, as another article does for general elections; permits the use of voting booths, guard rails, and ballot boxes which by other statutes are provided for general elections; requires the officials of primary elections to take the same oath as officials at the general elections; defines the powers of judges at primary elections; provides elaborately for the purity of the ballot box; commands that the sealed ballot boxes be delivered to the county clerk after the election * * *; and confers jurisdiction of election contests upon district courts * * *. A perusal of these provisions, so it is said, will convince that the state has prescribed and regulated party primaries as fully as general elections, and has made those who manage the primaries state officers subject to state direction and control.

While it is true that Texas has, by its laws, elaborately provided for the expression of party preference as to nominees, has required that preference to be expressed in a certain form of voting, and has attempted in minute detail to protect the suffrage of the members of the organization against fraud, it is equally true that the primary is a party primary; the expenses of it are not borne by the state, but by members of the party seeking nomination; the ballots are furnished not by the state, but by the agencies of the party; the votes are counted and the returns made by instrumentalities created by the party; and the state recognizes the state convention as the organ of the party for the declaration of principles and the formulation of policies. * * *

In *Bell* v. *Hill*, 74 S.W.(2d) 113 [(Tex. 1934)], the [Supreme Court of Texas] concluded that [political] parties in the State of Texas arise from the exercise of the free will and liberty of the citizens composing them; that they are voluntary associations for political action, and are not the creatures of the state, and further decided that * * * the State Constitution guaranteed to citizens the liberty of forming political associations, and the only limitation upon this right to be found in that instrument is the clause which requires the maintenance of a republican form of government. The statutes regulating the nomination of candidates by primaries * * * were held not to extend to the denial of the right of citizens to form a political party and to determine who might associate with them as members thereof. The court declared that a proper view of the election laws of Texas, and their history, required the conclusion that the Democratic party in that state is a voluntary political association, and, by its representatives assembled in convention, has the power to determine who shall be eligible for membership and, as such, eligible to participate in the party's primaries. * * * In the light of the principles so announced, we are unable to characterize the managers of the primary election as state officers in such sense that any action taken by them in obedience to the mandate of the state convention respecting eligibility to participate in the organization's deliberations is state action. * * *

The complaint states that * * * in Texas, nomination by the Democratic party is equivalent to election. These facts (the truth of which the demurrer assumes) the petitioner insists, without more, make out a forbidden discrimination. * * * The argument is that, as a negro may not be denied a ballot at a general election on account of his race or color, if exclusion from the primary renders his vote at the general election insignificant and useless, the result is to deny him the suffrage altogether. So to say is to confuse the privilege of membership in a party with the right to vote for one who is to hold a public office. With the former, the state need have no concern; with the latter, it is bound to concern itself, for the general election is a function of the state government, and discrimination by the state as respects participation by negroes on account of their race or color is prohibited by the Federal Constitution. * * *

We find no ground for holding that the respondent has, in obedience to the mandate of the law of Texas, discriminated against the petitioner or denied him any right guaranteed by the Fourteenth and Fifteenth Amendments.

Judgment affirmed.

Notes and Questions

1. Consider the effect of Texas state law on the outcome of *Grovey*. The Supreme Court of the United States concluded that the Texas Democratic Party was not a state actor (itself a federal question) principally because the Supreme Court of Texas concluded that state law limited the extent to which the Texas

Legislature could regulate party membership.[b] Thus, under *Grovey*, a party's status as a state actor or private entity appeared to be dependent on the control the state exercised over it. In other words, the opinion did not treat political parties as necessarily private entities; rather, the Texas Democratic Party was a private entity because Texas law allowed it to have the requisite autonomy.

2.   Relatedly, it is important to recognize that *Grovey* did not establish a First Amendment right of parties to be free from state control. The Texas Democratic Party was a private entity not because it had a constitutional right to control its own membership, but because Texas state law allowed it to control its own membership. We will discuss parties' constitutional rights to autonomy from state regulation later in this Chapter.

3.   Between *Grovey* and the next case to consider Texas's white primary, the Court decided *United States v. Classic*, 313 U.S. 299 (1941). *Classic* was a criminal case, in which the defendants, commissioners of elections in Louisiana, were accused of fraudulently altering ballots and improperly certifying the results of a Democratic primary election for Congress. The fraud was alleged to have violated two federal statutes making it a crime to deprive a person of rights protected by the United States Constitution. The defendants argued that, because the primary election was a proceeding of a private voluntary association, no constitutional right was violated.

The Court rejected the argument in an opinion by then-Justice Stone, without so much as citing *Grovey*. In the Court's view, the right to vote for Congress was protected by the Constitution, and Congress could protect that right by ensuring that primaries were not tainted by fraud. As the Court explained,

> That the free choice by the people of representatives in Congress, subject only to the restrictions to be found in §§ 2 and 4 of Article I and elsewhere in the Constitution, was one of the great purposes of our constitutional scheme of government cannot be doubted. We cannot regard it as any the less the constitutional purpose, or its words as any the less guarantying the integrity of that choice, when a state, exercising its privilege in the absence of Congressional action, changes the mode of choice from a single step, a general election, to two, of which the first is the choice at a primary of those candidates from whom, as a second step, the representative in Congress is to be chosen at the election.

313 U.S. at 316–17. Further, the Court concluded that a contrary interpretation would enable states to undercut the constitutionally protected right to vote by placing important electoral decisions in the hands of "private" entities: "It is hardly the performance of the judicial function to construe a statute which, in terms, protects a right secured by the Constitution, here the right to choose a representative in Congress, as applying to an election whose only function is to ratify a choice already made at the primary, but as having no application to the primary which is

---

[b] Of course, that state-law limitation did not stop the Texas Legislature from passing the 1923 statute at issue in *Nixon v. Herndon*, 273 U.S. 536 (1927). That statute, you will recall, prohibited blacks from participating in primary elections, whatever the desires of the party. It was struck down not because it violated state law, but because it violated the Fourteenth Amendment.

the only effective means of choice." *Id.* at 324. Accordingly, the Court held that the defendants' fraud in a primary election interfered with voters' constitutional rights, within the meaning of the statutes, and that the statutes were themselves constitutional exercises of congressional power.

Did *Classic* undermine *Grovey*, or can the two cases be reconciled? The government, in arguing *Classic*, noted that the Louisiana primary, unlike the Texas primary at issue in *Grovey*, was conducted by state officials and at public expense. Do those differences suffice to explain the different outcomes? The following case, factually identical in all relevant respects to *Grovey*, relies on *Classic* in overruling the earlier case.

SMITH v. ALLWRIGHT
Supreme Court of the United States
321 U.S. 649, 64 S. Ct. 757, 88 L. Ed. 987 (1944)

MR. JUSTICE REED delivered the opinion of the Court [in which MR. CHIEF JUSTICE STONE, MR. JUSTICE BLACK, MR. JUSTICE DOUGLAS, MR. JUSTICE MURPHY, MR. JUSTICE JACKSON, and MR. JUSTICE RUTLEDGE join].

This writ of certiorari brings here for review a claim for damages in the sum of $5,000 on the part of petitioner, a Negro citizen of the 48th precinct of Harris County, Texas, for the refusal of respondents, election and associate election judges, respectively, of that precinct, to give petitioner a ballot or to permit him to cast a ballot in the primary election of July 27, 1940, for the nomination of Democratic candidates for the United States Senate and House of Representatives, and Governor and other state officers. The refusal is alleged to have been solely because of the race and color of the proposed voter. * * *

The Democratic party, on May 24, 1932, in a state convention adopted the following resolution, which has not since been "amended, abrogated, annulled or avoided": "Be it resolved that all white citizens of the State of Texas who are qualified to vote under the Constitution and laws of the State shall be eligible to membership in the Democratic party and, as such, entitled to participate in its deliberations." It was by virtue of this resolution that the respondents refused to permit the petitioner to vote.

* * * Respondents * * * defended on the ground that the Democratic party of Texas is a voluntary organization, with members banded together for the purpose of selecting individuals of the group representing the common political beliefs as candidates in the general election. As such a voluntary organization, it was claimed, the Democratic party is free to select its own membership and limit to whites participation in the party primary. Such action, the answer asserted, does not violate the Fourteenth, Fifteenth or Seventeenth Amendment, as officers of government cannot be chosen at primaries, and the Amendments are applicable only to general elections, where governmental officers are actually elected. Primaries, it is said, are political party affairs, handled by party, not governmental, officers. * * *

Since *Grovey* v. *Townsend* [295 U.S. 45 (1935)] [p. 422] and prior to the present suit, no case from Texas involving primary elections has been before this Court. We did decide, however, *United States* v. *Classic*, 313 U.S. 299 [(1941)]. We there held that § 4 of Article I of the Constitution authorized Congress to regulate primary, as well as general, elections "where the primary is by law made an integral part of the election machinery." 313 U.S., at 318. Consequently, in the *Classic* case, * * * corrupt acts of election officers were subjected to Congressional sanctions because that body had power to protect rights of Federal suffrage secured by the Constitution in primary as in general elections. This decision depended, too, on the determination that, under the Louisiana statutes, the primary was a part of the procedure for choice of Federal officials. * * * The fusing by the *Classic* case of the primary and general elections into a single instrumentality for choice of officers has a definite bearing on the permissibility under the Constitution of excluding Negroes from primaries. This is not to say that the *Classic* case cuts directly into the rationale of *Grovey* v. *Townsend.* This latter case was not mentioned in the opinion. *Classic* bears upon *Grovey* v. *Townsend* not because exclusion of Negroes from primaries is any more or less state action by reason of the unitary character of the electoral process, but because the recognition of the place of the primary in the electoral scheme makes clear that state delegation to a party of the power to fix the qualifications of primary elections is delegation of a state function that may make the party's action the action of the state. When *Grovey* v. *Townsend* was written, the Court looked upon the denial of a vote in a primary as a mere refusal by a party of party membership. As the Louisiana statutes for holding primaries are similar to those of Texas, our ruling in *Classic* as to the unitary character of the electoral process calls for a reexamination as to whether or not the exclusion of Negroes from a Texas party primary was state action.

The statutes of Texas relating to primaries and the resolution of the Democratic party of Texas extending the privileges of membership to white citizens only are the same in substance and effect today as they were when *Grovey* v. *Townsend* was decided by a unanimous Court. The question as to whether the exclusionary action of the party was the action of the State persists as the determinative factor. In again entering upon consideration of the inference to be drawn as to state action from a substantially similar factual situation, it should be noted that *Grovey* v. *Townsend* upheld exclusion of Negroes from primaries through the denial of party member-ship by a party convention. A few years before [in *Nixon* v. *Condon*, 286 U.S. 73 (1932)], this Court refused approval of exclusion by the State Executive Committee of the party. A different result was reached on the theory that the Committee action was state authorized, and the Convention action was unfettered by statutory control. Such a variation in the result from so slight a change in form influences us to consider anew the legal validity of the distinction which has resulted in barring Negroes from participating in the nominations of candidates of the Democratic party in Texas. * * *

We are thus brought to an examination of the qualifications for Democratic primary electors in Texas, to determine whether state action or private action has excluded Negroes from participation. * * * Texas requires electors in a primary to pay a poll tax. Every person who does so pay and who has the qualifications of age and residence is an acceptable voter for the primary. * * * Texas requires by the law the election of the county officers of a party. These compose the county executive committee. The county chairmen so selected are members of the district executive committee and choose the chairman for the district. Precinct primary election officers are named by the county executive committee. Statutes provide for the election by the voters of precinct delegates to the county convention of a party and the selection of delegates to the district and state conventions by the county convention. The state convention selects the state executive committee. No convention may place in platform or resolution any demand for specific legislation without endorsement of such legislation by the voters in a primary. Texas thus directs the selection of all party officers.

Primary elections are conducted by the party under state statutory authority. The county executive committee selects precinct election officials and the county, district or state executive committees, respectively, canvass the returns. These party committees or the state convention certify the party's candidates to the appropriate officers for inclusion on the official ballot for the general election. No name which has not been so certified may appear upon the ballot for the general election as a candidate of a political party. No other name may be printed on the ballot which has not been placed in nomination by qualified voters who must take oath that they did not participate in a primary for the selection of a candidate for the office for which the nomination is made.

The state courts are given exclusive original jurisdiction of contested elections and of mandamus proceedings to compel party officers to perform their statutory duties.

We think that this statutory system for the selection of party nominees for inclusion on the general election ballot makes the party which is required to follow these legislative directions an agency of the state in so far as it determines the participants in a primary election. The party takes its character as a state agency from the duties imposed upon it by state statutes; the duties do not become matters of private law because they are performed by a political party. The plan of the Texas primary follows substantially that of Louisiana, with the exception that, in Louisiana, the state pays the cost of the primary, while Texas assesses the cost against candidates. In numerous instances, the Texas statutes fix or limit the fees to be charged. Whether paid directly by the state or through state requirements, it is state action which compels. When primaries become a part of the machinery for choosing officials, state and national, as they have here, the same tests to determine the character of discrimination or abridgement should be applied to the primary as are applied to the general election. If the state requires a certain electoral procedure, prescribes a general election ballot made up of party nominees so chosen and limits the choice of the electorate in general elections for state offices, practically speaking, to those whose names appear on such a ballot, it endorses, adopts and enforces the discrimination against Negroes, practiced by a party entrusted by Texas law with the determination of the qualifications of participants in the primary. This is state action within the meaning of the Fifteenth Amendment.

The United States is a constitutional democracy. Its organic law grants to all citizens a right to participate in the choice of elected officials without restriction by any state because of race. This grant to the people of the opportunity for choice is not to be nullified by a state through casting its electoral process in a form which permits a private organization to practice racial discrimination in the election.

Constitutional rights would be of little value if they could be thus indirectly denied.

The privilege of membership in a party may be, as this Court said in *Grovey* v. *Townsend*, 295 U.S. 45, 55, no concern of a state. But when, as here, that privilege is also the essential qualification for voting in a primary to select nominees for a general election, the state makes the action of the party the action of the state. In reaching this conclusion, we are not unmindful of the desirability of continuity of decision in constitutional questions. However, when convinced of former error, this Court has never felt constrained to follow precedent. In constitutional questions, where correction depends upon amendment, and not upon legislative action, this Court throughout its history has freely exercised its power to reexamine the basis of its constitutional decisions. This has long been accepted practice, and this practice has continued to this day. This is particularly true when the decision believed erroneous is the application of a constitutional principle, rather than an interpretation of the Constitution to extract the principle itself. Here, we are applying, contrary to the recent decision in *Grovey* v. *Townsend*, the well established principle of the Fifteenth Amendment, forbidding the abridgement by a state of a citizen's right to vote. *Grovey* v. *Townsend* is overruled.

Judgment reversed.

MR. JUSTICE FRANKFURTER concurs in the result [without opinion].

MR. JUSTICE ROBERTS [dissenting]. * * *

[*Grovey* v. *Townsend*] received the attention and consideration which the questions involved demanded, and the opinion represented the views of all the justices. It appears that those views do not now commend themselves to the court. I shall not restate them. They are exposed in the opinion, and must stand or fall on their merits. Their soundness, however, is not a matter which presently concerns me.

The reason for my concern is that the instant decision, overruling that announced about nine years ago, tends to bring adjudications of this tribunal into the same class as a restricted railroad ticket, good for this day and train only. I have no assurance, in view of current decisions, that the opinion announced today may not shortly be repudiated and overruled by justices who deem they have new light on the subject. * * *

[T]he court below relied, as it was bound to, upon our previous decision. As that court points out, the statutes of Texas have not been altered since *Grovey* v. *Townsend* was decided. The same resolution is involved as was drawn in question in *Grovey* v. *Townsend*. Not a fact differentiates that case from this except the names of the parties. * * *

It is regrettable that, in an era marked by doubt and confusion, an era whose greatest need is steadfastness of thought and purpose, this court, which has been looked to as exhibiting consistency in adjudication and a steadiness which would hold the balance even in the face of temporary ebbs and flows of opinion, should now itself become the breeder of fresh doubt and confusion in the public mind as to the stability of our institutions.

Notes and Questions

1. Consider the changes in the Court's membership between *Grovey* and *Smith*. Only Harlan Fiske Stone (who was elevated to Chief Justice by President Franklin Roosevelt) and Owen J. Roberts remained from 1935. The other seven Justices were appointed to the Court by Roosevelt. Consider, too, the historical context of the case. *Smith* was argued in the midst of World War II, at a time when it might have been particularly troubling to permit American states to make racial distinctions in excluding people from the political process. *Cf. Shelley v. Kraemer*, 334 U.S. 1 (1948) (finding state action satisfied by judicial enforcement of a racially restrictive covenant governing the sale of real estate). For a discussion of *Smith v. Allwright*'s practical success in granting blacks political power, see Michael J. Klarman, *The White Primary Rulings: A Case Study in the Consequences of Supreme Court Decisionmaking*, 29 FLA. ST. U. L. REV. 55 (2001) (arguing that *Smith* was more successful in altering societal practice than were the roughly contemporaneous decisions involving criminal procedure and school desegregation).

2. What difference is there between the regulation of state parties under Texas law, and the regulation of business corporations (which are generally not state actors) in every state's corporate law? *See Morse v. Republican Party of Virginia*, 517 U.S. 186, 274 n.15 (1996) (Thomas, J., dissenting); *Jackson v. Metropolitan Edison Co.*, 419 U.S. 345, 357–59 (1974) (holding that corporations are not state actors unless they enjoy a special relationship with the state, and further holding that a state-conferred utility monopoly does not qualify as such a relationship). Does the analogy indicate that the state-action question should be determined based on considerations other than the degree of state control over party procedures?

3. The state-action cases can be seen as trying to maintain two delicate distinctions. First, some nominally private entities carrying out functions related to elections should be considered state actors, but certainly not every group that holds political power can be a state actor. Otherwise, an influential group of friends might be a state actor only because of that influence. Second, as uncomfortable as most people are with parties' racial discrimination, a party's identity and membership are inextricably connected with its message. If a party cannot discriminate against people with an alternative message, then its ability to communicate its message will have been compromised. For example, the mission of the Right to Life Party might be imperiled if it was obligated to accept abortion-rights advocates as members. Those twin concerns are at play in many of the cases in the remainder of this Chapter.

4. *Problem.* The Court held in *Smith* that the party is "an agency of the state *in so far as it determines the participants in a primary election*" (emphasis added). Does it make sense that the party might be considered an agency of the state for some purposes but not for others? In what actions other than selecting the qualifications for primary voters might the party be a state actor? In what actions might it be merely a private actor? Consider whether a party should be considered

a state actor in carrying out the following functions:

    a.   Setting qualifications for party membership.

    b.   Setting qualifications for voting for party officials.

    c.   Setting qualifications for voting on the party platform.

    d.   Setting qualifications for voting in party elections to set any of the qualifications listed in (a)–(c).

    5.   Note 4 asks whether the party's status as a state actor might depend on the function it is performing. Might it depend also (or instead) on which provision of the Constitution it is alleged to have violated? Thus, might we be more inclined to treat a party as a state actor when it seeks to discriminate by race in violation of the Fourteenth or Fifteenth Amendment, as opposed to when it seeks to discriminate by viewpoint in alleged violation of the First Amendment (as incorporated through the Fourteenth Amendment for state parties)? We will return to this question when we consider *LaRouche v. Fowler*, 152 F.3d 974 (D.C. Cir. 1998) [p. 492], later in this Chapter.

TERRY v. ADAMS
Supreme Court of the United States
345 U.S. 461, 73 S. Ct. 809, 97 L. Ed. 1152 (1953)

MR. JUSTICE BLACK announced the judgment of the Court and an opinion in which MR. JUSTICE DOUGLAS and MR. JUSTICE BURTON join.

* * * This case raises questions concerning the constitutional power of a Texas county political organization called the Jaybird Democratic Association or Jaybird Party to exclude Negroes from its primaries on racial grounds. The Jaybirds deny that their racial exclusions violate the Fifteenth Amendment. They contend that the Amendment applies only to elections or primaries held under state regulation, that their association is not regulated by the state at all, and that it is not a political party, but a self-governing voluntary club. The District Court held the Jaybird racial discriminations invalid, and entered judgment accordingly. The Court of Appeals reversed, holding that there was no constitutional or congressional bar to the admitted discriminatory exclusion of Negroes, because Jaybird's primaries were not to any extent state controlled. We granted certiorari. * * *

The Jaybird Association or Party was organized in 1889. Its membership was then and always has been limited to white people; they are automatically members if their names appear on the official list of county voters. It has been run like other political parties, with an executive committee named from the county's voting precincts. Expenses of the party are paid by the assessment of candidates for office in its primaries. Candidates for county offices submit their names to the Jaybird Committee in accordance with the normal practice followed by regular political parties all over the country. Advertisements and posters proclaim that these candidates are running subject to the action of the Jaybird primary. While there is no legal compulsion on successful Jaybird candidates to enter Democratic primaries, they have nearly always done so, and, with few exceptions since 1889, have run and won without opposition in the Democratic primaries and the general elections that followed.[1] Thus, the party has been the dominant political group in the county since organization, having endorsed every county-wide official elected since 1889.

It is apparent that Jaybird activities follow a plan purposefully designed to exclude Negroes from voting and, at the same time, to escape the Fifteenth Amendment's command that the right of citizens to vote shall neither be denied nor abridged on account of race. These were the admitted party purposes according to the * * * testimony of the Jaybird's president[.] * * *

* * * The [Fifteenth] Amendment bans racial discrimination in voting by both state and nation. * * * Clearly the Amendment includes any election in which public issues are decided or public officials selected. Just as clearly, the Amendment excludes social or business clubs. And the statute shows the congressional mandate against discrimination whether the voting on public issues and officials is conducted in community, state or nation. Size is not a standard.

It is significant that precisely the same qualifications as those prescribed by Texas entitling electors to vote at county-operated primaries are adopted as the sole qualifications entitling electors to vote at the county-wide Jaybird primaries with a single proviso — Negroes are excluded. Everyone concedes that such a proviso in the county-operated primaries would be unconstitutional. The Jaybird Party thus brings into being and holds precisely the kind of election that the Fifteenth Amendment seeks to prevent. When it produces the equivalent of the prohibited election, the damage has been done.

For a state to permit such a duplication of its election processes is to permit a flagrant abuse of those processes to defeat the purposes of the Fifteenth Amendment. The use of the county-operated primary to ratify the result of the prohibited election merely compounds the offense. It violates the Fifteenth Amendment for a state, by such circumvention, to permit within its borders the use of any device that produces an equivalent of the prohibited election.

The only election that has counted in this Texas county for more than fifty years has been that held by the Jaybirds from which Negroes were excluded. The Democratic primary and the general election have become no more than the perfunctory ratifiers of the choice that has already been made in Jaybird elections from which Negroes have been excluded. It is immaterial that the state does not control that part of this elective process which it leaves for the Jaybirds to manage. The Jaybird primary has become an integral part, indeed the only effective part, of the elective process that determines who shall rule and govern in the county. The effect of the whole procedure, Jaybird primary plus Democratic primary plus general election, is to do precisely that which the Fifteenth Amendment forbids — strip Negroes of every vestige of influence in selecting the officials who control the local county matters that intimately touch the daily lives of citizens.

---

[1] * * * Here, Jaybird nominees are not put on any ballot as Jaybird nominees; they enter their own names as candidates in the Democratic primary. This distinction is not one of substance, but of form, and a statement of this Court in *Smith* v. *Allwright*, [321 U.S. 649, 661 (1944)] [p. 450], seems appropriate: *"Such a variation in the result from so slight a change in form* influences us to consider anew the legal validity of the distinction which has resulted in barring Negroes from participating in the nominations of candidates of the Democratic party in Texas." (Emphasis supplied.) * * * [Relocated. — Eds.]

We reverse the Court of Appeals' judgment reversing that of the District Court. * * * The case is remanded to the District Court to enter such orders and decrees as are necessary and proper * * *. In exercising this jurisdiction, the Court is left free to hold hearings to consider and determine what provisions are essential to afford Negro citizens of Fort Bend County full protection from future discriminatory Jaybird-Democratic-general election practices which deprive citizens of voting rights because of their color.

Reversed and remanded.

Mr. Justice Frankfurter. * * *

This case is for me by no means free of difficulty. Whenever the law draws a line between permissive and forbidden conduct, cases are bound to arise which are not obviously on one side or the other. * * * To find a denial or abridgment of the [Fifteenth-Amendment-]guaranteed voting right to colored citizens of Texas solely because they are colored, one must find that the State has had a hand in it.

The State, in these situations, must mean not private citizens, but those clothed with the authority and the influence which official position affords. The application of the prohibition of the Fifteenth Amendment to "any State" is translated by legal jargon to read "state action." This phrase gives rise to a false direction in that it implies some impressive machinery or deliberative conduct normally associated with what orators call a sovereign state. The vital requirement is State responsibility — that somewhere, somehow, to some extent, there be an infusion of conduct by officials, panoplied with State power, into any scheme by which colored citizens are denied voting rights merely because they are colored.

As the action of the entire white voting community, the Jaybird primary is, as a practical matter, the instrument of those few in this small county who are politically active — the officials of the local Democratic party and, we may assume, the elected officials of the county. As a matter of practical politics, those charged by State law with the duty of assuring all eligible voters an opportunity to participate in the selection of candidates at the primary — the county election officials who are normally leaders in their communities — participate by voting in the Jaybird primary. They join the white voting community in proceeding with elaborate formality, in almost all respects parallel to the procedures dictated by Texas law for the primary itself, to express their preferences in a wholly successful effort to withdraw significance from the State-prescribed primary, to subvert the operation of what is formally the law of the State for primaries in this county. * * *

The State of Texas has entered into a comprehensive scheme of regulation of political primaries, including procedures by which election officials shall be chosen. The county election officials are thus clothed with the authority of the State to secure observance of the State's interest in "fair methods and a fair expression" of preferences in the selection of nominees. If the Jaybird Association, although not a political party, is a device to defeat the law of Texas regulating primaries, and if the electoral officials, clothed with State power in the county, share in that subversion, they cannot divest themselves of the State authority and help as participants in the scheme. [H]ere, the county election officials aid in this subversion of the State's official scheme of which they are trustees, by helping as participants in the scheme.

This is not a case of occasional efforts to mass voting strength. Nor is this a case of boss control, whether crudely or subtly exercised. Nor is this a case of spontaneous efforts by citizens to influence votes or even continued efforts by a fraction of the electorate in support of good government. This is a case in which county election officials have participated in and condoned a continued effort effectively to exclude Negroes from voting. Though the action of the Association as such may not be proscribed by the Fifteenth Amendment, its role in the entire scheme to subvert the operation of the official primary brings it "within reach of the law. . . . [T]hey are bound together as the parts of a single plan. The plan may make the parts unlawful."

The State here devised a process for primary elections. The right of all citizens to share in it, and not to be excluded by unconstitutional bars, is emphasized by the fact that, in Texas, nomination in the Democratic primary is tantamount to election. The exclusion of the Negroes from meaningful participation in the only primary scheme set up by the State was not an accidental, unsought consequence of the exercise of civic rights by voters to make their common viewpoint count. It was the design, the very purpose, of this arrangement that the Jaybird primary in May exclude Negro participation in July. That it was the action in part of the election officials charged by Texas law with the fair administration of the primaries, brings it within the reach of the law. The officials made themselves party to means whereby the machinery with which they are entrusted does not discharge the functions for which it was designed.

It does not follow, however, that the relief granted below was proper. * * * [A] federal court cannot require that petitioners be allowed to vote in the Jaybird primary. * * * To say that Negroes should be allowed to vote in the Jaybird primary would be to say that the State is under a duty to see to it that Negroes may vote in that primary. We cannot tell the State that it must participate in and regulate this primary; we cannot tell the State what machinery it will use. But a court of equity can free the lawful political agency from the combination that subverts its capacity to function. What must be done is that this county be rid of the means by which the unlawful "usage" in this case asserts itself.

MR. JUSTICE CLARK, with whom THE CHIEF JUSTICE [VINSON], MR. JUSTICE REED, and MR. JUSTICE JACKSON join, concurring [in the judgment]. * * *

* * * Not every private club, association or league organized to influence public candidacies or political action must conform to the Constitution's restrictions on political parties. Certainly a large area of freedom permits peaceable assembly and concerted private action for political purposes to be exercised separately by white and colored citizens alike. More, however, is involved here.

The record discloses that the Jaybird Democratic Association operates as part and parcel of the Democratic Party, an organization existing under the auspices of Texas law. Each maintains the same basic qualification for membership: eligibility to vote under Texas law. Although the state Democratic Party in Texas, since *Smith* v. *Allwright*, no longer can restrict its membership to whites, the Jaybird

Democratic Association bars Negroes from its ranks. In May of each election year, it conducts a full-scale white primary in which each candidate campaigns for his candidacy subject to the action of that primary *and the Democratic primary of July*, linking the two primaries together. After gaining the Jaybird Democratic Association's endorsement, the announced winners after full publicity then file in the July Democratic primary. * * * Significantly, since 1889, the winners of the Jaybird Democratic Association balloting, with but a single exception shown by this record, ran unopposed and invariably won in the Democratic July primary and the subsequent general elections for county-wide office.

Quite evidently, the Jaybird Democratic Association operates as an auxiliary of the local Democratic Party organization, selecting its nominees and using its machinery for carrying out an admitted design of destroying the weight and effect of Negro ballots in Fort Bend County. To be sure, the Democratic primary and the general election are nominally open to the colored elector. But his must be an empty vote cast after the real decisions are made. And because the Jaybird-indorsed nominee meets no opposition in the Democratic primary, the Negro minority's vote is nullified at the sole stage of the local political process where the bargaining and interplay of rival political forces would make it count.

The Jaybird Democratic Association device, as a result, strikes to the core of the electoral process in Fort Bend County. Whether viewed as a separate political organization or as an adjunct of the local Democratic Party, the Jaybird Democratic Association is the decisive power in the county's recognized electoral process. Over the years, its balloting has emerged as the locus of effective political choice. * * * [W]hen a state structures its electoral apparatus in a form which devolves upon a political organization the uncontested choice of public officials, that organization itself, in whatever disguise, takes on those attributes of government which draw the Constitution's safeguards in play.

In sum, we believe that the activities of the Jaybird Democratic Association fall within the broad principle laid down in *Smith* v. *Allwright*. For that reason we join the judgment of the Court.

MR. JUSTICE MINTON, dissenting.

I am not concerned in the least as to what happens to the Jaybirds or their unworthy scheme. I am concerned about what this Court says is "state action" within the meaning of the Fifteenth Amendment to the Constitution. For, after all, this Court has power to redress a wrong under that Amendment only if the wrong is done by the State. * * *

As I understand MR. JUSTICE BLACK's opinion, he would have this Court redress the wrong even if it was individual action alone. I can understand that praiseworthy position, but it seems to me it is not in accord with the Constitution. State action must be shown.

MR. JUSTICE FRANKFURTER recognizes that it must be state action, but he seems to think it is enough to constitute state action if a state official participates in the Jaybird primary. That I cannot follow. For it seems clear to me that everything done by a person who is an official is not done officially, and as a representative of the

State. However, I find nothing in this record that shows the state or county officials participating in the Jaybird primary.

Mr. Justice Clark seems to recognize that state action must be shown. He finds state action in assumption, not in facts. This record will be searched in vain for one iota of state action sufficient to support an anemic inference that the Jaybird Association is in any way associated with, or forms a part of or cooperates in any manner with, the Democratic Party of the County or State, or with the State. It calls itself the Jaybird Democratic Association because its interest is only in the candidates of the Democratic Party in the county, a position understandable in Texas. * * *

Neither is there any more evidence that the Jaybird Association avails itself of or conforms in any manner to any law of the State of Texas [regulating political parties]. * * *

However, its action is not forbidden by the law of the State of Texas. Does such failure of the State to act to prevent individuals from doing what they have the right as individuals to do amount to state action? I venture the opinion it does not. * * *

[T]he Jaybird Association * * * neither files, certifies, nor supplies anything for the primary or election. The winner of the poll in the Jaybird Association contest files in the Democratic primary, where he may and sometimes has received opposition, and successful opposition, in precinct contests for County Commissioner, Justice of the Peace, and Constable. There is no rule of the Jaybird Association that requires the successful party in its poll to file in the Democratic primary or elsewhere. It is all individual, voluntary action. Neither the State nor the Democratic Party avails itself of the action of or cooperates in any manner with the Jaybird Association. * * *

* * * What the Jaybird Association did here was to conduct as individuals, separate and apart from the Democratic Party or the State, a straw vote as to who should receive the Association's endorsement for county and precinct offices. It has been successful in seeing that those who receive its endorsement are nominated and elected. That is true of concerted action by any group. In numbers there is strength. In organization there is effectiveness. * * *

I do not understand that concerted action of individuals which is successful somehow becomes state action. However, the candidates endorsed by the Jaybird Association have several times been defeated in primaries and elections. Usually, but not always, since 1938, only the Jaybird-endorsed candidate has been on the Democratic official ballot in the County.

In the instant case, the State of Texas has provided for elections and primaries. This is separate and apart and wholly unrelated to the Jaybird Association's activities. Its activities are confined to one County where a group of citizens have appointed themselves the censors of those who would run for public offices. Apparently, so far they have succeeded in convincing the voters of this County in most instances that their supported candidates should win. This seems to differ very little from situations common in many other places far north of the Mason-Dixon line, such as areas where a candidate must obtain the approval of a religious group. In other localities, candidates are carefully selected by both parties to give proper weight to Jew, Protestant, and Catholic, and certain posts are considered the sole possession of certain ethnic groups. The propriety of these practices is something the courts sensibly have left to the good or bad judgment of the electorate. It must be recognized that elections and other public business are influenced by all sorts of pressures from carefully organized groups. We have pressure from labor unions, from the National Association of Manufacturers, from the Silver Shirts, from the National Association for the Advancement of Colored People, from the Ku Klux Klan, and others. Far from the activities of these groups being properly labeled as state action, under either the Fourteenth or the Fifteenth Amendment, they are to be considered as attempts to influence or obtain state action.

The courts do not normally pass upon these pressure groups, whether their causes are good or bad, highly successful or only so-so. It is difficult for me to see how this Jaybird Association is anything but such a pressure group. Apparently it is believed in by enough people in Fort Bend County to obtain a majority of the votes for its approved candidates. This differs little from the situation in many parts of the "Bible Belt" where a church stamp of approval or that of the Anti-Saloon League must be put on any candidate who does not want to lose the election.

The State of Texas, in its elections and primaries, takes no cognizance of this Jaybird Association. The State treats its decisions apparently with the same disdain as it would the approval or condemnation of judicial candidates by a bar association poll of its members.

In this case, the majority have found that this pressure group's work does constitute state action. The basis of this conclusion is rather difficult to ascertain. Apparently it derives mainly from a dislike of the goals of the Jaybird Association. I share that dislike. I fail to see how it makes state action. I would affirm.

Notes and Questions

1.   With no opinion commanding a majority of the Justices, making sense of the Court's decision in *Terry* requires one to assess the views of each individual Justice. What divided the eight Justices who voted to reverse? What test does each opinion employ to determine whether the Jaybirds' discrimination violated the Fifteenth Amendment?

2.   During the Term when *Terry* was argued and decided, future-Chief Justice William Rehnquist was one of Justice Jackson's law clerks. Consider the following memorandum that Rehnquist wrote to Jackson concerning the various draft opinions in *Terry*:

Re: Opinions of Black and FF in Terry v. Adams

If you are going to dissent, I should think you might combine the ideas which you expressed last week with an attack on the reasoning of the two "majority opinions."

(1) Black — simply assumes the whole point in issue. The 15th Amendment requires state action, and certainly Congress under its power to "enforce" the amendment cannot drastically enlarge its scope. Yet the Black opinion utterly fails to face the problem of state

action. He says rather that the effect of the Fifteenth Amendment is to prevent the states from discriminating against Negroes in official elections; the result here is to accomplish that result "by indirection;" therefore that result is bad. * * * Surely the justices of this Court do not sit here to ruthlessly frustrate results which they consider undesirable, regardless of the wording of the constitution.

(2) FF — places the weight of the decision on the rather skimpy support to be found in his discovery of "state action": the county election officials voted in the Jaybird primary. In the first place, they voted not in their capacity as election officials, but as private citizens. Secondly, it was not their voting which effected the discrimination; it was the previously adopted rules, with which they may have had nothing to do. Thirdly, if this is the vice why not simply enjoin the officials from voting? When one must strain this hard to reach a result, the chances are that something is the matter with the result * * *.

(3) Your ideas — the constitution does not prevent the majority from banding together, nor does it attaint success in the effort. It is about time the Court faced the fact that the white people in the South don't like the colored people; the constitution restrains them from effecting this dislike thru state action, but it most assuredly did not appoint the Court as a sociological watchdog to rear up every time private discrimination raises its admittedly ugly head. To the extent that this decision advances the frontier of state action and "social gain", it pushes back the frontier of freedom of association and majority rule. Liberals should be the first to realize, after the past twenty years, that it does not do to push blindly through towards one constitutional goal without paying attention to other equally desirable values that are being trampled on in the process.

This is a position that I am sure ought to be stated; but if stated by Vinson, Minton, or Reed it just won't sound the same way as if you state it.

whr

William H. Rehnquist memo Re: Opinions of Black and Frankfurter, Robert Jackson Papers, Box 179, Library of Congress Manuscript Division (typographical errors corrected). Do you agree with the future Chief Justice's criticisms of Justice Black's and Justice Frankfurter's positions? Do you agree that an expansive interpretation of state action threatens associational freedoms? *Cf.* Herbert Wechsler, *Toward Neutral Principles of Constitutional Law*, 73 HARV. L. REV. 1, 33 (1959) (criticizing *Brown v. Board of Education*, 347 U.S. 483 (1954), as undermining whites' freedom not to associate with blacks).

3.   What differentiated the Jaybirds from any other influential interest group? Do you agree with Justice Clark that the "decisive power" of the Jaybirds made the association a state actor? Under this view, the state-action question seems intermingled with the substantive right being protected. For example, Justice Clark noted that the Jaybird primary allowed a black person's vote to be "nullified at the

sole stage of the local political process where the bargaining and interplay of rival political forces would make it count." Thus, in Justice Clark's view (as well as Justice Black's), state-action doctrine should not be interpreted to permit the purposes of the Fifteenth Amendment to be undermined. Or do you agree with Justice Minton that the actions of an interest group should not "somehow become[] state action" simply because of its "success[]"?

4. What did Justice Black mean when he concludes that states must not "permit" the "duplication of its election processes"? If the state had no role in creating the duplicative process, why would the Fifteenth Amendment require its abolishment? What could the state have done without infringing on the Jaybirds' First Amendment rights?

5. Does *Terry* have any applicability in a jurisdiction with competitive general elections? That is, if the Jaybirds exerted substantial influence over the nomination of Democrats, but if Republicans presented a viable alternative in the general election, would the Jaybirds still be state actors?

6. *Problem.* Bluecollarville is a city of 50,000 people. Acme, Inc., is by far the biggest employer in the community, with virtually every Bluecollarville family having at least one member employed at the local plant. The plant is unionized, and the city council has been dominated by Democratic candidates approved by the local chapter of the union representing the workers at the plant. In fact, in the last fifty years, no candidate who has failed to win the endorsement of the union has won a seat on the council. The union makes its endorsement decisions by secret ballot after debating the candidates at a regular union meeting approximately one month before the Democratic primary. Should the union be considered a state actor when it restricts participation in its meetings and votes to union members? Would it make any difference if the union's membership policies were racially discriminatory? What if they discriminated on another ground, such as gender, age, or political viewpoint?

7. After the remand to the district court, blacks were permitted to vote in the Jaybird primary, and influenced the outcomes of some races in 1954, 1956, and 1958. Was it appropriate for the court to order the integration of the association? No longer able to serve its purpose once integrated, the primary was discontinued in 1959. *See* Pauline Yelderman, The Jaybird Democratic Association of Fort Bend County (1979).

8. Are party *conventions* equivalent to primaries for purposes of state action? In *Morse v. Republican Party of Virginia*, 517 U.S. 186 (1996), plaintiffs challenged the fee that the Party charged for taking part in the convention that would select the Republican nominee for United States Senator. All voters were permitted to participate as delegates to the convention, provided that they paid a registration fee of $35 or $45 (depending on the date of registration) and declared loyalty to the Party. In determining that the fee was subject to § 5 of the Voting Rights Act (constitutional claims were brought in the district court but were not at issue on appeal), the Court concluded that the Party qualified as a "State or political subdivision" within the meaning of the Act. The Court was severely split, however, and it is difficult to know what conclusions to draw from *Morse* about state action.

Justice Stevens, writing also for Justice Ginsburg, relied on the White Primary Cases and equated the "State or political subdivision" language with the Fifteenth Amendment's state-action requirement. Accordingly, for those two Justices, requiring a fee for participating in a convention would constitute action of the state, just as would the imposition of a poll tax or other discrimination in admitting voters to a primary election. *See id.* at 214–15 (opinion of Stevens, J.).

Justice Breyer, in an opinion expressing the views of Justices O'Connor and Souter, as well as his own, agreed with Justice Stevens that the language of the Voting Rights Act encompassed the action of the Party in charging the fee. Justice Breyer cautioned that parties may have First Amendment rights to be free from governmental regulation as to some aspects of "the workings of a political party convention," *id.* at 239 (Breyer, J., concurring in the judgment), but concluded that the fee in this particular case qualified as state action because the party was open to any voter paying the fee, and therefore "resembles a primary about as closely as one could imagine." *Id.* at 238.

The four dissenting Justices concluded that the Party was not a "State or political subdivision." Justice Kennedy would have held that the statutory language did not include the party, but was unwilling to discuss whether in his view the Constitution's state-action requirement reached further than the VRA, *see id.* at 250 (Kennedy, J., dissenting). Justice Thomas, however, speaking for himself as well as Chief Justice Rehnquist and Justice Scalia, argued that the Party was not a state actor under the Constitution. *See id.* at 266–76 (Thomas, J., dissenting). Justice Thomas distinguished *Terry* by noting that in that case "the Jaybird primary was the *de facto* general election and * * * Texas consciously permitted it to serve as such." *Id.* at 269. In *Morse*, by contrast, the state did not use the Republicans' convention to subvert constitutional requirements, and the Republican Party in no way dominated the state in the manner that the Democratic Party dominated Texas at the time of the White Primary Cases. *See id.* at 269–70.

Are you convinced by Justice Thomas's attempt to distinguish *Terry*? Is there any limiting principle in the analyses of Justice Stevens and Justice Breyer that would leave some party operations free of constitutional constraints?

9. *Problem.* Rule 6(C) of the Democratic Party's rules for selecting delegates to its National Convention provides that "[s]tate Delegate Selection Plans shall provide for equal division between delegate men and delegate women and alternate men and alternate women within the state's entire convention delegation." The United States Attorney for the District of West Dakota brings a declaratory-judgment action to bar the party from enforcing Rule 6(C), arguing that the rule violates the Equal Protection Clause. The national and state parties defend on the ground that they are not state actors, and therefore cannot violate the Equal Protection Clause. What result? *Cf. O'Brien v. Brown*, 409 U.S. 1, 5 (1972).

10. *Problem.* A group of Republicans favoring gay rights seeks to publicize its views by leasing a booth at the state party convention and taking out an advertisement in the convention program. The Party, however, refuses to permit the group to take either action because of the Party's opposition to the group's message. Is the Party violating the Constitution? (You may assume that such viewpoint-based action by the state would violate the First Amendment.) *See Republican Party of*

Texas v. Dietz, 940 S.W.2d 86 (Tex. 1997).

11.   *Problem.* New Jersey State Senator Alene Ammond was elected as a Democrat, but "the Terror of Trenton" was excluded from the Democratic Caucus in retaliation for public criticisms she made about the Caucus and its members. Does the exclusion violate the Constitution? Would the result change if Ammond were excluded because of her race? *See Ammond v. McGahn*, 390 F. Supp. 655 (D.N.J. 1975), *rev'd on other grounds* 532 F.2d 325 (3d Cir. 1976). *See also Gewertz v. Jackman*, 467 F. Supp. 1047 (D.N.J. 1979) (denying a preliminary injunction where a state legislator complained that he was removed from a committee in retaliation for his opposition to the party leadership, but stating in dicta that there was no constitutional barrier to granting such an injunction in a case where the plaintiff were likely to succeed on the merits). *Cf. Vander Jagt v. O'Neill*, 699 F.2d 1166 (D.C. Cir. 1983) (refusing to enjoin Congress to allocate committee seats proportionally by party); *Davids v. Akers*, 549 F.2d 120 (9th Cir. 1977) (same as applied to a state legislature).

C.   ASSOCIATIONAL RIGHTS OF PARTIES

An association's right to define itself extends not only to creating and advancing a mission, but also to establishing qualifications for taking part in its activities. The participation of those who do not share the association's goals can hinder its achievement of those goals and interfere with its ability to send a clear message concerning what its goals are. *See Boy Scouts of America v. Dale*, 530 U.S. 640, 653–59 (2000); *Hurley v. Irish-American Gay, Lesbian and Bisexual Group of Boston, Inc.*, 515 U.S. 557, 570, 580–81 (1995). On the other hand, as the state-action materials illustrated, parties' central role in the electoral process means that individuals excluded from participation in parties may be excluded from the most meaningful and consequential political debates and decisions.

The following materials concern challenges to state regulation of parties, and cases are presented in chronological order. This sequencing allows one more easily to track the Justices' developing approaches to questions of what a political party is and who should be able to speak on its behalf. Because the issues presented in each of the cases may appear only slightly different from each other, however, the doctrinal rules that result from these cases may appear confusing. In reading the cases, therefore, separate in your mind two types of challenges. In the first type, the state regulation has the effect of limiting the party's associations. Thus, in *Tashjian v. Republican Party of Connecticut*, 479 U.S. 208 (1986) [p. 449], and *Clingman v. Beaver*, 544 U.S. 581 (2005) [p. 470], the parties wished to allow more people to vote in their primaries than state law allowed.

In the second type of challenge, the state regulation expands the party's association beyond those with whom the party would prefer to associate. Thus, in *Democratic Party of the United States v. Wisconsin ex rel. La Follette*, 450 U.S. 107 (1981) [p. 442], *California Democratic Party v. Jones*, 530 U.S. 567 (2000) [p. 460], and *Washington State Grange v. Washington State Republican Party*, 552 U.S. 442 (2008) [p. 481], the parties wished to limit the class of persons eligible to vote in their primaries to a smaller group than provided for by state law. (Where both state law and the parties wish to exclude a non-member from voting in a primary, such individual's right to vote does not extend to such an election. *See Nader v. Schaffer*, 417 F. Supp. 837 (D. Conn.), *summarily aff'd*, 429 U.S. 989 (1976).)

Whether a party challenges a state law because it invites the participation of too many or too few primary voters, the basis for the challenge is the same. The parties claim that their right of association encompasses a right of self-definition, which is itself dependent on the ability to determine the persons with whom the party will associate. *See, e.g., Democratic Party*, 450 U.S. at 122.[c] As you read these cases, consider whether that claim is weaker or stronger depending on whether the party is attempting to expand or contract its associations, and whether the justifications for interfering with the party's choices are sufficiently weighty as to overcome First Amendment objections.

Finally, also bear in mind the question of which bodies should be permitted to exercise the rights of the party. We might think of parties as distinct entities, but the parties themselves, like business corporations, may take actions only through humans. The class of persons making up "the party" is the entire membership (*cf. Nixon v. Condon*, 286 U.S. 73, 84 (1932), discussed at page 445, *supra*), but the entire membership is unlikely to be able to make many decisions concerning the way the party operates. Rather, decisions are often made by committees of the party, within the confines of state law created in large part by party members who hold office in government. But the committees and office-holders may not represent accurately the preferences of the party membership. Be wary, therefore, when you encounter claims that a certain law interferes with "the party's" rights.

DEMOCRATIC PARTY OF THE UNITED STATES v. WISCONSIN EX REL. LA FOLLETTE
Supreme Court of the United States
450 U.S. 107, 101 S. Ct. 1010, 67 L. Ed. 2d 82 (1981)

JUSTICE STEWART delivered the opinion of the Court [in which CHIEF JUSTICE BURGER, JUSTICE BRENNAN, JUSTICE WHITE, JUSTICE MARSHALL, and JUSTICE STEVENS join].

The charter of the appellant Democratic Party of the United States (National Party) provides that delegates to its National Convention shall be chosen through procedures in which only Democrats can participate. * * * The question on this appeal is whether Wisconsin may successfully insist that its delegates to the Convention be seated, even though those delegates are chosen through a process that includes a binding state preference primary election in which voters do not declare their party affiliation. * * *

Rule 2A of the Democratic Selection Rules for the 1980 National Convention states: "Participation in the delegate selection process in primaries or caucuses shall be restricted to Democratic voters only who publicly declare their party preference and have that preference publicly recorded." Under National Party rules, the "delegate selection process" includes any procedure by which delegates to

---

[c] As we will see in *Eu v. San Francisco County Democratic Central Committee*, 489 U.S. 214 (1989) [p. 478], parties' right of self-definition extends beyond controlling their membership to controlling their own internal procedures and deliberations as well.

the Convention are bound to vote for the nomination of particular candidates.

The election laws of Wisconsin allow non-Democrats — including members of other parties and independents — to vote in the Democratic primary without regard to party affiliation and without requiring a public declaration of party preference. The voters in Wisconsin's "open" primary express their choice among Presidential candidates for the Democratic Party's nomination; they do not vote for delegates to the National Convention. Delegates to the National Convention are chosen separately, after the primary, at caucuses of persons who have stated their affiliation with the Party. But these delegates, under Wisconsin law, are bound to vote at the National Convention in accord with the results of the open primary election. Accordingly, while Wisconsin's open Presidential preference primary does not itself violate National Party rules, the State's mandate that the results of the primary shall determine the allocation of votes cast by the State's delegates at the National Convention does.

In May, 1979, the Democratic Party of Wisconsin (State Party) submitted to the Compliance Review Commission of the National Party its plan for selecting delegates to the 1980 National Convention. The plan incorporated the provisions of the State's open primary laws, and, as a result, the Commission disapproved it as violating Rule 2A. Since compliance with Rule 2A was a condition of participation at the Convention, for which no exception could be made, the National Party indicated that Wisconsin delegates who were bound to vote according to the results of the open primary would not be seated.

The State Attorney General then brought an original action in the Wisconsin Supreme Court[, which] entered a judgment declaring that the State's system of selecting delegates to the Democratic National Convention is constitutional and binding on the appellants. * * * The National Party and the Democratic National Committee then brought this appeal[.] * * *

Rule 2A can be traced to efforts of the National Party to study and reform its nominating procedures and internal structure after the 1968 Democratic National Convention.[14] The Convention, the Party's highest governing authority, directed the Democratic National Committee (DNC) to establish a Commission on Party Structure and Delegate Selection (McGovern/Fraser Commission). This Commission concluded that a major problem faced by the Party was that rank-and-file Party members had been underrepresented at its Convention, and * * * expressed the concern that "a full opportunity for all Democrats to participate is diluted if members of other political parties are allowed to participate in the selection of delegates to the Democratic National Convention."

* * * In 1974, the National Party adopted its charter[, according to which] "The National Convention shall be composed of delegates who are chosen through processes which * * * *restrict participation to Democrats only. . . .* " (emphasis added).

---

[14] Wisconsin's open primary system * * * was adopted in 1903, and * * * is employed in Wisconsin not only to express preference for Presidential candidates, but to choose "partisan . . . state and local candidates . . . and an extensive array of nonpartisan officers" as well. * * *

Rule 2A took its present form in 1976. Consistent with the charter, it restricted participation in the delegate selection process in primaries or caucuses to "Democratic voters only who publicly declare their party preference and have that preference publicly recorded." But the 1976 Delegate Selection Rules allowed for an exemption from any rule, including Rule 2A, that was inconsistent with state law if the state party was unable to secure changes in the law. * * *

[A] study, assessing the Wisconsin Democratic primaries from 1964 to 1972, found that crossover voters comprised 26% to 34% of the primary voters; that the voting patterns of crossover voters differed significantly from those of participants who identified themselves as Democrats; and that crossover voters altered the composition of the delegate slate chosen from Wisconsin.[18] [Relying in part on this study, another commission established by the Party in 1975] specifically recommended that "participation in the delegate selection process in primaries or caucuses . . . be restricted to Democratic voters only who publicly declare their party preference and have that preference publicly recorded." Accordingly, the text of Rule 2A was retained, but a new Rule, 2B, was added, prohibiting any exemptions from Rule 2A.

The question in this case is not whether Wisconsin may conduct an open primary election if it chooses to do so, or whether the National Party may require Wisconsin to limit its primary election to publicly declared Democrats. Rather, the question is whether, once Wisconsin has opened its Democratic Presidential preference primary to voters who do not publicly declare their party affiliation, it may then bind the National Party to honor the binding primary results, even though those results were reached in a manner contrary to National Party rules.

The Wisconsin Supreme Court considered the question before it to be the constitutionality of the "open" feature of the state primary election law, as such. Concluding that the open primary serves compelling state interests by encouraging voter participation, the court held the state open primary constitutionally valid. Upon this issue, the Wisconsin Supreme Court may well be correct. In any event, there is no need to question its conclusion here. For the rules of the National Party do not challenge the authority of a State to conduct an open primary, so long as it is not binding on the National Party Convention. The issue is whether the State may compel the National Party to seat a delegation chosen in a way that violates the rules of the Party. * * *

"[T]he National Democratic Party and its adherents enjoy a constitutionally protected right of political association." This First Amendment freedom to gather in association for the purpose of advancing shared beliefs is protected by the Fourteenth Amendment from infringement by any State. And the freedom to associate for the "common advancement of political beliefs" necessarily presupposes the freedom to identify the people who constitute the association, and to limit the association to those people only. * * *

Here, the members of the National Party, speaking through their rules, chose to define their associational rights by limiting those who could participate in the

---

[18] A crossover primary is one that permits nonadherents of a party to "cross over" and vote in that party's primary.

processes leading to the selection of delegates to their National Convention. On several occasions, this Court has recognized that the inclusion of persons unaffiliated with a political party may seriously distort its collective decisions — thus impairing the party's essential functions — and that political parties may accordingly protect themselves "from intrusion by those with adverse political principles."[23] * * *

The State argues that its law places only a minor burden on the National Party. The National Party argues that the burden is substantial, because it prevents the Party from "screen[ing] out those whose affiliation is . . . slight, tenuous, or fleeting," and that such screening is essential to build a more effective and responsible Party. But it is not for the courts to mediate the merits of this dispute. For even if the State were correct,[25] a State, or a court, may not constitutionally substitute its own judgment for that of the Party. A political party's choice among the various ways of determining the makeup of a State's delegation to the party's national convention is protected by the Constitution. And as is true of all expressions of First Amendment freedoms, the courts may not interfere on the ground that they view a particular expression as unwise or irrational.

We must consider, finally, whether the State has compelling interests that justify the imposition of its will upon the appellants. * * * The State asserts a compelling interest in preserving the overall integrity of the electoral process, providing secrecy of the ballot, increasing voter participation in primaries, and preventing harassment of voters. But all those interests go to the conduct of the Presidential preference primary — not to the imposition of voting requirements upon those who, in a separate process, are eventually selected as delegates. Therefore, the interests advanced by the State do not justify its substantial intrusion into the associational freedom of members of the National Party.

The State has a substantial interest in the manner in which its elections are conducted, and the National Party has a substantial interest in the manner in which the delegates to its National Convention are selected. But these interests are not incompatible, and, to the limited extent they clash in this case, both interests can be preserved. The National Party rules do not forbid Wisconsin to conduct an open primary. But if Wisconsin does open its primary, it cannot require that Wisconsin delegates to the National Party Convention vote there in accordance with the primary results if to do so would violate Party rules. Since the Wisconsin Supreme Court has declared that the National Party cannot disqualify delegates who are bound to vote in accordance with the results of the Wisconsin open primary, its judgment is reversed.

---

[23] The extent to which "raiding" is a motivation of Wisconsin voters matters not. * * * The concern of the National Party is, rather, with crossover voters in general, regardless of their motivation.

[25] It may be the case, of course, that the public avowal of party affiliation required by Rule 2A provides no more assurance of party loyalty than does Wisconsin's requirement that a person vote in no more than one party's primary. But the stringency, and wisdom, of membership requirements is for the association and its members to decide — not the courts — so long as those requirements are otherwise constitutionally permissible.

It so ordered.

JUSTICE POWELL, with whom JUSTICE BLACKMUN and JUSTICE REHNQUIST join, dissenting.

* * * The question in this case is whether, in light of the National Party's rule that only publicly declared Democrats may have a voice in the nomination process, Wisconsin's open primary law infringes the National Party's First Amendment rights of association. Because I believe that this law does not impose a substantial burden on the associational freedom of the National Party, and actually promotes the free political activity of the citizens of Wisconsin, I dissent. * * *

* * * All that Wisconsin has done is to require the major parties to allow voters to affiliate with them — for the limited purpose of participation in a primary — *secretly*, in the privacy of the voting booth.[2] The Democrats remain free to require public affiliation from anyone wishing any greater degree of participation in party affairs. * * *

In evaluating the constitutional significance of this relatively minimal state regulation of party membership requirements, I am unwilling — at least in the context of a claim by one of the two major political parties — to conclude that every conflict between state law and party rules concerning participation in the nomination process creates a burden on associational rights. Instead, I would look closely at the nature of the intrusion, in light of the nature of the association involved, to see whether we are presented with a real limitation on First Amendment freedoms.

* * * If appellant National Party were an organization with a particular ideological orientation or political mission, perhaps this regulation would present a different question. In such a case, the state law might well open the organization to participation by persons with incompatible beliefs, and interfere with the associational rights of its founders.

The Democratic Party, however, is not organized around the achievement of defined ideological goals. Instead, the major parties in this country "have been characterized by a fluidity and overlap of philosophy and membership." *Rosario* v. *Rockefeller*, 410 U.S. 752, 769 (1973) (POWELL, J., dissenting). It can hardly be denied that this Party generally has been composed of various elements reflecting most of the American political spectrum.[4] The Party does take positions on public

---

[2] It is not fully accurate to say, as the Court does, that the "election laws of Wisconsin allow non-Democrats — including members of other parties and independents — to vote in the Democratic primary." The Wisconsin statute [allows voters] "* * * to express their preference for the person to be the presidential candidate *of their party*" (emphasis added). Thus, the act of voting in the Democratic primary fairly can be described as an act of affiliation with the Democratic Party. The real issue in this case is whether the Party has the right to decide that only publicly affiliated voters may participate.

The situation might be different in those States with "blanket" primaries — *i.e.*, those where voters are allowed to participate in the primaries of more than one party on a single occasion, selecting the primary they wish to vote in with respect to each individual elective office.

[4] The Charter of the National Democratic Party states that it is "open to all who desire to support the party and . . . be known as Democrats."

This perception need not be taken as a criticism of the American party structure. The major parties have played a key role in forming coalitions and creating consensus on national issues. "Broad-based

issues, but these positions vary from time to time, and there never has been a serious effort to establish for the Party a monolithic ideological identity by excluding all those with differing views. As a result, it is hard to see what the Democratic Party has to fear from an open primary plan. Wisconsin's law may influence to some extent the outcome of a primary contest by allowing participation by voters who are unwilling to affiliate with the Party publicly. It is unlikely, however, that this influence will produce a delegation with preferences that differ from those represented by a substantial number of delegates from other parts of the country. Moreover, it seems reasonable to conclude that, insofar as the major parties do have ideological identities, an open primary merely allows relatively independent voters to cast their lot with the party that speaks to their present concerns. By attracting participation by relatively independent-minded voters, the Wisconsin plan arguably may enlarge the support for a party at the general election. * * *

In sum, I would hold that the National Party has failed to make a sufficient showing of a burden on its associational rights.[9] * * *

Notes and Questions

1. If the rules of the Democratic Party had forbidden open primaries altogether, could the state demand that one be held? What if the party had decided to choose all its delegates by caucuses? Could the state require the party to hold some kind of primary? Would it make a difference if the party wanted to hold a primary, and the state demanded caucuses? *See American Party of Texas v. White*, 415 U.S. 767, 781 (1974) (stating that it was "too plain for argument" that states could require parties to select their nominees through either primaries or conventions, as the states chose). Could *Congress* require states to use primaries to select presidential nominees? *See* Richard L. Hasen, *"Too Plain for Argument?": The Uncertain Congressional Power to Require Parties to Choose Presidential Nominees Through Direct and Equal Primaries*, 102 Nw. U. L. Rev. 2009 (2008).

2. The Court stated that Wisconsin's allegedly compelling interests "go to the conduct of the Presidential preference primary," rather than to the requirement that delegates vote in accordance with the primary results. But why would the state bother to hold an open primary (and why would voters bother to participate) if the party was entitled to disregard the results?

3. Should it matter that the Democratic Party is "relatively nonideological"? Is it? Do you think Justice Powell's view of the Party was a product of his background or of the behavior and commitments of the Party? Justice Powell was a Richmond, Virginia, Democrat, but politically moderate and nominated to the Court by a

---

political parties supply an essential coherence and flexibility to the American political scene. They serve as coalitions of different interests that combine to seek national goals." * * *

[9] Of course, the National Party could decide that it no longer wishes to be a relatively nonideological party, but it has not done so. Such a change might call into question the institutionalized status achieved by the two major parties in state and federal law. * * * Arguably, the special status of the major parties is an additional factor favoring state regulation of the electoral process even in the face of a claim by such a party that this regulation has interfered with its First Amendment rights.

Republican President (Nixon) and confirmed by a Democratic Senate. (Then-Justice Rehnquist, however, who joined Justice Powell's opinion, was a lifelong conservative Republican.) Around the time of Justice Powell's nomination and of this case, the Democratic Party contained elements as disparate as George McGovern and James Eastland. Today, however, most observers believe the two major parties are much more ideologically homogenous. Should such a shift in ideological orientation affect the constitutionality of state laws mandating open primaries?

4.   As noted in *Democratic Party*, the Party's rule excluding non-Democrats was prompted by the McGovern/Fraser Commission, which the Party formed after the tumultuous 1968 Democratic National Convention. The Commission found that the participation of non-Democrats in the nominating process lessened Democrats' influence in choosing the nominees of their own party, and led to the selection of nominees who were more moderate than the ones who would have been chosen by Democrats alone. Both Senator George McGovern and Representative Donald Fraser, the chairmen of the Commission, were quite liberal — which was to be expected because the Commission's members were chosen by the chairman of the Democratic National Committee. Not coincidentally, the rules championed by the Commission favored ideologically extreme candidates, and McGovern himself won the Democratic nomination for President in 1972, the first year under the new rules. Ideologically extreme candidates are at a disadvantage in the general election, however, as McGovern and the Democrats found out that fall when Richard Nixon won reelection by capturing 49 out of 50 states.

5.   *Problem.* Recall from the Problem in Note 9 on page 464 that Rule 6(C) of the Democratic Party's rules for selecting delegates provides that "[s]tate Delegate Selection Plans shall provide for equal division between delegate men and delegate women and alternate men and alternate women within the state's entire convention delegation." East Dakota state law prohibits sex-based quotas, and the attorney general brings a declaratory-judgment action to ensure that the Party complies with the law. The Party argues that it has the right under the First Amendment to select delegates in the manner it chooses. Further, it argues, the tenets of the Democratic Party evince a commitment to gender equality such that Rule 6(C) is an important reflection of the Party's ideology. Does the First Amendment require the state to exempt the Party from the anti-quota law? *See Bachur v. Democratic National Party*, 836 F.2d 837 (4th Cir. 1987); *cf. O'Brien v. Brown*, 409 U.S. 1, 5 (1972).

6.   *Problem.* The Republican Party wishes to allocate delegates to its national convention not merely on the basis of state populations, but with "victory bonuses" that provide additional delegates to states voting Republican in past elections. Will the Party be able successfully to raise a First Amendment defense against a one-person, one-vote challenge? *See Ripon Society, Inc. v. National Republican Party*, 525 F.2d 567 (D.C. Cir. 1975) (en banc).

TASHJIAN v. REPUBLICAN PARTY OF CONNECTICUT
Supreme Court of the United States
479 U.S. 208, 107 S. Ct. 544, 93 L. Ed. 2d 514 (1986)

JUSTICE MARSHALL delivered the opinion of the Court [in which JUSTICE BRENNAN, JUSTICE WHITE, JUSTICE BLACKMUN, and JUSTICE POWELL join].

Appellee Republican Party of the State of Connecticut in 1984 adopted a Party rule which permits independent voters — registered voters not affiliated with any political party — to vote in Republican primaries for federal and statewide offices. Appellant Julia Tashjian, the Secretary of the State of Connecticut, is charged with the administration of the State's election statutes, which include a provision requiring voters in any party primary to be registered members of that party. Conn. Gen. Stat. § 9-431. Appellees, who in addition to the Party include the Party's federal officeholders and the Party's state chairman, challenged this eligibility provision on the ground that it deprives the Party of its First Amendment right to enter into political association with individuals of its own choosing. The District Court granted summary judgment in favor of appellees. The Court of Appeals affirmed. We noted probable jurisdiction, and now affirm. * * *

The Party here contends that § 9-431 impermissibly burdens the right of its members to determine for themselves with whom they will associate, and whose support they will seek, in their quest for political success. The Party's attempt to broaden the base of public participation in and support for its activities is conduct undeniably central to the exercise of the right of association. As we have said, the freedom to join together in furtherance of common political beliefs "necessarily presupposes the freedom to identify the people who constitute the association." *Democratic Party of United States* v. *Wisconsin ex rel. La Follette*, 450 U.S. 107, 122 (1981) [p. 442].

A major state political party necessarily includes individuals playing a broad spectrum of roles in the organization's activities. Some of the Party's members devote substantial portions of their lives to furthering its political and organizational goals, others provide substantial financial support, while still others limit their participation to casting their votes for some or all of the Party's candidates. Considered from the standpoint of the Party itself, the act of formal enrollment or public affiliation with the Party is merely one element in the continuum of participation in Party affairs, and need not be in any sense the most important.

Were the State to restrict by statute financial support of the Party's candidates to Party members, or to provide that only Party members might be selected as the Party's chosen nominees for public office, such a prohibition of potential association with nonmembers would clearly infringe upon the rights of the Party's members under the First Amendment to organize with like-minded citizens in support of common political goals. As we have said, "[a]ny interference with the freedom of a party is simultaneously an interference with the freedom of its adherents." *Democratic Party, supra,* at 122.[6] The statute here places limits upon the group of

---

[6] It is this element of potential interference with the rights of the Party's members which distinguishes the present case from others in which we have considered claims by nonmembers of a party

registered voters whom the Party may invite to participate in the "basic function" of selecting the Party's candidates. The State thus limits the Party's associational opportunities at the crucial juncture at which the appeal to common principles may be translated into concerted action, and hence to political power in the community.[7]
* * *

* * * Appellant contends that the Party's rule would require the purchase of additional voting machines, the training of additional poll workers, and potentially the printing of additional ballot materials specifically intended for independents voting in the Republican primary. In essence, appellant claims that the administration of the system contemplated by the Party rule would simply cost the State too much.

[T]he possibility of future increases in the cost of administering the election system is not a sufficient basis here for infringing appellees' First Amendment rights. Costs of administration would likewise increase if a third major party should come into existence in Connecticut, thus requiring the State to fund a third major-party primary. Additional voting machines, poll workers, and ballot materials would all be necessary under these circumstances as well. But the State could not forever protect the two existing major parties from competition solely on the ground that two major parties are all the public can afford. While the State is of course entitled to take administrative and financial considerations into account in choosing whether or not to have a primary system at all, it can no more restrain the Republican Party's freedom of association for reasons of its own administrative convenience than it could on the same ground limit the ballot access of a new major party.

Appellant argues that § 9-431 is justified as a measure to prevent raiding, a practice "whereby voters in sympathy with one party designate themselves as voters of another party so as to influence or determine the results of the other

---

seeking to vote in that party's primary despite the party's opposition. In this latter class of cases, the nonmember's desire to participate in the party's affairs is overborne by the countervailing and legitimate right of the party to determine its own membership qualifications. See *Rosario* v. *Rockefeller*, 410 U.S. 752 (1973); *Nader* v. *Schaffer*, 417 F. Supp. 837 (Conn.), summarily aff'd, 429 U.S. 989 (1976). Similarly, the Court has upheld the right of national political parties to refuse to seat at their conventions delegates chosen in state selection processes which did not conform to party rules. See *Democratic Party*; *Cousins* v. *Wigoda*, 419 U.S. 477 (1975). These situations are analytically distinct from the present case, in which the Party and its members seek to provide enhanced opportunities for participation by willing nonmembers. Under these circumstances, there is no conflict between the associational interests of members and nonmembers.

[7] Appellant contends that any infringement of the associational right of the Party or its members is *de minimis*, because Connecticut law, as amended during the pendency of this litigation, provides that any previously unaffiliated voter may become eligible to vote in the Party's primary by enrolling as a Party member as late as noon on the last business day preceding the primary. Thus, appellant contends, any independent voter wishing to participate in any Party primary may do so.

This is not a satisfactory response to the Party's contentions for two reasons. First, * * * the formal affiliation process is one which individual voters may employ in order to associate with the Party, but it provides no means by which the members of the Party may choose to broaden opportunities for joining the association by their own act, without any intervening action by potential voters. Second, and more importantly, the requirement of public affiliation with the Party in order to vote in the primary conditions the exercise of the associational right upon the making of a public statement of adherence to the Party which the State requires regardless of the actual beliefs of the individual voter. * * *

party's primary." *Rosario* v. *Rockefeller*, 410 U.S., [at] 760. While we have recognized that "a State may have a legitimate interest in seeking to curtail 'raiding,' since that practice may affect the integrity of the electoral process," that interest is not implicated here. The statute as applied to the Party's rule prevents independents, who otherwise cannot vote in any primary, from participating in the Republican primary. Yet a raid on the Republican Party primary by independent voters * * * is not impeded by § 9-431; the independent raiders need only register as Republicans and vote in the primary. * * *

Appellant's next argument in support of § 9-431 is that the closed primary system avoids voter confusion. Appellant contends that "[t]he legislature could properly find that it would be difficult for the general public to understand what a candidate stood for who was nominated in part by an unknown amorphous body outside the party, while nevertheless using the party name." * * *

As we have said, "[t]here can be no question about the legitimacy of the State's interest in fostering informed and educated expressions of the popular will in a general election." *Anderson* v. *Celebrezze*, 460 U.S. [780], 796 [(1983)] [p. 517]. To the extent that party labels provide a shorthand designation of the views of party candidates on matters of public concern, the identification of candidates with particular parties plays a role in the process by which voters inform themselves for the exercise of the franchise. Appellant's argument depends upon the belief that voters can be "misled" by party labels. But "[o]ur cases reflect a greater faith in the ability of individual voters to inform themselves about campaign issues." *Id.*, at 797. * * *

In arguing that the Party rule interferes with educated decisions by voters, appellant also disregards the substantial benefit which the Party rule provides to the Party and its members in seeking to choose successful candidates. Given the numerical strength of independent voters in the State, one of the questions most likely to occur to Connecticut Republicans in selecting candidates for public office is how can the Party most effectively appeal to the independent voter? By inviting independents to assist in the choice at the polls between primary candidates selected at the Party convention, the Party rule is intended to produce the candidate and platform most likely to achieve that goal. The state statute is said to decrease voter confusion, yet it deprives the Party and its members of the opportunity to inform themselves as to the level of support for the Party's candidates among a critical group of electors. "A State's claim that it is enhancing the ability of its citizenry to make wise decisions by restricting the flow of information to them must be viewed with some skepticism." *Anderson* v. *Celebrezze, supra*, at 798. The State's legitimate interests in preventing voter confusion and providing for educated and responsible voter decisions in no respect "make it necessary to burden the [Party's] rights."

Finally, appellant contends that § 9-431 furthers the State's compelling interest in protecting the integrity of the two-party system and the responsibility of party government. Appellant argues vigorously and at length that the closed primary system chosen by the state legislature promotes responsiveness by elected officials and strengthens the effectiveness of the political parties.

The relative merits of closed and open primaries have been the subject of substantial debate since the beginning of this century, and no consensus has as yet emerged. Appellant invokes a long and distinguished line of political scientists and public officials who have been supporters of the closed primary. But our role is not to decide whether the state legislature was acting wisely in enacting the closed primary system in 1955, or whether the Republican Party makes a mistake in seeking to depart from the practice of the past 30 years. * * *

* * * [We have upheld statutes that seek to protect the party against raiding by outsiders, but those cases are of little help to the State here, where] the state statute is defended on the ground that it protects the integrity of the Party against the Party itself.

Under these circumstances, the views of the State, which to some extent represent the views of the one political party transiently enjoying majority power, as to the optimum methods for preserving party integrity lose much of their force. The State argues that its statute is well designed to save the Republican Party from undertaking a course of conduct destructive of its own interests. But on this point "even if the State were correct, a State, or a court, may not constitutionally substitute its own judgment for that of the Party." *Democratic Party*, 450 U.S., at 123–124. The Party's determination of the boundaries of its own association, and of the structure which best allows it to pursue its political goals, is protected by the Constitution. "And as is true of all expressions of First Amendment freedoms, the courts may not interfere on the ground that they view a particular expression as unwise or irrational."[13]

We conclude that the State's enforcement, under these circumstances, of its closed primary system burdens the First Amendment rights of the Party. The interests which the appellant adduces in support of the statute are insubstantial, and accordingly the statute, as applied to the Party in this case, is unconstitutional. * * *

* * * The judgment of the Court of Appeals is

Affirmed.

JUSTICE STEVENS, with whom JUSTICE SCALIA joins, dissenting. * * *

[JUSTICE STEVENS noted that "the plain language of the Constitution requires that voters in congressional and senatorial elections 'shall have' the qualifications of voters in elections to the state legislature." Accordingly, he concluded that Connecticut could not constitutionally permit the Republicans to hold primaries for congressional elections in which independents were able to participate if a smaller class of voters (only Republicans) were eligible to participate in primaries for state

---

[13] Our holding today does not establish that state regulation of primary voting qualifications may never withstand challenge by a political party or its membership. A party seeking, for example, to open its primary to all voters, including members of other parties, would raise a different combination of considerations. Under such circumstances, the effect of one party's broadening of participation would threaten other parties with the disorganization effects which the statutes in *Storer* v. *Brown*, 415 U.S. 724 (1974) [p. 536], and *Rosario* v. *Rockefeller* were designed to prevent. * * *

legislative elections. In an omitted portion of the majority opinion, the Court held that the constitutional requirement did apply to primary elections, but was satisfied so long as every person qualified to vote for the state legislature was permitted to vote for Congress.]

JUSTICE SCALIA, with whom THE CHIEF JUSTICE [REHNQUIST] and JUSTICE O'CONNOR join, dissenting. * * *

In my view, the Court's opinion exaggerates the importance of the associational interest at issue, if indeed it does not see one where none exists. There is no question here of restricting the Republican Party's ability to recruit and enroll Party members by offering them the ability to select Party candidates; Conn. Gen. Stat. § 9-56 permits an independent voter to join the Party as late as the day before the primary. Nor is there any question of restricting the ability of the Party's members to select whatever candidate they desire. Appellees' only complaint is that the Party cannot leave the selection of its candidate to persons who are *not* members of the Party, and are unwilling to become members. It seems to me fanciful to refer to this as an interest in freedom of association between the members of the Republican Party and the putative independent voters. The Connecticut voter who, while steadfastly refusing to register as a Republican, casts a vote in the Republican primary, forms no more meaningful an "association" with the Party than does the independent or the registered Democrat who responds to questions by a Republican Party pollster. If the concept of freedom of association is extended to such casual contacts, it ceases to be of any analytic use.

The ability of the members of the Republican Party to select their own candidate, on the other hand, unquestionably implicates an associational freedom — but it can hardly be thought that that freedom is unconstitutionally impaired here. The Party is entirely free to put forward, if it wishes, that candidate who has the highest degree of support among Party members and independents combined. The State is under no obligation, however, to let its party primary be used, instead of a party-funded opinion poll, as the means by which the party identifies the relative popularity of its potential candidates among independents. Nor is there any reason apparent to me why the State cannot insist that this decision to support what might be called the independents' choice be taken *by the party membership in a democratic fashion*, rather than through a process that permits the members' votes to be diluted — and perhaps even absolutely outnumbered — by the votes of outsiders.

The Court's opinion characterizes this, disparagingly, as an attempt to "protec[t] the integrity of the Party against the Party itself." There are two problems with this characterization. The first, and less important, is that it is not true. We have no way of knowing that a majority of the Party's members is in favor of allowing ultimate selection of its candidates for federal and statewide office to be determined by persons outside the Party. That decision was not made by democratic ballot, but by the Party's state convention — which, for all we know, may have been dominated by officeholders and office seekers whose evaluation of the merits of assuring election of the Party's candidates, vis-à-vis the merits of proposing candidates faithful to the Party's political philosophy, diverged significantly from the views of the Party's rank and file. I had always thought it was a major purpose of state-imposed party primary requirements to protect the general party membership against this sort of minority control. Second and more important, however, *even if* it were the fact that the majority of the Party's members wanted its candidates to be determined by outsiders, there is no reason why the State is bound to honor that desire — any more than it would be bound to honor a party's democratically expressed desire that its candidates henceforth be selected by convention rather than by primary, or by the party's executive committee in a smoke-filled room. In other words, the validity of the state-imposed primary requirement itself, which we have hitherto considered "too plain for argument," *American Party of Texas* v. *White*, 415 U.S. 767, 781 (1974), presupposes that the State *has* the right "to protect the Party against the Party itself." Connecticut may lawfully require that significant elements of the democratic election process be democratic — whether the Party wants that or not. It is beyond my understanding why the Republican Party's delegation of its democratic choice to a Republican Convention can be proscribed, but its delegation of that choice to nonmembers of the Party cannot. * * *

I respectfully dissent.

Notes and Questions

1.   The Court frequently invoked the rights and interests of "the Party," but which individuals comprised the Party? Which individuals comprised the Party in the view of Justice Scalia?

2.   Should an organization (or members of an organization) have a constitutional right to associate with non-members?

3.   Did Connecticut law prevent the Party from associating with independents? Or is this merely a case where the state has refused to provide the party with special assistance in associating with outsiders?

4.   In Justice Scalia's view, the state's power to require parties to choose their nominees by primaries depends on the state having the right "to protect the Party against the Party itself." As such, it makes little sense to condemn closed primaries as paternalistic when the primary requirement itself is paternalistic. Is there a reason that a state would have the power to require primaries, but not have the power to determine the qualifications for voting in the primaries? What does *Democratic Party* say about that question?

5.   The Court, in footnote 13, suggests that while a party has the right to invite independents to vote in its primary (in other words, selecting a "semi-closed" primary over the state's choice of a "closed" one), a party may not have the right to invite members of other parties to vote in its primary (which would make the primary an "open" one). Should a party have the right to invite members of other parties to vote in its primary? Should a party have the right to associate with members of other parties in different ways, such as by soliciting financial support, sending invitations to meetings, or the like?

EU v. SAN FRANCISCO COUNTY
DEMOCRATIC CENTRAL COMMITTEE
Supreme Court of the United States
489 U.S. 214, 109 S. Ct. 1013, 103 L. Ed. 2d 271 (1989)

JUSTICE MARSHALL delivered the opinion of the Court [in which JUSTICE BRENNAN, JUSTICE WHITE, JUSTICE BLACKMUN, JUSTICE STEVENS, JUSTICE O'CONNOR, JUSTICE SCALIA, and JUSTICE KENNEDY join]. * * *

* * * The California Elections Code (Code) provides that the "official governing bodies" for [every "ballot-qualified"[1]] party are its "state convention," "state central committee," and "county central committees," and that these bodies are responsible for conducting the party's campaigns. At the same time, the Code provides that the official governing bodies "shall not endorse, support, or oppose, any candidate for nomination by that party for partisan office in the direct primary election." * * *

Although the official governing bodies of political parties are barred from issuing endorsements, other groups are not. Political clubs affiliated with a party, labor organizations, political action committees, other politically active associations, and newspapers frequently endorse primary candidates. With the official party organizations silenced by the ban, it has been possible for a candidate with views antithetical to those of her party nevertheless to win its primary.

In addition to restricting the primary activities of the official governing bodies of political parties, California also regulates their internal affairs. Separate statutory provisions dictate the size and composition of the state central committees; set forth rules governing the selection and removal of committee members; fix the maximum term of office for the chair of the state central committee; require that the chair rotate between residents of northern and southern California; specify the time and place of committee meetings; and limit the dues parties may impose on members. Violations of these provisions are criminal offenses punishable by fine and imprisonment.

Various [party members and committees] brought this action in federal court against state officials responsible for enforcing the Code. * * *

The District Court granted summary judgment for the plaintiffs * * *, ruling that the ban on primary endorsements * * * violated the First Amendment as applied to the States through the Fourteenth Amendment. * * * [T]he court [also] ruled that the laws prescribing the composition of state central committees, limiting the committee chairs' terms of office, and designating that the chair rotate between residents of northern and southern California violate the First Amendment. The court denied summary judgment with respect to the statutory provisions establish-

---

[1] A "ballot-qualified" party is eligible to participate in any primary election because: (a) during the last gubernatorial election, one of its candidates for state-wide office received two percent of the vote; (b) one percent of the State's voters are registered with the party; or (c) a petition establishing the party has been filed by ten percent of the State's voters.

In the interest of simplicity, we use the terms "ballot-qualified party" and "political party" interchangeably.

ing the time and place of committee meetings and the amount of dues.

The Court of Appeals for the Ninth Circuit affirmed. * * *

* * * To assess the constitutionality of a state election law, we first examine whether it burdens rights protected by the First and Fourteenth Amendments. If the challenged law burdens the rights of political parties and their members, it can survive constitutional scrutiny only if the State shows that it advances a compelling state interest and is narrowly tailored to serve that interest.

We first consider California's prohibition on primary endorsements by the official governing bodies of political parties. California concedes that its ban implicates the First Amendment, but contends that the burden is "miniscule." We disagree. The ban directly affects speech which "is at the core of our electoral process and of the First Amendment freedoms." * * *

California's ban on primary endorsements * * * prevents party governing bodies from stating whether a candidate adheres to the tenets of the party or whether party officials believe that the candidate is qualified for the position sought. This prohibition directly hampers the ability of a party to spread its message and hamstrings voters seeking to inform themselves about the candidates and the campaign issues. A "highly paternalistic approach" limiting what people may hear is generally suspect, but it is particularly egregious where the State censors the political speech a political party shares with its members.

Barring political parties from endorsing and opposing candidates not only burdens their freedom of speech but also infringes upon their freedom of association. * * * Freedom of association means not only that an individual voter has the right to associate with the political party of her choice, but also that a political party has a right to "identify the people who constitute the association" and to select a "standard bearer who best represents the party's ideologies and preferences."

Depriving a political party of the power to endorse suffocates this right. The endorsement ban prevents parties from promoting candidates "at the crucial juncture at which the appeal to common principles may be translated into concerted action, and hence to political power in the community." *Tashjian* [v. *Republican Party of Connecticut*], 479 U.S. [208], 216 [(1986)] [p. 449]. Even though individual members of the state central committees and county central committees are free to issue endorsements, imposing limitations "on individuals wishing to band together to advance their views on a ballot measure, while placing none on individuals acting alone, is clearly a restraint on the right of association." *Citizens Against Rent Control/Coalition for Fair Housing* v. *Berkeley*, 454 U.S. 290, 296 (1981).

Because the ban burdens appellees' rights to free speech and free association, it can only survive constitutional scrutiny if it serves a compelling governmental interest.[15] The State offers two: stable government and protecting voters from

---

[15] California contends that it need not show that its endorsement ban serves a compelling state interest, because the political parties have "consented" to it. In support of this claim, California observes that the legislators who could repeal the ban belong to political parties, that the bylaws of some parties prohibit primary endorsements, and that parties continue to participate in state-run primaries.

This argument is fatally flawed in several respects. We have never held that a political party's consent

confusion and undue influence. Maintaining a stable political system is, unquestionably, a compelling state interest. California, however, never adequately explains how banning parties from endorsing or opposing primary candidates advances that interest. There is no showing, for example, that California's political system is any more stable now than it was in 1963, when the legislature enacted the ban. Nor does the State explain what makes the California system so peculiar that it is virtually the only State that has determined that such a ban is necessary.

The only explanation the State offers is that its compelling interest in stable government embraces a similar interest in party stability. The State relies heavily on *Storer* v. *Brown*, [415 U.S. 724, 730 (1974)] [p. 512], where we stated that because "splintered parties and unrestrained factionalism may do significant damage to the fabric of government," States may regulate elections to ensure that "some sort of order, rather than chaos . . . accompan[ies] the democratic processes." Our decision in *Storer*, however, does not stand for the proposition that a State may enact election laws to mitigate intraparty factionalism during a primary campaign. To the contrary, *Storer* recognized that "contending forces within the party employ the primary campaign and the primary election to finally settle their differences." *Id.*, at 735. A primary is not hostile to intraparty feuds; rather it is an ideal forum in which to resolve them. * * *

It is no answer to argue, as does the State, that a party that issues primary endorsements risks intraparty friction which may endanger the party's general election prospects. Presumably a party will be motivated by self-interest and not engage in acts or speech that run counter to its political success. However, even if a ban on endorsements saves a political party from pursuing self-destructive acts, that would not justify a State substituting its judgment for that of the party. Because preserving party unity during a primary is not a compelling state interest, we must look elsewhere to justify the challenged law.

---

will cure a statute that otherwise violates the First Amendment. Even aside from this fundamental defect, California's consent argument is contradicted by the simple fact that the official governing bodies of various political parties have joined this lawsuit. * * *

There are other flaws in the State's argument. Simply because a legislator belongs to a political party does not make her at all times a representative of party interests. In supporting the endorsement ban, an individual legislator may be acting on her understanding of the public good or her interest in reelection. The independence of legislators from their parties is illustrated by the California Legislature's frequent refusal to amend the election laws in accordance with the wishes of political parties. Moreover, the State's argument ignores those parties with negligible, if any, representation in the legislature.

That the bylaws of some parties prohibit party primary endorsements also does not prove consent. These parties may have chosen to reflect state election law in their bylaws, rather than permit or require conduct prohibited by law. Nor does the fact that parties continue to participate in the state-run primary process indicate that they favor each regulation imposed upon that process. A decision to participate in state-run primaries more likely reflects a party's determination that ballot participation is more advantageous than the alternatives, that is, supporting independent candidates or conducting write-in campaigns. *See Storer* v. *Brown*, 415 U.S. 724, 745 (1974) [p. 536]; *Anderson* v. *Celebrezze*, 460 U.S. 780, 799, n.26 (1983) [p. 540].

Finally, the State's focus on the parties' alleged consent ignores the independent First Amendment rights of the parties' members. It is wholly undemonstrated that the members authorized the parties to consent to infringements of members' rights.

The State's second justification for the ban on party endorsements and statements of opposition is that it is necessary to protect primary voters from confusion and undue influence. Certainly the State has a legitimate interest in fostering an informed electorate. However, "[a] State's claim that it is enhancing the ability of its citizenry to make wise decisions by restricting the flow of information to them must be viewed with some skepticism." *Tashjian, supra,* at 221. While a State may regulate the flow of information between political associations and their members when necessary to prevent fraud and corruption, there is no evidence that California's ban on party primary endorsements serves that purpose.[19]

Because the ban on primary endorsements by political parties burdens political speech while serving no compelling governmental interest, we hold that [it] violate[s] the First and Fourteenth Amendments.

We turn next to California's restrictions on the organization and composition of official governing bodies, the limits on the term of office for state central committee chair, and the requirement that the chair rotate between residents of northern and southern California. These laws directly implicate the associational rights of political parties and their members. As we noted in *Tashjian,* a political party's "determination . . . of the structure which best allows it to pursue its political goals, is protected by the Constitution." 479 U.S., at 224. Freedom of association also encompasses a political party's decisions about the identity of, and the process for electing, its leaders.

The laws at issue burden these rights. By requiring parties to establish official governing bodies at the county level, California prevents the political parties from governing themselves with the structure they think best. * * * Each restriction * * * limits a political party's discretion in how to organize itself, conduct its affairs, and select its leaders. Indeed, the associational rights at stake are much stronger than those we credited in *Tashjian.* There, we found that a party's right to free association embraces a right to allow registered voters who are not party members to vote in the party's primary. Here, party members do not seek to associate with nonparty members, but only with one another in freely choosing their party leaders.[21]

Because the challenged laws burden the associational rights of political parties and their members, the question is whether they serve a compelling state interest. A State indisputably has a compelling interest in preserving the integrity of its election process. Toward that end, a State may enact laws that interfere with a party's internal affairs when necessary to ensure that elections are fair and honest. *Storer* v. *Brown,* 415 U.S., at 730. For example, a State may impose certain eligibility requirements for voters in the general election even though they limit parties' ability to garner support and members. We have also recognized that a State may impose restrictions that promote the integrity of primary elections. None

---

[19] The State suggested at oral argument that the endorsement ban prevents fraud by barring party officials from misrepresenting that they speak for the party. To the extent that the State suggests that only the primary election results can constitute a party endorsement, it confuses an endorsement from the official governing bodies that may influence election results with the results themselves. * * *

[21] By regulating the identity of the parties' leaders, the challenged statutes may also color the parties' message and interfere with the parties' decisions as to the best means to promote that message.

of these restrictions, however, involved direct regulation of a party's leaders. Rather, the infringement on the associational rights of the parties and their members was the indirect consequence of laws necessary to the successful completion of a party's external responsibilities in ensuring the order and fairness of elections.

In the instant case, the State has not shown that its regulation of internal party governance is necessary to the integrity of the electoral process. Instead, it contends that the challenged laws serve a compelling "interest in the 'democratic management of the political party's internal affairs.' " This, however, is not a case where intervention is necessary to prevent the derogation of the civil rights of party adherents. Cf. *Smith* v. *Allwright*, 321 U.S. 649 (1944) [p. 426]. Moreover, as we have observed, the State has no interest in "protect[ing] the integrity of the Party against the Party itself." *Tashjian*, 479 U.S., at 224. The State further claims that limiting the term of the state central committee chair and requiring that the chair rotate between residents of northern and southern California helps "prevent regional friction from reaching a 'critical mass.' " However, a State cannot substitute its judgment for that of the party as to the desirability of a particular internal party structure, any more than it can tell a party that its proposed communication to party members is unwise.

In sum, a State cannot justify regulating a party's internal affairs without showing that such regulation is necessary to ensure an election that is orderly and fair. Because California has made no such showing here, the challenged laws cannot be upheld.

* * * Accordingly, the judgment of the Court of Appeals is

Affirmed.

CHIEF JUSTICE REHNQUIST took no part in the consideration or decision of this case.

[JUSTICE STEVENS joined the Court's opinion but wrote to express "reservations" about the Court's use of strict scrutiny, which he believed might be thought to foreordain a conclusion of unconstitutionality.]

Notes and Questions

1. *Whose* First Amendment rights were abridged by the ban on endorsements by parties' official governing bodies? The parties and their members certainly have the First Amendment right to endorse candidates, but is that right being abridged here? How do we know which candidates the members prefer? Likewise, the individual members of the governing bodies have a First Amendment right to endorse candidates, but the endorsements here at issue are not those of any individuals, but of the bodies collectively. Finally, the endorsements may be considered to reflect the views of the governing bodies. But it is unclear why the governing bodies as such should have a right to endorse primary candidates.

Consider, in this regard, a party whose members are torn between nominating Apollo and Bacchus. The membership prefers Apollo by a small margin, but the governing body prefers Bacchus and wishes to endorse him publicly. Is it permissible in such a case to view the governing body as acting for the party?

2. The Court held unconstitutional California's attempt to regulate the internal governing structure of the Party. But did not *Smith v. Allwright*, 321 U.S. 649 (1944) [p. 426], *demand* that states regulate the internal governing structure of parties to ensure against racial discrimination? Did *Eu* adequately distinguish *Smith*?

3. In holding that parties have a right to endorse candidates in primary elections, the Court necessarily conceived of parties of having an existence and a purpose independent of their candidates. Such a conception matters not only in identifying and defining a party's right to association, but also in assessing the place of parties within campaign finance regulation. If parties have the right to create and disseminate a message independent of state interference — the basis of the right-of-association cases considered in this section — then we might expect to treat parties' campaign fund-raising and expenditures just as we would that of interest groups. On the other hand, parties exist largely, if not completely, to elect their candidates. Certainly in the stage between nomination and general election, parties are focused most intently on electing their candidates, and so there is a great degree of overlap between the interests of the parties and those of their candidates.

In *Federal Election Commission v. Colorado Republican Federal Campaign Committee*, 533 U.S. 431 (2001), the Supreme Court considered the constitutionality of the federal limit on parties' coordinated expenditures — expenditures, that is, that are coordinated with their candidates. The Party argued that because the job of parties is to secure the election of its candidates, parties are "joined at the hip" with their candidates. Accordingly, the parties argued, coordinated expenditures should be viewed as appropriate and desirable, rather than as a source of corruption.

In a 5-4 decision, the Court disagreed. The Court held that parties' coordinated expenditures could be limited because such expenditures did raise the risk of corruption — specifically, the risk that parties would act as bagmen for special interests or wealthy donors who would give money to parties with the expectation that their contributions would be funneled to the grateful candidates. *See id.* at 452 ("[Parties] act as agents for spending on behalf of those who seek to produce obligated officeholders."). The Court noted that parties had the right to make unlimited *independent* expenditures in support of its candidates, but that coordinated expenditures by parties (like coordinated expenditures by other groups) could lead to the same kind of corruption sought to be prevented by limits on contributions. In permitting coordinated expenditures to be limited, did the Court place too little weight on parties' rights to associate with their candidates?

CALIFORNIA DEMOCRATIC PARTY v. JONES
Supreme Court of the United States
530 U.S. 567, 120 S. Ct. 2402, 147 L. Ed. 2d 502 (2000)

JUSTICE SCALIA delivered the opinion of the Court [in which CHIEF JUSTICE REHNQUIST, JUSTICE O'CONNOR, JUSTICE KENNEDY, JUSTICE SOUTER, JUSTICE THOMAS, and JUSTICE BREYER join].

This case presents the question whether the State of California may, consistent with the First Amendment to the United States Constitution, use a so-called "blanket" primary to determine a political party's nominee for the general election.

Under California law, a candidate for public office has two routes to gain access to the general ballot for most state and federal elective offices. He may receive the nomination of a qualified political party by winning its primary; or he may file as an independent by obtaining (for a statewide race) the signatures of one percent of the State's electorate or (for other races) the signatures of three percent of the voting population of the area represented by the office in contest.

Until 1996, to determine the nominees of qualified parties California held what is known as a "closed" partisan primary, in which only persons who are members of the political party — *i.e.*, who have declared affiliation with that party when they register to vote — can vote on its nominee. In 1996 the citizens of California adopted by initiative Proposition 198. Promoted largely as a measure that would "weaken" party "hard-liners" and ease the way for "moderate problem-solvers," ([quoting from a] ballot pamphlet distributed to voters), Proposition 198 changed California's partisan primary from a closed primary to a blanket primary. Under the new system, "all persons entitled to vote, including those not affiliated with any political party, shall have the right to vote . . . for any candidate regardless of the candidate's political affiliation." Whereas under the closed primary each voter received a ballot limited to candidates of his own party, as a result of Proposition 198 each voter's primary ballot now lists every candidate regardless of party affiliation and allows the voter to choose freely among them. It remains the case, however, that the candidate of each party who wins the greatest number of votes "is the nominee of that party at the ensuing general election."

Petitioners in this case are four political parties — the California Democratic Party, the California Republican Party, the Libertarian Party of California, and the Peace and Freedom Party — each of which has a rule prohibiting persons not members of the party from voting in the party's primary. Petitioners brought suit in the United States District Court for the Eastern District of California against respondent California Secretary of State, alleging, *inter alia*, that California's blanket primary violated their First Amendment rights of association, and seeking declaratory and injunctive relief. * * * [T]he District Court held that the burden on petitioners' rights of association was not a severe one, and was justified by state interests ultimately reducing to this: "enhancing the democratic nature of the election process and the representativeness of elected officials." The Ninth Circuit, adopting the District Court's opinion as its own, affirmed. We granted certiorari. * * *

We have recognized, of course, that States have a major role to play in structuring and monitoring the election process, including primaries. * * * What we have not held, however, is that the processes by which political parties select their nominees are, as respondents would have it, wholly public affairs that States may regulate freely. To the contrary, we have continually stressed that when States regulate parties' internal processes they must act within limits imposed by the Constitution. See, *e.g.*, *Eu* v. *San Francisco County Democratic Central Comm.*, 489 U.S. 214 (1989) [p. 455]; *Democratic Party of United States* v. *Wisconsin ex rel. La Follette*, 450 U.S. 107 (1981) [p. 442]. In this regard, respondents' reliance on

Smith v. *Allwright*, 321 U.S. 649 (1944) [p. 426], and *Terry* v. *Adams*, 345 U.S. 461 (1953) [p. 431], is misplaced. In *Allwright*, we invalidated the Texas Democratic Party's rule limiting participation in its primary to whites; in *Terry*, we invalidated the same rule promulgated by the Jaybird Democratic Association, a "self-governing voluntary club." These cases held only that, when a State prescribes an election process that gives a special role to political parties, it "endorses, adopts and enforces the discrimination against Negroes," that the parties (or, in the case of the Jaybird Democratic Association, organizations that are "part and parcel" of the parties, see 345 U.S., at 482 (Clark, J., concurring)) bring into the process — so that the parties' discriminatory action becomes state action under the Fifteenth Amendment. *Allwright, supra,* at 664; see also *Terry*, 345 U.S., at 484 (Clark, J., concurring); 345 U.S., at 469 (opinion of Black, J.). They do not stand for the proposition that party affairs are public affairs, free of First Amendment protections — and our later holdings make that entirely clear.[5] See, *e.g., Tashjian* [v. *Republican Party of Connecticut*, 479 U.S. 208 (1986)] [p. 449].

Representative democracy in any populous unit of governance is unimaginable without the ability of citizens to band together in promoting among the electorate candidates who espouse their political views. * * * [T]he Court has recognized that the First Amendment protects "the freedom to join together in furtherance of common political beliefs," which "necessarily presupposes the freedom to identify the people who constitute the association, and to limit the association to those people only," *La Follette*, 450 U.S., at 122. That is to say, a corollary of the right to associate is the right not to associate. "Freedom of association would prove an empty guarantee if associations could not limit control over their decisions to those who share the interests and persuasions that underlie the association's being." 450 U.S., at 122 n.22.

In no area is the political association's right to exclude more important than in the process of selecting its nominee. That process often determines the party's positions on the most significant public policy issues of the day, and even when those positions are predetermined it is the nominee who becomes the party's ambassador to the general electorate in winning it over to the party's views. Some political parties — such as President Theodore Roosevelt's Bull Moose Party, the La Follette Progressives of 1924, the Henry Wallace Progressives of 1948, and the George Wallace American Independent Party of 1968 — are virtually inseparable

---

[5] The dissent is therefore wrong to conclude that *Allwright* and *Terry* demonstrate that "the protections that the First Amendment affords to the internal processes of a political party do not encompass a right to exclude nonmembers from voting in a state-required, state-financed primary election." Those cases simply prevent exclusion that violates some independent constitutional proscription. The closest the dissent comes to identifying such a proscription in this case is its reference to "the First Amendment associational interests" of citizens to participate in the primary of a party to which they do not belong, and the "fundamental right" of citizens "to cast a meaningful vote for the candidate of their choice." As to the latter: Selecting a candidate is quite different from voting for the candidate of one's choice. If the "fundamental right" to cast a meaningful vote were really at issue in this context, Proposition 198 would be not only constitutionally permissible but constitutionally required, which no one believes. As for the associational "interest" in selecting the candidate of a group to which one does not belong, that falls far short of a constitutional right, if indeed it can even fairly be characterized as an interest. It has been described in our cases as a "desire" — and rejected as a basis for disregarding the First Amendment right to exclude.

from their nominees (and tend not to outlast them).

Unsurprisingly, our cases vigorously affirm the special place the First Amendment reserves for, and the special protection it accords, the process by which a political party "selects a standard bearer who best represents the party's ideologies and preferences." *Eu*, 489 U.S., at 224. The moment of choosing the party's nominee, we have said, is "the crucial juncture at which the appeal to common principles may be translated into concerted action, and hence to political power in the community." *Tashjian*, 479 U.S., at 216.

In *La Follette*, the State of Wisconsin conducted an open presidential preference primary.[6] Although the voters did not select the delegates to the Democratic Party's National Convention directly — they were chosen later at caucuses of party members — Wisconsin law required these delegates to vote in accord with the primary results. Thus allowing nonparty members to participate in the selection of the party's nominee conflicted with the Democratic Party's rules. We held that, whatever the strength of the state interests supporting the open primary itself, they could not justify this "substantial intrusion into the associational freedom of members of the National Party."[7] 450 U.S., at 126.

California's blanket primary violates the principles set forth in these cases. Proposition 198 forces political parties to associate with — to have their nominees, and hence their positions, determined by — those who, at best, have refused to affiliate with the party, and, at worst, have expressly affiliated with a rival. In this respect, it is qualitatively different from a closed primary. Under that system, even when it is made quite easy for a voter to change his party affiliation the day of the primary, and thus, in some sense, to "cross over," at least he must formally *become a member of the party*; and once he does so, he is limited to voting for candidates of that party.[8]

---

[6] An open primary differs from a blanket primary in that, although as in the blanket primary any person, regardless of party affiliation, may vote for a party's nominee, his choice is limited to that party's nominees *for all offices*. He may not, for example, support a Republican nominee for Governor and a Democratic nominee for attorney general.

[7] The dissent, in attempting to fashion its new rule — that the right not to associate does not exist with respect to primary elections — rewrites *La Follette* to stand merely for the proposition that a political party has a First Amendment right to "defin[e] the organization and composition of its governing units." In fact, however, the state-imposed burden at issue in *La Follette* was "the intrusion by those with adverse political principles" upon the selection of the party's nominee (in that case its presidential nominee). 450 U.S., at 122. * * *

Not only does the dissent's principle of no right to exclude conflict with our precedents, but it also leads to nonsensical results. In *Tashjian*, we held that the First Amendment protects a party's right to invite independents to participate in the primary. Combining *Tashjian* with the dissent's rule affirms a party's constitutional right to allow outsiders to select its candidates, but denies a party's constitutional right to reserve candidate selection to its own members. The First Amendment would thus guarantee a party's right to lose its identity, but not to preserve it.

[8] In this sense, the blanket primary also may be constitutionally distinct from the open primary, in which the voter is limited to one party's ballot. See *La Follette, supra*, at 130, n.2 (Powell, J., dissenting) ("[T]he act of voting in the Democratic primary fairly can be described as an act of affiliation with the Democratic Party. . . . The situation might be different in those States with 'blanket' primaries — *i.e.*, those where voters are allowed to participate in the primaries of more than one party on a single occasion, selecting the primary they wish to vote in with respect to each individual elective office"). This

The evidence in this case demonstrates that under California's blanket primary system, the prospect of having a party's nominee determined by adherents of an opposing party is far from remote — indeed, it is a clear and present danger. For example, in one 1997 survey of California voters 37 percent of Republicans said that they planned to vote in the 1998 Democratic gubernatorial primary, and 20 percent of Democrats said they planned to vote in the 1998 Republican United States Senate primary. Those figures are comparable to the results of studies in other States with blanket primaries. One expert testified, for example, that in Washington the number of voters crossing over from one party to another can rise to as high as 25 percent, and another that only 25 to 33 percent of all Washington voters limit themselves to candidates of one party throughout the ballot. The impact of voting by nonparty members is much greater upon minor parties, such as the Libertarian Party and the Peace and Freedom Party. In the first primaries these parties conducted following California's implementation of Proposition 198, the total votes cast for party candidates in some races was more than *double* the total number of *registered party members*.

The record also supports the obvious proposition that these substantial numbers of voters who help select the nominees of parties they have chosen not to join often have policy views that diverge from those of the party faithful. The 1997 survey of California voters revealed significantly different policy preferences between party members and primary voters who "crossed over" from another party. One expert went so far as to describe it as "inevitable [under Proposition 198] that parties will be forced in some circumstances to give their official designation to a candidate who's not preferred by a majority or even plurality of party members." * * *

[T]he deleterious effects of Proposition 198 are not limited to altering the identity of the nominee. Even when the person favored by a majority of the party members prevails, he will have prevailed by taking somewhat different positions — and, should he be elected, will continue to take somewhat different positions in order to be renominated. As respondents' own expert concluded, "the policy positions of Members of Congress elected from blanket primary states are . . . more moderate, both in an absolute sense and relative to the other party, and so are more reflective of the preferences of the mass of voters at the center of the ideological spectrum." It is unnecessary to cumulate evidence of this phenomenon, since, after all, the whole *purpose* of Proposition 198 was to favor nominees with "moderate" positions. It encourages candidates — and officeholders who hope to be renominated — to curry favor with persons whose views are more "centrist" than those of the party base. In effect, Proposition 198 has simply moved the general election one step earlier in the process, at the expense of the parties' ability to perform the "basic function" of choosing their own leaders. * * *

In sum, Proposition 198 forces petitioners to adulterate their candidate-selection process — the "basic function of a political party" — by opening it up to persons wholly unaffiliated with the party. Such forced association has the likely outcome — indeed, in this case the *intended* outcome — of changing the parties' message. We can think of no heavier burden on a political party's associational freedom. Proposition 198 is therefore unconstitutional unless it is narrowly tailored to serve

case does not require us to determine the constitutionality of open primaries.

a compelling state interest. It is to that question which we now turn.

Respondents proffer seven state interests they claim are compelling. Two of them — producing elected officials who better represent the electorate and expanding candidate debate beyond the scope of partisan concerns — are simply circumlocution for producing nominees and nominee positions other than those the parties would choose if left to their own devices. [But requiring speakers to modify the content of their expression is impermissible.] * * *

Respondents' third asserted compelling interest is that the blanket primary is the only way to ensure that disenfranchised persons enjoy the right to an effective vote. By "disenfranchised," respondents do not mean those who cannot vote; they mean simply independents and members of the minority party in "safe" districts. These persons are disenfranchised, according to respondents, because under a closed primary they are unable to participate in what amounts to the determinative election — the majority party's primary; the only way to ensure they have an "effective" vote is to force the party to open its primary to them. This also appears to be nothing more than reformulation of an asserted state interest we have already rejected — recharacterizing nonparty members' keen desire to participate in selection of the party's nominee as "disenfranchisement" if that desire is not fulfilled. We have said, however, that a "nonmember's desire to participate in the party's affairs is overborne by the countervailing and legitimate right of the party to determine its own membership qualifications." *Tashjian*, 479 U.S., at 215–216, n.6. The voter's desire to participate does not become more weighty simply because the State supports it. Moreover, even if it were accurate to describe the plight of the non-party-member in a safe district as "disenfranchisement," Proposition 198 is not needed to solve the problem. The voter who feels himself disenfranchised should simply join the party. That may put him to a hard choice, but it is not a state-imposed restriction upon *his* freedom of association, whereas compelling party members to accept his selection of their nominee *is* a state-imposed restriction upon theirs.

Respondents' remaining four asserted state interests — promoting fairness, affording voters greater choice, increasing voter participation, and protecting privacy — are not, like the others, automatically out of the running; but neither are they, *in the circumstances of this case*, compelling. That determination is not to be made in the abstract, by asking whether fairness, privacy, etc., are highly significant values; but rather by asking whether the *aspect* of fairness, privacy, etc., addressed by the law at issue is highly significant. And for all four of these asserted interests, we find it not to be.

The aspect of fairness addressed by Proposition 198 is presumably the supposed inequity of not permitting nonparty members in "safe" districts to determine the party nominee. If that is unfair at all (rather than merely a consequence of the eminently democratic principle that — except where constitutional imperatives intervene — the majority rules), it seems to us less unfair than permitting nonparty members to hijack the party. As for affording voters greater choice, it is obvious that the net effect of this scheme — indeed, its avowed purpose — is to *reduce* the scope of choice, by assuring a range of candidates who are all more "centrist." This may well be described as broadening the range of choices *favored by the majority*

— but that is hardly a compelling state interest, if indeed it is even a legitimate one. The interest in increasing voter participation is just a variation on the same theme (more choices favored by the majority will produce more voters), and suffers from the same defect. As for the protection of privacy: The specific privacy interest at issue is not the confidentiality of medical records or personal finances, but confidentiality of one's party affiliation. Even if (as seems unlikely) a scheme for administering a closed primary could not be devised in which the voter's declaration of party affiliation would not be public information, we do not think that the State's interest in assuring the privacy of this piece of information in all cases can conceivably be considered a "compelling" one. If such information were generally so sacrosanct, federal statutes would not require a declaration of party affiliation as a condition of appointment to certain offices [including commissions for which no more than a certain number of members may be of the same party].

Finally, we may observe that even if all these state interests were compelling ones, Proposition 198 is not a narrowly tailored means of furthering them. Respondents could protect them all by resorting to a *nonpartisan* blanket primary. Generally speaking, under such a system, the State determines what qualifications it requires for a candidate to have a place on the primary ballot — which may include nomination by established parties and voter-petition requirements for independent candidates. Each voter, regardless of party affiliation, may then vote for any candidate, and the top two vote getters (or however many the State prescribes) then move on to the general election. This system has all the characteristics of the partisan blanket primary, save the constitutionally crucial one: Primary voters are not choosing a party's nominee. Under a nonpartisan blanket primary, a State may ensure more choice, greater participation, increased "privacy," and a sense of "fairness" — all without severely burdening a political party's First Amendment right of association.

* * * The burden Proposition 198 places on petitioners' rights of political association is both severe and unnecessary. The judgment for the Court of Appeals for the Ninth Circuit is reversed.

It is so ordered.

[JUSTICE KENNEDY joined the Court's opinion and wrote separately to argue that upholding the blanket primary would "compound[]" the interference with parties' First Amendment rights that he believed would result from the Court's acceptance of limits on parties' expenditures made in coordination with candidates. That doctrine is discussed in Chapter 9, *infra*.]

JUSTICE STEVENS, with whom JUSTICE GINSBURG joins * * *, dissenting. * * *

A State's power to determine how its officials are to be elected is a quintessential attribute of sovereignty. This case is about the State of California's power to decide who may vote in an election conducted, and paid for, by the State. The United States Constitution imposes constraints on the States' power to limit access to the polls, but we have never before held or suggested that it imposes any constraints on States' power to authorize additional citizens to participate in any state election for a state office. In my view, principles of federalism require us to respect the policy choice made by the State's voters in approving Proposition 198.

The blanket primary system instituted by Proposition 198 does not abridge "the ability of citizens to band together in promoting among the electorate candidates who espouse their political views." The Court's contrary conclusion rests on the premise that a political party's freedom of expressive association includes a "right not to associate," which in turn includes a right to exclude voters unaffiliated with the party from participating in the selection of that party's nominee in a primary election. In drawing this conclusion, however, the Court blurs two distinctions that are critical: (1) the distinction between a private organization's right to define itself and its messages, on the one hand, and the State's right to define the obligations of citizens and organizations performing public functions, on the other; and (2) the distinction between laws that abridge participation in the political process and those that encourage such participation.

When a political party defines the organization and composition of its governing units, when it decides what candidates to endorse, and when it decides whether and how to communicate those endorsements to the public, it is engaged in the kind of private expressive associational activity that the First Amendment protects.[3] * * *

[H]owever, the associational rights of political parties are neither absolute nor as comprehensive as the rights enjoyed by wholly private associations. I think it clear — though the point has never been decided by this Court — "that a State may require parties to use the primary format for selecting their nominees." The reason a State may impose this significant restriction on a party's associational freedoms is that both the general election and the primary are quintessential forms of state action. It is because the primary is state action that an organization — whether it calls itself a political party or just a "Jaybird" association — may not deny non-Caucasians the right to participate in the selection of its nominees. *Terry* v. *Adams*; *Smith* v. *Allwright*. The Court is quite right in stating that those cases "do not stand for the proposition that party affairs are [*wholly*] public affairs, free of First Amendment protections." They do, however, stand for the proposition that primary elections, unlike most "party affairs," are state action. The protections that the First Amendment affords to the "internal processes" of a political party do not encompass a right to exclude nonmembers from voting in a state-required, state-financed primary election.

The so-called "right not to associate" that the Court relies upon, then, is simply inapplicable to participation in a state election. A political party, like any other association, may refuse to allow non-members to participate in the party's decisions when it is conducting its own affairs; California's blanket primary system does not infringe this principle. But an election, unlike a convention or caucus, is a public affair. Although it is true that we have extended First Amendment protection to a party's right to invite independents to participate in its primaries, *Tashjian*, neither that case nor any other has held or suggested that the "right not to associate"

---

[3] * * * *La Follette* is a case about state regulation of internal party processes, not about regulation of primary elections. State-mandated intrusion upon either delegate selection or delegate voting would surely implicate the affected party's First Amendment right to define the organization and composition of its governing units, but it is clear that California intrudes upon neither in this case. * * *

imposes a limit on the State's power to open up its primary elections to all voters eligible to vote in a general election. In my view, while state rules abridging participation in its elections should be closely scrutinized, the First Amendment does not inhibit the State from acting to broaden voter access to state-run, state-financed elections. When a State acts not to limit democratic participation but to expand the ability of individuals to participate in the democratic process, it is acting not as a foe of the First Amendment but as a friend and ally.

Although I would not endorse it, I could at least understand a constitutional rule that protected a party's associational rights by allowing it to refuse to select its candidates through state-regulated primary elections. A meaningful "right not to associate," if there is such a right in the context of limiting an electorate, ought to enable a party to insist on choosing its nominees at a convention or caucus where non-members could be excluded. In the real world, however, anyone can "join" a political party merely by asking for the appropriate ballot at the appropriate time or (at most) by registering within a state-defined reasonable period of time before an election; neither past voting history nor the voter's race, religion, or gender can provide a basis for the party's refusal to "associate" with an unwelcome new member. There is an obvious mismatch between a supposed constitutional right "not to associate" and a rule that turns on nothing more than the state-defined timing of the new associate's application for membership.

The Court's reliance on a political party's "right not to associate" as a basis for limiting a State's power to conduct primary elections will inevitably require it either to draw unprincipled distinctions among various primary configurations or to alter voting practices throughout the Nation in fundamental ways. [Three States presently have blanket primaries, while an additional 21 States have open primaries and 8 States have semi-closed primaries in which independents may participate.] * * * Given that open primaries are supported by essentially the same state interests that the Court disparages today and are not as "narrow" as nonpartisan primaries, there is surely a danger that open primaries will fare no better against a First Amendment challenge than blanket primaries have. * * *[8]

In my view, the First Amendment does not mandate that a putatively private association be granted the power to dictate the organizational structure of state-run, state-financed primary elections. It is not this Court's constitutional function to choose between the competing visions of what makes democracy work — party autonomy and discipline versus progressive inclusion of the entire electorate in the process of selecting their public officials — that are held by the litigants in this case. That choice belongs to the people.

---

[8] When coupled with our decision in *Tashjian* that a party may require a State to open up a closed primary, this intrusion has even broader implications. It is arguable that, under the Court's reasoning combined with *Tashjian*, the only nominating options open for the States to choose without party consent are: (1) not to have primary elections, or (2) to have what the Court calls a "nonpartisan primary" — a system presently used in Louisiana — in which candidates previously nominated by the various political parties and independent candidates compete. These two options are the same in practice because the latter is not actually a "primary" in the common, partisan sense of that term at all. Rather, it is a general election with a runoff that has few of the benefits of democratizing the party nominating process that led the Court to declare the State's ability to require nomination by primary "too plain for argument."

Even if the "right not to associate" did authorize the Court to review the State's policy choice, its evaluation of the competing interests at stake is seriously flawed. * * * The Court's glib rejection of the State's interest in increasing voter participation is particularly regrettable. In an era of dramatically declining voter participation, States should be free to experiment with reforms designed to make the democratic process more robust by involving the entire electorate in the process of selecting those who will serve as government officials. Opening the nominating process to all and encouraging voters to participate in any election that draws their interest is one obvious means of achieving this goal. I would also give some weight to the First Amendment associational interests of nonmembers of a party seeking to participate in the primary process, to the fundamental right of such nonmembers to cast a meaningful vote for the candidate of their choice, and to the preference of almost 60% of California voters — including a majority of registered Democrats and Republicans — for a blanket primary. In my view, a State is unquestionably entitled to rely on this combination of interests in deciding who may vote in a primary election conducted by the State. It is indeed strange to find that the First Amendment forecloses this decision. * * *

Notes and Questions

1. The Court suggested in footnote 8 that *open* primaries might be distinguishable from *blanket* primaries, such that the former might survive a First Amendment challenge. Do you find the distinction plausible?

2. The Court noted that the "forced association" effected by blanket primaries "has the likely outcome — indeed, in this case the *intended* outcome — of changing the parties' message." That effect, which occurs in open primaries as well as blanket ones, is sometimes subtle and sometimes dramatic. One of the dramatic episodes occurred in the 2014 Mississippi Republican primary for U.S. Senate. The incumbent, Thad Cochran, succeeded in narrowly defeating his more-conservative challenger, Chris McDaniel, by appealing to Democrats and in particular to black Democrats, who turned out in record numbers. *See* Jonathan Weisman & Campbell Robertson, *Blacks Regain Sway at Polls in Mississsippi*, N.Y. TIMES (June 25, 2014), *at* http://www.nytimes.com/2014/06/26/us/politics/blacks-regain-sway-at-polls-in-mississippi.html?_r=0.

3. Does *California Democratic Party* or *Eu*, or both, mean that state-mandated primary elections themselves are unconstitutional?

4. *Problem.* Virginia permits parties to choose their nominees by a variety of methods, including primaries, caucuses, conventions, and unassembled caucuses known as "firehouse primaries." The parties themselves may select the method of nominating their candidates, except that an incumbent member of the state legislature may designate the method to be employed in determining the party's nominee for his or her seat. Thus, if a party wishes to nominate its state-legislative candidates by convention, but an incumbent legislator would prefer the party to hold a primary, there will be a primary and the party will nominate the winner of that primary. Does such a system violate the party's associational rights? Does it violate any other provision of the Constitution? *See Miller v. Brown*, 503 F.3d 360 (4th Cir. 2007).

5. What does *California Democratic Party* say about whether the constitutional right to vote extends to primaries?

6. Recall that *Tashjian v. Republican Party* involved the constitutionality of a state-mandated closed primary, *i.e.*, one as to which independents were barred, while *California Democratic Party* involved the constitutionality of a state-mandated blanket primary. Footnote 13 of *Tashjian* left open the constitutionality of state statutes mandating *semiclosed* primaries, *i.e.*, those as to which members of the party and independents may participate, but as to which members of *other* parties are barred. The next case considered that issue.

CLINGMAN v. BEAVER
Supreme Court of the United States
544 U.S. 581, 125 S. Ct. 2029, 161 L. Ed. 2d 920 (2005)

JUSTICE THOMAS delivered the opinion of the Court [in which CHIEF JUSTICE REHNQUIST, JUSTICE O'CONNOR, JUSTICE SCALIA, JUSTICE KENNEDY, and JUSTICE BREYER join], except as to Part II-A [in which CHIEF JUSTICE REHNQUIST, JUSTICE SCALIA, and JUSTICE KENNEDY join]. * * *

I

Oklahoma's election laws provide that only registered members of a political party may vote in the party's primary, unless the party opens its primary to registered Independents as well. In May 2000, the LPO [Libertarian Party of Oklahoma] notified the secretary of the Oklahoma State Election Board that it wanted to open its upcoming primary to all registered Oklahoma voters, without regard to their party affiliation. Pursuant to [Okla. Stat. Ann., Tit. 26] § 1-104, the secretary agreed as to Independent voters, but not as to voters registered with other political parties. The LPO and several Republican and Democratic voters then sued for declaratory and injunctive relief * * *, alleging that Oklahoma's semiclosed primary law unconstitutionally burdens their First Amendment right to freedom of political association. [The District Court held the semiclosed primary constitutional, but the Tenth Circuit reversed.] * * *

II

* * *

In *Tashjian* [v. *Republican Party of Connecticut*, 479 U.S. 208, 225 (1986)] [p. 449], this Court struck down, as inconsistent with the First Amendment, a closed primary system that prevented a political party from inviting Independent voters to vote in the party's primary. This case presents a question that *Tashjian* left open: whether a State may prevent a political party from inviting registered voters of other parties to vote in its primary. *Id.*, at 224, n.13. * * * We are persuaded that any burden Oklahoma's semiclosed primary imposes is minor and justified by legitimate state interests.

A

*   *   *

[T]he Republican and Democratic voters who have brought this action do not want to associate with the LPO, at least not in any formal sense. They wish to remain registered with the Republican, Democratic, or Reform parties, and yet to assist in selecting the Libertarian Party's candidates for the general election. Their interest is in casting a vote for a Libertarian candidate in a particular primary election, rather than in banding together with fellow citizens committed to the LPO's political goals and ideas. And the LPO is happy to have their votes, if not their membership on the party rolls.

However, a voter who is unwilling to disaffiliate from another party to vote in the LPO's primary forms little "association" with the LPO — nor the LPO with him. See *Tashjian, supra,* at 235 (SCALIA, J., dissenting). That same voter might wish to participate in numerous party primaries, or cast ballots for several candidates, in any given race. The issue is not "dual associations," [as JUSTICE O'CONNOR claims], but seemingly boundless ones. * * *

Oklahoma's semiclosed primary system imposes an even slighter burden on voters than on the LPO. * * * In Oklahoma, registered members of the Republican, Democratic, and Reform Parties who wish to vote in the LPO primary simply need to file a form with the county election board secretary to change their registration. Voters are not "locked in" to an unwanted party affiliation because with only nominal effort they are free to vote in the LPO primary. For this reason, too, the registration requirement does not unduly hinder the LPO from associating with members of other parties. To attract members of other parties, the LPO need only persuade voters to make the minimal effort necessary to switch parties.

B

Respondents argue that this case is no different from *Tashjian.* According to respondents, the burden imposed by Oklahoma's semiclosed primary system is no less severe than the burden at issue in *Tashjian,* and hence we must apply strict scrutiny as we did in *Tashjian.* We disagree. * * * As an initial matter, *Tashjian* applied strict scrutiny with little discussion of the magnitude of the burdens imposed by Connecticut's closed primary on parties' and voters' associational rights. But not every electoral law that burdens associational rights is subject to strict scrutiny. Instead, as our cases since *Tashjian* have clarified, strict scrutiny is appropriate only if the burden is severe. In *Tashjian* itself, Independent voters could join the Connecticut Republican Party as late as the day before the primary. As explained above, requiring voters to register with a party prior to participating in the party's primary minimally burdens voters' associational rights.

Nevertheless, *Tashjian* is distinguishable. Oklahoma's semiclosed primary imposes an even less substantial burden than did the Connecticut closed primary at issue in *Tashjian.* In *Tashjian,* this Court identified two ways in which Connecticut's closed primary limited citizens' freedom of political association. The first and most important was that it required Independent voters to affiliate publicly with a party to vote in its primary. That is not true in this case. At issue here are voters who have *already* affiliated publicly with one of Oklahoma's political parties. These voters need not register as Libertarians to vote in the LPO's primary; they need only declare themselves Independents, which would leave them free to participate in any party primary that is open to registered Independents.

The second and less important burden imposed by Connecticut's closed primary system was that political parties could not "broaden opportunities for joining . . . by their own act, without any intervening action by potential voters." *Tashjian*, 479 U.S., at 216, n.7. Voters also had to act by registering themselves in a particular party. That is equally true of Oklahoma's semiclosed primary system: Voters must register as Libertarians or Independents to participate in the LPO's primary. However, *Tashjian* did not characterize this burden alone as severe, and with good reason. Many electoral regulations, including voter registration generally, require that voters take some action to participate in the primary process. Election laws invariably "affect — at least to some degree — the individual's right to vote and his right to associate with others for political ends." *Anderson* v. *Celebrezze*, 460 U.S. 780, 788 (1983) [p. 517].

These minor barriers between voter and party do not compel strict scrutiny. To deem ordinary and widespread burdens like these severe would subject virtually every electoral regulation to strict scrutiny, hamper the ability of States to run efficient and equitable elections, and compel federal courts to rewrite state electoral codes. The Constitution does not require that result, for it is beyond question "that States may, and inevitably must, enact reasonable regulations of parties, elections, and ballots to reduce election- and campaign-related disorder." *Timmons* [v. *Twin Cities Area New Party*, 520 U.S. 351, 358 (1997)] [p. 534]; *Storer* v. *Brown*, 415 U.S. 724, 730 (1974) [p. 513]. Oklahoma's semiclosed primary system does not severely burden the associational rights of the State's citizenry.

C

When a state electoral provision places no heavy burden on associational rights, "a State's important regulatory interests will usually be enough to justify reasonable, nondiscriminatory restrictions." *Timmons, supra,* at 358; *Anderson, supra,* at 788. Here, Oklahoma's semiclosed primary advances a number of regulatory interests that this Court recognizes as important: It "preserves [political] parties as viable and identifiable interest groups"; enhances parties' electioneering and party-building efforts; and guards against party raiding and "sore loser" candidacies by spurned primary contenders.

First, as Oklahoma asserts, its semiclosed primary "preserves the political parties as viable and identifiable interest groups, insuring that the results of a primary election, in a broad sense, accurately reflect the voting of the party members." The LPO wishes to open its primary to registered Republicans and Democrats, who may well vote in numbers that dwarf the roughly 300 registered LPO voters in Oklahoma. If the LPO is permitted to open its primary to all registered voters regardless of party affiliation, the candidate who emerges from the LPO primary may be "unconcerned with, if not . . . hostile to," the political preferences of the majority of the LPO's members. It does not matter that the LPO is willing to risk the surrender of its identity in exchange for electoral success. Oklahoma's interest is independent and concerns the integrity of its primary system. The State wants to "avoid primary election outcomes which would tend to confuse or mislead the general voting population to the extent [it] relies on party labels as representative of certain ideologies."

Moreover, this Court has found that "in facilitating the effective operation of [a] democratic government, a state might reasonably classify voters or candidates according to political affiliations." But for that classification to mean much, Oklahoma must be allowed to limit voters' ability to roam among parties' primaries. * * * Opening the LPO's primary to all voters not only would render the LPO's *imprimatur* an unreliable index of its candidate's actual political philosophy, but it also "would make registered party affiliations significantly less meaningful in the Oklahoma primary election system." Oklahoma reasonably has concluded that opening the LPO's primary to all voters regardless of party affiliation would undermine the crucial role of political parties in the primary process.

Second, Oklahoma's semiclosed primary system, by retaining the importance of party affiliation, aids in parties' electioneering and party-building efforts. "It is common experience that direct solicitation of party members — by mail, telephone, or face-to-face contact, and by the candidates themselves or by their active supporters — is part of any primary election campaign." Yet parties' voter turnout efforts depend in large part on accurate voter registration rolls.

When voters are no longer required to disaffiliate before participating in other parties' primaries, voter registration rolls cease to be an accurate reflection of voters' political preferences. And without registration rolls that accurately reflect likely or potential primary voters, parties risk expending precious resources to turn out party members who may have decided to cast their votes elsewhere. If encouraging citizens to vote is an important state interest, then Oklahoma is entitled to protect parties' ability to plan their primaries for a stable group of voters.

Third, Oklahoma has an interest in preventing party raiding, or "the organized switching of blocs of voters from one party to another in order to manipulate the outcome of the other party's primary election." For example, if the outcome of the Democratic Party primary were not in doubt, Democrats might vote in the LPO primary for the candidate most likely to siphon off votes from the Republican candidate in the general election. Or a Democratic primary contender who senses defeat might launch a "sore loser" candidacy by defecting to the LPO primary, taking with him loyal Democratic voters, and thus undermining the Democratic Party in the general election. Oklahoma has an interest in "tempering the destabilizing effects" of precisely this sort of "party splintering and excessive factionalism." Oklahoma's semiclosed primary system serves that interest by discouraging voters from temporarily defecting from another party to vote in the LPO primary. While the State's interest will not justify "unreasonably exclusionary restrictions," *Timmons*, 520 U.S., at 367, we have "repeatedly upheld reasonable, politically neutral regulations" like Oklahoma's semiclosed primary law, *id.*, at 369. * * *

Oklahoma remains free to allow the LPO to invite registered voters of other parties to vote in its primary. But the Constitution leaves that choice to the democratic process, not to the courts. The judgment of the Court of Appeals is reversed, and the case is remanded for further proceedings.

It is so ordered.

JUSTICE O'CONNOR, with whom JUSTICE BREYER joins * * *, concurring in part and concurring in the judgment.

I join the Court's opinion except for Part II-A. * * *

The plurality questions whether the LPO and voters registered with another party have any constitutionally cognizable interest in associating with one another through the LPO's primary. Its doubts on this point appear to stem from two implicit premises: first, that a voter forms a cognizable association with a political party only by registering with that party; and second, that a voter can only form a cognizable association with one party at a time. Neither of these premises is sound, in my view. As to the first, registration with a political party surely may signify an important personal commitment, which may be accompanied by faithful voting and even activism beyond the polls. But for many voters, registration serves principally as a mandatory (and perhaps even ministerial) prerequisite to participation in the party's primaries. The act of casting a ballot in a given primary may, for both the voter and the party, constitute a form of association that is at least as important as the act of registering. The fact that voting is episodic does not, in my judgment, undermine its associational significance; it simply reflects the special character of the electoral process, which allows citizens to join together at regular intervals to shape government through the choice of public officials.

As to the question of dual associations, I fail to see why registration with one party should negate a voter's First Amendment interest in associating with a second party. We surely would not say, for instance, that a registered Republican or Democrat has no protected interest in associating with the Libertarian Party by attending meetings or making political contributions. The validity of voters' and parties' interests in dual associations seems particularly clear where minor parties are concerned. For example, a voter may have a longstanding affiliation with a major party that she wishes to maintain, but she may nevertheless have a substantial interest in associating with a minor party during particular election cycles or in elections for particular offices. The voter's refusal to disaffiliate from the major party may reflect her abiding commitment to that party (which is not necessarily inconsistent with her desire to associate with a second party), the objective costs of disaffiliation, or both. The minor party, for its part, may have a significant interest in augmenting its voice in the political process by associating with sympathetic members of the major parties.

None of this is to suggest that the State does not have a superseding interest in restricting certain forms of association. We have never questioned, for example, the States' authority to restrict voters' public registration to a single party or to limit each voter to participating in a single party's primary. But the fact that a State's regulatory authority may ultimately trump voters' or parties' associational interests in a particular context is no reason to dismiss the validity of those interests. As a more general matter, I question whether judicial inquiry into the genuineness, intensity, or duration of a given voter's association with a given party is a fruitful way to approach constitutional challenges to regulations like the one at issue here. Primary voting is an episodic and sometimes isolated act of association, but it is a vitally important one and should be entitled to some level of constitutional protection. Accordingly, where a party invites a voter to participate in its primary and the voter seeks to do so, we should begin with the premise that there are significant associational interests at stake. From this starting point, we can then ask to what extent and in what manner the State may justifiably restrict those interests. * * *

* * * [A]ssuming the availability of reasonable reregistration procedures, a party's inability to persuade a voter to disaffiliate from a rival party would suggest not the presence of anticompetitive regulatory restrictions, but rather the party's failure to win the voter's allegiance. The semiclosed primary law, standing alone, does not impose a significant obstacle to participation in the LPO's primary, nor does it indicate partisan self dealing or a lockup of the political process that would warrant heightened judicial scrutiny.

For essentially the reasons explained by the Court, I agree that Oklahoma has a legitimate interest in requiring voters to disaffiliate from one party before participating in another party's primary. On the record before us, I also agree that the State's regulatory interests are adequate to justify the limited burden the semiclosed primary law imposes on respondents' freedom of association. And finally, I agree that this case is distinguishable from *Tashjian*. I joined the dissent in that case, and I think the Court's application of strict scrutiny there is difficult to square with the flexible standard of review articulated in our more recent cases. But *Tashjian* is entitled to respect under principles of *stare decisis*, and it can be fairly distinguished on the grounds that the closed primary law in that case imposed a greater burden on associational interests than does Oklahoma's semiclosed primary law, while the State's regulatory interests in *Tashjian* were weaker than they are here. * * *

JUSTICE STEVENS, with whom JUSTICE GINSBURG joins, and with whom JUSTICE SOUTER joins as to Parts I, II, and III, dissenting.

The Court's decision today diminishes the value of two important rights protected by the First Amendment: the individual citizen's right to vote for the candidate of her choice and a political party's right to define its own mission. No one would contend that a citizen's membership in either the Republican or the Democratic Party could disqualify her from attending political functions sponsored by another party, or from voting for a third party's candidate in a general election. If a third party invites her to participate in its primary election, her right to support the candidate of her choice merits constitutional protection, whether she elects to make a speech, to donate funds, or to cast a ballot. The importance of vindicating that individual right far outweighs any public interest in punishing registered Republicans or Democrats for acts of disloyalty. The balance becomes even more lopsided when the individual right is reinforced by the right of the Libertarian Party of Oklahoma (LPO) to associate with willing voters.

In concluding that the State's interests override those important values, the

Court focuses on interests that are not legitimate. States do not have a valid interest in manipulating the outcome of elections, in protecting the major parties from competition, or in stunting the growth of new parties. While States do have a valid interest in conducting orderly elections and in encouraging the maximum participation of voters, neither of these interests overrides (or, indeed, even conflicts with) the valid interests of both the LPO and the voters who wish to participate in its primary.

In the final analysis, this case is simple. Occasionally, a political party's interest in defining its platform and its procedures for selecting and supporting its candidates conflicts with the voters' interest in participating in the selection of their elected representatives. If those values do conflict, we may be faced with difficult choices. But when, as in this case, those values reinforce one another a decision should be easy. Oklahoma has enacted a statute that impairs both; it denies a party the right to invite willing voters to participate in its primary elections. I would therefore affirm the Court of Appeals' judgment.

I

In rejecting the individual respondents' claims, the majority focuses on their associational interests. While the voters in this case certainly have an interest in associating with the LPO, they are primarily interested in voting for a particular candidate, who happens to be in the LPO. Indeed, I think we have lost sight of the principal purpose of a primary: to nominate a candidate for office.

Because our recent cases have focused on the associational interest of voters, rather than the right to vote itself, it is important to identify three basic precepts. First, it is clear that the right to vote includes the right to vote in a primary election. See *United States* v. *Classic*, 313 U.S. 299, 318 (1941); *Terry* v. *Adams*, 345 U.S. 461 (1953) [p. 431]. When the State makes the primary an "integral part of the procedure of choice," every eligible citizen's right to vote should receive the same protection as in the general election. Second, the right to vote, whether in the primary or the general election, is the right to vote "for the candidate of one's choice." Finally, in assessing burdens on that right — burdens that are not limited to absolute denial of the right — we should focus on the realities of the situation, not on empty formalism.

Here, the impact of the Oklahoma statute on the voters' right to vote for the candidate of their choosing is not a mere "burden"; it is a prohibition.[1] By virtue of the fact that their preferred candidate is a member of a different party, respondents are absolutely precluded from voting for him or her in the primary election. It is not an answer that the voters could participate in another primary (*i.e.*, the primary for the party with which they are registered) since the individual for whom they wish to vote is not a candidate in that primary. If the so-called "white primary" cases

---

[1] It is not enough that registered members of other parties may simply change their registration. Changing one's political party is not simply a matter of filing a form with the State; for many individuals it can be a significant decision. A view that party membership is merely a label demeans for many the personal significance of party identification and illustrates what little weight the majority actually gives to the associational interests in this case.

make anything clear, it is that the denial of the right to vote cannot be cured by the ability to participate in a subsequent or different election. Just as the "only election that has counted" in *Terry* was the Jaybird primary, since it was there that the public official was selected in any meaningful sense, the only primary that counts here is the one in which the candidate respondents want to vote for is actually running.

This is not to say that voters have an absolute right to participate in whatever primary they desire. For instance, the parties themselves have a strong associational interest in determining which individuals may vote in their primaries, and that interest will normally outweigh the interest of the uninvited voter.[2] But in the ordinary case the State simply has no interest in classifying voters by their political party and in limiting the elections in which voters may participate as a result of that classification. * * *

II

*   *   *

In concluding that the Oklahoma statute is constitutional, the majority argues that associational interests between the LPO and registered members of other parties are either nonexistent or not heavily burdened by the Oklahoma scheme. * * * [O]ur decision in *Tashjian* rejected these arguments.

In *Tashjian* we held that the State could not prohibit Republicans from inviting voters who were not registered with a political party to participate in the Republican primary. We recognized that "the Party's attempt to broaden the base of public participation in and support for its activities is conduct undeniably central to the exercise of the right of association." 479 U.S., at 214. Importantly, we rejected the notion that the associational interest was somehow diminished because the voters the party sought to include were not formally registered as Republicans. *Id.*, at 215. We reasoned that a State could not prohibit independents from contributing financial support to a Republican candidate or from participating in the party's events; it would be anomalous if it were able to prohibit participation by independents in the "basic function" of the party. Because of the importance of those interests, we carefully examined the interests asserted by the State, and finding them lacking, struck down the prohibition on independents' participation in the Republican primary.

Virtually identical interests are at stake in this case. It is the LPO's belief that attracting a more diverse group of voters in its primary would enable it to select a more mainstream candidate who would be more viable in the general election. Like the Republicans in *Tashjian*, the LPO is cognizant of the fact that in order to enjoy success at the voting booth it must have support from voters who identify themselves as independents, Republicans, or Democrats. * * *

---

[2] The voters' interest may still prevail if, as was the case in *Terry* v. *Adams* and *Smith* v. *Allwright*, the party primary is the *de facto* election. In part because of this Court's refusal to intervene in political gerrymandering cases, *Davis* v. *Bandemer*, 478 U.S. 109 (1986), an increasing number of districts are becoming "safe districts" in which one party effectively controls the outcome of the election.

III

As justification for the State's abridgment of the constitutionally protected interests asserted by the LPO and the voters, the majority relies on countervailing state interests that are either irrelevant or insignificant. Neither separately nor in the aggregate do these interests support the Court's decision.

First, the Court makes the remarkable suggestion that by opening up its primary to Democrats and Republicans, the LPO will be saddled with so many nonlibertarian voters that the ultimate candidate will not be, in any sense, "libertarian." But the LPO is *seeking* the crossover voting of Republicans and Democrats. Rightly or wrongly, the LPO feels that the best way to produce a viable candidate is to invite voters from other parties to participate in its primary. That may dilute what the Court believes to be the core of the Libertarian philosophy, but it is no business of the State to tell a political party what its message should be, how it should select its candidates, or how it should form coalitions to ensure electoral success.

Second, the majority expresses concern that crossover voting may create voter confusion. This paternalistic concern is belied by the District Court's finding that no significant voter confusion would occur.

Third, the majority suggests that crossover voting will impair the State's interest in properly classifying candidates and voters. As an empirical matter, a crossover voter may have a lesser commitment to the party with which he is registered if he votes in another party's primary. Nevertheless, the State does not have a valid interest in defining what it means to be a Republican or a Democrat, or in attempting to ensure the political orthodoxy of party members simply for the convenience of those parties. Even if participation in the LPO's primary causes a voter to be a less committed "Democrat" or "Republican" (a proposition I reject[7]), the dilution of that commitment does not justify abridgment of the fundamental rights at issue in this case. While party identity is important in our political system, it should not be immunized from the risk of change.

Fourth, the majority argues that opening up the LPO primary to members of the Republican and Democratic Parties might interfere with electioneering and party-building efforts. It is clear, of course, that the majority here is concerned only with the Democratic and Republican Parties, since party building is precisely what the LPO is attempting to accomplish. Nevertheless, that concern is misplaced. Even if, as the majority claims, the Republican and Democratic voter rolls, mailing lists, and phone banks are not as accurate as they would otherwise be,[9] the administrative inconvenience of the major parties does not outweigh the right to vote or the

---

[7] Allowing a potential crossover voter to vote in the LPO primary would not change the level of commitment he has toward his party of registration; it would simply give him an outlet to express the views he already holds.

[9] The majority's argument is that voters who would otherwise vote in the Republican or Democratic primaries would vote in the LPO primary, and that the Democratic and Republican lists would not be an accurate indicator of who is likely to vote in those primaries, and of which voters to spend party resources on. First, I find it doubtful that those voters who vote in the LPO primary would have voted in the Democratic or Republican primary; rather, they probably would not have been sufficiently motivated to

associational interests of those voters and the LPO. At its core, this argument is based on a fear that the LPO might be successful in convincing Democratic or Republican voters to participate more fully in the LPO. Far from being a compelling interest, it is an impermissible one.

Finally, the majority warns against the possibility of raiding, by which voters of another party maliciously vote in a primary in order to change the outcome of the primary, either to nominate a particularly weak candidate, a "sore-loser" candidate, or a candidate who would siphon votes from another party. * * * [H]owever, * * * [i]f the LPO is willing to take the risk that its party may be "hijacked" by individuals who hold views opposite to their own, the State has little interest in second-guessing the LPO's decision. * * *

In the end, the balance of interests clearly favors the LPO and those voters who wish to participate in its primary. The associational interests asserted — the right to select a standard bearer that the party thinks has the best chance of success, the ability to associate at the crucial juncture of selecting a candidate, and the desire to reach out to voters of other parties — are substantial and undoubtedly burdened by Oklahoma's statutory scheme. Any doubt about that fact is clearly answered by *Tashjian*. On the other side, the interests asserted by the State are either entirely speculative or simply protectionist measures that benefit the parties in power. No matter what the standard, they simply do not outweigh the interests of the LPO and its voters. * * *

Notes and Questions

1. Is Justice Stevens correct that the Court's analysis is inconsistent with *Tashjian*, or do you agree with the Court that *Tashjian* is distinguishable? Note that zero members of the *Tashjian* majority remained on the Court at the time of *Beaver*, while each of the four *Tashjian* dissenters was still on the Court as of 2004. (Justice Stevens's *Tashjian* dissent, however, did not indicate disagreement with *Tashjian*'s First Amendment analysis, and as a result it is not entirely surprising that he voted in *Beaver* to strike down Oklahoma's semiclosed primary.)

2. In her concurrence, Justice O'Connor suggested that states may restrict voters' and parties' associational rights by prohibiting persons from being members of more than one party, or from voting in more than one primary. Why? If she is correct that parties and voters can form "dual associations," what justification does a state have in limiting the activities that can comprise that association? *See American Party of Texas v. White*, 415 U.S. 767, 786 (1974):

> We have previously held that to protect the integrity of party primary elections, States may establish waiting periods before voters themselves may be permitted to change their registration and participate in another party's primary. *Rosario* v. *Rockefeller*, 410 U.S. 752 (1973). Likewise, it seems to us that the State may determine that it is essential to the integrity of the nominating process to confine voters to supporting one party and its

---

vote at all. Further, this would actually give Republicans and Democrats additional information as to which of their voters have Libertarian leanings.

candidates in the course of the same nominating process. [W]e see nothing invidious in disqualifying those who have voted at a party primary from signing petitions for another party seeking ballot position for its candidates for the same offices.

To take examples offered by Justice O'Connor and Justice Stevens, could a state prohibit persons from attending meetings of multiple parties or from donating money to more than one party? If not, what difference explains Justice O'Connor's view that states may restrict party membership and primary voting?

3.   Justice Stevens rested his analysis principally on the right to vote, rather than on parties' or voters' right of association. Why? Is he correct that the right to vote extends to primaries? Should such a right extend to participation in party caucuses and conventions as well? Should there be a fundamental right to be a member of one's chosen political party? How might one balance those rights against the party's right *not* to associate with the individual?

4.   *Problem.* Mississippi opens its primaries to those voters who "intend[] to support the nominations made in the primary in which [they] participate[]." It is not necessary, however, for voters to be members of the party in whose primary they wish to vote. The Mississippi Democratic Party challenges the law as creating the opportunity for non-Democrats to vote in its primary. Is the law unconstitutional? *See Mississippi State Democratic Party v. Barbour*, 491 F. Supp. 2d 641 (N.D. Miss. 2007), *vacated as unripe*, 529 F.3d 538 (5th Cir. 2008).

5.   *Problem.* State law provides that individuals eighteen years and older may vote in primary and general elections. The major parties wish to permit those persons who are seventeen at the time of the primary but who will turn eighteen by the date of the general election to vote in the primaries. Must the state permit them to vote? What if the parties wished to permit sixteen year-olds to vote in the primaries? What if the parties wish to exclude all persons under age 21? *See* Lisa Rein, *Pushing to Restore a Vote at 17*, WASH. POST Dec. 18, 2007, at B01.

6.   After *California Democratic Party* held that state's blanket primary unconstitutional, the State of Washington replaced its blanket primary with a "top-two" primary similar to the Louisiana system that *California Democratic Party* concluded would be constitutional. Under Louisiana's system, the candidates in the primary election were not identified by party, and the two candidates receiving the most votes, regardless of party, advanced to the general election. Washington's system added a twist: While the primary candidates were not identified as members of parties and were not running for the nomination of parties, the candidates were permitted to indicate on the ballot their party "preference." The next case explored whether that change tipped the constitutional balance.

WASHINGTON STATE GRANGE v. WASHINGTON STATE REPUBLICAN PARTY

Supreme Court of the United States
552 U.S. 442, 128 S. Ct. 1184, 170 L. Ed. 2d 151 (2008)

JUSTICE THOMAS delivered the opinion of the Court [in which CHIEF JUSTICE ROBERTS, JUSTICE STEVENS, JUSTICE SOUTER, JUSTICE GINSBURG, JUSTICE BREYER, and JUSTICE ALITO join].

In 2004, voters in the State of Washington passed an initiative changing the State's primary election system. The People's Choice Initiative of 2004, or Initiative 872 (I-872), provides that candidates for office shall be identified on the ballot by their self-designated "party preference"; that voters may vote for any candidate; and that the top two votegetters for each office, regardless of party preference, advance to the general election. The Court of Appeals for the Ninth Circuit held I-872 facially invalid as imposing an unconstitutional burden on state political parties' First Amendment rights. Because I-872 does not on its face impose a severe burden on political parties' associational rights, and because respondents' arguments to the contrary rest on factual assumptions about voter confusion that can be evaluated only in the context of an as-applied challenge, we reverse. * * *

Under I-872, all elections for "partisan offices" are conducted in two stages: a primary and a general election. To participate in the primary, a candidate must file a "declaration of candidacy" form, on which he declares his "major or minor party preference, or independent status." Each candidate and his party preference (or independent status) is in turn designated on the primary election ballot. A political party cannot prevent a candidate who is unaffiliated with, or even repugnant to, the party from designating it as his party of preference. In the primary election, voters may select "any candidate listed on the ballot, regardless of the party preference of the candidates or the voter."

The candidates with the highest and second-highest vote totals advance to the general election, regardless of their party preferences. Thus, the general election may pit two candidates with the same party preference against one another. Each candidate's party preference is listed on the general election ballot, and may not be changed between the primary and general elections. * * *

* * * Respondents argue that I-872 is unconstitutional under [*California Democratic Party* v.] *Jones* [530 U.S. 567 (2000)] [p. 460] because it has the same "constitutionally crucial" infirmity that doomed California's blanket primary: it allows primary voters who are unaffiliated with a party to choose the party's nominee. Respondents claim that candidates who progress to the general election under I-872 will become the *de facto* nominees of the parties they prefer, thereby violating the parties' right to choose their own standard-bearers and altering their messages. * * *

The flaw in this argument is that, unlike the California primary, the I-872 primary does not, by its terms, choose parties' nominees. The essence of nomination — the choice of a party representative — does not occur under I-872. The law never refers to the candidates as nominees of any party, nor does it treat them as such. To the contrary, the election regulations specifically provide that the primary "does not serve to determine the nominees of a political party but serves to winnow the number of candidates to a final list of two for the general election." The top two candidates from the primary election proceed to the general election regardless of their party preferences. Whether parties nominate their own candidates outside the state-run primary is simply irrelevant. In fact, parties may now nominate candidates by whatever mechanism they choose because I-872 repealed Washington's prior regulations governing party nominations.[7]

Respondents counter that, even if the I-872 primary does not actually choose parties' nominees, it nevertheless burdens their associational rights because voters will assume that candidates on the general election ballot are the nominees of their preferred parties. This brings us to the heart of respondents' case — and to the fatal flaw in their argument. At bottom, respondents' objection to I-872 is that voters will be confused by candidates' party-preference designations. Respondents' arguments are largely variations on this theme. Thus, they argue that even if voters do not assume that candidates on the general election ballot are the nominees of their parties, they will at least assume that the parties associate with, and approve of, them. This, they say, compels them to associate with candidates they do not endorse, alters the messages they wish to convey, and forces them to engage in counterspeech to disassociate themselves from the candidates and their positions on the issues.

We reject each of these contentions for the same reason: They all depend, not on any facial requirement of I-872, but on the possibility that voters will be confused as to the meaning of the party-preference designation. But respondents' assertion that voters will misinterpret the party-preference designation is sheer speculation. * * * There is simply no basis to presume that a well-informed electorate will interpret a candidate's party-preference designation to mean that the candidate is the party's chosen nominee or representative or that the party associates with or approves of the candidate. This strikes us as especially true here, given that it was the voters of Washington themselves, rather than their elected representatives, who enacted I-872.

Of course, it is *possible* that voters will misinterpret the candidates' party-preference designations as reflecting endorsement by the parties. But these cases involve a facial challenge, and we cannot strike down I-872 on its face based on the mere possibility of voter confusion. Because respondents brought their suit as a facial challenge, we have no evidentiary record against which to assess their assertions that voters will be confused. Indeed, because I-872 has never been implemented, we do not even have ballots indicating how party preference will be displayed. It stands to reason that whether voters will be confused by the party-preference designations will depend in significant part on the form of the ballot. * * * [W]e must, in fairness to the voters of the State of Washington who

---

[7] It is true that parties may no longer indicate their nominees on the ballot, but that is unexceptionable: The First Amendment does not give political parties a right to have their nominees designated as such on the ballot. See *Timmons* v. *Twin Cities Area New Party*, 520 U.S. 351, 362–363 (1997) [p. 557]. Parties do not gain such a right simply because the State affords candidates the opportunity to indicate their party preference on the ballot. "Ballots serve primarily to elect candidates, not as forums for political expression." *Id.*, at 363.

enacted I-872 and in deference to the executive and judicial officials who are charged with implementing it, ask whether the ballot could conceivably be printed in such a way as to eliminate the possibility of widespread voter confusion and with it the perceived threat to the First Amendment.

It is not difficult to conceive of such a ballot. For example, petitioners propose that the actual I-872 ballot could include prominent disclaimers explaining that party preference reflects only the self-designation of the candidate and not an official endorsement by the party. They also suggest that the ballots might note preference in the form of a candidate statement that emphasizes the candidate's personal determination rather than the party's acceptance of the candidate, such as "my party preference is the Republican Party." Additionally, the State could decide to educate the public about the new primary ballots through advertising or explanatory materials mailed to voters along with their ballots. We are satisfied that there are a variety of ways in which the State could implement I-872 that would eliminate any real threat of voter confusion. And without the specter of widespread voter confusion, respondents' arguments about forced association and compelled speech fall flat. * * *

Because we have concluded that I-872 does not severely burden respondents, the State need not assert a compelling interest. The State's asserted interest in providing voters with relevant information about the candidates on the ballot is easily sufficient to sustain I-872.

* * * We accordingly hold that I-872 is facially constitutional. The judgment of the Court of Appeals is reversed.

It is so ordered.

CHIEF JUSTICE ROBERTS, with whom JUSTICE ALITO joins, concurring.

I share JUSTICE SCALIA's concern that permitting a candidate to identify his political party preference on an official election ballot — regardless of whether the candidate is endorsed by the party or is even a member — may effectively force parties to accept candidates they do not want, amounting to forced association in violation of the First Amendment.

* * * Voter perceptions matter, [however,] and if voters do not actually believe the parties and the candidates are tied together, it is hard to see how the parties' associational rights are adversely implicated. After all, individuals frequently claim to favor this or that political party; these preferences, without more, do not create an unconstitutional forced association. * * *

If the ballot is designed in such a manner that no reasonable voter would believe that the candidates listed there are nominees or members of, or otherwise associated with, the parties the candidates claimed to "prefer," the I-872 primary system would likely pass constitutional muster. I cannot say on the present record that it would be impossible for the State to design such a ballot. * * * On the other hand, if the ballot merely lists the candidates' preferred parties next to the candidates' names, or otherwise fails clearly to convey that the parties and the candidates are not necessarily associated, the I-872 system would not survive a First Amendment challenge.

JUSTICE SCALIA complains that * * * a particular candidate's "endorsement" of a party might alter the party's message, and this violates the party's freedom of association.

But there is no general right to stop an individual from saying, "I prefer this party," even if the party would rather he not. Normally, the party protects its message in such a case through responsive speech of its own. What makes this case different of course is that the State controls the content of the ballot, which we have never considered a public forum. Neither the candidate nor the party dictates the message conveyed by the ballot. In such a case, it is important to know what the ballot actually says — both about the candidate and about the party's association with the candidate. It is possible that no reasonable voter in Washington State will regard the listed candidates as members of, or otherwise associated with, the political parties the candidates claim to prefer. Nothing in my analysis requires the parties to produce studies regarding voter perceptions on this score, but I would wait to see what the ballot says before deciding whether it is unconstitutional.

Still, I agree with JUSTICE SCALIA that the history of the challenged law suggests the State is not particularly interested in devising ballots that meet these constitutional requirements. But this record simply does not allow us to say with certainty that the election system created by I-872 is unconstitutional. Accordingly, I agree with the Court that respondents' present challenge to the law must fail, and I join the Court's opinion.

JUSTICE SCALIA, with whom JUSTICE KENNEDY joins, dissenting.

The electorate's perception of a political party's beliefs is colored by its perception of those who support the party; and a party's defining act is the selection of a candidate and advocacy of that candidate's election by conferring upon him the party's endorsement. When the state-printed ballot for the general election causes a party to be associated with candidates who may not fully (if at all) represent its views, it undermines both these vital aspects of political association. The views of the self-identified party supporter color perception of the party's message, and that self-identification on the ballot, with no space for party repudiation or party identification of its own candidate, impairs the party's advocacy of its standard bearer. Because Washington has not demonstrated that this severe burden upon parties' associational rights is narrowly tailored to serve a compelling interest — indeed, because it seems to me Washington's only plausible interest is precisely to reduce the effectiveness of political parties — I would find the law unconstitutional. * * *

The State of Washington need not like, and need not favor, political parties. It is entirely free to decline running primaries for the selection of party nominees and to hold nonpartisan general elections in which party labels have no place on the ballot. Parties would then be left to their own devices in both selecting and publicizing their candidates. But Washington has done more than merely decline to make its electoral machinery available for party building. Recognizing that parties draw support for their candidates by giving them the party imprimatur, Washington seeks to reduce the effectiveness of that endorsement by allowing *any* candidate to use the ballot for drawing upon the goodwill that a party has developed, while preventing the party from using the ballot to reject the claimed association or to identify the genuine candidate of its choice. This does not merely place the ballot off limits for party building; it makes the ballot an instrument by which party building is impeded, permitting unrebutted associations that the party itself does not approve. * * *

The Court makes much of the fact that the party names shown on the Washington ballot may be billed as mere statements of candidate "preference." To be sure, the party is not *itself* forced to display favor for someone it does not wish to associate with, * * * as the political parties were arguably forced to do by lending their ballot-endorsement as party nominee in *Jones*. But thrusting an unwelcome, self-proclaimed association upon the party on the election ballot itself is amply destructive of the party's associational rights. An individual's endorsement of a party shapes the voter's view of what the party stands for, no less than the party's endorsement of an individual shapes the voter's view of what the individual stands for. * * * And because the ballot is the only document voters are guaranteed to see, and the last thing they see before casting their vote, there is "no means of replying" that "would be equally effective with the voter."

Not only is the party's message distorted, but its goodwill is hijacked. There can be no dispute that candidate acquisition of party labels on Washington's ballot — even if billed as self-identification — is a means of garnering the support of those who trust and agree with the party. The "I prefer the D's" and "I prefer the R's" will not be on the ballot for esthetic reasons; they are designed to link candidates to unwilling parties (or at least parties who are unable to express their revulsion) and to encourage voters to cast their ballots based in part on the trust they place in the party's name and the party's philosophy. These harms will be present no matter how Washington's law is implemented. There is therefore "no set of circumstances" under which Washington's law would not severely burden political parties, and no good reason to wait until Washington has undermined its political parties to declare that it is forbidden to do so. * * *

* * * I assuredly do not share THE CHIEF JUSTICE's view that the First Amendment will be satisfied so long as the ballot "is designed in such a manner that no reasonable voter would believe that the candidates listed there are nominees or members of, or otherwise associated with, the parties the candidates claimed to 'prefer.'" To begin with, it seems to me quite impossible for the ballot to satisfy a reasonable voter that the candidate is not "associated with" the party for which he has expressed a preference. He has associated *himself* with the party by his very expression of a preference — and that indeed is the whole purpose of allowing the preference to be expressed. If all THE CHIEF JUSTICE means by "associated with" is that the candidate "does not speak on the party's behalf or with the party's approval," none of my analysis in this opinion relies upon that misperception, nor upon the misperception that the candidate is a member or the nominee of the party. Avoiding those misperceptions is far from enough. Is it enough to say on the ballot that a notorious and despised racist who says that the party is his choice does not speak with the party's approval? Surely not. His unrebutted association of that

party with his views distorts the image of the party nonetheless. And the fact that the candidate who expresses a "preference" for one or another party is shown not to be the nominee of that party does not deprive him of the boost from the party's reputation which the party wishes to confer only on its nominee. * * *

The majority opinion and THE CHIEF JUSTICE's concurrence also endorse a wait-and-see approach on the grounds that it is not yet evident how the law will affect voter perception of the political parties. But contrary to the Court's suggestion, it is not incumbent on the political parties to adduce "evidence" that forced association affects their ability to advocate for their candidates and their causes. We have never put expressive groups to this perhaps-impossible task. Rather, we accept their own assessments of the matter. * * * [I]n *Jones,* * * * we [did not] require the political parties to demonstrate either that voters would incorrectly perceive the "nominee" labels on the ballot to be the products of party elections or that the labels would change voter perceptions of the party. It does not take a study to establish that when statements of party connection are the sole information listed next to candidate names on the ballot, those statements will affect voters' perceptions of what the candidate stands for, what the party stands for, and whom they should elect.

Since I conclude that Washington's law imposes a severe burden on political parties' associational rights, I would uphold the law only if it were "narrowly tailored" to advance "a compelling state interest." Neither the Court's opinion nor the State's submission claims that Washington's law passes such scrutiny. The State argues only that it "has a rational basis" for "providing voters with a modicum of relevant information about the candidates." This is the only interest the Court's opinion identifies as well.

But "rational basis" is the *least* demanding of our tests * * *. It falls far, far short of establishing the compelling state interest that the First Amendment requires. And to tell the truth, here even the existence of a rational basis is questionable. Allowing candidates to identify themselves with particular parties on the ballot displays the State's view that adherence to party philosophy is "an important — perhaps paramount — consideration in the citizen's choice." If that is so, however, it seems to me irrational not to allow the party to disclaim that self-association, or to identify its own endorsed candidate.

It is no mystery what is going on here. There is no state interest behind this law except the Washington Legislature's dislike for bright-colors partisanship, and its desire to blunt the ability of political parties with noncentrist views to endorse and advocate their own candidates. * * * I dissent from the Court's conclusion that the Constitution permits this sabotage.

Notes and Questions

1. Consider various forms the Washington ballot might take. If the ballot said simply "Joe Smith (R)" and "Sally Jones (D)," with a notation at the bottom of the ballot saying that the party indications were expressions of party preferences of candidates, and did not necessarily indicate party membership or the parties' endorsements, would such a ballot be constitutional? What if, as the Court

suggested, the explanation were provided in a document provided with the ballot, but not on the ballot itself? After *Grange*, the Washington Secretary of State published a list of frequently asked questions for voters, which provided this explanation of the party preference: "Each candidate for partisan office may state a political party that he or she prefers. A candidate's preference does not imply that the candidate is nominated or endorsed by the party, or that the party approves of or associates with that candidate." Should the document make any difference to the constitutional question?

2.   If the disclaimer were to appear on the ballot, how detailed should the disclaimer have to be? If the ballot had a column next to the candidates' names that was labeled simply as "party preference," would that be constitutional? For the 2008 election, Washington chose to identify party preference on the ballot using this language:

JOHN SMITH
(Prefers Example Party)

or

JOHN SMITH
(States No Party Preference)

Sam Reed, Washington Secretary of State, *State Proposes Ballot Language for Top 2 Primary*, Apr. 16, 2008, *at* http://www.secstate.wa.gov/office/osos_ news.aspx?i= V22ztlROa18W%2FvuTy7o2Mw%3D%3D. Does that language obviate the constitutional concern?

The Ninth Circuit upheld Washington's top-two primary against a constitutional challenge in *Washington State Republican Party v. Washington State Grange*, 676 F.3d 784 (9th Cir.), *cert. denied*, 133 S. Ct. 110 (2012); *see also Rubin v. Bowen*, No. RG11605301 (Cal. Super. Ct. 2013), *available at* http://electionlawblog.org/wp-content/uploads/11-Order-Amended-Corrected.pdf (upholding California's top-two primary). The court held that the manner in which Washington implemented the primary was unlikely to lead to widespread voter confusion. In addition to the ballot notation described above, the ballots contained the following notice: "READ: Each candidate for partisan office may state a political party that he or she prefers. A candidate's preference does not imply that the candidate is nominated or endorsed by the party, or that the party approves of or associates with that candidate." Furthermore, the state mailed a notice to voters and aired advertisements explaining the new ballots.

3.   In an as-applied challenge to the Washington law, how should a court assess a ballot's capacity to confuse voters? Chief Justice Roberts suggested the appropriate test should be whether "no reasonable voter would believe that the candidates listed [on the ballot] are nominees or members of, or otherwise associated with, the parties the candidates claimed to 'prefer.' " Is the level of confusion a factual question to be decided by a jury? Should the question be whether the ballot is likely to mislead a "reasonable voter"? Whether confusion of actual voters (how many?) is possible? Probable? Should we limit our assessment to the "well-informed electorate," to which the majority referred? Why? What kind of evidence would be sufficient to support an argument that the ballot is too confusing?

4.   Should states be able to use non-partisan ballots, which include no reference to the candidates' party affiliations? Should the state have to demonstrate an interest in promoting the image of the officeholder as non-partisan? Does it matter whether the election is for judicial office or for a "political" one? *See Ohio Council 8 American Federation of State, County, and Municipal Employees v. Brunner,* 24 F. Supp. 3d 680 (S.D. Ohio 2014) (upholding Ohio's non-partisan ballot for judicial offices).

We close this section with two lower-court cases that involve issues of party identity and associational rights that have been featured throughout the cases we have read already. In both, a nominee objectionable to the party leadership sought the party's nomination, only to be told that his views were antithetical to the principles of the party.

DUKE v. MASSEY
United States Court of Appeals for the Eleventh Circuit
87 F.3d 1226 (11th Cir. 1996)

HATCHETT, CIRCUIT JUDGE [with whom HENDERSON, SENIOR CIRCUIT JUDGE, and MILLS, DISTRICT JUDGE, join]: * * *

David Duke, a controversial political figure, sought the Republican Party's nomination for President of the United States for the 1992 election. In pursuing the Republican Party nomination, Duke participated in presidential primaries in various states throughout the nation. In December 1991, Georgia's Secretary of State, Max Cleland, prepared and published a list of potential candidates for Georgia's presidential preference primary. Duke's name appeared on the Georgia list of presidential candidates for the Republican Party nomination. The Secretary submitted his initial list of presidential primary candidates to the presidential candidate selection committee (Committee) for the Republican Party, the committee that is responsible for representing the Republican Party in selecting the [R]epublican candidates to appear on the presidential preference primary ballot, according to section 21-2-193(a) of the Georgia Code.

On December 16, 1991, the Committee, consisting of Georgia's Republican Party Chairperson Alec Poitevint, Senate Minority Leader Tom Phillips, and House Minority Leader Paul Heard, met to discuss the Secretary's list of potential presidential candidates. Pursuant to their authority under O.C.G.A. § 21-2-193(a), the Committee deleted Duke's name from the list of potential [R]epublican presidential candidates.[3] Following the Committee's decision, the Secretary of State published a list of presidential candidates that did not include Duke's name. * * *

On January 15, 1992, Duke and voters who desired an opportunity to vote for him filed this lawsuit * * *, seeking a temporary restraining order, a preliminary

----

[3] Under Georgia law, "each person designated by the Secretary of State as a presidential candidate shall appear upon the ballot of the appropriate political party or body unless all committee members of the same political party or body as the candidate agree to delete such candidate's name from the ballot." O.C.G.A. § 21-2-193(a).

injunction, and a permanent injunction * * * to prevent the printing of primary ballots for the 1992 Georgia [R]epublican presidential preference primary without Duke's name being listed as a candidate. In their complaint, the appellants alleged that [O.G.C.A. § 21-2-193 and] the Committee's decision to exclude Duke's name from the primary ballot deprived them of their right to free speech, right to association, right to due process, right of equal protection, right to run for office and the right to vote, in violation of the First and Fourteenth Amendments to the United States Constitution. * * * The district court granted the appellees' motion for summary judgment finding that the state had a compelling interest in protecting political parties' right to define their identity and finding that the statute was narrowly tailored to advance the state's compelling interest. * * *

Since we have determined [in an earlier appeal] that the Committee's decision to exclude Duke from the primary ballot constituted state action, we now assess the purported interests that Duke and the voters alleged were infringed and the state's interests for enacting O.C.G.A. § 21-2-193. * * *

* * * Duke contends that because the statute grants the committee members "unfettered discretion" to grant or deny ballot access it is unconstitutional in that it allows the Committee members to exclude candidates based on the content of their speech. Duke argues that the statute also infringes his right to freedom of association.

* * * Although Duke is correct in identifying his First and Fourteenth Amendment interests, those interests do not trump the Republican Party's right to identify its membership based on political beliefs nor the state's interests in protecting the Republican Party's right to define itself. Therefore, the Committee, acting as representatives of the Republican Party under O.C.G.A. § 21-2-193, did not heavily burden Duke's First Amendment and Fourteenth Amendment rights when it excluded him from the Republican Party's presidential primary ballot.

The voters, supporters of Duke, claim that O.C.G.A. § 21-2-193 burdens their associational rights and their right to vote for a candidate of their choice [because] the Committee has unfettered discretion to decide who is fit and who is not fit to run as a [R]epublican. The Supreme Court has recognized that a free and open debate on the qualifications of candidates is "integral to the operation of the system of government established by our Constitution," and that burdens on candidate access to the ballot directly burden the voters' ability to voice preferences. In this case, however, the voters have failed to offer any authority suggesting that they have a right to vote for their candidate of choice as a [R]epublican in a nonbinding primary. In fact, * * * any burden on these voters is "considerably attenuated" and possibly nonexistent. * * *

Although we do not believe that Duke and the voters' rights were heavily burdened as a result of the Committee's decision under O.C.G.A. § 21-2-193, we will apply strict scrutiny as the district court did in order to err on the side of caution. Undeniably, Duke has a First Amendment right to express his political beliefs free from state discrimination no matter how repugnant his beliefs may be to others. It is equally clear, however, that he does not have a First Amendment right to express his beliefs as a presidential candidate for the Republican Party. The Republican Party has a First Amendment right to freedom of association and an attendant right to identify those who constitute the party based on political beliefs. [*Democratic Party of the United States v. La Follette*, 450 U.S. 107, 122 (1981)] [p. 442.] Therefore, the Committee acting in a representative capacity for the Republican Party did not have to accept Duke as a [R]epublican presidential candidate. Duke does not have the right to associate with an "unwilling partner." Likewise, Duke supporters do not have a First Amendment right to associate with him as a Republican Party presidential candidate. Duke's supporters were not foreclosed from supporting him * * * as a third-party candidate in the primary or as a write-in candidate in the primary or general election.

The state has a compelling interest in protecting political parties' right to define their membership. Moreover, states have a significant interest in structuring and regulating elections in order to facilitate order, honesty and fairness. Common sense dictates that states must regulate elections and that the regulations will necessarily impose some burden upon voters and parties. We believe that O.C.G.A. § 21-2-193 is narrowly tailored to further Georgia's compelling state interests. Under the statute, three party leaders are appointed to serve on the Committee.[8] Although the Committee's decision to exclude a candidate from the presidential primary ballot is unreviewable by the entire membership of the party, these committee members are leaders in the Republican Party and are ultimately held accountable for their decisions by the membership of the Republican Party. Under the terms of O.C.G.A. [§] 21-2-193, a person cannot serve on the Committee unless the membership of the Republican Party has placed them [*sic*] in a key leadership position. Surely, these persons are aware of the principles and platform of the Republican Party and can decide what presidential candidates are aligned with the party's views. Therefore, as leaders the membership of the party elected, they have been entrusted with the authority to make decisions for the party, and O.C.G.A. § 21-2-193 recognizes that these party leaders are in the best position to decide who should appear on Georgia's Republican Party presidential primary ballot.

* * * Under the Georgia statute, * * * any single member of the Committee may unilaterally place an excluded candidate's name on the presidential primary ballot. Therefore, the Georgia statute provides each of the committee members the ability to act as a check against arbitrary and capricious decisions. Duke and the voters argue that the operation of the Georgia statute actually undermined its purported interest in protecting a political party's ability to define itself because it allows the committee members to make decisions that the party membership may not review. This argument suggests that the full party should have the right to determine what names appear on the ballot for a presidential primary. As the district court aptly pointed out, a system that would require a full party vote to put candidates on the presidential primary ballot would likely duplicate the results of the primary itself and also of the Committee. We hold that O.C.G.A. § 21-2-103 is narrowly tailored as it provides the state an efficient and effective means of furthering its compelling interest of protecting a political party's right to exclude persons with "adverse political principles."

---

[8] It is difficult to imagine composing a committee of party leaders who are in a better position to determine how a presidential candidate lines up with the views of the party than the State Chairperson of the party and the Majority and Minority leaders of both the state house and senate.

Because we find that neither Duke nor his supporters' First or Fourteenth Amendment rights were heavily burdened and that O.C.G.A. § 21-2-193 is narrowly tailored to serve a compelling state interest, the district court did not err in granting summary judgment.

AFFIRMED.

Notes and Questions

1.   Reconsider *Nixon v. Condon*, 286 U.S. 73 (1932), discussed in § B of this Chapter. Note that in *Duke*, as in *Nixon II*, state law provided a political party's committee with certain power. In both cases, there was state action because of the involvement of the government. In *Nixon II*, the committee's decision to exclude blacks was held unconstitutional. Here, however, the decision to exclude Duke because of his viewpoint was upheld; indeed, the court held that the state had a "compelling interest of protecting a political party's right to exclude persons with 'adverse political principles.' " Is the distinction between racial and viewpoint discrimination a coherent one? Does it make sense to prohibit a racist party from excluding members of the hated race, but to protect the party's right to exclude persons who support tolerance toward that race?

2.   Would the result in *Duke* change if O.G.C.A. § 21-2-193(a) permitted a simple majority of the Committee to exclude candidates?

3.   Does a state have a compelling interest in permitting parties to discriminate along dimensions other than viewpoint? If the Amazon Party wants to exclude men, or the Family Values Party wants to exclude gays, would such exclusion be unconstitutional? If state law prohibits such exclusion, would those parties have a constitutional right to determine their membership qualifications irrespective of the law?

4.   *Duke* misdirects the reader away from the crucial issue, and towards platitudes as to which nobody disagrees. For example, nobody disputes that states can regulate some aspects of elections, and nobody disputes that parties have a First Amendment right to associate. The critical question is *who* shall be permitted to act in the name of the party. In other words, can the *committee*, exercising power conferred by the state, decide the candidates with whom the party will or will not associate? Or is it the province of the party membership as a whole to determine which candidates best express the values animating the party? Are you troubled by the court's observation that if the right to associate rests with the entire party membership, an expression of the membership's desires would "duplicate the results of the primary itself"?

Isn't the whole purpose of a primary election to ascertain the preferences of the party membership? In other words, the court assumes that there must be some proceeding preceding the primary to winnow the potential candidates, but that conclusion may not be self-evident. Would primary elections be unmanageable if party committees were unable to shorten the list of potential nominees? If such a function is indeed necessary, should the committees be limited in the criteria on which they base their decisions, for example, by considering popular support but not ideology?

LAROUCHE v. FOWLER
United States Court of Appeals for the District of Columbia Circuit
152 F.3d 974 (D.C. Cir. 1998)

GARLAND, *CIRCUIT JUDGE* [with whom SILBERMAN and SENTELLE, *CIRCUIT JUDGES*, join]:

This case arises out of Lyndon H. LaRouche, Jr.'s unsuccessful quest for the Democratic Party's 1996 nomination for President. The Party's application of certain of its internal rules deprived LaRouche of two delegates to the 1996 Democratic National Convention. LaRouche contends that application of those rules * * * violated his rights under the Constitution. * * * We affirm the dismissal of LaRouche's constitutional claims.

LaRouche declared his candidacy for the Democratic Party's 1996 nomination for President on August 7, 1993. On March 12, 1994, the Democratic National Committee (DNC) adopted its Delegate Selection Rules for the 1996 Democratic National Convention. Rule 11(K) provided:

> For purposes of these rules, a Democratic candidate for President must be registered to vote, must be a declared Democrat, and must, as determined by the Chairman of the Democratic National Committee, have established a bona fide record of public service, accomplishment, public writings and/or public statements affirmatively demonstrating that he or she has the interests, welfare and success of the Democratic Party of the United States at heart and will participate in the Convention in good faith.

In January 1995, the DNC adopted the "Call to the 1996 Democratic National Convention," which in Article VI defined "presidential candidate" as:

> any person who, as determined by the National Chairperson of the Democratic National Committee, has accrued delegates in the nominating process and plans to seek the nomination, has established substantial support for his or her nomination as the Democratic candidate for the Office of the President of the United States, is a bona fide Democrat whose record of public service, accomplishment, public writings and/or public statements affirmatively demonstrates that he or she is faithful to the interests, welfare and success of the Democratic Party of the United States, and will participate in the Convention in good faith.

By the spring of 1996, LaRouche had qualified for a position on the Democratic Party primary ballot in numerous states. On January 5, 1996, however, before the first primary was held, DNC Chairman Donald L. Fowler issued a letter addressed to the chairpersons of all state Democratic Party organizations. Expressly exercising his authority under Rule 11(K) and Article VI, Fowler determined that:

> Lyndon Larouche [sic] is not a bona fide Democrat and does not possess a record affirmatively demonstrating that he is faithful to, or has at heart, the interests, welfare and success of the Democratic Party of the United States. This determination is based on Mr. Larouche's expressed political beliefs, including beliefs which are explicitly racist and anti-Semitic, and otherwise utterly contrary to the fundamental beliefs . . . of the Demo-

cratic Party and . . . on his past activities including exploitation of and defrauding contributors and voters.

Following this determination, Fowler instructed the state parties that:

> Accordingly, Mr. Larouche [sic] is not to be considered a qualified candidate for nomination of the Democratic Party for President. . . . Therefore, state parties . . . should disregard any votes that might be cast for Mr. Larouche, should not allocate delegate positions to Mr. Larouche and should not recognize the selection of delegates pledged to him at any stage of the Delegate Selection Process.

> Further, Mr. Larouche will not be entitled to have his name placed in nomination for the office of President at the 1996 Democratic National Convention. No certification of a delegate pledged to [him] will be accepted by the Secretary of the DNC. * * *

LaRouche was not excluded from any primary ballot because of Fowler's letter. He appeared on Democratic Party primary ballots in twenty-six states, receiving a total of 597,853 votes. He alleges that under the otherwise operative party rules, he won sufficient support in Louisiana's Democratic Party primary and in Virginia's Democratic Party caucuses to be entitled to one national convention delegate from each state. The respective state party chairpersons, however, carried out the instructions in the Fowler letter and ruled that LaRouche was not entitled to the two delegates. * * *

On August 2, 1996, less than one month before the Democratic National Convention, LaRouche [and his supporters brought suit seeking] compensatory and punitive damages, declarations that the DNC rules and Fowler's actions were * * * unconstitutional, and injunctions ordering defendants to seat his delegates at the convention and prohibiting the DNC from reenacting Rule 11(K) or any similar rule for future conventions. * * *

On August 15, 1996, the district court * * * dismissed the entire complaint, with prejudice as to all defendants[.] * * *

[The court of appeals considered whether Fowler's behavior amounted to state action, ultimately assuming without deciding that state action was present. The court then went on to discuss LaRouche's argument that strict scrutiny should be applied to evaluate his constitutional claim.] * * * LaRouche and his supporters plainly do have First Amendment interests at stake. But if the restrictions imposed on plaintiffs are viewed from the standpoint of the "state's" electoral process as a whole — that is, as a combination of ballot access provided through both political party nomination and independent candidacy — it is not necessarily clear that the restrictions on plaintiffs were "severe." LaRouche's adherents still retained the right to express their political views by supporting other Democratic nominees, even if they could not nominate LaRouche. And LaRouche retained the right to run, and his supporters the right to vote for him, as either a third-party or independent candidate. Nor is there any reason to believe that LaRouche's ultimate chances of becoming President would have been measurably lessened by taking those routes than by seeking nomination at the Democratic National Convention — where by his own count he would have had only two of 4320 delegates. Accordingly, even if the specific burden imposed on LaRouche by the DNC Rules were "severe," the overall burden imposed by the "state" may not have been severe enough to require strict scrutiny under *Burdick* [v. *Takushi*, 504 U.S. 428 (1992)] [p. 525].

More importantly, we are not persuaded that the *Burdick* test is appropriate for application to this case. That test, after all, was designed for a challenge to a state law *by* a citizen or political party asserting First Amendment rights, and hence weighs the state's interests against the rights protected by the Amendment. It was not designed for a case in which the First Amendment weighs on both sides of the balance. The application of judicial strict scrutiny to the internal rules of a political party (setting aside, because they are not at issue here, party rules that effectively control state-run primary ballots) simply raises too many troubling questions.

May a court require a political party — itself a First Amendment creature — to show a compelling justification before it may limit a putative candidate's ability to associate himself with the party? May a court require a political party to show that such a limitation is narrowly tailored to meet that compelling justification? The difficulty of the issue is made manifest by holding it up to a mirror: if a state, finding Rule 11(K) unfair, were to adopt LaRouche's position by statute (by, for example, outlawing "litmus tests" for party nominees), could the Party be required to show a compelling interest for its rule to invalidate the statute? We already know the Supreme Court's likely answer to this question, as *Cousins* [v. *Wigoda*, 419 U.S. 477 (1975)] and [*Democratic Party of the United States v. Wisconsin ex rel.*] *LaFollette* [450 U.S. 107 (1981)] [p. 442] presented similar situations. The answer is that the DNC would not have the burden of justifying its rule. To the contrary, it is the state that would have to show that its interest was "compelling . . . to justify the . . . abridgment of the exercise by . . . the National Democratic Party of [its] constitutionally protected rights."

But if a state cannot, at the behest of a plaintiff like LaRouche, require a political party to change its rules unless it can show a compelling reason for retaining them, then should it make a difference if a federal court is asked to impose the same requirement? The federal courts, after all, act with the authority of the "state" (i.e., the federal government), and their intrusion into the First Amendment rights of a political party can be as invasive as that of any state. * * *

There is yet another reason for rejecting the applicability of strict scrutiny to intra-party rules. One of the principal triggers for such scrutiny in the usual First Amendment context is viewpoint discrimination. Yet that trigger is of doubtful applicability in the political party context. In this case, for example, one of LaRouche's complaints is that "[t]he very nature of the 'test' which is embodied in Rule 11(K)" — a test limiting candidates to "bona fide Democrats" — is by definition "an invasion of the free speech of candidates." Indeed, were the State of Louisiana to adopt a similar rule for the general election — for example, by limiting the ballot to bona fide Democrats, or to Democrats and Republicans while excluding independents — there can be little doubt that the State's law would fall.

But it is also obvious that viewpoint discrimination by a political party is quite another matter. Indeed, it is the *sine qua non* of a political party that it represent a particular political viewpoint. And it is the purpose of a party convention to decide on that viewpoint, in part by deciding which candidate will bear its standard: the liberal or the conservative, the free trader or the protectionist, the internationalist or the isolationist. Unlike a state, which is largely barred from making such decisions, a political party must make these decisions. Since in the end there will be only one Democratic and one Republican Party candidate on the general election ballot, their conventions ultimately *must* choose a political viewpoint. Surely even plaintiffs would agree that if the Democratic Party had chosen LaRouche over President Clinton as its candidate in 1996, the choice would have constituted the expression of a particular political point of view.

In sum, we conclude that even if a political party is a state actor, the presence of First Amendment interests on both sides of the equation makes inapplicable the test applied to electoral restrictions where the First Amendment weighs on only one side. [Rather, we shall ask whether the party's rules] "rationally advance some legitimate interest of the party in winning elections or otherwise achieving its political goals." [T]his test * * * best effectuates the Supreme Court's direction to approach judicial intervention in this area "with great caution and restraint," and to recognize "the large public interest in allowing the political processes to function free from judicial supervision." *O'Brien* [v. Brown], 409 U.S. [1,] 4–5 [(1972)].

[T]he Party interest at issue is a "legitimate" one. "There are no racial or other invidious classifications here" as there were in the White Primary Cases. There is, of course, viewpoint discrimination at play. But as we have already noted, there is nothing illegitimate about that kind of discrimination in a political party's nomination process.

Moreover, the Party's interest is not merely legitimate. Here, the associational rights of the Democratic National Party are at their zenith. The Party's ability to define who is a "bona fide Democrat" is nothing less than the Party's ability to define itself. * * *

The Party's effort to limit the list of candidates who can represent themselves to the voters as Democrats "rationally advance[s the] legitimate interest of the party in winning elections." By narrowing the field of those who represent it, the Party seeks to define its values, distinguish them from those of its competitors, and thereby attract like-minded voters. At the same time, it seeks to prevent confusion among those voters by excluding from its list of potential presidential nominees those who do not share those values. It advances the Party's ability to "achiev[e] its political goals" in other ways as well. As the Court said in *LaFollette*, when barring Wisconsin from requiring the Democratic Party to accept delegates selected through the state's open primary:

> * * * [T]he inclusion of persons unaffiliated with a political party may seriously distort its collective decisions — thus impairing the party's essential functions — and * * * political parties may accordingly protect themselves from intrusion by those with adverse political principles.

450 U.S. at 122.

LaRouche, of course, would dispute the applicability of this passage, arguing that unlike the open primary voters in Wisconsin, he is not "unaffiliated" with the Democratic Party and does not have "adverse political principles." But the Party itself obviously disagrees — and vociferously so. Nor is the Party required to accept

LaRouche's self-designation as the final word on the matter. Rather, the Party's "freedom to join together in furtherance of common political beliefs 'necessarily presupposes the freedom to identify the people who constitute the association.' " *Tashjian*, 479 U.S. at 214 (quoting *LaFollette*, 450 U.S. at 122).

LaRouche makes clear that his fundamental complaint is not so much with the Party's right to define itself, but rather with the "unfair" manner in which he contends it has done so. * * *

The answer to this aspect of LaRouche's complaint is that the Party's First Amendment rights extend not only to defining itself, but also to determining how to define itself. The Supreme Court made this point in both *Cousins* and *LaFollette* by upholding the Party's right to determine who could select its delegates, notwithstanding the states' views that a different process would be more appropriate. The Court faced a similar question again in *Eu*, where the California Elections Code dictated, among other things, the organization and composition of the state parties' official governing bodies. * * *

A party may, of course, pay heavily at the polls for the perception that it treats its members, delegates, or candidates unfairly. But that is a matter for the party to weigh, and for the people to decide in the general election. It is not a basis upon which a court can intervene as long as the party's processes rationally advance its legitimate interests. * * *

[*Affirmed.*]

Notes and Questions

1.   Recall from our discussion in § B of this Chapter that the White Primary Cases presented a quandary: Parties are state actors in adopting and applying racially discriminatory qualifications for voting in primaries, but the very function of a political party requires it to articulate and advocate a message. That fact requires parties to engage in "viewpoint discrimination," which the First Amendment ordinarily forbids. *LaRouche* attempts to solve this quandary not by treating parties as state actors for some purposes and not for others, nor by holding that the viewpoint discrimination constitutes a compelling interest that would survive strict scrutiny, but by holding that parties' viewpoint discrimination will be subject only to the rational-basis test. What is the court's justification for applying the rational-basis test? Do you think that is the appropriate test to use?

2.   Whereas usually the rational-basis test analyzes state action for its relationship to a "legitimate government interest," here the court asked whether the Democratic Party's viewpoint discrimination was rationally related to "some legitimate interest of the party in winning elections or otherwise achieving its political goals." Thus, it was the interest of the *party*, and not of the state as a whole, that was relevant. Should a state actor be permitted to engage in viewpoint discrimination when the only justification for doing so is to advance a partisan end? *Cf. Elrod v. Burns*, 427 U.S. 347, 362 (1976) [p. 726] (plurality opinion) (holding unconstitutional patronage-based firings of public employees) ("In the instant case, care must be taken not to confuse the interest of partisan organizations with

governmental interests. Only the latter will suffice.").

3.   If a state passed a law prohibiting the kind of viewpoint discrimination involved in *LaRouche*, would the law be constitutional?

4.   Is there any way to distinguish *Duke* from *LaRouche*? That is, is there an argument that one, but not the other, is correctly decided?

5.   *Problem.* Texas law permits parties to determine which of its candidates shall appear on the primary ballot. May a party require candidates, as a condition of appearing on the primary ballot, to sign a statement pledging the candidate's full support of whichever candidate receives the nomination? *See Kucinich v. Texas Democratic Party*, 563 F.3d 161, 166 (5th Cir. 2009). *Cf. Ray v. Blair*, 343 U.S. 214 (1952) (permitting parties to require potential presidential electors to pledge support for the parties' nominees). May the party enforce the same requirement as to persons wishing to *vote* in primaries?

D.   THIRD PARTIES, INDEPENDENT CANDIDATES, AND BALLOT ACCESS

The constitutional law surrounding the regulation of minor parties and independent candidates presents a conflict between states' interest in providing an orderly, stable election process that is easy for the public to understand and for voters to use, on the one hand, and the third parties' interest in raising challenges to the existing political structure and public policies, on the other. The Supreme Court has recognized that "as a practical matter, there must be a substantial regulation of elections if they are to be fair and honest and if some sort of order, rather than chaos, is to accompany the democratic processes." *Storer v. Brown*, 415 U.S. 724, 730 (1974) [p. 513]. Nevertheless, politicians' self-interest suggests that, without constitutional constraints, the members of the two major parties who hold public office will use electoral regulations to continue the dominance of those parties. *See, e.g., Munro v. Socialist Workers Party*, 479 U.S. 189, 201 (1986) (Marshall, J., dissenting).

WILLIAMS v. RHODES
Supreme Court of the United States
393 U.S. 23, 89 S. Ct. 5, 21 L. Ed. 2d 24 (1968)

MR. JUSTICE BLACK delivered the opinion of the Court [in which MR. JUSTICE DOUGLAS, MR. JUSTICE BRENNAN, MR. JUSTICE FORTAS, and MR. JUSTICE MARSHALL join].

The State of Ohio in a series of election laws has made it virtually impossible for a new political party, even though it has hundreds of thousands of members, or an old party, which has a very small number of members, to be placed on the state ballot to choose electors pledged to particular candidates for the Presidency and Vice Presidency of the United States.

Ohio Revised Code, § 3517.01, requires a new party to obtain petitions signed by qualified electors totaling 15% of the number of ballots cast in the last preceding gubernatorial election. The detailed provisions of other Ohio election laws result in the imposition of substantial additional burdens * * *.[1] Together these various restrictive provisions make it virtually impossible for any party to qualify on the ballot except the Republican and Democratic Parties. These two Parties face substantially smaller burdens because they are allowed to retain their positions on the ballot simply by obtaining 10% of the votes in the last gubernatorial election and need not obtain any signature petitions. Moreover, Ohio laws make no provision for ballot position for independent candidates as distinguished from political parties. * * *

* * * In determining whether or not a state law violates the Equal Protection Clause, we must consider the facts and circumstances behind the law, the interests which the State claims to be protecting, and the interests of those who are disadvantaged by the classification. In the present situation the state laws place burdens on two different, although overlapping, kinds of rights — the right of individuals to associate for the advancement of political beliefs, and the right of qualified voters, regardless of their political persuasion, to cast their votes effectively. * * *

No extended discussion is required to establish that the Ohio laws before us give the two old, established parties a decided advantage over any new parties struggling for existence and thus place substantially unequal burdens on both the right to vote and the right to associate. The right to form a party for the advancement of political goals means little if a party can be kept off the election ballot and thus denied an equal opportunity to win votes. So also, the right to vote is heavily burdened if that vote may be cast only for one of two parties at a time when other parties are clamoring for a place on the ballot. In determining whether the State has power to place such unequal burdens on minority groups where rights of this kind are at stake, the decisions of this Court have consistently held that "only a compelling state interest in the regulation of a subject within the State's constitutional power to regulate can justify limiting First Amendment freedoms."

The State has here failed to show any "compelling interest" which justifies

---

[1] Judge Kinneary describes, in his dissenting opinion below, the legal obstacles placed before a would-be third party even after the 15% signature requirement has been fulfilled:

"*First*, at the primary election, the new party, or any political party, is required to elect a state central committee consisting of two members from each congressional district and county central committees for each county in Ohio. *Second*, at the primary election the new party must elect delegates and alternates to a national convention. Since [an Ohio statute] prohibits a candidate from seeking the office of delegate to the national convention or committeeman if he voted as a member of a different party at a primary election in the preceding four year period, the new party would be required to have over twelve hundred members who had not previously voted in another party's primary, and who would be willing to serve as committeemen and delegates. *Third*, the candidates for nomination in the primary would have to file petitions signed by qualified electors. The term 'qualified electors' is not adequately defined in the Ohio Revised Code, but a related section provides that a qualified elector at a primary election of a political party is one who, (1) voted for a majority of that party's candidates at the last election, or, (2) has never voted in any election before. Since neither of the political party plaintiffs had any candidates at the last preceding regular state election, they would, of necessity, have to seek out members who had never voted before to sign the nominating petitions, and it would be only these persons who could vote in the primary election of the new party."

imposing such heavy burdens on the right to vote and to associate.

The State * * * claims that [it] may validly promote a two-party system in order to encourage compromise and political stability. The fact is, however, that the Ohio system does not merely favor a "two-party system"; it favors two particular parties — the Republicans and the Democrats — and in effect tends to give them a complete monopoly. There is, of course, no reason why two parties should retain a permanent monopoly on the right to have people vote for or against them. Competition in ideas and governmental policies is at the core of our electoral process and of the First Amendment freedoms. New parties struggling for their place must have the time and opportunity to organize in order to meet reasonable requirements for ballot position, just as the old parties have had in the past.

Ohio makes a variety of other arguments to support its very restrictive election laws. It points out, for example, that if three or more parties are on the ballot, it is possible that no one party would obtain 50% of the vote, and the runner-up might have been preferred to the plurality winner by a majority of the voters. Concededly, the State does have an interest in attempting to see that the election winner be the choice of a majority of its voters. But to grant the State power to keep all political parties off the ballot until they have enough members to win would stifle the growth of all new parties working to increase their strength from year to year. Considering these Ohio laws in their totality, this interest cannot justify the very severe restrictions on voting and associational rights which Ohio has imposed. * * *

The State also argues that its requirement of a party structure and an organized primary insures that those who disagree with the major parties and their policies "will be given a choice of leadership as well as issues" since any leader who attempts to capitalize on the disaffection of such a group is forced to submit to a primary in which other, possibly more attractive, leaders can raise the same issues and compete for the allegiance of the disaffected group. But while this goal may be desirable, Ohio's system cannot achieve it. Since the principal policies of the major parties change to some extent from year to year, and since the identity of the likely major party nominees may not be known until shortly before the election, this disaffected "group" will rarely if ever be a cohesive or identifiable group until a few months before the election. Thus, Ohio's burdensome procedures, requiring extensive organization and other election activities by a very early date, operate to prevent such a group from ever getting on the ballot and the Ohio system thus denies the "disaffected" not only a choice of leadership but a choice on the issues as well.

Finally Ohio claims that its highly restrictive provisions are justified because without them a large number of parties might qualify for the ballot, and the voters would then be confronted with a choice so confusing that the popular will could be frustrated. But the experience of many States, including that of Ohio prior to 1948, demonstrates that no more than a handful of parties attempts to qualify for ballot positions even when a very low number of signatures, such as 1% of the electorate, is required.[9] It is true that the existence of multitudinous fragmentary groups

---

[9] Forty-two States require third parties to obtain the signatures of only 1% or less of the electorate in order to appear on the ballot. It appears that no significant problem has arisen in these States which

might justify some regulatory control but in Ohio at the present time this danger seems to us no more than "theoretically imaginable." No such remote danger can justify the immediate and crippling impact on the basic constitutional rights involved in this case.

* * * [T]he totality of the Ohio restrictive laws taken as a whole imposes a burden on voting and associational rights which we hold is an invidious discrimination, in violation of the Equal Protection Clause. * * *

MR. JUSTICE DOUGLAS. * * *

In our political life, third parties are often important channels through which political dissent is aired: "All political ideas cannot and should not be channeled into the programs of our two major parties. History has amply proved the virtue of political activity by minority, dissident groups, which innumerable times have been in the vanguard of democratic thought and whose programs were ultimately accepted. . . . The absence of such voices would be a symptom of grave illness in our society." *Sweezy* v. *New Hampshire*, 354 U.S. 234, 250–251 [(1957)] (opinion of WARREN, C.J.).

The Equal Protection Clause * * * protects voting rights and political groups, as well as economic units, racial communities, and other entities. When "fundamental rights and liberties" are at issue, a State has less leeway in making classifications than when it deals with economic matters. I would think that a State has precious little leeway in making it difficult or impossible for citizens to vote for whomsoever they please and to organize campaigns for any school of thought they may choose, whatever part of the spectrum it reflects.

Cumbersome election machinery can effectively suffocate the right of association, the promotion of political ideas and programs of political action, and the right to vote. The totality of Ohio's requirements has those effects. * * *

Hence I concur in today's decision; and, while my emphasis is different from the Court's, I join its opinion.

MR. JUSTICE HARLAN, concurring in the result.

* * * Ohio's statutory scheme violates the basic right of political association assured by the First Amendment which is protected against state infringement under the Due Process Clause of the Fourteenth Amendment. It is true that Ohio has not directly limited appellants' right to assemble or discuss public issues or solicit new members. Instead, by denying the appellants any opportunity to participate in the procedure by which the President is selected, the State has eliminated the basic incentive that all political parties have for conducting such activities, thereby depriving appellants of much of the substance, if not the form, of their protected rights. The right to have one's voice heard and one's views considered by the appropriate governmental authority is at the core of the right of political association. * * * Just as a political group has a right to organize effectively

---

have relatively lenient requirements for obtaining ballot position.

so that its position may be heard in court; so it has the right to place its candidate for the Presidency before whatever body has the power to make the State's selection of Electors. * * *

Of course, the State may limit the right of political association by invoking an impelling policy justification for doing so. But as my Brother BLACK's opinion demonstrates, Ohio has been able to advance no such justification for denying almost half a million of its citizens their fundamental right to organize effectively for political purposes. Consequently, it may not exclude them from the process by which Presidential Electors are selected.

In deciding this case of first impression, I think it unnecessary to draw upon the Equal Protection Clause [which is of dubious applicability to Presidential elections because of the inequalities the Constitution prescribes in the allocation of Presidential Electors]. * * *

A word should be added about the constitutional status of Ohio's requirement that a third party, to qualify for ballot position, must collect the signatures of eligible voters in a number equal to 15% of those voting at the last gubernatorial election. * * *

In my view, this requirement, even when regarded in isolation, must fall. As my Brother BLACK's opinion suggests, the only legitimate interest the State may invoke in defense of this barrier to third-party candidacies is the fear that, without such a barrier, candidacies will proliferate in such numbers as to create a substantial risk of voter confusion.[8] Ohio's requirement cannot be said to be reasonably related to this interest. Even in the unprecedented event of a complete and utter popular disaffection with the two established parties, Ohio law would permit as many as six additional party candidates to compete with the Democrats and Republicans only if popular support should be divided relatively evenly among the new groups. And with fundamental freedoms at stake, such an unlikely hypothesis cannot support an incursion upon protected rights, especially since the presence of eight candidacies cannot be said, in light of experience, to carry a significant danger of voter confusion. As both Ohio's electoral history and the actions taken by the overwhelming majority of other States suggest, opening the ballot to this extent is perfectly consistent with the effective functioning of the electoral process. In sum, I think that Ohio has fallen far short of showing the compelling state interest necessary to overcome this otherwise protected right of political association.

---

[8] My Brother STEWART is, of course, quite right in pointing out that the presence of third parties may on occasion result in the election of the major candidate who is in reality less preferred by the majority of the voters. It seems clear to me, however, that many constitutional electoral structures could be designed which would accommodate this valid state interest, without depriving other political organizations of the right to participate effectively in the political process. A runoff election may be mandated if no party gains a majority, or the decision could be left to the State Legislature in such a case. Alternatively, the voter could be given the right, at the general election, to indicate both his first and his second choice for the Presidency — if no candidate received a majority of first-choice votes, the second-choice votes could then be considered. Finally, Electors could be chosen on a district-by-district rather than an at-large basis, thereby apportioning the electoral vote in a way more nearly approximating the popular vote. I would conclude that, with the substantial variety of less restrictive alternatives that are available, this interest cannot support Ohio's 15% requirement.

Since Ohio's requirement is so clearly disproportionate to the magnitude of the risk that it may properly act to prevent, I need not reach the question of the size of the signature barrier a State may legitimately raise against third parties on this ground. This should be left to the Ohio Legislature in the first instance.

Mr. Justice Stewart, dissenting[.] * * *

* * * I concede that the Fourteenth Amendment imposes some limitations upon a state legislature's freedom to choose a method for the appointment of electors. A State may not, for example, adopt a system that discriminates on grounds of religious or political belief. But I cannot agree that Ohio's system violates the Fourteenth Amendment in any way. * * *

* * * By preventing parties that have not demonstrated timely and widespread support from gaining places on its ballot, Ohio's provisions tend to guard against the possibility that small-party candidates will draw enough support to prevent either of the major contenders from obtaining an absolute majority of votes — and against the consequent possibility that election may be secured by candidates who gain a plurality but who are, vis-à-vis their principal opponents, preferred by less than half of those voting. Surely the attainment of these objectives is well within the scope of a State's authority under our Constitution. One may perhaps disagree with the political theory on which the objectives are based, but it is inconceivable to me that the Constitution imposes on the States a political philosophy under which they must be satisfied to award election on the basis of a plurality rather than a majority vote.[12]

In pursuing this interest Ohio has, at the same time, not completely prevented new parties from gaining access to that State's ballot. It has authorized ballot position for parties that can demonstrate by petition the support of 15% of the voting public 90 days before a primary election is to be held. My Brethren seem to suggest that the percentage figure is set too high, and the date too early. But I cannot join in this kind of second-guessing. While necessarily arbitrary, Ohio's standards can only be taken to represent reasonable attempts at accommodating the conflicting interests involved.[9]

Although Ohio's provisions do not freeze the Republican and Democratic Parties into the State's election structure by specific reference to those parties, it is true that established parties, once they become participants in the electoral process, continue to enjoy ballot position so long as they have polled 10% of the vote in the most recent Ohio gubernatorial election. It is suggested that the disparity between this figure and the 15% requirement applicable to new parties is invidiously

---

[12] My Brother Harlan suggests that Ohio's interest may be protected in "less restrictive" ways. * * * [E]ach of the methods mentioned by Mr. Justice Harlan appears to me to entail consequences which arguably would frustrate other legitimate state interests. Nor do all of them serve as effectively to promote the interest in question here as does the statutory scheme the Ohio Legislature has in fact enacted. I do not think problems such as those raised in this case can be solved by means of facile and unelaborated suggestions of "less restrictive alternatives"; issues of legislative policy are too complex for such easy answers to be satisfactory. [Relocated. — Eds.]

[9] The date specified, for instance, is related to Ohio's requirement that all political parties hold primary elections — another provision that is, it seems to me, well within the State's power to enact.

discriminatory. But I cannot accept the theory that Ohio is constitutionally compelled to apply precisely the same numerical test in determining whether established parties enjoy widespread support as it applies in determining that question with regard to new parties. * * *

The Court's opinion appears to concede that the State's interest in attempting to ensure that a minority of voters do not thwart the will of the majority is a legitimate one, but summarily asserts that this legitimate interest cannot constitutionally be vindicated. That assertion seems to echo the claim of my concurring Brethren — a claim not made by the appellants — that Ohio's statutory requirements in some way infringe upon First Amendment rights. I cannot agree. * * *

* * * Ohio's ballot requirements have [no] substantial impact on the attempts of political dissidents to organize effectively. Such persons are entirely free to assemble, speak, write, and proselytize as they see fit. They are free either to attempt to modify the character of the established major parties or to go their own way and set up separate political organizations. And if they can timely demonstrate that they have substantial support within the State — according to Ohio's reasonable standards for deciding that question — they may secure ballot position for the candidates they support. Ohio has restricted only their ability to secure ballot position without demonstrating that support. To me the conclusion that that single disability in any way significantly impairs their First Amendment rights is sheer speculation. [T]he present two-party system in this country is the product of social and political forces rather than of legal restrictions on minority parties. This Court has been shown neither that in States with minimal ballot restrictions third parties have flourished, nor that in States with more difficult requirements they are moribund. Mere speculation ought not to suffice to strike down a State's duly enacted laws. * * *

Mr. Justice White, dissenting * * *.

I agree with much of what my Brother Stewart says in his dissenting opinion[.] * * * Why a majority of the Court insists on holding the primary petition requirement impermissible, not on its own demerits, but because it appears in the statute books with more questionable provisions is the major mystery of the majority position. Neither the Independent nor the Socialist Labor Party is entitled to relief in this Court.

Mr. Chief Justice Warren, dissenting.

We have had but seven days to consider the important constitutional questions presented by these cases. * * * Appellants' belated requests for extraordinary relief have compelled all members of this Court to decide cases of this magnitude without the unhurried deliberation which is essential to the formulation of sound constitutional principles. * * *

Both the opinion of this Court and that of the District Court leave unresolved what restrictions, if any, a State can impose. Although both opinions treat the Ohio statutes as a "package," giving neither Ohio nor the courts any guidance, each contains intimations that a State can by reasonable regulation condition ballot position upon at least three considerations — a substantial showing of voter interest in the candidate seeking a place on the ballot, a requirement that this interest be evidenced sometime prior to the election, and a party structure demonstrating some degree of political organization. With each of these propositions I can agree. * * *

Whatever may be the applicable constitutional principles, appellants and the State of Ohio are entitled to know whether any of the various provisions attacked in this litigation do comport with constitutional standards. * * * Given the magnitude of the questions presented and the need for unhurried deliberation, I would dispose of appellants' request for declaratory relief * * * by a remand to the District Court for a clearer determination of the serious constitutional questions raised in these cases. * * *

Notes and Questions

1. Exactly what was the Court's holding? What was held unconstitutional? If you were advising the Ohio legislature about how to revise its statutes after *Williams*, what would you recommend?

2. *Williams* applied strict scrutiny, even though the Ohio laws did not explicitly favor any particular ideological view and did not discriminate against a suspect class. The laws certainly placed a greater burden on third parties than on major parties, but a law's disparate impact is not enough to trigger strict scrutiny, even where the harmed group is a racial minority. *See Washington v. Davis*, 426 U.S. 229 (1976). Should the Court have required the plaintiffs to prove Ohio's discriminatory *purpose* in passing these laws?

3. Justice Harlan argued that ballot access is constitutionally protected because it permits parties to make their views known to the electorate. How would such a conception of the First Amendment affect other cases we have confronted?

JENNESS v. FORTSON
Supreme Court of the United States
403 U.S. 431, 91 S. Ct. 1970, 29 L. Ed. 2d 554 (1971)

MR. JUSTICE STEWART delivered the opinion of the Court [in which MR. CHIEF JUSTICE BURGER, MR. JUSTICE DOUGLAS, MR. JUSTICE BRENNAN, MR. JUSTICE WHITE, MR. JUSTICE MARSHALL, and MR. JUSTICE BLACKMUN join].

Under Georgia law a candidate for elective public office who does not enter and win a political party's primary election can have his name printed on the ballot at the general election only if he has filed a nominating petition signed by at least 5% of the number of registered voters at the last general election for the office in question. * * * [A]ppellants, who were prospective candidates and registered voters, [challenged the constitutionality of the petition requirement. The District Court held it valid.] * * *

The basic structure of the pertinent provisions of the Georgia Election Code is relatively uncomplicated. Any political organization whose candidate received 20% or more of the vote at the most recent gubernatorial or presidential election is a "political party." Any other political organization is a "political body." "Political parties" conduct primary elections, regulated in detail by state law, and only the name of the candidate for each office who wins this primary election is printed on the ballot at the subsequent general election, as his party's nominee for the office in question. A nominee of a "political body" or an independent candidate, on the other hand, may have his name printed on the ballot at the general election by filing a nominating petition. This petition must be signed by "a number of electors of not less than five per cent. of the total number of electors eligible to vote in the last election for the filling of the office the candidate is seeking. . . . " The total time allowed for circulating a nominating petition is 180 days, and it must be filed on the second Wednesday in June, the same deadline that a candidate filing in a party primary must meet.

It is to be noted that these procedures relate only to the right to have the name of a candidate or the nominee of a "political body" printed on the ballot. There is no limitation whatever, procedural or substantive, on the right of a voter to write in on the ballot the name of the candidate of his choice and to have that write-in vote counted.

In this litigation the appellants have mounted their attack upon Georgia's nominating-petition requirement on two different but related constitutional fronts. First, they say that to require a nonparty candidate to secure the signatures of a certain number of voters before his name may be printed on the ballot is to abridge the freedoms of speech and association guaranteed to that candidate and his supporters by the First and Fourteenth Amendments. Secondly, they say that when Georgia requires a nonparty candidate to secure the signatures of 5% of the voters before printing his name on the ballot, yet prints the names of those candidates who have won nomination in party primaries, it violates the Fourteenth Amendment by denying the nonparty candidate the equal protection of the laws. * * *

[*Williams* v. *Rhodes*, 393 U.S. 23 (1968)] [p. 497], it is clear, presented a statutory scheme vastly different from the one before us here. Unlike Ohio, Georgia freely provides for write-in votes. Unlike Ohio, Georgia does not require every candidate to be the nominee of a political party, but fully recognizes independent candidacies. Unlike Ohio, Georgia does not fix an unreasonably early filing deadline for candidates not endorsed by established parties. Unlike Ohio, Georgia does not impose upon a small party or a new party the Procrustean requirement of establishing elaborate primary election machinery. Finally, and in sum, Georgia's election laws, unlike Ohio's, do not operate to freeze the political status quo. In this setting we cannot say that Georgia's 5% petition requirement violates the Constitution.

Anyone who wishes, and who is otherwise eligible, may be an independent candidate for any office in Georgia. Any political organization, however new or however small, is free to endorse any otherwise eligible person as its candidate for whatever elective public office it chooses. So far as the Georgia election laws are concerned, independent candidates and members of small or newly formed political organizations are wholly free to associate, to proselytize, to speak, to write, and to organize campaigns for any school of thought they wish. They may confine themselves to an appeal for write-in votes. Or they may seek, over a six months' period, the signatures of 5% of the eligible electorate for the office in question. If they choose the latter course, the way is open. For Georgia imposes no suffocating restrictions whatever upon the free circulation of nominating petitions. A voter may sign a petition even though he has signed others, and a voter who has signed the petition of a nonparty candidate is free thereafter to participate in a party primary. The signer of a petition is not required to state that he intends to vote for that candidate at the election. A person who has previously voted in a party primary is fully eligible to sign a petition, and so, on the other hand, is a person who was not even registered at the time of the previous election. No signature on a nominating petition need be notarized.

The open quality of the Georgia system is far from merely theoretical. For the stipulation of facts in this record informs us that a candidate for Governor in 1966 and a candidate for President in 1968, gained ballot designation by nominating petitions, and each went on to win a plurality of the votes cast at the general election.

In a word, Georgia in no way freezes the status quo, but implicitly recognizes the potential fluidity of American political life. Thus, any political body that wins as much as 20% support at an election becomes a "political party" with its attendant ballot position rights and primary election obligations, and any "political party" whose support at the polls falls below that figure reverts to the status of a "political body" with its attendant nominating petition responsibilities and freedom from primary election duties. We can find in this system nothing that abridges the rights of free speech and association secured by the First and Fourteenth Amendments.

The appellants' claim under the Equal Protection Clause of the Fourteenth Amendment fares no better. * * * The fact is, of course, that from the point of view of one who aspires to elective public office in Georgia, alternative routes are available to getting his name printed on the ballot. He may enter the primary of a political party, or he may circulate nominating petitions either as an independent candidate or under the sponsorship of a political organization.[25] We cannot see how Georgia has violated the Equal Protection Clause of the Fourteenth Amendment by making available these two alternative paths, neither of which can be assumed to be inherently more burdensome than the other.

Insofar as we deal here with the claims of a "political body," as contrasted with those of an individual aspirant for public office or an individual voter, the situation is somewhat different. For it is true that a "political party" in Georgia is assured of having the name of its nominee — the primary election winner — printed on the ballot, whereas the name of the nominee of a "political body" will be printed only if nominating petitions have been filed that contain the requisite number of signatures. But we can hardly suppose that a small or a new political organization could seriously urge that its interests would be advanced if it were forced by the State to establish all of the elaborate statewide, county-by-county, organizational paraphernalia required of a "political party" as a condition for conducting a primary election.

---

[25] The argument that the first alternative route is not realistically open to a candidate with unorthodox or "radical" views is hardly valid in the light of American political history. Time after time established political parties, at local, state, and national levels, have, while retaining their old labels, changed their ideological direction because of the influence and leadership of those with unorthodox or "radical" views.

Indeed, a large reason for the Court's invalidation of the Ohio election laws in *Williams* v. *Rhodes* was precisely that Ohio *did* impose just such requirements on small and new political organizations.

The fact is that there are obvious differences in kind between the needs and potentials of a political party with historically established broad support, on the one hand, and a new or small political organization on the other. Georgia has not been guilty of invidious discrimination in recognizing these differences and providing different routes to the printed ballot. Sometimes the grossest discrimination can lie in treating things that are different as though they were exactly alike, a truism well illustrated in *Williams* v. *Rhodes*.

There is surely an important state interest in requiring some preliminary showing of a significant modicum of support before printing the name of a political organization's candidate on the ballot — the interest, if no other, in avoiding confusion, deception, and even frustration of the democratic process at the general election. The 5% figure is, to be sure, apparently somewhat higher than the percentage of support required to be shown in many States as a condition for ballot position, but this is balanced by the fact that Georgia has imposed no arbitrary restrictions whatever upon the eligibility of any registered voter to sign as many nominating petitions as he wishes. Georgia in this case has insulated not a single potential voter from the appeal of new political voices within its borders.

The judgment is affirmed.

Mr. Justice Black and Mr. Justice Harlan concur in the result [without opinion].

Notes and Questions

1.   Did *Jenness* do anything to clarify *Williams*'s holding? Are you satisfied with the Court's use of factors, rather than rules, in these cases? Is it possible to construct sensible rules for determining the constitutionality of ballot-access restrictions, or must such determinations be made on a case-by-case basis?

2.   The Court explains that Georgia was not required to grant "political bodies" the automatic ballot access enjoyed by "political parties" at least in part because "political parties" were required to comply with additional burdens not faced by "political bodies." Do you believe Georgia would be able, constitutionally, to require minor parties "to establish all of the elaborate statewide, county-by-county, organizational paraphernalia" that Georgia law required of "political parties"? *Cf. Eu v. San Francisco County Democratic Central Committee*, 489 U.S. 214 (1989) [p. 455]. If not, how could the state deny "political bodies" the automatic ballot position enjoyed by "political parties"? Should "political bodies" have the choice whether to establish the organizational structure of "parties" and gain the automatic ballot position that comes with that status, on the one hand, or to forego the organizational structure at the cost of having to endure the petition requirement, on the other?

3.   In what circumstances might a 5% petition requirement be unconstitutional? Could a population be large enough that the number of people needed to reach 5% is unconstitutionally high *per se*? California has 17,153,012 registered voters. *See*

California Secretary of State, *15-Day Report of Registration*, May 4, 2009, *available at http://www.sos.ca.gov/elections/ror/ror-pages/15day-stwdsp-09/hist-reg-stats.pdf.* A 5% requirement applied to that population would mean the signatures of 857,651 people.

4. *Jenness* held that the state interest "in avoiding confusion, deception, and even frustration of the democratic process" sufficed to allow states to require "some preliminary showing of a significant modicum of support." The Court further discussed this authority in *Munro v. Socialist Workers Party*, 479 U.S. 189 (1986), in which it upheld a requirement that minor-party candidates receive 1% of the vote in Washington's blanket primary to have their names appear on the general-election ballot. As against the claim that there had been no voter confusion necessitating such a limitation on ballot access, the Court (over a dissent by Justice Marshall, joined by Justice Brennan) responded as follows:

> To require States to prove actual voter confusion, ballot overcrowding, or the presence of frivolous candidacies as a predicate to the imposition of reasonable ballot access restrictions would invariably lead to endless court battles over the sufficiency of the "evidence" marshaled by a State to prove the predicate. Such a requirement would necessitate that a State's political system sustain some level of damage before the legislature could take corrective action. Legislatures, we think, should be permitted to respond to potential deficiencies in the electoral process with foresight rather than reactively, provided that the response is reasonable and does not significantly impinge on constitutionally protected rights.

Id. at 195–96. Is such a deferential approach appropriate?

5. Should a write-in alternative *by itself* be sufficient to insulate ballot-access restrictions from constitutional attack? *See Lubin v. Panish*, 415 U.S. 709, 719 n.5 (1974) (dictum) ("The realities of the electoral process * * * strongly suggest that 'access' via write-in votes falls far short of access in terms of having the name of the candidate on the ballot. * * * [A write-in candidate] would be forced to rest his chances solely upon those voters who would remember his name and take the affirmative step of writing it on the ballot."); *cf. U.S. Term Limits, Inc. v. Thornton*, 514 U.S. 779, 828–36 (1995) [p. 550] (holding unconstitutional a law indirectly imposing term limits by denying long-serving representatives a place on the ballot).

BULLOCK v. CARTER
Supreme Court of the United States
405 U.S. 134, 92 S. Ct. 849, 31 L. Ed. 2d 92 (1972)

MR. CHIEF JUSTICE BURGER delivered the opinion of the Court [in which MR. JUSTICE DOUGLAS, MR. JUSTICE BRENNAN, MR. JUSTICE STEWART, MR. JUSTICE WHITE, MR. JUSTICE MARSHALL, and MR. JUSTICE BLACKMUN join].

Under Texas law, a candidate must pay a filing fee as a condition to having his name placed on the ballot in a primary election. [Three candidates for different offices were denied places on the Democratic Party's primary ballots because they were unable to pay the filing fees. They challenged the constitutionality of the filing-fee requirement.] * * *

Under the Texas statute, payment of the filing fee is an absolute prerequisite to a candidate's participation in a primary election. There is no alternative procedure by which a potential candidate who is unable to pay the fee can get on the primary ballot by way of petitioning voters,[5] and write-in votes are not permitted in primary elections for public office. Any person who is willing and able to pay the filing fee and who meets the basic eligibility requirements for holding the office sought can run in a primary.

Candidates for most district, county, and precinct offices must pay their filing fee to the county executive committee of the political party conducting the primary; the committee also determines the amount of the fee. The party committee must make an estimate of the total cost of the primary and apportion it among the various candidates "as in their judgment is just and equitable." The committee's judgment is to be guided by "the importance, emolument, and term of office for which the nomination is to be made." In counties with populations of one million or more, candidates for offices of two-year terms can be assessed up to 10% of their aggregate annual salary, and candidates for offices of four-year terms can be assessed up to 15% of their aggregate annual salary. In smaller counties there are no such percentage limitations.

The record shows that the fees required of the candidates in this case are far from exceptional in their magnitude. The size of the filing fees is plainly a natural consequence of a statutory system that places the burden of financing primary elections on candidates rather than on the governmental unit, and that imposes a particularly heavy burden on candidates for local office. The filing fees required of candidates seeking nomination for state offices and offices involving statewide primaries are more closely regulated by statute and tend to be appreciably smaller. * * *

The filing-fee requirement is limited to party primary elections, but the mechanism of such elections is the creature of state legislative choice and hence is "state action" within the meaning of the Fourteenth Amendment. *Gray* v. *Sanders*, 372 U.S. 368 (1963) [p. 163]; *Nixon* v. *Herndon*, 273 U.S. 536 (1927). * * * The question presented in this case is whether a state law that prevents potential candidates for public office from seeking the nomination of their party due to their inability to pay a portion of the cost of conducting the primary election is state action that unlawfully discriminates against the candidates so excluded or the voters who wish to support them.

The threshold question to be resolved is whether the filing-fee system should be sustained if it can be shown to have some rational basis, or whether it must withstand a more rigid standard of review. * * *

The initial and direct impact of filing fees is felt by aspirants for office, rather than voters, and the Court has not heretofore attached such fundamental status to candidacy as to invoke a rigorous standard of review. However, the rights of voters and the rights of candidates do not lend themselves to neat separation; laws that

---

[5] Texas law does permit the names of independent candidates to appear on the official ballot in the general election if a proper application containing a voter petition is submitted. * * * No fees are assessed against candidates in general elections.

affect candidates always have at least some theoretical, correlative effect on voters. Of course, not every limitation or incidental burden on the exercise of voting rights is subject to a stringent standard of review. Texas does not place a condition on the exercise of the right to vote, nor does it quantitatively dilute votes that have been cast. Rather, the Texas system creates barriers to candidate access to the primary ballot, thereby tending to limit the field of candidates from which voters might choose. The existence of such barriers does not of itself compel close scrutiny. In approaching candidate restrictions, it is essential to examine in a realistic light the extent and nature of their impact on voters.

Unlike a filing-fee requirement that most candidates could be expected to fulfill from their own resources or at least through modest contributions, the very size of the fees imposed under the Texas system gives it a patently exclusionary character. Many potential office seekers lacking both personal wealth and affluent backers are in every practical sense precluded from seeking the nomination of their chosen party, no matter how qualified they might be, and no matter how broad or enthusiastic their popular support. The effect of this exclusionary mechanism on voters is neither incidental nor remote. Not only are voters substantially limited in their choice of candidates, but also there is the obvious likelihood that this limitation would fall more heavily on the less affluent segment of the community, whose favorites may be unable to pay the large costs required by the Texas system. * * * Appellants do not dispute that this is endemic to the system. This disparity in voting power based on wealth cannot be described by reference to discrete and precisely defined segments of the community as is typical of inequities challenged under the Equal Protection Clause, and there are doubtless some instances of candidates representing the views of voters of modest means who are able to pay the required fee. But we would ignore reality were we not to recognize that this system falls with unequal weight on voters, as well as candidates, according to their economic status.

Because the Texas filing-fee scheme has a real and appreciable impact on the exercise of the franchise, and because this impact is related to the resources of the voters supporting a particular candidate, we conclude * * * that the laws must be "closely scrutinized" and found reasonably necessary to the accomplishment of legitimate state objectives in order to pass constitutional muster.

Appellants contend that the filing fees required by the challenged statutes are necessary both to regulate the ballot in primary elections and to provide a means for financing such elections.

The Court has recognized that a State has a legitimate interest in regulating the number of candidates on the ballot. In so doing, the State understandably and properly seeks to prevent the clogging of its election machinery, avoid voter confusion, and assure that the winner is the choice of a majority, or at least a strong plurality, of those voting, without the expense and burden of runoff elections. Although we have no way of gauging the number of candidates who might enter primaries in Texas if access to the ballot were unimpeded by the large filing fees in question here, we are bound to respect the legitimate objectives of the State in avoiding overcrowded ballots. Moreover, a State has an interest, if not a duty, to protect the integrity of its political processes from frivolous or fraudulent candidacies.

There is no escape from the conclusion that the imposition of filing fees ranging as high as $8,900 [approximately $50,100 in today's dollars — Eds.] tends to limit the number of candidates entering the primaries. However, even under conventional standards of review, a State cannot achieve its objectives by totally arbitrary means; the criterion for differing treatment must bear some relevance to the object of the legislation. To say that the filing-fee requirement tends to limit the ballot to the more serious candidates is not enough. There may well be some rational relationship between a candidate's willingness to pay a filing fee and the seriousness with which he takes his candidacy, but the candidates in this case affirmatively alleged that they were unable, not simply unwilling, to pay the assessed fees, and there was no contrary evidence. It is uncontested that the filing fees exclude legitimate as well as frivolous candidates. And even assuming that every person paying the large fees required by Texas law takes his own candidacy seriously, that does not make him a "serious candidate" in the popular sense. If the Texas fee requirement is intended to regulate the ballot by weeding out spurious candidates, it is extraordinarily ill-fitted to that goal; other means to protect those valid interests are available.

Instead of arguing for the reasonableness of the exclusion of some candidates, appellants rely on the fact that the filing-fee requirement is applicable only to party primaries, and point out that a candidate can gain a place on the ballot in the general election without payment of fees by submitting a proper application accompanied by a voter petition. Apart from the fact that the primary election may be more crucial than the general election in certain parts of Texas, we can hardly accept as reasonable an alternative that requires candidates and voters to abandon their party affiliations in order to avoid the burdens of the filing fees imposed by state law. Appellants have not demonstrated that their present filing-fee scheme is a necessary or reasonable tool for regulating the ballot.

In addition to the State's purported interest in regulating the ballot, the filing fees serve to relieve the State treasury of the cost of conducting the primary elections, and this is a legitimate state objective; in this limited sense it cannot be said that the fee system lacks a rational basis. But under the standard of review we consider applicable to this case, there must be a showing of necessity. * * *

We also reject the theory that since the candidates are availing themselves of the primary machinery, it is appropriate that they pay that share of the cost that they have occasioned. The force of this argument is diluted by the fact that candidates for offices requiring statewide primaries are generally assessed at a lower rate than candidates for local office, although the statewide primaries undoubtedly involve a greater expense.[29] More importantly, the costs do not arise because candidates decide to enter a primary or because the parties decide to conduct one, but because the State has, as a matter of legislative choice, directed that party primaries be held. The State has presumably chosen this course more to benefit the voters than the candidates.

Appellants seem to place reliance on the self-evident fact that if the State must

---

[29] This would be a different case if the fees approximated the cost of processing a candidate's application for a place on the ballot, a cost resulting from the candidate's decision to enter a primary. The term *filing* fee has long been thought to cover the cost of filing, that is, the cost of placing a particular document on the public record.

assume the cost, the voters, as taxpayers, will ultimately be burdened with the expense of the primaries. But it is far too late to make out a case that the party primary is such a lesser part of the democratic process that its cost must be shifted away from the taxpayers generally. The financial burden for general elections is carried by all taxpayers and appellants have not demonstrated a valid basis for distinguishing between these two legitimate costs of the democratic process. It seems appropriate that a primary system designed to give the voters some influence at the nominating stage should spread the cost among all of the voters in an attempt to distribute the influence without regard to wealth. Viewing the myriad governmental functions supported from general revenues, it is difficult to single out any of a higher order than the conduct of elections at all levels to bring forth those persons desired by their fellow citizens to govern. Without making light of the State's interest in husbanding its revenues, we fail to see such an element of necessity in the State's present means of financing primaries as to justify the resulting incursion on the prerogatives of voters.

Since the State has failed to establish the requisite justification for this filing-fee system, we hold that it results in a denial of equal protection of the laws. It must be emphasized that nothing herein is intended to cast doubt on the validity of reasonable candidate filing fees or licensing fees in other contexts. By requiring candidates to shoulder the costs of conducting primary elections through filing fees and by providing no reasonable alternative means of access to the ballot, the State of Texas has erected a system that utilizes the criterion of ability to pay as a condition to being on the ballot, thus excluding some candidates otherwise qualified and denying an undetermined number of voters the opportunity to vote for candidates of their choice. These salient features of the Texas system are critical to our determination of constitutional invalidity.

Affirmed.

Mr. Justice Powell and Mr. Justice Rehnquist took no part in the consideration or decision of this case.

Notes and Questions

1. *Problem.* A state statute requires each candidate for certain offices to pay a filing fee to participate in primary elections or to run as a write-in candidate at the general election. No candidate may win election unless he or she has paid the fee. The fee is 2% of the salary of the office sought. Sharon wants to run for County Supervisor, but is unable to pay the filing fee, which is $3500. Is the requirement constitutional? What if the statute required payment of the filing fee as a prerequisite to appearing on the ballot, but one could be a write-in candidate without paying the fee? What if potential candidates were permitted to obtain a certain number of signatures on a petition in lieu of paying the fee? *See Lubin v. Panish*, 415 U.S. 709 (1974).

2. If there had been no statute requiring a fee, and the parties themselves decided to impose an assessment on persons running for their endorsement, would

such an assessment be unconstitutional? Is such a situation in fact any different from the one in *Carter* itself?

3.   Would it be constitutional to impose a fee to seek a nomination in a party *caucus or convention*? Would it be constitutional for a state to *forbid* a party from imposing a fee on a candidate seeking a nomination in a party caucus or convention?

4.   *Problem.* In order to appear on the general-election ballot, minor party candidates in Pencilonia must submit petitions with a number of signatures equal to two percent of the number of votes received by any elected candidate for statewide office in the most recent election (which has usually meant 20,000–25,000 signatures). Major-party candidates, by contrast, must compete in primary elections, which they can do by filing two thousand (for president, United States senator, and governor) or one thousand signatures (for state treasurer, auditor general, and attorney general).

In Pencilonia the judiciary oversees challenges to the validity of minor-party candidates' petition signatures. (In all other states, such challenges are handled by an administrative agency in the executive branch.) In the event of a challenge, the court will require the challenger and the candidate to provide workers to review the signatures. Based on that review, the challenger and the candidate stipulate to the validity or invalidity of as many signatures as possible, and the court resolves any remaining disputes. The court may award costs "as it shall deem just," and some courts in recent years have required candidates to pay challengers' costs (totaling as much as $80,000) where there has been extensive fraud and deception in gathering signatures.

Minor parties and candidates challenge the law, arguing that it places an unconstitutional burden on their ability to run for office, and on voters' correlative right to vote for them. They argue that the costs associated with defending their signatures are significant deterrents to running for office, and the threat of having to pay for challengers' costs is an even stronger deterrent. The state responds that the law is distinguishable from *Bullock v. Carter* in that there is no mandatory fee and candidates can avoid having to pay challengers' costs simply by not submitting improper signatures. Is it unconstitutional to force minor parties to defend their signatures in court?

STORER v. BROWN
Supreme Court of the United States
415 U.S. 724, 94 S. Ct. 1274, 39 L. Ed. 2d 714 (1974)

MR. JUSTICE WHITE delivered the opinion of the Court [in which MR. CHIEF JUSTICE BURGER, MR. JUSTICE STEWART, MR. JUSTICE BLACKMUN, MR. JUSTICE POWELL, and MR. JUSTICE REHNQUIST join].

The California Elections Code forbids ballot position to an independent candidate for elective public office if he voted in the immediately preceding primary, § 6830(c), or if he had a registered affiliation with a qualified political party at any time within one year prior to the immediately preceding primary election. § 6830(d).
* * *

Prior to the 1972 elections, appellants [including two independent candidates for Congress, Storer and Frommhagen, who had left the Democratic Party within the year before the 1972 primary elections] filed their actions to have the above sections of the Elections Code declared unconstitutional and their enforcement enjoined. * * *

A three-judge District Court concluded that the statutes served a sufficiently important state interest to sustain their constitutionality and dismissed the complaints. * * * We affirm[.] * * *

In challenging § 6830(d), appellants rely on *Williams* v. *Rhodes* [393 U.S. 23 (1968)] [p. 497] and assert that under that case and subsequent cases dealing with exclusionary voting and candidate qualifications, *e.g.*, *Dunn* v. *Blumstein*, 405 U.S. 330 (1972) [p. 93]; *Bullock* v. *Carter*, 405 U.S. 134 (1972) [p. 508]; *Kramer* v. *Union Free School District*, 395 U.S. 621 (1969) [p. 62], substantial burdens on the right to vote or to associate for political purposes are constitutionally suspect and invalid under the First and Fourteenth Amendments and under the Equal Protection Clause unless essential to serve a compelling state interest. These cases, however, do not necessarily condemn § 6830(d). It has never been suggested that the *Williams-Kramer-Dunn* rule automatically invalidates every substantial restriction on the right to vote or to associate. Nor could this be the case under our Constitution where the States are given the initial task of determining the qualifications of voters who will elect members of Congress. Art. I, § 2, cl. 1. Also Art. I, § 4, cl. 1, authorizes the States to prescribe "the Times, Places and Manner of holding Elections for Senators and Representatives." Moreover, as a practical matter, there must be a substantial regulation of elections if they are to be fair and honest and if some sort of order, rather than chaos, is to accompany the democratic processes. In any event, the States have evolved comprehensive, and in many respects complex, election codes regulating in most substantial ways, with respect to both federal and state elections, the time, place, and manner of holding primary and general elections, the registration and qualifications of voters, and the selection and qualification of candidates.

It is very unlikely that all or even a large portion of the state election laws would fail to pass muster under our cases; and the rule fashioned by the Court to pass on constitutional challenges to specific provisions of election laws provides no litmus-paper test for separating those restrictions that are valid from those that are invidious under the Equal Protection Clause. The rule is not self-executing and is no substitute for the hard judgments that must be made. Decision in this context, as in others, is very much a "matter of degree," *Dunn* v. *Blumstein*, *supra*, at 348, very much a matter of "consider[ing] the facts and circumstances behind the law, the interests which the State claims to be protecting, and the interests of those who are disadvantaged by the classification." *Williams* v. *Rhodes*, *supra*, at 30; *Dunn* v. *Blumstein*, *supra*, at 335. What the result of this process will be in any specific case may be very difficult to predict with great assurance. * * *

[W]e have no hesitation in sustaining § 6830(d). In California, the independent candidacy route to obtaining ballot position is but a part of the candidate-nominating process, an alternative to being nominated in one of the direct party primaries. The independent candidate need not stand for primary election but must qualify for the ballot by demonstrating substantial public support in another way. Otherwise, the qualifications required of the independent candidate are very similar to, or identical with, those imposed on party candidates. Section 6401 imposes a flat disqualification upon any candidate seeking to run in a party primary if he has been "registered as affiliated with a political party other than that political party the nomination of which he seeks within 12 months immediately prior to the filing of the declaration." Moreover, §§ 6402 and 6611 provide that a candidate who has been defeated in a party primary may not be nominated as an independent or be a candidate of any other party; and no person may file nomination papers for a party nomination and an independent nomination for the same office, or for more than one office at the same election.

The requirement that the independent candidate not have been affiliated with a political party for a year before the primary is expressive of a general state policy aimed at maintaining the integrity of the various routes to the ballot. It involves no discrimination against independents. * * *

* * * The direct party primary in California is not merely an exercise or warm-up for the general election but an integral part of the entire election process, the initial stage in a two-stage process by which the people choose their public officers. It functions to winnow out and finally reject all but the chosen candidates. The State's general policy is to have contending forces within the party employ the primary campaign and primary election to finally settle their differences. The general election ballot is reserved for major struggles; it is not a forum for continuing intraparty feuds. The provision against defeated primary candidates running as independents effectuates this aim, the visible result being to prevent the losers from continuing the struggle and to limit the names on the ballot to those who have won the primaries and those independents who have properly qualified. The people, it is hoped, are presented with understandable choices and the winner in the general election with sufficient support to govern effectively.

Section 6830(d) carries very similar credentials. It protects the direct primary process by refusing to recognize independent candidates who do not make early plans to leave a party and take the alternative course to the ballot. It works against independent candidacies prompted by short-range political goals, pique, or personal quarrel. It is also a substantial barrier to a party fielding an "independent" candidate to capture and bleed off votes in the general election that might well go to another party.

A State need not take the course California has, but California apparently believes with the Founding Fathers that splintered parties and unrestrained factionalism may do significant damage to the fabric of government. See The Federalist, No. 10 (Madison). It appears obvious to us that the one-year disaffiliation provision furthers the State's interest in the stability of its political system. We also consider that interest as not only permissible, but compelling and as outweighing the interest the candidate and his supporters may have in making a late rather than an early decision to seek independent ballot status. Nor do we have reason for concluding that the device California chose, § 6830(d), was not an essential part of its overall mechanism to achieve its acceptable goals. [T]he Constitution does not require the State to choose ineffectual means to achieve its aims. To conclude otherwise might sacrifice the political stability of the system of the State, with profound consequences for the entire citizenry, merely in the interest of particular candidates and their supporters having instantaneous access to the ballot.

We conclude that § 6830(d) is not unconstitutional, and Storer and Frommhagen were properly barred from the ballot as a result of its application. * * *

[*Affirmed.*]

Mr. Justice Brennan, with whom Mr. Justice Douglas and Mr. Justice Marshall concur, dissenting. * * *

The California statute absolutely denies ballot position to independent candidates who, at any time within 12 months prior to the immediately preceding primary election, were registered as affiliated with a qualified political party. Intertwined with [California's requirement that] primary elections [] be held five months before the general election, § 6830(d) plainly places a significant burden upon independent candidacy — and therefore effectively burdens as well the rights of potential supporters and voters to associate for political purposes and to vote — because potential independent candidates, currently affiliated with a recognized party, are required to take affirmative action toward candidacy fully *17 months* before the general election. Thus, such candidates must make that decision at a time when, as a matter of the realities of our political system, they cannot know either who will be the nominees of the major parties, or what the significant election issues may be. * * *

The Court acknowledges the burdens imposed by § 6830(d) upon fundamental personal liberties, but agrees with the State's assertion that the burdens are justified by the State's compelling interest in the stability of its political system. Without § 6830(d), the argument runs, the party's primary system, an integral part of the election process, is capable of subversion by a candidate who first opts to participate in that method of ballot access, and later abandons the party and its candidate-selection process, taking with him his party supporters. Thus, in sustaining the validity of § 6830(d), the Court finds compelling the State's interests in preventing splintered parties and unrestricted factionalism and protecting the direct-primary system.

But the identification of these compelling state interests, which I accept, does not end the inquiry. There remains the necessity of determining whether these vital state objectives "cannot be served equally well in significantly less burdensome ways." * * *

I have searched in vain for even the slightest evidence in the records of these cases of any effort on the part of the State to demonstrate the absence of reasonably less burdensome means of achieving its objectives. This crucial failure cannot be remedied by the Court's conjecture that other means "*might* sacrifice the political stability of the system of the State" (emphasis added). When state legislation burdens fundamental constitutional rights, as conceded here, we are not at liberty to speculate that the State might be able to demonstrate the absence of less burdensome means; the burden of affirmatively demonstrating this is upon the State.

Moreover, less drastic means — which would not require the State to give appellants "instantaneous access to the ballot" — seem plainly available to achieve California's objectives. First, requiring party disaffiliation 12 months before the primary elections is unreasonable on its face. There is no evidence that splintering and factionalism of political parties will result unless disaffiliation is effected that far in advance of the primaries. To the contrary, whatever threat may exist to party stability is more likely to surface only shortly before the primary, when the identities of the potential field of candidates and issues become known. Thus, the State's interests would be adequately served and the rights of the appellants less burdened if the date when disaffiliation must be effected were set significantly closer to the primaries. Second, the requirement of party disaffiliation could be limited to those independent candidates who actually run in a party primary. Section 6830(d) sweeps far too broadly in its application to potential independent candidates who, though registered as affiliated with a recognized party, do not run for the party's nomination. Such an independent candidate plainly poses no threat of utilizing the party machinery to run in the primary, and then declaring independent candidacy, thereby splitting the party. * * *

ANDERSON v. CELEBREZZE
Supreme Court of the United States
460 U.S. 780, 103 S. Ct. 1564, 75 L. Ed. 2d 547 (1983)

JUSTICE STEVENS delivered the opinion of the Court [in which CHIEF JUSTICE BURGER, JUSTICE BRENNAN, JUSTICE MARSHALL, and JUSTICE BLACKMUN join].

On April 24, 1980, petitioner John Anderson announced that he was an independent candidate for the office of President of the United States. * * * On April 24, however, it was already too late for Anderson to qualify for a position on the ballot in Ohio and certain other states because the statutory deadlines for filing a statement of candidacy had already passed.[2] The question presented by this case is whether Ohio's early filing deadline placed an unconstitutional burden on the voting and associational rights of Anderson's supporters.

The facts are not in dispute. On May 16, 1980, Anderson's supporters tendered a nominating petition containing approximately 14,500 signatures and a statement of candidacy to respondent Celebrezze, the Ohio Secretary of State. These documents would have entitled Anderson to a place on the ballot if they had been filed on or before March 20, 1980. Respondent refused to accept the petition solely because it had not been filed within the time required by § 3513.257 of the Ohio Revised Code. Three days later Anderson and three voters * * * commenced this action * * *, challenging the constitutionality of Ohio's early filing deadline for independent candidates. The District Court granted petitioners' motion for sum-

---

[2] Anderson's name had been entered in the Republican primary in Ohio and 26 other States before he made his decision to run as an independent, and he actually competed unsuccessfully in nine Republican primaries. Nevertheless, the parties agree that his timely withdrawal from the Ohio primary avoided the application of the State's "sore loser" statute, which disqualifies a candidate who ran unsuccessfully in a party primary from running as an independent in the general election. [Relocated. — Eds.]

mary judgment and ordered respondent to place Anderson's name on the general election ballot. * * *

[The Court of Appeals reversed, but t]he election was held while the appeal was pending. In Ohio Anderson received 254,472 votes, or 5.9 percent of the votes cast; nationally, he received 5,720,060 votes or approximately 6.6 percent of the total. * * *

After a date toward the end of March, even if intervening events create unanticipated political opportunities, no independent candidate may enter the Presidential race and seek to place his name on the Ohio general election ballot. Thus the direct impact of Ohio's early filing deadline falls upon aspirants for office. Nevertheless, as we have recognized, "the rights of voters and the rights of candidates do not lend themselves to neat separation; laws that affect candidates always have at least some theoretical, correlative effect on voters." *Bullock* v. *Carter*, 405 U.S. 134, 143 (1972) [p. 508]. Our primary concern is with the tendency of ballot access restrictions "to limit the field of candidates from which voters might choose." Therefore, "[i]n approaching candidate restrictions, it is essential to examine in a realistic light the extent and nature of their impact on voters." *Ibid.*

The impact of candidate eligibility requirements on voters implicates basic constitutional rights.[7] * * * The right to vote is "heavily burdened" if that vote may be cast only for major-party candidates at a time when other parties or other candidates are "clamoring for a place on the ballot." The exclusion of candidates also burdens voters' freedom of association, because an election campaign is an effective platform for the expression of views on the issues of the day, and a candidate serves as a rallying-point for like-minded citizens.

Although these rights of voters are fundamental, not all restrictions imposed by the States on candidates' eligibility for the ballot impose constitutionally-suspect burdens on voters' rights to associate or to choose among candidates. We have recognized that, "as a practical matter, there must be a substantial regulation of elections if they are to be fair and honest and if some sort of order, rather than chaos, is to accompany the democratic processes." *Storer* v. *Brown*, 415 U.S. 724, 730 (1974) [p. 513]. To achieve these necessary objectives, States have enacted comprehensive and sometimes complex election codes. Each provision of these schemes, whether it governs the registration and qualifications of voters, the selection and eligibility of candidates, or the voting process itself, inevitably affects — at least to some degree — the individual's right to vote and his right to associate with others for political ends. Nevertheless, the State's important regulatory interests are generally sufficient to justify reasonable, nondiscriminatory restrictions.

Constitutional challenges to specific provisions of a State's election laws therefore cannot be resolved by any "litmus-paper test" that will separate valid from

---

[7] In this case, we base our conclusions directly on the First and Fourteenth Amendments and do not engage in a separate Equal Protection Clause analysis. We rely, however, on the analysis in a number of our prior election cases resting on the Equal Protection Clause of the Fourteenth Amendment. These cases, applying the "fundamental rights" strand of equal protection analysis, have identified the First and Fourteenth Amendment rights implicated by restrictions on the eligibility of voters and candidates, and have considered the degree to which the State's restrictions further legitimate state interests.

invalid restrictions. Instead, a court must * * * first consider the character and magnitude of the asserted injury to the rights protected by the First and Fourteenth Amendments that the plaintiff seeks to vindicate. It then must identify and evaluate the precise interests put forward by the State as justifications for the burden imposed by its rule. In passing judgment, the Court must not only determine the legitimacy and strength of each of those interests; it also must consider the extent to which those interests make it necessary to burden the plaintiff's rights. Only after weighing all these factors is the reviewing court in a position to decide whether the challenged provision is unconstitutional. The results of this evaluation will not be automatic; as we have recognized, there is "no substitute for the hard judgments that must be made."

An early filing deadline may have a substantial impact on independent-minded voters. In election campaigns, particularly those which are national in scope, the candidates and the issues simply do not remain static over time. Various candidates rise and fall in popularity; domestic and international developments bring new issues to center stage and may affect voters' assessments of national problems. Such developments will certainly affect the strategies of candidates who have already entered the race; they may also create opportunities for new candidacies. Yet Ohio's filing deadline prevents persons who wish to be independent candidates from entering the significant political arena established in the State by a Presidential election campaign — and creating new political coalitions of Ohio voters — at any time after mid-to-late March. At this point developments in campaigns for the major-party nominations have only begun, and the major parties will not adopt their nominees and platforms for another five months. Candidates and supporters within the major parties thus have the political advantage of continued flexibility; for independents, the inflexibility imposed by the March filing deadline is a correlative disadvantage because of the competitive nature of the electoral process.

If the State's filing deadline were later in the year, a newly-emergent independent candidate could serve as the focal point for a grouping of Ohio voters who decide, after mid-March, that they are dissatisfied with the choices within the two major parties. As we recognized in *Williams* v. *Rhodes*, 393 U.S. [23], 33 [(1968)] [p. 497], "[s]ince the principal policies of the major parties change to some extent from year to year, and since the identity of the likely major party nominees may not be known until shortly before the election, this disaffected 'group' will rarely if ever be a cohesive or identifiable group until a few months before the election." Indeed, several important third-party candidacies in American history were launched after the two major parties staked out their positions and selected their nominees at national conventions during the summer. But under § 3513.257, a late-emerging Presidential candidate outside the major parties, whose positions on the issues could command widespread community support, is excluded from the Ohio general election ballot. * * *

It is clear, then, that the March filing deadline places a particular burden on an identifiable segment of Ohio's independent-minded voters. * * * A burden that falls unequally on new or small political parties or on independent candidates impinges, by its very nature, on associational choices protected by the First Amendment. It discriminates against those candidates and — of particular importance — against those voters whose political preferences lie outside the existing political parties. By limiting the opportunities of independent-minded voters to associate in the electoral arena to enhance their political effectiveness as a group, such restrictions threaten to reduce diversity and competition in the marketplace of ideas. Historically political figures outside the two major parties have been fertile sources of new ideas and new programs; many of their challenges to the status quo have in time made their way into the political mainstream. In short, the primary values protected by the First Amendment — "a profound national commitment to the principle that debate on public issues should be uninhibited, robust, and wide-open," *New York Times Co.* v. *Sullivan*, 376 U.S. 254, 270 (1964) [p. 574] — are served when election campaigns are not monopolized by the existing political parties. * * *

The State identifies three separate interests that it seeks to further by its early filing deadline for independent Presidential candidates: voter education, equal treatment for partisan and independent candidates, and political stability. * * *

There can be no question about the legitimacy of the State's interest in fostering informed and educated expressions of the popular will in a general election. * * * We are persuaded, however, that the State's important and legitimate interest in voter education does not justify the specific restriction on participation in a Presidential election that is at issue in this case.

* * * [T]oday even trivial details about national candidates are instantaneously communicated nationwide in both verbal and visual form[, and] the vast majority of the electorate not only is literate but is informed on a day-to-day basis about events and issues that affect election choices and about the ever-changing popularity of individual candidates. In the modern world it is somewhat unrealistic to suggest that it takes more than seven months to inform the electorate about the qualifications of a particular candidate simply because he lacks a partisan label. * * *

We also find no merit in the State's claim that the early filing deadline serves the interest of treating all candidates alike. It is true that a candidate participating in a primary election must declare his candidacy on the same date as an independent. But both the burdens and the benefits of the respective requirements are materially different, and the reasons for requiring early filing for a primary candidate are inapplicable to independent candidates in the general election.

The consequences of failing to meet the statutory deadline are entirely different for party primary participants and independents. The name of the nominees of the Democratic and Republican parties will appear on the Ohio ballot in November even if they did not decide to run until after Ohio's March deadline had passed, but the independent is simply denied a position on the ballot if he waits too long. Thus, under Ohio's scheme, the major parties may include all events preceding their national conventions in the calculus that produces their respective nominees and campaign platforms, but the independent's judgment must be based on a history that ends in March. The early filing deadline for a candidate in a party's primary election is adequately justified by administrative concerns. Seventy-five days appears to be a reasonable time for processing the documents submitted by candidates and preparing the ballot. The primary date itself must be set sufficiently in advance of the general election; furthermore, a Presidential preference primary must precede the national convention, which is regularly held during the summer. Finally, the successful participant in a party primary generally acquires the automatic support of an experienced political organization; in the Presidential contest, he obtains the support of convention delegates.

Neither the administrative justification nor the benefit of an early filing deadline is applicable to an independent candidate. Ohio does not suggest that the March deadline is necessary to allow petition signatures to be counted and verified or to permit November general election ballots to be printed. In addition, the early deadline does not correspond to a potential benefit for the independent, as it does for the party candidate. After filing his statement of candidacy, the independent does not participate in a structured intraparty contest to determine who will receive organizational support; he must develop support by other means. In short, "equal treatment" of partisan and independent candidates simply is not achieved by imposing the March filing deadline on both. As we have written, "[s]ometimes the grossest discrimination can lie in treating things that are different as though they were exactly alike." *Jenness* v. *Fortson*, 403 U.S. 431, 442 (1971) [p. 504]. * * *

Ohio's asserted interest in political stability amounts to a desire to protect existing political parties from competition — competition for campaign workers, voter support, and other campaign resources — generated by independent candidates who have previously been affiliated with the party. * * * [But] protecting the Republican and Democratic parties from external competition cannot justify the virtual exclusion of other political aspirants from the political arena. * * *

[T]he early filing deadline is not precisely drawn to protect the parties from "intraparty feuding," whatever legitimacy that state goal may have in a Presidential election. If the deadline is designed to keep intraparty competition within the party structure, its coverage is both too broad and too narrow. It is true that in this case § 3513.257 was applied to a candidate who had previously competed in party primaries and then sought to run as an independent. But the early deadline applies broadly to independent candidates who have not been affiliated in the recent past with any political party. On the other hand, as long as the decision to run is made before the March deadline, Ohio does not prohibit independent candidacies by persons formerly affiliated with a political party, or currently participating in intraparty competition in other States — regardless of the effect on the political party structure. * * *

We began our inquiry by noting that our primary concern is not the interest of candidate Anderson, but rather, the interests of the voters who chose to associate together to express their support for Anderson's candidacy and the views he espoused. Under any realistic appraisal, the "extent and nature" of the burdens Ohio has placed on the voters' freedom of choice and freedom of association, in an election of nationwide importance, unquestionably outweigh the State's minimal interest in imposing a March deadline.

The judgment of the Court of Appeals is

Reversed.

Justice Rehnquist, with whom Justice White, Justice Powell, and Justice O'Connor join, dissenting. * * *

On the record before us, the effect of the Ohio filing deadline is quite easily summarized: it requires that a candidate, who has already decided to run for President, decide by March 20 which route his candidacy will take. He can become a nonparty candidate by filing a nominating petition with 5,000 signatures and assure himself a place on the general election ballot. Or, he can become a party candidate and take his chances in securing a position on the general election ballot by seeking the nomination of a party's national convention. Anderson chose the latter route and submitted in a timely fashion his nominating petition for Ohio's Republican Primary. Then, realizing that he had no chance for the Republican nomination, Anderson sought to change the form of this candidacy. The Ohio filing deadline prevented him from making this change. Quite clearly, rather than prohibiting him from seeking the Presidency, the filing deadline only prevented Anderson from having two shots at it in the same election year. * * *

Underlying the Court's entire opinion is the idea that "independent candidates" are treated differently than candidates fielded by the "major parties." But this observation is no more productive than comparing apples and oranges and wondering at the difference between them.

First of all, *any political party, major, minor, or otherwise*, can qualify for a position on Ohio's general election ballot and have that position held open until later in the election year. The reasonableness of this approach is fairly obvious. Political parties have, or at least hope to have, a continuing existence, representing particular philosophies. Each party has an interest in finding the best candidate to advance its philosophy in each election. The Court suggests that if such a procedure is so important for political parties, then followers of a particular candidate should also have more time. This argument simply does not wash. Any group of like-minded voters, if they are of sufficient numbers, is free to form a political party and ensure more time in selecting a candidate to express their views. But followers of a particular candidate need no time to find such a representative; they are organized around that candidate. Such followers have no real organized existence in the absence of that particular candidate. * * *

* * * The Court's opinion draws no line; I presume that a State must wait until all party nominees are chosen and then allow all unsuccessful party candidates to refight their party battles by forming an "independent" candidacy. I find nothing in the Constitution which requires this result. * * *

Notes and Questions

1. Can *Anderson* be squared with *Jenness v. Fortson* and *Storer v. Brown*?

2. Does the Court's opinion imply that ballot-access restrictions will be evaluated under heightened scrutiny whether third parties and major parties are subject to the same or different rules?

3. Professor Lowenstein has suggested that *Anderson* represents "a sort of antidoctrine. It calls for judges to consider all of the factors that bear on a particular problem, giving each due weight under the particular circumstances." Daniel H. Lowenstein, *The Supreme Court Has No Theory of Politics — and Be Thankful for Small Favors, in* THE U.S. SUPREME COURT AND THE ELECTORAL PROCESS 283, 295

(David K. Ryden ed., 2d ed. 2002). *See also Nader v. Keith*, 385 F.3d 729, 735 (7th Cir. 2004) (noting that because "[r]estrictions on candidacy must be considered together rather than separately," and because "there is great variance among the states' schemes," it is "difficult to rely heavily on precedent in evaluating such restrictions"). Do you agree?

4. According to *Anderson*, "discriminatory" restrictions disadvantaging independent candidates trigger strict scrutiny as a matter of First Amendment law — not just as a matter of equal protection. *See* footnote 7. But as the *Anderson* dissent makes clear, what one person views as discrimination, another may view as equity. Additionally, even where it is conceded that a regulation acts unequally on different people, reasonable arguments can often be constructed about whether such distinctions are justified. *Cf. Michael M. v. Superior Court*, 450 U.S. 464 (1981) (concluding that it was constitutional to distinguish between the sexes in the punishment of statutory rape). Indeed, as the Court in *Anderson* noted, the Constitution may *require* different treatment for groups that are in different circumstances. Do you believe Ohio treated independent candidates differently from party candidates? Do you think such treatment was appropriate?

5. *Problem.* Illinois requires independent candidates to obtain the signatures of 25,000 qualified voters and requires the submission of those signatures 134 days before the election — an earlier deadline than is imposed by every other state except Texas and Arizona. Are the two requirements constitutional when considered cumulatively? Is either requirement unconstitutional standing alone?

6. *Problem.* Independents wishing to appear on Hawaii's presidential-election ballot must obtain the signatures of 1% of the number of votes cast in the last presidential election. To form a new party, however, supporters must obtain signatures from only 0.1% of the state's registered voters. Is the disparity justified as compensating for earlier filing deadlines and primaries that are applicable to party candidates? *See Nader v. Cronin*, 2008 U.S. Dist. LEXIS 9272 (D. Haw. 2008); *Peroutka v. Cronin*, 179 P.3d 1050 (Haw. 2008). What if the state required more signatures from supporters of the new party than from independent candidates? *See Green Party of Arkansas v. Daniels*, 445 F. Supp. 2d 1056 (D. Ark. 2006).

7. *Problem.* Ballots often contain information about candidates beside their names. Such information may include a candidate's party affiliation, current occupation, and status as an incumbent or challenger. States often limit the sort of information that can appear on a ballot, however. Consider the following limitations. Do they unconstitutionally interfere with the right to vote?

A. Arkanzona permits each candidate to designate his or her political party affiliation, but only if the candidate is affiliated with a "recognized party." Recognized parties are those that polled at least 5% in the last gubernatorial election or that have filed a petition signed by registered voters numbering at least 1% of the number of voters in the last gubernatorial election. Candidates belonging to unrecognized parties and those belonging to no party must leave the space for party designation blank. The limitation is challenged by a candidate unaffiliated with a party who wishes to be identified as "Independent." *See Rosen v. Brown*, 970 F.2d 169 (6th Cir. 1992).

B. Bostonia permits candidates to designate their affiliations with "recognized parties," defined as in Arkanzona. Candidates who are unaffiliated, as well as candidates who are affiliated with an unrecognized party, are designated on the ballot as "Independent." The law is challenged by a candidate who is a member of an unrecognized party who wishes to have the ballot designate the name of his party. *See Schrader v. Blackwell*, 241 F.3d 783 (6th Cir. 2001); *Dart v. Brown*, 717 F.2d 1491 (5th Cir. 1983).

C. Connifornia permits candidates to designate their current occupations, but does not permit ballots to display "status" designations, except that incumbents may identify themselves as such. Charlie Candidate wishes to have the ballot identify him as a "peace activist." The state refuses to permit such a designation, citing the vagueness of the term and the potential for voter confusion. *See Rubin v. City of Santa Monica*, 308 F.3d 1008 (9th Cir. 2002).

8. *Problem.* West Vermont holds closed primaries, in which each party's primary is restricted to members of that party (subject to *Tashjian*'s requirement that parties can invite the participation of independents if the parties so desire). The state, however, imposes a deadline on persons wishing to register with a party. All such registrations must be filed at least thirty days before the general election, and take effect only after the election. (Exceptions are made, however, for those legally incapable of registering by the deadline, such as new residents and persons turning eighteen between the deadline and the election.) Thus, a person wishing to vote in the 2011 primary must register with that party no later than the beginning of October, 2010. The state defends this deadline as justified by the interest in preventing party raiding. Is it constitutional? Should the deadline be evaluated under strict scrutiny? *See Rosario v. Rockefeller*, 410 U.S. 752 (1973).

What if the state forbade participation in a primary unless the voter refrained from participating in a different party's primary for the preceding twenty-three months? *See Kusper v. Pontikes*, 414 U.S. 51 (1973).

9. *Problem.* New York Election Law §§ 5-304(2) and 5-304(3) provide that a registered voter wishing to establish or change membership in a political party must do so at least twenty-five days before the general election to be eligible to vote in the following year's primary election. Sections 5-201(1) and 5-201(3), however, establish that a person *not* registered to vote may vote in the primary if he registers and joins a party as late as twenty-five days before the primary election itself. The state justifies the law on the ground that it encourages non-registered voters to register, without severely burdening the rights of voters who were already registered. Does the statutory scheme violate the Equal Protection Clause or the First Amendment rights of registered voters? Should a court apply strict or rational-basis scrutiny? *See Van Wie v. Pataki*, 87 F. Supp. 2d 148 (N.D.N.Y. 2000), *vacated as moot* 267 F.3d 109 (2d Cir. 2001).

10. In North Carolina, groups that wish to qualify as new parties and to have their nominees appear on the ballot must submit petitions by May 17 signed by 2% of the number of voters who voted for governor in the last election. In *Pisano v. Strech*, 743 F.3d 927 (4th Cir. 2014), the Fourth Circuit upheld North Carolina's May 17 petition deadline against a challenge that it unconstitutionally interfered with

minor parties' ability to nominate presidential candidates. The court noted that the deadline left the parties with plenty of time — three and one-half years — in which to gather the signatures. Minor parties complained, arguing that the deadline was significantly in advance of the time when the major parties would choose their presidential nominees at their conventions in August and September. Accordingly, argued the minor parties, it was difficult to gather the signatures at such an early date because the public was not yet paying attention to politics. The court rejected this argument, explaining that North Carolina's deadline occurred *after* that state's primary, and so there was plenty of opportunity for the minor parties to take advantage of the citizens' political awareness during primary season.

11. One critical basis of disagreement concerning laws affecting third parties is the purpose served by their candidacies. Should minor parties have a First Amendment right of ballot access so they might "expand and affect political debate"? *Munro v. Socialist Workers Party*, 479 U.S. 189, 202 (1986) (Marshall, J., dissenting). *See also Williams v. Rhodes*, 393 U.S. 23, 39 (1968) [p. 497] (Douglas, J., concurring) (quoting *Sweezy v. New Hampshire*, 354 U.S. 234, 250–51 (1957) (opinion of Warren, C.J.)). Or should we think of the ballot as strictly a means to determine winners of elections? These questions have been in the background of the cases we have encountered so far. The next two cases bring them to the foreground.

BURDICK v. TAKUSHI
Supreme Court of the United States
504 U.S. 428, 112 S. Ct. 2059, 119 L. Ed. 2d 245 (1992)

JUSTICE WHITE delivered the opinion of the Court [in which CHIEF JUSTICE REHNQUIST, JUSTICE O'CONNOR, JUSTICE SCALIA, JUSTICE SOUTER, and JUSTICE THOMAS join].

The issue in this case is whether Hawaii's prohibition on write-in voting unreasonably infringes upon its citizens' rights under the First and Fourteenth Amendments. * * *

Petitioner is a registered voter in the city and county of Honolulu. In 1986, only one candidate filed nominating papers to run for the seat representing petitioner's district in the Hawaii House of Representatives. Petitioner wrote to state officials inquiring about Hawaii's write-in voting policy and received a copy of an opinion letter issued by the Hawaii Attorney General's Office stating that the State's election law made no provision for write-in voting. Petitioner then filed this lawsuit, claiming that he wished to vote in the primary and general elections for a person who had not filed nominating papers and that he wished to vote in future elections for other persons whose names might not appear on the ballot. * * * [The Hawaii Supreme Court, answering questions certified to it by the District Court, confirmed] that Hawaii's election laws barred write-in voting and that these measures were consistent with the State's Constitution. * * *

Petitioner proceeds from the erroneous assumption that a law that imposes any burden upon the right to vote must be subject to strict scrutiny. Our cases do not so hold.

It is beyond cavil that "voting is of the most fundamental significance under our constitutional structure." It does not follow, however, that the right to vote in any manner and the right to associate for political purposes through the ballot are absolute. The Constitution provides that States may prescribe "[t]he Times, Places and Manner of holding Elections for Senators and Representatives," Art. I, § 4, cl. 1, and the Court therefore has recognized that States retain the power to regulate their own elections. Common sense, as well as constitutional law, compels the conclusion that government must play an active role in structuring elections; "as a practical matter, there must be a substantial regulation of elections if they are to be fair and honest and if some sort of order, rather than chaos, is to accompany the democratic processes." *Storer* v. *Brown*, 415 U.S. 724, 730 (1974) [p. 513].

Election laws will invariably impose some burden upon individual voters. Each provision of a code, "whether it governs the registration and qualifications of voters, the selection and eligibility of candidates, or the voting process itself, inevitably affects — at least to some degree — the individual's right to vote and his right to associate with others for political ends." Consequently, to subject every voting regulation to strict scrutiny and to require that the regulation be narrowly tailored to advance a compelling state interest, as petitioner suggests, would tie the hands of States seeking to assure that elections are operated equitably and efficiently. Accordingly, the mere fact that a State's system "creates barriers . . . tending to limit the field of candidates from which voters might choose . . . does not of itself compel close scrutiny." *Bullock* v. *Carter*, 405 U.S. 134, 143 (1972) [p. 508].

Instead, * * * a more flexible standard applies. A court considering a challenge to a state election law must weigh "the character and magnitude of the asserted injury to the rights protected by the First and Fourteenth Amendments that the plaintiff seeks to vindicate" against "the precise interests put forward by the State as justifications for the burden imposed by its rule," taking into consideration "the extent to which those interests make it necessary to burden the plaintiff's rights." *Anderson* v. *Celebrezze*, 460 U.S. 780, 789 (1983) [p. 517]; *Tashjian* v. *Republican Party*, 479 U.S. 208, 213–214 (1986) [p. 449].

Under this standard, the rigorousness of our inquiry into the propriety of a state election law depends upon the extent to which a challenged regulation burdens First and Fourteenth Amendment rights. Thus, as we have recognized when those rights are subjected to "severe" restrictions, the regulation must be "narrowly drawn to advance a state interest of compelling importance." *Norman* v. *Reed*, 502 U.S. 279, 289 (1992). But when a state election law provision imposes only "reasonable, nondiscriminatory restrictions" upon the First and Fourteenth Amendment rights of voters, "the State's important regulatory interests are generally sufficient to justify" the restrictions. We apply this standard in considering petitioner's challenge to Hawaii's ban on write-in ballots.

There is no doubt that the Hawaii election laws, like all election regulations, have an impact on the right to vote, but it can hardly be said that the laws at issue here unconstitutionally limit access to the ballot by party or independent candidates or unreasonably interfere with the right of voters to associate and have candidates of their choice placed on the ballot. Indeed, petitioner understandably does not challenge the manner in which the State regulates candidate access to the ballot.

To obtain a position on the November general election ballot, a candidate must participate in Hawaii's open primary, "in which all registered voters may choose in which party primary to vote." The State provides three mechanisms through which a voter's candidate-of-choice may appear on the primary ballot.

First, a party petition may be filed 150 days before the primary by any group of persons who obtain the signatures of one percent of the State's registered voters. Then, 60 days before the primary, candidates must file nominating papers certifying, among other things, that they will qualify for the office sought and that they are members of the party that they seek to represent in the general election. The nominating papers must contain the signatures of a specified number of registered voters: 25 for candidates for statewide or federal office; 15 for state legislative and county races. The winner in each party advances to the general election. * * *

The second method through which candidates may appear on the Hawaii primary ballot is the established party route. Established parties that have qualified by petition for three consecutive elections and received a specified percentage of the vote in the preceding election may avoid filing party petitions for 10 years. The Democratic, Republican, and Libertarian Parties currently meet Hawaii's criteria for established parties. Like new party candidates, established party contenders are required to file nominating papers 60 days before the primary.

The third mechanism by which a candidate may appear on the ballot is through the designated nonpartisan ballot. Nonpartisans may be placed on the nonpartisan primary ballot simply by filing nominating papers containing 15 to 25 signatures, depending upon the office sought, 60 days before the primary. To advance to the general election, a nonpartisan must receive 10 percent of the primary vote or the number of votes that was sufficient to nominate a partisan candidate, whichever number is lower. During the 10 years preceding the filing of this action, 8 of 26 nonpartisans who entered the primary obtained slots on the November ballot.

Although Hawaii makes no provision for write-in voting in its primary or general elections, the system outlined above provides for easy access to the ballot until the cutoff date for the filing of nominating petitions, two months before the primary. Consequently, any burden on voters' freedom of choice and association is borne only by those who fail to identify their candidate of choice until days before the primary. But in *Storer* v. *Brown*, we gave little weight to "the interest the candidate and his supporters may have in making a late rather than an early decision to seek independent ballot status." 415 U.S., at 736. We think the same reasoning applies here and therefore conclude that any burden imposed by Hawaii's write-in vote prohibition is a very limited one. "To conclude otherwise might sacrifice the political stability of the system of the State, with profound consequences for the entire citizenry, merely in the interest of particular candidates and their supporters having instantaneous access to the ballot." *Ibid.*[7]

---

[7] The dissent complains that, because primary voters are required to opt for a specific partisan or nonpartisan ballot, they are foreclosed from voting in those races in which no candidate appears on their chosen ballot and in those races in which they are dissatisfied with the available choices. But this is generally true of primaries; voters are required to select a ticket, rather than choose from the universe of candidates running on all party slates. * * *

If the dissent were correct in suggesting that requiring primary voters to select a specific ballot impermissibly burdened the right to vote, it is clear under our decisions that the availability of a write-in

Because he has characterized this as a voting rights rather than ballot access case, petitioner submits that the write-in prohibition deprives him of the opportunity to cast a meaningful ballot, conditions his electoral participation upon the waiver of his First Amendment right to remain free from espousing positions that he does not support, and discriminates against him based on the content of the message he seeks to convey through his vote. At bottom, he claims that he is entitled to cast and Hawaii required to count a "protest vote" for Donald Duck, and that any impediment to this asserted "right" is unconstitutional.

Petitioner's argument is based on two flawed premises. First, in *Bullock* v. *Carter*, we minimized the extent to which voting rights cases are distinguishable from ballot access cases, stating that "the rights of voters and the rights of candidates do not lend themselves to neat separation." 405 U.S., at 143. Second, the function of the election process is "to winnow out and finally reject all but the chosen candidates," *Storer*, 415 U.S., at 735, not to provide a means of giving vent to "short-range political goals, pique, or personal quarrel[s]." Attributing to elections a more generalized expressive function would undermine the ability of States to operate elections fairly and efficiently.

Accordingly, we have repeatedly upheld reasonable, politically neutral regulations that have the effect of channeling expressive activity at the polls. Petitioner offers no persuasive reason to depart from these precedents. Reasonable regulation of elections *does not* require voters to espouse positions that they do not support; it *does* require them to act in a timely fashion if they wish to express their views in the voting booth. And there is nothing content based about a flat ban on all forms of write-in ballots.

* * * [W]e conclude that, in light of the adequate ballot access afforded under Hawaii's election code, the State's ban on write-in voting imposes only a limited burden on voters' rights to make free choices and to associate politically through the vote.

We turn next to the interests asserted by Hawaii to justify the burden imposed by its prohibition of write-in voting. Because we have already concluded that the burden is slight, the State need not establish a compelling interest to tip the constitutional scales in its direction. Here, the State's interests outweigh petitioner's limited interest in waiting until the eleventh hour to choose his preferred candidate.

* * * The prohibition on write-in voting is a legitimate means of averting divisive sore-loser candidacies. Hawaii further promotes the two-stage, primary-general election process of winnowing out candidates by permitting the unopposed victors in certain primaries to be designated office-holders. This focuses the attention of voters upon contested races in the general election. This would not be possible, absent the write-in voting ban.

Hawaii also asserts that its ban on write-in voting at the primary stage is necessary to guard against "party raiding." Party raiding is generally defined as

---

option would not provide an adequate remedy. *Anderson*, 460 U.S., at 799, n.26; *Lubin* v. *Panish*, 415 U.S. 709, 719, n.5 (1974).

"the organized switching of blocs of voters from one party to another in order to manipulate the outcome of the other party's primary election." Petitioner suggests that, because Hawaii conducts an open primary, this is not a cognizable interest. We disagree. While voters may vote on any ticket in Hawaii's primary, the State requires that party candidates be "member[s] of the party," and prohibits candidates from filing "nomination papers both as a party candidate and as a nonpartisan candidate." Hawaii's system could easily be circumvented in a party primary election by mounting a write-in campaign for a person who had not filed in time or who had never intended to run for election. It could also be frustrated at the general election by permitting write-in votes for a loser in a party primary or for an independent who had failed to get sufficient votes to make the general election ballot. The State has a legitimate interest in preventing these sorts of maneuvers, and the write-in voting ban is a reasonable way of accomplishing this goal.[9]

We think these legitimate interests asserted by the State are sufficient to outweigh the limited burden that the write-in voting ban imposes upon Hawaii's voters.[10]

Indeed, the foregoing leads us to conclude that when a State's ballot access laws pass constitutional muster as imposing only reasonable burdens on First and Fourteenth Amendment rights — as do Hawaii's election laws — a prohibition on write-in voting will be presumptively valid, since any burden on the right to vote for the candidate of one's choice will be light and normally will be counterbalanced by the very state interests supporting the ballot access scheme.

In such situations, the objection to the specific ban on write-in voting amounts to nothing more than the insistence that the State record, count, and publish individual protests against the election system or the choices presented on the ballot through the efforts of those who actively participate in the system. There are other means available, however, to voice such generalized dissension from the electoral process; and we discern no adequate basis for our requiring the State to provide and to finance a place on the ballot for recording protests against its constitutionally valid election laws.

[T]he right to vote is the right to participate in an electoral process that is necessarily structured to maintain the integrity of the democratic system. We think that Hawaii's prohibition on write-in voting, considered as part of an electoral scheme that provides constitutionally sufficient ballot access, does not impose an

---

[9] The State also supports its ban on write-in voting as a means of enforcing nominating requirements, combating fraud, and "fostering informed and educated expressions of the popular will."

[10] Although the dissent purports to agree with the standard we apply in determining whether the right to vote has been restricted, and implies that it is analyzing the write-in ban under some minimal level of scrutiny, the dissent actually employs strict scrutiny. This is evident from its invocation of quite rigid narrow tailoring requirements. For instance, the dissent argues that the State could adopt a less drastic means of preventing sore-loser candidacies, and that the State could screen out ineligible candidates through postelection disqualification rather than a write-in voting ban.

It seems to us that limiting the choice of candidates to those who have complied with state election law requirements is the prototypical example of a regulation that, while it affects the right to vote, is eminently reasonable. The dissent's suggestion that voters are entitled to cast their ballots for unqualified candidates appears to be driven by the assumption that an election system that imposes any restraint on voter choice is unconstitutional. This is simply wrong.

unconstitutional burden upon the First and Fourteenth Amendment rights of the State's voters. Accordingly, the judgment of the Court of Appeals is affirmed.

It is so ordered.

JUSTICE KENNEDY, with whom JUSTICE BLACKMUN and JUSTICE STEVENS join, dissenting. * * *

* * * In the election that triggered this lawsuit, petitioner did not wish to vote for the one candidate who ran for state representative in his district. Because he could not write in the name of a candidate he preferred, he had no way to cast a meaningful vote. Petitioner's dilemma is a recurring, frequent phenomenon in Hawaii because of the State's ballot access rules and the circumstance that one party, the Democratic Party, is predominant. * * *

Aside from constraints related to ballot access restrictions, the write-in ban limits voter choice in another way. Write-in voting can serve as an important safety mechanism in those instances where a late-developing issue arises or where new information is disclosed about a candidate late in the race. In these situations, voters may become disenchanted with the available candidates when it is too late for other candidates to come forward and qualify for the ballot. The prohibition on write-in voting imposes a significant burden on voters, forcing them either to vote for a candidate whom they no longer support or to cast a blank ballot. Write-in voting provides a way out of the quandary, allowing voters to switch their support to candidates who are not on the official ballot. * * *

* * * The right at stake here is the right to cast a meaningful vote for the candidate of one's choice. Petitioner's right to freedom of expression is not implicated. His argument that the First Amendment confers upon citizens the right to cast a protest vote and to have government officials count and report this vote is not persuasive. As the majority points out, the purpose of casting, counting, and recording votes is to elect public officials, not to serve as a general forum for political expression.

I agree as well with the careful statement the Court gives of the test to be applied in this case to determine if the right to vote has been constricted. As the Court phrases it, we must "weigh 'the character and magnitude of the asserted injury to the rights protected by the First and Fourteenth Amendments that the plaintiff seeks to vindicate' against 'the precise interests put forward by the State as justifications for the burden imposed by its rule,' taking into consideration 'the extent to which those interests make it necessary to burden the plaintiff's rights.' " I submit the conclusion must be that the write-in ban deprives some voters of any substantial voice in selecting candidates for the entire range of offices at issue in a particular election. * * *

[S]ome voters cannot vote for the candidate of their choice without a write-in option. In effect, a write-in ban, in conjunction with other restrictions, can deprive the voter of the opportunity to cast a meaningful ballot. As a consequence, write-in prohibitions can impose a significant burden on voting rights. * * * The fact that write-in candidates are longshots more often than not makes no difference; the right to vote for one's preferred candidate exists regardless of the likelihood that the candidate will be successful.

Based on the foregoing reasoning, I cannot accept the majority's presumption that write-in bans are permissible if the State's ballot access laws are otherwise constitutional. The presumption is circular, for it fails to take into account that we must consider the availability of write-in voting, or the lack thereof, as a factor in determining whether a State's ballot access laws considered as a whole are constitutional. * * *

* * * The liberality of a State's ballot access laws is one determinant of the extent of the burden imposed by the write-in ban; it is not, though, an automatic excuse for forbidding all write-in voting. In my view, a State that bans write-in voting in some or all elections must justify the burden on individual voters by putting forth the precise interests that are served by the ban. A write-in prohibition should not be presumed valid in the absence of any proffered justification by the State. * * *

Because Hawaii's write-in ban, when considered in conjunction with the State's ballot access laws, imposes a significant burden on voters such as petitioner, it must put forward the state interests which justify the burden so that we can assess them. I do not think it necessary here to specify the level of scrutiny that should then be applied because, in my view, the State has failed to justify the write-in ban under any level of scrutiny. The interests proffered by the State, some of which are puzzling, are not advanced to any significant degree by the write-in prohibition. I consider each of the interests in turn.

The interest that has the best potential for acceptance, in my view, is that of preserving the integrity of party primaries by preventing sore loser candidacies during the general election. * * * A write-in ban does serve this interest to some degree by eliminating one mechanism which could be used by sore loser candidates. But I do not agree that this interest provides "adequate justification" for the ban. As an initial matter, the interest can at best justify the write-in prohibition for general elections; it cannot justify Hawaii's complete ban in both the primary and the general election. And with respect to general elections, a write-in ban is a very overinclusive means of addressing the problem; it bars legitimate candidacies as well as undesirable sore loser candidacies. If the State desires to prevent sore loser candidacies, it can implement a narrow provision aimed at that particular problem.

The second interest advanced by the State is enforcing its policy of permitting the unopposed victors in certain primaries to be designated as officeholders without having to go through the general election. The majority states that "[t]his would not be possible, absent the write-in voting ban." This makes no sense. As petitioner's counsel acknowledged during oral argument, "[t]o the degree that Hawaii has abolished general elections in these circumstances, there is no occasion to cast a write-in ballot." If anything, the argument cuts the other way because this provision makes it all the more important to allow write-in voting in the primary elections because primaries are often dispositive.

Hawaii justifies its write-in ban in primary elections as a way to prevent party raiding. Petitioner argues that this alleged interest is suspect because the State created the party raiding problem in the first place by allowing open primaries. I agree. It is ironic for the State to raise this concern when the risk of party raiding is a feature of the open primary system the State has chosen. The majority suggests that write-in voting presents a particular risk of circumventing the primary system because state law requires candidates in party primaries to be members of the party. Again, the majority's argument is not persuasive. If write-in voters mount a campaign for a candidate who does not meet state-law requirements, the candidate would be disqualified from the election.

The State also cites its interest in promoting the informed selection of candidates, an interest it claims is advanced by "flushing candidates into the open a reasonable time before the election." I think the State has it backwards. The fact that write-in candidates often do not conduct visible campaigns seems to me to make it more likely that voters who go to the trouble of seeking out these candidates and writing in their names are well informed. The state interest may well cut the other way.

The State cites interests in combating fraud and enforcing nomination requirements. But the State does not explain how write-in voting presents a risk of fraud in today's polling places. As to the State's interest in making sure that ineligible candidates are not elected, petitioner's counsel pointed out at argument that approximately 20 States require write-in candidates to file a declaration of candidacy and verify that they are eligible to hold office a few days before the election.

In sum, the State's proffered justifications for the write-in prohibition are not sufficient under any standard to justify the significant impairment of the constitutional rights of voters such as petitioner. I would grant him relief.

Notes and Questions

1. What are the implications of the Court's unanimous conclusion that, in Justice Kennedy's words, the "right to freedom of expression is not implicated" by Hawaii's ban on write-in voting? *See also Timmons v. Twin Cities Area New Party*, 520 U.S. 351, 363 (1997) [p. 534] ("Ballots serve primarily to elect candidates, not as forums for political expression."); *Rubin v. City of Santa Monica*, 308 F.3d 1008, 1016 (9th Cir. 2002) ("A ballot is a ballot, not a bumper sticker."). Is that concession consistent with Justice Kennedy's claim that "the right to vote for one's preferred candidate exists regardless of the likelihood that the candidate will be successful"? *See also United States v. Classic*, 313 U.S. 299, 318 (1941) ("The right to participate in the choice of representatives for Congress includes * * * the right to cast a ballot and to have it counted * * * *whether for the successful candidate or not*" (emphasis added)). Recall that the constitutional right to vote recognized in *Classic* is based on Article I, § 2's implication that members of Congress be chosen by elections (*see* p. 425, *supra*); what is the basis for a right to have a vote for a *losing* candidate counted?

If voting's sole purpose is to serve as a mechanism for choosing between candidates (and deciding on ballot questions), then is voting a fundamental *individual* right at all? *See Reynolds v. Sims*, 377 U.S. 533, 561 (1964) (referring to the rights protected by the one-person, one-vote standard as "individual and personal in nature"); Pamela S. Karlan, *The Rights to Vote: Some Pessimism About Formalism*, 71 TEX. L. REV. 1705 (1993) (arguing that there are several "rights to vote," some of which are individual rights and some of which are group rights); Martin Shapiro, *Gerrymandering, Unfairness, and the Supreme Court*, 33 UCLA L. REV. 227, 232 (1985) (arguing that voting is an individual right, but the right to fair "representation" is a group right).[d]

2. Justice Kennedy would have held that Hawaii's write-in ban violated Burdick's "right to cast a meaningful vote for the candidate of [his] choice." What did Justice Kennedy mean by "meaningful"? In what respect would a vote for a candidate be meaningful if the candidate had no realistic chance of winning the election?

3. Under the Court's analysis in *Anderson v. Celebrezze*, 460 U.S. 780 (1983) [p. 517], and *Burdick*, which election regulations will be subject to strict scrutiny, and which will be subject to a more permissive standard? The Court in *Burdick*, quoting *Anderson*, says "reasonable, nondiscriminatory restrictions" will generally be justified by states' "important regulatory interests." What does the Court mean by "reasonable"? Was Ohio's filing deadline "reasonable"? Was Hawaii's write-in ban?

4. "Severe" restrictions are subjected to strict scrutiny. Is "severe" in this context the opposite of "reasonable"? Or can a "reasonable" restriction create a "severe" impairment on First and Fourteenth Amendment rights? Does *Burdick* mean that the rational-basis test applies for all non-severe burdens on the right to vote? In *Crawford v. Marion County Election Board*, 553 U.S. 181 (2008) [p. 1032], six Justices appeared to agree that, under *Burdick*, even non-severe restrictions must be justified by "relevant and legitimate state interests 'sufficiently weighty to justify the limitation.'" 128 S. Ct. at 1616 (opinion of Stevens, J., joined by Roberts, C.J., and Kennedy, J.) (quoting *Norman v. Reed*, 502 U.S. 279, 288–89 (1992); *id.* at 1628 (Souter, J., joined by Ginsburg, J., dissenting); *id.* at 1643 (Breyer, J., dissenting) (urging invalidation of Indiana's Voter ID law because of its "disproportionate burden" on certain voters). Thus, the Court has established a sliding scale, with the level of scrutiny varying depending on the extent of the burden on constitutional rights.

5. Do you agree with one commentator that "the severe burden test is nebulous and unclear, resulting in vague decisions that fail to distinguish between constitutional and unconstitutional state election regulations"? Joshua A. Douglas, Note, *A Vote for Clarity: Updating the Supreme Court's Severe Burden Test for State Election Regulations that Adversely Impact an Individual's Right to Vote*, 75 GEO. WASH. L. REV. 372, 373 (2007). Douglas suggested replacing the "nebulous" test with an empirical one drawn from the provisions of the Voting Rights Act requiring

---

[d] As discussed in Chapter 5, much of the recent scholarly discussion on the group or individual character of the right to vote has concerned the nature of the right under § 2 of the Voting Rights Act of members of minority groups to the same opportunity "to participate in the political process and to elect representatives of their choice" as held by "other members of the electorate," 52 U.S.C. § 10301(b), as well as the constitutional right under the *Shaw v. Reno*, 509 U.S. 630 (1993) [p. 379], line of cases to have districts drawn without the "predominant" consideration of race. *See, e.g.*, p. 405, *supra*; *Shaw v. Hunt*, 517 U.S. 899, 917 (1996) (stating that the right to an undiluted vote belongs to the individual members of a minority group, rather than to the group as a whole).

certain jurisdictions to provide assistance for voters who do not understand English: whether the challenged regulation affects more than 10,000, or five percent, of the voters in the jurisdiction. "If the regulation imposes a burden that exceeds either of these triggers, the regulation is per se severe and must survive strict scrutiny review." *Id.* at 386. Otherwise, rational-basis scrutiny would apply. *See id.* at 386–87. Is such a test an improvement over the existing one?

TIMMONS v. TWIN CITIES AREA NEW PARTY
Supreme Court of the United States
520 U.S. 351, 117 S. Ct. 1364, 137 L. Ed. 2d 589 (1997)

CHIEF JUSTICE REHNQUIST delivered the opinion of the Court [in which JUSTICE O'CONNOR, JUSTICE SCALIA, JUSTICE KENNEDY, JUSTICE THOMAS, and JUSTICE BREYER join].

Most States prohibit multiple-party, or "fusion," candidacies for elected office.[1] The Minnesota laws challenged in this case prohibit a candidate from appearing on the ballot as the candidate of more than one party. We hold that such a prohibition does not violate the First and Fourteenth Amendments to the United States Constitution.

Respondent is a chartered chapter of the national New Party. Petitioners are Minnesota election officials. In April 1994, Minnesota State Representative Andy Dawkins was running unopposed in the Minnesota Democratic-Farmer-Labor Party's (DFL) primary. That same month, New Party members chose Dawkins as their candidate for the same office in the November 1994 general election. Neither Dawkins nor the DFL objected, and Dawkins signed the required affidavit of candidacy for the New Party. Minnesota, however, prohibits fusion candidacies. Because Dawkins had already filed as a candidate for the DFL's nomination, local election officials refused to accept the New Party's nominating petition.

The New Party filed suit in United States District Court, contending that Minnesota's antifusion laws violated the Party's associational rights under the First and Fourteenth Amendments. The District Court granted summary judgment for the state defendants * * *. The Court of Appeals reversed. * * * We granted certiorari, and now reverse.

Fusion was a regular feature of Gilded Age American politics * * * in part because political parties, rather than local or state governments, printed and distributed their own ballots. These ballots contained only the names of a particular party's candidates, and so a voter could drop his party's ticket in the ballot box without even knowing that his party's candidates were supported by other parties as well. But after the 1888 presidential election, which was widely regarded as having been plagued by fraud, many States moved to the "Australian ballot system." Under that system, an official ballot, containing the names of all the candidates legally nominated by all the parties, was printed at public expense and distributed by public officials at polling places. By 1896, use of the Australian ballot was

---

[1] "Fusion," also called "cross-filing" or "multiple-party nomination," is * * * "the nomination by more than one political party of the same candidate for the same office in the same general election."

widespread. During the same period, many States enacted other election-related reforms, including bans on fusion candidacies. Minnesota banned fusion in 1901. This trend has continued and, in this century, fusion has become the exception, not the rule. Today, multiple-party candidacies are permitted in just a few States, and fusion plays a significant role only in New York.

The First Amendment protects the right of citizens to associate and to form political parties for the advancement of common political goals and ideas. As a result, political parties' government, structure, and activities enjoy constitutional protection. On the other hand, it is also clear that States may, and inevitably must, enact reasonable regulations of parties, elections, and ballots to reduce election- and campaign-related disorder. * * *

When deciding whether a state election law violates First and Fourteenth Amendment associational rights, we weigh the "character and magnitude" of the burden the State's rule imposes on those rights against the interests the State contends justify that burden, and consider the extent to which the State's concerns make the burden necessary. *Burdick* [v. *Takushi*, 504 U.S. 428], 434 [(1992)] [p. 525] (quoting *Anderson* v. *Celebrezze*, 460 U.S. 780, 789 (1983) [p. 517]). Regulations imposing severe burdens on plaintiffs' rights must be narrowly tailored and advance a compelling state interest. Lesser burdens, however, trigger less exacting review, and a State's "important regulatory interests" will usually be enough to justify "reasonable, nondiscriminatory restrictions." *Burdick, supra*, at 434 (quoting *Anderson, supra*, at 788). No bright line separates permissible election-related regulation from unconstitutional infringements on First Amendment freedoms.

The New Party's claim that it has a right to select its own candidate is uncontroversial, so far as it goes. That is, the New Party, and not someone else, has the right to select the New Party's "standard bearer." It does not follow, though, that a party is absolutely entitled to have its nominee appear on the ballot as that party's candidate. A particular candidate might be ineligible for office, unwilling to serve, or, as here, another party's candidate. That a particular individual may not appear on the ballot as a particular party's candidate does not severely burden that party's associational rights.

* * * The ban, which applies to major and minor parties alike, simply precludes one party's candidate from appearing on the ballot, as that party's candidate, if already nominated by another party. Respondent is free to try to convince Representative Dawkins to be the New Party's, not the DFL's, candidate. Whether the Party still wants to endorse a candidate who, because of the fusion ban, will not appear on the ballot as the Party's candidate, is up to the Party. * * *

The Court of Appeals emphasized its belief that, without fusion-based alliances, minor parties cannot thrive. This is a predictive judgment which is by no means self-evident. But, more importantly, the supposed benefits of fusion to minor parties do not require that Minnesota permit it. Many features of our political system — *e.g.*, single-member districts, "first past the post" elections, and the high costs of campaigning — make it difficult for third parties to succeed in American politics. But the Constitution does not require States to permit fusion any more than it requires them to move to proportional-representation elections or public financing of campaigns. * * *

It is true that Minnesota's fusion ban prevents the New Party from using the ballot to communicate to the public that it supports a particular candidate who is already another party's candidate. In addition, the ban shuts off one possible avenue a party might use to send a message to its preferred *candidate* because, with fusion, a candidate who wins an election on the basis of two parties' votes will likely know more — if the parties' votes are counted separately — about the particular wishes and ideals of his constituency. We are unpersuaded, however, by the Party's contention that it has a right to use the ballot itself to send a particularized message, to its candidate and to the voters, about the nature of its support for the candidate. Ballots serve primarily to elect candidates, not as forums for political expression. See *Burdick*, 504 U.S., at 438; *id.*, at 445 (KENNEDY, J., dissenting). Like all parties in Minnesota, the New Party is able to use the ballot to communicate information about itself and its candidate to the voters, so long as that candidate is not already someone else's candidate. The Party retains great latitude in its ability to communicate ideas to voters and candidates through its participation in the campaign, and Party members may campaign for, endorse, and vote for their preferred candidate even if he is listed on the ballot as another party's candidate.

In sum, Minnesota's laws do not restrict the ability of the New Party and its members to endorse, support, or vote for anyone they like. The laws do not directly limit the Party's access to the ballot. They are silent on parties' internal structure, governance, and policymaking. Instead, these provisions reduce the universe of potential candidates who may appear on the ballot as the Party's nominee only by ruling out those few individuals who both have already agreed to be another party's candidate and also, if forced to choose, themselves prefer that other party. They also limit, slightly, the Party's ability to send a message to the voters and to its preferred candidates. We conclude that the burdens Minnesota imposes on the Party's First and Fourteenth Amendment associational rights — though not trivial — are not severe. * * *

* * * [Accordingly], the State's asserted regulatory interests need only be "sufficiently weighty to justify the limitation" imposed on the Party's rights. * * * Minnesota argues here that its fusion ban is justified by its interests in avoiding voter confusion, promoting candidate competition (by reserving limited ballot space for opposing candidates), preventing electoral distortions and ballot manipulations, and discouraging party splintering and "unrestrained factionalism."

States certainly have an interest in protecting the integrity, fairness, and efficiency of their ballots and election processes as means for electing public officials. Petitioners contend that a candidate or party could easily exploit fusion as a way of associating his or its name with popular slogans and catchphrases. For example, members of a major party could decide that a powerful way of "sending a message" via the ballot would be for various factions of that party to nominate the major party's candidate as the candidate for the newly-formed "No New Taxes," "Conserve Our Environment," and "Stop Crime Now" parties. In response, an opposing major party would likely instruct its factions to nominate that party's candidate as the "Fiscal Responsibility," "Healthy Planet," and "Safe Streets" parties' candidate.

Whether or not the putative "fusion" candidates' names appeared on one or four ballot lines, such maneuvering would undermine the ballot's purpose by transforming it from a means of choosing candidates to a billboard for political advertising. The New Party responds to this concern, ironically enough, by insisting that the State could avoid such manipulation by adopting more demanding ballot-access standards rather than prohibiting multiple-party nomination. However, as we stated above, because the burdens the fusion ban imposes on the Party's associational rights are not severe, the State need not narrowly tailor the means it chooses to promote ballot integrity. The Constitution does not require that Minnesota compromise the policy choices embodied in its ballot-access requirements to accommodate the New Party's fusion strategy.

Relatedly, petitioners urge that permitting fusion would undercut Minnesota's ballot-access regime by allowing minor parties to capitalize on the popularity of another party's candidate, rather than on their own appeal to the voters, in order to secure access to the ballot. That is, voters who might not sign a minor party's nominating petition based on the party's own views and candidates might do so if they viewed the minor party as just another way of nominating the same person nominated by one of the major parties. Thus, Minnesota fears that fusion would enable minor parties, by nominating a major party's candidate, to bootstrap their way to major-party status in the next election and circumvent the State's nominating-petition requirement for minor parties. The State surely has a valid interest in making sure that minor and third parties who are granted access to the ballot are bona fide and actually supported, on their own merits, by those who have provided the statutorily required petition or ballot support.

States also have a strong interest in the stability of their political systems. This interest does not permit a State to completely insulate the two-party system from minor parties' or independent candidates' competition and influence, nor is it a paternalistic license for States to protect political parties from the consequences of their own internal disagreements. That said, the States' interest permits them to enact reasonable election regulations that may, in practice, favor the traditional two-party system, and that temper the destabilizing effects of party-splintering and excessive factionalism. The Constitution permits the Minnesota Legislature to decide that political stability is best served through a healthy two-party system. And while an interest in securing the perceived benefits of a stable two-party system will not justify unreasonably exclusionary restrictions, States need not remove all of the many hurdles third parties face in the American political arena today. * * *

We conclude that the burdens Minnesota's fusion ban imposes on the New Party's associational rights are justified by "correspondingly weighty" valid state interests in ballot integrity and political stability.[13] In deciding that Minnesota's fusion ban does not unconstitutionally burden the New Party's First and Fourteenth Amendment rights, we express no views on the New Party's policy-based arguments concerning the wisdom of fusion. It may well be that, as support for new political parties increases, these arguments will carry the day in some States' legislatures. But the Constitution does not require Minnesota, and the approxi-

---

[13] * * * [The] supposed interest [in "avoiding voter confusion"] * * * plays no part in our analysis today.

mately 40 other States that do not permit fusion, to allow it. The judgment of the Court of Appeals is reversed.

It is so ordered.

JUSTICE STEVENS, with whom JUSTICE GINSBURG joins, and with whom JUSTICE SOUTER joins as to Parts I and II, dissenting. * * *

The Court's conclusion that the Minnesota statute prohibiting multiple-party candidacies is constitutional rests on three dubious premises: (1) that the statute imposes only a minor burden on the Party's right to choose and to support the candidate of its choice; (2) that the statute significantly serves the State's asserted interests in avoiding ballot manipulation and factionalism; and (3) that, in any event, the interest in preserving the two-party system justifies the imposition of the burden at issue in this case. I disagree with each of these premises.

I

The members of a recognized political party unquestionably have a constitutional right to select their nominees for public office and to communicate the identity of their nominees to the voting public. Both the right to choose and the right to advise voters of that choice are entitled to the highest respect.

The Minnesota statutes place a significant burden on both of those rights. The Court's recital of burdens that the statute does not inflict on the Party does nothing to minimize the severity of the burdens that it does impose. The fact that the Party may nominate its second choice surely does not diminish the significance of a restriction that denies it the right to have the name of its first choice appear on the ballot. Nor does the point that it may use some of its limited resources to publicize the fact that its first choice is the nominee of some other party provide an adequate substitute for the message that is conveyed to every person who actually votes when a party's nominees appear on the ballot.

As to the first point, the State contends that the fusion ban in fact limits by only a few candidates the range of individuals a party may nominate, and that the burden is therefore quite small. But the *number* of candidates removed from the Party's reach cannot be the determinative factor. The ban leaves the Party free to nominate any eligible candidate except the particular "standard bearer who best represents the party's ideologies and preferences." *Eu* v. *San Francisco County Democratic Central Comm.*, 489 U.S. 214, 224 (1989) [p. 455].

The Party could perhaps choose to expend its resources supporting a candidate who was not in fact the best representative of its members' views. But a party's choice of a candidate is the most effective way in which that party can communicate to the voters what the party represents and, thereby, attract voter interest and support.[1] * * *

---

[1] The burden on the Party's right to nominate its first-choice candidate, by limiting the Party's ability to convey through its nominee what the Party represents, risks impinging on another core element of any political party's associational rights — the right to "broaden the base of public participation in and

The State next argues that — instead of nominating a second-choice candidate — the Party could remove itself from the ballot altogether, and publicly endorse the candidate of another party. But the right to be on the election ballot is precisely what separates a political party from any other interest group. The Court relies on the fact that the New Party remains free "to spread its message to all who will listen," through fora other than the ballot. Given the limited resources available to most minor parties, and the less-than-universal interest in the messages of third parties, it is apparent that the Party's message will, in this manner, reach a much smaller audience than that composed of all voters who can read the ballot in the polling booth.

The majority rejects as unimportant the limits that the fusion ban may impose on the Party's ability to express its political views, relying on our decision in *Burdick* v. *Takushi*, in which we noted that "the purpose of casting, counting, and recording votes is to elect public officials, not to serve as a general forum for political expression." But [o]ur conclusion that the ballot is not principally a forum for the individual expression of political sentiment through the casting of a vote does not justify the conclusion that the ballot serves no expressive purpose for the parties who place candidates on the ballot. Indeed, the long-recognized right to choose a "standard bearer who best represents the party's ideologies and preferences," *Eu*, 489 U.S., at 224, is inescapably an expressive right. * * *

II

Minnesota argues that the statutory restriction on the New Party's right to nominate the candidate of its choice is justified by the State's interests in avoiding voter confusion, preventing ballot clutter and manipulation, encouraging candidate competition, and minimizing intraparty factionalism. None of these rationales can support the fusion ban because the State has failed to explain how the ban actually serves the asserted interests.

I believe that the law significantly abridges First Amendment freedoms and that the State therefore must shoulder a correspondingly heavy burden of justification if the law is to survive judicial scrutiny. But even accepting the majority's view that the burdens imposed by the law are not weighty, the State's asserted interests must at least bear some plausible relationship to the burdens it places on political parties. * * *

* * * The possibility that members of the major parties will begin to create dozens of minor parties with detailed, issue-oriented titles for the sole purpose of nominating candidates under those titles is entirely hypothetical. * * * If the State wants to make it more difficult for any group to achieve the legal status of being a

---

support for its activities." *Tashjian* v. *Republican Party of Conn.*, 479 U.S. 208, 214 (1986) [p. 472]. * * * A fusion ban burdens the right of a minor party to broaden its base of support because of the political reality that the dominance of the major parties frequently makes a vote for a minor party or independent candidate a "wasted" vote. When minor parties can nominate a candidate also nominated by a major party, they are able to present their members with an opportunity to cast a vote for a candidate who will actually be elected. Although this aspect of a party's effort to broaden support is distinct from the ability to nominate the candidate who best represents the party's views, it is important to note that the party's right to broaden the base of its support is burdened in both ways by the fusion ban.

political party, it can do so within reason and still not run up against the First Amendment. * * * But once the State has established a standard for achieving party status, forbidding an acknowledged party from putting on the ballot its chosen candidate clearly frustrates core associational rights.

The State argues that the fusion ban promotes political stability by preventing intraparty factionalism and party raiding. States do certainly have an interest in maintaining a stable political system. But the State has not convincingly articulated how the fusion ban will prevent the factionalism it fears. * * * Indeed, the activity banned by Minnesota's law is the formation of coalitions, not the division and dissension of "splintered parties and unrestrained factionalism."

As for the State's argument that the fusion ban encourages candidate competition, this claim treats "candidates" as fungible goods, ignoring entirely each party's interest in nominating not just any candidate, but the candidate who best represents the party's views. Minnesota's fusion ban simply cannot be justified with reference to this or any of the above-mentioned rationales. I turn, therefore, to what appears to be the true basis for the Court's holding — the interest in preserving the two-party system.

III

* * *

* * * In most States, perhaps in all, there are two and only two major political parties. It is not surprising, therefore, that most States have enacted election laws that impose burdens on the development and growth of third parties. The law at issue in this case is undeniably such a law. The fact that the law was both intended to disadvantage minor parties and has had that effect is a matter that should weigh against, rather than in favor of, its constitutionality. * * *

Nothing in the Constitution prohibits the States from maintaining single-member districts with winner-take-all voting arrangements. And these elements of an election system do make it significantly more difficult for third parties to thrive. But these laws are different in two respects from the fusion bans at issue here. First, the method by which they hamper third-party development is not one that impinges on the associational rights of those third parties; minor parties remain free to nominate candidates of their choice, and to rally support for those candidates. The small parties' relatively limited likelihood of ultimate success on election day does not deprive them of the right to try. Second, the establishment of single-member districts correlates directly with the States' interests in political stability. Systems of proportional representation, for example, may tend toward factionalism and fragile coalitions that diminish legislative effectiveness. In the context of fusion candidacies, the risks to political stability are extremely attenuated. * * *

In some respects, the fusion candidacy is the best marriage of the virtues of the minor party challenge to entrenched viewpoints and the political stability that the two-party system provides. The fusion candidacy does not threaten to divide the legislature and create significant risks of factionalism, which is the principal risk proponents of the two-party system point to. But it does provide a means by which voters with viewpoints not adequately represented by the platforms of the two major parties can indicate to a particular candidate that — in addition to his support for the major party views — he should be responsive to the views of the minor party whose support for him was demonstrated where political parties demonstrate support — on the ballot. * * *

* * * I respectfully dissent.

JUSTICE SOUTER, dissenting.

I join parts I and II of JUSTICE STEVENS's dissent, agreeing as I do that none of the concerns advanced by the State suffices to justify the burden of the challenged statutes on petitioners' First Amendment interests. * * *

I am, however, unwilling to go the further distance of considering and rejecting the majority's "preservation of the two-party system" rationale. For while Minnesota has made no such argument before us, I cannot discount the possibility of a forceful one. There is considerable consensus that party loyalty among American voters has declined significantly in the past four decades, and that the overall influence of the parties in the political process has decreased considerably. In the wake of such studies, it may not be unreasonable to infer that the two-party system is in some jeopardy.

Surely the majority is right that States "have a strong interest in the stability of their political systems," that is, in preserving a political system capable of governing effectively. If it could be shown that the disappearance of the two-party system would undermine that interest, and that permitting fusion candidacies poses a substantial threat to the two-party scheme, there might well be a sufficient predicate for recognizing the constitutionality of the state action presented by this case. Right now, however, no State has attempted even to make this argument, and I would therefore leave its consideration for another day.

Notes and Questions

1. The greatest impediment to minor parties' electoral success is not ballot access. Rather, the prevalence in American jurisdictions of the plurality-winner, first-past-the-post system of elections all but ensures that over the long-term two parties representing views close to the political center will dominate. We discuss alternative election systems in Chapter 11, at p. 1096. For present purposes, it suffices to note that systems exist that would make it easier for minorities (including ideological minorities) to achieve representation in legislatures.

In light of the importance of vote-counting systems to third-party electoral chances, should courts be suspicious of states' decisions to adopt plurality systems? Should an understanding of alternative voting structures affect courts' review of ballot-access restrictions?

2. Is a ban on fusion "nondiscriminatory," given that a candidate forced to choose between nominations of a major party and a minor party would be unlikely to choose the latter? The Court notes that the Minnesota's ban "applies to major and minor parties alike," but is this a situation where "the grossest discrimination

can lie in treating things that are different as though they were exactly alike"? *Jenness v. Fortson*, 403 U.S. 431, 442 (1971) [p. 504].

3. Is the preservation of the two-party system a compelling interest? Is it a legitimate interest? If party loyalty weakened to the point where the two-party system were in "jeopardy," would that argue for upholding or striking down state laws designed to perpetuate the two-party system?

4. *Timmons* upheld a law limiting candidates to appearing on the ballot as the nominee of only one party. May states forbid candidates from appearing on the ballot for more than one *office*? Kentucky and Florida currently have such a law, and unless Kentucky's is changed, it could present a problem for U.S. Senator (and potential 2016 presidential candidate) Rand Paul. The statute, Ky. R.S. § 118.405, reads as follows: "No candidate's name shall appear on any voting machine or absentee ballot more than once, except that a candidate's name may appear twice if he is a candidate for a primary or a regular election and also a candidate to fill a vacancy in the same office required to be filled at a special election, when the special election to fill a vacancy is scheduled for the regular election day." Paul's term ends in January 2017. Accordingly, the law might bar him from appearing on the ballot in the 2016 presidential election as he is seeking reelection to the Senate. Kentucky Republicans are trying to change the law, and they are arguing that the law bans candidates from appearing on the ballot for multiple *state* offices.

It is relatively common for candidates to run for multiple offices. For example, Vice President Biden was simultaneously elected to the vice presidency and reelected to the U.S. Senate in 2008, and Paul Ryan, who attempted to unseat Biden in 2012, was reelected to the House of Representatives despite losing his vice-presidential bid. Several states appear to have followed Texas's lead after the Lone Star State amended its law in 1960 to allow Lyndon Johnson to pursue the vice presidency and reelection to the U.S. Senate. Delaware, curiously, is considering changing its law to *ban* multiple candidacies, even as Kentucky is considering loosening its restriction.

Regardless of the outcome of these legislative debates, should the government have the power to bar multiple candidacies, even for state offices? For example, could a state prohibit a state senator from simultaneously pursuing reelection and the governorship? Could it prohibit a sitting judge from simultaneously running for reelection and pursuing a higher judicial office? Could it prohibit a district attorney from simultaneously running for reelection and seeking to become a judge? Aside from the constitutional question, are such bans good policy?

The final case in this section incorporates themes that have animated our consideration of each of the issues in this Chapter. This First Amendment challenge to New York's convention method of selecting judicial candidates requires us to consider the right of party autonomy; individuals' rights to vote and run for office; the place of the two-party system in politics; and the appropriate roles of states, parties, judges, and the Constitution in establishing fair systems of selecting public officials.

NEW YORK STATE BOARD OF ELECTIONS v. LOPEZ TORRES

Supreme Court of the United States
552 U.S. 196, 128 S. Ct. 791, 169 L. Ed. 2d 665 (2008)

JUSTICE SCALIA delivered the opinion of the Court [in which CHIEF JUSTICE ROBERTS, JUSTICE STEVENS, JUSTICE SOUTER, JUSTICE THOMAS, JUSTICE GINSBURG, JUSTICE BREYER, and JUSTICE ALITO join].

The State of New York requires that political parties select their nominees for Supreme Court Justice at a convention of delegates chosen by party members in a primary election. We consider whether this electoral system violates the First Amendment rights of prospective party candidates.

The Supreme Court of New York is the State's trial court of general jurisdiction * * *. Under New York's current Constitution, the State is divided into 12 judicial districts, and Supreme Court Justices are elected to 14-year terms in each such district. * * *

Over the years, New York has changed the method by which Supreme Court Justices are selected several times. Under the New York Constitution of 1821, all judicial officers, except Justices of the Peace, were appointed by the Governor with the consent of the Senate. In 1846, New York amended its Constitution to require popular election of the Justices of the Supreme Court (and also the Judges of the New York Court of Appeals). In the early years under that regime, the State allowed political parties to choose their own method of selecting the judicial candidates who would bear their endorsements on the general-election ballot. The major parties opted for party conventions, the same method then employed to nominate candidates for other state offices.

In 1911, the New York Legislature enacted a law requiring political parties to select Supreme Court nominees * * * through direct primary elections. The primary system came to be criticized as a "device capable of astute and successful manipulation by professionals," and the Republican candidate for Governor in 1920 campaigned against it as "a fraud" that "offered the opportunity for two things, for the demagogue and the man with money." A law enacted in 1921 required parties to select their candidates for the Supreme Court by a convention composed of delegates elected by party members.

New York retains this system of choosing party nominees for Supreme Court Justice to this day. Section 6-106 of New York's election law sets forth its basic operation: "Party nominations for the office of justice of the supreme court shall be made by the judicial district convention." A "party" is any political organization whose candidate for Governor received 50,000 or more votes in the most recent election. In a September "delegate primary," party members elect delegates from each of New York's 150 assembly districts to attend the party's judicial convention for the judicial district in which the assembly district is located. An individual may run for delegate by submitting to the Board of Elections a designating petition signed by 500 enrolled party members residing in the assembly district, or by five percent of such enrolled members, whichever is less. These signatures must be gathered within a 37-day period preceding the filing deadline, which is approximately two months before the delegate primary. The delegates elected in these primaries are uncommitted; the primary ballot does not specify the judicial nominee whom they will support.

The nominating conventions take place one to two weeks after the delegate primary. Each of the 12 judicial districts has its own convention to nominate the party's Supreme Court candidate or candidates who will run at large in that district in the general election. The general election takes place in November. The nominees from the party conventions appear automatically on the general-election ballot. They may be joined on the general-election ballot by independent candidates and candidates of political organizations that fail to meet the 50,000 vote threshold for "party" status; these candidates gain access to the ballot by submitting timely nominating petitions with (depending on the judicial district) 3,500 or 4,000 signatures from voters in that district or signatures from five percent of the number of votes cast for Governor in that district in the prior election, whichever is less.

Respondent López Torres was elected in 1992 to the civil court for Kings County — a court with more limited jurisdiction than the Supreme Court — having gained the nomination of the Democratic Party through a primary election. She claims that soon after her election, party leaders began to demand that she make patronage hires, and that her consistent refusal to do so caused the local party to oppose her unsuccessful candidacy at the Supreme Court nominating conventions in 1997, 2002, and 2003. The following year, López Torres — together with other candidates who had failed to secure the nominations of their parties, voters who claimed to have supported those candidates, and the New York branch of a public-interest organization called Common Cause — brought suit in federal court against the New York Board of Elections, which is responsible for administering and enforcing the New York election law. They contended that New York's election law burdened the rights of challengers seeking to run against candidates favored by the party leadership, and deprived voters and candidates of their rights to gain access to the ballot and to associate in choosing their party's candidates. As relevant here, they sought a declaration that New York's convention system for selecting Supreme Court Justices violates their First Amendment rights, and an injunction mandating the establishment of a direct primary election to select party nominees for Supreme Court Justice.

The District Court issued a preliminary injunction granting the relief requested, [and a] unanimous panel of the United States Court of Appeals for the Second Circuit affirmed. * * *

A political party has a First Amendment right to limit its membership as it wishes, and to choose a candidate-selection process that will in its view produce the nominee who best represents its political platform. * * * In the present case, however, * * * [r]espondents are in no position to rely on the right that the First Amendment confers on political parties to structure their internal party processes and to select the candidate of the party's choosing. Indeed, both the Republican and Democratic state parties have intervened from the very early stages of this litigation to defend New York's electoral law. The weapon wielded by these plaintiffs is their *own* claimed associational right not only to join, but to have a certain degree of influence in, the party. They contend that New York's electoral system does not go far enough — does not go as far as the Constitution demands — in assuring that they will have a fair chance of prevailing in their parties' candidate-selection process.

This contention finds no support in our precedents. We have indeed acknowledged an individual's associational right to vote in a party primary without undue state-imposed impediment. [See *Kusper* v. *Pontikes*, 414 U.S. 51, 57 (1973).] [But] respondents do not claim that they have been excluded from voting in the primary. Moreover, even if we extended *Kusper* to cover not only the right to vote in the party primary but also the right to run, the requirements of the New York law (a 500-signature petition collected during a 37-day window in advance of the primary) are entirely reasonable. * * *

Respondents' real complaint is not that they cannot vote in the election for delegates, nor even that they cannot run in that election, but that the convention process that follows the delegate election does not give them a realistic chance to secure the party's nomination. The party leadership, they say, inevitably garners more votes for its slate of delegates (delegates uncommitted to any judicial nominee) than the unsupported candidate can amass for himself. And thus the leadership effectively determines the nominees. But this says nothing more than that the party leadership has more widespread support than a candidate not supported by the leadership. No New York law compels election of the leadership's slate — or, for that matter, compels the delegates elected on the leadership's slate to vote the way the leadership desires. And no state law prohibits an unsupported candidate from attending the convention and seeking to persuade the delegates to support her. * * * Here respondents complain not of the state law, but of the voters' (and their elected delegates') preference for the choices of the party leadership.

To be sure, we have * * * permitted States to set their faces against "party bosses" by requiring party-candidate selection through processes more favorable to insurgents, such as primaries. But to say that the State can require this is a far cry from saying that the Constitution demands it. None of our cases establishes an individual's constitutional right to have a "fair shot" at winning the party's nomination. And with good reason. What constitutes a "fair shot" is a reasonable enough question for legislative judgment, which we will accept so long as it does not too much infringe upon the party's associational rights. But it is hardly a manageable constitutional question for judges — especially for judges in our legal system, where traditional electoral practice gives no hint of even the existence, much less the content, of a constitutional requirement for a "fair shot" at party nomination. Party conventions, with their attendant "smoke-filled rooms" and domination by party leaders, have long been an accepted manner of selecting party candidates. * * * Selection by convention has never been thought unconstitutional, even when the delegates were not selected by primary but by party caucuses. * * *

Respondents put forward, as a special factor which gives them a First Amendment right to revision of party processes in the present case, the assertion that party loyalty in New York's judicial districts renders the general-election ballot "uncompetitive." They argue that the existence of entrenched "one-party rule" demands that the First Amendment be used to impose additional competition in the nominee-selection process of the parties. (The asserted "one-party rule," we may observe, is that of the Democrats in some judicial districts, and of the Republicans in others.) This is a novel and implausible reading of the First Amendment. * * *

The reason one-party rule is entrenched may be (and usually is) that voters approve of the positions and candidates that the party regularly puts forward. It is no function of the First Amendment to require revision of those positions or candidates. The States can, within limits (that is, short of violating the parties' freedom of association), discourage party monopoly — for example, by refusing to show party endorsement on the election ballot. But the Constitution provides no authority for federal courts to prescribe such a course. The First Amendment creates an open marketplace where ideas, most especially political ideas, may compete without government interference. It does not call on the federal courts to manage the market by preventing too many buyers from settling upon a single product.

Limiting respondents' court-mandated "fair shot at party endorsement" to situations of one-party entrenchment merely multiplies the impracticable lines courts would be called upon to draw. It would add to those alluded to earlier, the line at which mere party popularity turns into "one-party dominance." In the case of New York's election system for Supreme Court Justices, that line would have to be drawn separately for each of the 12 judicial districts — and in those districts that are "competitive" the current system would presumably remain valid. But why limit the remedy to *one*-party dominance? Does not the dominance of two parties similarly stifle competing opinions? Once again, we decline to enter the morass.

* * *

New York State has thrice (in 1846, 1911, and 1921) displayed a willingness to reconsider its method of selecting Supreme Court Justices. If it wishes to return to the primary system that it discarded in 1921, it is free to do so; but the First Amendment does not compel that. We reverse the Second Circuit's contrary judgment.

It is so ordered.

Justice Stevens, with whom Justice Souter joins, concurring.

While I join Justice Scalia's cogent resolution of the constitutional issues raised by this case, I think it appropriate to emphasize the distinction between constitutionality and wise policy. Our holding with respect to the former should not be misread as endorsement of the electoral system under review, or disagreement with the findings of the District Court that describe glaring deficiencies in that system and even lend support to the broader proposition that the very practice of electing judges is unwise. But as I recall my esteemed former colleague, Thurgood Marshall, remarking on numerous occasions: "The Constitution does not prohibit legislatures from enacting stupid laws."

JUSTICE KENNEDY, * * * concurring in the judgment. * * *

* * * Were the state-mandated-and-designed nominating convention the sole means to attain access to the general election ballot there would be considerable force, in my view, to respondents' contention that the First Amendment prohibits the State from requiring a delegate selection mechanism with the rigidities and difficulties attendant upon this one. The system then would be subject to scrutiny from the standpoint of a "reasonably diligent independent candidate," *Storer* v. *Brown*, 415 U.S. 724, 742 (1974) [p. 513]. * * *

As the Court is careful to note, however, New York has a second mechanism for placement on the final election ballot. One who seeks to be a Justice of the New York Supreme Court may qualify by a petition process. The petition must be signed by the lesser of (1) 5 percent of the number of votes last cast for Governor in the judicial district or (2) either 3,500 or 4,000 voters (depending on the district). This requirement has not been shown to be an unreasonable one, a point respondents appear to concede. True, the candidate who gains ballot access by petition does not have a party designation; but the candidate is still considered by the voters.

The petition alternative changes the analysis.

This is not to say an alternative route to the general election exempts the delegate primary/nominating convention from all scrutiny. * * * But there is a dynamic relationship between, in this case, the convention system and the petition process; higher burdens at one stage are mitigated by lower burdens at the other. * * * On the particular facts and circumstances of this case, then, I reach the same conclusion the Court does.

Notes and Questions

1.   Was the Court right to dismiss López Torres's argument that the convention system violated her rights because of the "one-party rule" that prevailed in many judicial districts? Suppose that the one-party domination of certain districts was the result, in part, of partisan gerrymandering. Would that fact undercut the Court's conclusion?

2.   What constitutional constraints limit the capacity of state law to privilege the choices of party bosses?

Chapter 7

TERM LIMITS

A. INTRODUCTION

Federal or state constitutions or statutes may place limits on the number of consecutive (or nonconsecutive) times a candidate may be reelected to the same office. Such term limits are not unknown in American law and politics. Indeed, at times there were various informal norms that certain political offices would be subject to rotation, even without formal term limits. For example, Abraham Lincoln served only one term in the U.S. House of Representatives in the 1840s due to such an informal agreement. Robert Struble, Jr., *House Turnover and the Principle of Rotation*, 94 POL. SCI. Q. 649 (1979–80) (discussing such norms in the U.S. House of Representatives in the nineteenth century). Until recently, most formal limits were restricted to executive offices. Most famously, the Twenty-Second Amendment to the U.S. Constitution limits Presidents to serving a maximum of two terms. The Amendment was adopted in 1951 after Franklin Roosevelt was elected four times, breaking the informal two-term tradition set by President Washington. Forty states place various term limits on their governors, and thirty-five percent of major cities place term limits on their mayors. Einer Elhauge, *Are Term Limits Undemocratic?*, 64 U. CHI. L. REV. 83, 87 n.9 (1997).

Support for term limits grew and became more controversial in the 1990s, when twenty-four states adopted limits for state legislators and some term-limited their Members of Congress as well. What accounted for the term-limit phenomenon in that decade? Support for term limits has always been supported by the notion that persons continually reelected to the same office unfairly or inappropriately aggrandize political power. Accordingly, the advantages of mandatory rotations are thought by some to outweigh the greater experience and seniority possessed by long-serving representatives, as well as the right of voters to elect whom they want to office. This notion gained particular currency in the past several decades for members of Congress and state legislators, who in that period enjoyed little turnover and high reelection rates. Many argued that limiting legislative terms would lead to, among other things, fewer professional politicians, greater devotion to the public good, less spending, and less capture by interest groups. Opponents of legislative term limits countered that such limits would degrade institutional memory and lead to the capture of less-experienced legislators by interest groups and bureaucrats, who are not effected by term limits. There was a lively popular and academic literature debating these points. *E.g.*, GEORGE F. WILL, RESTORATION: CONGRESS, TERM LIMITS, AND THE RECOVERY OF DELIBERATIVE DEMOCRACY (1992); Elizabeth Garrett, *Term Limitations and the Myth of the Citizen-Legislator*, 81 CORNELL L. REV. 623 (1996).

Inevitably, legal challenges were mounted to the new wave of legislative term limits, as the balance of this Chapter describes. As you consider the legal and policy issues confronting the courts in these challenges, consider also the scholarly literature that has examined the efficacy of the new limits. That literature to date does not provide much comfort for supporters of term limits. For example, some studies show that states with term limits spend *more* than states without. H. Abbie Erler, *Legislative Term Limits and State Spending*, 133 PUB. CHOICE 479 (2007) (offering speculations for this counterintuitive result, including that term limits open up the budgetary process in ways that lead to more participation by legislators and interest groups, which leads to more spending). Other studies suggest that term limits have had little effect on the type of people elected to office, but has (at least in the opinion of surveyed legislators) led to some of the ills forecast by critics of term limits, and to increased power of governors vis-à-vis legislatures. John M. Carey, et al., *The Effects of Term Limits on State Legislators: A New Survey of the 50 States*, 31 LEGIS. STUD. Q. 105 (2006).[a] One term-limits sympathizer has described the empirical studies of the effects of the limits as a "mixed bag of positives and negatives." LARRY J. SABATO, A MORE PERFECT CONSTITUTION 51 (2007). To what extent, if at all, should federal and state judges take into account such studies when pondering challenges to term limits?

B. THE CONSTITUTIONALITY OF TERM-LIMITING MEMBERS OF CONGRESS

The Constitution requires that members of the House of Representatives and of the Senate be at least twenty-five and thirty years old, respectively; citizens of the United States for seven and nine years, respectively; and inhabitants of the states from which they are elected. For decades, states have added qualifications, including term limits, to those requirements. Throughout the twentieth century, federal and state courts routinely struck down these additional requirements. *U.S. Term Limits, Inc. v. Thornton*, 514 U.S. 779, 798–800 (1995) (listing cases). The issue resurfaced in the 1990s and was resolved by the Supreme Court in the next case.

U.S. TERM LIMITS, INC. v. THORNTON
Supreme Court of the United States
514 U.S. 779, 115 S. Ct. 1842, 131 L. Ed. 2d 881 (1995)

JUSTICE STEVENS delivered the opinion of the Court [in which JUSTICE KENNEDY, JUSTICE SOUTER, JUSTICE GINSBURG, and JUSTICE BREYER join].

The Constitution sets forth qualifications for membership in the Congress of the

---

[a] For a sample of the large scholarly literature, see, e.g., Timothy Besley & Anne Case, *Does Electoral Accountability Affect Economic Policy Choices? Evidence from Gubernatorial Term Limits*, 110 Q. J. ECON. 769 (1995); Bruce E. Cain & Marc A. Levin, *Term Limits*, 2 ANN. REV. POL. SCI. 163 (1999); Andrew B. Hall, *Partisan Effects of Legislative Term Limits*, 39 LEGIS. STUD. Q. 407 (2014); Edward J. López, *Term Limits: Causes and Consequences*, 114 PUB. CHOICE 1 (2003); Susan M. Miller, et al., *Reexamining the Institutional Effects of Term Limits in U.S. State Legislatures*, 36 LEGIS. STUD. Q. 71 (2012).

United States. Article I, § 2, cl. 2, which applies to the House of Representatives, provides:

> "No Person shall be a Representative who shall not have attained to the Age of twenty five Years, and been seven Years a Citizen of the United States, and who shall not, when elected, be an Inhabitant of that State in which he shall be chosen."

Article I, § 3, cl. 3, which applies to the Senate, similarly provides:

> "No Person shall be a Senator who shall not have attained to the Age of thirty Years, and been nine Years a Citizen of the United States, and who shall not, when elected, be an Inhabitant of that State for which he shall be chosen."

* * *

At the general election on November 3, 1992, the voters of Arkansas adopted Amendment 73 to their State Constitution. Proposed as a "Term Limitation Amendment," its preamble stated:

> "The people of Arkansas find and declare that elected officials who remain in office too long become preoccupied with reelection and ignore their duties as representatives of the people. Entrenched incumbency has reduced voter participation and has led to an electoral system that is less free, less competitive, and less representative than the system established by the Founding Fathers. Therefore, the people of Arkansas, exercising their reserved powers, herein limit the terms of elected officials."

The limitations in Amendment 73 apply to three categories of elected officials. * * * Section 3, the provision at issue in these cases, applies to the Arkansas Congressional Delegation. It provides:

> "(a) Any person having been elected to three or more terms as a member of the United States House of Representatives from Arkansas shall not be certified as a candidate and shall not be eligible to have his/her name placed on the ballot for election to the United States House of Representatives from Arkansas.

> "(b) Any person having been elected to two or more terms as a member of the United States Senate from Arkansas shall not be certified as a candidate and shall not be eligible to have his/her name placed on the ballot for election to the United States Senate from Arkansas."

* * *

[T]he constitutionality of Amendment 73 depends critically on the resolution of two distinct issues. The first is whether the Constitution forbids States to add to or alter the qualifications specifically enumerated in the Constitution. The second is, if the Constitution does so forbid, whether the fact that Amendment 73 is formulated as a ballot access restriction rather than as an outright disqualification is of constitutional significance. Our resolution of these issues draws upon our prior resolution of a related but distinct issue: whether Congress has the power to add to or alter the qualifications of its Members.

Twenty-six years ago, in *Powell* v. *McCormack*, 395 U.S. 486 (1969), we reviewed the history and text of the Qualifications Clauses in a case involving an attempted exclusion of a duly elected Member of Congress. The principal issue was whether the power granted to each House in Art. I, § 5, cl. 1, to judge the "Qualifications of its own Members" includes the power to impose qualifications other than those set forth in the text of the Constitution. In an opinion by Chief Justice Warren for eight Members of the Court, we held that it does not. * * * We * * * conclude now, as we did in *Powell*, that history shows that, with respect to Congress, the Framers intended the Constitution to establish fixed qualifications. * * *

In *Powell*, of course, we did not rely solely on an analysis of the historical evidence, but instead complemented that analysis with "an examination of the basic principles of our democratic system." We noted that allowing Congress to impose additional qualifications would violate that "fundamental principle of our representative democracy . . . 'that the people should choose whom they please to govern them.'"

Our opinion made clear that this broad principle incorporated at least two fundamental ideas.[10] First, we emphasized the egalitarian concept that the opportunity to be elected was open to all. We noted in particular Madison's statement in The Federalist [No. 52] that "[u]nder these reasonable limitations [enumerated in the Constitution], the door of this part of the federal government is open to merit of every description, whether native or adoptive, whether young or old, and without regard to poverty or wealth, or to any particular profession of religious faith." Similarly, we noted that Wilson Carey Nicholas defended the Constitution against the charge that it "violated democratic principles" by arguing: "It has ever been considered a great security to liberty, that very few should be excluded from the right of being chosen to the legislature. This Constitution has amply attended to this idea. We find no qualifications required except those of age and residence."

Second, we recognized the critical postulate that sovereignty is vested in the people, and that sovereignty confers on the people the right to choose freely their representatives to the National Government. * * * Thus, in *Powell*, we agreed * * * "[t]hat the right of the electors to be represented by men of their own choice, was so essential for the preservation of all their other rights, that it ought to be considered as one of the most sacred parts of our constitution." * * *

Our reaffirmation of *Powell* does not necessarily resolve the specific questions presented in these cases. For petitioners argue that whatever the constitutionality of additional qualifications for membership imposed by Congress, the historical and textual materials discussed in *Powell* do not support the conclusion that the Constitution prohibits additional qualifications imposed by States. In the absence of such a constitutional prohibition, petitioners argue, the Tenth Amendment and the principle of reserved powers require that States be allowed to add such qualifications. * * * We disagree for two independent reasons. First, we conclude that the power to add qualifications is not within the "original powers" of the States, and thus is not reserved to the States by the Tenth Amendment. Second, even if States

---

[10] The principle also incorporated the more practical concern that reposing the power to adopt qualifications in Congress would lead to a self-perpetuating body to the detriment of the new Republic.

possessed some original power in this area, we conclude that the Framers intended the Constitution to be the exclusive source of qualifications for Members of Congress, and that the Framers thereby "divested" States of any power to add qualifications. * * *

Contrary to petitioners' assertions, the power to add qualifications is not part of the original powers of sovereignty that the Tenth Amendment reserved to the States. Petitioners' Tenth Amendment argument misconceives the nature of the right at issue because that Amendment could only "reserve" that which existed before. As Justice Story recognized [in his *Commentaries on the Constitution of the United States*], "the states can exercise no powers whatsoever, which exclusively spring out of the existence of the national government, which the constitution does not delegate to them. . . . No state can say, that it has reserved, what it never possessed." * * *

With respect to setting qualifications for service in Congress, no such right existed before the Constitution was ratified. * * * [E]lecting representatives to the National Legislature was a new right, arising from the Constitution itself. The Tenth Amendment thus provides no basis for concluding that the States possess reserved power to add qualifications to those that are fixed in the Constitution. Instead, any state power to set the qualifications for membership in Congress must derive not from the reserved powers of state sovereignty, but rather from the delegated powers of national sovereignty. In the absence of any constitutional delegation to the States of power to add qualifications to those enumerated in the Constitution, such a power does not exist.

Even if we believed that States possessed as part of their original powers some control over congressional qualifications, the text and structure of the Constitution, the relevant historical materials, and, most importantly, the "basic principles of our democratic system" all demonstrate that the Qualifications Clauses were intended to preclude the States from exercising any such power and to fix as exclusive the qualifications in the Constitution. * * *

As we noted earlier, the *Powell* Court recognized that an egalitarian ideal — that election to the National Legislature should be open to all people of merit — provided a critical foundation for the constitutional structure. This egalitarian theme echoes throughout the constitutional debates. In The Federalist No. 57, for example, Madison wrote:

> "Who are to be the objects of popular choice? Every citizen whose merit may recommend him to the esteem and confidence of his country. *No qualification of wealth, of birth, of religious faith, or of civil profession is permitted to fetter the judgment or disappoint the inclination of the people.*" The Federalist No. 57, at 351 [(C. Rossiter ed. 1961)] (emphasis added).

* * * Additional qualifications pose the same obstacle to open elections whatever their source. The egalitarian ideal, so valued by the Framers, is thus compromised to the same degree by additional qualifications imposed by States as by those imposed by Congress.

Similarly, we believe that state-imposed qualifications, as much as congressionally imposed qualifications, would undermine the second critical idea recognized in *Powell*: that an aspect of sovereignty is the right of the people to vote for whom they wish. Again, the source of the qualification is of little moment in assessing the qualification's restrictive impact.

Finally, state-imposed restrictions, unlike the congressionally imposed restrictions at issue in *Powell*, violate a third idea central to this basic principle: that the right to choose representatives belongs not to the States, but to the people. From the start, the Framers recognized that the "great and radical vice" of the Articles of Confederation was "the principle of LEGISLATION for STATES or GOVERN-MENTS, in their CORPORATE or COLLECTIVE CAPACITIES, and as contra-distinguished from the INDIVIDUALS of whom they consist." The Federalist No. 15, at 108 (Hamilton). Thus the Framers, in perhaps their most important contribution, conceived of a Federal Government directly responsible to the people, possessed of direct power over the people, and chosen directly, not by States, but by the people. * * *

Consistent with these views, the constitutional structure provides for a uniform salary to be paid from the national treasury, allows the States but a limited role in federal elections, and maintains strict checks on state interference with the federal election process. The Constitution also provides that the qualifications of the representatives of each State will be judged by the representatives of the entire Nation. The Constitution thus creates a uniform national body representing the interests of a single people.

Permitting individual States to formulate diverse qualifications for their representatives would result in a patchwork of state qualifications, undermining the uniformity and the national character that the Framers envisioned and sought to ensure. * * * Such a patchwork would also sever the direct link that the Framers found so critical between the National Government and the people of the United States.[32] * * *

Petitioners argue that, even if States may not add qualifications, Amendment 73 is constitutional because it is not such a qualification, and because Amendment 73 is a permissible exercise of state power to regulate the "Times, Places and Manner of holding Elections." We reject these contentions.

Unlike §§ 1 and 2 of Amendment 73, which create absolute bars to service for long-term incumbents running for state office, § 3 merely provides that certain Senators and Representatives shall not be certified as candidates and shall not have their names appear on the ballot. They may run as write-in candidates and, if elected, they may serve. Petitioners contend that only a legal bar to service creates an impermissible qualification, and that Amendment 73 is therefore consistent with the Constitution. * * *

---

[32] There is little significance to the fact that Amendment 73 was adopted by a popular vote, rather than as an Act of the state legislature. In fact, none of the petitioners argues that the constitutionality of a state law would depend on the method of its adoption. This is proper, because the voters of Arkansas, in adopting Amendment 73, were acting as citizens of the State of Arkansas, and not as citizens of the National Government. The people of the State of Arkansas have no more power than does the Arkansas Legislature to supplement the qualifications for service in Congress. * * *

We need not decide whether petitioners' narrow understanding of qualifications is correct because, even if it is, Amendment 73 may not stand. As we have often noted, "[c]onstitutional rights would be of little value if they could be . . . indirectly denied." *Harman* v. *Forssenius*, 380 U.S. 528, 540 (1965), quoting *Smith* v. *Allwright*, 321 U.S. 649, 664 (1944) [p. 426]. The Constitution "nullifies sophisticated as well as simple-minded modes" of infringing on constitutional protections. *Lane* v. *Wilson*, 307 U.S. 268, 275 (1939).

In our view, Amendment 73 is an indirect attempt to accomplish what the Constitution prohibits Arkansas from accomplishing directly. As the plurality opinion of the Arkansas Supreme Court recognized, Amendment 73 is an "effort to dress eligibility to stand for Congress in ballot access clothing," because the "intent and the effect of Amendment 73 are to disqualify congressional incumbents from further service." We must, of course, accept the state court's view of the purpose of its own law: We are thus authoritatively informed that the sole purpose of § 3 of Amendment 73 was to attempt to achieve a result that is forbidden by the Federal Constitution. Indeed, it cannot be seriously contended that the intent behind Amendment 73 is other than to prevent the election of incumbents. * * *

Petitioners make the related argument that Amendment 73 merely regulates the "Manner" of elections, and that the amendment is therefore a permissible exercise of state power under Article I, § 4, cl. 1 (the Elections Clause), to regulate the "Times, Places and Manner" of elections. We cannot agree. * * *

The Elections Clause gives States authority "to enact the numerous requirements as to procedure and safeguards which experience shows are necessary in order to enforce the fundamental right involved." *Smiley* v. *Holm*, 285 U.S. [355], 366 [(1932)]. However, "[t]he power to regulate the time, place, and manner of elections does not justify, without more, the abridgment of fundamental rights." *Tashjian* v. *Republican Party of Conn.*, 479 U.S. 208, 217 (1986) [p. 449]. States are thus entitled to adopt "generally applicable and evenhanded restrictions that protect the integrity and reliability of the electoral process itself." *Anderson* v. *Celebrezze*, 460 U.S. 780, 788, n.9 (1983) [p. 517]. * * *

The provisions at issue in [these] cases were thus constitutional because they regulated election *procedures* and did not even arguably impose any substantive qualification rendering a class of potential candidates ineligible for ballot position. They served the state interest in protecting the integrity and regularity of the election process, an interest independent of any attempt to evade the constitutional prohibition against the imposition of additional qualifications for service in Congress. And they did not involve measures that exclude candidates from the ballot without reference to the candidates' support in the electoral process. Our cases upholding state regulations of election procedures thus provide little support for the contention that a state-imposed ballot access restriction is constitutional when it is undertaken for the twin goals of disadvantaging a particular class of candidates and evading the dictates of the Qualifications Clauses. * * *

The merits of term limits, or "rotation," have been the subject of debate since the formation of our Constitution, when the Framers unanimously rejected a proposal to add such limits to the Constitution. The cogent arguments on both sides of the question that were articulated during the process of ratification largely retain their force today. Over half the States have adopted measures that impose such limits on some offices either directly or indirectly, and the Nation as a whole, notably by constitutional amendment, has imposed a limit on the number of terms that the President may serve. Term limits, like any other qualification for office, unquestionably restrict the ability of voters to vote for whom they wish. On the other hand, such limits may provide for the infusion of fresh ideas and new perspectives, and may decrease the likelihood that representatives will lose touch with their constituents. It is not our province to resolve this longstanding debate.

We are, however, firmly convinced that allowing the several States to adopt term limits for congressional service would effect a fundamental change in the constitutional framework. Any such change must come not by legislation adopted either by Congress or by an individual State, but rather — as have other important changes in the electoral process — through the amendment procedures set forth in Article V. The Framers decided that the qualifications for service in the Congress of the United States be fixed in the Constitution and be uniform throughout the Nation. That decision reflects the Framers' understanding that Members of Congress are chosen by separate constituencies, but that they become, when elected, servants of the people of the United States. They are not merely delegates appointed by separate, sovereign States; they occupy offices that are integral and essential components of a single National Government. In the absence of a properly passed constitutional amendment, allowing individual States to craft their own qualifications for Congress would thus erode the structure envisioned by the Framers, a structure that was designed, in the words of the Preamble to our Constitution, to form a "more perfect Union."

The judgment is affirmed.

It is so ordered.

JUSTICE KENNEDY, concurring. * * *

Federalism was our Nation's own discovery. The Framers split the atom of sovereignty. It was the genius of their idea that our citizens would have two political capacities, one state and one federal, each protected from incursion by the other. The resulting Constitution created a legal system unprecedented in form and design, establishing two orders of government, each with its own direct relationship, its own privity, its own set of mutual rights and obligations to the people who sustain it and are governed by it. * * *

Of course, because the Framers recognized that state power and identity were essential parts of the federal balance, the Constitution is solicitous of the prerogatives of the States, even in an otherwise sovereign federal province. The Constitution uses state boundaries to fix the size of congressional delegations, Art. I, § 2, cl. 3, ensures that each State shall have at least one representative, *ibid.*, grants States certain powers over the times, places, and manner of federal elections (subject to congressional revision), Art. I, § 4, cl. 1, requires that when the President is elected by the House of Representatives, the delegations from each State have one vote, Art. II, § 1, cl. 3, and Amdt. 12, and allows States to appoint electors for the

President, Art. II, § 1, cl. 2. Nothing in the Constitution or The Federalist Papers, however, supports the idea of state interference with the most basic relation between the National Government and its citizens, the selection of legislative representatives. * * *

Not the least of the incongruities in the position advanced by Arkansas is the proposition, necessary to its case, that it can burden the rights of resident voters in federal elections by reason of the manner in which they earlier had exercised it. If the majority of the voters had been successful in selecting a candidate, they would be penalized from exercising that same right in the future. Quite apart from any First Amendment concerns, see *Williams* v. *Rhodes*, 393 U.S. 23, 30 (1968) [p. 497]; *Anderson* v. *Celebrezze*, 460 U.S., [at] 786–788, neither the law nor federal theory allows a State to burden the exercise of federal rights in this manner. * * *

* * * There can be no doubt, if we are to respect the republican origins of the Nation and preserve its federal character, that there exists a federal right of citizenship, a relationship between the people of the Nation and their National Government, with which the States may not interfere. Because the Arkansas enactment intrudes upon this federal domain, it exceeds the boundaries of the Constitution.

JUSTICE THOMAS, with whom THE CHIEF JUSTICE [REHNQUIST], JUSTICE O'CONNOR, and JUSTICE SCALIA join, dissenting.

It is ironic that the Court bases today's decision on the right of the people to "choose whom they please to govern them." Under our Constitution, there is only one State whose people have the right to "choose whom they please" to represent Arkansas in Congress. The Court holds, however, that neither the elected legislature of that State nor the people themselves (acting by ballot initiative) may prescribe any qualifications for those representatives. The majority therefore defends the right of the people of Arkansas to "choose whom they please to govern them" by invalidating a provision that won nearly 60% of the votes cast in a direct election and that carried every congressional district in the State.

I dissent. Nothing in the Constitution deprives the people of each State of the power to prescribe eligibility requirements for the candidates who seek to represent them in Congress. The Constitution is simply silent on this question. And where the Constitution is silent, it raises no bar to action by the States or the people.

Because the majority fundamentally misunderstands the notion of "reserved" powers, I start with some first principles. Contrary to the majority's suggestion, the people of the States need not point to any affirmative grant of power in the Constitution in order to prescribe qualifications for their representatives in Congress, or to authorize their elected state legislators to do so. * * *

* * * The Federal Government and the States * * * face different default rules: Where the Constitution is silent about the exercise of a particular power — that is, where the Constitution does not speak either expressly or by necessary implication — the Federal Government lacks that power and the States enjoy it.

These basic principles are enshrined in the Tenth Amendment, which declares that all powers neither delegated to the Federal Government nor prohibited to the States "are reserved to the States respectively, or to the people." With this careful last phrase, the Amendment avoids taking any position on the division of power between the state governments and the people of the States: It is up to the people of each State to determine which "reserved" powers their state government may exercise. But the Amendment does make clear that powers reside at the state level except where the Constitution removes them from that level. All powers that the Constitution neither delegates to the Federal Government nor prohibits to the States are controlled by the people of each State. * * *

Any ambiguity in the Tenth Amendment's use of the phrase "the people" is cleared up by the body of the Constitution itself. Article I begins by providing that the Congress of the United States enjoys "[a]ll legislative Powers herein granted," § 1, and goes on to give a careful enumeration of Congress' powers, § 8. It then concludes by enumerating certain powers that are *prohibited* to the States. The import of this structure is the same as the import of the Tenth Amendment: If we are to invalidate Arkansas' Amendment 73, we must point to something in the Federal Constitution that deprives the people of Arkansas of the power to enact such measures.

The majority disagrees that it bears this burden. But its arguments are unpersuasive.

The majority begins by announcing an enormous and untenable limitation on the principle expressed by the Tenth Amendment. According to the majority, the States possess only those powers that the Constitution affirmatively grants to them or that they enjoyed before the Constitution was adopted; the Tenth Amendment "could only 'reserve' that which existed before." From the fact that the States had not previously enjoyed any powers over the particular institutions of the Federal Government established by the Constitution, the majority derives a rule precisely opposite to the one that the Amendment actually prescribes. * * *

The majority's essential logic is that the state governments could not "reserve" any powers they did not control at the time the Constitution was drafted. But it was not the state governments that were doing the reserving. The Constitution derives its authority instead from the consent of *the* people of the States. Given the fundamental principle that all governmental powers stem from the people of the States, it would simply be incoherent to assert that the people of the States could not reserve any powers that they had not previously controlled. * * *

I take it to be established, then, that the people of Arkansas do enjoy "reserved" powers over the selection of their representatives in Congress. Purporting to exercise those reserved powers, they have agreed among themselves that the candidates covered by § 3 of Amendment 73 — those whom they have already elected to three or more terms in the House of Representatives or to two or more terms in the Senate — should not be eligible to appear on the ballot for reelection, but should nonetheless be returned to Congress if enough voters are sufficiently enthusiastic about their candidacy to write in their names. Whatever one might think of the wisdom of this arrangement, we may not override the decision of the people of Arkansas unless something in the Federal Constitution deprives them of the power to enact such measures.

The majority settles on "the Qualifications Clauses" as the constitutional provisions that Amendment 73 violates. Because I do not read those provisions to impose any unstated prohibitions on the States, it is unnecessary for me to decide whether the majority is correct to identify Arkansas' ballot-access restriction with laws fixing true term limits or otherwise prescribing "qualifications" for congressional office. [T]he Qualifications Clauses are merely straightforward recitations of the minimum eligibility requirements that the Framers thought it essential for every Member of Congress to meet. They restrict state power only in that they prevent the States from abolishing all eligibility requirements for membership in Congress. * * *

* * * This restriction on state power reflects the fact that when the people of one State send immature, disloyal, or unknowledgeable representatives to Congress, they jeopardize not only their own interests but also the interests of the people of other States. Because Congress wields power over all the States, the people of each State need some guarantee that the legislators elected by the people of other States will meet minimum standards of competence. The Qualifications Clauses provide that guarantee: They list the requirements that the Framers considered essential to protect the competence of the National Legislature.

If the people of a State decide that they would like their representatives to possess additional qualifications, however, they have done nothing to frustrate the policy behind the Qualifications Clauses. Anyone who possesses all of the constitutional qualifications, plus some qualifications required by state law, still has all of the federal qualifications. Accordingly, the fact that the Constitution specifies certain qualifications that the Framers deemed necessary to protect the competence of the National Legislature does not imply that it strips the people of the individual States of the power to protect their own interests by adding other requirements for their own representatives. * * *

The majority responds that "a patchwork of state qualifications" would "undermin[e] the uniformity and the national character that the Framers envisioned and sought to ensure." Yet the Framers thought it perfectly consistent with the "national character" of Congress for the Senators and Representatives from each State to be chosen by the legislature or the people of that State. The majority never explains why Congress' fundamental character permits this state-centered system, but nonetheless prohibits the people of the States and their state legislatures from setting any eligibility requirements for the candidates who seek to represent them.

As for the majority's related assertion that the Framers intended qualification requirements to be uniform, this is a conclusion, not an argument. Indeed, it is a conclusion that the Qualifications Clauses themselves contradict. At the time of the framing, and for some years thereafter, the Clauses' citizenship requirements incorporated laws that varied from State to State. Thus, the Qualifications Clauses themselves made it possible that a person would be qualified to represent State A in Congress even though a similarly situated person would not be qualified to represent State B. * * *

Although the Qualifications Clauses neither state nor imply the prohibition that it finds in them, the majority infers from the Framers' "democratic principles" that the Clauses must have been generally understood to preclude the people of the

States and their state legislatures from prescribing any additional qualifications for their representatives in Congress. But the majority's evidence on this point establishes only two more modest propositions: (1) the Framers did not want the Federal Constitution itself to impose a broad set of disqualifications for congressional office, and (2) the Framers did not want the Federal Congress to be able to supplement the few disqualifications that the Constitution does set forth. The logical conclusion is simply that the Framers did not want the people of the States and their state legislatures to be constrained by too many qualifications imposed at the national level. The evidence does not support the majority's more sweeping conclusion that the Framers intended to bar the people of the States and their state legislatures from adopting additional eligibility requirements to help narrow their own choices. * * *

* * * One reason why the Framers decided not to let Congress prescribe the qualifications of its own Members was that incumbents could have used this power to perpetuate themselves or their ilk in office. As Madison pointed out at the Philadelphia Convention, Members of Congress would have an obvious conflict of interest if they could determine who may run against them. But neither the people of the States nor the state legislatures would labor under the same conflict of interest when prescribing qualifications for Members of Congress, and so the Framers would have had to use a different calculus in determining whether to deprive them of this power.

As the majority argues, democratic principles also contributed to the Framers' decision to withhold the qualification-setting power from Congress. But the majority is wrong to suggest that the same principles must also have led the Framers to deny this power to the people of the States and the state legislatures. In particular, it simply is not true that "the source of the qualification is of little moment in assessing the qualification's restrictive impact." There is a world of difference between a self-imposed constraint and a constraint imposed from above.

Congressional power over qualifications would have enabled the representatives from some States, acting collectively in the National Legislature, to prevent the people of another State from electing their preferred candidates. * * *

Yet this is simply to say that qualifications should not be set at the national level for offices whose occupants are selected at the state level. The majority never identifies the democratic principles that would have been violated if a state legislature, in the days before the Constitution was amended to provide for the direct election of Senators, had imposed some limits of its own on the field of candidates that it would consider for appointment. Likewise, the majority does not explain why democratic principles prohibit the people of a State from adopting additional eligibility requirements to help narrow their choices among candidates seeking to represent them in the House of Representatives. Indeed, the invocation of democratic principles to invalidate Amendment 73 seems particularly difficult in the present case, because Amendment 73 remains fully within the control of the people of Arkansas. If they wanted to repeal it (despite the 20-point margin by which they enacted it less than three years ago), they could do so by a simple majority vote. * * * When the people of a State themselves decide to restrict the field of candidates whom they are willing to send to Washington as their representatives, they simply have not violated the principle that "the people should choose whom they please to govern them." * * *

It is radical enough for the majority to hold that the Constitution implicitly precludes the people of the States from prescribing any eligibility requirements for the congressional candidates who seek their votes. This holding, after all, does not stop with negating the term limits that many States have seen fit to impose on their Senators and Representatives.[39] Today's decision also means that no State may disqualify congressional candidates whom a court has found to be mentally incompetent, who are currently in prison, or who have past vote-fraud convictions. Likewise, after today's decision, the people of each State must leave open the possibility that they will trust someone with their vote in Congress even though they do not trust him with *a* vote in the election for Congress.

In order to invalidate § 3 of Amendment 73, however, the majority must go further. The bulk of the majority's analysis * * * addresses the issues that would be raised if Arkansas had prescribed "genuine, unadulterated, undiluted term limits." But as the parties have agreed, Amendment 73 does not actually create this kind of disqualification. It does not say that covered candidates may not serve any more terms in Congress if reelected, and it does not indirectly achieve the same result by barring those candidates from seeking reelection. It says only that if they are to win reelection, they must do so by write-in votes. * * *

The majority suggests that this does not matter, because Amendment 73 itself says that it has the purpose of "evading the requirements of the Qualifications Clauses." * * * (I am not sure why the intent behind a law should affect our analysis under the Qualifications Clauses. If a law does not in fact add to the constitutional qualifications, the mistaken expectations of the people who enacted it would not seem to affect whether it violates the alleged exclusivity of those Clauses.) In any event, inquiries into legislative intent are even more difficult than usual when the legislative body whose unified intent must be determined consists of 825,162 Arkansas voters.

The majority nonetheless thinks it clear that the goal of § 3 is "to prevent the election of incumbents." In reaching this conclusion at the summary-judgment stage, however, the majority has given short shrift to petitioners' contrary claim. Petitioners do not deny that § 3 of Amendment 73 intentionally handicaps a class of candidates, in the sense that it decreases their pre-existing electoral chances. But petitioners do deny that § 3 is intended to (or will in fact) "prevent" the covered candidates from winning reelection, or "disqualify" them from further service. One of petitioners' central arguments is that congressionally conferred advantages have artificially inflated the pre-existing electoral chances of the covered candidates, and

---

[39] Going into the November 1994 elections, eight States [(Colorado, Michigan, Missouri, Montana, Ohio, Oregon, South Dakota, and Utah)] had adopted "pure" term limits of one sort or another. Eight other States [(Arizona, Arkansas, California, Florida, North Dakota, Oklahoma, Washington, and Wyoming)] had enacted "ballot access" provisions triggered by long-term incumbency or multiple prior terms in Congress. In the 1994 elections, six more States — Alaska, Idaho, Maine, Massachusetts, Nebraska, and Nevada — enacted term-limit or ballot-access measures, bringing to 22 the total number of States with such provisions. In 21 of these States, the measures have been enacted by direct vote of the people.

that Amendment 73 is merely designed to level the playing field on which challengers compete with them.

To understand this argument requires some background. Current federal law (enacted, of course, by congressional incumbents) confers numerous advantages on incumbents, and these advantages are widely thought to make it "significantly more difficult" for challengers to defeat them. For instance, federal law gives incumbents enormous advantages in building name recognition and good will in their home districts. See, e.g., 39 U.S.C. § 3210 (permitting Members of Congress to send "franked" mail free of charge); 2 U.S.C. §§ 61-1, 72a, 332 (permitting Members to have sizable taxpayer-funded staffs); 2 U.S.C. § 123b (establishing the House Recording Studio and the Senate Recording and Photographic Studios). At the same time that incumbent Members of Congress enjoy these in-kind benefits, Congress imposes spending and contribution limits in congressional campaigns that "can prevent challengers from spending more . . . to overcome their disadvantage in name recognition." Many observers believe that the campaign-finance laws also give incumbents an "enormous fund-raising edge" over their challengers by giving a large financing role to entities with incentives to curry favor with incumbents. In addition, the internal rules of Congress put a substantial premium on seniority, with the result that each Member's already plentiful opportunities to distribute benefits to his constituents increase with the length of his tenure. In this manner, Congress effectively "fines" the electorate for voting against incumbents. * * *

At the same time that incumbents enjoy the electoral advantages that they have conferred upon themselves, they also enjoy astonishingly high reelection rates. * * *

The voters of Arkansas evidently believe that incumbents would not enjoy such overwhelming success if electoral contests were truly fair — that is, if the government did not put its thumb on either side of the scale. The majority offers no reason to question the accuracy of this belief. Given this context, petitioners portray § 3 of Amendment 73 as an effort at the state level to offset the electoral advantages that congressional incumbents have conferred upon themselves at the federal level. * * *

* * * [T]oday's decision reads the Qualifications Clauses to impose substantial implicit prohibitions on the States and the people of the States. I would not draw such an expansive negative inference * * *. Rather, I would read the Qualifications Clauses to do no more than what they say. I respectfully dissent.

Notes and Questions

1. Both the majority and dissenting opinions in *U.S. Term Limits* spend a considerable amount of time discussing democratic principles to place their legal analyses in context. Einer Elhauge, in his article, *Are Term Limits Undemocratic?*, 64 U. Chi. L. Rev. 83 (1997), revisited those principles and confronted the apparent paradox that the same voters who frequently support term limits nonetheless also frequently vote to keep incumbent officeholders. There is no contradiction, Elhauge argued, because voters who — at least sometimes — wish to oust incumbents (keeping with the ethos of term limits) face a collective-action problem. Any individual political jurisdiction that has term limits is at a disadvantage to

jurisdictions that do not, since the latter keep seniority and other political advantages for their incumbents. In contrast, he suggested, the justification for the more established term limits for Presidents, governors, and mayors may reflect the need to deal with high barriers of political entry to run for such positions. He concluded that these rationales provided the better reasons to find term limits to be prodemocratic. How persuasive are Elhauge's arguments? Do they provide a better basis to support term limits at the state (and sub-state) level as opposed to those for federal officeholders, or vice-versa?

2.   The majority in *U.S. Term Limits* took pains to distinguish "procedural" regulations that protect the "integrity and regularity of the election process" from "substantive" restrictions such as those enacted by Arkansas. In other contexts, the Supreme Court has upheld various state-imposed qualifications for being placed on the ballot, including ones that fall more onerously on independent candidates. *E.g., Storer v. Brown*, 415 U.S. 724 (1974) [p. 513] (upholding provisions of California law which made independent candidates ineligible for placement on the general-election ballot if they had been members of an existing political party in the past primary season). Could these and similar state restrictions be attacked under *U.S. Term Limits*, at least for elections to federal offices? In *Campbell v. Davidson*, 233 F.3d 1229 (10th Cir. 2000), the court struck down provisions of Colorado law which required seekers of federal office to be registered voters in that state before the beginning of the term of office. Following *U.S. Term Limits* and distinguishing cases like *Storer*, the court concluded that the requirements did not merely winnow candidates for the ballot but impermissibly excluded certain types of candidates.

3.   Is there a constitutional difference between the people of a state acting collectively to add to the constitutionally specified qualifications — the effort struck down in *U.S. Term Limits* — and the people acting individually by voting against any candidate not possessing the additional qualifications? If a state legislature were to choose presidential electors (or, before the Seventeenth Amendment, United States Senators), could it constitutionally restrict its choice to those candidates with certain experience, or who are members of the majority party in the legislature?

4.   While *U.S. Term Limits* places considerable weight on the Qualifications Clauses of the Constitution, do the broader principles applied by the Court suggest that term limits for *state* officials also violate the Constitution? One court answered in the negative, concluding that lifetime term limits in California were constitutional, and that *U.S. Term Limits* was limited to congressional offices. *Bates v. Jones*, 131 F.3d 843, 847 n.1 (9th Cir. 1997) (en banc). In contrast, the dissent argued that the broader analysis of *U.S. Term Limits* suggested that it had implications for attacks on state term limits. *Id.* at 868–72 (Fletcher, J., dissenting).

5.   The vast majority of legislative term limits adopted in states in the 1990s were by popular initiative or referendum, not by state legislatures. Michael J. Klarman, *Majoritarian Judicial Review: The Entrenchment Problem*, 85 GEO. L.J. 491, 510 (1997). Why have state legislatures largely not enacted these limits? To what extent, if at all, should the method of enactment of term limits affect judicial review of such provisions?

6. Term limits are themselves sometimes limited or repealed, as support for the measures ebbs despite initial enthusiasm. For example, since the widespread adoption of such limits for state legislatures in the 1990s, two have been repealed by legislatures (Idaho and Utah), and others have been ruled unconstitutional by state supreme courts (Massachusetts, Oregon, Washington, and Wyoming). For other examples, see David W. Chen & Michael Barbaro, *Across Country, New Challenges to Term Limits*, N.Y. TIMES, Sept. 10, 2008, at A1. A high-profile example of the controversy that continues to surround term limits was the extension of the two-term limit for New York City's mayor to three terms in 2008. The extension survived a legal challenge, *Molinari v. Bloomberg*, 564 F.3d 587 (2d Cir. 2009), but it proved a political liability for incumbent Mayor Michael Bloomberg, the beneficiary of the change. Michael Barbaro, *Change to Term Limits Dogs Mayor*, N.Y. TIMES, Oct. 4, 2009, at A17. He nonetheless won reelection.

7. How does *U.S. Term Limits* apply to other state regulation of the election process for federal office? For example, should it invalidate state laws that permit the recall of members of Congress? For an affirmative answer, see *Comm. to Recall Robert Menendez v. Wells*, 7 A.3d 720 (N.J. 2010). The court struck down a state constitutional provision permitting the recall of any elected official representing the state in Congress on the basis of *U.S. Term Limits*. While many state provisions — a few explicitly, and more implicitly — appeared to permit the recall of members of Congress, the court noted that the consensus of scholarly authority, and the opinions of many state attorneys general, was that such provisions were unenforceable.

COOK v. GRALIKE
Supreme Court of the United States
531 U.S. 510, 121 S. Ct. 1029, 149 L. Ed. 2d 44 (2001)

JUSTICE STEVENS delivered the opinion of the Court [in which JUSTICE SCALIA, JUSTICE KENNEDY, JUSTICE SOUTER, JUSTICE THOMAS, JUSTICE GINSBURG, and JUSTICE BREYER join]. * * *

Article VIII [of the Missouri Constitution] "instruct[s]" each Member of Missouri's congressional delegation "to use all of his or her delegated powers to pass the Congressional Term Limits Amendment" set forth in § 16 of the Article. That proposed amendment would limit service in the United States Congress to three terms in the House of Representatives and two terms in the Senate.

Three provisions in Article VIII combine to advance its purpose. Section 17 prescribes that the statement "DISREGARDED VOTERS' INSTRUCTION ON TERM LIMITS" be printed on all primary and general ballots adjacent to the name of a Senator or Representative who fails to take any one of eight legislative acts in support of the proposed amendment. Section 18 provides that the statement "DECLINED TO PLEDGE TO SUPPORT TERM LIMITS" be printed on all primary and general election ballots next to the name of every nonincumbent congressional candidate who refuses to take a "Term Limit" pledge that commits the candidate, if elected, to performing the legislative acts enumerated in § 17. And § 19 directs the Missouri Secretary of State to determine and declare, pursuant to

§§ 17 and 18, whether either statement should be printed alongside the name of each candidate for Congress.

Respondent Don Gralike was a nonincumbent candidate for election in 1998 to the United States House of Representatives from Missouri's Third Congressional District. A month after Article VIII was amended, Gralike brought suit * * * to enjoin petitioner, the Secretary of State of Missouri, from implementing the Article, which the complaint alleges violates several provisions of the Federal Constitution. * * *

The federal offices at stake "aris[e] from the Constitution itself." *U.S. Term Limits, Inc.* v. *Thornton*, 514 U.S. [779], 805 [(1995)] [p. 550]. Because any state authority to regulate election to those offices could not precede their very creation by the Constitution, such power "had to be delegated to, rather than reserved by, the States." *Id.*, at 804. * * * Through the Elections Clause, the Constitution delegated to the States the power to regulate the "Times, Places and Manner of holding Elections for Senators and Representatives," subject to a grant of authority to Congress to "make or alter such Regulations." Art. I, § 4, cl. 1. No other constitutional provision gives the States authority over congressional elections, and no such authority could be reserved under the Tenth Amendment. By process of elimination, the States may regulate the incidents of such elections, including balloting, only within the exclusive delegation of power under the Elections Clause.

With respect to the Elections Clause, petitioner argues that Article VIII "merely regulates the manner in which elections are held by disclosing information about congressional candidates." As such, petitioner concludes, Article VIII is a valid exercise of Missouri's delegated power.

We disagree. To be sure, the Elections Clause grants to the States "broad power" to prescribe the procedural mechanisms for holding congressional elections. *Tashjian* v. *Republican Party of Conn.*, 479 U.S. 208, 217 (1986) [p. 449]; see also *Smiley* v. *Holm*, 285 U.S. 355, 366 (1932). Nevertheless, Article VIII falls outside of that grant of authority. As we made clear in *U.S. Term Limits*, "the Framers understood the Elections Clause as a grant of authority to issue procedural regulations, and not as a source of power to dictate electoral outcomes, to favor or disfavor a class of candidates, or to evade important constitutional restraints." 514 U.S., at 833–834. Article VIII is not a procedural regulation. It does not regulate the time of elections; it does not regulate the place of elections; nor, we believe, does it regulate the manner of elections. As to the last point, Article VIII bears no relation to the "manner" of elections as we understand it, for in our commonsense view that term encompasses matters like "notices, registration, supervision of voting, protection of voters, prevention of fraud and corrupt practices, counting of votes, duties of inspectors and canvassers, and making and publication of election returns." *Smiley*, 285 U.S., at 366; see also *U.S. Term Limits, Inc.* v. *Thornton*, 514 U.S., at 833. In short, Article VIII is not among "the numerous requirements as to procedure and safeguards which experience shows are necessary in order to enforce the fundamental right involved," *Smiley*, 285 U.S., at 366, ensuring that elections are "fair and honest," and that "some sort of order, rather than chaos, is to accompany the democratic process," *Storer* v. *Brown*, 415 U.S. 724, 730 (1974) [p. 513].

Rather, Article VIII is plainly designed to favor candidates who are willing to support the particular form of a term limits amendment set forth in its text and to disfavor those who either oppose term limits entirely or would prefer a different proposal. As noted, the state provision does not just "instruct" each member of Missouri's congressional delegation to promote in certain ways the passage of the specified term limits amendment. It also attaches a concrete consequence to noncompliance — the printing of the statement "DISREGARDED VOTERS' INSTRUCTIONS ON TERM LIMITS" by the candidate's name on all primary and general election ballots. Likewise, a nonincumbent candidate who does not pledge to follow the instruction receives the ballot designation "DECLINED TO PLEDGE TO SUPPORT TERM LIMITS."

In describing the two labels, the courts below have employed terms such as "pejorative," "negative," "derogatory," "intentionally intimidating," "particularly harmful," "politically damaging," "a serious sanction," "a penalty," and "official denunciation." The general counsel to petitioner's office, no less, has denominated the labels as "the Scarlet Letter." We agree with the sense of these descriptions. They convey the substantial political risk the ballot labels impose on current and prospective congressional members who, for one reason or another, fail to comply with the conditions set forth in Article VIII for passing its term limits amendment. Although petitioner now claims that the labels "merely" inform Missouri voters about a candidate's compliance with Article VIII, she has acknowledged under oath that the ballot designations would handicap candidates for the United States Congress. To us, that is exactly the intended effect of Article VIII.

Indeed, it seems clear that the adverse labels handicap candidates "at the most crucial stage in the election process — the instant before the vote is cast." *Anderson* v. *Martin*, 375 U.S. 399, 402 (1964). At the same time, "by directing the citizen's attention to the single consideration" of the candidates' fidelity to term limits, the labels imply that the issue "is an important — perhaps paramount — consideration in the citizen's choice, which may decisively influence the citizen to cast his ballot" against candidates branded as unfaithful. *Ibid.* While the precise damage the labels may exact on candidates is disputed between the parties, the labels surely place their targets at a political disadvantage to unmarked candidates for congressional office. Thus, far from regulating the procedural mechanisms of elections, Article VIII attempts to "dictate electoral outcomes." *U.S. Term Limits, Inc.* v. *Thornton*, 514 U.S., at 833–834. Such "regulation" of congressional elections simply is not authorized by the Elections Clause.

Accordingly, the judgment of the Court of Appeals is affirmed.

It is so ordered.

JUSTICE KENNEDY, concurring.

I join the opinion of the Court * * *. It seems appropriate, however, to add these brief observations * * *. The Court does not say the States are disabled from requesting specific action from Congress or from expressing their concerns to it. As the Court holds, however, the mechanism the State seeks to employ here goes well beyond this prerogative.

A State is not permitted to interpose itself between the people and their National Government as it seeks to do here. Whether a State's concern is with the proposed enactment of a constitutional amendment or an ordinary federal statute it simply lacks the power to impose any conditions on the election of Senators and Representatives, save neutral provisions as to the time, place, and manner of elections pursuant to Article I, § 4. * * * The Court rules, as it must, that the amendments to Article VIII of the Missouri Constitution do not regulate the time or place of federal elections; rather, those provisions are an attempt to control the actions of the State's congressional delegation.

The dispositive principle in this case is fundamental to the Constitution, to the idea of federalism, and to the theory of representative government. The principle is that Senators and Representatives in the National Government are responsible to the people who elect them, not to the States in which they reside. The Constitution was ratified by Conventions in the several States, not by the States themselves, U.S. Const., Art. VII, a historical fact and a constitutional imperative which underscore the proposition that the Constitution was ordained and established by the people of the United States. U.S. Const., preamble. The idea of federalism is that a National Legislature enacts laws which bind the people as individuals, not as citizens of a State; and, it follows, freedom is most secure if the people themselves, not the States as intermediaries, hold their federal legislators to account for the conduct of their office. If state enactments were allowed to condition or control certain actions of federal legislators, accountability would be blurred, with the legislators having the excuse of saying that they did not act in the exercise of their best judgment but simply in conformance with a state mandate. As noted in the concurring opinion in *Thornton*, "[n]othing in the Constitution or The Federalist Papers . . . supports the idea of state interference with the most basic relation between the National Government and its citizens, the selection of legislative representatives." 514 U.S., at 842. Yet that is just what Missouri seeks to do through its law — to wield the power granted to it by the Elections Clause to handicap those who seek federal office by affixing pejorative labels next to their names on the ballot if they do not pledge to support the State's preferred position on a certain issue. Neither the design of the Constitution nor sound principles of representative government are consistent with the right or power of a State to interfere with the direct line of accountability between the National Legislature and the people who elect it. For these reasons Article VIII is void.

This said, it must be noted that when the Constitution was enacted, respectful petitions to legislators were an accepted mode of urging legislative action. This right is preserved to individuals (the people) in the First Amendment. Even if a State, as an entity, is not itself protected by the Petition Clause, there is no principle prohibiting a state legislature from following a parallel course and by a memorial resolution requesting the Congress of the United States to pay heed to certain state concerns. From the earliest days of our Republic to the present time, States have done so in the context of federal legislation. See, *e.g.*, 22 Annals of Cong. 153–154 (1811) (reprinting a resolution by the General Assembly of the Commonwealth of Pennsylvania requesting that the charter of the Bank of the United States not be renewed); 2000 Ala. Acts 66 (requesting targeted relief for Medicare cuts); 2000 Kan. Sess. Laws, ch. 186 (urging Congress to allow state-inspected meat to be shipped in interstate commerce). Indeed, the situation was even more complex in the early days of our Nation, when Senators were appointed by state legislatures rather than directly elected. At that time, it appears that some state legislatures followed a practice of instructing the Senators whom they had appointed to pass legislation, while only requesting that the Representatives, who had been elected by the people, do so. See 22 Annals of Cong., at 153–154. I do not believe that the situation should be any different with respect to a proposed constitutional amendment, and indeed history bears this out. See, *e.g.*, 13 Annals of Cong. 95–96 (1803) (reprinting a resolution from the State of Vermont and the Commonwealth of Massachusetts requesting that Congress propose to the legislatures of the States a constitutional amendment akin to the Twelfth Amendment). The fact that the Members of the First Congress decided not to codify a right to instruct legislative representatives does not, in my view, prove that they intended to prohibit nonbinding petitions or memorials by the State as an entity.

If there are to be cases in which a close question exists regarding whether the State has exceeded its constitutional authority in attempting to influence congressional action, this case is not one of them. In today's case the question is not close. Here the State attempts to intrude upon the relationship between the people and their congressional delegates by seeking to control or confine the discretion of those delegates, and the interference is not permissible.

With these observations, I concur in the Court's opinion.

JUSTICE THOMAS, concurring * * *.

I continue to believe that, because they possess "reserved" powers, "the people of the States need not point to any affirmative grant of power in the Constitution in order to prescribe qualifications for their representatives in Congress, or to authorize their elected state legislators to do so." *U.S. Term Limits, Inc.* v. *Thornton*, 514 U.S., [at] 846 (THOMAS, J., dissenting). For this reason, I disagree with the Court's premise, derived from *U.S. Term Limits*, that the States have no authority to regulate congressional elections except for the authority that the Constitution expressly delegates to them. Nonetheless, the parties conceded the validity of this premise, and I therefore concur.

CHIEF JUSTICE REHNQUIST, with whom JUSTICE O'CONNOR joins, concurring in the judgment.

I would affirm the judgment of the Court of Appeals, but on the ground that Missouri's Article VIII violates the First Amendment to the United States Constitution. Specifically, I believe that Article VIII violates the First Amendment right of a political candidate, once lawfully on the ballot, to have his name appear unaccompanied by pejorative language required by the State. Our ballot access cases based on First Amendment grounds have rarely distinguished between the rights of candidates and the rights of voters. In *Bullock* v. *Carter*, 405 U.S. 134, 143 (1972) [p. 508], we said: "[T]he rights of voters and the rights of candidates do not lend themselves to neat separation; laws that affect candidates always have at least some theoretical, correlative effect on voters." And in *Anderson* v. *Celebrezze*, 460

U.S. 780, 787 (1983) [p. 517], we said that "voters can assert their preferences only through candidates or parties or both." Actions such as the present one challenging ballot provisions have in most instances been brought by the candidates themselves, and no one questions the standing of respondents Gralike and Harmon to raise a First Amendment challenge to such laws.[*]

Article I, § 4, provides that "[t]he Times, Places and Manner of holding Elections for Senators and Representatives, shall be prescribed in each State by the Legislature thereof. . . . " Missouri justifies Article VIII as a "time, place, and manner" regulation of election. Restrictions of this kind are valid "provided that they are justified without reference to the content of the regulated speech, that they are narrowly tailored to serve a significant governmental interest, and that they leave open ample alternative channels for communication of the information." *Clark v. Community for Creative Non-Violence*, 468 U.S. 288, 293 (1984). Missouri's Article VIII flunks two of these three requirements. Article VIII is not only not content neutral, but it actually discriminates on the basis of viewpoint because only those candidates who fail to conform to the State's position receive derogatory labels. The result is that the State injects itself into the election process at an absolutely critical point — the composition of the ballot, which is the last thing the voter sees before he makes his choice — and does so in a way that is not neutral as to issues or candidates. The candidates who are thus singled out have no means of replying to their designation which would be equally effective with the voter.

In *Anderson* v. *Martin*, we held that a Louisiana statute requiring the designation of a candidate's race on the ballot violated the Equal Protection Clause. In describing the effect of such a designation, the Court said: "[B]y directing the citizen's attention to the single consideration of race or color, the State indicates that a candidate's race or color is an important — perhaps paramount — consideration in the citizen's choice, which may decisively influence the citizen to cast his ballot along racial lines." *Id.*, at 402. So, too, here the State has chosen one and only one issue to comment on the position of the candidates. During the campaign, they may debate tax reform, Social Security, national security, and a host of other issues; but when it comes to the ballot on which one or the other of them is chosen, the State is saying that the issue of term limits is paramount. Although uttered in a different context, what we said in *Police Dept. of Chicago* v. *Mosley*, 408 U.S. 92, 96 (1972), is equally applicable here: "[Government] may not select which issues are worth discussing or debating."

If other Missouri officials feel strongly about the need for term limits, they are free to urge rejection of candidates who do not share their view and refuse to "take the pledge." Such candidates are able to respond to that sort of speech with speech of their own. But the State itself may not skew the ballot listings in this way without violating the First Amendment.

---

[*] The Court of Appeals upheld their First Amendment claim, but based its reasoning on the view that the ballot statements were "compelled speech" by the candidate, and therefore ran afoul of cases such as *Wooley* v. *Maynard*, 430 U.S. 705 (1977). I do not agree with the reasoning of the Court of Appeals. I do not believe a reasonable voter, viewing the ballot labeled as Article VIII requires, would think that the candidate in question chose to characterize himself as having "disregarded voters' instructions" or as "having declined to pledge" to support term limits.

Notes and Questions

1. How does *Gralike* apply to other state regulations of federal elections? Justice Kennedy said it was not a close case, but how are close cases evaluated under *Gralike*? For example, states frequently list the political parties of candidates on ballots for federal office. Can a candidate object under *Gralike*? For a general discussion of other ballot restrictions in light of *Gralike*, see Matthew M. Mannix, Comment, *Opening Ballot Access to Political Outsiders: How Third Parties Could Use* Cook v. Gralike *to Challenge the Dominance of America's Two-Party System*, 11 ROGER WILLIAMS U. L. REV. 273 (2005).

2. Does or should *Gralike* apply to *state* elections? How would the authors of the concurring opinions resolve that issue?

3. Why do you think Justice Scalia joined the majority opinion in *Gralike* after dissenting in *U.S. Term Limits*?

4. It has been argued that even without the Qualifications Clauses and the First Amendment, the result in *Gralike* should be the same, since the structural provisions of "a representative democracy — plainly contemplated by the Constitution's provisions for the federal legislature and federal elections — is dependent on the operation of elections unbiased by the existing government." Vicki C. Jackson, Cook v. Gralike: *Easy Cases and Structural Reasoning*, 2001 SUP. CT. REV. 299, 300; *cf. National Endowment for the Arts v. Finley*, 524 U.S. 569, 598 n.3 (1998) (Scalia, J., concurring in the judgment) ("I suppose it would be unconstitutional for the government to give money to an organization devoted to the promotion of candidates nominated by the Republican party — but it would be just as unconstitutional for the government itself to promote candidates nominated by the Republican party, and I do not think that that unconstitutionality has anything to do with the First Amendment."). But if Article VIII of the Missouri Constitution did not violate the Qualifications Clauses or the First Amendment, by what authority could the Supreme Court invalidate it?

Chapter 8

POLITICAL SPEECH

A. INTRODUCTION

The First Amendment "has its fullest and most urgent application * * * to the conduct of campaigns for political office." *Monitor Patriot Co. v. Roy*, 401 U.S. 265, 272 (1971). Accordingly, the constitutional protections of "the freedom of speech, [and] of the press" are particularly important in election law. Elections provide the clearest opportunity for the people to exercise the power of self-governance in a republic, and the power of the vote can be effective only if, and to the extent that, voters can inform themselves about the candidates and issues to be considered at elections. *See, e.g.*, ALEXANDER MEIKLEJOHN, FREE SPEECH AND ITS RELATIONSHIP TO SELF GOVERNMENT (1948).

Yet the importance of elections to the democratic process, and of speech to elections, means that disinformation can produce particularly severe negative consequences. Additionally, free-speech protections allow persons to exert influence commensurate with their ability to articulate a persuasive message and distribute it to an audience. Because some people are better than others at producing and distributing speech, and because some people can devote more resources to the effort than can others, free speech can result in inequality of political influence. Thus, ironically, elections present both a compelling context for protecting free speech, and a compelling context for limiting it.

This Chapter considers several different areas in which free-speech questions arise. Though our focus will be on election-related speech, some of the cases included here do not deal overtly with elections. Each case is significant, however, for what it says about the constitutional protection granted to speech on matters of public concern, and thereby forms a foundation for our understanding of the First Amendment's application to electoral politics.

The summary in this section, and the coverage in this Chapter, leave undiscussed many important areas of First Amendment doctrine, including some that relate to the expression of political speech and the communication of ideas that have the potential to shape politics. Thus, the Supreme Court's treatment of subversive speech and symbolic expression, for example, are not analyzed here; rather, we seek to present those portions of First Amendment law that have the largest impact on speech in campaigns.

The First Amendment applies by its terms only to congressional laws that abridge the listed freedoms, but the other branches of the federal government are also required to respect its strictures. Further, the Court has long considered First Amendment rights to be fundamental, and accordingly has interpreted the Fourteenth Amendment as extending the First Amendment's protections to the states. *See Fiske v. Kansas*, 274 U.S. 380, 386–87 (1927) (incorporating the First Amendment's protection of the freedom of speech); *Gitlow v. New York*, 268 U.S. 652, 666 (1925) (announcing the same principle in dictum). Thus, whether the challenged abridgement of speech is the result of state or federal action, it will be deemed constitutional only if it passes strict scrutiny — *i.e.*, if the restriction on speech is narrowly tailored to serve a compelling governmental interest.

Before one can determine that strict scrutiny is appropriate, however, it is necessary to determine whether a regulation implicates the right. As a general matter, "content-based" regulations trigger strict scrutiny, while "content-neutral" regulations concerning the time, place, or manner of speech are evaluated under a more forgiving test. If a regulation is motivated by a purpose unrelated to the content of the speech, it will be upheld if significant government interests outweigh the incidental restriction on speech. *See* RONALD D. ROTUNDA & JOHN E. NOWAK, 5 TREATISE ON CONSTITUTIONAL LAW § 20.47(a) at 461 (4th ed. 2008).

A content-based restriction is one where the harm the government seeks to prevent is related to the message of the speaker; the government must assess the content of the message to ascertain whether it risks the harm the government is trying to avoid. A content-neutral restriction, by contrast, seeks to achieve a result unrelated to the message of a given speaker. A ban on sound trucks, for example, limits the expression of speech, but does so in a content-neutral way because the harm the government seeks to prevent — the disturbances caused by noise — are unrelated to the message conveyed by the sound truck. Whether the sound truck carries a speech by a mayoral candidate, an advertisement about a ballot issue, a commercial advertisement, or a public-service announcement, the harm is the same. Content-neutral regulations are more apt to be constitutional than are content-based restrictions, but they must still be reasonable. The government cannot simply ban all speech within a certain area and defend on the ground that the ban is content-neutral. *See Board of Airport Commissioners v. Jews for Jesus, Inc.*, 482 U.S. 569 (1987).

"Viewpoint-based" restrictions are a subset of content-based ones. Viewpoint-based restrictions not only apply to speech depending on what message is conveyed in the speech, but use the power of the government to advantage one side in a debate. Thus, a regulation applying to speech "about the National Football League" would be content-based because the government would need to assess the speech to determine if the NFL were the subject of the speech. A regulation applying to speech "promoting the National Football League," however, would not only be content-based but would be viewpoint-based as well, because it would leave unregulated speech denigrating the League. Viewpoint-based regulations are almost always unconstitutional.

Certain categories of language have traditionally not been considered to be part of "the freedom of speech," and therefore the government can limit the use of such language without triggering the strict-scrutiny test. These categories include obscenity, fighting words, and libel. *See Chaplinsky v. New Hampshire*, 315 U.S. 568, 571–72 (1942). Even as to such "low-value speech," however, the Constitution may provide some protection — especially if a government regulation may in practice chill not only those kinds of speech, but other expression as well. In *New York Times Co v. Sullivan*, 376 U.S. 254 (1964) [p. 574], for example, the Court struck down a libel judgment against a newspaper as inconsistent with the First Amendment. The Court reasoned that even if libel is constitutionally unprotected, speakers would refrain from exercising their rights if they knew that a false statement would subject them to liability. Accordingly, the Court held that a state may award damages for libel only where the defendant's false statements were made with knowledge of their falsity, or with reckless disregard for whether they were false or not. *See id.* at 280.

Libel prohibitions are only one kind of regulation affecting speech about public affairs and public figures. Media outlets have occasionally been targets of governmental "fairness" regulation when regulators fear that media coverage has the capacity to slant the public's perception of candidates or issues. For the most part, such restrictions have failed to survive constitutional review. An exception exists, however, for regulation of broadcast media. Whereas regulation of newspapers' editorializing has been held flatly unconstitutional, *see Miami Herald Publishing Co. v. Tornillo*, 418 U.S. 241 (1974) [p. 631], the Supreme Court upheld the FCC's (since-repealed) requirement that radio and television broadcasters provide criticized persons an opportunity to respond to attacks. *See Red Lion Broadcasting Co. v. Federal Communications Commission*, 395 U.S. 367 (1969) [p. 605]. Broadcast media were different, the Court concluded, because the scarcity of available broadcast frequencies prevented each potential speaker from having access to the airwaves. Accordingly, broadcasters could constitutionally be considered to hold their licenses in the public interest, and obligated to permit other members of the public access to their stations when necessary to give the public a balanced presentation of issues.

Government is usually prohibited from imposing civil or criminal penalties for political speech, and may not interfere with the speech of candidates for public office. *See Brown v. Hartlage*, 456 U.S. 45 (1982) [p. 585]. Where a state's electoral process incorporates a role for petitions (often as a prerequisite to ballot-access for third parties or initiatives), the circulation of such petitions involves "core political speech." *See Meyer v. Grant*, 486 U.S. 414, 420–22 (1986) [p. 678]. Even judicial candidates possess a First Amendment right to announce their views in campaigns, though states may be able to restrict judicial campaign speech more than they can restrict speech in other types of campaigns. *See Republican Party of Minnesota v. White*, 536 U.S. 765, 783 (2002) [p. 756]. Political speakers are also protected from being forced to disclose their identities when speaking. *See McIntyre v. Ohio Elections Commission*, 514 U.S. 334 (1995). As we will see in Chapter 9, however, the Court has upheld campaign-finance laws that require donors to disclose their identities. *See Citizens United v. Federal Election Commission*, 558 U.S. 310, 366–71 (2010) [p. 1022]; *Buckley v. Valeo*, 424 U.S. 1, 74–82 (1976) [p. 1011] (*per curiam*).

When government acts not as a regulator but as an employer, it may sometimes condition employment on the employee's agreement not to engage in political speech — provided that the employee's speech would adversely affect job performance. Where an individual's job performance is unaffected by the speech, government may not discipline an employee for speech that opposes the government's viewpoint. *See Pickering v. Board of Education*, 391 U.S. 563 (1968) [p. 706]. In a series of cases upholding limitations on government employees' political activity, however, the Court has indicated that the government may impose limits on employees' First Amendment freedoms where public confidence in government demands that workers not be seen as having their jobs depend on their support for the party or politicians in power. *See Broadrick v. Oklahoma*, 413 U.S. 601 (1973); *Civil Service Commission v. National Association of Letter Carriers*, 413 U.S. 548 (1973) [p. 712]; *United Public Workers v. Mitchell*, 330 U.S. 75 (1947) [p. 698].

The dangers of a partisan government workforce are so acute that the Court has not only authorized limits on employees' speech, but has also held that the First Amendment itself requires government to refrain from making certain employment decisions on a patronage basis. Patronage persists to some degree, of course, but the Court has stated that party loyalty may be the basis for personnel decisions relating only to those positions for which "party affiliation is an appropriate requirement for the effective performance of the public office involved." *Branti v. Finkel*, 445 U.S. 507, 518–20 (1980).

One particular type of political speech — campaign finance — is the subject of its own Chapter. As you read the materials in this one, however, you should consider how the principles developed here should apply in evaluating the constitutionality of restrictions on raising or spending money in campaigns.

B. DEFAMATION AND THE PROBLEM OF FALSE STATEMENTS

We begin with perhaps the most famous First Amendment case in American history. *New York Times Co. v. Sullivan* constitutionalized the "actual malice" standard for libel, holding that the First Amendment prohibited states from awarding tort damages to public officials for libelous statements unless the defendant knew the statements were false, or unless the defendant acted in reckless disregard for whether the statements were false or not. The case has had a tremendous influence on political discourse because of its determination that even some false and damaging speech should receive constitutional protection so as to avoid "chilling" more worthy expression.

NEW YORK TIMES CO. v. SULLIVAN
Supreme Court of the United States
376 U.S. 254, 84 S. Ct. 710, 11 L. Ed. 2d 686 (1964)

MR. JUSTICE BRENNAN delivered the opinion of the Court [in which MR. CHIEF JUSTICE WARREN, MR. JUSTICE CLARK, MR. JUSTICE HARLAN, MR. JUSTICE STEWART, and MR. JUSTICE WHITE join].

We are required in this case to determine for the first time the extent to which the constitutional protections for speech and press limit a State's power to award damages in a libel action brought by a public official against critics of his official conduct.[1]

Respondent L.B. Sullivan is one of the three elected Commissioners of the City of Montgomery, Alabama. He testified that he was "Commissioner of Public Affairs and the duties are supervision of the Police Department, Fire Department, Department of Cemetery and Department of Scales." He brought this civil libel action [and a] jury in the Circuit Court of Montgomery County awarded him damages of $500,000 * * *.

Respondent's complaint alleged that he had been libeled by statements in a full-page advertisement that was carried in the New York Times on March 29, 1960. Entitled "Heed Their Rising Voices," the advertisement began by stating that "As the whole world knows by now, thousands of Southern Negro students are engaged in widespread non-violent demonstrations in positive affirmation of the right to live in human dignity as guaranteed by the U.S. Constitution and the Bill of Rights." It went on to charge that "in their efforts to uphold these guarantees, they are being met by an unprecedented wave of terror by those who would deny and negate that document which the whole world looks upon as setting the pattern for modern freedom. . . . " Succeeding paragraphs purported to illustrate the "wave of terror" by describing certain alleged events. The text concluded with an appeal for funds for three purposes: support of the student movement, "the struggle for the right-to-vote," and the legal defense of Dr. Martin Luther King, Jr., leader of the movement, against a perjury indictment then pending in Montgomery.

The text appeared over the names of 64 persons, many widely known for their activities in public affairs, religion, trade unions, and the performing arts. Below these names, and under a line reading "We in the south who are struggling daily for dignity and freedom warmly endorse this appeal," appeared the names of the four individual petitioners and of 16 other persons, all but two of whom were identified as clergymen in various Southern cities. The advertisement was signed at the bottom of the page by the "Committee to Defend Martin Luther King and the Struggle for Freedom in the South," and the officers of the Committee were listed.

Of the 10 paragraphs of text in the advertisement, the third and a portion of the sixth were the basis of respondent's claim of libel. They read as follows:

Third paragraph:

> "In Montgomery, Alabama, after students sang 'My Country, 'Tis of Thee' on the State Capitol steps, their leaders were expelled from school, and truckloads of police armed with shotguns and tear-gas ringed the Alabama State College Campus. When the entire student body protested to state authorities by refusing to re-register, their dining hall was padlocked in an attempt to starve them into submission."

Sixth paragraph:

---

[1] [The First Amendment governs state action and not private action, but t]hat proposition has no application to this case. Although this is a civil lawsuit between private parties, the Alabama courts have applied a state rule of law which petitioners claim to impose invalid restrictions on their constitutional freedoms of speech and press. [Relocated from text. — Eds.]

"Again and again the Southern violators have answered Dr. King's peaceful protests with intimidation and violence. They have bombed his home almost killing his wife and child. They have assaulted his person. They have arrested him seven times — for 'speeding,' 'loitering' and similar 'offenses.' And now they have charged him with 'perjury' — a *felony* under which they could imprison him for *ten years.* * * *"

Although neither of these statements mentions respondent by name, he contended that the word "police" in the third paragraph referred to him as the Montgomery Commissioner who supervised the Police Department, so that he was being accused of "ringing" the campus with police. He further claimed that the paragraph would be read as imputing to the police, and hence to him, the padlocking of the dining hall in order to starve the students into submission. As to the sixth paragraph, he contended that since arrests are ordinarily made by the police, the statement "They have arrested [Dr. King] seven times" would be read as referring to him; he further contended that the "They" who did the arresting would be equated with the "They" who committed the other described acts and with the "Southern violators." Thus, he argued, the paragraph would be read as accusing the Montgomery police, and hence him, of answering Dr. King's protests with "intimidation and violence," bombing his home, assaulting his person, and charging him with perjury. Respondent and six other Montgomery residents testified that they read some or all of the statements as referring to him in his capacity as Commissioner.

It is uncontroverted that some of the statements contained in the two paragraphs were not accurate descriptions of events which occurred in Montgomery. Although Negro students staged a demonstration on the State Capital steps, they sang the National Anthem and not "My Country, 'Tis of Thee." Although nine students were expelled by the State Board of Education, this was not for leading the demonstration at the Capitol, but for demanding service at a lunch counter in the Montgomery County Courthouse on another day. Not the entire student body, but most of it, had protested the expulsion, not by refusing to register, but by boycotting classes on a single day; virtually all the students did register for the ensuing semester. The campus dining hall was not padlocked on any occasion, and the only students who may have been barred from eating there were the few who had neither signed a preregistration application nor requested temporary meal tickets. Although the police were deployed near the campus in large numbers on three occasions, they did not at any time "ring" the campus, and they were not called to the campus in connection with the demonstration on the State Capitol steps, as the third paragraph implied. Dr. King had not been arrested seven times, but only four; and although he claimed to have been assaulted some years earlier in connection with his arrest for loitering outside a courtroom, one of the officers who made the arrest denied that there was such an assault.

On the premise that the charges in the sixth paragraph could be read as referring to him, respondent was allowed to prove that he had not participated in the events described. Although Dr. King's home had in fact been bombed twice when his wife and child were there, both of these occasions antedated respondent's tenure as Commissioner, and the police were not only not implicated in the bombings, but had made every effort to apprehend those who were. Three of Dr.

King's four arrests took place before respondent became Commissioner. Although Dr. King had in fact been indicted (he was subsequently acquitted) on two counts of perjury, each of which carried a possible five-year sentence, respondent had nothing to do with procuring the indictment.

Respondent made no effort to prove that he suffered actual pecuniary loss as a result of the alleged libel.[3] * * *

* * * The manager of the [Times'] Advertising Acceptability Department testified that he had approved the advertisement for publication because he knew nothing to cause him to believe that anything in it was false, and because it bore the endorsement of "a number of people who are well known and whose reputation" he "had no reason to question." Neither he nor anyone else at the Times made an effort to confirm the accuracy of the advertisement, either by checking it against recent Times news stories relating to some of the described events or by any other means. * * *

Under Alabama law as applied in this case, a publication is "libelous per se" if the words "tend to injure a person . . . in his reputation" or to "bring [him] into public contempt[.]" * * * The jury must find that the words were published "of and concerning" the plaintiff, but where the plaintiff is a public official his place in the governmental hierarchy is sufficient evidence to support a finding that his reputation has been affected by statements that reflect upon the agency of which he is in charge. Once "libel per se" has been established, the defendant has no defense as to stated facts unless he can persuade the jury that they were true in all their particulars. His privilege of "fair comment" for expressions of opinion depends on the truth of the facts upon which the comment is based. Unless he can discharge the burden of proving truth, general damages are presumed, and may be awarded without proof of pecuniary injury. A showing of actual malice is apparently a prerequisite to recovery of punitive damages, and the defendant may in any event forestall a punitive award by a retraction meeting the statutory requirements. Good motives and belief in truth do not negate an inference of malice, but are relevant only in mitigation of punitive damages if the jury chooses to accord them weight.

The question before us is whether this rule of liability, as applied to an action brought by a public official against critics of his official conduct, abridges the freedom of speech and of the press that is guaranteed by the First and Fourteenth Amendments.

Respondent relies heavily, as did the Alabama courts, on statements of this Court to the effect that the Constitution does not protect libelous publications. Those statements do not foreclose our inquiry here. None of the cases sustained the use of libel laws to impose sanctions upon expression critical of the official conduct of public officials. * * * [L]ibel can claim no talismanic immunity from constitutional limitations. It must be measured by standards that satisfy the First Amendment. * * *

---

[3] Approximately 394 copies of the edition of the Times containing the advertisement were circulated in Alabama. Of these, about 35 copies were distributed in Montgomery County. The total circulation of the Times for that day was approximately 650,000 copies.

[W]e consider this case against the background of a profound national commitment to the principle that debate on public issues should be uninhibited, robust, and wide-open, and that it may well include vehement, caustic, and sometimes unpleasantly sharp attacks on government and public officials. The present advertisement, as an expression of grievance and protest on one of the major public issues of our time, would seem clearly to qualify for the constitutional protection. The question is whether it forfeits that protection by the falsity of some of its factual statements and by its alleged defamation of respondent.

Authoritative interpretations of the First Amendment guarantees have consistently refused to recognize an exception for any test of truth — whether administered by judges, juries, or administrative officials — and especially one that puts the burden of proving truth on the speaker. The constitutional protection does not turn upon "the truth, popularity, or social utility of the ideas and beliefs which are offered." As Madison said, "Some degree of abuse is inseparable from the proper use of every thing; and in no instance is this more true than in that of the press." In *Cantwell* v. *Connecticut*, 310 U.S. 296, 310 [(1940)], the Court declared:

> "In the realm of religious faith, and in that of political belief, sharp differences arise. In both fields the tenets of one man may seem the rankest error to his neighbor. To persuade others to his own point of view, the pleader, as we know, at times, resorts to exaggeration, to vilification of men who have been, or are, prominent in church or state, and even to false statement. But the people of this nation have ordained in the light of history, that, in spite of the probability of excesses and abuses, these liberties are, in the long view, essential to enlightened opinion and right conduct on the part of the citizens of a democracy."

[E]rroneous statement is inevitable in free debate, and [] it must be protected if the freedoms of expression are to have the "breathing space" that they "need . . . to survive[.]" * * *

Injury to official reputation error affords no more warrant for repressing speech that would otherwise be free than does factual error. * * * Criticism of [government officials'] official conduct does not lose its constitutional protection merely because it is effective criticism and hence diminishes their official reputations.

If neither factual error nor defamatory content suffices to remove the constitutional shield from criticism of official conduct, the combination of the two elements is no less inadequate. This is the lesson to be drawn from the great controversy over the Sedition Act of 1798, 1 Stat. 596, which first crystallized a national awareness of the central meaning of the First Amendment. That statute made it a crime, punishable by a $5,000 fine and five years in prison, "if any person shall write, print, utter or publish . . . any false, scandalous and malicious writing or writings against the government of the United States, or either house of the Congress . . . , or the President . . . , with intent to defame . . . or to bring them, or either of them, into contempt or disrepute; or to excite against them, or either or any of them, the hatred of the good people of the United States." The Act allowed the defendant the defense of truth, and provided that the jury were to be judges both of the law and the facts. Despite these qualifications, the Act was vigorously condemned as unconstitutional in an attack joined in by Jefferson and Madison. * * *

Although the Sedition Act was never tested in this Court, the attack upon its validity has carried the day in the court of history. * * * [The Court recounted expressions of Members of Congress, President Jefferson, Supreme Court Justices, and commentators to the effect that the Act was unconstitutional.] These views reflect a broad consensus that the Act, because of the restraint it imposed upon criticism of government and public officials, was inconsistent with the First Amendment. * * * What a State may not constitutionally bring about by means of a criminal statute is likewise beyond the reach of its civil law of libel. * * *

The state rule of law is not saved by its allowance of the defense of truth. * * * A rule compelling the critic of official conduct to guarantee the truth of all his factual assertions — and to do so on pain of libel judgments virtually unlimited in amount — leads to a comparable "self-censorship." Allowance of the defense of truth, with the burden of proving it on the defendant, does not mean that only false speech will be deterred.[19] Even courts accepting this defense as an adequate safeguard have recognized the difficulties of adducing legal proofs that the alleged libel was true in all its factual particulars. Under such a rule, would-be critics of official conduct may be deterred from voicing their criticism, even though it is believed to be true and even though it is in fact true, because of doubt whether it can be proved in court or fear of the expense of having to do so. They tend to make only statements which "steer far wider of the unlawful zone." The rule thus dampens the vigor and limits the variety of public debate. It is inconsistent with the First and Fourteenth Amendments.

The constitutional guarantees require, we think, a federal rule that prohibits a public official from recovering damages for a defamatory falsehood relating to his official conduct unless he proves that the statement was made with "actual malice" — that is, with knowledge that it was false or with reckless disregard of whether it was false or not. * * * We hold today that the Constitution delimits a State's power to award damages for libel in actions brought by public officials against critics of their official conduct. Since this is such an action,[23] the rule requiring proof of actual malice is applicable. While Alabama law apparently requires proof of actual malice for an award of punitive damages, where general damages are concerned malice is "presumed." Such a presumption is inconsistent with the federal rule. * * *

Since respondent may seek a new trial, we deem that considerations of effective judicial administration require us to review the evidence in the present record to determine whether it could constitutionally support a judgment for respondent. * * * [W]e consider that the proof presented to show actual malice lacks the convincing clarity which the constitutional standard demands, and hence that it

---

[19] Even a false statement may be deemed to make a valuable contribution to public debate, since it brings about "the clearer perception and livelier impression of truth, produced by its collision with error." Mill, On Liberty (Oxford: Blackwell, 1947), at 15; see also Milton, Areopagitica, in Prose Works (Yale, 1959), Vol. II, at 561.

[23] We have no occasion here to determine how far down into the lower ranks of government employees the "public official" designation would extend for purposes of this rule, or otherwise to specify categories of persons who would or would not be included. Nor need we here determine the boundaries of the "official conduct" concept. It is enough for the present case that respondent's position as an elected city commissioner clearly made him a public official, and that the allegations in the advertisement concerned what was allegedly his official conduct as Commissioner in charge of the Police Department. * * *

would not constitutionally sustain the judgment for respondent under the proper rule of law. The case of the individual petitioners requires little discussion. Even assuming that they could constitutionally be found to have authorized the use of their names on the advertisement, there was no evidence whatever that they were aware of any erroneous statements or were in any way reckless in that regard. The judgment against them is thus without constitutional support.

As to the Times, we similarly conclude that the facts do not support a finding of actual malice. * * * We think the evidence against the Times supports at most a finding of negligence in failing to discover the misstatements, and is constitutionally insufficient to show the recklessness that is required for a finding of actual malice.

We also think the evidence was constitutionally defective in another respect: it was incapable of supporting the jury's finding that the allegedly libelous statements were made "of and concerning" respondent. * * *

There was no reference to respondent in the advertisement, either by name or official position. * * * The statements upon which respondent principally relies as referring to him are the two allegations that did concern the police or police functions: that "truckloads of police . . . ringed the Alabama State College Campus" after the demonstration on the State Capitol steps, and that Dr. King had been "arrested . . . seven times." * * * Although the statements may be taken as referring to the police, they did not on their face make even an oblique reference to respondent as an individual. Support for the asserted reference must, therefore, be sought in the testimony of respondent's witnesses. But none of them suggested any basis for the belief that respondent himself was attacked in the advertisement beyond the bare fact that he was in overall charge of the Police Department and thus bore official responsibility for police conduct[.] * * * [T]he evidence was constitutionally insufficient to support a finding that the statements referred to respondent. * * *

Reversed and remanded.

MR. JUSTICE BLACK, with whom MR. JUSTICE DOUGLAS joins, concurring [in the judgment].

[T]he Court holds that "the Constitution delimits a State's power to award damages for libel in actions brought by public officials against critics of their official conduct." I base my vote to reverse on the belief that the First and Fourteenth Amendments not merely "delimit" a State's power to award damages to "public officials against critics of their official conduct" but completely prohibit a State from exercising such a power. The Court goes on to hold that a State can subject such critics to damages if "actual malice" can be proved against them. "Malice," even as defined by the Court, is an elusive, abstract concept, hard to prove and hard to disprove. The requirement that malice be proved provides at best an evanescent protection for the right critically to discuss public affairs and certainly does not measure up to the sturdy safeguard embodied in the First Amendment. Unlike the Court, therefore, I vote to reverse exclusively on the ground that the Times and the individual defendants had an absolute, unconditional constitutional right to publish in the Times advertisement their criticisms of the Montgomery agencies and officials. * * *

[S]tate libel laws threaten the very existence of an American press virile enough to publish unpopular views on public affairs and bold enough to criticize the conduct of public officials. * * * In my opinion the Federal Constitution has dealt with this deadly danger to the press in the only way possible without leaving the free press open to destruction — by granting the press an absolute immunity for criticism of the way public officials do their public duty. Stopgap measures like those the Court adopts are in my judgment not enough. * * *

* * * This Nation, I suspect, can live in peace without libel suits based on public discussions of public affairs and public officials. But I doubt that a country can live in freedom where its people can be made to suffer physically or financially for criticizing their government, its actions, or its officials. * * * An unconditional right to say what one pleases about public affairs is what I consider to be the minimum guarantee of the First Amendment.

I regret that the Court has stopped short of this holding indispensable to preserve our free press from destruction.

MR. JUSTICE GOLDBERG, with whom MR. JUSTICE DOUGLAS joins, concurring in the result. * * *

In my view, the First and Fourteenth Amendments to the Constitution afford to the citizen and to the press an absolute, unconditional privilege to criticize official conduct despite the harm which may flow from excesses and abuses. The prized American right "to speak one's mind" about public officials and affairs needs "breathing space to survive." The right should not depend upon a probing by the jury of the motivation of the citizen or press. The theory of our Constitution is that every citizen may speak his mind and every newspaper express its view on matters of public concern and may not be barred from speaking or publishing because those in control of government think that what is said or written is unwise, unfair, false, or malicious. In a democratic society, one who assumes to act for the citizens in an executive, legislative, or judicial capacity must expect that his official acts will be commented upon and criticized. Such criticism cannot, in my opinion, be muzzled or deterred by the courts at the instance of public officials under the label of libel. * * *

* * * It may be urged that deliberately and maliciously false statements have no conceivable value as free speech. That argument, however, is not responsive to the real issue presented by this case, which is whether that freedom of speech which all agree is constitutionally protected can be effectively safeguarded by a rule allowing the imposition of liability upon a jury's evaluation of the speaker's state of mind. If individual citizens may be held liable in damages for strong words, which a jury finds false and maliciously motivated, there can be little doubt that public debate and advocacy will be constrained. And if newspapers, publishing advertisements dealing with public issues, thereby risk liability, there can also be little doubt that the ability of minority groups to secure publication of their views on public affairs and to seek support for their causes will be greatly diminished. * * *

This is not to say that the Constitution protects defamatory statements directed against the private conduct of a public official or private citizen. Freedom of press and of speech insures that government will respond to the will of the people and that changes may be obtained by peaceful means. Purely private defamation has little to do with the political ends of a self-governing society. The imposition of liability for private defamation does not abridge the freedom of public speech or any other freedom protected by the First Amendment. * * *

Notes and Questions

1. Do you agree with the Court that chilled speech represents a greater harm than do the false statements protected by the actual-malice standard? In the context of an electoral campaign, what harm can predictably result from *New York Times*? Consider *Dun & Bradstreet, Inc. v. Greenmoss Builders*, 472 U.S. 749, 767–69 (1985) (White, J., concurring in the judgment):

> I joined the judgment and opinion in *New York Times* [v. *Sullivan*]. I also joined later decisions extending the *New York Times* standard to other situations. But I came to have increasing doubts about the soundness of the Court's approach and about some of the assumptions underlying it. * * * I have * * * become convinced that the Court struck an improvident balance in the *New York Times* case between the public's interest in being fully informed about public officials and public affairs and the competing interest of those who have been defamed in vindicating their reputation.
>
> In a country like ours, where the people purport to be able to govern themselves through their elected representatives, adequate information about their government is of transcendent importance. That flow of intelligence deserves full First Amendment protection. Criticism and assessment of the performance of public officials and of government in general are not subject to penalties imposed by law. But these First Amendment values are not at all served by circulating false statements of fact about public officials. On the contrary, erroneous information frustrates these values. They are even more disserved when the statements falsely impugn the honesty of those men and women and hence lessen the confidence in government. As the Court said in *Gertz* [v. *Robert Welch, Inc*, 418 U.S. 323, 340 (1974)]: "[T]here is no constitutional value in false statements of fact. Neither the intentional lie nor the careless error materially advances society's interest in 'uninhibited, robust, and wide-open' debate on public issues." Yet in *New York Times* cases, the public official's complaint will be dismissed unless he alleges and makes out a jury case of a knowing or reckless falsehood. Absent such proof, there will be no jury verdict or judgment of any kind in his favor, even if the challenged publication is admittedly false. The lie will stand, and the public continue to be misinformed about public matters. * * *[2] [The public's] only chance of

---

[2] * * * It might be suggested that courts, as organs of the government, cannot be trusted to discern what the truth is. But the logical consequence of that view is that the First Amendment forbids all libel and slander suits, for in each such suit, there will be no recovery unless the court finds the publication at issue to be factually false. Of course, no forum is perfect, but that is not a justification for leaving whole

being accurately informed is measured by the public official's ability himself to counter the lie, unaided by the courts. That is a decidedly weak reed to depend on for the vindication of First Amendment interests — "it is the rare case where the denial overtakes the original charge. Denials, retractions, and corrections are not 'hot' news, and rarely receive the prominence of the original story."

Also, by leaving the lie uncorrected, the *New York Times* rule plainly leaves the public official without a remedy for the damage to his reputation. * * * The upshot is that the public official must suffer the injury, often cannot get a judgment identifying the lie for what it is, and has very little, if any, chance of countering that lie in the public press.

The *New York Times* rule thus countenances two evils: first, the stream of information about public officials and public affairs is polluted and often remains polluted by false information; and second, the reputation and professional life of the defeated plaintiff may be destroyed by falsehoods that might have been avoided with a reasonable effort to investigate the facts. In terms of the First Amendment and reputational interests at stake, these seem grossly perverse results.

2.   Should false statements be protected only to encourage the dissemination of truth, or is there value in the false statements themselves?

3.   The Court expounded on the privilege created by *New York Times* in *Garrison v. Louisiana*, 379 U.S. 64 (1964), and *Monitor Patriot Co. v. Roy*, 401 U.S. 265 (1971). *Garrison* held that criticism of a judge was protected even if the criticism reflected on the office holder's private character. *Roy* made explicit that the *New York Times* standard applied to candidates for public office as well as officeholders.

St. Amant v. Thompson, 390 U.S. 727 (1968), clarified the meaning of "actual malice" — in particular its focus on "reckless disregard" of a statement's falsity:

[R]eckless conduct is not measured by whether a reasonably prudent man would have published, or would have investigated before publishing. There must be sufficient evidence to permit the conclusion that the defendant in fact entertained serious doubts as to the truth of his publication. Publishing with such doubts shows reckless disregard for truth or falsity and demonstrates actual malice.

It may be said that such a test puts a premium on ignorance, encourages the irresponsible publisher not to inquire, and permits the issue to be determined by the defendant's testimony that he published the statement in good faith and unaware of its probable falsity. Concededly the reckless disregard standard may permit recovery in fewer situations than would a

---

classes of defamed individuals without redress or a realistic opportunity to clear their names. We entrust to juries and the courts the responsibility of decisions affecting the life and liberty of persons. It is perverse indeed to say that these bodies are incompetent to inquire into the truth of a statement of fact in a defamation case. I can therefore discern nothing in the Constitution which forbids a plaintiff to obtain a judicial decree that a statement is false — a decree he can then use in the community to clear his name and to prevent further damage from a defamation already published.

rule that publishers must satisfy the standard of the reasonable man or the prudent publisher. But *New York Times* and succeeding cases have emphasized that the stake of the people in public business and the conduct of public officials is so great that neither the defense of truth nor the standard of ordinary care would protect against self-censorship and thus adequately implement First Amendment policies. Neither lies nor false communications serve the ends of the First Amendment, and no one suggests their desirability or further proliferation. But to insure the ascertainment and publication of the truth about public affairs, it is essential that the First Amendment protect some erroneous publications as well as true ones. We adhere to this view and to the line which our cases have drawn between false communications which are protected and those which are not.

The defendant in a defamation action brought by a public official cannot, however, automatically insure a favorable verdict by testifying that he published with a belief that the statements were true. The finder of fact must determine whether the publication was indeed made in good faith. Professions of good faith will be unlikely to prove persuasive, for example, where a story is fabricated by the defendant, is the product of his imagination, or is based wholly on an unverified anonymous telephone call. Nor will they be likely to prevail when the publisher's allegations are so inherently improbable that only a reckless man would have put them in circulation. Likewise, recklessness may be found where there are obvious reasons to doubt the veracity of the informant or the accuracy of his reports.

Id. at 731–32. Do you agree that an objective negligence standard regarding falsity would undermine "First Amendment policies"? Should there be an obligation to investigate the truth of statements, at least where a reasonable person would have doubt? One state supreme court recently held that a plaintiff's defamation action, based on political advertising, failed because of lack of evidence of actual malice. *Bertrand v. Mullin*, 846 N.W.2d 884 (Iowa), *cert. denied*, 135 S. Ct. 373 (2014).

4.   Proclaiming that campaigning for public office is "not for the thin-skinned or the faint-hearted, to use two apropos clichés," the court in *Schatz v. Republican State Leadership Committee*, 669 F.3d 50 (1st Cir. 2012), held that an unsuccessful candidate who filed a defamation action against the opposing political party, based on allegedly false statements in political ads, failed to allege actual malice by the defendants. The ads accused Schatz, a town selectman, of voting to give $10,000 of taxpayers' money to a "political organization." The charge was true, but left out details — such as the fact that voters had authorized the expenditure, which was for the purpose of countering a school-consolidation measure — that would have made the expenditure appear less sinister. Similarly, the ads accused Schatz of voting to cancel an Independence Day fireworks display. The selectmen did in fact cancel the display, but Schatz voted the other way — a fact not disclosed in the newspaper report on which the ad was based. The court conceded that the complaint "used actual malice buzzwords," *id.* at 56, but failed adequately to allege facts to back up those legal conclusions. *See id.* at 57–58. Given the rigor with which cases like *Schatz*

apply the actual-malice standard, how likely is this sort of defamation claim to succeed?

BROWN v. HARTLAGE
Supreme Court of the United States
456 U.S. 45, 102 S. Ct. 1523, 71 L. Ed. 2d 732 (1982)

JUSTICE BRENNAN delivered the opinion of the Court [in which JUSTICE WHITE, JUSTICE MARSHALL, JUSTICE BLACKMUN, JUSTICE POWELL, JUSTICE STEVENS, and JUSTICE O'CONNOR join]. * * *

I

This case involves a challenge to an application of the Kentucky Corrupt Practices Act. The parties were opposing candidates in the 1979 general election for the office of Jefferson County Commissioner, "C" District. Petitioner, Carl Brown, was the challenger; respondent, Earl Hartlage, was the incumbent. On August 15, 1979, in the course of the campaign, Brown held a televised press conference together with Bill Creech, the "B" District candidate on the same party ticket. * * *

On behalf of himself and his running mate, Creech pledged the taxpayers some relief:

> "We abhor the commissioners' outrageous salaries. And to prove the strength of our convictions, one of our first official acts as county commissioners will be to lower our salary to a more realistic level. We will lower our salaries, saving the taxpayers $36,000 during our first term of office, by $3,000 each year."

[Brown himself reiterated the pledge.]

Shortly after the press conference, Brown and Creech learned that their commitment to lower their salaries arguably violated the Kentucky Corrupt Practices Act. On August 19, 1979, they issued a joint statement retracting their earlier pledge:

> "We are men enough to admit when we've made a mistake.

> "We have discovered that there are Kentucky court decisions and Attorney General opinions which indicate that our pledge to reduce our salaries if elected may be illegal. . . .

> ". . . [We] do hereby formally rescind our pledge to reduce the County Commissioner's salary if elected and instead pledge to seek corrective legislation in the next session of the General Assembly, to correct this silly provision of State Law."

In the November 6, 1979, election, Brown defeated Hartlage by 10,151 votes. Creech was defeated.

Hartlage then filed this action * * *, alleging that Brown had violated the Corrupt Practices Act and seeking to have the election declared void and the office of Jefferson County Commissioner, "C" District, vacated by Brown. [Ky. Rev. Stat.

§ 121.055], upon which Hartlage based his claim, provides:

> "Candidates prohibited from making expenditure, loan, promise, agreement, or contract as to action when elected, in consideration for vote. — No candidate for nomination or election to any state, county, city or district office shall * * * promise, agree or make a contract with any person to vote for or support any particular individual, thing or measure, in consideration for the vote or the financial or moral support of that person in any election, primary or nominating convention, and no person shall require that any candidate make such a promise, agreement or contract."

[The Kentucky Court of Appeals held that Brown violated the Corrupt Practices Act, and, imposing the statutorily prescribed remedy, ordered a new election.]

II

We begin our analysis of § 121.055 by acknowledging that the States have a legitimate interest in preserving the integrity of their electoral processes. Just as a State may take steps to ensure that its governing political institutions and officials properly discharge public responsibilities and maintain public trust and confidence, a State has a legitimate interest in upholding the integrity of the electoral process itself. But when a State seeks to uphold that interest by restricting speech, the limitations on state authority imposed by the First Amendment are manifestly implicated. * * *

The free exchange of ideas provides special vitality to the process traditionally at the heart of American constitutional democracy — the political campaign. "[If] it be conceded that the First Amendment was 'fashioned to assure the unfettered interchange of ideas for the bringing about of political and social changes desired by the people,' then it can hardly be doubted that the constitutional guarantee has its fullest and most urgent application precisely to the conduct of campaigns for political office." *Monitor Patriot Co.* v. *Roy*, 401 U.S. 265, 271–272 (1971). The political candidate does not lose the protection of the First Amendment when he declares himself for public office. Quite to the contrary:

> "The candidate, no less than any other person, has a First Amendment right to engage in the discussion of public issues and vigorously and tirelessly to advocate his own election and the election of other candidates. Indeed, it is of particular importance that candidates have the unfettered opportunity to make their views known so that the electorate may intelligently evaluate the candidates' personal qualities and their positions on vital public issues before choosing among them on election day. * * *"
> *Buckley* v. *Valeo* 424 U.S. 1, 52–53 (1976) *(per curiam)*.

When a State seeks to restrict directly the offer of ideas by a candidate to the voters, the First Amendment surely requires that the restriction be demonstrably supported by not only a legitimate state interest, but a compelling one, and that the restriction operate without unnecessarily circumscribing protected expression.

III

* * * We discern three bases upon which the application of the statute to Brown's promise might conceivably be justified: first, as a prohibition on buying votes; second, as facilitating the candidacy of persons lacking independent wealth; and third, as an application of the State's interests and prerogatives with respect to factual misstatements. We consider these possible justifications in turn.

A

* * * No body politic worthy of being called a democracy entrusts the selection of leaders to a process of auction or barter. And as a State may prohibit the giving of money or other things of value to a voter in exchange for his support, it may also declare unlawful an agreement embodying the intention to make such an exchange. Although agreements to engage in illegal conduct undoubtedly possess some element of association, the State may ban such illegal agreements without trenching on any right of association protected by the First Amendment. The fact that such an agreement necessarily takes the form of words does not confer upon it, or upon the underlying conduct, the constitutional immunities that the First Amendment extends to speech. * * *

It is thus plain that *some* kinds of promises made by a candidate to voters, and *some* kinds of promises elicited by voters from candidates, may be declared illegal without constitutional difficulty. But it is equally plain that there are constitutional limits on the State's power to prohibit candidates from making promises in the course of an election campaign. Some promises are universally acknowledged as legitimate, indeed "indispensable to decisionmaking in a democracy"; and the "maintenance of the opportunity for free political discussion to the end that government may be responsive to the will of the people and that changes may be obtained by lawful means . . . is a fundamental principle of our constitutional system." Candidate commitments enhance the accountability of government officials to the people whom they represent, and assist the voters in predicting the effect of their vote. The fact that some voters may find their self-interest reflected in a candidate's commitment does not place that commitment beyond the reach of the First Amendment. We have never insisted that the franchise be exercised without taint of individual benefit; indeed, our tradition of political pluralism is partly predicated on the expectation that voters will pursue their individual good through the political process, and that the summation of these individual pursuits will further the collective welfare.[7] So long as the hoped-for personal benefit is to be achieved through the normal processes of government, and not through some private arrangement, it has always been, and remains, a reputable basis upon which to cast one's ballot.

It remains to determine the standards by which we might distinguish between those "private arrangements" that are inconsistent with democratic government, and those candidate assurances that promote the representative foundation of our political system. We hesitate before attempting to formulate some test of constitu-

---

[7] See The Federalist No. 10. * * *

tional legitimacy: the precise nature of the promise, the conditions upon which it is given, the circumstances under which it is made, the size of the audience, the nature and size of the group to be benefited, all might, in some instance and to varying extents, bear upon the constitutional assessment. But acknowledging the difficulty of rendering a concise formulation, or recognizing the possibility of borderline cases, does not disable us from identifying cases far from any troublesome border.

It is clear that the statements of petitioner Brown in the course of the August 15 press conference were very different in character from the corrupting agreements and solicitations historically recognized as unprotected by the First Amendment. Notably, Brown's commitment to serve at a reduced salary was made openly, subject to the comment and criticism of his political opponent and to the scrutiny of the voters. We think the fact that the statement was made in full view of the electorate offers a strong indication that the statement contained nothing fundamentally at odds with our shared political ethic.

The Kentucky Court of Appeals analogized Brown's promise to a bribe. But however persuasive that analogy might be as a matter of state law, there is no *constitutional* basis upon which Brown's pledge to reduce his salary might be equated with a candidate's promise to pay voters for their support from his own pocketbook. * * * [D]espite the Kentucky courts' characterization of the promise to serve at a reduced salary as an offer "to reduce pro tanto the amount of taxes each individual taxpayer must pay, and thus . . . an offer to the voter of pecuniary gain," it is impossible to discern in Brown's generalized commitment any invitation to enter into an agreement that might place the statement outside the realm of unequivocal protection that the Constitution affords to political speech. Not only was the source of the promised benefit the public fisc, but that benefit was to extend beyond those voters who cast their ballots for Brown, to all taxpayers and citizens. Even if Brown's commitment could in some sense have been deemed an "offer," it scarcely contemplated a particularized acceptance or a *quid pro quo* arrangement. It was to be honored, "if elected"; it was conditioned not on any particular vote or votes, but entirely on the *majority's* vote.

In sum, Brown did not offer some private payment or donation in exchange for voter support; Brown's statement can only be construed as an expression of his intention to exercise public power in a manner that he believed might be acceptable to some class of citizens. If Brown's expressed intention had an individualized appeal to some taxpayers who felt themselves the likely beneficiaries of his form of fiscal restraint, that fact is of little constitutional significance. The benefits of most public policy changes accrue not only to the undifferentiated "public," but more directly to particular individuals or groups. Like a promise to lower taxes, to increase efficiency in government, or indeed to increase taxes in order to provide some group with a desired public benefit or public service, Brown's promise to reduce his salary cannot be deemed beyond the reach of the First Amendment, or considered as inviting the kind of corrupt arrangement the appearance of which a State may have a compelling interest in avoiding.

A State may insist that candidates seeking the approval of the electorate work within the framework of our democratic institutions, and base their appeal on assertions of fitness for office and statements respecting the means by which they intend to further the public welfare. But a candidate's promise to confer some ultimate benefit on the voter, *qua* taxpayer, citizen, or member of the general public, does not lie beyond the pale of First Amendment protection.

B

* * * The State might legitimately fear that [an] emphasis on free public service might result in persons of independent wealth but less ability being chosen over those who, though better qualified, could not afford to serve at a reduced salary.[8] But if § 121.055 was designed to further this interest, it chooses a means unacceptable under the First Amendment.[9] In barring certain public statements with respect to this issue, the State ban runs directly contrary to the fundamental premises underlying the First Amendment as the guardian of our democracy. That Amendment embodies our trust in the free exchange of ideas as the means by which the people are to choose between good ideas and bad, and between candidates for political office. The State's fear that voters might make an ill-advised choice does not provide the State with a compelling justification for limiting speech. It is simply not the function of government to "select which issues are worth discussing or debating" in the course of a political campaign.

C

[Section] 121.055 * * * bars promises to serve at a reduced salary only when the salary of the official has been "fixed by law," and where the promise cannot, therefore, be delivered. Of course, demonstrable falsehoods are not protected by the First Amendment in the same manner as truthful statements. But "erroneous statement is inevitable in free debate, and . . . it must be protected if the freedoms of expression are to have the 'breathing space' that they 'need . . . to survive,' " *New York Times Co.* v. *Sullivan*, 376 U.S. 254, 271–272 (1964) [p. 574], quoting *NAACP* v. *Button*, 371 U.S. 415, 433 (1963). Section 121.055, as applied in this case, has not afforded the requisite "breathing space."

The Commonwealth of Kentucky has provided that a candidate for public office forfeits his electoral victory if he errs in announcing that he will, if elected, serve at a reduced salary. As the Kentucky courts have made clear in this case, a candidate's liability under § 121.055 for such an error is absolute: His election victory must be

---

[8] [The Kentucky Court of Appeals feared that allowing candidates to promise to serve without remuneration]

"* * * would permit the various elective public offices to become filled by those who would purchase their election thereto by making the most extravagant bid. The auction method of choosing a public officer would supplant the personal fitness test. Eventually most of the public offices would be occupied by the opulent, who could afford to serve without pay, or by the ambitious, who would serve only for the pittance of honor attached to the office, or by the designing grafter, who would surely obtain his remuneration by methods which would not bear scrutiny. Under such a system good government would certainly vanish from every subdivision of the state." * * *

[Relocated. — Eds.]

[9] A State could address this concern by prohibiting the reduction of a public official's salary during his term of office, as Kentucky has done here. * * *

voided even if the offending statement was made in good faith and was quickly repudiated. The chilling effect of such absolute accountability for factual misstatements in the course of political debate is incompatible with the atmosphere of free discussion contemplated by the First Amendment in the context of political campaigns. Although the state interest in protecting the political process from distortions caused by untrue and inaccurate speech is somewhat different from the state interest in protecting individuals from defamatory falsehoods, the principles underlying the First Amendment remain paramount. Whenever compatible with the underlying interests at stake, under the regime of that Amendment "we depend for . . . correction not on the conscience of judges and juries but on the competition of other ideas." In a political campaign, a candidate's factual blunder is unlikely to escape the notice of, and correction by, the erring candidate's political opponent. The preferred First Amendment remedy of "more speech, not enforced silence," thus has special force. There has been no showing in this case that petitioner made the disputed statement other than in good faith and without knowledge of its falsity, or that he made the statement with reckless disregard as to whether it was false or not. Moreover, petitioner retracted the statement promptly after discovering that it might have been false. Under these circumstances, nullifying petitioner's election victory was inconsistent with the atmosphere of robust political debate protected by the First Amendment.

[Reversed and remanded.]

THE CHIEF JUSTICE [BURGER] concurs in the judgment [without opinion].

JUSTICE REHNQUIST, concurring in the result.

I agree that the provision of the Kentucky Corrupt Practices Act discussed by the Court in its opinion impermissibly limits freedom of speech on the part of political candidates in violation of the First and Fourteenth Amendments to the United States Constitution. Because on different facts I think I would give more weight to the State's interest in preventing corruption in elections, I am unable to join the Court's analogy between such laws and state defamation laws. * * *

Notes and Questions

1. *Problem.* Hawaii establishes a "Code of Fair Campaign Practices" establishing rules for conducting campaigns. Among the rules are that candidates "shall not use campaign material relating to any candidate's election which misrepresents, distorts, or otherwise falsifies the facts regarding the candidate," and that candidates "shall refrain from the use of personal vilification, character defamation, or any other form of scurrilous personal attacks on any candidate or his family." Candidates need not sign the Code, but a list of candidates endorsing the Code and a list of candidates refusing to endorse the Code are made public at a website maintained by the state's Campaign Spending Commission. Candidates who sign the Code and then breach it are subject to censure.

A candidate challenging the incumbent state senator signs the pledge and, during the campaign, distributes a flyer containing a cartoon depicting his opponent in a pocket labeled "Special Interests." The flyer also alleges that the incumbent's law firm had received one million dollars from one particular interest, and cited a newspaper story. The Commission censures the candidate, reasoning that he had no facts upon which to allege that the incumbent's position in the senate resulted in any gain for the incumbent or his firm. Is the censure constitutional? If the statement is protected under *New York Times* and *Brown v. Hartlage*, may the candidate waive that First Amendment protection by signing the Code? Would the result change if the state did not publicize the names of the non-signatories by maintaining the website? *See Ancheta v. Watada*, 135 F. Supp. 2d 1114 (D. Haw. 2001).

2. *Problem.* Roy Cooper, candidate for North Carolina Attorney General, sponsors a television advertisement, in which he criticizes his opponent, Dan Boyce. The audio portion of the advertisement is as follows:

> Dan Boyce — his law firm sued the state, charging $28,000 an hour in lawyer fees to the taxpayers. The Judge said it shocks the conscience. Dan Boyce's law firm wanted more than a police officer's salary for each hour's work. Dan Boyce, wrong for Attorney General.

In reality, the law firm carrying Boyce's name, Boyce & Isley, did not come into existence until after the institution of the suit, so the advertisement was arguably deceptive and defamatory in that it alleged that Boyce's law firm "sued the state." Further, the attorneys' fee was requested — not "charged" — by Boyce and was a contingency fee for successfully prosecuting a $150 million class-action suit.

Boyce, his partners, and the firm sued Cooper for defamation. Does the First Amendment permit the plaintiffs to recover? *See Boyce & Isley, PLLC v. Cooper*, 568 S.E.2d 893 (N.C. Ct. App. 2002).

3. *Problem.* A candidate running in the 2006 Republican primary publicizes some complimentary remarks other public officials made about him in 2004. In the campaign advertisement, the candidate reprints the text of the remarks accurately, and also notes in small print that they were made in 2004. Nevertheless, he is fined by a state agency charged with administering a law barring the use of endorsements without the approval of the endorsing party. Here, because the candidate never received permission from the public officials who made the statements, he violated the statute. Is the statute constitutional as applied to him? Would the statute be constitutional as applied to a candidate who accurately reprinted the text of the remarks, but nowhere indicated the date the remarks were made? Would the statute be constitutional as applied to a candidate who materially misrepresented the remarks that were made? The next case may prove useful in answering the last question.

UNITED STATES v. ALVAREZ
Supreme Court of the United States
567 U.S. —, 132 S. Ct. 2537, 183 L. Ed. 2d 574 (2012)

JUSTICE KENNEDY announced the judgment of the Court and delivered an opinion, in which THE CHIEF JUSTICE [ROBERTS], JUSTICE GINSBURG, and JUSTICE SOTOMAYOR join.

Lying was his habit. Xavier Alvarez, the respondent here, lied when he said that he played hockey for the Detroit Red Wings and that he once married a starlet from Mexico. But when he lied in announcing he held the Congressional Medal of Honor, respondent ventured onto new ground; for that lie violates a federal criminal statute, the Stolen Valor Act of 2005. 18 U.S.C. § 704. [Under the Act, anyone who "falsely represents himself or herself, verbally or in writing, to have been awarded any decoration or medal authorized by Congress for the Armed Forces of the United States" may be punished by a fine, six months' imprisonment, or both. Violators who claim to have won the Congressional Medal of Honor are subject to a heightened penalty — a fine, one year's imprisonment, or both.]

In 2007, respondent attended his first public meeting as a board member of the Three Valley Water District Board. The board is a governmental entity with headquarters in Claremont, California. He introduced himself as follows: "I'm a retired marine of 25 years. I retired in the year 2001. Back in 1987, I was awarded the Congressional Medal of Honor. I got wounded many times by the same guy." None of this was true. For all the record shows, respondent's statements were but a pathetic attempt to gain respect that eluded him. The statements do not seem to have been made to secure employment or financial benefits or admission to privileges reserved for those who had earned the Medal.

Respondent was indicted under the Stolen Valor Act for lying about the Congressional Medal of Honor at the meeting. The United States District Court for the Central District of California rejected his claim that the statute is invalid under the First Amendment. Respondent pleaded guilty to one count, reserving the right to appeal on his First Amendment claim. The United States Court of Appeals for the Ninth Circuit, in a decision by a divided panel, found the Act invalid under the First Amendment and reversed the conviction. * * *

* * * [C]ontent-based restrictions on speech have been permitted, as a general matter, only when confined to the few "historic and traditional categories [of expression] long familiar to the bar." Among these categories are advocacy intended, and likely, to incite imminent lawless action; obscenity; defamation; speech integral to criminal conduct; so-called "fighting words"; child pornography; fraud; true threats; and speech presenting some grave and imminent threat the government has the power to prevent, although a restriction under the last category is most difficult to sustain. These categories have a historical foundation in the Court's free speech tradition. The vast realm of free speech and thought always protected in our tradition can still thrive, and even be furthered, by adherence to those categories and rules.

Absent from those few categories where the law allows content-based regulation of speech is any general exception to the First Amendment for false statements.

This comports with the common understanding that some false statements are inevitable if there is to be an open and vigorous expression of views in public and private conversation, expression the First Amendment seeks to guarantee.

The Government disagrees with this proposition. It cites language from some of this Court's precedents to support its contention that false statements have no value and hence no First Amendment protection. * * * These quotations all derive from cases discussing defamation, fraud, or some other legally cognizable harm associated with a false statement, such as an invasion of privacy or the costs of vexatious litigation. In those decisions the falsity of the speech at issue was not irrelevant to our analysis, but neither was it determinative. The Court has never endorsed the categorical rule the Government advances: that false statements receive no First Amendment protection. Our prior decisions have not confronted a measure, like the Stolen Valor Act, that targets falsity and nothing more.

Even when considering some instances of defamation and fraud, moreover, the Court has been careful to instruct that falsity alone may not suffice to bring the speech outside the First Amendment. The statement must be a knowing or reckless falsehood. The Government thus seeks * * * to convert a rule that limits liability even in defamation cases where the law permits recovery for tortious wrongs into a rule that expands liability in a different, far greater realm of discourse and expression. That inverts the rationale for the exception. The requirements [sic] of a knowing falsehood or reckless disregard for the truth as the condition for recovery in certain defamation cases exists to allow more speech, not less. A rule designed to tolerate certain speech ought not blossom to become a rationale for a rule restricting it. * * *

The probable, and adverse, effect of the Act on freedom of expression illustrates, in a fundamental way, the reasons for the Law's distrust of content-based speech prohibitions.

The Act by its plain terms applies to a false statement made at any time, in any place, to any person. * * * Here the lie was made in a public meeting, but the statute would apply with equal force to personal, whispered conversations within a home. The statute seeks to control and suppress all false statements on this one subject in almost limitless times and settings. And it does so entirely without regard to whether the lie was made for the purpose of material gain.

Permitting the government to decree this speech to be a criminal offense, whether shouted from the rooftops or made in a barely audible whisper, would endorse government authority to compile a list of subjects about which false statements are punishable. That governmental power has no clear limiting principle. * * * Were this law to be sustained, there could be an endless list of subjects the National Government or the States could single out. Where false claims are made to effect a fraud or secure moneys or other valuable considerations, say offers of employment, it is well established that the Government may restrict speech without affronting the First Amendment. But the Stolen Valor Act is not so limited in its reach. Were the Court to hold that the interest in truthful discourse alone is sufficient to sustain a ban on speech, absent any evidence that the speech was used to gain a material advantage, it would give government a broad censorial power unprecedented in this Court's cases or in our constitutional tradition. The mere potential for the exercise of that power casts a chill, a chill the First Amendment cannot permit if free speech, thought, and discourse are to remain a foundation of our freedom. * * *

* * * The Government's interest in protecting the integrity of the Medal of Honor is beyond question. But to recite the Government's compelling interests is not to end the matter. The First Amendment requires that the Government's chosen restriction on the speech at issue be "actually necessary" to achieve its interest. There must be a direct causal link between the restriction imposed and the injury to be prevented. * * * The Government points to no evidence to support its claim that the public's general perception of military awards is diluted by false claims such as those made by Alvarez. * * *

[Further, t]he Government has not shown, and cannot show, why counterspeech would not suffice to achieve its interest. The facts of this case indicate that the dynamics of free speech, of counterspeech, of refutation, can overcome the lie. Respondent lied at a public meeting. Even before the FBI began investigating him for his false statements "Alvarez was perceived as a phony." Once the lie was made public, he was ridiculed online, his actions were reported in the press, and a fellow board member called for his resignation. There is good reason to believe that a similar fate would befall other false claimants. See Brief for Reporters Committee for Freedom of the Press et al. as *Amici Curiae* 30–33 (listing numerous examples of public exposure of false claimants). Indeed, the outrage and contempt expressed for respondent's lies can serve to reawaken and reinforce the public's respect for the Medal, its recipients, and its high purpose. The acclaim that recipients of the Congressional Medal of Honor receive also casts doubt on the proposition that the public will be misled by the claims of charlatans or become cynical of those whose heroic deeds earned them the Medal by right.

The remedy for speech that is false is speech that is true. This is the ordinary course in a free society. The response to the unreasoned is the rational; to the uninformed, the enlightened; to the straight-out lie, the simple truth. * * * The First Amendment itself ensures the right to respond to speech we do not like, and for good reason. Freedom of speech and thought flows not from the beneficence of the state but from the inalienable rights of the person. And suppression of speech by the government can make exposure of falsity more difficult, not less so. Society has the right and civic duty to engage in open, dynamic, rational discourse. These ends are not well served when the government seeks to orchestrate public discussion through content-based mandates. * * *

It is a fair assumption that any true holders of the Medal who had heard of Alvarez's false claims would have been fully vindicated by the community's expression of outrage, showing as it did the Nation's high regard for the Medal. The same can be said for the Government's interest. The American people do not need the assistance of a government prosecution to express their high regard for the special place that military heroes hold in our tradition. Only a weak society needs government protection or intervention before it pursues its resolve to preserve the truth. Truth needs neither handcuffs nor a badge for its vindication.

In addition, when the Government seeks to regulate protected speech, the restriction must be the "least restrictive means among available, effective alternatives." There is, however, at least one less speech-restrictive means by which the Government could likely protect the integrity of the military awards system. A Government-created database could list Congressional Medal of Honor winners. Were a database accessible through the Internet, it would be easy to verify and expose false claims. * * *

The judgment of the Court of Appeals is affirmed.

It is so ordered.

JUSTICE BREYER, with whom JUSTICE KAGAN joins, concurring in the judgment.

I agree with the plurality that the Stolen Valor Act of 2005 violates the First Amendment. But I do not rest my conclusion upon a strict categorical analysis. Rather, I base that conclusion upon the fact that the statute works First Amendment harm, while the Government can achieve its legitimate objectives in less restrictive ways.

In determining whether a statute violates the First Amendment, this Court has often found it appropriate to examine the fit between statutory ends and means. In doing so, it has examined speech-related harms, justifications, and potential alternatives. In particular, it has taken account of the seriousness of the speech-related harm the provision will likely cause, the nature and importance of the provision's countervailing objectives, the extent to which the provision will tend to achieve those objectives, and whether there are other, less restrictive ways of doing so. Ultimately the Court has had to determine whether the statute works speech-related harm that is out of proportion to its justifications. * * *

The statute before us * * * creates a significant risk of First Amendment harm. As written, it applies in family, social, or other private contexts, where lies will often cause little harm. It also applies in political contexts, where although such lies are more likely to cause harm, the risk of censorious selectivity by prosecutors is also high. Further, given the potential haziness of individual memory along with the large number of military awards covered (ranging from medals for rifle marksmanship to the Congressional Medal of Honor), there remains a risk of chilling that is not completely eliminated by *mens rea* requirements; a speaker might still be worried about being *prosecuted* for a careless false statement, even if he does not have the intent required to render him liable. And so the prohibition may be applied where it should not be applied, for example, to bar stool braggadocio or, in the political arena, subtly but selectively to speakers that the Government does not like. These considerations lead me to believe that the statute as written risks significant First Amendment harm.

Like both the plurality and the dissent, I believe the statute nonetheless has substantial justification. It seeks to protect the interests of those who have sacrificed their health and life for their country. The statute serves this interest by seeking to preserve intact the country's recognition of that sacrifice in the form of military honors. To permit those who have not earned those honors to claim otherwise dilutes the value of the awards. Indeed, the Nation cannot fully honor those who have sacrificed so much for their country's honor unless those who claim to have received its military awards tell the truth. Thus, the statute risks harming protected interests but only in order to achieve a substantial countervailing objective.

We must therefore ask whether it is possible substantially to achieve the Government's objective in less burdensome ways. In my view, the answer to this question is "yes." * * * For example, not all military awards are alike. Congress might determine that some warrant greater protection than others. And a more finely tailored statute might, as other kinds of statutes prohibiting false factual statements have done, insist upon a showing that the false statement caused specific harm or at least was material, or focus its coverage on lies most likely to be harmful or on contexts where such lies are most likely to cause harm.

* * * And an accurate, publicly available register of military awards, easily obtainable by political opponents, may well adequately protect the integrity of an award against those who would falsely claim to have earned it. And so it is likely that a more narrowly tailored statute combined with such information-disseminating devices will effectively serve Congress' end.

The Government has provided no convincing explanation as to why a more finely tailored statute would not work. In my own view, such a statute could significantly reduce the threat of First Amendment harm while permitting the statute to achieve its important protective objective. That being so, I find the statute as presently drafted works disproportionate constitutional harm. It consequently fails intermediate scrutiny, and so violates the First Amendment.

For these reasons, I concur in the Court's judgment.

JUSTICE ALITO, with whom JUSTICE SCALIA and JUSTICE THOMAS join, dissenting. * * *

Congress passed the Stolen Valor Act in response to a proliferation of false claims concerning the receipt of military awards. For example, in a single year, *more than 600* Virginia residents falsely claimed to have won the Medal of Honor. An investigation of the 333 people listed in the online edition of Who's Who as having received a top military award revealed that fully a third of the claims could not be substantiated. When the Library of Congress compiled oral histories for its Veterans History Project, 24 of the 49 individuals who identified themselves as Medal of Honor recipients had not actually received that award. The same was true of 32 individuals who claimed to have been awarded the Distinguished Service Cross and 14 who claimed to have won the Navy Cross. Notorious cases brought to Congress' attention included the case of a judge who falsely claimed to have been awarded *two* Medals of Honor and displayed counterfeit medals in his courtroom; a television network's military consultant who falsely claimed that he had received the Silver Star; and a former judge advocate in the Marine Corps who lied about receiving the Bronze Star and a Purple Heart.

As Congress recognized, the lies proscribed by the Stolen Valor Act inflict substantial harm. In many instances, the harm is tangible in nature: Individuals often falsely represent themselves as award recipients in order to obtain financial or other material rewards, such as lucrative contracts and government benefits. An investigation of false claims in a single region of the United States, for example, revealed that 12 men had defrauded the Department of Veterans Affairs out of more than $1.4 million in veteran's benefits. In other cases, the harm is less tangible, but nonetheless significant. The lies proscribed by the Stolen Valor Act tend to debase the distinctive honor of military awards. And legitimate award recipients and their families have expressed the harm they endure when an imposter takes credit for heroic actions that he never performed. One Medal of Honor recipient described the feeling as a "slap in the face of veterans who have paid the price and earned their medals."

It is well recognized in trademark law that the proliferation of cheap imitations of luxury goods blurs the " 'signal' given out by the purchasers of the originals." In much the same way, the proliferation of false claims about military awards blurs the signal given out by the actual awards by making them seem more common than they really are, and this diluting effect harms the military by hampering its efforts to foster morale and esprit de corps. Surely it was reasonable for Congress to conclude that the goal of preserving the integrity of our country's top military honors is at least as worthy as that of protecting the prestige associated with fancy watches and designer handbags.

Both the plurality and JUSTICE BREYER argue that Congress could have preserved the integrity of military honors by means other than a criminal prohibition, but Congress had ample reason to believe that alternative approaches would not be adequate. The chief alternative that is recommended is the compilation and release of a comprehensive list or database of actual medal recipients. If the public could readily access such a resource, it is argued, imposters would be quickly and easily exposed, and the proliferation of lies about military honors would come to an end.

This remedy, unfortunately, will not work. The Department of Defense has explained that the most that it can do is to create a database of recipients of certain top military honors awarded since 2001.[13]

Because a sufficiently comprehensive database is not practicable, lies about military awards cannot be remedied by what the plurality calls "counterspeech." Without the requisite database, many efforts to refute false claims may be thwarted, and some legitimate award recipients may be erroneously attacked. In addition, a steady stream of stories in the media about the exposure of imposters would tend to increase skepticism among members of the public about the entire awards system. This would only exacerbate the harm that the Stolen Valor Act is meant to prevent.

The plurality and the concurrence also suggest that Congress could protect the system of military honors by enacting a narrower statute. The plurality recommends a law that would apply only to lies that are intended to "secure moneys or other valuable considerations." In a similar vein, the concurrence comments that "a more finely tailored statute might . . . insist upon a showing that the false statement caused specific harm." But much damage is caused, both to real award recipients and to the system of military honors, by false statements that are not

---

[13] In addition, since the Department may not disclose the Social Security numbers or birthdates of recipients, this database would be of limited use in ascertaining the veracity of a claim involving a person with a common name.

linked to any financial or other tangible reward. Unless even a small financial loss — say, a dollar given to a homeless man falsely claiming to be a decorated veteran — is more important in the eyes of the First Amendment than the damage caused to the very integrity of the military awards system, there is no basis for distinguishing between the Stolen Valor Act and the alternative statutes that the plurality and concurrence appear willing to sustain. * * *

Time and again, this Court has recognized that as a general matter false factual statements possess no intrinsic First Amendment value. Consistent with this recognition, many kinds of false factual statements have long been proscribed without "rais[ing] any Constitutional problem." Laws prohibiting fraud, perjury, and defamation, for example, were in existence when the First Amendment was adopted, and their constitutionality is now beyond question.

We have also described as falling outside the First Amendment's protective shield certain false factual statements that were neither illegal nor tortious at the time of the Amendment's adoption. The right to freedom of speech has been held to permit recovery for the intentional infliction of emotional distress by means of a false statement, see [*Hustler Magazine, Inc.* v.] *Falwell*, [485 U.S. 46,] 56 [(1988)], even though that tort did not enter our law until the late 19th century. And in [*Time, Inc.* v.] *Hill*, [385 U.S. 374,] 390 [(1967)], the Court concluded that the free speech right allows recovery for the even more modern tort of false-light invasion of privacy.

In line with these holdings, it has long been assumed that the First Amendment is not offended by prominent criminal statutes with no close common-law analog. The most well known of these is probably 18 U.S.C. § 1001, which makes it a crime to "knowingly and willfully" make any "materially false, fictitious, or fraudulent statement or representation" in "any matter within the jurisdiction of the executive, legislative, or judicial branch of the Government of the United States." Unlike perjury, § 1001 is not limited to statements made under oath or before an official government tribunal. Nor does it require any showing of "pecuniary or property loss to the government." Instead, the statute is based on the need to protect "agencies from the perversion which *might* result from the deceptive practices described."

Still other statutes make it a crime to falsely represent that one is speaking on behalf of, or with the approval of, the Federal Government. See, *e.g.*, 18 U.S.C. § 912 (making it a crime to falsely impersonate a federal officer); § 709 (making it a crime to knowingly use, without authorization, the names of enumerated federal agencies, such as "Federal Bureau of Investigation," in a manner reasonably calculated to convey the impression that a communication is approved or authorized by the agency). We have recognized that § 912, like § 1001, does not require a showing of pecuniary or property loss and that its purpose is to "maintain the general good repute and dignity" of Government service. All told, there are more than 100 federal criminal statutes that punish false statements made in connection with areas of federal agency concern.

These examples amply demonstrate that false statements of fact merit no First Amendment protection in their own right. It is true, as JUSTICE BREYER notes, that many in our society either approve or condone certain discrete categories of false statements, including false statements made to prevent harm to innocent victims and so-called "white lies." But respondent's false claim to have received the Medal of Honor did not fall into any of these categories. * * * Respondent's claim, like all those covered by the Stolen Valor Act, served no valid purpose. * * *

* * * [T]here are broad areas in which any attempt by the state to penalize purportedly false speech would present a grave and unacceptable danger of suppressing truthful speech. Laws restricting false statements about philosophy, religion, history, the social sciences, the arts, and other matters of public concern would present such a threat. The point is not that there is no such thing as truth or falsity in these areas or that the truth is always impossible to ascertain, but rather that it is perilous to permit the state to be the arbiter of truth.

Even where there is a wide scholarly consensus concerning a particular matter, the truth is served by allowing that consensus to be challenged without fear of reprisal. Today's accepted wisdom sometimes turns out to be mistaken. * * *

Allowing the state to proscribe false statements in these areas also opens the door for the state to use its power for political ends. Statements about history illustrate this point. If some false statements about historical events may be banned, how certain must it be that a statement is false before the ban may be upheld? And who should make that calculation? [T]he potential for abuse of power in these areas is simply too great.

In stark contrast to hypothetical laws prohibiting false statements about history, science, and similar matters, the Stolen Valor Act presents no risk at all that valuable speech will be suppressed. The speech punished by the Act is not only verifiably false and entirely lacking in intrinsic value, but it also fails to serve any instrumental purpose that the First Amendment might protect. Tellingly, when asked at oral argument what truthful speech the Stolen Valor Act might chill, even respondent's counsel conceded that the answer is none.

Notes and Questions

1.   Note that the plurality and the dissent started from different premises. Justice Kennedy treated categories of unprotected speech as limited exceptions to the general rule banning content-based suppression of speech. Justice Alito, by contrast, treated those categories as establishing the principle that false speech is worthy of protection only when attempts to ban it would also suppress truthful speech. Which approach was more faithful to the Court's precedents?

2.   Justice Breyer argued that the Stolen Valor Act chilled some "careless" speech, despite its (imputed) *mens rea* requirement, because speakers might fear *prosecution* even if a *conviction* would be impossible. (The plurality likewise cited the Act's potential to chill speech as a reason for striking it down.) If such a concern were taken seriously, would that require that we protect defamatory speech made with "actual malice"?

3.   Do you agree with Justice Breyer that the statute's coverage was constitutionally problematic because it applied "in family, social, or other private contexts, where lies will often cause little harm"? When *Alvarez* was denied rehearing *en*

banc by the Ninth Circuit, Chief Judge Kozinski wrote a concurring opinion arguing that it was necessary to provide constitutional protection for "the white lies, exaggerations and deceptions that are an integral part of human intercourse." *United States v. Alvarez*, 638 F.3d 666, 673 (9th Cir. 2011) (denying reh'g *en banc*) (Kozinski, C.J., concurring). He then provided examples of such untruths:

> We lie to protect our privacy ("No, I don't live around here"); to avoid hurt feelings ("Friday is my study night"); to make others feel better ("Gee you've gotten skinny"); to avoid recriminations ("I only lost $10 at poker"); to prevent grief ("The doc says you're getting better"); to maintain domestic tranquility ("She's just a friend"); to avoid social stigma ("I just haven't met the right woman"); for career advancement ("I'm sooo lucky to have a smart boss like you"); to avoid being lonely ("I love opera"); to eliminate a rival ("He has a boyfriend"); to achieve an objective ("But I love you so much"); to defeat an objective ("I'm allergic to latex"); to make an exit ("It's not you, it's me"); to delay the inevitable ("The check is in the mail"); to communicate displeasure ("There's nothing wrong"); to get someone off your back ("I'll call you about lunch"); to escape a nudnik ("My mother's on the other line"); to namedrop ("We go way back"); to set up a surprise party ("I need help moving the piano"); to buy time ("I'm on my way"); to keep up appearances ("We're not talking divorce"); to avoid taking out the trash ("My back hurts"); to duck an obligation ("I've got a headache"); to maintain a public image ("I go to church every Sunday"); to make a point ("Ich bin ein Berliner"); to save face ("I had too much to drink"); to humor ("Correct as usual, King Friday"); to avoid embarrassment ("That wasn't me"); to curry favor ("I've read all your books"); to get a clerkship ("You're the greatest living jurist"); to save a dollar ("I gave at the office"); or to maintain innocence ("There are eight tiny reindeer on the rooftop").

Id. at 674–75. Are these statements harmless? After *Alvarez*, is there anything the legal system can do to punish one who, for example, uses "she's just a friend" to conceal a long-running affair from his wife? More generally, should false campaign speech be entitled to any more — or any less — protection than false speech about other topics?

Does the First Amendment permit the government "to determine the truth and falsity in political debate"? In *Pestrak v. Ohio Elections Commission*, 926 F.2d 573 (6th Cir. 1991), the Sixth Circuit confronted a challenge to the Commission's authority to discourage speakers from making false statements by "proclaim[ing] to the electorate the truth [or falsity] of various campaign allegations." *Id.* at 579. The court held that this "truth-declaring" function was

> closely comparable to those now carried on by many agencies of government. Thus, we regularly see: various high officials of the executive and legislative branches asserting the untruth of statements made by political opponents and the veracity of statements with which they agree; members of Congress, following hearings at which testimony may be compelled, issue reports declaring the truth or falsity of matters of the utmost importance to public policy and election campaigns; government agencies declare the

truth or falsity of statements with regard to apparently "technical" matters such as the inflation rate, the unemployment rate, energy reserves, infant mortality rates, or the population of the United States and its political subdivisions; and, government funded and sponsored news media, such as National Public Radio and the Corporation for Public Broadcasting/Public Broadcasting System regularly issue statements as to the truth or falsity of statements made by public officials. * * * All of this "speech" can have the most direct effect on governmental activities, as well as influencing public debate and election campaigns.

Id. Are you convinced by the Sixth Circuit's analogy between the common governmental announcements and the Commission's truth declarations?

4.   Ohio's ban on false statements made it to the Supreme Court in 2014, with the Court deciding only the procedural question of whether certain advocacy groups had alleged sufficient threat of harm to make their constitutional challenge justiciable. *Susan B. Anthony List v. Driehaus*, 134 S. Ct. 2334 (2014). The challenged provision prohibited "[m]ak[ing] a false statement concerning the voting record of a candidate or public official" and "disseminat[ing] a false statement concerning a candidate, either knowing the same to be false or with reckless disregard of whether it was false or not, if the statement is designed to promote the election, nomination, or defeat of the candidate."

In *Susan B. Anthony List*, a panel of the Ohio Elections Commission concluded that there was probable cause to believe that the group had violated the statute when it criticized an incumbent congressman for "vot[ing] for a health care bill that includes taxpayer-funded abortion." The statement was literally true, as the congressman in question voted for the Affordable Care Act, which does use tax dollars to pay for certain abortions, such as those that are the result of rape. The statement might have been thought to be misleading, however, as some people reading the statement might have inferred that the Act provided money for elective abortions. Accordingly, it is possible that the group in that case could have won an as-applied challenge to the law based on the statement's literal truth.

More important for future cases, however, is whether the Ohio law is *facially* constitutional, *i.e.*, whether it could be applied even in cases where the speech in question is demonstrably false. Do the facts of the *Susan B. Anthony* case change your idea of whether it is constitutional to have a government agency assessing the truth or falsity of political speech?

5.   The *Alvarez* plurality accepted longstanding limitations on political speech, including the law of defamation approved by *New York Times Co. v. Sullivan* and its progeny. Should the Court treat lies about ballot measures as analogous to defamation, or are they akin to the law struck down in *Alvarez*? On the one hand, lies about ballot measures do not harm any individual in the way that defamation harms the person defamed. On the other hand, perhaps statements about ballot measures are unlikely to trigger the "counterspeech" that could inform the public about the truth. *See Rickert v. Public Disclosure Comm'n*, 168 P.3d 826 (Wash. 2007) (striking down a false-statements prohibition in candidate elections); *Washington ex rel. Public Disclosure Comm'n v. 119 Vote No! Comm.*, 957 P.2d 691

(Wash. 1998) (striking down a false-statements prohibition concerning ballot measures).

In *281 Care Committee v. Arneson*, 638 F.3d 621 (8th Cir. 2011), *cert. denied*, 133 S. Ct. 61 (2012), the Eighth Circuit held that knowing or reckless false statements about ballot questions were constitutionally protected in the absence of a compelling reason for their suppression. (The court remanded for the application of strict scrutiny.) *Id.* at 636. The Supreme Court denied certiorari the day after it decided *Alvarez*. Do *281 Care Committee* and *Alvarez* grant constitutional protection to campaign "dirty tricks"?

6. *Problem.* Because Justice Kennedy's opinion garnered only four votes, Justice Breyer's opinion states the controlling rule. Thus, it is important to consider what other, narrower, statutes banning false or misleading speech might survive Justice Breyer's test of proportionality. Consider the following questions, the first two of which were raised by Justice Breyer in a portion of his opinion not reprinted here:

   a. May a political organization be punished for infringing the trademark of a different organization? *See United We Stand America, Inc. v. United We Stand America New York, Inc.*, 128 F.3d 86 (2d Cir. 1997).

   b. May a state prohibit candidates from falsely claiming to be incumbents? *See Hoy v. Fox*, 389 N.W.2d 446 (Mich. Ct. App. 1986).

   c. May a state criminalize lies about the voting process that are designed to trick people into staying away from the polls? *See* Richard L. Hasen, *Has SCOTUS OK'd Campaign Dirty Tricks?*, Politico, July 10, 2012, http://www.politico.com/news/stories/0712/78342.html; Eugene Volokh, *Freedom of Speech and Knowing Falsehoods*, Volokh Conspiracy, June 28, 2012, http://www.volokh.com/2012/06/28/freedom-of-speech-and-knowing-falsehoods/.

C. MEDIA COVERAGE

The First Amendment's protection of "the freedom of speech, [and] of the press" extends not just to candidates, but to the institutional media as well, and, indeed, everyone else. The press has been viewed as fulfilling a watchdog function, informing the public about candidates and public officials, among other issues of the day. Accordingly, the Court has been reluctant to permit government oversight of this institution, which is supposed to oversee government. Nevertheless, First Amendment rights are not absolute, and the permissible scope of government regulation depends on the medium and the policies pursued by the regulation.

The Supreme Court has refused to permit states to limit the editorial discretion of newspapers, reasoning that people upset with the policies of existing papers can start their own. Broadcast media, however, present a different picture, so to speak. Because the broadcast spectra are necessarily limited, the Court has treated broadcasters as fulfilling a public function and accordingly has permitted far more government intervention in the editorial policies of broadcasters than would be permissible in the case of newspapers. The Court upheld the so-called "fairness doctrine" in *Red Lion Broadcasting Co. v. FCC*, 395 U.S. 367 (1969) [p. 605], but the decision has been subject to criticism since then — in part due to technological innovations that many see as weakening the distinction the Court drew between print and broadcast media. The FCC's repeal of the doctrine in 1987, *see In re Syracuse Peace Council*, 2 F.C.C. Rcd. 5043 (1987), *upheld* 867 F.2d 654 (D.C. Cir. 1989), has made it unnecessary for the Court to revisit *Red Lion* head-on, but it remains a vitally important case in assessing the constitutional limits of government attempts to advance the "public interest" through regulations of broadcasters.

MILLS v. ALABAMA
Supreme Court of the United States
384 U.S. 214, 86 S. Ct. 1434, 16 L. Ed. 2d 484 (1966)

MR. JUSTICE BLACK delivered the opinion of the Court [in which MR. CHIEF JUSTICE WARREN, MR. JUSTICE DOUGLAS, MR. JUSTICE CLARK, MR. JUSTICE BRENNAN, MR. JUSTICE STEWART, MR. JUSTICE WHITE, and MR. JUSTICE FORTAS join].

The question squarely presented here is whether a State, consistently with the United States Constitution, can make it a crime for the editor of a daily newspaper to write and publish an editorial *on election day* urging people to vote a certain way on issues submitted to them.

On November 6, 1962, Birmingham, Alabama, held an election for the people to decide whether they preferred to keep their existing city commission form of government or replace it with a mayor-council government. On election day the Birmingham Post-Herald, a daily newspaper, carried an editorial written by its editor, appellant, James E. Mills, which strongly urged the people to adopt the mayor-council form of government. Mills was later arrested on a complaint charging that by publishing the editorial *on election day* he had violated § 285 of the Alabama Corrupt Practices Act, which makes it a crime "to do any electioneering or to solicit any votes * * * in support of or in opposition to any proposition that is being voted on on the day on which the election affecting such candidates or propositions is being held." * * *

Whatever differences may exist about interpretations of the First Amendment, there is practically universal agreement that a major purpose of that Amendment was to protect the free discussion of governmental affairs. This of course includes discussions of candidates, structures and forms of government, the manner in which government is operated or should be operated, and all such matters relating to political processes. The Constitution specifically selected the press, which includes not only newspapers, books, and magazines, but also humble leaflets and circulars, to play an important role in the discussion of public affairs. Thus the press serves and was designed to serve as a powerful antidote to any abuses of power by governmental officials and as a constitutionally chosen means for keeping officials elected by the people responsible to all the people whom they were selected to serve. Suppression of the right of the press to praise or criticize governmental agents and to clamor and contend for or against change, which is all that this editorial did, muzzles one of the very agencies the Framers of our Constitution thoughtfully and deliberately selected to improve our society and keep it free. The Alabama Corrupt Practices Act by providing criminal penalties for publishing editorials such as the one here silences the press at a time when it can be most effective. It is difficult to conceive of a more obvious and flagrant abridgment of the constitutionally guaranteed freedom of the press.

Admitting that the state law restricted a newspaper editor's freedom to publish editorials on election day, the Alabama Supreme Court nevertheless sustained the constitutionality of the law on the ground that the restrictions on the press were only "reasonable restrictions" or at least "within the field of reasonableness." The court reached this conclusion because it thought the law imposed only a minor limitation on the press — restricting it only on election days — and because the court thought the law served a good purpose. It said:

> "It is a salutary legislative enactment that protects the public from confusive last-minute charges and countercharges and the distribution of propaganda in an effort to influence voters on an election day; when as a practical matter, because of lack of time, such matters cannot be answered or their truth determined until after the election is over."

This argument, even if it were relevant to the constitutionality of the law, has a fatal flaw. The state statute leaves people free to hurl their campaign charges up to the last minute of the day before election. The law held valid by the Alabama Supreme Court then goes on to make it a crime to answer those "last-minute" charges on election day, the only time they can be effectively answered. Because the law prevents any adequate reply to these charges, it is wholly ineffective in protecting the electorate "from confusive last-minute charges and countercharges." We hold that no test of reasonableness can save a state law from invalidation as a violation of the First Amendment when that law makes it a crime for a newspaper editor to do no more than urge people to vote one way or another in a publicly held election.

The judgment of the Supreme Court of Alabama is reversed and the case is remanded for further proceedings not inconsistent with this opinion.

It is so ordered.

[MR. JUSTICE DOUGLAS's concurring opinion is omitted.]

Separate opinion of MR. JUSTICE HARLAN. * * *

* * * I agree with the Court that the decision below cannot stand. But I would rest reversal on the ground that the relevant provision of the Alabama statute — "to do any electioneering or to solicit any votes [on election day] * * * in support of or in opposition to any proposition that is being voted on on the day on which the election affecting such candidates or propositions is being held" — did not give the appellant * * * fair warning that the publication of an editorial of this kind was reached by the foregoing provisions of the Alabama Corrupt Practices Act. I deem a broader holding unnecessary.

Notes and Questions

1. *Problem.* A Virgin Islands statute prohibits candidates and their campaign staffs from engaging in political activity after 2:00 a.m. on election day. Is such a prohibition distinguishable from *Mills*? *See Abiff v. Virgin Islands Legislature*, 216 F. Supp. 2d 455 (D.V.I. 2002).

2. *Problem.* An Arizona statute requires any PAC wishing to promote the election or defeat of a candidate within ten days before an election to mail a copy of the advertisement to the opposition candidate twenty-four hours before its publication. The state defends the statute as "necessary to an informed electorate because it affords candidates an opportunity to respond to last-minute negative 'hit pieces' that may confuse or misinform voters." Is the statute constitutional? *See Arizona Right to Life Political Action Committee v. Bayless*, 320 F.3d 1002 (9th Cir. 2003). Would it make any difference if, instead of requiring PACs to mail advertisements to the opposition candidate, the statute required PACs to mail advertisements to a government agency, which would then investigate the accuracy of the advertisements' claims and issue press releases correcting any misleading or false assertions?

3. *Problem.* May a state ban exit polling within three hundred feet of a polling place? *See Daily Herald Co. v. Munro*, 758 F.2d 350 (9th Cir. 1984); *American Broadcasting Co. v. Blackwell*, 479 F. Supp. 2d 719 (S.D. Ohio 2006); *CBS v. Smith*, 681 F. Supp. 794 (S.D. Fla. 1988); *National Broadcasting Co. v. Colburg*, 699 F. Supp. 241 (D. Mont. 1988); *National Broadcasting Co. v. Cleland*, 697 F. Supp. 1204 (N.D. Ga. 1988); *Firestone v. News-Press Publishing Co.*, 538 So. 2d 457 (Fla. 1989). What if a state permitted the media to *conduct* exit polls, but prohibited the *announcement of the results* until the polls closed, reasoning that potential voters will be dissuaded from voting if they believe the election has, for practical purposes, been decided? *See CBS, Inc. v. Growe*, 15 MEDIA L. REP. 2275 (D. Minn. 1988).

RED LION BROADCASTING CO. v. FEDERAL COMMUNICATIONS COMMISSION

Supreme Court of the United States
395 U.S. 367, 89 S. Ct. 1764, 23 L. Ed. 2d 371 (1969)

MR. JUSTICE WHITE delivered the opinion of the Court [in which MR. CHIEF JUSTICE WARREN, MR. JUSTICE BLACK, MR. JUSTICE HARLAN, MR. JUSTICE BRENNAN, MR. JUSTICE STEWART, and MR. JUSTICE MARSHALL join].

The Federal Communications Commission has for many years imposed on radio and television broadcasters the requirement that discussion of public issues be presented on broadcast stations, and that each side of those issues must be given fair coverage. This is known as the fairness doctrine, which originated very early in the history of broadcasting and has maintained its present outlines for some time. It is an obligation whose content has been defined in a long series of FCC rulings in particular cases, and which is distinct from the statutory requirement of § 315 of the Communications Act[1] that equal time be allotted all qualified candidates for

---

[1] Communications Act of 1934, 47 U.S.C. § 301 *et seq.* Section 315 now reads:

public office. Two aspects of the fairness doctrine, relating to personal attacks in the context of controversial public issues and to political editorializing, were codified more precisely in the form of FCC regulations in 1967. The two cases before us * * * challenge the constitutional and statutory bases of the doctrine and component rules. *Red Lion* involves the application of the fairness doctrine to a particular broadcast, and *RTNDA* [*United States* v. *Radio Television News Directors Association*] arises as an action to review the FCC's 1967 promulgation of the personal attack and political editorializing regulations, which were laid down after the *Red Lion* litigation had begun.

The Red Lion Broadcasting Company is licensed to operate a Pennsylvania radio station, WGCB. On November 27, 1964, WGCB carried a 15-minute broadcast by the Reverend Billy James Hargis as part of a "Christian Crusade" series. A book by Fred J. Cook entitled "Goldwater — Extremist on the Right" was discussed by Hargis, who said that Cook had been fired by a newspaper for making false charges against city officials; that Cook had then worked for a Communist-affiliated publication; that he had defended Alger Hiss and attacked J. Edgar Hoover and the Central Intelligence Agency; and that he had now written a "book to smear and destroy Barry Goldwater." When Cook heard of the broadcast he concluded that he had been personally attacked and demanded free reply time, which the station refused. * * *

Not long after the *Red Lion* litigation was begun, the FCC [promulgated rules] with an eye to making the personal attack aspect of the fairness doctrine more precise and more readily enforceable, and to specifying its rules relating to political editorials. * * *

As they now stand amended, the regulations read as follows:

"Personal attacks; political editorials.

"(a) When, during the presentation of views on a controversial issue of public importance, an attack is made upon the honesty, character, integrity or like personal qualities of an identified person or group, the licensee shall,

---

"315. Candidates for public office; facilities; rules.

"(a) If any licensee shall permit any person who is a legally qualified candidate for any public office to use a broadcasting station, he shall afford equal opportunities to all other such candidates for that office in the use of such broadcasting station: Provided, That such licensee shall have no power of censorship over the material broadcast under the provisions of this section. No obligation is imposed upon any licensee to allow the use of its station by any such candidate. Appearance by a legally qualified candidate on any —

"(1) bona fide newscast,

"(2) bona fide news interview,

"(3) bona fide news documentary (if the appearance of the candidate is incidental to the presentation of the subject or subjects covered by the news documentary), or

"(4) on-the-spot coverage of bona fide news events (including but not limited to political conventions and activities incidental thereto),

shall not be deemed to be use of a broadcasting station within the meaning of this subsection. * * *

"(b) The charges made for the use of any broadcasting station for any of the purposes set forth in this section shall not exceed the charges made for comparable use of such station for other purposes. * * *"

within a reasonable time and in no event later than 1 week after the attack, transmit to the person or group attacked (1) notification of the date, time and identification of the broadcast; (2) a script or tape (or an accurate summary if a script or tape is not available) of the attack, and (3) an offer of a reasonable opportunity to respond over the licensee's facilities.

"(b) The provisions of paragraph (a) of this section shall not be applicable (1) to attacks on foreign groups or foreign public figures; (2) to personal attacks which are made by legally qualified candidates, their authorized spokesmen, or those associated with them in the campaign, on other such candidates, their authorized spokesmen, or persons associated with the candidates in the campaign; and (3) to bona fide newscasts, bona fide news interviews, and on-the-spot coverage of a bona fide news event (including commentary or analysis contained in the foregoing programs, but the provisions of paragraph (a) of this section shall be applicable to editorials of the licensee). * * *

"(c) Where a licensee, in an editorial, (i) endorses or (ii) opposes a legally qualified candidate or candidates, the licensee shall, within 24 hours after the editorial, transmit to respectively (i) the other qualified candidate or candidates for the same office or (ii) the candidate opposed in the editorial (1) notification of the date and the time of the editorial; (2) a script or tape of the editorial; and (3) an offer of a reasonable opportunity for a candidate or a spokesman of the candidate to respond over the licensee's facilities: Provided, however, That where such editorials are broadcast within 72 hours prior to the day of the election, the licensee shall comply with the provisions of this paragraph sufficiently far in advance of the broadcast to enable the candidate or candidates to have a reasonable opportunity to prepare a response and to present it in a timely fashion."

[RTNDA challenged the rules' constitutionality.]

Believing that the specific application of the fairness doctrine in *Red Lion*, and the promulgation of the regulations in *RTNDA*, are both authorized by Congress and enhance rather than abridge the freedoms of speech and press protected by the First Amendment, we hold them valid and constitutional[.] * * *

The broadcasters challenge the fairness doctrine and its specific manifestations in the personal attack and political editorial rules on conventional First Amendment grounds, alleging that the rules abridge their freedom of speech and press. Their contention is that the First Amendment protects their desire to use their allotted frequencies continuously to broadcast whatever they choose, and to exclude whomever they choose from ever using that frequency. No man may be prevented from saying or publishing what he thinks, or from refusing in his speech or other utterances to give equal weight to the views of his opponents. This right, they say, applies equally to broadcasters.

Although broadcasting is clearly a medium affected by a First Amendment interest, differences in the characteristics of new media justify differences in the First Amendment standards applied to them. * * *

Just as the Government may limit the use of sound-amplifying equipment potentially so noisy that it drowns out civilized private speech, so may the Government limit the use of broadcast equipment. The right of free speech of a broadcaster, the user of a sound truck, or any other individual does not embrace a right to snuff out the free speech of others.

When two people converse face to face, both should not speak at once if either is to be clearly understood. But the range of the human voice is so limited that there could be meaningful communications if half the people in the United States were talking and the other half listening. Just as clearly, half the people might publish and the other half read. But the reach of radio signals is incomparably greater than the range of the human voice and the problem of interference is a massive reality. The lack of know-how and equipment may keep many from the air, but only a tiny fraction of those with resources and intelligence can hope to communicate by radio at the same time if intelligible communication is to be had, even if the entire radio spectrum is utilized in the present state of commercially acceptable technology. * * *

Where there are substantially more individuals who want to broadcast than there are frequencies to allocate, it is idle to posit an unabridgeable First Amendment right to broadcast comparable to the right of every individual to speak, write, or publish. If 100 persons want broadcast licenses but there are only 10 frequencies to allocate, all of them may have the same "right" to a license; but if there is to be any effective communication by radio, only a few can be licensed and the rest must be barred from the airwaves. It would be strange if the First Amendment, aimed at protecting and furthering communications, prevented the Government from making radio communication possible by requiring licenses to broadcast and by limiting the number of licenses so as not to overcrowd the spectrum.

This has been the consistent view of the Court. Congress unquestionably has the power to grant and deny licenses and to eliminate existing stations. No one has a First Amendment right to a license or to monopolize a radio frequency; to deny a station license because "the public interest" requires it "is not a denial of free speech." * * *

This is not to say that the First Amendment is irrelevant to public broadcasting. * * * Because of the scarcity of radio frequencies, the Government is permitted to put restraints on licensees in favor of others whose views should be expressed on this unique medium. But the people as a whole retain their interest in free speech by radio and their collective right to have the medium function consistently with the ends and purposes of the First Amendment. It is the right of the viewers and listeners, not the right of the broadcasters, which is paramount. * * *

Rather than confer frequency monopolies on a relatively small number of licensees, in a Nation of 200,000,000, the Government could surely have decreed that each frequency should be shared among all or some of those who wish to use it, each being assigned a portion of the broadcast day or the broadcast week. The ruling and regulations at issue here do not go quite so far. They assert that under specified circumstances, a licensee must offer to make available a reasonable amount of broadcast time to those who have a view different from that which has already been expressed on his station. The expression of a political endorsement, or of a personal attack while dealing with a controversial public issue, simply triggers this time sharing. As we have said, the First Amendment confers no right on licensees to prevent others from broadcasting on "their" frequencies and no right to an unconditional monopoly of a scarce resource which the Government has denied others the right to use.

In terms of constitutional principle, and as enforced sharing of a scarce resource, the personal attack and political editorial rules are indistinguishable from the equal-time provision of § 315, a specific enactment of Congress requiring stations to set aside reply time under specified circumstances and to which the fairness doctrine and these constituent regulations are important complements. That provision, which has been part of the law since 1927, has been held valid by this Court as an obligation of the licensee relieving him of any power in any way to prevent or censor the broadcast, and thus insulating him from liability for defamation. The constitutionality of the statute under the First Amendment was unquestioned. *Farmers Educ. & Coop. Union* v. *WDAY*, 360 U.S. 525 (1959).

Nor can we say that it is inconsistent with the First Amendment goal of producing an informed public capable of conducting its own affairs to require a broadcaster to permit answers to personal attacks occurring in the course of discussing controversial issues, or to require that the political opponents of those endorsed by the station be given a chance to communicate with the public. Otherwise, station owners and a few networks would have unfettered power to make time available only to the highest bidders, to communicate only their own views on public issues, people and candidates, and to permit on the air only those with whom they agreed. There is no sanctuary in the First Amendment for unlimited private censorship operating in a medium not open to all. * * *

It is strenuously argued, however, that if political editorials or personal attacks will trigger an obligation in broadcasters to afford the opportunity for expression to speakers who need not pay for time and whose views are unpalatable to the licensees, then broadcasters will be irresistibly forced to self-censorship and their coverage of controversial public issues will be eliminated or at least rendered wholly ineffective. Such a result would indeed be a serious matter, for should licensees actually eliminate their coverage of controversial issues, the purposes of the doctrine would be stifled.

At this point, however, as the Federal Communications Commission has indicated, that possibility is at best speculative. The communications industry, and in particular the networks, have taken pains to present controversial issues in the past, and even now they do not assert that they intend to abandon their efforts in this regard. It would be better if the FCC's encouragement were never necessary to induce the broadcasters to meet their responsibility. And if experience with the administration of those doctrines indicates that they have the net effect of reducing rather than enhancing the volume and quality of coverage, there will be time enough to reconsider the constitutional implications. The fairness doctrine in the past has had no such overall effect.

That this will occur now seems unlikely, however, since if present licensees should suddenly prove timorous, the Commission is not powerless to insist that they give adequate and fair attention to public issues. * * *

It is argued that even if at one time the lack of available frequencies for all who wished to use them justified the Government's choice of those who would best serve the public interest by acting as proxy for those who would present differing views, or by giving the latter access directly to broadcast facilities, this condition no longer prevails so that continuing control is not justified. To this there are several answers.

Scarcity is not entirely a thing of the past. Advances in technology, such as microwave transmission, have led to more efficient utilization of the frequency spectrum, but uses for that spectrum have also grown apace. Portions of the spectrum must be reserved for vital uses unconnected with human communication, such as radio-navigational aids used by aircraft and vessels. * * * Among the various uses for radio frequency space, including marine, aviation, amateur, military, and common carrier users, there are easily enough claimants to permit use of the whole with an even smaller allocation to broadcast radio and television uses than now exists.

Comparative hearings between competing applicants for broadcast spectrum space are by no means a thing of the past. The radio spectrum has become so congested that at times it has been necessary to suspend new applications. The very high frequency television spectrum is, in the country's major markets, almost entirely occupied * * *.

The rapidity with which technological advances succeed one another to create more efficient use of spectrum space on the one hand, and to create new uses for that space by ever growing numbers of people on the other, makes it unwise to speculate on the future allocation of that space. It is enough to say that the resource is one of considerable and growing importance whose scarcity impelled its regulation by an agency authorized by Congress. Nothing in this record, or in our own researches, convinces us that the resource is no longer one for which there are more immediate and potential uses than can be accommodated, and for which wise planning is essential. This does not mean, of course, that every possible wavelength must be occupied at every hour by some vital use in order to sustain the congressional judgment. The substantial capital investment required for many uses, in addition to the potentiality for confusion and interference inherent in any scheme for continuous kaleidoscopic reallocation of all available space may make this unfeasible. The allocation need not be made at such a breakneck pace that the objectives of the allocation are themselves imperiled.

Even where there are gaps in spectrum utilization, the fact remains that existing broadcasters have often attained their present position because of their initial government selection in competition with others before new technological advances opened new opportunities for further uses. Long experience in broadcasting, confirmed habits of listeners and viewers, network affiliation, and other advantages in program procurement give existing broadcasters a substantial advantage over new entrants, even where new entry is technologically possible. These advantages are the fruit of a preferred position conferred by the Government. Some present possibility for new entry by competing stations is not enough, in itself, to render unconstitutional the Government's effort to assure that a broadcaster's programming ranges widely enough to serve the public interest.

In view of the scarcity of broadcast frequencies, the Government's role in allocating those frequencies, and the legitimate claims of those unable without governmental assistance to gain access to those frequencies for expression of their views, we hold the regulations and ruling at issue here are both authorized by statute and constitutional.[28] * * *

Not having heard oral argument in these cases, MR. JUSTICE DOUGLAS took no part in the Court's decision.[a]

Notes and Questions

1.   Before its repeal by the FCC in 1987, *see In re Syracuse Peace Council*, 2 F.C.C. Rcd. 5043 (1987), *upheld* 867 F.2d 654 (D.C. Cir. 1989), the fairness doctrine required broadcasters to provide for the equal airing of differing views, and the equal-time provisions continue to require broadcasters to make their facilities available on an equal basis. Suppose a broadcaster decides to adhere to a policy of strict neutrality: Nobody may use the facilities to discuss public issues. Does that satisfy the broadcaster's obligations? In *Columbia Broadcasting System, Inc. v. Democratic National Committee*, 412 U.S. 94 (1973), the Court upheld a Federal Communications Commission ruling that broadcasters need not accept any editorial advertisements, *if* they are otherwise satisfying their obligation to act in the "public interest" by providing full and fair coverage of public issues.

2.   Are the equal-time provisions in 47 U.S.C. § 315 (quoted in footnote 1 in *Red Lion*) appropriate means of ensuring broadcast neutrality? Are the exemptions for newscasts, interviews, documentaries, and on-the-spot coverage too broad? Not broad enough? *See, e.g.*, Anne Kramer Ricchiuto, *The End of Time for Equal Time?: Revealing the Statutory Myth of Fair Election Coverage*, 38 IND. L. REV. 267 (2005); Randy Dotinga, *Latest Path Around Soft-Money Ban: Buy a TV Station*, CHRISTIAN SCI. MONITOR, Dec. 17, 2003, USA section, at 2.

3.   May the government require broadcasters to provide free air time for candidates to discuss their views? *See, e.g.*, LILLIAN BEVIER, IS FREE TV FOR FEDERAL CANDIDATES CONSTITUTIONAL? (1999); Joel M. Gora, Buckley v. Valeo: *A Landmark of Political Freedom*, 33 AKRON L. REV. 7, 38 (1999) (citing "severe, and perhaps insurmountable, constitutional difficulties"); Cass R. Sunstein, *Television and the Public Interest*, 88 CALIF. L. REV. 499 (2000); Seth Grossman, Note, *Creating Competitive and Informative Campaigns: A Comprehensive Approach to "Free Air Time" for Political Candidates*, 22 YALE L. & POL'Y REV. 351 (2004).

---

[28] We need not deal with the argument that even if there is no longer a technological scarcity of frequencies limiting the number of broadcasters, there nevertheless is an economic scarcity in the sense that the Commission could or does limit entry to the broadcasting market on economic grounds and license no more stations than the market will support. Hence, it is said, the fairness doctrine or its equivalent is essential to satisfy the claims of those excluded and of the public generally. A related argument, which we also put aside, is that quite apart from scarcity of frequencies, technological or economic, Congress does not abridge freedom of speech or press by legislation directly or indirectly multiplying the voices and views presented to the public through time sharing, fairness doctrines, or other devices which limit or dissipate the power of those who sit astride the channels of communication with the general public.

[a] Justice Fortas resigned before the decision was announced; only seven Justices participated. [— Eds.]

4.   Have technological innovations since 1969 undercut *Red Lion*? Or has the increased dominance of national and international media empires further underscored the potential manipulative power of a relatively small number of broadcasters? In 2004, Sinclair Broadcasting Group, the country's largest owner and operator of television stations, planned to preempt regular programming to broadcast a documentary attacking presidential candidate John Kerry. Sinclair ultimately decided, however, to forego the plan after receiving strong opposition. Does freedom for broadcasters risk overwhelming the speech of persons and groups with opposing political views? *See* Elizabeth Jensen, *Conservative TV Group to Air Anti-Kerry Film*, L.A. TIMES, Oct. 9, 2004, at A1. If the FCC reinstituted the fairness doctrine today, would it be constitutional?

5.   In upholding the fairness doctrine, the Court argued that broadcasters benefited from a "preferred position conferred by the Government," *i.e.*, the initial conferral of a broadcast license. As a result, the Court was not sympathetic to broadcasters' claims that once the government granted a license it should not be able to influence the editorial content of programming. Should the "greater" power to deny a license altogether include the "lesser" power to regulate content?

6.   What other potential speakers have benefited from a "preferred position conferred by the Government"? Are all corporations in that category, as the corporate form provides limited liability and potentially perpetual life? *Cf. Citizens United v. Federal Election Commission*, 558 U.S. 310 , 175 L. Ed. 2d 753 (2010); *Austin v. Michigan Chamber of Commerce*, 494 U.S. 652, 658–60 (1990).

7.   As with much of constitutional law, analyses of the fairness doctrine can turn as much on the procedural question *who* decides the fairness question as on the substantive question whether there should be an obligation of fair coverage. Do you trust the FCC to adjudicate questions of fairness? What can we learn about that issue from the cases we have read so far in this Chapter?

8.   The fairness doctrine did not require *fair* coverage per se. Rather, it provided "attack[ed]" persons and groups with an opportunity for reply. As a result, skittish broadcasters could avoid triggering the right-of-reply obligation simply by not engaging in such attacks. Such a result may not be "fair" at all, however. Imaging that a broadcaster wishes to criticize Candidate X, who is running for mayor against Candidate Y. The fairness doctrine might discourage such criticism, but perhaps the criticism was well grounded and otherwise "fair." Are you troubled that such fair criticism might be silenced? Are you troubled by a right of reply to a fair criticism? Does such a right imply that the attack and the defense are equally weighty? Do you think the risks of broadcasters' editorial freedom exceed any harm caused by stifling proper attacks?

9.   Would the *scope* of a renewed fairness doctrine raise constitutional concerns? If the FCC were to reinstitute the fairness doctrine and apply it to (largely conservative) talk radio, but exempt standard news programs (which conservatives allege to have a liberal bias), would such a distinction be defensible as permitting the doctrine to reach only "editorial" or "commentary"?

10.   Should entertainment programs be exempt from the fairness doctrine? Studies demonstrate that many people — particularly young people — receive

information from late-night talk shows and other programs besides the traditional network newscasts. *See, e.g.*, Pew Research Center for the People & the Press, *Internet's Broader Role in Campaign 2008*, Jan. 11, 2008, *available at* http://people-press.org/report/384/. If that is an accurate reflection of modern American society, does that argue for an expanded fairness doctrine, or for the doctrine's eternal entombment?

11.   How might the FCC determine whether *Hannity*, the *O'Reilly Factor*, the *Rush Limbaugh Show*, *Paul Harvey News and Comment*, *Countdown with Keith Olbermann*, or *60 Minutes* are "bona fide newscasts" or "interviews," rather than editorials or commentary?

12.   *Problem.* Assuming that a renewed fairness doctrine were to apply to shows such as *Hannity & Colmes* and the *Colbert Report*, how should the FCC determine whether the shows were meeting their obligation of fairness? In *Hannity & Colmes*, one host was conservative and one was liberal, but Hannity took the stronger role (and is now the sole host of the successor program). Could the FCC justifiably conclude that the show overall favors conservative viewpoints? The *Colbert Report* is a satirical news program in which the host mocks conservative commentators by adopting a caricatured persona of one. Should *Colbert* have to give liberals or conservatives a right of reply to the Colbert character's exaggerated version of a conservative position?

MIAMI HERALD PUBLISHING CO. v. TORNILLO
Supreme Court of the United States
418 U.S. 241, 94 S. Ct. 2831, 41 L. Ed. 2d 730 (1974)

MR. CHIEF JUSTICE BURGER delivered the opinion of the Court [in which MR. JUSTICE DOUGLAS, MR. JUSTICE BRENNAN, MR. JUSTICE STEWART, MR. JUSTICE WHITE, MR. JUSTICE MARSHALL, MR. JUSTICE BLACKMUN, MR. JUSTICE POWELL, and MR. JUSTICE REHNQUIST join].

The issue in this case is whether a state statute granting a political candidate a right to equal space to reply to criticism and attacks on his record by a newspaper violates the guarantees of a free press.

In the fall of 1972, appellee, Executive Director of the Classroom Teachers Association, apparently a teachers' collective-bargaining agent, was a candidate for the Florida House of Representatives. On September 20, 1972, and again on September 29, 1972, appellant printed editorials critical of appellee's candidacy. In response to these editorials appellee demanded that appellant print verbatim his replies, defending the role of the Classroom Teachers Association and the organization's accomplishments for the citizens of Dade County. Appellant declined to print the appellee's replies and appellee brought suit * * *. The action was premised on Florida Statute § 104.38, a "right of reply" statute which provides that if a candidate for nomination or election is assailed regarding his personal character or official record by any newspaper, the candidate has the right to demand that the newspaper print, free of cost to the candidate, any reply the candidate may make to the newspaper's charges. The reply must appear in as conspicuous a place and in the same kind of type as the charges which prompted the reply, provided it does not take up more space than the charges. Failure to comply with the statute constitutes a first-degree misdemeanor. * * *

The appellee and supporting advocates of an enforceable right of access to the press vigorously argue that government has an obligation to ensure that a wide variety of views reach the public. * * * It is urged that at the time the First Amendment to the Constitution was ratified in 1791 as part of our Bill of Rights the press was broadly representative of the people it was serving. While many of the newspapers were intensely partisan and narrow in their views, the press collectively presented a broad range of opinions to readers. Entry into publishing was inexpensive; pamphlets and books provided meaningful alternatives to the organized press for the expression of unpopular ideas and often treated events and expressed views not covered by conventional newspapers. A true marketplace of ideas existed in which there was relatively easy access to the channels of communication.

Access advocates submit that although newspapers of the present are superficially similar to those of 1791 the press of today is in reality very different from that known in the early years of our national existence. * * * Newspapers have become big business and there are far fewer of them to serve a larger literate population. Chains of newspapers, national newspapers, national wire and news services, and one-newspaper towns, are the dominant features of a press that has become noncompetitive and enormously powerful and influential in its capacity to manipulate popular opinion and change the course of events. Major metropolitan newspapers have collaborated to establish news services national in scope. Such national news organizations provide syndicated "interpretive reporting" as well as syndicated features and commentary, all of which can serve as part of the new school of "advocacy journalism."

The elimination of competing newspapers in most of our large cities, and the concentration of control of media that results from the only newspaper's being owned by the same interests which own a television station and a radio station, are important components of this trend toward concentration of control of outlets to inform the public.

The result of these vast changes has been to place in a few hands the power to inform the American people and shape public opinion. Much of the editorial opinion and commentary that is printed is that of syndicated columnists distributed nationwide and, as a result, we are told, on national and world issues there tends to be a homogeneity of editorial opinion, commentary, and interpretive analysis. The abuses of bias and manipulative reportage are, likewise, said to be the result of the vast accumulations of unreviewable power in the modern media empires. In effect, it is claimed, the public has lost any ability to respond or to contribute in a meaningful way to the debate on issues. The monopoly of the means of communication allows for little or no critical analysis of the media except in professional journals of very limited readership. * * *

The obvious solution, which was available to dissidents at an earlier time when entry into publishing was relatively inexpensive, today would be to have additional newspapers. But the same economic factors which have caused the disappearance of vast numbers of metropolitan newspapers, have made entry into the marketplace of ideas served by the print media almost impossible. It is urged that the claim of newspapers to be "surrogates for the public" carries with it a concomitant fiduciary obligation to account for that stewardship. From this premise it is reasoned that the only effective way to insure fairness and accuracy and to provide for some accountability is for government to take affirmative action. The First Amendment interest of the public in being informed is said to be in peril because the "marketplace of ideas" is today a monopoly controlled by the owners of the market. * * *

* * * The clear implication [of our prior cases] has been that any such a compulsion to publish that which " 'reason' tells them should not be published" is unconstitutional. A responsible press is an undoubtedly desirable goal, but press responsibility is not mandated by the Constitution and like many other virtues it cannot be legislated.

Appellee's argument that the Florida statute does not amount to a restriction of appellant's right to speak because "the statute in question here has not prevented the *Miami Herald* from saying anything it wished" begs the core question. Compelling editors or publishers to publish that which " 'reason' tells them should not be published" is what is at issue in this case. The Florida statute operates as a command in the same sense as a statute or regulation forbidding appellant to publish specified matter. Governmental restraint on publishing need not fall into familiar or traditional patterns to be subject to constitutional limitations on governmental powers. The Florida statute exacts a penalty on the basis of the content of a newspaper. The first phase of the penalty resulting from the compelled printing of a reply is exacted in terms of the cost in printing and composing time and materials and in taking up space that could be devoted to other material the newspaper may have preferred to print. It is correct, as appellee contends, that a newspaper is not subject to the finite technological limitations of time that confront a broadcaster but it is not correct to say that, as an economic reality, a newspaper can proceed to infinite expansion of its column space to accommodate the replies that a government agency determines or a statute commands the readers should have available.

Faced with the penalties that would accrue to any newspaper that published news or commentary arguably within the reach of the right-of-access statute, editors might well conclude that the safe course is to avoid controversy. Therefore, under the operation of the Florida statute, political and electoral coverage would be blunted or reduced. Government-enforced right of access inescapably "dampens the vigor and limits the variety of public debate," *New York Times Co.* v. *Sullivan*, 376 U.S. 254, 279 (1964) [p. 574]. * * *

Even if a newspaper would face no additional costs to comply with a compulsory access law and would not be forced to forgo publication of news or opinion by the inclusion of a reply, the Florida statute fails to clear the barriers of the First Amendment because of its intrusion into the function of editors. A newspaper is more than a passive receptacle or conduit for news, comment, and advertising. The choice of material to go into a newspaper, and the decisions made as to limitations on the size and content of the paper, and treatment of public issues and public officials — whether fair or unfair — constitute the exercise of editorial control and judgment. It has yet to be demonstrated how governmental regulation of this crucial process can be exercised consistent with First Amendment guarantees of a free press as they have evolved to this time. Accordingly, the judgment of the Supreme Court of Florida is reversed.

It is so ordered.

MR. JUSTICE BRENNAN, with whom MR. JUSTICE REHNQUIST joins, concurring.

I join the Court's opinion which, as I understand it, addresses only "right of reply" statutes and implies no view upon the constitutionality of "retraction" statutes affording plaintiffs able to prove defamatory falsehoods a statutory action to require publication of a retraction.

MR. JUSTICE WHITE, concurring.

* * * We have learned, and continue to learn, from what we view as the unhappy experiences of other nations where government has been allowed to meddle in the internal editorial affairs of newspapers. Regardless of how beneficent-sounding the purposes of controlling the press might be, we prefer "the power of reason as applied through public discussion" and remain intensely skeptical about those measures that would allow government to insinuate itself into the editorial rooms of this Nation's press. * * *

Of course, the press is not always accurate, or even responsible, and may not present full and fair debate on important public issues. But the balance struck by the First Amendment with respect to the press is that society must take the risk that occasionally debate on vital matters will not be comprehensive and that all viewpoints may not be expressed. * * * Any other accommodation — any other system that would supplant private control of the press with the heavy hand of government intrusion — would make the government the censor of what the people may read and know. * * * Whatever power may reside in government to influence the publishing of certain narrowly circumscribed categories of material, we have never thought that the First Amendment permitted public officials to dictate to the press the contents of its news columns or the slant of its editorials.

But though a newspaper may publish without government censorship, it has never been entirely free from liability for what it chooses to print. Among other things, the press has not been wholly at liberty to publish falsehoods damaging to individual reputation. At least until today, we have cherished the average citizen's reputation interest enough to afford him a fair chance to vindicate himself in an action for libel characteristically provided by state law. He has been unable to force the press to tell his side of the story or to print a retraction, but he has had at least the opportunity to win a judgment if he has been able to prove the falsity of the damaging publication, as well as a fair chance to recover reasonable damages for his injury. * * *

Notes and Questions

1.   Tornillo argued that the "communications revolution" in the half-century before 1974 had changed the media in such a way as to make right-of-reply statutes necessary to ensure that a wide variety of views were made available to the public. In making this argument, Tornillo focused on the consolidation of media ownership, including the diminution in the number of newspapers produced in many markets and cross-ownership between media, as well as the tendency of media to focus on national news and report it in a similar way. Nevertheless, other developments in the "communications revolution" arguably cut the other way, demonstrating that modern technology was making it easier to publicize diverse views without the assistance of right-of-reply statutes. Do you see how?

2.   In the years since 1974, communications technology has continued to improve, and ownership of media conglomerates has continued to become more centralized. How should such developments affect the attitude of the courts to right-of-reply statutes?

3.   Does the majority opinion affect laws requiring newspapers to print retractions to correct misstatements of fact? Would a state be able to require that such retractions "appear in as conspicuous a place and in the same kind of type as the" misstatements? Would it matter if the misstatements were made negligently, recklessly, intentionally, or through no fault of the newspaper?

4.   *Red Lion* and *Tornillo* represent opposing poles concerning First Amendment protection of media. While the Court has all but immunized newspapers' editorial decisions from government regulation, broadcasters have been granted less autonomy. The next two cases involve public broadcasting and concern the extent to which the government may exercise editorial control of the broadcast media in the name of the "public interest." As you read them, consider whether there remains (and whether there ever was) sufficient justification for drawing a bright line between the editorial freedom of newspaper publishers and that of broadcasters.

FEDERAL COMMUNICATIONS COMMISSION v. LEAGUE OF WOMEN VOTERS
Supreme Court of the United States
468 U.S. 364, 104 S. Ct. 3106, 82 L. Ed. 2d 278 (1984)

JUSTICE BRENNAN delivered the opinion of the Court [in which JUSTICE MARSHALL, JUSTICE BLACKMUN, JUSTICE POWELL, and JUSTICE O'CONNOR join].

Moved to action by a widely felt need to sponsor independent sources of broadcast programming as an alternative to commercial broadcasting, Congress set out in 1967 to support and promote the development of noncommercial, educational broadcasting stations. A keystone of Congress' program was the Public Broadcasting Act of 1967, 47 U.S.C. § 390 *et seq.*, which established the Corporation for Public Broadcasting, a nonprofit corporation authorized to disburse federal funds to noncommercial television and radio stations in support of station operations and educational programming. Section 399 of that Act forbids any "noncommercial educational broadcasting station which receives a grant from the Corporation" to "engage in editorializing." In this case, we are called upon to decide whether Congress, by imposing that restriction, has passed a "law . . . abridging the freedom of speech, or of the press" in violation of the First Amendment of the Constitution. * * *

Appellee Pacifica Foundation is a nonprofit corporation that owns and operates several noncommercial educational broadcasting stations in five major metropolitan areas. Its licensees have received and are presently receiving grants from the Corporation and are therefore prohibited from editorializing by the terms of § 399 * * *. In April 1979, appellees brought this suit in the United States District Court for the Central District of California challenging the constitutionality of former § 399 [which prohibited all "noncommercial educational broadcasting station[s]" from editorializing and endorsing candidates]. * * * While the suit was pending before the District Court, Congress * * * amended § 399 by confining the ban on editorializing to noncommercial stations that receive Corporation grants and by separately prohibiting all noncommercial stations from making political endorsements, irrespective of whether they receive federal funds. Subsequently, appellees amended their complaint to reflect this change, challenging only the ban on editorializing.[9]

The District Court granted summary judgment in favor of appellees, holding that § 399's ban on editorializing violated the First Amendment. * * * The FCC appealed from the District Court judgment directly to this Court pursuant to 28 U.S.C. § 1252. [W]e now affirm.

* * * Section 399 plainly operates to restrict the expression of editorial opinion on matters of public importance, and, as we have repeatedly explained, communication of this kind is entitled to the most exacting degree of First Amendment protection. *E.g.*, *Minneapolis Star & Tribune Co.* v. *Minnesota Commissioner of Revenue*, 460 U.S. 575, 585 (1983); *First National Bank of Boston* v. *Bellotti*, 435 U.S. 765, 776–777 (1978) [p. 895]; *Buckley* v. *Valeo*, 424 U.S. 1, 14 (1976) [p. 799]; *Thornhill* v. *Alabama*, 310 U.S. 88, 101–102 (1940). Were a similar ban on editorializing applied to newspapers and magazines, we would not hesitate to strike it down as violative of the First Amendment. *E.g.*, *Mills* v. *Alabama*, 384 U.S. 214 (1966) [p. 603]. But, as the Government correctly notes, because broadcast regulation involves unique considerations, our cases have not followed precisely the same approach that we have applied to other media and have never gone so far as to demand that such regulations serve "compelling" governmental interests. At the same time, we think the Government's argument loses sight of concerns that are important in this area and thus misapprehends the essential meaning of our prior decisions concerning the reach of Congress' authority to regulate broadcast communication.

The fundamental principles that guide our evaluation of broadcast regulation are by now well established. First, we have long recognized that Congress, acting

---

[9] In their amended complaint, appellees did not challenge the provision in § 399 prohibiting all noncommercial educational broadcasting stations from "[supporting] or [opposing] any candidate for public office." * * * We therefore express no view of the constitutionality of [that provision].

pursuant to the Commerce Clause, has power to regulate the use of this scarce and valuable national resource. * * *[11]

Second, Congress may, in the exercise of this power, seek to assure that the public receives through this medium a balanced presentation of information on issues of public importance that otherwise might not be addressed if control of the medium were left entirely in the hands of those who own and operate broadcasting stations. Although such governmental regulation has never been allowed with respect to the print media, *Miami Herald Publishing Co.* v. *Tornillo*, 418 U.S. 241 (1974) [p. 613], we have recognized that "differences in the characteristics of new media justify differences in the First Amendment standards applied to them." *Red Lion Broadcasting Co.* v. *FCC*, 395 U.S. 367, 386 (1969) [p. 605]. The fundamental distinguishing characteristic of the new medium of broadcasting that, in our view, has required some adjustment in First Amendment analysis is that "[broadcast] frequencies are a scarce resource [that] must be portioned out among applicants." *Columbia Broadcasting System, Inc.* v. *Democratic National Committee*, 412 U.S. 94, 101 (1973). Thus, our cases have taught that, given spectrum scarcity, those who are granted a license to broadcast must serve in a sense as fiduciaries for the public by presenting "those views and voices which are representative of [their] community and which would otherwise, by necessity, be barred from the airwaves." *Red Lion, supra*, at 389. * * *

Finally, although the Government's interest in ensuring balanced coverage of public issues is plainly both important and substantial, we have, at the same time, made clear that broadcasters are engaged in a vital and independent form of communicative activity. As a result, the First Amendment must inform and give shape to the manner in which Congress exercises its regulatory power in this area. Unlike common carriers, broadcasters are "entitled under the First Amendment to exercise 'the widest journalistic freedom consistent with their public [duties].' " *CBS, Inc.* v. *FCC*, 453 U.S. 367, 395 (1981) (quoting *Columbia Broadcasting System, Inc.* v. *Democratic National Committee, supra*, at 110). Indeed, if the public's interest in receiving a balanced presentation of views is to be fully served, we must necessarily rely in large part upon the editorial initiative and judgment of the broadcasters who bear the public trust. * * *

Thus, although the broadcasting industry plainly operates under restraints not imposed upon other media, the thrust of these restrictions has generally been to secure the public's First Amendment interest in receiving a balanced presentation of views on diverse matters of public concern. As a result of these restrictions, of course, the absolute freedom to advocate one's own positions without also presenting opposing viewpoints — a freedom enjoyed, for example, by newspaper publishers and soapbox orators — is denied to broadcasters. But, as our cases attest, these restrictions have been upheld only when we were satisfied that the

---

[11] The prevailing rationale for broadcast regulation based on spectrum scarcity has come under increasing criticism in recent years. Critics, including the incumbent Chairman of the FCC, charge that with the advent of cable and satellite television technology, communities now have access to such a wide variety of stations that the scarcity doctrine is obsolete. We are not prepared, however, to reconsider our longstanding approach without some signal from Congress or the FCC that technological developments have advanced so far that some revision of the system of broadcast regulation may be required.

restriction is narrowly tailored to further a substantial governmental interest, such as ensuring adequate and balanced coverage of public issues, *e.g.*, *Red Lion*, 395 U.S., at 377. Making that judgment requires a critical examination of the interests of the public and broadcasters in light of the particular circumstances of each case. * * *

In seeking to defend the prohibition on editorializing imposed by § 399, the Government urges that the statute was aimed at preventing two principal threats to the overall success of the Public Broadcasting Act of 1967. According to this argument, the ban was necessary, first, to protect noncommercial educational broadcasting stations from being coerced, as a result of federal financing, into becoming vehicles for Government propagandizing or the objects of governmental influence; and, second, to keep these stations from becoming convenient targets for capture by private interest groups wishing to express their own partisan viewpoints. By seeking to safeguard the public's right to a balanced presentation of public issues through the prevention of either governmental or private bias, these objectives are, of course, broadly consistent with the goals identified in our earlier broadcast regulation cases. But, in sharp contrast to the restrictions upheld in *Red Lion* or in *CBS, Inc.* v. *FCC*, which left room for editorial discretion and simply required broadcast editors to grant others access to the microphone, § 399 directly prohibits the broadcaster from speaking out on public issues even in a balanced and fair manner. The Government insists, however, that the hazards posed in the "special" circumstances of noncommercial educational broadcasting are so great that § 399 is an indispensable means of preserving the public's First Amendment interests. We disagree.

When Congress first decided to provide financial support for the expansion and development of noncommercial educational stations, all concerned agreed that this step posed some risk that these traditionally independent stations might be pressured into becoming forums devoted solely to programming and views that were acceptable to the Federal Government. That Congress was alert to these dangers cannot be doubted. It sought through the Public Broadcasting Act to fashion a system that would provide local stations with sufficient funds to foster their growth and development while preserving their tradition of autonomy and community-orientation. * * *

The intended role of § 399 in achieving these purposes, however, is not as clear. * * * Indeed, it appears that, as the House Committee Report frankly admits, § 399 was added not because Congress thought it was essential to preserving the autonomy and vitality of local stations, but rather "[out] of an abundance of caution."[18]

---

[18] The legislative history surrounding § 399 also suggests that a variety of reasons lay behind the decision to include it as part of the Act. Although some supporters of § 399 plainly were concerned that permitting editorializing might create a risk that noncommercial stations would be subjected to undue governmental influence and thereby become vehicles for governmental propaganda, other supporters of the provision appear to have been more concerned with preventing the possibility that these stations would criticize Government officials. Representative Springer, the provision's chief sponsor and the ranking minority member of the House Committee that reported out the bill containing § 399, explained that his concerns were due at least in part to the fact that "[t]here are some of us who have very strong feelings because they have been editorialized against." * * *

More importantly, an examination of both the overall legislative scheme established by the 1967 Act and the character of public broadcasting demonstrates that the interest asserted by the Government is not substantially advanced by § 399. First, to the extent that federal financial support creates a risk that stations will lose their independence through the bewitching power of governmental largesse, the elaborate structure established by the Public Broadcasting Act already operates to insulate local stations from governmental interference. Congress not only mandated that the new Corporation for Public Broadcasting would have a private, bipartisan structure, but also imposed a variety of important limitations on its powers. The Corporation was prohibited from owning or operating any station, it was required to adhere strictly to a standard of "objectivity and balance" in disbursing federal funds to local stations, and it was prohibited from contributing to or otherwise supporting any candidate for office.

The Act also established a second layer of protections which serve to protect the stations from governmental coercion and interference. Thus, in addition to requiring the Corporation to operate so as to "assure the maximum freedom [of local stations] from interference with or control of program content or other activities," the Act expressly forbids "any department, agency, officer, or employee of the United States to exercise any direction, supervision, or control over educational television or radio broadcasting, or over the Corporation or any of its grantees or contractors . . . ," § 398(a). Subsequent amendments to the Act * * * have provided long-term appropriations authority for public broadcasting, rather than allowing funding to depend upon yearly appropriations; have strictly defined the percentage of appropriated funds that must be disbursed by the Corporation to local stations; and have defined objective criteria under which local television and radio stations receive basic grants from the Corporation to be used at the discretion of the station. The principal thrust of the amendments, therefore, has been to assure long-term appropriations for the Corporation and, more importantly, to insist that it pass specified portions of these funds directly through to local stations to give them greater autonomy in defining the uses to which those funds should be put. Thus, in sharp contrast to § 399, the unifying theme of these various statutory provisions is that they substantially reduce the risk of governmental interference with the editorial judgments of local stations without restricting those stations' ability to speak on matters of public concern.[19]

Even if these statutory protections were thought insufficient to the task, however, suppressing the particular category of speech restricted by § 399 is simply not likely, given the character of the public broadcasting system, to reduce substantially the risk that the Federal Government will seek to influence or put pressure on local stations. An underlying supposition of the Government's argument

---

[19] Furthermore, the risk that federal coercion or influence will be brought to bear against local stations as a result of federal financing is considerably attenuated by the fact that CPB grants account for only [23.4%] of total public broadcasting income. The vast majority of financial support comes instead from state and local governments, as well as a wide variety of private sources, including foundations, businesses, and individual contributions * * *. Given this diversity of funding sources and the decentralized manner in which funds are secured, the threat that improper federal influence will be exerted over local stations is not so pressing as to require the total suppression of editorial speech by these stations.

in this regard is that individual noncommercial stations are likely to speak so forcefully on particular issues that Congress, the ultimate source of the stations' federal funding, will be tempted to retaliate against these individual stations by restricting appropriations for all of public broadcasting. But, as the District Court recognized, the character of public broadcasting suggests that such a risk is speculative at best. There are literally hundreds of public radio and television stations in communities scattered throughout the United States and its territories. Given that central fact, it seems reasonable to infer that the editorial voices of these stations will prove to be as distinctive, varied, and idiosyncratic as the various communities they represent. More importantly, the editorial focus of any particular station can fairly be expected to focus largely on issues affecting only its community. Accordingly, absent some showing by the Government to the contrary, the risk that local editorializing will place all of public broadcasting in jeopardy is not sufficiently pressing to warrant § 399's broad suppression of speech. * * *

Furthermore, the manifest imprecision of the ban imposed by § 399 reveals that its proscription is not sufficiently tailored to the harms it seeks to prevent to justify its substantial interference with broadcasters' speech. Section 399 includes within its grip a potentially infinite variety of speech, most of which would not be related in any way to governmental affairs, political candidacies, or elections. Indeed, the breadth of editorial commentary is as wide as human imagination permits. But the Government never explains how, say, an editorial by local station management urging improvements in a town's parks or museums will so infuriate Congress or other federal officials that the future of public broadcasting will be imperiled unless such editorials are suppressed. Nor is it explained how the suppression of editorials alone serves to reduce the risk of governmental retaliation and interference when it is clear that station management is fully able to broadcast controversial views so long as such views are not labeled as its own. * * *

Finally, although the Government certainly has a substantial interest in ensuring that the audiences of noncommercial stations will not be led to think that the broadcaster's editorials reflect the official view of the Government, this interest can be fully satisfied by less restrictive means that are readily available. To address this important concern, Congress could simply require public broadcasting stations to broadcast a disclaimer every time they editorialize which would state that the editorial represents only the view of the station's management and does not in any way represent the views of the Federal Government or any of the station's other sources of funding. Such a disclaimer — similar to those often used in commercial and noncommercial programming of a controversial nature — would effectively and directly communicate to the audience that the editorial reflected only the views of the station rather than those of the Government. Furthermore, such disclaimers would have the virtue of clarifying the responses that might be made under the fairness doctrine by opponents of the station's position, since those opponents would know with certainty that they were responding only to the station's views and not in any sense to the Government's position.

In sum, § 399's broad ban on all editorializing by every station that receives CPB funds far exceeds what is necessary to protect against the risk of governmental interference or to prevent the public from assuming that editorials by public broadcasting stations represent the official view of government. The regulation impermissibly sweeps within its prohibition a wide range of speech by wholly private stations on topics that do not take a directly partisan stand or that have nothing whatever to do with federal, state, or local government.

Assuming that the Government's second asserted interest in preventing noncommercial stations from becoming a "privileged outlet for the political and ideological opinions of station owners and managers" is legitimate, the substantiality of this asserted interest is dubious. The patent overinclusiveness and underinclusiveness of § 399's ban "undermines the likelihood of a genuine [governmental] interest" in preventing private groups from propagating their own views via public broadcasting. If it is true, as the Government contends, that noncommercial stations remain free, despite § 399, to broadcast a wide variety of controversial views through their power to control program selection, to select which persons will be interviewed, and to determine how news reports will be presented, then it seems doubtful that § 399 can fairly be said to advance any genuinely substantial governmental interest in keeping controversial or partisan opinions from being aired by noncommercial stations. Indeed, since the very same opinions that cannot be expressed by the station's management may be aired so long as they are communicated by a commentator or by a guest appearing at the invitation of the station during an interview, § 399 clearly "provides only ineffective or remote support for the government's purpose."

In short, § 399 does not prevent the use of noncommercial stations for the presentation of partisan views on controversial matters; instead, it merely bars a station from specifically communicating such views on its own behalf or on behalf of its management. If the vigorous expression of controversial opinions is, as the Government assures us, affirmatively encouraged by the Act, and if local licensees are permitted under the Act to exercise editorial control over the selection of programs, controversial or otherwise, that are aired on their stations, then § 399 accomplishes only one thing — the suppression of editorial speech by station management. It does virtually nothing, however, to reduce the risk that public stations will serve solely as outlets for expression of narrow partisan views. * * *

Finally, the public's interest in preventing public broadcasting stations from becoming forums for lopsided presentations of narrow partisan positions is already secured by a variety of other regulatory means that intrude far less drastically upon the "journalistic freedom" of noncommercial broadcasters. The requirements of the FCC's fairness doctrine, for instance, which apply to commercial and noncommercial stations alike, ensure that such editorializing would maintain a reasonably balanced and fair presentation of controversial issues. Thus, even if the management of a noncommercial educational station were inclined to seek to further only its own partisan views when editorializing, it simply could not do so. Indeed, in considering the constitutionality of the FCC's fairness doctrine, the Court in *Red Lion* considered precisely the same justification invoked by the Government today in support of § 399: that without some requirement of fairness and balance, "station owners . . . would have unfettered power . . . to communicate only their own views on public issues . . . and to permit on the air only those with whom they agreed." 395 U.S., at 392. The solution to this problem offered by § 399, however, is precisely the opposite of the remedy prescribed by the FCC and endorsed by the Court in *Red Lion*. Rather than requiring noncommercial broadcasters who express editorial opinions on controversial subjects to permit *more speech* on such subjects to ensure that the public's First Amendment interest in receiving a balanced account of the issue is met, § 399 simply silences all editorial speech by such broadcasters. Since the breadth of § 399 extends so far beyond what is necessary to accomplish the goals identified by the Government, it fails to satisfy the First Amendment standards that we have applied in this area.

We therefore hold that even if some of the hazards at which § 399 was aimed are sufficiently substantial, the restriction is not crafted with sufficient precision to remedy those dangers that may exist to justify the significant abridgment of speech worked by the provision's broad ban on editorializing. The statute is not narrowly tailored to address any of the Government's suggested goals. Moreover, the public's "paramount right" to be fully and broadly informed on matters of public importance through the medium of noncommercial educational broadcasting is not well served by the restriction, for its effect is plainly to diminish rather than augment "the volume and quality of coverage" of controversial issues. *Red Lion*, 395 U.S., at 393. Nor do we see any reason to deny noncommercial broadcasters the right to address matters of public concern on the basis of merely speculative fears of adverse public or governmental reactions to such speech.

* * * Relying upon our recent decision in *Regan* v. *Taxation With Representation of Washington*, 461 U.S. 540 (1983), the Government argues that by prohibiting noncommercial educational stations that receive CPB grants from editorializing, Congress has, in the proper exercise of its spending power, simply determined that it "will not subsidize public broadcasting station editorials." In *Taxation With Representation*, the Court found that Congress could, in the exercise of its spending power, reasonably refuse to subsidize the lobbying activities of tax-exempt charitable organizations by prohibiting such organizations from using tax-deductible contributions to support their lobbying efforts. In so holding, however, we explained that such organizations remained free "to receive [tax-deductible] contributions to support nonlobbying [activities]." 461 U.S., at 545. Thus, a charitable organization could create, under § 501(c)(3) of the Internal Revenue Code, an affiliate to conduct its nonlobbying activities using tax-deductible contributions, and, at the same time, establish, under § 501(c)(4), a separate affiliate to pursue its lobbying efforts without such contributions. 461 U.S., at 544. Given that statutory alternative, the Court concluded that "Congress has not infringed any First Amendment rights or regulated any First Amendment activity; [it] has simply chosen not to pay for TWR's lobbying." *Id.*, at 546.

In this case, however, unlike the situation faced by the charitable organization in *Taxation With Representation*, a noncommercial educational station that receives only 1% of its overall income from CPB grants is barred absolutely from all editorializing. Therefore, in contrast to the appellee in *Taxation With Representation*, such a station is not able to segregate its activities according to the source of its funding. The station has no way of limiting the use of its federal funds to all noneditorializing activities, and, more importantly, it is barred from using even wholly private funds to finance its editorial activity. * * *[27]

---

[27] JUSTICE REHNQUIST's effort to prop up his position by relying on our decisions upholding certain

In conclusion, we emphasize that our disposition of this case rests upon a narrow proposition. We do not hold that the Congress or the FCC is without power to regulate the content, timing, or character of speech by noncommercial educational broadcasting stations. Rather, we hold only that the specific interests sought to be advanced by § 399's ban on editorializing are either not sufficiently substantial or are not served in a sufficiently limited manner to justify the substantial abridgment of important journalistic freedoms which the First Amendment jealously protects. Accordingly, the judgment of the District Court is

Affirmed.

Justice White: Believing that the editorializing and candidate endorsement proscription stand or fall together and being confident that Congress may condition use of its funds on abstaining from political endorsements, I join Justice Rehnquist's dissenting opinion.

Justice Rehnquist, with whom The Chief Justice [Burger] and Justice White join, dissenting.

* * * Congress in enacting § 399 of the Public Broadcasting Act has simply determined that public funds shall not be used to subsidize noncommercial, educational broadcasting stations which engage in "editorializing" or which support

---

provisions of the Hatch Act, 5 U.S.C. § 7324 *et seq.*, only reveals his misunderstanding of what is at issue in *this* case. For example, in both *United Public Workers* v. *Mitchell*, 330 U.S. 75 (1947) [p. 699], and *CSC* v. *Letter Carriers*, 413 U.S. 548 (1973) [p. 713], the Court has upheld § 9(a) of the Hatch Act — a provision that differs from § 399 in three fundamental respects: first, the statute only prohibits Government employees from "active participation in political management and political campaigns," and, accordingly, "[expressions], public or private, on public affairs, personalities and matters of public interest" are not proscribed, *id.*, at 556; second, the constitutionality of that restriction is grounded in the Government's substantial and important interest in ensuring effective job performance by its own employees, *id.*, at 564–565; and, finally, these restrictions evolved over a century of governmental experience with less restrictive alternatives that proved to be inadequate to maintain the effective operation of government, *id.*, at 557–563. Here, by contrast, the editorializing ban in § 399 directly suppresses not only political endorsements but all editorial expression on matters of public importance; it applies to independent, nongovernmental entities rather than to the Government's own employees; and, it is not grounded in any prior governmental experience with less restrictive means.

More importantly, in neither of those cases did the Court even consider that the restrictions could be justified simply because these employees were receiving Government funds, nor did it find that a lesser degree of judicial scrutiny was required simply because Government funds were involved.

Justice Rehnquist's reliance upon *Oklahoma* v. *CSC*, 330 U.S. 127 (1947), is also misplaced. There, a principal issue addressed by the Court was Oklahoma's claim that § 12 of the Hatch Act invaded the State's sovereignty in violation of the Tenth Amendment, because it authorized the Civil Service Commission to withhold federal funds from States whose officers violated the Act. * * * After citing *Mitchell* for the proposition that the Act did not impermissibly interfere with an employee's freedom of expression in political matters, 330 U.S., at 142, the Court explained: "While the United States is not concerned with, and has no power to regulate, local political activities as such of state officials, it does have power to fix the terms upon which its money allotments to states shall be disbursed. *The Tenth Amendment does not forbid the exercise of this power in the way that Congress has proceeded in this case.*" *Id.*, at 143 (emphasis added). Thus, it was only in the context of rejecting Oklahoma's Tenth Amendment claim that the Court used the language cited by the dissent. Just as in *Mitchell*, and *Letter Carriers*, therefore, the Court never intimated in *Oklahoma* v. *CSC* that the mere presence of Government funds was a sufficient reason to uphold the Hatch Act's restrictions on employee freedoms on the basis of relaxed First Amendment standards.

or oppose any political candidate. I do not believe that anything in the First Amendment to the United States Constitution prevents Congress from choosing to spend public moneys in that manner. * * *

Last Term, in *Regan* v. *Taxation With Representation of Washington*, we upheld a provision of the Internal Revenue Code which deprives an otherwise eligible organization of its tax-exempt status and its right to receive tax-deductible contributions if it engages in lobbying. We squarely rejected the contention that Congress' decision not to subsidize lobbying violates the First Amendment, even though we recognized that the right to lobby is constitutionally protected. * * * [T]he Court today seeks to avoid the thrust of that opinion by pointing out that a public broadcasting station is barred from editorializing with its nonfederal funds even though it may receive only a minor fraction of its income from CPB grants. * * *

But to me there is no distinction between § 399 and the statute which we upheld in *Oklahoma* v. *CSC*. Section 12(a) of the Hatch Act totally prohibits any local or state employee who is employed in any activity which receives partial or total financing from the United States from taking part in any political activities. One might just as readily denounce such congressional action as prohibiting employees of a state or local government receiving even a minor fraction of that government's income from federal assistance from exercising their First Amendment right to speak. But not surprisingly this Court upheld the Hatch Act provision in *Oklahoma* v. *CSC*, succinctly stating: "While the United States is not concerned with, and has no power to regulate, local political activities as such of state officials, it does have power to fix the terms upon which its money allotments to states shall be disbursed." *Id.*, at 143. See also *CSC* v. *Letter Carriers*; *United Public Workers* v. *Mitchell*.

The Court seems to believe that Congress actually subsidizes editorializing only if a station uses federal money specifically to cover the expenses that the Court believes can be isolated as editorializing expenses. But to me the Court's approach ignores economic reality. CPB's unrestricted grants are used for salaries, training, equipment, promotion, etc. — financial expenditures which benefit all aspects of a station's programming, including management's editorials. Given the impossibility of compartmentalizing programming expenses in any meaningful way, it seems clear to me that the only effective means for preventing the use of public moneys to subsidize the airing of management's views is for Congress to ban a subsidized station from all on-the-air editorializing. * * *

This is not to say that the Government may attach *any* condition to its largess; it is only to say that when the Government is simply exercising its power to allocate its own public funds, we need only find that the condition imposed has a rational relationship to Congress' purpose in providing the subsidy and that it is not primarily "aimed at the suppression of dangerous ideas." In this case Congress' prohibition is directly related to its purpose in providing subsidies for public broadcasting, and it is plainly rational for Congress to have determined that taxpayer moneys should not be used to subsidize management's views or to pay for management's exercise of partisan politics. Indeed, it is entirely rational for Congress to have wished to avoid the appearance of Government sponsorship of a particular view or a particular political candidate. Furthermore, Congress' prohibition is strictly neutral. In no sense can it be said that Congress has prohibited only editorial views of one particular ideological bent. Nor has it prevented public stations from airing programs, documentaries, interviews, etc. dealing with controversial subjects, so long as management itself does not expressly endorse a particular viewpoint. And Congress has not prevented station management from communicating its own views on those subjects through any medium other than subsidized public broadcasting. * * *

Here, in my view, Congress has rationally concluded that the bulk of taxpayers whose moneys provide the funds for grants by the CPB would prefer not to see the management of public stations engage in editorializing or the endorsing or opposing of political candidates. Because Congress' decision to enact § 399 is a rational exercise of its spending powers and strictly neutral, I would hold that nothing in the First Amendment makes it unconstitutional. Accordingly, I would reverse the judgment of the District Court.

JUSTICE STEVENS, dissenting.

The court jester who mocks the King must choose his words with great care. An artist is likely to paint a flattering portrait of his patron. The child who wants a new toy does not preface his request with a comment on how fat his mother is. Newspaper publishers have been known to listen to their advertising managers. Elected officials may remember how their elections were financed. By enacting the statutory provision that the Court invalidates today, a sophisticated group of legislators expressed a concern about the potential impact of Government funds on pervasive and powerful organs of mass communication. * * *

* * * The quality of the interest in maintaining government neutrality in the free market of ideas — of avoiding subtle forms of censorship and propaganda — outweigh the impact on expression that results from this statute. Indeed, by simply terminating or reducing funding, Congress could curtail much more expression with no risk whatever of a constitutional transgression. * * *

In my judgment the interest in keeping the Federal Government out of the propaganda arena is of overriding importance. That interest is of special importance in the field of electronic communication, not only because that medium is so powerful and persuasive, but also because it is the one form of communication that is licensed by the Federal Government. When the Government already has great potential power over the electronic media, it is surely legitimate to enact statutory safeguards to make sure that it does not cross the threshold that separates neutral regulation from the subsidy of partisan opinion.[11]

---

[11] The "fairness doctrine" is no answer to the concern that Government-funded organs of mass communication will, overall, take a pro-Government slant in editorializing and thereby create a distortion in the marketplace of ideas. First, the "fairness doctrine" is itself enforced by the Government. Second, that doctrine does not guarantee other speakers access to the microphone if they disagree with editorial opinion expressed by the station on public policy issues. No other voice need be heard if the Government determines that the station's editorial "fairly" presented the substance of "the" opposing view. Moreover, as appellees argue, editorials from an institution which the public may hold in high regard may carry

The Court does not question the validity of the basic interests served by § 399. Instead, it suggests that the statute does not substantially serve those interests because the Public Broadcasting Act operates in many other respects to insulate local stations from governmental interference. In my view, that is an indication of nothing more than the strength of the governmental interest involved here — Congress enacted many safeguards because the evil to be avoided was so grave. * * * No safeguard is foolproof; and the fact that funds are dispensed according to largely "objective" criteria certainly is no guarantee. Individuals must always make judgments in allocating funds, and pressure can be exerted in subtle ways as well as through outright fund-cutoffs.

Members of Congress, not members of the Judiciary, live in the world of politics. When they conclude that there is a real danger of political considerations influencing the dispensing of this money and that this provision is necessary to insulate grantees from political pressures in addition to the other safeguards, that judgment is entitled to our respect.

* * * No matter how great or how small the immediate risk may be, there surely is more than a theoretical possibility that future grantees might be influenced by the ever present tie of the political purse strings, even if those strings are never actually pulled. * * *

I respectfully dissent.

Notes and Questions

1. As the Court noted, the Corporation for Public Broadcasting itself was "prohibited from contributing to or otherwise supporting any candidate for office." Are those prohibitions constitutional? Are they distinguishable from similar restrictions applied to ordinary business corporations? *See Citizens United v. FEC*, 558 U.S. 310, 175 L. Ed. 2d 753 (2009).

2. The Court criticized the Act's "imprecision," arguing that few editorials would prompt congressional retaliation. How could Congress more narrowly tailor a ban without creating an unconstitutional content-based distinction?

3. Should the Court have deferred to Congress's judgment about the need to insulate public broadcasters from political influence, as Justice Stevens claimed, or should the Court have been suspicious that the desire to insulate broadcasters from political influence was itself motivated by politics, as the Court implied in footnote 18?

---

added weight in the marketplace of ideas. That fact, however, magnifies the evil sought to be avoided, for the danger is that pro-Government views that are not actually shared by that institution will be parroted to curry favor with its benefactor. [Relocated. -Eds.]

ARKANSAS EDUCATIONAL TELEVISION COMMISSION v. FORBES

Supreme Court of the United States

523 U.S. 666, 118 S. Ct. 1633, 140 L. Ed. 2d 875 (1998)

JUSTICE KENNEDY delivered the opinion of the Court [in which CHIEF JUSTICE REHNQUIST, JUSTICE O'CONNOR, JUSTICE SCALIA, JUSTICE THOMAS, and JUSTICE BREYER join].

A state-owned public television broadcaster sponsored a candidate debate from which it excluded an independent candidate with little popular support. The issue before us is whether, by reason of its state ownership, the station had a constitutional obligation to allow every candidate access to the debate. We conclude that, unlike most other public television programs, the candidate debate was subject to constitutional constraints applicable to nonpublic fora under our forum precedents. Even so, the broadcaster's decision to exclude the candidate was a reasonable, viewpoint-neutral exercise of journalistic discretion.

Petitioner, the Arkansas Educational Television Commission (AETC), is an Arkansas state agency owning and operating a network of five noncommercial television stations. * * * In the spring of 1992, AETC staff began planning a series of debates between candidates for federal office in the November 1992 elections. AETC decided to televise a total of five debates, scheduling one for the Senate election and one for each of the four congressional elections in Arkansas. Working in close consultation with Bill Simmons, Arkansas Bureau Chief for the Associated Press, AETC staff developed a debate format allowing about 53 minutes during each 1-hour debate for questions to and answers by the candidates. Given the time constraint, the staff and Simmons "decided to limit participation in the debates to the major party candidates or any other candidate who had strong popular support."

On June 17, 1992, AETC invited the Republican and Democratic candidates for Arkansas' Third Congressional District to participate in the AETC debate for that seat. Two months later, after obtaining the 2,000 signatures required by Arkansas law, respondent Ralph Forbes was certified as an independent candidate qualified to appear on the ballot for the seat. Forbes was a perennial candidate who had sought, without success, a number of elected offices in Arkansas. On August 24, 1992, he wrote to AETC requesting permission to participate in the debate for his district, scheduled for October 22, 1992. On September 4, AETC Executive Director Susan Howarth denied Forbes' request, explaining that AETC had "made a bona fide journalistic judgement that our viewers would best be served by limiting the debate" to the candidates already invited.

On October 19, 1992, Forbes filed suit against AETC, seeking injunctive and declaratory relief as well as damages. * * * At trial, AETC professional staff testified Forbes was excluded because he lacked any campaign organization, had not generated appreciable voter support, and was not regarded as a serious candidate by the press covering the election. The jury made express findings that AETC's decision to exclude Forbes had not been influenced by political pressure or disagreement with his views. The District Court entered judgment for AETC.

The Court of Appeals * * * reversed. The court acknowledged that AETC's decision to exclude Forbes "was made in good faith" and was "exactly the kind of journalistic judgment routinely made by newspeople." The court asserted, nevertheless, that AETC had "opened its facilities to a particular group — candidates running for the Third District Congressional seat." AETC's action, the court held, made the debate a public forum, to which all candidates "legally qualified to appear on the ballot" had a presumptive right of access. Applying strict scrutiny, the court determined that AETC's assessment of Forbes' "political viability" was neither a "compelling nor [a] narrowly tailored" reason for excluding him from the debate. * * * We now reverse. * * *

As a general rule, the nature of editorial discretion counsels against subjecting broadcasters to claims of viewpoint discrimination. Programming decisions would be particularly vulnerable to claims of this type because even principled exclusions rooted in sound journalistic judgment can often be characterized as viewpoint based. To comply with their obligation to air programming that serves the public interest, broadcasters must often choose among speakers expressing different viewpoints. * * * Much like a university selecting a commencement speaker, a public institution selecting speakers for a lecture series, or a public school prescribing its curriculum, a broadcaster by its nature will facilitate the expression of some viewpoints instead of others. Were the judiciary to require, and so to define and approve, pre-established criteria for access, it would risk implicating the courts in judgments that should be left to the exercise of journalistic discretion.

When a public broadcaster exercises editorial discretion in the selection and presentation of its programming, it engages in speech activity. Although programming decisions often involve the compilation of the speech of third parties, the decisions nonetheless constitute communicative acts. * * *

Although public broadcasting as a general matter does not lend itself to scrutiny under the forum doctrine, candidate debates present the narrow exception to the rule. For two reasons, a candidate debate like the one at issue here is different from other programming. First, unlike AETC's other broadcasts, the debate was by design a forum for political speech by the candidates. Consistent with the long tradition of candidate debates, the implicit representation of the broadcaster was that the views expressed were those of the candidates, not its own. The very purpose of the debate was to allow the candidates to express their views with minimal intrusion by the broadcaster. In this respect the debate differed even from a political talk show, whose host can express partisan views and then limit the discussion to those ideas.

Second, in our tradition, candidate debates are of exceptional significance in the electoral process. "[I]t is of particular importance that candidates have the . . . opportunity to make their views known so that the electorate may intelligently evaluate the candidates' personal qualities and their positions on vital public issues before choosing among them on election day." *CBS, Inc. v. FCC*, 453 U.S. 367, 396 (1981). Deliberation on the positions and qualifications of candidates is integral to our system of government, and electoral speech may have its most profound and widespread impact when it is disseminated through televised debates. * * *

The special characteristics of candidate debates support the conclusion that the

AETC debate was a forum of some type. * * * Forbes argues, and the Court of Appeals held, that the debate was a public forum to which he had a First Amendment right of access. Under our precedents, however, the debate was a nonpublic forum, from which AETC could exclude Forbes in the reasonable, viewpoint-neutral exercise of its journalistic discretion.

For our purposes, it will suffice to employ the categories of speech fora already established and discussed in our cases. "[T]he Court [has] identified three types of fora: the traditional public forum, the public forum created by government designation, and the nonpublic forum." Traditional public fora are defined by the objective characteristics of the property, such as whether, "by long tradition or by government fiat," the property has been "devoted to assembly and debate." The government can exclude a speaker from a traditional public forum "only when the exclusion is necessary to serve a compelling state interest and the exclusion is narrowly drawn to achieve that interest."

Designated public fora, in contrast, are created by purposeful governmental action. "The government does not create a [designated] public forum by inaction or by permitting limited discourse, but only by intentionally opening a nontraditional public forum for public discourse." Hence "the Court has looked to the policy and practice of the government to ascertain whether it intended to designate a place not traditionally open to assembly and debate as a public forum." If the government excludes a speaker who falls within the class to which a designated public forum is made generally available, its action is subject to strict scrutiny.

Other government properties are either nonpublic fora or not fora at all. The government can restrict access to a nonpublic forum "as long as the restrictions are reasonable and [are] not an effort to suppress expression merely because public officials oppose the speaker's view."

In summary, traditional public fora are open for expressive activity regardless of the government's intent. The objective characteristics of these properties require the government to accommodate private speakers. The government is free to open additional properties for expressive use by the general public or by a particular class of speakers, thereby creating designated public fora. Where the property is not a traditional public forum and the government has not chosen to create a designated public forum, the property is either a nonpublic forum or not a forum at all.

The parties agree the AETC debate was not a traditional public forum. The Court has rejected the view that traditional public forum status extends beyond its historic confines; and even had a more expansive conception of traditional public fora been adopted, the almost unfettered access of a traditional public forum would be incompatible with the programming dictates a television broadcaster must follow. The issue, then, is whether the debate was a designated public forum or a nonpublic forum.

Under our precedents, the AETC debate was not a designated public forum. To create a forum of this type, the government must intend to make the property "generally available" to a class of speakers. * * * A designated public forum is not created when the government allows selective access for individual speakers rather than general access for a class of speakers. * * *

* * * By recognizing the distinction [between the "general access" characteristic of a designated public forum and the "selective access" of a nonpublic forum], we encourage the government to open its property to some expressive activity in cases where, if faced with an all-or-nothing choice, it might not open the property at all. That this distinction turns on governmental intent does not render it unprotective of speech. Rather, it reflects the reality that, with the exception of traditional public fora, the government retains the choice of whether to designate its property as a forum for specified classes of speakers.

Here, the debate did not have an open-microphone format. * * * AETC made candidate-by-candidate determinations as to which of the eligible candidates would participate in the debate. "Such selective access, unsupported by evidence of a purposeful designation for public use, does not create a public forum." Thus the debate was a nonpublic forum.

[T]he Court of Appeals' holding would result in less speech, not more. In ruling that the debate was a public forum open to all ballot-qualified candidates, the Court of Appeals would place a severe burden upon public broadcasters who air candidates' views. In each of the 1988, 1992, and 1996 Presidential elections, for example, no fewer than 19 candidates appeared on the ballot in at least one State. In the 1996 congressional elections, it was common for 6 to 11 candidates to qualify for the ballot for a particular seat. On logistical grounds alone, a public television editor might, with reason, decide that the inclusion of all ballot-qualified candidates would "actually undermine the educational value and quality of debates."

Were it faced with the prospect of cacophony, on the one hand, and First Amendment liability, on the other, a public television broadcaster might choose not to air candidates' views at all. * * * These concerns are more than speculative. As a direct result of the Court of Appeals' decision in this case, the Nebraska Educational Television Network canceled a scheduled debate between candidates in Nebraska's 1996 United States Senate race. A First Amendment jurisprudence yielding these results does not promote speech but represses it.

The debate's status as a nonpublic forum, however, did not give AETC unfettered power to exclude any candidate it wished. * * * To be consistent with the First Amendment, the exclusion of a speaker from a nonpublic forum must not be based on the speaker's viewpoint and must otherwise be reasonable in light of the purpose of the property.

In this case, the jury found Forbes' exclusion was not based on "objections or opposition to his views." The record provides ample support for this finding, demonstrating as well that AETC's decision to exclude him was reasonable. AETC Executive Director Susan Howarth testified Forbes' views had "absolutely" no role in the decision to exclude him from the debate. She further testified Forbes was excluded because (1) "the Arkansas voters did not consider him a serious candidate"; (2) "the news organizations also did not consider him a serious candidate"; (3) "the Associated Press and a national election result reporting service did not plan to run his name in results on election night"; (4) Forbes "apparently had little, if any, financial support, failing to report campaign finances to the Secretary of State's office or to the Federal Election Commission"; and (5) "there [was] no 'Forbes for Congress' campaign headquarters other than his house." Forbes himself described his campaign organization as "bedlam" and the media coverage of his campaign as "zilch." It is, in short, beyond dispute that Forbes was excluded not because of his viewpoint but because he had generated no appreciable public interest. * * *

Nor did AETC exclude Forbes in an attempted manipulation of the political process. The evidence provided powerful support for the jury's express finding that AETC's exclusion of Forbes was not the result of "political pressure from anyone inside or outside [AETC]." There is no serious argument that AETC did not act in good faith in this case. AETC excluded Forbes because the voters lacked interest in his candidacy, not because AETC itself did.

The broadcaster's decision to exclude Forbes was a reasonable, viewpoint-neutral exercise of journalistic discretion consistent with the First Amendment. The judgment of the Court of Appeals is

Reversed.

JUSTICE STEVENS, with whom JUSTICE SOUTER and JUSTICE GINSBURG join, dissenting.

The Court has decided that a state-owned television network has no "constitutional obligation to allow every candidate access to" political debates that it sponsors. I do not challenge that decision. The judgment of the Court of Appeals should nevertheless be affirmed. * * *

No written criteria cabined the discretion of the AETC staff. Their subjective judgment about a candidate's "viability" or "newsworthiness" allowed them wide latitude either to permit or to exclude a third participant in any debate.[14] Moreover, in exercising that judgment they were free to rely on factors that arguably should favor inclusion as justifications for exclusion. Thus, the fact that Forbes had little financial support was considered as evidence of his lack of viability when that factor might have provided an independent reason for allowing him to share a free forum with wealthier candidates.[15] * * *

The reasons that support the need for narrow, objective, and definite standards to guide licensing decisions apply directly to the wholly subjective access decisions made by the staff of AETC.[18] The importance of avoiding arbitrary or viewpoint-

---

[14] It is particularly troubling that AETC excluded the only independent candidate but invited all the major-party candidates to participate in the planned debates, regardless of their chances of electoral success. As this Court has recognized, "political figures outside the two major parties have been fertile sources of new ideas and new programs; many of their challenges to the status quo have in time made their way into the political mainstream."

[15] Lack of substantial financial support apparently was not a factor in the decision to invite a major-party candidate with even less financial support than Forbes.

[18] Ironically, it is the standardless character of the decision to exclude Forbes that provides the basis for the Court's conclusion that the debates were a nonpublic forum rather than a limited public forum. The Court explains that "[a] designated public forum is not created when the government allows selective access for individual speakers rather than general access for a class of speakers." If, as AETC claims, it did invite either the entire class of "viable" candidates, or the entire class of "newsworthy" candidates, under the Court's reasoning, it created a designated public forum.

based exclusions from political debates militates strongly in favor of requiring the controlling state agency to use (and adhere to) preestablished, objective criteria to determine who among qualified candidates may participate. * * * A constitutional duty to use objective standards — *i.e.*, "neutral principles" — for determining whether and when to adjust a debate format would impose only a modest requirement that would fall far short of a duty to grant every multiple-party request. Such standards would also have the benefit of providing the public with some assurance that state-owned broadcasters cannot select debate participants on arbitrary grounds. * * *

Notes and Questions

1.   The Court essentially held that there is no requirement that public entities sponsoring debates adhere to preexisting criteria in inviting candidates to participate. As long as the decision to exclude a certain candidate is not motivated by disagreement with the candidate's viewpoint and is otherwise reasonable, the exclusion is constitutional. Justice Stevens argued that such a rule created too much opportunity for abuse, and that the public entity should not be permitted to limit participation in debates through an *ad hoc* process.

Despite the Court's holding that preexisting criteria are not a constitutional necessity, would you advise such entities to adopt them anyway? Why or why not?

2.   Is Justice Stevens's approach workable in other contexts? Would he require a state university to adhere to preexisting criteria in selecting a commencement speaker? What constitutional constraints would apply to such a situation under the Court's analysis?

3.   The Court opined that debates are different from programs such as "political talk shows" because debates are designed to feature the views of the candidates, whereas talk shows feature the views and agendas of the hosts. As a result, talk shows can be seen as expressing the viewpoints of the station, and the Court suggests that the First Amendment presents no barrier to the expression of such opinion, even when dissenters are not provided an opportunity to respond. Does this discussion indicate skepticism on the part of the Court with *Red Lion*?

4.   The *AETC* Court argued that treating debates as public fora would result in less speech because broadcasters would decline to hold debates if the only alternative were to provide access to every ballot-qualified candidate. Is that analysis consistent with *Red Lion*?

D.   ANONYMOUS SPEECH

BROWN v. SOCIALIST WORKERS '74 CAMPAIGN COMMITTEE (OHIO)
Supreme Court of the United States
459 U.S. 87, 103 S. Ct. 416, 74 L. Ed. 2d 250 (1982)

JUSTICE MARSHALL delivered the opinion of the Court [in which CHIEF JUSTICE BURGER, JUSTICE BRENNAN, JUSTICE WHITE, and JUSTICE POWELL join, and in which JUSTICE BLACKMUN joins as to Parts I, III, and IV]. * * *

I

The Socialist Workers Party (SWP) is a small political party with approximately 60 members in the State of Ohio. The Party states in its constitution that its aim is "the abolition of capitalism and the establishment of a workers' government to achieve socialism." As the District Court found, the SWP does not advocate the use of violence. It seeks instead to achieve social change through the political process, and its members regularly run for public office. The SWP's candidates have had little success at the polls. In 1980, for example, the Ohio SWP's candidate for the United States Senate received fewer than 77,000 votes, less than 1.9% of the total vote. Campaign contributions and expenditures in Ohio have averaged about $15,000 annually since 1974.

In 1974 appellees instituted a class action * * * challenging the constitutionality of the disclosure provisions of the Ohio Campaign Expense Reporting Law. The Ohio statute requires every candidate for political office to file a statement identifying each contributor and each recipient of a disbursement of campaign funds. The "object or purpose" of each disbursement must also be disclosed. The lists of names and addresses of contributors and recipients are open to public inspection for at least six years. Violations of the disclosure requirements are punishable by fines of up to $1,000 for each day of violation.

* * * [T]he three-judge court concluded that under *Buckley* v. *Valeo*, 424 U.S. 1 (1976) [p. 1011], the Ohio disclosure requirements are unconstitutional as applied to appellees. * * *

II

The Constitution protects against the compelled disclosure of political associations and beliefs. Such disclosures "can seriously infringe on privacy of association and belief guaranteed by the First Amendment." *Buckley* v. *Valeo*, *supra*, at 64. "Inviolability of privacy in group association may in many circumstances be indispensable to preservation of freedom of association, particularly where a group espouses dissident beliefs." *NAACP* v. *Alabama*, [357 U.S. 449], 462 [(1958)]. The right to privacy in one's political associations and beliefs will yield only to a "subordinating interest of the State [that is] compelling," *NAACP* v. *Alabama*, *supra*, at 463, and then only if there is a "substantial relation between the information sought and [an] overriding and compelling state interest."

In *Buckley* v. *Valeo* this Court upheld against a First Amendment challenge the reporting and disclosure requirements imposed on political parties by the Federal Election Campaign Act of 1971. The Court found three government interests sufficient in general to justify requiring disclosure of information concerning campaign contributions and expenditures: enhancement of voters' knowledge about a candidate's possible allegiances and interests, deterrence of corruption, and the enforcement of contribution limitations. The Court stressed, however, that in certain circumstances the balance of interests requires exempting minor political parties from compelled disclosures. The government's interests in compelling disclosures are "diminished" in the case of minor parties. Minor party candidates "usually represent definite and publicized viewpoints" well known to the public, and the improbability of their winning reduces the dangers of corruption and vote-buying. At the same time, the potential for impairing First Amendment interests is substantially greater:

> "We are not unmindful that the damage done by disclosure to the associational interests of the minor parties and their members and to supporters of independents could be significant. These movements are less likely to have a sound financial base and thus are more vulnerable to falloffs in contributions. In some instances fears of reprisal may deter contributions to the point where the movement cannot survive. The public interest also suffers if that result comes to pass, for there is a consequent reduction in the free circulation of ideas both within and without the political arena." [424 U.S.], at 71.

We concluded that in some circumstances the diminished government interests furthered by compelling disclosures by minor parties does not justify the greater threat to First Amendment values.

Buckley v. *Valeo* set forth the following test for determining when the First Amendment requires exempting minor parties from compelled disclosures:

> "The evidence offered need show only a reasonable probability that the compelled disclosure of a party's contributors' names will subject them to threats, harassment, or reprisals from either Government officials or private parties." *Id.*, at 74.

The Court acknowledged that "unduly strict requirements of proof could impose a heavy burden" on minor parties. *Ibid.* Accordingly, the Court emphasized that "[minor] parties must be allowed sufficient flexibility in the proof of injury." *Ibid.*

> "The proof may include, for example, specific evidence of past or present harassment of members due to their associational ties, or of harassment directed against the organization itself. A pattern of threats or specific manifestations of public hostility may be sufficient. New parties that have no history upon which to draw may be able to offer evidence of reprisals and threats directed against individuals or organizations holding similar views." *Ibid.*

Appellants concede that the *Buckley* test for exempting minor parties governs the disclosure of the names of *contributors*, but they contend that the test has no application to the compelled disclosure of names of *recipients* of campaign disbursements. Appellants assert that the State has a substantial interest in preventing the misuse of campaign funds.[10] They also argue that the disclosure of the names of recipients of campaign funds will have no significant impact on First Amendment rights, because, unlike a contribution, the mere receipt of money for commercial services does not affirmatively express political support.

We reject appellants' unduly narrow view of the minor-party exemption recognized in *Buckley*. Appellants' attempt to limit the exemption to laws requiring disclosure of contributors is inconsistent with the rationale for the exemption stated in *Buckley*. The Court concluded that the government interests supporting disclosure are weaker in the case of minor parties, while the threat to First Amendment values is greater. Both of these considerations apply not only to the disclosure of campaign contributors but also to the disclosure of recipients of campaign disbursements. * * *[11]

Moreover, appellants seriously understate the threat to First Amendment rights that would result from requiring minor parties to disclose the recipients of campaign disbursements. Expenditures by a political party often consist of reimbursements, advances, or wages paid to party members, campaign workers, and supporters, whose activities lie at the very core of the First Amendment. Disbursements may also go to persons who choose to express their support for an unpopular cause by providing services rendered scarce by public hostility and suspicion. Should their involvement be publicized, these persons would be as vulnerable to threats, harassment, and reprisals as are contributors whose connection with the party is solely financial.[14] Even individuals who receive disbursements

---

[10] This is one of three government interests identified in *Buckley*. Appellants do not contend that the other two interests, enhancing voters' ability to evaluate candidates and enforcing contribution limitations, support the disclosure of the names of recipients of campaign disbursements.

[11] The partial dissent suggests that the government interest in the disclosure of recipients of expenditures is not significantly diminished in the case of minor political parties, since parties with little likelihood of electoral success might nevertheless finance improper campaign activities merely to gain recognition. * * * [But m]ost of the limited resources of minor parties will typically be needed to pay for the ordinary fixed costs of conducting campaigns, such as filing fees, travel expenses, and the expenses incurred in publishing and distributing campaign literature and maintaining offices. * * * We cannot agree, therefore, that minor parties are as likely as major parties to make significant expenditures in funding dirty tricks or other improper campaign activities. Moreover, the expenditure by minor parties of even a substantial portion of their limitod [*sic*] funds on illegal activities would be unlikely to have a substantial impact.

Furthermore, the mere possibility that minor parties will resort to corrupt or unfair tactics cannot justify the substantial infringement on First Amendment interests that would result from compelling the disclosure of recipients of expenditures. * * * We * * * recognized [in *Buckley*] that the distorting influence of large contributors on elections may not be entirely absent in the context of minor parties. Nevertheless, because we concluded that the government interest in disclosing contributors is substantially reduced in the case of minor parties, we held that minor parties are entitled to an exemption from requirements that contributors be disclosed where they can show a reasonable probability of harassment. 424 U.S., at 70. Because we similarly conclude that the government interest in requiring the disclosure of recipients of expenditures is substantially reduced in the case of minor parties, we hold that the minor-party exemption recognized in *Buckley* applies to compelled disclosure of expenditures as well.

[14] The fact that some or even many recipients of campaign expenditures may not be exposed to the risk of public hostility does not detract from the serious threat to the exercise of First Amendment rights

for "merely" commercial transactions may be deterred by the public enmity attending publicity, and those seeking to harass may disrupt commercial activities on the basis of expenditure information. Because an individual who enters into a transaction with a minor party purely for commercial reasons lacks any ideological commitment to the party, such an individual may well be deterred from providing services by even a small risk of harassment.[16] Compelled disclosure of the names of such recipients of expenditures could therefore cripple a minor party's ability to operate effectively and thereby reduce "the free circulation of ideas both within and without the political arena." *Buckley*, 424 U.S., at 71.

We hold, therefore, that the test announced in *Buckley* for safeguarding the First Amendment interests of minor parties and their members and supporters applies not only to the compelled disclosure of campaign contributors but also to the compelled disclosure of recipients of campaign disbursements.

III

The District Court properly applied the *Buckley* test to the facts of this case. The District Court found "substantial evidence of both governmental and private hostility toward and harassment of SWP members and supporters." Appellees introduced proof of specific incidents of private and government hostility toward the SWP and its members within the four years preceding the trial. These incidents, many of which occurred in Ohio and neighboring States, included threatening phone calls and hate mail, the burning of SWP literature, the destruction of SWP members' property, police harassment of a party candidate, and the firing of shots at an SWP office. There was also evidence that in the 12-month period before trial 22 SWP members, including 4 in Ohio, were fired because of their party membership. Although appellants contend that two of the Ohio firings were not politically motivated, the evidence amply supports the District Court's conclusion that "private hostility and harassment toward SWP members make it difficult for them to maintain employment."

The District Court also found a past history of Government harassment of the SWP. * * * Until at least 1976, the FBI employed various covert techniques to obtain information about the SWP, including information concerning the sources of its funds and the nature of its expenditures. The District Court specifically found that the FBI had conducted surveillance of the Ohio SWP and had interfered with its activities within the State. Government surveillance was not limited to the FBI. The

---

of those who are so exposed. We cannot agree with the partial dissent's assertion that disclosures of disbursements paid to campaign workers and supporters will not increase the probability that they will be subjected to harassment and hostility. Apart from the fact that individuals may work for a candidate in a variety of ways without publicizing their involvement, the application of a disclosure requirement results in a dramatic increase in public exposure. Under Ohio law a person's affiliation with the party will be recorded in a document that must be kept open to inspection by any one who wishes to examine it for a period of at least six years. The preservation of unorthodox political affiliations in public records substantially increases the potential for harassment above and beyond the risk that an individual faces simply as a result of having worked for an unpopular party at one time.

[16] Moreover, it would be hard to think of many instances in which the state interest in preventing vote-buying and improper campaign activities would be furthered by the disclosure of payments for routine commercial services.

United States Civil Service Commission also gathered information on the SWP, the YSA, and their supporters, and the FBI routinely distributed its reports to Army, Navy and Air Force Intelligence, the United States Secret Service, and the Immigration and Naturalization Service.

The District Court properly concluded that the evidence of private and Government hostility toward the SWP and its members establishes a reasonable probability that disclosing the names of contributors and recipients will subject them to threats, harassment, and reprisals. There were numerous instances of recent harassment of the SWP both in Ohio and in other States.[20] There was also considerable evidence of past Government harassment. Appellants challenge the relevance of this evidence of Government harassment in light of recent efforts to curb official misconduct. Notwithstanding these efforts, the evidence suggests that hostility toward the SWP is ingrained and likely to continue. All this evidence was properly relied on by the District Court.

IV

The First Amendment prohibits a State from compelling disclosures by a minor party that will subject those persons identified to the reasonable probability of threats, harassment, or reprisals. Such disclosures would infringe the First Amendment rights of the party and its members and supporters. In light of the substantial evidence of past and present hostility from private persons and Government officials against the SWP, Ohio's campaign disclosure requirements cannot be constitutionally applied to the Ohio SWP.

The judgment of the three-judge District Court for the Southern District of Ohio is affirmed.

It is so ordered.

Justice Blackmun, concurring in part and concurring in the judgment.

[Justice Blackmun argued that the case did not properly present the question whether the anonymity of campaign disbursements should be subject to the same

---

[20] Some of the recent episodes of threats, harassment, and reprisals agains the SWP and its members occurred outside of Ohio. Anti-SWP occurrences in places such as Chicago (SWP office vandalized) and Pittsburgh (shots fired at SWP building) are certainly relevant to the determination of the public's attitude toward the SWP in Ohio. * * *

Appellants point to the lack of direct evidence linking the Ohio statute's disclosure requirements to the harassment of campaign contributors or recipients of disbursements. In *Buckley*, however, we rejected such "unduly strict requirements of proof" in favor of "flexibility in the proof of injury." [*Ibid.*] We thus rejected requiring a minor party to "come forward with witnesses who are too fearful to contribute but not too fearful to testify about their fear" or prove that "chill and harassment [are] directly attributable to the specific disclosure from which the exemption is sought." *Ibid.* We think that these considerations are equally applicable to the proof required to establish a reasonable probability that recipients will be subjected to threats and harassment if their names are disclosed. While the partial dissent appears to agree, its "separately focused inquiry" in reality requires evidence of chill and harassment directly attributable to the expenditure-disclosure requirement.

constitutional standard as the one applicable to contributions. Assuming, however, that the *Buckley* standard applied to both, he agreed that the Ohio law could not constitutionally be applied against the SWP, either as to contributions or expenditures.]

JUSTICE O'CONNOR, with whom JUSTICE REHNQUIST and JUSTICE STEVENS join, concurring in part and dissenting in part.

I concur in the judgment that the Socialist Workers Party has sufficiently demonstrated a reasonable probability that disclosure of contributors will subject those persons to threats, harassment, or reprisals, and thus under *Buckley* v. *Valeo* the State of Ohio cannot constitutionally compel the disclosure. Further, I agree that the broad concerns of *Buckley* apply to the required disclosure of recipients of campaign expenditures. But, as I view the record presented here, the SWP has failed to carry its burden of showing that there is a reasonable probability that disclosure of recipients of expenditures will subject the recipients themselves or the SWP to threats, harassment, or reprisals. Moreover, the strong public interest in fair and honest elections outweighs any damage done to the associational rights of the party and its members by application of the State's expenditure disclosure law. * * *

[T]here are important differences between disclosure of contributors and disclosure of recipients of campaign expenditures — differences that * * * compel me to conclude that the balance should not necessarily be calibrated identically. First, unlike the government's interest in disclosure of contributions, its interest in disclosure of expenditures does not decrease significantly for small parties. The Court in *Buckley* recognized that knowing the identity of contributors would not significantly increase the voters' ability to determine the political ideology of the minor-party candidate, for the stance of the minor-party candidate is usually well known. Nor would identifying a minor party's contributors further the interest in preventing the "buying" of a candidate, because of the improbability of the minor-party candidate's winning the election. Thus, these two major government interests in disclosure of contributions are significantly reduced for minor parties.[3]

In sharp contrast, however, the governmental interest in disclosure of expenditures remains significant for minor parties. The purpose of requiring parties to disclose expenditures is to deter improper influencing of voters. Corruption of the electoral process can take many forms: the actual buying of votes; the use of "slush funds;" dirty tricks; and bribes of poll watchers and other election officials. Certainly, a "persuasive" campaign worker on election day can corral voters for his minor-party candidate with even a modest "slush fund." Even though such improper practices are unlikely to be so successful as to attract enough votes to elect the minor-party candidate, a minor party, whose short-term goal is merely recognition, may be as tempted to resort to impermissible methods as are major parties, and the resulting deflection of votes can determine the outcome of the election of other

---

[3] [T]he third governmental interest articulated in *Buckley* — using disclosures to police limitations on contributions and expenditures — has no application to either contributions or expenditures in Ohio, since the Ohio statute sets no limitations on them.

candidates. The requirement of a *full* and *verifiable* report of expenditures is important in deterring such practices, for otherwise the party could hide the improper transactions through an accounting sleight of hand.[6]

On the other side of the balance, disclosure of recipients of expenditures will have a lesser impact on a minority party's First Amendment interests than will disclosure of contributors. * * * Many expenditures of the minority party will be for quite mundane purposes to persons not intimately connected with the organization. Payments for such things as office supplies, telephone service, bank charges, printing and photography costs would generally fall in this category. The likelihood that such business transactions would dry up if disclosed is remote at best. Unlike silent contributors, whom disclosure would reveal to the public as supporters of the party's ideological positions, persons providing business services to a minor party are not generally perceived by the public as supporting the party's ideology, and thus are unlikely to be harassed if their names are disclosed. Consequently, the party's associational interests are unlikely to be affected by disclosure of recipients of such expenditures.

Other recipients of expenditures may have closer ideological ties to the party. The majority suggests that campaign workers receiving per diem, travel, or room expenses may fit in this category. It is certainly conceivable that such persons may be harassed or threatened for their conduct. Laws requiring disclosure of recipients of expenditures, however, are not likely to contribute to this harassment. Once an individual has openly shown his close ties to the organization by campaigning for it, disclosure of receipt of expenditures is unlikely to increase the degree of harassment so significantly as to deter the individual from campaigning for the party. Further, in striking the balance, the governmental concerns are greatest precisely for the actions of campaign workers that might improperly influence voters. Thus, whatever marginal deterrence that may arise from disclosure of expenditures is outweighed by the heightened governmental interest.

In sum, the heightened governmental interest in disclosure of expenditures and the reduced marginal deterrent effect on associational interests demand a separately focused inquiry into whether there exists a reasonable probability that disclosure will subject recipients or the party itself to threats, harassment, or reprisals.

Turning to the evidence in this case, it is important to remember that, even though proof requirements must be flexible, *Buckley, supra,* at 74, the minor party carries the burden of production and persuasion to show that its First Amendment interests outweigh the governmental interests. Additionally, the application of the *Buckley* standard to the historical evidence is most properly characterized as a mixed question of law and fact, for which we normally assess the record independently to determine if it supports the conclusion of unconstitutionality as applied.[8]

---

[6] I therefore disagree with the majority's suggestion that the government interest in deterring corruption is not furthered by disclosure of all expenditures, including those for commercial services. Even if improprieties are unlikely to occur in expenditures for commercial services, full and verifiable disclosure is needed to ensure that other, improper expenditures are not hidden in commercial accounts.

[8] The majority does not clearly articulate the standard of review it is applying. By determining that

Here, there is no direct evidence of harassment of either contributors or recipients of expenditures. Rather, as the majority accurately represents it, the evidence concerns harassment and reprisals of visible party members, including violence at party headquarters and loss of jobs. I concur in the majority's conclusion that this evidence, viewed in its entirety, supports the conclusion that there will be a reasonable probability of harassment of contributors if their names are disclosed. This evidence is sufficiently linked to disclosure of contributors in large part because any person publicly known to support the SWP's unpopular ideological position may suffer the reprisals that this record shows active party members suffer, and the disclosure of contributors may lead the public to presume these people support the party's ideology.

In contrast, the record, read in its entirety, does not suggest that disclosure of recipients of expenditures would lead to harassment of recipients or reprisals to the party or its members. Appellees gave no breakdown of the types of expenditures they thought would lead to harassment if disclosed. The record does contain the expenditure statements of the SWP, which itemize each expenditure with its purpose while usually omitting the name and address of the recipient. The majority of expenditures, both in number and dollar amount, are for business transactions such as office supplies, food, printing, photographs, telephone service, and books. There is virtually no evidence that disclosure of the recipients of these expenditures will impair the SWP's ability to obtain needed services. Even if we assume that a portion of expenditures went to temporary campaign workers or others whom the public might identify as supporting the party's ideology, these persons have already publicly demonstrated their support by their campaign work. There is simply no basis for inferring that such persons would *thereafter* be harassed or threatened or otherwise deterred from working for the party by virtue of inclusion of their names in later expenditure reports, or that if any such remote danger existed, it would outweigh the concededly important governmental interests in disclosure of recipients of expenditures.

It is plain that appellees did not carry their burden of production and persuasion insofar as they challenge the expenditure disclosure provisions. I would therefore uphold the constitutionality of those portions of the Ohio statute that require the SWP to disclose the recipients of expenditures.

Notes and Questions

1. *Socialist Workers* was an as-applied challenge. How much evidence must a minor party produce to demonstrate a "reasonable probability of threats, harassment, or reprisals" so as to exclude it from reporting requirements?

At about the same time that it began pursuing the above litigation against the State of Ohio, the SWP also initiated litigation against the Federal Election Commission, seeking an exemption from the reporting requirements of the Federal Election Campaign Act, then 2 U.S.C. § 434(c), now 52 U.S.C. § 30104 (c). *Socialist Workers 1974 National Campaign Committee v. Federal Election Commission,*

---

the District Court "properly concluded" that the evidence established a reasonable probability of harassment, the majority seems to apply an independent-review standard.

Civil Action No. 74-1338 (D.D.C. 1974). In 1979, the parties entered into a consent decree which required the committees supporting the SWP candidates to maintain records in accordance with the Act and to file reports in a timely manner, but exempting the committees from the provisions requiring the disclosure of names, addresses, occupations, and principal places of business of contributors to SWP committees; of political committees or candidates supported by SWP committees; of lenders, endorsers, or guarantors of loans to the SWP committees; and of persons to whom the SWP committees made expenditures. The decree stated that its provisions would apply through 1984, and permitted the SWP to apply for extensions of its terms. Using the Advisory Opinion process of 2 U.S.C. § 437f (now 52 U.S.C. §30108), the FEC has voted on five occasions to extend the SWP's exemption. Although earlier extensions were granted unanimously, since 2003, each of three extensions has drawn at least one dissenting vote.

In 2003, the Commission extended the exemption by only a 4-2 vote. The evidence of ongoing harassment provided to the FEC by the SWP that year included statements from party officials and candidates that potential supporters feared public identification with the SWP, party workers claiming that they had difficulty selling subscriptions to the party newspaper because of fears their names would be placed on FBI watch lists, and statements from party fundraisers that long-time donors would refuse to contribute again if their names would be made public. What weight should the FEC, or perhaps a judge, place on such (self-serving?) statements? Might some potential donors say such things as excuses rather than giving an outright no to requests for support?

The SWP also supplied a number of examples of alleged harassment. Two typical examples: "SWP supporters were campaigning outside a factory in Newark when a man who identified himself as the factory's owner ripped a leaflet out of one of the supporter's hands, threatened to 'f*** up' the supporters, told them to 'get the f*** off his property' and repeatedly shoved them"; and "SWP supporters were staffing a table in the garment district of New York City [when] a man who said he owned the storefront business there told the SWP supporters they would have to move, and as they were moving he threatened to turn over the table." *See* Advisory Opinion 2003-02 (April 3, 2003). Are such incidents sufficient to demonstrate a need for an exemption? Are such episodes atypical of those faced by many demonstrators, picketers, leafletters, and volunteers for major-party campaigns?

If we wish to encourage more participation in politics, how much "harassment" and threats should be people be expected to accept as normal? Does it matter that the government requires individuals to provide for public consumption the information that may lead to their harassment?

2.   In addition to the level of threats and harassment, the Court in *Socialist Workers* focused on the fact that the SWP is a minor party. Why does this matter? At what point would a party cease to be a minor party? In 1996, the Reform Party nominee for President, Ross Perot, received 8.4% of the national popular vote. In 1998, Reform Party nominee Jessie Ventura was elected governor of Minnesota. Would the Reform Party have been considered a minor party heading into the 2000 election cycle?

3. Should minor party status matter, as opposed to the level of threats and harassment? After the 2004 presidential elections, various contributors to major-party candidates found their names and addresses listed as "targets" on a website maintained by an extremist animal-rights organization called Stop Huntingdon Animal Cruelty ("SHAC"), under the heading "Now You Know Where to Find Them." Members of SHAC had previously assaulted and vandalized property of various individuals working for Huntingdon Life Sciences, a London-based lab that used animals for drug testing. SHAC was listed as a domestic terrorist threat by the FBI. SHAC had compiled the list by searching the FEC's public database of donors who worked for companies that did business with Huntingdon Life Sciences. *See* Bradley A. Smith, *In Defense of Political Anonymity*, 20 CITY J. 74, 76–77 (2010).

In 2008, after California passed Proposition 8, a state constitutional amendment that prohibited state recognition of same-sex marriage, many financial supporters of the Amendment found their businesses and employers boycotted or vandalized; others were fired or forced to resign from their jobs. These supporters were identified from information gleaned from mandatory disclosure reports. *Id.* at 77. Is it appropriate for government to force people to provide information that may subject them to harassment, vandalism, threats, and loss of employment? Alternatively, assuming lawful, non-violent means are used, is there any reason why people shouldn't be held "accountable" for their beliefs and votes? Is this merely part of the public's legitimate "right to know"? *See Hollingsworth v. Perry*, 558 U.S. 183 (2010) (staying an order allowing cameras in the courtroom in a challenge to Proposition 8's validity).

4. In footnote 3 of her *Socialist Workers* opinion concurring in part and dissenting in part, Justice O'Connor notes that because Ohio at that time had no limits on contributions, reporting the names of contributors was not necessary for the government to police limits on contributions. How much should the state's interest in enforcing contribution limits matter? Couldn't the state require reporting to the state, without making the information public (as with tax returns)? How much does it matter if the alleged threat of harassment comes from the government itself, in the form of official retaliation or surveillance?

MCINTYRE v. OHIO ELECTIONS COMMISSION
Supreme Court of the United States
514 U.S. 334, 115 S. Ct. 1511, 131 L. Ed. 2d 426 (1995)

JUSTICE STEVENS delivered the opinion of the Court [in which JUSTICE O'CONNOR, JUSTICE KENNEDY, JUSTICE SOUTER, JUSTICE GINSBURG, and JUSTICE BREYER join].

The question presented is whether an Ohio statute that prohibits the distribution of anonymous campaign literature is a "law . . . abridging the freedom of speech" within the meaning of the First Amendment.

On April 27, 1988, Margaret McIntyre distributed leaflets to persons attending a public meeting at the Blendon Middle School in Westerville, Ohio. At this meeting, the superintendent of schools planned to discuss an imminent referendum on a proposed school tax levy. The leaflets expressed Mrs. McIntyre's opposition to the levy. There is no suggestion that the text of her message was false, misleading, or libelous. She had composed and printed it on her home computer and had paid a professional printer to make additional copies. Some of the handbills identified her as the author; others merely purported to express the views of "CONCERNED PARENTS AND TAX PAYERS." Except for the help provided by her son and a friend, who placed some of the leaflets on car windshields in the school parking lot, Mrs. McIntyre acted independently.

While Mrs. McIntyre distributed her handbills, an official of the school district, who supported the tax proposal, advised her that the unsigned leaflets did not conform to the Ohio election laws. Undeterred, Mrs. McIntyre appeared at another meeting on the next evening and handed out more of the handbills.

The proposed school levy was defeated at the next two elections, but it finally passed on its third try in November 1988. Five months later, the same school official filed a complaint with the Ohio Elections Commission charging that Mrs. McIntyre's distribution of unsigned leaflets violated § 3599.09(A) of the Ohio Code.[3] The commission agreed and imposed a fine of $100. * * *

Ohio maintains that the statute under review is a reasonable regulation of the electoral process. The State does not suggest that all anonymous publications are pernicious or that a statute totally excluding them from the marketplace of ideas would be valid. This is a wise (albeit implicit) concession, for the anonymity of an author is not ordinarily a sufficient reason to exclude her work product from the protections of the First Amendment.

"Anonymous pamphlets, leaflets, brochures and even books have played an important role in the progress of mankind." Great works of literature have frequently been produced by authors writing under assumed names.[4] Despite readers' curiosity and the public's interest in identifying the creator of a work of art, an author generally is free to decide whether or not to disclose his or her true identity. The decision in favor of anonymity may be motivated by fear of economic or official retaliation, by concern about social ostracism, or merely by a desire to preserve as much of one's privacy as possible. Whatever the motivation may be, at least in the field of literary endeavor, the interest in having anonymous works enter the marketplace of ideas unquestionably outweighs any public interest in requiring disclosure as a condition of entry. Accordingly, an author's decision to remain

---

[3] [The statute prohibits, *inter alia*, the printing or distribution of "any . . . publication which is designed to promote the nomination or election or defeat of a candidate, or to promote the adoption or defeat of any issue, or to influence the voters in any election, or make an expenditure for the purpose of financing political communications . . . unless there appears on such form of publication in a conspicuous place or is contained within said statement the name and residence or business address of the chairman, treasurer, or secretary of the organization issuing the same, or the person who issues, makes, or is responsible therefor."].

[4] American names such as Mark Twain (Samuel Langhorne Clemens) and O. Henry (William Sydney Porter) come readily to mind. Benjamin Franklin employed numerous different pseudonyms. Distinguished French authors such as Voltaire (Francois Marie Arouet) and George Sand (Amandine Aurore Lucie Dupin), and British authors such as George Eliot (Mary Ann Evans), Charles Lamb (sometimes wrote as "Elia"), and Charles Dickens (sometimes wrote as "Boz"), also published under assumed names. Indeed, some believe the works of Shakespeare were actually written by the Earl of Oxford rather than by William Shaksper of Stratford-on-Avon.

anonymous, like other decisions concerning omissions or additions to the content of a publication, is an aspect of the freedom of speech protected by the First Amendment.

The freedom to publish anonymously extends beyond the literary realm. In *Talley* [v. *California*, 362 U.S. 60 (1960)], the Court held that the First Amendment protects the distribution of unsigned handbills urging readers to boycott certain Los Angeles merchants who were allegedly engaging in discriminatory employment practices. Writing for the Court, Justice Black noted that "[p]ersecuted groups and sects from time to time throughout history have been able to criticize oppressive practices and laws either anonymously or not at all." *Id.*, at 64. * * * On occasion, quite apart from any threat of persecution, an advocate may believe her ideas will be more persuasive if her readers are unaware of her identity. Anonymity thereby provides a way for a writer who may be personally unpopular to ensure that readers will not prejudge her message simply because they do not like its proponent. Thus, even in the field of political rhetoric, where "the identity of the speaker is an important component of many attempts to persuade," *City of Ladue* v. *Gilleo*, 512 U.S. 43, 56 (1994), the most effective advocates have sometimes opted for anonymity. The specific holding in *Talley* related to advocacy of an economic boycott, but the Court's reasoning embraced a respected tradition of anonymity in the advocacy of political causes. This tradition is perhaps best exemplified by the secret ballot, the hard-won right to vote one's conscience without fear of retaliation.

California had defended the Los Angeles ordinance at issue in *Talley* as a law "aimed at providing a way to identify those responsible for fraud, false advertising and libel." We rejected that argument because nothing in the text or legislative history of the ordinance limited its application to those evils. * * * The Ohio statute likewise contains no language limiting its application to fraudulent, false, or libelous statements; to the extent, therefore, that Ohio seeks to justify § 3599.09(A) as a means to prevent the dissemination of untruths, its defense must fail for the same reason given in *Talley*. As the facts of this case demonstrate, the ordinance plainly applies even when there is no hint of falsity or libel.

Ohio's statute does, however, contain a different limitation: It applies only to unsigned documents designed to influence voters in an election. In contrast, the Los Angeles ordinance prohibited all anonymous handbilling "in any place under any circumstances." For that reason, Ohio correctly argues that *Talley* does not necessarily control the disposition of this case. We must, therefore, decide whether and to what extent the First Amendment's protection of anonymity encompasses documents intended to influence the electoral process.

Ohio places its principal reliance on cases such as *Anderson* v. *Celebrezze*, 460 U.S. 780 (1983) [p. 517]; *Storer v. Brown*, 415 U.S. 724 (1974) [p. 513]; and *Burdick* v. *Takushi*, 504 U.S. 428 (1992) [p. 525], in which we reviewed election code provisions governing the voting process itself. In those cases we * * * considered the relative interests of the State and the injured voters, and we evaluated the extent to which the State's interests necessitated the contested restrictions. * * *

* * * Unlike the statutory provisions challenged in *Storer* and *Anderson*, § 3599.09(A) of the Ohio Code does not control the mechanics of the electoral process. It is a regulation of pure speech. Moreover, even though this provision

applies evenhandedly to advocates of differing viewpoints,[8] it is a direct regulation of the content of speech. * * * Furthermore, the category of covered documents is defined by their content — only those publications containing speech designed to influence the voters in an election need bear the required markings. Consequently, we are not faced with an ordinary election restriction; this case "involves a limitation on political expression subject to exacting scrutiny."

Indeed, as we have explained on many prior occasions, the category of speech regulated by the Ohio statute occupies the core of the protection afforded by the First Amendment:

> "Discussion of public issues and debate on the qualifications of candidates are integral to the operation of the system of government established by our Constitution. * * * In a republic where the people are sovereign, the ability of the citizenry to make informed choices among candidates for office is essential, for the identities of those who are elected will inevitably shape the course that we follow as a nation. '[I]t can hardly be doubted that the constitutional guarantee has its fullest and most urgent application precisely to the conduct of campaigns for political office.'" *Buckley* v. *Valeo*, 424 U.S. 1, 14–15 (1976) *(per curiam)* [p. 1011].

Of course, core political speech need not center on a candidate for office. The principles enunciated in *Buckley* extend equally to issue-based elections such as the school tax referendum that Mrs. McIntyre sought to influence through her handbills. See *First Nat. Bank of Boston* v. *Bellotti*, 435 U.S. 765, 776–777 (1978) [p. 895] (speech on income tax referendum "is at the heart of the First Amendment's protection"). Indeed, the speech in which Mrs. McIntyre engaged — handing out leaflets in the advocacy of a politically controversial viewpoint — is the essence of First Amendment expression. That this advocacy occurred in the heat of a controversial referendum vote only strengthens the protection afforded to Mrs. McIntyre's expression: Urgent, important, and effective speech can be no less protected than impotent speech, lest the right to speak be relegated to those instances when it is least needed. No form of speech is entitled to greater constitutional protection than Mrs. McIntyre's.

When a law burdens core political speech, we apply "exacting scrutiny," and we uphold the restriction only if it is narrowly tailored to serve an overriding state interest. * * * Ohio judges its interest in preventing fraudulent and libelous statements and its interest in providing the electorate with relevant information to be sufficiently compelling to justify the anonymous speech ban. * * *

Insofar as the interest in informing the electorate means nothing more than the provision of additional information that may either buttress or undermine the argument in a document, we think the identity of the speaker is no different from other components of the document's content that the author is free to include or exclude. We have already held that the State may not compel a newspaper that prints editorials critical of a particular candidate to provide space for a reply by the

---

[8] Arguably, the disclosure requirement places a more significant burden on advocates of unpopular causes than on defenders of the status quo. For purposes of our analysis, however, we assume the statute evenhandedly burdens all speakers who have a legitimate interest in remaining anonymous.

candidate. *Miami Herald Publishing Co.* v. *Tornillo*, 418 U.S. 241 (1974) [p. 613]. The simple interest in providing voters with additional relevant information does not justify a state requirement that a writer make statements or disclosures she would otherwise omit. Moreover, in the case of a handbill written by a private citizen who is not known to the recipient, the name and address of the author add little, if anything, to the reader's ability to evaluate the document's message. Thus, Ohio's informational interest is plainly insufficient to support the constitutionality of its disclosure requirement.

The state interest in preventing fraud and libel stands on a different footing. We agree with Ohio's submission that this interest carries special weight during election campaigns when false statements, if credited, may have serious adverse consequences for the public at large. Ohio does not, however, rely solely on § 3599.09(A) to protect that interest. Its Election Code includes detailed and specific prohibitions against making or disseminating false statements during political campaigns. These regulations apply both to candidate elections and to issue-driven ballot measures. Thus, Ohio's prohibition of anonymous leaflets plainly is not its principal weapon against fraud.[13] Rather, it serves as an aid to enforcement of the specific prohibitions and as a deterrent to the making of false statements by unscrupulous prevaricators. Although these ancillary benefits are assuredly legitimate, we are not persuaded that they justify § 3599.09(A)'s extremely broad prohibition.

As this case demonstrates, the prohibition encompasses documents that are not even arguably false or misleading. It applies not only to the activities of candidates and their organized supporters, but also to individuals acting independently and using only their own modest resources. It applies not only to elections of public officers, but also to ballot issues that present neither a substantial risk of libel nor any potential appearance of corrupt advantage. It applies not only to leaflets distributed on the eve of an election, when the opportunity for reply is limited, but also to those distributed months in advance. It applies no matter what the character or strength of the author's interest in anonymity. Moreover, as this case also demonstrates, the absence of the author's name on a document does not necessarily protect either that person or a distributor of a forbidden document from being held responsible for compliance with the Election Code. Nor has the State explained why it can more easily enforce the direct bans on disseminating false documents against anonymous authors and distributors than against wrongdoers who might use false names and addresses in an attempt to avoid detection. We recognize that a State's enforcement interest might justify a more limited identification requirement, but Ohio has shown scant cause for inhibiting the leafletting at issue here.

Finally, Ohio vigorously argues that our opinions in *First Nat. Bank of Boston* v. *Bellotti* and *Buckley* v. *Valeo* amply support the constitutionality of its disclosure

---

[13] The same can be said with regard to "libel," as many * * * Election Code provisions prohibit false statements about candidates. To the extent those provisions may be underinclusive, Ohio courts also enforce the common-law tort of defamation. Like other forms of election fraud, then, Ohio directly attacks the problem of election-related libel; to the extent that the anonymity ban serves the same interest, it is merely a supplement.

requirement. Neither case is controlling[.][a] * * * In *Bellotti,* * * * although we commented in dicta on the prophylactic effect of requiring identification of the source of corporate advertising ["so that the people will be able to evaluate the arguments to which they are being subjected," 435 U.S., at 792 n.32], that footnote did not necessarily apply to independent communications by an individual like Mrs. McIntyre.

Our * * * comments concerned contributions to the candidate or expenditures authorized by the candidate or his responsible agent. They had no reference to the kind of independent activity pursued by Mrs. McIntyre. Required disclosures about the level of financial support a candidate has received from various sources are supported by an interest in avoiding the appearance of corruption that has no application to this case.

True, in another portion of the *Buckley* opinion we expressed approval of a requirement that even "independent expenditures" in excess of a threshold level be reported to the Federal Election Commission. But that requirement entailed nothing more than an identification to the Commission of the amount and use of money expended in support of a candidate. Though such mandatory reporting undeniably impedes protected First Amendment activity, the intrusion is a far cry from compelled self-identification on all election-related writings. A written election-related document — particularly a leaflet — is often a personally crafted statement of a political viewpoint. Mrs. McIntyre's handbills surely fit that description. As such, identification of the author against her will is particularly intrusive; it reveals unmistakably the content of her thoughts on a controversial issue. Disclosure of an expenditure and its use, without more, reveals far less information. It may be information that a person prefers to keep secret, and undoubtedly it often gives away something about the spender's political views. Nonetheless, even though money may "talk," its speech is less specific, less personal, and less provocative than a handbill — and as a result, when money supports an unpopular viewpoint it is less likely to precipitate retaliation. * * *

Under our Constitution, anonymous pamphleteering is not a pernicious, fraudulent practice, but an honorable tradition of advocacy and of dissent. Anonymity is a shield from the tyranny of the majority. It thus exemplifies the purpose behind the Bill of Rights, and of the First Amendment in particular: to protect unpopular individuals from retaliation — and their ideas from suppression — at the hand of an intolerant society. The right to remain anonymous may be abused when it shields fraudulent conduct. But political speech by its nature will sometimes have unpalatable consequences, and, in general, our society accords greater weight to the value of free speech than to the dangers of its misuse. Ohio has not shown that its interest in preventing the misuse of anonymous election-related speech justifies a prohibition of all uses of that speech. The State may, and does, punish fraud directly. But it cannot seek to punish fraud indirectly by indiscriminately outlawing a category of speech, based on its content, with no necessary relationship to the

---

[a] *First National Bank of Boston* held unconstitutional a ban on corporation-funded electoral advocacy concerning a ballot measure. *Buckley* struck down portions of the Federal Election Campaign Act, but upheld other portions including one mandating disclosure of campaign contributors. Both cases are extensively discussed in Chapter 9. — Eds.

danger sought to be prevented. One would be hard pressed to think of a better example of the pitfalls of Ohio's blunderbuss approach than the facts of the case before us.

The judgment of the Ohio Supreme Court is reversed.

It is so ordered.

JUSTICE GINSBURG, concurring. * * *

In for a calf is not always in for a cow. The Court's decision finds unnecessary, overintrusive, and inconsistent with American ideals the State's imposition of a fine on an individual leafleteer who, within her local community, spoke her mind, but sometimes not her name. We do not thereby hold that the State may not in other, larger circumstances require the speaker to disclose its interest by disclosing its identity. Appropriately leaving open matters not presented by McIntyre's handbills, the Court recognizes that a State's interest in protecting an election process "might justify a more limited identification requirement." But the Court has convincingly explained why Ohio lacks "cause for inhibiting the leafletting at issue here."

JUSTICE THOMAS, concurring in the judgment.

I agree with the majority's conclusion that Ohio's election law is inconsistent with the First Amendment. I would apply, however, a different methodology to this case. Instead of asking whether "an honorable tradition" of anonymous speech has existed throughout American history, or what the "value" of anonymous speech might be, we should determine whether the phrase "freedom of speech, or of the press," as originally understood, protected anonymous political leafletting. I believe that it did. * * *

Unfortunately, we have no record of discussions of anonymous political expression either in the First Congress, which drafted the Bill of Rights, or in the state ratifying conventions. Thus, our analysis must focus on the practices and beliefs held by the Founders concerning anonymous political articles and pamphlets. * * *

There is little doubt that the Framers engaged in anonymous political writing. The essays in the Federalist Papers, published under the pseudonym of "Publius," are only the most famous example of the outpouring of anonymous political writing that occurred during the ratification of the Constitution. Of course, the simple fact that the Framers engaged in certain conduct does not necessarily prove that they forbade its prohibition by the government. In this case, however, the historical evidence indicates that Founding-era Americans opposed attempts to require that anonymous authors reveal their identities on the ground that forced disclosure violated the "freedom of the press."

For example, the earliest and most famous American experience with freedom of the press, the 1735 Zenger trial, centered around anonymous political pamphlets. The case involved a printer, John Peter Zenger, who refused to reveal the anonymous authors of published attacks on the Crown Governor of New York. When the Governor and his council could not discover the identity of the authors, they prosecuted Zenger himself for seditious libel. Although the case set the Colonies afire for its example of a jury refusing to convict a defendant of seditious libel against Crown authorities, it also signified at an early moment the extent to which anonymity and the freedom of the press were intertwined in the early American mind.

During the Revolutionary and Ratification periods, the Framers' understanding of the relationship between anonymity and freedom of the press became more explicit. In 1779, for example, the Continental Congress attempted to discover the identity of an anonymous article in the Pennsylvania Packet signed by the name "Leonidas." Leonidas, who actually was Dr. Benjamin Rush, had attacked the Members of Congress for causing inflation throughout the States and for engaging in embezzlement and fraud. Elbridge Gerry, a delegate from Massachusetts, moved to haul the printer of the newspaper before Congress to answer questions concerning Leonidas. Several Members of Congress then rose to oppose Gerry's motion on the ground that it invaded the freedom of the press. * * * In the end, these arguments persuaded the assembled delegates, who "sat mute" in response to Gerry's motion. Neither the printer nor Dr. Rush ever appeared before Congress to answer for their publication.

At least one of the state legislatures shared Congress' view that the freedom of the press protected anonymous writing. Also in 1779, the upper house of the New Jersey State Legislature attempted to punish the author of a satirical attack on the Governor and the College of New Jersey (now Princeton) who had signed his work "Cincinnatus." Attempting to enforce the crime of seditious libel, the State Legislative Council ordered Isaac Collins — the printer and editor of the newspaper in which the article had appeared — to reveal the author's identity. Refusing, Collins declared: "Were I to comply . . . I conceive I should betray the trust reposed in me, and be far from acting as a faithful guardian of the Liberty of the Press." Apparently, the State Assembly agreed that anonymity was protected by the freedom of the press, as it voted to support the editor and publisher by frustrating the council's orders. * * *

To be sure, there was some controversy among newspaper editors over publishing anonymous articles and pamphlets. But this controversy was resolved in a manner that indicates that the freedom of the press protected an author's anonymity. The tempest began when a Federalist, writing anonymously himself, expressed fear that "emissaries" of "foreign enemies" would attempt to scuttle the Constitution by "fill[ing] the press with objections" against the proposal. He called upon printers to refrain from publishing when the author "chooses to remain concealed." Benjamin Russell, the editor of the prominent Federalist newspaper the Massachusetts Centinel, immediately adopted a policy of refusing to publish Anti-Federalist pieces unless the author provided his identity to be "handed to the publick, if required." A few days later, the Massachusetts Gazette announced that it would emulate the example set by the Massachusetts Centinel. * * * Federalists expressed similar thoughts in Philadelphia.

Ordinarily, the fact that some founding-era editors as a matter of policy decided not to publish anonymous articles would seem to shed little light upon what the Framers thought the *government* could do. The widespread criticism raised by the

Anti-Federalists, however, who were the driving force behind the demand for a Bill of Rights, indicates that they believed the freedom of the press to include the right to author anonymous political articles and pamphlets. That most other Americans shared this understanding is reflected in the Federalists' hasty retreat before the withering criticism of their assault on the liberty of the press [with the Centinel publishing anonymous Anti-Federalist essays and the Gazette refusing to release the names of Anti-Federalist authors]. * * *

The controversy over Federalist attempts to prohibit anonymous political speech is significant for several reasons. First, the Anti-Federalists clearly believed the right to author and publish anonymous political articles and pamphlets was protected by the liberty of the press. Second, although printers' editorial policies did not constitute state action, the Anti-Federalists believed that the Federalists were merely flexing the governmental powers they would fully exercise upon the Constitution's ratification. Third, and perhaps most significantly, it appears that the Federalists agreed with the Anti-Federalist critique. * * * When Federalist attempts to ban anonymity are followed by a sharp, widespread Anti-Federalist defense in the name of the freedom of the press, and then by an open Federalist retreat on the issue, I must conclude that both Anti-Federalists and Federalists believed that the freedom of the press included the right to publish without revealing the author's name. * * *

The large quantity of newspapers and pamphlets the Framers produced during the various crises of their generation show the remarkable extent to which the Framers relied upon anonymity. During the break with Great Britain, the revolutionaries employed pseudonyms both to conceal their identity from Crown authorities and to impart a message. * * *

If the practice of publishing anonymous articles and pamphlets fell into disuse after the Ratification, one might infer that the custom of anonymous political speech arose only in response to the unusual conditions of the 1776–1787 period. After all, the Revolution and the Ratification were not "elections," *per se*, either for candidates or for discrete issues. Records from the first federal elections indicate, however, that anonymous political pamphlets and newspaper articles remained the favorite media for expressing views on candidates. * * *

The use of anonymous writing extended to issues as well as candidates. The ratification of the Constitution was not the only issue discussed via anonymous writings in the press. James Madison and Alexander Hamilton, for example, resorted to pseudonyms in the famous "Helvidius" and "Pacificus" debates over President Washington's declaration of neutrality in the war between the British and French. Anonymous writings continued in such Republican papers as the Aurora and Federalists organs such as the Gazette of the United States at least until the election of Thomas Jefferson. * * *

While, like JUSTICE SCALIA, I am loath to overturn a century of practice shared by almost all of the States, I believe the historical evidence from the framing outweighs recent tradition. * * * Because the majority has adopted an analysis that is largely unconnected to the Constitution's text and history, I concur only in the judgment.

JUSTICE SCALIA, with whom THE CHIEF JUSTICE [REHNQUIST] joins, dissenting. * * *

The question posed by the present case is not the easiest sort to answer for those who adhere to the Court's (and the society's) traditional view that the Constitution bears its original meaning and is unchanging. * * * That technique is simple of application when government conduct that is claimed to violate the Bill of Rights or the Fourteenth Amendment is shown, upon investigation, to have been engaged in without objection at the very time the Bill of Rights or the Fourteenth Amendment was adopted. There is no doubt, for example, that laws against libel and obscenity do not violate "the freedom of speech" to which the First Amendment refers; they existed and were universally approved in 1791. Application of the principle of an unchanging Constitution is also simple enough at the other extreme, where the government conduct at issue was *not* engaged in at the time of adoption, and there is ample evidence that the *reason* it was not engaged in is that it was thought to violate the right embodied in the constitutional guarantee. Racks and thumbscrews, well-known instruments for inflicting pain, were not in use because they were regarded as cruel punishments.

The present case lies between those two extremes. Anonymous electioneering was not prohibited by law in 1791 or in 1868. In fact, it was widely practiced at the earlier date, an understandable legacy of the revolutionary era in which political dissent could produce governmental reprisal. * * * The practice of anonymous electioneering may have been less general in 1868, when the Fourteenth Amendment was adopted, but at least as late as 1837 it was respectable enough to be engaged in by Abraham Lincoln.

But to prove that anonymous electioneering was used frequently is not to establish that it is a constitutional right. Quite obviously, not every restriction upon expression that did not exist in 1791 or in 1868 is *ipso facto* unconstitutional, or else modern election laws such as those involved in *Burson* v. *Freeman*, 504 U.S. 191 (1992) [p. 1054] [limiting electioneering within a certain distance of polling places], and *Buckley* v. *Valeo* would be prohibited, as would (to mention only a few other categories) modern antinoise regulation * * * and modern parade-permitting regulation[.] * * *

[JUSTICE THOMAS's] concurrence recounts * * * pre- and post-Revolution examples of defense of anonymity in the name of "freedom of the press," but not a single one involves the context of restrictions imposed in connection with a free, democratic election, which is all that is at issue here. For many of them, moreover, * * * the issue of anonymity was incidental to the (unquestionably free-speech) issue of whether criticism of the government could be *punished* by the state.

Thus, the sum total of the historical evidence marshaled by the concurrence for the principle of *constitutional entitlement* to anonymous electioneering is partisan claims in the debate on ratification (which was *almost* like an election) that a viewpoint-based restriction on anonymity by newspaper editors violates freedom of speech. * * *

What we have, then, is the most difficult case for determining the meaning of the Constitution. No accepted existence of governmental restrictions of the sort at issue here demonstrates their constitutionality, but neither can their nonexistence clearly be attributed to constitutional objections. In such a case, constitutional adjudication necessarily involves not just history but judgment: judgment as to whether the government action under challenge is consonant with the concept of the protected freedom (in this case, the freedom of speech and of the press) that existed when the constitutional protection was accorded. In the present case, *absent other indication*, I would be inclined to agree with the concurrence that a society which used anonymous political debate so regularly would not regard as constitutional even moderate restrictions made to improve the election process. (I would, however, want further evidence of common practice in 1868, since I doubt that the Fourteenth Amendment time-warped the post-Civil War States back to the Revolution.)

But there *is* other indication, of the most weighty sort: the widespread and longstanding traditions of our people. Principles of liberty fundamental enough to have been embodied within constitutional guarantees are not readily erased from the Nation's consciousness. A governmental practice that has become general throughout the United States, and particularly one that has the validation of long, accepted usage, bears a strong presumption of constitutionality. And that is what we have before us here. Ohio Rev. Code Ann. § 3599.09(A) was enacted by the General Assembly of the State of Ohio almost 80 years ago. Even at the time of its adoption, there was nothing unique or extraordinary about it. The earliest statute of this sort was adopted by Massachusetts in 1890, little more than 20 years after the Fourteenth Amendment was ratified. No less than 24 States had similar laws by the end of World War I, and today every State of the Union except California has one, as does the District of Columbia, and as does the Federal Government where advertising relating to candidates for federal office is concerned. Such a universal and long-established American legislative practice must be given precedence, I think, over historical and academic speculation regarding a restriction that assuredly does not go to the heart of free speech. * * *

The Court says that the State has not explained "why it can more easily enforce the direct bans on disseminating false documents against anonymous authors and distributors than against wrongdoers who might use false names and addresses in an attempt to avoid detection." I am not sure what this complicated comparison means. I am sure, however, that (1) a person who is required to put his name to a document is much less likely to lie than one who can lie anonymously, and (2) the distributor of a leaflet which is unlawful because it is anonymous runs much more risk of immediate detection and punishment than the distributor of a leaflet which is unlawful because it is false. Thus, people will be more likely to observe a signing requirement than a naked "no falsity" requirement; and, having observed that requirement, will then be significantly less likely to lie in what they have signed.

But the usefulness of a signing requirement lies not only in promoting observance of the law against campaign falsehoods (though that alone is enough to sustain it). It lies also in promoting a civil and dignified level of campaign debate — which the State has no power to command, but ample power to encourage by such undemanding measures as a signature requirement. Observers of the past few national elections have expressed concern about the increase of character assassination — "mudslinging" is the colloquial term — engaged in by political candidates and their supporters to the detriment of the democratic process. Not all of this, in fact not much of it, consists of actionable untruth; most is innuendo, or demeaning characterization, or mere disclosure of items of personal life that have no bearing upon suitability for office. Imagine how much all of this would increase if it could be done anonymously. The principal impediment against it is the reluctance of most individuals and organizations to be publicly associated with uncharitable and uncivil expression. Consider, moreover, the increased potential for "dirty tricks." It is not unheard-of for campaign operatives to circulate material over the name of their opponents or their opponents' supporters (a violation of election laws) in order to attract or alienate certain interest groups. How much easier — and sanction free! — it would be to circulate anonymous material (for example, a *really* tasteless, though not actionably false, attack upon one's own candidate) with the hope and expectation that it will be attributed to, and held against, the other side.

The Court contends that demanding the disclosure of the pamphleteer's identity is no different from requiring the disclosure of any other information that may reduce the persuasiveness of the pamphlet's message. It cites *Miami Herald Publishing Co.* v. *Tornillo*, which held it unconstitutional to require a newspaper that had published an editorial critical of a particular candidate to furnish space for that candidate to reply. But it is not *usual* for a speaker to put forward the best arguments against himself, and it is a great imposition upon free speech to make him do so. Whereas it is quite usual — it is expected — for a speaker to *identify* himself, and requiring that is (at least when there are no special circumstances present) virtually no imposition at all.

We have approved much more onerous disclosure requirements in the name of fair elections. In *Buckley* v. *Valeo*, we upheld provisions of the Federal Election Campaign Act that required private individuals to report to the Federal Election Commission independent expenditures made for communications advocating the election or defeat of a candidate for federal office. Our primary rationale for upholding this provision was that it served an "informational interest" by "increas-[ing] the fund of information concerning those who support the candidates." The provision before us here serves the same informational interest, as well as more important interests, which I have discussed above. * * *

I respectfully dissent.

Notes and Questions

1. *Problem.* Mac Marga, a successful local businessman, has asked your advice. His state has a law identical to that in *McIntyre*. The school district covering his city of 200,000 people has placed a proposed school tax levy on the ballot. Marga believes that the District does not really need the money, and that high taxes are destroying the city's economic base and could force his company to relocate. He wants his corporation, the Marga Corporation, to spend $70,000 on radio, television, and newspaper ads to help defeat the levy. Marga's children attend public schools in the District, however, and he is concerned that if he is associated with efforts to defeat the levy, his children will be discriminated against by teachers and administrators when competing for spots on athletic teams, in other extra-curricular activities, and in grades. He wants to know if he can simply list the ads as having been paid for by "Concerned Taxpayers." What if Marga makes the expenditures as an individual, rather than through his corporation?

2. *Problem.* Tony Teacher has announced his candidacy for school board. A former president of the local teachers union affiliate, he has the support of most of the teachers in the district. He strongly supports higher taxes to improve the school district's education programs. Sally, a small business owner, thinks taxes are already too high. She wishes to spend $2,500 on leaflets urging Teacher's defeat, but she is concerned about having her name on the leaflets, as required by state law, because her husband is a teacher in the same school as Tony Teacher. She wants to know if she must comply with the law requiring all campaign material to include the name of the person paying for it.

3. Why do you think the school officials might have waited until after the levy had passed to file a complaint against Ms. McIntyre? What interest were they attempting to vindicate? What harm, if any, was caused by listing the flyers as paid for by "Concerned Parents and Taxpayers" (which McIntyre and her husband were) rather than her own name?

4. Even as it ruled for McIntyre, the Supreme Court suggested that the state had a legitimate interest in preventing fraudulent speech. Does this interest still exist in light of *United States v. Alvarez*, 132 S. Ct. 2537 (2012) [p. 592]?

5. As the problems in Notes 1 and 2 demonstrate, *McIntyre* leaves many unanswered questions about its scope. Is it limited to its particular facts? Does it apply only to individuals? To individuals, such as McIntyre, engaged in small scale activities? How small? Does it apply in candidate races, or only in ballot issue campaigns?

As you will see in Chapter 9, except for the exception for minor parties facing harassment that was granted in *Brown v. Socialist Workers Party '74 Campaign Comm.* [p. 635], the Supreme Court has consistently upheld mandatory disclosure of donors to candidate committees. However, the law on persons who contribute to organizations that discuss candidates and issues without specifically advocating the election or defeat of a candidate, or who make only occasional expenditures advocating the election or defeat or a candidate, is rather mixed. In the following case, Richard Posner and Frank Easterbrook, two of the most respected judges on the U.S. Courts of Appeals, attempt to deal with some of the apparent conflicts developing in the law of anonymous speech.

MAJORS v. ABELL
United States Court of Appeals for the Seventh Circuit
361 F.3d 349 (7th Cir. 2004)

POSNER, *CIRCUIT JUDGE* [with whom BAUER, *CIRCUIT JUDGE*, joins].

An Indiana statute, challenged in this suit as an infringement of free speech, requires that political advertising that "expressly advocat[es] the election or defeat of a clearly identified candidate" contain "a disclaimer that appears and is presented in a clear and conspicuous manner to give the reader or observer adequate notice of the identity of persons who paid for . . . the communication," and makes violation a misdemeanor. "Disclaimer" is a misnomer; the correct word would be "disclosure"

— but as we'll see, that word has been appropriated to describe a reporting requirement. * * *

Although [*McIntyre v. Ohio Elections Commission*, 514 U.S. 334 (1995)] [p. 644] held that government may not forbid the distribution of anonymous campaign literature, several subsequent decisions upheld statutes similar to the Indiana statute interpreted to reach all persons. *Federal Election Comm'n v. Public Citizen*, 268 F.3d 1283, 1287–91 (11th Cir. 2001) (per curiam); *Gable v. Patton*, 142 F.3d 940, 944–45 (6th Cir. 1998); *Kentucky Right to Life, Inc. v. Terry*, 108 F.3d 637, 646–48 (6th Cir. 1997). Those cases point out that the statute struck down in *McIntyre* applied to issue referenda as well as to candidate elections and that only issue referenda were before the Court, a difference on which *McIntyre* had relied to distinguish *Buckley v. Valeo*, 424 U.S. 1, 80 (1976) (per curiam), which had upheld a provision of the federal campaign finance law that was similar to these state statutes. * * * The opinions that distinguish *McIntyre* also point out that Ohio had defended its statute only on the basis that knowing the author of a document helps one to evaluate its truthfulness, whereas a weightier ground is that "disclosure protects the integrity of the electoral process by ensuring that the words of an independent group are not mistakenly understood as having come from the mouth of a candidate." It also deters corruption by identifying large contributors who may be seeking a quid pro quo and — a related point — it provides information helpful to the enforcement of the provisions of election campaign law, both also being purposes that had been emphasized in *Buckley*, 424 U.S. at 66–68. * * *

The constitutional issue * * * is difficult because it entails a balancing of imponderables. On the one hand, forbidding anonymous political advertising reduces the amount of political advertising because some would-be advertisers are unwilling to reveal their identity. On the other hand, the quality of the political advertising that continues to be produced and disseminated under such a regime is enhanced because the advertising contains additional information useful to the consumer. The avidity with which candidates for public office seek endorsements is evidence (as if any were needed) that the identity of a candidate's supporters — and opponents — is information that the voting public values highly. In areas of inquiry where logic or exact observation is unavailing, a speaker's credibility often depends crucially on who he is. As Aristotle said, "persuasion is achieved by the speaker's personal character when the speech is so spoken as to make us think him credible. We believe good men more fully and more readily than others: this is true generally whatever the question is, and absolutely true where exact certainty is impossible and opinions are divided." Aristotle, *Rhetoric*, in 2 *The Complete Works of Aristotle* 2152, 2155 (Jonathan Barnes ed. 1984). "Where exact certainty is impossible and opinions are divided" is a pretty good description of politics.

Can we get help in answering the thorny question presented by this appeal from the case law, and in particular from the Supreme Court's recent and very lengthy opinions in [*McConnell v. Federal Election Comm'n*, 540 U.S. 93 (2003)] [pp. 865, 923, 1019]? The provision of the Bipartisan Campaign Reform Act that is analogous to the Indiana statute regulates "electioneering communications," which are advertisements broadcast within 60 days of a general election or 30 days of a primary that refer to a candidate for federal office. 2 U.S.C. § 434(f)(3)(A)(i). Individuals who spend more than $10,000 producing such communications, or contribute at least $1,000 to an organization that produces them, must report (in the case of the contributions it is the recipient who must report) their identities to the Federal Election Commission. 2 U.S.C. §§ 434(f)(1)–(2). Without attempting to narrow the class of covered "individuals," the Supreme Court upheld this provision on the ground that it served "important state interests . . . [in] providing the electorate with information, deterring actual corruption and avoiding any appearance thereof, and gathering the data necessary to enforce more substantive electioneering restrictions." Like the Indiana statute, the provision of the Bipartisan Campaign Reform Act that the Court upheld requires identifying *any* person who contributes to the making of the ad, even if the person is not a candidate or a member of the candidate's campaign staff.

True, what is required is disclosure to an agency rather than disclosure in the political ad itself, though, as is apparent from the Court's reference to "providing the electorate with information," the identity of the contributor is available to the public rather than secreted by the FEC. 2 U.S.C. §§ 434(a)(11)–(12), (d)(2). That may not seem a big difference from the standpoint of protecting the advertiser from retaliation, but the Court had earlier indicated that having to identify itself to the entire audience for the ad has as a practical matter a greater inhibiting effect than just a reporting requirement does because it broadcasts the advertiser's name to the entire electoral community. *Buckley v. American Constitutional Law Foundation, Inc.*, 525 U.S. 182, 197–200 (1999) [p. 681]. The reaction may not be "retaliation" in any strong sense, but there is a weak sense as well; there may be a degree of social ostracism, some dirty looks, a few snide comments, and such, and we and other courts have long recognized that mild forms of retaliation can be effective in deterring the exercise of free speech.

The Court in *McIntyre* thought "the intrusion" on freedom of political advocacy brought about by a reporting requirement was "a far cry from compelled self-identification on all election-related writings," 514 U.S. at 355, which is what we have here — and what the Bipartisan Campaign Reform Act does not have; it does not even require identifying the specific ads financed by the reporting contributor. But of course the very thing that makes reporting less inhibiting than notice in the ad itself — fewer people are likely to see the report than the notice — makes reporting a less effective method of conveying information that by hypothesis the voting public values. It's as if cigarette companies, instead of having to disclose the hazards of smoking in their ads, had only to file a disclosure statement with the Food and Drug Administration.

The only reference to *McIntyre* by the majority in *McConnell* appears in a footnote that distinguishes "genuine issue ads" from "regulation of campaign speech" and assumes that restrictions constitutionally applicable to the latter, such as the restrictions both in the Bipartisan Campaign Reform Act and in the Indiana statute, might not be applicable to the former; *McIntyre* is cited noncommittally as having invalidated a "statute banning the distribution of anonymous campaign literature." 540 U.S. at 206 n.88. Remember that *McIntyre* had only been about issue referenda, where there are no candidates and so, it might be thought, "campaign literature" is more likely to consist of "genuine issue ads." Thus the Court may have so far narrowed *McIntyre* (one of the dissenting opinions said the Court had overruled it) that it no longer overlaps the Indiana statute.

An alternative interpretation, however, is that because the Bipartisan Campaign Reform Act and therefore the *McConnell* decision are about campaign financing, the decision is inapplicable to people who pay for political ads themselves, since they are not engaged in fund-raising. On that reading, *McIntyre*, which was such a case, is unaffected by *McConnell*, and so the Indiana statute, which is also about requiring self-financiers to identity themselves, is condemned by *McIntyre*'s holding. But campaign financing and fund-raising are not synonyms, as the argument assumes; and the Bipartisan Campaign Reform Act is not just about fund-raising — the relevant provision that the Court upheld applies equally to self-financed and other-financed ads. The disclosure statement must be filed by "every person who makes a disbursement for the direct costs of producing and airing electioneering communications in an aggregate amount in excess of $10,000 during any calendar year," whether he produces the ad himself or gives the money to someone else to produce it, 2 U.S.C. § 434(f)(1); and sections 434(a)(6)(B) and (E) expressly impose a requirement of reporting campaign disbursements by a candidate from his personal funds. And the first governmental interest that the Court recited in upholding the provision — that it would provide the electorate with information — is applicable to self-financed ads. An ad might seem disinterested, but if the voting public knew who had paid for it — maybe it was an interest group that the candidate was known to have done favors for — the existence of an interest might be revealed. To draw the constitutional line between self- and other-financed campaign ads would be to deliver a gratuitous benefit to wealthy candidates and wealthy supporters of candidates.

But what must give us considerable pause, in light of the distinction the Supreme Court has drawn between "disclosure" (reporting one's identity to a public agency) and "disclaimer" (placing that identity in the ad itself), is the fact that the Indiana statute requires the latter and not merely the former. *Buckley v. American Constitutional Law Foundation, Inc.*, *supra*, 525 U.S. at 197–200, invalidated a state law that required people who circulated petitions for issue referenda (actually initiatives, but the only and irrelevant difference is that a referendum asks the people to vote on a law proposed by the legislature, while in an initiative the proposal has not been before the legislature) to wear identification badges. But the requirement was inapplicable to elections of candidates. *Federal Election Comm'n v. Public Citizen*, *supra*, 268 F.3d at 1287–91, interpreting a provision of the previous federal campaign finance law, upheld a requirement of a disclaimer in a candidate election. But all that had to be disclaimed (for once, the word was apt) was that the advertiser was independent of the candidate — yet the court assumed that a separate requirement, that the identity of the advertiser be disclosed in the ad, was also valid. *Id.* at 1290. There is a similar assumption in *McConnell*. See 540 U.S. at 231. A statute quite like the Indiana statute was invalidated in *Citizens for Responsible Government State Political Action Comm. v. Davidson*, 236 F.3d 1174, 1198–1200 and n.10 (10th Cir. 2000) — and upheld in *Gable v. Patton*, *supra*, 142 F.3d at 944–45, and *Kentucky Right to Life, Inc. v. Terry*, *supra*, 108 F.3d at 646–48. Several cases, signally *McIntyre* itself, expressly or implicitly contrast the fragility of the small independent participant in political campaigns with large corporations or other organizations.

The Indiana Supreme Court, recognizing this last point, did a bit of judicial legerdemain, expanding the statutory exemption for mailings of up to 100 pieces of "mail" that are "substantially similar," Ind. Code § 3-9-3-2.5(a)(9), "to include any form of delivery of any written material, including personal delivery or use of some service other than use of the United States Postal Service," with the result that "Indiana's law permits some individual pamphleteering and applies only to candidate elections." The statutory exemption as expanded by judicial interpretation protects the most vulnerable independent contributors to political advocacy. And as we said earlier, to require only the reporting of the advertiser's name to a public agency, while it would as a practical matter allay some of the anxieties of potential advertisers, would at the same time reduce the amount of information possessed by voters. Both sides of the First Amendment balance would be depressed. We cannot say that the net effect of invalidating the Indiana statute would be to promote political speech.

As an original matter it could be objected that speech and the press would no longer be free if the government could insist that every speaker and every writer add to his message information that the government deems useful to the intended audience for the message, and that it is arbitrary for the government to single out the identity of the writer or speaker and decree that that information, though no other that potential voters might value as much or more, must be disclosed. But the Supreme Court crossed that Rubicon in *McConnell*. Reluctant, without clearer guidance from the Court, to interfere with state experimentation in the baffling and conflicted field of campaign finance law without guidance from authoritative precedent, we hold that the Indiana statute is constitutional.

The decision of the district court * * * is AFFIRMED.

EASTERBROOK, *Circuit Judge*, dubitante.[b]

Four decisions of the Supreme Court hold or strongly imply that the ability to speak anonymously — and thus with less concern for repercussions — is part of the "freedom of speech" protected by the first amendment against governmental interference. *Talley v. California*, 362 U.S. 60 (1960); *McIntyre v. Ohio Elections Commission*; *Buckley v. American Constitutional Law Foundation*; *Watchtower Bible & Tract Society of New York, Inc. v. Stratton*, 536 U.S. 150, 166–67 (2002). See Jonathan Turley, *Registering Publius: The Supreme Court and the Right to Anonymity*, 2001-02 Cato Sup. Ct. Rev. 57. * * *

There have been times and places in the United States when opposing elected political officials risked both wealth and health. Decisions such as *O'Hare Truck Service, Inc. v. Northlake*, 518 U.S. 712 (1996), and *Rutan v. Republican Party of Illinois*, 497 U.S. 62 (1990) [p. 741], hold that government is not entitled to retaliate, but what people do in fact often differs from what they should do, and litigation after the fact is no cure-all. It is no cure at all for retaliation by private actors, who are free to penalize those whose political views they do not accept, provided only that they do not cross the line into violence — and that line has not always been observed; think of persons whose candidates were the "wrong" race. Anonymity

---

[b] "Dubitante" is a rarely used label by a judge who expresses doubt, but does not dissent from the Court's opinion. [— Eds.]

thus may be especially valuable when opposing entrenched actors. Disclosure also makes it easier to see who has not done his bit for the incumbents, so that arms may be twisted and pockets tapped. Labor law deems it improper for employers to nose out union adherents' names; judges and members of the NLRB perceive that knowledge may facilitate retaliation and that fear of this outcome will stifle speech. Yet although union organizers may operate in secret, and everyone may vote in secret (our adoption of the Australian ballot came from awareness that disclosure could affect political support), political advocates must disclose their identities. Today the court holds that a state may require persons engaged in core political speech to identify themselves so that the officeholders and their allies can pinpoint their critics. How can this be?

According to my colleagues, the answer lies in the fact that *McConnell v. Federal Election Commission* rejected a constitutional challenge to § 201 of the Bipartisan Campaign Reform Act of 2002, which amended § 304 of the Federal Election Campaign Act. Section 304 as amended requires any person who makes disbursements exceeding $10,000 in any year for speech in federal campaigns, or who donates $1,000 or more to another person or group engaged in advocacy, to disclose his identity to the Federal Election Commission. Indiana's law differs — it starts from a lower threshold (100 sheets of paper) and requires disclosure to the public in the electioneering literature rather than to an agency — but once it is settled that speakers must reveal their identities directly to the political establishment, five Justices may think that everything else is mere detail.

Still, the Justices' failure to discuss *McIntyre*, or even to cite *Talley, American Constitutional Law Foundation*, or *Watchtower*, makes it impossible for courts at our level to make an informed decision — for the Supreme Court has not told us what principle to apply. Does *McConnell* apply to all electioneering? All speakers? To primary communications (as opposed to notices sent to agencies)? The Supreme Court wrote that § 304 is valid because it is (in the view of five Justices) a wise balance among competing interests. Yet the function of the first amendment is to put the regulation of speech off limits to government *even if* regulation is deemed wise. For the judiciary to say that a law is valid to the extent that it is good is to operate as a council of revision and to deny the power of a written constitution to constrain contemporary legislation supported by the social class from which judges are drawn. And when, as in *McConnell*, the judgment is supported by a one-vote margin, any Justice's conclusion that a particular extension is unwise will reverse the constitutional outcome. How can legislators or the judges of other courts determine what is apt to tip the balance?

Footnote 88 to the lead opinion in *McConnell* hints that one or more members of the majority may believe that the validity of the federal statute depends on its entire complement of rules. This footnote — the only place in which a majority opinion discusses *McIntyre* (though not when dealing with § 304!) — says that "BCRA's fidelity to those imperatives" sets it apart from the law held invalid in *McIntyre*. This treats the statute as a unit. It is difficult to say that the Indiana legislation at issue today displays "fidelity" to the "imperatives" of curtailing public corruption while allowing room for expression. As far as I can see, it has nothing to do with the risk of subtle bribery, and it attaches no weight to the risks borne by supporters of unpopular candidates. The majority in *McConnell* emphasized that the disclosure to the agency did *not* include the content of the advertisement. In Indiana the disclosure is affixed to the speech; the association is unavoidable; does this make a difference? My colleagues think not; I am not so sure.

Doubtless "a speaker's credibility often depends crucially on who he is." But how does this support *obligatory* disclosure? Speakers who prefer concealment in order to reduce their personal risks, and who accept the discount that readers attach to advocacy from unnamed sources, do not impose burdens on strangers. What then is the justification for regulation? "People are intelligent enough to evaluate the source of an anonymous writing. They can see it is anonymous. They know it is anonymous. They can evaluate its anonymity along with its message, as long as they are permitted, as they must be, to read that message." *McIntyre*, 514 U.S. at 348 n.11. Arguments that speech may be regulated to protect the audience from misunderstanding should fare poorly and outside of electioneering *have* fared poorly. See, e.g., *Virginia State Board of Pharmacy v. Virginia Citizens Consumer Council, Inc.*, 425 U.S. 748, 769–70 (1976). Anyway, we must consider the possibility that anonymity promotes a focus on the strength of the argument rather than the identity of the speaker; this is a reason why Madison, Hamilton, and Jay chose to publish *The Federalist* anonymously. Instead of having to persuade New Yorkers that his roots in Virginia should be overlooked, Madison could present the arguments and let the reader evaluate them on merit.

Trade associations and other interest groups will have little difficulty complying with Indiana's law. Factions that hope to secure political favors enjoy legal counsel who specialize in election matters. Professionals in the field not only will assure compliance but also will exploit the inevitable loopholes. The identity of these interest groups is no mystery; many operate from marble-clad buildings and deploy full-time lobbyists. Statutes such as Indiana's have their real bite when flushing small groups, political clubs, or solitary speakers into the limelight, or reducing them to silence. Indiana's statute, which requires disclosure from the first dollar of speech, bears especially heavily on political outsiders. Indiana has essentially forbidden *all* spontaneous political speech, perhaps all electioneering by individuals and small groups. Before favoring or opposing any candidate, a would-be speaker must navigate a thicket of rules. * * *

Often the Supreme Court says that even a small fee or tax, or a short delay in obtaining a free license (as in *Watchtower*), is an unacceptable burden on speech. Yet in *McConnell* the Court was sanguine about the delays, and non-trivial legal expenses, entailed in complying with complex rules for campaign speech. These outlays come on top of the costs that must be borne by persons who back the wrong horse and incur the enmity of elected officials — for the winners now are entitled to learn all of their vocal opponents' identities. Maybe these effects can be justified with respect to electioneering at the national level by deep-pocket interest groups — though I think that the Justices have been too ready to equate political support to bribery — but for local elections the equation is impossible to sustain.

Indiana does not contend that requiring disclosure by plaintiffs Carol Antun, Perry Metzger, and Bruce Martin — who want to use their own resources to speak on behalf of candidates of the Libertarian Party (and oppose incumbents, for libertarians do not occupy any major office in Indiana) — is essential to avert a material risk of underground favor-trading or bribery. Nor does the state try to justify mandatory disclosure by any truly independent speaker. Instead Indiana contends that it is entitled to regulate *all* electioneering by *every* speaker in order to avoid drawing lines. Given *McConnell*, I cannot be confident that my colleagues are wrong in thinking that five Justices will go along. But I also do not understand how that position can be reconciled with established principles of constitutional law.

Notes and Questions

1.   If Aristotle, quoted in Judge Posner's opinion for the Court, is correct, and "we believe good men more fully and more readily," is that an argument against permitting anonymous speech? Or does it suggest that voters will discount anonymous speech accordingly, leaving no need for mandated disclosure?

2.   At the close of his opinion, Judge Easterbrook noted that the speakers in *Majors* wished to oppose incumbent officeholders. What is the relevance of this observation?

3.   *Majors* discusses at length *McConnell v. FEC*, a campaign finance case to which we will return in Chapter 9. Since World War II, the Supreme Court has generally been strong in upholding the right to anonymous speech in a wide variety of situations. In addition to those covered in this book, such cases include *Thomas v. Collins*, 323 U.S. 516 (1945) (union organizer could not be required to obtain license before speaking); *NAACP v. Alabama*, 357 U.S. 449 (1958) (NAACP could not be forced to disclose donor and member lists in state investigation into corporate status); *Bates v. Little Rock*, 361 U.S. 516 (1960) (NAACP could not be required to turn over donor and member information as a condition of doing business in the city); *Talley v. California*, 362 U.S. 60 (1960) (picketers could not be required to put name and address of funders on handbills); and *Watchtower Bible & Tract Society v. Village of Stratton*, 536 U.S. 150 (2002) (door to door religious canvassers could not be required to register with government). However, as the *Majors* majority noted, the Supreme Court has been trending in the other direction on campaign finance cases. What factors might explain the different directions in the Court's jurisprudence? What reasons might there be to treat campaign finance cases differently than other political speech cases? In the long run, will the tendency toward more disclosure in campaign finance cases undercut the Court's commitment to protecting anonymity for other speakers?

The next case is the Supreme Court's most recent major effort at analyzing a compelled-disclosure claim. Does it answer some of the questions raised by Judges Posner and Easterbrook in *Majors*?

DOE v. REED

Supreme Court of the United States
561 U.S. 186, 130 S. Ct. 2811, 177 L. Ed. 2d 493 (2010)

CHIEF JUSTICE ROBERTS delivered the opinion of the Court [in which JUSTICE KENNEDY, JUSTICE GINSBURG, JUSTICE BREYER, JUSTICE ALITO, and JUSTICE SOTOMAYOR join].

The State of Washington allows its citizens to challenge state laws by referendum. * * * This case arises out of a state law extending certain benefits to same-sex couples, and a corresponding referendum petition to put that law to a popular vote. [The referendum, R-71, appeared on the November 2009 ballot. By a margin of 53% to 47%, the voters approved the law.] Respondent intervenors invoked the [Washington Public Records Act (PRA)] to obtain copies of the petition, with the names and addresses of the signers. Certain petition signers and the petition sponsor objected, arguing that such public disclosure would violate their rights under the First Amendment.

The course of this litigation, however, has framed the legal question before us more broadly. The issue at this stage of the case is not whether disclosure of this particular petition would violate the First Amendment, but whether disclosure of referendum petitions in general would do so. We conclude that such disclosure does not as a general matter violate the First Amendment, and we therefore affirm the judgment of the Court of Appeals. We leave it to the lower courts to consider in the first instance the signers' more focused claim concerning disclosure of the information on this particular petition, which is pending before the District Court. * * *

The compelled disclosure of signatory information on referendum petitions is subject to review under the First Amendment. An individual expresses a view on a political matter when he signs a petition under Washington's referendum procedure. In most cases, the individual's signature will express the view that the law subject to the petition should be overturned. Even if the signer is agnostic as to the merits of the underlying law, his signature still expresses the political view that the question should be considered "by the whole electorate." *Meyer* v. *Grant*, 486 U.S. 414, 421 (1988) [p. 678]. In either case, the expression of a political view implicates a First Amendment right. * * *

Respondents counter that signing a petition is a legally operative legislative act and therefore "does not involve any significant expressive element." It is true that signing a referendum petition may ultimately have the legal consequence of requiring the secretary of state to place the referendum on the ballot. But we do not see how adding such legal effect to an expressive activity somehow deprives that activity of its expressive component, taking it outside the scope of the First Amendment. * * *

We have a series of precedents considering First Amendment challenges to disclosure requirements in the electoral context. These precedents have reviewed such challenges under what has been termed "exacting scrutiny." See, *e.g.*, *Buckley* v. *Valeo*, 424 U.S. 1, 64 (1976) [p. 799] (*per curiam*).

That standard "requires a 'substantial relation' between the disclosure requirement and a 'sufficiently important' governmental interest." To withstand this scrutiny, "the strength of the governmental interest must reflect the seriousness of the actual burden on First Amendment rights." *Davis* [v. *Davis* [v. *Federal Election Comm'n*, 554 U.S. 724, 744 (2008)].[1]

Respondents assert two interests to justify the burdens of compelled disclosure under the PRA on First Amendment rights: (1) preserving the integrity of the electoral process by combating fraud, detecting invalid signatures, and fostering government transparency and accountability; and (2) providing information to the electorate about who supports the petition. Because we determine that the State's interest in preserving the integrity of the electoral process suffices to defeat the argument that the PRA is unconstitutional with respect to referendum petitions in general, we need not, and do not, address the State's "informational" interest.

The State's interest in preserving the integrity of the electoral process is undoubtedly important. * * * The State's interest is particularly strong with respect to efforts to root out fraud, which not only may produce fraudulent outcomes, but has a systemic effect as well: It "drives honest citizens out of the democratic process and breeds distrust of our government." *Purcell* v. *Gonzalez*, 549 U.S. 1, 4 (2006) (*per curiam*); see also *Crawford* v. *Marion County Election Bd.*, 553 U.S. 181, 196 (2008) [p. 1032] (opinion of STEVENS, J.). The threat of fraud in this context is not merely hypothetical; respondents and their *amici* cite a number of cases of petition-related fraud across the country to support the point.

But the State's interest in preserving electoral integrity is not limited to combating fraud. That interest extends to efforts to ferret out invalid signatures caused not by fraud but by simple mistake, such as duplicate signatures or signatures of individuals who are not registered to vote in the State. That interest also extends more generally to promoting transparency and accountability in the electoral process, which the State argues is "essential to the proper functioning of a democracy."

Plaintiffs contend that the disclosure requirements of the PRA are not "sufficiently related" to the interest of protecting the integrity of the electoral process. They argue that disclosure is not necessary because the secretary of state is already charged with verifying and canvassing the names on a petition, advocates and opponents of a measure can observe that process, and any citizen can challenge the secretary's actions in court. They also stress that existing criminal penalties reduce the danger of fraud in the petition process.

But the secretary's verification and canvassing will not catch all invalid signatures: The job is large and difficult (the secretary ordinarily checks "only 3 to 5%

---

[1] JUSTICE SCALIA doubts whether petition signing is entitled to any First Amendment protection at all. His skepticism is based on the view that petition signing has "legal effects" in the legislative process, while other aspects of political participation — with respect to which we have held there is a First Amendment interest — do not. That line is not as sharp as JUSTICE SCALIA would have it; he himself recognizes "the existence of a First Amendment interest in voting," which of course also can have legal effect. The distinction becomes even fuzzier given that only *some* petition signing has legal effect, and any such legal effect attaches only well after the expressive act of signing, if the secretary determines that the petition satisfies the requirements for inclusion on the ballot. Petitions that do not qualify for the ballot of course carry no legal effect.

of signatures"), and the secretary can make mistakes, too. Public disclosure can help cure the inadequacies of the verification and canvassing process.

Disclosure also helps prevent certain types of petition fraud otherwise difficult to detect, such as outright forgery and "bait and switch" fraud, in which an individual signs the petition based on a misrepresentation of the underlying issue. The signer is in the best position to detect these types of fraud, and public disclosure can bring the issue to the signer's attention.

Public disclosure thus helps ensure that the only signatures counted are those that should be, and that the only referenda placed on the ballot are those that garner enough valid signatures. Public disclosure also promotes transparency and accountability in the electoral process to an extent other measures cannot. In light of the foregoing, we reject plaintiffs' argument and conclude that public disclosure of referendum petitions in general is substantially related to the important interest of preserving the integrity of the electoral process.

Plaintiffs' more significant objection is that "the strength of the governmental interest" does not "reflect the seriousness of the actual burden on First Amendment rights." According to plaintiffs, the objective of those seeking disclosure of the R-71 petition is not to prevent fraud, but to publicly identify those who had validly signed and to broadcast the signers' political views on the subject of the petition. Plaintiffs allege, for example, that several groups plan to post the petitions in searchable form on the Internet, and then encourage other citizens to seek out the R-71 signers.

Plaintiffs explain that once on the Internet, the petition signers' names and addresses "can be combined with publicly available phone numbers and maps," in what will effectively become a blueprint for harassment and intimidation. To support their claim that they will be subject to reprisals, plaintiffs cite examples from the history of a similar proposition in California and from the experience of one of the petition sponsors in this case.

In related contexts, we have explained that those resisting disclosure can prevail under the First Amendment if they can show "a reasonable probability that the compelled disclosure [of personal information] will subject them to threats, harassment, or reprisals from either Government officials or private parties." *Buckley, supra,* at 74; see also *Citizens United* [v. *Federal Election Comm'n*], 558 U.S., at 367, 130 S. Ct. 876 , 175 L. Ed. 2d 753 [(2010)] [p. 1022]. The question before us, however, is not whether PRA disclosure violates the First Amendment with respect to those who signed the R-71 petition, or other particularly controversial petitions. The question instead is whether such disclosure in general violates the First Amendment rights of those who sign referendum petitions.

The problem for plaintiffs is that their argument rests almost entirely on the specific harm they say would attend disclosure of the information on the R-71 petition, or on similarly controversial ones. But typical referendum petitions "concern tax policy, revenue, budget, or other state law issues." Voters care about such issues, some quite deeply — but there is no reason to assume that any burdens imposed by disclosure of typical referendum petitions would be remotely like the burdens plaintiffs fear in this case.

Plaintiffs have offered little in response. They have provided us scant evidence or argument beyond the burdens they assert disclosure would impose on R-71 petition signers or the signers of other similarly controversial petitions. Indeed, what little plaintiffs do offer with respect to typical petitions in Washington hurts, not helps: Several other petitions in the State "have been subject to release in recent years," plaintiffs tell us, but apparently that release has come without incident.

Faced with the State's unrebutted arguments that only modest burdens attend the disclosure of a typical petition, we must reject plaintiffs' broad challenge to the PRA. In doing so, we note — as we have in other election law disclosure cases — that upholding the law against a broad-based challenge does not foreclose a litigant's success in a narrower one. See *Buckley, supra*, at 74 ("minor parties" may be exempt from disclosure requirements if they can show "a reasonable probability that the compelled disclosure of a party's contributors' names will subject them to threats, harassment, or reprisals from either Government officials or private parties"); *Citizens United, supra*, at 370 (disclosure "would be unconstitutional as applied to an organization if there were a reasonable probability that the group's members would face threats, harassment, or reprisals if their names were disclosed"). * * *

[*Affirmed.*]

JUSTICE BREYER, concurring.

In circumstances where, as here, "a law significantly implicates competing constitutionally protected interests in complex ways," the Court balances interests. *Nixon* v. *Shrink Missouri Government PAC*, 528 U.S. 377, 402 (2000) [p. 834] (BREYER, J., concurring). * * * As I read their opinions, this is what both the Court and JUSTICE STEVENS do. And for the reasons stated in those opinions (as well as many of the reasons discussed by JUSTICE SOTOMAYOR), I would uphold the statute challenged in this case. With this understanding, I join the opinion of the Court and JUSTICE STEVENS' opinion.

JUSTICE ALITO, concurring.

The Court holds that the disclosure under the Washington Public Records Act (PRA) of the names and addresses of persons who sign referendum petitions does not as a general matter violate the First Amendment, and I agree with that conclusion. Many referendum petitions concern relatively uncontroversial matters, and plaintiffs have provided no reason to think that disclosure of signatory information in those contexts would significantly chill the willingness of voters to sign. Plaintiffs' facial challenge therefore must fail.

Nonetheless, facially valid disclosure requirements can impose heavy burdens on First Amendment rights in individual cases. * * * The possibility of prevailing in an as-applied challenge provides adequate protection for First Amendment rights only if (1) speakers can obtain the exemption sufficiently far in advance to avoid chilling protected speech and (2) the showing necessary to obtain the exemption is not overly burdensome. With respect to the first requirement, the as-applied exemption becomes practically worthless if speakers cannot obtain the exemption quickly and well in advance of speaking. To avoid the possibility that a disclosure requirement might chill the willingness of voters to sign a referendum petition (and thus burden a circulator's ability to collect the necessary number of signatures), voters must have some assurance *at the time when they are presented with the petition* that their names and identifying information will not be released to the public. The only way a circulator can provide such assurance, however, is if the circulator has sought and obtained an as-applied exemption from the disclosure requirement well before circulating the petition. Otherwise, the best the circulator could do would be to tell voters that an exemption might be obtained at some point in the future. Such speculation would often be insufficient to alleviate voters' concerns about the possibility of being subjected to threats, harassment, or reprisals.

Additionally, speakers must be able to obtain an as-applied exemption without clearing a high evidentiary hurdle. We acknowledged as much in Buckley, where we noted that "unduly strict requirements of proof could impose a heavy burden" on speech. 424 U.S., at 74. Recognizing that speakers "must be allowed sufficient flexibility in the proof of injury to assure a fair consideration of their claim," we emphasized that speakers "need show only a *reasonable probability*" that disclosure will lead to threats, harassment, or reprisals. *Ibid.* (emphasis added). * * *

In light of those principles, the plaintiffs in this case have a strong argument that the PRA violates the First Amendment as applied to the Referendum 71 petition.

* * * The widespread harassment and intimidation suffered by supporters of California's Proposition 8 provides strong support for an as-applied exemption in the present case. * * *

What is more, when plaintiffs return to the District Court, they will have the opportunity to develop evidence of intimidation and harassment of Referendum 71 supporters * * *. For example, plaintiffs allege that the campaign manager for one of the plaintiff groups received threatening e-mails and phone calls, and that the threats were so severe that the manager filed a complaint with the local sheriff and had his children sleep in an interior room of his home. * * *

As-applied challenges to disclosure requirements play a critical role in protecting First Amendment freedoms. To give speech the breathing room it needs to flourish, prompt judicial remedies must be available well before the relevant speech occurs and the burden of proof must be low. In this case — both through analogy and through their own experiences — plaintiffs have a strong case that they are entitled to as-applied relief, and they will be able to pursue such relief before the District Court.

JUSTICE SOTOMAYOR, with whom JUSTICE STEVENS and JUSTICE GINSBURG join, concurring. * * *

The Court today confirms that the State of Washington's decision to make referendum petition signatures available for public inspection falls squarely within the realm of permissible election-related regulations. Public disclosure of the identity of petition signers, which is the rule in the overwhelming majority of States that use initiatives and referenda, advances States' vital interests in "[p]reserving the integrity of the electoral process, preventing corruption, and sustaining the active, alert responsibility of the individual citizen in a democracy for the wise conduct of government." * * *

On the other side of the ledger, I view the burden of public disclosure on speech and associational rights as minimal in this context. As this Court has observed with respect to campaign-finance regulations, "disclosure requirements . . . 'do not prevent anyone from speaking.' " *Citizens United*, 558 U.S., at 366. When it comes to initiatives and referenda, the impact of public disclosure on expressive interests is even more attenuated. While campaign-finance disclosure injects the government into what would otherwise have been private political activity, the process of legislating by referendum is inherently public. To qualify a referendum for the ballot, citizens are required to sign a petition and supply identifying information to the State. The act of signing typically occurs in public, and the circulators who collect and submit signatures ordinarily owe signers no guarantee of confidentiality. For persons with the "civic courage" to participate in this process, the State's decision to make accessible what they voluntarily place in the public sphere should not deter them from engaging in the expressive act of petition signing. Disclosure of the identity of petition signers, moreover, in no way directly impairs the ability of anyone to speak and associate for political ends either publicly or privately.

Given the relative weight of the interests at stake and the traditionally public nature of initiative and referendum processes, the Court rightly rejects petitioners' constitutional challenge to the State of Washington's petition disclosure regulations. These same considerations also mean that any party attempting to challenge particular applications of the State's regulations will bear a heavy burden. Even when a referendum involves a particularly controversial subject and some petition signers fear harassment from nonstate actors, a State's important interests in "protect[ing] the integrity and reliability of the initiative process" remain undiminished, and the State retains significant discretion in advancing those interests. Likewise, because the expressive interests implicated by the act of petition signing are always modest, I find it difficult to see how any incremental disincentive to sign a petition would tip the constitutional balance. Case-specific relief may be available when a State selectively applies a facially neutral petition disclosure rule in a manner that discriminates based on the content of referenda or the viewpoint of petition signers, or in the rare circumstance in which disclosure poses a reasonable probability of serious and widespread harassment that the State is unwilling or unable to control. Cf. *NAACP* v. *Alabama ex rel. Patterson*, 357 U.S. 449 (1958). Allowing case-specific invalidation under a more forgiving standard would unduly diminish the substantial breathing room States are afforded to adopt and implement reasonable, nondiscriminatory measures like the disclosure requirement now at issue. Accordingly, courts presented with an as-applied challenge to a regulation authorizing the disclosure of referendum petitions should be deeply skeptical of any assertion that the Constitution, which embraces political transparency, compels States to conceal the identity of persons who seek to participate in lawmaking through a state-created referendum process. With this understanding, I join the opinion of the Court.

Justice Stevens, with whom Justice Breyer joins, concurring in part and concurring in the judgment.

This is not a hard case. It is not about a restriction on voting or on speech and does not involve a classic disclosure requirement. Rather, the case concerns a neutral, nondiscriminatory policy of disclosing information already in the State's possession that, it has been alleged, might one day indirectly burden petition signatories. The burden imposed by Washington's application of the PRA to referendum petitions in the vast majority, if not all, its applications is not substantial. And the State has given a more than adequate justification for its choice. * * *

[A]ny effect on speech that disclosure might have is minimal. The PRA does not necessarily make it more difficult to circulate or obtain signatures on a petition, or to communicate one's views generally. Regardless of whether someone signs a referendum petition, that person remains free to say anything to anyone at any time. If disclosure indirectly burdens a speaker, "the amount of speech covered" is small — only a single, narrow message conveying one fact in one place. And while the democratic act of casting a ballot or signing a petition does serve an expressive purpose, the act does not involve any "interactive communication" and is "not principally" a method of "individual expression of political sentiment."

Weighed against the possible burden on constitutional rights are the State's justifications for its rule. In this case, the State has posited a perfectly adequate justification: an interest in deterring and detecting petition fraud.[2] * * *

There remains the issue of petitioners' as-applied challenge. * * * Any burden on speech that petitioners posit is speculative as well as indirect. For an as-applied challenge to a law such as the PRA to succeed, there would have to be a significant threat of harassment directed at those who sign the petition that cannot be mitigated by law enforcement measures.[5] Moreover, the character of the law challenged in a referendum does not, in itself, affect the analysis. Debates about tax policy and regulation of private property can become just as heated as debates about domestic partnerships. And as a general matter, it is very difficult to show that by later disclosing the names of petition signatories, individuals will be less willing to sign petitions. Just as we have in the past, I would demand strong evidence before concluding that an indirect and speculative chain of events imposes a substantial burden on speech. * * *

Accordingly, I concur with the opinion of the Court to the extent that it is not inconsistent with my own, and I concur in the judgment.

---

[2] Washington also points out that its disclosure policy informs voters about who supports the particular referendum. In certain election-law contexts, this informational rationale (among others) may provide a basis for regulation; in this case, there is no need to look beyond the State's quite obvious antifraud interest.

[5] A rare case may also arise in which the level of threat to any individual is not quite so high but a State's disclosure would substantially limit a group's ability to "garner the number of signatures necessary to place [a] matter on the ballot," thereby "limiting [its] ability to make the matter the focus of statewide discussion." *Meyer* v. *Grant*, 486 U.S., [at] 423.

JUSTICE SCALIA, concurring in the judgment. * * *

* * * Our Nation's longstanding traditions of legislating and voting in public refute the claim that the First Amendment accords a right to anonymity in the performance of an act with governmental effect. * * *

The filing of a [valid] referendum petition * * * has two legal effects: (1) It requires the secretary to place the measure referred to the people on the ballot at the next general election; and (2) it suspends operation of the measure, causing it only to have effect 30 days after it is approved during that election. A voter who signs a referendum petition is therefore exercising legislative power because his signature, somewhat like a vote for or against a bill in the legislature, seeks to affect the legal force of the measure at issue.[2]

Plaintiffs point to no precedent from this Court holding that legislating is protected by the First Amendment. Nor do they identify historical evidence demonstrating that "the freedom of speech" the First Amendment codified encompassed a right to legislate without public disclosure. This should come as no surprise; the exercise of lawmaking power in the United States has traditionally been public. * * *

Moreover, even when the people *asked* Congress for legislative changes — by exercising their constitutional right to "to petition the Government for a redress of grievances" — they did so publicly. The petition was read aloud in Congress. The petitioner's name (when large groups were not involved), his request, and what action Congress had taken on the petition were consistently recorded in the House and Senate Journals. Even when the people exercised legislative power directly, they did so not anonymously, but openly in town hall meetings.

Petitioning the government and participating in the traditional town meeting were precursors of the modern initiative and referendum. * * * Plaintiffs' argument implies that the public nature of these practices, so longstanding and unquestioned, violated the freedom of speech. There is no historical support for such a claim.

Legislating was not the only governmental act that was public in America. Voting was public until 1888 when the States began to adopt the Australian secret ballot. * * * Initially, the Colonies mostly continued the English traditions of voting by a show of hands or by voice — *viva voce* voting. * * *

Although there was variation, the election official would ordinarily compile a poll with the name and residence of each voter, and the name of the candidate for whom he voted. To prevent fraud, the Colonies in Rhode Island, New York, and New Jersey adopted the English rule that "copies of the poll must be delivered on demand to persons who were willing to pay a reasonable charge for the labor of writing them." Some colonies allowed candidates to demand a copy of the poll and required the legislature to examine the poll in a contested election. Thus, as in this

---

[2] The Court notes that "only *some* petition signing has legal effect." That is true. Some petitions may never be submitted to the secretary; they are irrelevant here, since they will never be subject to the PRA. But some petitions that are submitted to the secretary may lack the requisite number of signatures. Even as to those, the petition signer has exercised *his portion* of the legislative power when he signs the petition, much like a legislator who casts a losing vote.

case, the government not only publicly collected identifying information about who voted and for which candidate, it also disclosed that information to the public.

Any suggestion that *viva voce* voting infringed the accepted understanding of the pre-existing freedom of speech to which the First Amendment's text refers is refuted by the fact that several state constitutions that required or authorized *viva voce* voting *also* explicitly guaranteed the freedom of speech. Surely one constitutional provision did not render the other invalid.

Of course the practice of *viva voce* voting was gradually replaced with the paper ballot, which was thought to reduce fraud and undue influence. There is no indication that the shift resulted from a sudden realization that public voting infringed voters' freedom of speech, and the manner in which it occurred suggests the contrary. States adopted the paper ballot at different times, and some States changed methods multiple times. * * *

The new paper ballots did not make voting anonymous. Initially, many States did not regulate the form of the paper ballot. Taking advantage of this, political parties began printing ballots with their candidates' names on them. They used brightly colored paper and other distinctive markings so that the ballots could be recognized from a distance, making the votes public. * * *

It was precisely discontent over the nonsecret nature of ballot voting, and the abuses that produced, which led to the States' adoption of the Australian secret ballot. * * * But I am aware of no contention that the Australian system was required by the First Amendment (or the state counterparts). That would have been utterly implausible, since the inhabitants of the Colonies, the States, and the United States had found public voting entirely compatible with "the freedom of speech" for several centuries. * * *

Plaintiffs raise concerns that the disclosure of petition signatures may lead to threats and intimidation. Of course nothing prevents the people of Washington from keeping petition signatures secret to avoid that — just as nothing prevented the States from moving to the secret ballot. But there is no constitutional basis for this Court to impose that course upon the States — or to insist (as today's opinion does) that it can only be avoided by the demonstration of a "sufficiently important governmental interest." And it may even be a bad idea to keep petition signatures secret. There are laws against threats and intimidation; and harsh criticism, short of unlawful action, is a price our people have traditionally been willing to pay for self-governance. Requiring people to stand up in public for their political acts fosters civic courage, without which democracy is doomed. * * *

JUSTICE THOMAS, dissenting. * * *

The expressive political activity of signing a referendum petition is a paradigmatic example of "the practice of persons sharing common views banding together to achieve a common end." *Citizens Against Rent Control/Coalition for Fair Housing* v. *Berkeley*, 454 U.S. 290, 294 (1981). A referendum supported by only one person's signature is a nullity; it will never be placed on the ballot. * * * For these reasons, signing a referendum petition amounts to "political association" protected by the First Amendment.

This Court has long recognized the "vital relationship between" political association "and privacy in one's associations," *NAACP* v. *Alabama ex rel. Patterson*, 357 U.S., [at] 462, and held that "[t]he Constitution protects against the compelled disclosure of political associations and beliefs," *Brown* v. *Socialist Workers '74 Campaign Comm. (Ohio)*, 459 U.S., [at] 91. This constitutional protection "yield[s] only to a subordinating interest of the State that is compelling, and then only if there is a substantial relation between the information sought and an overriding and compelling state interest." *Id.*, at 91–92. Thus, unlike the Court, I read our precedents to require application of strict scrutiny to laws that compel disclosure of protected First Amendment association. Under that standard, a disclosure requirement passes constitutional muster only if it is narrowly tailored — *i.e.*, the least restrictive means — to serve a compelling state interest.

Washington's application of the PRA to a referendum petition does not survive strict scrutiny.

Washington first contends that it has a compelling interest in "transparency and accountability," which it claims encompasses several subordinate interests: preserving the integrity of its election process, preventing corruption, deterring fraud, and correcting mistakes by the secretary of state or by petition signers.

It is true that a State has a substantial interest in regulating its referendum and initiative processes "to protect the[ir] integrity and reliability." But Washington points to no precedent from this Court recognizing "correcting errors" as a distinct compelling interest that could support disclosure regulations. And our cases strongly suggest that preventing corruption and deterring fraud bear less weight in this particular electoral context: the signature-gathering stage of a referendum or initiative drive. The Court has twice observed that "the risk of fraud or corruption, or the appearance thereof, is more remote at the petition stage of an initiative than at the time of balloting." [*Buckley* v. *American Constitutional Law Foundation*, 525 U.S. 182], 203 [(1999)] (quoting *Meyer* v. *Grant*, 486 U.S., [at] 427). * * *

We should not abandon those principles merely because Washington and its amici can point to a mere eight instances of initiative-related fraud. If anything, these meager figures reinforce the conclusion that the risks of fraud or corruption in the initiative and referendum process are remote and thereby undermine Washington's claim that those two interests should be considered compelling for purposes of strict scrutiny.

Thus, I am not persuaded that Washington's interest in protecting the integrity and reliability of its referendum process, as the State has defined that interest, is compelling. But I need not answer that question here. Even assuming the interest is compelling, on-demand disclosure of a referendum petition to any person under the PRA is "a blunderbuss approach" to furthering that interest, not the least restrictive means of doing so. The events that prompted petitioners' complaint in this case demonstrate as much.

As Washington explained during oral argument, after the secretary of state receives signed referendum petitions, his "first step . . . is to take them to his archiving section and to have them digitized. As soon as they're digitized, they're available on disks for anyone who requests them" under the PRA. In this case, two organizations announced their intention to obtain the digitized names and addresses of referendum signers and post them "online, in a searchable format."

There is no apparent reason why Washington must broadly disclose referendum signers' names and addresses in this manner to vindicate the interest that it invokes here. Washington * * * could put the names and addresses of referendum signers into a similar electronic database that state employees could search *without* subjecting the name and address of each signer to wholesale public disclosure. The secretary could electronically cross-reference the referendum database against the "statewide voter registration list" contained in Washington's "statewide voter registration database," to ensure that each referendum signer meets Washington's residency and voter registration requirements. Doing so presumably would drastically reduce or eliminate possible errors or mistakes that Washington argues the secretary *might* make, since it would allow the secretary to verify virtually all of the signatures instead of the mere "3 to 5%" he "ordinarily checks."

An electronic referendum database would also enable the secretary to determine whether multiple entries correspond to a single registered voter, thereby detecting whether a voter had signed the petition more than once. In addition, the database would protect victims of "forgery" or " 'bait and switch' fraud." In Washington, "a unique identifier is assigned to each legally registered voter in the state." Washington could create a Web site, linked to the electronic referendum database, where a voter concerned that his name had been fraudulently signed could conduct a search using his unique identifier to ensure that his name was absent from the database — without requiring disclosure of the names and addresses of all the voluntary, legitimate signers. * * *

Washington nevertheless contends that its citizens must "have access to public records . . . to independently evaluate whether the Secretary properly determined to certify or not to certify a referendum to the ballot." * * * But Washington's Election Code already gives Washington voters access to referendum petition data. Under [Washington law], "[t]he verification and canvass of signatures on the [referendum] petition may be observed by persons representing the advocates and opponents of the proposed measure so long as they make no record of the names, addresses, or other information on the petitions or related records except upon" court order. Each side is entitled to at least two such observers[.] * * *

It is readily apparent that Washington can vindicate its stated interest in "transparency and accountability" through a number of more narrowly tailored means than wholesale public disclosure. Accordingly, this interest cannot justify applying the PRA to a referendum petition.

Washington also contends that it has a compelling interest in "providing relevant information to Washington voters," and that on-demand disclosure to the public is a narrowly tailored means of furthering that interest. This argument is easily dispatched, since this Court has already rejected it in [*McIntyre* v. *Ohio Elections Comm'n*, 514 U.S. 334 (1995)] [p. 644]. * * *

* * * People are intelligent enough to evaluate the merits of a referendum without knowing who supported it. Thus, just as this informational interest did not

justify the Ohio law in *McIntyre*, it does not justify applying the PRA to referendum petitions. * * *

The difficulty in predicting which referendum measures will prove controversial — combined with Washington's default position that signed referendum petitions will be disclosed on-demand, thereby allowing anyone to place this information on the Internet for broad dissemination — raises the significant probability that today's decision will "inhibit the exercise of legitimate First Amendment activity" with respect to referendum and initiative petitions.

Notes and Questions

1. Justice Alito suggested that as-applied challenges, to be useful, must be handled on a timely basis and should not face a "high evidentiary" hurdle. Justice Sotomayor countered that courts should be "deeply skeptical" of any as-applied challenge, and Justice Stevens argued that proving an as-applied challenge will be "very difficult" and should require "strong evidence." Which approach makes the most sense? If the Sotomayor/Stevens approach is correct about the burdens facing an as-applied challenge, should the Court have been more willing to make a facial determination of unconstitutionality?

2. In May of 2010, a few weeks before *Doe* was decided, a multi-jurisdictional drug task force raided a "medical marijuana dispensary" near Tacoma, Washington, in the process seizing numerous completed petitions for a ballot initiative that would "remove state civil and criminal penalties for persons eighteen years or older who cultivate, possess, transport, sell, or use marijuana" in the state. Supporters of the initiative claimed that police intended to intimidate people out of signing petitions. Gavin Dahl, *Seized Marijuana Legalization Petitions Missing*, RAW STORY, May 26, 2010, *at* http://rawstory.com/rs/2010/0526/case-marijuana-legalization-petitions-seized-drug-raid/. After *Doe*, police can simply obtain information on petition signatories through the Public Records Act. Would (should) a complaint based on such actions meet the Alito standard for obtaining as-applied relief? The Sotomayor/Stevens standard? Does this set of facts cause you to rethink your views on *Doe*?

3. Justice Scalia argued that disclosure statutes encourage "civic courage, without which democracy is doomed." Others, however, have expressed concern that there is little rational reason for voters to engage in learning about political issues. *See* JAMES BUCHANAN & GORDON TULLOCK, THE CALCULUS OF CONSENT: LOGICAL FOUNDATIONS OF A CONSTITUTIONAL DEMOCRACY (1962). Buchanan and Tullock focused on the fact that any one person's vote was extremely unlikely to determine the outcome of an election, but it seems equally true that any one person's signature is unlikely to determine whether an initiative or referendum appears on the ballot. Likewise, any one person's financial contribution to a campaign is unlikely to determine the outcome. Given the often tenuous incentives to participate in civic life, should we demand that the minority who do participate also exhibit "civic courage" that goes beyond the norm?

In the wake of California's Proposition 8, which amended the state constitution to define marriage as being between a man and a woman, there were many reports of harassment and vandalism against supporters of the initiative. Relying on mandatory-disclosure laws, opponents of the measure publicized the names and address of supporters, organized boycotts, and in some cases published on the Internet maps to donors' homes. Said one leader opposed to Proposition 8, "Years ago we would never have been able to get a blacklist that fast and quickly." *See* Bradley A. Smith, *In Defense of Political Anonymity*, 20 CITY J. 74, 77 (2010). Assuming that private boycotts are a legitimate tool for attempting to create social change — indeed, one itself protected by the First Amendment, *see NAACP v. Alabama ex rel. Patterson*, 357 U.S. 449, 460–66 (1958), should the state nonetheless be constitutionally prohibited from compelling the potential targets to disclose information that facilitates such boycotts and blacklists? Or is the proper balance between providing voters with information and protecting voters from harassment a classic matter for legislative balancing?

4.   Justice Thomas argued that there are less restrictive means available for the state to fulfill its anti-fraud goals. Yet some of these means, such as creating and maintaining a searchable website, would cost the state money. In an era of tight state budgets, to what extent should least-restrictive-means analysis take into account the financial costs to the state of providing a less restrictive alternative?

5.   On remand, the district court held that the names of petition-signers could be made public. *Doe v. Reed*, 823 F. Supp. 2d 1195 (W.D. Wash. 2011). The court noted that by the time of the decision, some of the identities of the referendum's supporters were publicly known, and concluded that the plaintiffs had failed to show that those persons had been subject to harassment. Plaintiffs sought an injunction against disclosure of their identities, but the injunction was denied by the district court, the Ninth Circuit, and the Supreme Court, the last over the dissent of Justice Alito, with Justice Kagan taking no part in the decision. 132 S. Ct. 449 (2011).

6.   Is the act of signing a petition "speech"? Justice Scalia characterized it as a legislative act and analogized petition-signing to "a vote for or against a bill in the legislature," while the Court suggested that acts having governmental effect could also be speech where they constitute "the expression of a political view." Nevertheless, in *Nevada Commission on Ethics v. Carrigan*, 131 S. Ct. 2343 (2011), an eight-Justice majority, in an opinion written by Justice Scalia, concluded that a vote in the legislature was not "speech" entitled to First Amendment protection:

> [A] legislator's vote is the commitment of his apportioned share of the legislature's power to the passage or defeat of a particular proposal. The legislative power thus committed is not personal to the legislator but belongs to the people; the legislator has no personal right to it. * * * In this respect, voting by a legislator is different from voting by a citizen. While "a voter's franchise is a personal right," "[t]he procedures for voting in legislative assemblies * * * pertain to legislators not as individuals but as political representatives executing the legislative process." *Coleman* v. *Miller*, 307 U.S. 433, 469–470 (1939) (opinion of Frankfurter, J.).

> * * * There are, to be sure, instances where action conveys a symbolic meaning — such as the burning of a flag to convey disagreement with a country's policies. But the act of voting symbolizes nothing. It *discloses*, to be sure, that the legislator wishes (for whatever reason) that the proposi-

tion on the floor be adopted, just as a physical assault discloses that the attacker dislikes the victim. But neither the one nor the other is an act of communication. * * *

Even if it were true that the vote itself could "express deeply held and highly unpopular views," the argument would still miss the mark. This Court has rejected the notion that the First Amendment confers a right to use governmental mechanics to convey a message. * * * [A] legislator has no right to use official powers for expressive purposes.

131 S. Ct. at 2350–51.

Is the analysis in *Carrigan* consistent with *Doe v. Reed*? Justice Alito, who concurred in the judgment on other grounds, thought not:

Voting has an expressive component in and of itself. * * * Just as the act of signing a petition is not deprived of its expressive character when the signature is given legal consequences, the act of voting is not drained of its expressive content when the vote has a legal effect. If an ordinary citizen casts a vote in a straw poll on an important proposal pending before a legislative body, that act indisputably constitutes a form of speech. If a member of the legislative body chooses to vote in the same straw poll, the legislator's act is no less expressive than that of an ordinary citizen. And if the legislator then votes on the measure in the legislative chamber, the expressive character of that vote is not eliminated simply because it may affect the outcome of the legislative process.

131 S. Ct at 2355 (Alito, J., concurring in part and concurring in the judgment). The Court responded that "[i]t is one thing to say that an inherently expressive act [*i.e.*, signing a petition] remains so despite its having governmental effect, but is altogether another thing to say that a governmental act becomes expressive simply because the governmental actor wishes it to be so." 131 S. Ct. at 2351 (opinion of the Court). Further, "[a] legislator voting on a bill is not fairly analogized to one simply discussing that bill or expressing an opinion for or against it. The former is performing a governmental act as a representative of his constituents; only the latter is exercising personal First Amendment rights." 131 S. Ct. at 2351 n.5.

Should there be a constitutional right to anonymity in voting, *i.e.*, a right to the Australian ballot? Every state provides for secret balloting, but the Supreme Court has never been asked to decide on its constitutional status. For what it is worth, John Stuart Mill argued that except in rare circumstances, balloting should not be in secret. He believed that public voting would encourage responsibility and accountability for one's vote. *See* JOHN STUART MILL, ON REPRESENTATIVE GOVERNMENT 323–29 (Everyman ed. 1993).

7. As the Notes following *Socialist Workers* illustrated, anonymity is often important to those who provide monetary support to campaigns. We will return to this topic in Chapter 9, when we discuss the constitutionality of rules that require disclosure of contributors' identities.

E. CIRCULATION OF PETITIONS

We encountered petition circulation in Chapter 6 when we studied the obstacles facing a third-party or independent candidate seeking to appear on the ballot. Petitions are a common requirement for the placement of initiatives on the ballot as well. In Chapter 6, our principal focus was on the extent to which states could demand a showing of support so as to prevent ballots from becoming unmanageable.

The simplest type of burden presented by petition requirements is the number of signatures that must be obtained. But, as *Williams v. Rhodes*, 393 U.S. 23 (1968) [p. 497], well illustrated, that is not the only hurdle for petitioners to surmount. Restrictions on *how* and *by whom* signatures may be collected, as well as on compensating signature-gatherers can have a significant impact on a petition's chances of meeting the signature threshold. Those burdens will be our primary concerns in this section.

MEYER v. GRANT
Supreme Court of the United States
486 U.S. 414, 108 S. Ct. 1886, 100 L. Ed. 2d 425 (1988)

JUSTICE STEVENS delivered the opinion of the Court [in which CHIEF JUSTICE REHNQUIST, JUSTICE BRENNAN, JUSTICE WHITE, JUSTICE MARSHALL, JUSTICE BLACKMUN, JUSTICE O'CONNOR, JUSTICE SCALIA, and JUSTICE KENNEDY join]. * * *

Colorado is one of several States that permits its citizens to place propositions on the ballot through an initiative process. Under Colorado law, proponents of an initiative measure must submit the measure to the State Legislative Council and the Legislative Drafting Office for review and comment. The draft is then submitted to a three-member title board, which prepares a title, submission clause, and summary. After approval of the title, submission clause, and summary, the proponents of the measure then have six months to obtain the necessary signatures, which must be in an amount equal to at least five percent of the total number of voters who cast votes for all candidates for the Office of Secretary of State at the last preceding general election. If the signature requirements are met, the petitions may be filed with the Secretary of State, and the measure will appear on the ballot at the next general election.

State law requires that the persons who circulate the approved drafts of the petitions for signature be registered voters. Before the signed petitions are filed with the Secretary of State, the circulators must sign affidavits attesting that each signature is the signature of the person whose name it purports to be and that, to the best of their knowledge and belief, each person signing the petition is a registered voter. The payment of petition circulators is punished as a felony.

Appellees are proponents of an amendment to the Colorado Constitution that would remove motor carriers from the jurisdiction of the Colorado Public Utilities Commission. In early 1984 they obtained approval of a title, submission clause, and summary for a measure proposing the amendment and began the process of obtaining the 46,737 signatures necessary to have the proposal appear on the November 1984 ballot. Based on their own experience as petition circulators, as well as that of other unpaid circulators, appellees concluded that they would need the assistance of paid personnel to obtain the required number of signatures within the allotted time. They then brought this action under 42 U.S.C. § 1983 against the Secretary of State and the Attorney General of Colorado seeking a declaration that the statutory prohibition against the use of paid circulators violates their rights under the First Amendment. [The District Court upheld the prohibition, but the en banc Court of Appeals reversed.] * * *

We fully agree with the Court of Appeals' conclusion that this case involves a limitation on political expression subject to exacting scrutiny. *Buckley* v. *Valeo*, 424 U.S. 1, 45 (1976) [p. 799]. * * * The circulation of an initiative petition of necessity involves both the expression of a desire for political change and a discussion of the merits of the proposed change. Although a petition circulator may not have to persuade potential signatories that a particular proposal should prevail to capture their signatures, he or she will at least have to persuade them that the matter is one deserving of the public scrutiny and debate that would attend its consideration by the whole electorate. This will in almost every case involve an explanation of the nature of the proposal and why its advocates support it. Thus, the circulation of a petition involves the type of interactive communication concerning political change that is appropriately described as "core political speech."

The refusal to permit appellees to pay petition circulators restricts political expression in two ways: First, it limits the number of voices who will convey appellees' message and the hours they can speak and, therefore, limits the size of the audience they can reach. Second, it makes it less likely that appellees will garner the number of signatures necessary to place the matter on the ballot, thus limiting their ability to make the matter the focus of statewide discussion. * * *

Appellants argue that even if the statute imposes some limitation on First Amendment expression, the burden is permissible because other avenues of expression remain open to appellees and because the State has the authority to impose limitations on the scope of the state-created right to legislate by initiative. Neither of these arguments persuades us that the burden imposed on appellees' First Amendment rights is acceptable.

That appellees remain free to employ other means to disseminate their ideas does not take their speech through petition circulators outside the bounds of First Amendment protection. Colorado's prohibition of paid petition circulators restricts access to the most effective, fundamental, and perhaps economical avenue of political discourse, direct one-on-one communication. That it leaves open "more burdensome" avenues of communication, does not relieve its burden on First Amendment expression. The First Amendment protects appellees' right not only to advocate their cause but also to select what they believe to be the most effective means for so doing.

* * * Colorado contends that because the power of the initiative is a state-created right, it is free to impose limitations on the exercise of that right. [But] the power to ban initiatives entirely [does not] include[] the power to limit discussion of political issues raised in initiative petitions. * * * We agree with the Court of Appeals' conclusion that the statute trenches upon an area in which the importance of First Amendment protections is "at its zenith." For that reason the burden that Colorado must overcome to justify this criminal law is well-nigh insurmountable.

We are not persuaded by the State's arguments that the prohibition is justified by its interest in making sure that an initiative has sufficient grass roots support to be placed on the ballot, or by its interest in protecting the integrity of the initiative process. As the Court of Appeals correctly held, the former interest is adequately protected by the requirement that no initiative proposal may be placed on the ballot unless the required number of signatures has been obtained.[7]

The State's interest in protecting the integrity of the initiative process does not justify the prohibition because the State has failed to demonstrate that it is necessary to burden appellees' ability to communicate their message in order to meet its concerns. The Attorney General has argued that the petition circulator has the duty to verify the authenticity of signatures on the petition and that compensation might provide the circulator with a temptation to disregard that duty. No evidence has been offered to support that speculation, however, and we are not prepared to assume that a professional circulator — whose qualifications for similar future assignments may well depend on a reputation for competence and integrity — is any more likely to accept false signatures than a volunteer who is motivated entirely by an interest in having the proposition placed on the ballot.

Other provisions of the Colorado statute deal expressly with the potential danger that circulators might be tempted to pad their petitions with false signatures. It is a crime to forge a signature on a petition, to make false or misleading statements relating to a petition, or to pay someone to sign a petition. Further, the top of each page of the petition must bear a statement printed in red ink warning potential signatories that it is a felony to forge a signature on a petition or to sign the petition when not qualified to vote and admonishing signatories not to sign the petition unless they have read and understand the proposed initiative. These provisions seem adequate to the task of minimizing the risk of improper conduct in the circulation of a petition, especially since the risk of fraud or corruption, or the appearance thereof, is more remote at the petition stage of an initiative than at the time of balloting.

* * * The Colorado statute prohibiting the payment of petition circulators imposes a burden on political expression that the State has failed to justify. The Court of Appeals correctly held that the statute violates the First and Fourteenth Amendments. Its judgment is therefore affirmed.

---

[7] Colorado also seems to suggest that it is permissible to mute the voices of those who can afford to pay petition circulators. "But the concept that government may restrict the speech of some elements of our society in order to enhance the relative voice of others is wholly foreign to the First Amendment." *Buckley* v. *Valeo*, 424 U.S., [at] 48–49. The concern that persons who can pay petition circulators may succeed in getting measures on the ballot when they might otherwise have failed cannot defeat First Amendment rights. As we said in *First National Bank of Boston* v. *Bellotti*, 435 U.S. 765, 790–791 (1978) [p. 895], paid advocacy "may influence the outcome of the vote; this would be its purpose. But the fact that advocacy may persuade the electorate is hardly a reason to suppress it. * * * [T]he people in our democracy are entrusted with the responsibility for judging and evaluating the relative merits of conflicting arguments."

It is so ordered.

BUCKLEY v. AMERICAN CONSTITUTIONAL LAW FOUNDATION, INC.

Supreme Court of the United States
525 U.S. 182, 119 S. Ct. 636, 142 L. Ed. 2d 599 (1999)

JUSTICE GINSBURG delivered the opinion of the Court [in which JUSTICE STEVENS, JUSTICE SCALIA, JUSTICE KENNEDY, and JUSTICE SOUTER join].

Colorado allows its citizens to make laws directly through initiatives placed on election ballots. We review in this case three conditions Colorado places on the ballot-initiative process: (1) the requirement that initiative-petition circulators be registered voters; (2) the requirement that they wear an identification badge bearing the circulator's name; and (3) the requirement that proponents of an initiative report the names and addresses of all paid circulators and the amount paid to each circulator. * * *

By constitutional amendment in 1980, and corresponding statutory change the next year, Colorado added to the requirement [not challenged in this action] that petition circulators be residents, the further requirement that they be registered voters. Registration, Colorado's Attorney General explained at oral argument, demonstrates "commit[ment] to the Colorado law-making process," and facilitates verification of the circulator's residence. Beyond question, Colorado's registration requirement drastically reduces the number of persons, both volunteer and paid, available to circulate petitions. We must therefore inquire whether the State's concerns warrant the reduction.

When this case was before the District Court, registered voters in Colorado numbered approximately 1.9 million. At least 400,000 persons eligible to vote were not registered. * * *

The Tenth Circuit reasoned that the registration requirement placed on Colorado's voter-eligible population produces a speech diminution of the very kind produced by the ban on paid circulators at issue in *Meyer* [v. *Grant*, 486 U.S. 414 (1988)] [p. 678]. We agree. The requirement that circulators be not merely voter eligible, but registered voters * * * decreases the pool of potential circulators as certainly as that pool is decreased by the prohibition of payment to circulators.[16] Both provisions "limi[t] the number of voices who will convey [the initiative proponents'] message" and, consequently, cut down "the size of the audience [proponents] can reach." In this case, as in *Meyer*, the requirement "imposes a burden on political expression that the State has failed to justify."

---

[16] Persons eligible to vote, we note, would not include "convicted drug felons who have been denied the franchise as part of their punishment," and could similarly be barred from circulating petitions. The dissent's concern that hordes of "convicted drug dealers," will swell the ranks of petition circulators, unstoppable by legitimate state regulation, is therefore undue. Even more imaginary is the dissent's suggestion that if the merely voter eligible are included among petition circulators, children and citizens of foreign lands will not be far behind. * * *

Colorado acknowledges that the registration requirement limits speech, but not severely, the State asserts, because "it is exceptionally easy to register to vote." The ease with which qualified voters may register to vote, however, does not lift the burden on speech at petition circulation time. Of course there are individuals who fail to register out of ignorance or apathy. But there are also individuals for whom, as the trial record shows, the choice not to register implicates political thought and expression. A lead plaintiff in this case, long active in ballot-initiative support — a party no doubt " 'able and willing' to convey a political message" — testified that his refusal to register is a "form of . . . private and public protest." Another initiative proponent similarly stated that some circulators refuse to register because "they don't believe that the political process is responsive to their needs." For these voter-eligible circulators, the ease of registration misses the point.

The State's dominant justification appears to be its strong interest in policing lawbreakers among petition circulators. Colorado seeks to ensure that circulators will be amenable to the Secretary of State's subpoena power, which in these matters does not extend beyond the State's borders. The interest in reaching law violators, however, is served by the requirement, upheld below, that each circulator submit an affidavit setting out, among several particulars, the "address at which he or she resides, including the street name and number, the city or town, [and] the county." This address attestation, we note, has an immediacy, and corresponding reliability, that a voter's registration may lack. The attestation is made at the time a petition section is submitted; a voter's registration may lack that currency.

ACLF did not challenge Colorado's right to require that all circulators be residents, a requirement that, the Tenth Circuit said, "more precisely achieved" the State's subpoena service objective. Nor was any eligible-to-vote qualification in contest in this lawsuit. Colorado maintains that it is more difficult to determine who is a state resident than it is to determine who is a registered voter. The force of that argument is diminished, however, by the affidavit attesting to residence that each circulator must submit with each petition section.

In sum, assuming that a residence requirement would be upheld as a needful integrity-policing measure — a question we * * * have no occasion to decide because the parties have not placed the matter of residence at issue — the added registration requirement is not warranted. That requirement cuts down the number of message carriers in the ballot-access arena without impelling cause.

Colorado enacted the provision requiring initiative-petition circulators to wear identification badges in 1993, five years after our decision in *Meyer*. The Tenth Circuit held the badge requirement invalid insofar as it requires circulators to display their names. The Court of Appeals did not rule on the constitutionality of other elements of the badge provision, namely, the "requirements that the badge disclose whether the circulator is paid or a volunteer, and if paid, by whom." Nor do we.

Evidence presented to the District Court, that court found, "demonstrated that compelling circulators to wear identification badges inhibits participation in the petitioning process." The badge requirement, a veteran ballot-initiative-petition organizer stated, "very definitely limited the number of people willing to work for us and the degree to which those who were willing to work would go out in public."

Another witness told of harassment he personally experienced as circulator of a hemp initiative petition. He also testified to the reluctance of potential circulators to face the recrimination and retaliation that bearers of petitions on "volatile" issues sometimes encounter: "[W]ith their name on a badge, it makes them afraid." Other petition advocates similarly reported that "potential circulators were not willing to wear personal identification badges."

Colorado urges that the badge enables the public to identify, and the State to apprehend, petition circulators who engage in misconduct. Here again, the affidavit requirement, unsuccessfully challenged below, is responsive to the State's concern; as earlier noted, each petition section must contain, along with the collected signatures of voters, the circulator's name, address, and signature. This notarized submission, available to law enforcers, renders less needful the State's provision for personal names on identification badges.

While the affidavit reveals the name of the petition circulator and is a public record, it is tuned to the speaker's interest as well as the State's. Unlike a name badge worn at the time a circulator is soliciting signatures, the affidavit is separated from the moment the circulator speaks. As the Tenth Circuit explained, the name badge requirement "forces circulators to reveal their identities at the same time they deliver their political message"; it operates when reaction to the circulator's message is immediate and "may be the most intense, emotional, and unreasoned." The affidavit, in contrast, does not expose the circulator to the risk of "heat of the moment" harassment.

Our decision in *McIntyre* v. *Ohio Elections Comm'n*, 514 U.S. 334 (1995) [p. 678], is instructive here. The complainant in *McIntyre* challenged an Ohio law that prohibited the distribution of anonymous campaign literature. * * * "Circulating a petition is akin to distributing a handbill," the Tenth Circuit observed in the decision now before us. Both involve a one-on-one communication. But the restraint on speech in this case is more severe than was the restraint in *McIntyre*. Petition circulation is the less fleeting encounter, for the circulator must endeavor to persuade electors to sign the petition. That endeavor, we observed in *Meyer*, "of necessity involves both the expression of a desire for political change and a discussion of the merits of the proposed change."

The injury to speech is heightened for the petition circulator because the badge requirement compels personal name identification at the precise moment when the circulator's interest in anonymity is greatest. For this very reason, the name badge requirement does not qualify for inclusion among the "more limited [election process] identification requirement[s]" to which we alluded in *McIntyre*. In contrast, the affidavit requirement * * *, which must be met only after circulators have completed their conversations with electors, exemplifies the type of regulation for which *McIntyre* left room.

In sum, we conclude * * * that Colorado's current badge requirement discourages participation in the petition circulation process by forcing name identification without sufficient cause. * * *

* * * Colorado requires ballot-initiative proponents who pay circulators to file both a final report when the initiative petition is submitted to the Secretary of State,

and monthly reports during the circulation period. The Tenth Circuit invalidated the final report provision only insofar as it compels disclosure of information specific to each paid circulator, in particular, the circulators' names and addresses and the total amount paid to each circulator. As modified by the Court of Appeals decision, the final report will reveal the amount paid per petition signature, and thus, effectively, the total amount paid to petition circulators. * * *

Mindful of *Buckley* [v. *Valeo*, 424 U.S. 1 (1976)] [p. 1011], which upheld disclosure provisions of the Federal Election Campaign Act], the Tenth Circuit * * * upheld the State's requirements for disclosure of *payors*, in particular, proponents' names and the total amount they have spent to collect signatures for their petitions. In this regard, the State and supporting *amici* stress the importance of disclosure as a control or check on domination of the initiative process by affluent special interest groups. Disclosure of the names of initiative sponsors, and of the amounts they have spent gathering support for their initiatives, responds to that substantial state interest.

Through the disclosure requirements that remain in place, voters are informed of the source and amount of money spent by proponents to get a measure on the ballot; in other words, voters will be told "who has proposed [a measure]," and "who has provided funds for its circulation." The added benefit of revealing the names of paid circulators and amounts paid to each circulator, the lower courts fairly determined from the record as a whole, is hardly apparent and has not been demonstrated.[22]

We note, furthermore, that ballot initiatives do not involve the risk of "*quid pro quo*" corruption present when money is paid to, or for, candidates. * * *

In sum, we agree with the Court of Appeals [*sic*] appraisal: Listing paid circulators and their income from circulation "forc[es] paid circulators to surrender the anonymity enjoyed by their volunteer counterparts"; no more than tenuously related to the substantial interests disclosure serves, Colorado's reporting require-ments, to the extent that they target paid circulators, "fai[l] exacting scrutiny." * * *

For the reasons stated, we conclude that the Tenth Circuit correctly separated necessary or proper ballot-access controls from restrictions that unjustifiably inhibit the circulation of ballot-initiative petitions. Therefore, the judgment of the Court of Appeals is

Affirmed.

JUSTICE THOMAS, concurring in the judgment.

When considering the constitutionality of a state election regulation that restricts core political speech or imposes "severe burdens" on speech or association,

---

[22] JUSTICE O'CONNOR states that "[k]nowing the names of paid circulators and the amounts paid to them [will] allo[w] members of the public to evaluate the sincerity or, alternatively, the potential bias of any circulator that approaches them." It is not apparent why or how this is so, for the reports containing the names of paid circulators would be filed with the Secretary of State and would not be at hand at the moment the circulators "approac[h]."

we have generally required that the law be narrowly tailored to serve a compelling state interest. But if the law imposes "lesser burdens," we have said that the State's important regulatory interests are generally sufficient to justify reasonable, nondiscriminatory restrictions. The Court today appears to depart from this now-settled approach. In my view, Colorado's badge, registration, and reporting requirements each must be evaluated under strict scrutiny. Judged by that exacting standard, I agree with the majority that each of the challenged regulations violates the First and Fourteenth Amendments, and accordingly concur only in the judgment. * * *

Colorado argues that its badge, registration, and reporting requirements impose "lesser" burdens, and consequently, each ought to be upheld as serving important state interests. I cannot agree.

The challenged badge requirement directly regulates the content of speech. The State requires that all petition circulators disclose, at the time they deliver their political message, their names and whether they were paid or unpaid. Therefore, the regulation must be evaluated under strict scrutiny. Moreover, the category of burdened speech is defined by its content — Colorado's badge requirement does not apply to those who circulate candidate petitions, only to those who circulate initiative or referendum proposals. Content-based regulation of speech typically must be narrowly tailored to a compelling state interest. The State's dominant justification for its badge requirement is that it helps the public to identify, and the State to apprehend, petition circulators who perpetrate fraud. Even assuming that this is a compelling interest, plainly, this requirement is not narrowly tailored. It burdens all circulators, whether they are responsible for committing fraud or not. In any event, the State has failed to satisfy its burden of demonstrating that fraud is a real, rather than a conjectural, problem.

Although Colorado's registration requirement does not *directly* regulate speech, it operates in the same fashion that Colorado's prohibition on paid circulators did in *Meyer* — the requirement reduces the voices available to convey political messages. We unanimously concluded in *Meyer* that initiative petition circulation was core political speech. * * * I see no reason to revisit our earlier conclusion. The aim of a petition is to secure political change, and the First Amendment, by way of the Fourteenth Amendment, guards against the State's efforts to restrict free discussions about matters of public concern.

Colorado primarily defends its registration requirement on the ground that it ensures that petition circulators are residents, which permits the State to more effectively enforce its election laws against those who violate them. The Tenth Circuit assumed, and so do I, that the State has a compelling interest in ensuring that all circulators are residents. Even so, it is clear, as the Court of Appeals decided, that the registration requirement is not narrowly tailored. A large number of Colorado's residents are not registered voters, as the majority points out, and the State's asserted interest could be more precisely achieved through a residency requirement. * * *

In my view, the burdens that the reporting requirement imposes on circulation are too attenuated to constitute a "severe burden" on core political speech. However, "compelled disclosure, in itself, can seriously infringe on privacy of association and belief guaranteed by the First Amendment." *Buckley* v. *Valeo*, 424 U.S., [at] 64 *(per curiam)*. In *Buckley*, because the disclosure requirements of the Federal Election Campaign Act of 1971 encroached on associational rights, we required that they pass a "strict test." *Id.*, at 66. The same associational interests are burdened by the State's reporting requirements here, and they must be evaluated under strict scrutiny.

* * * Even assuming that Colorado has a compelling interest in identifying circulators, its law does not serve that interest. The State requires that proponents identify only the names of *paid* circulators, not *all* circulators. The interest in requiring a report as to the money paid to each circulator by name, as the majority points out, has not been demonstrated.

The State contends that its asserted interest in providing the press and the electorate with information as to how much money is spent by initiative proponents to advance a particular measure is similar to the governmental interests in providing the electorate with information about how money is spent by a candidate and where it comes from, and in deterring actual corruption and avoiding the appearance of corruption that we recognized in *Buckley*. However, we have suggested that ballot initiatives and candidate elections involve different considerations. [*First National Bank of Boston* v. *Bellotti*, 435 U.S. 765, 787 n.26 (1978) [p. 895]; *Citizens Against Rent Control* v. *Berkeley*, 454 U.S. 290, 296–300 (1981).] Indeed, we recognized in *Meyer* that "the risk of improper conduct . . . is more remote at the petition stage of an initiative." Similarly, I would think, at the very least, the State's interest in informing the public of the financial interests behind an initiative proposal is not compelling during the petitioning stage. * * *

JUSTICE O'CONNOR, with whom JUSTICE BREYER joins, concurring in the judgment in part and dissenting in part.

Petition circulation undoubtedly has a significant political speech component. * * * [W]e held in [*Meyer* v. *Grant*] that regulations directly burdening the one-on-one, communicative aspect of petition circulation are subject to strict scrutiny.

Not all circulation-related regulations target this aspect of petition circulation, however. Some regulations govern the electoral process by directing the manner in which an initiative proposal qualifies for placement on the ballot. These latter regulations may indirectly burden speech but are a step removed from the communicative aspect of petitioning and are necessary to maintain an orderly electoral process. Accordingly, these regulations should be subject to a less exacting standard of review. * * *

I agree with the Court that requiring petition circulators to wear identification badges, specifically name badges, should be subject to, and fails, strict scrutiny. * * *

Unlike the majority, however, I believe that the requirement that initiative petition circulators be registered voters is a permissible regulation of the electoral process. It is indeed a classic example of this type of regulation * * * [that] only indirectly and incidentally burdens the communicative aspects of petition circulation. By its terms, the requirement does not directly prohibit otherwise qualified initiative petition circulators from circulating petitions. Moreover, * * * this requirement can be satisfied quite easily. * * *

Because the registration requirement indirectly and incidentally burdens the one-on-one, communicative aspect of petition circulation, [it must] advance [only] a legitimate state interest to be a reasonable regulation of the electoral process. Colorado maintains that the registration requirement is necessary to enforce its laws prohibiting circulation fraud and to guarantee the State's ability to exercise its subpoena power over those who violate these laws, two patently legitimate interests. In the past, Colorado has had difficulty enforcing its prohibition on circulation fraud, in particular its law against forging petition signatures, because violators fled the State. Colorado has shown that the registration requirement is an easy and a verifiable way to ensure that petition circulators fall under the State's subpoena power. For these reasons, I would uphold the requirement as a reasonable regulation of Colorado's electoral process.

Most disturbing is the Court's holding that Colorado's disclosure provisions are partially unconstitutional. * * * Colorado's disclosure provision is a step removed from the one-on-one, communicative aspects of petition circulation, and it burdens this communication in only an incidental manner. Like the mandatory affidavit that must accompany every set of signed petitions, the required disclosure reports "revea[l] the name of the petition circulator and [are] public record[s] . . . [, but are] separated from the moment the circulator speaks." This characteristic indeed makes the disclosure reports virtually indistinguishable from the affidavit requirement, which the Court suggests is a permissible regulation of the electoral process, and similarly lessens any chilling effect the reports might have on speech. If anything, the disclosure reports burden speech less directly than the affidavits because the latter are completed by the petition circulator, while the former are completed by the initiative proponent and thus are a step removed from petition circulation. In fact, the Court does not suggest that there is any record evidence tending to show that such remote disclosure will deter the circulation of initiative petitions. To the extent the disclosure requirements burden speech, the burden must be viewed as incremental and insubstantial in light of the affidavit requirement, which also reveals the identity of initiative petition circulators.

As a regulation of the electoral process with an indirect and insignificant effect on speech, the disclosure provision should be upheld so long as it advances a legitimate government interest. Colorado's asserted interests in combating fraud and providing the public with information about petition circulation are surely sufficient to survive this level of review. * * * Disclosure deters circulation fraud and abuse by encouraging petition circulators to be truthful and self-disciplined. The disclosure required here advances Colorado's interest in law enforcement by enabling the State to detect and to identify on a timely basis abusive or fraudulent circulators. Moreover, like election finance reporting generally, Colorado's disclosure reports provide facts useful to voters who are weighing their options. Members of the public deciding whether to sign a petition or how to vote on a measure can discover who has proposed it, who has provided funds for its circulation, and to whom these funds have been provided. Knowing the names of paid circulators and the amounts paid to them also allows members of the public to evaluate the sincerity or, alternatively, the potential bias of any circulator that approaches them. In other words, if one knows a particular circulator is well paid, one may be less likely to believe the sincerity of the circulator's statements about the initiative proposal. The monthly disclosure reports are public records available to the press and public, are "contemporaneous with circulation," and are more accessible than the other "masses of papers filed with the petitions."

It is apparent from the preceding discussion that, to combat fraud and to inform potential signatories in a timely manner, disclosure must be made at the time people are being asked to sign petitions and before any subsequent vote on a measure that qualifies for the ballot. * * * Accordingly, the monthly reports, which are disseminated during the circulation period and are available to the press, uniquely advance Colorado's interests. The affidavit requirement is not an effective substitute because the affidavits are not completed until after all signatures have been collected and thus after the time that the information is needed. In addition, the public's access to the affidavits is generally more restricted than its access to monthly disclosure reports, for as the District Court found, the public will have "greater difficulty in finding [the] names and addresses [of petition circulators] in the masses of papers filed with the petitions as compared with the monthly reports."

To be sure, Colorado requires disclosure of financial information about only paid circulators. But, contrary to the Court's assumption, this targeted disclosure is permissible because the record suggests that paid circulators are more likely to commit fraud and gather false signatures than other circulators. The existence of occasional fraud in Colorado's petitioning process is documented in the record. An elections officer for the State of Colorado testified that only paid circulators have been involved in recent fraudulent activity. Likewise, respondent William C. Orr, the executive director of the American Constitutional Law Foundation, Inc., while examining a witness, explained to the trial court that "volunteer organizations, they're self-policing and there's not much likelihood of fraud. . . . Paid circulators are perhaps different."

Because the legitimate interests asserted by Colorado are advanced by the disclosure provision and outweigh the incidental and indirect burden that disclosure places on political speech, I would uphold the provision as a reasonable regulation of the electoral process. Colorado's interests are more than legitimate, however. We have previously held that they are substantial. See *Buckley* v. *Valeo*, at 67, 68. Therefore, even if I thought more exacting scrutiny were required, I would uphold the disclosure requirements.

Because I feel the Court's decision invalidates permissible regulations that are vitally important to the integrity of the political process, and because the decision threatens the enforceability of other important and permissible regulations, I concur in the judgment only in part and dissent in part.

CHIEF JUSTICE REHNQUIST, dissenting. * * *

* * * [T]he Court today holds that a State cannot require that those who circulate the petitions to get initiatives on the ballot be electors, and that a State is constitutionally required to instead allow those who make no effort to register to

vote — political dropouts — and convicted drug dealers [denied the franchise as part of their punishment] to engage in this electoral activity.[1] Although the Court argues that only those eligible to vote may now circulate candidate petitions, there is no Colorado law to this effect. Such a law would also be even harder to administer than one which limited circulation to residents, because eligible Colorado voters are that subset of Colorado residents who have fulfilled the requirements for registration, and have not committed a felony or been otherwise disqualified from the franchise. A State would thus have to perform a background check on circulators to determine if they are not felons. And one of the reasons the State wished to limit petition circulation to electors in the first place was that it is far easier to determine who is an elector from who is a resident, much less who is "voter eligible." * * *

State ballot initiatives are a matter of state concern, and a State should be able to limit the ability to circulate initiative petitions to those people who can ultimately vote on those initiatives at the polls. If eligible voters make the conscious decision not to register to vote on the grounds that they reject the democratic process, they should have no right to complain that they cannot circulate initiative petitions to people who *are* registered voters. And the idea that convicted drug felons who have lost the right to vote under state law nonetheless have a constitutional right to circulate initiative petitions scarcely passes the "laugh test."

But the implications of today's holding are even more stark than its immediate effect. Under the Court's interpretation of *Meyer*, any ballot initiative regulation is unconstitutional if it either diminishes the pool of people who can circulate petitions or makes it more difficult for a given issue to ultimately appear on the ballot. Thus, while today's judgment is ostensibly circumscribed in scope, it threatens to invalidate a whole host of historically established state regulations of the electoral process in general. Indeed, while the Court is silent with respect to whether a State can limit initiative petition circulation to state residents, the implication of its reading of *Meyer* * * * is that under today's decision, a State cannot limit the ability to circulate issues of local concern to its own residents.

May a State prohibit children or foreigners from circulating petitions, where such restrictions would also limit the number of voices who could carry the proponents' message and thus cut down on the size of the audience the initiative proponents could reach? And if initiative petition circulation cannot be limited to electors, it would seem that a State can no longer impose an elector or residency requirement on those who circulate petitions to place candidates on ballots, either. At least 19 States plus the District of Columbia explicitly require that candidate petition circulators be electors, and at least one other State requires that its petition circulators be state residents. Today's decision appears to place each of these laws in serious constitutional jeopardy. * * *

As to the other two laws struck down by the Court, I agree that the badge requirement for petition circulators is unconstitutional. * * * I disagree, however, that the First Amendment renders the disclosure requirements unconstitutional.

---

[1] The respondents also presented the example of children who wished to circulate petitions. * * * Because the Court of Appeals held that the age restriction on petition circulation was constitutional, it is unnecessary to point out the absurdity of the respondents' minority argument. [Relocated. — Eds.]

The Court affirms the Court of Appeals' invalidation of only the portion of the law that requires final reports to disclose information specific to each paid circulator — the name, address, and amount paid to each. Important to the Court's decision is the idea that there is no risk of "*quid pro quo*" corruption when money is paid to ballot initiative circulators, and that paid circulators should not have to surrender the anonymity enjoyed by their volunteer counterparts. I disagree with this analysis because, under Colorado law, *all* petition circulators must surrender their anonymity under the affidavit requirement. Colorado law requires that each circulator must submit an affidavit which must include the circulator's "name, the address at which he or she resides, including the street name and number, the city or town, [and] the county." This affidavit requirement was upheld by the Tenth Circuit as not significantly burdening political expression, and is relied upon by the Court in holding that the registered voter requirement is unconstitutional. The only additional piece of information for which the disclosure requirement asks is thus the amount paid to each circulator. Since even after today's decision the identity of the circulators as well as the total amount of money paid to circulators will be a matter of public record, I do not believe that this additional requirement is sufficient to invalidate the disclosure requirements as a whole. They serve substantial interests and are sufficiently narrowly tailored to satisfy the First Amendment. * * *

Notes and Questions

1.   The Court repeatedly noted that ACLF did not challenge a state's ability to set residency requirements for signature-gatherers, but challenged only the further requirement that they be registered voters. Is this a sign that the residency requirement, too, would be unconstitutional? Or was the registration requirement unconstitutional because the residency requirement was a less restrictive means of satisfying the state's interests? *See Yes on Term Limits, Inc. v. Savage*, 550 F.3d 1023 (10th Cir. 2008); *Nader v. Brewer*, 531 F.3d 1028 (9th Cir. 2008); *Chandler v. City of Arvada*, 292 F.3d 1236 (10th Cir. 2002); *Initiative & Referendum Institute v. Jaeger*, 241 F.3d 614 (8th Cir. 2001); *Krislov v. Rednour*, 226 F.3d 851 (7th Cir. 2000). Could a state ban other election-related speech, such as television advertising, by out-of-staters concerning state-law issues?

2.   Suppose that the speech at issue related to a national matter and not a state one. For example, imagine that Congress proposes a Twenty-Eighth Amendment to the Constitution, and the states are considering whether to ratify it. May a state constitutionally prohibit citizens of other states from speaking about the matter? What if the state prohibited election-related speech by citizens of foreign countries?

3.   Might out-of-state-resident petition-circulators have claims under the Privileges and Immunities Clause, Art. IV, § 2, cl. 1, and the dormant Commerce Clause, Art I, § 8, cl. 3, (because such a prohibition would prevent out-of-staters from competing for jobs as petition-circulators), in addition to claims under the First Amendment? The Clauses generally operate to prevent states from privileging their own citizens as to fundamental liberties and economic opportunities, respectively. Nevertheless, states are permitted to favor their own citizens if they have a good

enough reason for doing so.[5] *See generally Supreme Court v. Piper*, 470 U.S. 274, 282 & n.13 (1985) (noting that the Privileges and Immunities Clause does not require states to forfeit their identities as sovereign political bodies, and that accordingly a state may restrict the privileges of voting and holding elective office to state residents); *Corfield v. Coryell*, 4 Wash. C.C. 371, Fed. Cas. No. 3,230 (1823).

4.   Should one's ability to speak, or the state's ability to require registration or disclosure, differ depending on whether the election is a ballot initiative or a candidate election?

5.   Chief Justice Rehnquist characterized the proposition that minors have a constitutional right to circulate petitions as "absurd[]," and the Court seemed to agree, saying that the suggestion was "imaginary." But why should minors not have such a right? Certainly minors generally possess a right to engage in expressive activity. *See, e.g., Tinker v. Des Moines Independent Community School District*, 393 U.S. 503 (1969). One of the few points on which a clear majority of the Court was able to agree in *McConnell v. Federal Election Commission*, 540 U.S. 93 (2003) [p. 865], was that the Bipartisan Campaign Reform Act's prohibition of contributions by minors, 2 U.S.C. § 441k, was unconstitutional. *See* 540 U.S. at 231–32. Should the same result obtain in the case of petition circulation?

6.   More broadly, why should a state be able to tie the ability to engage in election-related *speech* to the ability to *vote*? Are you comfortable calling petition circulation "speech," or should it receive less protection under the First Amendment than, for example, distributing leaflets? In *Empower Our Neighboroods v. Guadagno*, 2014 N.J. Super. Unpub. LEXIS 764 (N.J. Super. Ct. Law Div. Mar. 31, 2014), the court noted that "circulating petitions is primarily a freedom of speech issue and does not necessarily implicate the right to vote," *id.* at *74, but nonetheless required, at least temporarily, that petition-circulators be eligible to vote — i.e., that they be at least age 18 and state residents. The court argued that such a requirement might be based on the need to have confidence in petition-circulators when they certify that they witnessed the signatures on the petition and that they believe that the signatories are registered voters in the district. The court struck down requirements that petition-circulators themselves be registered voters and that they reside in the district.

7.   Does it abridge the First Amendment right of petition-circulators to require that each section of an initiative petition contain the circulator's name? In *Chula Vista Citizens for Jobs and Fair Competition v. Norris*, 755 F.3d 671 (9th Cir. 2014), a divided panel of the Ninth Circuit struck down such a requirement. The court held that the requirement failed exacting scrutiny, noting that initiative proponents were already required to disclose their identities twice: in filing with the city clerk a notice of intent to circulate a petition, and in publishing that notice in a newspaper.

8.   *Problem.* May a state prohibit initiative supporters from paying signature-

---

[5] Discrimination in favor of state residents will be upheld against a Privileges-and-Immunities-Clause challenge if it is "closely related to the advancement of a substantial state interest." *Supreme Court v. Friedman*, 487 U.S. 59, 65 (1988). The test under the dormant Commerce Clause is whether the state law "serves a legitimate local purpose" that "could not be served as well by nondiscriminatory means." *Maine v. Taylor*, 477 U.S. 131, 138 (1986).

gatherers by the signature? The state argues that the prohibition guards against fraud; the opponents argue that the prohibition makes it more expensive and inefficient to gather signatures. *See Citizens for Tax Reform v. Deters*, 518 F.3d 375 (6th Cir. 2008); *Prete v. Bradbury*, 438 F.3d 949 (9th Cir. 2006); *Initiative & Referendum Inst. v. Jaeger*, 241 F.3d 614 (8th Cir. 2001).

9. *Problem.* Many New England towns employ the "open town-hall meeting" style of governing, according to which all registered voters are empowered to legislate, in an exercise of direct, rather than representative, democracy. Debate at town-hall meetings is presided over by a moderator, who is elected by the voters of the town. All registered voters may speak at the meetings, but non-registered voters may speak only if the moderator permits them to do so. Does such a system abridge the First Amendment rights of non-registered voters who reside in the town? *See Curnin v. Town of Egremont*, 510 F.3d 24 (1st Cir. 2007). What if non-registered voters were absolutely barred from speaking, leaving the moderator without discretion? What if non-registered voters were prohibited from speaking at a public-comment portion of a representative body's meeting? *See Mesa v. White*, 197 F.3d 1041 (10th Cir. 1999); *Piscottano v. Town of Somers*, 396 F. Supp. 2d 187 (D. Conn. 2005); *Scroggins v. City of Topeka*, 2 F. Supp. 2d 1362 (D. Kan. 1998); *Pesek v. City of Brunswick*, 794 F. Supp. 768 (N.D. Ohio 1992).

F. GOVERNMENT SPEECH

The government can, and often does, speak to us. From statutory directives to agency web sites, and from "Just Say No" campaigns to town newsletters, we are confronted daily with government speech. Such speech rarely raises a constitutional question, even if the government is discriminating on the basis of viewpoint in creating its message — after all, the expression of a viewpoint is often the whole purpose of speaking. *See, e.g., Rust v. Sullivan*, 500 U.S. 173 (1991). Government speech in the context of elections, however, raises more serious questions. The next case explores whether the First Amendment, or any other portion of the Constitution, prohibits the government from taking sides in an electoral contest.

KIDWELL v. CITY OF UNION
United States Court of Appeals for the Sixth Circuit
462 F.3d 620 (6th Cir. 2006), *cert. denied*, 550 U.S. 935 (2007)

JULIA SMITH GIBBONS, CIRCUIT JUDGE. * * *

This case arises from a series of disputed ballot initiatives beginning in 1997 relating to the creation and funding of a fire department in the City of Union[, Ohio]. In 1997, Union's fire and emergency services (along with those of other neighboring communities) were provided by the neighboring township of Randolph. The combination of the restructuring of the townships and the perceived inadequacy in Union's emergency services led to changes in the fire department structure. The Union Council * * * ultimately passed an emergency resolution establishing a town fire department. The new fire department became effective on January 1, 1998.

The resolution establishing a Union fire department was challenged by the plaintiffs via a ballot initiative requiring a referendum. The referendum was preceded by a lively campaign in which the plaintiffs organized a "Vote Yes" campaign to retain the extant fire districts. The Council supported the opposite position and used public funds to disseminate information supporting its position to citizens [by] the hanging of "Vote No" banners, mailing of leaflets to residents, advertising in local newspapers, and using the town newsletter to support the Council's position. The referendum occurred in November 1997, and the Council's decision was ratified. Voters funded the new fire department in a May 1998 referendum. [Plaintiffs brought suit under 42 U.S.C. § 1983, arguing that the City's advocacy violated the First and Fourteenth Amendments. The District Court granted summary judgment to the defendants.] * * *

This case presents the rare instance when public citizens seek to limit the speech of a governmental entity rather than the reverse. The scenarios in which citizens may halt a government's speech are limited. * * * The government's power to fund its speech is similarly limited, however. In *NAACP v. Hunt*, 891 F.2d 1555, 1565–66 (11th Cir. 1990), the Eleventh Circuit identified three categories of government actions that courts have determined to be unconstitutional infringement of free speech: (1) abridgment of equality in the field of ideas by granting differential access to public fora based on viewpoint; (2) monopolization of the "marketplace of ideas"; and (3) compulsion of citizens "to support candidates, parties, ideologies, or causes that they are against." Plaintiffs assert that Union's actions violated two of these categories by denying them access to a public forum (the town newsletter and town treasury) and compelling them to support causes to which they are adverse. Plaintiffs urge us to find that government speech relating to elections is a form of unconstitutional compelled speech by distinguishing between governing and campaigning.

Turning first to the issue of differential access to public fora, plaintiffs argue that Union unconstitutionally denied them access to two public fora — the town newsletter and the town treasury — to which others had been granted access. A government abridges "equality in the field of ideas" when it grants "the use of a [public] forum to people whose views it finds acceptable, but [denies its] use to those wishing to express less favored or more controversial views." *Police Dept. of City of Chicago v. Mosley*, 408 U.S. 92, 96 (1972).

Plaintiffs assert that they were denied access to the town newsletter, but * * * they provide no evidence that they asked for or were refused access to that forum, even if it was public. Plaintiffs have similarly failed to present evidence that any other private group was given access to the newsletter other than a single quote about the contested issue that was responsive to another quote advocating the contrary position. "[W]hen government property is not dedicated to open communication the government may — without further justification — restrict use to those who participate in the forum's official business." *Perry Educ. Ass'n v. Perry Local Educators' Ass'n*, 460 U.S. 37, 53 (1983). The single quotation cannot be construed as opening the newsletter as a public forum. Further, "when the government determines an overarching message and retains power to approve every word disseminated at its behest, the message must be attributed to the government for First Amendment purposes." Here, Union approved the message delivered in the town newsletter, so its content must be considered that of the city itself, not that of the quoted private citizen. Plaintiffs thus cannot prevail on their public forum claim relating to the newsletter.

The town treasury is not a public forum; it is not "by tradition or designation a forum for public communication." *Perry*, 460 U.S. at 46. Nor is the treasury a limited purpose public forum; Union has not opened that treasury to the public by making any town funds available to private individuals or groups. Union has used the treasury for its own speech — a use that has no effect on the treasury as a public forum. To hold that Union's advocacy converts its treasury to a public forum would severely limit the town's ability to self-regulate and would be tantamount to a heckler's veto, where the government could not speak for fear of opening its treasury to the public. This argument is therefore baseless, and the plaintiffs' public forum challenge cannot succeed.

As to the plaintiffs' second claim regarding compelled speech, governments cannot compel citizens to support positions with which they disagree. *Wooley v. Maynard*, 430 U.S. 705, 715 (1977). This case, however, presents a compelled subsidy — not a compelled speech — claim because the plaintiffs were not themselves required to speak in any manner. * * *

The Supreme Court has held in several instances that compelled subsidies may violate the First Amendment rights of citizens. *See Abood v. Detroit Bd. of Ed.*, 431 U.S. 209 (1977) (labor union political action); *Keller v. State Bar of Cal.*, 496 U.S. 1 (1990) (bar dues for political action); *Board of Regents of Univ. of Wis. Sys. v. Southworth*, 529 U.S. 217 (2000) (student activities fund for extracurricular activity). All of the cases in which the Supreme Court has held a compelled subsidy to be a First Amendment violation have involved subsidies of speech by private organizations rather than by the government itself. Governmental subsidies are distinguishable from the labor union, state bar, and state university contexts because it is imperative that government be free to make unpopular decisions without opening the public fisc to opposing views. The Supreme Court recognized this distinction in *Southworth*: "The government, as a general rule, may support valid programs and policies by taxes or other exactions binding on protesting parties. Within this broader principle it seems inevitable that funds raised by the government will be spent for speech and other expression to defend its own policies." 529 U.S. at 229. More recently, in *Johanns v. Livestock Mktg. Ass'n*, 544 U.S. [550,] 559 [(2005)], the Court addressed a compelled subsidy directly in the governmental context:

> Our compelled-subsidy cases have consistently respected the principle that "[c]ompelled support of a private association is fundamentally different from compelled support of government." "Compelled support of government" — even those programs of government one does not approve — is of course perfectly constitutional, as every taxpayer must attest. And some government programs involve, or entirely consist of, advocating a position.

Here, the plaintiffs have challenged the expenditure of tax dollars by a governmental entity to advocate a position — a case that the Supreme Court deemed "perfectly constitutional" in *Johanns*. Though the plaintiffs acknowledge that the speech in this case is attributable to the government, they argue that the power of the government to compel subsidies for its speech is not as broad as the Supreme Court suggested in *Johanns*. Because the asserted subsidy arose in the context of an election, the plaintiffs argue that this court should find Union's speech to be unconstitutionally compulsive.

As the dissent recognizes, elections raise unique constitutional issues because they are the very foundation of a democratic system: where the government uses its official voice in an attempt to affect the identity of the people's elected representatives, it can undermine its legitimacy as a champion of the people's will and thereby subvert one of the principles underlying democratic society. Although these principles require some limit on the government's power to advocate during elections, they do not support a bright line rule barring such speech, at least where the government speaks within the scope of its governance functions. Governments must serve their citizens in myriad ways, including by provision of emergency services, and these activities require funding through taxation. Union's speech related to emergency service and tax initiatives thus fits squarely within its competence as governor and was made in the context of "advocat[ing] and defend[ing] its own policies." The issues on which the city advocated were thus germane to the mechanics of its function, and are clearly distinguishable from the hypothetical cases of government speech in support of particular candidates suggested by the dissent. Where speech is not so directed, the result may be different: in *Mountain States Legal Foundation v. Denver School District No. 1*, by contrast, the court ruled illegal a *local* school board's use of public funds for advocacy in a *statewide* initiative regarding education funding. 459 F. Supp. 357, 361 (D. Colo. 1978). Unlike Union's actions, the school board's advocacy in *Mountain States* was not directly related to its governance functions and was struck down.

In this case, Ohio's home rule system made Union's policies subject to acceptance or rejection by ballot. In this context, a limit on government speech during elections would allow hecklers to silence the government on issues in which it has an interest and expertise — and on which citizens have an interest in hearing their government's perspective. Because Union's speech in this case was germane to its role as governor, plaintiffs have failed to show that democratic legitimacy is threatened or that Union's compelled subsidy of its speech violates the Constitution.

The natural outcome of government speech is that some constituents will be displeased by the stance their government has taken. Displeasure does not necessarily equal unconstitutional compulsion, however, and in most cases the electoral process — not First Amendment litigation — is the appropriate recourse for such displeasure. The needs of effective governance command that the bar limiting government speech be high. The plaintiffs in this case have failed to show that the City of Union's expenditures crossed the line separating a valid compelled subsidy from an unconstitutional one, and valid advocacy from prescription of orthodoxy.

For the foregoing reasons, we affirm the district court decision.

BOYCE F. MARTIN, JR., Circuit Judge, dissenting.

* * * Although local governmental expenditures to advocate in an election may seem commonplace and uninspiring, I take the position that governmental campaigning in elections is implicitly prohibited by our constitutional design and republican form of government. "Free and honest elections are the very foundation of our republican form of government," and when the government uses tax dollars to enter an electoral contest and advocate in favor of a position or candidate, it distorts the very check on governmental power so central to our constitutional design — the next election — that I must conclude such activity is unconstitutional. * * *

* * * I concede that the government may ordinarily speak to advocate and defend its own policies. The caveat, however, is always that the citizens' remedy is at the ballot box in the next election. [Here], however, the government is distorting the *only* check on its power. I am not sure I would limit this argument to the confines of the First Amendment; rather, to me, it is more of a structural argument regarding democratic principles and the structure and purpose of the [C]onstitution. * * *

I believe that the Constitution properly prohibits the government from having a horse in the race when it comes to elections. When government advocates on one side of an issue, the ultimate source of governing power is shifted away from the people and the threat of official doctrine exists. Of course, the threat is not as omnipresent today in the United States as it is in some other countries. There is no real evidence in any of these cases on point that the government as speaker crowded out private speech. There is no evidence that the government sought to suppress or in any way discourage other speech of a contrary nature. The absence of this evidence, however, does not in my opinion cure the underlying evil — that is, ordinary democratic controls are insufficient as a remedy in situations where governmental influence threatens to undermine the independent political process. Governmental advocacy and campaign expenditures could arguably threaten to undermine free and fair elections, could be coercive, and could reasonably undermine the reliability and outcome of elections where the government acts as a participant.

Moreover, it could be argued that when the government takes sides in an election, it gives a content or viewpoint based subsidy to those advocating the position the government chooses to side with. In the ordinary case of governmental action outside of an election, political controls can remedy citizen disagreement with governmental actions. Citizens can make their voices known at the ballot box in the next election by voting current officeholders out. Governmental electioneering, however, diminishes the effectiveness of the political response and threatens underlying constitutional values and democratic principles. The outcome of elections ideally should reflect the pure will of the people unpolluted by government electioneering. Where the political response cannot provide an adequate remedy, it can be argued that courts must step in.

Thus, I would hold that the Constitution requires governmental neutrality in elections — that is, the Constitution permits the government to educate and inform the public, but it may not cross the line into advocacy. Thus, government could provide factual information in newsletters and other forms of communication with the electorate. [I]t would not always be easy finding the line of demarcation between informing and advocacy, but courts should look closely at the facts of each case, including the words used, the tone of the communication, the timing, and any other relevant factors. Moreover, government may provide equal access to a forum (as it does in so many other contexts) allowing both sides of the debate to advance their positions. Thus, a governmental newsletter such as the one at issue in this case could grant equal space to competing factions to make their best case to the electorate. This position, I think, would more appropriately reflective [sic] of the balance the Framers sought to strike in our democratic structure and goes a long way to ensuring that the true power remains with the people.

For these reasons, I must respectfully dissent from today's majority opinion.

Notes and Questions

1. Is this case more appropriately resolved on the basis of the First Amendment or the general "structural" features of the Constitution referenced in Judge Martin's dissent? *Cf. National Endowment for the Arts v. Finley*, 524 U.S. 569, 598 n.3 (1998) (Scalia, J., concurring in the judgment) ("I suppose it would be unconstitutional for the government to give money to an organization devoted to the promotion of candidates nominated by the Republican Party — but it would be just as unconstitutional for the government itself to promote candidates nominated by the Republican Party, and I do not think that that unconstitutionality has anything to do with the First Amendment."). Are there judicially manageable standards for enforcing these "structural" features? Are there other reasons courts should not enforce guarantees not protected by (relatively) specific constitutional text?[b] In a portion of the dissent not reprinted here, Judge Martin suggested that "[p]erhaps th[e] day has come" to revisit the Supreme Court's conclusion that the Guarantee Clause is nonjusticiable. *See* 462 F.3d at 635 n.5 (Martin, J., dissenting). Is his invocation of an undefined "structural" protection against governmental electoral advocacy simply a ruse to evade binding precedent?

2. Is there an administrable line between government speech that governs, informs and educates, on the one hand, and that which advocates electoral results, on the other? Is there an administrable line between advocacy of government policies, which Judge Martin concedes is permissible, and advocacy of electoral results, which he argues is not?

In Chapter 9, we will address the constitutionality of certain restrictions on "electioneering communications." The bright-line definition adopted in the Bipartisan Campaign Reform Act and upheld in *McConnell v. Federal Election Commis-*

---

[b] If you believe that courts are without power to enforce the structural guarantee of democracy without a clause in the Constitution specifically protecting it, do you reach the same conclusion with regard to the Court's holdings enforcing implicit constitutional limitations on governmental structure stemming from concerns about federalism and the separation of powers? *See, e.g., Alden v. Maine*, 527 U.S. 706 (1999); *Seminole Tribe v. Florida*, 517 U.S. 44 (1996); *National League of Cities v. Usery*, 426 U.S. 833 (1976), *overruled by Garcia v. San Antonio Metropolitan Transportation Authority*, 469 U.S. 528 (1985); *United States v. Nixon*, 418 U.S. 683 (1974); *Myers v. United States*, 272 U.S. 52 (1926).

sion, 540 U.S. 93 (2003) [p. 923] (but called into some question by *Federal Election Commission v. Wisconsin Right to Life, Inc.*, 551 U.S. 449 (2007)), treated all advertisements that referred to a "clearly identified candidate for Federal office," were made within sixty days before a general election or thirty days before a primary election, and could be received by 50,000 or more persons in the district as "electioneering communications," and subject to restrictions on their financing. The bright-line definition was adopted to avoid perceived problems of "sham" issue advocacy, where advertisements would ostensibly discuss issues, but would in reality encourage voters to support or oppose certain candidates.

Do Judge Martin's proposed distinctions create the same potential for subterfuge? How would he address the constitutionality of a governmentally sponsored advertisement discussing the advantages of "the Smith-Jones Health Care Act"? What about the commonplace signs at state borders that welcome travelers and gratuitously include the name of the incumbent governor? Suppose a legislator were to use his privilege to send free mail to his constituents telling of all the great things he has accomplished during his term — just in case any of the voters were to find such information relevant in deciding whom to support in the election the following month. Is such action unconstitutional?

3.   What limits are there on the majority's willingness to tolerate governmentally sponsored electoral speech? The majority says that perhaps a government could not speak on a matter that is far afield from its governing role, but doesn't government speech pose the greatest threat to democracy when it *is* directly related to its governing function?

4.   The court argued that restricting government's electoral speech would deprive citizens of the ability to "hear[] their government's perspective." Are you troubled by the implication that the government has a perspective independent of the citizenry?

5.   Are you concerned that government speech can overwhelm opposing messages, or do you believe that government speech will affect elections only if the voters agree with it? In other words, does government speech honor the public's capacity to reason or seek to subvert it? We will return to the issue of the persuasive power of campaign speech in Chapter 9.

G. PUBLIC EMPLOYEES

Government employees may be particularly interested in public affairs, and their knowledge may be invaluable to the rest of us in assessing the performance of government. As a result, the political participation of those employees may be especially valuable both for them and for everyone else. On the other hand, however, there are also more pressing reasons to restrict the political activities of government workers than apply to the rest of us. We want to be sure that civil servants will apply the law impartially, and if we think that they are using the law to their political advantage, then our confidence in government will be undermined. Additionally, we may view restrictions on workers' political activity as protection for the workers themselves — if an employee is forbidden from taking part in a political campaign, then we can be sure that a supervisor will not pressure the employee to do so on behalf of the supervisor's (or the governing administration's) preferred candidate. The cases in this section explore the extent to which public employment can limit employees' First Amendment right to participate in politics.

UNITED PUBLIC WORKERS OF AMERICA (C.I.O.) v. MITCHELL
Supreme Court of the United States
330 U.S. 75, 67 S. Ct. 556, 91 L. Ed. 754 (1947)

MR. JUSTICE REED delivered the opinion of the Court [in which MR. CHIEF JUSTICE VINSON, MR. JUSTICE FRANKFURTER, and MR. JUSTICE BURTON join]. * * *

[Appellants brought this constitutional challenge to the second sentence of § 9(a) of the Hatch Act, which] reads, "No officer or employee in the executive branch of the Federal Government * * * shall take any active part in political management or in political campaigns."[2]

* * * It is alleged that the individuals desire to engage in acts of political management and in political campaigns. * * *[11] From the affidavits it is plain, and

---

[2] 18 U.S.C. § 61h, as amended:

"(a) It shall be unlawful for any person employed in the executive branch of the Federal Government, or any agency or department thereof, to use his official authority or influence for the purpose of interfering with an election or affecting the result thereof. No officer or employee in the executive branch of the Federal Government, or any agency or department thereof, except a part-time officer or part-time employee without compensation * * * shall take any active part in political management or in political campaigns. All such persons shall retain the right to vote as they may choose and to express their opinions on all political subjects and candidates. For the purposes of this section the term 'officer' or 'employee' shall not be construed to include (1) the President and Vice President of the United States; (2) persons whose compensation is paid from the appropriation for the office of the President; (3) heads and assistant heads of executive departments; (4) officers who are appointed by the President, by and with the advice and consent of the Senate, and who determine policies to be pursued by the United States in its relations with foreign powers or in the Nationwide administration of Federal Laws. * * *

"(b) Any person violating the provisions of this section shall be immediately removed from the position or office held by him, and thereafter no part of the funds appropriated by any Act of Congress for such position or office shall be used to pay the compensation of such person."

[Relocated. Note that the Hatch Act, including the penalty provision, has been amended. It now permits the offending employee to be suspended without pay for no less than thirty days. 5 U.S.C. § 7326. — Eds.]

[11] "In discharge of their duties of citizenship, of their right to vote, and in exercise of their constitutional rights of freedom of speech, of the press, of assembly, and the right to engage in political activity, the individual plaintiffs desire to engage in the following acts: write for publication letters and articles in support of candidates for office; be connected editorially with publications which are identified with the legislative program of UFWA [former name of the present union appellant] and candidates who support it; solicit votes, aid in getting out voters, act as accredited checker, watcher, or challenger; transport voters to and from the polls without compensation therefor; participate in and help in organizing political parades; initiate petitions, and canvass for the signatures of others on such petitions; serve as party ward committeeman or other party official; and perform any and all acts not prohibited by any provision of law other than the second sentence of Section 9(a) and Section 15 of the Hatch Act, which constitute taking an active part in political management and political campaigns."

we so assume, that these activities will be carried on completely outside of the hours of employment. Appellants challenge the second sentence of § 9(a) as [violating the First Amendment's protections of freedom of speech, of the press, and of assembly; the Ninth and Tenth Amendments; and the Fifth Amendment's Due Process Clause, this last owing to the Act's alleged vagueness and its allegedly arbitrary distinctions between the employees subject to the restrictions of the Act and the employees not so restricted]. * * *

None of the appellants, except George P. Poole, has violated the provisions of the Hatch Act. They wish to act contrary to its provisions * * * and desire a declaration of the legally permissible limits of regulation. * * * The District Court * * * determined that the questioned provision of the Hatch Act was valid * * *. It accordingly dismissed the complaint and granted summary judgment to defendants. * * *

[The Supreme Court first held that each of the appellants' claims, other than Poole's, was unripe. The Court then turned to the merits of Poole's claim:]

[Poole] was a ward executive committeeman of a political party and was politically active on election day as a worker at the polls and a paymaster for the services of other party workers. * * * We accept appellants' contention that the nature of political rights reserved to the people by the Ninth and Tenth Amendments are involved. The right claimed as inviolate may be stated as the right of a citizen to act as a party official or worker to further his own political views. * * * And, if we look upon due process as a guarantee of freedom in those fields, there is a corresponding impairment of that right under the Fifth Amendment. Appellants' objections under the Amendments are basically the same.

We do not find persuasion in appellants' argument that such activities during free time are not subject to regulation even though admittedly political activities cannot be indulged in during working hours. The influence of political activity by government employees, if evil in its effects on the service, the employees or people dealing with them, is hardly less so because that activity takes place after hours. Of course, the question of the need for this regulation is for other branches of government rather than the courts. Our duty in this case ends if the Hatch Act provision under examination is constitutional.

Of course, it is accepted constitutional doctrine that these fundamental human rights are not absolutes. * * * The essential rights of the First Amendment in some instances are subject to the elemental need for order without which the guarantees of civil rights to others would be a mockery. * * * Again this Court must balance the extent of the guarantees of freedom against a congressional enactment to protect a democratic society against the supposed evil of political partisanship by classified employees of government. * * *

* * * Congress and the President are responsible for an efficient public service. If, in their judgment, efficiency may be best obtained by prohibiting active participation by classified employees in politics as party officers or workers, we see no constitutional objection.

Another Congress may determine that on the whole, limitations on active political management by federal personnel are unwise. The teaching of experience has evidently led Congress to enact the Hatch Act provisions. To declare that the present supposed evils of political activity are beyond the power of Congress to redress would leave the nation impotent to deal with what many sincere men believe is a material threat to the democratic system. Congress is not politically naive or regardless of public welfare or that of the employees. It leaves untouched full participation by employees in political decisions at the ballot box and forbids only the partisan activity of federal personnel deemed offensive to efficiency. With that limitation only, employees may make their contributions to public affairs or protect their own interests, as before the passage of the act.

The argument that political neutrality is not indispensable to a merit system for federal employees may be accepted. But because it is not indispensable does not mean that it is not desirable or permissible. Modern American politics involves organized political parties. Many classifications of Government employees have been accustomed to work in politics — national, state and local — as a matter of principle or to assure their tenure. Congress may reasonably desire to limit party activity of federal employees so as to avoid a tendency toward a one-party system. It may have considered that parties would be more truly devoted to the public welfare if public servants were not overactive politically.

Appellants urge that federal employees are protected by the Bill of Rights and that Congress may not "enact a regulation providing that no Republican, Jew or Negro shall be appointed to federal office, or that no federal employee shall attend Mass or take any active part in missionary work." None would deny such limitations on Congressional power but because there are some limitations it does not follow that a prohibition against acting as ward leader or worker at the polls is invalid. A reading of the Act * * * shows the wide range of public activities with which there is no interference by the legislation. It is only partisan political activity that is interdicted. It is active participation in political management and political campaigns. Expressions, public or private, on public affairs, personalities and matters of public interest, not an objective of party action, are unrestricted by law so long as the Government employee does not direct his activities toward party success.

It is urged, however, that Congress has gone further than necessary in prohibiting political activity to all types of classified employees. It is pointed out by appellants "that the impartiality of many of these is a matter of complete indifference to the effective performance" of their duties. Mr. Poole would appear to be a good illustration for appellants' argument. The complaint states that he is a roller in the Mint. We take it this is a job calling for the qualities of a skilled mechanic and that it does not involve contact with the public. Nevertheless, if in free time he is engaged in political activity, Congress may have concluded that the activity may promote or retard his advancement or preferment with his superiors. Congress may have thought that Government employees are handy elements for leaders in political policy to use in building a political machine. For regulation of employees it is not necessary that the act regulated be anything more than an act reasonably deemed by Congress to interfere with the efficiency of the public service. There are hundreds of thousands of United States employees with positions no more influential upon policy determination than that of Mr. Poole. Evidently what Congress feared was the cumulative effect on employee morale of political activity by all employees who could be induced to participate actively. It does not seem to us an unconstitutional basis for legislation.

There is a suggestion that administrative workers may be barred, constitutionally, from political management and political campaigns while the industrial workers may not be barred, constitutionally, without an act "narrowly drawn to define and punish specific conduct." A ready answer, it seems to us, lies in the fact that * * * Congress has determined that the presence of government employees, whether industrial or administrative, in the ranks of political party workers is bad. Whatever differences there may be between administrative employees of the Government and industrial workers in its employ are differences in detail so far as the constitutional power under review is concerned. Whether there are such differences and what weight to attach to them, are all matters of detail for Congress. We do not know whether the number of federal employees will expand or contract; whether the need for regulation of their political activities will increase or diminish. The use of the constitutional power of regulation is for Congress, not for the courts.

We have said that Congress may regulate the political conduct of Government employees "within reasonable limits," even though the regulation trenches to some extent upon unfettered political action. The determination of the extent to which political activities of governmental employees shall be regulated lies primarily with Congress. Courts will interfere only when such regulation passes beyond the general existing conception of governmental power. That conception develops from practice, history, and changing educational, social and economic conditions. The regulation of such activities as Poole carried on has the approval of long practice by the Commission, court decisions upon similar problems and a large body of informed public opinion. Congress and the administrative agencies have authority over the discipline and efficiency of the public service. When actions of civil servants in the judgment of Congress menace the integrity and the competency of the service, legislation to forestall such danger and adequate to maintain its usefulness is required. The Hatch Act is the answer of Congress to this need. We cannot say with such a background that these restrictions are unconstitutional.

* * * The activities of Mr. Poole, as ward executive committeeman and a worker at the polls, obviously fall within the prohibitions of § 9 of the Hatch Act against taking an active part in political management and political campaigns. * * * We need to examine no further at this time into the validity of the definition of political activity * * *.

The judgment of the District Court is accordingly affirmed.

Affirmed.

MR. JUSTICE MURPHY and MR. JUSTICE JACKSON took no part in the consideration or decision of this case.

MR. JUSTICE RUTLEDGE dissents as to Poole for the reasons stated by MR. JUSTICE BLACK. He does not pass upon the constitutional questions presented by the other appellants for the reason that he feels the controversy as to them is not yet appropriate for the discretionary exercise of declaratory judgment jurisdiction.

Mr. Justice Frankfurter, concurring.

[T]his case should be dismissed for want of jurisdiction [because the appeal was not timely docketed]. * * * But under compulsion of the Court's assumption of jurisdiction, I reach the merits and join in Mr. Justice Reed's opinion.

Mr. Justice Black, dissenting. * * *

* * * Legislation which muzzles several million citizens threatens popular government, not only because it injures the individuals muzzled, but also, because of its harmful effect on the body politic in depriving it of the political participation and interest of such a large segment of our citizens. * * *

It is argued that it is in the interest of clean politics to suppress political activities of federal and state employees. It would hardly seem to be imperative to muzzle millions of citizens because some of them, if left their constitutional freedoms, might corrupt the political process. All political corruption is not traceable to state and federal employees. Therefore, it is possible that other groups may later be compelled to sacrifice their right to participate in political activities for the protection of the purity of the Government of which they are a part.

It may be true, as contended, that some higher employees, unless restrained, might coerce their subordinates or that Government employees might use their official position to coerce other citizens. But is such a possibility of coercion of a subordinate by his employer limited to governmental employer-employee relationships? The same quality of argument would support a law to suppress the political freedom of all employees of private employers, and particularly of employers who borrow money or draw subsidies from the Government. * * * If the possibility exists that some * * * public employees may, by reason of their more influential positions, coerce other public employees or other citizens, laws can be drawn to punish the coercers. It hardly seems consistent with our system of equal justice to all to suppress the political and speaking freedom of millions of good citizens because a few bad citizens might engage in coercion.

It may also be true, as contended, that if public employees are permitted to exercise a full freedom to express their views in political campaigns, some public officials will discharge some employees and grant promotion to others on a political rather than on a merit basis. For the same reasons other public officials, occupying positions of influence, may use their influence to have their own political supporters appointed or promoted. But here again, if the practice of making discharges, promotions or recommendations for promotions on a political basis is so great an evil as to require legislation, the law could punish those public officials who engage in the practice. To punish millions of employees and to deprive the nation of their contribution to public affairs, in order to remove temptation from a proportionately small number of public officials, seems at the least to be a novel method of suppressing what is thought to be an evil practice. * * *

Mr. Justice Douglas, dissenting in part. * * *

* * * Poole is not in the administrative category of civil service. He is an industrial worker — a roller in the mint, a skilled laborer or artisan whose work or functions in no way affect the policy of the agency nor involve relationships with the public. * * *

* * * Political fortunes of parties will ebb and flow; top policy men in administrations will come and go; new laws will be passed and old ones amended or repealed. But those who give continuity to administration, those who contribute the basic skill and efficiency to the daily work of government, and those on whom the new as well as the old administration is dependent for smooth functioning of the complicated machinery of modern government are the core of the civil service. If they are beneficiaries of political patronage rather than professional careerists, serious results might follow — or so Congress could reasonably believe. Public confidence in the objectivity and integrity of the civil service system might be so weakened as to jeopardize the effectiveness of administrative government. Or it might founder on the rocks of incompetency, if every change in political fortunes turned out the incumbents, broke the continuity of administration, and thus interfered with the development of expert management at the technical levels. Or if the incumbents were political adventurers or party workers, partisanship might color or corrupt the processes of administration of law with which most of the administrative agencies are entrusted.

The philosophy is to develop a civil service which can and will serve loyally and equally well any political party which comes into power.

Those considerations might well apply to the entire group of civil servants in the administrative category — whether they are those in the so-called expert classification or are clerks, stenographers and the like. They are the ones who have access to the files, who meet the public, who arrange appointments, who prepare the basic data on which policy decisions are made. Each may be a tributary, though perhaps a small one, to the main stream which we call policy making or administrative action. If the element of partisanship enters into the official activities of any member of the group it may have its repercussions or effect throughout the administrative process. Thus in that type of case there would be much to support the view of the Court that Congress need not undertake to draw the line to include only the more important offices but can take the precaution of protecting the whole by insulating even the lowest echelon from partisan activities.

So, I think that if the issues tendered by Poole were tendered by an administrative employee, we would have quite a different case. For Poole claims the right to work as a ward executive committeeman, *i.e.*, as an officeholder in a political party.

But Poole, being an industrial worker, is as remote from contact with the public or from policy making or from the functioning of the administrative process as a charwoman. The fact that he is in the classified civil service is not, I think, relevant to the question of the degree to which his political activities may be curtailed. He is in a position not essentially different from one who works in the machine shop of a railroad or steamship which the Government runs, or who rolls aluminum in a manufacturing plant which the Government owns and operates. Can all of those categories of industrial employees constitutionally be insulated from American political life? If at some future time it should come to pass in this country, as it has in England, that a broad policy of state ownership of basic industries is inaugurated, does this decision mean that all of the hundreds of thousands of industrial workers affected could be debarred from the normal political activity which is one of our valued traditions?

The evils of the "spoils" system do not, of course, end with the administrative group of civil servants. History shows that the political regimentation of government industrial workers produces its own crop of abuses. Those in top policy posts or others in supervisory positions might seek to knit the industrial workers in civil service into a political machine. As a weapon they might seek to make the advancement of industrial workers dependent on political loyalty, on financial contributions, or on other partisan efforts. Or political activities of these workers might take place on government premises, on government time, or otherwise at government expense. These are specific evils which would require a specific treatment.

There is, however, no showing of any such abuse here. What Poole did, he did on his own without compulsion or suggestion or invitation from any one higher up. Nor does it appear that what he did was done on government time or on government premises. Moreover, as MR. JUSTICE BLACK points out, laws can be drawn to punish those who use such coercion. Such activity is more than the exercise of political prerogatives; it is the use of official power as well, and hence can be restrained or punished.

The question is whether a permissible remedy is complete or partial political sterilization of the industrial group. * * * The difficulty lies in attempting to preserve our democratic way of life by measures which deprive a large segment of the population of all political rights except the right to vote. Absent coercion, improper use of government position or government funds, or neglect or inefficiency in the performance of duty, federal employees have the same rights as other citizens under the Constitution. They are not second class citizens. If, in exercise of their rights, they find common political interests and join with each other or other groups in what they conceive to be their interests or the interests of the nation, they are simply doing what any other group might do. In other situations where the balance was between constitutional rights of individuals and a community interest which sought to qualify those rights, we have insisted that the statute be "narrowly drawn to define and punish specific conduct as constituting a clear and present danger to a substantial interest" of government.

That seems to me the proper course to follow here. The prohibition in § 9(a) of the Hatch Act against government employees taking an "active part in political management or in political campaigns" applies without discrimination to all employees whether industrial or administrative. The same is true of the Civil Service Rules. But the supposed evils are both different and narrower in case of industrial workers than they are in the case of the administrative group. The public interest in the political activity of a machinist or elevator operator or charwoman is a distinct and different problem. In those cases the public concern is in the preservation of an unregimented industrial group, in a group free from political pressures of superiors who use their official power for a partisan purpose. Then official power is misused, perverted. The Government is corrupted by making its industrial workers political captives, victims of bureaucratic power, agents for perpetuating one party in power.

Offset against that public concern are the interests of the employees in the exercise of cherished constitutional rights. * * * If those rights are to be qualified by the larger requirements of modern democratic government, the restrictions should be narrowly and selectively drawn to define and punish the specific conduct which constitutes a clear and present danger to the operations of government. It seems plain to me that that evil has its roots in the coercive activity of those in the hierarchy who have the power to regiment the industrial group or who undertake to do so. To sacrifice the political rights of the industrial workers goes far beyond any demonstrated or demonstrable need. Those rights are too basic and fundamental in our democratic political society to be sacrificed or qualified for anything short of a clear and present danger to the civil service system. No such showing has been made in the case of these industrial workers,[14] which justifies their political sterilization as distinguished from selective measures aimed at the coercive practices on which the spoils system feeds.

Notes and Questions

1.   Who is protected, and who is harmed, by the Hatch Act? If you believe that the employees themselves are helped (by removing pressure to conform to supervisors' political preferences), do you think the First Amendment permits such paternalism?

2.   As a consumer of government services, would you fear unfair treatment if your postal carrier was wearing a button supporting a political candidate you opposed? What if the IRS agent auditing your tax return did the same thing? What if you appeared before a judge who was supporting a candidate you opposed?

3.   In any of the above examples, do you worry about bias because the employee *holds* a political opinion, or because the employee has made his political opinion *known*? In other words, if the postal carrier, the IRS agent, or the judge held the same political views, but kept those views to himself or herself, is the threat of bias any less significant? We will return to these questions when we consider speech of judicial candidates in connection with *Republican Party of Minnesota v. White*, 536 U.S. 765 (2002) [p. 756], later in this Chapter.

4.   Between *Mitchell* and *Civil Service Commission v. National Association of Letter Carriers*, 413 U.S. 548 (1973) [p. 713], in which the Court again considered the constitutionality of the Hatch Act, the Court significantly expanded the First Amendment protections of government employees. In 1892, Justice Holmes, then serving on the Massachusetts Supreme Judicial Court, famously wrote that an individual fired from the police force because of his membership in a political

---

[14] Whether the Act, being unconstitutional as applied to Poole, could be separably applied to civil service employees in other categories is a question I do not reach.

committee "may have a constitutional right to talk politics, but he has no constitutional right to be a policeman." *McAuliffe v. Mayor of New Bedford*, 29 N.E. 517, 517 (Mass. 1892). The Court has since rejected that view, and has extended First Amendment protections to public employees, though the Court has maintained that certain restrictions on the rights of employees are necessary to the employment relationship, and are therefore constitutional. The following case is the seminal case concerning the free-speech rights of public employees. As you read it, consider whether its reasoning undercuts *Mitchell*'s holding.

PICKERING v. BOARD OF EDUCATION
Supreme Court of the United States
391 U.S. 563, 88 S. Ct. 1731, 20 L. Ed. 2d 811 (1968)

MR. JUSTICE MARSHALL delivered the opinion of the Court [in which MR. CHIEF JUSTICE WARREN, MR. JUSTICE HARLAN, MR. JUSTICE BRENNAN, MR. JUSTICE STEWART, and MR. JUSTICE FORTAS join].

Appellant Marvin L. Pickering, a teacher in Township High School District 205, Will County, Illinois, was dismissed from his position by the appellee Board of Education for sending a letter to a local newspaper in connection with a recently proposed tax increase that was critical of the way in which the Board and the district superintendent of schools had handled past proposals to raise new revenue for the schools. * * * For the reasons detailed below, we [hold] that appellant's rights to freedom of speech were violated * * *.

In February of 1961, the appellee Board of Education asked the voters of the school district to approve a bond issue to raise $4,875,000 to erect two new schools. The proposal was defeated. Then, in December of 1961, the Board submitted another bond proposal to the voters which called for the raising of $5,500,000 to build two new schools. This second proposal passed, and the schools were built with the money raised by the bond sales. In May of 1964, a proposed increase in the tax rate to be used for educational purposes was submitted to the voters by the Board and was defeated. Finally, on September 19, 1964, a second proposal to increase the tax rate was submitted by the Board, and was likewise defeated. It was in connection with this last proposal of the School Board that appellant wrote the letter to the editor * * * that resulted in his dismissal. * * *

The letter constituted, basically, an attack on the School Board's handling of the 1961 bond issue proposals and its subsequent allocation of financial resources between the schools' educational and athletic programs. It also charged the superintendent of schools with attempting to prevent teachers in the district from opposing or criticizing the proposed bond issue.

The Board dismissed Pickering for writing and publishing the letter. Pursuant to Illinois law, the Board was then required to hold a hearing on the dismissal. At the hearing, the Board charged that numerous statements in the letter were false, and that the publication of the statements unjustifiably impugned the "motives, honesty, integrity, truthfulness, responsibility and competence" of both the Board and the school administration. The Board also charged that the false statements damaged the professional reputations of its members and of the school administrators, would be disruptive of faculty discipline, and would tend to foment "controversy, conflict and dissension" among teachers, administrators, the Board of Education, and the residents of the district. * * *

The Illinois courts * * * rejected Pickering's claim that, on the facts of this case, he could not constitutionally be dismissed from his teaching position.

* * * "[T]he theory that public employment which may be denied altogether may be subjected to any conditions, regardless of how unreasonable, has been uniformly rejected." *Keyishian* v. *Board of Regents*, [385 U.S. 589,] 605–606 [(1967)]. At the same time, it cannot be gainsaid that the State has interests as an employer in regulating the speech of its employees that differ significantly from those it possesses in connection with regulation of the speech of the citizenry in general. The problem in any case is to arrive at a balance between the interests of the teacher, as a citizen, in commenting upon matters of public concern and the interest of the State, as an employer, in promoting the efficiency of the public services it performs through its employees.

The Board contends that "the teacher by virtue of his public employment has a duty of loyalty to support his superiors in attaining the generally accepted goals of education and that, if he must speak out publicly, he should do so factually and accurately, commensurate with his education and experience." Appellant, on the other hand, argues that the test applicable to defamatory statements directed against public officials by persons having no occupational relationship with them, namely, that statements to be legally actionable must be made "with knowledge that [they were] . . . false or with reckless disregard of whether [they were] . . . false or not," *New York Times Co.* v. *Sullivan*, 376 U. S. 254, 280 (1964) [p. 574], should also be applied to public statements made by teachers. Because of the enormous variety of fact situations in which critical statements by teachers and other public employees may be thought by their superiors, against whom the statements are directed, to furnish grounds for dismissal, we do not deem it either appropriate or feasible to attempt to lay down a general standard against which all such statements may be judged. However, in the course of evaluating the conflicting claims of First Amendment protection and the need for orderly school administration in the context of this case, we shall indicate some of the general lines along which an analysis of the controlling interests should run.

An examination of the statements in appellant's letter objected to by the Board reveals that they, like the letter as a whole, consist essentially of criticism of the Board's allocation of school funds between educational and athletic programs, and of both the Board's and the superintendent's methods of informing, or preventing the informing of, the district's taxpayers of the real reasons why additional tax revenues were being sought for the schools. The statements are in no way directed towards any person with whom appellant would normally be in contact in the course of his daily work as a teacher. Thus, no question of maintaining either discipline by immediate superiors or harmony among coworkers is presented here. Appellant's employment relationships with the Board and, to a somewhat lesser extent, with the superintendent are not the kind of close working relationships for which it can persuasively be claimed that personal loyalty and confidence are necessary to their proper functioning. Accordingly, to the extent that the Board's position here can be taken to suggest that even comments on matters of public concern that are substantially correct * * * may furnish grounds for dismissal if they are sufficiently critical in tone, we unequivocally reject it.[3]

We next consider the statements in appellant's letter which we agree to be false. [Such misstatements reported incorrectly some particulars concerning the amount of money spent on athletic programs. According to the Court, the misstatements were "perfectly consistent with good-faith error, and there is no evidence in the record to show that anything other than carelessness or insufficient information was responsible for their being made."] * * *

[T]he question whether a school system requires additional funds is a matter of legitimate public concern on which the judgment of the school administration, including the School Board, cannot, in a society that leaves such questions to popular vote, be taken as conclusive. On such a question free and open debate is vital to informed decisionmaking by the electorate. Teachers are, as a class, the members of a community most likely to have informed and definite opinions as to how funds allotted to the operation of the schools should be spent. Accordingly, it is essential that they be able to speak out freely on such questions without fear of retaliatory dismissal.

In addition, the amounts expended on athletics which Pickering reported erroneously were matters of public record on which his position as a teacher in the district did not qualify him to speak with any greater authority than any other taxpayer. The Board could easily have rebutted appellant's errors by publishing the accurate figures itself, either via a letter to the same newspaper or otherwise. We are thus not presented with a situation in which a teacher has carelessly made false statements about matters so closely related to the day-to-day operations of the schools that any harmful impact on the public would be difficult to counter because of the teacher's presumed greater access to the real facts. Accordingly, we have no occasion to consider at this time whether, under such circumstances, a school board could reasonably require that a teacher make substantial efforts to verify the accuracy of his charges before publishing them.

What we do have before us is a case in which a teacher has made erroneous public statements upon issues then currently the subject of public attention, which are critical of his ultimate employer but which are neither shown nor can be presumed to have in any way either impeded the teacher's proper performance of his daily duties in the classroom or to have interfered with the regular operation of the schools generally. In these circumstances, we conclude that the interest of the school administration in limiting teachers' opportunities to contribute to public

---

[3] It is possible to conceive of some positions in public employment in which the need for confidentiality is so great that even completely correct public statements might furnish a permissible ground for dismissal. Likewise, positions in public employment in which the relationship between superior and subordinate is of such a personal and intimate nature that certain forms of public criticism of the superior by the subordinate would seriously undermine the effectiveness of the working relationship between them can also be imagined. We intimate no views as to how we would resolve any specific instances of such situations, but merely note that significantly different considerations would be involved in such cases.

debate is not significantly greater than its interest in limiting a similar contribution by any member of the general public.

* * * It is * * * perfectly clear that, were appellant a member of the general public, the State's power to afford the appellee Board of Education or its members any legal right to sue him for writing the letter at issue here would be limited by the requirement that the letter be judged by the standard laid down in *New York Times*. * * *

While criminal sanctions and damage awards have a somewhat different impact on the exercise of the right to freedom of speech from dismissal from employment, it is apparent that the threat of dismissal from public employment is nonetheless a potent means of inhibiting speech. * * * [I]n a case such as the present one, in which the fact of employment is only tangentially and insubstantially involved in the subject matter of the public communication made by a teacher, we conclude that it is necessary to regard the teacher as the member of the general public he seeks to be.

In sum, we hold that, in a case such as this, absent proof of false statements knowingly or recklessly made by him, a teacher's exercise of his right to speak on issues of public importance may not furnish the basis for his dismissal from public employment. Since no such showing has been made in this case regarding appellant's letter, his dismissal for writing it cannot be upheld and the judgment of the Illinois Supreme Court must, accordingly, be reversed and the case remanded for further proceedings not inconsistent with this opinion.

It is so ordered.

MR. JUSTICE DOUGLAS, with whom MR. JUSTICE BLACK joins, concurs in the judgment of the Court [on the ground that First Amendment protections should extend to discussions of all public issues, irrespective of judicial "balancing" of the interests involved].

MR. JUSTICE WHITE, concurring in part and dissenting in part. * * *

* * * As I see it, a teacher may be fired without violation of the First Amendment for knowingly or recklessly making false statements regardless of their harmful impact on the schools. As the Court holds, however, in the absence of special circumstances he may not be fired if his statements were true or only negligently false, even if there is some harm to the school system. I therefore see no basis or necessity for the Court's foray into fact-finding with respect to whether the record supports a finding as to injury. If Pickering's false statements were either knowingly or recklessly made, injury to the school system becomes irrelevant, and the First Amendment would not prevent his discharge. For the State to be constitutionally precluded from terminating his employment, reliance on some other constitutional provision would be required. * * *

Notes and Questions

1. *Pickering* remains the seminal case in a line of decisions balancing the First Amendment rights of public employees to comment on matters of public concern against the government employers' interest in the efficient operation of their offices. Subsequent decisions have upheld the firing of an assistant district attorney who, upset about a transfer, distributed a questionnaire to other employees seeking their opinion about "transfer policy, office morale, the need for a grievance committee, the level of confidence in supervisors, and whether employees felt pressured to work in political campaigns," *Connick v. Myers*, 461 U.S. 138 (1983); and upheld the firing of a nurse who made critical comments about a supervisor, *Waters v. Churchill*, 511 U.S. 661 (1994), but held unconstitutional the firing of a clerical employee in a county constable's office who, upon hearing of an assassination attempt on President Reagan, remarked, "if they go for him again, I hope they get him," *Rankin v. McPherson*, 483 U.S. 378 (1987).

More recently, in *Garcetti v. Ceballos*, 547 U.S. 410 (2006), the Court upheld the imposition of discipline against a deputy district attorney who became involved in a confrontation with employees of the sheriff's department and ultimately testified for the defense in a case where he believed the investigation had been improperly conducted. The Court applied a two-part test to determine whether the discipline was constitutionally imposed. First, the employee's speech must be on a matter of public concern. Private matters — such as complaints about most internal office policies — do not give rise to First Amendment protection against discipline. Second, if the speech is about a matter of public concern, discipline may be imposed only where the speech has the potential of adversely affecting the operations of the office. In other words, government may restrict the speech of employees on matters of public concern only if there is a justification for treating their speech differently from the speech of a nonemployee. *Id.* at 418. The Court in *Ceballos* held that because the deputy was acting pursuant to his official duties, that his speech could not be considered to be "on a matter of public concern." *Id.* at 421. In *Lane v. Franks*, 134 S. Ct. 2369 (2014), the Court held that under *Pickering* and *Garcetti*, a public employee's sworn testimony under subpoena, outside the scope of his ordinary job duties, is entitled to First Amendment protection.

2. If challenges such as *Mitchell* were to be evaluated under this two-part test, an individual's speech at political conventions or contributions to political candidates, etc., would satisfy the "public concern" part of the test. The controversial part of the analysis would be in assessing whether the interests of the government employer outweigh the interests of the speaker. In that vein, consider *McPherson*'s rationale for holding that the county constable was prohibited from firing the employee who professed hope for the President's assassination:

> While McPherson's statement was made at the workplace, there is no evidence that it interfered with the efficient functioning of the office. The Constable was evidently not afraid that McPherson had disturbed or interrupted other employees — he did not inquire to whom respondent had made the remark and testified that he "was not concerned who she had made it to." * * *

Nor was there any danger that McPherson had discredited the office by making her statement in public. McPherson's speech took place in an area to which there was ordinarily no public access; her remark was evidently made in a private conversation with another employee. There is no suggestion that any member of the general public was present or heard McPherson's statement. * * *

* * * Evidently because McPherson had made the statement, and because the Constable believed that she "meant it," he decided that she was not a suitable employee to have in a law enforcement agency. But in weighing the State's interest in discharging an employee based on any claim that the content of a statement made by the employee somehow undermines the mission of the public employer, some attention must be paid to the responsibilities of the employee within the agency. The burden of caution employees bear with respect to the words they speak will vary with the extent of authority and public accountability the employee's role entails. Where, as here, an employee serves no confidential, policymaking, or public contact role, the danger to the agency's successful functioning from that employee's private speech is minimal. We cannot believe that every employee in Constable Rankin's office, whether computer operator, electrician, or file clerk, is equally required, on pain of discharge, to avoid any statement susceptible of being interpreted by the Constable as an indication that the employee may be unworthy of employment in his law enforcement agency. At some point, such concerns are so removed from the effective functioning of the public employer that they cannot prevail over the free speech rights of the public employee.

This is such a case. McPherson's employment-related interaction with the Constable was apparently negligible. Her duties were purely clerical * * *. There is no indication that she would ever be in a position to further — or indeed to have any involvement with — the minimal law enforcement activity engaged in by the Constable's office. Given the function of the agency, McPherson's position in the office, and the nature of her statement, we are not persuaded that Rankin's interest in discharging her outweighed her rights under the First Amendment.

483 U.S. at 388–92. Justice Scalia, joined by Chief Justice Rehnquist and Justices White and O'Connor, dissented, arguing that "no law enforcement agency is required by the First Amendment to permit one of its employees to 'ride with the cops and cheer for the robbers.'" *Id.* at 394 (Scalia, J., dissenting). He further argued that the Court's distinction between policymaking employees and others was misguided: "Nonpolicymaking employees * * * can hurt working relationships and undermine public confidence in an organization every bit as much as policymaking employees." *Id.* at 400 (Scalia, J., dissenting).

3. Do decisions such as *Pickering* and its progeny indicate that *Mitchell*'s understanding of the First Amendment is out of step with modern jurisprudence? The following case thought not.

UNITED STATES CIVIL SERVICE COMMISSION v.
NATIONAL ASSOCIATION OF
LETTER CARRIERS, AFL-CIO
Supreme Court of the United States
413 U.S. 548, 93 S. Ct. 2880, 37 L. Ed. 2d 796 (1973)

MR. JUSTICE WHITE delivered the opinion of the Court [in which MR. CHIEF JUSTICE BURGER, MR. JUSTICE STEWART, MR. JUSTICE BLACKMUN, MR. JUSTICE POWELL, and MR. JUSTICE REHNQUIST join].

[This case] present[s] the single question whether the prohibition in § 9(a) of the Hatch Act, now codified in 5 U.S.C. § 7324(a)(2), against federal employees taking "an active part in political management or in political campaigns," is unconstitutional on its face. * * *

[Plaintiffs — the National Association of Letter Carriers, six individual federal employees and certain local Democratic and Republican political committees — filed a complaint, claiming that the Act prevented them from engaging in certain political activity, including running for public office, holding office in a political club, campaigning for others, and writing letters to newspapers.]

We unhesitatingly reaffirm the [United Public Workers v.] Mitchell [330 U.S. 75 (1947)] [p. 699] holding that Congress had, and has, the power to prevent Mr. Poole and others like him from holding a party office, working at the polls, and acting as party paymaster for other party workers. An Act of Congress going no farther would in our view unquestionably be valid. So would it be if, in plain and understandable language, the statute forbade activities such as organizing a political party or club; actively participating in fund-raising activities for a partisan candidate or political party; becoming a partisan candidate for, or campaigning for, an elective public office; actively managing the campaign of a partisan candidate for public office; initiating or circulating a partisan nominating petition or soliciting votes for a partisan candidate for public office; or serving as a delegate, alternate or proxy to a political party convention. Our judgment is that neither the First Amendment nor any other provision of the Constitution invalidates a law barring this kind of partisan political conduct by federal employees. * * *

Until now, the judgment of Congress, the Executive, and the country appears to have been that partisan political activities by federal employees must be limited if the Government is to operate effectively and fairly, elections are to play their proper part in representative government, and employees themselves are to be sufficiently free from improper influences. The restrictions so far imposed on federal employees are not aimed at particular parties, groups, or points of view, but apply equally to all partisan activities of the type described. They discriminate against no racial, ethnic, or religious minorities. Nor do they seek to control political opinions or beliefs, or to interfere with or influence anyone's vote at the polls.

But, as the Court held in *Pickering* v. *Board of Education*, 391 U.S. 563, 568 (1968) [p. 707], the government has an interest in regulating the conduct and "the speech of its employees that differ[s] significantly from those it possesses in connection with regulation of the speech of the citizenry in general. The problem in any case is to arrive at a balance between the interests of the [employee], as a citizen, in commenting upon matters of public concern and the interest of the [government], as an employer, in promoting the efficiency of the public services it performs through its employees." Although Congress is free to strike a different balance than it has, if it so chooses, we think the balance it has so far struck is sustainable by the obviously important interests sought to be served by the limitations on partisan political activities now contained in the Hatch Act.

It seems fundamental in the first place that employees in the Executive Branch of the Government, or those working for any of its agencies, should administer the law in accordance with the will of Congress, rather than in accordance with their own or the will of a political party. They are expected to enforce the law and execute the programs of the Government without bias or favoritism for or against any political party or group or the members thereof. A major thesis of the Hatch Act is that to serve this great end of Government — the impartial execution of the laws — it is essential that federal employees, for example, not take formal positions in political parties, not undertake to play substantial roles in partisan political campaigns, and not run for office on partisan political tickets. Forbidding activities like these will reduce the hazards to fair and effective government.

There is another consideration in this judgment: it is not only important that the Government and its employees in fact avoid practicing political justice, but it is also critical that they appear to the public to be avoiding it, if confidence in the system of representative Government is not to be eroded to a disastrous extent.

Another major concern of the restriction against partisan activities by federal employees was perhaps the immediate occasion for enactment of the Hatch Act in 1939. That was the conviction that the rapidly expanding Government work force should not be employed to build a powerful, invincible, and perhaps corrupt political machine. The experience of the 1936 and 1938 campaigns convinced Congress that these dangers were sufficiently real that substantial barriers should be raised against the party in power — or the party out of power, for that matter — using the thousands or hundreds of thousands of federal employees, paid for at public expense, to man its political structure and political campaigns.

A related concern, and this remains as important as any other, was to further serve the goal that employment and advancement in the Government service not depend on political performance, and at the same time to make sure that Government employees would be free from pressure and from express or tacit invitation to vote in a certain way or perform political chores in order to curry favor with their superiors rather than to act out their own beliefs. It may be urged that prohibitions against coercion are sufficient protection; but for many years the joint judgment of the Executive and Congress has been that to protect the rights of federal employees with respect to their jobs and their political acts and beliefs it is not enough merely to forbid one employee to attempt to influence or coerce another.[12] * * * Perhaps Congress at some time will come to a different view of the

---

[12] In the 1940 debate over amendments to the Hatch Act, it was frequently stated that the only objectionable provisions were those restrictions in § 9 and the proposed § 12 against voluntary political activity. In response to the inquiry whether he was condemning those "who, without any coercion, voluntarily desire to take a part in politics," Senator Hatch replied that he "would draw the line if it could be drawn; but I defy . . . [anyone] to draw that line."

realities of political life and Government service; but that is its current view of the matter, and we are not now in any position to dispute it. Nor, in our view, does the Constitution forbid it.

Neither the right to associate nor the right to participate in political activities is absolute in any event. Nor are the management, financing, and conduct of political campaigns wholly free from governmental regulation. We agree with the basic holding of *Mitchell* that plainly identifiable acts of political management and political campaigning on the part of federal employees may constitutionally be prohibited. * * *

[The Court lastly concluded that the challenged prohibitions were not unconstitutionally vague or overbroad, relying on administrative regulations specifying the prohibited activities. The Court also noted that employees in doubt as to the legality of certain activities may request and receive advisory opinions from the Commission.]

For the foregoing reasons, the judgment of the District Court is reversed.

So ordered.

MR. JUSTICE DOUGLAS, with whom MR. JUSTICE BRENNAN and MR. JUSTICE MARSHALL concur, dissenting.

The Hatch Act by § 9(a) prohibits federal employees from taking "an active part in political management or in political campaigns." * * * There is no definition of what "an active part . . . in political campaigns" means. The Act incorporates over 3,000 rulings of the Civil Service Commission between 1886 and 1940, and many hundreds of rulings since 1940. But even with that gloss on the Act, the critical phrases lack precision. In 1971, the Commission published a three-volume work entitled Political Activities Reporter which contains over 800 of its decisions since the enactment of the Hatch Act. One can learn from studying those volumes that it is not "political activity" to march in a band during a political parade or to wear political badges or to "participate fully in public affairs, except as prohibited by law, in a manner which does not materially compromise his efficiency or integrity as an employee or the neutrality, efficiency, or integrity of his agency." 5 CFR § 733.111(a)(13).

That is to say, some things, like marching in a band, are clear. Others are pregnant with ambiguity as "participate fully in public affairs, except as prohibited by law, in a manner which does not materially compromise," etc. * * *

The chilling effect of these vague and generalized prohibitions is so obvious as not to need elaboration. That effect would not be material to the issue of constitutionality if only the normal contours of the police power were involved. On the run of social and economic matters the "rational basis" standard which *United Public Workers* v. *Mitchell* applied would suffice. But what may have been unclear to some in *Mitchell* should be now be abundantly clear to all. We deal here with a First Amendment right to speak, to propose, to publish, to petition Government, to assemble. Time and place are obvious limitations. Thus no one could object if employees were barred from using office time to engage in outside activities whether political or otherwise. But it is of no concern of Government what an employee does in his spare time, whether religion, recreation, social work, or politics is his hobby — unless what he does impairs efficiency or other facets of the merits of his job. Some things, some activities do affect or may be thought to affect the employee's job performance. But his political creed, like his religion, is irrelevant. In the areas of speech, like religion, it is of no concern what the employee says in private to his wife or to the public in Constitution Hall. If Government employment were only a "privilege," then all sorts of conditions might be attached. But it is now settled that Government employment may not be denied or penalized "on a basis that infringes [the employee's] constitutionally protected interests — especially, his interest in freedom of speech." If Government, as the majority stated in *Mitchell*, may not condition public employment on the basis that the employee will not "take any active part in missionary work," it is difficult to see why it may condition employment on the basis that the employee not take "an active part . . . in political campaigns." For speech, assembly, and petition are as deeply embedded in the First Amendment as proselytizing a religious cause.

Free discussion of governmental affairs is basic in our constitutional system. Laws that trench on that area must be narrowly and precisely drawn to deal with precise ends. * * * The present Act cannot be appropriately narrowed to meet the need for narrowly drawn language not embracing First Amendment speech or writing without substantial revision. * * *

The Commission, on a case-by-case approach, has listed 13 categories of prohibited activities, starting with the catch-all "include but are not limited to." So the Commission ends up with open-end discretion to penalize X or not to penalize him. For example, a "permissible" activity is the employee's right to "[e]xpress his opinion as an individual privately and publicly on political subjects and candidates." Yet "soliciting votes" is prohibited. Is an employee safe from punishment if he expresses his opinion that candidate X is the best and candidate Y the worst? Is that crossing the forbidden line of soliciting votes?

A nursing assistant at a veterans' hospital put an ad in a newspaper reading:

> "To All My Many Friends of Poplar Bluff and Butler County I want to take this opportunity to ask your vote and support in the election, TUESDAY, AUGUST 7th. A very special person is seeking the Democratic nomination for Sheriff. I do not have to tell you of his qualifications, his past records stand.

> "This person is my dad, Lester (Less) Massingham.

> "THANK YOU

> "WALLACE (WALLY) MASSINGHAM"

He was held to have violated the Act.

Is a letter a permissible "expression" of views or a prohibited "solicitation?" The Solicitor General says it is a "permissible" expression; but the Commission ruled otherwise. For an employee who does not have the Solicitor General as counsel great consequences flow from an innocent decision. He may lose his job. Therefore the most prudent thing is to do nothing. Thus is self-imposed censorship imposed on many nervous people who live on narrow economic margins.

I would strike this provision of the law down as unconstitutional so that a new start may be made on this old problem that confuses and restricts nearly five million federal, state, and local public employees today that live under the present Act.

Notes and Questions

1. *Letter Carriers* involved the constitutionality of restrictions on federal employees. On the day *Letter Carriers* was decided, the Court upheld similar restrictions on state employees as well. *Broadrick v. Oklahoma*, 413 U.S. 601 (1973).

2. In 1993, the Hatch Act was amended to permit government employees to engage in more political activity. The current version of the Act, 5 U.S.C. §§ 7321–7326, permits most employees to "take an active part in political management or in political campaigns" when off duty, but employees may not solicit or receive political contributions, and may not run for "a partisan political office." 5 U.S.C. §§ 7323(a), 7324(a)(1). While the employee is on duty, however, he or she "may not engage in political activity." 5 U.S.C. § 7324(a)(1). Employees' political activity is also forbidden in government buildings and vehicles, as well as when the employees are wearing government uniforms. 5 U.S.C. §§ 7324(a)(2)–(4).

3. *Problem.* May this amended statute be applied constitutionally to forbid grade-school teachers from wearing political buttons while working? *See Weingarten v. Board of Education*, 591 F. Supp. 2d 511 (S.D.N.Y. 2008). May a public university apply the same prohibition to its faculty? Would the ban on political buttons be constitutional as applied to an industrial worker, like Mr. Poole, who has little or no contact with the public? *See* 5 C.F.R. § 734.306.

4. *Problem.* Does the amended statute forbid a postal worker from attaching a political poster to the employee union bulletin board in a non-public area of a post office? *See Burrus v. Vegliante*, 336 F.3d 82 (2d Cir. 2003). If so, it is constitutional? May a teacher be forbidden from posting political material on a bulletin board in an area closed to students? *See Weingarten, supra.*

UNITED STATES v.
NATIONAL TREASURY EMPLOYEES UNION
Supreme Court of the United States
513 U.S. 454, 115 S. Ct. 1003, 130 L. Ed. 2d 964 (1995)

JUSTICE STEVENS delivered the opinion of the Court [in which JUSTICE KENNEDY, JUSTICE SOUTER, JUSTICE GINSBURG, and JUSTICE BREYER join].

In 1989 Congress enacted a law that broadly prohibits federal employees from accepting any compensation for making speeches or writing articles. The prohibition applies even when neither the subject of the speech or article nor the person or group paying for it has any connection with the employee's official duties. We must decide whether that statutory prohibition comports with the Constitution's command that "Congress shall make no law . . . abridging the freedom of speech." We hold that it does not.

In 1967 Congress authorized the appointment every four years of a special Commission on Executive, Legislative, and Judicial Salaries, whose principal function would be to recommend appropriate levels of compensation for the top positions in all three branches of the Federal Government. * * *

The 1989 Quadrennial Commission's report noted that inflation had decreased the salary levels for senior Government officials, measured in constant dollars, by approximately 35% since 1969. The report

> "also found that because their salaries are so inadequate, many members of Congress are supplementing their official compensation by accepting substantial amounts of 'honoraria' for meeting with interest groups which desire to influence their votes. Albeit to a less troubling extent, the practice of accepting honoraria also extends to top officials of the Executive and Judicial branches."

Accordingly, the Commission recommended that "salary levels for top officials be set at approximately the same amount in constant dollars" as those in effect in 1969 and further that "Congress enact legislation abolishing the practice of accepting honoraria in all three branches."

The President's Commission on Federal Ethics Law Reform subsequently issued a report that endorsed the Quadrennial Commission's views. * * *

Although not adopted in their entirety, the two Commissions' recommendations echo prominently in the Ethics Reform Act of 1989. Section 703 of that Act provided a 25% pay increase to Members of Congress, federal judges, and certain high-level Executive Branch employees above the salary grade GS-15. Another section — the one at issue here — amended § 501(b) of the Ethics in Government Act of 1978 to create an "Honoraria Prohibition," which reads: "An individual may not receive any honorarium while that individual is a Member, officer or employee."

Section 505 of the Ethics Reform Act defined "officer or employee" to include nearly all employees of the Federal Government[.] * * * [The Act, as amended in 1992, also defined "honorarium"] as follows:

> "(3) The term 'honorarium' means a payment of money or any thing of value for an appearance, speech or article (including a series of appearances, speeches, or articles if the subject matter is directly related te [*sic*] the individual's official duties or the payment is made because of the individual's status with the Government) by a Member, officer or employee, excluding any actual and necessary travel expenses incurred by such individual (and one relative) to the extent that such expenses are paid or reimbursed * * *."

Section 503(2) of the Ethics Reform Act provides that the statutory provisions governing honoraria for employees of the Executive Branch shall be subject to rules and regulations issued by the Office of Government Ethics (OGE) and administered by designated agency ethics officials. OGE's regulations permit reimbursement of certain expenses associated with appearances, speeches, and articles. The regulations also confine the reach of each of those terms. Thus, a performance using "an artistic, athletic or other such skill or talent" is not an "appearance"; reading a part in a play or delivering a sermon is not a "speech"; and works of "fiction, poetry, lyrics, or script" are not "article[s]." The regulations permit teaching a course involving multiple presentations at an accredited program or institution. * * *

Each of the individual respondents alleges that he or she has in the past received compensation for writing or speaking on various topics in full compliance with earlier ethics regulations. The record contains a number of affidavits describing respondents' past activities that the honoraria ban would now prohibit. A mail handler employed by the Postal Service in Arlington, Virginia, had given lectures on the Quaker religion for which he received small payments * * *. An aerospace engineer employed at the Goddard Space Flight Center in Greenbelt, Maryland, had lectured on black history for a fee of $100 per lecture. A microbiologist at the Food and Drug Administration had earned almost $3,000 per year writing articles and making radio and television appearances reviewing dance performances. A tax examiner employed by the Internal Revenue Service in Ogden, Utah, had received comparable pay for articles about the environment.

The District Court granted respondents' motion for summary judgment, held the statute "unconstitutional insofar as it applies to Executive Branch employees of the United States government," and enjoined the Government from enforcing the statute against any Executive Branch employee. * * * The Court of Appeals affirmed. * * *

Federal employees who write for publication in their spare time have made significant contributions to the marketplace of ideas. They include literary giants like Nathaniel Hawthorne and Herman Melville, who were employed by the Customs Service; Walt Whitman, who worked for the Departments of Justice and Interior; and Bret Harte, an employee of the Mint. Respondents have yet to make comparable contributions to American culture, but they share with these great artists important characteristics that are relevant to the issue we confront.

Even though respondents work for the Government, they have not relinquished "the First Amendment rights they would otherwise enjoy as citizens to comment on matters of public interest." *Pickering* v. *Board of Ed.*, 391 U.S. 563, 568 (1968) [p. 707]. They seek compensation for their expressive activities in their capacity as citizens, not as Government employees. They claim their employment status has no more bearing on the quality or market value of their literary output than it did on that of Hawthorne or Melville. With few exceptions, the content of respondents' messages has nothing to do with their jobs and does not even arguably have any adverse impact on the efficiency of the offices in which they work. They do not address audiences composed of co-workers or supervisors; instead, they write or speak for segments of the general public. Neither the character of the authors, the subject matter of their expression, the effect of the content of their expression on their official duties, nor the kind of audiences they address has any relevance to their employment.

In *Pickering* and a number of other cases we have recognized that Congress may impose restraints on the job-related speech of public employees that would be plainly unconstitutional if applied to the public at large. When a court is required to determine the validity of such a restraint, it must "arrive at a balance between the interests of the [employee], as a citizen, in commenting upon matters of public concern and the interest of the State, as an employer, in promoting the efficiency of the public services it performs through its employees." *Pickering*, 391 U.S., at 568.

In such cases, which usually have involved disciplinary actions taken in response to a government employee's speech, we have applied *Pickering*'s balancing test only when the employee spoke *"as a citizen* upon matters of public concern" rather than *"as an employee* upon matters only of personal interest." *Connick* v. *Myers*, 461 U.S. 138, 147 (1983) (emphasis added). Thus, private speech that involves nothing more than a complaint about a change in the employee's own duties may give rise to discipline without imposing any special burden of justification on the government employer. If, however, the speech does involve a matter of public concern, the government bears the burden of justifying its adverse employment action. Respondents' expressive activities in this case fall within the protected category of citizen comment on matters of public concern rather than employee comment on matters related to personal status in the workplace. The speeches and articles for which they received compensation in the past were addressed to a public audience, were made outside the workplace, and involved content largely unrelated to their government employment. * * *

Although § 501(b) neither prohibits any speech nor discriminates among speakers based on the content or viewpoint of their messages, its prohibition on compensation unquestionably imposes a significant burden on expressive activity. Publishers compensate authors because compensation provides a significant incentive toward more expression. By denying respondents that incentive, the honoraria ban induces them to curtail their expression if they wish to continue working for the Government.

The ban imposes a far more significant burden on respondents than on the relatively small group of lawmakers whose past receipt of honoraria motivated its enactment. The absorbing and time-consuming responsibilities of legislators and policymaking executives leave them little opportunity for research or creative expression on subjects unrelated to their official responsibilities. Such officials often receive invitations to appear and talk about subjects related to their work because of their official identities. In contrast, invitations to rank-and-file employees usually depend only on the market value of their messages. The honoraria ban is unlikely to reduce significantly the number of appearances by high-ranking officials as long as travel expense reimbursement for the speaker and one relative is available as an alternative form of remuneration. In contrast, the denial of compensation for lower paid, nonpolicymaking employees will inevitably diminish their expressive output.

The large-scale disincentive to Government employees' expression also imposes a significant burden on the public's right to read and hear what the employees would otherwise have written and said. We have no way to measure the true cost of that burden, but we cannot ignore the risk that it might deprive us of the work of a future Melville or Hawthorne.[16] The honoraria ban imposes the kind of burden that abridges speech under the First Amendment.

---

[16] These authors' familiar masterworks would survive the honoraria ban as currently administered. Besides exempting all books, the OGE regulations protect fiction and poetry from the ban's coverage, although the statute's language is not so clear. But great artists deal in fact as well as fiction, and some deal in both.

Because the vast majority of the speech at issue in this case does not involve the subject matter of Government employment and takes place outside the workplace, the Government is unable to justify § 501(b) on the grounds of immediate workplace disruption asserted in *Pickering* and the cases that followed it. Instead, the Government submits that the ban comports with the First Amendment because the prohibited honoraria were "reasonably deemed by Congress to interfere with the efficiency of the public service." *Public Workers* v. *Mitchell*, 330 U.S. 75, 101 (1947) [p. 699].

In *Mitchell* we upheld the prohibition of the Hatch Act on partisan political activity by all classified federal employees, including, for example, a skilled mechanic at the mint named Poole who had no policymaking authority. We explained that "[t]here are hundreds of thousands of United States employees with positions no more influential upon policy determination than that of Mr. Poole. Evidently what Congress feared was the cumulative effect on employee morale of political activity by all employees who could be induced to participate actively." 330 U.S., at 101. In *Civil Service Comm'n* v. *Letter Carriers*, 413 U.S. 548 (1973) [p. 713], we noted that enactment of the Hatch Act in 1939 reflected "the conviction that the rapidly expanding Government work force should not be employed to build a powerful, invincible, and perhaps corrupt political machine." *Id.*, at 565. An equally important concern was

> "to further serve the goal that employment and advancement in the Government service not depend on political performance, and at the same time to make sure that Government employees would be free from pressure and from express or tacit invitation to vote in a certain way or perform political chores in order to curry favor with their superiors rather than to act out their own beliefs." *Id.*, at 566.

Thus, the Hatch Act aimed to *protect* employees' rights, notably their right to free expression, rather than to restrict those rights. Like the Hatch Act, the honoraria ban affects hundreds of thousands of federal employees. Unlike partisan political activity, however, honoraria hardly appear to threaten employees' morale or liberty. Moreover, Congress effectively designed the Hatch Act to combat demonstrated ill effects of Government employees' partisan political activities. In contrast, the Government has failed to show how it serves the interests it asserts by applying the honoraria ban to respondents.

The Government's underlying concern is that federal officers not misuse or appear to misuse power by accepting compensation for their unofficial and nonpolitical writing and speaking activities. This interest is undeniably powerful, but the Government cites no evidence of misconduct related to honoraria in the vast rank and file of federal employees below grade GS-16.[18] Instead of a concern about

---

[18] The Government cites a report of the General Accounting Office (GAO) to support its assertion that the ban is necessary to prevent widespread improprieties. * * * The GAO Report's examples of instances that gave rise to serious concerns about real or apparent impropriety were two cases in which high-level employees (a chemist and a physicist) engaged in consulting activities related to the subject matter of their jobs. Its 112 pages contain not one mention of any real or apparent impropriety related to a lower level employee or to any employee engaged in writing or speaking or in any conduct unrelated to his or her Government job.

the "cumulative effect" of a widespread practice that Congress deemed to "menace the integrity and the competency of the service," *Mitchell*, 330 U.S., at 103, the Government relies here on limited evidence of actual or apparent impropriety by legislators and high-level executives, together with the purported administrative costs of avoiding or detecting lower level employees' violations of established policies.

[T]he Government has based its defense of the ban on abuses of honoraria by Members of Congress. Congress reasonably could assume that payments of honoraria to judges or high-ranking officials in the Executive Branch might generate a similar appearance of improper influence. Congress could not, however, reasonably extend that assumption to all federal employees below grade GS-16, an immense class of workers with negligible power to confer favors on those who might pay to hear them speak or to read their articles. A federal employee, such as a supervisor of mechanics at the Mint, might impair efficiency and morale by using political criteria to judge the performance of his or her staff. But one can envision scant harm, or appearance of harm, resulting from the same employee's accepting pay to lecture on the Quaker religion or to write dance reviews.

Although operational efficiency is undoubtedly a vital governmental interest, features of the honoraria ban's text cast serious doubt on the Government's submission that Congress perceived honoraria as so threatening to the efficiency of the entire federal service as to render the ban a reasonable response to the threat. The first is the rather strange parenthetical reference to "a series of appearances, speeches, or articles" * * * in the definition of the term "honorarium." The amended definition excludes such a series from the prohibited category unless "the subject matter is directly related to the individual's official duties or the payment is made because of the individual's status with the Government." In other words, accepting pay for a *series* of articles is prohibited if, and only if, a nexus exists between the author's employment and either the subject matter of the expression or the identity of the payor. For an *individual* article or speech, in contrast, pay is taboo even if neither the subject matter nor the payor bears any relationship at all to the author's duties.

Congress' decision to provide a total exemption for all unrelated series of speeches undermines application of the ban to individual speeches and articles with no nexus to Government employment. Absent such a nexus, no corrupt bargain or even appearance of impropriety appears likely. The Government's only argument against a general nexus limitation is that a wholesale prophylactic rule is easier to enforce than one that requires individual nexus determinations. The nexus limitation for series, however, unambiguously reflects a congressional judgment that agency ethics officials and the OGE can enforce the statute when it includes a nexus test. A blanket burden on the speech of nearly 1.7 million federal employees requires a much stronger justification than the Government's dubious claim of administrative convenience.

The definition's limitation of "honoraria" to expressive activities also undermines the Government's submission that the breadth of § 501 is reasonably necessary to protect the efficiency of the public service. * * * One might reasonably argue that expressive activities, because they occupy a favored position in the constitutional firmament, should be exempt from even a comprehensive ban on outside income. Imposing a greater burden on speech than on other off-duty activities assumed to pose the same threat to the efficiency of the federal service is, at best, anomalous. * * *

* * * The speculative benefits the honoraria ban may provide the Government are not sufficient to justify this crudely crafted burden on respondents' freedom to engage in expressive activities. Section 501(b) violates the First Amendment. * * *

JUSTICE O'CONNOR, concurring in the judgment in part and dissenting in part. * * *

* * * I agree with the Court that § 501 is unconstitutional insofar as it bars the respondent class of Executive Branch employees from receiving honoraria for non-work-related speeches, appearances, and articles. In contrast to the Court, I would hold § 501 invalid only to that extent.

CHIEF JUSTICE REHNQUIST, with whom JUSTICE SCALIA and JUSTICE THOMAS join, dissenting. * * *

* * * I cannot say that the balance that Congress has struck between its interests and the interests of its employees to receive compensation for their First Amendment expression is unreasonable. * * *

* * * There is little doubt that Congress reasonably could conclude that its interests in preventing impropriety and the appearance of impropriety in the federal work force outweigh the employees' interests in receiving compensation for expression that has a nexus to their Government employment. * * *

The Court concedes that in light of the abuses of honoraria by its Members, Congress could reasonably assume that "payments of honoraria to judges or high-ranking officials in the Executive Branch might generate a similar appearance of improper influence," but it concludes that Congress could not extend this presumption to federal employees below grade GS-16. The theory underlying the Court's distinction — that federal employees below grade GS-16 have negligible power to confer favors on those who might pay to hear them speak or to read their articles — is seriously flawed. Tax examiners, bank examiners, enforcement officials, or any number of federal employees have substantial power to confer favors even though their compensation level is below grade GS-16.

Furthermore, we rejected the same distinction in *Public Workers* v. *Mitchell*: "* * * Whatever differences there may be between administrative employees of the government and industrial workers in its employ are differences in detail so far as the constitutional power under review is concerned. Whether there are such differences and what weight to attach to them, are all matters of detail for Congress." 330 U.S., at 102. Congress was not obliged to draw an infinitely filigreed statute to deal with every subtle distinction between various groups of employees.

The Court dismisses the Hatch Act experience as irrelevant, because it aimed to *protect* employees' rights, notably their right to free expression, rather than to restrict those rights. This is, indeed, a strange characterization of § 9(a) of the Hatch Act. * * * [I]t can hardly be said that the Act *protected* the rights of workers who wished to engage in partisan political activity. One of the purposes of the Act was assuredly to free employees who did not wish to become engaged in politics from requests by their superiors to contribute money or time, but to the extent the Act protected these employees it undoubtedly limited the First Amendment rights of those who did wish to take an active part in politics. * * *

The Court observes that because a nexus limitation is retained for a series of speeches, it cannot be that difficult to enforce. The exception that the honoraria ban makes for a "series of appearances, speeches, or articles," far from undermining the statute's basic purpose, demonstrates that Congress was sensitive to the need for inhibiting as little speech consistent with its responsibility of ensuring that its employees perform their duties impartially and that there is no appearance of impropriety. One is far less likely to undertake a "series" of speeches or articles without being paid than he is to make a single speech or write a single article without being paid. Congress reasonably could have concluded that the number of cases where an employee wished to deliver a "series" of speeches would be much smaller than the number of requests to give individual speeches or write individual articles.

Unlike our prototypical application of *Pickering* which normally involves a response to the content of employee speech, the honoraria ban prohibits no speech and is unrelated to the message or the viewpoint expressed by the Government employee. Furthermore, the honoraria ban exempts from its prohibition travel and other expenses related to employee speech. Because there is only a limited burden on respondents' First Amendment rights, Congress reasonably could have determined that its paramount interests in preventing impropriety and the appearance of impropriety in its work force justified the honoraria ban. * * *

Notes and Questions

1. Can *Treasury Employees* be distinguished from *Letter Carriers*? In distinguishing the Court's analysis of the Hatch Act, *Treasury Employees* cited the "demonstrated ill effects" of employees' unregulated political activities. 513 U.S. at 471. Similarly, Justice O'Connor, in an omitted portion of her opinion, noted that the Court upheld the Hatch Act "only after canvassing nearly a century of concrete experience with the evils of the political spoils system." *Id.* at 483 (O'Connor, J., concurring in the judgment in part and dissenting in part). Does this mean that the country should have to experience a century of evils before taking action? Should the experience be relevant in assessing the constitutionality of either the Hatch Act or the honorarium ban?

2. *Problem.* After *Treasury Employees*, imagine that Congress redrafts the definition of honorarium to apply to all payments to employees "for an appearance, speech, or article (including a series of appearances, speeches, or articles), if the subject matter is directly related to the individual's official duties or the payment is made because of the individual's status with the Government." Is the amended statute constitutional? Would it be constitutional to apply the amended statute to employees hired after the effective date of the amendment, *even after they have left government service*?

3. *Problem.* May the following governmental officials be banned from taking honoraria? In each, assume that a statute prohibits payment for such endeavors.

a. Oliver Wendell Douglas, an accomplished author and farmer before his appointment to the Seventh Circuit, wishes to write books and give speeches about the law, literature, and life on the prairie.

b. Miss Teri Story, a Supreme Court Justice, wishes to publish a treatise on constitutional law and to teach a course on the subject at the Harvard Law School.

c. Sandy Beach, a member of Congress and a former college professor of government, wishes to write about the power of interest groups and the influence they have with legislators.

d. Marvin Pickling, a schoolteacher, wishes to give lectures concerning the expenditure of funds in the school system.

4. *Treasury Employees* holds not only that certain government employees must be permitted to speak, but that they must be permitted to receive payment for speaking. Yet under *Mitchell* and *Letter Carriers*, they can be prohibited from speaking or taking actions that have too close an association with partisan politics. Is the line between those two types of cases too fuzzy? Suppose the employee in *Treasury Employees* who gave lectures on black history were to mention his view of President Obama or the historical significance of his election. Would such a speech fall within the constitutional protection established by *Treasury Employees*? Should it?

5. Should a speech's constitutional protection depend on the location where it is delivered? Would, for example, a government employee's speech be protected if given on a street corner but not if given at a political convention? Would such a result violate the speaker's, or the party's, constitutional rights?

6. So-called "resign-to-run" statutes prohibit an office-holder from pursuing a different position unless he or she resigns the first office. Such statutes, like the Hatch Act and the employment discipline at issue in *Pickering*, discourage government employees from participating in politics. Resign-to-run statutes, however, impose restrictions on persons already holding office (rather than on unelected employees) and do not interfere with office-holders' right to speak. These differences caused the Court, in *Clements v. Fashing*, 457 U.S. 957 (1982), to conclude that resign-to-run statutes do not severely interfere with First Amendment rights, and to uphold them under the rational-basis test.

Are resign-to-run statutes good policy? Would it be a good idea to institute them on the national level, requiring, for example, Members of Congress to resign their offices before running for President, or requiring Representatives to resign before running for the Senate? Should sitting Senators be ineligible for judicial nominations?

Suppose that instead of requiring an office-holder to resign his or her office before running for a different post, a state law made an office-holder ineligible for any other office until the expiry of his or her term. *Cf.* U.S. CONST. art. I, § 6, cl. 2 ("No Senator or Representative shall, during the Time for which he was elected, be appointed to any civil Office under the Authority of the United States, which shall have been created, or the Emoluments whereof shall have been encreased during such time; and no Person holding any Office under the United States, shall be a Member of either House during his Continuance in Office."). Does a state have a sufficiently important interest in requiring ambitious office-holders to complete their terms so as to overcome the impact such a law has on the First Amendment rights of such would-be candidates and the voters who would support them? *See Fashing*, 457 U.S. at 966–69 (plurality opinion). What if the disqualification continued for a period *after* the term of office expired?

H. PATRONAGE

In the *Divine Comedy*'s Eighth Circle of Hell, Dante finds the Simoniacs, who had sold Church offices. He speaks to one, Pope Nicholas III, who is stuck upside-down in a rock, with only his feet and legs up to the calf visible and the soles of his feet afire. Nicholas admits to using his power to advance his family and his own wealth, provoking Dante's condemnation:

> *Well, tell me now: what was the sum of money*
> *that holy Peter had to pay our Lord*
> *before He gave the keys into his keeping?*
> *Certainly He asked no more than "Follow me."*
> *Nor did Peter or the rest extort gold coins*
> *or silver from Matthias when he was picked to fill the place the evil one*
> *[Judas Iscariot] had lost.*
> *So stay stuck there, for you are rightly punished * * *.*

Inferno, Canto XIX (Mark Musa trans., Penguin Books 1971). The following cases also condemn the dispensation of offices according to considerations other than merit, though the punishment is considerably less severe.

ELROD v. BURNS
Supreme Court of the United States
427 U.S. 347, 96 S. Ct. 2673, 49 L. Ed. 2d 547 (1976)

MR. JUSTICE BRENNAN announced the judgment of the Court and delivered an opinion in which MR. JUSTICE WHITE and MR. JUSTICE MARSHALL joined.

This case presents the question whether public employees who allege that they were discharged or threatened with discharge solely because of their partisan political affiliation or nonaffiliation state a claim for deprivation of constitutional rights secured by the First and Fourteenth Amendments. * * *

In December 1970, the Sheriff of Cook County, [Illinois,] a Republican, was replaced by Richard Elrod, a Democrat. At that time, respondents, all Republicans, were employees of the Cook County Sheriff's Office. They were non-civil-service employees and, therefore, not covered by any statute, ordinance, or regulation protecting them from arbitrary discharge. One respondent, John Burns, was Chief Deputy of the Process Division and supervised all departments of the Sheriff's Office working on the seventh floor of the building housing that office. Frank Vargas was a bailiff and security guard at the Juvenile Court of Cook County. Fred L. Buckley was employed as a process server in the office. Joseph Dennard was an employee in the office.

It has been the practice of the Sheriff of Cook County, when he assumes office from a Sheriff of a different political party, to replace non-civil-service employees of the Sheriffs' Office with members of his own party when the existing employees lack or fail to obtain requisite support from, or fail to affiliate with, that party. Consequently, subsequent to Sheriff Elrod's assumption of office, respondents * * * were discharged from their employment solely because they did not support and were not members of the Democratic Party and had failed to obtain the sponsorship of one of its leaders. * * *

The Cook County Sheriff's practice of dismissing employees on a partisan basis is but one form of the general practice of political patronage. The practice also includes placing loyal supporters in government jobs that may or may not have been made available by political discharges. Nonofficeholders may be the beneficiaries of lucrative government contracts for highway construction, buildings, and supplies. Favored wards may receive improved public services. Members of the judiciary may even engage in the practice through the appointment of receiverships, trusteeships, and refereeships. Although political patronage comprises a broad range of activities, we are here concerned only with the constitutionality of dismissing public employees for partisan reasons.

Patronage practice is not new to American politics. It has existed at the federal level at least since the Presidency of Thomas Jefferson, although its popularization and legitimation primarily occurred later, in the Presidency of Andrew Jackson. The practice is not unique to American politics. It has been used in many European countries, and in darker times, it played a significant role in the Nazi rise to power in Germany and other totalitarian states. More recent times have witnessed a strong decline in its use, particularly with respect to public employment. Indeed, only a few decades after Andrew Jackson's administration, strong discontent with the corruption and inefficiency of the patronage system of public employment eventuated in the Pendleton Act, the foundation of modern civil service. And on the state and local levels, merit systems have increasingly displaced the practice. * * *

The decline of patronage employment is not, of course, relevant to the question of its constitutionality. It is the practice itself, not the magnitude of its occurrence, the constitutionality of which must be determined. Nor for that matter does any unacceptability of the practice signified by its decline indicate its unconstitutionality. Our inquiry does not begin with the judgment of history, though the actual operation of a practice viewed in retrospect may help to assess its workings with respect to constitutional limitations. Rather, inquiry must commence with identification of the constitutional limitations implicated by a challenged governmental practice. * * *

The cost of the practice of patronage is the restraint it places on freedoms of belief and association. In order to maintain their jobs, respondents were required to pledge their political allegiance to the Democratic Party, work for the election of other candidates of the Democratic Party, contribute a portion of their wages to the Party, or obtain the sponsorship of a member of the Party, usually at the price of one of the first three alternatives. Regardless of the incumbent party's identity, Democratic or otherwise, the consequences for association and belief are the same.

An individual who is a member of the out-party maintains affiliation with his own party at the risk of losing his job. He works for the election of his party's candidates and espouses its policies at the same risk. The financial and campaign assistance that he is induced to provide to another party furthers the advancement of that party's policies to the detriment of his party's views and ultimately his own beliefs, and any assessment of his salary is tantamount to coerced belief. See *Buckley* v. *Valeo*, 424 U.S. 1, 19 (1976) [p. 799]. Even a pledge of allegiance to another party, however ostensible, only serves to compromise the individual's true beliefs. Since the average public employee is hardly in the financial position to support his party and another, or to lend his time to two parties, the individual's ability to act according to his beliefs and to associate with others of his political persuasion is constrained, and support for his party is diminished.

It is not only belief and association which are restricted where political patronage is the practice. The free functioning of the electoral process also suffers. Conditioning public employment on partisan support prevents support of competing political interests. Existing employees are deterred from such support, as well as the multitude seeking jobs. As government employment, state or federal, becomes more pervasive, the greater the dependence on it becomes, and therefore the greater becomes the power to starve political opposition by commanding partisan support, financial and otherwise. Patronage thus tips the electoral process in favor of the incumbent party, and where the practice's scope is substantial relative to the size of the electorate, the impact on the process can be significant.

Our concern with the impact of patronage on political belief and association does not occur in the abstract, for political belief and association constitute the core of those activities protected by the First Amendment. * * * Patronage, therefore, to the extent it compels or restrains belief and association, is inimical to the process which undergirds our system of government and is "at war with the deeper traditions of democracy embodied in the First Amendment." As such, the practice unavoidably confronts decisions by this Court either invalidating or recognizing as invalid government action that inhibits belief and association through the conditioning of public employment on political faith.

The Court recognized in *United Public Workers* v. *Mitchell*, 330 U.S. 75, 100 (1947) [p. 699], that "Congress may not 'enact a regulation providing that no Republican, Jew or Negro shall be appointed to federal office. . . .'" This principle was reaffirmed in *Wieman* v. *Updegraff*, 344 U.S. 183 (1952), which held that a State could not require its employees to establish their loyalty by extracting an oath denying past affiliation with Communists. And in *Cafeteria Workers* v. *McElroy*, 367 U.S. 886, 898 (1961), the Court recognized again that the government could not deny employment because of previous membership in a particular party.

Particularly pertinent to the constitutionality of the practice of patronage dismissals are *Keyishian* v. *Board of Regents*, 385 U.S. 589 (1967), and *Perry* v. *Sindermann*, 408 U.S. 593 (1972). In *Keyishian*, the Court invalidated New York statutes barring employment merely on the basis of membership in "subversive" organizations. *Keyishian* squarely held that political association alone could not, consistently with the First Amendment, constitute an adequate ground for denying public employment. In *Perry*, the Court broadly rejected the validity of limitations on First Amendment rights as a condition to the receipt of a governmental benefit, stating that the government "may not deny a benefit to a person on a basis that infringes his constitutionally protected interests — especially, his interest in freedom of speech. For if the government could deny a benefit to a person because of his constitutionally protected speech or associations, his exercise of those freedoms would in effect be penalized and inhibited. This would allow the government to 'produce a result which [it] could not command directly.' Such interference with constitutional rights is impermissible."

Patronage practice falls squarely within the prohibitions of *Keyishian* and *Perry*. Under that practice, public employees hold their jobs on the condition that they provide, in some acceptable manner, support for the favored political party. The threat of dismissal for failure to provide that support unquestionably inhibits protected belief and association, and dismissal for failure to provide support only penalizes its exercise. The belief and association which government may not ordain directly are achieved by indirection.[13] And regardless of how evenhandedly these restraints may operate in the long run, after political office has changed hands several times, protected interests are still infringed and thus the violation remains. * * *

Although the practice of patronage dismissals clearly infringes First Amendment interests, our inquiry is not at an end, for the prohibition on encroachment of First Amendment protections is not an absolute. Restraints are permitted for appropriate reasons. [Petitioners suggest] that because there is no right to a government benefit, such as public employment, the benefit may be denied for any reason. *Perry*, however, emphasized that "[f]or at least a quarter-century, this Court has made clear that even though a person has no 'right' to a valuable governmental benefit and even though the government may deny him the benefit for any number of reasons, there are some reasons upon which the government may not rely." *Perry* and *Keyishian* properly recognize one such impermissible reason: The denial of a public benefit may not be used by the government for the purpose of creating an incentive enabling it to achieve what it may not command directly. "[T]he theory that public employment which may be denied altogether may be subjected to any conditions, regardless of how unreasonable, has been uniformly rejected." "It is too late in the day to doubt that the liberties of religion and expression may be infringed by the denial of or placing of conditions upon a benefit or privilege." *Sherbert* v. *Verner*, 374 U.S. 398, 404 (1963). "[T]his Court now has rejected the concept that

---

[13] The increasingly pervasive nature of public employment provides officials with substantial power through conditioning jobs on partisan support, particularly in this time of high unemployment. Since the government, however, may not seek to achieve an unlawful end either directly or indirectly, the inducement afforded by placing conditions on a benefit need not be particularly great in order to find that rights have been violated. Rights are infringed both where the government fines a person a penny for being a Republican and where it withholds the grant of a penny for the same reason.

Petitioners contend that even though the government may not provide that public employees may retain their jobs only if they become affiliated with or provide support for the in-party, respondents here have waived any objection to such requirements. The difficulty with this argument is that it completely swallows the rule. Since the qualification may not be constitutionally imposed absent an appropriate justification, to accept the waiver argument is to say that the government may do what it may not do. A finding of waiver in this case, therefore, would be contrary to our view that a partisan job qualification abridges the First Amendment.

constitutional rights turn upon whether a governmental benefit is characterized as a 'right' or as a 'privilege.' " *Sugarman* v. *Dougall*, 413 U.S. 634, 644 (1973).

* * * It is firmly established that a significant impairment of First Amendment rights must survive exacting scrutiny. * * * Thus encroachment "cannot be justified upon a mere showing of a legitimate state interest." The interest advanced must be paramount, one of vital importance, and the burden is on the government to show the existence of such an interest. In the instant case, care must be taken not to confuse the interest of partisan organizations with governmental interests. Only the latter will suffice. Moreover, it is not enough that the means chosen in furtherance of the interest be rationally related to that end. The gain to the subordinating interest provided by the means must outweigh the incurred loss of protected rights, and the government must "emplo[y] means closely drawn to avoid unnecessary abridgment. . . . " * * * In short, if conditioning the retention of public employment on the employee's support of the in-party is to survive constitutional challenge, it must further some vital government end by a means that is least restrictive of freedom of belief and association in achieving that end, and the benefit gained must outweigh the loss of constitutionally protected rights.

One interest which has been offered in justification of patronage is the need to insure effective government and the efficiency of public employees. It is argued that employees of political persuasions not the same as that of the party in control of public office will not have the incentive to work effectively and may even be motivated to subvert the incumbent administration's efforts to govern effectively. We are not persuaded. The inefficiency resulting from the wholesale replacement of large numbers of public employees every time political office changes hands belies this justification. And the prospect of dismissal after an election in which the incumbent party has lost is only a disincentive to good work. Further, it is not clear that dismissal in order to make room for a patronage appointment will result in replacement by a person more qualified to do the job since appointment often occurs in exchange for the delivery of votes, or other party service, not job capability. More fundamentally, however, the argument does not succeed because it is doubtful that the mere difference of political persuasion motivates poor performance; nor do we think it legitimately may be used as a basis for imputing such behavior. The Court has consistently recognized that mere political association is an inadequate basis for imputing disposition to ill-willed conduct. Though those cases involved affiliation with the Communist Party, we do not "consider these [respondents'] interest in freely associating with members of the [Republican] Party less worthy of protection than [other] employees' interest in associating with Communists or former Communists." At all events, less drastic means for insuring government effectiveness and employee efficiency are available to the State. Specifically, employees may always be discharged for good cause, such as insubordination or poor job performance, when those bases in fact exist.

Even if the first argument that patronage serves effectiveness and efficiency be rejected, it still may be argued that patronage serves those interests by giving the employees of an incumbent party the incentive to perform well in order to insure their party's incumbency and thereby their jobs. Patronage, according to the argument, thus makes employees highly accountable to the public. But the ability of officials more directly accountable to the electorate to discharge employees for cause and the availability of merit systems, growth in the use of which has been quite significant, convince us that means less intrusive than patronage still exist for achieving accountability in the public work force and, thereby, effective and efficient government. The greater effectiveness of patronage over these less drastic means, if any, is at best marginal, a gain outweighed by the absence of intrusion on protected interests under the alternatives.

The lack of any justification for patronage dismissals as a means of furthering government effectiveness and efficiency distinguishes this case from *CSC* v. *Letter Carriers*, 413 U.S. 548 (1973) [p. 713], and *United Public Workers* v. *Mitchell*. In both of those cases, legislative restraints on political management and campaigning by public employees were upheld despite their encroachment on First Amendment rights because, *inter alia*, they did serve in a necessary manner to foster and protect efficient and effective government. Interestingly, the activities that were restrained by the legislation involved in those cases are characteristic of patronage practices. As the Court observed in *Mitchell*: "The conviction that an actively partisan governmental personnel threatens good administration has deepened since [1882]. Congress recognizes danger to the service in that political rather than official effort may earn advancement and to the public in that governmental favor may be channeled through political connections."

A second interest advanced in support of patronage is the need for political loyalty of employees, not to the end that effectiveness and efficiency be insured, but to the end that representative government not be undercut by tactics obstructing the implementation of policies of the new administration, policies presumably sanctioned by the electorate. The justification is not without force, but is nevertheless inadequate to validate patronage wholesale. Limiting patronage dismissals to policymaking positions is sufficient to achieve this governmental end. Nonpolicymaking individuals usually have only limited responsibility and are therefore not in a position to thwart the goals of the in-party.

No clear line can be drawn between policymaking and nonpolicymaking positions. While nonpolicymaking individuals usually have limited responsibility, that is not to say that one with a number of responsibilities is necessarily in a policymaking position. The nature of the responsibilities is critical. Employee supervisors, for example, may have many responsibilities, but those responsibilities may have only limited and well-defined objectives. An employee with responsibilities that are not well defined or are of broad scope more likely functions in a policymaking position. In determining whether an employee occupies a policymaking position, consideration would also be given to whether the employee acts as an adviser or formulates plans for the implementation of broad goals. Thus, the political loyalty "justification is a matter of proof, or at least argument, directed at particular kinds of jobs." Since, as we have noted, it is the government's burden to demonstrate an overriding interest in order to validate an encroachment on protected interests, the burden of establishing this justification as to any particular respondent will rest on the petitioners on remand, cases of doubt being resolved in favor of the particular respondent.

It is argued that a third interest supporting patronage dismissals is the preservation of the democratic process. According to petitioners, "we have contrived no system for the support of party that does not place considerable reliance on patronage. The party organization makes a democratic government work and charges a price for its services." The argument is thus premised on the centrality of partisan politics to the democratic process.

Preservation of the democratic process is certainly an interest protection of which may in some instances justify limitations on First Amendment freedoms. But however important preservation of the two-party system or any system involving a fixed number of parties may or may not be,[22] we are not persuaded that the elimination of patronage practice or, as is specifically involved here, the interdiction of patronage dismissals, will bring about the demise of party politics. Political parties existed in the absence of active patronage practice prior to the administration of Andrew Jackson, and they have survived substantial reduction in their patronage power through the establishment of merit systems.

Patronage dismissals thus are not the least restrictive alternative to achieving the contribution they may make to the democratic process. The process functions as well without the practice, perhaps even better, for patronage dismissals clearly also retard that process. Patronage can result in the entrenchment of one or a few parties to the exclusion of others. And most indisputably, as we recognized at the outset, patronage is a very effective impediment to the associational and speech freedoms which are essential to a meaningful system of democratic government. Thus, if patronage contributes at all to the elective process, that contribution is diminished by the practice's impairment of the same. Indeed, unlike the gain to representative government provided by the Hatch Act in *CSC* v. *Letter Carriers* and *United Public Workers* v. *Mitchell*, the gain to representative government provided by the practice of patronage, if any, would be insufficient to justify its sacrifice of First Amendment rights.

To be sure, *Letter Carriers* and *Mitchell* upheld Hatch Act restraints sacrificing political campaigning and management, activities themselves protected by the First Amendment. But in those cases it was the Court's judgment that congressional subordination of those activities was permissible to safeguard the core interests of individual belief and association. Subordination of some First Amendment activity was permissible to protect other such activity. Today, we hold that subordination of other First Amendment activity, that is, patronage dismissals, not only is permissible, but also is mandated by the First Amendment. And since patronage dismissals fall within the category of political campaigning and management, this conclusion irresistibly flows from *Mitchell* and *Letter Carriers*. For if the First Amendment did not place individual belief and association above political campaigning and management, at least in the setting of public employment, the restraints on those latter

---

[22] Partisan politics bears the imprimatur only of tradition, not the Constitution.

"It may be correct that the patronage system has been followed for 'almost two hundred years' and therefore was in existence when the Constitution was adopted. However, the notoriety of the practice in the administration of Andrew Jackson in 1828 implies that it was not prevalent theretofore; we are not aware of any discussion of the practice during the drafting of the Constitution or the First Amendment. In any event, if the age of a pernicious practice were a sufficient reason for its continued acceptance, the constitutional attack on racial discrimination would, of course, have been doomed to failure." *Illinois State Employees Union* v. *Lewis*, 473 F.2d 561, 568 n.14 (CA7 1972) [(Stevens, J.)].

activities could not have been judged permissible in *Mitchell* and *Letter Carriers*.[27]

It is apparent that at bottom we are required to engage in the resolution of conflicting interests under the First Amendment. The constitutional adjudication called for by this task is well within our province. The illuminating source to which we turn in performing the task is the system of government the First Amendment was intended protect, a democratic system whose proper functioning is indispensably dependent on the unfettered judgment of each citizen on matters of political concern. Our decision in obedience to the guidance of that source does not outlaw political parties or political campaigning and management. Parties are free to exist and their concomitant activities are free to continue. We require only that the rights of every citizen to believe as he will and to act and associate according to his beliefs be free to continue as well.

In summary, patronage dismissals severely restrict political belief and association. Though there is a vital need for government efficiency and effectiveness, such dismissals are on balance not the least restrictive means for fostering that end. There is also a need to insure that policies which the electorate has sanctioned are effectively implemented. That interest can be fully satisfied by limiting patronage dismissals to policymaking positions. Finally, patronage dismissals cannot be justified by their contribution to the proper functioning of our democratic process through their assistance to partisan politics since political parties are nurtured by other, less intrusive and equally effective methods. More fundamentally, however, any contribution of patronage dismissals to the democratic process does not suffice to override their severe encroachment on First Amendment freedoms. We hold, therefore, that the practice of patronage dismissals is unconstitutional under the First and Fourteenth Amendments, and that respondents thus stated a valid claim for relief. * * *

The judgment of the Court of Appeals is

Affirmed.

MR. JUSTICE STEVENS did not participate in the consideration or decision of this case.

MR. JUSTICE STEWART, with whom MR. JUSTICE BLACKMUN joins, concurring in the judgment. * * *

This case does not require us to consider the broad contours of the so-called patronage system, with all its variations and permutations. In particular, it does not require us to consider the constitutional validity of a system that confines the hiring

---

[27] The judgment that the First Amendment interests in political campaigning and management must, in the setting of public employment, give way to the First Amendment interests in individual belief and association does not necessarily extend to other contexts. Restraining political campaigning and management in the area of public employment leaves it free to continue in other settings. The consequence of no such restraint, however, is the complete restriction of individual belief and association for each public employee affected.

of some governmental employees to those of a particular political party, and I would intimate no views whatever on that question.

The single substantive question involved in this case is whether a nonpolicymaking, nonconfidential government employee can be discharged or threatened with discharge from a job that he is satisfactorily performing upon the sole ground of his political beliefs. I agree with the plurality that he cannot.

MR. CHIEF JUSTICE BURGER, dissenting.

The Court's decision today represents a significant intrusion into the area of legislative and policy concerns[.] * * * Constant inroads on the powers of the States to manage their own affairs cannot fail to complicate our system and centralize more power in Washington. * * *

MR. JUSTICE POWELL, with whom THE CHIEF JUSTICE and MR. JUSTICE REHNQUIST join, dissenting.

The Court holds unconstitutional a practice as old as the Republic, a practice which has contributed significantly to the democratization of American politics. This decision is urged on us in the name of First Amendment rights, but in my view the judgment neither is constitutionally required nor serves the interest of a representative democracy. It also may well disserve rather than promote core values of the First Amendment. I therefore dissent. * * *

Partisan politics, as we now know them, did not assume a prominent role in national politics immediately after the adoption of the Constitution. Nonetheless, [President] Washington tended to confine appointments even of customs officials and postmasters to Federalists, as opposed to anti-Federalists. As the role of parties expanded, partisan considerations quickly influenced employment decisions. John Adams removed some Republicans from minor posts, and Jefferson, the first President to succeed a President of an opposing party, made significant patronage use of the appointment and removal powers. The administrations of Madison, Monroe, and John Quincy Adams provided no occasion for conspicuous patronage practice in employment, as each succeeded a copartisan. Jackson, of course, used patronage extensively when he became the first President since Jefferson to succeed an antagonistic administration.

It thus appears that patronage employment practices emerged on the national level at an early date, and that they were conspicuous during Jackson's Presidency largely because of their necessary dormancy during the long succession of Republican Presidents. During that period, however, patronage in hiring was practiced widely in the States, especially in New York and Pennsylvania. This afforded a theoretical and popular legitimacy to patronage, helping to lay the groundwork for acceptance of Jackson's actions on the national level.

It is recognized that patronage in employment played a significant role in democratizing American politics. Before patronage practices developed fully, an "aristocratic" class dominated political affairs, a tendency that persisted in areas where patronage did not become prevalent. Patronage practices broadened the base of political participation by providing incentives to take part in the process, thereby increasing the volume of political discourse in society. Patronage also strengthened parties, and hence encouraged the development of institutional responsibility to the electorate on a permanent basis. * * *

In many situations patronage employment practices also entailed costs to government efficiency. These costs led eventually to reforms placing most federal and state civil service employment on a nonpatronage basis. But the course of such reform is of limited relevance to the task of constitutional adjudication in this case. It is pertinent to note, however, that a perceived impingement on employees' political beliefs by the patronage system was not a significant impetus to such reform. * * *

[Petitioners] apparently accepted patronage jobs knowingly and willingly, while fully familiar with the "tenure" practices long prevailing in the Sheriff's Office. Such employees have benefited from their political beliefs and activities; they have not been penalized for them. In these circumstances, I am inclined to [believe] that beneficiaries of a patronage system may not be heard to challenge it when it comes their turn to be replaced. * * * In any event, I am forced to turn to the question addressed by the plurality * * *.

* * * In concluding that patronage hiring practices are unconstitutional, the plurality seriously underestimates the strength of the government interest especially at the local level in allowing some patronage hiring practices, and it exaggerates the perceived burden on First Amendment rights.

As indicated above, patronage hiring practices have contributed to American democracy by stimulating political activity and by strengthening parties, thereby helping to make government accountable.[6] It cannot be questioned seriously that these contributions promote important state interests. * * *

We also have recognized the strong government interests in encouraging stable political parties and avoiding excessive political fragmentation. Through the medium of established parties the "people . . . are presented with understandable choices and the winner in the general election with sufficient support to govern effectively," *Storer* v. *Brown*, 415 U.S. 724, 735 (1974) [p. 513], while "splintered parties and unrestrained factionalism [might] do significant damage to the fabric of government."

Without analysis, however, the plurality opinion disparages the contribution of patronage hiring practices in advancing these state interests. It merely asserts that such practices cause the "free functioning of the electoral process [to suffer]," and that "we are not persuaded that the elimination of . . . patronage dismissals, will bring about the demise of party politics." One cannot avoid the impression, however, that even a threatened demise of parties would not trouble the plurality. In my view,

---

[6] Some commentators have believed that patronage hiring practices promote other social interests as well: "Patronage is peculiarly important for minority groups, involving much more than the mere spoils of office. Each first appointment given a member of any underdog element is a boost in that element's struggle for social acceptance. It means that another barrier to their advance has been lifted, another shut door has swung open." S. Lubell, The Future of American Politics 76–77 (1952).

this thinking reflects a disturbing insensitivity to the political realities relevant to the disposition of this case.

The complaining parties are or were employees of the Sheriff. In many communities, the sheriff's duties are as routine as process serving, and his election attracts little or no general public interest. * * * Unless the candidates for these offices are able to dispense the traditional patronage that has accrued to the offices, they also are unlikely to attract donations of time or money from voluntary groups. * * * Long experience teaches that at this local level traditional patronage practices contribute significantly to the democratic process. The candidates for these offices derive their support at the precinct level, and their modest funding for publicity, from cadres of friends and political associates who hope to benefit if their "man" is elected. The activities of the latter are often the principal source of political information for the voting public. The "robust" political discourse that the plurality opinion properly emphasizes is furthered — not restricted — by the time-honored system.

Patronage hiring practices also enable party organizations to persist and function at the local level. Such organizations become visible to the electorate at large only at election time, but the dull periods between elections require ongoing activities: precinct organizations must be maintained; new voters registered; and minor political "chores" performed for citizens who otherwise may have no practical means of access to officeholders. In some communities, party organizations and clubs also render helpful social services.

It is naive to think that these types of political activities are motivated at these levels by some academic interest in "democracy" or other public service impulse. For the most part, as every politician knows, the hope of some reward generates a major portion of the local political activity supporting parties. It is difficult to overestimate the contributions to our system by the major political parties, fortunately limited in number compared to the fractionalization that has made the continued existence of democratic government doubtful in some other countries. Parties generally are stable, high-profile, and permanent institutions. When the names on a long ballot are meaningless to the average voter, party affiliation affords a guidepost by which voters may rationalize a myriad of political choices. Voters can and do hold parties to long-term accountability, and it is not too much to say that, in their absence, responsive and responsible performance in low-profile offices, particularly, is difficult to maintain.

It is against decades of experience to the contrary, then, that the plurality opinion concludes that patronage hiring practices interfere with the "free functioning of the electoral process." This *ad hoc* judicial judgment runs counter to the judgments of the representatives of the people in state and local governments, representatives who have chosen, in most instances, to retain some patronage practices in combination with a merit-oriented civil service. One would think that elected representatives of the people are better equipped than we to weigh the need for some continuation of patronage practices in light of the interests above identified, and particularly in view of local conditions.[10] Against this background,

---

[10] The judgment today is limited to nonpolicymaking positions. A "policy-making" exception, however,

the assertion in the plurality opinion that "[p]atronage dismissals . . . are not the least restrictive alternative to achieving [any] contribution they may make to the democratic process" is unconvincing, especially since no alternative to some continuation of patronage practices is suggested.

I thus conclude that patronage hiring practices sufficiently serve important state interests, including some interests sought to be advanced by the First Amendment, to justify a tolerable intrusion on the First Amendment interests of employees or potential employees.

* * * This case differs materially from previous cases involving the imposition of political conditions on employment, see, *e.g.*, *Garner* v. *Los Angeles Board of Public Works*, 341 U.S. 716 (1951), cases where there was an attempt to exclude "a minority group . . . odious to the majority." In that context there was a danger that governmental action was directed toward the elimination of political beliefs by penalizing adherents to them. But patronage hiring practices have been consistent historically with vigorous ideological competition in the political "marketplace." And even after one becomes a beneficiary, the system leaves significant room for individual political expression. Employees, regardless of affiliation, may vote freely[11] and express themselves on some political issues. The principal intrusion of patronage hiring practices on First Amendment interests thus arises from the coercion on associational choices that may be created by one's desire initially to obtain employment. This intrusion, while not insignificant, must be measured in light of the limited role of patronage hiring in most government employment. The pressure to abandon one's beliefs and associations to obtain government employment — especially employment of such uncertain duration — does not seem to me to assume impermissible proportions in light of the interests to be served. * * *[12]

---

will not allow substantial advancement of the state interests undercut by the Court's holding, as it is doubtful that any significant number of employees can be identified as policymakers in a sheriff's office. States have chosen to provide for the election of many local officials who have little or no genuine policymaking functions, and the subordinates of such officials are even less likely to have such functions. It thus is predictable that the holding today will terminate almost completely the contributions of patronage hiring practices to the democratic process. The probability of this result is increased to the extent that the needs of efficiency in local government require that policymaking positions be included in a merit-oriented, nonpolitical civil service.

[11] It appears that before the adoption of the Australian ballot, one's access to or retention of a government job sometimes could depend on voting "correctly." Today this ultimate core of political expression is beyond the reach of any coercive effects of the patronage system.

[12] In concluding that the Constitution does not require the invalidation of state and local patronage systems, I wish to make clear that approval of any particular type of system or of the practice in any particular State, city, or community is not implied. I believe that the prevailing practice is to establish a broad base of merit-oriented civil service, but to leave some room for the operation of traditional patronage. I must say that the "mix" in Cook County (where only about half of the employees in the Sheriff's Office are within the merit system) seems disproportionate. On the other hand, there are smaller communities — *e.g.*, where nonpartisan, council-manager forms of government exist — in which the merit system embraces the vast majority of public employees. Political scientists and students of government differ, and their views also have varied from time to time, as to the best means of structuring state and local government employment in the public interest. Nor is the answer necessarily the same for every community without regard to its size, form of government, or other local conditions. My conviction, as indicated in the opinion above, is that we should not foreclose local options in the name of a constitutional right perceived to be applicable for the first time after nearly two centuries.

Notes and Questions

1.   Who is in a better position to assess the wisdom of patronage hiring practices — elected officials, as Justice Powell argued, or electorally unaccountable judges, as the plurality implied?

2.   Four years after *Elrod*, the Court was presented with the question whether assistant public defenders could be discharged because of their political affiliations or sympathies. The Court held that they could not, but in so doing the Court appeared to revise the *Elrod* standard for determining which employees could be dismissed on political grounds. While *Elrod* had focused on whether the position had "policymaking" responsibilities or required confidentiality, *Branti v. Finkel*, 445 U.S. 507, 518–20 (1980), asked whether "party affiliation is an appropriate requirement for the effective performance of the public office involved":

> [I]t is not always easy to determine whether a position is one in which political affiliation is a legitimate factor to be considered. Under some circumstances, a position may be appropriately considered political even though it is neither confidential nor policymaking in character. As one obvious example, if a State's election laws require that precincts be supervised by two election judges of different parties, a Republican judge could be legitimately discharged solely for changing his party registration. That conclusion would not depend on any finding that the job involved participation in policy decisions or access to confidential information. Rather, it would simply rest on the fact that party membership was essential to the discharge of the employee's governmental responsibilities.
>
> It is equally clear that party affiliation is not necessarily relevant to every policymaking or confidential position. The coach of a state university's football team formulates policy, but no one could seriously claim that Republicans make better coaches than Democrats, or vice versa, no matter which party is in control of the state government. On the other hand, it is equally clear that the Governor of a State may appropriately believe that the official duties of various assistants who help him write speeches, explain his views to the press, or communicate with the legislature cannot be performed effectively unless those persons share his political beliefs and party commitments. In sum, the ultimate inquiry is not whether the label "policymaker" or "confidential" fits a particular position; rather, the question is whether the hiring authority can demonstrate that party affiliation is an appropriate requirement for the effective performance of the public office involved.
>
> Having thus framed the issue, it is manifest that the continued employment of an assistant public defender cannot properly be conditioned upon his allegiance to the political party in control of the county government. The primary, if not the only, responsibility of an assistant public defender is to represent individual citizens in controversy with the State. * * *
>
> Thus, whatever policymaking occurs in the public defender's office must relate to the needs of individual clients and not to any partisan political interests. Similarly, although an assistant is bound to obtain access to

confidential information arising out of various attorney-client relationships, that information has no bearing whatsoever on partisan political concerns. Under these circumstances, it would undermine, rather than promote, the effective performance of an assistant public defender's office to make his tenure dependent on his allegiance to the dominant political party.

Justice Powell, in a dissent joined by then-Justice Rehnquist and in part by Justice Stewart, criticized the Court for going beyond *Elrod* in holding that even some policymaking officials would be insulated from patronage dismissals if their political affiliation was not relevant to the job. He further argued that the "appropriate[ness]" standard was so vague as to raise the possibility of litigation over a wide range of jobs, making the judiciary the "final arbiters as to who federal, state, and local governments may employ." *Id.* at 525 (Powell, J., dissenting). In a portion of the dissent joined only by then-Justice Rehnquist, Justice Powell reiterated the view he expressed in *Elrod* that patronage was valuable in supporting the two-party system. He further argued that "[b]ecause voters certainly may elect governmental officials [including public defenders and their assistants] on the basis of party ties, it is difficult to perceive a constitutional reason for prohibiting them from delegating that same authority to legislators and appointed officials." *Id.* at 533–34 (Powell, J., dissenting). Justice Stewart also filed a dissenting opinion, in which he argued that the "confidential" nature of the job of an assistant public defender distinguished *Branti* from *Elrod. See id.* at 520–21 (Stewart, J., dissenting).

3.   What explains Chief Justice Burger's switch from dissenting in *Elrod* to joining the *Branti* majority?

4.   Lower courts have consistently held that in evaluating whether an employee may be dismissed for political reasons, the responsibilities specified in the job description, rather than the duties that the employee customarily performed, are controlling. As explained in *Sanders v. Montoya*, 982 P.2d 1064 (N.M. Ct. App. 1999), focusing on the job description lessens the burden on courts by making it unnecessary to reevaluate every job whenever there is a shift in the way office administration is handled. Further, the job-description approach provides certainty to litigants and allows the new administration to fill certain positions with political allies, regardless of the ways in which the prior administration had been using its employees.

5.   Should the First Amendment provide protection against dismissal for an employee who is running for election against her boss? In *Carver v. Dennis*, 104 F.3d 847 (6th Cir. 1997), the plaintiff was a deputy county clerk. She was fired because she planned to run against the incumbent county clerk. The court held that there was a distinction between dismissals based on one's political affiliation, political beliefs, or the expression of those beliefs, on the one hand, and one's political candidacy, on the other. The court concluded that only the first category received protection under *Elrod* and *Branti*: "This was not a patronage dismissal. It was not a dismissal because of political beliefs or affiliations. It was not a dismissal based on politics at all, except to the extent that running for public office is a political exercise in its broad sense." *Id.* at 850. *See also Wilbur v. Mahan*, 3 F.3d 214 (7th Cir. 1993); *Bart v. Telford*, 677 F.2d 622 (7th Cir. 1982). Does this

explanation understate the importance to democracy of running for office? *See Click v. Copeland*, 970 F.2d 106, 112 (5th Cir. 1992). Is there a constitutional difference between firing the employee and subjecting him or her to retaliatory harassment? *See Wallace v. Benware*, 67 F.3d 655, 661 (7th Cir. 1995) (holding that a sheriff could dismiss or demote a deputy who had run against him, but could not subject him to "a campaign of petty harassment").

6. Judge Easterbrook of the Seventh Circuit has argued that the Supreme Court's decisions upholding the Hatch Act and resign-to-run statutes, *see supra* § G, foreclose the possibility that public employees would be protected from dismissal based on their decision to run for office. *See Wilbur*, 3 F.3d at 219–21 (Easterbrook, J., concurring in judgment). The majority, in an opinion by Judge Posner, responded that "it would be rather a stretch of the Hatch Act cases to interpret them as authorizing a public official selectively to apply a 'resign to run' provision to his political enemies." *Id.* at 216 (opinion of the court). Judge Easterbrook countered that a public official is not behaving selectively when he discharges every employee who runs against him — "[a]nyone running for his seat is an incumbent's enemy" — and that it would be ironic to encourage, in the name of the First Amendment, a policy *mandating* dismissal of employees who run for office. *Id.* at 220 (Easterbrook, J., concurring in judgment). Who has the better of the argument?

7. Would the result change if the employee were running for Congress, rather than for the boss's position? *See Newcomb v. Brennan*, 558 F.2d 825 (7th Cir. 1977).

What if the candidate were not the employee herself, but her son? Would the employee receive protection from the employer's decision to fire her because of her son's candidacy? *See Smith v. Frye*, 488 F.3d 263 (4th Cir.), *cert. denied*, 552 U.S. 1039 (2007). What if an employee is subject to retaliation neither for her political affiliation nor for her relative's candidacy *per se*, but for her campaigning on behalf of her relative who was running against a candidate supported by her superiors? *See Riddell v. Gordon*, 2008 U.S. Dist. LEXIS 88410 (D. Del. 2008).

Suppose instead that after an election for county clerk in which the incumbent is defeated, the new office-holder fires an employee who is the wife of his former opponent. *See Lowe v. Padgett*, 740 F. Supp. 481 (E.D. Tenn. 1989), *aff'd* 897 F.2d 529 (6th Cir. 1990). *Cf. McCabe v. Sharrett*, 12 F.3d 1558 (11th Cir. 1994) (holding that a police chief acted constitutionally when he transferred his secretary because he feared the secretary's marriage to another police officer might compromise her loyalty and her ability to keep confidences).

8. *Problem.* Barney Fife, deputy sheriff of Mayberry, decides to challenge incumbent sheriff Andy Taylor in the next election. Another deputy, Floyd D. Barber, and jailer Otis Campbell decide to support Fife, and spend off-duty time distributing leaflets and otherwise campaigning for him. Taylor is upset at the challenge, and fires Fife as well as Barber and Campbell. Should the Constitution be interpreted to provide all three employees with the same protection, or are there significant distinctions owing to their positions or their activities? *See Jantzen v. Hawkins*, 188 F.3d 1247 (10th Cir. 1999).

RUTAN v. REPUBLICAN PARTY OF ILLINOIS
Supreme Court of the United States
497 U.S. 62, 110 S. Ct. 2729, 111 L. Ed. 2d 52 (1990)

Justice Brennan delivered the opinion of the Court [in which Justice White, Justice Marshall, Justice Blackmun, and Justice Stevens join].

To the victor belong only those spoils that may be constitutionally obtained. *Elrod* v. *Burns*, 427 U.S. 347 (1976) [p. 726], and *Branti* v. *Finkel*, 445 U.S. 507 (1980), decided that the First Amendment forbids government officials to discharge or threaten to discharge public employees solely for not being supporters of the political party in power, unless party affiliation is an appropriate requirement for the position involved. Today we are asked to decide the constitutionality of several related political patronage practices — whether promotion, transfer, recall, and hiring decisions involving low-level public employees may be constitutionally based on party affiliation and support. We hold that they may not.

The petition and cross-petition before us arise from a lawsuit protesting certain employment policies and practices instituted by Governor James Thompson of Illinois. On November 12, 1980, the Governor issued an executive order proclaiming a hiring freeze for every agency, bureau, board, or commission subject to his control. The order prohibits state officials from hiring any employee, filling any vacancy, creating any new position, or taking any similar action. It affects approximately 60,000 state positions. More than 5,000 of these become available each year as a result of resignations, retirements, deaths, expansions, and reorganizations. The order proclaims that "*no* exceptions" are permitted without the Governor's "express permission after submission of appropriate requests to [his] office."

Requests for the Governor's "express permission" have allegedly become routine. Permission has been granted or withheld through an agency expressly created for this purpose, the Governor's Office of Personnel (Governor's Office). Agencies have been screening applicants under Illinois' civil service system, making their personnel choices, and submitting them as requests to be approved or disapproved by the Governor's Office. Among the employment decisions for which approvals have been required are new hires, promotions, transfers, and recalls after layoffs.

By means of the freeze, according to petitioners and cross-respondents, the Governor has been using the Governor's Office to operate a political patronage system to limit state employment and beneficial employment-related decisions to those who are supported by the Republican Party. In reviewing an agency's request that a particular applicant be approved for a particular position, the Governor's Office has looked at whether the applicant voted in Republican primaries in past election years, whether the applicant has provided financial or other support to the Republican Party and its candidates, whether the applicant has promised to join and work for the Republican Party in the future, and whether the applicant has the support of Republican Party officials at state or local levels.

Five people (including the three petitioners) brought suit * * * alleg[ing] that they had suffered discrimination with respect to state employment because they had not been supporters of the State's Republican Party and that this discrimination violates the First Amendment. Cynthia B. Rutan has been working for the State since 1974 as a rehabilitation counselor. She claims that since 1981 she has been repeatedly denied promotions to supervisory positions for which she was qualified because she had not worked for or supported the Republican Party. Franklin Taylor, who operates road equipment for the Illinois Department of Transportation, claims that he was denied a promotion in 1983 because he did not have the support of the local Republican Party. Taylor also maintains that he was denied a transfer to an office nearer to his home because of opposition from the Republican Party chairmen in the counties in which he worked and to which he requested a transfer. James W. Moore claims that he has been repeatedly denied state employment as a prison guard because he did not have the support of Republican Party officials. The two other plaintiffs, before the Court as cross-respondents, allege that they were not recalled after layoffs because they lacked Republican credentials. * * *

The District Court dismissed the complaint with prejudice[.] * * * Noting that this Court had previously determined that the patronage practice of discharging public employees on the basis of their political affiliation violates the First Amendment, the Court of Appeals held that other patronage practices violate the First Amendment only when they are the "substantial equivalent of a dismissal." The court explained that an employment decision is equivalent to a dismissal when it is one that would lead a reasonable person to resign. * * *

* * * We granted certiorari to decide the important question whether the First Amendment's proscription of patronage dismissals recognized in *Elrod* and *Branti* extends to promotion, transfer, recall, or hiring decisions involving public employment positions for which party affiliation is not an appropriate requirement.

We first address the claims of the four current or former employees. Respondents urge us to view *Elrod* and *Branti* as inapplicable because the patronage dismissals at issue in those cases are different in kind from failure to promote, failure to transfer, and failure to recall after layoff. Respondents initially contend that the employee[s'] First Amendment rights have not been infringed because they have no entitlement to promotion, transfer, or rehire. We rejected just such an argument in *Elrod* and *Branti*, as both cases involved state workers who were employees at will with no legal entitlement to continued employment. In *Perry* [v. *Sindermann*, 408 U.S. 593 (1972)] we held explicitly that the plaintiff teacher's lack of a contractual or tenure right to re-employment was immaterial to his First Amendment claim. We explained the viability of his First Amendment claim as follows:

> "For at least a quarter-century, this Court has made clear that even though a person has no 'right' to a valuable governmental benefit and even though the government may deny him the benefit for any number of reasons, *there are some reasons upon which the government may not rely. It may not deny a benefit to a person on a basis that infringes his constitutionally protected interests — especially, his interest in freedom of speech.* For if the government could deny a benefit to a person because of his constitutionally protected speech or associations, his exercise of those freedoms would in effect be penalized and inhibited. This would allow the government to

'produce a result which [it] could not command directly.' Such interference with constitutional rights is impermissible." (emphasis added).

Likewise, we find the assertion here that the employee petitioners and cross-respondents had no legal entitlement to promotion, transfer, or recall beside the point.

Respondents next argue that the employment decisions at issue here do not violate the First Amendment because the decisions are not punitive, do not in any way adversely affect the terms of employment, and therefore do not chill the exercise of protected belief and association by public employees. This is not credible. Employees who find themselves in dead-end positions due to their political backgrounds *are* adversely affected. They will feel a significant obligation to support political positions held by their superiors, and to refrain from acting on the political views they actually hold, in order to progress up the career ladder. Employees denied transfers to workplaces reasonably close to their homes until they join and work for the Republican Party will feel a daily pressure from their long commutes to do so. And employees who have been laid off may well feel compelled to engage in whatever political activity is necessary to regain regular paychecks and positions corresponding to their skill and experience.[7]

The same First Amendment concerns that underlay our decisions in *Elrod* and *Branti* are implicated here. Employees who do not compromise their beliefs stand to lose the considerable increases in pay and job satisfaction attendant to promotions, the hours and maintenance expenses that are consumed by long daily commutes, and even their jobs if they are not rehired after a "temporary" layoff. These are significant penalties and are imposed for the exercise of rights guaranteed by the First Amendment. Unless these patronage practices are narrowly tailored to further vital government interests, we must conclude that they impermissibly encroach on First Amendment freedoms.

We find, however, that our conclusions in *Elrod* and *Branti* are equally applicable to the patronage practices at issue here. A government's interest in securing effective employees can be met by discharging, demoting, or transferring staff members whose work is deficient. A government's interest in securing employees who will loyally implement its policies can be adequately served by choosing or dismissing certain high-level employees on the basis of their political views. Likewise, the "preservation of the democratic process" is no more furthered by the patronage promotions, transfers, and rehires at issue here than it is by patronage dismissals. First, "political parties are nurtured by other, less intrusive and equally effective methods." Political parties have already survived the substantial decline in patronage employment practices in this century. Second, patronage decidedly impairs the elective process by discouraging free political expression by public employees. Respondents, who include the Governor of Illinois and other state officials, do not suggest any other overriding government interest in favoring Republican Party supporters for promotion, transfer, and rehire.

---

[7] The complaint in this case states that Dan O'Brien was driven to do exactly this. After being rejected for recall by the Governor's Office, he allegedly pursued the support of a Republican Party official, despite his previous interest in the Democratic Party.

We therefore determine that promotions, transfers, and recalls after layoffs based on political affiliation or support are an impermissible infringement on the First Amendment rights of public employees. * * * The First Amendment is not a tenure provision, protecting public employees from actual or constructive discharge. [But it] prevents the government, except in the most compelling circumstances, from wielding its power to interfere with its employees' freedom to believe and associate, or to not believe and not associate. * * *

Petitioner James W. Moore presents the closely related question whether patronage hiring violates the First Amendment. Patronage hiring places burdens on free speech and association similar to those imposed by the patronage practices discussed above. A state job is valuable. Like most employment, it provides regular paychecks, health insurance, and other benefits. In addition, there may be openings with the State when business in the private sector is slow. There are also occupations for which the government is a major (or the only) source of employment, such as social workers, elementary school teachers, and prison guards. Thus, denial of a state job is a serious privation.

Nonetheless, respondents contend that the burden imposed is not of constitutional magnitude. Decades of decisions by this Court belie such a claim. We premised *Torcaso* v. *Watkins*, 367 U.S. 488 (1961), on our understanding that loss of a job opportunity for failure to compromise one's convictions states a constitutional claim. We held that Maryland could not refuse an appointee a commission for the position of notary public on the ground that he refused to declare his belief in God, because the required oath "unconstitutionally invades the appellant's freedom of belief and religion." *Id.*, at 496. In *Keyishian* v. *Board of Regents of Univ. of New York*, 385 U.S. 589, 609–610 (1967), we held a law affecting appointment and retention of teachers invalid because it premised employment on an unconstitutional restriction of political belief and association. In *Elfbrandt* v. *Russell*, 384 U.S. 11, 19 (1966), we struck down a loyalty oath which was a prerequisite for public employment.

Almost half a century ago, this Court made clear that the government "may not enact a regulation providing that no Republican . . . shall be appointed to federal office." *Public Workers* v. *Mitchell*, 330 U.S. 75, 100 (1947) [p. 699]. What the First Amendment precludes the government from commanding directly, it also precludes the government from accomplishing indirectly. Under our sustained precedent, conditioning hiring decisions on political belief and association plainly constitutes an unconstitutional condition, unless the government has a vital interest in doing so. We find no such government interest here, for the same reasons that we found that the government lacks justification for patronage promotions, transfers, or recalls. * * *

We hold that the rule of *Elrod* and *Branti* extends to promotion, transfer, recall, and hiring decisions based on party affiliation and support and that all of the petitioners and cross-respondents have stated claims upon which relief may be granted.

[Affirmed in part, reversed in part, and remanded.]

[The concurring opinion of JUSTICE STEVENS, responding to JUSTICE SCALIA's dissent, is omitted.]

JUSTICE SCALIA, with whom THE CHIEF JUSTICE [REHNQUIST] and JUSTICE KENNEDY join, and with whom JUSTICE O'CONNOR joins as to Parts II and III, dissenting.

Today the Court establishes the constitutional principle that party membership is not a permissible factor in the dispensation of government jobs, except those jobs for the performance of which party affiliation is an "appropriate requirement." It is hard to say precisely (or even generally) what that exception means, but if there is any category of jobs for whose performance party affiliation is not an appropriate requirement, it is the job of being a judge, where partisanship is not only unneeded but positively undesirable. It is, however, rare that a federal administration of one party will appoint a judge from another party. And it has always been rare. Thus, the new principle that the Court today announces will be enforced by a corps of judges (the Members of this Court included) who overwhelmingly owe their office to its violation. Something must be wrong here, and I suggest it is the Court.

The merit principle for government employment is probably the most favored in modern America, having been widely adopted by civil service legislation at both the state and federal levels. But there is another point of view * * *. As the merit principle has been extended and its effects increasingly felt[,] * * * we find that political leaders at all levels increasingly complain of the helplessness of elected government, unprotected by "party discipline," before the demands of small and cohesive interest groups.

The choice between patronage and the merit principle — or, to be more realistic about it, the choice between the desirable mix of merit and patronage principles in widely varying federal, state, and local political contexts — is not so clear that I would be prepared, as an original matter, to chisel a single, inflexible prescription into the Constitution. Fourteen years ago, in *Elrod* v. *Burns*, the Court did that. *Elrod* was limited however, as was the later decision of *Branti* v. *Finkel*, to patronage firings, leaving it to state and federal legislatures to determine when and where political affiliation could be taken into account in hirings and promotions. Today the Court makes its constitutional civil service reform absolute, extending to all decisions regarding government employment. Because the First Amendment has never been thought to require this disposition, which may well have disastrous consequences for our political system, I dissent.

I

The restrictions that the Constitution places upon the government in its capacity as lawmaker, *i.e.*, as the regulator of private conduct, are not the same as the restrictions that it places upon the government in its capacity as employer. We have recognized this in many contexts, with respect to many different constitutional guarantees. * * * With regard to freedom of speech in particular: Private citizens cannot be punished for speech of merely private concern, but government employees can be fired for that reason. *Connick* v. *Myers*, 461 U.S. 138, 147 (1983). Private citizens cannot be punished for partisan political activity, but federal and state employees can be dismissed and otherwise punished for that reason. *Public Workers* v. *Mitchell*, 330 U.S. 75, 101 (1947); *Civil Service Comm'n* v. *Letter Carriers*, 413 U.S. 548, 556 (1973) [p. 713]; *Broadrick* v. *Oklahoma*, 413 U.S. 601, 616–617 (1973).

Once it is acknowledged that the Constitution's prohibition against laws "abridging the freedom of speech" does not apply to laws enacted in the government's capacity as employer in the same way that it does to laws enacted in the government's capacity as regulator of private conduct, it may sometimes be difficult to assess what employment practices are permissible and what are not. That seems to me not a difficult question, however, in the present context. The provisions of the Bill of Rights were designed to restrain transient majorities from impairing long-recognized personal liberties. They did not create by implication novel individual rights overturning accepted political norms. Thus, when a practice not expressly prohibited by the text of the Bill of Rights bears the endorsement of a long tradition of open, widespread, and unchallenged use that dates back to the beginning of the Republic, we have no proper basis for striking it down.[1] Such a venerable and accepted tradition is not to be laid on the examining table and scrutinized for its conformity to some abstract principle of First Amendment adjudication devised by this Court. To the contrary, such traditions are themselves the stuff out of which the Court's principles are to be formed. They are, in these uncertain areas, the very points of reference by which the legitimacy or illegitimacy of *other* practices are to be figured out. When it appears that the latest "rule," or "three-part test," or "balancing test" devised by the Court has placed us on a collision course with such a landmark practice, it is the former that must be recalculated by us, and not the latter that must be abandoned by our citizens. I know of no other way to formulate a constitutional jurisprudence that reflects, as it should, the principles adhered to, over time, by the American people, rather than those favored by the personal (and necessarily shifting) philosophical dispositions of a majority of this Court.

I will not describe at length the claim of patronage to landmark status as one of our accepted political traditions. Justice Powell discussed it in his dissenting opinions in *Elrod* and *Branti*. Suffice it to say that patronage was, without any thought that it could be unconstitutional, a basis for government employment from the earliest days of the Republic until *Elrod* — and has continued unabated *since Elrod*, to the extent still permitted by that unfortunate decision. Given that unbroken tradition regarding the application of an ambiguous constitutional text,

---

[1] The customary invocation of *Brown* v. *Board of Education*, 347 U.S. 483 (1954), as demonstrating the dangerous consequences of this principle, is unsupportable. I argue for the role of tradition in giving content only to *ambiguous* constitutional text; no tradition can supersede the Constitution. In my view the Fourteenth Amendment's requirement of "equal protection of the laws," combined with the Thirteenth Amendment's abolition of the institution of black slavery, leaves no room for doubt that laws treating people differently because of their race are invalid. Moreover, even if one does not regard the Fourteenth Amendment as crystal clear on this point, a tradition of *unchallenged* validity did not exist with respect to the practice in *Brown*. To the contrary, in the 19th century the principle of "separate-but-equal" had been vigorously opposed on constitutional grounds, litigated up to this Court, and upheld only over the dissent of one of our historically most respected Justices. See *Plessy* v. *Ferguson*, 163 U.S. 537, 555–556 (1896) (Harlan, J., dissenting).

there was in my view no basis for holding that patronage-based dismissals violated the First Amendment — much less for holding, as the Court does today, that even patronage hiring does so.

II

Even accepting the Court's own mode of analysis, however, and engaging in "balancing" a tradition that ought to be part of the scales, *Elrod*, *Branti*, and today's extension of them seem to me wrong.

The Court limits patronage on the ground that the individual's interest in uncoerced belief and expression outweighs the systemic interests invoked to justify the practice. The opinion indicates that the government may prevail only if it proves that the practice is "narrowly tailored to further vital government interests."

That strict-scrutiny standard finds no support in our cases. Although our decisions establish that government employees do not lose all constitutional rights, we have consistently applied a lower level of scrutiny when "the governmental function operating . . . [is] not the power to regulate or license, as lawmaker, an entire trade or profession, or to control an entire branch of private business, but, rather, as proprietor, to manage [its] internal operatio[ns]. . . . " *Cafeteria & Restaurant Workers* v. *McElroy*, 367 U.S. 886, 896 (1961). When dealing with its own employees, the government may not act in a manner that is "patently arbitrary or discriminatory," but its regulations are valid if they bear a "rational connection" to the governmental end sought to be served, *Kelley* v. *Johnson*, 425 U.S. 238, 247 (1976).

In particular, restrictions on speech by public employees are not judged by the test applicable to similar restrictions on speech by nonemployees. We have said that "[a] governmental employer may subject its employees to such special restrictions on free expression as are reasonably necessary to promote effective government." *Brown* v. *Glines*, 444 U.S. 348, 356, n.13 (1980). In *Public Workers* v. *Mitchell*, 330 U.S., at 101, upholding provisions of the Hatch Act which prohibit political activities by federal employees, we said that "it is not necessary that the act regulated be anything more than an act reasonably deemed by Congress to interfere with the efficiency of the public service." We reaffirmed *Mitchell* in *Civil Service Comm'n* v. *Letter Carriers*, over a dissent by Justice Douglas arguing against application of a special standard to Government employees, except insofar as their "job performance" is concerned. We did not say that the Hatch Act was narrowly tailored to meet the government's interest, but merely deferred to the judgment of Congress, which we were not "in any position to dispute." Indeed, we recognized that the Act was not indispensably necessary to achieve those ends, since we repeatedly noted that "Congress at some time [may] come to a different view." In *Broadrick* v. *Oklahoma*, we upheld similar restrictions on state employees, though directed "at political expression which if engaged in by private persons would plainly be protected by the First and Fourteenth Amendments."

To the same effect are cases that specifically concern adverse employment action taken against public employees because of their speech. In *Pickering* v. *Board of*

Education of Township High School Dist., 391 U.S. 563, 568 (1968) [p. 707], we recognized:

> "[T]he State has interests as an employer in regulating the speech of its employees that differ significantly from those it possesses in connection with regulation of the speech of the citizenry in general. The problem in any case is to arrive at a balance between the interests of the [employee], as a citizen, in commenting upon matters of public concern and the interest of the State, as an employer, in promoting the efficiency of the public services it performs through its employees."

Because the restriction on speech is more attenuated when the government conditions employment than when it imposes criminal penalties, and because "government offices could not function if every employment decision became a constitutional matter," we have held that government employment decisions taken on the basis of an employee's speech do not "abridg[e] the freedom of speech" merely because they fail the narrow-tailoring and compelling-interest tests applicable to direct regulation of speech. We have not subjected such decisions to strict scrutiny, but have accorded "a wide degree of deference to the employer's judgment" that an employee's speech will interfere with close working relationships.

When the government takes adverse action against an employee on the basis of his political affiliation (an interest whose constitutional protection is derived from the interest in speech), the same analysis applies. That is why both the *Elrod* plurality, and the opinion concurring in the judgment, as well as *Branti*, and the Court today, rely on *Perry* v. *Sindermann*, 408 U.S. 593 (1972), a case that applied the test announced in *Pickering*, not the strict-scrutiny test applied to restrictions imposed on the public at large. Since the government may dismiss an employee for political *speech* "reasonably deemed by Congress to interfere with the efficiency of the public service," *Public Workers* v. *Mitchell*, it follows, *a fortiori*, that the government may dismiss an employee for political *affiliation* if "reasonably necessary to promote effective government."

While it is clear from the above cases that the normal "strict scrutiny" that we accord to government regulation of speech is not applicable in this field, the precise test that replaces it is not so clear; we have used various formulations. The one that appears in the case dealing with an employment practice closest in its effects to patronage is whether the practice could be "reasonably deemed" by the enacting legislature to further a legitimate goal. *Public Workers* v. *Mitchell*. For purposes of my ensuing discussion, however, I will apply a less permissive standard that seems more in accord with our general "balancing" test: Can the governmental advantages of this employment practice reasonably be deemed to outweigh its "coercive" effects? * * *

* * * The Court holds that the governmental benefits of patronage cannot reasonably be thought to outweigh its "coercive" effects (even the lesser "coercive" effects of patronage hiring as opposed to patronage firing) not merely in 1990 in the State of Illinois, but at any time in any of the numerous political subdivisions of this vast country. It seems to me that that categorical pronouncement reflects a naive vision of politics and an inadequate appreciation of the systemic effects of patronage

in promoting political stability and facilitating the social and political integration of previously powerless groups.

The whole point of my dissent is that the desirability of patronage is a policy question to be decided by the people's representatives; I do not mean, therefore, to endorse that system. But in order to demonstrate that a legislature could reasonably determine that its benefits outweigh its "coercive" effects, I must describe those benefits as the proponents of patronage see them: As Justice Powell discussed at length in his *Elrod* dissent, patronage stabilizes political parties and prevents excessive political fragmentation — both of which are results in which States have a strong governmental interest. Party strength requires the efforts of the rank and file, especially in "the dull periods between elections," to perform such tasks as organizing precincts, registering new voters, and providing constituent services. Even the most enthusiastic supporter of a party's program will shrink before such drudgery, and it is folly to think that ideological conviction alone will motivate sufficient numbers to keep the party going through the off years. * * *

The Court simply refuses to acknowledge the link between patronage and party discipline, and between that and party success. * * * It is unpersuasive to claim, as the Court does, that party workers are obsolete because campaigns are now conducted through media and other money-intensive means. Those techniques have supplemented but not supplanted personal contacts. Certainly they have not made personal contacts unnecessary in campaigns for the lower level offices that are the foundations of party strength, nor have they replaced the myriad functions performed by party regulars not directly related to campaigning. And to the extent such techniques have replaced older methods of campaigning (partly in response to the limitations the Court has placed on patronage), the political system is not clearly better off. Increased reliance on money-intensive campaign techniques tends to entrench those in power much more effectively than patronage — but without the attendant benefit of strengthening the party system. A challenger can more easily obtain the support of party workers (who can expect to be rewarded even if the candidate loses — if not this year, then the next) than the financial support of political action committees (which will generally support incumbents, who are likely to prevail).

It is self-evident that eliminating patronage will significantly undermine party discipline; and that as party discipline wanes, so will the strength of the two-party system. But, says the Court, "[p]olitical parties have already survived the substantial decline in patronage employment practices in this century." This is almost verbatim what was said in *Elrod.* Fourteen years later it seems much less convincing. Indeed, now that we have witnessed, in 18 of the last 22 years, an Executive Branch of the Federal Government under the control of one party while the Congress is entirely or (for two years) partially within the control of the other party; now that we have undergone the most recent federal election, in which 98% of the incumbents, of whatever party, were returned to office; and now that we have seen elected officials changing their political affiliation with unprecedented readiness, the statement that "political parties have already survived" has a positively whistling-in-the-graveyard character to it. Parties have assuredly survived — but as what? As the forges upon which many of the essential compromises of American political life are hammered out? Or merely as convenient vehicles for the conducting of national Presidential elections?

The patronage system does not, of course, merely foster political parties in general; it fosters the two-party system in particular. When getting a job, as opposed to effectuating a particular substantive policy, is an available incentive for party workers, those attracted by that incentive are likely to work for the party that has the best chance of displacing the "ins," rather than for some splinter group that has a more attractive political philosophy but little hope of success. Not only is a two-party system more likely to emerge, but the differences between those parties are more likely to be moderated, as each has a relatively greater interest in appealing to a majority of the electorate and a relatively lesser interest in furthering philosophies or programs that are far from the mainstream. The stabilizing effects of such a system are obvious. In the context of electoral laws we have approved the States' pursuit of such stability, and their avoidance of the "splintered parties and unrestrained factionalism [that] may do significant damage to the fabric of government." *Storer* v. *Brown*, 415 U.S. 724, 736 (1974) [p. 513] (upholding law disqualifying persons from running as independents if affiliated with a party in the past year).

Equally apparent is the relatively destabilizing nature of a system in which candidates cannot rely upon patronage-based party loyalty for their campaign support, but must attract workers and raise funds by appealing to various interest groups. * * *

Patronage, moreover, has been a powerful means of achieving the social and political integration of excluded groups. By supporting and ultimately dominating a particular party "machine," racial and ethnic minorities have — on the basis of their politics rather than their race or ethnicity — acquired the patronage awards the machine had power to confer. No one disputes the historical accuracy of this observation, and there is no reason to think that patronage can no longer serve that function. The abolition of patronage, however, prevents groups that have only recently obtained political power, especially blacks, from following this path to economic and social advancement. * * *

While the patronage system has the benefits argued for above, it also has undoubted disadvantages. It facilitates financial corruption, such as salary kickbacks and partisan political activity on government-paid time. It reduces the efficiency of government, because it creates incentives to hire more and less-qualified workers and because highly qualified workers are reluctant to accept jobs that may only last until the next election. And, of course, it applies some greater or lesser inducement for individuals to join and work for the party in power.

To hear the Court tell it, this last is the greatest evil. That is not my view, and it has not historically been the view of the American people. Corruption and inefficiency, rather than abridgment of liberty, have been the major criticisms leading to enactment of the civil service laws — for the very good reason that the patronage system does not have as harsh an effect upon conscience, expression, and association as the Court suggests. As described above, it is the nature of the pragmatic, patronage-based, two-party system to build alliances and to suppress rather than foster ideological tests for participation in the division of political "spoils." What the patronage system ordinarily demands of the party worker is loyalty to, and activity on behalf of, the organization itself rather than a set of political beliefs. He is generally free to urge *within the organization* the adoption of any political position; but if that position is rejected he must vote and work for the party nonetheless. The diversity of political expression (other than expression of party loyalty) is channeled, in other words, to a different stage — to the contests for party endorsement rather than the partisan elections. It is undeniable, of course, that the patronage system entails some constraint upon the expression of views, particularly at the partisan-election stage, and considerable constraint upon the employee's right to associate with the other party. It greatly exaggerates these, however, to describe them as a general "coercion of belief." Indeed, it greatly exaggerates them to call them "coercion" at all, since we generally make a distinction between inducement and compulsion. The public official offered a bribe is not "coerced" to violate the law, and the private citizen offered a patronage job is not "coerced" to work for the party. In sum, I do not deny that the patronage system influences or redirects, perhaps to a substantial degree, individual political expression and political association. But like the many generations of Americans that have preceded us, I do not consider that a significant impairment of free speech or free association.

In emphasizing the advantages and minimizing the disadvantages (or at least minimizing one of the disadvantages) of the patronage system, I do not mean to suggest that that system is best. It may not always be; it may never be. To oppose our *Elrod-Branti* jurisprudence, one need not believe that the patronage system is *necessarily* desirable; nor even that it is always and everywhere *arguably* desirable; but merely that it is a political arrangement that may sometimes be a reasonable choice, and should therefore be left to the judgment of the people's elected representatives. The choice in question, I emphasize, is not just between patronage and a merit-based civil service, but rather among various combinations of the two that may suit different political units and different eras: permitting patronage hiring, for example, but prohibiting patronage dismissal; permitting patronage in most municipal agencies but prohibiting it in the police department; or permitting it in the mayor's office but prohibiting it everywhere else. I find it impossible to say that, always and everywhere, all of these choices fail our "balancing" test.

The last point explains why *Elrod* and *Branti* should be overruled, rather than merely not extended. Even in the field of constitutional adjudication, where the pull of *stare decisis* is at its weakest, one is reluctant to depart from precedent. But when that precedent is not only wrong, not only recent, not only contradicted by a long prior tradition, but also has proved unworkable in practice, then all reluctance ought to disappear. In my view that is the situation here. Though unwilling to leave it to the political process to draw the line between desirable and undesirable patronage, the Court has neither been prepared to rule that no such line exists (*i.e.*, that *all* patronage is unconstitutional) nor able to design the line itself in a manner that judges, lawyers, and public employees can understand. *Elrod* allowed patronage dismissals of persons in "policymaking" or "confidential" positions. *Branti* retreated from that formulation, asking instead "whether the hiring authority can demonstrate that party affiliation is an appropriate requirement for the effective performance of the public office involved." What that means is anybody's guess. * * *

Since the current doctrine leaves many employees utterly in the dark about whether their jobs are protected, they are likely to play it safe. On the other side, the exception was designed to permit the government to implement its electoral mandate. But unless the government is fairly sure that dismissal is permitted, it will leave the politically uncongenial official in place, since an incorrect decision will expose it to lengthy litigation and a large damages award, perhaps even against the responsible officials personally.

This uncertainty and confusion are not the result of the fact that *Elrod*, and then *Branti*, chose the wrong "line." My point is that there is no right line — or at least no right line that can be nationally applied and that is known by judges. Once we reject as the criterion a long political tradition showing that party-based employment is entirely permissible, yet are unwilling (as any reasonable person must be) to replace it with the principle that party-based employment is entirely impermissible, we have left the realm of law and entered the domain of political science, seeking to ascertain when and where the undoubted benefits of political hiring and firing are worth its undoubted costs. The answer to that will vary from State to State, and indeed from city to city, even if one rejects out of hand (as the *Branti* line does) the benefits associated with party stability. Indeed, the answer will even vary from year to year. During one period, for example, it may be desirable for the manager of a municipally owned public utility to be a career specialist, insulated from the political system. During another, when the efficient operation of that utility or even its very existence has become a burning political issue, it may be desirable that he be hired and fired on a political basis. The appropriate "mix" of party-based employment is a political question if there ever was one, and we should give it back to the voters of the various political units to decide, through civil service legislation crafted to suit the time and place, which mix is best.

III

Even were I not convinced that *Elrod* and *Branti* were wrongly decided, I would hold that they should not be extended beyond their facts, viz., actual discharge of employees for their political affiliation. Those cases invalidated patronage firing in order to prevent the "restraint it places on freedoms of belief and association." The loss of one's current livelihood is an appreciably greater constraint than such other disappointments as the failure to obtain a promotion or selection for an uncongenial transfer. * * *

Notes and Questions

1. Justices Brennan, Powell, and Scalia engaged in a lively debate in *Elrod*, *Branti*, and *Rutan* over the importance of patronage for the well-being of political parties. Who had the better of that argument? In that regard, consider Cynthia Grant Bowman, *"We Don't Want Anybody Anybody Sent": The Death of Patronage Hiring in Chicago*, 86 Nw. U. L. REV. 57 (1991), which contends that in practice, political patronage has not been generally beneficial to political parties. For example, Bowman argues that, in many cities, political patronage often did not aid disadvantaged immigrant and minority groups, in part due to the limited number of jobs that could be filled by such patronage.

2.   In their dissenting opinions, Justice Powell and Justice Scalia made much of the capacity of patronage to promote the two-party system. How significant do you think the government interest is in limiting the number of competing parties? We consider that question more extensively in Chapter 6, § D.

3.   Assuming it is proper for the government to promote a stable two-party system, is patronage necessary to achieve that end? Duverger's Law holds that an electoral structure of single-member districts with plurality winners itself encourages the development of two (and only two) centrist parties. The "Law" is not universal — regional parties have been successful in nations that use single-member, first-past-the-post systems — but perhaps it indicates that the viability of the two-party system is not jeopardized by the *Elrod/Branti/Rutan* holdings. *See generally* William H. Riker, *The Two-Party System and Duverger's Law: An Essay on the History of Political Science*, 76 AM. POL. SCI. REV. 753 (1982); Maurice Duverger, *Factors in a Two-Party and Multiparty System, in* PARTY POLITICS AND PRESSURE GROUPS 23 (1972).

4.   In the latter part of the twentieth century, many political campaigns at the national, state, and local levels have been characterized as being candidate-driven with regard to strategy, fund-raising, and the mobilization of workers, with the party itself taking a largely secondary role. Is it fair to attribute, even in part, this decline of the power of political parties to cases like *Elrod* and its progeny? Or did these cases mainly follow rather than cause this trend? For an argument in favor of the latter view, see Richard L. Hasen, *Patronage, in* 4 ENCYCLOPEDIA OF THE AMERICAN CONSTITUTION 1885, 1886 (Leonard W. Levy & Kenneth L. Karst eds., 2d ed. 2000).

5.   Whatever the precise linkage between patronage and the health of political parties, one apparent effect of *Elrod* and its progeny was to route patronage away from government jobs and toward government contracts with private firms. This trend was exacerbated by stagnation or declines in public employment, and increasing efforts to privatize certain traditionally governmental functions. Cynthia Grant Bowman, *The Supreme Court's Patronage Decisions and the Theory and Practice of Politics, in* THE U.S. SUPREME COURT AND THE ELECTORAL PROCESS 126, 140–42 (David K. Ryden ed., 2d ed. 2002). Should patronage contracting be treated the same way as patronage in employment?

The Supreme Court confronted this issue in the companion cases of *Board of County Commissioners, Wabaunsee County v. Umbehr*, 518 U.S. 668 (1996), and *O'Hare Truck Service v. City of Northlake*, 518 U.S. 712 (1996). In *Umbehr*, the Court held that when a county cancelled a trash-hauling contract, allegedly because of the hauler's criticism of the county, the hauler had a cause of action for violation of his First Amendment rights. In *O'Hare*, the Court held that an independent contractor, allegedly dropped from a regularly used list due to the failure to make campaign contributions to the mayor, also had a cause of action for violation of free-speech rights. In both cases, the Court engaged in a case-by-case balancing of the interests of the government to contract, and of the free-speech rights of contractors, drawing in part on cases such as *Pickering v. Board of Education*, 391 U.S. 563 (1968) [p. 707], involving public employees. The Court held (in *O'Hare*) that such a balancing of interests had not been appropriate in *Elrod* or *Branti*, since in those cases there had been a "raw test of political affiliation." Justice Scalia, joined by Justice Thomas, dissented in both *Umbehr* and *O'Hare*. Chief Justice Rehnquist, Justice Kennedy, and Justice O'Connor, each of whom had dissented in *Rutan*, were in the majority in both cases; the latter two Justices wrote the majority opinions in *O'Hare* and *Umbehr*, respectively. In his dissent, Justice Scalia approved of the use of a *Pickering*-type balancing test to resolve those cases, but argued that *Umbehr* and *O'Hare* were incoherent in attempting to distinguish intrusions on rights of "free speech" (to which balancing applied) and of political affiliation (to which the *Elrod/Branti/Rutan* rules applied).

6. In *Rutan*, Justice Scalia pointed out the difficulties in determining the jobs for which political affiliation would be a relevant qualification. Consider how one court has grappled with this issue. The United States Court of Appeals for the Sixth Circuit considered the following government jobs to fall within the exception: (1) positions specifically named in law to which discretionary authority is granted concerning law enforcement or policy "of political concern"; (2) positions to which a significant amount of such discretionary authority has been explicitly or implicitly delegated; (3) confidential advisors to such position-holders; or (4) positions that are filled by balancing out political party representation or by balancing out selections made by government parties. *McCloud v. Testa*, 97 F.3d 1536, 1557 (6th Cir. 1996). A court should consider the inherent duties of a position, rather than the actual tasks undertaken by an employee, and a position need not fit perfectly into one of these categories in order to fit under the exception. *Silberstein v. City of Dayton*, 440 F.3d 306, 319 (6th Cir. 2006). How easy or difficult is it to apply these multi-factor tests?

7. *Problem.* Analyze whether persons holding the following government positions should receive First Amendment protection against patronage-based dismissals:

A. Assistant County Attorneys, charged with "representing the County in court cases and in the performance of other legal work." *See Gordon v. County of Rockland*, 110 F.3d 886 (2d Cir. 1997); *Fazio v. City and County of San Francisco*, 125 F.3d 1328 (9th Cir. 1997); *Finkelstein v. Bergna*, 924 F.2d 1449 (9th Cir. 1991). *See also Shade v. Rackauckas*, 2004 Cal. App. Unpub. LEXIS 7691 (Cal. Ct. App. 2004) (drawing a distinction between "assistant district attorneys" and "senior deputy district attorneys" and characterizing only the former as possessing policymaking responsibilities).

B. An attorney employed by a private firm that does work for the City Attorney, fired after public officials told the firm that it would lose City work unless the plaintiff's political opposition to the mayor were stopped. *See Biggs v. Best*, 189 F.3d 989 (9th Cir. 1999).

C. Deputy sheriff. *Compare Hall v. Tollett*, 128 F.3d 418 (6th Cir. 1997) (granting protection), *with Cutcliffe v. Cochran*, 117 F.3d 1353 (11th Cir. 1997), *and Upton v. Thompson*, 930 F.2d 1209 (7th Cir. 1991) (denying it). *See also DiRuzza v. County of Tehama*, 206 F.3d 1304 (9th Cir. 2000).

D. Chief deputy sheriff, which differs from the position of deputy sheriff only in that the chief deputy would assume the responsibilities of the sheriff if the sheriff were unable to perform. *See Hall,* 128 F.3d at 425–26.

E. Correctional officer. *See Flenner v. Sheahan,* 107 F.3d 459 (7th Cir. 1997).

F. Administrative assistant to the mayor. *Faughender v. City of North Olmsted,* 927 F.2d 909 (6th Cir. 1991).

G. Administrative assistants in the County Prosecutor's Office. *See Hobler v. Brueher,* 325 F.3d 1145 (9th Cir. 2003).

H. Administrative assistant to the county engineer or the state Department of Transportation. *See Smith v. Sushka,* 117 F.3d 965 (6th Cir. 1997); *Rice v. Ohio Department of Transportation,* 14 F.3d 1133 (6th Cir. 1994).

I. Director of administrative services for the State Treasurer's Office. *See Garcia-Montoya v. State Treasurer's Office,* 16 P.3d 1084 (N.M. 2001).

8. In his dissent in *Rutan,* Justice Scalia wryly observed that federal judges, many of whom themselves were nominated by Presidents based on political affiliation, were now holding that public officials could not hire or fire based on such affiliations. If *state* judges are appointed based, in whole or in part, on their political affiliation, does that violate the rights of lawyers, wishing to be considered for such appointments, who do not share such affiliations? In Ohio, for example, judges are selected via competitive, non-partisan elections. The governor is granted unfettered authority in the Ohio constitution to fill judicial vacancies, and the appointee, to retain his office, must then run in the next election. There is considerable evidence that, with very few exceptions, Ohio governors have filled such vacancies based on political affiliation, that is, restricting consideration to lawyers from their parties.

In *Newman v. Voinovich,* 986 F.2d 159 (6th Cir. 1993), a Democratic lawyer was not considered to fill a vacancy by a Republican governor. (Note: One of the authors of this casebook served as co-counsel for the plaintiff.) The court held that this practice did not state a claim under *Elrod* and *Branti.* State judges, the court held, fell under the exception of those cases, since "judges are policymakers because their political beliefs influence and dictate their decisions on important jurisprudential matters." *Id.* at 163. Is this a proper application of the exception as described in *Branti*? Is "party affiliation . . . an appropriate requirement for the effective performance" of a judicial office? Should it matter that judges work in a branch of government separate from the appointer? Or that a state has, in effect, chosen to permit the governor to take political considerations into account in filling judicial vacancies? Or that Ohio law provides that judicial elections be officially non-partisan? For discussion, see Michael E. Solimine, *Constitutional Restrictions on the Partisan Appointment of Federal and State Judges,* 61 U. Cin. L. Rev. 955 (1993).

9. Relatedly, does the First Amendment protect administrative law judges from dismissal based on political ideology or affiliation? *See Roldan-Plumey v. Cerezo-Suarez,* 115 F.3d 58 (1st Cir. 1997). What about domestic-relations-court referees? *See Mumford v. Zieba,* 4 F.3d 429 (6th Cir. 1993).

10. *Public Workers v. Mitchell* opined that "a regulation providing that no Republican . . . shall be appointed to federal office" would be unconstitutional. If you think the Court was wrong in *Elrod*, *Branti*, and *Rutan* to construct a constitutional right against the use of patronage as a qualification for certain types of government service, do you also disagree with *Mitchell*'s dictum?

I. JUDICIAL CANDIDATES' SPEECH

Thirty-nine states elect some or all of their judges, either in contested elections or "retention" elections. Within the former category, some states use partisan elections, in which the candidates' parties are identified on the ballot, while other states use nonpartisan elections. Even in states with nonpartisan ballots, however, parties (just like every other private association) may endorse and campaign for candidates. *See Geary v. Renne*, 911 F.2d 280 (9th Cir. 1990) (en banc). In retention elections, a sitting judge (initially selected by appointment) appears unopposed on the ballot, and voters are asked whether he or she should be retained in office. The appointment/retention system is known alternately as the Missouri Plan, after the state that first implemented it, or, misleadingly, as "merit selection." *See* Michael R. Dimino, *The Futile Quest for a System of Judicial "Merit" Selection*, 67 ALB. L. REV. 803, 803 (2004) (calling "merit selection "a propagandistic misnomer [because] nothing ensures that judges chosen under that plan will be better than judges under any other system").

Despite the fact that the vast majority of state judges must face the voters to continue in office, judicial candidates until recently had been restricted in their campaign speech by state codes of judicial conduct. Drafters of the codes reasoned that judicial candidates' appeals to voters are inconsistent with the judicial function — judges should seek to apply the law rather than to achieve results that will be popular with the electorate. Opponents saw the restrictions not only as paternalistic and inconsistent with the very idea of electing judges, but as a means to promote the continuance in office of judges with unpopular views. The following case struck down one limitation on judicial campaign speech, but the constitutionality of other speech restrictions remains to be decided.

REPUBLICAN PARTY OF MINNESOTA v. WHITE
Supreme Court of the United States
536 U.S. 765, 122 S. Ct. 2528, 153 L. Ed. 2d 694 (2002)

JUSTICE SCALIA delivered the opinion of the Court [in which CHIEF JUSTICE REHNQUIST, JUSTICE O'CONNOR, JUSTICE KENNEDY, and JUSTICE THOMAS join].

The question presented in this case is whether the First Amendment permits the Minnesota Supreme Court to prohibit candidates for judicial election in that State from announcing their views on disputed legal and political issues.

I

Since Minnesota's admission to the Union in 1858, the State's Constitution has provided for the selection of all state judges by popular election. Since 1912, those elections have been nonpartisan. Since 1974, they have been subject to a legal restriction which states that a "candidate for a judicial office, including an incumbent judge," shall not "announce his or her views on disputed legal or political issues." This prohibition, promulgated by the Minnesota Supreme Court and based on Canon 7(B) of the 1972 American Bar Association (ABA) Model Code of Judicial Conduct, is known as the "announce clause." Incumbent judges who violate it are subject to discipline, including removal, censure, civil penalties, and suspension without pay. Lawyers who run for judicial office also must comply with the announce clause. Those who violate it are subject to, *inter alia*, disbarment, suspension, and probation. * * *

[Gregory] Wersal [a candidate for the Minnesota Supreme Court in 1996 and 1998] filed this lawsuit * * *, seeking, *inter alia*, a declaration that the announce clause violates the First Amendment and an injunction against its enforcement. Wersal alleged that he was forced to refrain from announcing his views on disputed issues during the 1998 campaign, to the point where he declined response to questions put to him by the press and public, out of concern that he might run afoul of the announce clause. Other plaintiffs in the suit, including the Minnesota Republican Party, alleged that, because the clause kept Wersal from announcing his views, they were unable to learn those views and support or oppose his candidacy accordingly. The parties filed cross-motions for summary judgment, and the District Court found in favor of respondents, holding that the announce clause did not violate the First Amendment. [T]he United States Court of Appeals for the Eighth Circuit affirmed. We granted certiorari.

II

Before considering the constitutionality of the announce clause, we must be clear about its meaning. * * * We know that "announcing . . . views" on an issue covers much more than *promising* to decide an issue a particular way. The prohibition extends to the candidate's mere statement of his current position, even if he does not bind himself to maintain that position after election. All the parties agree this is the case, because the Minnesota Code contains a so-called "pledges or promises" clause, which *separately* prohibits judicial candidates from making "pledges or promises of conduct in office other than the faithful and impartial performance of the duties of the office" — a prohibition that is not challenged here and on which we express no view.

There are, however, some limitations that the Minnesota Supreme Court has placed upon the scope of the announce clause that are not (to put it politely) immediately apparent from its text. The statements that formed the basis of the complaint against Wersal in 1996 included criticism of past decisions of the Minnesota Supreme Court. One piece of campaign literature stated that "the Minnesota Supreme Court has issued decisions which are marked by their disregard for the Legislature and a lack of common sense." It went on to criticize a decision excluding from evidence confessions by criminal defendants that were not tape-recorded, asking "should we conclude that because the Supreme Court does not trust police, it allows confessed criminals to go free?" It criticized a decision striking down a state law restricting welfare benefits, asserting that "it's the

Legislature which should set our spending policies." And it criticized a decision requiring public financing of abortions for poor women as "unprecedented" and a "pro-abortion stance." Although one would think that all of these statements touched on disputed legal or political issues, they did not (or at least do not now) fall within the scope of the announce clause. The Judicial Board issued an opinion stating that judicial candidates may criticize past decisions, and the Lawyers Board refused to discipline Wersal for the foregoing statements because, in part, it thought they did not violate the announce clause. The Eighth Circuit relied on the Judicial Board's opinion in upholding the announce clause, and the Minnesota Supreme Court recently embraced the Eighth Circuit's interpretation.

There are yet further limitations upon the apparent plain meaning of the announce clause: In light of the constitutional concerns, the District Court construed the clause to reach only disputed issues that are likely to come before the candidate if he is elected judge. The Eighth Circuit accepted this limiting interpretation by the District Court, and in addition construed the clause to allow general discussions of case law and judicial philosophy. The Supreme Court of Minnesota adopted these interpretations as well * * *.

It seems to us, however, that — like the text of the announce clause itself — these limitations upon the text of the announce clause are not all that they appear to be. First, respondents acknowledged at oral argument that statements critical of past judicial decisions are *not* permissible if the candidate also states that he is against *stare decisis*. Thus, candidates must choose between stating their views critical of past decisions and stating their views in opposition to *stare decisis*. Or, to look at it more concretely, they may state their view that prior decisions were erroneous only if they do not assert that they, if elected, have any power to eliminate erroneous decisions. Second, limiting the scope of the clause to issues likely to come before a court is not much of a limitation at all. One would hardly expect the "disputed legal or political issues" raised in the course of a state judicial election to include such matters as whether the Federal Government should end the embargo of Cuba. Quite obviously, they will be those legal or political disputes that are the proper (or by past decisions have been made the improper) business of the state courts. And within that relevant category, "there is almost no legal or political issue that is unlikely to come before a judge of an American court, state or federal, of general jurisdiction." Third, construing the clause to allow "general" discussions of case law and judicial philosophy turns out to be of little help in an election campaign. At oral argument, respondents gave, as an example of this exception, that a candidate is free to assert that he is a "strict constructionist." But that, like most other philosophical generalities, has little meaningful content for the electorate unless it is exemplified by application to a particular issue of construction likely to come before a court — for example, whether a particular statute runs afoul of any provision of the Constitution. Respondents conceded that the announce clause would prohibit the candidate from exemplifying his philosophy in this fashion. Without such application to real-life issues, all candidates can claim to be "strict constructionists" with equal (and unhelpful) plausibility.

In any event, it is clear that the announce clause prohibits a judicial candidate from stating his views on any specific nonfanciful legal question within the province of the court for which he is running, except in the context of discussing past decisions — and in the latter context as well, if he expresses the view that he is not bound by *stare decisis*.[5]

Respondents contend that this still leaves plenty of topics for discussion on the campaign trail. These include a candidate's "character," "education," "work habits," and "how [he] would handle administrative duties if elected." Indeed, the Judicial Board has printed a list of preapproved questions which judicial candidates are allowed to answer. These include how the candidate feels about cameras in the courtroom, how he would go about reducing the caseload, how the costs of judicial administration can be reduced, and how he proposes to ensure that minorities and women are treated more fairly by the court system. Whether this list of preapproved subjects, and other topics not prohibited by the announce clause, adequately fulfill the First Amendment's guarantee of freedom of speech is the question to which we now turn.

III

As the Court of Appeals recognized, the announce clause both prohibits speech on the basis of its content and burdens a category of speech that is "at the core of our First Amendment freedoms" — speech about the qualifications of candidates for public office. The Court of Appeals concluded that the proper test to be applied to determine the constitutionality of such a restriction is what our cases have called strict scrutiny; the parties do not dispute that this is correct. Under the strict-scrutiny test, respondents have the burden to prove that the announce clause is (1) narrowly tailored, to serve (2) a compelling state interest. *E.g.*, *Eu* v. *San Francisco County Democratic Central Comm.*, 489 U.S. 214, 222 (1989) [p. 455]. In order for respondents to show that the announce clause is narrowly tailored, they must demonstrate that it does not "unnecessarily circumscribe protected expression." *Brown* v. *Hartlage*, 456 U.S. 45, 54 (1982) [p. 585].

The Court of Appeals concluded that respondents had established two interests as sufficiently compelling to justify the announce clause: preserving the impartiality of the state judiciary and preserving the appearance of the impartiality of the state judiciary. Respondents reassert these two interests before us, arguing that the first is compelling because it protects the due process rights of litigants, and that the second is compelling because it preserves public confidence in the judiciary. Respondents are rather vague, however, about what they mean by "impartiality."
* * *

---

[5] In 1990, in response to concerns that its 1972 Model Canon — which was the basis for Minnesota's announce clause — violated the First Amendment, the ABA replaced that canon with a provision that prohibits a judicial candidate from making "statements that commit or appear to commit the candidate with respect to cases, controversies or issues that are likely to come before the court." ABA Model Code of Judicial Conduct, Canon 5(A)(3)(d)(ii) (2000). At oral argument, respondents argued that the limiting constructions placed upon Minnesota's announce clause by the Eighth Circuit, and adopted by the Minnesota Supreme Court, render the scope of the clause no broader than the ABA's 1990 canon. * * * We do not know whether the announce clause (as interpreted by state authorities) and the 1990 ABA canon are one and the same. No aspect of our constitutional analysis turns on this question.

A

One meaning of "impartiality" in the judicial context — and of course its root meaning — is the lack of bias for or against either *party* to the proceeding. Impartiality in this sense assures equal application of the law. That is, it guarantees a party that the judge who hears his case will apply the law to him in the same way he applies it to any other party. This is the traditional sense in which the term is used. It is also the sense in which it is used in the cases cited by respondents and *amici* for the proposition that an impartial judge is essential to due process. *Tumey* v. *Ohio*, 273 U.S. 510, 523, 531–534 (1927) (judge violated due process by sitting in a case in which it would be in his financial interest to find against one of the parties); *Aetna Life Ins. Co.* v. *Lavoie*, 475 U.S. 813, 822–825 (1986) (same); *Ward* v. *Monroeville*, 409 U.S. 57, 58–62 (1972) (same).

We think it plain that the announce clause is not narrowly tailored to serve impartiality (or the appearance of impartiality) in this sense. Indeed, the clause is barely tailored to serve that interest *at all*, inasmuch as it does not restrict speech for or against particular *parties*, but rather speech for or against particular *issues*. To be sure, when a case arises that turns on a legal issue on which the judge (as a candidate) had taken a particular stand, the party taking the opposite stand is likely to lose. But not because of any bias against that party, or favoritism toward the other party. *Any* party taking that position is just as likely to lose. The judge is applying the law (as he sees it) evenhandedly.

B

It is perhaps possible to use the term "impartiality" in the judicial context (though this is certainly not a common usage) to mean lack of preconception in favor of or against a particular *legal view*. This sort of impartiality would be concerned, not with guaranteeing litigants equal application of the law, but rather with guaranteeing them an equal chance to persuade the court on the legal points in their case. Impartiality in this sense may well be an interest served by the announce clause, but it is not a *compelling* state interest, as strict scrutiny requires. A judge's lack of predisposition regarding the relevant legal issues in a case has never been thought a necessary component of equal justice, and with good reason. For one thing, it is virtually impossible to find a judge who does not have preconceptions about the law. As then-JUSTICE REHNQUIST observed of our own Court: "Since most Justices come to this bench no earlier than their middle years, it would be unusual if they had not by that time formulated at least some tentative notions that would influence them in their interpretation of the sweeping clauses of the Constitution and their interaction with one another. It would be not merely unusual, but extraordinary, if they had not at least given opinions as to constitutional issues in their previous legal careers." *Laird* v. *Tatum*, 409 U.S. 824, 835 (1972) (memorandum opinion). Indeed, even if it were possible to select judges who did not have preconceived views on legal issues, it would hardly be desirable to do so. "Proof that a Justice's mind at the time he joined the Court was a complete *tabula rasa* in the area of constitutional adjudication would be evidence of lack of qualification, not lack of bias." *Ibid.* * * * And since avoiding judicial preconceptions on legal issues is neither possible nor desirable, pretending otherwise by attempting to preserve the "appearance" of that type of impartiality can hardly be a compelling state interest either.

C

A third possible meaning of "impartiality" (again not a common one) might be described as openmindedness. This quality in a judge demands, not that he have no preconceptions on legal issues, but that he be willing to consider views that oppose his preconceptions, and remain open to persuasion, when the issues arise in a pending case. This sort of impartiality seeks to guarantee each litigant, not an *equal* chance to win the legal points in the case, but at least *some* chance of doing so. It may well be that impartiality in this sense, and the appearance of it, are desirable in the judiciary, but we need not pursue that inquiry, since we do not believe the Minnesota Supreme Court adopted the announce clause for that purpose.

Respondents argue that the announce clause serves the interest in openmindedness, or at least in the appearance of openmindedness, because it relieves a judge from pressure to rule a certain way in order to maintain consistency with statements the judge has previously made. The problem is, however, that statements in election campaigns are such an infinitesimal portion of the public commitments to legal positions that judges (or judges-to-be) undertake, that this object of the prohibition is implausible. Before they arrive on the bench (whether by election or otherwise) judges have often committed themselves on legal issues that they must later rule upon. More common still is a judge's confronting a legal issue on which he has expressed an opinion while on the bench. Most frequently, of course, that prior expression will have occurred in ruling on an earlier case. But judges often state their views on disputed legal issues outside the context of adjudication — in classes that they conduct, and in books and speeches. Like the ABA Codes of Judicial Conduct, the Minnesota Code not only permits but encourages this. That is quite incompatible with the notion that the need for openmindedness (or for the appearance of openmindedness) lies behind the prohibition at issue here.

The short of the matter is this: In Minnesota, a candidate for judicial office may not say "I think it is constitutional for the legislature to prohibit same-sex marriages." He may say the very same thing, however, up until the very day before he declares himself a candidate, and may say it repeatedly (until litigation is pending) after he is elected. As a means of pursuing the objective of openmindedness that respondents now articulate, the announce clause is so woefully underinclusive as to render belief in that purpose a challenge to the credulous.

Justice Stevens asserts that statements made in an election campaign pose a special threat to openmindedness because the candidate, when elected judge, will have a *particular* reluctance to contradict them. That might be plausible, perhaps, with regard to campaign *promises*. A candidate who says "If elected, I will vote to uphold the legislature's power to prohibit same-sex marriages" will positively be breaking his word if he does not do so (although one would be naive not to recognize that campaign promises are — by long democratic tradition — the least binding form of human commitment). But, as noted earlier, the Minnesota Supreme Court has adopted a separate prohibition on campaign "pledges or promises," which is not challenged here. The proposition that judges feel significantly greater compulsion, or appear to feel significantly greater compulsion, to maintain consistency with *nonpromissory* statements made during a judicial campaign than with such statements made before or after the campaign is not self-evidently true. * * * In any event, it suffices to say that respondents have not carried the burden imposed by our strict-scrutiny test to establish this proposition (that campaign statements are uniquely destructive of openmindedness) on which the validity of the announce clause rests.

Moreover, the notion that the special context of electioneering justifies an *abridgment* of the right to speak out on disputed issues sets our First Amendment jurisprudence on its head. "Debate on the qualifications of candidates" is "at the core of our electoral process and of the First Amendment freedoms," not at the edges. *Eu*, 489 U.S., at 222–223. "The role that elected officials play in our society makes it all the more imperative that they be allowed freely to express themselves on matters of current public importance." "It is simply not the function of government to select which issues are worth discussing or debating in the course of a political campaign." *Brown*, 456 U.S., at 60. We have never allowed the government to prohibit candidates from communicating relevant information to voters during an election.

JUSTICE GINSBURG would do so — and much of her dissent confirms rather than refutes our conclusion that the purpose behind the announce clause is not openmindedness in the judiciary, but the undermining of judicial elections. She contends that the announce clause must be constitutional because due process would be denied if an elected judge sat in a case involving an issue on which he had previously announced his view. She reaches this conclusion because, she says, such a judge would have a "direct, personal, substantial, and pecuniary interest" in ruling consistently with his previously announced view, in order to reduce the risk that he will be "voted off the bench and thereby lose [his] salary and emoluments." But elected judges — regardless of whether they have announced any views beforehand — *always* face the pressure of an electorate who might disagree with their rulings and therefore vote them off the bench. Surely the judge who frees Timothy McVeigh places his job much more at risk than the judge who (horror of horrors!) reconsiders his previously announced view on a disputed legal issue. So if, as JUSTICE GINSBURG claims, it violates due process for a judge to sit in a case in which ruling one way rather than another increases his prospects for reelection, then — quite simply — the practice of electing judges is itself a violation of due process. It is not difficult to understand how one with these views would approve the election-nullifying effect of the announce clause. They are not, however, the views reflected in the Due Process Clause of the Fourteenth Amendment, which has coexisted with the election of judges ever since it was adopted.

JUSTICE GINSBURG devotes the rest of her dissent to attacking arguments we do not make. For example, * * * we neither assert nor imply that the First Amendment requires campaigns for judicial office to sound the same as those for legislative office. What we do assert, and what JUSTICE GINSBURG ignores, is that, *even if* the First Amendment allows greater regulation of judicial election campaigns than legislative election campaigns, the announce clause still fails strict scrutiny because it is woefully underinclusive, prohibiting announcements by judges (and would-be judges) only at certain times and in certain forms. We rely on the cases involving speech during elections only to make the obvious point that this underinclusiveness cannot be explained by resort to the notion that the First Amendment provides less protection during an election campaign than at other times.[11]

But in any case, JUSTICE GINSBURG greatly exaggerates the difference between judicial and legislative elections. She asserts that "the rationale underlying unconstrained speech in elections for political office — that representative government depends on the public's ability to choose agents who will act at its behest — does not carry over to campaigns for the bench." This complete separation of the judiciary from the enterprise of "representative government" might have some truth in those countries where judges neither make law themselves nor set aside the laws enacted by the legislature. It is not a true picture of the American system. Not only do state-court judges possess the power to "make" common law, but they have the immense power to shape the States' constitutions as well. Which is precisely why the election of state judges became popular.[12]

IV

*   *   *

There is an obvious tension between the article of Minnesota's popularly approved Constitution which provides that judges shall be elected, and the Minnesota Supreme Court's announce clause which places most subjects of interest to the voters off limits. (The candidate-speech restrictions of all the other States that have them are also the product of judicial fiat.) The disparity is perhaps unsurprising, since the ABA, which originated the announce clause, has long been an opponent of judicial elections. That opposition may be well taken (it certainly had the support of the Founders of the Federal Government), but the First Amendment does not permit it to achieve its goal by leaving the principle of elections in place while preventing candidates from discussing what the elections are about. "The greater power to dispense with elections altogether does not include the lesser power to conduct elections under conditions of state-imposed voter ignorance. If the State chooses to tap the energy and the legitimizing power of the democratic process, it must accord the participants in that process . . . the First Amendment rights that attach to their roles." *Renne* v. *Geary*, 501 U.S. 312, 349 (1991) (Marshall, J., dissenting).

The Minnesota Supreme Court's canon of judicial conduct prohibiting candidates for judicial election from announcing their views on disputed legal and political

---

[11] Nor do we assert that candidates for judicial office should be *compelled* to announce their views on disputed legal issues. Thus, JUSTICE GINSBURG's repeated invocation of instances in which nominees to this Court declined to announce such views during Senate confirmation hearings is pointless. [T]he practice of *voluntarily* demurring does not establish the legitimacy of *legal compulsion* to demur * * *.

[12] * * * Even if the policymaking capacity of judges were limited to courts of last resort, that would only prove that the announce clause fails strict scrutiny [because] the announce clause * * * applies to high- and low-court candidates alike. In fact, however, the judges of inferior courts *often* "make law," since the precedent of the highest court does not cover every situation, and not every case is reviewed. * * *

issues violates the First Amendment. Accordingly, we reverse the grant of summary judgment to respondents and remand the case for proceedings consistent with this opinion.

It is so ordered.

JUSTICE O'CONNOR, concurring.

I join the opinion of the Court but write separately to express my concerns about judicial elections generally. Respondents claim that "the Announce Clause is necessary . . . to protect the State's compelling governmental interest in an actual and perceived . . . impartial judiciary." I am concerned that, even aside from what judicial candidates may say while campaigning, the very practice of electing judges undermines this interest.

* * * Elected judges cannot help being aware that if the public is not satisfied with the outcome of a particular case, it could hurt their reelection prospects. Even if judges were able to suppress their awareness of the potential electoral conse-quences of their decisions and refrain from acting on it, the public's confidence in the judiciary could be undermined simply by the possibility that judges would be unable to do so.

Moreover, contested elections generally entail campaigning. And campaigning for a judicial post today can require substantial funds. * * * Yet relying on campaign donations may leave judges feeling indebted to certain parties or interest groups. Even if judges were able to refrain from favoring donors, the mere possibility that judges' decisions may be motivated by the desire to repay campaign contributors is likely to undermine the public's confidence in the judiciary. * * *

Minnesota has chosen to select its judges through contested popular elections instead of through an appointment system or a combined appointment and retention election system along the lines of the Missouri Plan. In doing so the State has voluntarily taken on the risks to judicial bias described above. As a result, the State's claim that it needs to significantly restrict judges' speech in order to protect judicial impartiality is particularly troubling. If the State has a problem with judicial impartiality, it is largely one the State brought upon itself by continuing the practice of popularly electing judges.

JUSTICE KENNEDY, concurring.

I agree with the Court that Minnesota's prohibition on judicial candidates' announcing their legal views is an unconstitutional abridgment of the freedom of speech. There is authority for the Court to apply strict scrutiny analysis to resolve some First Amendment cases, and the Court explains in clear and forceful terms why the Minnesota regulatory scheme fails that test. So I join its opinion.

I adhere to my view, however, that content-based speech restrictions that do not fall within any traditional exception should be invalidated without inquiry into narrow tailoring or compelling government interests. * * * The political speech of candidates is at the heart of the First Amendment, and direct restrictions on the content of candidate speech are simply beyond the power of government to impose. * * *

Minnesota may choose to have an elected judiciary. It may strive to define those characteristics that exemplify judicial excellence. It may enshrine its definitions in a code of judicial conduct. It may adopt recusal standards more rigorous than due process requires, and censure judges who violate these standards. What Minnesota may not do, however, is censor what the people hear as they undertake to decide for themselves which candidate is most likely to be an exemplary judicial officer. Deciding the relevance of candidate speech is the right of the voters, not the State. See *Brown* v. *Hartlage*, 456 U.S., [at] 60. The law in question here contradicts the principle that unabridged speech is the foundation of political freedom. * * *

* * * The State may not regulate the content of candidate speech merely because the speakers are candidates. This case does not present the question whether a State may restrict the speech of judges because they are judges — for example, as part of a code of judicial conduct; the law at issue here regulates judges only when and because they are candidates. Whether the rationale of [cases concerning the speech of government employees] could be extended to allow a general speech restriction on sitting judges — regardless of whether they are campaigning — in order to promote the efficient administration of justice, is not an issue raised here.

Petitioner Gregory Wersal was not a sitting judge but a challenger; he had not voluntarily entered into an employment relationship with the State or surrendered any First Amendment rights. His speech may not be controlled or abridged in this manner. Even the undoubted interest of the State in the excellence of its judiciary does not allow it to restrain candidate speech by reason of its content. Minnesota's attempt to regulate campaign speech is impermissible.

JUSTICE STEVENS, with whom JUSTICE SOUTER, JUSTICE GINSBURG, and JUSTICE BREYER join, dissenting. * * *

There is a critical difference between the work of the judge and the work of other public officials. In a democracy, issues of policy are properly decided by majority vote; it is the business of legislators and executives to be popular. But in litigation, issues of law or fact should not be determined by popular vote; it is the business of judges to be indifferent to unpopularity. * * *

Consistent with that fundamental attribute of the office, countless judges in countless cases routinely make rulings that are unpopular and surely disliked by at least 50 percent of the litigants who appear before them. It is equally common for them to enforce rules that they think unwise, or that are contrary to their personal predilections. For this reason, opinions that a lawyer may have expressed before becoming a judge, or a judicial candidate, do not disqualify anyone for judicial service because every good judge is fully aware of the distinction between the law and a personal point of view. It is equally clear, however, that such expressions after a lawyer has been nominated to judicial office shed little, if any, light on his capacity for judicial service. Indeed, to the extent that such statements seek to enhance the popularity of the candidate by indicating how he would rule in specific cases if elected, they evidence a lack of fitness for the office.

Of course, any judge who faces reelection may believe that he retains his office only so long as his decisions are popular. Nevertheless, the elected judge, like the lifetime appointee, does not serve a constituency while holding that office. He has a duty to uphold the law and to follow the dictates of the Constitution. If he is not a judge on the highest court in the State, he has an obligation to follow the precedent of that court, not his personal views or public opinion polls.[2] He may make common law, but judged on the merits of individual cases, not as a mandate from the voters.

By recognizing a conflict between the demands of electoral politics and the distinct characteristics of the judiciary, we do not have to put States to an all or nothing choice of abandoning judicial elections or having elections in which anything goes. * * * [A] judicial candidate, who announces his views in the context of a campaign, is effectively telling the electorate: "Vote for me because I believe X, and I will judge cases accordingly." Once elected, he may feel free to disregard his campaign statements, but that does not change the fact that the judge announced his position on an issue likely to come before him *as a reason to vote for him.* Minnesota has a compelling interest in sanctioning such statements. * * *

The Court boldly asserts that respondents have failed to carry their burden of demonstrating "that campaign statements are uniquely destructive of openmindedness." But the very purpose of most statements prohibited by the announce clause is to convey the message that the candidate's mind is not open on a particular issue. The lawyer who writes an article advocating harsher penalties for polluters surely does not commit to that position to the same degree as the candidate who says "vote for me because I believe all polluters deserve harsher penalties." At the very least, such statements obscure the appearance of openmindedness. More importantly, like the reasoning in the Court's opinion, they create the false impression that the standards for the election of political candidates apply equally to candidates for judicial office.[4] * * *

JUSTICE GINSBURG, with whom JUSTICE STEVENS, JUSTICE SOUTER, and JUSTICE BREYER join, dissenting.

Whether state or federal, elected or appointed, judges perform a function fundamentally different from that of the people's elected representatives. Legislative and executive officials act on behalf of the voters who placed them in office; "judges represent the Law." *Chisom* v. *Roemer*, 501 U.S. 380, 411 (1991) (SCALIA, J., dissenting). Unlike their counterparts in the political branches, judges are expected to refrain from catering to particular constituencies or committing themselves on controversial issues in advance of adversarial presentation. Their mission is to

---

[2] The Court largely ignores the fact that judicial elections are not limited to races for the highest court in the State. Even if announcing one's views in the context of a campaign for the State Supreme Court might be permissible, the same statements are surely less appropriate when one is running for an intermediate or trial court judgeship. * * *

[4] JUSTICE KENNEDY would go even further and hold that no content-based restriction of a judicial candidate's speech is permitted under the First Amendment. While he does not say so explicitly, this extreme position would preclude even Minnesota's prohibition against "pledges or promises" by a candidate for judicial office. A candidate could say "vote for me because I promise to never reverse a rape conviction," and the Board could do nothing to formally sanction that candidate. The unwisdom of this proposal illustrates why the same standards should not apply to speech in campaigns for judicial and legislative office.

decide "individual cases and controversies" on individual records, neutrally applying legal principles, and, when necessary, "standing up to what is generally supreme in a democracy: the popular will," Scalia, *The Rule of Law as a Law of Rules*, 56 U. Chi. L. Rev. 1175, 1180 (1989). * * *

The speech restriction must fail, in the Court's view, because an electoral process is at stake; if Minnesota opts to elect its judges, the Court asserts, the State may not rein in what candidates may say. I do not agree with this unilocular, "an election is an election," approach. * * *

* * * Even when they develop common law or give concrete meaning to constitutional text, judges act only in the context of individual cases, the outcome of which cannot depend on the will of the public. Thus, the rationale underlying unconstrained speech in elections for political office — that representative government depends on the public's ability to choose agents who will act at its behest — does not carry over to campaigns for the bench. * * *

All parties to this case agree that, whatever the validity of the Announce Clause, the State may constitutionally prohibit judicial candidates from pledging or promising certain results. The reasons for this agreement are apparent. Pledges or promises of conduct in office, however commonplace in races for the political branches, are inconsistent "with the judge's obligation to decide cases in accordance with his or her role." This judicial obligation to avoid prejudgment corresponds to the litigant's right, protected by the Due Process Clause of the Fourteenth Amendment, to "an impartial and disinterested tribunal in both civil and criminal cases." The proscription against pledges or promises thus represents an accommodation of "constitutionally protected interests [that] lie on both sides of the legal equation." *Nixon* v. *Shrink Missouri Government PAC*, 528 U.S. 377, 400 (2000) [p. 834] (BREYER, J., concurring). Balanced against the candidate's interest in free expression is the litigant's "powerful and independent constitutional interest in fair adjudicative procedure." * * *

[I]n *Tumey* v. *Ohio*, we held that due process was violated where a judge received a portion of the fines collected from defendants whom he found guilty. Such an arrangement, we said, gave the judge a "direct, personal, substantial[, and] pecuniary interest" in reaching a particular outcome and thereby denied the defendant his right to an impartial arbiter. [273 U.S.], at 523. *Ward* v. *Monroeville* extended *Tumey*'s reasoning, holding that due process was similarly violated where fines collected from guilty defendants constituted a large part of a village's finances, for which the judge, who also served as the village mayor, was responsible. Even though the mayor did not personally share in those fines, we concluded, he "perforce occupied two practically and seriously inconsistent positions, one partisan and the other judicial." 409 U.S., at 60.

We applied the principle of *Tumey* and *Ward* most recently in *Aetna Life Ins. Co.* v. *Lavoie*. That decision invalidated a ruling of the Alabama Supreme Court written by a justice who had a personal interest in the resolution of a dispositive issue. The Alabama Supreme Court's ruling was issued while the justice was pursuing a separate lawsuit in an Alabama lower court, and its outcome "had the clear and immediate effect of enhancing both the legal status and the settlement value" of that separate suit. [475 U.S.], at 824. As in *Ward* and *Tumey*, we held, the justice therefore had an interest in the outcome of the decision that unsuited him to participate in the judgment. It mattered not whether the justice was actually influenced by this interest; "the Due Process Clause," we observed, "may sometimes bar trial by judges who have no actual bias and who would do their very best to weigh the scales of justice equally between contending parties." *Id.*, at 825.

These cases establish three propositions important to this dispute. First, a litigant is deprived of due process where the judge who hears his case has a "direct, personal, substantial, and pecuniary" interest in ruling against him. Second, this interest need not be as direct as it was in *Tumey*, where the judge was essentially compensated for each conviction he obtained; the interest may stem, as in *Ward*, from the judge's knowledge that his success and tenure in office depend on certain outcomes. "The test," we have said, "is whether the . . . situation is one 'which would offer a possible temptation to the average man as a judge [that] might lead him not to hold the balance nice, clear, and true.' " *Ward*, 409 U.S., at 60 (quoting *Tumey*, 273 U.S., at 532). And third, due process does not require a showing that the judge is actually biased as a result of his self-interest. Rather, our cases have "always endeavored to prevent even the probability of unfairness." * * *

The justification for the pledges or promises prohibition follows from these principles. When a judicial candidate promises to rule a certain way on an issue that may later reach the courts, the potential for due process violations is grave and manifest. If successful in her bid for office, the judicial candidate will become a judge, and in that capacity she will be under pressure to resist the pleas of litigants who advance positions contrary to her pledges on the campaign trail. If the judge fails to honor her campaign promises, she will not only face abandonment by supporters of her professed views, she will also "risk being assailed as a dissembler," willing to say one thing to win an election and to do the opposite once in office. A judge in this position therefore may be thought to have a "direct, personal, substantial, [and] pecuniary interest" in ruling against certain litigants, for she may be voted off the bench and thereby lose her salary and emoluments unless she honors the pledge that secured her election. * * *

In addition to protecting litigants' due process rights, * * * [p]rohibiting a judicial candidate from pledging or promising certain results if elected directly promotes the State's interest in preserving public faith in the bench. When a candidate makes such a promise during a campaign, the public will no doubt perceive that she is doing so in the hope of garnering votes. And the public will in turn likely conclude that when the candidate decides an issue in accord with that promise, she does so at least in part to discharge her undertaking to the voters in the previous election and to prevent voter abandonment in the next. The perception of that unseemly *quid pro quo* — a judicial candidate's promises on issues in return for the electorate's votes at the polls — inevitably diminishes the public's faith in the ability of judges to administer the law without regard to personal or political self-interest.[4]

---

[4] The author of the Court's opinion declined on precisely these grounds to tell the Senate whether he would overrule a particular case: "Let us assume that I have people arguing before me to do it or not to do it. I think it is quite a thing to be arguing to somebody who you know has made a representation in the course of his confirmation hearings, and that is, by way of condition to his being confirmed, that he will do this or do that. I think I would be in a very bad position to adjudicate the case without being

* * *

Uncoupled from the Announce Clause, the ban on pledges or promises is easily circumvented. By prefacing a campaign commitment with the caveat, "although I cannot promise anything," or by simply avoiding the language of promises or pledges altogether, a candidate could declare with impunity how she would decide specific issues. Semantic sanitizing of the candidate's commitment would not, however, diminish its pernicious effects on actual and perceived judicial impartiality. * * *

By targeting statements that do not technically constitute pledges or promises but nevertheless "publicly make known how [the candidate] would decide" legal issues, the Announce Clause prevents this end run around the letter and spirit of its companion provision. No less than the pledges or promises clause itself, the Announce Clause is an indispensable part of Minnesota's effort to maintain the health of its judiciary, and is therefore constitutional for the same reasons. * * *

Notes and Questions

1. The Court avoids addressing whether judicial openmindedness and the appearance of judicial openmindedness are compelling state interests because, the Court concludes, Minnesota did not adopt the announce clause for those purposes. Why should it matter whether the state had the purpose of achieving certain compelling interests, if the statute does in fact serve them? In the Court's view, the prohibition was "so woefully underinclusive" that it would fail the narrow-tailoring portion of the strict-scrutiny analysis even if openmindedness and its appearance were compelling interests. Could a speech limitation be drafted so as to advance judicial openmindedness in a narrowly tailored way?

2. *Is* openmindedness a compelling interest? Is it of compelling importance for judges to remain open to persuasion by the most frivolous arguments? *See* Michael R. Dimino, *Pay No Attention to that Man Behind the Robe: Judicial Elections, the First Amendment, and Judges as Politicians*, 21 YALE L. & POL'Y REV. 301, 343–46 (2003).

3. The Court in *Republican Party v. White* proclaimed that it was not taking any position on the constitutionality of bans on judicial candidates' pledging and promising particular conduct in office. Are such restrictions constitutional? How can one distinguish "pledges or promises" from announcements of legal or political views, so as not to chill the exercise of protected speech?

4. Is it constitutional for a state (taking a cue from the 1990 ABA Model Code of Judicial Conduct) to ban judicial candidates from making statements that "commit or appear to commit" them with respect to issues likely to come before the court? Is there any way for a candidate to announce his views on a "disputed legal or political issue" without "appearing to commit" himself to such a view?

5. Restrictions on judicial conduct and campaign speech do not prevent judges

accused of having a less than impartial view of the matter." (hearings before the Senate Judiciary Committee on the nomination of then—Judge Scalia).

or judicial candidates from *holding* views on legal or political issues; rather, they prevent others from *discovering* those views. Accordingly, the principal benefit of such restrictions is not in promoting judicial neutrality, but in promoting an *image* of judicial neutrality. Is that interest compelling? *Compare* Charles Gardner Geyh, *Straddling the Fence Between Truth and Pretense: The Role of Law and Preference in Judicial Decision Making and the Future of Judicial Independence*, 22 NOTRE DAME J.L., ETHICS & PUB. POL'Y 435, 448 (2008), *with* Dimino, *Pay No Attention*, *supra*, at 346. Does respect for the courts depend on the public's belief that judges do not have views on such matters? *See* James L. Gibson, *Challenges to the Impartiality of State Supreme Courts: Legitimacy Theory and "New-Style" Judicial Campaigns*, 102 AM. POL. SCI. REV. 59 (2008). If promoting respect for the courts is a compelling state interest, would promoting respect for other branches of government justify restrictions on speech in, say, legislative or presidential campaigns? *Cf.* Sedition Act, 1 Stat. 596 (1798) (forbidding the publication of "any false, scandalous and malicious writing or writings against the government of the United States, or either house of the Congress of the United States, or the President of the United States, with intent to defame the[m] * * *, or to bring them, or either of them, into contempt or disrepute * * *").

6. Why do you suppose that Justice Souter, who usually was quite solicitous of First Amendment claims, and Chief Justice Rehnquist, who was usually not, flipped sides in this case? *See* Michael R. Dimino, *Counter-Majoritarian Power and Judges' Political Speech*, 58 FLA. L. REV. 53 (2006).

7. Should the Court have treated elected judges as government employees, with restrictions on their political activities evaluated under *United Public Workers v. Mitchell*, 330 U.S. 75 (1947)? May states restrict the speech of *appointed* judges on a government-employment theory? May states restrict the speech of lawyers on the theory that the license to practice law is a state-conferred benefit that may be conditioned on maintaining public respect for the legal system?

8. The dissenters argued that states should be able to adopt a middle road between fully competitive elections and appointive systems. Thus, in Justice Stevens's words, the Court unwisely "put States to an all or nothing choice of abandoning judicial elections or having elections in which anything goes." 536 U.S. at 800 (Stevens, J., dissenting). The majority, by contrast, adopted the view that "the greater power to dispense with elections altogether does not include the lesser power to conduct elections under conditions of state-imposed voter ignorance." Throughout this course you have seen and will see many variants of the greater-includes-the-lesser argument. Usually the argument runs into difficulty where the "lesser" power isn't really part of the greater one, but is instead a different power. For example, a state need not have elected school boards, but if it chooses to have them, the elections must comply with the constitutional guarantee of equality. *See Kramer v. Union Free School District No. 15*, 395 U.S. 621, 628–30 & n.11 (1969) [p. 62]. Likewise here, the power to appoint judges may not be the same as the power to limit speech by or about judges.

Do you agree with the dissenters that a middle road is possible? Do you think that a state could adopt such a middle approach for presidential elections, on the rationale that the state legislature need not have popular elections for presidential electors at all? *See McPherson v. Blacker*, 146 U.S. 1, 27 (1892). Would it be constitutional for a state to hold judicial elections, but to deviate from the requirements of one-person, one-vote? *See Wells v. Edwards*, 347 F. Supp. 453 (M.D. La. 1972), *aff'd* 409 U.S. 1095 (*per curiam*) (holding judicial elections immune from one person, one vote).

9.   Underlying the dissenters' argument is the conviction that states are entitled to treat judicial offices differently from "political" ones because of the differences in their respective duties. Should states be able to make this choice for the people? That is, should a state be able to restrict speech in judicial elections because it wants the judicial function to be (and to be recognized as) non-political, if the people want to vote based on campaign statements? *See generally* Dimino, *Pay No Attention*, *supra*.

10.   If you agree with the dissenters in *White*, how much freedom do you believe states should be given to define the independence of state offices? Should states be able to adopt a Burkean approach to the legislature or executive, and argue that undue electioneering risks pandering to the public, which could destroy the officials' ability to exercise their own consciences? Which officials in the executive and legislative branches have an obligation to apply the law irrespective of public opinion? *See, e.g.*, U.S. CONST. art. II, § 3 (providing that the President "shall take Care that the Laws be faithfully executed"); *United States v. Nixon*, 418 U.S. 683 (1974) (requiring the President to comply with a subpoena); *Cooper v. Aaron*, 358 U.S. 1, 18–19 (1959) (requiring states to abide by the Court's decision in *Brown v. Board of Education*, 347 U.S. 483 (1954)); *Marbury v. Madison*, 5 U.S. (1 Cranch) 137, 168 (1803) (stating that the Jefferson administration's refusal to provide Marbury his commission "is a plain violation" of Marbury's right to the document, "for which the laws of his country afford him a remedy"). Would the *White* dissenters uphold restrictions on campaign speech in elections for district attorney, secretary of state, or coroner?

11.   As you will see in Chapter 9, Justice Ginsburg's argument that the announce clause is necessary to prevent evasion of the pledges-and-promises clause is analogous to the argument that stringent campaign-finance restrictions are necessary to ensure that other limits are not evaded. Such house-that-Jack-built arguments are not limited to election law. *Cf. Wickard v. Filburn*, 317 U.S. 111, 127–29 (1942); *M'Culloch v. Maryland*, 17 U.S. (4 Wheat.) 316, 417 (1819).

12.   Is the entire enterprise of electing judges inconsistent with the ideal of an independent judiciary that can defend the rule of law? *See, e.g.*, Steven P. Croley, *The Majoritarian Difficulty: Elective Judiciaries and the Rule of Law*, 62 U. CHI. L. REV. 689 (1995); Michael R. Dimino, Sr., *Accountability Before the Fact*, 22 NOTRE DAME J.L., ETHICS & PUB. POL'Y 451 (2008); Charles Gardner Geyh, *Why Judicial Elections Stink*, 64 OHIO ST. L.J. 43 (2003); David E. Pozen, *The Irony of Judicial Elections*, 108 COLUM. L. REV. 265 (2008). Consider *New York Board of Elections v. López Torres*, 552 U.S. 196, 212 (2008) [p. 543] (Kennedy, J., joined by Breyer, J., concurring in the judgment):

> When one considers that elections require candidates to conduct campaigns and to raise funds in a system designed to allow for competition among interest groups and political parties, the persisting question is

whether that process is consistent with the perception and the reality of judicial independence and judicial excellence. The rule of law, which is a foundation of freedom, presupposes a functioning judiciary respected for its independence, its professional attainments, and the absolute probity of its judges. And it may seem difficult to reconcile these aspirations with elections.

Still, though the Framers did not provide for elections of federal judges, most States have made the opposite choice, at least to some extent. In light of this longstanding practice and tradition in the States, the appropriate practical response is not to reject judicial elections outright but to find ways to use elections to select judges with the highest qualifications. A judicial election system presents the opportunity, indeed the civic obligation, for voters and the community as a whole to become engaged in the legal process. Judicial elections, if fair and open, could be an essential forum for society to discuss and define the attributes of judicial excellence and to find ways to discern those qualities in the candidates. The organized bar, the legal academy, public advocacy groups, a principled press, and all the other components of functioning democracy must engage in this process.

Justice Stevens more bluntly suggested that problems observed in judicial elections "lend support to the * * * proposition that the very practice of electing judges is unwise." *Id.* at 209 (Stevens, J., joined by Souter, J., concurring). Ultimately, however, Justice Stevens concluded that "[t]he Constitution does not prohibit legislatures from enacting stupid laws." *Id.*

For additional commentary on state judicial elections, from a variety of perspectives, see CHRIS W. BONNEAU & MELINDA GANN HALL, IN DEFENSE OF JUDICIAL ELECTIONS (1999), *reviewed in* Michael E. Solimine, *Independence, Accountability, and the Case for State Judicial Elections*, 9 ELECTION L.J. 215 (2010); JED HANDELSMAN SHUGERMAN, THE PEOPLE'S COURTS: PURSUING JUDICIAL INDEPENDENCE IN AMERICA (2012); James J. Sample, *Retention Elections 2.010*, 46 U.S.F. L. REV. 383 (2011); and Rebecca D. Gill, *Beyond High Hopes and Unmet Expectations: Judicial Selection Reforms in the States*, 96 JUDICATURE 278 (2013).

13.   Despite the Court's apparently unanimous view in *López Torres* that states may constitutionally select their judges by popular elections, *Caperton v. A.T. Massey Coal Co.*, 556 U.S. 868 , 129 S. Ct. 2252 (2009), decided the following year by a 5-4 margin, may indicate that there are constitutional concerns surrounding the election of judges. In *Caperton*, the Court held that the Due Process Clause required the recusal of an elected state-supreme-court justice in a case reviewing the legality of a $50 million judgment. The CEO of the company against which the judgment was entered had spent $3 million in support of the judge's election. Almost all of the $3 million was spent independently of the judge's campaign, however, and the company itself spent nothing. The Court held that due process was compromised, but was careful to state that the "extreme" facts of *Caperton* should serve to differentiate that case from more common instances in which litigants have supported the selection of judges hearing their cases. The Court's test for determining when the Due Process Clause has been violated, however, was vague:

> We conclude that there is a serious risk of actual bias — based on objective and reasonable perceptions — when a person with a personal stake in a particular case had a significant and disproportionate influence in placing the judge on the case by raising funds or directing the judge's election campaign when the case was pending or imminent. The inquiry centers on the contribution's relative size in comparison to the total amount of money contributed to the campaign, the total amount spent in the election, and the apparent effect such contribution had on the outcome of the election.

129 S. Ct. at 2263–64. Are you satisfied that judicial elections can continue after *Caperton*, or will recusal motions hamper the effective operation of elected courts?

14.   Does recusal unconstitutionally burden the First Amendment rights of a candidate's supporters? *Nevada Commission on Ethics v. Carrigan*, 131 S. Ct. 2343 (2011), involved a state law requiring legislators to recuse themselves from voting on measures when their private commitments would call into question their "independence of judgment." The Supreme Court held that the First Amendment right of free speech did not extend to casting a legislative vote, but did not address whether the recusal provision unconstitutionally burdened campaign speech.

In a concurring opinion, Justice Kennedy suggested that legislative recusal provisions may well violate the constitutional rights of persons who offer their support to candidates:

> As a general matter, citizens voice their support and lend their aid because they wish to confer the powers of public office on those whose positions correspond with their own. That dynamic, moreover, links the principles of participation and representation at the heart of our democratic government. Just as candidates announce positions in exchange for citizens' votes, *Brown* v. *Hartlage*, 456 U.S. 45, 55–56 (1982) [p. 585], so too citizens offer endorsements, advertise their views, and assist political campaigns based upon bonds of common purpose. These are the mechanisms that sustain representative democracy.

131 S. Ct. at 2353 (Kennedy, J., concurring).

Nevertheless, Justice Kennedy suggested that requiring recusal of *judges* might be different:

> The differences between the role of political bodies in formulating and enforcing public policy, on the one hand, and the role of courts in adjudicating individual disputes according to law, on the other, may call for a different understanding of the responsibilities attendant upon holders of those respective offices and of the legitimate restrictions that may be imposed upon them.

131 S. Ct. at 2353. *See also* 131 S. Ct. at 2349 n.3 (opinion of the Court) (noting that "[t]here are of course differences between a legislator's vote and a judge's, and thus between legislative and judicial recusal rules," and contrasting a judge's vote while on the bench (which is not part of the freedom of speech protected by the First Amendment) to his or her "speech during elections" (which was held in *Republican Party of Minnesota v. White* to be protected)).

Is Justice Kennedy's proposed distinction between judges and legislators consistent with the reasoning of *Republican Party of Minnesota v. White*?

15. In 2015, the Supreme Court revisited the First Amendment's applicability to judicial campaigns, emphatically concluding that judicial elections are *not* like those for "political" offices. This time the issue was the constitutionality of an ethical canon prohibiting judicial candidates from personally soliciting campaign funds.

WILLIAMS-YULEE v. FLORIDA BAR
Supreme Court of the United States
575 U.S. —, 135 S. Ct. 1656 (2015)

CHIEF JUSTICE ROBERTS delivered the opinion of the Court, except as to Part II.[c]

* * * In an effort to preserve public confidence in the integrity of their judiciaries, many * * * States prohibit judges and judicial candidates from personally soliciting funds for their campaigns. We must decide whether the First Amendment permits such restrictions on speech.

We hold that it does. Judges are not politicians, even when they come to the bench by way of the ballot. And a State's decision to elect its judiciary does not compel it to treat judicial candidates like campaigners for political office. A State may assure its people that judges will apply the law without fear or favor — and without having personally asked anyone for money. * * *

I * * *

Canon 7C(1) [of the Florida Code of Judicial Conduct] governs fundraising in judicial elections. The Canon, which is based on a provision in the American Bar Association's Model Code of Judicial Conduct, provides:

> "A candidate, including an incumbent judge, for a judicial office that is filled by public election between competing candidates shall not personally solicit campaign funds, or solicit attorneys for publicly stated support, but may establish committees of responsible persons to secure and manage the expenditure of funds for the candidate's campaign and to obtain public statements of support for his or her candidacy. Such committees are not prohibited from soliciting campaign contributions and public support from any person or corporation authorized by law."

Florida statutes impose additional restrictions on campaign fundraising in judicial elections. Contributors may not donate more than $1,000 per election to a trial court candidate or more than $3,000 per retention election to a Supreme Court justice. Campaign committee treasurers must file periodic reports disclosing the names of contributors and the amount of each contribution.

Judicial candidates can seek guidance about campaign ethics rules from the

---

[c] JUSTICES BREYER, SOTOMAYOR, and KAGAN join this opinion in its entirety. JUSTICE GINSBURG joins all except Part II. [— Eds.]

Florida Judicial Ethics Advisory Committee. The Committee has interpreted Canon 7 to allow a judicial candidate to serve as treasurer of his own campaign committee, learn the identity of campaign contributors, and send thank you notes to donors.

Like Florida, most other States prohibit judicial candidates from soliciting campaign funds personally, but allow them to raise money through committees. According to the American Bar Association, 30 of the 39 States that elect trial or appellate judges have adopted restrictions similar to Canon 7C(1).

Lanell Williams-Yulee, who refers to herself as Yulee, has practiced law in Florida since 1991. In September 2009, she decided to run for a seat on the county court for Hillsborough County, a jurisdiction of about 1.3 million people that includes the city of Tampa. Shortly after filing paperwork to enter the race, Yulee drafted a letter announcing her candidacy. The letter described her experience and desire to "bring fresh ideas and positive solutions to the Judicial bench." The letter then stated:

> "An early contribution of $25, $50, $100, $250, or $500, made payable to 'Lanell Williams-Yulee Campaign for County Judge', will help raise the initial funds needed to launch the campaign and get our message out to the public. I ask for your support [i]n meeting the primary election fund raiser goals. Thank you in advance for your support."

Yulee signed the letter and mailed it to local voters. She also posted the letter on her campaign Web site.

Yulee's bid for the bench did not unfold as she had hoped. She lost the primary to the incumbent judge. Then the Florida Bar filed a complaint against her [for violating] the ban on personal solicitation of campaign funds in Canon 7C(1).

Yulee admitted that she had signed and sent the fundraising letter. But she argued that the Bar could not discipline her for that conduct because the First Amendment protects a judicial candidate's right to solicit campaign funds in an election. The Florida Supreme Court * * * publicly reprimanded [Yulee] and ordered [her] to pay the costs of the proceeding ($1,860).

II

* * * The parties agree that Canon 7C(1) restricts Yulee's speech on the basis of its content by prohibiting her from soliciting contributions to her election campaign. The parties disagree, however, about the level of scrutiny that should govern our review.

* * * As we have long recognized, speech about public issues and the qualifications of candidates for elected office commands the highest level of First Amendment protection. See *Eu* v. *San Francisco County Democratic Central Comm.*, 489 U.S. 214, 223 (1989) [p. 455]. Indeed, in our only prior case concerning speech restrictions on a candidate for judicial office, this Court and both parties assumed that strict scrutiny applied. *Republican Party of Minn.* v. *White*, 536 U.S. 765, 774 (2002). * * * [W]e hold today what we assumed in *White*: A State may restrict the speech of a judicial candidate only if the restriction is narrowly tailored to serve a compelling interest.

III

* * * Canon 7C(1) advances the State's compelling interest in preserving public confidence in the integrity of the judiciary, and it does so through means narrowly tailored to avoid unnecessarily abridging speech. This is therefore one of the rare cases in which a speech restriction withstands strict scrutiny.

A

The Florida Supreme Court adopted Canon 7C(1) to promote the State's interests in "protecting the integrity of the judiciary" and "maintaining the public's confidence in an impartial judiciary." The way the Canon advances those interests is intuitive: Judges, charged with exercising strict neutrality and independence, cannot supplicate campaign donors without diminishing public confidence in judicial integrity. * * * Simply put, Florida and most other States have concluded that the public may lack confidence in a judge's ability to administer justice without fear or favor if he comes to office by asking for favors.

The interest served by Canon 7C(1) has firm support in our precedents. We have recognized the "vital state interest" in safeguarding "public confidence in the fairness and integrity of the nation's elected judges." *Caperton* v. *A.T. Massey Coal Co.*, 556 U.S. 868, 889 (2009). The importance of public confidence in the integrity of judges stems from the place of the judiciary in the government. Unlike the executive or the legislature, the judiciary "has no influence over either the sword or the purse; . . . neither force nor will but merely judgment." The Federalist No. 78, p. 465 (C. Rossiter ed. 1961) (A. Hamilton) (capitalization altered). The judiciary's authority therefore depends in large measure on the public's willingness to respect and follow its decisions. * * * It follows that public perception of judicial integrity is "a state interest of the highest order." *Caperton*, 556 U.S., at 889. * * *

The parties devote considerable attention to our cases analyzing campaign finance restrictions in political elections. But a State's interest in preserving public confidence in the integrity of its judiciary extends beyond its interest in preventing the appearance of corruption in legislative and executive elections. As we explained in *White*, States may regulate judicial elections differently than they regulate political elections, because the role of judges differs from the role of politicians. 536 U.S., at 783; *id.*, at 805 (GINSBURG, J., dissenting). Politicians are expected to be appropriately responsive to the preferences of their supporters. Indeed, such "responsiveness is key to the very concept of self-governance through elected officials." The same is not true of judges. In deciding cases, a judge is not to follow the preferences of his supporters, or provide any special consideration to his campaign donors. * * * As in *White*, therefore, our precedents applying the First Amendment to political elections have little bearing on the issues here. * * *

* * * Moreover, personal solicitation by a judicial candidate "inevitably places the solicited individuals in a position to fear retaliation if they fail to financially support that candidate." Potential litigants then fear that "the integrity of the judicial system has been compromised, forcing them to search for an attorney in part based upon the criteria of which attorneys have made the obligatory contributions." A

State's decision to elect its judges does not require it to tolerate these risks. The Florida Bar's interest is compelling.

B

Yulee acknowledges the State's compelling interest in judicial integrity. She argues, however, that the Canon's failure to restrict other speech equally damaging to judicial integrity and its appearance undercuts the Bar's position. In particular, she notes that Canon 7C(1) allows a judge's campaign committee to solicit money, which arguably reduces public confidence in the integrity of the judiciary just as much as a judge's personal solicitation. Yulee also points out that Florida permits judicial candidates to write thank you notes to campaign donors, which ensures that candidates know who contributes and who does not. * * *

* * * Canon 7C(1) raises no fatal underinclusivity concerns. The solicitation ban aims squarely at the conduct most likely to undermine public confidence in the integrity of the judiciary: personal requests for money by judges and judicial candidates. The Canon applies evenhandedly to all judges and judicial candidates, regardless of their viewpoint or chosen means of solicitation. And unlike some laws that we have found impermissibly underinclusive, Canon 7C(1) is not riddled with exceptions. Indeed, the Canon contains zero exceptions to its ban on personal solicitation.

Yulee relies heavily on the provision of Canon 7C(1) that allows solicitation by a candidate's campaign committee. But Florida, along with most other States, has reasonably concluded that solicitation by the candidate personally creates a categorically different and more severe risk of undermining public confidence than does solicitation by a campaign committee. The identity of the solicitor matters, as anyone who has encountered a Girl Scout selling cookies outside a grocery store can attest. When the judicial candidate himself asks for money, the stakes are higher for all involved. The candidate has personally invested his time and effort in the fundraising appeal; he has placed his name and reputation behind the request. The solicited individual knows that, and also knows that the solicitor might be in a position to singlehandedly make decisions of great weight: The same person who signed the fundraising letter might one day sign the judgment. This dynamic inevitably creates pressure for the recipient to comply, and it does so in a way that solicitation by a third party does not. Just as inevitably, the personal involvement of the candidate in the solicitation creates the public appearance that the candidate will remember who says yes, and who says no.

In short, personal solicitation by judicial candidates implicates a different problem than solicitation by campaign committees. However similar the two solicitations may be in substance, a State may conclude that they present markedly different appearances to the public. Florida's choice to allow solicitation by campaign committees does not undermine its decision to ban solicitation by judges.

Likewise, allowing judicial candidates to write thank you notes to campaign donors does not detract from the State's interest in preserving public confidence in the integrity of the judiciary. Yulee argues that permitting thank you notes heightens the likelihood of actual bias by ensuring that judicial candidates know who supported their campaigns, and ensuring that the supporter knows that the candidate knows. Maybe so. But the State's compelling interest is implicated most directly by the candidate's personal solicitation itself. A failure to ban thank you notes for contributions not solicited by the candidate does not undercut the Bar's rationale. * * *

Taken to its logical conclusion, the position advanced by Yulee and the principal dissent is that Florida may ban the solicitation of funds by judicial candidates only if the State bans *all* solicitation of funds in judicial elections. The First Amendment does not put a State to that all-or-nothing choice. We will not punish Florida for leaving open more, rather than fewer, avenues of expression, especially when there is no indication that the selective restriction of speech reflects a pretextual motive.

C * * *

* * * Yulee concedes — and the principal dissent seems to agree — that Canon 7C(1) is valid in numerous applications. Yulee acknowledges that Florida can prohibit judges from soliciting money from lawyers and litigants appearing before them. In addition, she says the State "might" be able to ban "direct one-to-one solicitation of lawyers and individuals or businesses that could reasonably appear in the court for which the individual is a candidate." She also suggests that the Bar could forbid "in person" solicitation by judicial candidates. But Yulee argues that the Canon cannot constitutionally be applied to her chosen form of solicitation: a letter posted online and distributed via mass mailing. No one, she contends, will lose confidence in the integrity of the judiciary based on personal solicitation to such a broad audience.

This argument misperceives the breadth of the compelling interest that under-lies Canon 7C(1). Florida has reasonably determined that personal appeals for money by a judicial candidate inherently create an appearance of impropriety that may cause the public to lose confidence in the integrity of the judiciary. That interest may be implicated to varying degrees in particular contexts, but the interest remains whenever the public perceives the judge personally asking for money.

Moreover, the lines Yulee asks us to draw are unworkable. Even under her theory of the case, a mass mailing would create an appearance of impropriety if addressed to a list of all lawyers and litigants with pending cases. So would a speech soliciting contributions from the 100 most frequently appearing attorneys in the jurisdiction. Yulee says she might accept a ban on one-to-one solicitation, but is the public impression really any different if a judicial candidate tries to buttonhole not one prospective donor but two at a time? Ten? Yulee also agrees that in person solicitation creates a problem. But would the public's concern recede if the request for money came in a phone call or a text message?

We decline to wade into this swamp. The First Amendment requires that Canon 7C(1) be narrowly tailored, not that it be "perfectly tailored." The impossibility of perfect tailoring is especially apparent when the State's compelling interest is as intangible as public confidence in the integrity of the judiciary. Yulee is of course correct that some personal solicitations raise greater concerns than others. A judge who passes the hat in the courthouse creates a more serious appearance of impropriety than does a judicial candidate who makes a tasteful plea for support on the radio. But most problems arise in greater and lesser gradations, and the First Amendment does not confine a State to addressing evils in their most acute form. Here, Florida has concluded that all personal solicitations by judicial candidates create a public appearance that undermines confidence in the integrity of the judiciary; banning all personal solicitations by judicial candidates is narrowly tailored to address that concern. * * *

Finally, Yulee contends that Florida can accomplish its compelling interest through the less restrictive means of recusal rules and campaign contribution limits. We disagree. A rule requiring judges to recuse themselves from every case in which a lawyer or litigant made a campaign contribution would disable many jurisdictions. And a flood of postelection recusal motions could "erode public confidence in judicial impartiality" and thereby exacerbate the very appearance problem the State is trying to solve. Moreover, the rule that Yulee envisions could create a perverse incentive for litigants to make campaign contributions to judges solely as a means to trigger their later recusal — a form of peremptory strike against a judge that would enable transparent forum shopping.

As for campaign contribution limits, Florida already applies them to judicial elections. A State may decide that the threat to public confidence created by personal solicitation exists apart from the amount of money that a judge or judicial candidate seeks. Even if Florida decreased its contribution limit, the appearance that judges who personally solicit funds might improperly favor their campaign donors would remain. Although the Court has held that contribution limits advance the interest in preventing *quid pro quo* corruption and its appearance in political elections, we have never held that adopting contribution limits precludes a State from pursuing its compelling interests through additional means. And in any event, a State has compelling interests in regulating judicial elections that extend beyond its interests in regulating political elections, because judges are not politicians.

In sum, because Canon 7C(1) is narrowly tailored to serve a compelling government interest, the First Amendment poses no obstacle to its enforcement in this case. As a result of our decision, Florida may continue to prohibit judicial candidates from personally soliciting campaign funds, while allowing them to raise money through committees and to otherwise communicate their electoral messages in practically any way. The principal dissent faults us for not answering a slew of broader questions, such as whether Florida may cap a judicial candidate's spending or ban independent expenditures by corporations. Yulee has not asked these questions, and for good reason — they are far afield from the narrow regulation actually at issue in this case. * * *

* * * Judicial candidates have a First Amendment right to speak in support of their campaigns. States have a compelling interest in preserving public confidence in their judiciaries. When the State adopts a narrowly tailored restriction like the one at issue here, those principles do not conflict. A State's decision to elect judges does not compel it to compromise public confidence in their integrity.

The judgment of the Florida Supreme Court is

Affirmed.

JUSTICE BREYER, concurring.

As I have previously said, I view this Court's doctrine referring to tiers of scrutiny as guidelines informing our approach to the case at hand, not tests to be mechanically applied. On that understanding, I join the Court's opinion.

JUSTICE GINSBURG, * * * concurring in part and concurring in the judgment.

I join the Court's opinion save for Part II. As explained in my dissenting opinion in *Republican Party of Minnesota* v. *White*, I would not apply exacting scrutiny to a State's endeavor sensibly to "differentiate elections for political offices . . . , from elections designed to select those whose office it is to administer justice without respect to persons." * * *

JUSTICE SCALIA, with whom JUSTICE THOMAS joins, dissenting.

An ethics canon adopted by the Florida Supreme Court bans a candidate in a judicial election from asking anyone, under any circumstances, for a contribution to his campaign. Faithful application of our precedents would have made short work of this wildly disproportionate restriction upon speech. Intent upon upholding the Canon, however, the Court flattens one settled First Amendment principle after another.

I * * *

* * * I do not for a moment question the Court's conclusion that States have different compelling interests when regulating judicial elections than when regulating political ones. Unlike a legislator, a judge must be impartial — without bias for or against any party or attorney who comes before him. I accept for the sake of argument that States have a compelling interest in ensuring that its judges are *seen* to be impartial. I will likewise assume that a judicial candidate's request to a litigant or attorney presents a danger of coercion that a political candidate's request to a constituent does not. But Canon 7C(1) does not narrowly target concerns about impartiality or its appearance; it applies even when the person asked for a financial contribution has no chance of ever appearing in the candidate's court. And Florida does not invoke concerns about coercion, presumably because the Canon bans solicitations regardless of whether their object is a lawyer, litigant, or other person vulnerable to judicial pressure. So Canon 7C(1) fails exacting scrutiny and infringes the First Amendment. This case should have been just that straightforward.

II

The Court concludes that Florida may prohibit personal solicitations by judicial candidates as a means of preserving "public confidence in the integrity of the judiciary." It purports to reach this destination by applying strict scrutiny, but it would be more accurate to say that it does so by applying the appearance of strict scrutiny.

A

The first sign that mischief is afoot comes when the Court describes Florida's compelling interest. The State must first identify its objective with precision before one can tell whether that interest is compelling and whether the speech restriction narrowly targets it. In *White*, for example, the Court did not allow a State to invoke hazy concerns about judicial impartiality in justification of an ethics rule against judicial candidates' announcing their positions on legal issues. The Court instead separately analyzed the State's concerns about judges' bias against parties, preconceptions on legal issues, and openmindedness, and explained why each concern (and each for a different reason) did not suffice to sustain the rule. [536 U.S.,] at 775–780.

In stark contrast to *White*, the Court today relies on Florida's invocation of an ill-defined interest in "public confidence in judicial integrity." The Court at first suggests that "judicial integrity" involves the "ability to administer justice without fear or favor." * * * When the Court explains how solicitation undermines confidence in judicial integrity, integrity starts to sound like saintliness. It involves independence from any "*possible* temptation" that "*might* lead" the judge, "even unknowingly," to favor one party. When the Court turns to distinguishing in-person solicitation from solicitation by proxy, the any-possible-temptation standard no longer helps and thus drops out. The critical factors instead become the "pressure" a listener feels during a solicitation and the "appearance that the candidate will remember who says yes, and who says no." But when it comes time to explain Florida's decision to allow candidates to write thank-you notes, the "appearance that the candidate . . . remember[s] who says yes" gets nary a mention. And when the Court confronts Florida's decision to prohibit mass-mailed solicitations, concern about pressure fades away. More outrageous still, the Court at times molds the interest in the perception that judges have integrity into an interest in the perception that judges do not solicit — for example when it says, "all personal solicitations by judicial candidates create a public appearance that undermines confidence in the integrity of the judiciary; banning all personal solicitations by judicial candidates is narrowly tailored to address that concern." This is not strict scrutiny; it is sleight of hand.

B

The Court's twistifications have not come to an end; indeed, they are just beginning. In order to uphold Canon 7C(1) under strict scrutiny, Florida must do more than point to a vital public objective brooding overhead. The State must also meet a difficult burden of demonstrating that the speech restriction substantially advances the claimed objective. * * *

* * * The Court announces, on the basis of its "intuiti[on]," that allowing personal solicitations will make litigants worry that "judges' decisions may be motivated by the desire to repay campaign contributions." But this case is not about whether

Yulee has the right to receive campaign contributions. It is about whether she has the right to *ask* for campaign contributions that Florida's statutory law already allows her to receive. Florida bears the burden of showing that banning *requests* for lawful contributions will improve public confidence in judges — not just a little bit, but significantly, because "the Government does not have a compelling interest in each marginal percentage point by which its goals are advanced."

Neither the Court nor the State identifies the slightest evidence that banning requests for contributions will substantially improve public trust in judges. Nor does common sense make this happy forecast obvious. [J]udicial elections in America date back more than two centuries — but rules against personal solicitations date back only to 1972. The peaceful coexistence of judicial elections and personal solicitations for most of our history calls into doubt any claim that allowing personal solicitations would imperil public faith in judges. Many States allow judicial candidates to ask for contributions even today, but nobody suggests that public confidence in judges fares worse in these jurisdictions than elsewhere. And in any event, if candidates' appeals for money are "characteristically intertwined" with discussion of qualifications and views on public issues, how can the Court be so sure that the public will regard them as improprieties rather than as legitimate instances of campaigning? In the final analysis, Florida comes nowhere near making the convincing demonstration required by our cases that the speech restriction in this case substantially advances its objective.

C

But suppose we play along with the premise that prohibiting solicitations will significantly improve the public reputation of judges. Even then, Florida must show that the ban restricts no more speech than necessary to achieve the objective.

Canon 7C(1) falls miles short of satisfying this requirement. The Court seems to accept Florida's claim that solicitations erode public confidence by creating the perception that judges are selling justice to lawyers and litigants. Yet the Canon prohibits candidates from asking for money from *anybody* — even from someone who is neither lawyer nor litigant, even from someone who (because of recusal rules) cannot possibly appear before the candidate as lawyer or litigant. Yulee thus may not call up an old friend, a cousin, or even her parents to ask for a donation to her campaign. The State has not come up with a plausible explanation of how soliciting someone who has no chance of appearing in the candidate's court will diminish public confidence in judges.

No less important, Canon 7C(1) bans candidates from asking for contributions even in messages that do not target any listener in particular — mass-mailed letters, flyers posted on telephone poles, speeches to large gatherings, and Web sites addressed to the general public. Messages like these do not share the features that lead the Court to pronounce personal solicitations a menace to public confidence in the judiciary. Consider online solicitations. They avoid "the spectacle of lawyers or potential litigants directly handing over money to judicial candidates." People who come across online solicitations do not feel "pressure" to comply with the request. Nor does the candidate's signature on the online solicitation suggest "that the candidate will remember who says yes, and who says no." Yet Canon 7C(1) prohibits these and similar solicitations anyway. This tailoring is as narrow as the Court's scrutiny is strict.

Perhaps sensing the fragility of the initial claim that *all* solicitations threaten public confidence in judges, the Court argues that "the lines Yulee asks [it] to draw are unworkable." That is a difficulty of the Court's own imagination. In reality, the Court could have chosen from a whole spectrum of workable rules. It could have held that States may regulate no more than solicitation of participants in pending cases, or solicitation of people who are likely to appear in the candidate's court, or even solicitation of any lawyer or litigant. And it could have ruled that candidates have the right to make fundraising appeals that are not directed to any particular listener (like requests in mass-mailed letters), or at least fundraising appeals plainly directed to the general public (like requests placed online). The Supreme Court of Florida has made similar accommodations in other settings. It allows sitting judges to solicit memberships in civic organizations if (among other things) the solicitee is not "likely ever to appear before the court on which the judge serves." And it allows sitting judges to accept gifts if (among other things) "the donor is not a party or other person . . . whose interests have come or are likely to come before the judge." It is not too much to ask that the State show election speech similar consideration.

The Court's accusation of unworkability also suffers from a bit of a pot-kettle problem. Consider the many real-world questions left open by today's decision. Does the First Amendment permit restricting a candidate's appearing at an event where somebody *else* asks for campaign funds on his behalf? Does it permit prohibiting the candidate's *family* from making personal solicitations? Does it allow prohibiting the candidate from participating in the creation of a Web site that solicits funds, even if the candidate's name does not appear next to the request? More broadly, could Florida ban thank-you notes to donors? Cap a candidate's campaign spending? Restrict independent spending by people other than the candidate? Ban independent spending by corporations? And how, by the way, are judges supposed to decide whether these measures promote public confidence in judicial integrity, when the Court does not even have a consistent theory about what it means by "judicial integrity"? For the Court to wring its hands about workability under these circumstances is more than one should have to bear.

D * * *

* * * Canon 7C(1)'s scope suggests that it has nothing to do with the appearances created by judges' asking for money, and everything to do with hostility toward judicial campaigning. How else to explain the Florida Supreme Court's decision to ban *all* personal appeals for campaign funds (even when the solicitee could never appear before the candidate), but to tolerate appeals for other kinds of funds (even when the solicitee will surely appear before the candidate)? It should come as no surprise that the ABA, whose model rules the Florida Supreme Court followed when framing Canon 7C(1), opposes judicial elections — preferring instead a system in which (surprise!) a committee of lawyers proposes candidates from among whom the Governor must make his selection.

The Court tries to strike a pose of neutrality between appointment and election of judges, but no one should be deceived. A Court that sees impropriety in a candidate's request for *any* contributions to his election campaign does not much like judicial selection by the people. One cannot have judicial elections without judicial campaigns, and judicial campaigns without funds for campaigning, and funds for campaigning without asking for them. When a society decides that its judges should be elected, it necessarily decides that selection by the people is more important than the oracular sanctity of judges, their immunity from the (shudder!) indignity of begging for funds, and their exemption from those shadows of impropriety that fall over the proletarian public officials who must run for office. * * * The prescription that judges be elected probably springs from the people's realization that their judges can become their rulers — and (it must be said) from just a deep-down feeling that members of the Third Branch will profit from a hearty helping of humble pie, and from a severe reduction of their great remove from the (ugh!) People. (It should not be thought that I myself harbor such irreverent and revolutionary feelings; but I think it likely — and year by year more likely — that those who favor the election of judges do so.) In any case, hostility to campaigning by judges entitles the people of Florida to amend their Constitution to replace judicial elections with the selection of judges by lawyers' committees; it does not entitle the Florida Supreme Court to adopt, or this Court to endorse, a rule of judicial conduct that abridges candidates' speech in the judicial elections that the Florida Constitution prescribes. * * *

I respectfully dissent.

JUSTICE KENNEDY, dissenting. * * *

With all due respect for the Court, it seems fair and necessary to say its decision rests on two premises, neither one correct. One premise is that in certain elections — here an election to choose the best qualified judge — the public lacks the necessary judgment to make an informed choice. Instead, the State must protect voters by altering the usual dynamics of free speech. The other premise is that since judges should be accorded special respect and dignity, their election can be subject to certain content-based rules that would be unacceptable in other elections. In my respectful view neither premise can justify the speech restriction at issue here. Although States have a compelling interest in seeking to ensure the appearance and the reality of an impartial judiciary, it does not follow that the State may alter basic First Amendment principles in pursuing that goal. * * *

It is not within our Nation's First Amendment tradition to abridge speech simply because the government believes a question is too difficult or too profound for voters. If the State is concerned about unethical campaign practices, it need not revert to the assumption that voters themselves are insensitive to ethics. Judicial elections were created to enable citizens to decide for themselves which judges are best qualified and which are most likely to "stand by the constitution of the State against the encroachment of power." The Court should not now presume citizens are unequipped for that task when it comes to judging for themselves who should judge them. * * *

* * * This law comes nowhere close to being narrowly tailored. And by saying that it survives that vital First Amendment requirement, the Court now writes what is literally a casebook guide to eviscerating strict scrutiny any time the Court

encounters speech it dislikes. On these premises, and for the reasons explained in more detail by JUSTICE SCALIA, it is necessary for me to file this respectful dissent.

JUSTICE ALITO, dissenting.

I largely agree with what I view as the essential elements of the dissents filed by JUSTICES SCALIA and KENNEDY. * * * Florida has a compelling interest in making sure that its courts decide cases impartially and in accordance with the law and that its citizens have no good reason to lack confidence that its courts are performing their proper role. But the Florida rule is not narrowly tailored to serve that interest.

Indeed, this rule is about as narrowly tailored as a burlap bag. It applies to all solicitations made in the name of a candidate for judicial office — including, as was the case here, a mass mailing. It even applies to an ad in a newspaper. It applies to requests for contributions in any amount, and it applies even if the person solicited is not a lawyer, has never had any interest at stake in any case in the court in question, and has no prospect of ever having any interest at stake in any litigation in that court. If this rule can be characterized as narrowly tailored, then narrow tailoring has no meaning, and strict scrutiny, which is essential to the protection of free speech, is seriously impaired.

Notes and Questions

1.   Are there sufficient reasons to distinguish between the First Amendment protection given to financing judicial campaigns, on the one hand, and financing legislative or executive campaigns, on the other? In both instances, restrictions on the funding would be justified by the need to prevent the actuality or appearance of impropriety. But the Court appears to have a different vision of impropriety for those different offices, as you will learn in the next Chapter. The Court seems to accept that "political" officials will show a certain favoritism for their supporters, while *Williams-Yulee* found a compelling interest in avoiding even the appearance that judges would favor theirs.

2.   Throughout this Chapter, we have explored several different areas of First Amendment doctrine that have application in campaigns and elections. Should states be able to impose greater restrictions on speech in those areas when *judicial* elections are involved? Would states, for example, have a sufficiently compelling interest in protecting the appearance of judicial integrity to allow them to permit judges to recover for defamatory falsehoods without satisfying the actual-malice standard?

3.   *Problem.* In the years since *Republican Party of Minnesota v. White* struck down the announce clause, there has been much controversy about the constitutionality of other restrictions on judicial campaign activity. *Williams-Yulee* is unlikely to resolve those controversies. Are the following restrictions narrowly tailored to serve a compelling interest?

    a.   Laws prohibiting judicial candidates from identifying themselves as members of political parties. *See Carey v. Wotnitzek*, 614 F.3d 189 (6th Cir. 2010); *Siefert v. Alexander*, 608 F.3d 974 (7th Cir. 2010), *cert. denied*, 131 S. Ct.

2872 (2011); *Republican Party of Minnesota v. White*, 416 F.3d 738 (8th Cir. 2005) (*en banc*) (on remand from the Supreme Court).

b. Laws prohibiting judicial candidates from pursuing party endorsements. *See Republican Party v. White, supra.*

c. Laws prohibiting judicial candidates from attending political gatherings. *See id.*

d. Laws prohibiting judicial candidates from speaking at political gatherings or speaking on behalf of political organizations. *See Bauer v. Shepard*, 620 F.3d 704 (7th Cir. 2010), *cert. denied*, 131 S. Ct. 2872 (2011).

e. Laws prohibiting judicial candidates from holding party office.

f. Laws prohibiting judicial candidates from endorsing or opposing candidates for public office. *See Wersal v. Sexton*, 613 F.3d 821 (8th Cir. 2010); *Siefert, supra; Bauer, supra.*

4. The Ninth Circuit recently (but before Williams-Yulee) invalidated several provisions of the Arizona Code of Judicial Conduct that restricted the speech of judicial candidates. *Wolfson v. Concannon*, 750 F.3d 1145 (9th Cir. 2014). The court held that the provisions — which banned the personal solicitation of campaign funds, as well as making speeches, raising funds, or otherwise supporting or opposing another's campaign — were not narrowly tailored to serve the compelling interests in the actuality and appearance of an impartial judiciary. Interestingly, the court invalidated several of the provisions only as applied to non-judge candidates, *i.e.*, persons running for judicial office but who were not incumbent judges. The court reasoned that the speech prohibitions were not narrowly tailored ways of protecting the impartiality of the judiciary when they applied to people who were not, and might never be, judges. The plaintiff, Wolfson, was a non-judge candidate, and the court held that he could not challenge the rules as applied to incumbent judges. *See Wolfson v. Brammer*, 616 F.3d 1045, 1064 (9th Cir. 2010). Are such speech restrictions constitutional as applied to incumbent judges running for re-election?

5. Ohio statutes, dating to the Progressive Era, prohibit the inclusion of judicial candidates' political party affiliations on Ohio's nonpartisan general election ballot. Does that prohibition violate the First Amendment rights of the candidate or of the party? A recent attack on the statute was rejected in *Ohio Council 8 American Federation of State, County, and Municipal Employees v. Brunner*, 24 F. Supp. 3d 680 (S.D. Ohio 2014). Is there a constitutional difference between (a) laws prohibiting judicial candidates from announcing their partisan affiliations, (b) laws prohibiting parties from endorsing their preferred judicial candidates, *see Sanders County Republican Central Comm. v. Bullock*, 698 F.3d 741 (9th Cir. 2012), and (c) laws prohibiting judicial candidates' partisan affiliations from appearing on the ballot?

Chapter 9

CAMPAIGN FINANCE

A. INTRODUCTION

Perhaps no issue in the field of election law has been so contentious for so long as that of campaign finance.

In a 1997 interview, former House Minority Leader Richard Gephardt (D-Mo.) stated, "What we have is two important values in direct conflict: freedom of speech, and our desire for healthy campaigns in a healthy democracy." Nancy Gibbs, *The Wake Up Call*, TIME, Feb. 3, 1997, at 22. Although Gephardt was often criticized for suggesting that these values were in conflict, in fact his comment well summed up the debate. There is virtually unanimous agreement that the purpose of the First Amendment is to "protect the free discussion of governmental affairs." *Mills v. Alabama*, 384 U.S. 214, 218 (1966). Yet many Americans are deeply concerned when politicians must solicit large sums of cash to finance their political campaigns. This system of campaign funding is perceived to foster political corruption and to create political inequality inconsistent with the principles "behind one person, one vote."

As you read through the cases in this Chapter, you should see that the tension between free speech on the one hand, and anti-corruption and equality concerns on the other, is a constant theme. The opinions often carry an edge rarely found in judicial writing. Perhaps this is because campaign finance brings to the surface deep disagreements not only about the proper mode of constitutional interpretation, but about theories of democratic representation, about the meaning of political equality, and about our fundamental attitudes towards government.

Further confusing the debate is that the goals Americans set for their campaign-finance system are often at cross-purposes. For example, caps on campaign spending reduce concerns created by candidate fundraising, but can also reduce the flow of information needed for a well informed electorate. Disclosure of campaign contributions provides information to the electorate but compromises privacy and perhaps even the notion of a secret ballot. And always, partisan politics hovers in the background, for few areas of law so directly affect partisan prospects. Is it best, then, to leave balancing of these concerns to the legislature, which claims particular familiarity with campaigns and elections? Or does the unique opportunity to manipulate the law for partisan or personal advantage suggest a particularly strong need for judicial skepticism of legislative enactments?

B. BASIC PRINCIPLES

At the core of most campaign-finance regulation systems are restrictions on contributions to political campaigns. Although a there have been some proposals to address political inequality, and even corruption, through public-financing plans that do not rely on limitations on contributions and spending, these are the exception. *See* Joel Fleishman & Pope McCorkle, *Level Up Rather than Level Down: Towards a New Theory of Campaign Finance*, 52 J.L. & POL. 211 (1984); BRUCE ACKERMAN & IAN AYRES, VOTING WITH DOLLARS: A NEW PARADIGM FOR CAMPAIGN FINANCE (2002). Most proposals for reform and more importantly, virtually all laws in the United States, have been built around restrictions on contributions to candidates, parties, campaigns, or other political organizations, and in some cases, around limits on expenditures.

For many years, the Supreme Court avoided the First Amendment issues raised by campaign-finance regulations. In *United States v. Newberry*, 256 U.S. 232 (1921), a lower court convicted Truman Newberry, a candidate in Michigan's Republican primary for the U.S. Senate, of violating the Corrupt Practices Act by contributing $100,000 (approximately $1.6 million in 2016 dollars) to his own campaign, in violation of limits existing in Michigan state law.[a] A divided Supreme Court reversed on the ground that the constitutional authority to regulate the "time, place, and manner" of elections did not extend to primaries, which it viewed as private affairs. (This holding would be overruled in *United States v. Classic*, 313 U.S. 299 (1941), one of the "White Primary Cases." *See* Chapter 6).

In *United States v. Congress of Industrial Organizations*, 335 U.S. 106 (1948), the lower court held that a provision of the Taft-Hartley Act, prohibiting corporations and unions from any type of spending on political campaigns, was unconstitutional insofar as it applied to political commentary, editorials, and endorsements in a newspaper published by a union for its members' benefit. The Supreme Court affirmed without reaching the constitutional issue. While four members of the Court — Justices Rutledge, Black, Douglas, and Murphy — would have found that the law did cover the publication in question and that it was unconstitutional, the majority, in an opinion authored by Justice Reed, concluded that the statute did not clearly prohibit "a trade journal, a house organ, or a newspaper published by a corporation, from expressing views on candidates or political proposals in the regular course of its publication."

In the following case, commonly referred to as *Auto Workers*, the Supreme Court again avoided ruling on the constitutionality of limitations on contributions and expenditures. However, the opinion, written by Justice Frankfurter, is important for the extensive history it presents of campaign-finance law. This history has been relied on by the Supreme Court in numerous later cases, though as the notes that follow discuss, in recent years it has fallen into some disrepute.

---

[a] Newberry, a founder of the Packard Automobile Company, defeated Ford Motor Company founder Henry Ford for the Republican nomination. Ford, however, also entered and won the Democratic primary, and Newberry defeated him a second time in the general election. Newberry was represented in the Supreme Court by former Justice and presidential candidate, and future Chief Justice, Charles Evans Hughes. Ford was a political ally of President Woodrow Wilson, who had defeated Hughes in the 1916 presidential race.

UNITED STATES v. INTERNATIONAL UNION UNITED AUTOMOBILE, AIRCRAFT AND AGRICULTURAL IMPLEMENT WORKERS OF AMERICA (UAW-CIO)
Supreme Court of the United States
352 U.S. 567, 77 S. Ct. 529, 1 L. Ed. 2d 563 (1957)

MR. JUSTICE FRANKFURTER delivered the opinion of the Court [in which MR. JUSTICE BURTON, MR. JUSTICE CLARK, MR. JUSTICE HARLAN, and MR. JUSTICE BRENNAN join].[b]

The issues tendered in this case are the construction and, ultimately, the constitutionality of 18 U.S.C. § 610, an Act of Congress that prohibits corporations and labor organizations from making "a contribution or expenditure in connection with" any election for federal office. * * *

Appreciation of the circumstances that begot this statute is necessary for its understanding, and understanding of it is necessary for adjudication of the legal problems before us. Speaking broadly, what is involved here is the integrity of our electoral process, and, not less, the responsibility of the individual citizen for the successful functioning of that process. This case thus raises issues not less than basic to a democratic society.

The concentration of wealth consequent upon the industrial expansion in the post-Civil War era had profound implications for American life. The impact of the abuses resulting from this concentration gradually made itself felt by a rising tide of reform protest in the last decade of the nineteenth century. The Sherman Law was a response to the felt threat to economic freedom created by enormous industrial combines. The income tax law of 1894 reflected congressional concern over the growing disparity of income between the many and the few.

No less lively, although slower to evoke federal action, was popular feeling that aggregated capital unduly influenced politics, an influence not stopping short of corruption. * * * In the [18]90's many States passed laws requiring candidates for office and their political committees to make public the sources and amounts of contributions to their campaign funds and the recipients and amounts of their campaign expenditures. The theory behind these laws was that the spotlight of publicity would discourage corporations from making political contributions and would thereby end their control over party policies. But these state publicity laws either became dead letters or were found to be futile. As early as 1894, the sober-minded Elihu Root saw the need for more effective legislation. He urged the Constitutional Convention of the State of New York to prohibit political contributions by corporations:

> "The idea is to prevent . . . the great railroad companies, the great insurance companies, the great telephone companies, the great aggregations of wealth from using their corporate funds, directly or indirectly, to send members of the legislature to these halls in order to vote for their protection and the advancement of their interests as against those of the public. It strikes at a constantly growing evil which has done more to shake

---

[b] This case was decided on March 11, 1957, before the Senate had confirmed Charles Whittaker to fill the seat vacated by Stanley Reed. Accordingly, only eight Justices participated. [— Eds.]

the confidence of the plain people of small means of this country in our political institutions than any other practice which has ever obtained since the foundation of our Government. And I believe that the time has come when something ought to be done to put a check to the giving of $50,000 or $100,000 by a great corporation toward political purposes upon the understanding that a debt is created from a political party to it."

Concern over the size and source of campaign funds so actively entered the presidential campaign of 1904 that it crystallized popular sentiment for federal action to purge national politics of what was conceived to be the pernicious influence of "big money" campaign contributions. * * * President Theodore Roosevelt quickly responded to this national mood. In his annual message to Congress on December 5, 1905, he recommended that:

"All contributions by corporations to any political committee or for any political purpose should be forbidden by law; directors should not be permitted to use stockholders' money for such purposes; and, moreover, a prohibition of this kind would be, as far as it went, an effective method of stopping the evils aimed at in corrupt practices acts."

Grist was added to the reformers' mill by the investigation of the great life insurance companies conducted by the Joint Committee of the New York Legislature, the Armstrong Committee, under the guidance of Charles Evans Hughes. The Committee's report, filed early in 1906, revealed that one insurance company alone had contributed almost $50,000 to a national campaign committee in 1904 and had given substantial amounts in preceding presidential campaigns. The Committee concluded:

"Contributions by insurance corporations for political purposes should be strictly forbidden. Neither executive officers nor directors should be allowed to use the moneys paid for purposes of insurance in support of political candidates or platforms. . . . Whether made for the purpose of supporting political views or with the desire to obtain protection for the corporation, these contributions have been wholly unjustifiable. * * * The frank admission that moneys have been obtained for use in State campaigns upon the expectation that candidates thus aided in their election would support the interests of the companies, has exposed both those who solicited the contributions and those who made them to severe and just condemnation."

Less than a month later the Committee on Elections of the House of Representatives began considering a number of proposals designed to cleanse the political process. Some bills prohibited political contributions by certain classes of corporations; some merely required disclosure of contributions; and others made bribery at elections a federal crime. The feeling of articulate reform groups was reflected at a public hearing held by the Committee. Perry Belmont, leader of a nation-wide organization advocating a federal publicity bill, stated:

". . . this thing has come to the breaking point. We have had enough of it. We don't want any more secret purchase of organizations, which nullifies platforms, nullifies political utterances and the pledges made by political leaders in and out of Congress."

This view found strong support in the testimony of Samuel Gompers, President of the American Federation of Labor, who said, with respect to the publicity bill:

"* * * It is doubtful to my mind if the contributions and expenditures of vast sums of money in the nominations and elections for our public offices can continue to increase without endangering the endurance of our Republic in its purity and in its essence.

". . . If the interests of any people are threatened by corruption in our public life or corruption in elections, surely it must of necessity be those, that large class of people, whom we for convenience term the wageworkers.

"[O]ne of the reasons for the absence of legislation of a liberal or sympathetic or just character, so far as it affects the interest of the wage-earners of America, can be fairly well traced with the growth of the corruption funds and the influences that are in operation during elections and campaigns. . . . I am under the impression that the patience of the American workingmen is about exhausted —

". . . [If] we are really determined that our elections shall be free from the power of money and its lavish use and expenditure without an accounting to the conscience and the judgment of the people of America, we will have to pass some measure of this kind."

President Roosevelt's annual message of 1906 listed as the first item of congressional business a law prohibiting political contributions by corporations. Shortly thereafter, in 1907, Congress provided:

"That it shall be unlawful for any national bank, or any corporation organized by authority of any laws of Congress, to make a money contribution in connection with any election to any political office. It shall also be unlawful for any corporation whatever to make a money contribution in connection with any election at which Presidential and Vice-Presidential electors or a Representative in Congress is to be voted for or any election by any State legislature of a United States Senator."

As the historical background of this statute indicates, its aim was not merely to prevent the subversion of the integrity of the electoral process. Its underlying philosophy was to sustain the active, alert responsibility of the individual citizen in a democracy for the wise conduct of government.

This Act of 1907 was merely the first concrete manifestation of a continuing congressional concern for elections "free from the power of money." The 1909 Congress witnessed unsuccessful attempts to amend the Act to proscribe the contribution of anything of value and to extend its application to the election of state legislatures. The Congress of 1910 translated popular demand for further curbs upon the political power of wealth into a publicity law that required committees operating to influence the results of congressional elections in two or more States to report all contributions and disbursements and to identify contributors and recipients of substantial sums. That law also required persons who spent more than

$50 annually for the purpose of influencing congressional elections in more than one State to report those expenditures if they were not made through a political committee. At the next session that Act was extended to require all candidates for the Senate and the House of Representatives to make detailed reports with respect to both nominating and election campaigns. The amendment also placed maximum limits on the amounts that congressional candidates could spend in seeking nomination and election, and forbade them from promising employment for the purpose of obtaining support. And in 1918 Congress made it unlawful either to offer or to solicit anything of value to influence voting.

This Court's decision in *Newberry* v. *United States*, 256 U.S. 232 [(1921)], invalidating federal regulation of Senate primary elections, led to the Federal Corrupt Practices Act of 1925, a comprehensive revision of existing legislation. The debates preceding that Act's passage reveal an attitude important to an understanding of the course of this legislation. Thus, Senator Robinson, one of the leaders of the Senate, said:

> "We all know . . . that one of the great political evils of the time is the apparent hold on political parties which business interests and certain organizations seek and sometimes obtain by reason of liberal campaign contributions. Many believe that when an individual or association of individuals makes large contributions for the purpose of aiding candidates of political parties in winning the elections, they expect, and sometimes demand, and occasionally, at least, receive, consideration by the beneficiaries of their contributions which not infrequently is harmful to the general public interest. It is unquestionably an evil which ought to be dealt with, and dealt with intelligently and effectively."

One of the means chosen by Congress to deal with this evil was § 313 of the 1925 Act, which strengthened the 1907 statute (1) by changing the phrase "money contribution" to "contribution" * * *; (2) by extending the prohibition on corporate contributions to the election to Congress of Delegates and Resident Commissioners; and (3) by penalizing the recipient of any forbidden contribution as well as the contributor.

When, in 1940, Congress moved to extend the Hatch Act, which was designed to free the political process of the abuses deemed to accompany the operation of a vast civil administration, its reforming zeal also led Congress to place further restrictions upon the political potentialities of wealth. Section 20 of the law amending the Hatch Act made it unlawful for any "political committee," as defined in the Act of 1925, to receive contributions of more than $3,000,000 or to make expenditures of more than that amount in any calendar year. And § 13 made it unlawful "for any person, directly or indirectly, to make contributions in an aggregate amount in excess of $5,000, during any calendar year, or in connection with any campaign for nomination or election, to or on behalf of any candidate for an elective Federal office" or any committee supporting such a candidate. The term "person" was defined to include any committee, association, organization or other group of persons. In offering § 13 from the Senate floor Senator Bankhead said:

> "We all know that money is the chief source of corruption. We all know that large contributions to political campaigns not only put the political party

under obligation to the large contributors, who demand pay in the way of legislation, but we also know that large sums of money are used for the purpose of conducting expensive campaigns through the newspapers and over the radio; in the publication of all sorts of literature, true and untrue; and for the purpose of paying the expenses of campaigners sent out into the country to spread propaganda, both true and untrue."

The need for unprecedented economic mobilization propelled by World War II enormously stimulated the power of organized labor and soon aroused consciousness of its power outside its ranks. Wartime strikes gave rise to fears of the new concentration of power represented by the gains of trade unionism. And so the belief grew that, just as the great corporations had made huge political contributions to influence governmental action or inaction, whether consciously or unconsciously, the powerful unions were pursuing a similar course, and with the same untoward consequences for the democratic process. Thus, in 1943, when Congress passed the Smith-Connally Act to secure defense production against work stoppages, contained therein was a provision extending to labor organizations, for the duration of the war. The testimony of Congressman Landis, author of this measure, before a subcommittee of the House Committee on Labor makes plain the dominant concern that evoked it:

"[P]ublic opinion toward the conduct of labor unions is rapidly undergoing a change. The public thinks, and has a right to think, that labor unions, as public institutions should be granted the same rights and no greater rights than any other public group. My bill seeks to put labor unions on exactly the same basis, insofar as their financial activities are concerned, as corporations have been on for many years.

"* * * One of the matters upon which I sensed that the public was taking a stand opposite to that of labor leaders was the question of the handling of funds of labor organizations. The public was aroused by many rumors of huge war chests being maintained by labor unions, of enormous fees and dues being extorted from war workers, of political contributions to parties and candidates which later were held as clubs over the head of high Federal officials. * * *

Despite § 313's wartime application to labor organizations, Congress was advised of enormous financial outlays said to have been made by some unions in connection with the national elections of 1944. The Senate's Special Committee on Campaign Expenditures investigated, *inter alia*, the role of the Political Action Committee of the Congress of Industrial Organizations. The Committee found "no clear-cut violation of the Corrupt Practices Act on the part of the Political Action Committee" on the ground that it had made direct contributions only to candidates and political committees involved in state and local elections and federal primaries, to which the Act did not apply, and had limited its participation in federal elections to political "expenditures," as distinguished from "contributions" to candidates or committees. The Committee also investigated, on complaint of Senator Taft, the Ohio C.I.O. Council's distribution to the public at large of 200,000 copies of a pamphlet opposing the re-election of Senator Taft and supporting his rival. In response to the C.I.O.'s assertion that this was not a proscribed "contribution" but merely an "expenditure of its own funds to state its position to the world, exercising its right of free speech," the Committee requested the Department of Justice to bring a test case on these facts. It also recommended extension of § 313 to cover primary campaigns and nominating conventions. A minority of the Committee, Senators Ball and Ferguson, advocated further amendment of § 313 to proscribe "expenditures" as well as "contributions" in order to avoid the possibility of emasculation of the statutory policy through a narrow judicial construction of "contributions."

The 1945 Report of the House Special Committee to Investigate Campaign Expenditures expressed concern over the vast amounts that some labor organizations were devoting to politics:

> "The scale of operations of some of these organizations is impressive. Without exception, they operate on a Nation-wide basis; and many of them have affiliated local organizations. One was found to have an annual budget for 'educational' work approximating $1,500,000, and among other things regularly supplies over 500 radio stations with 'briefs for broadcasters.' Another, with an annual budget of over $300,000 for political 'education,' has distributed some 80,000,000 pieces of literature, including a quarter million copies of one article. Another, representing an organized labor membership of 5,000,000, has raised $700,000 for its national organizations in union contributions for political 'education' in a few months, and a great deal more has been raised for the same purpose and expended by its local organizations."

Like the Senate Committee, it advocated extension of § 313 to primaries and nominating conventions, and noted the existence of a controversy over the scope of "contribution." The following year the House Committee made a further study of the activities of organizations attempting to influence the outcome of federal elections. It found that the Brotherhood of Railway Trainmen and other groups employed professional political organizers, sponsored partisan radio programs and distributed campaign literature. It concluded that:

> "The intent and purpose of the provision of the act prohibiting any corporation or labor organization making any contribution in connection with any election would be wholly defeated if it were assumed that the term 'making any contribution' related only to the donating of money directly to a candidate, and excluded the vast expenditures of money in the activities herein shown to be engaged in extensively. Of what avail would a law be to prohibit the contributing direct to a candidate and yet permit the expenditure of large sums in his behalf?

> "The committee is firmly convinced, after a thorough study of the provisions of the act, the legislative history of the same, and the debates on the said provisions when it was pending before the House, that the act was intended to prohibit such expenditures."

Accordingly, to prevent further evasion of the statutory policy, the Committee attached to its recommendation that the prohibition of contributions by labor organizations be made permanent the additional proposal that the statute "be clarified so as to specifically provide that expenditures of money for salaries to organizers, purchase of radio time, and other expenditures by the prohibited organizations in connection with elections, constitute violations of the provisions of said section, whether or not said expenditures are with or without the knowledge or consent of the candidates."

Early in 1947 the Special Committee to Investigate Senatorial Campaign Expenditures in the 1946 elections, the Ellender Committee, urged similar action to "plug the existing loophole." * * *

Shortly thereafter, Congress again acted to protect the political process from what it deemed to be the corroding effect of money employed in elections by aggregated power. Section 304 of the labor bill introduced into the House by Representative Hartley in 1947, like the Ellender bill, embodied the changes recommended in the reports of the Senate and House Committees on Campaign Expenditures. It sought to amend § 313 of the Corrupt Practices Act to proscribe any "expenditure" as well as "any contribution," to make permanent § 313's application to labor organizations and to extend its coverage to federal primaries and nominating conventions. * * * In explaining § 304 to his colleagues, Senator Taft * * * said:

"* * * In this instance the words of the Smith-Connally Act have been somewhat changed in effect so as to plug up a loophole which obviously developed, and which, if the courts had permitted advantage to be taken of it, as a matter of fact, would absolutely have destroyed the prohibition against political advertising by corporations. If 'contribution' does not mean 'expenditure,' then a candidate for office could have his corporation friends publish an advertisement for him in the newspapers every day for a month before election. I do not think the law contemplated such a thing, but it was claimed that it did, at least when it applied to labor organizations. So, all we are doing here is plugging up the hole which developed, following the recommendation by our own Elections Committee, in the Ellender bill."

[T]he bill subsequently became law despite the President's veto. It is this section of the statute that the District Court held did not reach the activities alleged in the indictment. * * *

[T]he indictment charged appellee with having used union dues to sponsor commercial television broadcasts designed to influence the electorate to select certain candidates for Congress in connection with the 1954 elections.

To deny that such activity, either on the part of a corporation or a labor organization, constituted an "expenditure in connection with any [federal] election" is to deny the long series of congressional efforts calculated to avoid the deleterious influences on federal elections resulting from the use of money by those who exercise control over large aggregations of capital. More particularly, this Court would have to ignore the history of the statute from the time it was first made applicable to labor organizations. As indicated by the reports of the Congressional Committees that investigated campaign expenditures, it was to embrace precisely the kind of indirect contribution alleged in the indictment that Congress amended § 313 to proscribe "expenditures." It is open to the Government to prove under this indictment activity by appellee that, except for an irrelevant difference in the medium of communication employed, is virtually indistinguishable from the Brotherhood of Railway Trainmen's purchase of radio time to sponsor candidates or the Ohio C.I.O.'s general distribution of pamphlets to oppose Senator Taft. Because such conduct was claimed to be merely "an expenditure [by the union] of its own funds to state its position to the world," the Senate and House Committees recommended and Congress enacted, as we have seen, the prohibition of "expenditures" as well as "contributions" to "plug the existing loophole." * * *

Appellee urges that if, as we hold, 18 U.S.C. § 610 embraces the activity alleged in the indictment, it offends several rights guaranteed by the Constitution.[2] The Government replies that the actual restraint upon union political activity imposed by the statute is so narrowly limited that Congress did not exceed its powers to protect the political process from undue influence of large aggregations of capital and to promote individual responsibility for democratic government. * * *

The wisdom of refraining from avoidable constitutional pronouncements * * * is peculiarly appropriate in the circumstances of this case. First of all, these questions come to us unillumined by the consideration of a single judge — we are asked to decide them in the first instance. [O]nly an adjudication on the merits can provide the concrete factual setting that sharpens the deliberative process especially demanded for constitutional decision. Finally, by remanding the case for trial it may well be that the Court will not be called upon to pass on the questions now raised. * * *

Allegations of the indictment hypothetically framed to elicit a ruling from this Court or based upon misunderstanding of the facts may not survive the test of proof. For example, was the broadcast paid for out of the general dues of the union membership or may the funds be fairly said to have been obtained on a voluntary basis? Did the broadcast reach the public at large or only those affiliated with appellee? Did it constitute active electioneering or simply state the record of particular candidates on economic issues? Did the union sponsor the broadcast with the intent to affect the results of the election? * * * We suggest the possibility of such questions, not to imply answers to problems of statutory construction, but merely to indicate the covert issues that may be involved in this case. * * *

Because the District Court's erroneous interpretation of the statute led it to stop the prosecution prematurely, its judgment must be reversed and the case must be remanded to it for further proceedings not inconsistent with this opinion.

---

[2] ". . . if such an expenditure is prohibited by 18 U.S.C. 610, * * * the statute (i) abridges freedom of speech and of the press and the right peaceably to assemble and to petition; (ii) abridges the right to choose senators and representatives guaranteed by Article I, § 2 and the Seventeenth Amendment; (iii) creates an arbitrary and unlawful classification and discriminates against labor organizations in violation of the Fifth Amendment, and (iv) is vague and indefinite and fails to provide a reasonably ascertainable standard of guilt in violation of the Fifth and Sixth Amendments." Brief for appellee, pp. 2–3.

Reversed and remanded.

MR. JUSTICE DOUGLAS, with whom THE CHIEF JUSTICE [WARREN] and MR. JUSTICE BLACK join, dissenting.

We deal here with a problem that is fundamental to the electoral process and to the operation of our democratic society. It is whether a union can express its views on the issues of an election and on the merits of the candidates, unrestrained and unfettered by the Congress. The principle at stake is not peculiar to unions. It is applicable as well to associations of manufacturers, retail and wholesale trade groups, consumers' leagues, farmers' unions, religious groups and every other association representing a segment of American life and taking an active part in our political campaigns and discussions. It is as important an issue as has come before the Court, for it reaches the very vitals of our system of government.

Under our Constitution it is We The People who are sovereign. The people have the final say. The legislators are their spokesmen. The people determine through their votes the destiny of the nation. It is therefore important — vitally important — that all channels of communication be open to them during every election, that no point of view be restrained or barred, and that the people have access to the views of every group in the community.

In *United States* v. *C.I.O.*, 335 U.S. 106, 144 [(1948)], Mr. Justice Rutledge spoke of the importance of the First Amendment rights — freedom of expression and freedom of assembly — to the integrity of our elections. "The most complete exercise of those rights," he said, "is essential to the full, fair and untrammeled operation of the electoral process. To the extent they are curtailed the electorate is deprived of information, knowledge and opinion vital to its function."

What the Court does today greatly impairs those rights. It sustains an indictment charging no more than the use of union funds for broadcasting television programs that urge and endorse the selection of certain candidates for the Congress of the United States. The opinion of the Court places that advocacy in the setting of corrupt practices. The opinion generates an environment of evil-doing and points to the oppressions and misdeeds that have haunted elections in this country.

Making a speech endorsing a candidate for office does not, however, deserve to be identified with antisocial conduct. Until today political speech has never been considered a crime. The making of a political speech up to now has always been one of the preferred rights protected by the First Amendment. It usually costs money to communicate an idea to a large audience. But no one would seriously contend that the expenditure of money to print a newspaper deprives the publisher of freedom of the press. Nor can the fact that it costs money to make a speech — whether it be hiring a hall or purchasing time on the air — make the speech any the less an exercise of First Amendment rights. Yet this statute, as construed and applied in this indictment, makes criminal any "expenditure" by a union for the purpose of expressing its views on the issues of an election and the candidates. * * *

I would affirm the judgment dismissing the indictment.

Notes and Questions

1. In recent years, scholars engaging in significant historical research have challenged Justice Frankfurter's "heroic" account of the development of campaign-finance law. The most direct analysis of Frankfurter's opinion has come from Professor Allison Hayward, who has argued that Justice Frankfurter's opinion "avoided political context and truncated political and legislative history. What emerges from a more complete account is a messy, complicated record, dictated by political opportunism. At each step, reform was a way to capitalize on public sentiment and restrict political rivals' access to financial resources, using little debated legislative vehicles and parliamentary skill." Allison R. Hayward, *Revisiting the Fable of Reform*, 45 HARV. J. ON LEGIS. 421, 422 (2008). In *Citizens United v. Federal Election Commission*, 558 U.S. 310 (2010) [p. 1022], the Supreme Court, relying Hayward's scholarship and an amicus brief filed by several campaign finance scholars, declared the *United Auto Workers'* history "flawed." *Id.* at 363.

Others have similarly argued that most reform is best explained by efforts to gain partisan or ideological advantage and to protect incumbent legislators. *See* JOHN SAMPLES, THE FALLACY OF CAMPAIGN FINANCE REFORM 189–232 (2006); RAYMOND J. LA RAJA, SMALL CHANGE: MONEY, POLITICAL PARTIES, AND CAMPAIGN FINANCE REFORM 43–80 (2008). Professor Adam Winkler has argued that the primary motivation for the Tillman Act and early publicity acts had little to do with battling political corruption or inequality, but rather with protecting the rights of corporate shareholders and the reserves of insurance companies. Adam Winkler, *Other People's Money: Corporations, Agency Costs, and Campaign Finance Law*, 92 GEO. L.J. 871 (2004).

Do the motivations of legislators matter when determining the constitutionality of campaign-finance laws? Should it matter if the history of the law in question demonstrated concern for the "wise conduct of government" (Frankfurter), or the absence of "any exercise of reasoned policy judgment" (Hayward)? Hayward, supra, at 454. Does this affect your attitude toward legislation in this area?

2. At the close of *Auto Workers*, Justice Frankfurter raised several issues that, he suggested, might be clarified by allowing the prosecution to continue. Do you agree that these issues could make a difference in determining the law's constitutionality? Why or why not?

3. Was Justice Frankfurter's cautious approach of avoiding constitutional adjudication the right choice? *Auto Workers* did not return to the Supreme Court. On November 6, 1957, a federal jury found the defendants not guilty on all counts. Hayward, *supra*, at 463. The failure of the prosecution in *Auto Workers* was, in fact, not atypical — in fact, between 1925 and 1971, there was not a single successful prosecution under the Federal Corrupt Practices Act. FRANK SORAUF, INSIDE CAMPAIGN FINANCE: MYTHS AND REALITIES 6 (1992).

In 1972, Congress completely revamped federal campaign-finance law with the passage of the Federal Election Campaign Act ("FECA").[c] In its original form, FECA relied primarily on disclosure of contributions rather than limits on contributions. However, the law had scarcely taken effect before the Watergate scandal broke. Although the new disclosure requirements of the FECA actually helped to break key parts of the Watergate scandal, *see* HERBERT E. ALEXANDER, FINANCING POLITICS: MONEY, ELECTIONS AND POLITICAL REFORM 30–32 (1992), the scandal provided the impetus for a more far-reaching law. The 1974 Amendments to the FECA effectively re-wrote the law from the ground up, including new limits on contributions and expenditures, new disclosure requirements, public financing of the presidential campaigns, and the creation of a new, independent federal agency, the Federal Election Commission, to oversee enforcement.

The law was immediately challenged by a conglomeration of plaintiffs from across the political spectrum, including former Democratic presidential candidate Eugene McCarthy, Conservative Party U.S. Senator James Buckley, the Libertarian Party, the Mississippi Republican Party, the New York branch of the American Civil Liberties Union, the American Conservative Union, and many others. The Court of Appeals upheld all major parts of the Act. 519 F.2d 821 (D.C. Cir. 1975). The ambitious scope of the law and the creation of a new enforcement commission made it difficult, if not impossible, for the Supreme Court to avoid the issues it had sidestepped in *Newberry*, *CIO*, and *Auto Workers*. The resulting decision, *Buckley v. Valeo*, is by some measures the longest Supreme Court opinion ever, and certainly the longest *per curiam* opinion. Forty years later, it remains the touchstone of campaign-finance law, and the starting point for virtually every Supreme Court or lower-court opinion on campaign finance. Below are substantial portions of the *Buckley* opinion, setting forth general principles and dealing with contribution and expenditure limits. Later in this Chapter, we will look at portions of *Buckley* dealing with public financing of campaigns and disclosure of contributions and expenditures.

BUCKLEY v. VALEO
Supreme Court of the United States
424 U.S. 1, 96 S. Ct. 612, 46 L. Ed. 2d 659 (1976)

PER CURIAM. [MR. JUSTICE BRENNAN, MR. JUSTICE STEWART, and MR. JUSTICE POWELL join this opinion in full, and MR. JUSTICE REHNQUIST joins all portions of the opinion excerpted here. MR. JUSTICE MARSHALL joins in all but Part I-C-2. MR. JUSTICE BLACKMUN joins in all but Part I-B. MR. CHIEF JUSTICE BURGER joins in Part I-C.]

These appeals present constitutional challenges to the key provisions of the Federal Election Campaign Act of 1971 (Act), and related provisions of the Internal Revenue Code of 1954, all as amended in 1974. * * *

---

[c] FECA was passed in February 1972, but is normally referred to as the Federal Election Campaign Act of 1971, when the bill was introduced.

I. CONTRIBUTION AND EXPENDITURE LIMITATIONS

The intricate statutory scheme adopted by Congress to regulate federal election campaigns includes restrictions on political contributions and expenditures that apply broadly to all phases of and all participants in the election process. The major contribution and expenditure limitations in the Act prohibit individuals from contributing more than $25,000 in a single year or more than $1,000 to any single candidate for an election campaign and from spending more than $1,000 a year "relative to a clearly identified candidate." Other provisions restrict a candidate's use of personal and family resources in his campaign and limit the overall amount that can be spent by a candidate in campaigning for federal office. * * *

A. General Principles

The Act's contribution and expenditure limitations operate in an area of the most fundamental First Amendment activities. Discussion of public issues and debate on the qualifications of candidates are integral to the operation of the system of government established by our Constitution. The First Amendment affords the broadest protection to such political expression in order "to assure [the] unfettered interchange of ideas for the bringing about of political and social changes desired by the people." *Roth* v. *United States*, 354 U.S. 476, 484 (1957). Although First Amendment protections are not confined to "the exposition of ideas," *Winters* v. *New York*, 333 U.S. 507, 510 (1948), "there is practically universal agreement that a major purpose of that Amendment was to protect the free discussion of governmental affairs, . . . of course includ[ing] discussions of candidates." *Mills* v. *Alabama*, 384 U.S. 214, 218 (1966) [p. 603]. This no more than reflects our "profound national commitment to the principle that debate on public issues should be uninhibited, robust, and wide-open," *New York Times Co.* v. *Sullivan*, 376 U.S. 254, 270 (1964) [p. 574]. In a republic where the people are sovereign, the ability of the citizenry to make informed choices among candidates for office is essential, for the identities of those who are elected will inevitably shape the course that we follow as a nation. As the Court observed in *Monitor Patriot Co.* v. *Roy*, 401 U.S. 265, 272 (1971), "it can hardly be doubted that the constitutional guarantee has its fullest and most urgent application precisely to the conduct of campaigns for political office."

The First Amendment protects political association as well as political expression. The constitutional right of association explicated in *NAACP* v. *Alabama*, 357 U.S. 449, 460 (1958), stemmed from the Court's recognition that "[e]ffective advocacy of both public and private points of view, particularly controversial ones, is undeniably enhanced by group association." Subsequent decisions have made clear that the First and Fourteenth Amendments guarantee "freedom to associate with others for the common advancement of political beliefs and ideas," a freedom that encompasses "[t]he right to associate with the political party of one's choice."

It is with these principles in mind that we consider the primary contentions of the parties with respect to the Act's limitations upon the giving and spending of money in political campaigns. Those conflicting contentions could not more sharply define the basic issues before us. Appellees contend that what the Act regulates is conduct, and that its effect on speech and association is incidental at most. Appellants respond that contributions and expenditures are at the very core of political speech, and that the Act's limitations thus constitute restraints on First Amendment liberty that are both gross and direct.

In upholding the constitutional validity of the Act's contribution and expenditure provisions on the ground that those provisions should be viewed as regulating conduct, not speech, the Court of Appeals relied upon *United States* v. *O'Brien*, 391 U.S. 367 (1968). The *O'Brien* case involved a defendant's claim that the First Amendment prohibited his prosecution for burning his draft card because his act was "symbolic speech" engaged in as a "demonstration against the war and against the draft." On the assumption that "the alleged communicative element in O'Brien's conduct [was] sufficient to bring into play the First Amendment," the Court sustained the conviction because it found "a sufficiently important governmental interest in regulating the nonspeech element" that was "unrelated to the suppression of free expression" and that had an "incidental restriction on alleged First Amendment freedoms . . . no greater than [was] essential to the furtherance of that interest." *Id.*, at 376–377. The Court expressly emphasized that *O'Brien* was not a case "where the alleged governmental interest in regulating conduct arises in some measure because the communication allegedly integral to the conduct is itself thought to be harmful." *Id.*, at 382.

We cannot share the view that the present Act's contribution and expenditure limitations are comparable to the restrictions on conduct upheld in *O'Brien*. The expenditure of money simply cannot be equated with such conduct as destruction of a draft card. Some forms of communication made possible by the giving and spending of money involve speech alone, some involve conduct primarily, and some involve a combination of the two. Yet this Court has never suggested that the dependence of a communication on the expenditure of money operates itself to introduce a nonspeech element or to reduce the exacting scrutiny required by the First Amendment. For example, in *Cox* v. *Louisiana*, 379 U.S. 559 (1965), the Court contrasted picketing and parading with a newspaper comment and a telegram by a citizen to a public official. The parading and picketing activities were said to constitute conduct "intertwined with expression and association," whereas the newspaper comment and the telegram were described as a "pure form of expression" involving "free speech alone" rather than "expression mixed with particular conduct." *Id.*, at 563–564.

Even if the categorization of the expenditure of money as conduct were accepted, the limitations challenged here would not meet the *O'Brien* test because the governmental interests advanced in support of the Act involve "suppressing communication." The interests served by the Act include restricting the voices of people and interest groups who have money to spend and reducing the overall scope of federal election campaigns. Although the Act does not focus on the ideas expressed by persons or groups subjected to its regulations, it is aimed in part at equalizing the relative ability of all voters to affect electoral outcomes by placing a ceiling on expenditures for political expression by citizens and groups. Unlike *O'Brien*, where the Selective Service System's administrative interest in the preservation of draft cards was wholly unrelated to their use as a means of communication, it is beyond dispute that the interest in regulating the alleged "conduct" of giving or spending money "arises in some measure because the communication allegedly integral to the conduct is itself thought to be harmful."

Nor can the Act's contribution and expenditure limitations be sustained * * * [as] reasonable time, place, and manner regulations, which do not discriminate among speakers or ideas, in order to further an important governmental interest unrelated to the restriction of communication. * * * [T]he present Act's contribution and expenditure limitations impose direct quantity restrictions on political communication and association by persons, groups, candidates, and political parties in addition to any reasonable time, place, and manner regulations otherwise imposed.[17]

A restriction on the amount of money a person or group can spend on political communication during a campaign necessarily reduces the quantity of expression by restricting the number of issues discussed, the depth of their exploration, and the size of the audience reached.[18] This is because virtually every means of communicating ideas in today's mass society requires the expenditure of money. The distribution of the humblest handbill or leaflet entails printing, paper, and circulation costs. Speeches and rallies generally necessitate hiring a hall and publicizing the event. The electorate's increasing dependence on television, radio, and other mass media for news and information has made these expensive modes of communication indispensable instruments of effective political speech.

The expenditure limitations contained in the Act represent substantial rather than merely theoretical restraints on the quantity and diversity of political speech. The $1,000 ceiling on spending "relative to a clearly identified candidate" would appear to exclude all citizens and groups except candidates, political parties, and the institutional press from any significant use of the most effective modes of communication.[20] Although the Act's limitations on expenditures by campaign organizations and political parties provide substantially greater room for discussion and debate, they would have required restrictions in the scope of a number of past congressional and Presidential campaigns and would operate to constrain campaigning by candidates who raise sums in excess of the spending ceiling.

By contrast with a limitation upon expenditures for political expression, a limitation upon the amount that any one person or group may contribute to a candidate or political committee entails only a marginal restriction upon the contributor's ability to engage in free communication. A contribution serves as a general expression of support for the candidate and his views, but does not communicate the underlying basis for the support. The quantity of communication by the contributor does not increase perceptibly with the size of his contribution, since the expression rests solely on the undifferentiated, symbolic act of contributing. At most, the size of the contribution provides a very rough index of the

---

[17] The nongovernmental appellees argue that just as the decibels emitted by a sound truck can be regulated consistently with the First Amendment, the Act may restrict the volume of dollars in political campaigns without impermissibly restricting freedom of speech. This comparison underscores a fundamental misconception. [A] decibel restriction * * * limit[s] the manner of operating a soundtruck, but not the extent of its proper use. By contrast, the Act's dollar ceilings restrict the extent of the reasonable use of virtually every means of communicating information. * * *

[18] Being free to engage in unlimited political expression subject to a ceiling on expenditures is like being free to drive an automobile as far and as often as one desires on a single tank of gasoline.

[20] The record indicates that, as of January 1, 1975, one full-page advertisement in a daily edition of a certain metropolitan newspaper cost $6,971.04 — almost seven times the annual limit on expenditures "relative to" a particular candidate imposed on the vast majority of individual citizens and associations.

intensity of the contributor's support for the candidate. A limitation on the amount of money a person may give to a candidate or campaign organization thus involves little direct restraint on his political communication, for it permits the symbolic expression of support evidenced by a contribution but does not in any way infringe the contributor's freedom to discuss candidates and issues. While contributions may result in political expression if spent by a candidate or an association to present views to the voters, the transformation of contributions into political debate involves speech by someone other than the contributor.

Given the important role of contributions in financing political campaigns, contribution restrictions could have a severe impact on political dialogue if the limitations prevented candidates and political committees from amassing the resources necessary for effective advocacy. There is no indication, however, that the contribution limitations imposed by the Act would have any dramatic adverse effect on the funding of campaigns and political associations.[23] The overall effect of the Act's contribution ceilings is merely to require candidates and political committees to raise funds from a greater number of persons and to compel people who would otherwise contribute amounts greater than the statutory limits to expend such funds on direct political expression, rather than to reduce the total amount of money potentially available to promote political expression.

The Act's contribution and expenditure limitations also impinge on protected associational freedoms. Making a contribution, like joining a political party, serves to affiliate a person with a candidate. In addition, it enables like-minded persons to pool their resources in furtherance of common political goals. The Act's contribution ceilings thus limit one important means of associating with a candidate or committee, but leave the contributor free to become a member of any political association and to assist personally in the association's efforts on behalf of candidates. And the Act's contribution limitations permit associations and candidates to aggregate large sums of money to promote effective advocacy. By contrast, the Act's $1,000 limitation on independent expenditures "relative to a clearly identified candidate" precludes most associations from effectively amplifying the voice of their adherents, the original basis for the recognition of First Amendment protection of the freedom of association. See *NAACP* v. *Alabama*, 357 U.S., at 460. The Act's constraints on the ability of independent associations and candidate campaign organizations to expend resources on political expression "is simultaneously an interference with the freedom of [their] adherents," *Sweezy* v. *New Hampshire*, 354 U.S. 234, 250 (1957) (plurality opinion).

In sum, although the Act's contribution and expenditure limitations both implicate fundamental First Amendment interests, its expenditure ceilings impose significantly more severe restrictions on protected freedoms of political expression and association than do its limitations on financial contributions.

---

[23] Statistical findings agreed to by the parties reveal that approximately 5.1% of the $73,483,613 raised by the 1,161 candidates for Congress in 1974 was obtained in amounts in excess of $1,000. In 1974, two major-party senatorial candidates, Ramsey Clark and Senator Charles Mathias, Jr., operated large-scale campaigns on contributions raised under a voluntarily imposed $100 contribution limitation.

B. Contribution Limitations

1. The $1,000 Limitation on Contributions by Individuals and Groups to Candidates and Authorized Campaign Committees

Section 608(b) provides, with certain limited exceptions, that "no person shall make contributions to any candidate with respect to any election for Federal office which, in the aggregate, exceed $1,000." The statute defines "person" broadly to include "an individual, partnership, committee, association, corporation or any other organization or group of persons." The limitation reaches a gift, subscription, loan, advance, deposit of anything of value, or promise to give a contribution, made for the purpose of influencing a primary election, a Presidential preference primary, or a general election for any federal office.[24] The $1,000 ceiling applies regardless of whether the contribution is given to the candidate, to a committee authorized in writing by the candidate to accept contributions on his behalf, or indirectly via earmarked gifts passed through an intermediary to the candidate.[25] The restriction applies to aggregate amounts contributed to the candidate for each election — with primaries, run-off elections, and general elections counted separately and all Presidential primaries held in any calendar year treated together as a single election campaign. * * *

Appellants contend that the $1,000 contribution ceiling unjustifiably burdens First Amendment freedoms, employs overbroad dollar limits, and discriminates against candidates opposing incumbent officeholders and against minor-party candidates in violation of the Fifth Amendment. We address each of these claims of invalidity in turn.

(a)

As the general discussion in Part I-A indicated, the primary First Amendment problem raised by the Act's contribution limitations is their restriction of one aspect of the contributor's freedom of political association. * * * In view of the fundamental nature of the right to associate, governmental "action which may have the effect of curtailing the freedom to associate is subject to the closest scrutiny." Yet, it is clear that "[n]either the right to associate nor the right to participate in political activities is absolute." *CSC* v. *Letter Carriers*, 413 U.S. 548, 567 (1973) [p. 713]. Even a " 'significant interference' with protected rights of political association" may be sustained if the State demonstrates a sufficiently important interest and employs means closely drawn to avoid unnecessary abridgment of associational freedoms.

Appellees argue that the Act's restrictions on large campaign contributions are justified by three governmental interests. According to the parties and *amici*, the primary interest served by the limitations and, indeed, by the Act as a whole, is the prevention of corruption and the appearance of corruption spawned by the real or

---

[24] The Act exempts from the contribution ceiling the value of all volunteer services provided by individuals to a candidate or a political committee and excludes the first $500 spent by volunteers on certain categories of campaign-related activities. * * *

[25] Expenditures by persons and associations that are "authorized or requested" by the candidate or his agents are treated as contributions under the Act.

imagined coercive influence of large financial contributions on candidates' positions and on their actions if elected to office. Two "ancillary" interests underlying the Act are also allegedly furthered by the $1,000 limits on contributions. First, the limits serve to mute the voices of affluent persons and groups in the election process and thereby to equalize the relative ability of all citizens to affect the outcome of elections. Second, it is argued, the ceilings may to some extent act as a brake on the skyrocketing cost of political campaigns and thereby serve to open the political system more widely to candidates without access to sources of large amounts of money.

It is unnecessary to look beyond the Act's primary purpose — to limit the actuality and appearance of corruption resulting from large individual financial contributions — in order to find a constitutionally sufficient justification for the $1,000 contribution limitation. Under a system of private financing of elections, a candidate lacking immense personal or family wealth must depend on financial contributions from others to provide the resources necessary to conduct a successful campaign. The increasing importance of the communications media and sophisticated mass-mailing and polling operations to effective campaigning make the raising of large sums of money an ever more essential ingredient of an effective candidacy. To the extent that large contributions are given to secure a political *quid pro quo* from current and potential office holders, the integrity of our system of representative democracy is undermined. Although the scope of such pernicious practices can never be reliably ascertained, the deeply disturbing examples surfacing after the 1972 election demonstrate that the problem is not an illusory one.

Of almost equal concern as the danger of actual *quid pro quo* arrangements is the impact of the appearance of corruption stemming from public awareness of the opportunities for abuse inherent in a regime of large individual financial contributions. In *CSC* v. *Letter Carriers* the Court found that the danger to "fair and effective government" posed by partisan political conduct on the part of federal employees charged with administering the law was a sufficiently important concern to justify broad restrictions on the employees' right of partisan political association. Here, as there, Congress could legitimately conclude that the avoidance of the appearance of improper influence "is also critical . . . if confidence in the system of representative Government is not to be eroded to a disastrous extent."

Appellants contend that the contribution limitations must be invalidated because bribery laws and narrowly drawn disclosure requirements constitute a less restrictive means of dealing with "proven and suspected *quid pro quo* arrangements." But laws making criminal the giving and taking of bribes deal with only the most blatant and specific attempts of those with money to influence governmental action. And while disclosure requirements serve the many salutary purposes discussed elsewhere in this opinion, Congress was surely entitled to conclude that disclosure was only a partial measure, and that contribution ceilings were a necessary legislative concomitant to deal with the reality or appearance of corruption inherent in a system permitting unlimited financial contributions, even when the identities of the contributors and the amounts of their contributions are fully disclosed.

The Act's $1,000 contribution limitation focuses precisely on the problem of large campaign contributions — the narrow aspect of political association where the actuality and potential for corruption have been identified — while leaving persons free to engage in independent political expression, to associate actively through volunteering their services, and to assist to a limited but nonetheless substantial extent in supporting candidates and committees with financial resources.[31] Significantly, the Act's contribution limitations in themselves do not undermine to any material degree the potential for robust and effective discussion of candidates and campaign issues by individual citizens, associations, the institutional press, candidates, and political parties.

We find that, under the rigorous standard of review established by our prior decisions, the weighty interests served by restricting the size of financial contributions to political candidates are sufficient to justify the limited effect upon First Amendment freedoms caused by the $1,000 contribution ceiling.

(b)

Appellants' first overbreadth challenge to the contribution ceilings rests on the proposition that most large contributors do not seek improper influence over a candidate's position or an officeholder's action. Although the truth of that proposition may be assumed, it does not undercut the validity of the $1,000 contribution limitation. Not only is it difficult to isolate suspect contributions but, more importantly, Congress was justified in concluding that the interest in safeguarding against the appearance of impropriety requires that the opportunity for abuse inherent in the process of raising large monetary contributions be eliminated.

A second, related overbreadth claim is that the $1,000 restriction is unrealistically low because much more than that amount would still not be enough to enable an unscrupulous contributor to exercise improper influence over a candidate or officeholder, especially in campaigns for statewide or national office. While the contribution limitation provisions might well have been structured to take account of the graduated expenditure limitations for Congressional and Presidential campaigns, Congress' failure to engage in such fine tuning does not invalidate the legislation. As the Court of Appeals observed, "[i]f it is satisfied that some limit on contributions is necessary, a court has no scalpel to probe, whether, say, a $2,000 ceiling might not serve as well as $1,000." Such distinctions in degree become significant only when they can be said to amount to differences in kind.

---

[31] While providing significant limitations on the ability of all individuals and groups to contribute large amounts of money to candidates, the Act's contribution ceilings do not foreclose the making of substantial contributions to candidates by some major special-interest groups through the combined effect of individual contributions from adherents or * * * political funds * * * authorized under the Act to contribute to candidates. As a prime example, § 610 permits corporations and labor unions to establish segregated funds to solicit voluntary contributions to be utilized for political purposes. Corporate and union resources without limitation may be employed to administer these funds and to solicit contributions from employees, stockholders, and union members. Each separate fund may contribute up to $5,000 per candidate per election so long as the fund qualifies as a political committee under § 608(b)(2). * * *

(c)

Apart from these First Amendment concerns, appellants argue that the contribution limitations work such an invidious discrimination between incumbents and challengers that the statutory provisions must be declared unconstitutional on their face. In considering this contention, it is important at the outset to note that the Act applies the same limitations on contributions to all candidates regardless of their present occupations, ideological views, or party affiliations. Absent record evidence of invidious discrimination against challengers as a class, a court should generally be hesitant to invalidate legislation which on its face imposes evenhanded restrictions.

There is no such evidence to support the claim that the contribution limitations in themselves discriminate against major-party challengers to incumbents. Challengers can and often do defeat incumbents in federal elections. Major-party challengers in federal elections are usually men and women who are well known and influential in their community or State. Often such challengers are themselves incumbents in important local, state, or federal offices. Statistics in the record indicate that major-party challengers as well as incumbents are capable of raising large sums for campaigning. Indeed, a small but nonetheless significant number of challengers have in recent elections outspent their incumbent rivals. And, to the extent that incumbents generally are more likely than challengers to attract very large contributions, the Act's $1,000 ceiling has the practical effect of benefiting challengers as a class.[d] Contrary to the broad generalization drawn by the appellants, the practical impact of the contribution ceilings in any given election will clearly depend upon the amounts in excess of the ceilings that, for various reasons, the candidates in that election would otherwise have received and the utility of these additional amounts to the candidates. To be sure, the limitations may have a significant effect on particular challengers or incumbents, but the record provides no basis for predicting that such adventitious factors will invariably and invidiously benefit incumbents as a class. Since the danger of corruption and the appearance of corruption apply with equal force to challengers and to incumbents, Congress had ample justification for imposing the same fundraising constraints upon both.

The charge of discrimination against minor-party and independent candidates is more troubling, but the record provides no basis for concluding that the Act invidiously disadvantages such candidates. As noted above, the Act on its face treats all candidates equally with regard to contribution limitations. And the restriction would appear to benefit minor-party and independent candidates relative to their major-party opponents because major-party candidates receive far more money in large contributions. * * * [T]he record is virtually devoid of support for the claim that the $1,000 contribution limitation will have a serious effect on the initiation and scope of minor-party and independent candidacies. Moreover, any attempt to exclude minor parties and independents en masse from the Act's contribution limitations overlooks the fact that minor-party candidates may win elective office or

---

[d] In fact, data made available by FECA's disclosure requirements have consistently shown that challengers receive a higher percentage of their total funds in contributions of $1000 or more. *See, e.g.,* Campaign Finance Institute, *Raising Limits Helps Non-Incumbents More Than Incumbents*, Mar. 26, 2001, available at http://www.cfinst.org/pr/prRelease.aspx?ReleaseID=35#tables. [— Eds.]

have a substantial impact on the outcome of an election.

In view of these considerations, we conclude that the impact of the Act's $1,000 contribution limitation on major-party challengers and on minor-party candidates does not render the provision unconstitutional on its face.

2. The $5,000 Limitation on Contributions by Political Committees

Section 608(b)(2) permits certain committees, designated as "political committees," to contribute up to $5,000 to any candidate with respect to any election for federal office. In order to qualify for the higher contribution ceiling, a group must have been registered with the Commission as a political committee for not less than six months, have received contributions from more than 50 persons and, except for state political party organizations, have contributed to five or more candidates for federal office. Appellants argue that these qualifications unconstitutionally discriminate against *ad hoc* organizations in favor of established interest groups and impermissibly burden free association. The argument is without merit. Rather than undermining freedom of association, the basic provision enhances the opportunity of bona fide groups to participate in the election process, and the registration, contribution, and candidate conditions serve the permissible purpose of preventing individuals from evading the applicable contribution limitations by labeling themselves committees.

3. Limitations on Volunteers' Incidental Expenses

The Act excludes from the definition of contribution "the value of services provided without compensation by individuals who volunteer a portion or all of their time on behalf of a candidate or political committee." Certain expenses incurred by persons in providing volunteer services to a candidate are exempt from the $1,000 ceiling only to the extent that they do not exceed $500. These expenses are expressly limited to (1) "the use of real or personal property and the cost of invitations, food, and beverages, voluntarily provided by an individual to a candidate in rendering voluntary personal services on the individual's residential premises for candidate-related activities"; "the sale of any food or beverage by a vendor for use in a candidate's campaign at a charge [at least equal to cost but] less than the normal comparable charge"; and (3) "any unreimbursed payment for travel expenses made by an individual who on his own behalf volunteers his personal services to a candidate."

If, as we have held, the basic contribution limitations are constitutionally valid, then surely these provisions are a constitutionally acceptable accommodation of Congress' valid interest in encouraging citizen participation in political campaigns while continuing to guard against the corrupting potential of large financial contributions to candidates. The expenditure of resources at the candidate's direction for a fundraising event at a volunteer's residence or the provision of in-kind assistance in the form of food or beverages to be resold to raise funds or consumed by the participants in such an event provides material financial assistance to a candidate. The ultimate effect is the same as if the person had contributed the dollar amount to the candidate and the candidate had then used the contribution to pay for the fundraising event or the food. Similarly, travel undertaken as a volunteer at the direction of the candidate or his staff is an expense of the campaign and may properly be viewed as a contribution if the volunteer absorbs the fare. Treating these expenses as contributions when made to the candidate's campaign or at the direction of the candidate or his staff forecloses an avenue of abuse without limiting actions voluntarily undertaken by citizens independently of a candidate's campaign.

4. The $25,000 Limitation on Total Contributions During any Calendar Year

In addition to the $1,000 limitation on the nonexempt contributions that an individual may make to a particular candidate for any single election, the Act contains an overall $25,000 limitation on total contributions by an individual during any calendar year. * * * The overall $25,000 ceiling does impose an ultimate restriction upon the number of candidates and committees with which an individual may associate himself by means of financial support. But this quite modest restraint upon protected political activity serves to prevent evasion of the $1,000 contribution limitation by a person who might otherwise contribute massive amounts of money to a particular candidate through the use of unearmarked contributions to political committees likely to contribute to that candidate, or huge contributions to the candidate's political party. The limited, additional restriction on associational freedom imposed by the overall ceiling is thus no more than a corollary of the basic individual contribution limitation that we have found to be constitutionally valid.

C. Expenditure Limitations

The Act's expenditure ceilings impose direct and substantial restraints on the quantity of political speech. The most drastic of the limitations restricts individuals and groups, including political parties that fail to place a candidate on the ballot, to an expenditure of $1,000 "relative to a clearly identified candidate during a calendar year." Other expenditure ceilings limit spending by candidates, their campaigns, and political parties in connection with election campaigns. It is clear that a primary effect of these expenditure limitations is to restrict the quantity of campaign speech by individuals, groups, and candidates. The restrictions, while neutral as to the ideas expressed, limit political expression "at the core of our electoral process and of the First Amendment freedoms."

1. The $1,000 Limitation on Expenditures "Relative to a Clearly Identified Candidate"

Section 608(e)(1) provides that "[n]o person may make any expenditure . . . relative to a clearly identified candidate during a calendar year which, when added to all other expenditures made by such person during the year advocating the election or defeat of such candidate, exceeds $1,000."[45] The plain effect of § 608(e)(1)

---

[45] * * * The statute provides some limited exceptions through various exclusions from the otherwise comprehensive definition of "expenditure." The most important exclusions are: (1) "any news story, commentary, or editorial distributed through the facilities of any broadcasting station, newspaper, magazine, or other periodical publication, unless such facilities are owned or controlled by any political

is to prohibit all individuals, who are neither candidates nor owners of institutional press facilities, and all groups, except political parties and campaign organizations, from voicing their views "relative to a clearly identified candidate" through means that entail aggregate expenditures of more than $1,000 during a calendar year. The provision, for example, would make it a federal criminal offense for a person or association to place a single one-quarter page advertisement "relative to a clearly identified candidate" in a major metropolitan newspaper.

Before examining the interests advanced in support of § 608(e)(1)'s expenditure ceiling, consideration must be given to appellants' contention that the provision is unconstitutionally vague. * * *[48] The test is whether the language of § 608(e)(1) affords the "[p]recision of regulation [that] must be the touchstone in an area so closely touching our most precious freedoms."

The key operative language of the provision limits "any expenditure . . . relative to a clearly identified candidate." Although "expenditure," "clearly identified," and "candidate" are defined in the Act, there is no definition clarifying what expenditures are "relative to" a candidate. The use of so indefinite a phrase as "relative to" a candidate fails to clearly mark the boundary between permissible and impermissible speech, unless other portions of § 608(e)(1) make sufficiently explicit the range of expenditures covered by the limitation. The section prohibits "any expenditure . . . relative to a clearly identified candidate during a calendar year which, *when added to all other expenditures . . . advocating the election or defeat of such candidate*, exceeds $1,000." (Emphasis added.) This context clearly permits, if indeed it does not require, the phrase "relative to" a candidate to be read to mean "advocating the election or defeat of" a candidate.

But while such a construction of § 608(e)(1) refocuses the vagueness question, the Court of Appeals was mistaken in thinking that this construction eliminates the problem of unconstitutional vagueness altogether. For the distinction between discussion of issues and candidates and advocacy of election or defeat of candidates may often dissolve in practical application. Candidates, especially incumbents, are intimately tied to public issues involving legislative proposals and governmental actions. Not only do candidates campaign on the basis of their positions on various public issues, but campaigns themselves generate issues of public interest. In an analogous context, this Court in *Thomas* v. *Collins*, 323 U.S. 516 (1945), observed:

> "[W]hether words intended and designed to fall short of invitation would miss that mark is a question both of intent and of effect. No speaker, in such circumstances, safely could assume that anything he might say upon the general subject would not be understood by some as an invitation. In short,

---

party, political committee, or candidate," and (2) "any communication by any membership organization or corporation to its members or stockholders, if such membership organization or corporation is not organized primarily for the purpose of influencing the nomination for election, or election, of any person to Federal office." * * *

[48] In such circumstances, vague laws may not only "trap the innocent by not providing fair warning" or foster "arbitrary and discriminatory application" but also operate to inhibit protected expression by inducing "citizens to 'steer far wider of the unlawful zone . . . than if the boundaries of the forbidden areas were clearly marked.'" "Because First Amendment freedoms need breathing space to survive, government may regulate in the area only with narrow specificity."

the supposedly clear-cut distinction between discussion, laudation, general advocacy, and solicitation puts the speaker in these circumstances wholly at the mercy of the varied understanding of his hearers and consequently of whatever inference may be drawn as to his intent and meaning.

"Such a distinction offers no security for free discussion. In these conditions it blankets with uncertainty whatever may be said. It compels the speaker to hedge and trim." *Id.* at 535.

The constitutional deficiencies described in *Thomas* v. *Collins* can be avoided only by reading § 608(e)(1) as limited to communications that include explicit words of advocacy of election or defeat of a candidate, much as the definition of "clearly identified" in § 608(e)(2) requires that an explicit and unambiguous reference to the candidate appear as part of the communication.[51] * * * [I]n order to preserve the provision against invalidation on vagueness grounds, § 608(e)(1) must be construed to apply only to expenditures for communications that in express terms advocate the election or defeat of a clearly identified candidate for federal office.[52]

We turn then to the basic First Amendment question — whether § 608(e)(1) even as thus narrowly and explicitly construed, impermissibly burdens the constitutional right of free expression. * * *

The discussion in Part I-A, *supra*, explains why the Act's expenditure limitations impose far greater restraints on the freedom of speech and association than do its contribution limitations. The markedly greater burden on basic freedoms caused by § 608(e)(1) thus cannot be sustained simply by invoking the interest in maximizing the effectiveness of the less intrusive contribution limitations. Rather, the constitutionality of § 608(e)(1) turns on whether the governmental interests advanced in its support satisfy the exacting scrutiny applicable to limitations on core First Amendment rights of political expression.

We find that the governmental interest in preventing corruption and the appearance of corruption is inadequate to justify § 608(e)(1)'s ceiling on independent expenditures. First, assuming, *arguendo*, that large independent expenditures pose the same dangers of actual or apparent *quid pro quo* arrangements as do large contributions, § 608(e)(1) does not provide an answer that sufficiently relates to the elimination of those dangers. Unlike the contribution limitations' total ban on the giving of large amounts of money to candidates, § 608(e)(1) prevents only some large expenditures. So long as persons and groups eschew expenditures that in express terms advocate the election or defeat of a clearly identified candidate, they are free to spend as much as they want to promote the candidate and his views. The exacting interpretation of the statutory language necessary to avoid unconstitutional vague-

---

[51] Section 608(e)(2) defines "clearly identified" to require that the candidate's name, photograph or drawing, or other unambiguous reference to his identity appear as part of the communication. Such other unambiguous reference would include use of the candidate's initials (*e.g.*, FDR), the candidate's nickname (*e.g.*, Ike), his office (*e.g.*, the President or the Governor of Iowa), or his status as a candidate (*e.g.*, the Democratic Presidential nominee, the senatorial candidate of the Republican Party of Georgia).

[52] This construction would restrict the application of § 608(e)(1) to communications containing express words of advocacy of election or defeat, such as "vote for," "elect," "support," "cast your ballot for," "Smith for Congress," "vote against," "defeat," "reject."

ness thus undermines the limitation's effectiveness as a loophole-closing provision by facilitating circumvention by those seeking to exert improper influence upon a candidate or officeholder. It would naively underestimate the ingenuity and resourcefulness of persons and groups desiring to buy influence to believe that they would have much difficulty devising expenditures that skirted the restriction on express advocacy of election or defeat but nevertheless benefited the candidate's campaign. Yet no substantial societal interest would be served by a loophole-closing provision designed to check corruption that permitted unscrupulous persons and organizations to expend unlimited sums of money in order to obtain improper influence over candidates for elective office.

Second, quite apart from the shortcomings of § 608(e)(1) in preventing any abuses generated by large independent expenditures, the independent advocacy restricted by the provision does not presently appear to pose dangers of real or apparent corruption comparable to those identified with large campaign contributions. The parties defending § 608(e)(1) * * * argue that expenditures controlled by or coordinated with the candidate and his campaign might well have virtually the same value to the candidate as a contribution and would pose similar dangers of abuse. Yet such controlled or coordinated expenditures are treated as contributions rather than expenditures under the Act. Section 608(b)'s contribution ceilings rather than § 608(e)(1)'s independent expenditure limitation prevent attempts to circumvent the Act through prearranged or coordinated expenditures amounting to disguised contributions. By contrast, § 608(e)(1) limits expenditures for express advocacy of candidates made totally independently of the candidate and his campaign. Unlike contributions, such independent expenditures may well provide little assistance to the candidate's campaign and indeed may prove counterproductive. The absence of prearrangement and coordination of an expenditure with the candidate or his agent not only undermines the value of the expenditure to the candidate, but also alleviates the danger that expenditures will be given as a *quid pro quo* for improper commitments from the candidate. Rather than preventing circumvention of the contribution limitations, § 608(e)(1) severely restricts all independent advocacy despite its substantially diminished potential for abuse.

While the independent expenditure ceiling thus fails to serve any substantial governmental interest in stemming the reality or appearance of corruption in the electoral process, it heavily burdens core First Amendment expression. * * * Advocacy of the election or defeat of candidates for federal office is no less entitled to protection under the First Amendment than the discussion of political policy generally or advocacy of the passage or defeat of legislation.

It is argued, however, that the ancillary governmental interest in equalizing the relative ability of individuals and groups to influence the outcome of elections serves to justify the limitation on express advocacy of the election or defeat of candidates imposed by § 608(e)(1)'s expenditure ceiling. But the concept that government may restrict the speech of some elements of our society in order to enhance the relative voice of others is wholly foreign to the First Amendment, which was designed "to secure 'the widest possible dissemination of information from diverse and antagonistic sources,' " and "to assure unfettered interchange of ideas for the bringing about of political and social changes desired by the people." The First Amendment's protection against governmental abridgment of free expression cannot properly be made to depend on a person's financial ability to engage in public discussion.[55] * * *

For the reasons stated, we conclude that § 608(e)(1)'s independent expenditure limitation is unconstitutional under the First Amendment.

2. Limitation on Expenditures by Candidates from Personal or Family Resources

The ceiling on personal expenditures by candidates on their own behalf, like the limitations on independent expenditures contained in § 608(e)(1), imposes a substantial restraint on the ability of persons to engage in protected First Amendment expression. The candidate, no less than any other person, has a First Amendment right to engage in the discussion of public issues and vigorously and tirelessly to advocate his own election and the election of other candidates. Indeed, it is of particular importance that candidates have the unfettered opportunity to make their views known so that the electorate may intelligently evaluate the candidates' personal qualities and their positions on vital public issues before choosing among them on election day. Mr. Justice Brandeis' observation that in our country "public discussion is a political duty," *Whitney* v. *California,* 274 U.S. 357, 375 (concurring), applies with special force to candidates for public office. Section 608(a)'s ceiling on personal expenditures by a candidate in furtherance of his own candidacy thus clearly and directly interferes with constitutionally protected freedoms.

The primary governmental interest served by the Act — the prevention of actual and apparent corruption of the political process — does not support the limitation on the candidate's expenditure of his own personal funds. As the Court of Appeals concluded: "Manifestly, the core problem of avoiding undisclosed and undue influence on candidates from outside interests has lesser application when the monies involved come from the candidate himself or from his immediate family." Indeed, the use of personal funds reduces the candidate's dependence on outside contributions and thereby counteracts the coercive pressures and attendant risks of abuse to which the Act's contribution limitations are directed.

The ancillary interest in equalizing the relative financial resources of candidates competing for elective office, therefore, provides the sole relevant rationale for § 608(a)'s expenditure ceiling. That interest is clearly not sufficient to justify the provision's infringement of fundamental First Amendment rights. First, the limitation may fail to promote financial equality among candidates. A candidate who spends less of his personal resources on his campaign may nonetheless outspend his

---

[55] * * * In *Red Lion Broadcasting Co.* v. *FCC,* 395 U.S. 367 (1969) [p. 605], the Court upheld the political-editorial and personal-attack portions of the Federal Communications Commission's fairness doctrine. That doctrine requires broadcast licensees to devote programming time to the discussion of controversial issues of public importance and to present both sides of such issues. *Red Lion* "makes clear that the broadcast media pose unique and special problems not present in the traditional free speech case," by demonstrating that "it is idle to posit an unabridgeable First Amendment right to broadcast comparable to the right of every individual to speak, write, or publish." *Red Lion* therefore undercuts appellees' claim that § 608(e)(1)'s limitations may permissibly restrict the First Amendment rights of individuals in this "traditional free speech case." Moreover, in contrast to the undeniable effect of § 608(e)(1), the presumed effect of the fairness doctrine is one of "enhancing the volume and quality of coverage" of public issues.

rival as a result of more successful fundraising efforts. Indeed, a candidate's personal wealth may impede his efforts to persuade others that he needs their financial contributions or volunteer efforts to conduct an effective campaign. Second, and more fundamentally, the First Amendment simply cannot tolerate § 608(a)'s restriction upon the freedom of a candidate to speak without legislative limit on behalf of his own candidacy. We therefore hold that § 608(a)'s restriction on a candidate's personal expenditures is unconstitutional.

3. Limitations on Campaign Expenditures

Section 608(c) places limitations on overall campaign expenditures by candidates seeking nomination for election and election to federal office. * * *

No governmental interest that has been suggested is sufficient to justify the restriction on the quantity of political expression imposed by § 608(c)'s campaign expenditure limitations. The major evil associated with rapidly increasing campaign expenditures is the danger of candidate dependence on large contributions. The interest in alleviating the corrupting influence of large contributions is served by the Act's contribution limitations and disclosure provisions rather than by § 608(c)'s campaign expenditure ceilings. The Court of Appeals' assertion that the expenditure restrictions are necessary to reduce the incentive to circumvent direct contribution limits is not persuasive. There is no indication that the substantial criminal penalties for violating the contribution ceilings combined with the political repercussion of such violations will be insufficient to police the contribution provisions. Extensive reporting, auditing, and disclosure requirements applicable to both contributions and expenditures by political campaigns are designed to facilitate the detection of illegal contributions. Moreover, as the Court of Appeals noted, the Act permits an officeholder or successful candidate to retain contributions in excess of the expenditure ceiling and to use these funds for "any other lawful purpose." This provision undercuts whatever marginal role the expenditure limitations might otherwise play in enforcing the contribution ceilings.

The interest in equalizing the financial resources of candidates competing for federal office is no more convincing a justification for restricting the scope of federal election campaigns. Given the limitation on the size of outside contributions, the financial resources available to a candidate's campaign, like the number of volunteers recruited, will normally vary with the size and intensity of the candidate's support. There is nothing invidious, improper, or unhealthy in permitting such funds to be spent to carry the candidate's message to the electorate. Moreover, the equalization of permissible campaign expenditures might serve not to equalize the opportunities of all candidates but to handicap a candidate who lacked substantial name recognition or exposure of his views before the start of the campaign.

The campaign expenditure ceilings appear to be designed primarily to serve the governmental interests in reducing the allegedly skyrocketing costs of political campaigns. * * * [T]he mere growth in the cost of federal election campaigns in and of itself provides no basis for governmental restrictions on the quantity of campaign spending and the resulting limitation on the scope of federal campaigns. The First Amendment denies government the power to determine that spending to promote one's political views is wasteful, excessive, or unwise. In the free society ordained by our Constitution it is not the government but the people — individually as citizens and candidates and collectively as associations and political committees — who must retain control over the quantity and range of debate on public issues in a political campaign.

For these reasons we hold that § 608(c) is constitutionally invalid.

In sum, the provisions of the Act that impose a $1,000 limitation on contributions to a single candidate, a $5,000 limitation on contributions by a political committee to a single candidate, and a $25,000 limitation on total contributions by an individual during any calendar year, are constitutionally valid. These limitations, along with the disclosure provisions, constitute the Act's primary weapons against the reality or appearance of improper influence stemming from the dependence of candidates on large campaign contributions. The contribution ceilings thus serve the basic governmental interest in safeguarding the integrity of the electoral process without directly impinging upon the rights of individual citizens and candidates to engage in political debate and discussion. By contrast, the First Amendment requires the invalidation of the Act's independent expenditure ceiling, its limitation on a candidate's expenditures from his own personal funds, and its ceilings on overall campaign expenditures. These provisions place substantial and direct restrictions on the ability of candidates, citizens, and associations to engage in protected political expression, restrictions that the First Amendment cannot tolerate. * * *

Mr. Justice Stevens took no part in the consideration or decision of these cases.

Mr. Chief Justice Burger, concurring in part and dissenting in part.

* * * [T]he Court's result does violence to the intent of Congress in this comprehensive scheme of campaign finance. By dissecting the Act bit by bit, and casting off vital parts, the Court fails to recognize that the whole of this Act is greater than the sum of its parts. Congress intended to regulate all aspects of federal campaign finances, but what remains after today's holding leaves no more than a shadow of what Congress contemplated. I question whether the residue leaves a workable program. * * *

I agree fully with that part of the Court's opinion that holds unconstitutional the limitations the Act puts on campaign expenditures * * *. which "place substantial and direct restrictions on the ability of candidates, citizens, and associations to engage in protected political expression, restrictions that the First Amendment cannot tolerate." Yet when it approves similarly stringent limitations on contributions, the Court ignores the reasons it finds so persuasive in the context of expenditures. For me contributions and expenditures are two sides of the same First Amendment coin.

* * * Limiting contributions, as a practical matter, will limit expenditures and will put an effective ceiling on the amount of political activity and debate that the Government will permit to take place. The argument that the ceiling is not, after all, very low as matters now stand gives little comfort for the future, since the Court elsewhere notes the rapid inflation in the cost of political campaigning.

The Court attempts to separate the two communicative aspects of political contributions — the "moral" support that the gift itself conveys, which the Court suggests is the same whether the gift is $10 or $10,000,[6] and the fact that money translates into communication. The Court dismisses the effect of the limitations on the second aspect of contributions: "[T]he transformation of contributions into political debate involves speech by someone other than the contributor." On this premise — that contribution limitations restrict only the speech of "someone other than the contributor" — rests the Court's justification for treating contributions differently from expenditures. The premise is demonstrably flawed; the contribution limitations will, in specific instances, limit exactly the same political activity that the expenditure ceilings limit, and at least one of the "expenditure" limitations the Court finds objectionable [*i.e.*, limits on a candidate's contributions to his own campaign] operates precisely like the "contribution" limitations.

The Court's attempt to distinguish the communication inherent in political contributions from the speech aspects of political expenditures simply "will not wash." We do little but engage in word games unless we recognize that people — candidates and contributors — spend money on political activity because they wish to communicate ideas, and their constitutional interest in doing so is precisely the same whether they or someone else utters the words.

The Court attempts to make the Act seem less restrictive by casting the problem as one that goes to freedom of association rather than freedom of speech. I have long thought freedom of association and freedom of expression were two peas from the same pod. The contribution limitations of the Act impose a restriction on certain forms of associational activity that are for the most part, as the Court recognizes, harmless in fact. And the restrictions are hardly incidental in their effect upon particular campaigns. Judges are ill-equipped to gauge the precise impact of legislation, but a law that impinges upon First Amendment rights requires us to make the attempt. It is not simply speculation to think that the limitations on contributions will foreclose some candidacies.[9] The limitations will also alter the nature of some electoral contests drastically.[10]

* * * If such restraints can be justified at all, they must be justified by the very strongest of state interests. With this much the Court clearly agrees; the Court even goes so far as to note that legislation cutting into these important interests must employ "means closely drawn to avoid unnecessary abridgment of associational freedoms."

---

[6] Whatever the effect of the limitation, it is clearly arbitrary — Congress has imposed the same ceiling on contributions to a New York or California senatorial campaign that it has put on House races in Alaska or Wyoming. Both the strength of support conveyed by the gift of $1,000 and the gift's potential for corruptly influencing the recipient will vary enormously from place to place. * * *

[9] Candidates who must raise large initial contributions in order to appeal for more funds to a broader audience will be handicapped. It is not enough to say that the contribution ceilings "merely . . . require candidates . . . to raise funds from a greater number of persons," where the limitations will effectively prevent candidates without substantial personal resources from doing just that.

[10] Under the Court's holding, candidates with personal fortunes will be free to contribute to their own campaigns as much as they like, since the Court chooses to view the Act's provisions in this regard as unconstitutional "expenditure" limitations rather than "contribution" limitations.

After a bow to the "weighty interests" Congress meant to serve, the Court then forsakes this analysis in one sentence: "Congress was surely entitled to conclude that disclosure was only a partial measure, and that contribution ceilings were a necessary legislative concomitant to deal with the reality or appearance of corruption. . . . " In striking down the limitations on campaign expenditures, the Court relies in part on its conclusion that other means — namely, disclosure and contribution ceilings — will adequately serve the statute's aim. It is not clear why the same analysis is not also appropriate in weighing the need for contribution ceilings in addition to disclosure requirements. Congress may well be entitled to conclude that disclosure was a "partial measure," but I had not thought until today that Congress could enact its conclusions in the First Amendment area into laws immune from the most searching review by this Court.

Finally, it seems clear to me that in approving these limitations on contributions the Court must rest upon the proposition that "pooling" money is fundamentally different from other forms of associational or joint activity. I see only two possible ways in which money differs from volunteer work, endorsements, and the like. Money can be used to buy favors, because an unscrupulous politician can put it to personal use; second, giving money is a less visible form of associational activity. With respect to the first problem, the Act does not attempt to do any more than the bribery laws to combat this sort of corruption. In fact, the Act does not reach at all, and certainly the contribution limits do not reach, forms of "association" that can be fully as corrupt as a contribution intended as a *quid pro quo* — such as the eleventh-hour endorsement by a former rival, obtained for the promise of a federal appointment. This underinclusiveness is not a constitutional flaw, but it demonstrates that the contribution limits do not clearly focus on this first distinction. To the extent Congress thought that the second problem, the lesser visibility of contributions, required that money be treated differently from other forms of associational activity, disclosure laws are the simple and wholly efficacious answer; they make the invisible apparent. * * *

MR. JUSTICE WHITE, concurring in part and dissenting in part.

I am * * * in agreement with the Court's judgment upholding the limitations on contributions. I dissent, however, from the Court's view that the expenditure limitations violate the First Amendment.

Concededly, neither the limitations on contributions nor those on expenditures directly or indirectly purport to control the content of political speech by candidates or by their supporters or detractors. What the Act regulates is giving and spending money, acts that have First Amendment significance not because they are themselves communicative with respect to their qualifications of the candidate, but because money may be used to defray the expenses of speaking or otherwise communicating about the merits or demerits of federal candidates for election. The act of giving money to political candidates, however, may have illegal or other undesirable consequences: it may be used to secure the express or tacit understanding that the giver will enjoy political favor if the candidate is elected. Both Congress and this Court's cases have recognized this as a mortal danger against which effective preventive and curative steps must be taken. * * *

It would make little sense to me and apparently made none to Congress, to limit the amounts an individual may give to a candidate or spend with his approval but fail to limit the amounts that could be spent on his behalf. Yet the Court permits the former while striking down the latter limitation. No more than $1,000 may be given to a candidate or spent at his request or with his approval or cooperation; but otherwise, apparently, a contributor is to be constitutionally protected in spending unlimited amounts of money in support of his chosen candidate or candidates. * * *

As an initial matter, the argument that money is speech and that limiting the flow of money to the speaker violates the First Amendment proves entirely too much. Compulsory bargaining and the right to strike, both provided for or protected by federal law, inevitably have increased the labor costs of those who publish newspapers, which are in turn an important factor in the recent disappearance of many daily papers. Federal and state taxation directly removes from company coffers large amounts of money that might be spent on larger and better newspapers. The antitrust laws are aimed at preventing monopoly profits and price fixing, which gouge the consumer. It is also true that general price controls have from time to time existed and have been applied to the newspapers or other media. But it has not been suggested, nor could it be successfully, that these laws, and many others, are invalid because they siphon off or prevent the accumulation of large sums that would otherwise be available for communicative activities. * * *

[E]xpenditure ceilings reinforce the contribution limits and help eradicate the hazard of corruption. The Court upholds the overall limit of $25,000 on an individual's political contributions in a single election year on the ground that it helps reinforce the limits on gifts to a single candidate. By the same token, the expenditure limit imposed on candidates plays its own role in lessening the chance that the contribution ceiling will be violated. Without limits on total expenditures, campaign costs will inevitably and endlessly escalate. Pressure to raise funds will constantly build and with it the temptation to resort in "emergencies" to those sources of large sums, who, history shows, are sufficiently confident of not being caught to risk flouting contribution limits. Congress would save the candidate from the predicament by establishing a reasonable ceiling on all candidates. This is a major consideration in favor of the limitation. It should be added that many successful candidates will also be saved from large, over-hanging campaign debts which must be paid off with money raised while holding public office and at a time when they are already preparing or thinking about the next campaign. The danger to the public interest in such situations is self-evident.

Besides backing up the contribution provisions, which are aimed at preventing untoward influence on candidates that are elected, expenditure limits have their own potential for preventing the corruption of federal elections themselves. For many years the law has required the disclosure of expenditures as well as contributions. * * * [T]he corrupt use of money by candidates is as much to be feared as the corrosive influence of large contributions. There are many illegal ways of spending money to influence elections. One would be blind to history to deny that unlimited money tempts people to spend it on *whatever* money can buy to influence an election. On the assumption that financing illegal activities is low on the campaign organization's priority list, the expenditure limits could play a substantial role in preventing unethical practices. There just would not be enough of "that kind of money" to go around.

I have little doubt in addition that limiting the total that can be spent will ease the candidate's understandable obsession with fundraising, and so free him and his staff to communicate in more places and ways unconnected with the fundraising function. There is nothing objectionable — indeed it seems to me a weighty interest in favor of the provision — in the attempt to insulate the political expression of federal candidates from the influence inevitably exerted by the endless job of raising increasingly large sums of money. * * *

It is also important to restore and maintain public confidence in federal elections. It is critical to obviate or dispel the impression that federal elections are purely and simply a function of money, that federal offices are bought and sold or that political races are reserved for those who have the facility — and the stomach — for doing whatever it takes to bring together those interests, groups, and individuals that can raise or contribute large fortunes in order to prevail at the polls. * * *

The holding perhaps is not that federal candidates have the constitutional right to purchase their election, but many will so interpret the Court's conclusion in this case. I cannot join the Court in this respect. * * *

Notes and Questions

1.   Congress's right to regulate campaign finance is well established in the Court's jurisprudence and generally assumed in *Buckley*. 424 U.S. at 14, n.16. Article I, § 4 of the Constitution, on which the Court relied, gives Congress the power to regulate the "Times, Places, and Manner of holding Elections for Senators and Representatives." Is "holding [an] Election[]" the same as campaigning, or has the Court wrongfully conflated "campaign" with "election?" *See* Robert G. Natelson, *The Original Scope of Congressional Power to Regulate Elections*, 13 U. PA. J. CONST. L. 1 (2010). Natelson argues that the clause was limited to provisions of public notice, establishing the time and place for voting, supervision of officers and election judges, management of poll lists, and similar voting mechanics — not to campaigning for office. *Id.* at 9–20. In a portion of his separate opinion concerning FECA's public-financing system for presidential campaigns, Chief Justice Burger noted that the government was not "polic[ing] the integrity of the electoral process" but instead was policing "political debate itself." 424 U.S. at 248.

2.   What are the constitutional interests at stake in campaign-finance regulation? Read *Buckley* carefully: Does it say, as some have suggested, say that "money is speech," *see* J. Skelly Wright, *Politics and the Constitution: Is Money Speech?*, 85 YALE L.J. 1001, 1005 (1976), or is its message slightly but significantly different — that money is necessary to speak widely, and that preventing dissemination of speech is a First Amendment problem? In either case, virtually everyone agrees that campaign-finance laws, in the Court's words, "operate in an area of the most fundamental First Amendment activities." Since *Buckley*, nineteen men and women have sat on the Court, and only Justice Stevens has argued that for constitutional purposes, campaign-contribution and expenditure limitations should be treated merely as restrictions on property. *See Nixon v. Shrink Missouri Government*

PAC, 528 U.S. 377, 398–99 [p. 834] (Stevens, J., concurring). What fundamental First Amendment activities are at stake?

3. The more difficult issue for the courts has not been whether the First Amendment is at issue, but whether or not, in the words of Justice Breyer, "constitutionally protected interests lie on both sides of the legal equation," *id.* at 400 (Breyer, J., concurring); *see also* STEPHEN BREYER, ACTIVE LIBERTY 49 (2005); Burt Neuborne, *Toward a Democracy Centered Reading of the First Amendment*, 93 NW. U. L. REV. 1055, 1058–59 (1999) (arguing that constitutional "values" support campaign finance limitations); Harold Leventhal, *Courts and Political Thickets*, 77 COLUM. L. REV. 345, 373 (1977), and, if so, what that means. Justice Breyer has argued that restrictions can enhance First Amendment interests. As a result, "a presumption against constitutionality is out of place." *Nixon*, 528 U.S. at 401 (Breyer, J., concurring). In what ways might campaign-finance regulations enhance free speech or other constitutional values? For arguments that "constitutionally protected interests" or "constitutional values" are poor substitutes for traditional First Amendment analysis, see Daniel D. Polsby, Buckley v. Valeo: *The Special Nature of Political Speech*, 1976 SUP. CT. REV. 1 (1976); Bradley A. Smith, *The John Roberts Salvage Company: After* McConnell, *a New Court Looks to Repair the Constitution*, 68 OHIO ST. L.J. 891, 904–907 (2007).

The dispute over the role of constitutional values and interests is not merely one of theory, but of empirical analysis as well. Critics of campaign-finance regulation have not only disputed whether there are constitutionally protected interests on both sides of the legal equation, but whether regulation in fact protects or enhances such interests. *See* RODNEY A. SMITH, MONEY, POWER & ELECTIONS: HOW CAMPAIGN FINANCE REFORM SUBVERTS AMERICAN DEMOCRACY (2006); BRADLEY A. SMITH, UNFREE SPEECH: THE FOLLY OF CAMPAIGN FINANCE REFORM 144–45 (2001).

4. For the most part, *Buckley* seems to recognize just one compelling government interest: prevention of "corruption or its appearance." The extent to which campaign contributions are truly a source of political corruption is hotly disputed in professional literature, *see* Stephen D. Ansolabehere, John M. de Figueiredo, & James M. Snyder, Jr., *Why Is There So Little Money in American Politics*, 17 J. ECON. PERSPECTIVES 105, 113–117 (2003) (compiling and reviewing thirty-six peer-reviewed studies between 1977 and 2002 and concluding, "after controlling for legislator ideology, [campaign] contributions have no detectable effects on the behavior of legislators"), but there is no question the public perceives contributions as corrupting, Nathaniel Persily & Kelli Lammi, *Perceptions of Corruption and Campaign Finance: When Public Opinion Determines Constitutional Law*, 153 U. PA. L. REV. 119 (2004).

But what did the Court mean by "corruption"? In a portion of the opinion joined by all justices except Justice Blackmun, who would have struck down contribution limits, *Buckley* defines corruption as "large contributions * * * given to secure a political quid pro quo" 424 U.S. at 26. In *Federal Election Commission v. National Conservative Political Action Committee*, 470 U.S. 480 (1985), then-Justice Rehnquist wrote for a seven-member majority:

> Corruption is a subversion of the political process. Elected officials are
> influenced to act contrary to their obligations of office by the prospect of

financial gain to themselves or infusions of money into their campaigns. The hallmark of corruption is the financial *quid pro quo*: dollars for political favors.

How satisfied are you with that definition?

In recent years, a number of scholars have attempted to broaden the meaning of "corruption" to include broader themes of disconnection between voters and officeholders. Professor Larry Lessig argues that large amounts of private money in campaigns breaks the "dependence" of the legislature on the will of the people. Lessig argues that this "dependence corruption" justifies new restraints on political speech, *see* Lawrence Lessig, *A Reply to Professor Hasen*, 126 Harv. L. Rev. 61 (2012). Indeed, Lessig goes so far as to argue that this constitutes "corruption" as the term would have been used at the founding. Larry Lessig, *What an Originalist Would Understand 'Corruption' to Mean*, 102 Cal. L. Rev. 1 (2014). Zephyr Teachout has made similar arguments, suggesting that the Constitution includes an inherent "anti-corruption" principle, which can be understood to authorize sweeping government regulation of political campaigns. Teachout, *The Anti-Corruption Principle*, 94 Cornell L. Rev. 341 (2009). For doubts that the framers' views on corruption can be shoehorned into modern analysis, see Bruce E. Cain, *Is 'Dependence Corruption' the Solution to America's Campaign Finance Problems?*, 102 Cal. L. Rev. 37 (2014). But assume that the founders would have understood "corruption" along the lines of Lessig's "dependence corruption" or Teachout's broad, overpowering "anti-corruption principle": would that substantially alter the constitutional analysis, which is based, at least in part, on the grounds that regulation suppresses speech in a manner contrary to the First Amendment? In other words, is the First Amendment merely a broad, aspirational statement of concern for free speech and prevention of corruption, or is it better understood as a constitutional constraint that purposefully defines and limits the approaches that government can take to try to stamp out corruption?

Robert Post refashions the problem as one not of "corruption," but "electoral integrity," in which the public loses "trust[] that representatives will be attentive to public opinion." Robert Post, Citizens Divided: Campaign Finance Reform and the Constitution (2014). How would a regime based on "electoral integrity" look different, if at all, from the law faced in *Buckley*? How would judges determine if "electoral integrity" had been violated? *See* Pamela Karlan, *Citizens Deflected: Electoral Integrity and Political Reforms*, in Post, Citizens Divided, *supra*, 141 (Robert C. Post, ed. 2014); Justin Levitt, *Electoral Integrity: The Confidence Game*, 89 N.Y.U. L. Rev. Online 70 (2014).

As we will see, the Court itself has sometimes wavered on its formulation of a corruption interest sufficient to justify restrictions on First Amendment activity. In *Austin v. Michigan State Chamber of Commerce*, 494 U.S. 652, 660 (1990) [p. 907] a six justice majority suggested another definition: "the corrosive and distorting effects of immense aggregation of wealth that are accumulated with the corporate form and that have little or no correlation to the public's support for the corporation's political ideas." What does this mean? Is it important that political ideas be disseminated only in proportion to their pre-existing levels of support in the larger public? And in *McConnell v. Federal Election Commission*, 540 U.S. 93,

150 (2003) [p. 865] the Court suggested that "access to high-level government officials" that might come with campaign contributions or expenditures constituted "corruption." However, both of these definitions were later rejected by the Court in *Citizens United*. Is "access" corrupting? Officeholders must divide their time — does it not make sense that they would meet with those who supported their election? Even the *McConnell Court* agreed that access did not necessarily "secure actual influence," let alone policy results. 540 U.S. at 150.

5. What is meant by "the appearance of corruption"? If there is actual corruption, why isn't that enough? If it refers to fears unsupported by evidence, Persily and Lammi, *supra*. at 124, note that irrational fears are one of the few reasons insufficient to pass the Court's lowest level of scrutiny, rational basis. *See Romer v. Evans*, 517 U.S. 620 (1996); *City of Cleburne v. Cleburne Living Center*, 473 U.S. 432 (1985). Does the "appearance of corruption" serve as a proxy for the difficulty of proving actual corruption? Is "appearance of corruption" a broad justification for campaign finance regulation, since it is always easy to find people dissatisfied with the quality or actions of government? Or is it tightly tied to what the Court holds to be actual corruption — the appearance of *quid pro quo* exchanges being made? *See* Bradley A. Smith, *Super PACs and the Role of 'Coordination' in Campaign Finance Law*, 49 WILLAMETTE L. REV. 603, 615–616 (2013).

6. One of the most oft-quoted passages of *Buckley* is its quick dismissal of the equality interest proffered by the government as "wholly foreign to the First Amendment." However, many scholars believe that the equality rationale is the more compelling reason to support limitations and restrictions. *See, e.g.*, J. Skelly Wright, *Money and the Pollution of Politics: Is the First Amendment an Obstacle to Political Equality?*, 82 COLUM. L. REV. 611 (1982); Owen Fiss, *Free Speech and Social Structure*, 71 IOWA L. REV. 1405, 1425 (1986); Cass R. Sunstein, *Political Equality and Unintended Consequences*, 94 COLUM. L. REV. 1390, 1398–99 (1994). The result of *Buckley*, however, is that arguments to the courts favoring campaign-finance regulation, regardless of their motivation, must be shoehorned into an anti-corruption rationale. *See* Elizabeth Garrett, *Justice Marshall's Jurisprudence on Law and Politics*, 52 HOW. L.J. 655, 665–679 (2009).

Did the Court err in rejecting the equality rationale? *Compare* Fiss, *supra*, at 1416, 1425 ("We should learn to recognize the state not only as an enemy, but also as a friend of speech. . . . [W]e may sometimes find it necessary to restrict the speech of some elements of our society in order to enhance the relative influence of others. . . . "), *with* Polsby, *supra*, at 43 ("Almost every country in the world, including those behind the iron curtain, can display a constitution that guarantees freedom of expression to the people — to the extent, of course, that the people's representatives deem proper. With *Buckley v. Valeo* in hand, we can boast that our Constitution protects something far scarcer in history than that sort of freedom. And with the knowledge of the caliber of people who sometimes get their hands on our government, it is well that this is so."). *See also* David A. Strauss, *What is the Goal of Campaign Finance Reform*, 1995 U. CHI. LEGAL F. 141; Bruce E. Cain, *Moralism & Realism in Campaign Finance Reform*, 1995 U. CHI. LEGAL F. 111; Daniel H. Lowenstein, *Campaign Contributions and Corruption*, 1995 U. CHI. LEGAL F. 163.

Buckley did recognize other state interests in the context of disclosure, which will be discussed later in this Chapter.

7.   What is the level of scrutiny that *Buckley* applies to expenditure limits? To limits on contributions? Read again *Buckley's* standard for contribution limits: A regulation "may be sustained if the State demonstrates a sufficiently important interest and employs means closely drawn to avoid unnecessary abridgment of associational freedoms." What does this mean? How does it compare to "exacting scrutiny" that the Court declares is the standard for reviewing expenditure limits? *See* Marlene A. Nicholson, *Political Campaign Expenditure Limitations and the Unconstitutional Conditions Doctrine*, 10 HASTINGS CONST. L.Q. 601, 607–08 (1983). Is "exacting scrutiny" the same as "strict scrutiny"? Note that the term "strict scrutiny" as a phrase for describing a heightened degree of judicial review only began to see regular use in the 1960s, and at the time of *Buckley* the justices on the Court still used a variety of terms to convey the concept of heightened scrutiny that today is generally referenced as "strict scrutiny." *See* Richard H. Fallon, Jr., *Strict Judicial Scrutiny*, 54 UCLA L. REV. 1267, 1273–85 (2007).

A concern voiced in *Buckley*, that will resurface regularly in the Court's later cases, is whether or not restrictions primarily serve to benefit incumbent office-holders seeking re-election. *See, e.g.*, MICHAEL J. MALBIN & THOMAS GAIS, THE DAY AFTER REFORM: SOBERING CAMPAIGN FINANCE LESSONS FROM THE STATES 144–45 (1998). Does this concern go to the level of scrutiny to be applied, or to the Court's analysis under whatever level of scrutiny is applied?

8.   Does *Buckley's* distinction between contributions and expenditures make sense? What are some of the consequences of that distinction? Perhaps the most obvious consequence of the Court's decision to uphold contribution limits while striking down expenditure limits is that the distinction leaves an unlimited demand for campaign money, while limiting the supply of campaign money available. Joel M. Gora, Book Review: *No Law Abridging . . .* , 24 HARV. J.L. & PUB. POL'Y 841, 859 (2001). What are some of the predictable results of constricting supply while leaving demand unlimited? *See* Samuel Issacharoff & Pamela S. Karlan, *The Hydraulics of Campaign Finance Reform*, 77 TEX. L. REV. 1705, 1710–11 (1999). Other commentators argue that the distinction is fundamentally flawed as a matter of constitutional law: The commentators include those both those who would allow limits on spending, Burt Neuborne, *The Supreme Court and Free Speech: Love and a Question*, 42 ST. LOUIS U. L. REV. 789, 796–97 (1996); William P. Marshall, *The Last Best Chance for Campaign Finance Reform*, 94 NW. U. L. REV. 335, 350–51 (2000), and those who would abolish limits on contributions, *see* Lillian R. BeVier, *Money & Politics: A Perspective on the First Amendment and Campaign Finance Reform*, 73 CAL. L. REV. 1045 (1985); Bradley A. Smith, *Money Talks: Speech, Corruption, Equality and Campaign Finance*, 86 GEO. L.J. 45 (1997).

Despite these criticisms, the contribution/expenditure distinction has remained remarkably durable. Professor Daniel Lowenstein has argued that "[c]ontribution limits address the conflict of interest problem more directly . . . than campaign spending limits, whereas spending limits restrict speech more directly than contribution limits." Also, "[a]lthough the jury of social scientists is still out, there is reason to believe that to the extent spending limits reduce spending more than contribution limits, this will tend to make spending limits more detrimental to electoral competition." Lowenstein concluded, however, that these distinctions are insufficient to "support a general principle that expenditure limits are nearly always unconstitutional while contribution limits are nearly always valid." Daniel H. Lowenstein, *A Patternless Mosaic: Campaign Finance and the First Amendment After* Austin, 21 CAP. U. L. REV. 381, 401–402 (1992). Eugene Volokh has offered a more vigorous defense, arguing that the distinction offers a realistic compromise between the public's concerns about corruption and equality and First Amendment demands that speakers retain "considerable opportunities to speak." Eugene Volokh, *Freedom of Speech and Speech About Political Candidates: The Unintended Consequences of Three Proposals*, 24 HARV. J.L. & PUB. POL'Y 47, 65 (2000); *see also* Eugene Volokh, *Why* Buckley v. Valeo *is Basically Right*, 34 ARIZ. ST. L.J. 1095 (2002).

9. Re-read *Buckley*'s footnote 52 and the accompanying text. Here the Court distinguished between what became commonly known as "express advocacy," that is, explicit exhortations for voters to vote for or against specific candidates; and "issue advocacy," the discussion of candidates and issues that stopped short of such explicit exhortations to vote in particular ways. In the decades after *Buckley*, this distinction would come to dominate many of the legal debates over the reach and propriety of campaign-finance laws.

Note on Political Committees

The Federal Election Campaign Act Amendments of 1974, in addition to placing limits on contributions and expenditures, defined a "political committee" as "any committee, club, association, or other group of persons which receives contributions aggregating in excess of $1,000 during a calendar year or which makes expenditures aggregating in excess of $1,000 during a calendar year * * *." 52 U.S.C. § 30101 (4).

This definition is critically important because once an organization or group is deemed to be a "political committee" under FECA, it is subject to a broad array of regulatory requirements. It must register with the FEC, and further

> it must appoint a treasurer; ensure that contributions are forwarded to the treasurer within 10 or 30 days of receipt, depending on the amount of contribution; see that its treasurer keeps an account of every contribution regardless of amount, the name and address of any person who makes a contribution in excess of $50, all contributions received from political committees, and the name and address of any person to whom a disbursement is made regardless of amount; and preserve receipts for all disbursements over $200 and all records for three years. [It] must file a statement of organization containing its name, address, the name of its custodian of records, and its banks, safety deposit boxes, or other depositories; must report any change in the above information within 10 days; and may dissolve only upon filing a written statement that it will no longer receive any contributions nor make disbursements, and that it has no outstanding debts or obligations.

Federal Election Commission v. Massachusetts Citizens for Life, 479 U.S. 238, 253 (1986) (citations omitted). On top of these organizational and record-keeping requirements, a political committee has to report to the FEC, for public disclosure, the name, address, and employer of all donors in excess of $200. Additionally, until altered by court decisions in 2010 (see p. 981, *infra*) all political committees were subject to limitations on the size of contributions they could accept, and the sources of those contributions.

In another part of the *Buckley* opinion that appears in Section G of this Chapter, *infra*, the Court held that FECA's broad definition of "political committee" was unconstitutionally vague for the same reasons it held that the definition of "expenditure" was unconstitutionally vague. Because "'political committee' is defined only in terms of amount of annual "contributions" and 'expenditures,' [it] could be interpreted to reach groups engaged purely in issue discussion * * *. To fulfill the purposes of the Act [the definition of 'political committee'] need only encompass organizations that are under the control of a candidate or the major purpose of which is the nomination or election of a candidate." *Buckley*, 424 U.S. at 79.

By narrowing the definition of "political committee" to organizations with a major purpose of nominating or electing candidates, the Court protected groups such as the American Civil Liberties Union, the U.S. Chamber of Commerce, the Sierra Club, and literally thousands of small citizens' groups around the country from having to register as political committees if they spent a small amount on direct political advocacy. But how would the "major purpose" of a group be ascertained? As a practical matter, the FEC held that a group had a "major purpose" of electing candidates if more than half of its activity consisted of making "contributions" or "expenditures" under FECA, as those terms were narrowed in definition by *Buckley. See Akins v. Federal Election Commission*, 101 F.3d 731, 734 (D.C. Cir. 1996), *vacated on other grds., Federal Election Commission v. Akins*, 524 U.S. 11 (1998).

FECA and FEC regulations provide for several types of political committees. An "authorized committee" is a campaign committee specifically authorized by a candidate for office to conduct the campaign. Every candidate must designate at least one authorized committee, and at least one "principle campaign committee" responsible for the campaign. Political parties are designated as "party committees."

Political committees that are not party committees or candidate committees are generally referred to as PACs, an acronym for "political action committee." A PAC is a method for individuals to pool their resources to support like-minded candidates. Basically, there are two types of PACs, "connected" and "unconnected." Connected PACs include PACs established by a corporation or labor union, which the Act calls "Separate Segregated Funds" (or "SSF") because the union or corporation must keep the funds separate from its general treasury. A "connected PAC" may also be established by a membership association (such as the Sierra Club or the National Rifle Association) or trade association (such as the National Association of Realtors). Though the rules governing these PACs, including who and how they can solicit contributions, are complex, a simplified explanation is that these

SSFs and other connected PACs can only solicit contributions from individuals associated with the connected or sponsoring organization. Unions can solicit members and their families for contributions; corporations can solicit PAC contributions from shareholders, officers, and management and their families; connected PACs solicit from members of the sponsoring organization. A "non-connected committee" — as the name suggests — is not sponsored by or connected to any such entity, and is free to solicit contributions from the general public. The big advantage of a Connected PAC is that the sponsoring organization can pay to organize and provide administrative support for the PAC. These costs — organizing the PAC, arranging fundraising events, maintaining mailing lists, complying with legal accounting and reporting requirements, soliciting contributions — are often quite substantial, and can easily eat up 40 to 50% or more of a PAC's revenues. A non-connected PAC must absorb these costs from contributions given to it. But it has the advantage of being able to solicit contributions from anyone.

As you read the following sections on contribution limits and especially expenditure limits, consider that in many cases what is at stake is not merely the ability of a group to make such contributions or expenditures — as we have just seen, *Buckley* makes clear that the government cannot limit expenditures — but whether the disbursements by a group will be deemed to be "contributions" or "expenditures" under the Act, thus becoming the group's "major purpose," and triggering political committee status, with the accompanying regulatory burdens and restrictions on fundraising.

Note on "Express Advocacy"/"Issue Advocacy" Distinction

Recall the distinction drawn by *Buckley* between "express advocacy" and "issue advocacy," *supra* [810–11], limiting the definition of "expenditure" to "express advocacy." Why does this matter, given that *Buckley* went on to hold that independent expenditures — express advocacy — could not be constitutionally limited? The reasons are a bit complex, but very helpful to understanding the development of campaign finance law.

First, although *Buckley* struck down limits on expenditures, and some of the plaintiffs were incorporated entities, it did not specifically address 52 U.S.C. § 30118, which prohibited corporate expenditures. After *Buckley* and until the Supreme Court decision in *Citizens United v. Federal Election Commission*, 558 U.S. 310 (2010) [p. 941] in 2010, the FEC and many states continued to hold that corporate expenditures were illegal, at least in candidate races. *See*, in addition to *Citizens United, First National Bank of Boston v. Bellotti*, 435 U.S. 765 (1978) [p. 895] and *Austin v. Michigan State Chamber of Commerce*, 494 U.S. 652 (1990) [p. 907]. Thus, corporate and union-funded expenditures were barred if they included "express advocacy," but not if they avoided "express advocacy."

Second, as explained in the previous Note on Political Committees [p. 824], *Buckley* held that political committee status would only accrue to "organizations that are under the control of a candidate or the major purpose of which is the nomination or election of a candidate." 424 U.S. at 79. But *Buckley* did not indicate how one might establish the "major purpose" of an organization. A narrow interpretation might have limited the definition to candidate committees, political parties, and PACs formed to contribute directly to candidates — that is, to organizations formed explicitly to engage in candidate elections. This approach would obviously have left many organizations making expenditures outside the ambit of political committee. Another approach would have focused on the organization's overall intent. But determining "intent" would seem to raise exactly the type of vagueness problem and chilling effect that the Court sought to avoid with the express advocacy standard in the first place. The FEC eventually adopted an approach of measuring primary purpose by expenditures — if a group devoted more than half its resources to "express advocacy" expenditures and contributions to candidates, it would be deemed a "political committee," subject to the full array of registration and reporting requirements, and also to limitations on the size and sources of contributions it could receive, including no corporate or labor funding. If it did not devote more than half its resources to contributions or express advocacy, it was free of such requirements. *See Akins v. Federal Election Commission*, 101 F.3d 731, 734 (D.C. Cir. 1996), *vacated on other grds., Federal Election Commission v. Akins*, 524 U.S. 11 (1998). (Eventually the U.S. Court of Appeals would rule that limiting the sources and size of contributions to organizations that only made independent expenditures was unconstitutional, but that decision would not come until nearly 35 years after *Buckley*. *See SpeechNow.org v. Federal Election Commission*, 599 F.3d 686 (D.C. Cir. 2010)).

Finally, if an organization or other spender were not a political committee and ran an ad expressly advocating the election or defeat of a candidate, it still had to report that particular expenditure to the FEC. But if the ad did not expressly advocate for or against a candidate, the organization or spender had no reporting obligations.

As a result of these administrative interpretations of *Buckley*, whether or not an organization was engaged in "express advocacy" was a very important issue and the FEC and advocacy groups engaged in an ongoing guerrilla war in the appellate courts throughout the 1980s and 1990s as to the definition of "express advocacy," with the FEC generally getting the worst of the battle. Consider the following three cases, which both typified and framed the battle:

• In *Federal Election Commission v. Central Long Island Tax Reform Immediately Committee*, 616 F.2d 45 (1980) (*CLITRIM*), CLITRIM, a local group loosely affiliated with Tax Reform Immediately (TRIM), a project of the national John Birch Society, spent $135 to hand out a four page pamphlet at local shopping malls, commuter railway stations, and at a local political meeting. The pamphlet

> furnished information on the general views of the organizations, identified the officers of the Committee, furnished information about the CLITRIM members and invited others to join. The remaining pages reported the voting record of Congressman Jerome A. Ambro, a local representative of central Long Island. These pages included a photograph of Congressman Ambro and a chart of 24 votes cast by him, 21 of which were characterized as for "Higher Taxes and More Government" and 3 as for "Lower Taxes and Less Government." CLITRIM's stand against higher taxes and "Big Government" in favor of lower taxes and "Less Government" was made clear by slogans and commentaries. However, the leaflet did not refer to

any federal election, to Congressman Ambro's political affiliation or candidacy, or to any electoral opponent of the Congressman.

Id. at 51. The pamphlet also stated, "[i]f your Representative consistently votes for measures that increase taxes, let him know how you feel. And thank him when he votes for lower taxes and less government." *Id.* at 53.Various complaints were filed against CLITRIM and other local TRIM affiliates, and the FEC investigated. The Court held the leaflets did not constitute "express advocacy."

- In *Federal Election Commission v. Furgatch*, 807 F. 2d 857 (9th Cir.) *cert denied* 484 U.S. 850 (1987), the FEC scored a rare victory in the express advocacy wars. Harvey Furgatch purchased a full page ad in the Boston Globe three days before the 1980 presidential election, headlined "Don't let him do it." The ad then provided a long list of allegations about the behavior of President Jimmy Carter. The ad concluded that Carter was "attempt[ing] to hide his own record, or lack of it. If he succeeds the country will be burdened with four more years of incoherencies, ineptness and illusion, as he leaves a legacy of low-level campaigning.

DON'T LET HIM DO IT." *Id.* at 858. The Court of Appeals held that Furgatch's ad did amount to "express advocacy," because it included a "clear plea for action" and that the only act a reader could take to "not let him do it" was to vote against Carter. But the Court stressed, "[w]e emphasize that if any reasonable alternative reading of speech can be suggested, it cannot be express advocacy." *Id* at 864–65. The case was, said the Court, "a close call." *Id.* at 861.

- The FEC's efforts to use *Furgatch* to broaden the definition of "express advocacy" beyond the type of examples described in *Buckley* was almost wholly unsuccessful, as indicated by *Federal Election Commission v. Christian Action Network*, 110 F.3d 1049 (4th Cir. 1997) (*CAN*). In that case, CAN ran a TV ad with the following text:

> Bill Clinton's vision for America includes job quotas for homosexuals, giving homosexuals special civil rights, allowing homosexuals in the armed forces. Al Gore supports homosexual couples' adopting children and becoming foster parents. Is this your vision for a better America? For more information on traditional family values, contact the Christian Action Network.

Id. at 1058. The FEC conceded that the ad did not advocate for the defeat of Bill Clinton in the 1992 presidential race, but argued that it could still be deemed express advocacy because, "considered as a whole with the imagery, music, film footage, and voice intonations, the advertisements' nonprescriptive language unmistakably conveyed a message expressly advocating the defeat of Governor Clinton." String citing to numerous defeats the FEC had suffered in court on the express advocacy question, the Court held that the FEC's argument lacked "substantial justification" and could not be "made in good faith." *Id.* at 1064. The Court took the unusual step of awarding attorney's fees against the FEC. *Id.*

These three cases illustrate how unwilling lower courts have been to extend the definition of "express advocacy" beyond the types of explicit phrases — "vote for," "elect," "support," "cast your ballot for," "Smith for Congress," "vote against," "defeat," "reject" — found in *Buckley*, 424 U.S. 1, at 44 fn. 52.

As you will see, the Supreme Court decision in *Citizens United, supra,* and the Court of Appeals decision in *SpeechNow.org v. Federal Election, supra,* and broad acquiescence in that decision by the FEC and other courts, have greatly reduced the importance of the "express advocacy"/"issue advocacy" distinction. But the "express advocacy" standard remains important for determining political committee status under federal law, with its added reporting and organizational requirements, and it remains embedded as well in many state laws. *See, e.g.,* Mich. Stat. Ann. 169.206(j); *State ex rel. Two Unnamed Petitioners v. Peterson,* 363 Wis. 2d 1 (2015). Understanding the distinction, and the narrow definition that the courts have given to "express advocacy," remains valuable both to understanding many of the cases that follow in this chapter, and to ongoing issues in campaign finance law.

C. LIMITS ON CONTRIBUTIONS

A key distinction in *Buckley* is that between limits on contributions, which are subjected to a lower standard of review and generally held constitutional, and limits on expenditures, which are given more rigorous scrutiny and were found unconstitutional in *Buckley*. Understanding this paradigm is basic to any understanding of campaign-finance law. In this and the following two sections, we will see how the case law regulating contributions and expenditures has developed, and consider the effects of this dichotomy on regulation.

Limits on contributions take two basic forms: source limitations, and amount limitations. For example, under the Federal Election Campaign Act, direct union and corporate contributions to candidates are prohibited. 52 U.S.C. § 30118. This is a source limitation. Contributions by individuals are allowed, but limited. 52 U.S.C. § 30117. This is an amount limitation. These limits are adjusted each election cycle for inflation, and published by the FEC. This all sounds simple enough, but the law provides a variety of often confusing limits for giving to and by different types of entities. The limits for the 2015–16 election cycle are show in the figure below:

	RECIPIENTS				
CONTRIBUTION LIMITS FOR 2015-2016 FEDERAL ELECTIONS					
DONORS	**Candidate Committee**	**PAC[1]** (SSF and Nonconnected)	**State/District/ Local Party Committee**	**National Party Committee**	**Additional National Party Committee Accounts[2]**
Individual	$2,700* per election	$5,000 per year	$10,000 per year (combined)	$33,400* per year	$100,200* per account, per year
Candidate Committee	$2,000 per election	$5,000 per year	Unlimited Transfers	Unlimited Transfers	
PAC-Multicandidate	$5,000 per election	$5,000 per year	$5,000 per year (combined)	$15,000 per year	$45,000 per account, per year
PAC-Nonmulticandidate	$2,700 per election	$5,000 per year	$10,000 per year (combined)	$33,400* per year	$100,200* per account, per year
State/District/Local Party Committee	$5,000 per election	$5,000 per year	Unlimited Transfers		
National Party Committee	$5,000 per election[3]	$5,000 per year			

*- Indexed for inflation in odd-numbered years.

[1] "PAC" here refers to a committee that makes contributions to other federal political committees. Independent-expenditure-only political committees (sometimes called "super PACs") may accept unlimited contributions, including from corporations and labor organizations.

[2] The limits in this column apply to a national party committee's accounts for: (i) the presidential nominating convention; (ii) election recounts and contests and other legal proceedings; and (iii) national party headquarters buildings. A party's national committee, Senate campaign committee and House campaign committee are each considered separate national party committees with separate limits. Only a national party committee, not the parties' national congressional campaign committees, may have an account for the presidential nominating convention.

[3] Additionally, a national party committee and its Senatorial campaign committee may contribute up to $46,800 combined per campaign to each Senate candidate.

Federal Election Commission, 999 E Street NW, Washington, DC 20463 (800) 424-9530; (202) 694-1100 info@fec.gov

Notes and Questions

1. In *California Medical Association v. Federal Election Commission*, 453 U.S. 182 (1981), the California Medical Association (CMA), an unincorporated association of physicians, formed the California Medical Political Action Committee, a federal political action committee (PAC) governed by the Federal Election Campaign Act. The CMA wanted to expend more than $5,000 to pay the administrative cost of operating the PAC. But while the Act allows corporations and unions to pay the expenses of connected PACs, it makes no such provision for an unincorporated organization such as CMA to do so. CMA argued that it could hardly "corrupt" its own PAC, and also that it violated equal protection that a corporation could pay the administrative expenses of its SSF, but an unincorporated organization could not.

The Court rejected both arguments, noting that if an unincorporated organization could pay all the administrative expenses, that would essentially free up other dollars to go to candidates, with the effect that the sponsoring organization would be circumventing the limits on its giving. As to the fact that corporations could pay those expenses, the Court noted that that fact aside, corporations faced far more restrictions on their political activity than an unincorporated entity such as the CMA.

2. In another early post-*Buckley* decision, *Federal Election Commission v. National Right to Work Committee*, 459 U.S. 197 (1982), the Court addressed the ability of a connected PAC to solicit contributions from the public. The National Right to Work Committee (NRWC) is a non-profit, non-stock corporation. The organization's articles of incorporation provided that the corporation "shall not have members." As an educational organization, NRWC regularly mailed millions of individuals from lists it had compiled or purchased, and such mailings typically included requests for financial support. Persons who responded to NRWC surveys and "action alerts," but did not contribute financially, were considered "supporting members." Those who contributed financially were called "active members." Both groups received acknowledgements and a membership card. However, such status gave them no voting rights or control over the organization, and there were no membership meetings or other member activities.

After FECA was passed, NRWC established a Separate Segregated Fund, or PAC, to receive donations and make contributions to candidates for federal office who shared the organizations goals. In accordance with FEC regulations, NRWC paid for the administration of the PAC from its general treasury. It solicited contributions for the PAC from some 267,000 past donors ("active members") to NRWC. The FEC argued that the persons solicited by NRWC were not actually "members" of the organization, and therefore were ineligible to contribute to the group's PAC. The Supreme Court, in a unanimous opinion, ruled that the solicited individuals were not "members" within the meaning of the statute, and thus could not be solicited to contribute to NRWC's PAC. The Court went on to dismiss NRWC's claim that the membership requirement violated its freedom of association, citing two justifications:

> The first purpose of § 441b, the government states, is to ensure that substantial aggregations of wealth amassed by the special advantages which go with the corporate form of organization should not be converted into political "war chests" which could be used to incur political debts from legislators who are aided by the contributions. * * * The second purpose of the provisions, petitioners argue, is to protect the individuals who have paid money into a corporation or union for purposes other than the support of candidates from having that money used to support political candidates to whom they may be opposed. * * *

> We agree with petitioners that these purposes are sufficient to justify the regulation at issue.

459 U.S. at 207–08.

3.   Do the results in *California Medical Association* and *NRWC* do anything to prevent corruption or its appearance? If so, how? The California Medical Association's desire to provide administrative support for its PAC from its general treasury was undoubtedly prompted by the cost of operating and maintaining a PAC. In addition to applicable limits on contributions to a PAC, PACs are subject to extensive and detailed organizational, reporting, and compliance requirements, including limits on who can be solicited for contributions to the PAC. For many PACs, the administrative and compliance costs can equal or even exceed the amount raised by the PAC for the purpose of making contributions to candidates. Title 52 U.S.C. § 30118 allows corporations and unions to pay these administrative and compliance costs without limit, thus increasing the amounts that can be spent on political races. *See* John M. de Figueiredo & Elizabeth Garrett, *Paying for Politics*, 78 S. Cal. L. Rev. 591, 603 (2005). Is this corrupting? Does it increase the potential for corruption from the PAC, which is still limited to contributing $5,000 to any one candidate?

Similarly, do either of the purposes cited by the Court in NRWC actually apply in that case? The Court expresses concern that large war chests might "be used to incur debts from legislators." But NRWC's "war chest" came from donations from members of the public. Is this a problem, given that limitations on contributions to the PAC assure that any "war chest" so accumulated will be the result of large numbers of people voluntarily making small contributions, and that NRWC's PAC itself is limited to contributing no more than $5,000 to any candidate in an election? Or, to put it differently, does it matter if the candidate feels a debt to a group when that debt is incurred because the group represents large numbers of people? Don't those large numbers reflect the popularity of the ideas in the public?

The Court also says that the "war chest" was accumulated thanks to "special advantages which go with the corporate form * * *." What "special advantages" did NRWC gain from the corporate form that it could convert into a "political 'war chest' "? Limited liability? But in fact, NRWC would still be liable to the full extent of its members' contributions (that is to say, to the full extent of its budget and retained capital, since its income came from contributions); and its members would not be liable beyond the scope of their contributions regardless of NRWC's legal form. If not limited liability, is there some other special benefit it obtained?

The Court's acceptance of the second interest offered by the state — protecting persons who have "paid money into a corporation or union" from having their "money used to support political candidates to whom they may be opposed" — is even more puzzling. Whatever the merits of that concern where members are required to join unions by law, *see Abood v. Detroit Bd. of Educ.*, 431 U.S. 209 (1977), or unable to sell corporate stock without significant sacrifice, *see* Stuart Taylor, *Congress Can Help Repair Ruling's Damage*, Nat'l J., Jan. 30, 2010, does it apply in the case of the National Right to Work Committee? Wouldn't most people who "paid money into the corporation" do so precisely because they favored the organization's political goals (note that the NRWC did not have capital stock, only members and donors)? Of course, donors may not agree with every decision of NRWC to endorse a candidate. But is it any more likely that a typical NRWC supporter would be upset if his money supported NRWC PAC administrative costs than if it went to lobby for a bill the donor did not support, or was used to criticize an officeholder whom the donor supported? In short, when you give to an organization based on ideological affinity, don't you always run the risk that you may not agree with some future action the organization takes?

4.   In the wake of *NRWC*, a good deal of an organization's ability to solicit and raise PAC funds will depend on the definition of "member." The Court suggested that to be considered "members" for purposes of PAC solicitations, individuals would need to have some ability to exercise control over an organization's administration and finance. How much control is enough? In 1993, the FEC adopted a regulation that limited the definition of "member" to those who either (i) had a "significant financial attachment" to the organization beyond "merely the payment of dues," (ii) paid regular dues and had the right to vote directly for at least one member of the organization's board, or (iii) had the right to vote directly for all members of the organization's board. 11 C.F.R. § 114.1(e) (1993). The United States Chamber of Commerce and the American Medical Association sued. The plaintiffs noted that under the FEC regulation, over 220,000 dues-paying members of the Chamber (all but 63 of their total membership) and approximately 44,500 of the AMA's 290,000 dues-paying physicians would not qualify as "members," meaning that the organization could not solicit them for PAC contributions or communicate with them on political matters, other than by using its PAC. The Court of Appeals held that the definition violated the First Amendment rights of the plaintiffs to communicate with their members. *United States Chamber of Commerce v. Federal Election Commission*, 69 F.3d 600 (D.C. Cir. 1995). The FEC then amended its rule to provide that anyone paying regular dues qualified as a "member" for purposes of the Act. 11 C.F.R. § 100.134(f).

5.   *Buckley* upheld limits on contributions, but can a donation be limited merely because it is a "contribution" to a political organization? In *Citizens Against Rent Control/Coalition for Fair Housing v. City of Berkeley*, 454 U.S. 290, 102 S. Ct. 434, 70 L. Ed. 2d 492 (1981), the City of Berkeley, California had enacted an ordinance prohibiting contributions in excess of $250 to any political committee, including those formed solely to support or oppose ballot measures. The Court declined to adopt a rigid, formal application of *Buckley* in which a contribution could be limited merely because it was a "contribution." Rather, the Court insisted that the limit must relate to the anti-corruption interest.

> *Buckley* identified a single narrow exception to the rule that limits on political activity were contrary to the First Amendment. The exception relates to the perception of undue influence of large contributors to a *candidate*. * * * "Referenda are held on issues, not candidates for public office. The risk of corruption perceived in cases involving candidate elections * * * simply is not present in a popular vote on a public issue."
> * * * [*First National Bank of Boston v. Bellotti*], 435 U.S. at 790 [p. 895].

454 U.S. at 296–298 (emphasis in original). The Court struck down the ordinance as applied to ballot committees.

6.   *Problem.* City Alderman Conrad Sweat nearly lost his seat in the last election when his opponent, a political neophyte and wealthy auto dealership owner, spent $100,000 of his own money on his campaign. This shattered the previous record for spending in a race for alderman, which had been just $54,000. The dealer

has publicly indicated that he may seek the office again in the near future. The City's campaign finance ordinance imposes a $500 limit on contributions to a campaign. Alderman Sweat has proposed an amendment to the ordinance, which would redefine an expenditure by a candidate as a "contribution" to his own campaign, thus subjecting it to the $500 limit. Is the Amendment constitutional? *See Nixon v. Shrink Missouri Government PAC*, 528 U.S. 377, 405 (2000) (Breyer, J. concurring).

7. The decisions in *California Medical Association, National Right to Work Committee*, and *Citizens Against Rent Control* aside, the first two decades of post-*Buckley* litigation largely concerned expenditures, rather than contributions. This is because *Buckley* clearly upheld limits on contributions to candidate committees and political parties. Recall also that the *Buckley* plaintiffs argued that the law was overbroad because the $1,000 limit — approximately $4,800 in 2015 inflation-adjusted dollars — was set at a level far below that creating any meaningful threat of corruption. The Court's response — "a court has no scalpel to probe, whether, say, a $2,000 ceiling might not serve as well as $1,000" — seemed to foreclose most challenges to limits as being too low. But *Buckley* did suggest that contribution limits could be challenged if it were shown that "the limitations prevented candidates and political committees from amassing the resources necessary for effective advocacy." As general rates of inflation gradually eroded the relative purchasing power of $1,000, it seemed only a matter of time before new challenges were brought to the level of limits on campaign contributions. Such a challenge reached the Supreme Court in 2000, in the following case. The case is also important for its discussion of the level of evidence that the state need put forth to justify the infringements on First Amendment rights.

NIXON v. SHRINK MISSOURI GOVERNMENT PAC
Supreme Court of the United States
528 U.S. 377, 120 S. Ct. 897, 145 L. Ed. 2d 886 (2000)

JUSTICE SOUTER delivered the opinion of the Court [in which CHIEF JUSTICE REHNQUIST, JUSTICE STEVENS, JUSTICE O'CONNOR, JUSTICE GINSBURG, and JUSTICE BREYER join].

The principal issues in this case are whether *Buckley* v. *Valeo*, 424 U.S. 1 (1976) [p. 799] *(per curiam)*, is authority for state limits on contributions to state political candidates and whether the federal limits approved in *Buckley*, with or without adjustment for inflation, define the scope of permissible state limitations today. We hold *Buckley* to be authority for comparable state regulation, which need not be pegged to *Buckley*'s dollars.

In 1994, the Legislature of Missouri enacted Senate Bill 650 to restrict the permissible amounts of contributions to candidates for state office. Mo. Rev. Stat. § 130.032. * * *

The statutory dollar amounts are baselines for an adjustment each even-numbered year, to be made "by multiplying the base year amount by the cumulative consumer price index . . . and rounded to the nearest twenty-five-dollar amount, for all years since January 1, 1995." § 130.032.2. When this suit was filed, the limits ranged from a high of $1,075 for contributions to candidates for statewide office (including state auditor) and for any office where the population exceeded 250,000, down to $275 for contributions to candidates for state representative or for any office for which there were fewer than 100,000 people represented.

Respondents Shrink Missouri Government PAC, a political action committee, and Zev David Fredman, a candidate for the 1998 Republican nomination for state auditor, sought to enjoin enforcement of the contribution statute as violating their First and Fourteenth Amendment rights (presumably those of free speech, association, and equal protection, although the complaint did not so state). Shrink Missouri gave $1,025 to Fredman's candidate committee in 1997, and another $50 in 1998. Shrink Missouri represented that, without the limitation, it would contribute more to the Fredman campaign. Fredman alleged he could campaign effectively only with more generous contributions than § 130.032.1 allowed.

[T]he District Court sustained the statute[, but t]he Court of Appeals for the Eighth Circuit [reversed]. * * *

Precision about the relative rigor of the standard to review contribution limits was not a pretense of the *Buckley per curiam* opinion. To be sure, in addressing the speech claim, we explicitly rejected both *O'Brien* intermediate scrutiny for communicative action, see *United States* v. *O'Brien*, 391 U.S. 367 (1968), and the similar standard applicable to merely time, place, and manner restrictions. * * * In distinguishing these tests, the discussion referred generally to "the exacting scrutiny required by the First Amendment," and added that "the constitutional guarantee has its fullest and most urgent application precisely to the conduct of campaigns for political office." * * *

We then, however, drew a line between expenditures and contributions, treating expenditure restrictions as direct restraints on speech, which nonetheless suffered little direct effect from contribution limits:

> "[A] limitation upon the amount that any one person or group may contribute to a candidate or political committee entails only a marginal restriction upon the contributor's ability to engage in free communication. A contribution serves as a general expression of support for the candidate and his views, but does not communicate the underlying basis for the support. The quantity of communication by the contributor does not increase perceptibly with the size of his contribution, since the expression rests solely on the undifferentiated symbolic act of contributing. At most, the size of the contribution provides a very rough index of the intensity of the contributor's support for the candidate. A limitation on the amount of money a person may give to a candidate or campaign organization thus involves little direct restraint on his political communication, for it permits the symbolic expression of support evidenced by a contribution but does not in any way infringe the contributor's freedom to discuss candidates and issues." [424 U.S.], at 20–21.

We thus said, in effect, that limiting contributions left communication significantly unimpaired.

We flagged a similar difference between expenditure and contribution limitations in their impacts on the association right. * * * "We have consistently held that restrictions on contributions require less compelling justification than restrictions on independent spending." It has, in any event, been plain ever since *Buckley* that contribution limits would more readily clear the hurdles before them. * * * Thus, under *Buckley's* standard of scrutiny, a contribution limit involving "significant interference" with associational rights could survive if the Government demonstrated that contribution regulation was "closely drawn" to match a "sufficiently important interest," though the dollar amount of the limit need not be "fine tun[ed]."

While we did not attempt to parse distinctions between the speech and association standards of scrutiny for contribution limits, we did make it clear that those restrictions bore more heavily on the associational right than on freedom to speak. We consequently proceeded on the understanding that a contribution limitation surviving a claim of associational abridgment would survive a speech challenge as well, and we held the standard satisfied by the contribution limits under review. * * *

In speaking of "improper influence" and "opportunities for abuse" in addition to "*quid pro quo* arrangements," we recognized a concern not confined to bribery of public officials, but extending to the broader threat from politicians too compliant with the wishes of large contributors. These were the obvious points behind our recognition that the Congress could constitutionally address the power of money "to influence governmental action" in ways less "blatant and specific" than bribery.

In defending its own statute, Missouri espouses those same interests of preventing corruption and the appearance of it that flows from munificent campaign contributions. Even without the authority of *Buckley*, there would be no serious question about the legitimacy of the interests claimed, which, after all, underlie bribery and antigratuity statutes. While neither law nor morals equate all political contributions, without more, with bribes, we spoke in *Buckley* of the perception of corruption "inherent in a regime of large individual financial contributions" to candidates for public office, as a source of concern "almost equal" to *quid pro quo* improbity. The public interest in countering that perception was, indeed, the entire answer to the overbreadth claim raised in the *Buckley* case. This made perfect sense. Leave the perception of impropriety unanswered, and the cynical assumption that large donors call the tune could jeopardize the willingness of voters to take part in democratic governance. Democracy works "only if the people have faith in those who govern, and that faith is bound to be shattered when high officials and their appointees engage in activities which arouse suspicions of malfeasance and corruption." *United States v. Mississippi Valley Generating Co.*, 364 U.S. 520 (1961).

Although respondents neither challenge the legitimacy of these objectives nor call for any reconsideration of *Buckley*, they take the State to task, as the Court of Appeals did, for failing to justify the invocation of those interests with empirical evidence of actually corrupt practices or of a perception among Missouri voters that unrestricted contributions must have been exerting a covertly corrosive influence. The state statute is not void, however, for want of evidence.

The quantum of empirical evidence needed to satisfy heightened judicial scrutiny of legislative judgments will vary up or down with the novelty and plausibility of the justification raised. *Buckley* demonstrates that the dangers of large, corrupt contributions and the suspicion that large contributions are corrupt are neither novel nor implausible. The opinion noted that "the deeply disturbing examples surfacing after the 1972 election demonstrate that the problem [of corruption] is not an illusory one." Although we did not ourselves marshal the evidence in support of the congressional concern, we referred to "a number of the abuses" detailed in the Court of Appeals's decision, which described how corporations, well-financed interest groups, and rich individuals had made large contributions, some of which were illegal under existing law, others of which reached at least the verge of bribery. * * *

While *Buckley*'s evidentiary showing exemplifies a sufficient justification for contribution limits, it does not speak to what may be necessary as a minimum. As to that, respondents are wrong in arguing that in the years since *Buckley* came down we have "supplemented" its holding with a new requirement that governments enacting contribution limits must "demonstrate that the recited harms are real, not merely conjectural[.]" * * *

* * * [T]his case does not present a close call requiring further definition of whatever the State's evidentiary obligation may be. While the record does not show that the Missouri Legislature relied on the evidence and findings accepted in *Buckley*,[6] * * * the substantiation of the congressional concerns reflected in *Buckley* has its counterpart supporting the Missouri law. Although Missouri does not preserve legislative history, the State presented an affidavit from State Senator Wayne Goode, the co-chair of the state legislature's Interim Joint Committee on Campaign Finance Reform at the time the State enacted the contribution limits, who stated that large contributions have "the real potential to buy votes." The District Court cited newspaper accounts of large contributions supporting inferences of impropriety. One report questioned the state treasurer's decision to use a certain bank for most of Missouri's banking business after that institution contributed $20,000 to the treasurer's campaign. Another made much of the receipt by a candidate for state auditor of a $40,000 contribution from a brewery and one for $20,000 from a bank. * * * [T]he Eighth Circuit itself * * * identified a $420,000 contribution to candidates in northern Missouri from a political action committee linked to an investment bank, and three scandals, including one in which a state representative was "accused of sponsoring legislation in exchange for kickbacks," and another in which Missouri's former attorney general pleaded guilty to charges of conspiracy to misuse state property, after being indicted for using a state workers' compensation fund to benefit campaign contributors. And although majority votes do not, as such, defeat First Amendment protections, the statewide vote on Proposition A [which imposed even stricter contribution limits than the ones enacted by the Missouri Legislature] certainly attested to the perception relied upon here: "[A]n overwhelming 74 percent of the voters of Missouri determined that contribution limits are necessary to combat corruption and the appearance thereof."

---

[6] Cf. *Renton* v. *Playtime Theatres, Inc.*, 475 U.S. 41, 51–52 (1986) ("The First Amendment does not require a city, before enacting . . . an ordinance, to conduct new studies or produce evidence independent of that already generated by other cities, so long as whatever evidence the city relies upon is reasonably believed to be relevant to the problem that the city addresses").

There might, of course, be need for a more extensive evidentiary documentation if respondents had made any showing of their own to cast doubt on the apparent implications of *Buckley*'s evidence and the record here, but the closest respondents come to challenging these conclusions is their invocation of academic studies said to indicate that large contributions to public officials or candidates do not actually result in changes in candidates' positions. Smith, *Money Talks: Speech, Corruption, Equality, and Campaign Finance*, 86 Geo. L.J. 45, 58 (1997); Smith, *Faulty Assumptions and Undemocratic Consequences of Campaign Finance Reform*, 105 Yale L.J. 1049, 1067–1068 (1995). Other studies, however, point the other way. F. Sorauf, Inside Campaign Finance 169 (1992); Hall & Wayman, *Buying Time: Moneyed Interests and the Mobilization of Bias in Congressional Committees*, 84 Am. Pol. Sci. Rev. 797 (1990); D. Magleby & C. Nelson, The Money Chase 78 (1990). Given the conflict among these publications, and the absence of any reason to think that public perception has been influenced by the studies cited by respondents, there is little reason to doubt that sometimes large contributions will work actual corruption of our political system, and no reason to question the existence of a corresponding suspicion among voters.

Nor do we see any support for respondents' various arguments that in spite of their striking resemblance to the limitations sustained in *Buckley*, those in Missouri are so different in kind as to raise essentially a new issue about the adequacy of the Missouri statute's tailoring to serve its purposes. Here, as in *Buckley*, "[t]here is no indication . . . that the contribution limitations imposed by the [law] would have any dramatic[ally] adverse effect on the funding of campaigns and political associations," and thus no showing that "the limitations prevented the candidates and political committees from amassing the resources necessary for effective advocacy." 424 U.S., at 21. The District Court found here that in the period since the Missouri limits became effective, "candidates for state elected office [have been] quite able to raise funds sufficient to run effective campaigns," and that "candidates for political office in the state are still able to amass impressive campaign war chests." * * *

These conclusions of the District Court and the supporting evidence also suffice to answer respondents' variant claim that the Missouri limits today differ in kind from *Buckley*'s owing to inflation since 1976. Respondents seem to assume that *Buckley* set a minimum constitutional threshold for contribution limits, which in dollars adjusted for loss of purchasing power are now well above the lines drawn by Missouri. But this assumption is a fundamental misunderstanding of what we held.

In *Buckley*, we specifically rejected the contention that $1,000, or any other amount, was a constitutional minimum below which legislatures could not regulate. As indicated above, we referred instead to the outer limits of contribution regulation by asking whether there was any showing that the limits were so low as to impede the ability of candidates to "amas[s] the resources necessary for effective advocacy." We asked, in other words, whether the contribution limitation was so radical in effect as to render political association ineffective, drive the sound of a candidate's voice below the level of notice, and render contributions pointless. Such being the test, the issue in later cases cannot be truncated to a narrow question about the power of the dollar, but must go to the power to mount a campaign with all the dollars likely to be forthcoming. [T]he dictates of the First Amendment are not mere functions of the Consumer Price Index.

* * * The judgment of the Court of Appeals is, accordingly, reversed, and the case is remanded for proceedings consistent with this opinion.

It is so ordered.

JUSTICE STEVENS, concurring.

* * * Money is property; it is not speech.

Speech has the power to inspire volunteers to perform a multitude of tasks on a campaign trail, on a battleground, or even on a football field. Money, meanwhile, has the power to pay hired laborers to perform the same tasks. It does not follow, however, that the First Amendment provides the same measure of protection to the use of money to accomplish such goals as it provides to the use of ideas to achieve the same results.

Our Constitution and our heritage properly protect the individual's interest in making decisions about the use of his or her own property. Governmental regulation of such decisions can sometimes be viewed either as "deprivations of liberty" or as "deprivations of property," *see, e.g., Moore v. East Cleveland,* 431 U.S. 494 (1977) (STEVENS, J., concurring in judgment). Telling a grandmother that she may not use her own property to provide shelter to a grandchild — or to hire mercenaries to work in that grandchild's campaign for public office — raises important constitutional concerns that are unrelated to the First Amendment. * * * Because I did not participate in the Court's decision in *Buckley,* I did not have the opportunity to suggest then that those property and liberty concerns adequately explain the Court's decision to invalidate the expenditure limitations in the 1974 Act.

* * * The right to use one's own money to hire gladiators, or to fund "speech by proxy," certainly merits significant constitutional protection. These property rights, however, are not entitled to the same protection as the right to say what one pleases.

JUSTICE BREYER, with whom JUSTICE GINSBURG joins, concurring.

The dissenters accuse the Court of weakening the First Amendment. They believe that failing to adopt a "strict scrutiny" standard "balance[s] away First Amendment freedoms." But the principal dissent oversimplifies the problem faced in the campaign finance context. It takes a difficult constitutional problem and turns it into a lopsided dispute between political expression and government censorship. Under the cover of this fiction and its accompanying formula, the dissent would make the Court absolute arbiter of a difficult question best left, in the main, to the political branches. * * *

[T]his is a case where constitutionally protected interests lie on both sides of the legal equation. For that reason there is no place for a strong presumption against constitutionality, of the sort often thought to accompany the words "strict scrutiny." Nor can we expect that mechanical application of the tests associated with "strict scrutiny" — the tests of "compelling interests" and "least restrictive means" — will properly resolve the difficult constitutional problem that campaign finance statutes pose. * * *

On the one hand, a decision to contribute money to a campaign is a matter of First Amendment concern — not because money *is* speech (it is not); but because it *enables* speech. Through contributions the contributor associates himself with the candidate's cause, helps the candidate communicate a political message with which the contributor agrees, and helps the candidate win by attracting the votes of similarly minded voters. * * * Both political association and political communication are at stake.

On the other hand, restrictions upon the amount any one individual can contribute to a particular candidate seek to protect the integrity of the electoral process — the means through which a free society democratically translates political speech into concrete governmental action. * * * Moreover, by limiting the size of the largest contributions, such restrictions aim to democratize the influence that money itself may bring to bear upon the electoral process. Cf. *Reynolds* v. *Sims*, 377 U.S. 533, 565 (1964) [p. 173] (in the context of apportionment, the Constitution "demands" that each citizen have "an equally effective voice"). In doing so, they seek to build public confidence in that process and broaden the base of a candidate's meaningful financial support, encouraging the public participation and open discussion that the First Amendment itself presupposes.

In service of these objectives, the statute imposes restrictions of degree. It does not deny the contributor the opportunity to associate with the candidate through a contribution, though it limits a contribution's size. Nor does it prevent the contributor from using money (alone or with others) to pay for the expression of the same views in other ways. Instead, it permits all supporters to contribute the same amount of money, in an attempt to make the process fairer and more democratic.

Under these circumstances, a presumption against constitutionality is out of place. I recognize that *Buckley* used language that could be interpreted to the contrary. It said, for example, that it rejected "the concept that government may restrict the speech of some elements of our society in order to enhance the relative voice of others." But those words cannot be taken literally. The Constitution often permits restrictions on the speech of some in order to prevent a few from drowning out the many — in Congress, for example, where constitutionally protected debate is limited to provide every Member an equal opportunity to express his or her views. Or in elections, where the Constitution tolerates numerous restrictions on ballot access, limiting the political rights of some so as to make effective the political rights of the entire electorate. See, *e.g.*, *Storer* v. *Brown*, 415 U.S. 724, 736 (1974) [p. 513]. Regardless, as the result in *Buckley* made clear, the statement does not automatically invalidate a statute that seeks a fairer electoral debate through contribution limits, nor should it forbid the Court to take account of the competing constitutional interests just mentioned.

In such circumstances — where a law significantly implicates competing constitutionally protected interests in complex ways — the Court has closely scrutinized the statute's impact on those interests, but refrained from employing a simple test that effectively presumes unconstitutionality. Rather, it has balanced interests. And in practice that has meant asking whether the statute burdens any one such interest in a manner out of proportion to the statute's salutary effects upon the others (perhaps, but not necessarily, because of the existence of a clearly superior, less restrictive alternative). Where a legislature has significantly greater institutional expertise, as, for example, in the field of election regulation, the Court in practice defers to empirical legislative judgments — at least where that deference does not risk such constitutional evils as, say, permitting incumbents to insulate themselves from effective electoral challenge. This approach is that taken in fact by *Buckley* for contributions, and is found generally where competing constitutional interests are implicated, such as privacy, see, *e.g.*, *Frisby* v. *Schultz*, 487 U.S. 474, 485–488 (1988) (balancing rights of privacy and expression); First Amendment interests of listeners or viewers, see, *e.g.*, *Turner Broadcasting System, Inc.* v. *FCC*, 520 U.S. 180, 192–194 (1997) (recognizing the speech interests of both viewers and cable operators); *Columbia Broadcasting System, Inc.* v. *Democratic National Committee*, 412 U.S. 94, 102–103 (1973) ("Balancing the various First Amendment interests involved in the broadcast media . . . is a task of a great delicacy and difficulty"); *Red Lion Broadcasting Co.* v. *FCC*, 395 U.S. 367, 389–390 (1969) [p. 605] (First Amendment permits the Federal Communications Commission to restrict the speech of some to enable the speech of others), and the integrity of the electoral process, see, *e.g.*, *Storer* v. *Brown*, *supra*, at 730 ("[T]here must be a substantial regulation of elections if they are to be fair and honest"). * * * Applying this approach to the present case, I would uphold the statute essentially for the reasons stated by the Court. * * *

JUSTICE KENNEDY, dissenting. * * *

Zev David Fredman asks us to evaluate his speech claim in the context of a system which favors candidates and officeholders whose campaigns are supported by soft money, usually funneled through political parties. The Court pays him no heed. The plain fact is that the compromise the Court invented in *Buckley* set the stage for a new kind of speech to enter the political system. It is covert speech. The Court has forced a substantial amount of political speech underground, as contributors and candidates devise ever more elaborate methods of avoiding contribution limits, limits which take no account of rising campaign costs. The preferred method has been to conceal the real purpose of the speech. Soft money may be contributed to political parties in unlimited amounts, see *Colorado Republican Federal Campaign Comm.* v. *Federal Election Comm'n*, 518 U.S. 604 (1996) [p. 984], and is used often to fund so-called issue advocacy, advertisements that promote or attack a candidate's positions without specifically urging his or her election or defeat. Issue advocacy, like soft money, is unrestricted, while straightforward speech in the form of financial contributions paid to a candidate, speech subject to full disclosure and prompt evaluation by the public, is not. Thus has the Court's decision given us covert speech. This mocks the First Amendment. The current system would be unfortunate, and suspect under the First Amendment, had it evolved from a deliberate legislative choice; but its unhappy origins are in our earlier decree in *Buckley*, which by accepting half of what Congress did (limiting contributions) but rejecting the other (limiting expenditures) created a misshapen system, one which distorts the meaning of speech.

The irony that we would impose this regime in the name of free speech ought to be sufficient ground to reject *Buckley*'s wooden formula in the present case. The wrong goes deeper, however. By operation of the *Buckley* rule, a candidate cannot oppose this system in an effective way without selling out to it first. Soft money must be raised to attack the problem of soft money. In effect, the Court immunizes its own erroneous ruling from change. Rulings of this Court must never be viewed with more caution than when they provide immunity from their own correction in the political process and in the forum of unrestrained speech. The melancholy history of campaign finance in *Buckley*'s wake shows what can happen when we intervene in the dynamics of speech and expression by inventing an artificial scheme of our own.

The case in one sense might seem unimportant. It appears that Mr. Fredman was an outsider candidate who may not have had much of a chance. Yet, by binding him to the outdated limit of $1,075 per contribution in a system where parties can raise soft money without limitation and a powerful press faces no restrictions on use of its own resources to back its preferred candidates, the Court tells Mr. Fredman he cannot challenge the status quo unless he first gives into it. This is not the First Amendment with which I am familiar.

To defend its extension of *Buckley* to present times, the Court, of course, recites the dangers of corruption, or the appearance of corruption, when an interested person contributes money to a candidate. What the Court does not do is examine and defend the substitute it has encouraged, covert speech funded by unlimited soft money. In my view that system creates dangers greater than the one it has replaced. The first danger is the one already mentioned: that we require contributors of soft money and its beneficiaries to mask their real purpose. Second, we have an indirect system of accountability that is confusing, if not dispiriting, to the voter. The very disaffection or distrust that the Court cites as the justification for limits on direct contributions has now spread to the entire political discourse. *Buckley* has not worked.

My colleagues in the majority, in my respectful submission, do much disservice to our First Amendment jurisprudence by failing to acknowledge or evaluate the whole operation of the system that we ourselves created in *Buckley*. Our First Amendment principles surely tell us that an interest thought to be the compelling reason for enacting a law is cast into grave doubt when a worse evil surfaces in the law's actual operation. And our obligation to examine the operation of the law is all the more urgent when the new evil is itself a distortion of speech. By these measures the law before us cannot pass any serious standard of First Amendment review.

Among the facts the Court declines to take into account is the emergence of cyberspace communication by which political contributions can be reported almost simultaneously with payment. The public can then judge for itself whether the candidate or the officeholder has so overstepped that we no longer trust him or her to make a detached and neutral judgment. This is a far more immediate way to assess the integrity and the performance of our leaders than through the hidden world of soft money and covert speech.

Officeholders face a dilemma inherent in the democratic process and one that has never been easy to resolve: how to exercise their best judgment while soliciting the continued support and loyalty of constituents whose interests may not always coincide with that judgment. Edmund Burke captured the tension in his Speeches at Bristol. "Your representative owes you, not his industry only, but his judgment; and he betrays instead of serving you, if he sacrifices it to your opinion." E. Burke, Speeches of the Right Hon. Edmund Burke (J. Burke ed. 1867). Whether our officeholders can discharge their duties in a proper way when they are beholden to certain interests both for reelection and for campaign support is, I should think, of constant concern not alone to citizens but to conscientious officeholders themselves. There are no easy answers, but the Constitution relies on one: open, robust, honest, unfettered speech that the voters can examine and assess in an ever-changing and more complex environment.

* * * It suffices here to say that the law in question does not come even close to passing any serious scrutiny. * * *

JUSTICE THOMAS, with whom JUSTICE SCALIA joins, dissenting.

In the process of ratifying Missouri's sweeping repression of political speech, the Court today adopts the analytic fallacies of our flawed decision in *Buckley* v. *Valeo*. Unfortunately, the Court is not content to merely adhere to erroneous precedent. Under the guise of applying *Buckley*, the Court proceeds to weaken the already enfeebled constitutional protection that *Buckley* afforded campaign contributions. In the end, the Court employs a *sui generis* test to balance away First Amendment freedoms.

Because the Court errs with each step it takes, I dissent. [O]ur decision in *Buckley* was in error, and I would overrule it. I would subject campaign contribution limitations to strict scrutiny, under which Missouri's contribution limits are patently unconstitutional.

I begin with a proposition that ought to be unassailable: Political speech is the primary object of First Amendment protection. * * * The Founders sought to protect the rights of individuals to engage in political speech because a self-governing people depends upon the free exchange of political information. And that free exchange should receive the most protection when it matters the most — during campaigns for elective office.* * *

I do not start with these foundational principles because the Court openly disagrees with them — it could not, for they are solidly embedded in our precedents. * * * Instead, I start with them because the Court today abandons them. For nearly half a century, this Court has extended First Amendment protection to a multitude of forms of "speech," such as making false defamatory statements, filing lawsuits, dancing nude, exhibiting drive-in movies with nudity, burning flags, and wearing military uniforms. Not surprisingly, the Courts of Appeals have followed our lead and concluded that the First Amendment protects, for example, begging, shouting obscenities, erecting tables on a sidewalk, and refusing to wear a necktie. In light of the many cases of this sort, today's decision is a most curious anomaly. Whatever the proper status of such activities under the First Amendment, I am confident that they are less integral to the functioning of our Republic than campaign contributions. Yet the majority today, rather than going out of its way to *protect* political speech, goes out of its way to *avoid* protecting it. [C]ontributions to political campaigns generate essential political speech. And contribution caps, which place a direct and substantial limit on core speech, should be met with the utmost skepticism and should receive the strictest scrutiny.

To justify its decision upholding contribution limitations while striking down expenditure limitations, the Court in *Buckley* explained that expenditure limits "represent substantial rather than merely theoretical restraints on the quantity and diversity of political speech," while contribution limits "entai[l] only a marginal restriction upon the contributor's ability to engage in free communication." In drawing this distinction, the Court in *Buckley* relied on the premise that contributing to a candidate differs qualitatively from directly spending money. It noted that "[w]hile contributions may result in political expression if spent by a candidate or an association to present views to the voters, the transformation of contributions into political debate involves speech by someone other than the contributor." * * *

But this was a faulty distinction *ab initio* because it ignored the reality of how speech of all kinds is disseminated:

> "Even in the case of a direct expenditure, there is usually some go-between that facilitates the dissemination of the spender's message — for instance, an advertising agency or a television station. To call a contribution 'speech by proxy' thus does little to differentiate it from an expenditure. The only possible difference is that contributions involve an extra step in the proxy chain. But again, that is a difference in form, not substance."

And, inasmuch as the speech-by-proxy argument was disconnected from the realities of political speech to begin with, it is not surprising that we have firmly rejected it since *Buckley*. In *Federal Election Comm'n* v. *National Conservative Political Action Comm.*, 470 U.S. 480 (1985), we cast aside the argument that a contribution does not represent the constitutionally protected speech of a contributor, recognizing "that the contributors obviously like the message they are hearing from these organizations and want to add their voices to that message; otherwise they would not part with their money." Though in that case we considered limitations on expenditures made by associations, our holding that the speech-by-proxy argument fails to diminish contributors' First Amendment rights is directly applicable to this case. In both cases, donors seek to disseminate information by giving to an organization controlled by others. Through contributing, citizens see to it that their views on policy and politics are articulated. In short, "they are aware that however great the confidence they may justly feel in their own good sense, their interests can be more effectually promoted by [another] than by themselves." The Federalist No. 35, p. 214 (C. Rossiter ed. 1961) (A. Hamilton).

Without the assistance of the speech-by-proxy argument, the remainder of *Buckley*'s rationales founder. Those rationales — that the "quantity of communication by the contributor does not increase perceptibly with the size of his contribution," that "the size of the contribution provides a very rough index of the intensity of the contributor's support for the candidate," and that "[a] contribution serves as a general expression of support for the candidate and his views, but does not communicate the underlying basis for the support" — still rest on the proposition that speech by proxy is not fully protected. These contentions simply ignore that a contribution, by amplifying the voice of the candidate, helps to ensure the dissemination of the messages that the contributor wishes to convey. Absent the ability to rest on the denigration of contributions as mere "proxy speech," the arguments fall apart.[3]

The decision of individuals to speak through contributions rather than through independent expenditures is entirely reasonable.[4] Political campaigns are largely candidate focused and candidate driven. Citizens recognize that the best advocate for a candidate (and the policy positions he supports) tends to be the candidate himself. And candidate organizations also offer other advantages to citizens wishing to partake in political expression. Campaign organizations offer a ready-built, convenient means of communicating for donors wishing to support and amplify political messages. Furthermore, the leader of the organization — the candidate — has a strong self-interest in efficiently expending funds in a manner that maximizes the power of the messages the contributor seeks to disseminate. Individual citizens understandably realize that they "may add more to political discourse by giving rather than spending, if the donee is able to put the funds to more productive use than can the individual." *Colorado Republican*, 518 U.S., at 636 (THOMAS, J., concurring in judgment and dissenting in part). * * *[5]

In the end, *Buckley*'s claim that contribution limits "d[o] not in any way infringe the contributor's freedom to discuss candidates and issues," ignores the distinct role

---

[3] If one were to accept the speech-by-proxy point and consider a contribution a mere symbolic gesture, *Buckley*'s auxiliary arguments still falter. The claim that a large contribution receives less protection because it only expresses the "intensity of the contributor's support for the candidate," fails under our jurisprudence because we have accorded full First Amendment protection to expressions of intensity. See *Cohen* v. *California*, 403 U.S. 15, 25–26 (1971) (protecting the use of an obscenity to stress a point). Equally unavailing is the claim that a contribution warrants less protection because it "does not communicate the underlying basis for the support." We regularly hold that speech is protected when the underlying basis for a position is not given. See, *e.g., City of Ladue* v. *Gilleo*, 512 U.S. 43, 46 (1994) (sign reading "For Peace in the Gulf"); *Tinker* v. *Des Moines Independent Community School Dist.*, 393 U.S. 503 (1969) (black armband signifying opposition to Vietnam war). * * *

[4] JUSTICE STEVENS asserts that "[m]oney is property; it is not speech," and contends that there is no First Amendment right "to hire mercenaries" and "to hire gladiators." These propositions are directly contradicted by many of our precedents. For example, in *Meyer* v. *Grant*, 486 U.S. 414 (1988) [p. 678] (opinion of the Court by STEVENS, J.), * * * [we] held that "[a state ban on payments to] petition circulators restricts political expression" by "limit[ing] the number of voices who will convey appellees' message and the hours they can speak and, therefore, limits the size of the audience they can reach." In short, the Court held that the First Amendment protects the right to pay others to help get a message out. In other cases, this Court extended such protection, holding that the First Amendment prohibits laws that do not ban, but instead only regulate, the terms upon which so-called mercenaries and gladiators are retained. See *Riley* v. *National Federation of Blind of N.C., Inc.*, 487 U.S. 781 (1988) (holding that the First Amendment prohibits state restriction on the amount a charity may pay a professional fundraiser). * * *

[5] Even if contributions to a candidate were not the most effective means of speaking — and contribution caps left political speech "significantly unimpaired" — an individual's choice of that mode of expression would still be protected. "The First Amendment protects [individuals'] right not only to advocate their cause but also to select what they believe to be the most effective means for so doing." *Meyer, supra,* at 424, (opinion of the Court by STEVENS, J.). See also *Glickman* v. *Wileman Brothers & Elliott, Inc.*, 521 U.S. 457, 488 (1997) (SOUTER, J., dissenting) (noting a "First Amendment interest in touting [one's] wares as he sees fit").

of candidate organizations as a means of individual participation in the Nation's civic dialogue.[6] The result is simply the suppression of political speech. By depriving donors of their right to speak through the candidate, contribution limits relegate donors' points of view to less effective modes of communication. Additionally, limiting contributions curtails individual participation. "Even for the affluent, the added costs in money or time of taking out a newspaper advertisement, handing out leaflets on the street, or standing in front of one's house with a hand-held sign may make the difference between participating and not participating in some public debate." *Buckley* completely failed in its attempt to provide a basis for permitting government to second-guess the individual choices of citizens partaking in quint-essentially democratic activities. "The First Amendment mandates that we presume that speakers, not the government, know best both what they want to say and how to say it."

The Court in *Buckley* denigrated the speech interests not only of contributors, but also of candidates * * * [by] focus[ing] exclusively on aggregate campaign funding. * * *

The Court's flawed and unsupported aggregate approach ignores both the rights and value of individual candidates. * * * [T]he right to free speech is a right held by each American, not by Americans en masse. The Court in *Buckley* provided no basis for suppressing the speech of an individual candidate simply because other candidates (or candidates in the aggregate) may succeed in reaching the voting public. And any such reasoning would fly in the face of the premise of our political system — liberty vested in individual hands safeguards the functioning of our democracy. In the case at hand, the Missouri scheme has a clear and detrimental effect on a candidate such as respondent Fredman, who lacks the advantages of incumbency, name recognition, or substantial personal wealth, but who has managed to attract the support of a relatively small number of dedicated supporters: It forbids his message from reaching the voters. * * *

In my view, the Constitution leaves it entirely up to citizens and candidates to determine who shall speak, the means they will use, and the amount of speech sufficient to inform and persuade. *Buckley*'s ratification of the government's attempt to wrest this fundamental right from citizens was error.

Today, the majority blindly adopts *Buckley*'s flawed reasoning without so much as pausing to consider the collapse of the speech-by-proxy argument or the reality that *Buckley*'s remaining premises fall when deprived of that support.

After ignoring these shortcomings, the Court proceeds to apply something less — much less — than strict scrutiny. Just how much less the majority never says.

---

[6] *Buckley*'s approach to associational freedom is also unsound. In defense of its decision, the Court in *Buckley* explained that contribution limits "leave the contributor free to become a member of any political association and to assist personally in the association's efforts on behalf of candidates." In essence, the Court accepted contribution limits because alternative channels of association remained open. This justification, however, is peculiar because we have rejected the notion that a law will pass First Amendment muster simply because it leaves open other opportunities. *Spence* v. *Washington*, 418 U.S. 405, 411, n.4 (1974) (Although a prohibition's effect may be "minuscule and trifling," a person "is not to have the exercise of his liberty of expression in appropriate places abridged on the plea that it may be exercised in some other place." * * *

The Court in *Buckley* at least purported to employ a test of "closest scrutiny." The Court's words were belied by its actions, however, and it never deployed the test in the fashion that the superlative instructs. * * * The Court today abandons even that pretense and reviews contributions under the *sui generis* "*Buckley's* standard of scrutiny," which fails to obscure the Court's ad hoc balancing away of First Amendment rights. Apart from its endorsement of *Buckley's* rejection of the intermediate standards of review used to evaluate expressive conduct and time, place, and manner restrictions, the Court makes no effort to justify its deviation from the tests we traditionally employ in free speech cases. * * *

* * * After hiding behind *Buckley's* discredited reasoning and invoking "*Buckley's* standard of scrutiny," the Court proceeds to significantly extend the holding in that case. The Court's substantive departure from *Buckley* begins with a revision of our compelling-interest jurisprudence. In *Buckley*, the Court indicated that the only interest that could qualify as "compelling" in this area was the government's interest in reducing actual and apparent corruption. And the Court repeatedly used the word "corruption" in the narrow *quid pro quo* sense, meaning "[p]erversion or destruction of integrity in the discharge of public duties by bribery or favour." 3 Oxford English Dictionary 974 (2d ed. 1989). See also Webster's Third New International Dictionary 512 (1976) ("inducement (as of a political official) by means of improper considerations (as bribery) to commit a violation of duty"). When the Court set forth the interest in preventing actual corruption, it spoke about "large contributions . . . given to secure a political *quid pro quo* from current and potential office holders." The Court used similar language when it set forth the interest in protecting against the appearance of corruption: "Of almost equal concern as the danger of actual *quid pro quo* arrangements is the impact of the appearance of corruption stemming from public awareness of the opportunities for abuse inherent in a regime of large individual financial contributions." Later, in discussing limits on independent expenditures, the Court yet again referred to the interest in protecting against the "dangers of actual or apparent *quid pro quo* arrangements." *See Buckley* at 47 (referring to "the danger that expenditures will be given as a *quid pro quo* for improper commitments"); *id.*, at 67 (corruption relates to "post-election special favors that may be given in return" for contributions). To be sure, after mentioning *quid pro quo* transactions, the Court went on to use more general terms such as "opportunities for abuse," "potential for abuse," "improper influence," "attempts . . . to influence," and "buy[ing] influence." But this general language acquires concrete meaning only in light of the preceding specific references to *quid pro quo* arrangements.

Almost a decade after *Buckley*, we reiterated that "corruption" has a narrow meaning with respect to contribution limitations on individuals:

> "Corruption is a subversion of the political process. Elected officials are influenced to act contrary to their obligations of office by the prospect of financial gain to themselves or infusions of money into their campaigns. The hallmark of corruption is the financial *quid pro quo*: dollars for political favors." [*National Conservative Political Action Committee*], 470 U.S. [480], 497 [(1985)]. * * *

The majority today, by contrast, separates "corruption" from its *quid pro quo* roots and gives it a new, far-reaching (and speech-suppressing) definition, something like "[t]he perversion of anything from an original state of purity." 3 Oxford English Dictionary, *supra*, at 974. * * * And the Court proceeds to define that state of purity, casting aspersions on "politicians too compliant with the wishes of large contributors." "But precisely what the 'corruption' may consist of we are never told with assurance." Presumably, the majority does not mean that politicians should be free of attachments to constituent groups.[9] * * * [W]ithout bothering to offer any elaboration, much less justification, the majority permits vague and unenumerated harms to suffice as a compelling reason for the government to smother political speech.

* * * The fact is that the majority ratifies a law with a much broader sweep than that approved in *Buckley*. In *Buckley*, the Court upheld contribution limits of $1,000 on individuals and $5,000 on political committees (in 1976 dollars). Here, by contrast, the Court approves much more restrictive contribution limitations, ranging from $250 to $1,000 (in 1995 dollars) for both individuals and political committees. Mo. Rev. Stat. § 130.032.1 (Supp.1999). The disparity between Missouri's caps and those upheld in *Buckley* is more pronounced when one takes into account some measure of inflation ([which has reduced the purchasing power of a dollar by two-thirds since 1976] when *Buckley* was decided). Yet the Court's opinion gives not a single indication that the two laws may differ in their tailoring. The Court fails to pay any regard to the drastically lower level of the limits here, fails to explain why political committees should be subjected to the same limits as individuals, and fails to explain why caps that vary with the size of political districts are tailored to corruption. I cannot fathom how a $251 contribution could pose a substantial risk of "secur[ing] a political *quid pro quo*." Thus, contribution caps set at such levels could never be "closely drawn," to preventing *quid pro quo* corruption. The majority itself undertakes no such defense.

The Court * * * persuad[es] itself that Missouri's limits do not suppress political speech because, prior to the enactment of contribution limits, "97.62 percent of all contributors to candidates for state auditor made contributions of $2,000 or less." But this statistical anecdote offers the Court no refuge and the citizenry no comfort. As an initial matter, the statistic provides no assurance that Missouri's law has not

---

[9] The Framers, of course, thought such attachments inevitable in a free society and that faction would infest the political process. As to controlling faction, James Madison explained, "There are again two methods of removing the causes of faction: the one, by destroying the liberty which is essential to its existence; the other, by giving to every citizen the same opinions, the same passions, and the same interests." The Federalist No. 10, p.78 (C. Rossiter ed. 1961). Contribution caps are an example of the first method, which Madison contemptuously dismissed:

"It could never be more truly said than of the first remedy that it was worse than the disease. Liberty is to faction what air is to fire, an aliment without which it instantly expires. But it could not be a less folly to abolish liberty, which is essential to political life, because it nourishes faction than it would be to wish the annihilation of air, which is essential to animal life, because it imparts to fire its destructive agency." *Ibid.*

The Framers preferred a political system that harnessed such faction for good, preserving liberty while also ensuring good government. Rather than adopting the repressive "cure" for faction that the majority today endorses, the Framers armed individual citizens with a remedy. "If a faction consists of less than a majority, relief is supplied by the republican principle, which enables the majority to defeat its sinister views by regular vote." *Id.*, at 80.

reduced the resources supporting political speech, since the largest contributors provide a disproportionate amount of funds. The majority conspicuously offers no data revealing the percentage of funds provided by large contributors. * * * If the majority's assumption is incorrect — *i.e.*, if Missouri's contribution limits actually do significantly reduce campaign speech — then the majority's calm assurance that political speech remains unaffected collapses. If the majority's assumption is correct — *i.e.*, if large contributions provide very little assistance to a candidate seeking to get out his message (and thus will not be missed when capped) — then the majority's reasoning still falters. For if large contributions offer as little help to a candidate as the Court maintains, then the Court fails to explain why a candidate would engage in "corruption" for such a meager benefit. The majority's statistical claim directly undercuts its constitutional defense that large contributions pose a substantial risk of corruption.

Given the majority's ill-advised and illiberal aggregate rights approach, it is unsurprising that the Court's *pro forma* hunt for suppressed speech proves futile. Such will always be the case, for courts have no yardstick by which to judge the proper amount and effectiveness of campaign speech. See, *e.g.*, Smith, *Faulty Assumptions and Undemocratic Consequences of Campaign Finance Reform*, 105 Yale L.J. 1049, 1061 (1996). I, however, would not fret about such matters. The First Amendment vests choices about the proper amount and effectiveness of political advocacy not in the government — whether in the legislatures or the courts — but in the people. * * *

Missouri does assert that its contribution caps are aimed at preventing actual and apparent corruption. * * * But the State's contribution limits are not narrowly tailored to that harm. The limits directly suppress the political speech of both contributors and candidates, and only clumsily further the governmental interests that they allegedly serve. They are crudely tailored because they are massively overinclusive, prohibiting all donors who wish to contribute in excess of the cap from doing so and restricting donations without regard to whether the donors pose any real corruption risk. * * * Moreover, the government has less restrictive means of addressing its interest in curtailing corruption. Bribery laws bar precisely the *quid pro quo* arrangements that are targeted here. And disclosure laws "deter actual corruption and avoid the appearance of corruption by exposing large contributions and expenditures to the light of publicity." * * *

In the end, contribution limitations find support only in the proposition that other means will not be as effective at rooting out corruption. But when it comes to a significant infringement on our fundamental liberties, that some undesirable conduct may not be deterred is an insufficient justification to sweep in vast amounts of protected political speech. * * *

* * * States are free to enact laws that directly punish those engaged in corruption and require the disclosure of large contributions, but they are not free to enact generalized laws that suppress a tremendous amount of protected speech along with the targeted corruption. * * *

I respectfully dissent.

Notes and Questions

1. *Shrink PAC*, as this decision is often called, is the first in a series of cases from the early 2000s reflecting an approach that Professor Hasen dubbed "the new deference." Richard L. Hasen, *Rethinking the Unconstitutionality of Contribution and Expenditure Limits in Ballot Measure Campaigns*, 78 S. CAL. L. REV. 885, 886 (2005). These cases — *Shrink PAC*; *Federal Election Commission v. Colorado Republican Federal Campaign Committee (Colorado II)*, 533 U.S. 431 (2001); *Federal Election Commission v. Beaumont*, 539 U.S. 146 (2003); and *McConnell v. Federal Election Commission*, 540 U.S. 93 (2003) [p. 923] — are marked by a high degree of deference to legislative judgment and expertise atypical of the Court's earlier campaign-finance decisions.

Consider the level of evidence that the Court found acceptable to justify Missouri's regulation in *Shrink PAC*: a handful of newspaper editorials, and affidavits submitted by supporters of the legislation. The Court held that the quantity of "empirical evidence needed to satisfy heightened judicial scrutiny of legislative judgments will vary up or down with the novelty and plausibility of the justification raised." One scholar has argued that in *Shrink PAC*, "since contribution limits do not seem to be narrowly tailored to the problem of eliminating corruption, the Court simply lowered the bar." J. Clark Kelso, Book Review, *Mr. Smith Goes to Washington*, 1 ELEC. L.J. 75, 78 (2002). Do you think that the evidence described in the Court's opinion would have been sufficient to carry the government's burden in *Buckley*, *CARC*, or *NCPAC*? Should it be? Compare the Court's approach here to its approach in non-political-speech cases, *e.g.*, *Greater New Orleans Broadcasting Ass'n v. United States*, 527 U.S. 173, 188 (1999) ("a governmental body seeking to sustain a restriction on commercial speech must demonstrate that the harms it recites are real and that its restriction will in fact alleviate them to a material degree") (quoting *Edenfield v. Fane*, 507 U.S. 761, 768 (1993)); *Rubin v. Coors Brewing Co.*, 514 U.S. 476, 487 (1995) ("this requirement [is] critical").

2. *Shrink PAC* was the first challenge to the size of a contribution limit to reach the Supreme Court since *Buckley*. Missouri's 1998 limit of $1075 was the equivalent of approximately $355 in 1976, when *Buckley* was decided. Upholding contribution limits generally, the *Buckley* court suggested that limits could nevertheless be unconstitutional if they "prevented candidates and political committees from amassing the resources necessary for effective advocacy." How would a court decide when or if this point were reached? Is there a realistic alternative to the posture of deference taken by the majority in *Shrink PAC*?

The majority relied on the District Court finding that "candidates for political office in the state are still able to amass impressive campaign war chests." The dissent focused specifically on the plaintiff, Zev Fredman, and his inability to compete under the Missouri limits. Which is more important to the First Amendment analysis — that most candidates can raise the funds needed to compete, or that some candidates cannot?

3. Justice Breyer suggested that the Court "in practice" defers to the legislature where it has "significantly greater institutional expertise, as, for example, in the field of election regulation." Is this true? Compare this to many of the cases that appear elsewhere in this book, *cf., e.g., Reynolds v. Sims*, 377 U.S. 533 (1964) [p. 173]

(population criteria for redistricting); *Shaw v. Reno*, 509 U.S. 630 (1993) [p. 354] (consideration of race in redistricting); *Tashjian v. Republican Party of Connecticut*, 479 U.S. 208 (1986) [p. 448] (closed primaries); *California Democratic Party v. Jones*, 530 U.S. 567 (2000) [p. 460] (blanket primaries); *Timmons v. Twin Cities Area New Party*, 520 U.S. 351 (1997) [p. 533] (party cross-endorsements); *Meyer v. Grant*, 486 U.S. 414 (1988) [p. 678] (gathering petition signatures); *Williams v. Rhodes*, 393 U.S. 23 (1968) [p. 497] (independent ballot access); *Republican Party of Minnesota v. White*, 536 U.S. 765 (2002) [p. 756] (speech in judicial elections), or *Buckley v. Valeo*, 424 U.S. 1 (1976) [p. 799] (independent expenditures in campaigns).

Justice Breyer did qualify his position by adding that deference has been accorded "at least where that deference does not risk such constitutional evils as, say, permitting incumbents to insulate themselves from effective electoral challenge." Do the cases listed above, and others in this book where the Court has not deferred to the legislature, hinge on incumbents insulating themselves from effective challenge? Or are there other evils, and if so, which evils should qualify as triggering a higher level of scrutiny, *i.e.*, less deference? In their separate *Shrink PAC* dissents, Justices Thomas and Kennedy both noted that Zev Fredman needed to accept larger contributions because he lacked the advantages of some other candidates, mainly incumbents. How is a Justice to tell, then, if a law allows incumbents to insulate themselves from challenge? One way might be through increased reliance on social-science research. *See* Richard L. Hasen, *The Newer Incoherence: Competition, Social Science, and Balancing in Campaign Finance Law after* Randall v. Sorrell, 68 Ohio St. L.J. 849 (2007). But does relying on social-science research merely put the judge exactly in the position of second-guessing legislative judgments? For a response to Professor Hasen, see Bradley A. Smith, *The John Roberts Salvage Company: After* McConnell, *a New Court Looks to Repair the Constitution*, 68 Ohio St. L.J. 891, 907–909 (2007).

4. *Shrink PAC* reveals deep divisions among the justices in their approach to campaign finance restrictions. Beginning with *Buckley*, every justice to serve on the Court had agreed that these were properly considered First Amendment cases. In *Shrink PAC*, Justice Stevens becomes the first justice to disavow that paradigm. *See* Bradley A. Smith, *McCutcheon v. Federal Election Commission: An Unlikely Blockbuster*, 9 NYU J.L. & Liberty 48, 50 (2015). Justices Thomas and Scalia, meanwhile, break in the other direction. They renounce *Buckley's* expenditure/contribution distinction and would hold limits on both unconstitutional, while Justice Kennedy stops just short of joining them. Meanwhile, Justice Breyer stakes out his claim that there "is no place for a strong presumption of unconstitutionality, of the sort often thought to accompany the words 'strict scrutiny' ", thus rejecting the *Buckley* test in his own way. Since *Shrink PAC*, 5-4 decisions became increasingly common in campaign finance cases heard by the Court. Smith, *supra* at 53, n.10.

In the next case, with Chief Justice Roberts and Justice Alito having replaced Chief Justice Rehnquist and Justice O'Connor from the *Shrink PAC* majority, the Court again faced the challenge of determining when, if ever, a contribution limit can be too low to withstand constitutional scrutiny. The Court was also asked to consider if spending limitations could be constitutional.

RANDALL v. SORRELL

Supreme Court of the United States

548 U.S. 230, 126 S. Ct. 2479, 165 L. Ed. 2d 482 (2006)

JUSTICE BREYER announced the judgment of the Court and delivered an opinion, in which THE CHIEF JUSTICE [ROBERTS] joins, and in which JUSTICE ALITO joins except as to Parts II-B-1 and II-B-2.

We here consider the constitutionality of a Vermont campaign finance statute that limits both (1) the amounts that candidates for state office may spend on their campaigns (expenditure limitations) and (2) the amounts that individuals, organizations, and political parties may contribute to those campaigns (contribution limitations). Vt. Stat. Ann., Tit. 17, § 2801 et seq. (2002). We hold that both sets of limitations are inconsistent with the First Amendment. Well-established precedent makes clear that the expenditure limits violate the First Amendment. *Buckley* v. *Buckley v. Valeo*. The contribution limits are unconstitutional because in their specific details (involving low maximum levels and other restrictions) they fail to satisfy the First Amendment's requirement of careful tailoring. *Id*. at 25–30. That is to say, they impose burdens upon First Amendment interests that (when viewed in light of the statute's legitimate objectives) are disproportionately severe.

I * * *

In 1997, Vermont enacted * * * Pub. Act No. 64 (hereinafter Act or Act 64), the statute at issue here. Act 64, which took effect immediately after the 1998 elections, imposes mandatory expenditure limits on the total amount a candidate for state office can spend during a "two-year general election cycle," *i.e.*, the primary plus the general election, in approximately the following amounts: governor, $300,000; lieutenant governor, $100,000; other statewide offices, $45,000; state senator, $4,000 (plus an additional $2,500 for each additional seat in the district); state representative (two-member district), $3,000; and state representative (single member district), $2,000. These limits are adjusted for inflation in odd-numbered years * * *. Incumbents seeking reelection * * * may spend no more than 90% of the above amounts. * * *

With certain minor exceptions, expenditures over $50 made on a candidate's behalf by others count against the candidate's expenditure limit if those expenditures are "intentionally facilitated by, solicited by or approved by" the candidate's campaign. These provisions apply so as to count against a campaign's expenditure limit any spending by political parties or committees that is coordinated with the campaign and benefits the candidate. And any party expenditure that "primarily benefits six or fewer candidates who are associated with the political party" is "presumed" to be coordinated with the campaign and therefore to count against the campaign's expenditure limit.

Act 64 also imposes strict contribution limits. The amount any single individual can contribute to the campaign of a candidate for state office during a "two-year general election cycle" is limited as follows: governor, lieutenant governor, and other statewide offices, $400; state senator, $300; and state representative, $200.

Unlike its expenditure limits, Act 64's contribution limits are not indexed for inflation.

A political committee is subject to these same limits. So is a political party, defined broadly to include "any subsidiary, branch or local unit" of a party, as well as any "national or regional affiliates" of a party (taken separately or together). Thus, for example, the statute treats the local, state, and national affiliates of the Democratic Party as if they were a single entity and limits their total contribution to a single candidate's campaign for governor (during the primary and the general election together) to $400.

The Act also imposes a limit of $2,000 upon the amount any individual can give to a political party during a 2-year general election cycle.

The Act defines "contribution" broadly in approximately the same way it defines "expenditure." Any expenditure made on a candidate's behalf counts as a contribution to the candidate if it is "intentionally facilitated by, solicited by or approved by" the candidate. And a party expenditure that "primarily benefits six or fewer candidates who are associated with the" party is "presumed" to count against the party's contribution limits.

There are a few exceptions. A candidate's own contributions to the campaign and those of the candidate's family fall outside the contribution limits. Volunteer services do not count as contributions. Nor does the cost of a meet-the-candidate function, provided that the total cost for the function amounts to $100 or less. * * *

[The Court determined that Vermont's limitations on expenditures were unconstitutional, and that it was not appropriate in this case to reconsider "so well established a precedent" as *Buckley v. Valeo*, 424 U.S. 1.] [*See* p. 888].

III

We turn now to a more complex question, namely, the constitutionality of Act 64's contribution limits. The parties, while accepting *Buckley*'s approach, dispute whether, despite *Buckley*'s general approval of statutes that limit campaign contributions, Act 64's contribution limits are so severe that in the circumstances its particular limits violate the First Amendment. * * *

[The *Buckley* Court held that] contribution limitations are permissible as long as the Government demonstrates that the limits are "closely drawn" to match a "sufficiently important interest." It found that the interest advanced in the case, "prevent[ing] corruption" and its "appearance," was "sufficiently important" to justify the statute's contribution limits.

The Court also found that the contribution limits before it were "closely drawn." It recognized that, in determining whether a particular contribution limit was "closely drawn," the amount, or level, of that limit could make a difference. Indeed, it wrote that "contribution restrictions could have a severe impact on political dialogue if the limitations prevented candidates and political committees from amassing the resources necessary for effective advocacy." But the Court added that such "distinctions in degree become significant only when they can be said to amount to differences in kind." Pointing out that it had "no scalpel to probe, whether, say, a $2,000 ceiling might not serve as well as $1,000," the Court found "no indication" that the $1,000 contribution limitations imposed by the Act would have "any dramatic adverse effect on the funding of campaigns." It therefore found the limitations constitutional.

Since *Buckley*, the Court has consistently upheld contribution limits in other statutes. * * * The Court has recognized, however, that contribution limits might *sometimes* work more harm to protected First Amendment interests than their anti-corruption objectives could justify. And individual Members of the Court have expressed concern lest too low a limit magnify the "reputation-related or media-related advantages of incumbency and thereby insulat[e] legislators from effective electoral challenge." [*Nixon v. Shrink Missouri Government PAC*, 528 U.S. 377, 395–397 (2000)] [p. 834]. In the cases before us, the petitioners challenge Act 64's contribution limits on that basis.

B

Following *Buckley*, we must determine whether Act 64's contribution limits prevent candidates from "amassing the resources necessary for effective [campaign] advocacy"; whether they magnify the advantages of incumbency to the point where they put challengers to a significant disadvantage; in a word, whether they are too low and too strict to survive First Amendment scrutiny. In answering these questions, we recognize, as *Buckley* stated, that we have "no scalpel to probe" each possible contribution level. We cannot determine with any degree of exactitude the precise restriction necessary to carry out the statute's legitimate objectives. In practice, the legislature is better equipped to make such empirical judgments, as legislators have "particular expertise" in matters related to the costs and nature of running for office. Thus ordinarily we have deferred to the legislature's determination of such matters.

Nonetheless, as *Buckley* acknowledged, we must recognize the existence of some lower bound. At some point the constitutional risks to the democratic electoral process become too great. After all, the interests underlying contribution limits, preventing corruption and the appearance of corruption, "directly implicate the integrity of our electoral process." Yet that rationale does not simply mean "the lower the limit, the better." That is because contribution limits that are too low can also harm the electoral process by preventing challengers from mounting effective campaigns against incumbent officeholders, thereby reducing democratic accountability. Were we to ignore that fact, a statute that seeks to regulate campaign contributions could itself prove an obstacle to the very electoral fairness it seeks to promote. Thus, we see no alternative to the exercise of independent judicial judgment as a statute reaches those outer limits. And, where there is strong indication in a particular case, *i.e.*, danger signs, that such risks exist (both present in kind and likely serious in degree), courts, including appellate courts, must review the record independently and carefully with an eye toward assessing the statute's "tailoring," that is, toward assessing the proportionality of the restrictions. * * *

We find those danger signs present here. As compared with the contribution limits upheld by the Court in the past, and with those in force in other States, Act 64's limits are sufficiently low as to generate suspicion that they are not closely drawn. The Act sets its limits per election cycle, which includes both a primary and a general election. Thus, in a gubernatorial race with both primary and final election contests, the Act's contribution limit amounts to $200 per election per candidate (with significantly lower limits for contributions to candidates for State Senate and House of Representatives). These limits apply both to contributions from individuals and to contributions from political parties, whether made in cash or in expenditures coordinated (or presumed to be coordinated) with the candidate.

These limits are well below the limits this Court upheld in *Buckley*. Indeed, in terms of real dollars (*i.e.*, adjusting for inflation), the Act's $200 per election limit on individual contributions to a campaign for governor is slightly more than one-twentieth of the limit on contributions to campaigns for federal office before the Court in *Buckley*. Adjusted to reflect its value in 1976 (the year *Buckley* was decided), Vermont's contribution limit on campaigns for statewide office (including governor) amounts to $113.91 per 2-year election cycle, or roughly $57 per election, as compared to the $1,000 per election limit on individual contributions at issue in *Buckley*. (The adjusted value of Act 64's limit on contributions from political parties to candidates for statewide office, again $200 per candidate per election, is just over one one-hundredth of the comparable limit before the Court in *Buckley*, $5,000 per election.) Yet Vermont's gubernatorial district — the entire State — is no smaller than the House districts to which *Buckley*'s limits applied. In 1976, the average congressional district contained a population of about 465,000. * * * Indeed, Vermont's population is 621,000 — about one-third *larger*. * * *

Moreover, considered as a whole, Vermont's contribution limits are the lowest in the Nation. Act 64 limits contributions to candidates for statewide office (including governor) to $200 per candidate per election. We have found no State that imposes a lower per election limit. Indeed, we have found only seven States that impose limits on contributions to candidates for statewide office at or below $500 per election, more than twice Act 64's limit. * * * We are aware of no State that imposes a limit on contributions from political parties to candidates for statewide office lower than Act 64's $200 per candidate per election limit. Similarly, we have found only three States that have limits on contributions to candidates for state legislature below Act 64's $150 and $100 per election limits. And we are aware of no State that has a lower limit on contributions from political parties to state legislative candidates.

Finally, Vermont's limit is well below the lowest limit this Court has previously upheld, the limit of $1,075 per election (adjusted for inflation every two years) for candidates for Missouri state auditor. *Shrink*. The comparable Vermont limit of roughly $200 per election, not adjusted for inflation, is less than one-sixth of Missouri's current inflation-adjusted limit ($1,275).

We recognize that Vermont's population is much smaller than Missouri's. Indeed, Vermont is about one-ninth of the size of Missouri. Statistical Abstract 21 (2006). Thus, *per citizen*, Vermont's limit is slightly more generous. As of 2006, the ratio of the contribution limit to the size of the constituency in Vermont is .00064, while Missouri's ratio is .00044, 31% lower.

But this does not necessarily mean that Vermont's limits are less objectionable than the limit upheld in *Shrink*. A campaign for state auditor is likely to be less costly than a campaign for governor; campaign costs do not automatically increase or decrease in precise proportion to the size of an electoral district. Moreover, Vermont's limits, unlike Missouri's limits, apply in the same amounts to contributions made by political parties. And, as we have said, Missouri's (current) $1,275 per election limit, unlike Vermont's $200 per election limit, is indexed for inflation.

The factors we have mentioned offset any neutralizing force of population differences. At the very least, they make it difficult to treat *Shrink*'s (then) $1,075 limit as providing affirmative support for the lawfulness of Vermont's far lower levels. *Cf.* 528 U.S., at 404 (BREYER, J., concurring) (The *Shrink* "limit . . . is low enough to raise . . . a [significant constitutional] question"). And even were that not so, Vermont's failure to index for inflation means that Vermont's levels would soon be far lower than Missouri's regardless of the method of comparison.

In sum, Act 64's contribution limits are substantially lower than both the limits we have previously upheld and comparable limits in other States. These are danger signs that Act 64's contribution limits may fall outside tolerable First Amendment limits. We consequently must examine the record independently and carefully to determine whether Act 64's contribution limits are "closely drawn" to match the State's interests.

Our examination of the record convinces us that, from a constitutional perspective, Act 64's contribution limits are too restrictive. We reach this conclusion based not merely on the low dollar amounts of the limits themselves, but also on the statute's effect on political parties and on volunteer activity in Vermont elections. *Taken together*, Act 64's substantial restrictions on the ability of candidates to raise the funds necessary to run a competitive election, on the ability of political parties to help their candidates get elected, and on the ability of individual citizens to volunteer their time to campaigns show that the Act is not closely drawn to meet its objectives. In particular, five factors together lead us to this decision.

First, the record suggests, though it does not conclusively prove, that Act 64's contribution limits will significantly restrict the amount of funding available for challengers to run competitive campaigns. For one thing, the petitioners' expert, Clark Bensen, conducted a race-by-race analysis of the 1998 legislative elections (the last to take place before Act 64 took effect) and concluded that Act 64's contribution limits would have reduced the funds available in 1998 to Republican challengers in competitive races in amounts ranging from 18% to 53% of their total campaign income. * * *

For another thing, the petitioners' expert witnesses produced evidence and analysis showing that Vermont political parties (particularly the Republican Party) "target" their contributions to candidates in competitive races, that those contributions represent a significant amount of total candidate funding in such races, and that the contribution limits will cut the parties' contributions to competitive races dramatically. Their statistics showed that the party contributions accounted for a significant percentage of the total campaign income in those races. And their studies showed that Act 64's contribution limits would cut the party contributions by between 85% (for the legislature on average) and 99% (for governor).

More specifically, Bensen pointed out that in 1998, the Republican Party made contributions to 19 Senate campaigns in amounts that averaged $2,001, which on average represented 16% of the recipient campaign's total income. Act 64 would reduce these contributions to $300 per campaign, an average reduction of about 85%. The party contributed to 50 House campaigns in amounts averaging $787, which on average represented 28% of the recipient campaign's total income. Act 64 would reduce these contributions to $200 per campaign, an average reduction of 74.5%. And the party contributed $40,600 to its gubernatorial candidate, an amount that accounted for about 16% of the candidate's funding. The Act would have reduced that contribution by 99%, to $400.

Bensen added that 57% of all 1998 Senate campaigns and 30% of all House campaigns exceeded Act 64's expenditure limits, which were enacted along with the statute's contribution limits. Moreover, 27% of all Senate campaigns and 10% of all House campaigns spent more than double those limits.

The respondents did not contest these figures. Rather, they presented evidence that focused, not upon *strongly contested* campaigns, but upon the funding amounts available for the *average* campaign. * * *

The respondents' evidence leaves the petitioners' evidence unrebutted in certain key respects. That is because the critical question concerns not simply the *average* effect of contribution limits on fundraising but, more importantly, the ability of a candidate running against an incumbent officeholder to mount an effective *challenge*. And information about *average* races, rather than *competitive* races, is only distantly related to that question, because competitive races are likely to be far more expensive than the average race. We concede that the record does contain some anecdotal evidence supporting the respondents' position, namely, testimony about a post-Act-64 competitive mayoral campaign in Burlington, which suggests that a challenger can "amas[s] the resources necessary for effective advocacy." But the facts of that particular election are not described in sufficient detail to offer a convincing refutation of the implication arising from the petitioners' experts' studies.

Rather, the petitioners' studies, taken together with low *average* Vermont campaign expenditures and the typically higher costs that a challenger must bear to overcome the name-recognition advantage enjoyed by an incumbent, raise a reasonable inference that the contribution limits are so low that they may pose a significant obstacle to candidates in competitive elections. Cf. Ornstein, *supra*, at 87–96 (In the 2000 U.S. House and Senate elections, successful challengers spent far more than the average candidate). Information about average races does not rebut that inference. Consequently, the inference amounts to one factor (among others) that here counts against the constitutional validity of the contribution limits.

Second, Act 64's insistence that political parties abide by *exactly* the same low contribution limits that apply to other contributors threatens harm to a particularly important political right, the right to associate in a political party. * * *

The Act applies its $200 to $400 limits — precisely the same limits it applies to an individual — to virtually all affiliates of a political party taken together as if they were a single contributor. That means, for example, that the Vermont Democratic Party, taken together with all its local affiliates, can make one contribution of at most $400 to the Democratic gubernatorial candidate, one contribution of at most $300 to a Democratic candidate for State Senate, and one contribution of at most $200 to a Democratic candidate for the State House of Representatives. The Act includes within these limits not only direct monetary contributions but also expenditures in kind: stamps, stationery, coffee, doughnuts, gasoline, campaign buttons, and so forth. Indeed, it includes all party expenditures "intended to promote the election of a specific candidate or group of candidates" as long as the candidate's campaign "facilitate[s]," "solicit[s]," or "approve[s]" them. And a party expenditure that "primarily benefits six or fewer candidates who are associated with the" party is "presumed" to count against the party's contribution limits.

In addition to the negative effect on "amassing funds" that we have described, the Act would severely limit the ability of a party to assist its candidates' campaigns by engaging in coordinated spending on advertising, candidate events, voter lists, mass mailings, even yard signs. And, to an unusual degree, it would discourage those who wish to contribute small amounts of money to a party, amounts that easily comply with individual contribution limits. Suppose that many individuals do not know Vermont legislative candidates personally, but wish to contribute, say, $20 or $40, to the State Republican Party, with the intent that the party use the money to help elect whichever candidates the party believes would best advance its ideals and interests — the basic object of a political party. Or, to take a more extreme example, imagine that 6,000 Vermont citizens each want to give $1 to the State Democratic Party because, though unfamiliar with the details of the individual races, they would like to make a small financial contribution to the goal of electing a Democratic state legislature. And further imagine that the party believes control of the legislature will depend on the outcome of three (and only three) House races. The Act prohibits the party from giving $2,000 (of the $6,000) to each of its candidates in those pivotal races. Indeed, it permits the party to give no more than $200 to each candidate, thereby thwarting the aims of the 6,000 donors from making a meaningful contribution to state politics by giving a small amount of money to the party they support. Thus, the Act would severely inhibit collective political activity by preventing a political party from using contributions by small donors to provide meaningful assistance to any individual candidate.

We recognize that we have previously upheld limits on contributions from political parties to candidates, in particular the federal limits on coordinated party spending. [*Federal Election Commission v. Colorado Republican Party*], 533 U.S. 431 [(2001)] (*Colorado II*). And we also recognize that any such limit will negatively affect *to some extent* the fund-allocating party function just described. But the contribution limits at issue in *Colorado II* were far less problematic, for they were significantly higher than Act 64's limits (at least $67,560 in coordinated spending and $5,000 in direct cash contributions for U.S. Senate candidates, at least $33,780 in coordinated spending and $5,000 in direct cash contributions for U.S. House candidates). And they were much higher than the federal limits on contributions from individuals to candidates, thereby reflecting an effort by Congress to balance (1) the need to allow individuals to participate in the political process by contributing to political parties that help elect candidates with (2) the need to prevent the use of political parties "to circumvent contribution limits that apply to individuals." Act 64, by placing identical limits upon contributions to candidates, whether made by an individual or by a political party, gives to the former consideration *no weight at all.* * * *

Third, the Act's treatment of volunteer services aggravates the problem. Like its federal statutory counterpart, the Act excludes from its definition of "contribution" all "services provided without compensation by individuals volunteering their time on behalf of a candidate." But the Act does not exclude the expenses those volunteers incur, such as travel expenses, in the course of campaign activities. The Act's broad definitions would seem to count those expenses against the volunteer's contribution limit, at least where the spending was facilitated or approved by campaign officials. And, unlike the Federal Government's treatment of comparable requirements, the State has not (insofar as we are aware) created an exception excluding such expenses. * * *

The absence of some such exception may matter in the present context, where contribution limits are very low. That combination, low limits and no exceptions, means that a gubernatorial campaign volunteer who makes four or five round trips driving across the State performing volunteer activities coordinated with the campaign can find that he or she is near, or has surpassed, the contribution limit. So too will a volunteer who offers a campaign the use of her house along with coffee and doughnuts for a few dozen neighbors to meet the candidate, say, two or three times during a campaign. Such supporters will have to keep careful track of all miles driven, postage supplied (500 stamps equals $200), pencils and pads used, and so forth. And any carelessness in this respect can prove costly, perhaps generating a headline, "Campaign laws violated," that works serious harm to the candidate.

These sorts of problems are unlikely to affect the constitutionality of a limit that is reasonably high. * * * But Act 64's contribution limits are so low, and its definition of "contribution" so broad, that the Act may well impede a campaign's ability effectively to use volunteers, thereby making it more difficult for individuals to associate in this way. * * * Again, the very low limits at issue help to transform differences in degree into difference in kind. And the likelihood of unjustified interference in the present context is sufficiently great that we must consider the lack of tailoring in the Act's definition of "contribution" as an added factor counting against the constitutional validity of the contribution limits before us.

Fourth, unlike the contribution limits we upheld in *Shrink,* Act 64's contribution limits are not adjusted for inflation. Its limits decline in real value each year. Indeed, in real dollars the Act's limits have already declined by about 20% ($200 in 2006 dollars has a real value of $160.66 in 1997 dollars). A failure to index limits means that limits which are already suspiciously low will almost inevitably become too low over time. It means that future legislation will be necessary to stop that almost inevitable decline, and it thereby imposes the burden of preventing the decline upon incumbent legislators who may not diligently police the need for changes in limit levels to ensure the adequate financing of electoral challenges.

Fifth, we have found nowhere in the record any special justification that might warrant a contribution limit so low or so restrictive as to bring about the serious associational and expressive problems that we have described. Rather, the basic justifications the State has advanced in support of such limits are those present in *Buckley.* The record contains no indication that, for example, corruption (or its appearance) in Vermont is significantly more serious a matter than elsewhere. Indeed, other things being equal, one might reasonably believe that a contribution of, say, $250 (or $450) to a candidate's campaign was less likely to prove a corruptive force than the far larger contributions at issue in the other campaign finance cases we have considered.

These five sets of considerations, taken together, lead us to conclude that Act 64's contribution limits are not narrowly tailored. * * *

IV

We conclude that * * * Act 64's contribution limits * * * violate the First Amendment, for they burden First Amendment interests in a manner that is disproportionate to the public purposes they were enacted to advance. * * *

[JUSTICE ALITO's opinion, concurring in part and concurring in the judgment, arguing that was not necessary to re-examine *Buckley* to decide the expenditure limits side of the case, is omitted.]

JUSTICE KENNEDY, concurring in the judgment. * * *

Viewed within the legal universe we have ratified and helped create, the result the plurality reaches is correct; given my own skepticism regarding that system and its operation, however, it seems to me appropriate to concur only in the judgment.

JUSTICE THOMAS, with whom JUSTICE SCALIA joins, concurring in the judgment. * * *

I continue to believe that *Buckley* provides insufficient protection to political speech, the core of the First Amendment. The illegitimacy of *Buckley* is further underscored by the continuing inability of the Court (and the plurality here) to apply *Buckley* in a coherent and principled fashion. As a result, *stare decisis* should pose no bar to overruling *Buckley* and replacing it with a standard faithful to the First Amendment. Accordingly, I concur only in the judgment. * * *

[JUSTICE STEVENS' dissenting opinion, arguing to overrule *Buckley* on expenditure limits, appears at p. 890.]

JUSTICE SOUTER, with whom JUSTICE GINSBURG joins, and with whom JUSTICE STEVENS joins as to Parts II and III, dissenting. * * *

[In Part I of his dissent, Justice Souter argued that *Buckley* did not "categorically foreclose the possibility that some spending limits might comport with the First Amendment" and that the case should be remanded for further development of the record.]

II

Although I would defer judgment on the merits of the expenditure limitations, I believe the Court of Appeals correctly rejected the challenge to the contribution limits. Low though they are, one cannot say that "the contribution limitation[s are] so radical in effect as to render political association ineffective, drive the sound of a candidate's voice below the level of notice, and render contributions pointless." *Shrink*, 528 U.S., [at] 397.

The limits set by Vermont are not remarkable departures either from those previously upheld by this Court or from those lately adopted by other States. The plurality concedes that on a per-citizen measurement Vermont's limit for statewide elections "is slightly more generous" than the one set by the Missouri statute approved by this Court in *Shrink*. Not only do those dollar amounts get more generous the smaller the district, they are consistent with limits set by the legislatures of many other States, all of them with populations larger than Vermont's, some significantly so. The point is not that this Court is bound by judicial sanctions of those numbers; it is that the consistency in legislative judgment tells us that Vermont is not an eccentric party of one, and that this is a case for the judicial deference that our own precedents say we owe here. * * *

To place Vermont's contribution limits beyond the constitutional pale, therefore, is to forget not only the facts of *Shrink*, but also our self-admonition against second-guessing legislative judgments about the risk of corruption to which contribution limits have to be fitted. And deference here would surely not be overly complaisant. Vermont's legislators themselves testified at length about the money that gets their special attention, see Act 64, H. 28, Legislative Findings and Intent (finding that "[s]ome candidates and elected officials, particularly when time is limited, respond and give access to contributors who make large contributions in preference to those who make small or no contributions"); testimony of Elizabeth Ready: "If I have only got an hour at night when I get home to return calls, I am much more likely to return [a donor's] call than I would [a non-donor's]. . . . [W]hen you only have a few minutes to talk, there are certain people that get access." * * * And testimony identified the amounts high enough to pay for effective campaigning in a State where the cost of running tends to be on the low side, see [*Landell v. Sorrell*, 118 F. Supp. 2d 459, 472 (Vt. 2000)] ("Vermont ranks 49th out of the 50 states in campaign spending. The majority of major party candidates for statewide office in the last three election cycles spent less than what the spending limits of Act 64 would allow. * * *").

Still, our cases do not say deference should be absolute. We can all imagine dollar limits that would be laughable, and per capita comparisons that would be meaningless because aggregated donations simply could not sustain effective campaigns. The plurality thinks that point has been reached in Vermont, and in particular that the low contribution limits threaten the ability of challengers to run effective races against incumbents. * * * [But t]he petitioners offered, and the plurality invokes, no evidence that the risk of a pro-incumbent advantage has been realized; in fact, * * * the experience of the Burlington race [where, the plurality concedes, a mayoral challenger was able to run a competitive campaign] is confirmed by recent empirical studies addressing this issue of incumbent's advantage. See, *e.g.*, Eom & Gross, *Contribution Limits and Disparity in Contributions Between Gubernatorial Candidates*, 59 Pol. Research Q. 99 (2006) ("Analyses of both the number of contributors and the dollar amount of contributions [to gubernatorial candidates] suggest no support for an increased bias in favor of incumbents resulting from the presence of campaign contribution limits. If anything, contribution limits can work to reduce the bias that traditionally works in favor of incumbents. Also, contribution limits do not seem to increase disparities between gubernatorial candidates in general") (emphasis deleted); Bardwell, *Money and Challenger Emergence in Gubernatorial Primaries*, 55 Pol. Research Q. 653 (2002) (finding that contribution limits favor neither incumbents nor challengers); Hogan, *The Costs of Representation in State Legislatures: Explaining Variations in Campaign Spending*, 81 Soc. Sci. Q. 941, 952 (2000) (finding that contribution limits reduce incumbent spending but have no effect on challenger or open-seat candidate spending). The Legislature of Vermont evidently tried to account for the realities of campaigning in Vermont, and I see no evidence of constitutional miscalculation sufficient to dispense with respect for its judgments.

III

* * * [I]ssues of detail call for some attention, the first being the requirement that a volunteer's expenses count against the person's contribution limit. The plurality certainly makes out the case that accounting for these expenses will be a colossal nuisance, but there is no case here that the nuisance will noticeably limit volunteering, or that volunteers whose expenses reach the limit cannot continue with their efforts subject to charging their candidates for the excess. Granted, if the provisions for contribution limits were teetering on the edge of unconstitutionality, Act 64's treatment of volunteers' expenses might be the finger-flick that gives the fatal push, but it has no greater significance than that.

Second, the failure of the Vermont law to index its limits for inflation is even less important. This challenge is to the law as it is, not to a law that may have a different impact after future inflation if the state legislature fails to bring it up to economic date.

Third, subjecting political parties to the same contribution limits as individuals does not condemn the Vermont scheme. What we said in *Federal Election Comm'n v. Colorado Republican Federal Campaign Comm.*, dealing with regulation of coordinated expenditures, goes here, too. The capacity and desire of parties to make large contributions to competitive candidates with uphill fights are shared by rich individuals, and the risk that large party contributions would be channels to evade individual limits cannot be eliminated. Nor are these reasons to support the party limits undercut by claims that the restrictions render parties impotent, for the parties are not precluded from uncoordinated spending to benefit their candidates. That said, I acknowledge the suggestions in the petitioners' briefs that such restrictions in synergy with other influences weakening party power would justify a wholesale reexamination of the situation of party organization today. But whether such a comprehensive reexamination belongs in courts or only in legislatures is not an issue presented by these cases. * * *

IV

Because * * * because I do not see the contribution limits as depressed to the level of political inaudibility, I respectfully dissent.

Notes and Questions

1. In campaign finance cases, it is rare for Justice Thomas and Justice Souter to agree, but the two agree (Justice Thomas in a portion of his opinion not reprinted above) that *Randall's* plurality opinion is not faithful to *Shrink PAC*. Indeed, Justice Souter seems rather appropriately vexed at the near disappearance of *Shrink PAC* from the plurality opinion in *Randall*. Do you agree that *Randall* turns its back on *Shrink PAC*? Consider, for example, *Shrink PAC's* rejection of the plaintiff's claim that limits should be adjusted for inflation, with the emphasis the *Randall* plurality places on the lack of inflation indexing in Vermont, and value of Vermont's limits with the limits in *Buckley* adjusted for inflation and population.

2. What is a contribution? One factor the Court considered in finding Vermont's contribution limits unconstitutionally low was the strict limit on volunteer activity. What types of volunteer activity can or should be considered contributions at all? Most citizens who volunteer for a campaign devote only a few hours to the effort. However, consider a law student who spends the summer volunteering for a campaign, devoting 10 weeks of full-time work. As a summer clerk at a local law firm, the student could earn $1000 per week. How should his volunteer work be valued? Similarly, the FEC's regulations on volunteer activity permit a major music artist to perform at a campaign rally on behalf of a candidate without charging a fee. *See* FEC Advisory Opinion 1980-42 (June 25, 1980). The value of such an appearance, of course might normally be many thousands of dollars.

Under the equality rationale for campaign finance, rejected by the Supreme Court in *Buckley* but favored by many academics and activists, does it make sense to exclude volunteer activity from the definition of "contribution"? Certainly such a construction allows a small number of people, mainly celebrities, to make contributions of enormous value that other citizens cannot match. Bradley A. Smith, *Faulty Assumptions and Undemocratic Consequences of Campaign Finance Reform*, 105 YALE L.J. 1049, 1078–81 (1996).

3. The ability of more and more people to create and upload videos for public viewing on the internet, or to devote blog sites to political activity, have created new dilemmas for the state's regulatory apparatus. In Advisory Opinion 1998-22 (Nov. 12, 1998), the FEC determined that a web site set up by an individual to support President Clinton had to be reported as an independent expenditure. By 2002, the FEC had changed its tune — writing regulations to implement the Bipartisan Campaign Reform Act, the Agency wrote a broad exemption for internet activity — so broad that a federal court struck it down as contrary to the Act. *See Shays v. Federal Election Commission*, 337 F. Supp. 2d 28 (D.D.C. 2004). The Agency's second effort at an internet regulation also exempted a substantial amount of internet activity, a decision that remains at once popular and controversial. *See* 71 Fed. Reg. 18589 (Apr. 12, 2006); Daniel W. Butrymowicz, *Loophole.com: How the FEC's Failure to Fully Regulate the Internet Undermines Campaign Finance Law*, 109 COLUM. L. REV. 1708 (2009).

4. The Federal Election Campaign Act, and most state laws, specifically exempt press editorializing and reporting from the definition of contribution or expenditure under campaign finance laws. Is such an exemption constitutionally required? In 2005, voters in Washington state were asked to consider Initiative 912 (I-912),

repealing a statewide gas tax enacted by the legislature. Two Seattle area radio hosts, Kirby Wilbur and John Carlson, were strongly critical of the gas tax, and began devoting substantial portions of their programs to advocating for repeal of the tax. They also encouraged listeners to contribute to No New Gas Tax (NNGT), the organization formed to support I-912, to circulate petitions to qualify the initiative for the ballot, and to visit NNGT's website and offices to obtain petitions. Officials in San Juan County and three Washington cities (all of whom stood to benefit from the gas tax revenue) filed a complaint with the state's Public Disclosure Commission, which enforces the state's campaign finance laws. The local governments complained that the on-air activities of Wilbur and Carlson constituted "contributions" to NNGT that were required to be publicly reported under state law. (The prosecutors also hired a private law firm — the bond counsel for the State of Washington, and thus a firm that stood to benefit from bonds issued on the strength of the gas tax revenues — to prosecute the matter). A trial court held for the local governments, agreeing with the complainants that the activity of the radio hosts and their station constituted political contributions rather than "commentary." The Washington Supreme Court reversed, holding that the activities were not a "contribution" under the Washington statute, but declining to rule on the question of whether such activities are constitutionally protected. *San Juan County v. No New Gas Tax*, 157 P.3d 831 (Wash. 2007).

Does the Constitution mandate a media exemption? If so, who is entitled to the exemption? Talk radio or television hosts, such as Kirby and Carlson, or Rush Limbaugh and Rachel Maddow? Politically oriented comedians such as Jon Stewart? What about bloggers? Newspapers? *See* Clifford A. Jones, *The Stephen Colbert Problem: The Media Exemption for Corporate Political Advocacy and the "Hail to the Cheese Stephen Colbert Nacho Cheese Doritos 2008 Presidential Campaign Coverage,"* 19 U. FLA. J. L. & PUB. POL'Y 295 (2008) (exploring the breakdown of traditional media categories in the modern era). *See also* Richard L. Hasen, *Campaign Finance Laws and the Rupert Murdoch Problem*, 77 TEX. L. REV. 1627 (1999) (arguing that the media exemption is "unjustifiable" and that limits on the press should be acceptable); Allison R. Hayward, *Regulation of Blog Campaign Advocacy on the Internet: Comparing U.S., German, and E.U. Approaches*, 16 CARDOZO J. INT'L & COMP. L. 379 (2008) (comparing and evaluating various approaches).

Should the activities of the radio commentators have been considered a contribution at all, any media exemption aside? Do you think their activities were a "contribution" to the I-912 campaign? The Washington state law defined contribution, in pertinent part, as "(i) A loan, gift, deposit, subscription, forgiveness of indebtedness, donation, advance, pledge, payment, transfer of funds between political committees, or *anything of value, including personal and professional services* for less than full consideration; * * *. (iii) The *financing* by a person of the dissemination, distribution, or republication, in whole or in part, *of broadcast*, written, graphic, or other form of *political advertising* or electioneering communication *prepared by a candidate, a political committee, or its authorized agent.*" Had Kirby and Wilber made "contributions" within the meaning of the statute? If so, is the statute constitutional under *Buckley v. Valeo*, media exemption aside?

5. *Problem. Randall* remains the only case in which the Supreme Court has overturned a contribution limit as unconstitutionally low. Does *Randall* provide a meaningful set of criteria for lower courts apply in determining if a limit is unconstitutionally low? You are the legislative aide to a state senator in Colorado, population 4.9 million. Concerned about heavy spending in state races, the senator wants to propose a bill reducing the maximum contribution in state races to $400 in all state races. Contributions to parties will be capped at $500 and parties will be limited to contributing $500 to candidates. Individuals will be subject to an overall cap of $2,500 per election cycle. Limits are not indexed for inflation, but all volunteer services are exempt. Following *Buckley*, independent expenditures are unlimited. The Senator wants your opinion as to whether the bill is constitutional under *Randall*.

6. The *Randall* plurality refers to "the right to associate with a political party" as "a particularly important political right." Just three years before *Randall*, however, the Court decided *McConnell v. Federal Election Commission*, 540 U.S. 93 (2003), taking a decidedly different attitude toward political parties, describing them more or less as bagmen for corrupt politicians, and discounting the associational rights of parties and their adherents to the point that one commenter argued that after *McConnell*, "the associational rights vindicated through parties * * * have little place in the constitutional law of campaign finance." Robert F. Bauer, *McConnell, Parties, and the Decline of the Right of Association*, 3 ELECTION L.J. 199, 204 (2004).

McCONNELL v. FEDERAL ELECTION COMMISSION
Supreme Court of the United States
540 U.S. 93, 124 S. Ct. 619. 157 L. Ed. 2d 491 (2003)

[In 2002, Congress passed the Bipartisan Campaign Reform Act, commonly known by its acronym "BCRA" or as "McCain-Feingold" after its primary sponsors in the Senate. BCRA was a wide ranging statute that purported to address numerous campaign finance issues, including contributions by minors, the definition of "coordinated" expenditures, and more, but its core provisions dealt with two perceived problems: "soft money" and "issue advocacy." The "issue advocacy" provisions attempted to limit certain types of expenditures close to an election, and are discussed in Part D of this chapter.

The Federal Election Campaign Act limited contributions to candidate committees, parties, and PACs made for the purpose of influencing federal elections. States, of course, remained free to set their own limits on contributions in connection with campaigns for state office. In an early advisory opinion, the Federal Election Commission permitted state political parties to accept contributions outside of FECA's source and amount limitations to be used in state and local elections. Advisory Opinion 1978-10, Fed. Elec. Camp. Fin. Guide (CCH) ¶ 5340. Later the FEC ruled that national parties could pay for activities affecting both state and federal elections, such as get-out-the-vote drives and generic party advertising (e.g. "Vote Republican") with a mix of both federal and non-federal money, Advisory Opinion 1979-17, Fed. Elec. Camp. Fin. Guide (CCH) ¶ 5416. Money raised under the limitations of FECA gradually became known as "federal" or "hard" money. Money raised outside of FECA's limits became known as "non-federal" or "soft" money. In 1995 the Commission determined that soft money could be used to fund ads that mentioned federal candidates, so long as they did not expressly advocate the election or defeat of a candidate. Advisory Opinion 1995-25, Fed. Elec. Camp. Fin. Guide (CCH) ¶ 6162. As the permissible uses of soft money expanded, so did the amount raised and spent. By the election of 2000, soft money accounted for roughly 42 percent of the spending by the national political parties. Much of this money was raised in very large amounts — 800 donors contributed almost $300 million to the national parties in the 2000 election cycle.

BCRA responded to the growth in soft money by prohibiting national parties from receiving or spending soft money, prohibiting national parties from soliciting or directing soft money contributions to other organizations, and sharply limiting the ability of state and local parties to use non-federal funds to pay for activities that might affect a federal election — such as voter registration and get-out-the-vote drives. All of these provisions and others in BCRA were challenged in *McConnell v. Federal Election Commission*, 540 U.S. 93 (2003). In a lengthy, sprawling opinion, a 5-4 Court majority upheld all key provisions of the Act.

In a joint opinion joined by Justices Breyer, Souter, and Ginsberg, Justices O'Connor and Stevens brushed aside claims that the statute was unconstitutionally overbroad. Particularly important was their view of the anti-corruption interest at stake.]

> Plaintiffs argue that without concrete evidence of an instance in which a federal officeholder has actually switched a vote (or, presumably, evidence of a specific instance where the public believes a vote was switched), Congress has not shown that there exists real or apparent corruption. But the record is to the contrary. The evidence connects soft money to manipulations of the legislative calendar, leading to Congress' failure to enact, among other things, generic drug legislation, tort reform, and tobacco legislation. * * *

> More importantly, plaintiffs conceive of corruption too narrowly. Our cases have firmly established that Congress' legitimate interest extends beyond preventing simple cash-for-votes corruption to curbing "undue influence on an officeholder's judgment, and the appearance of such influence." [*Federal Election Commission v. Colorado Republican Federal Campaign Committee*, 533 U.S. 431 (2001)] [*Colorado II*]. Many of the "deeply disturbing examples" of corruption cited by this Court in *Buckley* to justify FECA's contribution limits were not episodes of vote buying, but evidence that various corporate interests had given substantial donations to gain access to high-level government officials. Even if that access did not secure actual influence, it certainly gave the "appearance of such influence." *Colorado II.* * * *

> The record in the present case is replete with similar examples of national party committees peddling access to federal candidates and officeholders in exchange for large soft-money donations. * * *

Despite this evidence and the close ties that candidates and officeholders have with their parties, Justice Kennedy would limit Congress' regulatory interest *only* to the prevention of the actual or apparent *quid pro quo* corruption "inherent in" contributions made directly to, contributions made at the express behest of, and expenditures made in coordination with, a federal officeholder or candidate. Regulation of any other donation or expenditure — regardless of its size, the recipient's relationship to the candidate or officeholder, its potential impact on a candidate's election, its value to the candidate, or its unabashed and explicit intent to purchase influence — would, according to Justice Kennedy, simply be out of bounds. This crabbed view of corruption, and particularly of the appearance of corruption, ignores precedent, common sense, and the realities of political fundraising exposed by the record in this litigation.

Justice Kennedy's interpretation of the First Amendment would render Congress powerless to address more subtle but equally dispiriting forms of corruption. Just as troubling to a functioning democracy as classic *quid pro quo* corruption is the danger that officeholders will decide issues not on the merits or the desires of their constituencies, but according to the wishes of those who have made large financial contributions valued by the office-holder. Even if it occurs only occasionally, the potential for such undue influence is manifest. And unlike straight cash-for-votes transactions, such corruption is neither easily detected nor practical to criminalize. The best means of prevention is to identify and to remove the temptation. * * *

Justice Kennedy likewise takes too narrow a view of the appearance of corruption. He asserts that only those transactions with "inherent corruption potential," which he again limits to contributions directly to candidates, justify the inference "that regulating the conduct will stem the appearance of real corruption." In our view, however, Congress is not required to ignore historical evidence regarding a particular practice or to view conduct in isolation from its context. To be sure, mere political favoritism or opportunity for influence alone is insufficient to justify regulation. As the record demonstrates, it is the manner in which parties have *sold* access to federal candidates and officeholders that has given rise to the appearance of undue influence. Implicit (and, as the record shows, sometimes explicit) in the sale of access is the suggestion that money buys influence. It is no surprise then that purchasers of such access unabashedly admit that they are seeking to purchase just such influence. It was not unwarranted for Congress to conclude that the selling of access gives rise to the appearance of corruption. * * *

540 U.S. at 149–153.

[The *McConnell* Court also rejected the plaintiffs claim that BCRA violated the equal protection component of the Due Process Clause of the Fifth Amendment by leaving interest groups free to undertake activities and raise funds prohibited to the parties:]

Congress is fully entitled to consider the real-world differences between political parties and interest groups when crafting a system of campaign finance regulation. * * * Interest groups do not select slates of candidates for elections. Interest groups do not determine who will serve on legislative committees, elect congressional leadership, or organize legislative caucuses. Political parties have influence and power in the legislature that vastly exceeds that of any interest group. As a result, it is hardly surprising that party affiliation is the primary way by which voters identify candidates, or that parties in turn have special access to and relationships with federal officeholders. Congress' efforts at campaign finance regulation may account for these salient differences.

Id. at 188.

Notes and Questions

1. The *McConnell* opinions constitute one of the longest — by some measures the longest — Supreme Court cases ever reported. At the time it was decided, *McConnell* looked like a blockbuster case that could soon replace *Buckley* as the lodestar of campaign finance jurisprudence. But *McConnell* did not hold up well. The majority opinion was heavily criticized even by many who agreed with the judgment, *see, e.g.*, Richard L. Hasen, Buckley *Is Dead, Long Live* Buckley: *The New Campaign Finance Incoherence of McConnell v. Federal Election Commission*, 153 U. PA. L. REV. 31, 32–33 (2004), and within a decade the case's key holdings on expenditures had been overruled in substantial part, and its broad definition of corruption largely rejected by the Court. *See* Part D, *infra*. *McConnell's* holding on the soft money ban, however, has held up against challenges. *Republican National Committee v. Federal Election Commission*, 698 F. Supp. 2d 150 (D.D.C.) *cert. den.* 561 U.S. 1040 (2010); *In re Cao*, 619 F. 3d 410 (5th Cir. 2010) *cert. den.* 131 S. Ct. 1718 (2011).

2. Perhaps the most significant element of the *McConnell* opinion is its definition of the corruption interest that the state may seek to address through reform. The Court holds that mere preferential access to contributors is enough to justify the ban on party soft-money. Richard Briffault, McConnell v. FEC *and the Transformation of Campaign Finance Law*, 3 ELECTION L.J. 147, 162–63 (2004), notes the effect:

> By focusing on special access, *McConnell* reframed the corruption analysis from the consideration of contributions on formal decisions to their effect on the opportunity to influence government actions. * * * [T]he Court treated preferential access as a problem in itself, and found that Congress could take steps to eliminate a campaign finance device that created special incentives to officeholders to give special access to donors.

The Court argued that contributions to parties could be limited, "[e]ven if that access did not secure actual influence." Since *Buckley*, of course, the Court had recognized a legitimate state interest that went beyond preventing quid prop quo corruption to include the "appearance of corruption." But in *McConnell*, the Court moved one step further, holding that the state may limit access that creates the opportunity for appearance of corruption. *See* Lillian R. BeVier, McConnell v. FEC: *Not Senator Buckley's First Amendment*, 3 ELECTION L.J. 127 (2004), for a critique of this and other elements of the decision.

3.   How big a problem is access? Consider:

> You get back from lunch. You've got fourteen phone messages on your desk. Thirteen of them are from constituents you've never heard of, and one of them is from a guy who just came to your fundraiser two weeks earlier and gave you $2,000. Which phone call are you going to return first?

PHILIP M. STERN, THE BEST CONGRESS MONEY CAN BUY 101 (1988) (quoting former congressman Michael Barnes). Certainly the idea that money buys access has a common sense appeal, and the *McConnell* Court relied heavily on anecdotal tales from BCRA's congressional supporters about money and access. *See also* MARTIN SCHRAM, SPEAKING FREELY (1995).

Several recent works, however, have challenged whether this common sense notion is empirically true. While there are no doubt anecdotal stories of access, these researchers argue that in fact constituents are more likely to gain access to members of Congress than are contributors. *See* John Samples, *Against Deference*, 12 NEXUS J. OP. 21, 28–31 (2007); Marie Hojnakni & David Kimball, *PAC Contributions and Lobbying Contacts in Congressional Committees*, 54 POL. RESEARCH Q. 176 (2001); Michelle L. Chin, Jon R. Bond & Nehemia Geva, *A Foot in the Door: An Experimental Study of PAC and Constituency Influence on Access*, 62 J. POL. 543 (2000). *But see* Richard Hall & Frank Wyman, *Buying Time: Moneyed Interests and the Mobilization of Bias in Congressional Committees*, 84 AMER. POL. SCI. REV. 797 (1990). *See also* Bradley A. Smith, *Money Talks: Speech, Corruption, Equality, and Campaign Finance*, 86 GEO. L. J. 45, 92–93 (1997) (arguing that eliminating access based on campaign contributions would not increase political equality or decrease the appearance of corruption).

4.   Contrary to many expectations, the national political parties were largely able to replace the soft money lost due to BCRA. Gary Jacobson, *A Collective Dilemma Solved: The Distribution of Party Campaign Resources in the 2006 and 2008 Congressional Elections*, (paper presented at UCLA Election Law Symposium, Jan. 29, 2010). Nevertheless, the effect of BCRA on the parties remains hotly disputed. Supporters of BCRA argued that even if party fundraising were curtailed, parties would benefit because they would be weaned from their addiction to television advertising and forced to work harder to recruit volunteers and small donors. *See* Nathaniel Persily, *The Law of American Party Finance* in Keith Ewing and Samuel Issacharoff, PARTY FUNDING AND CAMPAIGN FINANCING IN INTERNATIONAL PERSPECTIVE, 212, 237–238 (2006) (citing *McConnell* defendants' expert). Others, however, argue that indeed parties have lost influence to non-party interest groups. *See e.g.* Jeff Brindle, *Real Reform Means Repealing BCRA and Strengthening Parties*, Campaigns and Elections (Sept. 30, 2012); PETER J. WALLISON AND JOEL M. GORA, BETTER PARTIES, BETTER GOVERNMENT: A REALISTIC PROGRAM FOR CAMPAIGN FINANCE REFORM (2009); RAYMOND J. LA RAJA, SMALL CHANGE: MONEY, POLITICAL PARTIES, AND CAMPAIGN FINANCE REFORM (2008).

5.   *McConnell*, following close on the heels of *Shrink PAC, Colorado Republican II*, and *Federal Election Commission v. Beaumont*, marks the apogee of judicial deference to congressional decision making. The majority argued that given

Congress's particular expertise in elections and in witnessing the effects of money on legislative behavior, judicial deference to congressional decisions in this area is particularly appropriate. Justice Scalia, dissenting, argued that given Congress's particular vested interest in elections, and thus the potential for witting or unwitting self-dealing, judicial deference to congressional decisions in this area is particularly inappropriate. Which view do you find more persuasive?

Is the legislature more knowledgeable, for better or worse, about campaign finance legislation than other bills? BCRA was passed after nearly a decade of vote trading in Congress, and revisions aimed at attracting the votes of specific legislators. *See* JOHN SAMPLES, THE FALLACY OF CAMPAIGN FINANCE REFORM 238–254 (2006). Eleven months after BCRA took effect, members of the House Committee on Rules and Administration, which has jurisdiction over campaign finance legislation, inquired as to whether the FEC might develop a program to explain the Act to members of Congress. Jennifer Yachnin, *House Admin Requests BCRA Symposium*, ROLL CALL, Oct. 30, 2003.

6. The *McConnell* opinion's strongly deferential tone suggested to many that the Court was prepared to accept campaign finance regulation going far beyond even that of BCRA. Yet within months, litigation was already underway that would soon cause the new *McConnell* paradigm to begin to unravel. The first of these lawsuits reached the Supreme Court in the fall of 2005. In *Wisconsin Right to Life v. Federal Election Commission*, 546 U.S. 410 (2006) *(WRTL I)*, the Supreme Court held, in a brief, 9-0 *per curiam* opinion, that *McConnell* did not preclude as-applied challenges to BCRA's electioneering communications provisions. *Randall v. Sorrell* [p. 852], decided months later, indicated that the Court was taking a reinvigorated look at campaign finance laws. While many of the Court's decisions since have dealt with the expenditure side of the law, or with public financing of campaigns, *see* Sections D and F, *infra*, in 2014 the Court issued a high profile decision striking down a federal contribution limit.

McCUTCHEON v. FEDERAL ELECTION COMMISSION
Supreme Court of the United States
__ U.S. __, 134 S. Ct. 1434, 188 L. Ed. 2d 468 (2014)

CHIEF JUSTICE ROBERTS announced the judgment of the Court and delivered an opinion, in which JUSTICE SCALIA, JUSTICE KENNEDY, and JUSTICE ALITO join.

* * *

In a series of cases over the past 40 years, we have spelled out how to draw the constitutional line between the permissible goal of avoiding corruption in the political process and the impermissible desire simply to limit political speech. We have said that government regulation may not target the general gratitude a candidate may feel toward those who support him or his allies, or the political access such support may afford. "Ingratiation and access . . . are not corruption." *Citizens United v. Federal Election Comm'n*, 558 U.S. 310, 360, 130 S. Ct. 876, 175 L. Ed. 2d 753 (2010) [p. 941]. They embody a central feature of democracy — that constituents support candidates who share their beliefs and interests, and candidates who are elected can be expected to be responsive to those concerns.

Any regulation must instead target what we have called "*quid pro quo*" corruption or its appearance. See *id.*, at 359. That Latin phrase captures the notion of a direct exchange of an official act for money. * * * "The hallmark of corruption is the financial *quid pro quo*: dollars for political favors." *Federal Election Comm'n v. National Conservative Political Action Comm.*, 470 U.S. 480, 497, 105 S. Ct. 1459, 84 L. Ed. 2d 455 (1985). Campaign finance restrictions that pursue other objectives, we have explained, impermissibly inject the Government "into the debate over who should govern." [*Arizona Free Enterprise Club's Freedom Club PAC v. Bennett*, 131 S. Ct. 2806, 2826 (2011).] [p. 1000] And those who govern should be the *last* people to help decide who *should* govern.

The statute at issue in this case imposes two types of limits on campaign contributions. The first, called base limits, restricts how much money a donor may contribute to a particular candidate or committee. 2 U.S.C. § 441a(a)(1). The second, called aggregate limits, restricts how much money a donor may contribute in total to all candidates or committees. § 441a(a)(3). This case does not involve any challenge to the base limits, which we have previously upheld as serving the permissible objective of combatting corruption. The Government contends that the aggregate limits also serve that objective, by preventing circumvention of the base limits. We conclude, however, that the aggregate limits do little, if anything, to address that concern, while seriously restricting participation in the democratic process. The aggregate limits are therefore invalid under the First Amendment.

* * *

Buckley held that the Government's interest in preventing *quid pro quo* corruption or its appearance was "sufficiently important," * * * so that the interest would satisfy even strict scrutiny. . . . [However] we must assess the fit between the stated governmental objective and the means selected to achieve that objective. Or to put it another way, if a law that restricts political speech does not "avoid unnecessary abridgement" of First Amendment rights, *Buckley*, 424 U.S., at 25, it cannot survive "rigorous" review.

Because we find a substantial mismatch between the Government's stated objective and the means selected to achieve it, the aggregate limits fail even under the "closely drawn" test. * * *

An aggregate limit on *how many* candidates and committees an individual may support through contributions is not a "modest restraint" at all. The Government may no more restrict how many candidates or causes a donor may support than it may tell a newspaper how many candidates it may endorse.

To put it in the simplest terms, the aggregate limits prohibit an individual from fully contributing to the primary and general election campaigns of ten or more candidates, even if all contributions fall within the base limits Congress views as adequate to protect against corruption. The individual may give up to $5,200 each to nine candidates, but the aggregate limits constitute an outright ban on further contributions to any other candidate (beyond the additional $1,800 that may be spent before reaching the $48,600 aggregate limit). At that point, the limits deny the individual all ability to exercise his expressive and associational rights by contributing to someone who will advocate for his policy preferences. A donor must limit the number of candidates he supports, and may have to choose which of several policy concerns he will advance — clear First Amendment harms that the dissent never acknowledges.

It is no answer to say that the individual can simply contribute less money to more people. To require one person to contribute at lower levels than others because he wants to support more candidates or causes is to impose a special burden on broader participation in the democratic process. And as we have recently admonished, the Government may not penalize an individual for "robustly exercis[ing]" his First Amendment rights.

The First Amendment burden is especially great for individuals who do not have ready access to alternative avenues for supporting their preferred politicians and policies. In the context of base contribution limits, *Buckley* observed that a supporter could vindicate his associational interests by personally volunteering his time and energy on behalf of a candidate. Such personal volunteering is not a realistic alternative for those who wish to support a wide variety of candidates or causes. Other effective methods of supporting preferred candidates or causes without contributing money are reserved for a select few, such as entertainers capable of raising hundreds of thousands of dollars in a single evening. * * *

[W]hile preventing corruption or its appearance is a legitimate objective, Congress may target only a specific type of corruption — "*quid pro quo*" corruption. As *Buckley* explained, Congress may permissibly seek to rein in "large contributions [that] are given to secure a political *quid pro quo* from current and potential office holders." 424 U.S., at 26. In addition to "actual *quid pro quo* arrangements," Congress may permissibly limit "the appearance of corruption stemming from public awareness of the opportunities for abuse inherent in a regime of large individual financial contributions" to particular candidates. *Id.*, at 27; see also *Citizens United*, 558 U.S., at 359 ("When *Buckley* identified a sufficiently important governmental interest in preventing corruption or the appearance of corruption, that interest was limited to *quid pro quo* corruption").

Spending large sums of money in connection with elections, but not in connection with an effort to control the exercise of an officeholder's official duties, does not give rise to such *quid pro quo* corruption. Nor does the possibility that an individual who spends large sums may garner "influence over or access to" elected officials or political parties. *Id.*, at 359. And because the Government's interest in preventing the appearance of corruption is equally confined to the appearance of *quid pro quo* corruption, the Government may not seek to limit the appearance of mere influence or access. * * *

The Government has a strong interest * * * in combatting corruption and its appearance. We have, however, held that this interest must be limited to a specific kind of corruption — *quid pro quo* corruption — in order to ensure that the Government's efforts do not have the effect of restricting the First Amendment right of citizens to choose who shall govern them. For the reasons set forth, we conclude that the aggregate limits on contributions do not further the only governmental interest this Court accepted as legitimate in *Buckley*. They instead intrude without justification on a citizen's ability to exercise "the most fundamental

First Amendment activities." *Buckley*, 424 U.S., at 14.

The judgment of the District Court is reversed.

JUSTICE THOMAS concurring in the judgment.

* * * Contributions and expenditures are simply "two sides of the same First Amendment coin," and our efforts to distinguish the two have produced mere "word games" rather than any cognizable principle of constitutional law. *Buckley, supra*, at 241, 244, (Burger, C.J., concurring in part and dissenting in part). For that reason, I would overrule *Buckley* and subject the aggregate limits in BCRA to strict scrutiny, which they would surely fail. * * *

JUSTICE BREYER, with whom JUSTICE GINSBURG, JUSTICE SOTOMAYOR, and JUSTICE KAGAN join, dissenting.

* * * The plurality's first claim — that large aggregate contributions do not "give rise" to "corruption" — is plausible only because the plurality defines "corruption" too narrowly. The plurality describes the constitutionally permissible objective of campaign finance regulation as follows: "Congress may target only a specific type of corruption — '*quid pro quo*' corruption." It then defines *quid pro quo* corruption to mean no more than "a direct exchange of an official act for money" — an act akin to bribery. It adds specifically that corruption does *not* include efforts to "garner 'influence over or access to' elected officials or political parties." Moreover, the Government's efforts to prevent the "appearance of corruption" are "equally confined to the appearance of *quid pro quo* corruption," as narrowly defined. In the plurality's view, a federal statute could not prevent an individual from writing a million dollar check to a political party (by donating to its various committees), because the rationale for any limit would "dangerously broade[n] the circumscribed definition of *quid pro quo* corruption articulated in our prior cases."

This critically important definition of "corruption" is inconsistent with the Court's prior case law (with the possible exception of *Citizens United*, . . .). It is virtually impossible to reconcile with this Court's decision in *McConnell* [v. *FEC*, 540 U.S. 93 (2003)], upholding the Bipartisan Campaign Reform Act of 2002 (BCRA). And it misunderstands the constitutional importance of the interests at stake. In fact, constitutional interests — indeed, First Amendment interests — lie on both sides of the legal equation.

In reality, as the history of campaign finance reform shows and as our earlier cases on the subject have recognized, the anticorruption interest that drives Congress to regulate campaign contributions is a far broader, more important interest than the plurality acknowledges. It is an interest in maintaining the integrity of our public governmental institutions. And it is an interest rooted in the Constitution and in the First Amendment itself.

Consider at least one reason why the First Amendment protects political speech. Speech does not exist in a vacuum. Rather, political communication seeks to secure government action. A politically oriented "marketplace of ideas" seeks to form a public opinion that can and will influence elected representatives.

This is not a new idea. Eighty-seven years ago, Justice Brandeis wrote that the First Amendment's protection of speech was "essential to effective democracy." *Whitney* v. *California*, 274 U.S. 357, 377, (1927) (concurring opinion). Chief Justice Hughes reiterated the same idea shortly thereafter: "A fundamental principle of our constitutional system" is the "maintenance of the opportunity for free political discussion *to the end* that government may be responsive to the will of the people." *Stromberg v. California*, 283 U.S. 359, 369 (1931) (emphasis added). In *Citizens United*, the Court stated that "[s]peech is an essential mechanism of democracy, for it is *the means* to hold officials accountable to the people."

The Framers had good reason to emphasize this same connection between political speech and governmental action. An influential 18th-century continental philosopher had argued that in a representative democracy, the people lose control of their representatives between elections, during which interim periods they were "in chains." J. Rousseau, An Inquiry Into the Nature of the Social Contract 265–266 (transl. 1791).

The Framers responded to this criticism both by requiring frequent elections to federal office, and by enacting a First Amendment that would facilitate a "chain of communication between the people, and those, to whom they have committed the exercise of the powers of government." J. Wilson, Commentaries on the Constitution of the United States of America 30–31 (1792). This "chain" would establish the necessary "communion of interests and sympathy of sentiments" between the people and their representatives, so that public opinion could be channeled into effective governmental action. The Federalist No. 57, p. 386 (J. Cooke ed. 1961) (J. Madison); accord, T. Benton, 1 Abridgement of the Debates of Congress, from 1789 to 1856, p. 141 (1857) (explaining that the First Amendment will strengthen American democracy by giving " 'the people' " a right to " 'publicly address their representatives,' " " 'privately advise them,' " or " 'declare their sentiments by petition to the whole body' " (quoting James Madison)). Accordingly, the First Amendment advances not only the individual's right to engage in political speech, but also the public's interest in preserving a democratic order in which collective speech *matters*.

What has this to do with corruption? It has everything to do with corruption. Corruption breaks the constitutionally necessary "chain of communication" between the people and their representatives. It derails the essential speech-to-government-action tie. Where enough money calls the tune, the general public will not be heard. Insofar as corruption cuts the link between political thought and political action, a free marketplace of political ideas loses its point.

That is one reason why the Court has stressed the constitutional importance of Congress' concern that a few large donation not drown out the voices of the many.
* * *

That is also why the Court has used the phrase "subversion of the political process" to describe circumstances in which "[e]lected officials are influenced to act contrary to their obligations of office by the prospect of financial gain to themselves or infusions of money into their campaigns." *NCPAC*, 470 U.S., at 497. *See also Federal Election Comm'n* v. *National Right to Work Comm.*, 459 U.S. 197, 208 (1982) (the Government's interests in preventing corruption "directly implicate the integrity of our electoral process" (internal quotation marks and citation omitted)). *See generally* R. Post, Citizens Divided: Campaign Finance Reform and the Constitution 7–16, 80–94 (forthcoming 2014) (arguing that the efficacy of American democracy depends on "electoral integrity" and the responsiveness of public officials to public opinion).

The "appearance of corruption" can make matters worse. It can lead the public to believe that its efforts to communicate with its representatives or to help sway public opinion have little purpose. And a cynical public can lose interest in political participation altogether. See *Nixon v. Shrink Missouri Government PAC*, 528 U.S. 377, 390 (2000) ("[T]he cynical assumption that large donors call the tune could jeopardize the willingness of voters to take part in democratic governance"). Democracy, the Court has often said, cannot work unless "the people have faith in those who govern." *United States* v. *Mississippi Valley Generating Co.*, 364 U.S. 520, 562 (1961).

The upshot is that the interests the Court has long described as preventing "corruption" or the "appearance of corruption" are more than ordinary factors to be weighed against the constitutional right to political speech. Rather, they are interests rooted in the First Amendment itself. They are rooted in the constitutional effort to create a democracy responsive to the people — a government where laws reflect the very thoughts, views, ideas, and sentiments, the expression of which the First Amendment protects. Given that end, we can and should understand campaign finance laws as resting upon a broader and more significant constitutional rationale than the plurality's limited definition of "corruption" suggests. We should see these laws as seeking in significant part to strengthen, rather than weaken, the First Amendment. To say this is not to deny the potential for conflict between (1) the need to permit contributions that pay for the diffusion of ideas, and (2) the need to limit payments in order to help maintain the integrity of the electoral process. But that conflict takes place within, not outside, the First Amendment's boundaries.
* * *

Notes and Questions

1.   During the 2014 election cycle, the aggregate limits faced by McCutcheon, a self-employed engineer from Alabama, were $48,600 in contributions to all federal candidates, and $74,600 to all other political committees, of which no more than $48,600 could be contributed to PACs and state and local party committees, for a total of $123,200 in contributions. Obviously, only a very small number of Americans can afford to make so many contributions. Indeed, during the 2012 election cycle, fewer than 600 contributors bumped up against the cap. For this and other reasons, the immediate effects of *McCutcheon* are likely to be less than earthshattering:

> The inevitable result * * * [of *McCutcheon* is] that a small number of wealthy donors would take money that is currently not spent on politics, or used for independent expenditures, and contribute it directly to candidates and parties. This would, at the margin, positively address two longstanding concerns of regulatory advocates. First, by making more money available from proven donors, it would provide slight relief from the burdens of fundraising for officeholders. Second, it could be expected to bring a small

percentage of independent expenditure dollars currently going to organizations with fewer disclosure obligations back to candidates and parties, which have the greatest disclosure obligations.

Bradley A. Smith, McCutcheon v. Federal Election Commission: *An Unlikely Blockbuster*, 9 N.Y.U. J. L. & Lib. 48, 51–52 (2015). Yet *McCutcheon*, like so many recent campaign finance decisions on the Court, was a 5-4 decision, with very lengthy opinions and a heated dissent. Why? Consider the concept of corruption used by the majority in *McConnell* [p. 865] versus the concept of corruption employed by the *McCutcheon* plurality. What is the impact of this difference on future cases?

2.   Notice that Justice Breyer's dissent shifts the paradigm: for Justice Breyer, the First Amendment is not about preserving individual liberty from government encroachment, but about enabling the government to create a more efficient "marketplace of ideas" that will "secure government action." This conception of the Amendment as a "collective" right is radically different from that of the majority. The majority sees the First Amendment protecting an individual right to speak and protecting the integrity of the electoral system from politicians themselves: incumbent officeholders are "the last people" we should trust to regulate political speech. What ramifications flow from each view? Who has the better argument?

3.   In upholding the limits against *McCutcheon's* challenge,

> [T]he District Court imagined a hypothetical scenario that might occur in a world without aggregate limits. A single donor might contribute the maximum amount under the base limits to nearly 50 separate committees, each of which might then transfer the money to the same single committee. That committee, in turn, might use all the transferred money for coordinated expenditures on behalf of a particular candidate, allowing the single donor to circumvent the base limit on the amount he may contribute to that candidate. The District Court acknowledged that "it may seem unlikely that so many separate entities would willingly serve as conduits" for the single donor's interests, but it concluded that such a scenario "is not hard to imagine."

134 S. Ct. at 1443–44. The *McCutcheon* dissent went much further down this path than the District Court, offering a series of hypothetical scenarios such as one in which over 500 candidate and party committees would coordinate all their activities, allowing a donor to write a single check for $3.6 million (which would then be redistributed to all the various candidate and party committees participating subject to the base limits on each committee), and then having each of the 500 plus recipient committees transfer money to a single candidate. 134 S. Ct. at 1473–87. Such hypotheticals were dismissed by the plurality as, in some cases, "illegal under current campaign finance laws," 134 S. Ct. at 1456, and in others as "highly implausible," "speculation," and "divorced from reality." 134 S. Ct. at 1452–56. *See also* Allen Dickerson, McCutcheon v. FEC *and the Supreme Court's Pivot to Buckley*, 2014 Cato Sup. Ct. Rev. 95, 121–25 (2014); *Id.* at 123 ("Notably, even in a world with aggregate limits, it would be possible for an individual conspiring with 15 PACs to funnel $74,600 to a single candidate. Yet, perhaps unsurprisingly, nobody appears to do this — because it would involve breaking an astounding number of

federal laws."); *see also* Zac Morgan, McCutcheon's *Wild Hypotheticals*, Center for Competitive Politics, Dec. 11, 2013 (*available at* http://www.campaignfreedom.org/2013/12/11/mccutcheons-wild-hypotheticals/) (analyzing hypotheticals raised by justices Kagan and Breyer at oral argument and discussing how those hypotheticals would violate the law even after a victory for the *McCutcheon* plaintiffs). Notice again the contrasting approaches of the two camps. In *Shrink Missouri Government PAC* [p. 834] the majority, upholding the regulation in question, had argued that the plausibility of government's rationale effectively lowered the evidentiary bar needed to justify the regulation. The *McCutcheon* plurality — *McConnell* dissenters Justices Scalia and Kennedy, with Chief Justice Roberts replacing *McConvell* dissenter Chief Justice Rehnquist, and Justice Alito replacing Justice O'Connor to flip the majority (with *McConnell* dissenter Justice Thomas concurring in the judgment) — effectively flips that standard. Under *McCutcheon*, claims of possible "circumvention" by the government must be considered plausible before they will be given credence as an important state interest by the Court. The plurality also rejected what it called a "prophylaxis-upon-prophylaxis" approach to preventing "circumvention" of the law. 134 S. Ct. at 1458. What is the importance of this change, going forward?

4.   The dissent also objected to the plurality's claim that the aggregate limits were not closely drawn to address the government's concerns.

> The plurality concludes that even if circumvention were a threat, the aggregate limits are "poorly tailored" to address it. *Ante*, at 1456–1457. The First Amendment requires " 'a fit that is * * * reasonable,' " and there is no such "fit" here because there are several alternative ways Congress could prevent evasion of the base limits. *Ibid.* * * * The plurality, however, does not show, or try to show, that these hypothetical alternatives could effectively replace aggregate contribution limits.

134 S. Ct. at 1479. Implicit in the plurality's approach is the assumption that it is up to the government to prove that its means are narrowly tailored — not up to the plaintiffs to prove that they are not. Who should have this burden? Why does it matter? How does it affect future cases?

5.   *Problem.* Consider the following scenarios in light of the foregoing case law on contributions:

a.   A state caps contributions to candidate committees at $2,000. However, if a candidate is being outraised by at least 20% by an opponent who spends at least $100,000 in personal funds, the limit on contributions to the candidate being outspent rises to $10,000. *See Davis v. Federal Election Commission*, 554 U.S. 724 (2008).

b.   A state legislator has discovered that a number of children, some as young as age seven, have made contributions of $500 or more to candidates. In each case, the child's parents had already contributed the legal maximum to a candidate. The legislator believes that these donations are really controlled by the parents, who use the children to circumvent the limits on contributions. He proposes a law prohibiting anyone under the age of 15 from contributing to a candidate. Is the law constitutional? *See McConnell v. Federal Election*, 540 U.S. 93, 231–32 (2003).

c. State law allows an individual to contribute up to $5,000 to a candidate for the primary election, and up to $5,000 for the general election. This is true even if the candidate has no primary opponent. State law also allows a candidate to transfer funds left over from past races to his current campaign account. Thus a candidate can transfer leftover primary funds to his general election account. Plaintiff Morgan Justice is a candidate state senate. A first time candidate for office, he has just survived a difficult and expensive primary to win his party's nomination, and now faces an incumbent in the general election. The incumbent had no primary opposition. Plaintiff Guy Rich did not contribute to any candidate in the primary because he had no strong preference between the three candidates in the primary; but now wishes to contribute $10,000 to Justice for the general election, as he strongly dislikes the incumbent and considers the race particularly important to his party's chances to gain a majority in the legislature. Justice and Rich have challenged the law. They do not challenge the total election cycle limit of $10,000, but argue that it is unconstitutional as a violation of the First Amendment and the Equal Protection Clause of the Fourteenth Amendment to force Rich to divide his contributions between the primary and general election. They argue that because the incumbent has no primary opposition, donors can effectively contribute $10,000 for the general election to the incumbent, but not to Justice. They also argue that if the incumbent is not "corrupted" by receiving $10,000 from a donor in an election year, neither is Justice. The state argues that the limits are per election, not per year or per candidate. It argues that while some candidates are unopposed in primaries, others are not. Further, in some races the primary may be hotly contested, but the winner of a particular party primary is almost certain to win the general election. Allowing a donor to contribute a full $10,000 in a hotly contested race may be enough to unduly sway a legislator and lead to quid pro quo corruption. What should be the result? *See Holmes v. Federal Election Commission*, 2015 U.S. Dist. LEXIS 51414, 1 (D.D.C. Apr. 20, 2015).

6. As part of the Bipartisan Campaign Reform Act of 2002 (BCRA), Congress enacted what became known as the "millionaire's amendment." The workings of the provision were exceedingly complex, but basically it provided that when a candidate was outspending his opponent by at least $350,000, and that margin was due to the candidate's spending his personal funds on the race, contribution limits for the outspent candidate would be trebled (from $2,300 to $6,900 at the time the provision was challenged). In *Davis v. Federal Election Commission*, 554 U.S. 724 (2008), the Court held the scheme unconstitutional. Justice Alito, writing for a 5-4 majority that included Chief Justice Roberts and Justices Scalia, Kennedy, and Thomas, argued that "while the [Amendment] does not impose a cap on a candidate's expenditure of personal funds, * * * it imposes an unprecedented penalty on any candidate who robustly exercises his First Amendment right. [The Millionaire's Amendment] requires a candidate to choose between the First Amendment right to engage in unfettered political speech and subjection to discriminatory fundraising limits." 554 U.S. at 738–39. The Court saw no anti-corruption interest serve by the Amendment. The dissent, Justice Stevens writing for himself and Justices Souter, Breyer, and Ginsburg, argued "Davis cannot show that the Millionaire's Amendment causes him

* * * any First Amendment injury whatsoever. The Millionaire's Amendment quiets no speech at all." *Id.* at 753.

What class of candidates do you think is most likely to benefit from the Millionaire's Amendment? (Hint: of the top 10 self-funded candidates for U.S. House and Senate in 2014, only one was an incumbent, Center for Responsive Politics, https://www.opensecrets.org/overview/topself.php). Historically, challengers are more reliant on large contributions than are incumbents, and the incumbent spending advantage more than doubled after passage of FECA's contribution limits in 1974. Most self-funded candidates are challengers.

Was the *Davis* dissent correct in suggesting that no one was silenced by the Millionaire's Amendment? After all, challenger Davis was still free to spend his money. Is there some other problem with the state attempting to equalize the race by different contribution limits for different candidates? If *Davis* had been decided differently, what limits do you think would have existed on the ability of legislatures to create differing limits? Consider: "[W]e have long recognized the strength of an independent governmental interest in reducing both the influence of wealth on the outcomes of elections, and the appearance that wealth alone dictates those results." *Davis*, 554 U.S. at 755 (Stevens, *dissenting*).

7.   One longstanding feature of federal law, and many state laws, is a ban on political contributions by government contractors. Is such a complete ban overbroad, at least as applied to individuals who hold small research or consulting contracts with the government? *See Wagner v. Federal Election Commission*, 793 F.3d 1 (D.C. Cir. 2015) (upholding ban). The plaintiffs in the case were two consultants earning approximately $600/day when consulting with the government, and a researcher with a $12,000 piece work contract.

8.   Do special circumstances exist for other classes of persons that may justify bans on contributions? *See* 17 C.F.R. 275.206(4) (barring an investment adviser who makes a political contribution to an elected official in a position to influence the selection of the adviser for two years from providing any advisory services to the government for compensation, either directly or through a fund.).

9.   *McCutcheon v. FEC* is, as of publication of this volume, the Supreme Court's most recent foray into the question of contribution limits. For many years, the constitutionality of contribution limits seemed to be one of the more settled questions in campaign finance law. However, with the decisions in *Randall v. Sorrell* [p. 852] and *McCutcheon*, it is no longer clear that this is the case. Two justices — Scalia and Thomas — have clearly indicated their view that *Buckley* should be overruled on the question of contribution limits, and limits held unconstitutional. Justice Kennedy has not made that open statement, but reading his dissenting opinion in *Shrink Missouri Government PAC v. FEC* and his brief concurrence in *Randall*, as well as his opinions in the expenditure cases to follow, many observers believe he, too, would vote to overrule *Buckley*. Justice Alito has also suggested, in a concurrence in *Randall*, that he would be open to reconsidering *Buckley* in the right case. Meanwhile, Chief Justice Roberts wrote the plurality opinions in both *Randall* and *McCutcheon*. Are there possibly five votes to overturn *Buckley* on contribution limits?

Regardless of how you count the votes for possibly overruling *Buckley*, do you think *Buckley's* distinction between contributions and expenditures can be justified, or are they truly, as Chief Justice Burger said, "two sides of the same coin"? And if so, is the Court too easy on contribution limits, or too hard on expenditure limits? How rigorous should the Court be in its examination of campaign contribution limits? And, what, of course, is a sufficiently important state interest to overcome the language of the First Amendment, which is written in absolutist terms? As we turn now to the constitutional treatment of expenditure limits, you might keep these questions in mind. You might also consider whether, constitutional issues aside, it makes sense to maintain contribution limits in a world of unlimited expenditures. Do they serve a purpose when expenditures are unlimited? What do you think would be the effect of removing — or dramatically raising — contribution limits? Consider that 12 states have either no limits on contributions at all, or no general limits on the size of individual contributions in state races. Those states are Alabama, Indiana, Iowa, Mississippi, Missouri, Nebraska, North Dakota, Oregon, Pennsylvania, Texas, Utah, and Virginia. Are you prepared to say that those states are better or more poorly governed than other states? That corruption is more or less of a problem than in other states? Are there any particular patterns or common traits in those states that seem relevant?

D. LIMITATIONS ON EXPENDITURES

Recall that in *Buckley v. Valeo* [p. 799], the Supreme Court subjected limitations on expenditures to an apparently higher degree of scrutiny than it did contributions, and ultimately struck down limitations on total spending by candidates and political committees, on a candidate's expenditures on his or her own campaign, and on the amounts that could be spent by individuals or groups acting independently of a campaign. Before reading further, you may find it useful to review that section of the *Buckley* opinion.

Limitations on expenditures raise many of the same big picture issues as limitations on contributions: What role, if any, should the First Amendment leave for government to try to equalize political influence or campaign expenditures? What is meant by "corruption" and "the appearance of corruption"? To what extent can we trust government actors to make and enforce fair rules governing political participation? Does the legislature merit more than the usual deference from the judiciary, due to its "particular expertise" in the field, or less, due to its apparent self-interest? What should be the standard of review? What is the empirical effect of money in campaigns — does it "drown out" voices, or allow voices to be heard?

While these and many other questions cut across the regulation of both contributions and expenditures, and the constitutional analysis of those regulations, and while many cases discussed in this chapter involved both contribution and expenditure limits, we believe it is useful to separate the analysis. First, that has been the approach taken by the Court ever since *Buckley*. Second, understanding the distinction *Buckley* made between contributions and expenditures, and how that has shaped regulatory efforts, is crucial to understanding campaign finance law at a practical — and practitioner's — level. As you consider the cases that follow, ask yourself whether the Court's constitutional distinction between contributions and expenditures makes sense, and perhaps more importantly, why they might make sense to a Court that is often pulled in two very different directions. Note that in the cases in this section, the presumption is that the spending is independent of a candidate — that is, it is not done at the request of a candidate, or after conferring with the candidate about the expenditure, its message, audience, timing, etc. In Section [E], we will discuss such "coordinated" expenditures.

FEDERAL ELECTION COMMISSION v. NATIONAL CONSERVATIVE POLITICAL ACTION COMMITTEE
Supreme Court of the United States
470 U.S. 480, 105 S. Ct. 1459, 84 L. Ed. 2d 455 (1985)

JUSTICE REHNQUIST delivered the opinion of the Court [in the entirety of which CHIEF JUSTICE BURGER, JUSTICE BLACKMUN, JUSTICE POWELL, and JUSTICE O'CONNOR join, and in Part II of which JUSTICE BRENNAN and JUSTICE STEVENS join].

The Presidential Election Campaign Fund Act (Fund Act), 26 U.S.C. § 9001 *et seq.*, offers the Presidential candidates of major political parties the option of receiving public financing for their general election campaigns. If a Presidential candidate elects public financing, § 9012(f) makes it a criminal offense for independent "political committees," such as appellees National Conservative Political Action Committee (NCPAC) and Fund For A Conservative Majority (FCM), to expend more than $1,000 to further that candidate's election. * * *

II

NCPAC is a nonprofit, nonmembership corporation formed under the District of Columbia Nonprofit Corporation Act in August 1975 and registered with the FEC as a political committee. Its primary purpose is to attempt to influence directly or indirectly the election or defeat of candidates for federal, state, and local offices by making contributions and by making its own expenditures. * * *

Both NCPAC and FCM are self-described ideological organizations with a conservative political philosophy. They solicited funds in support of President Reagan's 1980 campaign, and they spent money on such means as radio and television advertisements to encourage voters to elect him President. On the record before us, these expenditures were "independent" in that they were not made at the request of or in coordination with the official Reagan election campaign committee or any of its agents. Indeed, there are indications that the efforts of these organizations were at times viewed with disfavor by the official campaign as counterproductive to its chosen strategy. NCPAC and FCM expressed their intention to conduct similar activities in support of President Reagan's reelection in 1984, and we may assume that they did so. * * *

There can be no doubt that the expenditures at issue in this case produce speech at the core of the First Amendment. * * * The PACs in this case, of course, are not lone pamphleteers or street corner orators in the Tom Paine mold; they spend substantial amounts of money in order to communicate their political ideas through sophisticated media advertisements. And of course the criminal sanction in question is applied to the expenditure of money to propagate political views, rather than to the propagation of those views unaccompanied by the expenditure of money. But for purposes of presenting political views in connection with a nationwide Presidential election, allowing the presentation of views while forbidding the expenditure of more than $1,000 to present them is much like allowing a speaker in a public hall to express his views while denying him the use of an amplifying system. * * *

We also reject the notion that the PACs' form of organization or method of solicitation diminishes their entitlement to First Amendment protection. The First Amendment freedom of association is squarely implicated in these cases. NCPAC and FCM are mechanisms by which large numbers of individuals of modest means can join together in organizations which serve to "[amplify] the voice of their adherents." *Buckley* v. *Valeo*, 424 U.S., at 22. It is significant that in 1979–1980 approximately 101,000 people contributed an average of $75 each to NCPAC and in 1980 approximately 100,000 people contributed an average of $25 each to FCM.

The FEC urges that these contributions do not constitute individual speech, but merely "speech by proxy," because the contributors do not control or decide upon the use of the funds by the PACs or the specific content of the PACs' advertisements and other speech. The plurality emphasized in that case, however, that nothing in the statutory provision in question "limits the amount [an unincorporated association] or any of its members may independently expend in order to advocate political views," but only the amount it may contribute to a multicandidate political committee. Unlike *California Medical Assn.* [v. *Federal Election Comm'n*, 453 U.S. 182 (1981)], the present cases involve limitations on expenditures by PACs, not on the contributions they receive; and in any event these contributions are predominantly small and thus do not raise the same concerns as the sizable contributions involved in *California Medical Assn.*

Another reason the "proxy speech" approach is not useful in this case is that the contributors obviously like the message they are hearing from these organizations and want to add their voices to that message; otherwise they would not part with their money. To say that their collective action in pooling their resources to amplify their voices is not entitled to full First Amendment protection would subordinate the voices of those of modest means as opposed to those sufficiently wealthy to be able to buy expensive media ads with their own resources.

* * *

In *Buckley* we struck down the FECA's limitation on individuals' independent expenditures because we found no tendency in such expenditures, uncoordinated with the candidate or his campaign, to corrupt or to give the appearance of corruption. For similar reasons, we also find § 9012(f)'s limitation on independent expenditures by political committees to be constitutionally infirm.

* * * It is contended that, because the PACs may by the breadth of their organizations spend larger amounts than the individuals in *Buckley*, the potential for corruption is greater. But precisely what the "corruption" may consist of we are never told with assurance. The fact that candidates and elected officials may alter or reaffirm their own positions on issues in response to political messages paid for by the PACs can hardly be called corruption, for one of the essential features of

democracy is the presentation to the electorate of varying points of view. It is of course hypothetically possible here, as in the case of the independent expenditures forbidden in *Buckley*, that candidates may take notice of and reward those responsible for PAC expenditures by giving official favors to the latter in exchange for the supporting messages. But here, as in *Buckley*, the absence of prearrangement and coordination undermines the value of the expenditure to the candidate, and thereby alleviates the danger that expenditures will be given as a *quid pro quo* for improper commitments from the candidate. On this record, such an exchange of political favors for uncoordinated expenditures remains a hypothetical possibility and nothing more. * * *

In the District Court, the FEC attempted to show actual corruption or the appearance of corruption by offering evidence of high-level appointments in the Reagan administration of persons connected with the PACs and newspaper articles and polls purportedly showing a public perception of corruption. The District Court excluded most of the proffered evidence as irrelevant to the critical elements to be proved: corruption of candidates or public perception of corruption of candidates. A tendency to demonstrate distrust of PACs is not sufficient. We * * * agree with the District Court that the evidence falls far short of being adequate [to show corruption or its appearance]. * * *

Here, * * * the groups and associations in question, designed expressly to participate in political debate, are quite different from the traditional corporations organized for economic gain. * * * § 9012(f) * * * indiscriminately lumps with corporations any "committee, association or organization." Indeed, the FEC in its briefs to this Court does not even make an effort to defend the statute under a construction limited in reach to corporations.

While in *NRWC* we held that the compelling governmental interest in preventing corruption supported the restriction of the influence of political war chests funneled through the corporate form, in the present cases we do not believe that a similar finding is supportable: when the First Amendment is involved, our standard of review is "rigorous," *Buckley* v. *Valeo*, 424 U.S., at 29, and the effort to link either corruption or the appearance of corruption to independent expenditures by PACs, whether large or small, simply does not pass this standard of review. Even assuming that Congress could fairly conclude that large-scale PACs have a sufficient tendency to corrupt, the overbreadth of § 9012(f) in these cases is so great that the section may not be upheld. We are not quibbling over fine-tuning of prophylactic limitations, but are concerned about wholesale restriction of clearly protected conduct. * * *

[*Affirmed.*]

[JUSTICE STEVENS's opinion concurring in part and dissenting in part briefly addresses a standing issue which we have omitted from the Court's opinion.]

JUSTICE WHITE * * *, dissenting. * * *

Today's holding * * * rests on [*Buckley's*] distinction between "independent" and "coordinated" expenditures. The Court was willing to accept that expenditures undertaken in consultation with a candidate or his committee should be viewed as contributions. But it rejected Congress' judgment that independent expenditures were matters of equal concern, concluding that they did not pose the danger of real or apparent corruption that supported limits on contributions. The distinction is not tenable. "Independent" PAC expenditures function as contributions. Indeed, a significant portion of them no doubt would be direct contributions to campaigns had the FECA not limited such contributions to $5,000. The growth of independent PAC spending has been a direct and openly acknowledged response to the contribution limits in the FECA. In general, then, the reasons underlying limits on contributions equally underly limits on such "independent" expenditures.

The credulous acceptance of the formal distinction between coordinated and independent expenditures blinks political reality. That the PACs' expenditures are not formally "coordinated" is too slender a reed on which to distinguish them from actual contributions to the campaign. The candidate cannot help but know of the extensive efforts "independently" undertaken on his behalf. In this realm of possible tacit understandings and implied agreements, I see no reason not to accept the congressional judgment that so-called independent expenditures must be closely regulated.

The PACs do not operate in an anonymous vacuum. There are significant contacts between an organization like NCPAC and candidates for, and holders of, public office. In addition, personnel may move between the staffs of candidates or officeholders and those of PACs. This is not to say that there has in the past been any improper coordination or political favors. We need not evaluate the accuracy of reports of such activities, or of the perception that large-scale independent PAC expenditures mean "the return of the big spenders whose money talks and whose gifts are not forgotten." *See* N.Y. Times, June 15, 1980, section 4, p. 20E, col. 1. It is enough to note that there is ample support for the congressional determination that the corrosive effects of large campaign contributions — not least among these a public perception of business as usual — are not eliminated solely because the "contribution" takes the form of an "independent expenditure." "Preserving the integrity of the electoral process [and] the individual citizen's confidence in government" "are interests of the highest importance." * * *

As in *Buckley*, I am convinced that it is pointless to limit the amount that can be contributed to a candidate or spent with his approval without also limiting the amounts that can be spent on his behalf.[9] In the Fund Act, Congress limited

---

[9] In a discussion with which I entirely agree, the Senate Committee supported the 1974 limits on "independent expenditures" as follows:

"[Such] controls are imperative if Congress is to enact meaningful limits on direct contributions. Otherwise, wealthy individuals limited to a $3,000 direct contribution could also purchase one hundred thousand dollars' worth of advertisements for a favored candidate. Such a loophole would render direct contribution limits virtually meaningless.

"Admittedly, expenditures made directly by an individual to urge support of a candidate pose First Amendment issues more vividly than do financial contributions to a campaign fund. Nevertheless, to prohibit a $60,000 direct contribution to be used for a TV spot commercial but then to permit the would-be contributor to purchase the time himself, and place a commercial endorsing the candidate, would exalt constitutional form over substance. Your Committee does not believe the First Amendment requires such a wooden construction." S. Rep. No. 93-689, pp. 18–19 (1974).

contributions, direct or coordinated, to zero. It is nonsensical to allow the purposes of this limitation to be entirely defeated by allowing the sort of "independent" expenditures at issue here, and the First Amendment does not require us to do so.
* * *

JUSTICE MARSHALL, dissenting.

* * *Although I joined the portion of the *Buckley per curiam* that distinguished contributions from independent expenditures for First Amendment purposes, I now believe that the distinction has no constitutional significance.

The contribution/expenditure distinction in *Buckley* was grounded on two factors. First, the Court reasoned that independent expenditures offer significantly less potential for abuse than contributions. * * *

Undoubtedly, when an individual interested in obtaining the proverbial ambassadorship had the option of either contributing directly to a candidate's campaign or doing so indirectly through independent expenditures, he gave money directly. It does not take great imagination, however, to see that, when the possibility for direct financial assistance is severely limited, as it is in light of *Buckley*'s decision to uphold the contribution limitation, such an individual will find other ways to financially benefit the candidate's campaign. It simply belies reality to say that a campaign will not reward massive financial assistance provided in the only way that is legally available. And the possibility of such a reward provides a powerful incentive to channel an independent expenditure into an area that a candidate will appreciate. Surely an eager supporter will be able to discern a candidate's needs and desires; similarly, a willing candidate will notice the supporter's efforts. To the extent that individuals are able to make independent expenditures as part of a *quid pro quo*, they succeed in undermining completely the first rationale for the distinction made in *Buckley*.

The second factor supporting the distinction between contributions and expenditures was the relative magnitude of the First Amendment interest at stake. The Court found that the constitutional interest implicated in the limitation on expenditures was the right to advocate the election or defeat of a particular candidate. This right, the Court reasoned, "is no less entitled to protection under the First Amendment than the discussion of political policy generally or advocacy of the passage or defeat of legislation." In contrast, the Court found that the limitation on contributions primarily implicated "the contributor's freedom of political association." Although the Court acknowledged that this right was a "fundamental" one, it concluded that the expenditure ceiling imposed significantly more severe restrictions on political freedoms than the contribution limitation.

I disagree that the limitations on contributions and expenditures have significantly different impacts on First Amendment freedoms. First, the underlying rights at issue — freedom of speech and freedom of association — are both core First Amendment rights. Second, in both cases the regulation is of the same form: It concerns the amount of money that can be spent for political activity. Thus, I do not see how one interest can be deemed more compelling than the other.

In summary, I am now unpersuaded by the distinction established in *Buckley*. I have come to believe that the limitations on independent expenditures challenged in that case and here are justified by the congressional interests in promoting "the reality and appearance of equal access to the political arena," and in eliminating political corruption and the appearance of such corruption. Therefore, I dissent * * *.

Notes and Questions

1.   Why was this case at the Court at all? Didn't *Buckley* decide this issue? *Buckley* struck down the general limitation on independent expenditures. NCPAC arises under a separate section of the law that limits independent expenditures when a presidential candidate has accepted government campaign subsidies from the Presidential Election Campaign Fund. The idea was that in return for a government campaign subsidy, the candidate could agree to restraints which might otherwise be unconstitutional. *See* Part F of this chapter, *infra*, [p 996]. It would seem odd, however, that the candidate, by his agreement to accept public funds, could bind other individuals and groups to surrender First Amendment rights. Still, it is somewhat surprising that neither the majority nor the dissent discuss the public financing aspect of the law.

2.   Is the debate between Justice White and the majority on the corrupting effect of independent expenditures largely empirical, or more a matter of law? The majority points to evidence that NCPAC's expenditures were looked upon with disfavor by the Reagan campaign as being inconsistent with the campaign's messaging strategy, and says that the lack of "prearrangement and coordination" reduces the opportunity for *quid pro quo* corruption. Justice White does not dispute the former, but would defer to Congressional judgment about the need to control the latter. But by not disputing the former, he seems to accept that at least some independent expenditures are unlikely to curry favor at all. And it is difficult to deny that the opportunities for corruption are fewer, and less certain, when the spenders and candidate do not coordinate their activities. After all, he does not deny the evidence that NCPAC's activities were viewed negatively by the Reagan campaign. At the same time, can the majority really deny with a straight face that "there is ample support for the congressional determination that the corrosive effects of large campaign contributions * * * are not eliminated solely because the "contribution" takes the form of an "independent expenditure"? Yet no one is suggesting that these determinations be made on a case by case basis depending on the particular record of each case. Would it be fair to say, then, that the two sides simply disagree as a legal matter on where to strike the balance between free speech and government's fears that this type of speech leads to corruption? Note as well their competing views of "corruption" and the majority's lack of concern that supporters of the victor might have been rewarded with government appointments.

3.   Justice Marshall suggests that "an eager supporter will be able to discern a candidate's needs and desires; similarly, a willing candidate will notice the supporter's efforts." Is that really corruption? If the possibility that a candidate, once elected, will reward his supporters is enough to limit an activity, is there any political activity that cannot be limited by the government? Isn't the reason people participate in politics because they expect to be rewarded, if only by enactment of

public policies that they favor? Should an officeholder be required to abandon the priorities of those who voted for him on the basis of his campaign platform?

In a recent study of campaign staff, candidates, and other political players, researchers found considerable frustration among campaign staff "at not being able to coordinate with the outside groups. For example, there was a common experience of being on the receiving end of an attack and wanting to respond with a particular message but lacking the resources. Meanwhile, an outside group wanting to support the campaign has the resources to respond but lacks the critical information or, from the campaign's perspective, gets the message wrong." DANIEL P. TOKAJI AND RENATA E.B. STRAUSE, THE NEW SOFT MONEY: OUTSIDE SPENDING IN CONGRESSIONAL ELECTIONS 64 (Election Law @ Moritz 2014). Respondents generally found it difficult to maximize efficiency with independent expenditures because of the lack of information. *Id. at* 62–68. Note also that federal law guarantees candidate expenditures the "lowest unit rate" from broadcasters. Independent spenders get no such favoritism, but must pay market rates. *See* 47 U.S.C. §315 (b).

4.   The potential negative ramifications of the majority's view are generally well known and often voiced: large independent expenditures; a fear that these expenditures warp the electoral process and ultimately public policy; a loss of public confidence in government; the possibility of official action being taken in gratitude for large independent expenditures, or the hope of future independent expenditures; and actual *quid pro quo* exchanges that are simply difficult to prove without an obvious "victim" to report the crime. Less discussed are the potential negative ramifications of the dissent. What are some of the ramifications of the dissent's view? Note that the limit on independent expenditures under FECA, as it stood before *Buckley*, was just $1,000. Does this effectively shut down most public participation in campaigns, except through direct financial support of the candidates? Justice White also would justify limits on independent expenditures because, even when the expenditure appears to be independent, "There are significant contacts between an organization like NCPAC and candidates for, and holders of, public office [and] personnel may move between the staffs of candidates or officeholders and those of PACs." Can citizens and the organizations they belong to really be forced to choose (or have the choice made for them by law) between contact with officeholders, and the right to speak and campaign for or against officeholders? What would such a political system look like? Under Justice Marshall's "equal access to the political arena" justification for limits, how would the government decide who had had enough access, and who needed more? Would there be limits on government's ability to try to reallocate political power by limiting the ability of some to speak? What might that regime look like? Can you anticipate "unanticipated" consequences?

5.   *NCPAC* was not the first post-*Buckley* decision to affirm *Buckley's* holding on spending limits. Previously, in *First National Bank of Boston v. Bellotti* [p. 895], the Supreme Court had upheld the right of a corporation to make expenditures in connection with a ballot issue.

In 1997, Vermont enacted Proposition 64, which included spending limitations. After a long, torturous journey through the lower courts, Proposition 64 reached the Supreme Court in 2006.

RANDALL v. SORRELL

Supreme Court of the United States

548 U.S. 230, 126 S. Ct. 2479, 165 L. Ed. 2d 482 (2006)

JUSTICE BREYER announced the judgment of the Court and delivered an opinion, in which THE CHIEF JUSTICE [ROBERTS] joins, and in which JUSTICE ALITO joins except as to Parts II-B-1 and II-B-2.

We here consider the constitutionality of a Vermont campaign finance statute that limits both * * * the amounts that candidates for state office may spend on their campaigns (expenditure limitations) * * *

II

We turn first to the Act's expenditure limits. Do those limits violate the *First Amendment's* free speech guarantees? * * *

B

1

The respondents recognize that, in respect to expenditure limits, *Buckley* appears to be a controlling — and unfavorable — precedent. They seek to overcome that precedent in two ways. First, they ask us in effect to overrule *Buckley*. Post-*Buckley* experience, they believe, has shown that contribution limits (and disclosure requirements) alone cannot effectively deter corruption or its appearance; hence experience has undermined an assumption underlying that case. Indeed, the respondents have devoted several pages of their briefs to attacking *Buckley*'s holding on expenditure limits.

Second, in the alternative, they ask us to limit the scope of *Buckley* significantly by distinguishing *Buckley* from the present case. They advance as a ground for distinction a justification for expenditure limitations that, they say, *Buckley* did not consider, namely, that such limits help to protect candidates from spending too much time raising money rather than devoting that time to campaigning among ordinary voters. We find neither argument persuasive.

2

The Court has often recognized the "fundamental importance" of *stare decisis*, the basic legal principle that commands judicial respect for a court's earlier decisions and the rules of law they embody. * * * [T]he rule of law demands that adhering to our prior case law be the norm. Departure from precedent is exceptional, and requires "special justification." * * * This is especially true where, as here, the principle has become settled through iteration and reiteration over a long period of time.

We can find here no such special justification that would require us to overrule

Buckley. Subsequent case law has not made *Buckley* a legal anomaly or otherwise undermined its basic legal principles. * * * We cannot find in the respondents' claims any demonstration that circumstances have changed so radically as to undermine *Buckley*'s critical factual assumptions. The respondents have not shown, for example, any dramatic increase in corruption or its appearance in Vermont; nor have they shown that expenditure limits are the only way to attack that problem. * * * At the same time, *Buckley* has promoted considerable reliance. Congress and state legislatures have used *Buckley* when drafting campaign finance laws. And, as we have said, this Court has followed *Buckley*, upholding and applying its reasoning in later cases. Overruling *Buckley* now would dramatically undermine this reliance on our settled precedent.

For all these reasons, we find this a case that fits the *stare decisis* norm. And we do not perceive the strong justification that would be necessary to warrant overruling so well established a precedent. We consequently decline the respondents' invitation to reconsider *Buckley*.

3

The respondents also ask us to distinguish these cases from *Buckley*. But we can find no significant basis for that distinction. Act 64's expenditure limits are not substantially different from those at issue in *Buckley*. In both instances the limits consist of a dollar cap imposed upon a candidate's expenditures. Nor is Vermont's primary justification for imposing its expenditure limits significantly different from Congress' rationale for the *Buckley* limits: preventing corruption and its appearance.

The sole basis on which the respondents seek to distinguish *Buckley* concerns a further supporting justification. They argue that expenditure limits are necessary in order to reduce the amount of time candidates must spend raising money. Increased campaign costs, together with the fear of a better-funded opponent, mean that, without expenditure limits, a candidate must spend too much time raising money instead of meeting the voters and engaging in public debate. *Buckley*, the respondents add, did not fully consider this justification. Had it done so, they say, the Court would have upheld, not struck down, FECA's expenditure limits.

In our view, it is highly unlikely that fuller consideration of this time protection rationale would have changed *Buckley*'s result. The *Buckley* Court was aware of the connection between expenditure limits and a reduction in fundraising time. In a section of the opinion dealing with FECA's public financing provisions, it wrote that Congress was trying to "free candidates from the rigors of fundraising." * * * The Court of Appeals' opinion and the briefs filed in this Court pointed out that a natural consequence of higher campaign expenditures was that "candidates were compelled to allow to fund raising increasing and extreme amounts of money and energy." *Buckley v. Valeo, 519 F.2d 821, 838 (CADC 1975)*. And, in any event, the connection between high campaign expenditures and increased fundraising demands seems perfectly obvious.

Under these circumstances, the respondents' argument amounts to no more than an invitation so to limit *Buckley*'s holding as effectively to overrule it. For the reasons set forth above, we decline that invitation as well. And, given *Buckley*'s continued authority, we must conclude that Act 64's expenditure limits violate the First Amendment. * * *

IV

We conclude that Act 64's expenditure limits violate the First Amendment as interpreted in *Buckley* v. *Valeo*. We also conclude that the specific details of Act 64's contribution limits require us to hold that those limits violate the First Amendment, for they burden First Amendment interests in a manner that is disproportionate to the public purposes they were enacted to advance. * * *

[Justice ALITO's opinion, concurring in part and concurring in the judgment, arguing that was not necessary to re-examine *Buckley* to decide the case, is omitted.]

[For Justice KENNEDY's opinion concurring in the judgment, see p. 860.]

[The opinion of Justice THOMAS, with whom Justice SCALIA joins, concurring in the judgment, is omitted]

JUSTICE STEVENS' dissenting

I am convinced that *Buckley*'s holding on expenditure limits is wrong, and that the time has come to overrule it.

I have not reached this conclusion lightly. As Justice Breyer correctly observes, *stare decisis* is a principle of " 'fundamental importance.' " But it is not an inexorable command, and several factors, taken together, provide special justification for revisiting the constitutionality of statutory limits on candidate expenditures.

To begin with, *Buckley*'s holding on expenditure limits itself upset a long-established practice. For the preceding 65 years, congressional races had been subject to statutory limits on both expenditures and contributions. See 37 Stat. 28; Federal Corrupt Practices Act of 1925, 43 Stat. 1073; Federal Election Campaign Finance Act of 1971, 86 Stat. 5; Federal Election Campaign Act Amendments of 1974, 88 Stat. 1263. * * * As the Court of Appeals had recognized in *Buckley v. Valeo*, 519 F.2d 821, 859 (CADC 1975) (en banc), our earlier jurisprudence provided solid support for treating these limits as permissible regulations of conduct rather than speech. * * * While *Buckley*'s holding on contribution limits was consistent with this backdrop, its holding on expenditure limits "involve[d] collision with a prior doctrine more embracing in its scope, intrinsically sounder, and verified by experience."

There are further reasons for reexamining *Buckley*'s holding on candidate expenditure limits that do not apply to its holding on candidate contribution limits. Although we have subsequently reiterated the line *Buckley* drew between these two types of limits, we have done so primarily in cases affirming the validity of contribution limits or their functional equivalents. * * * In contrast, these are our first post-*Buckley* cases that raise the constitutionality of expenditure limits on the amounts that candidates for office may spend on their own campaigns. * * *

As Justice White recognized, it is quite wrong to equate money and speech. *Buckley*, 424 U.S., at 263 (opinion concurring in part and dissenting in part). To the contrary:

> "The burden on actual speech imposed by limitations on the spending of money is minimal and indirect. All rights of direct political expression and advocacy are retained. Even under the campaign laws as originally enacted, everyone was free to spend as much as they chose to amplify their views on general political issues, just not specific candidates. The restrictions, to the extent they do affect speech, are viewpoint-neutral and indicate no hostility to the speech itself or its effects." *National Conservative Political Action Comm.*, 470 U.S., at 508–509 (White, J., dissenting).

Accordingly, these limits on expenditures are far more akin to time, place, and manner restrictions than to restrictions on the content of speech. Like Justice White, I would uphold them "so long as the purposes they serve are legitimate and sufficiently substantial."

Buckley's conclusion to the contrary relied on the following oft-quoted metaphor: "Being free to engage in unlimited political expression subject to a ceiling on expenditures is like being free to drive an automobile as far and as often as one desires on a single tank of gasoline."

But, of course, while a car cannot run without fuel, a candidate can speak without spending money. And while a car can only travel so many miles per gallon, there is no limit on the number of speeches or interviews a candidate may give on a limited budget. Moreover, provided that this budget is above a certain threshold, a candidate can exercise due care to ensure that her message reaches all voters. Just as a driver need not use a Hummer to reach her destination, so a candidate need not flood the airways with ceaseless sound-bites of trivial information in order to provide voters with reasons to support her.

Indeed, the examples of effective speech in the political arena that did not depend on any significant expenditure by the campaigner are legion. It was the content of William Jennings Bryan's comments on the "Cross of Gold" — and William McKinley's responses delivered from his front porch in Canton, Ohio — rather than any expenditure of money that appealed to their cost-free audiences. Neither Abraham Lincoln nor John F. Kennedy paid for the opportunity to engage in the debates with Stephen Douglas and Richard Nixon that may well have determined the outcomes of Presidential elections. When the seasoned campaigners who were Members of the Congress that endorsed the expenditure limits in the Federal Election Campaign Act Amendments of 1974 concluded that a modest budget would not preclude them from effectively communicating with the electorate, they necessarily rejected the *Buckley* metaphor.

These campaigners also identified significant government interests favoring the imposition of expenditure limits. Not only do these limits serve as an important complement to corruption-reducing contribution limits, * * * but they also "protect equal access to the political arena, [and] free candidates and their staffs from the interminable burden of fundraising." *Colorado Republican Federal Campaign Comm. v. Federal Election Comm'n*, 518 U.S. 604, 649–650 *(1996)* (Stevens, J., dissenting). These last two interests are particularly acute. When campaign costs are so high that only the rich have the reach to throw their hats into the ring, we fail "to protect the political process from undue influence of large aggregations of capital and to promote individual responsibility for democratic government." *Automobile Workers*. States have recognized this problem, but *Buckley*'s perceived ban on expenditure limits severely limits their options in dealing with it.

The interest in freeing candidates from the fundraising straitjacket is even more compelling. Without expenditure limits, fundraising devours the time and attention of political leaders, leaving them too busy to handle their public responsibilities effectively. That fact was well recognized by backers of the legislation reviewed in *Buckley*, by the Court of Appeals judges who voted to uphold the expenditure limitations in that statute, and by Justice White — who not incidentally had personal experience as an active participant in a Presidential campaign. * * * The validity of their judgment has surely been confirmed by the mountains of evidence that has been accumulated in recent years concerning the time that elected officials spend raising money for future campaigns and the adverse effect of fundraising on the performance of their official duties.

Additionally, there is no convincing evidence that these important interests favoring expenditure limits are fronts for incumbency protection. *Buckley*'s cursory suggestion to the contrary failed to take into account the mixed evidence before it on this issue. * * * And only by "permit[ting] States nationwide to experiment with these critically needed reforms" — as 18 States urge us to do--will we enable further research on how expenditure limits relate to our incumbent reelection rates.[4] In the meantime, a legislative judgment that "enough is enough" should command the greatest possible deference from judges interpreting a constitutional provision that, at best, has an indirect relationship to activity that affects the quantity — rather than the quality or the content — of repetitive speech in the marketplace of ideas. * * *

JUSTICE SOUTER, with whom JUSTICE GINSBURG joins, * * * dissenting.

We said in *Buckley* that "expenditure limitations impose far greater restraints on the freedom of speech and association than do . . . contribution limitations," but the *Buckley* Court did not categorically foreclose the possibility that some spending

---

[4] Indeed, the example of the city of Albuquerque suggests that concerns about incumbent entrenchment are unfounded. In 1974, the city set expenditure limits on municipal elections. A 2-year interlude aside, these limits applied until 2001, when they were successfully challenged by municipal candidates. *Homans v. Albuquerque*, 217 F. Supp. 2d 1197, aff'd, 366 F.3d 900 (CA10), cert. denied, 543 U.S. 1002 (2004). In its findings of fact, the Federal District Court determined that "[n]ationwide, eighty-eight percent (88%) of incumbent Mayors successfully sought reelection in 1999. In contrast, since 1974, the City has had a zero percent (0%) success rate for Mayors seeking reelection." 217 F. Supp. 2d, at 1200. The court further concluded that the "system of unlimited spending has deleterious effects on the competitiveness of elections because it gives incumbent candidates an electoral advantage." While far from conclusive, this example cuts against the view that there is a slam-dunk correlation between expenditure limits and incumbent advantage. See also Brief for Center for Democracy and Election Management at American University as *Amicus Curiae* (concluding that Canada, the United Kingdom, New Zealand, and Malta — all of which have campaign expenditure limits — have more electoral competition than the United States, Jamaica, Ireland, and Australia — all of which lack such limits).

limit might comport with the First Amendment. Instead, *Buckley* held that the constitutionality of an expenditure limitation "turns on whether the governmental interests advanced in its support satisfy the [applicable] exacting scrutiny." In applying that standard in *Buckley* itself, the Court gave no indication that it had given serious consideration to an aim that Vermont's statute now pursues: to alleviate the drain on candidates' and officials' time caused by the endless fundraising necessary to aggregate many small contributions to meet the opportunities for ever more expensive campaigning. * * *

The legislature's findings are surely significant enough to justify the Court of Appeals's remand to the District Court to decide whether Vermont's spending limits are the least restrictive means of accomplishing what the court unexceptionably found to be worthy objectives. * * *

Notes and Questions

1.   Act 64 was passed, in part, specifically "to provoke a test case to overrule *Buckley* with regard to expenditure limitations." *See Landell v. Sorrell*, 382 F. 3d 91, 156 (2002) (Winter, J. *dissenting*), *reversed sub nom. Randall v. Sorrell*. For a fuller explication of the "time protection rationale" offered by the state in support of spending limits, *see* Mark C. Alexander, *Let Them Do Their Jobs: The Compelling Government Interest in Protecting the Time of Candidates and Elected Officials*, 37 Loy. U. Chi. L. J. 669 (2006); Vincent Blasi, *Free Speech and the Widening Gyre of Fund-Raising: Why Campaign Spending Limits May Not Violate the First Amendment After All*, 94 Colum. L. Rev. 1281 (1994).

One author of this casebook has argued that the state's evidence in Randall was "a fraud." *See* Bradley A. Smith, *Fooling the Court*, ElectionLaw@Moritz, Mar. 1, 2006 (*available at* http://moritzlaw.osu.edu/electionlaw/etable06/060301-smith01.php) (noting that none of the Vermont lawmakers supporting the legislation either admitted to or identified any specific acts of corruption, and that the state's Attorney General admitted he had never prosecuted a politician for corruption in over a decade on the job; and further noting that Vermont's legislators earned $8,000 annually for their part-time service, while the average cost of running for the legislature was $4,000; assuming the part-time legislators have other sources of income, a typical legislator could fund his or her campaign using just one-quarter of his salary, and never spend any time fundraising.)

2.   After *Randall*, is *Buckley* "superprecedent?" *See* Allison R. Hayward, *The Per Curiam Opinion of Steel:* Buckley v. Valeo *as Superprecedent?: Clues from Wisconsin and Vermont*, 2005–06 Cato Sup. Ct. Rev. 195 (2006). Justice Breyer's plurality opinion devotes very little to rebutting the state's time protection argument, or arguments that contribution limits alone are insufficient to deter corruption or its appearance. Rather it deals with the question of spending limits primarily by clinging to precedent. Why do you think this is?

3.   In arguing for not disturbing the *Buckley* precedent on expenditure limitations, Justice Breyer suggests that states have relied on *Buckley* when drafting legislation. Does this argument make sense? Would you have encouraged, or expected, more states to follow Vermont's lead and pass laws in direct defiance of the

Court's constitutional ruling in *Buckley*? If the Court had reversed *Buckley* on expenditure limits, in what way would states have been harmed by their past reliance?

4. Justice Stevens' argument that "[f]or the preceding 65 years, congressional races had been subject to statutory limits on both expenditures and contributions. See 37 Stat. 28; Federal Corrupt Practices Act of 1925, 43 Stat. 1073" is misleading. As the Court of Appeals in *Buckley* noted, "In the only prosecution ever brought thereunder, ceilings were held unconstitutional as applied to primary elections, on the ground that a party primary was not a federal election. *Newberry v. United States*, 256 U.S. 232, 247, 258, 41 S. Ct. 469, 65 L. Ed. 913 (1921). * * * After *Newberry*, Congress acted to update federal election law, and enacted the Federal Corrupt Practices Act, which contained expenditure ceilings for general elections." *Buckley v. Valeo*, 519 F. 2d 821, 859 (D.C. Cir. 1975) (en banc). The statute was never challenged on First Amendment grounds, for obvious reasons:

> It applied only to contributions within the "knowledge" of the candidates, who naturally arranged matters so that they "knew" nothing — only finance committees and their treasurers "knew." This statute was totally ignored, and not a single prosecution was even attempted from its birth to repeal.

ROBERT E. DENTON, JR., POLITICAL COMMUNICATION ETHICS: AN OXYMORON 181 (2000). At the time of its repeal in 1971, the Corrupt Practices Act limited spending on Senate races to $25,000, and on House races to $5,000. Although spending in the 1970 election is difficult to determine because of the lack of effective reporting, in 1972 the median House race cost over $60,000. Gary C. Jacobson, *Partisanship, Money and Competition: Elections and the Transformation of Congress Since the 1970s*, in Lawrence C. Dodd and Bruce I. Oppenheimer, eds., CONGRESS RECONSIDERED 117, 127 (2013).

Justice Stevens also cites Williams McKinley as an example of "effective speech . . . that did not depend on any significant expenditure * * *." In fact, in inflation-adjusted dollars spent per votes cast, McKinley's 1896 campaign remains the most expensive in U.S. history. Seth Masket, *Spending on Presidential Elections*, Feb. 23, 2012, posted *at* http://enikrising.blogspot.com/2012/02/spending-on-presidential-elections.html#.T0bO8lmiw0U.twitter.

5. Justice Stevens argues that unlimited spending merely encourages "ceaseless sound-bites of trivial information." Compare Stevens' view to Justice Kennedy's in *Shrink PAC*: "a self-governing people depends upon the free exchange of political information." Do these differing views of the value of campaign speech explain the Court's divisions?

————

If general limits on expenditures are unconstitutional, may the characteristics of certain entities justify a limit or prohibition on expenditures by a particular class of speakers? And in particular, may corporate speech be limited?

The earliest state laws regulating campaign expenditures were prohibitions on corporate contributions passed in the 1890s. The first federal campaign finance law was the Tillman Act, passed in 1907 and named for its primary Senate sponsor, the fiery, controversial South Carolina Senator "Pitchfork" Ben Tillman. *See* Bradley A. Smith, Unfree Speech: The Folly of Campaign Finance Reform 23–24 (2001); Robert Mutch, Campaigns, Congresses and Courts: The Making of Federal Campaign Finance Law 2–6 (1988). Corporations soon learned, however, that they could escape the effects of the ban simply by making "expenditures" rather than "contributions." In 1947, Congress extended the ban to prohibit corporations (and unions) from using general treasury funds for campaign expenditures. Enforcement of these laws was lax, however, and they were readily circumvented in any case. Smith, *supra* at 24–30. The prohibition on corporate and union spending from general treasury funds was renewed as part of the 1974 amendments to FECA. 2 U.S.C. § 441b. However, even though several of the *Buckley* plaintiffs, such as the American Civil Liberties Union, were incorporated entities, and though *Buckley* struck down limits on expenditures, this anti-corporate provision was not explicitly challenged in *Buckley*.

As you read the following cases, consider the extent to which the debate is shaped not only by the principles of campaign finance, but by differing views of the role of corporations in American life and, indeed, the legal status of corporations. Are corporations "creatures of the state," imbued with special rights granted by the state and therefore subject to limitation by the state, or are they voluntary associations of individuals, whose legal protections are nothing less than the protections of individual rights of association, contract, property, and speech?

FIRST NATIONAL BANK OF BOSTON v. BELLOTTI
Supreme Court of the United States
435 U.S. 765, 98 S. Ct. 1407, 55 L. Ed. 2d 707 (1978)

Mr. Justice Powell delivered the opinion of the Court [in which Mr. Chief Justice Burger, Mr. Justice Stewart, Mr. Justice Blackmun, and Mr. Justice Stevens join]. * * *

The statute at issue, Mass. Gen. Laws Ann., ch. 55, § 8, prohibits appellants, two national banking associations and three business corporations, from making contributions or expenditures "for the purpose of . . . influencing or affecting the vote on any question submitted to the voters, other than one materially affecting any of the property, business or assets of the corporation." The statute further specifies that "[no] question submitted to the voters solely concerning the taxation of the income, property or transactions of individuals shall be deemed materially to affect the property, business or assets of the corporation." A corporation that violates § 8 may receive a maximum fine of $50,000; a corporate officer, director, or agent who violates the section may receive a maximum fine of $10,000 or imprisonment for up to one year, or both.

Appellants wanted to spend money to publicize their views on a proposed constitutional amendment that was to be submitted to the voters as a ballot question at a general election on November 2, 1976. The amendment would have permitted the legislature to impose a graduated tax on the income of individuals . . . . [Appellants] brought this action seeking to have the statute declared unconstitutional. [The Massachusetts Supreme Judicial Court upheld the statute.] * * *

The court below framed the principal question in this case as whether and to what extent corporations have First Amendment rights.[15] We believe that the court posed the wrong question. The Constitution often protects interests broader than those of the party seeking their vindication. The First Amendment, in particular, serves significant societal interests. The proper question therefore is not whether corporations "have" First Amendment rights and, if so, whether they are coextensive with those of natural persons. Instead, the question must be whether § 8 abridges expression that the First Amendment was meant to protect. We hold that it does. * * *

If the speakers here were not corporations, no one would suggest that the State could silence their proposed speech. [14] It is the type of speech indispensable to decisionmaking in a democracy, and this is no less true because the speech comes from a corporation rather than an individual. The inherent worth of the speech in terms of its capacity for informing the public does not depend upon the identity of its source, whether corporation, association, union, or individual. * * *

Yet appellee suggests that First Amendment rights generally have been afforded only to corporations engaged in the communications business or through which individuals express themselves, and the court below apparently accepted the "materially affecting" theory as the conceptual common denominator between appellee's position and the precedents of this Court. It is true that the "materially affecting" requirement would have been satisfied in the Court's decisions affording protection to the speech of media corporations and corporations otherwise in the business of communication or entertainment, and to the commercial speech of business corporations. * * * In such cases, the speech would be connected to the corporation's business almost by definition. But the effect on the business of the corporation was not the governing rationale in any of these decisions. None of them

---

[15] It has been settled for almost a century that corporations are persons within the meaning of the *Fourteenth Amendment. Santa Clara County v. Southern Pacific R. Co.*, 118 U.S. 394 (1886). [Relocated — Eds.].

[14] The Massachusetts court did not go so far as to accept appellee's argument that corporations, as creatures of the State, have only those rights granted them by the State. The court below recognized that such an extreme position could not be reconciled either with the many decisions holding state laws invalid under the *Fourteenth Amendment* when they infringe protected speech by corporate bodies, or with decisions affording corporations the protection of constitutional guarantees other than the First Amendment. * * *

In cases where corporate speech has been denied the shelter of the *First Amendment*, there is no suggestion that the reason was because a corporation rather than an individual or association was involved. Corporate identity has been determinative in several decisions denying corporations certain constitutional rights, such as the privilege against compulsory self-incrimination, or equality with individuals in the enjoyment of a right to privacy, but this is not because the States are free to define the rights of their creatures without constitutional limit. Otherwise, corporations could be denied the protection of all constitutional guarantees, including due process and the equal protection of the laws. Certain "purely personal" guarantees, such as the privilege against compulsory self-incrimination, are unavailable to corporations and other organizations because the "historic function" of the particular guarantee has been limited to the protection of individuals. Whether or not a particular guarantee is "purely personal" or is unavailable to corporations for some other reason depends on the nature, history, and purpose of the particular constitutional provision. [Relocated.— Eds.]

mentions, let alone attributes significance to, the fact that the subject of the challenged communication materially affected the corporation's business. * * *

Nor do our recent commercial speech cases lend support to appellee's business interest theory. They illustrate that the First Amendment goes beyond protection of the press and the self-expression of individuals to prohibit government from limiting the stock of information from which members of the public may draw. A commercial advertisement is constitutionally protected not so much because it pertains to the seller's business as because it furthers the societal interest in the "free flow of commercial information." * * * [20]

We thus find no support in the First or Fourteenth Amendment, or in the decisions of this Court, for the proposition that speech that otherwise would be within the protection of the First Amendment loses that protection simply because its source is a corporation that cannot prove, to the satisfaction of a court, a material effect on its business or property. * * *

Section 8 permits a corporation to communicate to the public its views on certain referendum subjects — those materially affecting its business — but not others. It also singles out one kind of ballot question — individual taxation — as a subject about which corporations may never make their ideas public. The legislature has drawn the line between permissible and impermissible speech according to whether there is a sufficient nexus, as defined by the legislature, between the issue presented to the voters and the business interests of the speaker.

In the realm of protected speech, the legislature is constitutionally disqualified from dictating the subjects about which persons may speak and the speakers who may address a public issue. * * * If a legislature may direct business corporations to "stick to business," it also may limit other corporations — religious, charitable, or civic — to their respective "business" when addressing the public. Such power in government to channel the expression of views is unacceptable under the First Amendment. [21] Especially where, as here, the legislature's suppression of speech suggests an attempt to give one side of a debatable public question an advantage in

---

[20] It is somewhat ironic that appellee seeks to reconcile these decisions with the "materially affecting" concept by noting that the commercial speaker would "have a direct financial interest in the speech." Until recently, the "purely commercial" nature of an advertisement was thought to undermine and even negate its entitlement to the sanctuary of the *First Amendment. Valentine v. Chrestensen, 316 U.S. 52 (1942);* * * * Appellee would invert the debate by giving constitutional significance to a corporation's "hawking of wares" while approving criminal sanctions for a bank's expression of opinion on a tax law of general public interest.

In emphasizing the societal interest and the fact that this Court's decisions have not turned on the effect upon the speaker's business interests, we do not say that such interests may not be relevant or important in a different context.

[21] Even assuming that the rationale behind the "materially affecting" requirement itself were unobjectionable, the limitation in § 8 would have an impermissibly restraining effect on protected speech. Much valuable information which a corporation might be able to provide would remain unpublished because corporate management would not be willing to risk the substantial criminal penalties — personal as well as corporate — provided for in § 8. * * * As the facts in this case illustrate, management never could be sure whether a court would disagree with its judgment as to the effect upon the corporation's business of a particular referendum issue. In addition, the burden and expense of litigating the issue — especially when what must be established is a complex and amorphous economic relationship

expressing its views to the people, [22] the First Amendment is plainly offended. Yet the State contends that its action is necessitated by governmental interests of the highest order. We next consider these asserted interests.

* * * Especially where, as here, a prohibition is directed at speech itself, and the speech is intimately related to the process of governing, "the State may prevail only upon showing a subordinating interest which is compelling," * * * "and the burden is on the government to show the existence of such an interest." * * * Even then, the State must employ means "closely drawn to avoid unnecessary abridgment . . . ." * * *

Appellee * * * advances two principal justifications for the prohibition of corporate speech. The first is the State's interest in sustaining the active role of the individual citizen in the electoral process and thereby preventing diminution of the citizen's confidence in government. The second is the interest in protecting the rights of shareholders whose views differ from those expressed by management on behalf of the corporation. However weighty these interests may be in the context of partisan candidate elections,[26] they either are not implicated in this case or are not served at all, or in other than a random manner, by the prohibition in § 8.

Preserving the integrity of the electoral process, preventing corruption, and "[sustaining] the active, alert responsibility of the individual citizen in a democracy for the wise conduct of government" are interests of the highest importance. * * * Preservation of the individual citizen's confidence in government is equally important. * * *

Appellee advances a number of arguments in support of his view that these interests are endangered by corporate participation in discussion of a referendum issue. They hinge upon the assumption that such participation would exert an undue

---

— would unduly impinge on the exercise of the constitutional right. "[The] free dissemination of ideas [might] be the loser." * * *

[22] * * * Our observation about the apparent purpose of the Massachusetts Legislature is not an endorsement of the legislature's factual assumptions about the views of corporations. We know of no documentation of the notion that corporations are likely to share a monolithic view on an issue such as the adoption of a graduated personal income tax. Corporations, like individuals or groups, are not homogeneous. They range from great multinational enterprises whose stock is publicly held and traded to medium-size public companies and to those that are closely held and controlled by an individual or family. It is arguable that small or medium-size corporations might welcome imposition of a graduated personal income tax that might shift a greater share of the tax burden onto wealthy individuals.

[26] * * * Appellants do not challenge the constitutionality of laws prohibiting or limiting corporate contributions to political candidates or committees, or other means of influencing candidate elections. * * *

The overriding concern behind the enactment of statutes such as the Federal Corrupt Practices Act was the problem of corruption of elected representatives through the creation of political debts. See *United States v. Automobile Workers*, [352 U.S. 567], 570–575 [(1957)] [p. 789]. The importance of the governmental interest in preventing this occurrence has never been doubted. The case before us presents no comparable problem, and our consideration of a corporation's right to speak on issues of general public interest implies no comparable right in the quite different context of participation in a political campaign for election to public office. Congress might well be able to demonstrate the existence of a danger of real or apparent corruption in independent expenditures by corporations to influence candidate elections. Cf. *Buckley v. Valeo, supra*; Comment, The Regulation of Union Political Activity: Majority and Minority Rights and Remedies, 126 U. Pa. L. Rev. 386, 408–410 (1977).

influence on the outcome of a referendum vote, and — in the end — destroy the confidence of the people in the democratic process and the integrity of government. According to appellee, corporations are wealthy and powerful and their views may drown out other points of view. If appellee's arguments were supported by record or legislative findings that corporate advocacy threatened imminently to undermine democratic processes, thereby denigrating rather than serving First Amendment interests, these arguments would merit our consideration. Cf. *Red Lion Broadcasting Co. v. FCC*, 395 U.S. 367 (1969) [p. 605]. But there has been no showing that the relative voice of corporations has been overwhelming or even significant in influencing referenda in Massachusetts, [28] or that there has been any threat to the confidence of the citizenry in government.

Nor are appellee's arguments inherently persuasive or supported by the precedents of this Court. Referenda are held on issues, not candidates for public office. The risk of corruption perceived in cases involving candidate elections, *supra* simply is not present in a popular vote on a public issue.[29] To be sure, corporate advertising may influence the outcome of the vote; this would be its purpose. But the fact that advocacy may persuade the electorate is hardly a reason to suppress it: The Constitution "protects expression which is eloquent no less than that which is unconvincing." * * * We noted only recently that "the concept that government may restrict the speech of some elements of our society in order to enhance the relative voice of others is wholly foreign to the First Amendment . . . ." *Buckley* [*v. Valeo*], 424 U.S. [1], 48–49 [(1976)].[30] Moreover, the people in our democracy are entrusted with the responsibility for judging and evaluating the relative merits of conflicting

---

[28] In his dissenting opinion, MR. JUSTICE WHITE relies on incomplete facts with respect to expenditures in the 1972 referendum election, in support of his perception as to the "domination of the electoral process by corporate wealth." The record shows only the extent of corporate and individual contributions to the two committees that were organized to support and oppose, respectively, the constitutional amendment. * * * The dissenting opinion makes no reference to the fact that amounts of money expended independently of organized committees need not be reported under Massachusetts law, and therefore remain unknown.

Even if viewed as material, any inference that corporate contributions "dominated" the electoral process on this issue is refuted by the 1976 election. There the voters again rejected the proposed constitutional amendment even in the absence of any corporate spending, which had been forbidden by the decision below.

[29] * * * Appellee contends that the State's interest in sustaining the active role of the individual citizen is especially great with respect to referenda because they involve the direct participation of the people in the lawmaking process. But far from inviting greater restriction of speech, the direct participation of the people in a referendum, if anything, increases the need for " 'the widest possible dissemination of information from diverse and antagonistic sources.' "

[30] MR. JUSTICE WHITE argues, without support in the record, that because corporations are given certain privileges by law they are able to "amass wealth" and then to "dominate" debate on an issue. He concludes from this generalization that the State has a subordinating interest in denying corporations access to debate and, correspondingly, in denying the public access to corporate views. The potential impact of this argument, especially on the news media, is unsettling. One might argue with comparable logic that the State may control the volume of expression by the wealthier, more powerful corporate members of the press in order to "enhance the relative voices" of smaller and less influential members.

Except in the special context of limited access to the channels of communication, see *Red Lion Broadcasting Co.* v. *FCC*, this concept contradicts basic tenets of First Amendment jurisprudence. We rejected a similar notion in *Miami Herald Publishing Co.* v. *Tornillo*, 418 U.S. 241 (1974) [p. 613].

arguments.[31] They may consider, in making their judgment, the source and credibility of the advocate.[32] But if there be any danger that the people cannot evaluate the information and arguments advanced by appellants, it is a danger contemplated by the Framers of the First Amendment. * * * In sum, "[a] restriction so destructive of the right of public discussion [as § 8], without greater or more imminent danger to the public interest than existed in this case, is incompatible with the freedoms secured by the First Amendment." *Thomas v. Collins*, 323 U.S. 516 (1945).

B

Finally, appellee argues that § 8 protects corporate shareholders, an interest that is both legitimate and traditionally within the province of state law. *Cort v. Ash*, 422 U.S. 66, 82–84 (1975). The statute is said to serve this interest by preventing the use of corporate resources in furtherance of views with which some shareholders may disagree. This purpose is belied, however, by the provisions of the statute, which are both underinclusive and overinclusive.

The underinclusiveness of the statute is self-evident. Corporate expenditures with respect to a referendum are prohibited, while corporate activity with respect to the passage or defeat of legislation is permitted, *supra*, even though corporations may engage in lobbying more often than they take positions on ballot questions submitted to the voters. Nor does § 8 prohibit a corporation from expressing its views, by the expenditure of corporate funds, on any public issue until it becomes the subject of a referendum, though the displeasure of disapproving shareholders is unlikely to be any less.

The fact that a particular kind of ballot question has been singled out for special treatment undermines the likelihood of a genuine state interest in protecting shareholders. It suggests instead that the legislature may have been concerned with silencing corporations on a particular subject. * * *

Nor is the fact that § 8 is limited to banks and business corporations without relevance. Excluded from its provisions and criminal sanctions are entities or organized groups in which numbers of persons may hold an interest or membership, and which often have resources comparable to those of large corporations. Minorities in such groups or entities may have interests with respect to institutional speech quite comparable to those of minority shareholders in a corporation. Thus the exclusion of Massachusetts business trusts, real estate investment trusts, labor unions, and other associations undermines the plausibility of the State's purported

---

[31] * * * The State's paternalism evidenced by this statute is illustrated by the fact that Massachusetts does not prohibit lobbying by corporations, which are free to exert as much influence on the people's representatives as their resources and inclinations permit. * * * If the First Amendment protects the right of corporations to petition legislative and administrative bodies, see *California Motor Transp. Co. v. Trucking Unlimited*, 404 U.S. 508–510–511 (1972); *Eastern Railroad Presidents Conf. v. Noerr Motor Freight, Inc.*, 365 U.S. 127, 137–138 (1961), there hardly can be less reason for allowing corporate views to be presented openly to the people when they are to take action in their sovereign capacity.

[32] Corporate advertising, unlike some methods of participation in political campaigns, is likely to be highly visible. Identification of the source of advertising may be required as a means of disclosure, so that the people will be able to evaluate the arguments to which they are being subjected. * * *

concern for the persons who happen to be shareholders in the banks and corporations covered by § 8.

The overinclusiveness of the statute is demonstrated by the fact that § 8 would prohibit a corporation from supporting or opposing a referendum proposal even if its shareholders unanimously authorized the contribution or expenditure. Ultimately shareholders may decide, through the procedures of corporate democracy, whether their corporation should engage in debate on public issues.[34] Acting through their power to elect the board of directors or to insist upon protective provisions in the corporation's charter, shareholders normally are presumed competent to protect their own interests. In addition to intracorporate remedies, minority shareholders generally have access to the judicial remedy of a derivative suit to challenge corporate disbursements alleged to have been made for improper corporate purposes or merely to further the personal interests of management.

Assuming, *arguendo*, that protection of shareholders is a "compelling" interest under the circumstances of this case, we find "no substantially relevant correlation between the governmental interest asserted and the State's effort" to prohibit appellants from speaking. * * *

V

Because that portion of § 8 challenged by appellants prohibits protected speech in a manner unjustified by a compelling state interest, it must be invalidated. The judgment of the Supreme Judicial Court is

Reversed.

---

[34] Appellee does not explain why the dissenting shareholder's wishes are entitled to such greater solicitude in this context than in many others where equally important and controversial corporate decisions are made by management or by a predetermined percentage of the shareholders. Mr. Justice White's repeatedly expressed concern for corporate shareholders who may be "coerced" into supporting "causes with which they disagree" apparently is not shared by appellants' shareholders. Not a single shareholder has joined appellee in defending the Massachusetts statute or, so far as the record shows, has interposed any objection to the right asserted by the corporations to make the proscribed expenditures. * * *

The dissent of Mr. Justice White relies heavily on *Abood v. Detroit Board of Education*, 431 U.S. 209 (1977), and *Machinists v. Street*, 367 U.S. 740 (1961). These decisions involved the First Amendment rights of employees in closed or agency shops not to be compelled, as a condition of employment, to support with financial contributions the political activities of other union members with which the dissenters disagreed.

Street and *Abood* are irrelevant to the question presented in this case. In those cases employees were required, either by state law or by agreement between the employer and the union, to pay dues or a "service fee" to the exclusive bargaining representative. To the extent that these funds were used by the union in furtherance of political goals, unrelated to collective bargaining, they were held to be unconstitutional because they compelled the dissenting union member " 'to furnish contributions of money for the propagation of opinions which he disbelieves . . . .' " *Abood, supra,* (Thomas Jefferson as quoted in I. Brant, James Madison: The Nationalist 354 (1948)).

The critical distinction here is that no shareholder has been "compelled" to contribute anything. Apart from the fact, noted by the dissent, that compulsion by the State is wholly absent, the shareholder invests in a corporation of his own volition and is free to withdraw his investment at any time and for any reason. * * *

MR. CHIEF JUSTICE BURGER, concurring. * * *

A disquieting aspect of Massachusetts' position is that it may carry the risk of impinging on the First Amendment rights of those who employ the corporate form — as most do — to carry on the business of mass communications, particularly the large media conglomerates. * * *

In terms of "unfair advantage in the political process" and "corporate domination of the electoral process," it could be argued that such media conglomerates * * * pose a much more realistic threat to valid interests than do appellants and similar entities not regularly concerned with shaping popular opinion on public issues. * * *

In terms of Massachusetts' other concern, the interests of minority shareholders, I perceive no basis for saying that the managers and directors of the media conglomerates are more or less sensitive to the views and desires of minority shareholders than are corporate officers generally. * * * Thus, no factual distinction has been identified as yet that would justify government restraints on the right of appellants to express their views without, at the same time, opening the door to similar restraints on media conglomerates with their vastly greater influence. * * *

Because the First Amendment was meant to guarantee freedom to express and communicate ideas, I can see no difference between the right of those who seek to disseminate ideas by way of a newspaper and those who give lectures or speeches and seek to enlarge the audience by publication and wide dissemination. "[T]he purpose of the Constitution was not to erect the press into a privileged institution but to protect all persons in their right to print what they will as well as to utter it. ' . . . the liberty of the press is no greater and no less . . . ' than the liberty of every citizen of the Republic." *Pennekamp v. Florida*, 328 U.S. 331, 364, 66 S. Ct. 1029, 1046, 90 L. Ed. 1295 (1946) (Frankfurter, J., concurring).

In short, the First Amendment does not "belong" to any definable category of persons or entities: It belongs to all who exercise its freedoms.

MR. JUSTICE WHITE, with whom MR. JUSTICE BRENNAN and MR. JUSTICE MARSHALL join, dissenting. * * *

By holding that Massachusetts may not prohibit corporate expenditures or contributions made in connection with referenda involving issues having no material connection with the corporate business, the Court not only invalidates a statute which has been on the books in one form or another for many years, but also casts considerable doubt upon the constitutionality of legislation passed by some 31 States restricting corporate political activity, as well as upon the Federal Corrupt Practices Act.

There is now little doubt that corporate communications come within the scope of the First Amendment. This, however, is merely the starting point of analysis, because an examination of the First Amendment values that corporate expression furthers and the threat to the functioning of a free society it is capable of posing reveals that it is not fungible with communications emanating from individuals and is subject to restrictions which individual expression is not. Indeed, what some have considered to be the principal function of the First Amendment, the use of communication as a means of self-expression, self-realization, and self-fulfillment, is not at all furthered by corporate speech. * * * Undoubtedly, as this Court has recognized, *NAACP v. Button,* 371 U.S. 415 (1963), there are some corporations formed for the express purpose of advancing certain ideological causes shared by all their members, or, as in the case of the press, of disseminating information and ideas. Under such circumstances, association in a corporate form may be viewed as merely a means of achieving effective self-expression. But this is hardly the case generally with corporations operated for the purpose of making profits. Shareholders in such entities do not share a common set of political or social views, and they certainly have not invested their money for the purpose of advancing political or social causes or in an enterprise engaged in the business of disseminating news and opinion. * * *

Thus when a profitmaking corporation contributes to a political candidate this does not further the self-expression or self-fulfillment of its shareholders in the way that expenditures from them as individuals would.[6]

The self-expression of the communicator is not the only value encompassed by the First Amendment. One of its functions, often referred to as the right to hear or receive information, is to protect the interchange of ideas. Any communication of ideas, and consequently any expenditure of funds which makes the communication of ideas possible, it can be argued, furthers the purposes of the First Amendment. This proposition does not establish, however, that the right of the general public to receive communications financed by means of corporate expenditures is of the same dimension as that to hear other forms of expression. * * * [C]orporate expenditures designed to further political causes lack the connection with individual self-expression which is one of the principal justifications for the constitutional protection of speech provided by the First Amendment. Ideas which are not a product of individual choice are entitled to less First Amendment protection. Secondly, the restriction of corporate speech concerned with political matters impinges much less severely upon the availability of ideas to the general public than do restrictions upon individual speech. Even the complete curtailment of corporate communications concerning political or ideological questions not integral to day-to-day business functions would leave individuals, including corporate shareholders, employees, and customers, free to communicate their thoughts. Moreover, it is unlikely that any significant communication would be lost by such a prohibition. These individuals would remain perfectly free to communicate any ideas which could be conveyed by means of the corporate form. Indeed, such individuals could even form associations for the very purpose of promoting political or ideological causes. * * *

It bears emphasis here that the Massachusetts statute forbids the expenditure of corporate funds in connection with referenda but in no way forbids the board of

---

[6] This distinguishes the regulation of corporate speech from the limitations upon individual political campaign expenditures invalidated in *Buckley v. Valeo.* The Court there struck down the limitations upon individual expenditures because they impermissibly restricted the right of individuals to speak their minds and make their views known. At the same time, however, the Court sustained limitations upon political contributions on the ground that such provisions entail a much lesser restriction upon the individual's ability to engage in free communication than expenditure restrictions. In the case of corporate political activities, we are not at all concerned with the self-expression of the communicator.

directors of a corporation from formulating and making public what it represents as the views of the corporation even though the subject addressed has no material effect whatsoever on the business of the corporation. These views could be publicized at the individual expense of the officers, directors, stockholders, or anyone else interested in circulating the corporate view on matters irrelevant to its business. * * *

The Court's opinion appears to recognize at least the possibility that fear of corporate domination of the electoral process would justify restrictions upon corporate expenditures and contributions in connection with referenda but brushes this interest aside by asserting that "there has been no showing that the relative voice of corporations has been overwhelming or even significant in influencing referenda in Massachusetts," and by suggesting that the statute in issue represents an attempt to give an unfair advantage to those who hold views in opposition to positions which would otherwise be financed by corporations. It fails even to allude to the fact, however, that Massachusetts' most recent experience with unrestrained corporate expenditures in connection with ballot questions establishes precisely the contrary. In 1972, a proposed amendment to the Massachusetts Constitution which would have authorized the imposition of a graduated income tax on both individuals and corporations was put to the voters. The Committee for Jobs and Government Economy, an organized political committee, raised and expended approximately $120,000 to oppose the proposed amendment, the bulk of it raised through large corporate contributions. Three of the present appellant corporations each contributed $3,000 to this committee. In contrast, the Coalition for Tax Reform, Inc., the only political committee organized to support the 1972 amendment, was able to raise and expend only approximately $7,000. Perhaps these figures reflect the Court's view of the appropriate role which corporations should play in the Massachusetts electoral process, but it nowhere explains why it is entitled to substitute its judgment for that of Massachusetts and other States,[11] as well as the United States, which have acted to correct or prevent similar domination of the electoral process by corporate wealth. * * *

There is an additional overriding interest related to the prevention of corporate domination which is substantially advanced by Massachusetts' restrictions upon corporate contributions: assuring that shareholders are not compelled to support and financially further beliefs with which they disagree where, as is the case here, the issue involved does not materially affect the business, property, or other affairs of the corporation. * * *

* * * In most contexts, of course, the views of the dissenting shareholder have little, if any, First Amendment significance. By purchasing interests in corporations shareholders accept the fact that corporations are going to make decisions

---

[11] California had the same experience in connection with a 1976 referendum measure which would have required legislative approval of nuclear generating plant sites. Two hundred and three corporations contributed approximately $2,530,000 in opposition to the amendment, which was defeated. Supporters of the measure collected altogether only approximately $1,600,000. California Fair Political Practices Comm'n, Campaign Contribution and Spending Report — June 8, 1976, Primary Election 289–298. Later in the same year a similar initiative measure was placed on the ballot in Montana. Corporations contributed approximately $144,000 in opposition to the measure, while its supporters were able to collect only $451. This measure was also defeated. Brief for State of Montana as *Amicus Curiae*.

concerning matters such as advertising integrally related to their business operations according to the procedures set forth in their charters and bylaws. Otherwise, corporations could not function. First Amendment concerns of stockholders are directly implicated, however, when a corporation chooses to use its privileged status to finance ideological crusades which are unconnected with the corporate business or property and which some shareholders might not wish to support. * * *

I would affirm the judgment of the Supreme Judicial Court for the Commonwealth of Massachusetts.

JUSTICE REHNQUIST, dissenting.* * *

A State grants to a business corporation the blessings of potentially perpetual life and limited liability to enhance its efficiency as an economic entity. It might reasonably be concluded that those properties, so beneficial in the economic sphere, pose special dangers in the political sphere. Furthermore, it might be argued that liberties of political expression are not at all necessary to effectuate the purposes for which States permit commercial corporations to exist. So long as the Judicial Branches of the State and Federal Governments remain open to protect the corporation's interest in its property, it has no need, though it may have the desire, to petition the political branches for similar protection. Indeed, the States might reasonably fear that the corporation would use its economic power to obtain further benefits beyond those already bestowed. I would think that any particular form of organization upon which the State confers special privileges or immunities different from those of natural persons would be subject to like regulation, whether the organization is a labor union, a partnership, a trade association, or a corporation.

One need not adopt such a restrictive view of the political liberties of business corporations to affirm the judgment of the Supreme Judicial Court in this case. * * * I can see no basis for concluding that the liberty of a corporation to engage in political activity with regard to matters having no material effect on its business is necessarily incidental to the purposes for which the Commonwealth permitted these corporations to be organized or admitted within its boundaries.

I would affirm the judgment of the Supreme Judicial Court.

Notes and Questions

1.   Do corporations have First Amendment rights? *Bellotti* argues that that is not the proper question; rather, it focuses on the public's right to hear, perhaps in an effort to avoid abstract questions of corporate personhood and First Amendment rights (*but see* fn. 15). What individuals have a right to hear cannot be denied them simply due to the identity of the speaker. This reasoning has been criticized: after all, the people of Massachusetts, through their legislature, decided they did not wish to hear from corporations. Carl E. Schneider, *Free Speech and Corporate Freedom: A Comment on First National Bank of Boston v. Bellotti*, 59 So. CAL. L. REV. 1227, 1235 (1986). But the constitution protects minority rights — even if only a minority of Massachusetts citizens want to hear from corporations, are they not entitled, under the First Amendment, to do so? Does it matter if the Courts focus on the speakers or the listeners?

2. Justice White suggests if corporate speech were prohibited, the individual shareholders, employees, and customers "could even form associations for the very purpose of promoting political or ideological causes." Suppose that the shareholders of a corporation agreed that the income tax proposal opposed by First National Bank was, indeed, a bad idea, because it was bad for their investments in the Bank. If they joined together, how might they organize? Might they form a corporation? A great many, if not most, political advocacy groups are incorporated. Should that be prohibited? If not, why force the First National Bank shareholders to form a second corporation to speak about the public policies that might affect their original corporation?

Justice White also suggests that the board of directors of a corporation could endorse a view and publicize it at their individual expense. Suppose that a state has placed on a ballot an initiative that a corporation's directors have concluded will cost the corporation $400 million over 10 years. They wish to spend $200,000 to try to defeat the initiative. Is that a good use of corporate funds? Is it realistic to ask the corporate president to pay that personally? If it were the rule that officers and directors had to pay for political advocacy to benefit the corporation from their personal funds, won't such anticipated expenses simply be included in future compensation packages?

3. Justices White and Burger engage in a lively debate over the meaning of the press, a discussion that has been highly truncated in the edited opinions above. Most newspapers and other publishers are incorporated, of course, and would therefore be covered by laws limiting corporate speech without the "press exemption" provided in the law. But what constitutes "the press." Justice Burger says it is an activity — publishing. Justice White believes it is an entity or trade — newspapers, broadcasters, etc. Under the latter view, would the press exemption apply to regularly published newsletters? *Cf. Phillips Publishing v. Federal Election Commission*, 517 F. Supp. 1308 (D.D.C. 1981). In 2004, the National Rifle Association launched its own satellite radio station, "NRA News," specifically to take advantage of the exemption for the press. Many overtly political magazines are published with little intent to ever make a profit, and are subsidized by wealthy individuals, foundations (which sometimes accept corporate contributions), or corporations. Would the exemption extend to a book or movie published or produced by a pro-life or pro-choice organization? *See* Bradley A. Smith, *The John Roberts Salvage Company: After* McConnell, *A New Court Looks to Repair the Constitution*, 68 OHIO ST. L. J. 891, 895–899 (2007). Does the exemption for press cover activities outside of direct publication, such as paid advertising by the publisher about the publication? *See Readers Digest Association v. Federal Election Commission*, 509 F. Supp. 1210 (S.D.N.Y. 1981). Read the language of the federal press exemption at 52 U.S.C. § 30101(9)(B)(i). Does it cover books and movies? If not, would the Constitution require it to do so? *See* Federal Election Commission, Advisory Op. 2004-30 (Citizens United) (Sept. 9, 2004) (Concurring Opinion of Commissioner Smith). Note that the Supreme Court has never held that the institutional press is constitutionally entitled to protections not available to all citizens wishing to publish their views.

4. At the core of *Bellotti* is *Buckley's* rejection of the equality rationale for limiting campaign spending. If advertising affects election results, "that would be

its purpose." If some have more money than others, and thus more opportunity to make their arguments, it is up to the voters to sort things out. Yet the Court makes this endorsement of *Buckley* only after a head fake towards the equality rationale — citing *Red Lion Broadcasting Co. v. FCC*, 395 U.S. 367 (1969), the Court suggests equality arguments would, "merit our consideration" if supported by legislative or record findings. The Court then seems to suggest that in ballot initiatives, where there is no candidate to be corrupted, there can never be a compelling state interest in limiting spending, by corporations or others. *Bellotti's* bottom line is that a state may not limit spending in ballot initiatives. But it also suggests that corporate speech is and should be protected beyond ballot initiatives, if not because of the rights of the corporation, then at least because of the rights of listeners to hear different points of view.

5. Though *Bellotti* seemed to settle the question of corporate spending on ballot initiatives, are there different compelling reasons that might justify limits on corporate (and union) independent expenditures in candidate races? The federal government instituted a prohibition on corporate expenditures in candidates races in 1947, and at the beginning of 2010, twenty-three states also had bans on corporate spending in candidate races. National Conference of State Legislatures, *Life After Citizens United*, Jan. 28, 2010 (*available at* http://www.ncsl.org/default. aspx?tabid=19607).

In *Federal Election Commission v. Massachusetts Citizens for Life, Inc.*, 479 U.S. 238 (1986) (*MCFL*), the Supreme Court held that the prohibition on corporate political expenditures was unconstitutional as applied to MCFL, a small, non-profit corporation. The Court stressed three features "essential to our holding": 1) the corporation was formed to promote political ideas, and did not engage in business activities; 2) it had no shareholders or others with a claim on its earnings; and 3) it was not established by another corporation, and accepted no corporate funds. Does the criteria in *MCFL* suggests that it is not the corporate form itself that should cause worry, but rather the type of corporation? After all, MCFL is very different from Exxon. Would a rule based along the lines of the Court's *MCFL* criteria be more effective at promoting the aims of campaign finance regulation and the First Amendment?

The next three cases address the question of corporate expenditures in a much broader context than did *MCFL*.

AUSTIN v. MICHIGAN STATE CHAMBER OF COMMERCE
Supreme Court of the United States
494 U.S. 652, 110 S. Ct. 1391, 108 L. Ed. 2d 652 (1990)

Justice Marshall delivered the opinion of the Court. * * *

Section 54(1) of the Michigan Campaign Finance Act prohibits corporations from making * * * independent expenditures in connection with state candidate elections. * * * The Act exempts from this general prohibition against corporate political spending any expenditure made from a segregated fund. A corporation may solicit contributions to its political fund only from an enumerated list of persons associated with the corporation. * * *

In June 1985 Michigan scheduled a special election to fill a vacancy in the Michigan House of Representatives. Although the Chamber had established and funded a separate political fund, it sought to use its general treasury funds to place in a local newspaper an advertisement supporting a specific candidate. * * *

The mere fact that the Chamber is a corporation does not remove its speech from the ambit of the First Amendment. See, *e.g., First National Bank of Boston* v. *Bellotti*, 435 U.S. 765, 777 (1978). * * *

The State contends that the unique legal and economic characteristics of corporations necessitate some regulation of their political expenditures to avoid corruption or the appearance of corruption. See *FEC* v. *National Conservative Political Action Committee*, 470 U.S. 480, 496–497 (1985) *(NCPAC)* ("[P]reventing corruption or the appearance of corruption are the only legitimate and compelling government interests thus far identified for restricting campaign finances"). State law grants corporations special advantages — such as limited liability, perpetual life, and favorable treatment of the accumulation and distribution of assets — that enhance their ability to attract capital and to deploy their resources in ways that maximize the return on their shareholders' investments. These state-created advantages not only allow corporations to play a dominant role in the Nation's economy, but also permit them to use "resources amassed in the economic marketplace" to obtain "an unfair advantage in the political marketplace." [*Federal Election Commission v. Massachusetts Citizens for Life*, 479 U.S. 238, 257 (1986)]. * * *

The Chamber argues that this concern about corporate domination of the political process is insufficient to justify a restriction on independent expenditures. Although this Court has distinguished these expenditures from direct contributions in the context of federal laws regulating individual donors, *Buckley* [*v. Valeo*], 424 U.S. [1], 47 [(1976)] [p. 799], it has also recognized that a legislature might demonstrate a danger of real or apparent corruption posed by such expenditures when made by corporations to influence candidate elections, *Bellotti, supra,* at 788, n. 26. Regardless of whether this danger of "financial *quid pro quo*" corruption, may be sufficient to justify a restriction on independent expenditures, Michigan's regulation aims at a different type of corruption in the political arena: the corrosive and distorting effects of immense aggregations of wealth that are accumulated with the help of the corporate form and that have little or no correlation to the public's support for the corporation's political ideas. The Act does not attempt "to equalize the relative influence of speakers on elections,"; rather, it ensures that expenditures reflect actual public support for the political ideas espoused by corporations. We emphasize that the mere fact that corporations may accumulate large amounts of wealth is not the justification for § 54; rather, the unique state-conferred corporate structure that facilitates the amassing of large treasuries warrants the limit on independent expenditures. Corporate wealth can unfairly influence elections when it is deployed in the form of independent expenditures, just as it can when it assumes the guise of political contributions. We therefore hold that the State has articulated a sufficiently compelling rationale to support its restriction on independent expenditures by corporations.

We next turn to the question whether the Act is sufficiently narrowly tailored to achieve its goal. We find that the Act is precisely targeted to eliminate the distortion caused by corporate spending while also allowing corporations to express their political views. Contrary to the dissents' critical assumptions, the Act does not impose an *absolute* ban on all forms of corporate political spending but permits corporations to make independent political expenditures through separate segregated funds. Because persons contributing to such funds understand that their money will be used solely for political purposes, the speech generated accurately reflects contributors' support for the corporation's political views.

The Chamber argues that § 54(1) is substantially overinclusive, because it includes within its scope closely held corporations that do not possess vast reservoirs of capital. We rejected a similar argument in *FEC* v. *National Right to Work Committee*, 459 U.S. 197 (1982), in the context of federal restrictions on the persons from whom corporations could solicit contributions to their segregated funds. The Court found that the federal campaign statute, 2 U. S. C. § 441b, "reflect[ed] a legislative judgment that the special characteristics of the corporate structure require particularly careful regulation. While § 441b restricts the solicitation of corporations and labor unions without great financial resources, as well as those more fortunately situated, we accept Congress' judgment that it is the *potential* for such influence that demands regulation." Although some closely held corporations, just as some publicly held ones, may not have accumulated significant amounts of wealth, they receive from the State the special benefits conferred by the corporate structure and present the potential for distorting the political process. This potential for distortion justifies § 54(1)'s general applicability to all corporations. The section therefore is not substantially overbroad. * * *

The Chamber also attacks § 54(1) as underinclusive because it does not regulate the independent expenditures of unincorporated labor unions. Whereas unincorporated unions, and indeed individuals, may be able to amass large treasuries, they do so without the significant state-conferred advantages of the corporate structure; corporations are "by far the most prominent example of entities that enjoy legal advantages enhancing their ability to accumulate wealth." The desire to counterbalance those advantages unique to the corporate form is the State's compelling interest in this case; thus, excluding from the statute's coverage unincorporated entities that also have the capacity to accumulate wealth "does not undermine its justification for regulating corporations."

Moreover, labor unions differ from corporations in that union members who disagree with a union's political activities need not give up full membership in the organization to avoid supporting its political activities. Although a union and an employer may require that all bargaining unit employees become union members, a union may not compel those employees to support financially "union activities beyond those germane to collective bargaining, contract administration, and grievance adjustment." *Communications Workers* v. *Beck*, 487 U.S. 735, 745 (1988). See also *Abood v. Detroit Bd. of Ed.*, 431 U.S. 209 (1977) (holding that compelling nonmember employees to contribute to union's political activities infringes employees' First Amendment rights). An employee who objects to a union's political activities thus can decline to contribute to those activities, while continuing to enjoy the benefits derived from the union's performance of its duties as the exclusive representative of the bargaining unit on labormanagement issues. As a result, the funds available for a union's political activities more accurately reflects members' support for the organization's political views than does a corporation's general treasury. Michigan's decision to exclude unincorporated labor unions from the scope of § 54(1) is therefore justified by the crucial differences between unions and corporations.

Because we hold that § 54(1) does not violate the First Amendment, we must address the Chamber's contention that the provision infringes its rights under the Fourteenth Amendment. The Chamber argues that the statute treats similarly situated entities unequally. Specifically, it contends that the State should also restrict the independent expenditures of unincorporated associations with the ability to accumulate large treasuries and of corporations engaged in the media business.

Because the right to engage in political expression is fundamental to our constitutional system, statutory classifications impinging upon that right must be narrowly tailored to serve a compelling governmental interest. * * * We find that, even under such strict scrutiny, the statute's classifications pass muster under the Equal Protection Clause. As we explained in the context of our discussions of whether the statute was overinclusive or underinclusive, the State's decision to regulate only corporations is precisely tailored to serve the compelling state interest of eliminating from the political process the corrosive effect of political "war chests" amassed with the aid of the legal advantages given to corporations.

Similarly, we find that the Act's exemption of media corporations from the expenditure restriction does not render the statute unconstitutional. The "media exception" excludes from the definition of "expenditure" any "expenditure by a broadcasting station, newspaper, magazine, or other periodical or publication for any news story, commentary, or editorial in support of or opposition to a candidate for elective office . . . in the regular course of publication or broadcasting," § 169.206(3)(d). * * * It is true that the exemption does not refer expressly to "media corporations." Nevertheless, the exception will undoubtedly result in the imposition of fewer restrictions on the expression of corporations that are in the media business. Thus, it cannot be regarded as neutral, and the distinction must be justified by a compelling state purpose.

Although all corporations enjoy the same state-conferred benefits inherent in the corporate form, media corporations differ significantly from other corporations in that their resources are devoted to the collection of information and its dissemination to the public. We have consistently recognized the unique role that the press plays in "informing and educating the public, offering criticism, and providing a forum for discussion and debate." *Bellotti*, 435 U.S., at 781. The Act's definition of "expenditure," conceivably could be interpreted to encompass election-related news stories and editorials. The Act's restriction on independent expenditures therefore might discourage incorporated news broadcasters or publishers from serving their crucial societal role. The media exception ensures that the Act does not hinder or prevent the institutional press from reporting on, and publishing editorials about, newsworthy events. * * * A valid distinction thus exists between corporations that are part of the media industry and other corporations that are not involved in the regular business of imparting news to the public. Although the press' unique societal role may not entitle the press to greater protection under the Constitution, it does provide a compelling reason for the State to exempt media corporations from the scope of political expenditure limitations. We therefore hold that the Act does not violate the Equal Protection Clause.

Michigan identified as a serious danger the significant possibility that corporate political expenditures will undermine the integrity of the political process, and it has implemented a narrowly tailored solution to that problem. By requiring corporations to make all independent political expenditures through a separate fund made up of money solicited expressly for political purposes, the Michigan Campaign Finance Act reduces the threat that huge corporate treasuries amassed with the aid of favorable state laws will be used to influence unfairly the outcome of elections. * * * We therefore reverse the decision of the Court of Appeals.

JUSTICE BRENNAN, concurring. * * *

The Chamber is first and foremost a business association, not a political advocacy organization. The Michigan statute advances the [government's legitimate] interest in two distinct ways, by preventing both the Chamber *and other business corporations* from using the funds of other persons for purposes that those persons may not support. First, the state law protects the small businessperson who does not wish his or her dues to be spent in support of political candidates, but who nevertheless wishes to maintain an association with the Chamber because of the myriad benefits it provides that are unrelated to its political activities. * * * To attract new members, Chamber advertisements promise a wide variety of services, including "regular and special publications, legislative briefings, group insurance, a business hot-line, and seminars." * * * A member faces significant disincentives to withdraw, even if he disagrees with the Chamber's expenditures in support of a particular candidate.

In addition, the Michigan law protects dissenting shareholders of business corporations that are members of the Chamber to the extent that such shareholders oppose the use of their money, paid as dues to the Chamber out of general corporate treasury funds, for political campaigns. The Michigan law prevents the Chamber from "serv[ing] as a conduit for corporate political spending."

JUSTICE STEVENS, concurring.

In my opinion the distinction between individual expenditures and individual contributions that the Court identified in *Buckley v. Valeo* should have little, if any, weight in reviewing corporate participation in candidate elections. In that context, I believe the danger of either the fact, or the appearance, of *quid pro quo* relationships provides an adequate justification for state regulation of both expenditures and contributions. Moreover, as we recognized in *First National Bank of Boston v. Bellotti*, there is a vast difference between lobbying and debating public issues on the one hand, and political campaigns for election to public office on the other. Accordingly, I join the Court's opinion and judgment.

JUSTICE SCALIA, dissenting.

"Attention all citizens. To assure the fairness of elections by preventing dispro-portionate expression of the views of any single powerful group, your Government has decided that the following associations of persons shall be prohibited from speaking or writing in support of any candidate: ___." In permitting Michigan to make private corporations the first object of this Orwellian announcement, the Court today endorses the principle that too much speech is an evil that the democratic majority can proscribe. I dissent because that principle is contrary to our case law and incompatible with the absolutely central truth of the First Amendment: that government cannot be trusted to assure, through censorship, the "fairness" of political debate.

The Court's opinion says that political speech of corporations can be regulated because "[s]tate law grants [them] special advantages," and because this "unique state-conferred corporate structure . . . facilitates the amassing of large treasur-ies." This analysis seeks to create one good argument by combining two bad ones. Those individuals who form that type of voluntary association known as a corporation are, to be sure, given special advantages — notably, the immunization of their personal fortunes from liability for the actions of the association — that the State is under no obligation to confer. But so are other associations and private individuals given all sorts of special advantages that the State need not confer, ranging from tax breaks to contract awards to public employment to outright cash subsidies. It is rudimentary that the State cannot exact as the price of those special advantages the forfeiture of First Amendment rights. * * * The categorical suspension of the right of any person, or of any association of persons, to speak out on political matters must be justified by a compelling state need. * * * That is why the Court puts forward its second bad argument, the fact that corporations "amas[s] large treasuries." But that alone is also not sufficient justification for the suppres-sion of political speech, unless one thinks it would be lawful to prohibit men and women whose net worth is above a certain figure from endorsing political candidates. Neither of these two flawed arguments is improved by combining them and saying, as the Court in effect does, that "since the State gives special advantages to these voluntary associations, and since they thereby amass vast wealth, they may be required to abandon their right of political speech."[*]

The Court's extensive reliance upon the fact that the objects of this speech restriction, corporations, receive "special advantages" is in stark contrast to our

---

[*] The Court's assertion that the Michigan law "does not impose an *absolute* ban on all forms of corporate political spending," is true only in a respect that is irrelevant for purposes of First Amendment analysis. A corporation is absolutely prohibited from spending its own funds on this form of political speech, and would be guilty of misrepresentation if it asserted that a particular candidate was supported or opposed by the corporation. This is to say that the corporation *as a corporation* is prohibited from speaking. What the Michigan law permits the corporation to do is to serve as the founder and treasurer of a different association of individuals that can endorse or oppose political candidates. The equivalent, where an individual rather than an association is concerned, would be to prohibit John D. Rockefeller from making political endorsements, but to permit him to form an association to which others (though not he himself) can contribute for the purpose of making political endorsements. Just as political speech by that association is not speech by John D. Rockefeller, so also speech by a corporate PAC that the Michigan law allows is not speech by the corporation itself.

opinion issued just six years ago in *FCC* v. *League of Women Voters of California*, 468 U.S. 364 (1984), * * * striking down a congressionally imposed ban upon editorializing by noncommercial broadcasting stations that receive federal funds[.] * * * Commercial corporations may not have a public *persona* as sympathetic as that of public broadcasters, but they are no less entitled to this Court's concern.

As for the second part of the Court's argumentation, the fact that corporations (or at least some of them) possess "massive wealth": Certain uses of "massive wealth" in the electoral process — whether or not the wealth is the result of "special advantages" conferred by the State — pose a substantial risk of corruption which constitutes a compelling need for the regulation of speech. Such a risk plainly exists when the wealth is given directly to the political candidate, to be used under his direction and control. We held in *Buckley* v. *Valeo*, however, that independent expenditures to express the political views of individuals and associations do not raise a sufficient threat of corruption to justify prohibition. Neither the Court's opinion nor either of the concurrences makes any effort to distinguish that case * * *. Section 608(e)(1) of the Federal Election Campaign Act of 1971, which we found unconstitutional in *Buckley*, was directed, like the Michigan law before us here, to expenditures made for the purpose of advocating the election or defeat of a particular candidate. It limited to $1,000 (a *lesser* restriction than the absolute prohibition at issue here) such expenditures not merely by "individuals," but by "persons," specifically defined to include corporations. The plaintiffs in the case included corporations, and we specifically discussed § 608(e)(1) as a restriction addressed not just to individuals but to "individuals and groups," "persons and groups," "persons and organizations," "person[s] [and] association[s]." In support of our determination that the restriction was "wholly at odds with the guarantees of the First Amendment" we cited *Miami Herald Publishing Co.* v. *Tornillo*, 418 U.S. 241 (1974) [p. 613], which involved limitations upon a corporation. * * *

Buckley v. *Valeo* should not be overruled, because it is entirely correct. The contention that prohibiting overt advocacy for or against a political candidate satisfies a "compelling need" to avoid "corruption" is easily dismissed. As we said in *Buckley*, "[i]t would naively underestimate the ingenuity and resourcefulness of persons and groups desiring to buy influence to believe that they would have much difficulty devising expenditures that skirted the restriction on express advocacy of election or defeat but nevertheless benefited the candidate's campaign." Independent advocacy, moreover, unlike contributions, "may well provide little assistance to the candidate's campaign and indeed may prove counterproductive," thus reducing the danger that it will be exchanged "as a *quid pro quo* for improper commitments from the candidate." The latter point seems even more plainly true with respect to corporate advocates than it is with respect to individuals. I expect I could count on the fingers of one hand the candidates who would generally welcome, much less negotiate for, a formal endorsement by AT&T or General Motors. The advocacy of such entities that have "amassed great wealth" will be effective only to the extent that it brings to the people's attention *ideas* which — despite the invariably self-interested and probably uncongenial source — strike them as true.

The Court does not try to defend the proposition that independent advocacy poses a substantial risk of political "corruption," as English speakers understand that term. Rather, it asserts that that concept (which it defines as " 'financial *quid pro quo'* corruption") is really just a narrow subspecies of a hitherto unrecognized genus of political corruption. "Michigan's regulation," we are told, "aims at a different type of corruption in the political arena: the corrosive and distorting effects of immense aggregations of wealth that are accumulated with the help of the corporate form and that have little or no correlation to the public's support for the corporations's political ideas." Under this mode of analysis, virtually anything the Court deems politically undesirable can be turned into political corruption — by simply describing its effects as politically "corrosive," which is close enough to "corruptive" to qualify. It is sad to think that the First Amendment will ultimately be brought down not by brute force but by poetic metaphor.

The Court's opinion ultimately rests upon that proposition whose violation constitutes the "New Corruption": Expenditures must "reflect actual public support for the political ideas espoused." This illiberal free-speech principle of "one man, one minute" was proposed and soundly rejected in *Buckley.* * * * But it can be said that I have not accurately quoted today's decision. It does not endorse the proposition that government may ensure that expenditures "reflect actual public support for the political ideas espoused," but only the more limited proposition that government may ensure that expenditures "reflect actual public support for the political ideas espoused *by corporations.*" The limitation is of course entirely irrational. Why is it perfectly all right if advocacy by an individual billionaire is out of proportion with "actual public support" for his positions? There is no explanation, except the effort I described at the outset of this discussion to make one valid proposition out of two invalid ones: When the vessel labeled "corruption" begins to founder under weight too great to be logically sustained, the argumentation jumps to the good ship "special privilege"; and when that in turn begins to go down, it returns to "corruption." Thus hopping back and forth between the two, the argumentation may survive but makes no headway towards port, where its conclusion waits in vain.

Justice Brennan's concurrence would have us believe that the prohibition adopted by Michigan and approved by the Court is a paternalistic measure to protect the corporate shareholders of America. It is designed, we are told, "to avert [the] danger" that "corporate funds drawn from the general treasury — which represents, after all, [the shareholder's] money," might be used on behalf of a political candidate he opposes. But such solicitude is a most implausible explanation for the Michigan statute, inasmuch as it permits corporations to take as many ideological and political positions as they please, so long as they are not "in assistance of, or in opposition to, the nomination or election of a candidate." Mich. Comp. Laws § 169.206(1) (1979). That is indeed the Court's sole basis for distinguishing *First National Bank of Boston v. Bellotti,* 435 U.S. 765 (1978), which invalidated restriction of a corporation's general political speech. The Michigan law appears to be designed, in other words, neither to protect shareholders, nor even (impermissibly) to "balance" general political debate, but to protect political candidates. Given the degree of political sophistication that ought to attend the exercise of our constitutional responsibilities, it is regrettable that this should come as a surprise.

But even if the object of the prohibition could plausibly be portrayed as the protection of shareholders (which the Court's opinion, at least, does not even assert), that would not suffice as a "compelling need" to support this blatant restriction upon core political speech. A person becomes a member of that form of association known as a for-profit corporation in order to pursue economic objectives, *i.e.*, to make money. Some corporate charters may specify the line of commerce to which the company is limited, but even that can be amended by shareholder vote. Thus, in joining such an association, the shareholder knows that management may take any action that is ultimately in accord with what the majority (or a specified supermajority) of the shareholders wishes, so long as that action is designed to make a profit. That is the deal. The corporate actions to which the shareholder exposes himself, therefore, include many things that he may find politically or ideologically uncongenial: investment in South Africa, operation of an abortion clinic, publication of a pornographic magazine, or even publication of a newspaper that adopts absurd political views and makes catastrophic political endorsements. His only protections against such assaults upon his ideological commitments are (1) his ability to persuade a majority (or the requisite minority) of his fellow shareholders that the action should not be taken, and ultimately (2) his ability to sell his stock. (The latter course, by the way, does not ordinarily involve the severe psychic trauma or economic disaster that Justice Brennan's opinion suggests.) It seems to me entirely fanciful, in other words, to suggest that the Michigan statute makes any significant contribution toward insulating the exclusively profit-motivated shareholder from the rude world of politics and ideology.

But even if that were not fanciful, it would be fanciful to think, as Justice Brennan's opinion assumes, that there is any difference between for-profit and not-for-profit corporations insofar as the need for protection of the individual member's ideological psyche is concerned. Would it be any more upsetting to a shareholder of General Motors that it endorsed the election of Henry Wallace (to stay comfortably in the past) than it would be to a member of the American Civil Liberties Union that it endorsed the election of George Wallace? I should think much less so. Yet in the one case as in the other, the only protection against association-induced trauma is the will of the majority and, in the last analysis, withdrawal from membership. * * *

C

Th[e] state interest [in "eliminating from the political process the corrosive effect of political 'war chests' amassed with the aid of the legal advantages given to corporations"] (assuming it is compelling) does indeed explain why the State chose to silence "only corporations" rather than wealthy individuals as well. But it does not explain (what "narrow tailoring" pertains to) why the State chose to silence *all* corporations, rather than just those that possess great wealth. If narrow tailoring means anything, surely it must mean that action taken to counter the effect of amassed "war chests" must be targeted, if possible, at amassed "war chests." And surely such targeting is possible — either in the manner accomplished by the provision that we invalidated in *Buckley,* *i.e.*, by limiting the prohibition to independent expenditures above a certain amount, or in some other manner, *e.g.*, by limiting the expenditures of only those corporations with more than a certain amount of net worth or annual profit. * * *

The Court thus holds, for the first time since Justice Holmes left the bench, that a direct restriction upon speech is narrowly enough tailored if it extends to speech that has the mere *potential* for producing social harm. * * * Today's reversal of field will require adjustment of a fairly large number of significant First Amendment holdings. Presumably the State may now convict individuals for selling books found to have a potentially harmful influence on minors, *Butler* v. *Michigan*, 352 U.S. 380 (1957), ban indecent telephone communications that have the potential for reaching minors, *Sable Communications of California* v. *FCC*, 492 U.S. 115 (1989), restrain the press from publishing information that has the potential for jeopardizing a criminal defendant's right to a fair trial, *Nebraska Press Assn.* v. *Stuart*, 427 U.S. 539 (1976), or the potential for damaging the reputation of the subject of an investigation, *Landmark Communications, Inc.* v. *Virginia*, 435 U.S. 829 (1978), compel publication of the membership lists of organizations that have a potential for illegal activity, see *NAACP* v. *Alabama ex rel. Patterson*, 357 U.S. 449, 464 (1958), and compel an applicant for bar membership to reveal her political beliefs and affiliations to eliminate the potential for subversive activity, *Baird* v. *State Bar of Arizona*, 401 U.S. 1 (1971).

Finally, a few words are in order concerning the Court's approval of the Michigan law's exception for "media corporations." This is all right, we are told, because of "the unique role that the press plays in 'informing and educating the public, offering criticism, and providing a forum for discussion and debate.'" But if one believes in the Court's rationale of "compelling state need" to prevent amassed corporate wealth from skewing the political debate, surely that "unique role" of the press does not give Michigan justification for *excluding* media corporations from coverage, but provides especially strong reason to *include* them. Amassed corporate wealth that regularly sits astride the ordinary channels of information is much more likely to produce the New Corruption (too much of one point of view) than amassed corporate wealth that is generally busy making money elsewhere. Such media corporations not only have vastly greater power to perpetrate the evil of overinforming, they also have vastly greater opportunity. General Motors, after all, will risk a stockholder suit if it makes a political endorsement that is not plausibly tied to its ability to make money for its shareholders. But media corporations make money *by* making political commentary, including endorsements. For them, unlike any other corporations, the whole world of politics and ideology is fair game. Yet the Court tells us that it is reasonable to *exclude* media corporations, rather than target them specially.

Members of the institutional press, despite the Court's approval of their illogical exemption from the Michigan law, will find little reason for comfort in today's decision. The theory of New Corruption it espouses is a dagger at their throats. The Court today holds merely that media corporations *may* be excluded from the Michigan law, not that they *must* be. * * * One must hope, I suppose, that Michigan will continue to provide this generous and voluntary exemption.

I would not do justice to the significance of today's decision to discuss only its lapses from case precedent and logic. Infinitely more important than that is its departure from long-accepted premises of our political system regarding the benevolence that can be expected of government in managing the arena of public debate, and the danger that is to be anticipated from powerful private institutions that compete with government, and with one another, within that arena.

Perhaps the Michigan law before us here has an unqualifiedly noble objective — to "equalize" the political debate by preventing disproportionate expression of corporations' points of view. But governmental abridgment of liberty is always undertaken with the very best of announced objectives (dictators promise to bring order, not tyranny), and often with the very best of genuinely intended objectives (zealous policemen conduct unlawful searches in order to put dangerous felons behind bars). The premise of our Bill of Rights, however, is that there are some things — even some seemingly *desirable* things — that government cannot be trusted to do. The very first of these is establishing the restrictions upon speech that will assure "fair" political debate. The incumbent politician who says he welcomes full and fair debate is no more to be believed than the entrenched monopolist who says he welcomes full and fair competition. Perhaps the Michigan Legislature was genuinely trying to assure a "balanced" presentation of political views; on the other hand, perhaps it was trying to give unincorporated unions (a not insubstantial force in Michigan) political advantage over major employers. Or perhaps it was trying to assure a "balanced" presentation because it knows that with evenly balanced speech incumbent officeholders generally win. The fundamental approach of the First Amendment, I had always thought, was to assume the worst, and to rule the regulation of political speech "for fairness' sake" simply out of bounds.

I doubt that those who framed and adopted the First Amendment would agree that avoiding the New Corruption, that is, calibrating political speech to the degree of public opinion that supports it, is even a *desirable* objective, much less one that is important enough to qualify as a compelling state interest. Those Founders designed, of course, a system in which popular ideas would ultimately prevail; but also, through the First Amendment, a system in which true ideas could readily become popular. For the latter purpose, the calibration that the Court today endorses is precisely backwards: To the extent a valid proposition has scant public support, it should have wider rather than narrower public circulation. I am confident, in other words, that Jefferson and Madison would not have sat at these controls; but if they did, they would have turned them in the opposite direction. * * *

Why should the Michigan voters in the 93d House District be deprived of the information that private associations owning and operating a vast percentage of the industry of the State, and employing a large number of its citizens, believe that the election of a particular candidate is important to their prosperity? Contrary to the Court's suggestion, the same point cannot effectively be made through corporate PACs to which individuals may voluntarily contribute. It is important to the message that it represents the views of Michigan's leading corporations *as corporations*, occupying the "lofty platform" that they do within the economic life of the State — not just the views of some *other* voluntary associations to which some of the corporations' shareholders belong.

Despite all the talk about "corruption and the appearance of corruption" — evils that are not significantly implicated and that can be avoided in many other ways — it is entirely obvious that the object of the law we have approved today is not to prevent wrongdoing but to prevent speech. Since those private associations known as corporations have so much money, they will speak so much more, and their views will be given inordinate prominence in election campaigns. This is not an argument

that our democratic traditions allow — neither with respect to individuals associated in corporations nor with respect to other categories of individuals whose
speech may be "unduly" extensive (because they are rich) or "unduly" persuasive
(because they are movie stars) or "unduly" respected (because they are clergymen).
The premise of our system is that there is no such thing as too much speech — that
the people are not foolish but intelligent, and will separate the wheat from the chaff.
As conceded in Lincoln's aphorism about fooling "all of the people some of the time,"
that premise will not invariably accord with reality; but it will assuredly do so much
more frequently than the premise the Court today embraces: that a healthy
democratic system can survive the legislative power to prescribe how much political
speech is too much, who may speak, and who may not. * * *

Because today's decision is inconsistent with unrepudiated legal judgments of
our Court, but even more because it is incompatible with the unrepealable political
wisdom of our First Amendment, I dissent.

JUSTICE KENNEDY, with whom JUSTICE O'CONNOR and JUSTICE SCALIA join, dissenting. * * *

(The proposed advertisement is reproduced in the Appendix to this opinion.) The
advertisement discussed the local economy and unemployment and explained why
the candidate supported by the Chamber would understand and improve local
economic conditions. This communication is banned by the law here in question, the
Michigan Campaign Finance Act (Act). * * *

In both practice and theory, the prohibition aims at the heart of political debate.
* * *

To create second-class speakers that can be stifled on the subject of candidate
qualifications is to silence some of the most significant participants in the American
public dialogue, as evidenced by the *amici* briefs filed on behalf of the Chamber of
Commerce by the American Civil Liberties Union, the Center for Public Interest
Law, the American Medical Association, the National Association of Realtors, the
American Insurance Association, the National Organization for Women, Green-
peace Action, the National Abortion Rights Action League, the National Right to
Work Committee, the Planned Parenthood Federation of America, the Fund for the
Feminist Majority, the Washington Legal Foundation, and the Allied Educational
Foundation. I reject any argument based on the idea that these groups and their
views are not of importance and value to the self-fulfillment and self-expression of
their members, and to the rich public dialogue that must be the mark of any free
society. To suggest otherwise is contrary to the American political experience and
our own judicial knowledge. * * *

By deciding to operate as a nonprofit corporation rather than an unincorporated
association, a group does not forfeit its First Amendment protection to participate
in political discourse. * * *

By constructing a rationale for the jurisprudence of this Court that prevents
distinguished organizations in public affairs from announcing that a candidate is
qualified or not qualified for public office, the Court imposes its own model of
speech, one far removed from economic and political reality. It is an unhappy

paradox that this Court, which has the role of protecting speech and of barring censorship from all aspects of political life, now becomes itself the censor. In the course of doing so, the Court reveals a lack of concern for speech rights that have the full protection of the First Amendment. I would affirm the judgment.

APPENDIX A

Michigan Needs Richard Bandstra To Help Us Be Job Competitive Again

The Michigan State Chamber of Commerce, an organization of over 8,000 member companies, associations and local chambers of commerce, is committed to making Michigan more competitive for business investment and job creation. With that goal in mind, we'd like to share some facts with the electors in the 93rd House District before they vote in tomorrow's special election.

To be job competitive, Michigan needs to have fair regulatory policies on business regarding such important issues as workers' compensation and we need to encourage greater efficiency in state government by lowering the state personal income tax.

Currently, workers' compensation costs are 20% higher in Michigan than those in neighboring states. Why? Our eligibility standards are not the same as most other states. Too many people are allowed to quality for too long a period of a time.

Many Grand Rapids businesses are competing with firms in other states having lower regulatory costs. Unless checked, this disadvantage may continue to cost Michigan jobs . . . jobs that are lost when businesses leave Michigan, expand out of state, or when out-state companies seeking to expand don't locate here in Michigan.

To ensure that Michigan is job competitive, we need legislators at the State Capitol who will show courage and stand up to special interests that advocate greater regulation and taxes.

The Michigan State Chamber of Commerce believes Richard Bandstra has the background and training to do the best job in Lansing for the people of the 93rd House District. We believe he will work to reduce workers' compensation costs and for an early rollback of the personal income tax rate.

The State Chamber is committed to job development in Michigan. We believe Richard Bandstra shares that commitment.

On Monday June 10th, Elect Richard Bandstra State Representative 93rd House District Special Election

Notes and Questions

1.   Look at the ad in question in *Austin*. Is the information of the type that could be valuable to voters? Would the ad have the same impact if funded by an individual business executive? Or is the sponsor part of the message and what gives it salience?

2.   *Austin* finds that the state ban on corporate expenditures is, in accordance with *Buckley*, attempting to address corruption. The Court refers to it as a "different type of corruption": "the corrosive and distortive effects of immense aggregations of wealth * * *." What does that mean? When people refer to government "corruption," do you think this is usually what they have in mind?

3.   The Court suggests that there is something wrong when political spending has "little or no correlation to the to the public's support for the corporation's political ideas." Is there any reason to think political spending should regularly correlate with the public's support for the donors' ideas? *See* Bradley A. Smith, *Searching for Corruption in All the Wrong Places*, 2002–2003 Cato Sup. Ct. Rev. 187, 204 (2003). Historically, unpopular causes are most reliant on large contributions. Bradley A. Smith, Unfree Speech: The Folly of Campaign Finance Reform 66–67 (2001).

As of April 2015, the Idaho legislature was dominated by Republicans, 57-13 in the House and 28-7 in the State Senate. It has been over twenty years since a Democrat received as much as 45% of the vote in a race for Governor. No Democrat has been elected to the U.S. Senate since 1974, or carried the state in a presidential race since 1964. Suppose the state adopted a public funding program for campaigns, which provided each major party candidate with the same amount of funds. Would this be problematic on the grounds that the funds did not correspond to the public's demonstrated support for the two parties' political ideas?

4.   Elizabeth Garrett, a clerk for Justice Marshall at the time of *Austin* and now President at Cornell University, notes that Justice Marshall approved of the equality rationale rejected in *Buckley*. Justice Marshall's majority opinion in *Austin*, according to Professor Garrett, "appropriated the language used to describe an egalitarian justification for campaign finance regulation, but * * * expressed that state interest in the acceptable corruption terminology." Elizabeth Garrett, *Influence and Legacy: The Future of the Post-Marshall Court: New Voices in Politics: Justice Marshall's Jurisprudence on Law and Politics*, 52 How. L. J. 655, 670–71, 675 (2009).

5.   Is the Court's distinction between unions and corporations for equal protection purposes persuasive? The Majority argues that while unions may amass large treasuries, they do so "without the significant state-conferred advantages of the corporate structure." Is that true? Consider the legislatively imposed rules governing labor relations that have, since the 1930s, replaced many common law doctrines in an open effort to confer advantages on unions, such as the statutory prohibition on "yellow dog" contracts, which required a worker to agree not to join a union as a condition of employment, limits on the use of injunctions against picketing that threatens violence, and requirements that corporations recognize unions, refrain from retaliation against or dismissal of employees for union activity, and negotiate with unions. *See* Richard A. Epstein, *A Common Law for Labor Relations: A*

Critique of the New Deal Labor Legislation, 92 YALE L. J. 1357 (1983).

6. Do "state-conferred advantages" really help companies amass large sums that can be used for political purposes? Not according to one corporate scholar:

> [M]anagers who divert corporate resources from profitmaking activities towards funding political campaigns on such a grand level as to warrant the characterization "corrosive and distorting" will find their firm's "large treasuries" shrinking as the firm becomes less competitive in its product and the capital markets. And perpetual life cuts in precisely the opposite direction than the Court supposed * * *. As a class, managers must always look forward to tomorrow's product and capital market competition.

> True, limited liability does help managers obtain capital. But it does so only by capping investors' personal liability to creditors of the corporation at the amount of the investors' investment. Limited liability does not shield the corporation itself from liability for its debts. So to suppose that limited liability will help an incorporated firm amass a huge treasury for use in electoral campaigns is to suppose investor irrationality. Who would invest in a company that, rather than promising handsome returns, merely hands over the corporate treasury to political candidates?

Robert H. Sitkoff, *Corporate Political Speech, Political Extortion, and the Competition for Corporate Charters*, 69 U. CHI. L. REV. 1103, 1109–10 (2002).

7. Only about 40% of firms in the Fortune 500 maintain PACs. Does this shed any light on the perceived value of corporate political spending? *See* Stephen D. Ansolabehere, John M. de Figueiredo, & James M. Snyder, Jr., *Why is There So Little Money in American Politics*, 17 J. ECON. PERSPECTIVES 105 (2003).

8. Recall that while *Buckley* prohibited limitations on expenditures, it reached that holding only after it first narrowed the FECA's definition of "expenditure" to apply only to "expenditures for communications that in express terms advocate the election or defeat of a clearly identified candidate for federal office." As the Court further explained in famous footnote 52 to the *Buckley* opinion, by this it meant "communications containing express words of advocacy of election or defeat, such as 'vote for,' 'elect,' 'support,' 'cast your ballot for,' 'Smith for Congress,' 'vote against,' 'defeat,' 'reject.' " See p. 811. Coupled with *Bellotti's* holding that corporations had a clear right to engage in issue speech, this meant that even after *Austin* corporations remained free to fund ads about issues — and to mention candidates in those ads so long as they avoided "express advocacy." By the mid-1990s, the Republican and Democratic Parties were raising substantial funds from corporations, unions, and wealthy individuals in order to fund "issue ads" that glowed with praise for their party candidates (or searing criticism of their opponents), but which avoided "express advocacy" of "election or defeat." Because they avoided "express advocacy," such funds, which became known as "soft money," and were not considered "contributions," and payments for the ads were not "expenditures," under the law. Additionally, non-party advocacy groups such as Planned Parenthood, the NAACP, the Club for Growth, and the National Rifle Association, often themselves incorporated, used money from corporate and union donations to fund similar issue ads. *See* Annenberg Public Policy Center, ISSUE ADVERTISING IN THE

1999–2000 ELECTION CYCLE (2001). Perhaps the most famous such "issue ad" was the "Bill Yellowtail" ad, the text of which is set forth in footnote 78 of the Court's opinion in *McConnell v. Federal Election Commission*, 540 U.S. 93, 193 (2003), below.

In 2002, Congress passed the Bipartisan Campaign Reform Act (BCRA), commonly known as "McCain-Feingold" for its principle Senate sponsors. Although the bill covered a broad array of perceived abuses, the core provisions dealt with "soft money." Title I of BCRA prohibited political parties from funding operations with "soft money." Title II made it illegal to use corporate or union funds for "electioneering communications," which were defined as broadcast ads that mention a candidate for office and air within 30 days of a primary election or caucus, or 60 days of a general election, with the potential to reach 50,000 or more voters. We have already seen how the Supreme Court in *McConnell v. FEC* resolved the challenge to the party soft money provision of Title I [see p. 865]. Below is an excerpt from the Court's opinions dealing with Title II.

McCONNELL v. FEDERAL ELECTION COMMISSION
Supreme Court of the United States
540 U.S. 93, 124 S. Ct. 619, 157 L. Ed. 2d 491 (2003)

JUSTICE STEVENS and JUSTICE O'CONNOR delivered the opinion of the Court with respect to BCRA Titles I and II.* * * *

[T]he term "electioneering communication" * * * is defined to encompass any "broadcast, cable, or satellite communication" that

"(I) refers to a clearly identified candidate for Federal office;

"(II) is made within—

     "(aa) 60 days before a general, special, or runoff election for the office sought by the candidate; or

     "(bb) 30 days before a primary or preference election, or a convention or caucus of a political party that has authority to nominate a candidate, for the office sought by the candidate; and

"(III) in the case of a communication which refers to a candidate other than President or Vice President, is targeted to the relevant electorate." 2 USC § 434(f)(3)(A)(i) (Supp. 2003).

New FECA § 304(f)(3)(C) further provides that a communication is " 'targeted to the relevant electorate' " if it "can be received by 50,000 or more persons" in the district or State the candidate seeks to represent. 2 USC § 434(f)(3)(C). * * *

The major premise of plaintiffs' challenge to BCRA's use of the term "electioneering communication" is that *Buckley* drew a constitutionally mandated line between express advocacy and so-called issue advocacy, and that speakers possess an inviolable First Amendment right to engage in the latter category of speech. Thus, plaintiffs maintain, Congress cannot constitutionally require disclosure of, or

---

*   JUSTICE SOUTER, JUSTICE GINSBURG, and JUSTICE BREYER join this opinion in its entirety.

regulate expenditures for, "electioneering communications" without making an exception for those "communications" that do not meet *Buckley*'s definition of express advocacy.

That position misapprehends our prior decisions, for the express advocacy restriction was an endpoint of statutory interpretation, not a first principle of constitutional law. In *Buckley* we began by examining then-18 USC § 608(e)(1) (1970 ed., Supp. IV), which restricted expenditures " 'relative to a clearly identified candidate,' " and we found that the phrase " 'relative to' " was impermissibly vague. We concluded that the vagueness deficiencies could "be avoided only by reading § 608(e)(1) as limited to communications that include explicit words of advocacy of election or defeat of a candidate." We provided examples of words of express advocacy, such as " 'vote for,' 'elect,' 'support,' . . . 'defeat,' [and] 'reject,' " and those examples eventually gave rise to what is now known as the "magic words" requirement.

We then considered FECA's disclosure provisions. * * * Finding that the "ambiguity of this phrase" posed "constitutional problems," we noted our "obligation to construe the statute, if that can be done consistent with the legislature's purpose, to avoid the shoals of vagueness." "To insure that the reach" of the disclosure requirement was "not impermissibly broad, we construe[d] 'expenditure' for purposes of that section in the same way we construed the terms of § 608(e) — to reach only funds used for communications that expressly advocate the election or defeat of a clearly identified candidate."

Thus, a plain reading of *Buckley* makes clear that the express advocacy limitation, in both the expenditure and the disclosure contexts, was the product of statutory interpretation rather than a constitutional command. In narrowly reading the FECA provisions in *Buckley* to avoid problems of vagueness and overbreadth, we nowhere suggested that a statute that was neither vague nor overbroad would be required to toe the same express advocacy line. * * *

Nor are we persuaded, independent of our precedents, that the First Amendment erects a rigid barrier between express advocacy and so-called issue advocacy. That notion cannot be squared with our longstanding recognition that the presence or absence of magic words cannot meaningfully distinguish electioneering speech from a true issue ad. Indeed, the unmistakable lesson from the record in this litigation * * * is that *Buckley*'s magic-words requirement is functionally meaningless. * * * Not only can advertisers easily evade the line by eschewing the use of magic words, but they would seldom choose to use such words even if permitted. And although the resulting advertisements do not urge the viewer to vote for or against a candidate in so many words, they are no less clearly intended to influence the election.[78] *Buckley*'s express advocacy line, in short, has not aided the legislative

---

[78] One striking example is an ad that a group called "Citizens for Reform" sponsored during the 1996 Montana congressional race, in which Bill Yellowtail was a candidate. The ad stated:

"Who is Bill Yellowtail? He preaches family values but took a swing at his wife. And Yellowtail's response? He only slapped her. But 'her nose was not broken.' He talks law and order . . . but is himself a convicted felon. And though he talks about protecting children, Yellowtail failed to make his own child support payments — then voted against child support enforcement. Call Bill Yellowtail. Tell him to support family values."

effort to combat real or apparent corruption, and Congress enacted BCRA to correct the flaws it found in the existing system.

Finally we observe that new FECA § 304(f)(3)'s definition of "electioneering communication" raises none of the vagueness concerns that drove our analysis in *Buckley*. The term "electioneering communication" applies only (1) to a broadcast (2) clearly identifying a candidate for federal office, (3) aired within a specific time period, and (4) targeted to an identified audience of at least 50,000 viewers or listeners. These components are both easily understood and objectively determinable. * * * Thus, the constitutional objection that persuaded the Court in *Buckley* to limit FECA's reach to express advocacy is simply inapposite here. * * *

Since our decision in *Buckley*, Congress' power to prohibit corporations and unions from using funds in their treasuries to finance advertisements expressly advocating the election or defeat of candidates in federal elections has been firmly embedded in our law. * * *

Section 203 of BCRA amends FECA § 316(b)(2) to extend this rule, which previously applied only to express advocacy, to all "electioneering communications" covered by the definition of that term in amended FECA § 304(f)(3), discussed above. Thus, under BCRA, corporations and unions may not use their general treasury funds to finance electioneering communications, but they remain free to organize and administer segregated funds, or PACs, for that purpose. Because corporations can still fund electioneering communications with PAC money, it is "simply wrong" to view the provision as a "complete ban" on expression rather than a regulation. * * *

* * * [P]laintiffs argue that the justifications that adequately support the regulation of express advocacy do not apply to significant quantities of speech encompassed by the definition of electioneering communications.

This argument fails to the extent that the issue ads broadcast during the 30- and 60-day periods preceding federal primary and general elections are the functional equivalent of express advocacy. The justifications for the regulation of express advocacy apply equally to ads aired during those periods if the ads are intended to influence the voters' decisions and have that effect. The precise percentage of issue ads that clearly identified a candidate and were aired during those relatively brief preelection time spans but had no electioneering purpose is a matter of dispute between the parties and among the judges on the District Court. Nevertheless, the vast majority of ads clearly had such a purpose. Moreover, whatever the precise percentage may have been in the past, in the future corporations and unions may finance genuine issue ads during those time frames by simply avoiding any specific reference to federal candidates, or in doubtful cases by paying for the ad from a segregated fund.

We are therefore not persuaded that plaintiffs have carried their heavy burden of proving that amended FECA § 316(b)(2) is overbroad. * * *

In addition * * * some plaintiffs contend that [BCRA § 316(b)(2)] unconstitution-

---

The notion that this advertisement was designed purely to discuss the issue of family values strains credulity.

ally discriminates in favor of media companies. FECA § 304(f)(3)(B)(i) excludes from the definition of electioneering communications any "communication appearing in a news story, commentary, or editorial distributed through the facilities of any broadcasting station, unless such facilities are owned or controlled by any political party, political committee, or candidate." 2 USC § 434(f)(3)(B)(i). Plaintiffs argue this provision gives free rein to media companies to engage in speech without resort to PAC money. Section 304(f)(3)(B)(i)'s effect, however, is much narrower than plaintiffs suggest. The provision excepts news items and commentary only; it does not afford *carte blanche* to media companies generally to ignore FECA's provisions. The statute's narrow exception is wholly consistent with First Amendment principles. "A valid distinction . . . exists between corporations that are part of the media industry and other corporations that are not involved in the regular business of imparting news to the public." *Austin* [*v. Michigan Chamber of Commerce*], 494 U.S. [652], 668 [(1990)] [p. 907]. Numerous federal statutes have drawn this distinction to ensure that the law "does not hinder or prevent the institutional press from reporting on, and publishing editorials about, newsworthy events." * * *

We affirm the District Court's judgment to the extent that it upheld the constitutionality of FECA § 316(b)(2).

* * *

Justice Scalia, concurring in part and dissenting in part. * * *

I wish to address three fallacious propositions that might be thought to justify some or all of the provisions of this legislation — only the last of which is explicitly embraced by the principal opinion for the Court, but all of which underlie, I think, its approach to these cases.

(a) Money is Not Speech * * *

In any economy operated on even the most rudimentary principles of division of labor, effective public communication requires the speaker to make use of the services of others. An author may write a novel, but he will seldom publish and distribute it himself. A freelance reporter may write a story, but he will rarely edit, print, and deliver it to subscribers. To a government bent on suppressing speech, this mode of organization presents opportunities: Control any cog in the machine, and you can halt the whole apparatus. License printers, and it matters little whether authors are still free to write. Restrict the sale of books, and it matters little who prints them. Predictably, repressive regimes have exploited these principles by attacking all levels of the production and dissemination of ideas. In response to this threat, we have interpreted the First Amendment broadly.

Division of labor requires a means of mediating exchange, and in a commercial society, that means is supplied by money. The publisher pays the author for the right to sell his book; it pays its staff who print and assemble the book; it demands payments from booksellers who bring the book to market. This, too, presents opportunities for repression: Instead of regulating the various parties to the enterprise individually, the government can suppress their ability to coordinate by regulating their use of money. What good is the right to print books without a right to buy works from authors? Or the right to publish newspapers without the right to pay deliverymen? The right to speak would be largely ineffective if it did not include the right to engage in financial transactions that are the incidents of its exercise. * * *

History and jurisprudence bear this out. The best early examples derive from the British efforts to tax the press after the lapse of licensing statutes by which the press was first regulated. The Stamp Act of 1712 imposed levies on all newspapers, including an additional tax for each advertisement. It was a response to unfavorable war coverage, * * * [and] succeeded in killing off approximately half the newspapers in England in its first year. In 1765, Parliament applied a similar Act to the Colonies. * * * The founding generation saw these taxes as grievous incursions on the freedom of the press.

We have kept faith with the Founders' tradition by prohibiting the selective taxation of the press. *Minneapolis Star & Tribune Co.* v. *Minnesota Comm'r of Revenue*, 460 U.S. 575 (1983) (ink and paper tax); *Grosjean* [v. *American Press Co.*, 297 U.S. 233 (1936)] (advertisement tax). And we have done so whether the tax was the product of illicit motive or not. These press-taxation cases belie the claim that regulation of money used to fund speech is not regulation of speech itself. A tax on a newspaper's advertising revenue does not prohibit anyone from saying anything; it merely appropriates part of the revenue that a speaker would otherwise obtain. That is even a step short of totally prohibiting advertising revenue — which would be analogous to the total prohibition of certain campaign-speech contributions in the present cases. Yet it is unquestionably a violation of the First Amendment.

Many other cases exemplify the same principle that an attack upon the funding of speech is an attack upon speech itself. In *Schaumburg* v. *Citizens for a Better Environment*, 444 U.S. 620, (1980), we struck down an ordinance limiting the amount charities could pay their solicitors. In *Simon & Schuster, Inc.* v. *Members of N. Y. State Crime Victims Bd.*, 502 U.S. 105 (1991), we held unconstitutional a state statute that appropriated the proceeds of criminals' biographies for payment to the victims. And in *Rosenberger* v. *Rector and Visitors of Univ. of Va.*, 515 U.S. 819 (1995), we held unconstitutional a university's discrimination in the disbursement of funds to speakers on the basis of viewpoint. Most notable, perhaps, is our famous opinion in *New York Times Co.* v. *Sullivan*, 376 U.S. 254 (1964), holding that paid advertisements in a newspaper were entitled to full First Amendment protection * * *.

It should be obvious, then, that a law limiting the amount a person can spend to broadcast his political views is a direct restriction on speech. That is no different from a law limiting the amount a newspaper can pay its editorial staff or the amount a charity can pay its leafletters. It is equally clear that a limit on the amount a candidate can *raise* from any one individual for the purpose of speaking is also a direct limitation on speech. That is no different from a law limiting the amount a publisher can accept from any one shareholder or lender, or the amount a newspaper can charge any one advertiser or customer.

(b) Pooling Money is Not Speech

Another proposition which could explain at least some of the results of today's opinion is that the First Amendment right to spend money for speech does not include the right to combine with others in spending money for speech. Such a proposition fits uncomfortably with the concluding words of our Declaration of Independence: "And for the support of this Declaration, . . . we mutually pledge to each other our Lives, *our Fortunes* and our sacred Honor." (Emphasis added.) The freedom to associate with others for the dissemination of ideas — not just by singing or speaking in unison, but by pooling financial resources for expressive purposes — is part of the freedom of speech. * * *

If it were otherwise, Congress would be empowered to enact legislation requiring newspapers to be sole proprietorships, banning their use of partnership or corporate form. That sort of restriction would be an obvious violation of the First Amendment, and it is incomprehensible why the conclusion should change when what is at issue is the pooling of funds for the most important (and most perennially threatened) category of speech: electoral speech. The principle that such financial association does not enjoy full First Amendment protection threatens the existence of all political parties.

(c) Speech by Corporations Can Be Abridged

The last proposition that might explain at least some of today's casual abridgment of free-speech rights is this: that the particular form of association known as a corporation does not enjoy full First Amendment protection. Of course the text of the First Amendment does not limit its application in this fashion, even though "[b]y the end of the eighteenth century the corporation was a familiar figure in American economic life." C. Cooke, Corporation, Trust and Company 92 (1951). Nor is there any basis in reason why First Amendment rights should not attach to corporate associations — and we have said so. [*see e.g. First Nat. Bank of Boston* v. *Bellotti*, 435 U.S. 765 (1978)] [p. 895]. * * *

* * * In the modern world, giving the government power to exclude corporations from the political debate enables it effectively to muffle the voices that best represent the most significant segments of the economy and the most passionately held social and political views. People who associate — who pool their financial resources — for purposes of economic enterprise overwhelmingly do so in the corporate form; and with increasing frequency, incorporation is chosen by those who associate to defend and promote particular ideas — such as the American Civil Liberties Union and the National Rifle Association, parties to these cases. Imagine, then, a government that wished to suppress nuclear power — or oil and gas exploration, or automobile manufacturing, or gun ownership, or civil liberties — and that had the power to prohibit corporate advertising against its proposals. To be sure, the individuals involved in, or benefited by, those industries, or interested in those causes, could (given enough time) form political action committees or other associations to make their case. But the organizational form in which those enterprises already *exist*, and in which they can most quickly and most effectively get their message across, is the corporate form. The First Amendment does not in my view permit the restriction of that political speech. And the same holds true for

corporate electoral speech: A candidate should not be insulated from the most effective speech that the major participants in the economy and major incorporated interest groups can generate.

* * * But let us not be deceived. While the Government's briefs and arguments before this Court focused on the horrible "appearance of corruption," the most passionate floor statements during the debates on this legislation pertained to so-called attack ads, which the Constitution surely protects, but which Members of Congress analogized to "crack cocaine," 144 Cong. Rec. S868 (Feb. 24, 1998) (remarks of Sen. Daschle), "drive-by shooting[s]," *id.*, at S879 (remarks of Sen. Durbin), and "air pollution, "143 Cong. Rec. 20505 (1997) (remarks of Sen. Dorgan). There is good reason to believe that the ending of negative campaign ads was the principal attraction of the legislation. A Senate sponsor said, "I hope that we will not allow our attention to be distracted from the real issues at hand — how to raise the tenor of the debate in our elections and give people real choices. No one benefits from negative ads. They don't aid our Nation's political dialog." *Id.*, at 20521–20522 (remarks of Sen. McCain). He assured the body that "[y]ou cut off the soft money, you are going to see a lot less of that [attack ads]. Prohibit unions and corporations, and you will see a lot less of that. If you demand full disclosure for those who pay for those ads, you are going to see a lot less of that . . . ." 147 Cong. Rec. S3116 (Mar. 29, 2001) (remarks of Sen. McCain). See also, *e.g.,* 148 Cong. Rec. S2117 (Mar. 20, 2002) (remarks of Sen. Cantwell) ("This bill is about slowing the ad war . . . . It is about slowing political advertising and making sure the flow of negative ads by outside interest groups does not continue to permeate the airwaves"); 143 Cong. Rec. 20746 (1997) (remarks of Sen. Boxer) ("These so-called issues ads are not regulated at all and mention candidates by name. They directly attack candidates without any accountability. It is brutal. . . . We have an opportunity in the McCain-Feingold bill to stop that . . . "); 145 Cong. Rec. S12606–S12607 (Oct. 14, 1999) (remarks of Sen. Wellstone) ("I think these issue advocacy ads are a nightmare. I think all of us should hate them. . . . [By passing the legislation], [w]e could get some of this poison politics off television").

Another theme prominent in the legislative debates was the notion that there is too much money spent on elections. The first principle of "reform" was that "there should be less money in politics." 147 Cong. Rec. S3236 (Apr. 2, 2001) (remarks of Sen. Murray). "The enormous amounts of special interest money that flood our political system have become a cancer in our democracy." 148 Cong. Rec. S2151 (Mar. 20, 2002) (remarks of Sen. Kennedy). "[L]arge sums of money drown out the voice of the average voter." *Id.*, at H373 (Feb. 13, 2002) (remarks of Rep. Langevin). The system of campaign finance is "drowning in money." *Id.*, at H404 (remarks of Rep. Menendez). And most expansively:

> "Despite the ever-increasing sums spent on campaigns, we have not seen an improvement in campaign discourse, issue discussion or voter education. More money does not mean more ideas, more substance or more depth. Instead, it means more of what voters complain about most. More 30-second spots, more negativity and an increasingly longer campaign period." *Id.* at S2150 (Mar. 20, 2002) (remarks of Sen. Kerry).

Perhaps voters do detest these 30-second spots — though I suspect they detest even more hour-long campaign-debate interruptions of their favorite entertainment programming. Evidently, however, these ads *do persuade* voters, or else they would not be so routinely used by sophisticated politicians of all parties. The point, in any event, is that it is not the proper role of those who govern us to judge which campaign speech has "substance" and "depth" (do you think it might be that which is least damaging to incumbents?) and to abridge the rest.

And what exactly are these outrageous sums frittered away in determining who will govern us? A report prepared for Congress concluded that the total amount, in hard and soft money, spent on the 2000 federal elections was between $2.4 and $2.5 billion. *All* campaign spending in the United States, including state elections, ballot initiatives, and judicial elections, has been estimated at $3.9 billion for 2000, which was a year that "shattered spending and contribution records." Even taking this last, larger figure as the benchmark, it means that Americans spent about half as much electing all their Nation's officials, state and federal, as they spent on movie tickets ($7.8 billion); about a fifth as much as they spent on cosmetics and perfume ($18.8 billion); and about a sixth as much as they spent on pork (the nongovernmental sort) ($22.8 billion). If our democracy is drowning from this much spending, it cannot swim.

* * * This litigation is about preventing criticism of the government. I cannot say for certain that many, or some, or even any, of the Members of Congress who voted for this legislation did so not to produce "fairer" campaigns, but to mute criticism of their records and facilitate reelection. Indeed, I will stipulate that all those who voted for the Act believed they were acting for the good of the country. There remains the problem of the Charlie Wilson Phenomenon, named after Charles Wilson, former president of General Motors, who is supposed to have said during the Senate hearing on his nomination as Secretary of Defense that "what's good for General Motors is good for the country." Those in power, even giving them the benefit of the greatest good will, are inclined to believe that what is good for them is good for the country. Whether in prescient recognition of the Charlie Wilson Phenomenon, or out of fear of good old-fashioned, malicious, self-interested manipulation, "[t]he fundamental approach of the First Amendment . . . was to assume the worst, and to rule the regulation of political speech 'for fairness' sake' simply out of bounds." Having abandoned that approach to a limited extent in *Buckley*, we abandon it much further today.

We will unquestionably be called upon to abandon it further still in the future. * * *

The first instinct of power is the retention of power, and, under a Constitution that requires periodic elections, that is best achieved by the suppression of election-time speech. * * * The federal election campaign laws, which are already (as today's opinions show) so voluminous, so detailed, so complex, that no ordinary citizen dare run for office, or even contribute a significant sum, without hiring an expert adviser in the field, can be expected to grow more voluminous, more detailed, and more complex in the years to come — and always, always, with the objective of reducing the excessive amount of speech.

JUSTICE THOMAS * * * concurring in the judgment in part and dissenting in part[.]

* * * Today's holding continues a disturbing trend: the steady decrease in the level of scrutiny applied to restrictions on core political speech. Although this trend is most obvious in the review of contribution limits, it has now reached what even this Court today would presumably recognize as a direct restriction on core political speech: limitations on independent expenditures. * * *

The chilling endpoint of the Court's reasoning is not difficult to foresee: outright regulation of the press. None of the rationales offered by the defendants, and none of the reasoning employed by the Court, exempts the press. * * * Media companies can run pro-candidate editorials as easily as non-media corporations can pay for advertisements. Candidates can be just as grateful to media companies as they can be to corporations and unions. In terms of "the corrosive and distorting effects" of wealth accumulated by corporations that has "little or no correlation to the public's support for the corporation's political ideas," *Austin*, 494 U.S. at 660, there is no distinction between a media corporation and a non-media corporation. Media corporations are influential. There is little doubt that the editorials and commentary they run can affect elections. Nor is there any doubt that media companies often wish to influence elections. One would think that the New York Times fervently hopes that its endorsement of Presidential candidates will actually influence people. What is to stop a future Congress from determining that the press is "too influential," and that the "appearance of corruption" is significant when media organizations endorse candidates or run "slanted" or "biased" news stories in favor of candidates or parties? Or, even easier, what is to stop a future Congress from concluding that the availability of unregulated media corporations creates a loophole that allows for easy "circumvention" of the limitations of the current campaign finance laws? * * *

Although today's opinion does not expressly strip the press of First Amendment protection, there is no principle of law or logic that would prevent the application of the Court's reasoning in that setting. The press now operates at the whim of Congress.

JUSTICE KENNEDY, [with whom THE CHIEF JUSTICE and JUSTICE SCALIA join], dissenting in part[.] * * *

Our precedents teach, above all, that Government cannot be trusted to moderate its own rules for suppression of speech. The dangers posed by speech regulations have led the Court to insist upon principled constitutional lines and a rigorous standard of review. The majority now abandons these distinctions and limitations. * * *

The Court * * * in effect interprets the anticorruption rationale to allow regulation not just of "actual or apparent *quid pro quo* arrangements," but of any conduct that wins goodwill from or influences a Member of Congress. * * * Access, in the Court's view, has the same legal ramifications as actual or apparent corruption of officeholders. This new definition of corruption sweeps away all protections for speech that lie in its path.

* * * Access in itself . . . shows only that in a general sense an officeholder favors

someone or that someone has influence on the officeholder. There is no basis, in law or in fact, to say favoritism or influence in general is the same as corrupt favoritism or influence in particular. By equating vague and generic claims of favoritism or influence with actual or apparent corruption, the Court adopts a definition of corruption that dismantles basic First Amendment rules, permits Congress to suppress speech in the absence of a *quid pro quo* threat, and moves beyond the rationale that is *Buckley*'s very foundation.

The generic favoritism or influence theory articulated by the Court is at odds with standard First Amendment analyses because it is unbounded and susceptible to no limiting principle. Any given action might be favored by any given person, so by the Court's reasoning political loyalty of the purest sort can be prohibited. There is no remaining principled method for inquiring whether a campaign finance regulation does in fact regulate corruption in a serious and meaningful way. We are left to defer to a congressional conclusion that certain conduct creates favoritism or influence.

Though the majority cites common sense as the foundation for its definition of corruption, in the context of the real world only a single definition of corruption has been found to identify political corruption successfully and to distinguish good political responsiveness from bad — that is *quid pro quo*. Favoritism and influence are not, as the Government's theory suggests, avoidable in representative politics. It is in the nature of an elected representative to favor certain policies, and, by necessary corollary, to favor the voters and contributors who support those policies. It is well understood that a substantial and legitimate reason, if not the only reason, to cast a vote for, or to make a contribution to, one candidate over another is that the candidate will respond by producing those political outcomes the supporter favors. Democracy is premised on responsiveness. *Quid pro quo* corruption has been, until now, the only agreed upon conduct that represents the bad form of responsiveness and presents a justiciable standard with a relatively clear limiting principle: Bad responsiveness may be demonstrated by pointing to a relationship between an official and a *quid*.

The majority attempts to mask its extension of *Buckley* under claims that BCRA prevents the appearance of corruption, even if it does not prevent actual corruption, since some assert that any donation of money to a political party is suspect. Under *Buckley*'s holding that Congress has a valid "interest in stemming the reality or appearance of corruption," however, the inquiry does not turn on whether some persons assert that an appearance of corruption exists. Rather, the inquiry turns on whether the Legislature has established that the regulated conduct has inherent corruption potential, thus justifying the inference that regulating the conduct will stem the appearance of real corruption. *Buckley* was guided and constrained by this analysis. In striking down expenditure limits the Court in *Buckley* did not ask whether people thought large election expenditures corrupt, because clearly at that time many persons, including a majority of Congress and the President, did. ("According to the parties and *amici*, the primary interest served . . . by the Act as a whole, is the prevention of corruption and the appearance of corruption"). Instead, the Court asked whether the Government had proved that the regulated conduct, the expenditures, posed inherent *quid pro quo* corruption potential.

The *Buckley* decision made this analysis even clearer in upholding contribution limitations. It stated that even if actual corrupt contribution practices had not been proved, Congress had an interest in regulating the appearance of corruption that is "inherent in a regime of large individual financial contributions." The *quid pro quo* nature of candidate contributions justified the conclusion that the contributions pose inherent corruption potential; and this in turn justified the conclusion that their regulation would stem the appearance of real corruption. * * *

The majority permits a new and serious intrusion on speech when it upholds § 203, the key provision in Title II that prohibits corporations and labor unions from using money from their general treasury to fund electioneering communications. The majority compounds the error made in *Austin* v. *Michigan Chamber of Commerce*, and silences political speech central to the civic discourse that sustains and informs our democratic processes. Unions and corporations, including nonprofit corporations, now face severe criminal penalties for broadcasting advocacy messages that "refe[r] to a clearly identified candidate," in an election season. Instead of extending *Austin* to suppress new and vibrant voices, I would overrule it and return our campaign finance jurisprudence to principles consistent with the First Amendment.

* * * I surmise that even the majority, along with the Government, appreciates [the] problems with *Austin*. That is why it invents a new justification. We are now told that "the government also has a compelling interest in insulating federal elections from the type of corruption arising from the real or apparent creation of political debts."

This rationale has no limiting principle. Were we to accept it, Congress would have the authority to outlaw even pure issue ads, because they, too, could endear their sponsors to candidates who adopt the favored positions. Taken to its logical conclusion, the alleged Government interest "in insulating federal elections from . . . the real or apparent creation of political debts" also conflicts with *Buckley*. If a candidate feels grateful to a faceless, impersonal corporation for making independent expenditures, the gratitude cannot be any less when the money came from the CEO's own pocket. *Buckley*, however, struck down limitations on independent expenditures and rejected the Government's corruption argument absent evidence of coordination. The Government's position would eviscerate the line between expenditures and contributions and subject both to the same "complaisant review under the First Amendment." *FEC* v. *Beaumont*, 123 S. Ct. 2200 (2003). * * *

These regulations are more than minor clerical requirements. Rather, they create major disincentives for speech, with the effect falling most heavily on smaller entities that often have the most difficulty bearing the costs of compliance. Even worse, for an organization that has not yet set up a PAC, spontaneous speech that "refers to a clearly identified candidate for Federal office" becomes impossible, even if the group's vital interests are threatened by a piece of legislation pending before Congress on the eve of a federal election. Couple the litany of administrative burdens with the categorical restriction limiting PACs' solicitation activities to "members," and it is apparent that PACs are inadequate substitutes for corporations in their ability to engage in unfettered expression.

Even if the newly formed PACs manage to attract members and disseminate their messages against these heavy odds, they have been forced to assume a false identity while doing so. * * * Forcing speech through an artificial "secondhand endorsement structure . . . debases the value of the voice of nonprofit corporate speakers . . . [because] PAC's are interim, ad hoc organizations with little continuity or responsibility." In contrast, their sponsoring organizations "have a continuity, a stability, and an influence" that allows "their members and the public at large to evaluate their . . . credibility."

The majority can articulate no compelling justification for imposing this scheme of compulsory ventriloquism. If the majority is concerned about corruption and distortion of the political process, it makes no sense to diffuse the corporate message and, under threat of criminal penalties, to compel the corporation to spread the blame to its ad hoc intermediary. * * *

Once we turn away from the distraction of the PAC option, the provision cannot survive strict scrutiny. * * *

The prohibition, with its crude temporal and geographic proxies, is a severe and unprecedented ban on protected speech. * * * Suppose a few Senators want to show their constituents in the logging industry how much they care about working families and propose a law, 60 days before the election, that would harm the environment by allowing logging in national forests. Under § 203, a nonprofit environmental group would be unable to run an ad referring to these Senators in their districts. The suggestion that the group could form and fund a PAC in the short time required for effective participation in the political debate is fanciful. For reasons already discussed, moreover, an ad hoc PAC would not be as effective as the environmental group itself in gaining credibility with the public. Never before in our history has the Court upheld a law that suppresses speech to this extent.

The group would want to refer to these Senators, either by name or by photograph, not necessarily because an election is at stake. It might be supposed the hypothetical Senators have had an impeccable environmental record, so the environmental group might have no previous or present interest in expressing an opinion on their candidacies. Or, the election might not be hotly contested in some of the districts, so whatever the group says would have no practical effect on the electoral outcome. The ability to refer to candidates and officeholders is important because it allows the public to communicate with them on issues of common concern. Section 203's sweeping approach fails to take into account this significant free speech interest. Under any conventional definition of overbreadth, it fails to meet strict scrutiny standards. It forces electioneering communications sponsored by an environmental group to contend with faceless and nameless opponents and consign their broadcast, as the NRA well puts it, to a world where politicians who threaten the environment must be referred to as " 'He Whose Name Cannot Be Spoken.' " * * *

We are supposed to find comfort in the knowledge that the ad is banned under § 203 only if it "is targeted to the relevant electorate," defined as communications that can be received by 50,000 or more persons in the candidate's district. This Orwellian criterion, however, is analogous to a law, unconstitutional under any known First Amendment theory, that would allow a speaker to say anything he chooses, so long as his intended audience could not hear him. * * * A central purpose of issue ads is to urge the public to pay close attention to the candidate's platform on the featured issues. By banning broadcast in the very district where the candidate is standing for election, § 203 shields information at the heart of the First Amendment from precisely those citizens who most value the right to make a responsible judgment at the voting booth.

In the end the Government and intervenor-defendants cannot dispute the looseness of the connection between § 203 and the Government's proffered interest in stemming corruption. * * * Instead, they defend § 203 on the ground that the targeted ads "may influence," are "likely to influence," or "will in all likelihood have the effect of influencing" a federal election. The mere fact that an ad may, in one fashion or another, influence an election is an insufficient reason for outlawing it. I should have thought influencing elections to be the whole point of political speech. Neither strict scrutiny nor any other standard the Court has adopted to date permits outlawing speech on the ground that it might influence an election, which might lead to greater access to politicians by the sponsoring organization, which might lead to actual corruption or the appearance of corruption. Settled law requires a real and close connection between end and means. The attenuated causation the majority endorses today is antithetical to the concept of narrow tailoring. * * *

As communities have grown and technology has evolved, concerted speech not only has become more effective than a single voice but also has become the natural preference and efficacious choice for many Americans. The Court, upholding multiple laws that suppress both spontaneous and concerted speech, leaves us less free than before. Today's decision breaks faith with our tradition of robust and unfettered debate.

Notes and Questions

1. *McConnell* upheld the restrictions on "electioneering communications" in part on the grounds that the distinction between "express advocacy" and "issue advocacy" was "functionally meaningless." Recall, however, that one reason the *Buckley* Court struck down limits on independent expenditures was that, having held that the term "expenditure" should be interpreted as applying only to express advocacy, the state had no interest in limiting expenditures, because "[i]t would naively underestimate the ingenuity and resourcefulness of persons and groups * * * to believe that they would have much difficulty devising expenditures that skirted the restriction on express advocacy * * * but nevertheless benefitted a candidate's campaign." 424 U.S. at 45. What, if anything, changed in the intervening years?

McConnell's description of the distinction between issue advocacy and express advocacy as "functionally meaningless" is one of the opinion's most notable phrases, appearing twice in the opinion. The second appearance of the phrase, however, includes a qualifier: "the line between express advocacy and issue advocacy is, *for Congress's purposes*, functionally meaningless." 540 U.S. at 217 (emphasis added). Did the distinction serve any purpose for persons other than Congress? Imagine that you are a lawyer, seeking to advise your client as to whether a particular ad is subject to regulation under FECA. Would the express advocacy standard be functionally meaningless, or would it be very meaningful?

Buckley drew the distinction between issue advocacy and express advocacy in order to remove the vagueness problem for the speaker. BCRA handled this vagueness problem by establishing a bright line based on the number of days prior to an election that an ad was run, and whether it mentioned a clearly identified candidate. This shifts the question from one of vagueness to one of overbreadth. The litigants hotly debated the meaning of two studies relied on by the government: CRAIG B. HOLMAN & LUKE P. MCLOUGHLIN, BUYING TIME 2000: TELEVISION ADVERTISEMENTS IN THE 2000 FEDERAL ELECTIONS (Brennan Center for Justice 2001), and JONATHAN S. KRASNO & DANIEL E. SELTZ, BUYING TIME 1998: TELEVISION ADVERTISEMENTS IN THE 1998 CONGRESSIONAL ELECTIONS (Brennan Center for Justice 2000), but in the end the Court was comfortable that most issue ads run within BCRA's electioneering communications time frame "clearly had such [an electioneering] purpose." The plaintiffs' expert has criticized the Court for "ignor[ing] the data and empirical issues." James L. Gibson, *BCRA's Assault on the First Amendment: The Death of the Overbreadth Doctrine?*, 3 ELECTION L.J. 245, 249 (2004). Professor David Magleby, who served as an expert for the government, counters that *McConnell* is unique in the attention paid by the Court to the record evidence. David B. Magleby, *The Importance of the Record in McConnell v. FEC*, 3 ELECTION L.J. 285 (2004),

Did *McConnell* underestimate the scope of BCRA's electioneering communications prohibitions? While the law's electioneering communications window appears to be limited to 90 days (30 days before the primary, 60 days before the general election), the fact that many media markets lap into multiple states means that at the presidential level, in many metropolitan areas the prohibition extends far beyond those time frames. *See* Bradley A. Smith & Jason Robert Owen, *Boundary-Based Restrictions in Boundless Broadcast Media Markets: McConnell v. FEC's Underinclusive Overbreadth Analysis*, 18 STAN. L. & POL'Y REV. 240 (2007) (studying numerous multi-state media markets and finding that in presidential elections the electioneering communications limitations applied for in excess of 120 days in all markets, and upwards of 200 days in many).

2.   Note that the distinction between express advocacy and issue advocacy remained an important part of the law after *McConnell*, because it would still determination the level of regulation of speech outside the "electioneering communications" windows of BCRA. Even after *Citizens United v. Federal Election Commission*, 558 U.S. 310 [*infra* p. 941] upheld the right of corporations to make express advocacy independent expenditures, the distinction remains important for purposes of reporting disclosure, as we will see in Part G of this Chapter.

3.   Are limits on corporate speech content neutral? Or do they reflect certain assumptions about the positions that corporations might take on public issues and campaigns?

4.   Justice Scalia suggests that much of the impetus for BCRA was to protect incumbent lawmakers from criticism, and cites numerous quotes from the Congressional Record. Is it legitimate to question the motives of lawmakers in this way? Does it matter, if the law can be supported on more neutral grounds, anyway? Is the possibility that incumbents will use campaign finance laws to help keep themselves

in power a reason to maintain a high level of judicial scrutiny and particular skepticism about the evils said to be addresses by legislation?

5.   At the time it was decided, *McConnell* was thought to mark the triumph of judicial deference in the realm of campaign finance. However, the Court's decision in *Randall v. Sorrell*, 548 U.S. 230 (2006) [p. 852] just two terms later marked a return to of judicial skepticism, and just three and a half years after being announced, *McConnell's* holding on independent expenditures was sharply trimmed back in *Federal Election Commission v. Wisconsin Right to Life, Inc. (WRTL II)*, 551 U.S. 449 (2007). The issue in *WRTL II* was an as-applied challenge to the very electioneering communications provisions of BCRA upheld against a facial challenge in *McConnell*. WRTL, a non-profit corporation that accepted contributions from for-profit corporations, sought to run a trio of radio ads urging senators to oppose filibusters of President Bush's judicial nominees. Here is the script of one of the ads, called "Wedding":

" 'PASTOR: And who gives this woman to be married to this man?

" 'BRIDE'S FATHER: Well, as father of the bride, I certainly could. But instead, I'd like to share a few tips on how to properly install drywall. Now you put the drywall up * * *

" 'VOICE-OVER: Sometimes it's just not fair to delay an important decision.

" 'But in Washington it's happening. A group of Senators is using the filibuster delay tactic to block federal judicial nominees from a simple "yes" or "no" vote. So qualified candidates don't get a chance to serve.

" 'It's politics at work, causing gridlock and backing up some of our courts to a state of emergency.

" 'Contact Senators Feingold and Kohl and tell them to oppose the filibuster.

" 'Visit: BeFair.org

" 'Paid for by Wisconsin Right to Life (befair.org), which is responsible for the content of this advertising and not authorized by any candidate or candidate's committee.' "

Id. at 458. Two other ads, "Loan" and "Waiting" were similar. The ads were prohibited by BCRA because they were to air within the 30 day pre-primary election window proscribed by BCRA for corporate funded ads naming a candidate. WRTL argued that the ads were not the "functional equivalent of express advocacy" as upheld in *McConnell*. The government argued that an ad should be considered the "functional equivalent of express advocacy" if they were intended to influence elections and could have that effect. The Court disagreed. Chief Justice Roberts, wrote the lead opinion:

Far from serving the values the First Amendment is meant to protect, an intent-based test would chill core political speech by opening the door to a trial on every ad within the terms of § 203, on the theory that the speaker actually intended to affect an election, no matter how compelling the indications that the ad concerned a pending legislative or policy issue. No reasonable speaker would choose to run an ad covered by BCRA if its only defense to a criminal prosecution would be that its motives were pure. An intent-based standard "blankets with uncertainty whatever may be said," and "offers no security for free discussion." * * *

[A] court should find that an ad is the functional equivalent of express advocacy only if the ad is susceptible of no reasonable interpretation other than as an appeal to vote for or against a specific candidate. Under this test, WRTL's three ads are plainly not the functional equivalent of express advocacy. First, their content is consistent with that of a genuine issue ad: The ads focus on a legislative issue, take a position on the issue, exhort the public to adopt that position, and urge the public to contact public officials with respect to the matter. Second, their content lacks indicia of express advocacy: The ads do not mention an election, candidacy, political party, or challenger; and they do not take a position on a candidate's character, qualifications, or fitness for office. * * *

BCRA § 203 can be constitutionally applied to WRTL's ads only if it is narrowly tailored to further a compelling interest. * * * This Court has never recognized a compelling interest in regulating ads, like WRTL's, that are neither express advocacy nor its functional equivalent.[9]

* * *

This Court has long recognized "the governmental interest in preventing corruption and the appearance of corruption" in election campaigns. This interest has been invoked as a reason for upholding *contribution* limits. We have suggested that this interest might also justify limits on electioneering *expenditures* because it may be that, in some circumstances, "large independent expenditures pose the same dangers of actual or apparent *quid pro quo* arrangements as do large contributions."

---

[9] The dissent stresses a number of points that, while not central to our decision, nevertheless merit a response. First, the dissent overstates its case when it asserts that the "PAC alternative" gives corporations a constitutionally sufficient outlet to speak. PACs impose well-documented and onerous burdens, particularly on small nonprofits. See *MCFL. McConnell* did conclude that segregated funds "provid[e] corporations and unions with a constitutionally sufficient opportunity to engage in express advocacy" and its functional equivalent, but that holding did not extend beyond functional equivalents — and if it did, the PAC option would justify regulation of all corporate speech, a proposition we have rejected, see *Bellotti.* Second, the response that a speaker should just take out a newspaper ad, or use a website, rather than complain that it cannot speak through a broadcast communication, is too glib. Even assuming for the sake of argument that the possibility of using a different medium of communication has relevance in determining the permissibility of a limitation on speech, newspaper ads and websites are not reasonable alternatives to broadcast speech in terms of impact and effectiveness. Third, we disagree with the dissent's view that corporations can still speak by changing what they say to avoid mentioning candidates. That argument is akin to telling Cohen that he cannot wear his jacket because he is free to wear one that says "I disagree with the draft," cf. *Cohen* v. *California*, 403 U.S. 15 (1971), or telling 44 Liquormart that it can advertise so long as it avoids mentioning prices, cf. *44 Liquormart, Inc.* v. *Rhode Island*, 517 U.S. 484 (1996). Such notions run afoul of "the fundamental rule of protection under the First Amendment, that a speaker has the autonomy to choose the content of his own message." *Hurley* v. *Irish-American Gay, Lesbian and Bisexual Group of Boston, Inc.*, 515 U.S. 557 (1995). [Relocated — Eds.]

McConnell arguably applied this interest — which this Court had only assumed could justify regulation of express advocacy — to ads that were the "functional equivalent" of express advocacy. But to justify regulation of WRTL's ads, this interest must be stretched yet another step to ads that are *not* the functional equivalent of express advocacy. Enough is enough. Issue ads like WRTL's are by no means equivalent to contributions, and the *quid-pro-quo* corruption interest cannot justify regulating them. To equate WRTL's ads with contributions is to ignore their value as political speech.

Appellants argue that an expansive definition of "functional equivalent" is needed to ensure that issue advocacy does not circumvent the rule against express advocacy, which in turn helps protect against circumvention of the rule against contributions. But such a prophylaxis-upon-prophylaxis approach to regulating expression is not consistent with strict scrutiny. * * *

[A]s is often the case in this Court's First Amendment opinions, we have gotten this far in the analysis without quoting the Amendment itself: "Congress shall make no law . . . abridging the freedom of speech." The Framers' actual words put these cases in proper perspective. Our jurisprudence over the past 216 years has rejected an absolutist interpretation of those words, but when it comes to drawing difficult lines in the area of pure political speech — between what is protected and what the Government may ban — it is worth recalling the language we are applying. *McConnell* held that express advocacy of a candidate or his opponent by a corporation shortly before an election may be prohibited, along with the functional equivalent of such express advocacy. We have no occasion to revisit that determination today. But when it comes to defining what speech qualifies as the functional equivalent of express advocacy subject to such a ban — the issue we *do* have to decide — we give the benefit of the doubt to speech, not censorship. The First Amendment's command that "Congress shall make no law . . . abridging the freedom of speech" demands at least that.

Id. at 468–482. Justice Roberts' opinion was joined only by Justice Alito. Justices Scalia, Kennedy, and Thomas concurred in the judgment, and would have used the case to reconsider (and presumably overrule) *McConnell*. The dissenting justices, in an opinion by Justice Souter, argued that Roberts' opinion was a *de facto* overruling of *McConnell* (an opinion shared by the three justices concurring in the judgment). Not surprisingly (at least in retrospect), much of Justice Souter's dissent foreshadowed arguments that the dissent would make three years later in *Citizens United v. FEC*.

6. *WRTL II* not only limited the reach of *McConnell*, but the lead opinion strikes a remarkably different tone from that in *McConnell*. *McConnell's* majority began by quoting turn of the century (20th century, that is) progressive statesman/politician Elihu Root about the need for regulation, and concluded by stating the Court had no illusions but that more regulation would be needed in the future. In contrast, Chief Justice Roberts' controlling opinion in *WRTL II* conspicuously concludes with a recitation of the First Amendment and claims as a rhetorical highlight the simple exclamation, "enough is enough." *WRTL II* evinces a skepti-

cism of government not seen since the Court's early decisions in *CARC*, *Bellotti*, and *Buckley* itself, and certainly different from *McConnell*:

> In both tone and substance, *Buckley* is an affirmation of free political speech, an expression of skepticism about legislative trustworthiness in regulating political campaign speech, and a concomitant rejection of all but the narrowest rationales for its regulation. Its animating premises are that speech about issues and candidates during election campaigns is of the utmost constitutional value; that limitations on contributions to and expenditures on such speech are the functional equivalent of regulations of speech itself; that limitations of both must be subjected to careful scrutiny * * *

> *McConnell* discarded *Buckley*'s underlying premises and almost entirely dismantled the limits it imposed on the power of legislatures to regulate speech during political campaigns. It appeared to regard the speech regulated by the BCRA as of negligible value, it expressed practically unconditional confidence in the legislature's trustworthiness in regulating it, and it embraced an expansive rationale for regulation.

See Lillian R. BeVier, McConnell v. FEC: *Not Senator Buckley's First Amendment*, 3 ELECTION L.J. 127, 128 (2004). Professor Hasen, from the other side of the debate, expands on the point:

> The *McConnell* opinion was full of language about legislative deference, flexibility, political reality, and the need to give Congress the room to address campaign finance problems step-by-step. It gave a long and fawning history tracing congressional efforts to limit big money, and especially corporate election spending, in the federal electoral process. It spoke of the ease of evading campaign finance laws, and the need for courts to take a functional, not formal, view of what counts as election-related speech. It minimized First Amendment concerns by noting alternative means for corporate influence over the electoral process, including PAC requirements, alternative means of communications, or even changing the content of the electoral message such as by omitting the name of the candidate mentioned in the advertisement.

> The tone of the principal opinion in WRTL II is the polar opposite of McConnell. There is no nod to legislative deference or recognition of Congress's need to react to the "hydraulic" effect of money. Rather than talk of a PAC alternative, the WRTL II principal opinion mentions a free speech "ban" (or variations on the word "ban") twelve times and a speech "blackout" seventeen times. It refers to corporate election broadcasting paid for from treasury funds as a "crime" twice. * * *

> The WRTL II principal opinion makes no mention of congressional deference (nor does it use the term "loophole," a term appearing ten times in the McConnell joint majority opinion), but the term "First Amendment" appears eighteen times and variations on the word "censor" three times. In contrast, the discussion of section 203 in McConnell's joint majority opinion mentioned the First Amendment merely three times, and never to cel-

ebrate the free speech principles behind the Amendment."

Richard L. Hasen, 92 MINN. L. REV. 1064, 1086–87 (2008). The tone of opinions in campaign finance cases also seem, to at least some observers, to be growing sharper, and more bitter.

> [T]he nub of the controversy lies in this: the majority and the dissents in *WRTL II* (or in any of the campaign finance cases that the Court has decided since *Austin*) occupy *no* common First Amendment ground. Though they disagree in good faith, both of their points of view cannot be right, and the differences that exist between them are at such a fundamental level that they leave scant room for compromise * * *

> Reading the differing opinions in search of an opening wedge for genuine engagement, one finds the justices talking past one another. They share neither empirical assumptions nor theoretical premises.

Lillian R. BeVier, *First Amendment Basics Redux:* Buckley v. Valeo *to* FEC v. Wisconsin Right to Life, 2006–07 CATO SUP. CT. REV. 77, 105 (2007).

7. The *WRTL II* dissent argues explicitly that the decision is not faithful to *McConnell*. The controlling opinion implies, and Justice Scalia's opinion argues explicitly, that *McConnell* was not faithful to *Buckley*. Do you agree? How much infidelity is going on at the Court? What impact should this have when considering the applicability of *stare decisis*, as the Court would do in the next case?

CITIZENS UNITED v. FEDERAL ELECTION COMMISSION
Supreme Court of the United States
558 U.S. 310, 130 S. Ct. 876, 175 L. Ed. 2d 753 (2010)

JUSTICE KENNEDY delivered the opinion of the Court [in the entirety of which CHIEF JUSTICE ROBERTS, JUSTICE SCALIA, and JUSTICE ALITO join; in which JUSTICE THOMAS joins except as to Part IV; and in which JUSTICE STEVENS, JUSTICE GINSBURG, JUSTICE BREYER, and JUSTICE SOTOMAYOR join as to Part IV].

Federal law prohibits corporations and unions from using their general treasury funds to make independent expenditures for speech defined as an "electioneering communication" or for speech expressly advocating the election or defeat of a candidate. 2 U.S.C. § 441b. Limits on electioneering communications were upheld in *McConnell* v. *Federal Election Comm'n*, 540 U.S. 93, 203–209 (2003) [p. 923]. The holding of *McConnell* rested to a large extent on an earlier case, *Austin* v. *Michigan Chamber of Commerce*, 494 U.S. 652 (1990) [p. 907]. *Austin* had held that political speech may be banned based on the speaker's corporate identity.

In this case we are asked to reconsider *Austin* and, in effect, *McConnell*.

I

Citizens United is a nonprofit corporation. It * * * has an annual budget of about $12 million. Most of its funds are from donations by individuals; but, in addition, it accepts a small portion of its funds from for-profit corporations.

In January 2008, Citizens United released a film entitled *Hillary: The Movie*. We refer to the film as *Hillary*. It is a 90-minute documentary about then-Senator Hillary Clinton, who was a candidate in the Democratic Party's 2008 Presidential primary elections. *Hillary* mentions Senator Clinton by name and depicts interviews with political commentators and other persons, most of them quite critical of Senator Clinton. *Hillary* was released in theaters and on DVD, but Citizens United wanted to increase distribution by making it available through video-on-demand.

Video-on-demand allows digital cable subscribers to select programming from various menus, including movies, television shows, sports, news, and music. The viewer can watch the program at any time and can elect to rewind or pause the program. In December 2007, a cable company offered, for a payment of $1.2 million, to make *Hillary* available on a video-on-demand channel called "Elections '08." Some video-on-demand services require viewers to pay a small fee to view a selected program, but here the proposal was to make *Hillary* available to viewers free of charge.

To implement the proposal, Citizens United was prepared to pay for the video-on-demand; and to promote the film, it produced two 10-second ads and one 30-second ad for *Hillary*. Each ad includes a short (and, in our view, pejorative) statement about Senator Clinton, followed by the name of the movie and the movie's Website address. Citizens United desired to promote the video-on-demand offering by running advertisements on broadcast and cable television.

Before the Bipartisan Campaign Reform Act of 2002 (BCRA), federal law prohibited — and still does prohibit — corporations and unions from using general treasury funds to make direct contributions to candidates or independent expenditures that expressly advocate the election or defeat of a candidate, through any form of media, in connection with certain qualified federal elections. 2 U.S.C. § 441b; BCRA § 203 amended § 441b to prohibit any "electioneering communication" as well. 2 U.S.C. § 441b(b)(2). An electioneering communication is defined as "any broadcast, cable, or satellite communication" that "refers to a clearly identified candidate for Federal office" and is made within 30 days of a primary or 60 days of a general election. § 434(f)(3)(A). * * * Corporations and unions * * * may establish, however, a "separate segregated fund" (known as a political action committee, or PAC) for [express advocacy or electioneering communications]. 2 U.S.C. § 441b(b)(2). The moneys received by the segregated fund are limited to donations from stockholders and employees of the corporation or, in the case of unions, members of the union. *Ibid.*

Citizens United wanted to make *Hillary* available through video-on-demand within 30 days of the 2008 primary elections. It feared, however, that both the film and the ads would be covered by § 441b's ban on corporate-funded independent expenditures, thus subjecting the corporation to civil and criminal penalties under § 437g. In December 2007, Citizens United sought declaratory and injunctive relief against the FEC. It argued that (1) § 441b is unconstitutional as applied to *Hillary*; and (2) BCRA's disclaimer and disclosure requirements, BCRA §§ 201 and 311, are unconstitutional as applied to *Hillary* and to the three ads for the movie. * * *

III * * *

* * * Section 441b makes it a felony for all corporations — including nonprofit advocacy corporations — either to expressly advocate the election or defeat of candidates or to broadcast electioneering communications within 30 days of a primary election and 60 days of a general election. Thus, the following acts would all be felonies under § 441b: The Sierra Club runs an ad, within the crucial phase of 60 days before the general election, that exhorts the public to disapprove of a Congressman who favors logging in national forests; the National Rifle Association publishes a book urging the public to vote for the challenger because the incumbent U.S. Senator supports a handgun ban; and the American Civil Liberties Union creates a Web site telling the public to vote for a Presidential candidate in light of that candidate's defense of free speech. These prohibitions are classic examples of censorship.

Section 441b is a ban on corporate speech notwithstanding the fact that a PAC created by a corporation can still speak. A PAC is a separate association from the corporation. So the PAC exemption from § 441b's expenditure ban, § 441b(b)(2), does not allow corporations to speak. Even if a PAC could somehow allow a corporation to speak — and it does not — the option to form PACs does not alleviate the First Amendment problems with § 441b. PACs are burdensome alternatives; they are expensive to administer and subject to extensive regulations. For example, every PAC must appoint a treasurer, forward donations to the treasurer promptly, keep detailed records of the identities of the persons making donations, preserve receipts for three years, and file an organization statement and report changes to this information within 10 days.

And that is just the beginning. PACs must file detailed monthly reports with the FEC, which are due at different times depending on the type of election that is about to occur:

> "These reports must contain information regarding the amount of cash on hand; the total amount of receipts, detailed by 10 different categories; the identification of each political committee and candidate's authorized or affiliated committee making contributions, and any persons making loans, providing rebates, refunds, dividends, or interest or any other offset to operating expenditures in an aggregate amount over $200; the total amount of all disbursements, detailed by 12 different categories; the names of all authorized or affiliated committees to whom expenditures aggregating over $200 have been made; persons to whom loan repayments or refunds have been made; the total sum of all contributions, operating expenses, outstanding debts and obligations, and the settlement terms of the retirement of any debt or obligation." [*McConnell*,] 540 U.S., at 331–332 [(opinion of KENNEDY, J.)] (quoting *MCFL*, *supra*, at 253–254).

PACs have to comply with these regulations just to speak. This might explain why fewer than 2,000 of the millions of corporations in this country have PACs. PACs, furthermore, must exist before they can speak. Given the onerous restrictions, a corporation may not be able to establish a PAC in time to make its views known regarding candidates and issues in a current campaign.

Section 441b's prohibition on corporate independent expenditures is thus a ban on speech. As a "restriction on the amount of money a person or group can spend on political communication during a campaign," that statute "necessarily reduces the quantity of expression by restricting the number of issues discussed, the depth of their exploration, and the size of the audience reached." *Buckley* v. *Valeo*, 424 U.S. 1, 19 (1976) *(per curiam).* * * * If § 441b applied to individuals, no one would believe that it is merely a time, place, or manner restriction on speech. Its purpose and effect are to silence entities whose voices the Government deems to be suspect.

Speech is an essential mechanism of democracy, for it is the means to hold officials accountable to the people. The right of citizens to inquire, to hear, to speak, and to use information to reach consensus is a precondition to enlightened self-government and a necessary means to protect it. * * *

For these reasons, political speech must prevail against laws that would suppress it, whether by design or inadvertence. Laws that burden political speech are "subject to strict scrutiny," which requires the Government to prove that the restriction "furthers a compelling interest and is narrowly tailored to achieve that interest." * * * Premised on mistrust of governmental power, the First Amendment stands against attempts to disfavor certain subjects or viewpoints. Prohibited, too, are restrictions distinguishing among different speakers, allowing speech by some but not others. See *First Nat. Bank of Boston* v. *Bellotti*, 435 U.S. 765, 784 (1978) [p. 895]. As instruments to censor, these categories are interrelated: Speech restrictions based on the identity of the speaker are all too often simply a means to control content.

Quite apart from the purpose or effect of regulating content, moreover, the Government may commit a constitutional wrong when by law it identifies certain preferred speakers. By taking the right to speak from some and giving it to others, the Government deprives the disadvantaged person or class of the right to use speech to strive to establish worth, standing, and respect for the speaker's voice. The Government may not by these means deprive the public of the right and privilege to determine for itself what speech and speakers are worthy of consideration. The First Amendment protects speech and speaker, and the ideas that flow from each.

The Court has upheld a narrow class of speech restrictions that operate to the disadvantage of certain persons, but these rulings were based on an interest in allowing governmental entities [such as schools, prisons, the military, and the civil service] to perform their functions. The corporate independent expenditures at issue in this case, however, would not interfere with governmental functions, so these cases are inapposite. These precedents stand only for the proposition that there are certain governmental functions that cannot operate without some restrictions on particular kinds of speech. By contrast, it is inherent in the nature of the political process that voters must be free to obtain information from diverse sources in order to determine how to cast their votes. At least before *Austin*, the Court had not allowed the exclusion of a class of speakers from the general public dialogue.

We find no basis for the proposition that, in the context of political speech, the

Government may impose restrictions on certain disfavored speakers. Both history and logic lead us to this conclusion.

The Court has recognized that First Amendment protection extends to corporations. *Bellotti, supra,* at 778, n.14. * * *

This protection has been extended by explicit holdings to the context of political speech. See, *e.g.,* [*NAACP* v.] *Button,* 371 U.S. [415], 428–429 [(1963)]; *Grosjean* v. *American Press Co.,* 297 U.S. 233, 244 (1936). Under the rationale of these precedents, political speech does not lose First Amendment protection "simply because its source is a corporation." *Bellotti, supra,* at 784; see *Pacific Gas & Elec. Co.* v. *Public Util. Comm'n of Cal.,* 475 U.S. 1, 8 (1986) (plurality opinion) ("The identity of the speaker is not decisive in determining whether speech is protected. Corporations and other associations, like individuals, contribute to the 'discussion, debate, and the dissemination of information and ideas' that the First Amendment seeks to foster" (quoting *Bellotti,* 435 U.S., at 783)). The Court has thus rejected the argument that political speech of corporations or other associations should be treated differently under the First Amendment simply because such associations are not "natural persons." *Id.,* at 776; see *id.,* at 780, n.16.

At least since the latter part of the 19th century, the laws of some States and of the United States imposed a ban on corporate direct contributions to candidates. *See* B. SMITH, UNFREE SPEECH: THE FOLLY OF CAMPAIGN FINANCE REFORM 23 (2001). Yet not until 1947 did Congress first prohibit independent expenditures by corporations and labor unions in § 304 of the Labor Management Relations Act 1947 (codified at 2 U.S.C. § 251). In passing this Act Congress overrode the veto of President Truman, who warned that the expenditure ban was a "dangerous intrusion on free speech."

For almost three decades thereafter, the Court did not reach the question whether restrictions on corporate and union expenditures are constitutional. * * *

In *Buckley,* the Court addressed various challenges to the Federal Election Campaign Act of 1971 (FECA) as amended in 1974. These amendments created 18 U.S.C. § 608(e), an independent expenditure ban * * * that applied to individuals as well as corporations and labor unions. * * *

The *Buckley* Court explained that the potential for *quid pro quo* corruption distinguished direct contributions to candidates from independent expenditures. The Court emphasized that "the independent expenditure ceiling . . . fails to serve any substantial governmental interest in stemming the reality or appearance of corruption in the electoral process," *id.,* at 47–48, because "[t]he absence of prearrangement and coordination . . . alleviates the danger that expenditures will be given as a *quid pro quo* for improper commitments from the candidate," *id.,* at 47. *Buckley* invalidated § 608(e)'s restrictions on independent expenditures, with only one Justice dissenting.

Buckley did not consider § 610's separate ban on corporate and union independent expenditures * * *. Had § 610 been challenged in the wake of *Buckley,* however, it could not have been squared with the reasoning and analysis of that precedent. The expenditure ban invalidated in *Buckley,* § 608(e), applied to corporations and unions; and some of the prevailing plaintiffs in *Buckley* were corporations, *id.*, at 8. * * *

Notwithstanding this precedent, Congress recodified § 610's corporate and union expenditure ban at 2 U.S.C. § 441b four months after *Buckley* was decided. Section 441b is the independent expenditure restriction challenged here.

Less than two years after *Buckley*, *Bellotti* reaffirmed the First Amendment principle that the Government cannot restrict political speech based on the speaker's corporate identity. *Bellotti* could not have been clearer when it struck down a state-law prohibition on corporate independent expenditures related to referenda issues:

> "We thus find no support in the First . . . Amendment, or in the decisions of this Court, for the proposition that speech that otherwise would be within the protection of the First Amendment loses that protection simply because its source is a corporation that cannot prove, to the satisfaction of a court, a material effect on its business or property. * * *

> "In the realm of protected speech, the legislature is constitutionally disqualified from dictating the subjects about which persons may speak and the speakers who may address a public issue." *Id.*, at 784–785.

It is important to note that the reasoning and holding of *Bellotti* did not rest on the existence of a viewpoint-discriminatory statute. It rested on the principle that the Government lacks the power to ban corporations from speaking.

Bellotti did not address the constitutionality of the State's ban on corporate independent expenditures to support candidates. In our view, however, that restriction would have been unconstitutional under *Bellotti*'s central principle: that the First Amendment does not allow political speech restrictions based on a speaker's corporate identity.

Thus the law stood until *Austin*. * * * There, the Michigan Chamber of Commerce sought to use general treasury funds to run a newspaper ad supporting a specific candidate. Michigan law, however, prohibited corporate independent expenditures that supported or opposed any candidate for state office. A violation of the law was punishable as a felony. The Court sustained the speech prohibition.

To bypass *Buckley* and *Bellotti*, the *Austin* Court identified a new governmental interest in limiting political speech: an antidistortion interest. *Austin* found a compelling governmental interest in preventing "the corrosive and distorting effects of immense aggregations of wealth that are accumulated with the help of the corporate form and that have little or no correlation to the public's support for the corporation's political ideas." 494 U.S., at 660.

The Court is thus confronted with conflicting lines of precedent: a pre-*Austin* line that forbids restrictions on political speech based on the speaker's corporate identity and a post-*Austin* line that permits them. No case before *Austin* had held that Congress could prohibit independent expenditures for political speech based on the speaker's corporate identity. * * *

In its defense of the corporate-speech restrictions in § 441b, the Government notes the antidistortion rationale on which *Austin* and its progeny rest in part, yet it all but abandons reliance upon it. It argues instead that two other compelling interests support *Austin*'s holding that corporate expenditure restrictions are constitutional: an anticorruption interest and a shareholder-protection interest. We consider the three points in turn.

As for *Austin*'s antidistortion rationale, the Government does little to defend it. And with good reason, for the rationale cannot support § 441b.

If the First Amendment has any force, it prohibits Congress from fining or jailing citizens, or associations of citizens, for simply engaging in political speech. If the antidistortion rationale were to be accepted, however, it would permit Government to ban political speech simply because the speaker is an association that has taken on the corporate form. The Government contends that *Austin* permits it to ban corporate expenditures for almost all forms of communication stemming from a corporation. If *Austin* were correct, the Government could prohibit a corporation from expressing political views in media beyond those presented here, such as by printing books. The Government responds "that the FEC has never applied this statute to a book," and if it did, "there would be quite [a] good as-applied challenge." This troubling assertion of brooding governmental power cannot be reconciled with the confidence and stability in civic discourse that the First Amendment must secure.

* * * *Austin* sought to defend the antidistortion rationale as a means to prevent corporations from obtaining "an unfair advantage in the political marketplace" by using "resources amassed in the economic marketplace." 494 U.S., at 659. But *Buckley* rejected the premise that the Government has an interest "in equalizing the relative ability of individuals and groups to influence the outcome of elections." 424 U.S., at 48; see *Bellotti, supra*, at 791, n.30. * * * The rule that political speech cannot be limited based on a speaker's wealth is a necessary consequence of the premise that the First Amendment generally prohibits the suppression of political speech based on the speaker's identity.

Either as support for its antidistortion rationale or as a further argument, the *Austin* majority undertook to distinguish wealthy individuals from corporations on the ground that "[s]tate law grants corporations special advantages — such as limited liability, perpetual life, and favorable treatment of the accumulation and distribution of assets." 494 U.S., at 658–659. This does not suffice, however, to allow laws prohibiting speech. "It is rudimentary that the State cannot exact as the price of those special advantages the forfeiture of First Amendment rights." *Id.*, at 680 (SCALIA, J., dissenting).

It is irrelevant for purposes of the First Amendment that corporate funds may "have little or no correlation to the public's support for the corporation's political ideas." *Id.*, at 660 (majority opinion). All speakers, including individuals and the media, use money amassed from the economic marketplace to fund their speech. The First Amendment protects the resulting speech, even if it was enabled by economic transactions with persons or entities who disagree with the speaker's ideas. See *id.*, at 707 (KENNEDY, J., dissenting) ("Many persons can trace their funds to corporations, if not in the form of donations, then in the form of dividends, interest, or salary").

Austin's antidistortion rationale would produce the dangerous, and unaccept-able, consequence that Congress could ban political speech of media corporations. Media corporations are now exempt from § 441b's ban on corporate expenditures. See 2 U.S.C. §§ 431(9)(B)(i), 434(f)(3)(B)(i). Yet media corporations accumulate wealth with the help of the corporate form, the largest media corporations have "immense aggregations of wealth," and the views expressed by media corporations often "have little or no correlation to the public's support" for those views. Thus, under the Government's reasoning, wealthy media corporations could have their voices diminished to put them on par with other media entities. There is no precedent for permitting this under the First Amendment.

The media exemption discloses further difficulties with the law now under consideration. There is no precedent supporting laws that attempt to distinguish between corporations which are deemed to be exempt as media corporations and those which are not. "We have consistently rejected the proposition that the institutional press has any constitutional privilege beyond that of other speakers." *Id.*, at 691 ((SCALIA, J., dissenting). With the advent of the Internet and the decline of print and broadcast media, moreover, the line between the media and others who wish to comment on political and social issues becomes far more blurred.

The law's exception for media corporations is, on its own terms, all but an admission of the invalidity of the antidistortion rationale. And the exemption results in a further, separate reason for finding this law invalid: Again by its own terms, the law exempts some corporations but covers others, even though both have the need or the motive to communicate their views. The exemption applies to media corporations owned or controlled by corporations that have diverse and substantial investments and participate in endeavors other than news. So even assuming the most doubtful proposition that a news organization has a right to speak when others do not, the exemption would allow a conglomerate that owns both a media business and an unrelated business to influence or control the media in order to advance its overall business interest. At the same time, some other corporation, with an identical business interest but no media outlet in its ownership structure, would be forbidden to speak or inform the public about the same issue. This differential treatment cannot be squared with the First Amendment.

There is simply no support for the view that the First Amendment, as originally understood, would permit the suppression of political speech by media corporations. The Framers may not have anticipated modern business and media corporations. Yet television networks and major newspapers owned by media corporations have become the most important means of mass communication in modern times. The First Amendment was certainly not understood to condone the suppression of political speech in society's most salient media. It was understood as a response to the repression of speech and the press that had existed in England and the heavy taxes on the press that were imposed in the colonies. The great debates between the Federalists and the Anti-Federalists over our founding document were published and expressed in the most important means of mass communication of that era — newspapers owned by individuals. At the founding, speech was open, comprehen-sive, and vital to society's definition of itself; there were no limits on the sources of speech and knowledge. The Framers may have been unaware of certain types of speakers or forms of communication, but that does not mean that those speakers and media are entitled to less First Amendment protection than those types of speakers and media that provided the means of communicating political ideas when the Bill of Rights was adopted.

Austin interferes with the "open marketplace" of ideas protected by the First Amendment. It permits the Government to ban the political speech of millions of associations of citizens. Most of these are small corporations without large amounts of wealth. See Congressional Research Service Report for Congress, Business Organizational Choices 10 (2009) (more than 75% of corporations whose income is taxed under federal law have less than $1 million in receipts per year). This fact belies the Government's argument that the statute is justified on the ground that it prevents the "distorting effects of immense aggregations of wealth." *Austin*, 494 U.S., at 660. It is not even aimed at amassed wealth.

The censorship we now confront is vast in its reach. The Government has "muffle[d] the voices that best represent the most significant segments of the economy." *McConnell, supra*, at 257–258 (opinion of (SCALIA, J.). And "the electorate [has been] deprived of information, knowledge and opinion vital to its function." By suppressing the speech of manifold corporations, both for-profit and nonprofit, the Government prevents their voices and viewpoints from reaching the public and advising voters on which persons or entities are hostile to their interests. Factions will necessarily form in our Republic, but the remedy of "destroying the liberty" of some factions is "worse than the disease." The Federalist No. 10, p. 130 (B. Wright ed. 1961) (J. Madison). Factions should be checked by permitting them all to speak, see *ibid.*, and by entrusting the people to judge what is true and what is false. * * *

Even if § 441b's expenditure ban were constitutional, wealthy corporations could still lobby elected officials, although smaller corporations may not have the resources to do so. And wealthy individuals and unincorporated associations can spend unlimited amounts on independent expenditures. Yet certain disfavored associations of citizens — those that have taken on the corporate form — are penalized for engaging in the same political speech.

When Government seeks to use its full power, including the criminal law, to command where a person may get his or her information or what distrusted source he or she may not hear, it uses censorship to control thought. This is unlawful. The First Amendment confirms the freedom to think for ourselves.

What we have said also shows the invalidity of other arguments made by the Government. For the most part relinquishing the antidistortion rationale, the Government falls back on the argument that corporate political speech can be banned in order to prevent corruption or its appearance. In *Buckley*, the Court found this interest "sufficiently important" to allow limits on contributions but did not extend that reasoning to expenditure limits. 424 U.S., at 25. * * *

* * * Limits on independent expenditures, such as § 441b, have a chilling effect extending well beyond the Government's interest in preventing *quid pro quo* corruption. The anticorruption interest is not sufficient to displace the speech here in question. Indeed, 26 States do not restrict independent expenditures by for-profit corporations. The Government does not claim that these expenditures have corrupted the political process in those States.

A single footnote in *Bellotti* purported to leave open the possibility that corporate independent expenditures could be shown to cause corruption. 435 U.S., at 788, n.26. For the reasons explained above, we now conclude that independent expenditures, including those made by corporations, do not give rise to corruption or the appearance of corruption. * * *

When *Buckley* identified a sufficiently important governmental interest in preventing corruption or the appearance of corruption, that interest was limited to *quid pro quo* corruption. The fact that speakers may have influence over or access to elected officials does not mean that these officials are corrupt:

> "Favoritism and influence are not . . . avoidable in representative politics. It is in the nature of an elected representative to favor certain policies, and, by necessary corollary, to favor the voters and contributors who support those policies. It is well understood that a substantial and legitimate reason, if not the only reason, to cast a vote for, or to make a contribution to, one candidate over another is that the candidate will respond by producing those political outcomes the supporter favors. Democracy is premised on responsiveness." *McConnell*, 540 U.S., at 297 (opinion of KENNEDY, J.).

Reliance on a "generic favoritism or influence theory . . . is at odds with standard First Amendment analyses because it is unbounded and susceptible to no limiting principle." *Id.*, at 296.

The appearance of influence or access, furthermore, will not cause the electorate to lose faith in our democracy. By definition, an independent expenditure is political speech presented to the electorate that is not coordinated with a candidate. The fact that a corporation, or any other speaker, is willing to spend money to try to persuade voters presupposes that the people have the ultimate influence over elected officials. This is inconsistent with any suggestion that the electorate will refuse "to take part in democratic governance" because of additional political speech made by a corporation or any other speaker. * * *

The *McConnell* record was "over 100,000 pages" long, yet it "does not have any direct examples of votes being exchanged for . . . expenditures." This confirms *Buckley*'s reasoning that independent expenditures do not lead to, or create the appearance of, *quid pro quo* corruption. In fact, there is only scant evidence that independent expenditures even ingratiate. Ingratiation and access, in any event, are not corruption. The BCRA record establishes that certain donations to political parties, called "soft money," were made to gain access to elected officials. This case, however, is about independent expenditures, not soft money. When Congress finds that a problem exists, we must give that finding due deference; but Congress may not choose an unconstitutional remedy. If elected officials succumb to improper influences from independent expenditures; if they surrender their best judgment; and if they put expediency before principle, then surely there is cause for concern. We must give weight to attempts by Congress to seek to dispel either the appearance or the reality of these influences. The remedies enacted by law, however, must comply with the First Amendment; and, it is our law and our tradition that more speech, not less, is the governing rule. An outright ban on corporate political speech during the critical preelection period is not a permissible remedy. Here

Congress has created categorical bans on speech that are asymmetrical to preventing *quid pro quo* corruption.

The Government contends further that corporate independent expenditures can be limited because of its interest in protecting dissenting shareholders from being compelled to fund corporate political speech. This asserted interest, like *Austin*'s antidistortion rationale, would allow the Government to ban the political speech even of media corporations. Assume, for example, that a shareholder of a corporation that owns a newspaper disagrees with the political views the newspaper expresses. Under the Government's view, that potential disagreement could give the Government the authority to restrict the media corporation's political speech. The First Amendment does not allow that power. There is, furthermore, little evidence of abuse that cannot be corrected by shareholders "through the procedures of corporate democracy." *Bellotti*, 435 U.S., at 794; see *id.*, at 794, n.34.

Those reasons are sufficient to reject this shareholder-protection interest; and, moreover, the statute is both underinclusive and overinclusive. As to the first, if Congress had been seeking to protect dissenting shareholders, it would not have banned corporate speech in only certain media within 30 or 60 days before an election. A dissenting shareholder's interests would be implicated by speech in any media at any time. As to the second, the statute is overinclusive because it covers all corporations, including nonprofit corporations and for-profit corporations with only single shareholders. As to other corporations, the remedy is not to restrict speech but to consider and explore other regulatory mechanisms. The regulatory mechanism here, based on speech, contravenes the First Amendment.

We need not reach the question whether the Government has a compelling interest in preventing foreign individuals or associations from influencing our Nation's political process. Cf. 2 U.S.C. § 441e (contribution and expenditure ban applied to "foreign national[s]"). Section 441b is not limited to corporations or associations that were created in foreign countries or funded predominately by foreign shareholders. Section 441b therefore would be overbroad even if we assumed, *arguendo*, that the Government has a compelling interest in limiting foreign influence over our political process.

Our precedent is to be respected unless the most convincing of reasons demonstrates that adherence to it puts us on a course that is sure error. "Beyond workability, the relevant factors in deciding whether to adhere to the principle of *stare decisis* include the antiquity of the precedent, the reliance interests at stake, and of course whether the decision was well reasoned." We have also examined whether "experience has pointed up the precedent's shortcomings."

These considerations counsel in favor of rejecting *Austin*, which itself contravened this Court's earlier precedents in *Buckley* and *Bellotti*. * * *

For the reasons above, it must be concluded that *Austin* was not well reasoned. The Government defends *Austin*, relying almost entirely on "the quid pro quo interest, the corruption interest or the shareholder interest," and not *Austin*'s expressed antidistortion rationale. When neither party defends the reasoning of a precedent, the principle of adhering to that precedent through *stare decisis* is diminished. *Austin* abandoned First Amendment principles, furthermore, by relying on language in some of our precedents that traces back to the [*United States* v.] *Automobile Workers* [352 U.S. 567, 570–584 (1957)] Court's flawed historical account of campaign finance laws, see Brief for Campaign Finance Scholars as *Amici Curiae*; Hayward, [Revisiting the Fable of Reform] 45 Harv. J. Legis. 421 (2008).

Austin is undermined by experience since its announcement. Political speech is so ingrained in our culture that speakers find ways to circumvent campaign finance laws. Our Nation's speech dynamic is changing, and informative voices should not have to circumvent onerous restrictions to exercise their First Amendment rights. * * * Corporations, like individuals, do not have monolithic views. On certain topics corporations may possess valuable expertise, leaving them the best equipped to point out errors or fallacies in speech of all sorts, including the speech of candidates and elected officials.

Rapid changes in technology — and the creative dynamic inherent in the concept of free expression — counsel against upholding a law that restricts political speech in certain media or by certain speakers. Today, 30-second television ads may be the most effective way to convey a political message. Soon, however, it may be that Internet sources, such as blogs and social networking Web sites, will provide citizens with significant information about political candidates and issues. Yet, § 441b would seem to ban a blog post expressly advocating the election or defeat of a candidate if that blog were created with corporate funds. The First Amendment does not permit Congress to make these categorical distinctions based on the corporate identity of the speaker and the content of the political speech.

No serious reliance interests are at stake. [R]eliance interests are important considerations in property and contract cases, where parties may have acted in conformance with existing legal rules in order to conduct transactions. Here, though, parties have been prevented from acting — corporations have been banned from making independent expenditures. Legislatures may have enacted bans on corporate expenditures believing that those bans were constitutional. This is not a compelling interest for *stare decisis*. If it were, legislative acts could prevent us from overruling our own precedents, thereby interfering with our duty "to say what the law is." *Marbury* v. *Madison*, [5 U.S. 137] 1 Cranch 137, 177 (1803).

Due consideration leads to this conclusion: *Austin* should be and now is overruled. We return to the principle established in *Buckley* and *Bellotti* that the Government may not suppress political speech on the basis of the speaker's corporate identity. No sufficient governmental interest justifies limits on the political speech of nonprofit or for-profit corporations. * * * Section 441b's restrictions on corporate independent expenditures are therefore invalid and cannot be applied to *Hillary*.

Given our conclusion we are further required to overrule the part of *McConnell* that upheld BCRA § 203's extension of § 441b's restrictions on corporate independent expenditures. See 540 U.S., at 203–209. The *McConnell* Court relied on the antidistortion interest recognized in *Austin* to uphold a greater restriction on speech than the restriction upheld in *Austin*, see 540 U.S., at 205, and we have found this interest unconvincing and insufficient. This part of *McConnell* is now overruled.

[Part IV, upholding BCRA's disclosure requirements for electioneering communications, is reprinted in Part H of this Chapter, *infra.*]

V

When word concerning the plot of the movie *Mr. Smith Goes to Washington* reached the circles of Government, some officials sought, by persuasion, to discourage its distribution. Under *Austin*, though, officials could have done more than discourage its distribution — they could have banned the film. After all, it, like *Hillary*, was speech funded by a corporation that was critical of Members of Congress. *Mr. Smith Goes to Washington* may be fiction and caricature; but fiction and caricature can be a powerful force.

Modern day movies, television comedies, or skits on Youtube.com might portray public officials or public policies in unflattering ways. Yet if a covered transmission during the blackout period creates the background for candidate endorsement or opposition, a felony occurs solely because a corporation, other than an exempt media corporation, has made the "purchase, payment, distribution, loan, advance, deposit, or gift of money or anything of value" in order to engage in political speech. 2 U.S.C. § 431(9)(A)(i). Speech would be suppressed in the realm where its necessity is most evident: in the public dialogue preceding a real election. Governments are often hostile to speech, but under our law and our tradition it seems stranger than fiction for our Government to make this political speech a crime. Yet this is the statute's purpose and design. * * *

The judgment of the District Court is reversed with respect to the constitutionality of 2 U.S.C. § 441b's restrictions on corporate independent expenditures. * * * The case is remanded for further proceedings consistent with this opinion.

It is so ordered.

CHIEF JUSTICE ROBERTS, with whom JUSTICE ALITO joins, concurring.

The Government urges us in this case to uphold a direct prohibition on political speech. It asks us to embrace a theory of the First Amendment that would allow censorship not only of television and radio broadcasts, but of pamphlets, posters, the Internet, and virtually any other medium that corporations and unions might find useful in expressing their views on matters of public concern. Its theory, if accepted, would empower the Government to prohibit newspapers from running editorials or opinion pieces supporting or opposing candidates for office, so long as the newspapers were owned by corporations — as the major ones are. First Amendment rights could be confined to individuals, subverting the vibrant public discourse that is at the foundation of our democracy.

The Court properly rejects that theory, and I join its opinion in full. The First Amendment protects more than just the individual on a soapbox and the lonely pamphleteer. * * *

The dissent advocates an approach to addressing Citizens United's claims that I find quite perplexing. It presumably agrees with the majority that Citizens United's narrower statutory and constitutional arguments lack merit — otherwise its conclusion that the group should lose this case would make no sense. Despite agreeing that these narrower arguments fail, however, the dissent argues that the majority should nonetheless latch on to one of them in order to avoid reaching the broader constitutional question of whether *Austin* remains good law. * * *

This approach is based on a false premise: that our practice of avoiding unnecessary (and unnecessarily broad) constitutional holdings somehow trumps our obligation faithfully to interpret the law. It should go without saying, however, that we cannot embrace a narrow ground of decision simply because it is narrow; it must also be right. Thus while it is true that "[i]f it is not necessary to decide more, it is necessary not to decide more," sometimes it *is* necessary to decide more. There is a difference between judicial restraint and judicial abdication. * * *

This is the first case in which we have been asked to overrule *Austin*, and thus it is also the first in which we have had reason to consider how much weight to give *stare decisis* in assessing its continued validity. The dissent erroneously declares that the Court "reaffirmed" *Austin*'s holding in subsequent cases — namely, *Federal Election Comm'n* v. *Beaumont*, 539 U.S. 146 (2003); *McConnell*; and *WRTL*. Not so. Not a single party in any of those cases asked us to overrule *Austin*, and as the dissent points out, the Court generally does not consider constitutional arguments that have not properly been raised. *Austin*'s validity was therefore not directly at issue in the cases the dissent cites. The Court's unwillingness to overturn *Austin* in those cases cannot be understood as a *reaffirmation* of that decision. * * *

* * * [*Austin*] was an "aberration" insofar as it departed from the robust protections we had granted political speech in our earlier cases. *Austin* undermined the careful line that *Buckley* drew to distinguish limits on contributions to candidates from limits on independent expenditures on speech. *Buckley* rejected the asserted government interest in regulating independent expenditures, conclud-ing that "restrict[ing] the speech of some elements of our society in order to enhance the relative voice of others is wholly foreign to the First Amendment." 424 U.S., at 48–49; see also *Bellotti*, [435 U.S.], at 790–791; *Citizens Against Rent Control/Coalition for Fair Housing* v. *Berkeley*, 454 U.S. 290, 295 (1981). *Austin*, however, allowed the Government to prohibit these same expenditures out of concern for "the corrosive and distorting effects of immense aggregations of wealth" in the marketplace of ideas. 494 U.S., at 660. *Austin*'s reasoning was — and remains — inconsistent with *Buckley*'s explicit repudiation of any government interest in "equalizing the relative ability of individuals and groups to influence the outcome of elections." 424 U.S., at 48–49.

Austin was also inconsistent with *Bellotti*'s clear rejection of the idea that "speech that otherwise would be within the protection of the First Amendment loses that protection simply because its source is a corporation." 435 U.S., at 784. The dissent correctly points out that *Bellotti* involved a referendum rather than a candidate election, and that *Bellotti* itself noted this factual distinction. But this distinction does not explain why corporations may be subject to prohibitions on speech in candidate elections when individuals may not.

Second, the validity of *Austin*'s rationale — itself adopted over two "spirited dissents" — has proved to be the consistent subject of dispute among Members of this Court ever since. The simple fact that one of our decisions remains controversial is, of course, insufficient to justify overruling it. But it does undermine the precedent's ability to contribute to the stable and orderly development of the law. In such circumstances, it is entirely appropriate for the Court — which in this case is squarely asked to reconsider *Austin*'s validity for the first time — to address the matter with a greater willingness to consider new approaches capable of restoring our doctrine to sounder footing.

Third, the *Austin* decision is uniquely destabilizing because it threatens to subvert our Court's decisions even outside the particular context of corporate express advocacy. The First Amendment theory underlying *Austin*'s holding is extraordinarily broad. *Austin*'s logic would authorize government prohibition of political speech by a category of speakers in the name of equality — a point that most scholars acknowledge (and many celebrate), but that the dissent denies.

It should not be surprising, then, that Members of the Court have relied on *Austin*'s expansive logic to justify greater incursions on the First Amendment, even outside the original context of corporate advocacy on behalf of candidates running for office. See, *e.g.*, *Davis* v. *Federal Election Comm'n*, 554 U.S. 724, 756 (2008) (STEVENS, J., concurring in part and dissenting in part) (relying on *Austin* and other cases to justify restrictions on campaign spending by individual candidates, explaining that "there is no reason that their logic — specifically, their concerns about the corrosive and distorting effects of wealth on our political process — is not equally applicable in the context of individual wealth"); *McConnell, supra*, at 203–209 (extending *Austin* beyond its original context to cover not only the "functional equivalent" of express advocacy by corporations, but also electioneering speech conducted by labor unions). The dissent in this case succumbs to the same temptation, suggesting that *Austin* justifies prohibiting corporate speech because such speech might unduly influence "the market for legislation." The dissent reads *Austin* to permit restrictions on corporate speech based on nothing more than the fact that the corporate form may help individuals coordinate and present their views more effectively. A speaker's ability to persuade, however, provides no basis for government regulation of free and open public debate on what the laws should be.

If taken seriously, *Austin*'s logic would apply most directly to newspapers and other media corporations. They have a more profound impact on public discourse than most other speakers. These corporate entities are, for the time being, not subject to § 441b's otherwise generally applicable prohibitions on corporate political speech. But this is simply a matter of legislative grace. The fact that the law currently grants a favored position to media corporations is no reason to overlook the danger inherent in accepting a theory that would allow government restrictions on their political speech.

These readings of *Austin* do no more than carry that decision's reasoning to its logical endpoint. In doing so, they highlight the threat *Austin* poses to First Amendment rights generally, even outside its specific factual context of corporate express advocacy. Because *Austin* is so difficult to confine to its facts — and because its logic threatens to undermine our First Amendment jurisprudence and the nature of public discourse more broadly — the costs of giving it *stare decisis* effect are unusually high.

Finally and most importantly, the Government's own effort to defend *Austin* — or, more accurately, to defend something that is not quite *Austin* — underscores its weakness as a precedent of the Court. The Government concedes that *Austin* "is not the most lucid opinion," yet asks us to reaffirm its holding. But while invoking *stare decisis* to support this position, the Government never once even *mentions* the compelling interest that *Austin* relied upon in the first place: the need to diminish "the corrosive and distorting effects of immense aggregations of wealth that are accumulated with the help of the corporate form and that have little or no correlation to the public's support for the corporation's political ideas." 494 U.S., at 660.

Instead of endorsing *Austin* on its own terms, the Government urges us to reaffirm *Austin*'s specific holding on the basis of two new and potentially expansive interests — the need to prevent actual or apparent *quid pro quo* corruption, and the need to protect corporate shareholders. Those interests may or may not support the *result* in *Austin*, but they were plainly not part of the *reasoning* on which *Austin* relied.

To its credit, the Government forthrightly concedes that *Austin* did not embrace either of the new rationales it now urges upon us. * * *

To the extent that the Government's case for reaffirming *Austin* depends on radically reconceptualizing its reasoning, that argument is at odds with itself. *Stare decisis* is a doctrine of preservation, not transformation. It counsels deference to past mistakes, but provides no justification for making new ones. There is therefore no basis for the Court to give precedential sway to reasoning that it has never accepted, simply because that reasoning happens to support a conclusion reached on different grounds that have since been abandoned or discredited. * * *

Because continued adherence to *Austin* threatens to subvert the "principled and intelligible" development of our First Amendment jurisprudence, I support the Court's determination to overrule that decision. * * *

JUSTICE SCALIA, with whom JUSTICE ALITO joins, and with whom JUSTICE THOMAS joins in part, concurring. * * *

I write separately to address JUSTICE STEVENS' discussion of *"Original Understandings."* This section of the dissent purports to show that today's decision is not supported by the original understanding of the First Amendment. The dissent attempts this demonstration, however, in splendid isolation from the text of the First Amendment. It never shows why "the freedom of speech" that was the right of Englishmen did not include the freedom to speak in association with other individuals, including association in the corporate form.

Instead of taking this straightforward approach to determining the Amendment's meaning, the dissent embarks on a detailed exploration of the Framers' views about the "role of corporations in society." The Framers didn't like corporations, the dissent concludes, and therefore it follows (as night the day) that corporations had no rights of free speech. Of course the Framers' personal affection or disaffection for corporations is relevant only insofar as it can be thought to be reflected in the understood meaning of the text they enacted — not, as the dissent suggests, as a freestanding substitute for that text. But the dissent's distortion of proper analysis is even worse than that. Though faced with a constitutional text that makes no distinction between types of speakers, the dissent feels no necessity to provide even an isolated statement from the founding era to the effect that corporations are *not* covered, but places the burden on petitioners to bring forward statements showing that they *are* ("there is not a scintilla of evidence to support the notion that anyone believed [the First Amendment] would preclude regulatory distinctions based on the corporate form").

Despite the corporation-hating quotations the dissent has dredged up, it is far from clear that by the end of the 18th century corporations were despised. If so, how came there to be so many of them? The dissent's statement that there were few business corporations during the eighteenth century — "only a few hundred during all of the 18th century" — is misleading. There were approximately 335 charters issued to business corporations in the United States by the end of the 18th century. * * * Moreover, what seems like a small number by today's standards surely does not indicate the relative importance of corporations when the Nation was considerably smaller. * * *

Even if we thought it proper to apply the dissent's approach of excluding from First Amendment coverage what the Founders disliked, and even if we agreed that the Founders disliked founding-era corporations; modern corporations might not qualify for exclusion. Most of the Founders' resentment towards corporations was directed at the state-granted monopoly privileges that individually chartered corporations enjoyed. Modern corporations do not have such privileges, and would probably have been favored by most of our enterprising Founders — excluding, perhaps, Thomas Jefferson and others favoring perpetuation of an agrarian society. Moreover, if the Founders' specific intent with respect to corporations is what matters, why does the dissent ignore the Founders' views about other legal entities that have more in common with modern business corporations than the founding-era corporations? At the time of the founding, religious, educational, and literary corporations were incorporated under general incorporation statutes, much as business corporations are today.[4] There were also small unincorporated business associations, which some have argued were the "true progenitors" of today's business corporations. Were all of these silently excluded from the protections of the First Amendment?

The lack of a textual exception for speech by corporations cannot be explained on the ground that such organizations did not exist or did not speak. To the contrary, colleges, towns and cities, religious institutions, and guilds had long been organized as corporations at common law and under the King's charter, and as I have discussed, the practice of incorporation only expanded in the United States. Both corporations and voluntary associations actively petitioned the Government and expressed their views in newspapers and pamphlets. For example: An antislavery Quaker corporation petitioned the First Congress, distributed pamphlets, and

---

[4] At times (though not always) the dissent seems to exclude such non-"business corporations" from its denial of free speech rights. Finding in a seemingly categorical text a distinction between the rights of business corporations and the rights of non-business corporations is even more imaginative than finding a distinction between the rights of *all* corporations and the rights of other associations.

communicated through the press in 1790. The New York Sons of Liberty sent a circular to colonies farther south in 1766. And the Society for the Relief and Instruction of Poor Germans circulated a biweekly paper from 1755 to 1757. The dissent offers no evidence — none whatever — that the First Amendment's unqualified text was originally understood to exclude such associational speech from its protection.

Historical evidence relating to the textually similar clause "the freedom of . . . the press" also provides no support for the proposition that the First Amendment excludes conduct of artificial legal entities from the scope of its protection. The freedom of "the press" was widely understood to protect the publishing activities of individual editors and printers. But these individuals often acted through newspapers, which (much like corporations) had their own names, outlived the individuals who had founded them, could be bought and sold, were sometimes owned by more than one person, and were operated for profit. Their activities were not stripped of First Amendment protection simply because they were carried out under the banner of an artificial legal entity. And the notion which follows from the dissent's view, that modern newspapers, since they are incorporated, have free-speech rights only at the sufferance of Congress, boggles the mind.[6] * * *

The dissent says that when the Framers "constitutionalized the right to free speech in the First Amendment, it was the free speech of individual Americans that they had in mind." That is no doubt true. All the provisions of the Bill of Rights set forth the rights of individual men and women — not, for example, of trees or polar bears. But the individual person's right to speak includes the right to speak *in association with other individual persons.* Surely the dissent does not believe that speech by the Republican Party or the Democratic Party can be censored because it is not the speech of "an individual American." It is the speech of many individual Americans, who have associated in a common cause, giving the leadership of the party the right to speak on their behalf. The association of individuals in a business corporation is no different — or at least it cannot be denied the right to speak on the simplistic ground that it is not "an individual American."[7]

---

[6] The dissent seeks to avoid this conclusion (and to turn a liability into an asset) by interpreting the Freedom of the Press Clause to refer to the institutional press (thus demonstrating, according to the dissent, that the Founders "did draw distinctions — explicit distinctions — between types of 'speakers,' or speech outlets or forms"). It is passing strange to interpret the phrase "the freedom of speech, or of the press" to mean, not everyone's right to speak or publish, but rather everyone's right to speak or the institutional press's right to publish. No one thought that is what it meant. Patriot Noah Webster's 1828 dictionary contains, under the word "press," the following entry:

"*Liberty of the press*, in civil policy, is the free right of publishing books, pamphlets, or papers without previous restraint; or the unrestrained right which every citizen enjoys of publishing his thoughts and opinions, subject only to punishment for publishing what is pernicious to morals or to the peace of the state."

As the Court's opinion describes, our jurisprudence agrees with Noah Webster and contradicts the dissent. * * *

[7] The dissent says that "speech" refers to oral communications of human beings, and since corporations are not human beings they cannot speak. This is sophistry. The authorized spokesman of a corporation is a human being, who speaks on behalf of the human beings who have formed that association — just as the spokesman of an unincorporated association speaks on behalf of its members. The power to publish thoughts, no less than the power to speak thoughts, belongs only to human beings,

But to return to, and summarize, my principal point, which is the conformity of today's opinion with the original meaning of the First Amendment. The Amendment is written in terms of "speech," not speakers. Its text offers no foothold for excluding any category of speaker, from single individuals to partnerships of individuals, to unincorporated associations of individuals, to incorporated associations of individuals — and the dissent offers no evidence about the original meaning of the text to support any such exclusion. We are therefore simply left with the question whether the speech at issue in this case is "speech" covered by the First Amendment. No one says otherwise. A documentary film critical of a potential Presidential candidate is core political speech, and its nature as such does not change simply because it was funded by a corporation. Nor does the character of that funding produce any reduction whatever in the "inherent worth of the speech" and "its capacity for informing the public." Indeed, to exclude or impede corporate speech is to muzzle the principal agents of the modern free economy. We should celebrate rather than condemn the addition of this speech to the public debate.

JUSTICE STEVENS, with whom JUSTICE GINSBURG, JUSTICE BREYER, and JUSTICE SOTOMAYOR join, concurring in part and dissenting in part.

The real issue in this case concerns how, not if, the appellant may finance its electioneering. Citizens United is a wealthy nonprofit corporation that runs a political action committee (PAC) with millions of dollars in assets. Under the Bipartisan Campaign Reform Act of 2002 (BCRA), it could have used those assets to televise and promote *Hillary: The Movie* wherever and whenever it wanted to. It also could have spent unrestricted sums to broadcast *Hillary* at any time other than the 30 days before the last primary election. Neither Citizens United's nor any other corporation's speech has been "banned." All that the parties dispute is whether Citizens United had a right to use the funds in its general treasury to pay for broadcasts during the 30-day period. The notion that the First Amendment dictates an affirmative answer to that question is, in my judgment, profoundly misguided. Even more misguided is the notion that the Court must rewrite the law relating to campaign expenditures by *for-profit* corporations and unions to decide this case. * * *

The Court's central argument for why *stare decisis* ought to be trumped is that it does not like *Austin*. The opinion "was not well reasoned," our colleagues assert, and it conflicts with First Amendment principles. This, of course, is the Court's merits argument, the many defects in which we will soon consider. I am perfectly willing to concede that if one of our precedents were dead wrong in its reasoning or irreconcilable with the rest of our doctrine, there would be a compelling basis for revisiting it. But neither is true of *Austin*, * * * and restating a merits argument with additional vigor does not give it extra weight in the *stare decisis* calculus.

* * * The Court proclaims that "*Austin* is undermined by experience since its announcement." * * * The majority has no empirical evidence with which to substantiate the claim; we just have its *ipse dixit* that the real world has not been

---

but the dissent sees no problem with a corporation's enjoying the freedom of the press. * * *

kind to *Austin*. Nor does the majority bother to specify in what sense *Austin* has been "undermined." * * *[18]

The majority also contends that the Government's hesitation to rely on *Austin's* antidistortion rationale "diminishe[s]" "the principle of adhering to that precedent." Why it diminishes the value of *stare decisis* is left unexplained. We have never thought fit to overrule a precedent because a litigant has taken any particular tack. Nor should we. Our decisions can often be defended on multiple grounds, and a litigant may have strategic or case-specific reasons for emphasizing only a subset of them. Members of the public, moreover, often rely on our bottom-line holdings far more than our precise legal arguments; surely this is true for the legislatures that have been regulating corporate electioneering since *Austin*. The task of evaluating the continued viability of precedents falls to this Court, not to the parties. * * *

We have recognized that "*[s]tare decisis* has special force when legislators or citizens 'have acted in reliance on a previous decision, for in this instance overruling the decision would dislodge settled rights and expectations or require an extensive legislative response.'" *Stare decisis* protects not only personal rights involving property or contract but also the ability of the elected branches to shape their laws in an effective and coherent fashion. Today's decision takes away a power that we have long permitted these branches to exercise. State legislatures have relied on their authority to regulate corporate electioneering, confirmed in *Austin*, for more than a century. The Federal Congress has relied on this authority for a comparable stretch of time, and it specifically relied on *Austin* throughout the years it spent developing and debating BCRA. The total record it compiled was *100,000 pages* long. Pulling out the rug beneath Congress after affirming the constitutionality of § 203 six years ago shows great disrespect for a coequal branch.

By removing one of its central components, today's ruling makes a hash out of BCRA's "delicate and interconnected regulatory scheme." *McConnell*, 540 U.S., at 172. Consider just one example of the distortions that will follow: Political parties are barred under BCRA from soliciting or spending "soft money," funds that are not subject to the statute's disclosure requirements or its source and amount limitations. 2 U.S.C. § 441i; *McConnell*, 540 U.S., at 122–126. Going forward, corporations and unions will be free to spend as much general treasury money as they wish on ads that support or attack specific candidates, whereas national parties will not be able to spend a dime of soft money on ads of any kind. The Court's ruling thus dramatically enhances the role of corporations and unions — and the narrow interests they represent — vis-à-vis the role of political parties — and the broad coalitions they represent — in determining who will hold public office.

---

[18] THE CHIEF JUSTICE suggests that *Austin* has been undermined by subsequent dissenting opinions. Under this view, it appears that the more times the Court stands by a precedent in the face of requests to overrule it, the weaker that precedent becomes. THE CHIEF JUSTICE further suggests that *Austin* "is uniquely destabilizing because it threatens to subvert our Court's decisions even outside" its particular facts, as when we applied its reasoning in *McConnell*. Once again, the theory seems to be that the more we utilize a precedent, the more we call it into question. For those who believe *Austin* was correctly decided — as the Federal Government and the States have long believed, as the majority of Justices to have served on the Court since *Austin* have believed, and as we continue to believe — there is nothing "destabilizing" about the prospect of its continued application. It is gutting campaign finance laws across the country, as the Court does today, that will be destabilizing.

Beyond the reliance interests at stake, the other *stare decisis* factors also cut against the Court. Considerations of antiquity are significant for similar reasons. *McConnell* is only six years old, but *Austin* has been on the books for two decades, and many of the statutes called into question by today's opinion have been on the books for a half-century or more. The Court points to no intervening change in circumstances that warrants revisiting *Austin*. Certainly nothing relevant has changed since we decided *WRTL* two Terms ago. And the Court gives no reason to think that *Austin* and *McConnell* are unworkable. * * *

In the end, the Court's rejection of *Austin* and *McConnell* comes down to nothing more than its disagreement with their results. Virtually every one of its arguments was made and rejected in those cases, and the majority opinion is essentially an amalgamation of resuscitated dissents. The only relevant thing that has changed since *Austin* and *McConnell* is the composition of this Court.

The So-Called "Ban"

Pervading the Court's analysis is the ominous image of a "categorical ba[n]" on corporate speech. * * * This characterization is highly misleading, and needs to be corrected.

* * * For starters, [the] statutes [upheld in *Austin* and *McConnell*] provide exemptions for PACs, separate segregated funds established by a corporation for political purposes. * * * A significant and growing number of corporations avail themselves of this option; during the most recent election cycle, corporate and union PACs raised nearly a billion dollars. Administering a PAC entails some administrative burden, but so does complying with the disclaimer, disclosure, and reporting requirements that the Court today upholds, and no one has suggested that the burden is severe for a sophisticated for-profit corporation. * * * Like all other natural persons, every shareholder of every corporation remains entirely free under *Austin* and *McConnell* to do however much electioneering she pleases outside of the corporate form. The owners of a "mom & pop" store can simply place ads in their own names, rather than the store's. If ideologically aligned individuals wish to make unlimited expenditures through the corporate form, they may utilize an *MCFL* organization that has policies in place to avoid becoming a conduit for business or union interests.

The laws upheld in *Austin* and *McConnell* leave open many additional avenues for corporations' political speech. Consider the statutory provision we are ostensibly evaluating in this case, BCRA § 203. It has no application to genuine issue advertising — a category of corporate speech Congress found to be far more substantial than election-related advertising — or to Internet, telephone, and print advocacy.[31] Like numerous statutes, it exempts media companies' news stories,

---

[31] Roaming far afield from the case at hand, the majority worries that the Government will use § 203 to ban books, pamphlets, and blogs. Yet by its plain terms, § 203 does not apply to printed material. And in light of the ordinary understanding of the terms "broadcast, cable, [and] satellite," coupled with Congress' clear aim of targeting "a virtual torrent of televised election-related ads," we highly doubt that § 203 could be interpreted to apply to a Web site or book that happens to be transmitted at some stage over airwaves or cable lines, or that the FEC would ever try to do so. If it should, the Government

commentaries, and editorials from its electioneering restrictions, in recognition of the unique role played by the institutional press in sustaining public debate.[32] See 2 U.S.C. § 434(f)(3)(B)(i). It also allows corporations to spend unlimited sums on political communications with their executives and shareholders, § 441b(b)(2)(A); 11 CFR § 114.3(a)(1), to fund additional PAC activity through trade associations, 2 U.S.C. § 441b(b)(4)(D), to distribute voting guides and voting records, 11 CFR §§ 114.4(c)(4)–(5), to underwrite voter registration and voter turnout activities, § 114.3(c)(4); § 114.4(c)(2), to host fundraising events for candidates within certain limits, § 114.4(c); § 114.2(f)(2), and to publicly endorse candidates through a press release and press conference, § 114.4(c)(6). * * *

In many ways, then, § 203 functions as a source restriction or a time, place, and manner restriction. It applies in a viewpoint-neutral fashion to a narrow subset of advocacy messages about clearly identified candidates for federal office, made during discrete time periods through discrete channels. In the case at hand, all Citizens United needed to do to broadcast *Hillary* right before the primary was to abjure business contributions or use the funds in its PAC, which by its own account is "one of the most active conservative PACs in America."

So let us be clear: Neither *Austin* nor *McConnell* held or implied that corporations may be silenced; the FEC is not a "censor"; and in the years since these cases were decided, corporations have continued to play a major role in the national dialogue. Laws such as § 203 target a class of communications that is especially likely to corrupt the political process, that is at least one degree removed from the views of individual citizens, and that may not even reflect the views of those who pay for it. Such laws burden political speech, and that is always a serious matter, demanding careful scrutiny. But the majority's incessant talk of a "ban" aims at a straw man.

Identity-Based Distinctions

The second pillar of the Court's opinion is its assertion that "the Government cannot restrict political speech based on the speaker's . . . identity." * * * Like its paeans to unfettered discourse, the Court's denunciation of identity-based distinctions may have rhetorical appeal but it obscures reality.

* * * The Government routinely places special restrictions on the speech rights of students, prisoners, members of the Armed Forces, foreigners, and its own employees. When such restrictions are justified by a legitimate governmental interest, they do not necessarily raise constitutional problems.[46] In contrast to the blanket rule that the majority espouses, our cases recognize that the Government's

---

acknowledges "there would be quite [a] good as-applied challenge."

[32] As the Government points out, with a media corporation there is also a lesser risk that investors will not understand, learn about, or support the advocacy messages that the corporation disseminates. Everyone knows and expects that media outlets may seek to influence elections in this way.

[46] The majority states that the cases just cited are "inapposite" because they "stand only for the proposition that there are certain governmental functions that cannot operate without some restrictions on particular kinds of speech." The majority's creative suggestion that these cases stand only for that one proposition is quite implausible. In any event, the proposition lies at the heart of this case, as Congress and half the state legislatures have concluded, over many decades, that their core functions of

interests may be more or less compelling with respect to different classes of speakers, and that the constitutional rights of certain categories of speakers, in certain contexts, "are not automatically coextensive with the rights" that are normally accorded to members of our society.

* * * It is fair to say that our First Amendment doctrine has "frowned on" certain identity-based distinctions, particularly those that may reflect invidious discrimination or preferential treatment of a politically powerful group. But it is simply incorrect to suggest that we have prohibited all legislative distinctions based on identity or content. Not even close.

The election context is distinctive in many ways, and the Court, of course, is right that the First Amendment closely guards political speech. But in this context, too, the authority of legislatures to enact viewpoint-neutral regulations based on content and identity is well settled. We have, for example, allowed state-run broadcasters to exclude independent candidates from televised debates. *Arkansas Ed. Television Comm'n v. Forbes*, 523 U.S. 666 (1998) [p. 629]. We have upheld statutes that prohibit the distribution or display of campaign materials near a polling place. *Burson v. Freeman*, 504 U.S. 191 (1992) [p. 1053]. Although we have not reviewed them directly, we have never cast doubt on laws that place special restrictions on campaign spending by foreign nationals. See, *e.g.*, 2 U.S.C. § 441e(a)(1). And we have consistently approved laws that bar Government employees, but not others, from contributing to or participating in political activities. These statutes burden the political expression of one class of speakers, namely, civil servants. Yet we have sustained them on the basis of longstanding practice and Congress' reasoned judgment that certain regulations which leave "untouched full participation . . . in political decisions at the ballot box," *Civil Service Comm'n v. Letter Carriers*, 413 U.S. 548, 556 (1973) [p. 712], help ensure that public officials are "sufficiently free from improper influences," *id.*, at 564, and that "confidence in the system of representative Government is not . . . eroded to a disastrous extent."

The same logic applies to this case with additional force because it is the identity of corporations, rather than individuals, that the Legislature has taken into account. As we have unanimously observed, legislatures are entitled to decide "that the special characteristics of the corporate structure require particularly careful regulation" in an electoral context. [*Federal Election Comm'n v. National Right to Work Comm.*], 459 U.S. [197], 209–210 [(1982)] [*(NRWC)*].[50] Not only has the distinctive potential of corporations to corrupt the electoral process long been recognized, but within the area of campaign finance, corporate spending is also "furthest from the core of political expression, since corporations' First Amendment speech and association interests are derived largely from those of their members and of the public in receiving information," *Beaumont*, 539 U.S., at 161, n.8. Campaign finance distinctions based on corporate identity tend to be less worrisome, in other words, because the "speakers" are not natural persons, much less

---

administering elections and passing legislation cannot operate effectively without some narrow restrictions on corporate electioneering paid for by general treasury funds.

[50] They are likewise entitled to regulate media corporations differently from other corporations "to ensure that the law 'does not hinder or prevent the institutional press from reporting on, and publishing editorials about, newsworthy events.'" *McConnell*, 540 U.S., at 208 (quoting *Austin*, 494 U.S., [at] 668).

members of our political community, and the governmental interests are of the highest order. Furthermore, when corporations, as a class, are distinguished from noncorporations, as a class, there is a lesser risk that regulatory distinctions will reflect invidious discrimination or political favoritism.

If taken seriously, our colleagues' assumption that the identity of a speaker has *no* relevance to the Government's ability to regulate political speech would lead to some remarkable conclusions. Such an assumption would have accorded the propaganda broadcasts to our troops by "Tokyo Rose" during World War II the same protection as speech by Allied commanders. More pertinently, it would appear to afford the same protection to multinational corporations controlled by foreigners as to individual Americans: To do otherwise, after all, could "enhance the relative voice" of some (*i.e.*, humans) over others (*i.e.*, nonhumans).[51] Under the majority's view, I suppose it may be a First Amendment problem that corporations are not permitted to vote, given that voting is, among other things, a form of speech.[52]

In short, the Court dramatically overstates its critique of identity-based distinctions, without ever explaining why corporate identity demands the same treatment as individual identity. Only the most wooden approach to the First Amendment could justify the unprecedented line it seeks to draw.

Our First Amendment Tradition

A third fulcrum of the Court's opinion is the idea that *Austin* and *McConnell* are radical outliers, "aberration[s]," in our First Amendment tradition. The Court has it exactly backwards. It is today's holding that is the radical departure from what had been settled First Amendment law. To see why, it is useful to take a long view.

1. Original Understandings

Let us start from the beginning. The Court invokes "ancient First Amendment principles" and original understandings to defend today's ruling, yet it makes only a perfunctory attempt to ground its analysis in the principles or understandings of those who drafted and ratified the Amendment. Perhaps this is because there is not a scintilla of evidence to support the notion that anyone believed it would preclude regulatory distinctions based on the corporate form. To the extent that the Framers' views are discernible and relevant to the disposition of this case, they would appear to cut strongly against the majority's position.

This is not only because the Framers and their contemporaries conceived of speech more narrowly than we now think of it, see Bork, Neutral Principles and

---

[51] The Court all but confesses that a categorical approach to speaker identity is untenable when it acknowledges that Congress might be allowed to take measures aimed at "preventing foreign individuals or associations from influencing our Nation's political process." * * * The notion that Congress might lack the authority to distinguish foreigners from citizens in the regulation of electioneering would certainly have surprised the Framers, whose "obsession with foreign influence derived from a fear that foreign powers and individuals had no basic investment in the well-being of the country." * * *

[52] Of course, voting is not speech in a pure or formal sense, but then again neither is a campaign expenditure; both are nevertheless communicative acts aimed at influencing electoral outcomes.

Some First Amendment Problems, 47 Ind. L.J. 1, 22 (1971), but also because they held very different views about the nature of the First Amendment right and the role of corporations in society. Those few corporations that existed at the founding were authorized by grant of a special legislative charter.[53] * * * Corporations were created, supervised, and conceptualized as quasi-public entities, "designed to serve a social function for the state." It was "assumed that [they] were legally privileged organizations that had to be closely scrutinized by the legislature because their purposes had to be made consistent with public welfare."

* * * General incorporation statutes, and widespread acceptance of business corporations as socially useful actors, did not emerge until the 1800's.

The Framers thus took it as a given that corporations could be comprehensively regulated in the service of the public welfare. Unlike our colleagues, they had little trouble distinguishing corporations from human beings, and when they constitutionalized the right to free speech in the First Amendment, it was the free speech of individual Americans that they had in mind.[55] * * * In light of these background practices and understandings, it seems to me implausible that the Framers believed "the freedom of speech" would extend equally to all corporate speakers, much less that it would preclude legislatures from taking limited measures to guard against corporate capture of elections.

The Court observes that the Framers drew on diverse intellectual sources, communicated through newspapers, and aimed to provide greater freedom of speech than had existed in England. From these (accurate) observations, the Court concludes that "[t]he First Amendment was certainly not understood to condone the suppression of political speech in society's most salient media." This conclusion is far from certain, given that many historians believe the Framers were focused on prior restraints on publication and did not understand the First Amendment to "prevent the subsequent punishment of such [publications] as may be deemed contrary to the public welfare." Yet, even if the majority's conclusion were correct, it would tell us only that the First Amendment was understood to protect political speech *in* certain media. It would tell us little about whether the Amendment was understood to protect general treasury electioneering expenditures *by* corporations, *and to what extent*.

As a matter of original expectations, then, it seems absurd to think that the First Amendment prohibits legislatures from taking into account the corporate identity of a sponsor of electoral advocacy. As a matter of original meaning, it likewise seems baseless — unless one evaluates the First Amendment's "principles" or its "purpose" at such a high level of generality that the historical understandings of the Amendment cease to be a meaningful constraint on the judicial task. This case

---

[53] Scholars have found that only a handful of business corporations were issued charters during the colonial period, and only a few hundred during all of the 18th century. * * * [Moreover, m]ore than half of the century's total business charters were issued between 1796 and 1800[, after the ratification of the First Amendment].

[55] In normal usage then, as now, the term "speech" referred to oral communications by individuals. * * * Given that corporations were conceived of as artificial entities and do not have the technical capacity to "speak," the burden of establishing that the Framers and ratifiers understood "the freedom of speech" to encompass corporate speech is, I believe, far heavier than the majority acknowledges.

sheds a revelatory light on the assumption of some that an impartial judge's application of an originalist methodology is likely to yield more determinate answers, or to play a more decisive role in the decisional process, than his or her views about sound policy.

JUSTICE SCALIA criticizes the foregoing discussion for failing to adduce statements from the founding era showing that corporations were understood to be excluded from the First Amendment's free speech guarantee. Of course, JUSTICE SCALIA adduces no statements to suggest the contrary proposition, or even to suggest that the contrary proposition better reflects the kind of right that the drafters and ratifiers of the Free Speech Clause thought they were enshrining. Although JUSTICE SCALIA makes a perfectly sensible argument that an individual's right to speak entails a right to speak with others for a common cause, he does not explain why those two rights must be precisely identical, or why that principle applies to electioneering by corporations that serve no "common cause." Nothing in his account dislodges my basic point that members of the founding generation held a cautious view of corporate power and a narrow view of corporate rights (not that they "despised" corporations), and that they conceptualized speech in individualistic terms. If no prominent Framer bothered to articulate that corporate speech would have lesser status than individual speech, that may well be because the contrary proposition — if not also the very notion of "corporate speech" — was inconceivable.

JUSTICE SCALIA also emphasizes the unqualified nature of the First Amendment text. Yet he would seemingly read out the Free Press Clause: How else could he claim that my purported views on newspapers must track my views on corporations generally?[57] * * * In any event, the text only leads us back to the questions who or what is guaranteed "the freedom of speech," and, just as critically, what that freedom consists of and under what circumstances it may be limited. JUSTICE SCALIA appears to believe that because corporations are created and utilized by individuals, it follows (as night the day) that their electioneering must be equally protected by the First Amendment and equally immunized from expenditure limits. That conclusion certainly does not follow as a logical matter, and JUSTICE SCALIA fails to explain why the original public meaning leads it to follow as a matter of interpretation. * * *

In fairness, our campaign finance jurisprudence has never attended very closely to the views of the Framers, whose political universe differed profoundly from that of today. We have long since held that corporations are covered by the First Amendment, and many legal scholars have long since rejected the concession theory of the corporation.[J] But "historical context is usually relevant," and in light

---

[57] In fact, the Free Press Clause might be turned against JUSTICE SCALIA, for two reasons. First, we learn from it that the drafters of the First Amendment did draw distinctions — explicit distinctions — between types of "speakers," or speech outlets or forms. Second, the Court's strongest historical evidence all relates to the Framers' views on the press, yet while the Court tries to sweep this evidence into the Free Speech Clause, the Free Press Clause provides a more natural textual home. The text and history highlighted by our colleagues suggests why one type of corporation, those that are part of the press, might be able to claim special First Amendment status, and therefore why some kinds of "identity"-based distinctions might be permissible after all. Once one accepts that much, the intellectual edifice of the majority opinion crumbles.

[J] According to concession theory, corporations are created by, and delegated power from, the state to

of the Court's effort to cast itself as guardian of ancient values, it pays to remember that nothing in our constitutional history dictates today's outcome. To the contrary, this history helps illuminate just how extraordinarily dissonant the decision is.

2. *Legislative and Judicial Interpretation*

A century of more recent history puts to rest any notion that today's ruling is faithful to our First Amendment tradition. At the federal level, the express distinction between corporate and individual political spending on elections stretches back to 1907, when Congress passed the Tillman Act, banning all corporate contributions to candidates. * * *

Over the years, the limitations on corporate political spending have been modified in a number of ways, as Congress responded to changes in the American economy and political practices that threatened to displace the commonweal. * * * The Taft-Hartley Act of 1947 is of special significance for this case. In that Act passed more than 60 years ago, Congress extended the prohibition on corporate support of candidates to cover not only direct contributions, but independent expenditures as well. * * *

By the time Congress passed FECA in 1971, the bar on corporate contributions and expenditures had become such an accepted part of federal campaign finance regulation that when a large number of plaintiffs, including several nonprofit corporations, challenged virtually every aspect of the Act in *Buckley*, no one even bothered to argue that the bar as such was unconstitutional. *Buckley* famously (or infamously) distinguished direct contributions from independent expenditures, but its silence on corporations only reinforced the understanding that corporate expenditures could be treated differently from individual expenditures. * * *

Thus, it was unremarkable, in a 1982 case holding that Congress could bar nonprofit corporations from soliciting nonmembers for PAC funds, that then-Justice Rehnquist wrote for a unanimous Court that Congress' "careful legislative adjustment of the federal electoral laws, in a cautious advance, step by step, to account for the particular legal and economic attributes of corporations . . . warrants considerable deference," and "reflects a permissible assessment of the dangers posed by those entities to the electoral process." *NRWC*, 459 U.S., at 209. * * *

The corporate/individual distinction was not questioned by the Court's disposition, in 1986, of a challenge to the expenditure restriction as applied to a distinctive type of nonprofit corporation. In [*Federal Election Commission v. Massachusetts Citizens for Life (MCFL)*, 479 U.S. 238 (1986)], we * * *held by a 5-to-4 vote was that a limited class of corporations must be allowed to use their general treasury funds for independent expenditures, because Congress' interests in protecting shareholders and "restrict[ing] 'the influence of political war chests funneled through the corporate form' " did not apply to corporations that were structurally insulated from those concerns. * * *

Four years later, in *Austin*, we considered whether corporations falling outside the *MCFL* exception could be barred from using general treasury funds to make

---

effectuate public purposes, even when that purpose is the carrying on of business. [— Eds.]

independent expenditures in support of, or in opposition to, candidates. We held they could be. * * * In light of the corrupting effects such spending might have on the political process, we permitted the State of Michigan to limit corporate expenditures on candidate elections to corporations' PACs, which rely on voluntary contributions and thus "reflect actual public support for the political ideals espoused by corporations," *ibid.* * * *

In the 20 years since *Austin*, we have reaffirmed its holding and rationale a number of times, see, *e.g.*, *Beaumont*, 539 U.S., at 153–156, most importantly in *McConnell*, where we upheld the provision challenged here, § 203 of BCRA.[62] * * *

When we asked in *McConnell* "whether a compelling governmental interest justifie[d]" § 203, we found the question "easily answered": "We have repeatedly sustained legislation aimed at 'the corrosive and distorting effects of immense aggregations of wealth that are accumulated with the help of the corporate form and that have little or no correlation to the public's support for the corporation's political ideas.'" 540 U.S., at 205 (quoting *Austin*, 494 U.S., at 660). These precedents "represent respect for the legislative judgment that the special characteristics of the corporate structure require particularly careful regulation." 540 U.S., at 205. "Moreover, recent cases have recognized that certain restrictions on corporate electoral involvement permissibly hedge against 'circumvention of [valid] contribution limits.'" *Ibid.* BCRA, we found, is faithful to the compelling governmental interests in "preserving the integrity of the electoral process, preventing corruption, . . . sustaining the active, alert responsibility of the individual citizen in a democracy for the wise conduct of the government," and maintaining "the individual citizen's confidence in government." 540 U.S., at 206–207, n.88. What made the answer even easier than it might have been otherwise was the option to form PACs, which give corporations, at the least, "a constitutionally sufficient opportunity to engage in" independent expenditures. 540 U.S., at 203.

Buckley and Bellotti

* * * In the Court's view, *Buckley* and *Bellotti* decisively rejected the possibility of distinguishing corporations from natural persons in the 1970's; it just so happens that in every single case in which the Court has reviewed campaign finance legislation in the decades since, the majority failed to grasp this truth. The Federal Congress and dozens of state legislatures, we now know, have been similarly deluded.

The majority emphasizes *Buckley's* statement that "[t]he concept that government may restrict the speech of some elements of our society in order to enhance the relative voice of others is wholly foreign to the First Amendment." But this elegant phrase cannot bear the weight that our colleagues have placed on it. For one thing, the Constitution does, in fact, permit numerous "restrictions on the speech of

---

[62] According to THE CHIEF JUSTICE, we are "erroneou[s]" in claiming that *McConnell* and *Beaumont* "reaffirmed" *Austin*. In both cases, the Court explicitly relied on *Austin* and quoted from it at length. The *McConnell* Court did so in the teeth of vigorous protests by Justices in today's majority that *Austin* should be overruled. Both Courts also heard criticisms of *Austin* from parties or *amici*. If this does not qualify as reaffirmation of a precedent, then I do not know what would.

some in order to prevent a few from drowning out the many": for example, restrictions on ballot access and on legislators' floor time. For another, the *Buckley* Court used this line in evaluating "the ancillary governmental interest in equalizing the relative ability of individuals and groups to influence the outcome of elections." 424 U.S., at 48. It is not apparent why this is relevant to the case before us. The majority suggests that *Austin* rests on the foreign concept of speech equalization, but we made it clear in *Austin* (as in several cases before and since) that a restriction on the way corporations spend their money is no mere exercise in disfavoring the voice of some elements of our society in preference to others. Indeed, we *expressly* ruled that the compelling interest supporting Michigan's statute was not one of "equaliz[ing] the relative influence of speakers on elections," but rather the need to confront the distinctive corrupting potential of corporate electoral advocacy financed by general treasury dollars.

For that matter, it should go without saying that when we made this statement in *Buckley*, we could not have been casting doubt on the restriction on corporate expenditures in candidate elections, which had not been challenged[.] * * *

The case on which the majority places even greater weight than *Buckley*, however, is *Bellotti*, claiming it "could not have been clearer" that *Bellotti*'s holding forbade distinctions between corporate and individual expenditures like the one at issue here. The Court's reliance is odd. The only thing about *Bellotti* that could not be clearer is that it declined to adopt the majority's position. *Bellotti* ruled, in an explicit limitation on the scope of its holding, that "our consideration of a corporation's right to speak on issues of general public interest implies no comparable right in the quite different context of participation in a political campaign for election to public office." 435 U.S., at 788, n.26; see also *id.*, at 787–788 (acknowledging that the interests in preserving public confidence in Government and protecting dissenting shareholders may be "weighty . . . in the context of partisan candidate elections"). *Bellotti*, in other words, did not touch the question presented in *Austin* and *McConnell*, and the opinion squarely disavowed the proposition for which the majority cites it.

The majority attempts to explain away the distinction *Bellotti* drew — between general corporate speech and campaign speech intended to promote or prevent the election of specific candidates for office — as inconsistent with the rest of the opinion and with *Buckley*. Yet the basis for this distinction is perfectly coherent: The anticorruption interests that animate regulations of corporate participation in candidate elections * * * do not apply equally to regulations of corporate participation in referenda. A referendum cannot owe a political debt to a corporation, seek to curry favor with a corporation, or fear the corporation's retaliation. * * * The Court's critique of *Bellotti*'s footnote 26 puts it in the strange position of trying to elevate *Bellotti* to canonical status, while simultaneously disparaging a critical piece of its analysis as unsupported and irreconcilable with *Buckley*. *Bellotti*, apparently, is both the font of all wisdom and internally incoherent.

The *Bellotti* Court confronted a dramatically different factual situation from the one that confronts us in this case: a state statute that barred business corporations' expenditures on some referenda but not others. Specifically, the statute barred a business corporation "from making contributions or expenditures 'for the purpose of . . . influencing or affecting the vote on any question submitted to the voters, other than one materially affecting any of the property, business or assets of the corporation,' " and it went so far as to provide that referenda related to income taxation would not "be deemed materially to affect the property, business or assets of the corporation," 435 U.S., at 768. As might be guessed, the legislature had enacted this statute in order to limit corporate speech on a proposed state constitutional amendment to authorize a graduated income tax. The statute was a transparent attempt to prevent corporations from spending money to defeat this amendment, which was favored by a majority of legislators but had been repeatedly rejected by the voters. We said that "where, as here, the legislature's suppression of speech suggests an attempt to give one side of a debatable public question an advantage in expressing its views to the people, the First Amendment is plainly offended." *Id.*, at 785–786.

Bellotti thus involved a *viewpoint-discriminatory* statute, created to effect a particular policy outcome. * * * To make matters worse, the law at issue did not make any allowance for corporations to spend money through PACs. This really was a complete ban on a specific, preidentified subject.

The majority grasps a quotational straw from *Bellotti*, that speech does not fall entirely outside the protection of the First Amendment merely because it comes from a corporation. Of course not, but no one suggests the contrary and neither *Austin* nor *McConnell* held otherwise. They held that even though the expenditures at issue were subject to First Amendment scrutiny, the restrictions on those expenditures were justified by a compelling state interest. We acknowledged in *Bellotti* that numerous "interests of the highest importance" can justify campaign finance regulation. 435 U.S., at 788–789. But we found no evidence that these interests were served by the Massachusetts law. *Id.*, at 789. * * *

Austin and *McConnell*, then, sit perfectly well with *Bellotti*. * * * The difference between the cases is not that *Austin* and *McConnell* rejected First Amendment protection for corporations whereas *Bellotti* accepted it. The difference is that the statute at issue in *Bellotti* smacked of viewpoint discrimination, targeted one class of corporations, and provided no PAC option; and the State has a greater interest in regulating independent corporate expenditures on candidate elections than on referenda, because in a functioning democracy the public must have faith that its representatives owe their positions to the people, not to the corporations with the deepest pockets. * * *

Having explained why this is not an appropriate case in which to revisit *Austin* and *McConnell* and why these decisions sit perfectly well with "First Amendment principles," I come at last to the interests that are at stake. * * *

The Anticorruption Interest

* * * Corruption can take many forms. Bribery may be the paradigm case. But the difference between selling a vote and selling access is a matter of degree, not kind. And selling access is not qualitatively different from giving special preference to those who spent money on one's behalf. Corruption operates along a spectrum, and the majority's apparent belief that *quid pro quo* arrangements can be neatly

demarcated from other improper influences does not accord with the theory or reality of politics. It certainly does not accord with the record Congress developed in passing BCRA, a record that stands as a remarkable testament to the energy and ingenuity with which corporations, unions, lobbyists, and politicians may go about scratching each other's backs — and which amply supported Congress' determination to target a limited set of especially destructive practices.

* * * As summarized [by one District Judge in the *McConnell* litigation]:

> The factual findings of the Court illustrate that corporations and labor unions routinely notify Members of Congress as soon as they air electioneering communications relevant to the Members' elections. The record also indicates that Members express appreciation to organizations for the airing of these election-related advertisements. Indeed, Members of Congress are particularly grateful when negative issue advertisements are run by these organizations, leaving the candidates free to run positive advertisements and be seen as 'above the fray.' Political consultants testify that campaigns are quite aware of who is running advertisements on the candidate's behalf, when they are being run, and where they are being run. Likewise, a prominent lobbyist testifies that these organizations use issue advocacy as a means to influence various Members of Congress.

> * * * Finally, a large majority of Americans (80%) are of the view that corporations and other organizations that engage in electioneering communications, which benefit specific elected officials, receive special consideration from those officials when matters arise that affect these corporations and organizations.

* * * [This] analysis shows the great difficulty in delimiting the precise scope of the *quid pro quo* category, as well as the adverse consequences that *all* such arrangements may have. There are threats of corruption that are far more destructive to a democratic society than the odd bribe. Yet the majority's understanding of corruption would leave lawmakers impotent to address all but the most discrete abuses. * * *

Quid pro Quo *Corruption*

The majority appears to think it decisive that the BCRA record does not contain "direct examples of votes being exchanged for . . . expenditures." It would have been quite remarkable if Congress had created a record detailing such behavior by its own Members. Proving that a specific vote was exchanged for a specific expenditure has always been next to impossible: Elected officials have diverse motivations, and no one will acknowledge that he sold a vote. Yet, even if "[i]ngratiation and access . . . are not corruption" themselves, they are necessary prerequisites to it; they can create both the opportunity for, and the appearance of, *quid pro quo* arrangements. The influx of unlimited corporate money into the electoral realm also creates new opportunities for the mirror image of *quid pro quo* deals: threats, both explicit and implicit. Starting today, corporations with large war chests to deploy on electioneering may find democratically elected bodies becoming much more attuned to their interests. * * *

Austin and Corporate Expenditures

Just as the majority gives short shrift to the general societal interests at stake in campaign finance regulation, it also overlooks the distinctive considerations raised by the regulation of *corporate* expenditures. The majority fails to appreciate that *Austin*'s antidistortion rationale is itself an anticorruption rationale, see 494 U.S., at 660 (describing "a different type of corruption"), tied to the special concerns raised by corporations. Understood properly, "antidistortion" is simply a variant on the classic governmental interest in protecting against improper influences on officeholders that debilitate the democratic process. It is manifestly not just an "equalizing" ideal in disguise.

1. *Antidistortion*

The fact that corporations are different from human beings might seem to need no elaboration, except that the majority opinion almost completely elides it. *Austin* set forth some of the basic differences. Unlike natural persons, corporations have "limited liability" for their owners and managers, "perpetual life," separation of ownership and control, "and favorable treatment of the accumulation and distribution of assets . . . that enhance their ability to attract capital and to deploy their resources in ways that maximize the return on their shareholders' investments." 494 U.S., at 658–659. Unlike voters in U.S. elections, corporations may be foreign controlled.[70] Unlike other interest groups, business corporations have been "effectively delegated responsibility for ensuring society's economic welfare"; they inescapably structure the life of every citizen. "[T]he resources in the treasury of a business corporation," furthermore, "are not an indication of popular support for the corporation's political ideas." *Id.*, at 659 (quoting *MCFL*, 479 U.S., at 258). "They reflect instead the economically motivated decisions of investors and customers. The availability of these resources may make a corporation a formidable political presence, even though the power of the corporation may be no reflection of the power of its ideas." 494 U.S., at 659 (quoting *MCFL*, 479 U.S., at 258).* * *

[S]ome corporations have affirmatively urged Congress to place limits on their electioneering communications. These corporations fear that officeholders will shake them down for supportive ads, that they will have to spend increasing sums on elections in an ever-escalating arms race with their competitors, and that public trust in business will be eroded. A system that effectively forces corporations to use their shareholders' money both to maintain access to, and to avoid retribution from, elected officials may ultimately prove more harmful than beneficial to many corporations. It can impose a kind of implicit tax. * * *

* * * Corporate "domination" of electioneering, *Austin*, 494 U.S., at 659, can generate the impression that corporations dominate our democracy. When citizens turn on their televisions and radios before an election and hear only corporate electioneering, they may lose faith in their capacity, as citizens, to influence public policy. A Government captured by corporate interests, they may come to believe, will be neither responsive to their needs nor willing to give their views a fair

---

[70] In state elections, even domestic corporations may be "foreign"-controlled in the sense that they are incorporated in another jurisdiction and primarily owned and operated by out-of-state residents.

hearing. The predictable result is cynicism and disenchantment * * *. To the extent that corporations are allowed to exert undue influence in electoral races, the speech of the eventual winners of those races may also be chilled. Politicians who fear that a certain corporation can make or break their reelection chances may be cowed into silence about that corporation. * * * At the least, I stress again, a legislature is entitled to credit these concerns and to take tailored measures in response.

The majority's unwillingness to distinguish between corporations and humans similarly blinds it to the possibility that corporations' "war chests" and their special "advantages" in the legal realm may translate into special advantages in the market for legislation. When large numbers of citizens have a common stake in a measure that is under consideration, it may be very difficult for them to coordinate resources on behalf of their position. * * * Corporations, [by contrast], are uniquely equipped to seek laws that favor their owners, not simply because they have a lot of money but because of their legal and organizational structure. * * *

* * * All of the majority's theoretical arguments turn on a proposition with undeniable surface appeal but little grounding in evidence or experience, "that there is no such thing as too much speech." If individuals in our society had infinite free time to listen to and contemplate every last bit of speech uttered by anyone, anywhere; and if broadcast advertisements had no special ability to influence elections apart from the merits of their arguments (to the extent they make any); and if legislators always operated with nothing less than perfect virtue; then I suppose the majority's premise would be sound. In the real world, we have seen, corporate domination of the airwaves prior to an election may decrease the average listener's exposure to relevant viewpoints, and it may diminish citizens' willingness and capacity to participate in the democratic process.

* * * *Austin*'s "concern about corporate domination of the political process" reflects more than a concern to protect governmental interests outside of the First Amendment. It also reflects a concern to *facilitate* First Amendment values by preserving some breathing room around the electoral "marketplace" of ideas, the marketplace in which the actual people of this Nation determine how they will govern themselves. The majority seems oblivious to the simple truth that laws such as § 203 do not merely pit the anticorruption interest against the First Amendment, but also pit competing First Amendment values against each other. There are, to be sure, serious concerns with any effort to balance the First Amendment rights of speakers against the First Amendment rights of listeners. But when the speakers in question are not real people and when the appeal to "First Amendment principles" depends almost entirely on the listeners' perspective, it becomes necessary to consider how listeners will actually be affected.

* * * Our colleagues have raised some interesting and difficult questions about Congress' authority to regulate electioneering by the press, and about how to define what constitutes the press. *But that is not the case before us.* Section 203 does not apply to media corporations, and even if it did, Citizens United is not a media corporation. * * *

2. *Shareholder Protection*

There is yet another way in which laws such as § 203 can serve First Amendment values. Interwoven with *Austin*'s concern to protect the integrity of the electoral process is a concern to protect the rights of shareholders from a kind of coerced speech: electioneering expenditures that do not "reflec[t] [their] support." 494 U.S., at 660–661. When corporations use general treasury funds to praise or attack a particular candidate for office, it is the shareholders, as the residual claimants, who are effectively footing the bill. Those shareholders who disagree with the corporation's electoral message may find their financial investments being used to undermine their political convictions.

The PAC mechanism, by contrast, helps assure that those who pay for an electioneering communication actually support its content and that managers do not use general treasuries to advance personal agendas. * * *

The Court dismisses this interest on the ground that abuses of shareholder money can be corrected "through the procedures of corporate democracy," and, it seems, through Internet-based disclosures.[76] I fail to understand how this addresses the concerns of dissenting union members, who will also be affected by today's ruling, and I fail to understand why the Court is so confident in these mechanisms. By "corporate democracy," presumably the Court means the rights of shareholders to vote and to bring derivative suits for breach of fiduciary duty. In practice, however, many corporate lawyers will tell you that "these rights are so limited as to be almost nonexistent," given the internal authority wielded by boards and managers and the expansive protections afforded by the business judgment rule.[k] Modern technology may help make it easier to track corporate activity, including electoral advocacy, but it is utopian to believe that it solves the problem. Most American households that own stock do so through intermediaries such as mutual funds and pension plans, which makes it more difficult both to monitor and to alter particular holdings. Studies show that a majority of individual investors make no trades at all during a given year. Moreover, if the corporation in question operates a PAC, an investor who sees the company's ads may not know whether they are being funded through the PAC or through the general treasury.

If and when shareholders learn that a corporation has been spending general treasury money on objectionable electioneering, they can divest. Even assuming that they reliably learn as much, however, this solution is only partial. The injury to the shareholders' expressive rights has already occurred; they might have preferred to keep that corporation's stock in their portfolio for any number of economic reasons; and they may incur a capital gains tax or other penalty from selling their shares, changing their pension plan, or the like. The shareholder protection rationale has been criticized as underinclusive, in that corporations also spend

---

[76] Legislatures remain free in their incorporation and tax laws to condition the types of activity in which corporations may engage, including electioneering activity, on specific disclosure requirements or on prior express approval by shareholders or members.

[k] The business-judgment rule insulates corporate directors from suit by presuming that corporate transactions have been undertaken with due care, in good faith, and in the belief that they are in the corporation's best interest. [— Eds.]

money on lobbying and charitable contributions in ways that any particular shareholder might disapprove. But those expenditures do not implicate the selection of public officials, an area in which "the interests of unwilling . . . corporate shareholders [in not being] forced to subsidize that speech" "are at their zenith." And in any event, the question is whether shareholder protection provides a basis for regulating expenditures in the weeks before an election, not whether additional types of corporate communications might similarly be conditioned on voluntariness. * * *

* * * At bottom, the Court's opinion is * * * a rejection of the common sense of the American people, who have recognized a need to prevent corporations from undermining self-government since the founding, and who have fought against the distinctive corrupting potential of corporate electioneering since the days of Theodore Roosevelt. It is a strange time to repudiate that common sense. While American democracy is imperfect, few outside the majority of this Court would have thought its flaws included a dearth of corporate money in politics.

I would affirm the judgment of the District Court.

Notes and Questions

1. After *Citizens United*, is it constitutional for Congress to ban foreign-owned U.S. corporations from making independent expenditures? (Note that another section of FECA already prohibits foreign corporations from making contributions or expenditures, 2 U.S.C. § 441e, 11 C.F.R. § 110.20). In *Bluman v. Federal Election Commission*, 800 F. Supp. 2d 281 (D.D.C. 2011), *sum. aff'd* 132 S. Ct. 1087, 181 L. Ed. 2d 726 (2012), a suit instituted shortly after *Citizens United* was decided, plaintiffs were a Canadian citizen who had resided in the U.S. for four years on student and work visas, and was eligible to remain for up five more years; and a dual Canadian-Israeli citizen living in the United States and working temporarily as a medical resident, with eligibility to remain in the U.S. for as much as seven more years. Each sought to contribute to various U.S. politicians, parties, and PACs that supported their views on a variety of issues, but were forbidden to do so by federal law, which prohibits non-permanent resident aliens from making contributions in connection with United States elections. A three judge panel of the federal district court upheld the prohibition and was summarily affirmed by the Supreme Court.

2. *Problem.* Consider the constitutionality of the following proposals:

a. A state imposes a ban on independent expenditures by corporations chartered in different states, or those corporations having a majority of shares owned by out-of-state residents.

b. A state limits a candidate's out-of-state contributions to $100,000.

c. A state limits a candidate's out-of-state contributions to a percentage of total contributions.

d. Congress limits the amount a candidate can receive from persons living outside the candidate's district.

e. Congress prohibits contributions from persons living outside the district.

3.   May Congress ban only large corporations from making independent expenditures? That is, if Congress made an exception for "mom-and-pop" corporations, would the rest of the ban be constitutional?

4.   Does a ban on corporate electioneering actually benefit corporations, in that it protects them from being pressured to support candidates? Compare to the discussion of restrictions on the political activities of government employees in Chapter 8, § G.

5.   One argument for preserving a ban on corporate spending is the protection of minority shareholders, who may not want their funds spent to support candidates with whom they disagree. While this issue was discussed in the opinions in *Bellotti*, *MCFL*, *Austin*, and *WRTL II*, it received an unusual amount of attention in the immediate aftermath of *Citizens United*. One view holds that unhappy shareholders can simply sell their stock. Others argue that this is not always a viable alternative. Consider, for example, that selling stock at a particular time may result in a major tax liability or a loss on the sale; or consider a public employee whose retirement contributions are invested in the state retirement system, which then invests in a company making political expenditures in support of candidates he opposes. Should such individuals be protected from such corporate expenditures? Consider that corporations frequently make charitable contributions with which some stockholders disagree, or business decisions with which they disagree (for example, to increase profits by skimping on pollution control equipment; or to temporarily decrease profits by spending more on safety). Generally speaking, under the business judgment rule corporate directors have broad discretion to make decisions, including contributions to charities, themes for corporate advertising (that may offend some shareholders) and the like. Does limiting that discretion in the area of political giving interfere with the rights of majority shareholders, either by muzzling their speech or creating management inefficiencies that would detract from shareholder value?

One leading corporate scholar argues that consideration of minority shareholders should not affect the First Amendment rights of corporations:

> [T]he shareholder-protection rationale for the current scheme of restrictions on corporate political activity depends on a showing that (1) shareholders incur agency costs from permitting corporate political activity * * * (2) that these costs outweigh benefits of permitting the managers to engage in corporate speech through the corporation * * * ; and (3) that the costs of leaving such protection to shareholder choice outweigh the benefits of doing so. Such a showing would be extraordinarily difficult to make.

Larry E. Ribstein, *Corporate Political Speech*, 49 WASH. & LEE L. REV. 109 (1992). For other commentary, *See also* Robert H. Sitkoff, *Corporate Political Speech, Political Extortion, and the Competition for Corporate Charters*, 69 U. CHI. L. REV. 1103 (2002) (the theory of shareholder protection "assumes that shareholders are locked into their investment, and further that in the absence of regulation all corporations will engage in political speech. But these assumptions depend on a paucity of investment opportunities and/or opaque securities markets. These assumptions are dubious.") For an opposing view that argues exactly those assumptions, *see* Victor Brudney, *Business Corporations and Stockholders' Rights under the First Amendment*, 91 YALE L. J. 235, 235–37 (1981). *See also* Adam Winkler, *Corporate Personhood and the Rights of Corporate Speech*, 30 SEA. U. L. REV. 863 (2007).

6. What are the state-conferred advantages of a corporation? The dissenters cite three advantages, the first of which is limited liability. How does limited liability help a corporation amass wealth? The corporation can still be sued for all its assets. Limited liability protects the assets of individual shareholders, not the corporation as an entity. Individual shareholders are still free to spend their funds or even to form other associations to spend their personal funds on political speech.

A second cited benefit is perpetual life. The law, of course, does not prohibit inherited wealth from being spent on political activity. And cannot unincorporated businesses be sold over generations? Corporate scholar Robert Sitkoff notes that "as a class, managers must always look forward to tomorrow's product and capital market competition." Thus perpetual life makes large political spending riskier than for an individual. "Managers who divert corporate resources from profit-making activities towards funding political campaigns on such a grand level as to warrant the characterization "corrosive and distorting" will find their firm's "large treasuries" shrinking as the firm becomes less competitive in its product and the capital markets." Because of perpetual life, managers are never in the "last period" situation, in which they can indulge their political desires because the "game" is ending. Robert H. Sifkoff, *Corporate Political Speech, Political Extortion, and the Competition for Corporate Charters*, 69 U. CHI. L. REV. 1103, 1109 (2002).

The third is general benefits from the state in taxation and the retention and distribution of assets. Doctors, lawyers, and other learned professions gain protection from competition through state licensing systems. Many of these professionals make a great deal of money. Can the state limit their political expenditures because of the benefits they receive from the state? By registering the deeds to homes with the state, homeowners gain certain advantages. Homeowners also receive favorable federal tax treatment. May the government compel homeowners to give up speech rights for these benefits?

The competing views of the majority and dissent, are substantially shaped by differing theories of what a corporation is. The dissenters in *Bellotti* and *Citizens United* (and the majority in *Austin*) appear to adhere to some version of the concession theory, in which the state retains presumptive authority to regulate the corporate entity. The majority in *Bellotti* and *Citizens United* (the dissent in *Austin*) appears to adhere to what is generally called contractarian theory, in which corporations are seen not as "creatures of the state" but as creations of the individuals who found, own, and manage them. These individuals are bound in an extensive web of express and implied contracts embodied in the corporation, and to regulate the corporation is to regulate the individuals who make up the corporation. For an overview of relevant corporate theory, see Anne Tucker, *Flawed Assumptions: A Corporate Law Analysis of Free Speech and Corporate Personhood in Citizens United*, 61 CASE W. RES. L. REV. 497, 501–506 (2010). For a small sampling of the literature on corporate governance, theory, and speech rights, see Stefan J. Padfeld, *The Silent Role of Corporate Theory in the Supreme Court's Campaign Finance Cases*, 15 U. PA. J. CONST. L. 831 (2013); Roger Coffin, *A Responsibility to*

Speak: Citizens United, Corporate Governance, and Managing Risks, 8 HASTINGS BUS. L. J. 103 (2012); Larry E. Ribstein, *The First Amendment and Corporate Governance*, 27 GA. ST. U. L. REV. 1019, 1021 (2011); Sifkoff, *supra*.

7. Does *Citizens United* undercut the rationale for restricting direct corporate contributions to candidates? The case that it does is at least superficially appealing. If, as *Citizens United* says (p. 1020), "government cannot restrict political speech based on the speaker's corporate identity," then one might question the justification for the outright prohibition on corporate contributions to candidates. Does a $2,600 contribution from a corporation really offer more opportunity for quid pro quo exchange than a $2,600 contribution from that corporation's CEO? Similarly, the Court's opinion noted that due to the costs and burden of maintaining a political action committee, "fewer than 2000 of the millions of corporations in this country have PACs" (p. 1018). If PACs are an inadequate substitute for corporate expenditures, should the Court extend this reasoning to hold that PACs are an inadequate substitute for most corporations to make contributions?

Apparently not. William Danielczyk was criminally prosecuted for, *inter alia*, using straw donors to contribute corporate funds to a campaign. Danielczyk argued that after *Citizens United*, a complete ban on corporate contributions was unconstitutional. The Court of Appeals, however, upheld the ban, and the Supreme Court denied certiorari. Are there justifications for banning corporate contributions that are not present in considering corporate expenditures? *United States v. Danielczyk*, 683 F.3d 611 (4th Cir. 2012), *cert denied* 133 S. Ct. 1459 (2013). Recall that *Buckley* held that a limit on independent expenditures was a greater First Amendment burden than a limit on contributions, and that contributions posed a greater danger of corruption than independent expenditures. Are these considerations enough to justify the difference? Is there an equal-protection claim? Should Congress have to treat all potential donors and spenders alike? Consider *Austin v. Michigan State Chamber of Commerce*, 494 U.S. 652 (1990) [p. 944], which held that the state could differentiate in its treatment of corporations, unions, and the press, and *California Medical Association v. FEC*, 453 U.S. 182 (1981) [p. 822], which upheld distinctions in the treatment of partnerships and corporations.

8. In *Western Tradition Partnership v. Bullock*, 271 P.3d 1 (Mont. 2011), the Montana Supreme Court upheld Montana's ban on independent corporate expenditures. The court interpreted *Citizens United* not to hold that a prohibition on independent expenditures was *per se* unconstitutional, but only that such a prohibition must be justified by the record. The court then relied on the following history as establishing a sufficiently compelling state interest to justify the ban:

> Examples of well-financed corruption abound. In the fight over mineral rights between entrepreneur F. Augustus Heinze and the Anaconda Company, then controlled by Standard Oil, Heinze managed to control the two State judges in Butte, who routinely decided cases in his favor. The Butte judges denied being bribed, but one of them admitted that Anaconda representatives had offered him $250,000 cash to sign an affidavit that Heinze had bribed him.
>
> In response to the legal conflicts with Heinze, in 1903 Anaconda/ Standard closed down all its industrial and mining operations (but not the

many newspapers it controlled), throwing 4/5 of the labor force of Montana out of work. Its price for sending its employees back to work was that the Governor call a special session of the Legislature to enact a measure that would allow Anaconda to avoid having to litigate in front of the Butte judges. The Governor and Legislature capitulated and the statute survives.

W.A. Clark, who had amassed a fortune from the industrial operations in Butte, set his sights on the United States Senate. In 1899, in the wake of a large number of suddenly affluent members, the Montana Legislature elected Clark to the U.S. Senate. Clark admitted to spending $272,000 in the effort and the estimated expense was over $400,000. Complaints of Clark's bribery of the Montana Legislature led to an investigation by the U.S. Senate in 1900. The Senate investigating committee concluded that Clark had won his seat through bribery and unseated him. The Senate committee "expressed horror at the amount of money which had been poured into politics in Montana elections * * * and expressed its concern with respect to the general aura of corruption in Montana." * * *

After the Anaconda Company cleared itself of opposition from Heinze and others, it controlled 90% of the press in the state and a majority of the legislature. By 1915 the company, after having acquired all of Clark's holdings as well as many others, "clearly dominated the Montana economy and political order . . . [and] local folks now found themselves locked in the grip of a corporation controlled from Wall Street and insensitive to their concerns." Even at that time it was evident that industrial corporations controlled the state "thus converting the state government into a political instrument for the furthering and accomplishment of legislation and the execution of laws favorable to the absentee stockholders of the large corporations and inimical to the economic interests of the wage earning and farming classes who constitute by far the larger percentage of the population in Montana."

In 1900 Clark himself testified in the United States Senate that "[m]any people have become so indifferent to voting" in Montana as a result of the "large sums of money that have been expended in the state. * * * "This naked corporate manipulation of the very government (Governor and Legislature) of the State ultimately resulted in populist reforms that are still part of Montana law. In 1906 the people voted to amend the state Constitution to allow for voter initiatives. Not long thereafter, in 1906 this new initiative power was used to enact reforms including * * * the Corrupt Practices Act, part of which survives as [the statute] at issue in this case

271 P.3d at 23–28 (citations omitted).

Read this history closely. How relevant is it to the constitutionality of the ban on independent corporate expenditures? Do its examples — bribery of judges and legislators, control of newspapers (which are exempt from the Montana prohibition on corporate expenditures), use of economic power to close factories, and allegations of legislative dominance a decade after the state prohibited corporate expenditures — support application of the Montana statute on independent campaign expenditures as necessary to prevent corruption? Do they demonstrate that corporate spending poses a threat of corruption, or do they fail to support the notion that corporate spending in campaigns corrupts the legislature? Does it make a difference to your thinking that during this period of alleged corporate domination, the state passed the reforms mentioned in the last quoted paragraph, including the ban on corporate political spending?

Could the statute be interpreted as an effort to by anti-Anaconda forces to improve their political position by limiting opposition speech? *See* Robert G. Natelson, *Montana's Supreme Court Relies on Erroneous History in Rejecting Citizens United* 8 (Center for Competitive Politics 2012). According to Natelson:

> Montana activists have a long history of adopting campaign finance "reforms" — even obviously unconstitutional ones — to promote their political agendas. Section 13-35-227 was just one example. Another arose in 1975, when "progressives" successfully banned corporate spending on ballot issues. A federal appeals court struck down the ban as unconstitutional. In 1996, they convinced the voters to pass I-125 — yet another ban on corporate spending in ballot issue campaigns. The purpose was to prevent mining companies from defending themselves against an anti-mining initiative (I-137), to be offered at the following general election. Two federal courts invalidated I-125.

> During oral argument on the Western Tradition case, the Montana justices communicated that they were deeply concerned about how corporate contributions might change electoral results — particularly in their own elections, where corporate money has heretofore been locked out and financing dominated by trial lawyers.

The U.S. Supreme Court, in a one page *per curiam* opinion, summarily reversed, 5-4, in *American Tradition Partnership v. Bullock*, 132 S. Ct. 2490 (2012). The Justices split along the same lines as in *Citizens United*.

Recall that in *Citizens United*, the Court wrote, "independent expenditures, including those made by corporations, do not give rise to corruption or the appearance of corruption." Is this an evidentiary judgment by the court, or a statement of what constitutes a "compelling government interest" for purposes of First Amendment law? Consider that in *American Tradition Partnership*, the Court did not discuss any of the evidence that the Montana court found persuasive, writing only, "[t]he question presented in this case is whether the holding of *Citizens United* applies to the Montana state law. There can be no serious doubt that it does. Montana's arguments in support of the judgment below either were already rejected in *Citizens United* or fail to meaningfully distinguish that case."

Note on "Superpacs"

Citizens United is often credited (or blamed) for the creation of what the Federal Election Commission recognizes as "Independent Expenditure Committees" but what have become colloquially known as "Super PACs." A Super PAC is simply a PAC, subject to the same organizational and reporting requirements as any other PAC. However, Super PACs make only independent expenditures — they do not contribute to parties, candidates, or traditional PACs.

As a result, Super PACs are permitted to receive contributions from any source, including corporations and unions, in any amount, without limit.

Super PACs are actually not a direct creation of *Citizens United*, but rather of a Court of Appeals case, *SpeechNow.org v. Federal Election Commission*, 599 F.3d 686 (D.C. Cir. 2010). In *SpeechNow*, an unincorporated group of individuals challenged the $5,000 personal limit on contributions to a political committee as applied to a committee that only made independent expenditures. The plaintiffs argued that if it were not corrupting for a single individual to finance independent expenditures without limit, it could not be corrupting if that same individual joined with others to make such expenditures. The Court of Appeals, relying heavily on *Citizens United* (decided just six days before oral argument in *SpeechNow*) ruled for the plaintiffs, and the government chose not to appeal. Since then, *SpeechNow* has largely been accepted as the law in all jurisdictions. Thus the two cases are interlocking: *Citizens United* holds that, as a matter of law, independent expenditures are not corrupting; *SpeechNow*, relying on that ruling, therefore allows speakers to pool their resources, without limit, to make independent expenditures; and *Citizens United* in turn permits corporations and unions to join in those pooling efforts. *SpeechNow* was quickly followed by several others courts and is generally treated as law nationwide. *See Republican Party of New Mexico v. King*, 741 F. 3d 1089 (10th Cir. 2013); *New York Progress and Protection PAC v. Walsh*, 733 F.3d 483 (2nd Cir. 2013); *Texans for Free Enterprise v. Texas Ethics Commission*, 732 F. 3d 535 (5th Cir. 2013); *Long Beach Area Chamber of Commerce v. City of Long Beach*, 603 F.3d 684 (9th Cir. 2010); *Michigan Chamber of Commerce v. Land*, 725 F. Supp. 2d 665 (W.D. Mich. 2010).

Despite some popular perception to the contrary, the substantial majority of contributions to Super PACs have come from individuals, not corporations or unions. *See* Adam Lioz & Blair Bowie, *Election Spending 2012: Post-Election Analysis of Federal Election Commission Data* (Nov. 9, 2012), http://www.demos. org/publication/election-spending-2012-post-election-analysis-federal-election-commission-data (finding just 11% from business, five percent from unions, and an additional 14% from sources that include a mix of union, corporate, and individual money).

Super PACs, however, are not the only way that persons can join together to speak. Non-profit "social welfare" organizations operating under § 501(c)(4) of the Internal Revenue Code, such as the NAACP Voter Education Fund, the Sierra Club, or the National Rifle Association, may also make independent expenditures. The same is true for trade associations organized under § 501(c)(6) of the Code, such as the U.S. Chamber of Commerce. These organizations can accept corporate and union contributions as well as individual contributions.

However, if political activity becomes such an organization's primary activity, it triggers two consequences: first, the group or organization could become a "political committee" as defined by the Federal Election Campaign Act, and thus subject to the full organizational and reporting requirements of the Act. Second, the group would jeopardize or lose its tax status — it would presumably be forced to reorganize under Section 527 of the Internal Revenue Code, the section used by political organizations. For political purposes, the major consequence of being reclassified under Section 527 is that such a group must publicly disclose its donors, either through the FEC reporting system (if it qualifies as a "political committee" under the Federal Election Campaign Act, meaning it makes $1,000 or more in express advocacy expenditures or takes in more than $1,000 in contributions for that purpose) or otherwise through the IRS. Non- profits and trade associations operating under Section 501(c) can keep the identity of their donors and members confidential. Alternatively, the organization may simply be taxed as a for-profit corporation.

What constitutes an organization's "primary purpose" has never been clearly resolved. Generally, most experts in the field assume an organization must simply devote less than half its resources to political activity to avoid that designation. But note further that lobbying does not count as political activity for making this determination. Thus a group can devote substantial sums to campaigning, and most or all the rest of its budget to lobbying. For a concise introduction to these issues, see Donald B. Tobin, *The Rise of 501(c)(4)'s in Campaign Activity: Are They as Clever as They Think?*, Election Law@Moritz, Oct. 5, 2010, *at* http://moritzlaw.osu.edu/electionlaw/comments/index.php?ID=7667.

The end result after *Citizens United* and various other decisions and statutes was that, as of the spring of 2012–2015, political organizers had several types of organizations available to them:

a. *Traditional PACs:* Traditional PACs register with the FEC and report all donors over $200. They may make contributions to candidates and party commit-tees, or make independent expenditures. They may be (and at the federal level are) subject to limits on the size of contributions they may receive, and the source of those contributions (no corporate or union money). Examples include Emily's List Political Action Committee and Microsoft Political Action Committee.

b. *Independent Expenditure Committees, or Super PACs:* Super PACs are subject to the same registration and reporting requirements as traditional PACs, but may only make independent expenditures. They may accept contributions without limit from individuals, corporations, and unions. Examples include Ameri-can Crossroads, formed by Republican strategist Karl Rove, and Priorities USA, a Super PAC formed to help re-elect President Obama.

c. *Non-PAC 527s:* A non-PAC 527 is an organization that is deemed by the IRS to have political activity as its primary purpose, but does not qualify as a "political committee" under FEC regulations. This comes about when the organization engages in "electioneering communications" or other political messages that do not include "express advocacy" (which is needed to trigger "committee" status under FECA, per *Buckley*) but are deemed sufficiently political by the IRS, which uses a broader definition of "political activity," to be ineligible for 501(c)(4) status. The organizations are not subject to contribution restrictions but must publicly disclose their donors through the Internal Revenue Service, and cannot engage in "express advocacy" communications. They may not contribute directly to parties or candi-dates. Such organizations, including Swift Boat Veterans for Truth and MoveOn.org in the 2004 presidential campaign, were popular in the past, but have declined in use since the advent of Super PACs. MoveOn has in recent years disbanded its 527 arm.

d. 501(c)(4) and (c)(6) organizations: These organizations cannot make direct contributions to candidates, but may make independent expenditures so long as those expenditures do not become their primary purpose. They do not have to disclose their donors to the public. The NAACP Voter Education Fund and the National Rifle Association are examples of non-profits operating under Section 501(c)(4); the U.S. Chamber of Commerce is a trade association operating under Section 501(c)(6).

It is possible for one umbrella organization to operate any combination of the above forms of organizations. For example, a 501(c)(4) non-profit group may establish a traditional PAC to contribute to directly to candidates, a Super PAC to make independent expenditures, and also make limited expenditures from its general treasury, allowing some donors to remain confidential, provided it keeps the various funds separate. *See Carey v. Federal Election Commission,* 791 F. Supp. 2d 121 (D.D.C. 2011).

In the 2011–2012, the Federal Election Commission reported that independent expenditures accounted for approximately 18.2% of total federal political spending, or $1.27 billion of $6.98 billion. Federal Election Commission, *Summary of Campaign Activity of 2011–12 Election Cycle,* Apr. 19, 2013, revised Mar. 27, 2014, http://www.fec.gov/press/press2013/20130419_2012-24m-Summary.shtml. In the non-presidential year 2014, independent spending accounted for approximately $788 million, including independent spending by political parties. That amounted to approximately 21% of approximately $3.77 billion in total spending. Super PACs accounted for approximately $339 million, or a bit under nine percent of total spending. *See* Federal Election Commission, *Statistical Summary of 24-Month Campaign Activity of the 2013–2014 Election Cycle,* Apr. 3, 2015, (*available at* http://www.fec.gov/press/press2015/news_releases/20150403release.shtml# search=2014%20spending%20totals).

Problem: Dick and Jane have approached you on behalf of an informal group of fifteen or so anti-war activists who gather each weekend to picket and pass out anti-war literature. The group wants to buy radio ads and put up billboards urging the defeat of their incumbent congressman, Hank Manley, whom they believe has been too supportive of the war. "We don't want to pull any punches," they tell you. "We want these ads to be hard hitting." To be effective, they believe they need to raise at least $120,000. The members of their informal group are middle class professionals — teachers, college professors, a yoga instructor, some small business owners and a few stay-at-home parents, and they doubt they can raise the $120,000 from within the group. But Jane has talked about their plans with her friend Joe Rich, a wealthy entrepreneur. Rich told Jane he would be willing to contribute up to $150,000 to help defeat Manley. However, since one of his companies has a number of government contracts, he doesn't want to upset Manley, who, if re-elected, might use his office to try to harm his government business. For tax purposes, he would also prefer to make the contribution through one of his corporations, if possible. (All his companies are privately held). How would you advise Dick and Jane to proceed?

E. COORDINATED EXPENDITURES

Recall that in *Buckley v. Valeo* the Supreme Court held that expenditures are entitled to greater protection than are contributions. It then struck down limitations both on expenditures by candidates, and on expenditures made independently of candidates. But the Court also noted that expenditures that are "controlled by or coordinated with" a campaign were treated under the Act as contributions to the campaign, and so subject to limitation. This creates a tremendously important issue for political advocates, candidates, and the lawyers who advise them: what does it mean to "coordinate," such that what would otherwise be an "expenditure" not subject to limits becomes a "contribution" subject to limits? Somewhat surprisingly, there is remarkably little judicial guidance on the subject, and what there is has largely been relegated to coordination between parties and candidates, with even less about what other organizations can do. The FEC, for its part, has wrestled for years with several different definitions of "coordination." We begin this section with what little guidance we have from the Supreme Court.

COLORADO REPUBLICAN FEDERAL CAMPAIGN COMMITTEE v. FEDERAL ELECTION COMMISSION
(Colorado Republican I)
Supreme Court of the United States
518 U.S. 604, 116 S. Ct. 2309, 135 L. Ed. 2d 795 (1996)

JUSTICE BREYER announced the judgment of the Court and delivered an opinion, in which JUSTICE O'CONNOR and JUSTICE SOUTER join.

In April 1986, before the Colorado Republican Party had selected its senatorial candidate for the fall's election, that party's Federal Campaign Committee bought radio advertisements attacking Timothy Wirth, the Democratic Party's likely candidate. The Federal Election Commission (FEC) charged that this "expenditure" exceeded the dollar limits that a provision of the Federal Election Campaign Act of 1971 (FECA or Act) imposes upon political party "expenditure[s] in connection with" a "general election campaign" for congressional office. 2 U.S.C. § 441a(d)(3). This case focuses upon the constitutionality of those limits as applied to this case. We conclude that the First Amendment prohibits the application of this provision to the kind of expenditure at issue here — an expenditure that the political party has made independently, without coordination with any candidate.

I * * *

* * * [W]ithout special treatment, political parties ordinarily would be subject to the general limitation on contributions by a "multicandidate political committee" * * * See § 441a(a)(4). That provision * * * limits annual contributions by a "multicandidate political committee" to no more than $5,000 to any candidate. * * * This contribution limit governs not only direct contributions but also indirect contributions that take the form of coordinated expenditures, defined as "expenditures made . . . in cooperation, consultation, or concert, with, or at the request or suggestion of, a candidate, his authorized political committees, or their agents."

§ 441a(a)(7)(B)(i). Thus, ordinarily, a party's coordinated expenditures would be subject to the $5,000 limitation.

However, FECA's special provision, which we shall call the "Party Expenditure Provision," creates a *general exception* from this contribution limitation, and from any other limitation on expenditures. * * * After exempting political parties from the general contribution and expenditure limitations of the statute, the Party Expenditure Provision then imposes a *substitute limitation* upon party "expenditures" in a senatorial campaign equal to the greater of $20,000 or "2 cents multiplied by the voting age population of the State," adjusted for inflation since 1974. The provision permitted a political party in Colorado in 1986 to spend about $103,000 in connection with the general election campaign of a candidate for the United States Senate. * * *

In January 1986, Timothy Wirth, then a Democratic Congressman, announced that he would run for an open Senate seat in November. In April, before either the Democratic primary or the Republican convention, the Colorado Republican Federal Campaign Committee (Colorado Party or Party), a petitioner here, bought radio advertisements attacking Congressman Wirth. The State Democratic Party complained to the FEC. It pointed out that the Colorado Party had previously assigned its $103,000 general election allotment to the National Republican Senatorial Committee, leaving it without any permissible spending balance. See *Federal Election Comm'n* v. *Democratic Senatorial Campaign Comm.*, 454 U.S. 27 (1981) (state party may appoint national senatorial campaign committee as agent to spend its Party Expenditure Provision allotment). It argued that the purchase of radio time was an "expenditure in connection with the general election campaign of a candidate for Federal office," which, consequently, exceeded the Party Expenditure Provision limits. * * *

The summary judgment record indicates that the expenditure in question is what this Court in *Buckley* called an "independent" expenditure, not a "coordinated" expenditure that other provisions of FECA treat as a kind of campaign "contribution." See *Buckley* [*v. Valeo*, 424 U.S. 1], 36–37, 46–47, 78 [(1978)] [p. 799] [(*per curiam*)]; [*Federal Election Comm'n v. National Conservative Political Action Comm.*, 470 U.S. 480, 498 (1985)] [p. 881]. * * * In a deposition, the Colorado Party's Chairman, Howard Callaway, pointed out that, at the time of the expenditure, the Party had not yet selected a senatorial nominee from among the three individuals vying for the nomination. He added that he arranged for the development of the script at his own initiative, that he, and no one else, approved it, that the only other politically relevant individuals who might have read it were the Party's executive director and political director, and that all relevant discussions took place at meetings attended only by Party staff.

* * * [Callaway stated] that it was the practice of the Party to "coordinate with the candidate" "campaign strategy," and for Callaway to be "as involved as [he] could be" with the individuals seeking the Republican nomination, by making available to them "all of the assets of the party." These latter statements, however, are general descriptions of Party practice. They do not refer to the advertising campaign at issue here or to its preparation. Nor do they conflict with, or cast significant doubt upon, the uncontroverted direct evidence that this advertising

campaign was developed by the Colorado Party independently and not pursuant to any general or particular understanding with a candidate. We can find no "genuine" issue of fact in this respect. * * * And we therefore treat the expenditure, for constitutional purposes, as an "independent" expenditure, not an indirect campaign contribution.

So treated, the expenditure falls within the scope of the Court's precedents that extend First Amendment protection to independent expenditures. Beginning with *Buckley*, the Court's cases have found a "fundamental constitutional difference between money spent to advertise one's views independently of the candidate's campaign and money contributed to the candidate to be spent on his campaign." *NCPAC, supra* at 497. * * *

Given these established principles, we do not see how a provision that limits a political party's independent expenditures can escape their controlling effect. A political party's independent expression not only reflects its members' views about the philosophical and governmental matters that bind them together, it also seeks to convince others to join those members in a practical democratic task, the task of creating a government that voters can instruct and hold responsible for subsequent success or failure. The independent expression of a political party's views is "core" First Amendment activity no less than is the independent expression of individuals, candidates, or other political committees. See, *e.g.*, *Eu* v. *San Francisco County Democratic Central Comm.*, 489 U.S. 214 (1989).

We are not aware of any special dangers of corruption associated with political parties that tip the constitutional balance in a different direction. * * *

* * * If anything, an independent expenditure made possible by a $20,000 donation, but controlled and directed by a party rather than the donor, would seem less likely to corrupt than the same (or a much larger) independent expenditure made directly by that donor. In any case, the constitutionally significant fact, present equally in both instances, is the lack of coordination between the candidate and the source of the expenditure. This fact prevents us from assuming, absent convincing evidence to the contrary, that a limitation on political parties' independent expenditures is necessary to combat a substantial danger of corruption of the electoral system. * * *

[T]he Government and supporting *amici* argue that the expenditure is "coordinated" because a party and its candidate are identical, *i.e.*, the party, in a sense, "is" its candidates. We cannot assume, however, that this is so. See, *e.g.*, W. Keefe, Parties, Politics, and Public Policy in America 59–74 (5th ed. 1988) (describing parties as "coalitions" of differing interests). Congress chose to treat candidates and their parties quite differently under the Act, for example, by regulating contributions from one to the other. And we are not certain whether a metaphysical identity would help the Government, for in that case one might argue that the absolute identity of views and interests eliminates any potential for corruption, as would seem to be the case in the relationship between candidates and their campaign committees. * * *

For these reasons, the judgment of the Court of Appeals is vacated, and the case is remanded for further proceedings.

JUSTICE KENNEDY, with whom THE CHIEF JUSTICE and JUSTICE SCALIA join, concurring in the judgment and dissenting in part. * * *

We had no occasion in *Buckley* to consider possible First Amendment objections to limitations on spending by parties. While our cases uphold contribution limitations on individuals and associations, * * * political party spending "in cooperation, consultation, or concert with" a candidate does not fit within our description of "contributions" in *Buckley*. In my view, we should not transplant the reasoning of cases upholding ordinary contribution limitations to a case involving FECA's restrictions on political party spending.

The First Amendment embodies a "profound national commitment to the principle that debate on public issues should be uninhibited, robust, and wide-open." Political parties have a unique role in serving this principle; they exist to advance their members' shared political beliefs. * * * A party performs this function, in part, by "identifying the people who constitute the association, and . . . limiting the association to those people only." *Democratic Party of United States* v. *Wisconsin ex rel. La Follette*, 450 U.S. 107, 122 (1981). Having identified its members, however, a party can give effect to their views only by selecting and supporting candidates. A political party has its own traditions and principles that transcend the interests of individual candidates and campaigns; but in the context of particular elections, candidates are necessary to make the party's message known and effective, and vice versa.

It makes no sense, therefore, to ask, as FECA does, whether a party's spending is made "in cooperation, consultation, or concert with" its candidate. The answer in most cases will be yes, but that provides more, not less, justification for holding unconstitutional the statute's attempt to control this type of party spending, which bears little resemblance to the contributions discussed in *Buckley*. Party spending "in cooperation, consultation, or concert with" its candidates of necessity "communicate[s] the underlying basis for the support," 424 U.S. at 21, *i.e.*, the hope that he or she will be elected and will work to further the party's political agenda.

The problem is not just the absence of a basis in our First Amendment cases for treating the party's spending as contributions. The greater difficulty posed by the statute is its stifling effect on the ability of the party to do what it exists to do. It is fanciful to suppose that limiting party spending of the type at issue here "does not in any way infringe the contributor's freedom to discuss candidates and issues," since it would be impractical and imprudent, to say the least, for a party to support its own candidates without some form of "cooperation" or "consultation." The party's speech, legitimate on its own behalf, cannot be separated from speech on the candidate's behalf without constraining the party in advocating its most essential positions and pursuing its most basic goals. The party's form of organization and the fact that its fate in an election is inextricably intertwined with that of its candidates cannot provide a basis for the restrictions imposed here.

We have a constitutional tradition of political parties and their candidates engaging in joint First Amendment activity; we also have a practical identity of interests between the two entities during an election. Party spending "in cooperation, consultation, or concert with" a candidate therefore is indistinguishable in substance from expenditures by the candidate or his campaign committee. We held in *Buckley* that the First Amendment does not permit regulation of the latter, and it should not permit this regulation of the former. Congress may have authority, consistent with the First Amendment, to restrict undifferentiated political party contributions which satisfy the constitutional criteria we discussed in *Buckley*, but that type of regulation is not at issue here.

I would resolve the Party's First Amendment claim in accord with these principles rather than remit the Party to further protracted proceedings. Because the principal opinion would do otherwise, I concur only in the judgment.

JUSTICE THOMAS, with whom THE CHIEF JUSTICE and JUSTICE SCALIA join * * * concurring in the judgment and dissenting in part. * * *

Were I convinced that the *Buckley* framework rested on a principled distinction between contributions and expenditures, which I am not, I would nevertheless conclude that § 441a(d)(3)'s limits on political parties violate the First Amendment. * * *

The Government asserts that the purpose of § 441a(d)(3) is to prevent the corruption of candidates and elected representatives by party officials. * * * As applied in the specific context of campaign funding by political parties, the anti-corruption rationale loses its force. What could it mean for a party to "corrupt" its candidate or to exercise "coercive" influence over him? The very aim of a political party is to influence its candidate's stance on issues and, if the candidate takes office or is reelected, his votes. When political parties achieve that aim, that achievement does not, in my view, constitute "a subversion of the political process." For instance, if the Democratic Party spends large sums of money in support of a candidate who wins, takes office, and then implements the Party's platform, that is not corruption; that is successful advocacy of ideas in the political marketplace and representative government in a party system. * * *

The structure of political parties is such that the theoretical danger of those groups actually engaging in *quid pro quos* with candidates is significantly less than the threat of individuals or other groups doing so. American political parties, generally speaking, have numerous members with a wide variety of interests, features necessary for success in majoritarian elections. Consequently, the influence of any one person or the importance of any single issue within a political party is significantly diffused. * * *

In sum, there is only a minimal threat of "corruption," as we have understood that term, when a political party spends to support its candidate or to oppose his competitor, whether ***648*** or not that expenditure is made in concert with the candidate. Parties and candidates have traditionally worked together to achieve their common goals, and when they engage in that work, there is no risk to the Republic. To the contrary, the danger to the Republic lies in Government suppression of such activity. Under *Buckley* and our subsequent cases, § 441a(d)(3)'s heavy burden on First Amendment rights is not justified by the threat of corruption at which it is assertedly aimed.

To conclude, I would find § 441a(d)(3) unconstitutional not just as applied to petitioners, but also on its face. * * *

JUSTICE STEVENS, with whom JUSTICE GINSBURG joins, dissenting.

In my opinion, all money spent by a political party to secure the election of its candidate for the office of United States Senator should be considered a "contribution" to his or her campaign. * * *

[T]hree interests provide a constitutionally sufficient predicate for federal limits on spending by political parties. First, such limits serve the interest in avoiding both the appearance and the reality of a corrupt political process. A party shares a unique relationship with the candidate it sponsors because their political fates are inextricably linked. That interdependency creates a special danger that the party — or the persons who control the party — will abuse the influence it has over the candidate by virtue of its power to spend. The provisions at issue are appropriately aimed at reducing that threat. The fact that the party in this case had not yet chosen its nominee at the time it broad-cast the challenged advertisements is immaterial to the analysis. Although the Democratic and Republican nominees for the 1996 Presidential race will not be selected until this summer, current advertising expenditures by the two national parties are no less contributions to the campaigns of the respective frontrunners than those that will be made in the fall.

Second, these restrictions supplement other spending limitations embodied in the Federal Election Campaign Act of 1971, which are likewise designed to prevent corruption. Individuals and certain organizations are permitted to contribute up to $1,000 to a candidate. Since the same donors can give up to $5,000 to party committees, if there were no limits on party spending, their contributions could be spent to benefit the candidate and thereby circumvent the $1,000 cap. * * *

Finally, I believe the Government has an important interest in leveling the electoral playing field by constraining the cost of federal campaigns. * * * It is quite wrong to assume that the net effect of limits on contributions and expenditures — which tend to protect equal access to the political arena, to free candidates and their staffs from the interminable burden of fund-raising, and to diminish the importance of repetitive 30-second commercials — will be adverse to the interest in informed debate protected by the First Amendment.

Congress surely has both wisdom and experience in these matters that is far superior to ours. I would therefore accord special deference to its judgment on questions related to the extent and nature of limits on campaign spending. Accordingly, I would affirm the judgment of the Court of Appeals.

Notes and Questions

1. *Coordination* is an elusive concept, made more difficult by the fact that most major interest groups have regular contacts with their advocates and supporters in the legislature. For example, a major interest group such as the Sierra Club or the National Association of Manufacturers will have meet frequently with allies in Congress to discuss legislation. In doing so, they may discuss the status of public opinion on issues of mutual concern, ways to move public opinion, and the general political climate as it relates to their issues. Later, when these candidates seek reelection or election to a higher office, these same interest groups may wish to

support their candidacies. At what point does their general political knowledge about the plans and messages of the candidates rise to the level of "coordination"?

This determination is made still more difficult by the fluidity of staffing in politics, and the relatively small number of skilled vendors. For example, it would not be uncommon for the legislative director of a pro-environmental protection congressman to accept a job with the Sierra Club; and then to leave the Sierra Club later to serve as campaign manager for her former boss's re-election effort, which the Sierra Club will seek to support. Given the staffer's knowledge of both the Sierra Club's and the candidate's campaigns, does this create coordination per se? Furthermore, there are a relatively small number of political consultants who handle most major campaigns. Suppose that Senator Jones has hired Political Admen, Inc. to handle media for her campaign, and that the Club for Growth, a group that lobbies for lower taxes and reduced government spending, also uses Political Admen, Inc., for its media needs. If the Club decides to make expenditures in support of Senator Jones, Political Admen will have access to the media and messaging strategies of both the Club and Senator Jones, as it advises each on how to spend campaign dollars. Does this constitute coordination?

Making this even more difficult is what some have called "independent coordination." That is, it is not generally difficult for political junkies to know which states, congressional districts, or portions of districts are particularly important. Similarly, it is relatively easy, simply through following the news, to learn of the key issues in a campaign, and the speeches and pronouncements of candidate. Moreover, campaigns will usually publicize upcoming campaign appearances, and the campaign may speak openly in the press about its strategies for winning. Indeed, because the law now requires ad buys to be made public, groups can even know of a candidate's advertising plans. Thus, an organization can typically gather all the information it needs to run a "coordinated" campaign without ever speaking to the candidate.

2. Prior to *Colorado Republican I*, the FEC considered all party expenditures to be *per se* coordinated with their candidates. Is it truly impossible for a party to make expenditures to influence a race without coordinating those expenditures with its candidates? Remember that the expenditures in *Colorado Republican I* were made before the Party had even selected its candidate. Yet both the opinions concurring in the judgment and dissenting seem to consider parties and candidates, in Justice Stevens' words, "inextricably linked." For the dissenters, that is an argument that party spending is not much different, or perhaps even more potentially corrupting, than other spending, and thus an argument for regulation; for the concurring justices, it is an argument that the regulation is unconstitutional, operating where there is no threat of corruption and making it impossible for the party to achieve the goals for which its members associate. The plurality opinion treats the parties much like any other spender, and like any other spender it can act independently of candidates. Which view of coordination do you think is most correct, and which set of consequences would you draw from that view? Is it possible that all three views expressed can be correct, depending on time and place?

3. *Problem:* Jeb Clinton, a former governor, senator, cabinet member, and member of a prominent political family, is widely expected to seek his party's

nomination for President in 2020. Through the winter and spring of 2019, Clinton makes a number of speeches around the country, travels extensively to meet with state party leaders, and actively raises money for the Party and various PACs that generally support his party. Public opinion surveys consistently show him to be a leading presidential contender. The Party, meanwhile, runs advertisements promoting a number of issues generally associated with Clinton. Clinton and Party officials have numerous discussions about the Party's messaging and attempt to coordinate Party activities with Clinton's visits to different states. Clinton has not declared himself a candidate for President. The first caucuses and primaries are eight or more months in the future, with the general election over 18 months off. Leaders of the opposing party have come to you, as counsel for that party, asking if it is worthwhile to file a complaint with the Federal Election Commission alleging illegal coordination between Clinton and the Party. If it is not possible to file a complaint immediately, they wonder if a complaint could be filed when and if Clinton declares his candidacy. Your advice?

4. While *Colorado Republican I* tells us what coordination is not in one particular situation, it tells us very little about what coordination is. Perhaps surprisingly, the courts have made very few forays into the discussion. One of the few (perhaps only) federal court decisions to examine the concept of coordination in depth is *FEC v. Christian Coalition*, 52 F. Supp. 2d 45 (D.D.C. 1999). The Court described the standard advocated by the FEC as one in which "any consultation between a potential spender and a federal candidate's campaign organization about the candidate's plans, projects, or needs renders any subsequent expenditures made for the purpose of influencing the election 'coordinated,' i.e. contributions." *Id.* at 89. The Court considered what it called this "insider trading" standard to be unconstitutionally overbroad:

> To be sure, the scenario the FEC paints to support its approach is plausible: A corporate or union representative meets with campaign staff on one or more occasions and receives non-public information about the campaign's strategy; the corporate or union representative learns that the campaign seeks to highlight one or more of the candidate's policy positions before a specific constituency; acting on the "tip," the corporation or union expends or "invests" considerable sums from its "war chest" to pay for communications highlighting said policy position(s) before said constituency; after the candidate is elected, the corporation or union seeks to profit from its investment by demanding special access to the elected official or a legislative *quid pro quo.* * * *

> Nonetheless, while this plausible scenario demonstrates that the potential for corruption flowing from coordinated expenditures is non-speculative, the prohibition on such expenditures must be narrowly tailored to meet this danger. An "insider trading" or conspiracy approach also sweeps in all attempts by corporations and unions to discuss policy matters with the candidate while these groups are contemporaneously funding communications directed at the same policy matters. *Cf. Clifton [v. Maine Right to Life Committee,]* 114 F.3d [1309], 1313 [(1st Cir. 1997)] (FEC's bar on oral contact regarding voter guides [defining inquiries as to a candidate's position, made to help compile a non-partisan voter guide, as "coordinated"]

is an overbroad prophylactic rule). The FEC believes that its concept of coordination is narrowly tailored to the anti-corruption interest because its definition "reaches only those expenditures that are made after consultation with a candidate concerning campaign strategy or activities, not mere lobbying or asking a candidate or incumbent where she stands on a particular policy issue or proposed legislation."

But as the facts of this case demonstrate, discussion of campaign strategy and discussion of policy issues are hardly two easily distinguished subjects. *See Buckley*, 424 U.S. at 249 ("Candidates, especially incumbents, are intimately tied to public issues involving legislative proposals and governmental actions."). The FEC's tidy distinction between discussion of campaign strategy and mere lobbying is cold comfort for those who seek to discuss with a candidate an issue that is at the time dominating the campaign. Indeed, the record in this case demonstrates that a candidate's decision when to take a stand, where to stand, and how to communicate the stand on a policy issue often are integral parts of campaign strategy. The facts further demonstrate that a candidate frequently listens to the concerns of sympathetic constituencies or factions before making those important strategic decisions. While the FEC's approach would certainly address the potential for corruption in the above-described scenario, it would do so only by heavily burdening the common, probably necessary, communications between candidates and constituencies during an election campaign.

Id. at 89–90.

The Court noted that it had pressed both parties to provide their proposed legal standard for defining the activities that would amount to "coordination" of expenditures, but "neither party was particularly responsive." *Id.* at 91. The Court thus supplied its own definition:

In the absence of a request or suggestion from the campaign, an expressive expenditure becomes "coordinated;" where the candidate or her agents can exercise control over, or where there has been substantial discussion or negotiation between the campaign and the spender over, a communication's: (1) contents; (2) timing; (3) location, mode, or intended audience (e.g., choice between newspaper or radio advertisement); or (4) "volume" (e.g., number of copies of printed materials or frequency of media spots). Substantial discussion or negotiation is such that the candidate and spender emerge as partners or joint venturers in the expressive expenditure, but the candidate and spender need not be equal partners.

Id. at 92. Applying that definition, the Court found that on the facts of the case no coordination had occurred.

5.   In response to *Colorado I* and *FEC v. Christian Coalition* (which it did not appeal), the FEC adopted a new definition of coordination in 2000, essentially adopting the *Christian Coalition* standard. 65 Fed. Reg. 76138 (Dec. 6, 2000). Campaign finance reform groups were concerned that this new FEC definition allowed too many opportunities for "coordinated" activities to pass unregulated.

Thus, extensive efforts were made to write a new, statutory definition of coordination into the Bipartisan Campaign Reform Act of 2002. Ultimately, however, Congress could not agree on a definition, and settled for repealing the existing FEC regulation and ordering the Agency to write a new definition. Pub. L. No. 107-155, § 214 (2002). Accordingly, the FEC adopted a new definition in 2002, but the lead House sponsors of BCRA challenged the FEC's regulations in Court as insufficiently rigorous, and they were struck down by a federal court in *Shays v. Federal Election Commission*, 337 F. Supp. 2d 28 (D.D.C. 2004), *aff'd* 414 F. 3d 76 (D.C. Cir. 2005) (*Shays I*). The Commission tried again, passing new rules in 2006, which were again successfully challenged in Court as insufficiently rigorous, *Shays v. FEC*, 508 F. Supp. 2d 10 (D.D.C. 2007), *aff'd* 528 F. 3d 914 (D.C. Cir. 2008) (*Shays II*). The FEC opened yet another rule making in the fall of 2009, seven years after passage of BCRA. *See* 74 Fed. Reg. 53893 (Oct. 21, 2009). No new final rule had been issued as of April 2015. Pursuant to the order in *Shays II*, the FEC's 2003 regulations remain in effect while the FEC works to promulgate new regulations.

6. The FEC coordination rule adopted in 2003, 11 C.F.R. § 109, includes both "conduct" and "content" standards. The former regulate the types of contacts and conduct that constitute "coordination." The latter limit findings of coordination based on expenditures for public communications to only certain communications — specifically, to communications including "express advocacy;" "electioneering communications" as defined in 52 U.S.C. § 30104(f) (essentially broadcast ads made within 30 days of a primary or caucus or 60 days of a general election); republication or distribution of a candidate's own campaign material; and certain other "public communications" that reference a candidate or party close to an election.

What is the purpose of including a "content" standard? Investigations into allegedly coordinated actions are among the most intrusive undertaken by the FEC. In order to determine if the coordination has taken place, the FEC typically probes into the number and content of communications between the candidate and his campaign staff, and the staff and leadership of the group alleged to be illegally coordinating its activities. This frequently involves substantial probing into the political strategy and tactics of both entities. *See* James Bopp, Jr. & Richard E. Colestrom, *The First Amendment Needs No Reform: Protecting Liberty from Campaign Finance Reformers*, 51 Cath. U. L. Rev. 785, 833 (2002). *See generally* Bradley A. Smith & Stephen M. Hoersting, *A Toothless Anaconda: Innovation, Impotence, and Overenforcement at the Federal Election Commission*, 1 Election L.J. 145, 167–169 (2002). Then consider the Supreme Court's decision in *Buckley*, narrowing the definition of "expenditure" to "express advocacy":

> [The Act contains] no definition clarifying what expenditures are "relative to" a candidate. The use of so indefinite a phrase as "relative to" a candidate fails to clearly mark the boundary between permissible and impermissible speech * * *.

> "[W]hether words intended and designed to fall short of invitation would miss that mark is a question both of intent and of effect. No speaker, in such circumstances, safely could assume that anything he might say upon the general subject would not be understood by some as an invitation. In short, the supposedly clear-cut distinction between discussion, laudation, general

advocacy, and solicitation puts the speaker in these circumstances wholly at the mercy of the varied understanding of his hearers and consequently of whatever inference may be drawn as to his intent and meaning.

"Such a distinction offers no security for free discussion. In these conditions it blankets with uncertainty whatever may be said. It compels the speaker to hedge and trim."

Buckley v. Valeo, 424 U.S. 1, 41–43 (1976) (citations omitted).

Does the vagueness problem go away merely because an expenditure is coordinated? Consider the following example: Senator Workman has made support for organized labor a major theme throughout his political career. Over the course of his term, representatives of the AFL-CIO meet regularly with Mr. Workman, whom they consider a key legislative ally, on a wide variety of issues of concern to labor. At times, the AFL-CIO runs advertisements attempting to build public support on matters of importance to organized labor, such as opposition to free trade agreements and support for workplace safety standards. In planning such campaigns, they often meet with Senator Workman to discuss the Senate's legislative agenda, which senators might be swayed in their vote by shifts in public opinion or calling greater public attention to their vote, and other issues of strategy. As such, the AFL-CIO obviously meets the "conduct" standards for coordination. But should the AFL-CIO's expenditures on labor issues, made after such consultations, be considered "campaign contributions"?

For a concise history of the effort to develop workable coordination rules from *Christian Coalition* through the FEC's first post-BCRA rulemaking, see Robert F. Bauer, *The McCain-Feingold Coordination Rules: The Ongoing Program to Keep Politics Under Control*, 32 FORDHAM URB. L. J. 507 (2005).

7.   In the wake of *Citizens United v. Federal Election Commission*, 558 U.S. 310 (2010) [p. 941] and *SpeechNow.org v. Federal Election Commission*, 599 F.3d 686 (D.C. Cir. 2010), and the ensuing creation of "Super PACs," there has been a good deal of criticism that Super PACs are not, as required by law, operating independently of the candidates they support. The concern is typically voiced that Super PACs are run by party operatives, former staffers, supporters, or friends of the candidate supported. *See e.g.* Richard Briffault, *Coordination Reconsidered*, 113 COLUM. L. REV. SIDEBAR 88 (2013); Kyle Langvardt, *The Sorry Case for* Citizens United, 6 CHARLESTON L. REV. 569, 574 (2012); Taylor Lincoln, *Super Connected: Outside Groups' Devotion to Individual Candidates and Political Parties Disproves the Supreme Court's Key Assumption in Citizens United That Unregulated Outside Spenders Would Be 'Independent'* (Public Citizen 2012). But who would you expect to run any political group that supported a candidate? Wouldn't it always be at least a "supporter"? For an argument as to why such contacts cannot constitutionally justify regulation as "coordinated" communications, see Bradley A. Smith, *Super PACs and the Role of 'Coordination' in Campaign Finance Law*, 49 WILLAMETTE L. REV. 603, 630–635 (2013).

8.   Given the difficulties in drawing a coordination standard that does not unduly limit protected independent expenditures, yet at the same time protects against corruption, is it even possible to draw a meaningful coordination standard? Michael

Gilbert and Brian Barnes argue that the concept of coordination simply cannot work. They argue that it is impossible to draw a coordination standard that is not both wildly underinclusive (failing to capture much corrupting behavior) and wildly overinclusive (prohibiting much non-corrupting speech), and that this is true regardless of the definition one gives to corruption. They conclude that "coordination [does not] relate[] in any operational way to corruption." Michael D. Gilbert and Brian Barnes, *The Coordination Fallacy*, __ FLA. ST. U. L. REV. __ (2016). Does this go too far? Note that if Gilbert and Barnes are correct, the implications are enormous. Absent some anti-coordination rule, contribution limits (at least so long as private expenditures are allowed) become all but meaningless — the candidate can simply ask someone else to pay the bills. Would a coordination rule that merely prohibited republication of campaign materials, direct payment of campaign bills, or expenditures made at a candidate's request, be operable?

9.   If you are wondering why the case is called *Colorado Republican I*, there is a *Colorado Republican II*. On remand, it was determined that the Party really did intend to engage in coordinated spending, and so the question the parties to the suit had originally raised — did limits on party coordinated spending violate the Constitution — finally returned to the Supreme Court in 2001. In *Federal Election Commission v. Colorado Republican Federal Campaign Committee*, 533 U.S. 431 (2001), the Supreme Court ruled, 5-4, that limits on party coordinated expenditures did not violate the Constitution. Since there was no question that the Party's expenditures were coordinated, the case has little to say about the standard for coordination.

Rather, *Colorado II* is most remarkable for the majority's searing assessment of the role of party. The majority described political parties as "instruments of some contributors whose object is * * * to support any candidate who will be obliged to the contributors"; "agents for spending on behalf of those who seek to produce obligated officeholders"; and as a vehicle used to "circumvent contribution limits * * * and thereby exacerbate the threat of corruption." *Id.* at 452–453. The dissenters (Justice Thomas writing, joined by Chief Justice Rehnquist and Justices Scalia and Kennedy), not surprisingly, offered a much more benign and indeed salutary interpretation of the role of parties. The two sides also engaged in a lengthy battle over the quantum and type of evidence the government should have to produce, mirroring the debate of *Nixon v. Shrink Missouri Government PAC*, 528 U.S. 377 (2000) [p. 834] one year earlier. For a book-length defense of the proposition that parties ought to receive favored status under the law, *see* PETER J. WALLISON & JOEL M. GORA, BETTER PARTIES, BETTER GOVERNMENT: A REALISTIC PROGRAM FOR CAMPAIGN FINANCE REFORM 87–111 (2009). They see parties as buffers between donors and the ultimate recipients of funds, as mediators between candidates and interest groups, and as a source that can direct funds to those races and candidates where they can be used most efficiently.

10.   "The . . . result of this pair of cases [*Colorado I* and *Colorado II*] is to drive a wedge between parties and candidates. Parties can spend unlimited sums to help their candidates, but only if they do so independently of the candidates — that is, without sharing information on the candidate's strengths and weaknesses, strategies, plans, polling data, and so forth." Bradley A. Smith, *A Moderate, Modern*

Campaign Finance Reform Agenda, 12 NEXUS J. OP. 3, 16 (2007). As a matter of policy, does this make sense?

F. GOVERNMENT FINANCING OF CAMPAIGNS

BUCKLEY v. VALEO
Supreme Court of the United States
424 U.S. 1, 96 S. Ct. 612, 46 L. Ed. 2d 659 (1976)

PER CURIAM. [MR. JUSTICE BRENNAN, MR. JUSTICE STEWART, and MR. JUSTICE POWELL join this opinion in full, and MR. JUSTICE MARSHALL and MR. JUSTICE BLACKMUN join all portions of the opinion excerpted here. MR. JUSTICE REHNQUIST joins in the portions excerpted here, except to the extent that Section III finds the treatment of minor parties and independent candidates to be constitutional. MR. CHIEF JUSTICE BURGER dissents from Section III of the opinion. MR. JUSTICE STEVENS took no part in the consideration or decision of these cases] * * *

* * * In the free society ordained by our Constitution it is not the government but the people — individually as citizens and candidates and collectively as associations and political committees — who must retain control over the quantity and range of debate on public issues in a political campaign.[65] * * *

III. PUBLIC FINANCING OF PRESIDENTIAL ELECTION CAMPAIGNS

[The Act] establishes a Presidential Election Campaign Fund (Fund), financed from general revenues in the aggregate amount designated by individual taxpayers, * * * who on their income tax returns may authorize payment to the Fund of one dollar of their tax liability in the case of an individual return or two dollars in the case of a joint return.[1] The Fund consists of three separate accounts to finance (1) party nominating conventions, (2) general election campaigns, and (3) primary campaigns. * * *

For expenses in the general election campaign, § 9004 (a)(1) entitles each major-party [Presidential] candidate to $20,000,000. This amount is * * * adjusted for inflation. To be eligible for funds the candidate must pledge not to incur expenses in excess of the entitlement under § 9004 (a)(1) and not to accept private contributions except to the extent that the fund is insufficient to provide the full entitlement. * * * New-party candidates receive no money prior to the general election, but any candidate receiving 5% or more of the popular vote in the election is entitled to post-election payments according to [a] formula applicable to minor-party candidates. * * *

[T]he Presidential Primary Matching Payment Account * * * is intended to aid

---

[65] For the reasons discussed in Part III, *infra*, Congress may engage in public financing of election campaigns and may condition acceptance of public funds on an agreement by the candidate to abide by specified expenditure limitations. Just as a candidate may voluntarily limit the size of the contributions he chooses to accept, he may decide to forgo private fundraising and accept public funding.

[1] Now $3 and $6, respectively. [— Eds.]

campaigns by candidates seeking Presidential nomination "by a political party," in "primary elections." The threshold eligibility requirement is that the candidate raise at least $5,000 in each of 20 States, counting only the first $250 from each person contributing to the candidate. In addition, the candidate must agree to abide by the spending limits. Funding is provided according to a matching formula: each qualified candidate is entitled to a sum equal to the total private contributions received, disregarding contributions from any person to the extent that total contributions to the candidate by that person exceed $250. Payments to any candidate under Chapter 96 may not exceed 50% of the overall expenditure ceiling accepted by the candidate. * * *

Appellants * * * argue that "by analogy" to the Religion Clauses of the First Amendment public financing of election campaigns, however meritorious, violates the First Amendment. * * * [T]he analogy is patently inapplicable to our issue here. Although "Congress shall make no law . . . abridging the freedom of speech, or of the press," [the public financing provision] is a congressional effort, not to abridge, restrict, or censor speech, but rather to use public money to facilitate and enlarge public discussion and participation in the electoral process, goals vital to a self-governing people. Thus, [the provision] furthers, not abridges, pertinent First Amendment values. * * *

It cannot be gainsaid that public financing as a means of eliminating the improper influence of large private contributions furthers a significant governmental interest. In addition, the limits on contributions necessarily increase the burden of fund-raising, and Congress properly regarded public financing as an appropriate means of relieving major-party Presidential candidates from the rigors of soliciting private contributions. * * *

MR. CHIEF JUSTICE BURGER, concurring in part and dissenting in part.

Since the turn of this century when the idea of Government subsidies for political campaigns first was broached, there has been no lack of realization that the use of funds from the public treasury to subsidize political activity of private individuals would produce substantial and profound questions about the nature of our democratic society. The Majority Leader of the Senate, although supporting such legislation in 1967, said that "the implications of these questions . . . go to the very heart and structure of the Government of the Republic." The Solicitor General in his amicus curiae brief states that "the issues involved here are of indisputable moment." He goes on to express his view that public financing will have "profound effects in the way candidates approach issues and each other." Public financing, he notes, "affects the role of the party in campaigns for office, changes the role of the incumbent government vis-a-vis all parties, and affects the relative strengths and strategies of candidates vis-a-vis each other and their party's leaders."

* * * The public monies at issue here are not being employed simply to police the integrity of the electoral process or to provide a forum for the use of all participants in the political dialogue, as would, for example, be the case if free broadcast time were granted. Rather, we are confronted with the Government's actual financing, out of general revenues, a segment of the political debate itself. * * *

* * * [T]he inappropriateness of subsidizing, from general revenues, the actual political dialogue of the people — the process which begets the Government itself — is as basic to our national tradition as the separation of church and state also deriving from the First Amendment, or the separation of civilian and military authority, neither of which is explicit in the Constitution but both of which have developed through case-by-case adjudication of express provisions of the Constitution. * * *

"[V]arying measures of control * * *," Lemon v. Kurtzman, supra, 403 U.S. [602], 621 [(1971)] * * * usually accompany grants from Government * * *. Up to now, the Court has always been extraordinarily sensitive, when dealing with First Amendment rights, to the risk that the "flag tends to follow the dollars."

Notes and Questions

1. Are Chief Justice Burger's fears well-grounded? The system of government financing for Presidential campaigns has been in effect for four decades, although in 2012, for the first time, both major party candidates chose to raise private funds rather than participate in the system. Have Justice Burger's worries come true? Can you think of ways that government financing might change candidate and party behavior? Consider: Candidates have long been entitled to the "lowest unit rate" — that is, the lowest charge made to other customer for similar broadcast time — by federal law. 47 U.S.C. § 315(b). As part of the Bipartisan Campaign Reform Act of 2002, federal candidates must appear in their broadcast ads, identify themselves, and state that they approve the message. 52 U.S.C. § 30120(d). Such a statement usually takes up to 10% or more of the typical television ad, forcing the candidate to forego saying something else. The provision is enforced not by penalizing the campaign directly but instead by depriving the non-complying candidate of the right to the lowest unit rate. A law passed in Arizona requires recipients of public funding to participate in at least one public debate. Does this suggest Burger was right, or that his worries are relatively trivial? If Congress sought to place too many restrictions on campaigns, could not the Courts step in on a case by case basis? For an elaboration of Burger's concerns, *see* Bradley A. Smith, *Separation of Campaign & State*, 81 GEO. WASH. L. REV. 2038 (2013).

2. *Problem:* Jim Chambers is running for state senate. A naturalized U.S. citizen for 23 years, born in Peru and given his Anglicized first name after his paternal great grandfather, an American who immigrated to Peru, Jim is 7/8ths Hispanic in his lineage, is of dark complexion, and speaks English with a slight accent. Jim is an accomplished physician, highly respected by his peers, and has served in several appointed, policy-making positions in state government, generally receiving high marks for his service. His voice, however, is high pitched and not always commanding. And Jim is not, shall we say gently, especially handsome. Jim fears that he does not do well on camera because of his appearance and voice. His district is one of the least racially diverse in the state, and for both ideological and electoral reasons Jim wishes to downplay his race in the campaign. For all these reasons, Jim appears only briefly, if at all, in his campaign's television advertisements.

The state has a system of public funding of campaigns. Jim believes that the incentives developed to encourage candidates to participate in the public financing system, including what he considers particularly burdensome reporting requirements and very low contribution limits placed on non-participating candidates, make it impossible for him to compete financially in the race if he does not participate in the public funding program. However, the program also requires candidates accepting public funds to participate in a series of three one-hour, televised debates, which Jim thinks could also doom his candidacy, given the electorate's superficial attraction to on-camera appearance and his concerns that some voters will voter against him on account of race. If Jim challenges of the public funding law as coercive in nature, what should be the result? *See* Ariz. Rev. Stat. Ann. §16-956 (A).

3. *Buckley* holds that candidate participation in a public funding system must be voluntary and not compelled. One of the rationales offered in favor of prohibitions on corporate campaign spending is the protection of dissenting shareholders. *See Austin v. Michigan State Chamber of Commerce*, 494 U.S. 652, 673–675 (1990) [p. 907]. *See also Abood v. Detroit Board of Education*, 431 U.S. 209 (1977) (union members entitled to refund of that portion of compulsory union fees spent on political activity). The Presidential Election Campaign Fund avoided the problem of forcing taxpayers to fund candidates with opposing views by earmarking funds designated for that purpose by taxpayers. Should states be permitted to adopt public-financing systems that use general tax revenues?

4. Contrary to the promise of footnote 65, Part III of the *Buckley* opinion never addressed why Congress could condition the receipt of public funds on a candidate's acceptance of expenditure limitations. Assuming that government can provide incentives to a candidate to participate in a voluntary system of public funding, at what point do those incentives become coercive in nature? For example, could a state set a maximum contribution of just $25, but offer the opportunity to participate in a generous public funding system as an alternative? With the notable exception of *Day v. Holahan*, 34 F.3d 1356 (8th Cir. 1994), most incentive plans for participation in government financing systems were upheld by federal courts prior to 2010. *See North Carolina Right to Life v. Leake*, 524 F.3d 427 (4th Cir.), *cert. denied sub. nom. Duke v. Leake*, 555 U.S. 994 (2008); *Daggett v. Commission on Governmental Ethics and Election Practices*, 205 F.3d 445 (1st Cir. 2000); *Gable v. Patton*, 142 F.3d 940 (6th Cir. 1998); *Rosenstiel v. Rodriguez*, 101 F.3d 1544 (8th Cir. 1996); *Vote Choice Inc. v. DiStefano*, 4 F.3d 26 (1st Cir. 1993). However, the Supreme Court's decision in *Davis v. Federal Election Commission*, 554 U.S. 724 (2008) [p. 878, note 6] cast considerable doubt on the ability of government to treat candidates differently for fundraising purposes, and in particular to "penalize" a candidate for raising or spending money by relaxing fundraising rules for that candidate's opponent. The Supreme Court's decision in the next case seems to have confirmed those doubts, and either overruled or raised serious questions about the validity of several of the Court of Appeals decisions cited above.

ARIZONA FREE ENTERPRISE CLUB'S
FREEDOM CLUB PAC v. BENNETT
Supreme Court of the United States
564 U.S. __, 131 S. Ct. 2806, 180 L. Ed. 2d 664 (2011)

CHIEF JUSTICE ROBERTS delivered the opinion of the Court [in which JUSTICE SCALIA, JUSTICE KENNEDY, JUSTICE THOMAS, and JUSTICE ALITO join]. * * *

The Arizona Citizens Clean Elections Act, passed by initiative in 1998, created a voluntary public financing system to fund the primary and general election campaigns of candidates for state office. All eligible candidates for Governor, secretary of state, attorney general, treasurer, superintendent of public instruction, the corporation commission, mine inspector, and the state legislature (both the House and Senate) may opt to receive public funding. Eligibility is contingent on the collection of a specified number of five-dollar contributions from Arizona voters, and the acceptance of certain campaign restrictions and obligations. Publicly funded candidates must agree, among other things, to limit their expenditure of personal funds to $500; * * * [and] adhere to an overall expenditure cap. * * *

In exchange for accepting these conditions, participating candidates are granted public funds to conduct their campaigns. In many cases, this initial allotment may be the whole of the State's financial backing of a publicly funded candidate. But when certain conditions are met, publicly funded candidates are granted additional "equalizing" or matching funds.

* * * [M]atching funds are triggered when a privately financed candidate's expenditures, combined with the expenditures of independent groups made in support of the privately financed candidate or in opposition to a publicly financed candidate, exceed the * * * allotment of state funds to the publicly financed candidate. * * * A privately financed candidate's expenditures of his personal funds are counted as contributions for purposes of calculating matching funds during a general election.

Once matching funds are triggered, each additional dollar that a privately financed candidate spends during the primary results in one dollar in additional state funding to his publicly financed opponent (less a 6% reduction meant to account for fundraising expenses). During a general election, every dollar that a candidate receives in contributions — which includes any money of his own that a candidate spends on his campaign — results in roughly one dollar in additional state funding to his publicly financed opponent. In an election where a privately funded candidate faces multiple publicly financed candidates, one dollar raised or spent by the privately financed candidate results in an almost one dollar increase in public funding to each of the publicly financed candidates.

Once the public financing cap is exceeded, * * * [s]pending by independent groups on behalf of a privately funded candidate, or in opposition to a publicly funded candidate, results in matching funds. Independent expenditures made in support of a publicly financed candidate can result in matching funds for other publicly financed candidates in a race. The matching funds provision is not activated, however, when independent expenditures are made in opposition to a privately financed candidate. Matching funds top out at two times the initial authorized grant of public funding to the publicly financed candidate. * * *

An example may help clarify how the Arizona matching funds provision operates. Arizona is divided into 30 districts for purposes of electing members to the State's House of Representatives. Each district elects two representatives to the House biannually. In the last general election, the number of candidates competing for the two available seats in each district ranged from two to seven. Arizona's Fourth District had three candidates for its two available House seats. Two of those candidates opted to accept public funding; one candidate chose to operate his campaign with private funds.

In that election, if the total funds contributed to the privately funded candidate, added to that candidate's expenditure of personal funds and the expenditures of supportive independent groups, exceeded $21,479 — the allocation of public funds for the general election in a contested State House race — the matching funds provision would be triggered. At that point, a number of different political activities could result in the distribution of matching funds. For example:

- If the privately funded candidate spent $1,000 of his own money to conduct a direct mailing, each of his publicly funded opponents would receive $940 ($1,000 less the 6% offset).

- If the privately funded candidate held a fundraiser that generated $1,000 in contributions, each of his publicly funded opponents would receive $940.

- If an independent expenditure group spent $1,000 on a brochure expressing its support for the privately financed candidate, each of the publicly financed candidates would receive $940 directly.

- If an independent expenditure group spent $1,000 on a brochure opposing one of the publicly financed candidates, but saying nothing about the privately financed candidate, the publicly financed candidates would receive $940 directly.

- If an independent expenditure group spent $1,000 on a brochure supporting one of the publicly financed candidates, the other publicly financed candidate would receive $940 directly, but the privately financed candidate would receive nothing.

- If an independent expenditure group spent $1,000 on a brochure opposing the privately financed candidate, no matching funds would be issued.

A publicly financed candidate would continue to receive additional state money in response to fundraising and spending by the privately financed candidate and independent expenditure groups until that publicly financed candidate received a total of $64,437 in state funds (three times the initial allocation for a State House race).

Petitioners * * * filed suit challenging the constitutionality of the matching funds provision. The candidates and independent expenditure groups argued that the matching funds provision unconstitutionally penalized their speech and burdened their ability to fully exercise their First Amendment rights. * * *

Although the speech of the candidates and independent expenditure groups that brought this suit is not directly capped by Arizona's matching funds provision, those parties contend that their political speech is substantially burdened by the state law in the same way that speech was burdened by the law we recently found invalid in *Davis* v. *Federal Election Comm'n*, 554 U.S. 724 (2008). In *Davis*, we considered a First Amendment challenge to the so-called "Millionaire's Amendment" of the Bipartisan Campaign Reform Act of 2002. Under that Amendment, if a candidate for the United States House of Representatives spent more than $350,000 of his personal funds, [his opponent] was permitted to collect individual contributions up to $6,900 per contributor — three times the normal contribution limit of $2,300. The candidate who spent more than the personal funds limit remained subject to the original contribution cap.

* * *

In addressing the constitutionality of the Millionaire's Amendment, we acknowledged that the provision did not impose an outright cap on a candidate's personal expenditures. We nonetheless concluded that the Amendment was unconstitutional because it forced a candidate "to choose between the First Amendment right to engage in unfettered political speech and subjection to discriminatory fundraising limitations." *Id.*, at 739. * * *

The logic of *Davis* largely controls our approach to this case. Much like the burden placed on speech in *Davis*, the matching funds provision "imposes an unprecedented penalty on any candidate who robustly exercises [his] First Amendment right[s]." Under that provision, "the vigorous exercise of the right to use personal funds to finance campaign speech" leads to "advantages for opponents in the competitive context of electoral politics." *Ibid.*

* * * If the law at issue in *Davis* imposed a burden on candidate speech, the Arizona law unquestionably does so as well.

The penalty imposed by Arizona's matching funds provision is different in some respects from the penalty imposed by the law we struck down in *Davis*. But those differences make the Arizona law *more* constitutionally problematic, not less. First, the penalty in *Davis* consisted of raising the contribution limits for one of the candidates. The candidate who benefited from the increased limits still had to go out and raise the funds. He may or may not have been able to do so. The other candidate, therefore, faced merely the possibility that his opponent would be able to raise additional funds, through contribution limits that remained subject to a cap. * * * Here the benefit to the publicly financed candidate is the direct and automatic release of public money. That is a far heavier burden than in *Davis*.

Second, * * * the matching funds provision can create a multiplier effect. In the Arizona Fourth District House election previously discussed, if the spending cap were exceeded, each dollar spent by the privately funded candidate would result in an additional dollar of campaign funding to each of that candidate's publicly financed opponents. In such a situation, the matching funds provision forces privately funded candidates to fight a political hydra of sorts. Each dollar they spend generates two adversarial dollars in response, * * * a markedly more significant burden than in *Davis*.

Third, unlike the law at issue in *Davis*, all of this is to some extent out of the privately financed candidate's hands. Even if that candidate opted to spend less than the initial public financing cap, any spending by independent expenditure groups to promote the privately financed candidate's election — regardless whether such support was welcome or helpful — could trigger matching funds. What is more, that state money would go directly to the publicly funded candidate to use as he saw fit. That disparity in control — giving money directly to a publicly financed candidate, in response to independent expenditures that cannot be coordinated with the privately funded candidate — is a substantial advantage for the publicly funded candidate. That candidate can allocate the money according to his own campaign strategy, which the privately financed candidate could not do with the independent group expenditures that triggered the matching funds.

The burdens that this regime places on independent expenditure groups are akin to those imposed on the privately financed candidates themselves. * * * [T]he more money spent on [a] candidate's behalf or in opposition to a publicly funded candidate, the more money the publicly funded candidate receives from the State. * * * [T]he effect of a dollar spent on election speech is a guaranteed financial payout to the publicly funded candidate the group opposes. Moreover, spending one dollar can result in the flow of dollars to multiple candidates the group disapproves of, dollars directly controlled by the publicly funded candidate or candidates.

In some ways, the burden the Arizona law imposes on independent expenditure groups is worse than the burden it imposes on privately financed candidates, and thus substantially worse than the burden we found constitutionally impermissible in *Davis*. If a candidate contemplating an electoral run in Arizona surveys the campaign landscape and decides that the burdens imposed by the matching funds regime make a privately funded campaign unattractive, he at least has the option of taking public financing. Independent expenditure groups, of course, do not.

Once the spending cap is reached, an independent expenditure group that wants to support a particular candidate — because of that candidate's stand on an issue of concern to the group — can only avoid triggering matching funds in one of two ways. The group can either opt to change its message from one addressing the merits of the candidates to one addressing the merits of an issue, or refrain from speaking altogether. * * * [F]orcing that choice — trigger matching funds, change your message, or do not speak — certainly contravenes "the fundamental rule of protection under the First Amendment, that a speaker has the autonomy to choose the content of his own message."[6] * * *

The State argues that the matching funds provision actually results in more speech by "increas[ing] debate about issues of public concern" in Arizona elections and "promot[ing] the free and open debate that the First Amendment was intended to foster." * * * Any increase in speech resulting from the Arizona law is of one kind

---

[6] The dissent sees "*chutzpah*" in candidates exercising their right not to participate in the public financing scheme, while objecting that the system violates their First Amendment rights. The charge is unjustified, but, in any event, it certainly cannot be leveled against the independent expenditure groups. The dissent barely mentions such groups in its analysis, and fails to address not only the distinctive burdens imposed on these groups — as set forth above — but also the way in which privately financed candidates are particularly burdened when matching funds are triggered by independent group speech.

and one kind only — that of publicly financed candidates. The burden imposed on privately financed candidates and independent expenditure groups reduces their speech. * * * Thus, even if the matching funds provision did result in more speech by publicly financed candidates and more speech in general, it would do so at the expense of impermissibly burdening (and thus reducing) the speech of privately financed candidates and independent expenditure groups. This sort of "beggar thy neighbor" approach to free speech — "restrict[ing] the speech of some elements of our society in order to enhance the relative voice of others" is "wholly foreign to the First Amendment." *Id.*, at 48–49.[7] * * *

The State also argues, and the Court of Appeals concluded, that any burden on privately financed candidates and independent expenditure groups is more analogous to the burden placed on speakers by the disclosure and disclaimer requirements we recently upheld in *Citizens United* [*v. Federal Election Comm'n*, 130 S. Ct. 876 (2010)] [p. 1022] than to direct restrictions on candidate and independent expenditures. This analogy is not even close. A political candidate's disclosure of his funding resources does not result in a cash windfall to his opponent, or affect their respective disclosure obligations. * * *

The State correctly asserts that the candidates and independent expenditure groups "do not . . . claim that a single lump sum payment to publicly funded candidates," equivalent to the maximum amount of state financing that a candidate can obtain through matching funds, would impermissibly burden their speech. The State reasons that if providing all the money up front would not burden speech, providing it piecemeal does not do so either. And the State further argues that such incremental administration is necessary to ensure that public funding is not under- or over-distributed.

These arguments miss the point. It is not the amount of funding that the State provides to publicly financed candidates that is constitutionally problematic in this case. It is the manner in which that funding is provided — in direct response to the political speech of privately financed candidates and independent expenditure groups. And the fact that the State's matching mechanism may be more efficient than other alternatives * * * is of no moment; "the First Amendment does not permit the State to sacrifice speech for efficiency."

The United States as *amicus* contends that "[p]roviding additional funds to petitioners' opponents does not make petitioners' own speech any less effective" and thus does not substantially burden speech. Of course it does. One does not have to subscribe to the view that electoral debate is zero sum to see the flaws in the United States' perspective. All else being equal, an advertisement supporting the election of a candidate that goes without a response is often more effective than an advertisement that is directly controverted. And even if the publicly funded

---

[7] The dissent also repeatedly argues that the Arizona matching funds regime results in "*more* political speech," but — given the logic of the dissent's position — that is only as a step to *less* speech. If the matching funds provision achieves its professed goal and causes candidates to switch to public financing, there will be less speech: no spending above the initial state-set amount by formerly privately financed candidates, and no associated matching funds for anyone. Not only that, the level of speech will depend on the State's judgment of the desirable amount, an amount tethered to available (and often scarce) state resources.

candidate decides to use his new money to address a different issue altogether, the end goal of that spending is to claim electoral victory over the opponent that triggered the additional state funding. * * *

There is a debate between the parties in this case as to what state interest is served by the matching funds provision. The privately financed candidates and independent expenditure groups contend that the provision works to "level[] electoral opportunities" by equalizing candidate "resources and influence." The State and the Clean Elections Institute counter that the provision "furthers Arizona's interest in preventing corruption and the appearance of corruption." * * *

We have repeatedly rejected the argument that the government has a compelling state interest in "leveling the playing field" that can justify undue burdens on political speech.

"Leveling electoral opportunities means making and implementing judgments about which strengths should be permitted to contribute to the outcome of an election," *Davis, supra*, at 742 — a dangerous enterprise and one that cannot justify burdening protected speech. * * * [S]uch basic intrusion by the government into the debate over who should govern goes to the heart of First Amendment values.

"Leveling the playing field" can sound like a good thing. But in a democracy, campaigning for office is not a game. It is a critically important form of speech. The First Amendment embodies our choice as a Nation that, when it comes to such speech, the guiding principle is freedom — the "unfettered interchange of ideas" — not whatever the State may view as fair.

* * * But even if the ultimate objective of the matching funds provision is to combat corruption — and not "level the playing field" — the burdens that the matching funds provision imposes on protected political speech are not justified.

Burdening a candidate's expenditure of his own funds on his own campaign does not further the State's anticorruption interest. Indeed, we have said that * * * "the use of personal funds reduces the candidate's dependence on outside contributions and thereby counteracts the coercive pressures and attendant risks of abuse" of money in politics. * * *

We have also held that "independent expenditures . . . do not give rise to corruption or the appearance of corruption." * * *

* * * Arizona already has some of the most austere contribution limits in the United States. * * * In the face of such ascetic contribution limits, strict disclosure requirements, and the general availability of public funding, it is hard to imagine what marginal corruption deterrence could be generated by the matching funds provision.

Perhaps recognizing that the burdens the matching funds provision places on speech cannot be justified in and of themselves, * * * the State and the Clean Elections Institute offer another argument: They contend that the provision indirectly serves the anticorruption interest, by ensuring that enough candidates participate in the State's public funding system, which in turn helps combat corruption. * * *

The flaw in the State's argument is apparent in what its reasoning would allow. By the State's logic it could grant a publicly funded candidate five dollars in matching funds for every dollar his privately financed opponent spent, or force candidates who wish to run on private funds to pay a $10,000 fine in order to encourage participation in the public funding regime. Such measures might well promote participation in public financing, but would clearly suppress or unacceptably alter political speech. How the State chooses to encourage participation in its public funding system matters, and we have never held that a State may burden political speech — to the extent the matching funds provision does — to ensure adequate participation in a public funding system. Here the State's chosen method is unduly burdensome and not sufficiently justified to survive First Amendment scrutiny. * * *

The judgment of the Court of Appeals for the Ninth Circuit is reversed.

JUSTICE KAGAN, with whom JUSTICE GINSBURG, JUSTICE BREYER, and JUSTICE SOTO-MAYOR join, dissenting. * * *

* * * Arizona's matching funds provision does not restrict, but instead subsidizes, speech. The law "impose[s] no ceiling on [speech] and do[es] not prevent anyone from speaking." *Citizens United*. By enabling participating candidates to respond to their opponents' expression, the statute expands public debate, in adherence to "our tradition that more speech, not less, is the governing rule." *Id.* What the law does — all the law does — is fund more speech.

* * *

[Petitioners] are making a novel argument: that Arizona violated *their* First Amendment rights by disbursing funds to *other* speakers even though they could have received (but chose to spurn) the same financial assistance. Some people might call that *chutzpah*.

Indeed, what petitioners demand is essentially a right to quash others' speech through the prohibition of a (universally available) subsidy program. Petitioners are able to convey their ideas without public financing — and they would prefer the field to themselves, so that they can speak free from response. * * *

* * * According to the Court, the special problem here lies in Arizona's matching funds mechanism, which the majority claims imposes a "substantia[l] burde[n]" on a privately funded candidate's speech. Sometimes, the majority suggests that this "burden" lies in the way the mechanism "diminish[es] the effectiveness" of the privately funded candidate's expression by enabling his opponent to respond. At other times, the majority indicates that the "burden" resides in the deterrent effect of the mechanism: The privately funded candidate "might not spend money" because doing so will trigger matching funds. Either way, the majority is wrong to see a substantial burden on expression.[5]

---

[5] The majority's error on this score extends both to candidates and to independent expenditure groups. Contrary to the majority's suggestion, nearly all of my arguments showing that the Clean Elections Act does not impose a substantial burden apply to both sets of speakers (and apply regardless

* * * [H]as the majority shown that the burden resulting from the Arizona statute is "substantial"? I will not quarrel with the majority's assertion that responsive speech by one candidate may make another candidate's speech less effective; that, after all, is the whole idea of the First Amendment, and a *benefit* of having more responsive speech. * * * And I will assume that the operation of this statute may on occasion deter a privately funded candidate from spending money, and conveying ideas by that means. * * * Still, does that effect count as a severe burden on expression? By the measure of our prior decisions — which have upheld campaign reforms with an equal or greater impact on speech — the answer is no.

Number one: *Any* system of public financing, including the lump-sum model upheld in *Buckley*, imposes a similar burden on privately funded candidates. Suppose Arizona were to do what all parties agree it could under *Buckley* — provide a single upfront payment (say, $150,000) to a participating candidate, rather than an initial payment (of $50,000) plus 94% of whatever his privately funded opponent spent, up to a ceiling (the same $150,000). That system would "diminis[h] the effectiveness" of a privately funded candidate's speech at least as much, and in the same way: It would give his opponent, who presumably would not be able to raise that sum on his own, more money to spend. And so too, a lump-sum system may deter speech. A person relying on private resources might well choose not to enter a race at all, because he knows he will face an adequately funded opponent. And even if he decides to run, he likely will choose to speak in different ways — for example, by eschewing dubious, easy-to-answer charges — because his opponent has the ability to respond. Indeed, privately funded candidates may well find the lump-sum system *more* burdensome than Arizona's (assuming the lump is big enough). Pretend you are financing your campaign through private donations. Would you prefer that your opponent receive a guaranteed, upfront payment of $150,000, or that he receive only $50,000, with the *possibility* — a possibility that you mostly get to control — of collecting another $100,000 somewhere down the road? Me too. * * *

Number two: Our decisions about disclosure and disclaimer requirements show the Court is wrong. Starting in *Buckley* and continuing through last Term, the Court has repeatedly declined to view these requirements as a substantial First Amendment burden, even though they discourage some campaign speech. * * * Like a disclosure rule, the matching funds provision may occasionally deter, but "impose[s] no ceiling" on electoral expression.

The majority breezily dismisses this comparison, labeling the analogy "not even close" because disclosure requirements result in no payment of money to a speaker's opponent. * * * But the majority does not tell us why this difference matters. Nor could it. The majority strikes down the matching funds provision because of its ostensible *effect* — most notably, that it may deter a person from spending money in an election. But this Court has acknowledged time and again

---

of whether independent or candidate expenditures trigger the matching funds). That is also true of every one of my arguments demonstrating the State's compelling interest in this legislation. But perhaps the best response to the majority's view that the Act inhibits independent expenditure groups lies in an empirical fact already noted: Expenditures by these groups have risen by 253% since Arizona's law was enacted. * * *

that disclosure obligations have the selfsame effect. * * *

Number three: Any burden that the Arizona law imposes does not exceed the burden associated with contribution limits, which we have also repeatedly upheld. * * * Rather than potentially deterring or "diminish[ing] the effectiveness" of expressive activity, these limits stop it cold. Yet we have never subjected these restrictions to the most stringent review. * * *

For all these reasons, the Court errs in holding that the government action in this case substantially burdens speech and so requires the State to offer a compelling interest. But in any event, Arizona has come forward with just such an interest, explaining that the Clean Elections Act attacks corruption and the appearance of corruption in the State's political system. * * *

* * * The Clean Elections Act, the State avers, "deters *quid pro quo* corruption and the appearance of corruption by providing Arizona candidates with an option to run for office without depending on outside contributions." And so Arizona, like many state and local governments, has implemented public financing on the theory (which this Court has previously approved), that the way to reduce political corruption is to diminish the role of private donors in campaigns.[11]

And that interest justifies the matching funds provision at issue because it is a critical facet of Arizona's public financing program. The provision is no more than a disbursement mechanism; but it is also the thing that makes the whole Clean Elections Act work. [P]ublic financing has an Achilles heel — the difficulty of setting the subsidy at the right amount. Too small, and the grant will not attract candidates to the program; and with no participating candidates, the program can hardly decrease corruption. Too large, and the system becomes unsustainable, or at the least an unnecessary drain on public resources. But finding the sweet-spot is near impossible because of variation, across districts and over time, in the political system. Enter the matching funds provision, which takes an ordinary lump-sum amount, divides it into thirds, and disburses the last two of these (to the extent necessary) via a self-calibrating mechanism. That provision is just a fine-tuning of the lump-sum program approved in *Buckley* — a fine-tuning, it bears repeating, that prevents no one from speaking and discriminates against no message. But that fine-tuning can make the difference between a wholly ineffectual program and one that removes corruption from the political system. * * *

I respectfully dissent.

---

[11] The majority briefly suggests that the State's "austere contribution limits" lessen the need for public financing, but provides no support for that dubious claim. As Arizona and other jurisdictions have discovered, contribution limits may not eliminate the risk of corrupt dealing between candidates and donors, * * * *Buckley* upheld *both* limits on contributions to federal candidates *and* public financing of presidential campaigns. Arizona, like Congress, was "surely entitled to conclude" that contribution limits were only a "partial measure," and that a functional public financing system was also necessary to eliminate political corruption. * * *

Notes and Questions

1. Was the Court correct that "[t]he logic of *Davis*" controlled the outcome of this case? How so? Or why not?

2. Does the majority adequately address the dissent's principle argument — that no one's speech is being limited, and the government is merely providing more avenues for speech?

3. As the dissent notes, if it would be legal for the government simply to provide a larger grant to participating candidates at the outset, why is it problematic to start participating candidates with a small grant and then raise the amount only if the participating candidate is being outspent? Isn't the latter actually a better situation for the non-participating candidate?

Does the problem relate to the horserace nature of elections and the trigger for added matching funds? A candidate must decide at the outset whether or not to participate. Once a candidate has decided to forego the subsidy, however, his calculation may be upset not by his own spending, but by the independent spending of others that may be of little advantage to him, or even unhelpful. Similarly, in a multi-candidate primary or race in which only one candidate was privately funded, independent expenditures supporting that candidate could trigger matching funds for each of his participating opponents, thus releasing more money to be spent against the favored candidate than the amount of the expenditure for that candidate. In such a situation, would you advocate that your client, a grassroots organization, make an independent expenditure in the race?

4. Justice Kagan argued that Arizona's interest in distributing matching funds was not the equalization of resources *per se*, but rather encouraging candidates to opt-in to the public- financing system by promising the candidates the funds necessary to wage competitive races. Encouraging participation in the public-financing system, in turn, was tied to the traditional anti-corruption interest. Is this meaningfully different from the equality argument, or is it simply a back-door way of promoting equality in anti-corruption garb?

5. One co-author of this casebook, noting Justice Kagan's point that the Arizona could simply have awarded the entire matching fund amount at the outset of the campaign, has argued that what truly disturbs the majority is not that speech is discouraged but that government financing generally requires the government to take sides in the election. If the government financing system is not effective if not enough candidates participate (particularly those most likely to win and eventually hold office), then the government must try to assure publicly financed candidates win a substantial portion of elections. Nor is such a commitment "content-neutral."

> The very act of subsidizing candidates who choose to raise funds in a particular manner is a way of choosing favorites. The plan in Arizona was referred to as "clean elections" and administered by the Citizens Clean Elections Commission. Participating candidates were, therefore, regularly referred to as "clean" candidates. It is hard to see this as anything but the "scarlet letter" approach properly rejected in [*Cook v.*] *Gralike* [531 U.S. 510, 525–526 (2001), striking down a state law that required ballots to state that a candidate had "disregarded voters' instruction" by refusing to

support specific legislation] [p. 564]. Even without this "scarlet letter," the government's decision to subsidize some candidates acts as an implicit endorsement of the candidates' means of financing the campaign. Campaign fundraising is part of the campaign itself. Campaigns craft messages with great care and follow a myriad of strategies. Some seek large numbers of small contributions, hoping to use the psychological commitment of having donated to assure strong support. Others rely on large contributions to save time and expense that would go into fundraising. Telling a campaign how to raise funds interferes with campaign strategy as much as if the government were to subsidize candidates for advertising in some media but not others. Giving to some the seal of approval — "clean" — while denying it to others is not neutral.

Furthermore, the propriety of spending tax money is itself an issue in a campaign. Once the government has decided it has an interest in drawing candidates into the government financing system, it has a vested interest in increasing their odds of winning. Of course, some candidates will nonetheless choose to stay out of the system, often for ideological reasons — most probably that they favor lower levels of spending or limited government power to dispense subsidies. Which type of candidate do you believe is most likely to turn down government funding: a candidate who believes, on ideological grounds, in small, limited government, or a candidate who believes in larger, more activist government? As Justice Kagan might answer, "me too."

See Bradley A. Smith, *Separation of Campaign & State*, 81 Geo. Wash. L. Rev. 2038, 2094 (2013).

6.   Although most government financing systems are accompanied by restrictions on contributions and expenditures, the government could simply provide funds to candidates with no strings attached. What would be some of the advantages or disadvantages to such an approach? *See* Joel Fleishman and Pope McCorkle, *Level Up Rather than Level Down: Towards a New Theory of Campaign Finance*, 52 J.L. & Pol. 211 (1984).

7.   Not surprisingly, there is voluminous literature about whether or not public financing addresses the problems it is intended to resolve. To a substantial extent, the many authors' views of public funding depend on the extent to which they see the present system as "corrupt" or "unequal," to their understanding of how politics does or should work in practice, and to normative views about equality and freedom. For a small taste of this literature, consider John Samples, *The Failure of Taxpayer Financing of Political Campaigns* in Welfare for Politicians? 213 (Samples, J., ed., 2005); Patrick Basham, *Taxpayer Financing in Comparative Perspective* in Welfare for Politicians? 275 (Samples, J., ed., 2005); Bruce Ackerman and Ian Ayres, Voting With Dollars: A New Paradigm for Campaign Finance (2002); Richard Briffault, *Public Funding and Democratic Elections*, 148 U. Pa. L. Rev. 563 (1999); Bradley A. Smith, *Some Problems with Taxpayer Funded Political Campaigns*, 148 U. Pa. L. Rev. 591 (1999).

G.   REPORTING AND DISCLOSURE OF CONTRIBUTIONS AND EXPENDITURES

New York passed the nation's first law requiring disclosure of campaign contributions and expenditures in 1890, and the first federal "publicity act" was passed in 1910. *See* EARL R. SIKES, STATE AND FEDERAL CORRUPT PRACTICES LEGISLATION 122, 284–291 (1928). Mandatory disclosure of campaign contributions and expenditures has been a mainstay of campaign finance law both in the United States and internationally, ever since. Joel W. Johnson, *Democracy and Disclosure: Electoral Systems and the Regulation of Political Finance*, 7 ELECTION L.J. 325 (2008).

As of 2008, every U.S. state had adopted laws requiring campaign contributions to be disclosed; only one state, North Dakota, did not require disclosure of campaign expenditures; and only six states did not require disclosure of independent expenditures. CALIFORNIA VOTER FOUNDATION, GRADING STATE DISCLOSURE 2, 19–20 (2008) (*available at* http://www.campaigndisclosure.org/gradingstate/GSD08.pdf.) Even many of the staunchest opponents of regulating campaign expenditures and contributions favor disclosure as an acceptable alternative to greater regulation. *See e.g.* JOHN SAMPLES, THE FALLACY OF CAMPAIGN FINANCE REFORM 272–286 (2006); Kathleen M. Sullivan, *Political Money and Freedom and Speech*, 30 U. C. DAVIS LAW REV. 1663, 1668 (1997). Indeed, so firmly rooted are disclosure laws in the regulatory landscape that one congressional reform advocate is reported to have declared that disclosure was "not regulation." *See* Bradley A. Smith, *In Defense of Political Anonymity*, 20 CITY J. 74, 75 (2010).

Yet disclosure laws are not free from controversy. In fact the Supreme Court has a long tradition of protecting anonymous speech, *see Thomas v. Collins*, 323 U.S. 516 (1945); *Talley v. California*, 362 U.S. 60 (1960); *McIntyre v. Ohio Elections Commission*, 514 U.S. 334 (1995); *Watchtower Bible & Tract Society v. Village of Stratton*, 536 U.S. 150 (2002); *see supra* Chapter 8, Part [D], p. [634–77]. It is not surprising then, that both *Buckley v. Valeo*, 424 U.S. 1 (1976), and *McConnell v. Federal Election Commission*, 540 U.S. 93 (2003) included challenges to disclosure provisions included as part of the Federal Election Campaign Act.

BUCKLEY v. VALEO
Supreme Court of the United States
424 U.S. 1 (1976)

PER CURIAM [MR. JUSTICE BRENNAN, MR. JUSTICE STEWART, and MR. JUSTICE POWELL join this opinion in full, and MR. JUSTICE REHNQUIST joins all portions of the opinion excerpted here. MR. JUSTICE MARSHALL joins in all but Part I-C-2. MR. JUSTICE BLACKMUN joins in all but Part I-B. MR. CHIEF JUSTICE BURGER joins in Part I-C. MR. JUSTICE STEVENS took no part in the consideration or decision of these cases.] * * *

II. REPORTING AND DISCLOSURE REQUIREMENTS

Unlike the limitations on contributions and expenditures imposed by 18 U.S.C. § 608, the disclosure requirements of the Act, 2 U.S.C. § 431 et seq., are not challenged by appellants as per se unconstitutional restrictions on the exercise of First Amendment freedoms of speech and association. Indeed, appellants argue that "narrowly drawn disclosure requirements are the proper solution to virtually all of the evils Congress sought to remedy." The particular requirements embodied in the Act are attacked as overbroad — both in their application to minor-party and independent candidates and in their extension to contributions as small as $11 or $101. Appellants also challenge the provision for disclosure by those who make independent contributions and expenditures, § 434 (e). The Court of Appeals found no constitutional infirmities in the provisions challenged here. We affirm the determination on overbreadth and hold that § 434 (e), if narrowly construed, also is within constitutional bounds. * * *

The Act presently under review replaced all prior disclosure laws. Its primary disclosure provisions impose reporting obligations on "political committees" and candidates. "Political committee" is defined in § 431 (d) as a group of persons that receives "contributions" or makes "expenditures" of over $1,000 in a calendar year. * * *

Each political committee is required to register with the Commission and to keep detailed records of both contributions and expenditures. These records must include the name and address of everyone making a contribution in excess of $10, along with the date and amount of the contribution. If a person's contributions aggregate more than $100, his occupation and principal place of business are also to be included.[m] These files are subject to periodic audits and field investigations by the Commission.

Each committee and each candidate also is required to file quarterly reports. The reports are to contain detailed financial information, including the full name, mailing address, occupation, and principal place of business of each person who has contributed over $100[1] in a calendar year, as well as the amount and date of the contributions. They are to be made available by the Commission "for public inspection and copying." Every candidate for federal office is required to designate a "principal campaign committee," which is to receive reports of contributions and expenditures made on the candidate's behalf from other political committees and to compile and file these reports, together with its own statements, with the Commission.

Every individual or group, other than a political committee or candidate, who makes "contributions" or "expenditures" of over $100[o] in a calendar year "other than by contribution to a political committee or candidate" is required to file a statement with the Commission. Any violation of these recordkeeping and reporting provisions is punishable by a fine * * * or a prison term * * * , or both.

---

[m] The thresholds in this paragraph are, as of 2015, $50 and $200, respectively. In inflation-adjusted terms, the first limit is almost equal to its 1974 value, while the second would be more than twice the current $200 threhhold. [— Eds.]

[1] $200 as of 2015. [— Eds.]

[o] $250 as of 2015. [— Eds.]

A. General Principles

Unlike the overall limitations on contributions and expenditures, the disclosure requirements impose no ceiling on campaign-related activities. But we have repeatedly found that compelled disclosure, in itself, can seriously infringe on privacy of association and belief guaranteed by the First Amendment. *E.g., Gibson v. Florida Legislative Comm.*, 372 U.S. 539 (1963); *NAACP v. Button*, 371 U.S. 415 (1963); *Shelton v. Tucker*, 364 U.S. 479 (1960); *Bates v. Little Rock*, 361 U.S. 516 (1960); *NAACP v. Alabama*, 357 U.S. 449 (1958).

We long have recognized that significant encroachments on First Amendment rights of the sort that compelled disclosure imposes cannot be justified by a mere showing of some legitimate governmental interest. Since *NAACP v. Alabama* we have required that the subordinating interests of the State must survive exacting scrutiny. We also have insisted that there be a "relevant correlation" or "substantial relation" between the governmental interest and the information required to be disclosed. This type of scrutiny is necessary even if any deterrent effect on the exercise of First Amendment rights arises, not through direct government action, but indirectly as an unintended but inevitable result of the government's conduct in requiring disclosure.

Appellees argue that the disclosure requirements of the Act differ significantly from those at issue in *NAACP v. Alabama* and its progeny because the Act only requires disclosure of the names of contributors and does not compel political organizations to submit the names of their members.

As we have seen, group association is protected because it enhances "[(e]ffective advocacy." The right to join together "for the advancement of beliefs and ideas," is diluted if it does not include the right to pool money through contributions, for funds are often essential if "advocacy" is to be truly or optimally "effective." Moreover, the invasion of privacy of belief may be as great when the information sought concerns the giving and spending of money as when it concerns the joining of organizations, for "[f]inancial transactions can reveal much about a person's activities, associations, and beliefs." Our past decisions have not drawn fine lines between contributors and members but have treated them interchangeably. In *Bates*, for example, we applied the principles of *NAACP vs. Alabama* and reversed convictions for failure to comply with a city ordinance that required the disclosure of "dues, assessments, and contributions paid, by whom and when paid."

The strict test established by *NAACP vs. Alabama* is necessary because compelled disclosure has the potential for substantially infringing the exercise of First Amendment rights. But we have acknowledged that there are governmental interests sufficiently important to outweigh the possibility of infringement, particularly when the "free functioning of our national institutions" is involved.

The governmental interests sought to be vindicated by the disclosure requirements are of this magnitude. They fall into three categories. First, disclosure provides the electorate with information "as to where political campaign money comes from and how it is spent by the candidate" in order to aid the voters in evaluating those who seek federal office. It allows voters to place each candidate in the political spectrum more precisely than is often possible solely on the basis of party labels and campaign speeches. The sources of a candidate's financial support also alert the voter to the interests to which a candidate is most likely to be responsive and thus facilitate predictions of future performance in office.

Second, disclosure requirements deter actual corruption and avoid the appearance of corruption by exposing large contributions and expenditures to the light of publicity. This exposure may discourage those who would use money for improper purposes either before or after the election. A public armed with information about a candidate's most generous supporters is better able to detect any post-election special favors that may be given in return. And, * * * Congress could reasonably conclude that full disclosure during an election campaign tends "to prevent the corrupt use of money to affect elections." In enacting these requirements it may have been mindful of Mr. Justice Brandeis' advice: "Publicity is justly commended as a remedy for social and industrial diseases. Sunlight is said to be the best of disinfectants; electric light the most efficient policeman."

Third, and not least significant, recordkeeping, reporting, and disclosure requirements are an essential means of gathering the data necessary to detect violations of the contribution limitations described above.

The disclosure requirements, as a general matter, directly serve substantial governmental interests. In determining whether these interests are sufficient to justify the requirements we must look to the extent of the burden that they place on individual rights.

It is undoubtedly true that public disclosure of contributions to candidates and political parties will deter some individuals who otherwise might contribute. In some instances, disclosure may even expose contributors to harassment or retaliation. These are not insignificant burdens on individual rights, and they must be weighed carefully against the interests which Congress has sought to promote by this legislation. In this process, we note and agree with appellants' concession that disclosure requirements — certainly in most applications — appear to be the least restrictive means of curbing the evils of campaign ignorance and corruption that Congress found to exist. Appellants argue, however, that the balance tips against disclosure when it is required of contributors to certain parties and candidates. We turn now to this contention.

B. Application to Minor Parties and Independents

Appellants contend that the Act's requirements are overbroad insofar as they apply to contributions to minor parties and independent candidates because the governmental interest in this information is minimal and the danger of significant infringement on First Amendment rights is greatly increased.

In *NAACP vs. Alabama* the organization had "made an uncontroverted showing that on past occasions revelation of the identity of its rank-and-file members [had] exposed these members to economic reprisal, loss of employment, threat of physical coercion, and other manifestations of public hostility," and the State was unable to show that the disclosure it sought had a "substantial bearing" on the issues it sought to clarify. Under those circumstances, the Court held that "whatever interest the State may have in [disclosure] has not been shown to be sufficient to overcome petitioner's constitutional objections." * * * [However], *NAACP vs. Alabama* is inapposite where, as here, any serious infringement on First Amendment rights brought about by the compelled disclosure of contributors is highly speculative.

It is true that the governmental interest in disclosure is diminished when the contribution in question is made to a minor party with little chance of winning an election. As minor parties usually represent definite and publicized viewpoints, there may be less need to inform the voters of the interests that specific candidates represent. Major parties encompass candidates of greater diversity. In many situations the label "Republican" or "Democrat" tells a voter little. The candidate who bears it may be supported by funds from the far right, the far left, or any place in between on the political spectrum. It is less likely that a candidate of, say, the Socialist Labor Party will represent interests that cannot be discerned from the party's ideological position.

The Government's interest in deterring the "buying" of elections and the undue influence of large contributors on officeholders also may be reduced where contributions to a minor party or an independent candidate are concerned, for it is less likely that the candidate will be victorious. But a minor party sometimes can play a significant role in an election. Even when a minor-party candidate has little or no chance of winning, he may be encouraged by major-party interests in order to divert votes from other major-party contenders.

We are not unmindful that the damage done by disclosure to the associational interests of the minor parties and their members and to supporters of independents could be significant. These movements are less likely to have a sound financial base and thus are more vulnerable to falloffs in contributions. In some instances fears of reprisal may deter contributions to the point where the movement cannot survive. The public interest also suffers if that result comes to pass, for there is a consequent reduction in the free circulation of ideas both within and without the political arena.

There could well be a case, similar to those before the Court in *NAACP vs. Alabama* and *Bates*, where the threat to the exercise of First Amendment rights is so serious and the state interest furthered by disclosure so insubstantial that the Act's requirements cannot be constitutionally applied. But no appellant in this case has tendered record evidence of the sort proffered in *NAACP vs. Alabama*. * * * On this record, the substantial public interest in disclosure identified by the legislative history of this Act outweighs the harm generally alleged. * * *

C. Section 434 (e)

Section 434 (e) requires "[e]very person (other than a political committee or candidate) who makes contributions or expenditures" aggregating over $100 in a calendar year "other than by contribution to a political committee or candidate" to file a statement with the Commission. Unlike the other disclosure provisions, this section does not seek the contribution list of any association. Instead, it requires direct disclosure of what an individual or group contributes or spends. * * *

* * * Section 434 (e) is part of Congress' effort to achieve "total disclosure" by reaching "every kind of political activity" in order to insure that the voters are fully informed and to achieve through publicity the maximum deterrence to corruption

and undue influence possible. The provision is responsive to the legitimate fear that efforts would be made, as they had been in the past, to avoid the disclosure requirements by routing financial support of candidates through avenues not explicitly covered by the general provisions of the Act.

In its effort to be all-inclusive, however, the provision raises serious problems of vagueness, particularly treacherous where, as here, the violation of its terms carries criminal penalties and fear of incurring these sanctions may deter those who seek to exercise protected First Amendment rights.

Section 434 (e) applies to "[e]very person . . . who makes contributions or expenditures." "Contributions" and "expenditures" are defined in parallel provisions in terms of the use of money or other valuable assets "for the purpose of . . . influencing" the nomination or election of candidates for federal office. It is the ambiguity of this phrase that poses constitutional problems. * * *

In Part I we discussed what constituted a "contribution" for purposes of the contribution limitations set forth in 18 U.S.C. § 608 (b). We construed that term to include not only contributions made directly or indirectly to a candidate, political party, or campaign committee, and contributions made to other organizations or individuals but earmarked for political purposes, but also all expenditures placed in cooperation with or with the consent of a candidate, his agents, or an authorized committee of the candidate. The definition of "contribution" in § 431 (e) for disclosure purposes parallels the definition in Title 18 almost word for word, and we construe the former provision as we have the latter. So defined, "contributions" have a sufficiently close relationship to the goals of the Act, for they are connected with a candidate or his campaign.

* * * The general requirement that "political committees" and candidates disclose their expenditures could raise * * * vagueness problems, for "political committee" is defined only in terms of amount of annual "contributions" and "expenditures," and could be interpreted to reach groups engaged purely in issue discussion. * * * To fulfill the purposes of the Act ["political committee"] need only encompass organizations that are under the control of a candidate or the major purpose of which is the nomination or election of a candidate. Expenditures of candidates and of "political committees" so construed can be assumed to fall within the core area sought to be addressed by Congress. They are, by definition, campaign related.

But when the maker of the expenditure is not within these categories — when it is an individual other than a candidate or a group other than a "political committee" — the relation of the information sought to the purposes of the Act may be too remote. To insure that the reach of § 434 (e) is not impermissibly broad, we construe "expenditure" for purposes of that section in the same way we construed the terms of § 608 (e) — to reach only funds used for communications that expressly advocate the election or defeat of a clearly identified candidate. This reading is directed precisely to that spending that is unambiguously related to the campaign of a particular federal candidate.

In summary, § 434(e) as construed, imposes independent reporting requirements on individuals and groups that are not candidates or political committees only in the following circumstances: (1) when they make contributions earmarked for political purposes or authorized or requested by a candidate or his agent, to some person other than a candidate or political committee, and (2) when they make expenditures for communications that expressly advocate the election or defeat of a clearly identified candidate.

[Section] 434 (e), as construed, bears a sufficient relationship to a substantial governmental interest. As narrowed, § 434 (e), * * * does not reach all partisan discussion for it only requires disclosure of those expenditures that expressly advocate a particular election result. This might have been fatal if the only purpose of § 434 (e) were to stem corruption or its appearance by closing a loophole in the general disclosure requirements. But the disclosure provisions, including § 434 (e), serve another, informational interest, and even as construed § 434 (e) increases the fund of information concerning those who support the candidates. It goes beyond the general disclosure requirements to shed the light of publicity on spending that is unambiguously campaign related but would not otherwise be reported because it takes the form of independent expenditures or of contributions to an individual or group not itself required to report the names of its contributors. * * * [I]t is not fatal that § 434 (e) encompasses purely independent expenditures uncoordinated with a particular candidate or his agent. The corruption potential of these expenditures may be significantly different, but the informational interest can be as strong as it is in coordinated spending, for disclosure helps voters to define more of the candidates' constituencies.

D. Thresholds

Appellants' third contention, based on alleged overbreadth, is that the monetary thresholds in the record-keeping and reporting provisions lack a substantial nexus with the claimed governmental interests, for the amounts involved are too low even to attract the attention of the candidate, much less have a corrupting influence.

The provisions contain two thresholds. Records are to be kept by political committees of the names and addresses of those who make contributions in excess of $10, § 432 (c)(2), and these records are subject to Commission audit, § 438 (a)(8). If a person's contributions to a committee or candidate aggregate more than $100, his name and address, as well as his occupation and principal place of business, are to be included in reports filed by committees and candidates with the Commission, § 434 (b)(2), and made available for public inspection, § 438 (a)(4). * * *

The $10 and $100 thresholds are indeed low. Contributors of relatively small amounts are likely to be especially sensitive to recording or disclosure of their political preferences. These strict requirements may well discourage participation by some citizens in the political process, a result that Congress hardly could have intended. Indeed, there is little in the legislative history to indicate that Congress focused carefully on the appropriate level at which to require recording and disclosure. Rather, it seems merely to have adopted the thresholds existing in similar disclosure laws since 1910. But we cannot require Congress to establish that it has chosen the highest reasonable threshold. The line is necessarily a judgmental decision, best left in the context of this complex legislation to congressional discretion. We cannot say, on this bare record, that the limits designated are wholly without rationality. * * *

In summary, we find no constitutional infirmities in the recordkeeping, reporting, and disclosure provisions of the Act.

Mr. Chief Justice Burger, concurring in part and dissenting in part. * * *

Disclosure is, in principle, the salutary and constitutional remedy for most of the ills Congress was seeking to alleviate. I therefore agree fully with the broad proposition that public disclosure of contributions by individuals and by entities — particularly corporations and labor unions — is an effective means of revealing the type of political support that is sometimes coupled with expectations of special favors or rewards. That disclosure impinges on First Amendment rights is conceded by the Court, but given the objectives to which disclosure is directed, I agree that the need for disclosure outweighs individual constitutional claims.

* * * The Court's theory, however, goes beyond permissible limits. Under the Court's view, disclosure serves broad informational purposes, enabling the public to be fully informed on matters of acute public interest. Forced disclosure of one aspect of a citizen's political activity, under this analysis, serves the public right to know. This open-ended approach is the only plausible justification for the otherwise irrationally low ceilings of $10 and $100 for anonymous contributions. The burdens of these low ceilings seem to me obvious, and the Court does not try to question this. With commendable candor, the Court acknowledges: "It is undoubtedly true that public disclosure of contributions to candidates and political parties will deter some individuals who otherwise might contribute."

Examples come readily to mind. Rank-and-file union members or rising junior executives may now think twice before making even modest contributions to a candidate who is disfavored by the union or management hierarchy. Similarly, potential contributors may well decline to take the obvious risks entailed in making a reportable contribution to the opponent of a well-entrenched incumbent. This fact of political life did not go unnoticed by the Congress: "The disclosure provisions really have in fact made it difficult for challengers to challenge incumbents." * * *

The public right to know ought not be absolute when its exercise reveals private political convictions. Secrecy, like privacy, is not per se criminal. On the contrary, secrecy and privacy as to political preferences and convictions are fundamental in a free society. For example, one of the great political reforms was the advent of the secret ballot as a universal practice. Similarly, the enlightened labor legislation of our time has enshrined the secrecy of choice of a bargaining representative for workers. * * *

* * * I would therefore hold unconstitutional the provisions requiring reporting of contributions of more than $10 and to make a public record of the name, address, and occupation of a contributor of more than $100.

McCONNELL v. FEDERAL ELECTION COMMISSION
Supreme Court of the United States
540 U.S. 93, 124 S. Ct. 619, 157 L. Ed. 2d 491 (2003)

JUSTICE STEVENS and JUSTICE O'CONNOR deliverd the opinion of the Court * * * in which JUSTICE SOUTER, JUSTICE GINSBURG, and JUSTICE BREYER join]. * * *

Under FECA § 304, as amended by BCRA §201], whenever any person makes disbursements totaling more than $10,000 during any calendar year for the direct costs of producing and airing electioneering communications, he must file a statement with the FEC identifying the pertinent elections and all persons sharing the costs of the disbursements. If the disbursements are made from a corporation's or labor union's segregated account, or by a single individual who has collected contributions from others, the statement must identify all persons who contributed $1,000 or more to the account or the individual during the calendar year. The statement must be filed within 24 hours of each "disclosure date" — a term defined to include the first date and all subsequent dates on which a person's aggregate undisclosed expenses for electioneering communications exceed $10,000 for that calendar year. Another subsection further provides that the execution of a contract to make a disbursement is itself treated as a disbursement for purposes of FECA's disclosure requirements.

In addition to the failed argument that BCRA's amendments to FECA § 304 improperly extend to both express and issue advocacy, plaintiffs challenge amended FECA § 304's disclosure requirements as unnecessarily (1) requiring disclosure of the names of persons who contributed $1,000 or more to the individual or group that paid for a communication, and (2) mandating disclosure of executory contracts for communications that have not yet aired. The District Court rejected the former submission but accepted the latter, finding invalid new FECA § 304(f)(5), which governs executory contracts. * * *

We agree with the District Court that the important state interests that prompted the *Buckley* Court to uphold FECA's disclosure requirements — providing the electorate with information, deterring actual corruption and avoiding any appearance thereof, and gathering the data necessary to enforce more substantive electioneering restrictions — apply in full to BCRA. Accordingly, *Buckley* amply supports application of FECA § 304's disclosure requirements to the entire range of "electioneering communications." * * *

* * * *Buckley* forecloses a facial attack on the new provision in § 304 that requires disclosure of the names of persons contributing $1,000 or more to segregated funds or individuals that spend more than $10,000 in a calendar year on electioneering communications. Like our earlier decision in *NAACP* v. *Alabama*, 357 U.S. 449 (1958), *Buckley* recognized that compelled disclosures may impose an unconstitutional burden on the freedom to associate in support of a particular cause. Nevertheless, *Buckley* rejected the contention that FECA's disclosure requirements could not constitutionally be applied to minor parties and independent candidates because the Government's interest in obtaining information from such parties was minimal and the danger of infringing their rights substantial. In

Buckley, unlike *NAACP*, we found no evidence that any party had been exposed to economic reprisals or physical threats as a result of the compelled disclosures. We acknowledged that such a case might arise in the future, however, and addressed the standard of proof that would then apply:

> "We recognize that unduly strict requirements of proof could impose a heavy burden, but it does not follow that a blanket exemption for minor parties is necessary. Minor parties must be allowed sufficient flexibility in the proof of injury to assure a fair consideration of their claim. The evidence offered need show only a reasonable probability that the compelled disclosure of a party's contributors' names will subject them to threats, harassment, or reprisals from either Government officials or private parties."

In this litigation the District Court applied *Buckley*'s evidentiary standard and found — consistent with our conclusion in *Buckley*, and in contrast to that in *Brown* — that the evidence did not establish the requisite "reasonable probability" of harm to any plaintiff group or its members. The District Court noted that some parties had expressed such concerns, but it found a "lack of specific evidence about the basis for these concerns." We agree, but we note that, like our refusal to recognize a blanket exception for minor parties in *Buckley*, our rejection of plaintiffs' facial challenge to the requirement to disclose individual donors does not foreclose possible future challenges to particular applications of that requirement.

We also are unpersuaded by plaintiffs' challenge to new FECA § 304(f)(5), which requires disclosure of executory contracts for electioneering communications. * * *

In our view, this provision serves an important purpose the District Court did not advance. BCRA's amendments to FECA § 304 mandate disclosure only if and when a person makes disbursements totaling more than $10,000 in any calendar year to pay for electioneering communications. Plaintiffs do not take issue with the use of a dollar amount, rather than the number or dates of the ads, to identify the time when a person paying for electioneering communications must make disclosures to the FEC. Nor do they question the need to make the contents of parties' disclosure statements available to curious voters in advance of elections. Given the relatively short time frames in which electioneering communications are made, the interest in assuring that disclosures are made promptly and in time to provide relevant information to voters is unquestionably significant. Yet fixing the deadline for filing disclosure statements based on the date when aggregate disbursements exceed $10,000 would open a significant loophole * * *. [P]olitical supporters could avoid preelection disclosures concerning ads slated to run during the final week of a campaign simply by making a preelection downpayment of less than $10,000, with the balance payable after the election. * * *.

The record contains little evidence identifying any harm that might flow from the enforcement of § 304(f)(5)'s "advance" disclosure requirement. * * * It is no doubt true that § 304(f)(5) will sometimes require the filing of disclosure statements in advance of the actual broadcast of an advertisement. But the same would be true in the absence of an advance disclosure requirement, if a television station insisted on advance payment for all of the ads covered by a contract. * * *

As the District Court observed, amended FECA § 304's disclosure requirements are constitutional because they " 'd[o] not prevent anyone from speaking.' " Moreover, the required disclosures " 'would not have to reveal the specific content of the advertisements, yet they would perform an important function in informing the public about various candidates' supporters *before* election day.' " Accordingly, we * * * [uphold] the disclosure requirements in amended FECA § 304. * * *

JUSTICE KENNEDY, [with whom THE CHIEF JUSTICE and JUSTICE SCALIA join,] concurring in the judgment in part and dissenting in part[.] * * *

[BCRA] § 201's advance disclosure requirement — the aspect of the provision requiring those who have contracted to speak to disclose their speech in advance — is, in my view, unconstitutional. Advance disclosure imposes real burdens on political speech that *post hoc* disclosure does not. It forces disclosure of political strategy by revealing where ads are to be run and what their content is likely to be (based on who is running the ad). It also provides an opportunity for the ad buyer's opponents to dissuade broadcasters from running ads. Against those tangible additional burdens, the Government identifies no additional interest uniquely served by advance disclosure. If Congress intended to ensure that advertisers could not flout these disclosure laws by running an ad before the election, but paying for it afterwards, see *ante*, at 693, then Congress should simply have required the disclosure upon the running of the ad. Burdening the First Amendment further by requiring advance disclosure is not a constitutionally acceptable alternative. To the extent § 201 requires advance disclosure, it finds no justification in its subordinating interests and imposes greater burdens than the First Amendment permits.

JUSTICE THOMAS, * * * dissenting in part [.]* * *

I must now address an issue on which I differ from all of my colleagues: the disclosure provisions in BCRA § 201, now contained in new FECA § 304(f). * * * [T]his Court has explicitly recognized that "the interest in having anonymous works enter the marketplace of ideas unquestionably outweighs any public interest in requiring disclosure as a condition of entry," and thus that "an author's decision to remain anonymous . . . is an aspect of the freedom of speech protected by the First Amendment. The Court now backs away from this principle, allowing the established right to anonymous speech to be stripped away based on the flimsiest of justifications.

The only plausible interest asserted by the defendants to justify the disclosure provisions is the interest in providing "information" about the speaker to the public. But we have already held that "[t]he simple interest in providing voters with additional relevant information does not justify a state requirement that a writer make statements or disclosures she would otherwise omit." [*McIntyre v Ohio Elections Comm'n*, 514 U.S. 334, 338 (1995)] [p. 644] Of course, *Buckley* upheld the disclosure requirement on expenditures for communications using words of express advocacy based on this informational interest. And admittedly, *McIntyre* purported to distinguish *Buckley*. But the two ways *McIntyre* distinguished *Buckley* — one, that the disclosure of "an expenditure and its use, without more, reveals far less information [than a forced identification of the author of a pamphlet,]"; and two, that in candidate elections, the "Government can identify a compelling state interest in avoiding the corruption that might result from campaign expenditures," — are inherently implausible. The first is simply wrong. The revelation of one's political expenditures for independent communications about candidates can be just as revealing as the revelation of one's name on a pamphlet for a noncandidate election. The second was outright rejected in *Buckley* itself, where the Court concluded that independent expenditures did not create any substantial risk of real or apparent corruption. Hence, the only reading of *McIntyre* that remains consistent with the principles it contains is that it overturned *Buckley* to the extent that *Buckley* upheld a disclosure requirement solely based on the governmental interest in providing information to the voters.

The right to anonymous speech cannot be abridged based on the interests asserted by the defendants. I would thus hold that the disclosure requirements of BCRA § 201 are unconstitutional. Because of this conclusion, the so-called advance disclosure requirement of § 201 necessarily falls as well. * * *

CITIZENS UNITED v. FEDERAL ELECTION COMMISSION
Supreme Court of the United States
558 U.S. 310, 130 S. Ct. 876, 175 L. Ed. 2d 753 (2010)

JUSTICE KENNEDY delivered the opinion of the Court [in which CHIEF JUSTICE ROBERTS, JUSTICE STEVENS, JUSTICE SCALIA, JUSTICE GINSBURG, JUSTICE BREYER, JUSTICE ALITO and JUSTICE SOTOMAYOR join as to the portion excerpted here.] * * *

Under BCRA § 311, televised electioneering communications funded by anyone other than a candidate must include a disclaimer that "_____ is responsible for the content of this advertising." 2 U.S.C. § 441d(d)(2). The required statement must be made in a "clearly spoken manner," and displayed on the screen in a "clearly readable manner" for at least four seconds. *Ibid.* It must state that the communication "is not authorized by any candidate or candidate's committee"; it must also display the name and address (or Web site address) of the person or group that funded the advertisement. § 441d(a)(3). Under BCRA § 201, any person who spends more than $10,000 on electioneering communications within a calendar year must file a disclosure statement with the FEC. 2 U.S.C. § 434(f)(1). That statement must identify the person making the expenditure, the amount of the expenditure, the election to which the communication was directed, and the names of certain contributors. § 434(f)(2).

Disclaimer and disclosure requirements may burden the ability to speak, but they "impose no ceiling on campaign-related activities," and "do not prevent anyone from speaking." The Court has subjected these requirements to "exacting scrutiny," which requires a "substantial relation" between the disclosure requirement and a "sufficiently important" governmental interest.

In *Buckley* [*v. Valeo*, 424 U.S. 1 (1976)] [p. 1011] the Court explained that disclosure could be justified based on a governmental interest in "provid[ing] the electorate with information" about the sources of election-related spending. The *McConnell* Court applied this interest in rejecting facial challenges to BCRA §§ 201 and 311. * * *

For the reasons stated below, we find the statute valid as applied to the ads for the movie and to the movie itself.

Citizens United sought to broadcast one 30-second and two 10-second ads to promote *Hillary*. * * * Citizens United argues that the disclaimer requirements in § 311 are unconstitutional as applied to its ads. It contends that the governmental interest in providing information to the electorate does not justify requiring disclaimers for any commercial advertisements, including the ones at issue here. We disagree. * * * At the very least, the disclaimers avoid confusion by making clear that the ads are not funded by a candidate or political party. * * *

Last, Citizens United argues that disclosure requirements can chill donations to an organization by exposing donors to retaliation. Some *amici* point to recent events in which donors to certain causes were blacklisted, threatened, or otherwise targeted for retaliation. In *McConnell* [*v. Federal Election Commission*, 540 U.S. 93 (2003)] [p. 1019], the Court recognized that § 201 would be unconstitutional as applied to an organization if there were a reasonable probability that the group's members would face threats, harassment, or reprisals if their names were disclosed. The examples cited by *amici* are cause for concern. Citizens United, however, has offered no evidence that its members may face similar threats or reprisals. To the contrary, Citizens United has been disclosing its donors for years and has identified no instance of harassment or retaliation.

Shareholder objections raised through the procedures of corporate democracy, see *Bellotti, supra,* at 794, and n.34, can be more effective today because modern technology makes disclosures rapid and informative. A campaign finance system that pairs corporate independent expenditures with effective disclosure has not existed before today. * * * With the advent of the Internet, prompt disclosure of expenditures can provide shareholders and citizens with the information needed to hold corporations and elected officials accountable for their positions and supporters. Shareholders can determine whether their corporation's political speech advances the corporation's interest in making profits, and citizens can see whether elected officials are " 'in the pocket' of so-called moneyed interests." The First Amendment protects political speech; and disclosure permits citizens and shareholders to react to the speech of corporate entities in a proper way. This transparency enables the electorate to make informed decisions and give proper weight to different speakers and messages.

For the same reasons we uphold the application of BCRA §§ 201 and 311 to the ads, we affirm their application to *Hillary*. We find no constitutional impediment to the application of BCRA's disclaimer and disclosure requirements to a movie broadcast via video-on-demand. And there has been no showing that, as applied in this case, these requirements would impose a chill on speech or expression.

JUSTICE THOMAS, concurring in part and dissenting in part. * * *

* * * The disclosure, disclaimer, and reporting requirements in BCRA §§ 201 and 311 are * * * unconstitutional.

[JUSTICE THOMAS related examples provided by *amici* of threats against persons whose support for a California anti-gay-marriage proposition was disclosed because of a California law similar to §§ 201 and 311.] These instances of retaliation sufficiently demonstrate why this Court should invalidate mandatory disclosure and reporting requirements. But *amici* present evidence of yet another reason to do so — the threat of retaliation from *elected officials*. As *amici*'s submissions make clear, this threat extends far beyond a single ballot proposition in California. For example, a candidate challenging an incumbent state attorney general reported that some members of the State's business community feared donating to his campaign because they did not want to cross the incumbent; in his words, "I go to so many people and hear the same thing: 'I sure hope you beat [the incumbent], but I can't afford to have my name on your records. He might come after me next.'" The incumbent won reelection in 2008.

My point is not to express any view on the merits of the political controversies I describe. Rather, it is to demonstrate — using real-world, recent examples — the fallacy in the Court's conclusion that "[d]isclaimer and disclosure requirements . . . impose no ceiling on campaign-related activities, and do not prevent anyone from speaking." Of course they do. Disclaimer and disclosure requirements enable private citizens and elected officials to implement political strategies *specifically calculated* to curtail campaign-related activity and prevent the lawful, peaceful exercise of First Amendment rights. * * *

I cannot endorse a view of the First Amendment that subjects citizens of this Nation to death threats, ruined careers, damaged or defaced property, or preemptive and threatening warning letters as the price for engaging in "core political speech, the 'primary object of First Amendment protection.'" Accordingly, I respectfully dissent from the Court's judgment upholding BCRA §§ 201 and 311.

Notes and Questions

1. *Buckley* and *McConnell* are two of the longest sets of opinions in Supreme Court history. Yet the discussion of disclosure is relatively brief in each case, with very little discussion of the evidence and arguments offered by the parties. How sound are the opinions?

The *Buckley* Court identified three government interests served by mandatory disclosure. To what extent does disclosure truly serve these interests?

The first government interest is in preventing corruption that falls short of bribery. The theory is that disclosure will embarrass both large donors and the candidates who accept them. Perry Belmont, *Publicity of Election Expenditures*, 180 N. AMER. REV. 166, 182 (1905). But can this justify the disclosure of modest contributions? How does this anti-corruption interest work? According to two skeptics:

> The theory of disclosure insists that voters will reject candidates at the polls when disclosure shows too much spending, misdirected spending, unsavory or disfavored financial sources, or excessive contributions. In elections, however, a citizen cannot express himself solely on campaign finance practices; his vote for a candidate is a decision about many other issues as well * * *. Voters do not and should not give campaign finance

practices heavy weight in making ballot choices, and therefore candidates rarely need fear that disclosure of such practices will result in political penalties at the polls.

David W. Adamany & George E. Agree, Political Money: A Strategy for Campaign Financing in America 103–12 (1975). In 2000, before the Bipartisan Campaign Reform Act prohibited unlimited soft money donations to parties, 800 individuals contributed an average of $375,000 to the national political parties. Richard Briffault, *The Future of Reform: Campaign Finance After the Bipartisan Campaign Reform Act of 2002*, 34 Ariz. St. L.J. 1179, 1183 (2002). Does this prove that Adamany and Agree were correct? At the same time, others express the concern, voiced by Justice Burger in *Buckley*, than many laws set the disclosure threshold so low as to capture contributions that are highly unlikely to have any improper influence on a candidate or officeholder. *See e.g.* William McGeveran, *Mrs. McIntyre's Checkbook: Privacy Costs of Political Contribution Disclosure*, 6 U. Pa. J. Const. L. 1, 30 (2003).

A second government interest recognized in *Buckley* is in providing the electorate with information. Is this true? Certainly public endorsements by interest groups and prominent individuals have value to voters. Does disclosure of information about contributions and expenditures add to that knowledge? Low disclosure thresholds may inhibit the effectiveness of disclosure laws in meeting the government's information interest, by drowning voters with data of little informational value. *Id.* at 28–29; *see also* Richard Briffault, *Campaign Finance Disclosure 2.0*, 9 Election L.J. 273 (2010). And voters, in fact, rarely seek out such information. Raymond J. LaRaja, *Sunshine Laws and the Press: The Effect of Campaign Disclosure on News Reporting*, 6 Election L.J. 236, 237 (2007). Others casting doubt on the informational benefits of disclosure include Benjamin Barr and Stephen R. Klein, *Publius Was Not a PAC: Reconciling Anonymous Political Speech, The First Amendment, and Campaign Finance Disclosure*, 14 Wyo. L. Rev. 253 (2014); Dick Carpenter and Jeffrey Milyo, *The Public's Right to Know Versus Compelled Speech: What Does Social Science Research Tell Us About the Benefits and Costs of Campaign Finance Disclosure in Non-Candidate Elections*, 40 Fordham Urb. L. J. 101 (2012).

Other studies suggest that compulsory disclosure discourages political participation. *See* Alexandre Courture Gagnon and Filip Palda, *The Price of Transparency: Do Campaign Finance Disclosure Law Discourage Political Participation by Citizens' Groups*, 146 Pub. Choice 353 (2011).

Finally, reporting of campaign contributions may aid the government in enforcing other limitations, such as those on contributions. Assuming that this is a valid government interest, does it serve to justify public disclosure of the information so reported?

2. Another interest? Bob Bauer, a prominent practitioner who served as General Counsel to the Obama for President campaign and later as White House Counsel, has suggested that in practice, the primary purpose of disclosure has become to generate news stories and press releases justifying further restrictions on contributions, spending, and other activity. Robert F. Bauer, *Not Just a Private Matter: The Purposes of Disclosure in an Expanded Regulatory System*, 6

ELECTION L.J. 38 (2007). Bauer expresses skepticism that disclosure serves the government interests identified in *Buckley*.

3. As recently as 1996, researchers or others interested in learning about donors to federal campaigns typically had to visit the office of the Federal Election Commission and manually poor over the records. Disclosure was overwhelmingly, therefore, a Washington, D.C. activity, with distribution of the information to the broader public mediated by reporters and a small number of public interest groups that sought to organize and publish the information. The rise of the internet and electronic filing and on-line publication of reports has dramatically changed the nature of disclosure, making it possible for anyone with internet access to pull up filing information at virtually zero cost, often within hours of contributions being made. Some prominent web sites, such as the Huffington Post and EightMaps.com, have linked the required disclosure information to mapping services, so that an interested person can find, within seconds, not only the names and addresses of donors, but maps to their homes. States have followed suit, and 49 states now post information on campaign contributors on the internet, 40 within two days of filing. CALIFORNIA VOTER FOUNDATION, GRADING STATE DISCLOSURE *supra* at 20.

As donor information has become widely available, tales of abuse of the information, including lost employment, commercial boycotts, physical threats, vandalism, and even death threats have surfaced with increasing frequency. *See ProtectMarriage.com v. Bowen*, 599 F. Supp. 2d 1197 (E.D. Ca. 2009); Elian Dashev, *Economic Boycotts as Harassment: The Threat to First Amendment Protected Speech in the Aftermath of* Doe v. Reed, 45 LOY. L.A. L. REV. 207 (2011); Bradley A. Smith, *In Defense of Political Anonymity*, 20 CITY J. 74, 76–77 (2010). Does this change the calculus from that set forth by the Court in *Buckley* and *McConnell*?

For more sanguine views on the costs and benefits of disclosure, *see e.g.* Lloyd Hitoshi Mayer, *Politics and the Public's Right to Know*, 13 ELECTION L.J. 138 (2014); Michael Kang, *Campaign Disclosure in Direct Democracy*, 97 MINN. L. REV. 1700 (2013); Jonathan C. Zellner, *Artificial Grassroots Advocacy and the Constitutionality of Legislative Identification and Control Measures*, 43 CONN. L. REV. 357 (2010).

4. The *McConnell* Court states that its ruling does not foreclose future as-applied challenges to the law. Review *Brown v. Socialist Workers '74 Campaign Committee*, 459 U.S. 87 (1982) [p. 634], for a pre-*McConnell* as applied challenge to the FEC's public reporting requirements. Also review *Doe v. Reed*, 561 U.S. 186 (2010) [p. 653]. *Doe* presented a facial challenge to another election related disclosure statute. Rejecting the facial challenge, the justices, in a set of opinions, discussed the level of evidence that ought to be necessary to win a future as-applied challenge. Were their standards consistent with *Brown*? On remand, the district court denied plaintiffs request for relief, and the Supreme Court eventually denied certiorari over an objection from Justice Alito, who wrote a dissent from the denial, arguing that "petitioners adduced evidence that some supporters of the referendum 'received death threats,' 'had their children threatened,' and suffered various indignities." *Doe v. Reed*, 132 S. Ct. 449 (2011). How much evidence must be put forward? How much do you think should have to be put forward?

5. *See Meyer v. Grant*, 486 U.S. 414 (1988) [p. 678] and *Buckley v. American Constitutional Law Foundation*, 525 U.S. 182 (1999) [p. 680] for the Supreme Court's treatment of compulsory disclosure in other ballot measure contexts.

6. Although one longstanding justification for disclosure laws is that they assist in preventing corruption, other commentators have noted that it is the very ability of candidates and officeholders to identify contributors (and non-contributors) that creates many of the public concerns about campaign contributions. Without the ability to identify donors (and non-donors), officeholders can neither be influenced by donations, nor can they abuse their office to extract, through threats of adverse government action, contributions from unwilling donors. In a much discussed book, Yale Law School Professors Bruce Ackerman and Ian Ayres argue that rather than compel disclosure of contributor information, the government should establish a system that prevents candidates from knowing who their donors are, similar to a blind trust. BRUCE ACKERMAN & IAN AYRES, VOTING WITH DOLLARS: A NEW PARADIGM FOR CAMPAIGN FINANCE (2002). Two law reviews held symposia, featuring many of the country's leading campaign finance and election law scholars, dedicated specifically to discussing the Ackerman/Ayres book. *See* 91 CAL. L. REV. 641–768 (2003); 37 U. RICH. L. REV. 935–1184 (2003). A strong critique of the Ackerman/Ayres proposal is Lillian R. BeVier, *What Ails Us?* (Book Review), 112 YALE L. J. 1135 (2003).

7. Dissenting in *McConnell*, Justice Thomas argues that neither *Buckley* nor *McConnell* can be harmonized with *McIntyre v. Ohio Elections Commission*, 514 U.S. 334 (1995). Do you agree? How would you make the attempt? *See Majors v. Abell*, 361 F.3d 349, 355 (7th Cir. 2004); *id.* at 356 (Easterbrook, J., *dubitante*); *Kentucky Right to Life, Inc. v. Terry*, 108 F.3d 637 (6th Cir.), *cert. denied sub nom. Kentucky Right to Life v. Stengel*, 522 U.S. 860 (1997).

8. In the wake of *Citizens United*, there has been a great deal of confusion about what campaign spending must be disclosed. Of course, disclosure rules for candidate and party committees and ballot committees will vary from state to state. However, most states follow the basic contours of federal law, with the major difference typically being the thresholds that trigger mandatory disclosure.

What a group or organization must disclose largely depends on its form of organization and the nature of its activities.

a. *Candidate committees, political parties, and political action committees ("PACs")*. These overt campaign organizations are subject to the greatest disclosure. At the federal level, they must disclose all donors in excess of $200 in aggregate giving. Many states have much lower thresholds, *see, e.g.*, Florida Stat. Title IX § 106.7(4)(a)(1) (2011) (requiring reporting of all contributions regardless of size). They also must file detailed reports on expenditures, by category and vendor. During election years reports are typically filed monthly, though expenditures or contributions close to the election can trigger added reporting requirements, often demanding reporting with 48 hours. *See* 2 U.S.C. §§ 432–434.

b. *Super PACs*. Super PACs are subject to the same organizational and reporting requirements as regular PACs. It has been argued, however, that if a non-profit membership corporation contributes to a Super PAC, voters would know that the non-profit funded the Super PAC, but may not know who funded the non-profit. *See*

Trevor Potter, *Five Myths About Super PACs*, WASH. POST, p. B2, Apr. 15, 2012. It is unclear, however, how great a concern this should be. Non-profit organizations have long been able to engage in limited political activity without disclosing their donors or membership, *see NAACP v. Alabama*, 357 U.S. 449 (1957), and have long done so. (Scripts of NAACP Voter Education Fund ads from 2000, for example, are available from Democracy in Action, *at* http://www.gwu.edu/~action/ads2/adnaacp.html (accessed June 29, 2012).)

One example that is suggested as demonstrating the need for greater disclosure by Super PACs is the case of W. Spann, LLC. The corporation was formed in March of 2011 and dissolved in July of that year. In between, its only business appears to have been donating $1 million to a Super PAC. Dan Eggen, *Mystery Firm's $1M Donation to Pro-Romney PAC Raises Concern Over Transparency*, WASH. POST, p. A2, Aug. 4, 2011. However, within three days the creator of W. Spann LLC was known — Edward Conard, a long-time supporter of presidential candidate Mitt Romney who was apparently advised by his estate planning attorney. Michael Isikoff, *Firm Gives $1 Million to Pro-Romney Group, Then Dissolves*, MSNBC, Aug. 4, 2011, *available at* http://www.msnbc.msn.com/id/44011308/. Federal law prohibits contributions in the name of another, which has been interpreted to include reimbursing or advancing the money for a contribution. 2 U.S.C. § 441f; 11 C.F.R. § 110.4. Knowing this, was the contribution from W. Spann LLC legal? Based on what you have heard about *Citizens United*, why would an attorney not experienced in campaign finance law think that this was legal? Consider this passage from a leading reform organization blog: "*Citizens United* created an environment in which it is perfectly legal for a shell non-profit corporation to engage in election-related spending on behalf of a hidden interest." Lisa Rosenberg, *Citizens United Decision Could Lead to Foreign Interests Influencing US Elections*, Sunlight Foundation Blog, Mar. 13, 2012, *available at* http://sunlightfoundation.com/blog/2012/03/13/citizens-united-decision-could-lead-to-foreign-interests-influencing-us-elections/. In light of 2 U.S.C. § 441f, is that a correct statement of the law? Could such comments create incorrect public perceptions of what the law allows?

c. *Non-PAC 527s*. By having a primary purpose of engaging in political activity, but avoiding express advocacy, a group qualifies as a Non-PAC 527, named for section 527 of the Internal Revenue Code, under which political committees operate. "527s" were a popular vehicle for campaign organizers in the 1990s through the election of 2004 because they could raise unlimited contributions from individuals, corporations, and unions. Because these groups did not make direct campaign contributions or engage in "express advocacy," they were exempt from the FECA's political committee disclosure provisions, per *Buckley*. In 2000, Congress required these organizations to disclose their donors to the Internal Revenue Service, or else pay taxes on undisclosed receipts. Pub. L. No. 06t-230 (2000). Non-PAC 527s have declined dramatically in use since *SpeechNow.org. v. Federal Election Commission* permitted the creation of Super PACs, and *Citizens United* made it possible for unions and corporations to fund express advocacy communications.

d. *Non-Profit Organizations*. Non-profit organizations operating under 26 U.S.C. §§ 501(c)(4) ("social welfare organizations") and (c)(6) ("business leagues") may engage in political activity so long as that does not become their primary purpose.

Even if political activity becomes their primary purpose, they may escape regulation as political committees under the FECA pursuant to *Federal Election Commission v. Massachusetts Citizens for Life, Inc.*, 479 U.S. 238 (1986) [p. 907, n. 5]. These groups still must file reports with the FEC when they make political expenditures, but they do not need to disclose who contributed to the organization unless the contributions were made to fund specific ads, which is rare. *See* 2 U.S.C. § 434(c)(1). Due to a quirk in the law, however, even though they do not need to disclose donors when making independent expenditures (*i.e.*, expenditures for express advocacy), these non-profits must disclose the names of individual donors when making "electioneering communications" (broadcast ads mentioning a candidate without express advocacy within 60 days of a general election or 30 days of a primary). *See* 2 U.S.C. § 434(f); *Van Hollen v. FEC*, 2012 U.S. App. LEXIS 10333 (D.C. Cir. May 14, 2012).

9. Note that in addition to the disclosures mentioned above, all broadcast ads and most print ads must also contain a disclosure notice stating the name of the individual or organization paying for the ad. Additionally, Federal Communication Commission regulations require broadcasters to maintain a "political file" that tracks all political ad buys, which is available for public inspection. 47 C.F.R. § 73.1212. However, while these reveal who bought the ad, they will not necessarily inform the listener or viewer as to who contributed the funds used by the organization to purchase the ad. Is this added information necessary? Does it rise to the level of a "compelling government interest"?

In addition to theoretical and constitutional issues about who should be compelled to disclose their political spending, and when, there are practical issues that make it much easier to call for disclosure than to devise a system that effectively informs the public. Consider the following problem, which is based on a real-world model of political activity.

10. *Problem.* In December 2016, the Acme Widget Company makes a $200,000 dues payment to the North American Chamber of Business ("NACB"). It makes another such payment in December of 2017. The NACB has a budget of $50 million annually, with thousands of member companies which pay dues based on their size and desired level of participation in the group. In March 2014, the NACB transfers $600,000 to the State Chamber of Business. The State Chamber of Business is independent from NACB, but NACB often works with various state groups, and transfers the $600,000 as part of a program in which it agrees to match money raised by state organizations to help elect pro-business candidates. The State Chamber of Business had raised another $600,000 for political activity from 157 member companies over the previous six months. In raising the money, it did not state any specific races in which it planned to spend money or make endorsements, and of course donors gave up all rights to the money contributed. In June of 2018, the State Chamber of Business transfers $1.1 million to Moving Our State Forward, a 501(c)(4) established by the State Chamber in 2005 to conduct lobbying, public education, and political activity. The State Chamber normally uses Moving Our State Forward as its primary vehicle for political action. In July 2018, Moving Our State Forward transfers $500,000 to the State Business Alliance, a Super PAC organized in February 2018 by various business groups in the state. The State Business Alliance receives donations from other trade and business associations and

corporations, and has a total budget for 2018 of $2.8 million. In September 2018, the State Business Alliance makes a $250,000 television ad buy attacking Congresswoman Banks. What should be disclosed? *See* Bradley A. Smith, *Disclosure in a Post-Citizens United Real World*, 6 U. St. Thomas J. L. & Pub. Pol'y 257 (2012).

Chapter 10

AT THE POLLS

A. INTRODUCTION

The constitutional protection of the right to vote is implicated throughout the electoral process. In Chapter 1 we began our discussion of the right by discussing attempts by states and municipalities to control *who* may exercise the right to vote. In subsequent Chapters we considered the impact on the right caused by, among other laws, the drawing of electoral districts and ballot-access limitations. The following cases concern challenges to state restrictions on *how* voters may exercise the right to vote and campaign. The cases struggle explicitly with the meaning and application of strict scrutiny in the electoral context, and provide an opportunity to consider the way the right to vote informs constitutional review of laws that affect all aspects of elections.

The right to vote is considered fundamental, but if strict scrutiny were applied to each law that limited the exercise of that right, it would be impossible to write rules for the orderly administration of elections. Thus, the Supreme Court has recognized that a lesser standard of scrutiny is appropriate when evaluating at least some election laws, lest elections descend into "chaos." The trick, of course, is in determining which regulations should be subject to more stringent scrutiny, and as to this issue the Court has not established a rule that is capable of consistent application.

The Court, instead, has used the balancing test from *Anderson v. Celebrezze*, 460 U.S. 780, 789 (1983) [p. 517], under which a reviewing court weighs the extent of the burden against the state's justifications for it. "Severe" burdens are constitutional only if they pass strict scrutiny, while lesser burdens are subject to less stringent review. While it appeared to some after *Burdick v. Takushi*, 504 U.S. 428 (1992) [p. 525], that "reasonable, nondiscriminatory" regulations presenting less than "severe" burdens on the right to vote would be subject to the lenient rational-basis test, it now seems that such lesser burdens will be evaluated on a continuum, with the most deferential scrutiny applying only to the most minimal burdens on voting rights.

One particularly controversial voting regulation has been the requirement that voters present identification before being permitted to vote. Critics claim that such a law disproportionately harms the poor, the elderly, and minorities, each of whom might be thought to favor liberal candidates. Defenders of the requirement cite the need to guard against fraud. The Court, in *Crawford v. Marion County Election Board*, 553 U.S. 181 (2008) [p. 1032], upheld a photo-identification requirement against a facial challenge, but did not foreclose the possibility that an as-applied challenge could succeed.

Sometimes government regulation, far from imposing burdens on casting ballots, seeks to alleviate them. Yet there, too, the regulations can cause constitutional problems. In *Burson v. Freeman*, 504 U.S. 191 (1992) [p. 1054], for example, the Court confronted a challenge to a state law that prohibited speech within one hundred feet of polling places. The Court upheld the speech restriction, reasoning that the state had compelling interests in protecting voters' access to the polls and ensuring against voter intimidation. Because strict scrutiny requires both a compelling interest and narrow tailoring, however, the Court had to assess whether a one-hundred-foot radius was narrow enough. The Court held that it was, but in so doing deferred substantially to the state's judgment and the judgment of history that such restrictions were necessary. As you work through these cases and as you review the other cases we have encountered in this course, consider how deferential courts should be to the choices legislatures make in constructing election laws.

B. BURDENS ON CASTING BALLOTS

The next case considers the constitutionality of requirements that voters prove their identities by presenting state- or federal-government-issued photo identification. Should such requirements be considered "severe" burdens on the right to vote and therefore subject to strict scrutiny? Afterwards, we take up the issue of vote trading, and consider whether such agreements are protected political speech or unprotected attempts to buy votes with reciprocal promises.

CRAWFORD v. MARION COUNTY ELECTION BOARD
Supreme Court of the United States
553 U.S. 181, 128 S. Ct. 1610, 170 L. Ed. 2d 574 (2008)

JUSTICE STEVENS announced the judgment of the Court and delivered an opinion in which THE CHIEF JUSTICE [ROBERTS] and JUSTICE KENNEDY join.

At issue in these cases is the constitutionality of an Indiana statute requiring citizens voting in person on election day, or casting a ballot in person at the office of the circuit court clerk prior to election day, to present photo identification issued by the government.

Referred to as either the "Voter ID Law" or "SEA [Senate Enrolled Act] 483," the statute applies to in-person voting at both primary and general elections. The requirement does not apply to absentee ballots submitted by mail, and the statute contains an exception for persons living and voting in a state-licensed facility such as a nursing home. A voter who is indigent or has a religious objection to being photographed may cast a provisional ballot that will be counted only if she executes an appropriate affidavit before the circuit court clerk within 10 days following the election. A voter who has photo identification but is unable to present that identification on election day may file a provisional ballot that will be counted if she brings her photo identification to the circuit county clerk's office within 10 days. No photo identification is required in order to register to vote, and the State offers free photo identification to qualified voters able to establish their residence and identity.
* * *

[Plaintiffs, including the Indiana Democratic Party and organizations representing elderly, disabled, poor, and minority voters,] allege that the new law substantially burdens the right to vote in violation of the Fourteenth Amendment; that it is neither a necessary nor appropriate method of avoiding election fraud; and that it will arbitrarily disfranchise qualified voters who do not possess the required identification and will place an unjustified burden on those who cannot readily obtain such identification.

After discovery, District Judge Barker * * * grant[ed] defendants' motion for summary judgment. * * * A divided panel of the Court of Appeals affirmed. * * *

In *Harper* v. *Virginia Bd. of Elections*, 383 U.S. 663 (1966) [p. 37], the Court held that Virginia could not condition the right to vote in a state election on the payment of a poll tax of $1.50. We rejected the dissenters' argument that the interest in promoting civic responsibility by weeding out those voters who did not care enough about public affairs to pay a small sum for the privilege of voting provided a rational basis for the tax. * * * Although the State's justification for the tax was rational, it was invidious because it was irrelevant to the voter's qualifications.

Thus, under the standard applied in *Harper*, even rational restrictions on the right to vote are invidious if they are unrelated to voter qualifications. In *Anderson* v. *Celebrezze*, 460 U.S. 780, 788 n.9 (1983) [p. 517], however, we confirmed the general rule that "evenhanded restrictions that protect the integrity and reliability of the electoral process itself" are not invidious and satisfy the standard set forth in *Harper*. Rather than applying any "litmus test" that would neatly separate valid from invalid restrictions, we concluded that a court must identify and evaluate the interests put forward by the State as justifications for the burden imposed by its rule, and then make the "hard judgment" that our adversary system demands.

In later election cases we have followed *Anderson's* balancing approach. Thus, in *Norman* v. *Reed*, 502 U.S. 279, 288–289 (1992), after identifying the burden Illinois imposed on a political party's access to the ballot, we "called for the demonstration of a corresponding interest sufficiently weighty to justify the limitation," and concluded that the "severe restriction" was not justified by a narrowly drawn state interest of compelling importance. Later, in *Burdick* v. *Takushi*, 504 U.S. 428 (1992) [p. 525], we applied *Anderson's* standard for "reasonable, nondiscriminatory restrictions," and upheld Hawaii's prohibition on write-in voting despite the fact that it prevented a significant number of "voters from participating in Hawaii elections in a meaningful manner." We reaffirmed *Anderson's* requirement that a court evaluating a constitutional challenge to an election regulation weigh the asserted injury to the right to vote against the "precise interests put forward by the State as justifications for the burden imposed by its rule."[8]

In neither *Norman* nor *Burdick* did we identify any litmus test for measuring the severity of a burden that a state law imposes on a political party, an individual

---

[8] Contrary to Justice Scalia's suggestion, our approach remains faithful to *Anderson* and *Burdick*. The *Burdick* opinion was explicit in its endorsement and adherence to *Anderson*, and repeatedly cited *Anderson*. To be sure, *Burdick* rejected the argument that strict scrutiny applies to all laws imposing a burden on the right to vote; but in its place, the Court applied the "flexible standard" set forth in *Anderson*. *Burdick* surely did not create a novel "deferential 'important regulatory interests' standard."

voter, or a discrete class of voters. However slight that burden may appear, as *Harper* demonstrates, it must be justified by relevant and legitimate state interests "sufficiently weighty to justify the limitation." We therefore begin our analysis of the constitutionality of Indiana's statute by focusing on those interests. * * *

[The State argues that the burdens imposed by the Voter ID Law are justified by the interests of deterring and detecting voter fraud, as well as safeguarding voter confidence.] The only kind of voter fraud that SEA 483 addresses is in-person voter impersonation at polling places. The record contains no evidence of any such fraud actually occurring in Indiana at any time in its history. Moreover, petitioners argue that provisions of the Indiana Criminal Code punishing such conduct as a felony provide adequate protection against the risk that such conduct will occur in the future. It remains true, however, that flagrant examples of such fraud in other parts of the country have been documented throughout this Nation's history by respected historians and journalists,[11] that occasional examples have surfaced in recent years,[12] and that Indiana's own experience with fraudulent voting in the 2003 Democratic primary for East Chicago Mayor — though perpetrated using absentee ballots and not in-person fraud — demonstrate that not only is the risk of voter fraud real but that it could affect the outcome of a close election.

There is no question about the legitimacy or importance of the State's interest in counting only the votes of eligible voters. Moreover, the interest in orderly administration and accurate recordkeeping provides a sufficient justification for carefully identifying all voters participating in the election process. While the most effective method of preventing election fraud may well be debatable, the propriety of doing so is perfectly clear.

In its brief, the State argues that the inflation of its voter rolls provides further support for its enactment of SEA 483. The record contains a November 5, 2000, newspaper article asserting that, as the result of [the National Voter Registration Act of 1993, which restricts the ability of states to remove names from lists of registered voters,] and "sloppy record keeping," Indiana's lists of registered voters included the names of thousands of persons who had either moved, died, or were not eligible to vote because they had been convicted of felonies. * * * Even though Indiana's own negligence may have contributed to the serious inflation of its registration lists when SEA 483 was enacted, the fact of inflated voter rolls does

---

[11] One infamous example is the New York City elections of 1868. William (Boss) Tweed set about solidifying and consolidating his control of the city. One local tough who worked for Boss Tweed, "Big Tim" Sullivan, insisted that his "repeaters" (individuals paid to vote multiple times) have whiskers:

> "When you've voted 'em with their whiskers on, you take 'em to a barber and scrape off the chin fringe. Then you vote 'em again with the side lilacs and a mustache. Then to a barber again, off comes the sides and you vote 'em a third time with the mustache. If that ain't enough and the box can stand a few more ballots, clean off the mustache and vote 'em plain face. That makes every one of 'em good for four votes."

[12] Judge Barker cited record evidence containing examples from California, Washington, Maryland, Wisconsin, Georgia, Illinois, Pennsylvania, Missouri, Miami, and St. Louis. * * * While * * * much of the fraud was actually absentee ballot fraud or voter registration fraud, there remain scattered instances of in-person voter fraud. For example, after a hotly contested gubernatorial election in 2004, Washington conducted an investigation of voter fraud and uncovered 19 "ghost voters." After a partial investigation of the ghost voting, one voter was confirmed to have committed in-person voting fraud.

provide a neutral and nondiscriminatory reason supporting the State's decision to require photo identification.

Finally, the State contends that it has an interest in protecting public confidence "in the integrity and legitimacy of representative government." While that interest is closely related to the State's interest in preventing voter fraud, public confidence in the integrity of the electoral process has independent significance, because it encourages citizen participation in the democratic process. * * *

States employ different methods of identifying eligible voters at the polls. Some merely check off the names of registered voters who identify themselves; others require voters to present registration cards or other documentation before they can vote; some require voters to sign their names so their signatures can be compared with those on file; and in recent years an increasing number of States have relied primarily on photo identification. A photo identification requirement imposes some burdens on voters that other methods of identification do not share. For example, a voter may lose his photo identification, may have his wallet stolen on the way to the polls, or may not resemble the photo in the identification because he recently grew a beard. Burdens of that sort arising from life's vagaries, however, are neither so serious nor so frequent as to raise any question about the constitutionality of SEA 483; the availability of the right to cast a provisional ballot provides an adequate remedy for problems of that character.

The burdens that are relevant to the issue before us are those imposed on persons who are eligible to vote but do not possess a current photo identification that complies with the requirements of SEA 483. The fact that most voters already possess a valid driver's license, or some other form of acceptable identification, would not save the statute under our reasoning in *Harper*, if the State required voters to pay a tax or a fee to obtain a new photo identification. But just as other States provide free voter registration cards, the photo identification cards issued by Indiana's BMV are also free. For most voters who need them, the inconvenience of making a trip to the BMV, gathering the required documents, and posing for a photograph surely does not qualify as a substantial burden on the right to vote, or even represent a significant increase over the usual burdens of voting.[17]

Both evidence in the record and facts of which we may take judicial notice, however, indicate that a somewhat heavier burden may be placed on a limited number of persons. They include elderly persons born out-of-state, who may have difficulty obtaining a birth certificate; persons who because of economic or other personal limitations may find it difficult either to secure a copy of their birth certificate or to assemble the other required documentation to obtain a state-issued identification; homeless persons; and persons with a religious objection to being photographed. If we assume, as the evidence suggests, that some members of these classes were registered voters when SEA 483 was enacted, the new identification requirement may have imposed a special burden on their right to vote.

---

[17] To obtain a photo identification card a person must present at least one "primary" document, which can be a birth certificate, certificate of naturalization, U.S. veterans photo identification, U.S. military photo identification, or a U.S. passport. Indiana, like most States, charges a fee for obtaining a copy of one's birth certificate. This fee varies by county and is currently between $3 and $12. Some States charge substantially more.

The severity of that burden is, of course, mitigated by the fact that, if eligible, voters without photo identification may cast provisional ballots that will ultimately be counted. To do so, however, they must travel to the circuit court clerk's office within 10 days to execute the required affidavit. It is unlikely that such a requirement would pose a constitutional problem unless it is wholly unjustified. And even assuming that the burden may not be justified as to a few voters,[19] that conclusion is by no means sufficient to establish petitioners' right to the relief they seek in this litigation.

Given the fact that petitioners have advanced a broad attack on the constitutionality of SEA 483, seeking relief that would invalidate the statute in all its applications, they bear a heavy burden of persuasion. * * *

Petitioners ask this Court, in effect, to perform a unique balancing analysis that looks specifically at a small number of voters who may experience a special burden under the statute and weighs their burdens against the State's broad interests in protecting election integrity. Petitioners urge us to ask whether the State's interests justify the burden imposed on voters who cannot afford or obtain a birth certificate and who must make a second trip to the circuit court clerk's office after voting. But on the basis of the evidence in the record it is not possible to quantify either the magnitude of the burden on this narrow class of voters or the portion of the burden imposed on them that is fully justified.

First, the evidence in the record does not provide us with the number of registered voters without photo identification * * *. Further, the deposition evidence presented in the District Court does not provide any concrete evidence of the burden imposed on voters who currently lack photo identification. * * * The record says virtually nothing about the difficulties faced by either indigent voters or voters with religious objections to being photographed. * * *

In sum, on the basis of the record that has been made in this litigation, we cannot conclude that the statute imposes "excessively burdensome requirements" on any class of voters.[20] * * * When we consider only the statute's broad application to all

---

[19] Presumably most voters casting provisional ballots will be able to obtain photo identifications before the next election. It is, however, difficult to understand why the State should require voters with a faith-based objection to being photographed to cast provisional ballots subject to later verification in every election when the BMV is able to issue these citizens special licenses that enable them to drive without any photo identification.

[20] Three comments on JUSTICE SOUTER's speculation about the non-trivial burdens that SEA 483 may impose on "tens of thousands" of Indiana citizens are appropriate. First, the fact that the District Judge estimated that when the statute was passed in 2005, 43,000 citizens did not have photo identification tells us nothing about the number of free photo identification cards issued since then. Second, the fact that public transportation is not available in some Indiana counties tells us nothing about how often elderly and indigent citizens have an opportunity to obtain a photo identification at the BMV, either during a routine outing with family or friends or during a special visit to the BMV arranged by a civic or political group such as the League of Women Voters or a political party. Further, nothing in the record establishes the distribution of voters who lack photo identification. To the extent that the evidence sheds any light on that issue, it suggests that such voters reside primarily in metropolitan areas, which are served by public transportation in Indiana * * *. Third, the indigent, elderly, or disabled need not "journey all the way to their county seat each time they wish to exercise the franchise" if they obtain a free photo identification card from the BMV. While it is true that obtaining a birth certificate carries with it a financial cost, the record does not provide even a rough estimate of how many indigent voters lack copies

Indiana voters we conclude that it "imposes only a limited burden on voters' rights." *Burdick*, 504 U.S., at 439. The "precise interests" advanced by the State are therefore sufficient to defeat petitioners' facial challenge to SEA 483. * * *

In their briefs, petitioners stress the fact that all of the Republicans in the General Assembly voted in favor of SEA 483 and the Democrats were unanimous in opposing it. * * * It is fair to infer that partisan considerations may have played a significant role in the decision to enact SEA 483. If such considerations had provided the only justification for a photo identification requirement, we may also assume that SEA 483 would suffer the same fate as the poll tax at issue in *Harper*.

But if a nondiscriminatory law is supported by valid neutral justifications, those justifications should not be disregarded simply because partisan interests may have provided one motivation for the votes of individual legislators. The state interests identified as justifications for SEA 483 are both neutral and sufficiently strong to require us to reject petitioners' facial attack on the statute. The application of the statute to the vast majority of Indiana voters is amply justified by the valid interest in protecting "the integrity and reliability of the electoral process."

The judgment of the Court of Appeals is affirmed.

It is so ordered.

Justice Scalia, with whom Justice Thomas and Justice Alito join, concurring in the judgment.

The lead opinion assumes petitioners' premise that the voter-identification law "may have imposed a special burden on" some voters, but holds that petitioners have not assembled evidence to show that the special burden is severe enough to warrant strict scrutiny. That is true enough, but for the sake of clarity and finality (as well as adherence to precedent), I prefer to decide these cases on the grounds that petitioners' premise is irrelevant and that the burden at issue is minimal and justified.

To evaluate a law respecting the right to vote — whether it governs voter qualifications, candidate selection, or the voting process — we use the approach set out in *Burdick* v. *Takushi*. This calls for application of a deferential "important regulatory interests" standard for nonsevere, nondiscriminatory restrictions, reserving strict scrutiny for laws that severely restrict the right to vote. The lead opinion resists the import of *Burdick* by characterizing it as simply adopting "the balancing approach" of *Anderson* v. *Celebrezze*. Although *Burdick* liberally quoted *Anderson*, *Burdick* forged *Anderson*'s amorphous "flexible standard" into something resembling an administrable rule. Since *Burdick*, we have repeatedly reaffirmed the primacy of its two-track approach. See *Timmons* v. *Twin Cities Area New Party*, 520 U.S. 351, 358 (1997) [p. 534]; *Clingman* v. *Beaver*, 544 U.S. 581, 586–587 (2005) [p. 470]. "[S]trict scrutiny is appropriate only if the burden is severe." *Id.*, at 592. Thus, the first step is to decide whether a challenged law

---

of their birth certificates. Supposition based on extensive Internet research is not an adequate substitute for admissible evidence subject to cross-examination in constitutional adjudication.

severely burdens the right to vote. Ordinary and widespread burdens, such as those requiring "nominal effort" of everyone, are not severe. See *id.*, at 591, 593–597. Burdens are severe if they go beyond the merely inconvenient.

Of course, we have to identify a burden before we can weigh it. The Indiana law affects different voters differently, but what petitioners view as the law's several light and heavy burdens are no more than the different *impacts* of the single burden that the law uniformly imposes on all voters. To vote in person in Indiana, *everyone* must have and present a photo identification that can be obtained for free. The State draws no classifications, let alone discriminatory ones, except to establish *optional* absentee and provisional balloting for certain poor, elderly, and institutionalized voters and for religious objectors. Nor are voters who already have photo identifications exempted from the burden, since those voters must maintain the accuracy of the information displayed on the identifications, renew them before they expire, and replace them if they are lost.

The Indiana photo-identification law is a generally applicable, nondiscriminatory voting regulation, and our precedents refute the view that individual impacts are relevant to determining the severity of the burden it imposes. In the course of concluding that the Hawaii laws at issue in *Burdick* "impose[d] only a limited burden on voters' rights to make free choices and to associate politically through the vote," we considered the laws and their reasonably foreseeable effect on *voters generally*. We did not discuss whether the laws had a severe effect on Mr. Burdick's own right to vote, given his particular circumstances. That was essentially the approach of the *Burdick* dissenters, who would have applied strict scrutiny to the laws because of their effect on "some voters." Subsequent cases have followed *Burdick*'s generalized review of nondiscriminatory election laws. Indeed, *Clingman*'s holding that burdens are not severe if they are ordinary and widespread would be rendered meaningless if a single plaintiff could claim a severe burden. * * *

Insofar as our election-regulation cases rest upon the requirements of the Fourteenth Amendment, weighing the burden of a nondiscriminatory voting law upon each voter and concomitantly requiring exceptions for vulnerable voters would effectively turn back decades of equal-protection jurisprudence. A voter complaining about such a law's effect on him has no valid equal-protection claim because, without proof of discriminatory intent, a generally applicable law with disparate impact is not unconstitutional. The Fourteenth Amendment does not regard neutral laws as invidious ones, *even when their burdens purportedly fall disproportionately on a protected class. A fortiori* it does not do so when, as here, the classes complaining of disparate impact are not even protected.[*]

Even if I thought that *stare decisis* did not foreclose adopting an individual-focused approach, I would reject it as an original matter. This is an area where the

---

[*] A number of our early right-to-vote decisions, purporting to rely upon the Equal Protection Clause, strictly scrutinized nondiscriminatory voting laws requiring the payment of fees. See, *e.g., Harper* v. *Virginia Bd. of Elections*, 383 U.S., [at] 670 (poll tax); *Bullock* v. *Carter*, 405 U.S. 134, 145 (1972) [p. 508] (ballot-access fee); *Lubin* v. *Panish*, 415 U.S. 709, 716–719 (1974) (ballot-access fee). To the extent those decisions continue to stand for a principle that *Burdick* does not already encompass, it suffices to note that we have never held that legislatures must calibrate *all* election laws, even those totally unrelated to money, for their impacts on poor voters or must otherwise accommodate wealth disparities.

dos and don'ts need to be known in advance of the election, and voter-by-voter examination of the burdens of voting regulations would prove especially disruptive. A case-by-case approach naturally encourages constant litigation. Very few new election regulations improve everyone's lot, so the potential allegations of severe burden are endless. A State reducing the number of polling places would be open to the complaint it has violated the rights of disabled voters who live near the closed stations. Indeed, it may even be the case that some laws already on the books are especially burdensome for some voters, and one can predict lawsuits demanding that a State adopt voting over the Internet or expand absentee balloting.

That sort of detailed judicial supervision of the election process would flout the Constitution's express commitment of the task to the States. See Art. I, § 4. It is for state legislatures to weigh the costs and benefits of possible changes to their election codes, and their judgment must prevail unless it imposes a severe and unjustified overall burden upon the right to vote, or is intended to disadvantage a particular class. Judicial review of their handiwork must apply an objective, uniform standard that will enable them to determine, *ex ante*, whether the burden they impose is too severe.

The lead opinion's record-based resolution of these cases, which neither rejects nor embraces the rule of our precedents, provides no certainty, and will embolden litigants who surmise that our precedents have been abandoned. There is no good reason to prefer that course.

The universally applicable requirements of Indiana's voter-identification law are eminently reasonable. The burden of acquiring, possessing, and showing a free photo identification is simply not severe, because it does not "even represent a significant increase over the usual burdens of voting." And the State's interests are sufficient to sustain that minimal burden. That should end the matter. That the State accommodates some voters by permitting (not requiring) the casting of absentee or provisional ballots, is an indulgence — not a constitutional imperative that falls short of what is required.

JUSTICE SOUTER, with whom JUSTICE GINSBURG joins, dissenting.

Indiana's "Voter ID Law" threatens to impose nontrivial burdens on the voting right of tens of thousands of the State's citizens, and a significant percentage of those individuals are likely to be deterred from voting. The statute is unconstitutional under the balancing standard of *Burdick* v. *Takushi*: a State may not burden the right to vote merely by invoking abstract interests, be they legitimate, or even compelling, but must make a particular, factual showing that threats to its interests outweigh the particular impediments it has imposed. The State has made no such justification here, and as to some aspects of its law, it has hardly even tried. I therefore respectfully dissent from the Court's judgment sustaining the statute.

Voting-rights cases raise two competing interests, the one side being the fundamental right to vote. As against the unfettered right, however, lies the "[c]ommon sense, as well as constitutional law . . . that government must play an active role in structuring elections; 'as a practical matter, there must be a substantial regulation of elections if they are to be fair and honest and if some sort of order, rather than chaos, is to accompany the democratic processes.' " [504 U.S.], at 433.

Given the legitimacy of interests on both sides, we have avoided pre-set levels of scrutiny in favor of a sliding-scale balancing analysis: the scrutiny varies with the effect of the regulation at issue. * * *

The first set of burdens shown in these cases is the travel costs and fees necessary to get one of the limited variety of federal or state photo identifications needed to cast a regular ballot under the Voter ID Law. The travel is required for the personal visit to a license branch of the Indiana Bureau of Motor Vehicles, which is demanded of anyone applying for a driver's license or nondriver photo identification. * * * Poor, old, and disabled voters who do not drive a car, however, may find the trip prohibitive[.][4] * * *

The burden of traveling to a more distant BMV office rather than a conveniently located polling place is probably serious for many of the individuals who lack photo identification. They almost certainly will not own cars, and public transportation in Indiana is fairly limited. [Twenty-one] of Indiana's 92 counties have no public transportation system at all, and as of 2000, nearly 1 in every 10 voters lived within 1 of these 21 counties. Among the counties with some public system, 21 provide service only within certain cities, and 32 others restrict public transportation to regional county service, leaving only 18 that offer countywide public transportation. * * *

Although making voters travel farther than what is convenient for most and possible for some does not amount to a "severe" burden under *Burdick*, that is no reason to ignore the burden altogether. It translates into an obvious economic cost (whether in work time lost, or getting and paying for transportation) that an Indiana voter must bear to obtain an ID.

For those voters who can afford the roundtrip, a second financial hurdle appears: in order to get photo identification for the first time, they need to present "a birth certificate, a certificate of naturalization, U.S. veterans photo identification, U.S. military photo identification, or a U.S. passport." As the lead opinion says, the two most common of these documents come at a price: Indiana counties charge anywhere from $3 to $12 for a birth certificate (and in some other States the fee is significantly higher), and that same price must usually be paid for a first-time passport, since a birth certificate is required to prove U.S. citizenship by birth. The

---

[4] The State asserts that the elderly and disabled are adequately accommodated through their option to cast absentee ballots, and so any burdens on them are irrelevant. But * * * there are crucial differences between the absentee and regular ballot. Voting by absentee ballot leaves an individual without the possibility of receiving assistance from poll workers, and thus increases the likelihood of confusion and error. More seriously, * * * Indiana law "treats absentee voters differently from the way it treats Election Day voters," in the important sense that "an absentee ballot may not be recounted in situations where clerical error by an election officer rendered it invalid." The State itself notes that "election officials routinely reject absentee ballots on suspicion of forgery." * * *

It is one thing (and a commendable thing) for the State to make absentee voting available to the elderly and disabled; but it is quite another to suggest that, because the more convenient but less reliable absentee ballot is available, the State may freely deprive the elderly and disabled of the option of voting in person.

total fees for a passport, moreover, are up to about $100. So most voters must pay at least one fee to get the ID necessary to cast a regular ballot. As with the travel costs, these fees are far from shocking on their face, but in the *Burdick* analysis it matters that both the travel costs and the fees are disproportionately heavy for, and thus disproportionately likely to deter, the poor, the old, and the immobile.

To be sure, Indiana has a provisional-ballot exception to the ID requirement for individuals the State considers "indigent" as well as those with religious objections to being photographed, and this sort of exception could in theory provide a way around the costs of procuring an ID. But Indiana's chosen exception does not amount to much relief.

The law allows these voters who lack the necessary ID to sign the poll book and cast a provisional ballot. As the lead opinion recognizes, though, that is only the first step; to have the provisional ballot counted, a voter must then appear in person before the circuit court clerk or county election board within 10 days of the election, to sign an affidavit attesting to indigency or religious objection to being photographed (or to present an ID at that point). Unlike the trip to the BMV (which, assuming things go smoothly, needs to be made only once every four years for renewal of nondriver photo identification), this one must be taken every time a poor person or religious objector wishes to vote, because the State does not allow an affidavit to count in successive elections. And unlike the trip to the BMV (which at least has a handful of license branches in the more populous counties), a county has only one county seat. Forcing these people to travel to the county seat every time they try to vote is particularly onerous for the reason noted already, that most counties in Indiana either lack public transportation or offer only limited coverage.
* * *

All of this suggests that provisional ballots do not obviate the burdens of getting photo identification. And even if that were not so, the provisional-ballot option would be inadequate for a further reason: the indigency exception by definition offers no relief to those voters who do not consider themselves (or would not be considered) indigent but as a practical matter would find it hard, for nonfinancial reasons, to get the required ID (most obviously the disabled).

Indiana's Voter ID Law thus threatens to impose serious burdens on the voting right, even if not "severe" ones, and the next question under *Burdick* is whether the number of individuals likely to be affected is significant as well. Record evidence and facts open to judicial notice answer yes.

Although the District Court found that petitioners failed to offer any reliable empirical study of numbers of voters affected, we may accept that court's rough calculation that 43,000 voting-age residents lack the kind of identification card required by Indiana's law. * * * To be sure, the 43,000 figure has to be discounted to some extent, residents of certain nursing homes being exempted from the photo identification requirement. But the State does not suggest that this narrow exception could possibly reduce 43,000 to an insubstantial number.[24]

---

[24] The State does imply that we should further discount the 43,000 estimate to exclude citizens who are not registered to vote, or who are registered but not planning to vote. But that argument is flatly contradicted by this Court's settled precedent. As our cases have recognized, disfranchisement is

The upshot is this. Tens of thousands of voting-age residents lack the necessary photo identification. A large proportion of them are likely to be in bad shape economically. The Voter ID Law places hurdles in the way of either getting an ID or of voting provisionally, and they translate into nontrivial economic costs. There is accordingly no reason to doubt that a significant number of state residents will be discouraged or disabled from voting. * * *

Because the lead opinion finds only "limited" burdens on the right to vote, it avoids a hard look at the State's claimed interests. But having found the Voter ID Law burdens far from trivial, I have to make a rigorous assessment of "the precise interests put forward by the State as justifications for the burden imposed by its rule, [and] the extent to which those interests make it necessary to burden the plaintiff's rights." *Burdick*, 504 U.S., at 434. * * *

[Justice Souter argued that the state's justifications were insufficient, largely because of the lack of in-person voter impersonation fraud.]

JUSTICE BREYER, dissenting.

Indiana's statute * * * imposes a burden upon some voters, but it does so in order to prevent fraud, to build confidence in the voting system, and thereby to maintain the integrity of the voting process. In determining whether this statute violates the Federal Constitution, I would balance the voting-related interests that the statute affects, asking "whether the statute burdens any one such interest in a manner out of proportion to the statute's salutary effects upon the others (perhaps, but not necessarily, because of the existence of a clearly superior, less restrictive alternative)." *Nixon* v. *Shrink Missouri Government PAC*, 528 U.S. 377, 402 (2000) [p. 834] (BREYER, J., concurring). Applying this standard, I believe the statute is unconstitutional because it imposes a disproportionate burden upon those eligible voters who lack a driver's license or other statutorily valid form of photo ID. * * *

Notes and Questions

1.   Count the votes in *Crawford*. If a single opinion commands the agreement of a majority of the participating Justices, then the opinion is "of the Court." Where no opinion commands a majority, then one must look more closely at the opinions of the Justices who agree in the ultimate disposition of the case (affirmance, reversal, vacatur, etc.). The opinion representing the views of the most Justices who agree in the judgment is referred to as the "plurality" opinion. In *Crawford*, however, there was no plurality opinion because the six Justices who agreed to affirm the judgment of the Court of Appeals were split 3-3. Justice Stevens's opinion became the "lead opinion" because he had greater seniority than did Justice Scalia, who wrote for the

---

disfranchisement, whether or not the disfranchised voter would have voted if given the choice. That is why in *Dunn* v. *Blumstein*, 405 U.S. 330 (1972) [p. 93], the Court did not ask whether any significant number of individuals deprived of the right to vote by durational residence requirements would actually have chosen to vote. And in *Harper* v. *Virginia Bd. of Elections*, the Court did not pause to consider whether any of the qualified voters deterred by the $1.50 poll tax would have opted to vote if there had been no fee. Our cases make clear that the Constitution protects an individual's ability to vote, not merely his decision to do so.

other group of three Justices, but the Stevens opinion is not entitled to any greater precedential weight because it comes first in the U.S. Reports.

Rather, the precedential weight of the opinions is assessed by analyzing the Court's rule from *Marks v. United States*, 430 U.S. 188 (1977). Under the *Marks* rule, "[w]hen a fragmented Court decides a case and no single rationale explaining the result enjoys the assent of five Justices, 'the holding of the Court may be viewed as that position taken by those Members who concurred in the judgments on the narrowest grounds. . . . ' " *Nichols v. United States*, 511 U.S. 738, 745 (1994). Thus, Justice Stevens's opinion will likely be given precedential weight because it is "narrowe[r]" than Justice Scalia's.

2. In *Crawford* there were six votes for reading *Burdick* as adopting an open-ended balancing test *à la Anderson*, rather than as dividing election regulations into those that present "severe" burdens on the right to vote and those that do not. Both the lead opinion and Justice Souter's dissent explicitly state that courts should balance the need for election regulations against the burdens the regulations impose, even when such burdens are less than "severe," and Justice Breyer also applies a balancing analysis in evaluating the ID law. Review *Anderson* and consider whether its standard is administrable or capable of being applied consistently. Is *Burdick*'s two-tiered test any better from a perspective of administrability?

3. Justice Stevens's distaste for the two-tiered standard of review that Justice Scalia saw in *Burdick* was predictable. Justice Stevens, of course, authored the Court's opinion in *Anderson*, and has called for the abandonment of the tiers of scrutiny in equal-protection analysis. *See Craig v. Boren*, 429 U.S. 190, 211 (1976) (Stevens, J., concurring) ("There is only one Equal Protection Clause."). *See also Karcher v. Daggett*, 462 U.S. 725, 749 (1983) (Stevens, J., concurring) (same). According to Justice Stevens, the preferable approach would be to apply a single standard under which states would be required to "govern impartially." Under such an analysis, the justifications for disparate treatment would have to be progressively more convincing as the discrimination became more severe, but state classifications and justifications would be evaluated on a continuum rather than according to tiers. Such an approach has an advantage in allowing courts to make finer assessments as to whether states' classifications are justified, but places a large amount of discretion in the courts.

4. Recall Justice Breyer's argument that campaign-finance restrictions promote political equality, and therefore "constitutionally protected interests lie on both sides of the legal equation." *Nixon v. Shrink Missouri Government PAC*, 528 U.S. 377, 400 (2000) [p. 834] (Breyer, J., concurring). Do constitutionally protected interests lie on both sides of the debate about voter-ID laws? That is, does the Constitution protect not only the right to vote, but also the "right for each voter not to have his legitimate vote diluted or cancelled by an illegal vote"? J. Kenneth Blackwell & Kenneth A. Klukowski, *The Other Voting Right: Protecting Every Citizen's Vote by Safeguarding the Integrity of the Ballot Box*, 28 YALE L. & POL'Y REV. 107, 109 (2009). For a defense of *Crawford* along that line, see *id.* at 116–17; *see also* Bradley A. Smith, *Broken Windows and Voting Rights*, 156 U. PENN L. REV. PENNUMBRA 241 (2007).

5.   A recurring question throughout election law is whether the government may limit individuals' rights to participate in politics because of a concern that the participation creates an appearance of impropriety. For example, limits on campaign fund-raising and judicial candidates' speech have been justified by such a concern, and appearances are significant in the law of electoral districting as well, as we saw in Chapter 5 when considering *Shaw v. Reno*, 509 U.S. 630 (1993) [p. 354], and its progeny.

In *Crawford*, Indiana relied in part on its belief that the voter-ID law served not only the interest in preventing *actual* fraud, but in strengthening the public's *faith* that the elections were not tainted by fraud. Justice Stevens agreed, and argued that "public confidence in the integrity of the electoral process" was important because it "encourages citizen participation in the democratic process." What significance should be given to the state's interest in preventing the *appearance* of voter fraud, even if Indiana could point to no instances of actual voter-impersonation fraud in the state's history? *See* Andrew N. DeLaney, Note, *Appearance Matters: Why the State Has an Interest in Preventing the Appearance of Voting Fraud*, 83 N.Y.U. L. Rev. 847 (2008); Joel A. Heller, Note, *Fearing Fear Itself: Photo Identification Laws, Fear of Fraud, and the Fundamental Right to Vote*, 62 Vand. L. Rev. 1871 (2009).

6.   Should one assess the severity of election regulations from the perspective of voters generally, or from that of the voters most inconvenienced by them? What do the Court's prior cases say about that question?

7.   Consider the footnote in Justice Scalia's opinion. Is he in effect arguing that *Harper* was wrongly decided? Are you convinced by his attempt to distinguish that case? In answering these questions, does it matter whether the challenge to the poll tax in *Harper* is characterized as a facial or an as-applied attack?

8.   Justice Souter argued in his footnote 24 that the number of persons burdened by the photo-ID requirement should include persons who would choose not to vote even if there were no such requirement, because "the Constitution protects an individual's ability to vote, not merely his decision to do so." In what respect, however, does any limitation on voting burden someone who would not exercise the franchise in the absence of the purported burden? Do the cases Justice Souter cited require counting those citizens who not only do not plan to vote, but who are unregistered? Note that the lead opinion points to the record as "not provid[ing] us with the number of *registered voters* without photo identification" (emphasis added).

9.   Since the start of 2011, 13 states — Alabama, Arkansas, Kansas, Mississippi, New Hampshire, North Carolina, Pennsylvania, Rhode Island, South Carolina, Tennessee, Texas, Virginia, and Wisconsin — have enacted voter-ID laws or amended existing laws to increase ID requirements to register or to vote. (Pennsylvania's law was struck down in state court, however.) A total of 34 states have enacted laws requiring some form of identification to vote, with 31 of those states having voter-ID laws that are currently in effect.

Note that these laws differ in important details, such as the acceptable forms of identification, whether a photo-ID is required or whether a non-photo-ID will suffice, and whether a voter without ID can cast a ballot after signing an affidavit at the polling place. A useful catalogue of states' laws by the National Conference of State Legislatures is *available at* http://www.ncsl.org/default.aspx?tabid=16602.

Lower-court challenges too many of the new laws — some based on state law and others based on federal law — have reached varying results. *Compare, e.g., Democratic Party of Georgia v. Perdue*, 707 S.E.2d 67 (Ga. 2011) (upholding Georgia's law) *and Frank v. Walker*, 768 F.3d 744 (7th Cir. 2014) (upholding Wisconsin's — and overturning a district-court judgment striking it down), *cert. denied*, 135 S. Ct. 1551 (2015) *with Applewhite v. Commonwealth*, 2014 Pa. Commw. LEXIS 62 (Pa. Commw. Ct. Jan. 17, 2014) (striking down Pennsylvania's law). Arkansas's law was struck down by a lower court, but the Arkansas Supreme Court vacated that judgment on procedural grounds. *See Arkansas State Board of Election Commissioners v. Pulaski County Election Commission*, 437 S.W.3d 80 (Ark. 2014).

Additionally, the new voter-ID legislation has led to controversy surrounding the Voting Rights Act's preclearance requirement. The Department of Justice granted preclearance to some states' laws, including those in New Hampshire and Virginia. DOJ initially denied South Carolina's application, but the D.C. District Court granted preclearance after South Carolina offered an interpretation that gutted the law of most of its significance. *South Carolina v. United States*, 898 F. Supp. 2d 30 (D.D.C. 2012). Under this interpretation, voters can continue to use non-photo voter registration cards, as long as they provide a reason for not having a photo ID. The D.C. District Court denied Texas's request for preclearance of its photo-ID law. *See Texas v. Holder*, 888 F. Supp. 2d 113 (D.D.C. 2012), *vacated and remanded*, 133 S. Ct. 2886 (2013).

With the Supreme Court's invalidation of the preclearance coverage formula in § 4 of the VRA in *Shelby County, Alabama v. Holder*, 133 S. Ct. 2612 (2013), it appears that preclearance will no longer be an obstacle for the formerly covered jurisdictions. North Carolina, portions of which had been covered under the formula struck down in *Shelby County*, has attempted to take advantage of that decision to enact a new voter-ID law, but the Justice Department has filed suit to stop it. DOJ is alleging that North Carolina's voter-ID law is intentionally discriminatory and thus unconstitutional. *See* Josh Gerstein, *Justice Department Challenges North Carolina Voter ID Law*, Politico (Sept. 30, 2013), *at* http://www.politico.com//story/2013/09/justice-department-north-carolina-voter-id-law-97542.html.

There is a move to use VRA § 3 to bail-in some of the formerly covered jurisdictions, and DOJ's suit against North Carolina asks for bail-in as well as for the invalidation of the photo-ID law. *See id.* To the extent such efforts are successful, preclearance will again be required for the areas bailed-in.

10. In *Arizona v. Inter Tribal Council of Arizona, Inc.*, 133 S. Ct. 2247 (2013), the Supreme Court considered an Arizona law that required voters to present proof of citizenship upon registration. The Court held that the law was pre-empted by the National Voter Registration Act, 52 U.S.C. § 20505(a)(1), because the Arizona law imposed an additional registration requirement beyond completion of the federal form that, according to the NVRA, states must "accept and use."

While thus an apparent victory for challengers of such laws, the full story is much more favorable to states. The Court opined that Congress's power to regulate the times, places and manner of federal elections does not include the power to decide "*who* may vote in [those] elections." (slip op. at 13). And the government conceded that the federal form should require sufficient information to permit state officials to determine if applicants satisfy state-law qualifications for registration. Accordingly, Arizona cannot require proof of citizenship in addition to the requirements listed on the federal form, but Arizona can likely demand that the federal form add a proof-of-citizenship requirement to its list of materials that prospective Arizona registrants must provide.

11. *Problem.* Indiana prohibits convicted sex offenders from coming within one thousand feet of schools, playgrounds, and similar areas. John Doe is a sex offender, having been convicted of child molestation, whose polling place is an elementary school. He may not request an absentee ballot because he will be within the county on Election Day, and does not satisfy any of the other conditions permitting use of an absentee ballot, such as hospitalization or status as an invalid. To comply with the prohibition and vote, he must appear in person before an absentee board in downtown Indianapolis. Is such a requirement constitutional? *See Does v. City of Indianapolis*, 2006 U.S. Dist. LEXIS 72865, *9–*10 (S.D. Ind. 2006). Would the result change if Doe were able to request and cast an absentee ballot by mail? As Justice Souter pointed out in footnote 4 of his dissenting opinion in *Crawford*, there are certain advantages to casting a ballot in-person, including the assistance of poll workers if necessary and the reduced chance that a ballot will be rejected upon suspicion of fraud.

PORTER v. BOWEN
United States Court of Appeals for the Ninth Circuit
496 F.3d 1009 (2007), *reh'g en banc denied*, 518 F.3d 1181 (9th Cir. 2008)[a]

FISHER, CIRCUIT JUDGE [with whom CLIFTON, CIRCUIT JUDGE, and MARTINEZ, DISTRICT JUDGE, join]: * * *

On October 26, 2000, less than two weeks before the upcoming national presidential election [between Republican George W. Bush, Democrat Al Gore, and Green Party candidate Ralph Nader], William J. Cody created a website called voteswap2000.com. The website's self-professed goal was "[t]o maximize the percentage of the popular vote that Nader receives, yet allow Gore to win the national election." To this end, the website contained links to various articles discussing the 2000 election and urging people to swap votes so that Gore would become President and Nader would receive at least five percent of the popular vote. [If Nader reached the five-percent threshold, his party would qualify for federal funding in future elections.] More relevant here, the website also included a matching system that put people who described themselves as "Nader voters in . . . swing states" in e-mail contact with people who described themselves as "Gore voters in blow-out states." Once paired, the individuals could exchange e-mails and

---

[a] Judge Kleinfeld's dissent, which appears at the end of this opinion, is from the order denying rehearing. [-Eds.]

agree to trade their votes. As the website put it, "the original Gore voter will vote for Nader, boosting his national popular totals, while the Nader voter will vote for Gore, which will hopefully prevent a Bush victory in that state." * * *

In total, 5,041 people were matched by the voteswap2000.com database. It is unknown, however, how many Nader and Gore votes were actually swapped after users were paired. Given secret balloting, whether either or both of the parties to a vote-swapping agreement followed through on their commitments could not be verified. There was therefore no assurance for users of voteswap2000.com that their counterparts voted in the manner they promised beyond the counterparts' word. As the website told paired individuals, "remember that this is just a friendly agreement, and you are taking their word that they will follow through."

On October 23, 2000, Alan Porter and Anand Ranganathan separately created a website called votexchange2000.com. Like voteswap2000.com, votexchange2000.com explained the dilemma facing third-party supporters in swing states, and advocated a vote-swapping solution whereby "[v]oters in a swing state who wish to vote for a third party candidate could swap their vote with voters in 'safe states' who would normally vote for a leading party candidate." Also as with voteswap2000.com, users of votexchange2000.com were given the e-mail address of an appropriate partner after identifying their own state of residency and voting intentions; at that point, "these two people [could] contact each other and satisfy each other that they [could] trust each other to vote the other's preferences." However, unlike voteswap2000.com, votexchange2000.com was not intended solely to match swing-state Nader supporters with safe-state Gore supporters; instead, *any* third-party supporter in a swing state could be matched with an appropriate major-party supporter in a safe state. Finally, votexchange2000.com included a warning that "[t]here is no way to be absolutely definitely certainly 100% sure" that a vote swap was actually consummated. While "trust[ing] in the innate goodness of people," the website recommended that users "take some reasonable measures to insure that you could trust the other person."

On October 30, 2000, four days after voteswap2000.com began operation (and eight days before the election), the website's owners received a letter from Bill Jones, then Secretary of State of California, informing them that their site was "engaged in criminal activity" [and threatening them with prosecution should the brokering of vote exchanges continue]. * * * Immediately after receiving Jones's letter, the owners of voteswap2000.com disabled their website's vote-swapping mechanism, barred Internet users outside California from accessing the website, posted a notice on the website about what had happened and e-mailed all people who had been matched about the potential illegality of vote swapping. These actions "satisfactorily resolve[d]" the issue as far as Jones was concerned. Even though they did not receive an analogous letter, the owners of votexchange2000.com also disabled their website's vote-swapping mechanism as soon as they found out about the voteswap2000.com letter. * * *

Cody, Porter, Patrick Kerr and Steven Lewis ("Appellants") filed the present lawsuit on November 2, 2000 (five days before the presidential election). Kerr is a California citizen who supported Nader but was worried about contributing to a Bush victory in his state; Lewis is a Massachusetts citizen who supported Gore but would have considered swapping his vote with a swing-state Nader supporter. Both Kerr and Lewis were interested in using the voteswapping mechanisms offered by voteswap2000.com and votexchange2000.com, but were unable to do so after those mechanisms were disabled. * * *

The first issue we must resolve is whether Jones' actions burdened any constitutionally protected speech or conduct. That is, did Appellants have a First Amendment interest in voteswap2000.com and votexchange2000's voteswapping mechanisms or the communication and vote swaps that the mechanisms enabled? Beginning with the voteswapping mechanisms themselves, we hold that they are entitled to at least some First Amendment protection. The mechanisms conveyed useful information to users by providing them with the e-mail addresses of appropriate counterparts with whom they could swap votes. Voteswap2000.com also offered data about states' political leanings, ballot situations and electoral systems as soon as users of the mechanism identified their states of residency.

As Appellants argue, the vote-swap mechanisms also expressed a reasonably clear message of support for third-party candidates and concern that winner-take-all systems might allow a candidate to receive all of a state's electoral votes even though he was opposed by a majority of the state's voters (as measured by the popular vote). * * *

Looking next at the communication and vote swaps that the mechanisms enabled between paired users, we agree with Appellants that they too constituted protected speech or conduct. As discussed above, after being matched by the websites' vote-swapping mechanisms, users were encouraged to contact each other by e-mail. It is reasonable to assume that the users' ensuing messages would have concerned their political preferences and, if the users reached a meeting of the minds, resulted in agreements to swap votes on election day. This kind of communication is clearly protected by the First Amendment. "[T]here is practically universal agreement that a major purpose of that Amendment was to protect the free discussion of governmental affairs," including "discussions of candidates." *Mills v. Alabama*, 384 U.S. 214, 218 (1966) [p. 603]; *see also Meyer v. Grant*, 486 U.S. 414, 422 (1988) [p. 678] ("[I]nteractive communication concerning political change . . . is appropriately described as 'core political speech.' "); *Buckley v. Valeo*, 424 U.S. 1, 14 (1976) [p. 799] ("Discussion of public issues and debate on the qualifications of candidates are . . . afford[ed] the broadest protection . . . .").

Any agreements that paired users may have reached about swapping votes were also constitutionally protected. Such agreements — like the e-mails that preceded them — involved people's opinions on "campaigns for political office," which are precisely where the First Amendment "has its fullest and most urgent application." *Monitor Patriot Co. v. Roy*, 401 U.S. 265, 272 (1971). Agreements whereby a swing-state third-party supporter and safe-state major-party supporter pledged to trade votes also would have expressed those voters' (1) support for a particular major-party candidate or (2) support for a particular third-party candidate, as well as (3) their concern that unless action was taken, the winner-take-all electoral system could result in the will of the swing state's popular-vote majority being overridden.

Whatever the wisdom of using vote-swapping agreements to communicate these positions, such agreements plainly differ from conventional (and illegal) vote buying, which conveys no message other than the parties' willingness to exchange votes for money (or some other form of private profit). The Supreme Court held in *Brown v. Hartlage*, 456 U.S. 45, 55 (1982) [p. 585], that vote buying may be banned "without trenching on any right of association protected by the First Amendment." Vote swapping, however, is more akin to the candidate's pledge in *Brown* to take a pay cut if elected, which the Court concluded was constitutionally protected, than to unprotected vote buying. Like the candidate's pledge, vote swapping involves a "promise to confer some ultimate benefit on the voter, *qua* . . . citizen[ ] or member of the general public" — i.e., another person's agreement to vote for a particular candidate. *Id.* at 58–59.[16] And unlike vote buying, vote swapping is not an "illegal exchange for *private* profit" since the only benefit a vote swapper can receive is a marginally higher probability that his preferred electoral outcome will come to pass. *Id.* at 55 (emphasis added).

Both the websites' vote-swapping mechanisms and the communication and vote swaps that they enabled were therefore constitutionally protected. At their core, they amounted to efforts by politically engaged people to support their preferred candidates and to avoid election results that they feared would contravene the preferences of a majority of voters in closely contested states. Whether or not one agrees with these voters' tactics, such efforts, when conducted honestly and without money changing hands, are at the heart of the liberty safeguarded by the First Amendment.

The Secretary asserts three interests to justify any alleged burdening of Appellants' protected activity: preventing corruption, preventing fraud and preventing the subversion of the Electoral College. * * * Preventing corruption and preventing fraud have both been repeatedly recognized as weighty government interests. However, as Appellants argue, no decision has ever recognized a state's interest in preventing the subversion of the Electoral College, let alone characterized such an interest as important or substantial. In any event, we need not decide whether preventing the subversion of the Electoral College is a legitimate government interest because, as we discuss below, even if it were, it was not furthered by Jones' actions. * * * We conclude that the Secretary's interests in preventing corruption and preventing the subversion of the Electoral College were not furthered at all by the threatened prosecution of the owners of voteswap2000.com and votexchange2000.com, and that the State's anti-fraud interest was not addressed in a sufficiently tailored manner.

Beginning with the State's anti-corruption interest, * * * we construe this interest to encompass only the prevention of illicit financial transactions such as the buying of votes or the contribution of large sums of money to legislators in exchange for political support. So defined, this interest was not advanced by the threatened prosecution of the owners of voteswap2000.com and votexchange2000.com. The websites did not encourage the trading of votes for money, or indeed for anything

---

[16] * * * In one respect, moreover, this case is easier than *Brown* because it does not involve any financial self-interest whatsoever. The voters in *Brown* could have expected to receive some (small) pecuniary advantage from the promised salary-saving. Here, in contrast, people agreed to swap votes without any promise at all of financial benefit. [Relocated. — Eds.]

other than other votes. Votexchange2000.com actually included a notation that "It *is* illegal to pay someone to vote on your behalf, or even get paid to vote yourself. Stay away from the money. Just vote" (emphasis in original). And there is no evidence in the record, nor has the Secretary argued, that any website users ever misused the voteswapping mechanisms by offering or accepting money for their votes.

The state's anti-fraud interest *was* furthered by Jones' threatened prosecution of the website owners. At least three kinds of fraud could have been perpetrated through those websites' vote-swapping mechanisms. People from other states (or even other countries) could have pretended to be third-party swing-state supporters or major-party safe-state supporters. Regardless of their location, people could have used the websites' vote-swapping mechanisms multiple times, thus trading their one vote (or zero votes) for several other votes. And even people who were truthful about their location and who only swapped votes once could have deliberately misrepresented their voting intentions. Threatening Appellants' websites with prosecution unless they disabled the vote-swapping mechanisms thus served the State's anti-fraud interest for the obvious reason that none of the above species of fraud could have been committed through mechanisms that were no longer in operation.

However, the Secretary has failed to demonstrate that the burden imposed on constitutionally protected activity by the disabling of the mechanisms was not "greater than [was] essential to the furtherance of [the State's anti-fraud] interest." First, the Secretary has not called our attention to, nor have we been able to locate, any evidence in the record that fraud actually took place during the brief period that the vote-swapping mechanisms were operational. No website users came forward with either admissions that they committed fraud or worries that their counterparts misrepresented their state of residency or voting intentions. The websites' owners also did not notice any suspicious online activity, such as the use of "obviously fake or multiple e-mail addresses," which voteswap2000.com stated it would try to eliminate if it occurred.

Second, as described above, both websites repeatedly warned users that fraud was possible and advised them to take steps to reassure themselves that they could trust their matched counterparts. Voteswap2000.com told users to "[u]se your own good judgement to determine if the person you are matched with is legitimate, and be aware that some people will try to abuse this system." Similarly, votexchange2000.com recommended that users "take some reasonable measures to insure that you could trust the other person." The Secretary has not explained why these warnings were insufficient, or what kind of language (if any) would have assuaged the State's concerns.

Third, the manner in which the vote-swapping mechanisms operated reduced the opportunities for widespread fraud. Any would-be fraudster would have had to exchange e-mails and come to a vote-swapping agreement separately with each intended victim. There was no way to "automate" the fraud, that is, to agree to trade votes without first making e-mail contact and offering specific representations (even if bogus) to the other party about the fraudster's identity, location and voting intentions.

Lastly, the Secretary has failed to establish (or, indeed, even to argue) that the

State's anti-fraud interest could not have been advanced as effectively through less restrictive means. * * * Appellants[] offer * * * at least two suggestions for preventing fraud short of disabling the websites' vote-swapping mechanisms altogether, neither of which was addressed by the Secretary. First, * * * "[m]ore stringent warnings" about the danger of fraud could have been posted on the websites, to even more clearly alert users of the need to exercise good judgment in trusting someone known only through the Internet. Second, * * * [i]f those who utilized the voteswapping mechanism had been required by law (or even simply the websites) to prove their identity and residency before they could have been matched with other users (perhaps by providing information such as a driver's license number or the voter registration number that is typically listed on voter identification cards), then the websites could have stopped users from swapping votes multiple times or from misrepresenting their state of residency. * * *

Finally, the State's interest in preventing the subversion of the Electoral College, assuming it to be a legitimate interest, was not furthered by Jones' actions. As a technical matter, Appellants are correct that the vote-swapping mechanisms did not enable users to cast their votes in states in which they were not registered, nor could the constitutionally prescribed arrangement for selecting the President have been undermined by the mechanisms. More fundamentally, the whole point of voteswap2000.com and votexchange2000.com was to prevent the preferences of a majority of a state's voters from being frustrated by the winner-take-all systems in place in most states. * * * Such an outcome would not have represented a subversion of the Electoral College, which would have continued to operate precisely as set forth in the Constitution. It also would not have undermined the state's electoral system, which would have still allocated all of the state's electoral votes to the candidate who received a plurality of the state's popular vote. All that the vote swapping would have done would have been to offset the anomalies that its advocates believe can result when more than two candidates face off in winner-take-all systems.

We therefore hold that Jones' threatened prosecution of the owners of voteswap2000.com and votexchange2000.com was unconstitutional[.] * * * We express no opinion on whether less severe measures — such as the verification methods suggested by Appellants — would pass muster[.] * * *

KLEINFELD, Circuit Judge, with whom Circuit Judges O'SCANNLAIN and BEA join, dissenting from denial of rehearing en banc:

I respectfully dissent.

This case is about whether the First Amendment protects from prosecution people who buy votes. Instead of cash, or beer and cigars, the buyers offered promises. * * * The deals were in the form, "if you promise to vote for my preferred candidate in your state, I will promise to vote for your preferred candidate in my state." * * *

Our panel decision holds that by sending the letter threatening criminal prosecution, the Secretary of State "violated Appellants' First Amendment rights." The theory seems to be that the sites expressed support for candidates, and the agreements they facilitated "involved" political opinions, so the solicitations were constitutionally protected speech. * * *

There is not much precedent on point, because few have had the chutzpah to argue that buying promises to vote for someone, or arranging for them, would be constitutionally protected. *Brown v. Hartlage*, the only case relied upon by the panel, says the opposite of what the panel decision uses it for.

In *Brown*, the Supreme Court says that the First Amendment does not shield speech to buy votes. The Court's language goes beyond the simple money-for-vote exchange, to exclude from First Amendment protection agreements for exchanges, and agreements for things of value other than money:

> [A] State may surely prohibit a candidate from buying votes. No body politic worthy of being called a democracy entrusts the selection of leaders to a process of auction or barter. And as a State may prohibit the giving of money or other things of value to a voter in exchange for his support, it may also declare unlawful an agreement embodying the intention to make such an exchange.

[456 U.S. at 54–55.] What the Court held to be unprotected is what we have in this case: a scheme to facilitate the exchange of something valuable, a promise, in exchange for a vote. The difference between the vote swapping scheme here and more traditional vote buying is that instead of one side to the transaction buying the vote and the other selling it, both are buying and both are selling.

Brown also speaks explicitly to the argument that the vote buying is mere words and not conduct. "The fact that [a vote buying] agreement necessarily takes the form of words does not confer upon it, or upon the underlying conduct, the constitutional immunities that the First Amendment extends to speech." [*Id.* at 55.]

The exchange of promises is an ordinary means of making a contract, whether legal or illegal, and no one has doubted for centuries that promises form consideration for contracts. Contracts are how people buy things of value, sometimes promises to sell goods in exchange for promises to pay, promises of quantity discounts, or, as in this case, promises to vote for the other person's preferred candidate. The panel considered it important that the vote-swaps operated "without money changing hands," but a promise is consideration whether it involves cash or not. The California statutes, like those of all the other states in this circuit, prohibit vote buying for consideration other than money, as well as for cash. Of course, the buyer of the vote may be cheated by secret nonperformance of the promise he bought, and have no legal remedy, but a promise is good consideration even if the promise is unenforceable, and even if it is "not binding or against public policy." [Restatement (Second) Contracts § 78 & cmt. a.]

* * * State-by-state voting is the system for which [article II, § 1 of the Constitution and the Twelfth Amendment] provide. The First Amendment does not prevent state prosecution of those who subvert it by making arrangements effectively to cast votes in other states. * * *

If people in one state want people in another state to vote a particular way, they can go there and ring doorbells, send them letters, buy advertisements on their media, publicize arguments on the internet, and otherwise explain to them why they ought to vote a particular way. But they do not have a constitutional right to buy their votes, with money or promises.

Notes and Questions

1. Are statutes prohibiting vote buying constitutional? Why does every state and the federal government (*see* 18 U.S.C. §§ 597, 598) prohibit the practice? Professor Richard Hasen has identified three main rationales for vote-buying prohibitions: equality (the poor will sell their votes more readily than will the wealthy), efficiency (votes will be purchased so that government could be employed for the benefit of the purchasers, rather than for the general public), and inalienability (votes should not be transferable). *See* Richard L. Hasen, *Vote Buying*, 88 CALIF. L. REV. 1323 (2000). Are any of these rationales persuasive reasons to prohibit vote buying?

2. Are vote swaps speech, expressive conduct, or neither?

3. If *Porter* is wrong, and these websites could lawfully be shut down, could a state constitutionally punish an agreement to trade votes if it was made without a website or another enabling mechanism? For example, could a state prohibit two relatives living in different states from agreeing on their own to trade votes?

4. The majority opinion states that there is an important interest in preventing the users of the website from being defrauded, but holds that shutting down the site was an inappropriate way of pursuing that objective. Are there other kinds of fraud that the state could seek to prevent by shutting down the sites?

5. The state attempted to justify its actions by invoking the interest in preventing corruption. What did the Court interpret this interest to mean? What do you think the state meant by "corruption" in this context?

6. *Problem.* New Yorkshire law provides that "no voter shall allow his ballot to be seen by any person with the intention of letting it be known how he is about to vote or how he has voted. This prohibition shall include taking a digital image or photograph of his marked ballot and distributing or sharing the image via social media or by any other means." The law undoubtedly implicates the First Amendment, as it prohibits a certain form of speech about politics, but the state contends that the law satisfies constitutional standards. The state defends its ban by pointing to the interest in preventing vote-buying — the same interest that underlies the adoption of the secret ("Australian") ballot. The photo ban, so the argument goes, prevents voters from being able to prove how they voted; and nobody would try to buy a vote when there is no way of proving that the voter has voted the "right" way. Voters can still claim to have voted for one candidate or another, but there is no way to be sure that the voter is telling the truth.

Does the photo ban trigger strict scrutiny? If it does, is the ban narrowly tailored to the goal of preventing vote-buying? Note that the ban applies to all displays of marked ballots — even when the voter did not sell his vote. Does the constitutionality of the ban depend on the prevalence of vote-buying? If so, how is a state supposed to demonstrate that vote-buying is a significant problem if the ban itself ensured that vote-buying could not take place? *See Rideout v. Gardner*, 2015 U.S. Dist. LEXIS 105194 (D.N.H. 2015) (striking down such a ban); Richard L. Hasen, *Why the Selfie Is a Threat to Democracy*, REUTERS , Aug. 18, 2015, at http://blogs. reuters.com/great-debate/2015/08/17/why-the-selfie-is-a-threat-to-democracy/ (criticizing *Rideout*).

C. CAMPAIGN-FREE ZONES AROUND POLLING PLACES

In Chapter 8, we discovered that the First Amendment's protection of "the freedom of speech" is most powerful when applied to speech concerning political campaigns. Nevertheless, the interests of free expression occasionally confront other powerful societal interests, and even other constitutional rights. The next case examines such a conflict, as it considers the constitutionality of a restriction of political speech near polling places.

BURSON v. FREEMAN
Supreme Court of the United States
504 U.S. 191, 112 S. Ct. 1846, 119 L. Ed. 2d 5 (1992)

JUSTICE BLACKMUN announced the judgment of the Court and delivered an opinion, in which THE CHIEF JUSTICE [REHNQUIST], JUSTICE WHITE, and JUSTICE KENNEDY join. * * *

The State of Tennessee has carved out an election-day "campaign-free zone" through § 2-7-111(b) of its election code. That section reads in pertinent part:

> "Within * * * [100 feet from the entrances], and the building in which the polling place is located, the display of campaign posters, signs or other campaign materials, distribution of campaign materials, and solicitation of votes for or against any person or political party or position on a question are prohibited."

Violation of § 2-7-111(b) is a Class C misdemeanor punishable by a term of imprisonment not greater than 30 days or a fine not to exceed $50, or both. * * *

[Section] 2-7-111(b) * * * bars [political] speech in quintessential public forums. These forums include those places "which by long tradition or by government fiat have been devoted to assembly and debate," such as parks, streets, and sidewalks.[2] * * * At the same time, however, expressive activity, even in a quintessential public forum, may interfere with other important activities for which the property is used. Accordingly, this Court has held that the government may regulate the time, place, and manner of the expressive activity, so long as such restrictions are content neutral, are narrowly tailored to serve a significant governmental interest, and leave open ample alternatives for communication.

The Tennessee restriction under consideration, however, is not a facially content-neutral time, place, or manner restriction. Whether individuals may exercise their free speech rights near polling places depends entirely on whether

---

[2] Testimony at trial established that at some Tennessee polling locations the campaign-free zone included sidewalks and streets adjacent to the polling places.

their speech is related to a political campaign. The statute does not reach other categories of speech, such as commercial solicitation, distribution, and display. This Court has held that the First Amendment's hostility to content-based regulation extends not only to a restriction on a particular viewpoint, but also to a prohibition of public discussion of an entire topic.

As a facially content-based restriction on political speech in a public forum, § 2-7-111(b) must be subjected to exacting scrutiny: The State must show that the "regulation is necessary to serve a compelling state interest and that it is narrowly drawn to achieve that end." * * *

Tennessee asserts that its campaign-free zone serves two compelling interests. First, the State argues that its regulation serves its compelling interest in protecting the right of its citizens to vote freely for the candidates of their choice. Second, Tennessee argues that its restriction protects the right to vote in an election conducted with integrity and reliability. The interests advanced by Tennessee obviously are compelling ones. * * *

To survive strict scrutiny, however, a State must do more than assert a compelling state interest — it must demonstrate that its law is necessary to serve the asserted interest. While we readily acknowledge that a law rarely survives such scrutiny, an examination of the evolution of election reform, both in this country and abroad, demonstrates the necessity of restricted areas in or around polling places. * * *

[T]he history of election regulation in this country reveals a persistent battle against two evils: voter intimidation and election fraud. After an unsuccessful experiment with an unofficial ballot system, all 50 States, together with numerous other Western democracies, settled on the same solution: a secret ballot secured in part by a restricted zone around the voting compartments. We find that this widespread and time-tested consensus demonstrates that some restricted zone is necessary in order to serve the States' compelling interests in preventing voter intimidation and election fraud.

Respondent and the dissent advance three principal challenges to this conclusion. First, respondent argues that restricted zones are overinclusive because States could secure these same compelling interests with statutes that make it a misdemeanor to interfere with an election or to use violence or intimidation to prevent voting. We are not persuaded. Intimidation and interference laws fall short of serving a State's compelling interests because they "deal with only the most blatant and specific attempts" to impede elections. Moreover, because law enforcement officers generally are barred from the vicinity of the polls to avoid any appearance of coercion in the electoral process, many acts of interference would go undetected. These undetected or less than blatant acts may nonetheless drive the voter away before remedial action can be taken.

Second, respondent and the dissent argue that Tennessee's statute is underinclusive because it does not restrict other types of speech, such as charitable and commercial solicitation or exit polling, within the 100-foot zone. We agree that distinguishing among types of speech requires that the statute be subjected to strict scrutiny. We do not, however, agree that the failure to regulate all speech renders the statute fatally underinclusive. * * * [T]here is, as summarized above, ample evidence that political candidates have used campaign workers to commit voter intimidation or electoral fraud. In contrast, there is simply no evidence that political candidates have used other forms of solicitation or exit polling to commit such electoral abuses. States adopt laws to address the problems that confront them. The First Amendment does not require States to regulate for problems that do not exist.

Finally, the dissent argues that we confuse history with necessity. Yet the dissent concedes that a secret ballot was necessary to cure electoral abuses. Contrary to the dissent's contention, the link between ballot secrecy and some restricted zone surrounding the voting area is not merely timing — it is common sense. The only way to preserve the secrecy of the ballot is to limit access to the area around the voter.[10] Accordingly, we hold that *some* restricted zone around the voting area is necessary to secure the State's compelling interest.

The real question then is *how large* a restricted zone is permissible or sufficiently tailored. Respondent and the dissent argue that Tennessee's 100-foot boundary is not narrowly drawn to achieve the State's compelling interest in protecting the right to vote. We disagree.

As a preliminary matter, the long, uninterrupted and prevalent use of these statutes makes it difficult for States to come forward with the sort of proof the dissent wishes to require. The majority of these laws were adopted originally in the 1890s, long before States engaged in extensive legislative hearings on election regulations. The prevalence of these laws, both here and abroad, then encouraged their reenactment without much comment. The fact that these laws have been in effect for a long period of time also makes it difficult for the States to put on witnesses who can testify as to what would happen without them. Finally, it is difficult to isolate the exact effect of these laws on voter intimidation and election fraud. Voter intimidation and election fraud are successful precisely because they are difficult to detect.

Furthermore, because a government has such a compelling interest in securing the right to vote freely and effectively, this Court never has held a State "to the burden of demonstrating empirically the objective effects on political stability that [are] produced" by the voting regulation in question. *Munro* v. *Socialist Workers Party*, 479 U.S. 189, 195 (1986).[11] Elections vary from year to year, and place to place. It is therefore difficult to make specific findings about the effects of a voting regulation. Moreover, the remedy for a tainted election is an imperfect one.

---

[10] The logical connection between ballot secrecy and restricted zones distinguishes this case from those cited by the dissent in which the Court struck down longstanding election regulations. In those cases, there was no rational connection between the asserted interest and the regulation. See, *e.g.*, *Harper* v. *Virginia Bd. of Elections*, 383 U.S. 663, 666 (1966) [p. 37] ("Voter qualifications have no relation to wealth nor to paying or not paying this or any other tax").

[11] This modified "burden of proof" does not apply to all cases in which there is a conflict between First Amendment rights and a State's election process — instead, it applies only when the First Amendment right threatens to interfere with the act of voting itself, *i.e.*, cases involving voter confusion from overcrowded ballots, like *Munro*, or cases such as this one, in which the challenged activity physically interferes with electors attempting to cast their ballots. Thus, for example, States must come forward with more specific findings to support regulations directed at intangible "influence," such as the ban on election-day editorials struck down in *Mills* v. *Alabama*, 384 U.S. 214 (1966) [p. 603].

Rerunning an election would have a negative impact on voter turnout. Thus, requiring proof that a 100-foot boundary is perfectly tailored to deal with voter intimidation and election fraud

> "would necessitate that a State's political system sustain some level of damage before the legislature could take corrective action. Legislatures, we think, should be permitted to respond to potential deficiencies in the electoral process with foresight rather than reactively, provided that the response is reasonable and does not *significantly impinge* on constitutionally protected rights." *Id.*, at 195–196 (emphasis added).

We do not think that the minor geographic limitation prescribed by § 2-7-111(b) constitutes such a significant impingement. Thus, we simply do not view the question whether the 100-foot boundary line could be somewhat tighter as a question of "constitutional dimension." Reducing the boundary to 25 feet, as suggested by the Tennessee Supreme Court, is a difference only in degree, not a less restrictive alternative in kind. As was pointed out in the dissenting opinion in the Tennessee Supreme Court, it "takes approximately 15 seconds to walk 75 feet." The State of Tennessee has decided that these last 15 seconds before its citizens enter the polling place should be their own, as free from interference as possible. We do not find that this is an unconstitutional choice.

At some measurable distance from the polls, of course, governmental regulation of vote solicitation could effectively become an impermissible burden akin to the statute struck down in *Mills* v. *Alabama*. In reviewing challenges to specific provisions of a State's election laws, however, this Court has not employed any " 'litmus-paper test' that will separate valid from invalid restrictions." *Anderson* v. *Celebrezze*, 460 U.S. [780], 789 [(1983)] [p. 517]. Accordingly, it is sufficient to say that in establishing a 100-foot boundary, Tennessee is on the constitutional side of the line.

In conclusion, we reaffirm that it is the rare case in which we have held that a law survives strict scrutiny. This, however, is such a rare case. Here, the State, as recognized administrator of elections, has asserted that the exercise of free speech rights conflicts with another fundamental right, the right to cast a ballot in an election free from the taint of intimidation and fraud. A long history, a substantial consensus, and simple common sense show that some restricted zone around polling places is necessary to protect that fundamental right. Given the conflict between these two rights, we hold that requiring solicitors to stand 100 feet from the entrances to polling places does not constitute an unconstitutional compromise.

The judgment of the Tennessee Supreme Court is reversed, and the case is remanded for further proceedings not inconsistent with this opinion.

It is so ordered.

JUSTICE THOMAS took no part in the consideration or decision of this case.

JUSTICE KENNEDY, concurring.

* * * Under what I deem the proper approach, neither a general content-based proscription of speech nor a content-based proscription of speech in a public forum can be justified unless the speech falls within one of a limited set of well-defined categories. [But the regulation at issue here is not content-based.] * * * "[G]overnment regulation of expressive activity is content neutral so long as it is *justified without reference to the content of the regulated speech*.' " *Ward* v. *Rock Against Racism*, 491 U.S. 781, 791 (1989).

[T]here is a narrow area in which the First Amendment permits freedom of expression to yield to the extent necessary for the accommodation of another constitutional right. That principle can apply here * * *; for under the statute the State acts to protect the integrity of the polling place where citizens exercise the right to vote. * * * The State is not using this justification to suppress legitimate expression. * * *

JUSTICE SCALIA, concurring in the judgment.

If the category of "traditional public forum" is to be a tool of analysis rather than a conclusory label, it must remain faithful to its name and derive its content from *tradition*. Because restrictions on speech around polling places on election day are as venerable a part of the American tradition as the secret ballot, § 2-7-111 does not restrict speech in a traditional public forum, and the "exacting scrutiny" that the plurality purports to apply is inappropriate. Instead, I believe that § 2-7-111, though content-based, is constitutional because it is a reasonable, viewpoint-neutral regulation of a nonpublic forum. I therefore concur in the judgment of the Court.

* * * Ever since the widespread adoption of the secret ballot in the late 19th century, viewpoint-neutral restrictions on election-day speech within a specified distance of the polling place — or on physical presence there — have been commonplace, indeed prevalent. By 1900, at least 34 of the 45 States (including Tennessee) had enacted such restrictions. It is noteworthy that most of the statutes banning election-day speech near the polling place specified the same distance set forth in § 2-7-111 (100 feet), and it is clear that the restricted zones often encompassed streets and sidewalks. Thus, the streets and sidewalks around polling places have traditionally *not* been devoted to assembly and debate. * * *

For the reasons that the plurality believes § 2-7-111 survives exacting scrutiny, I believe it is at least reasonable; and respondent does not contend that it is viewpoint discriminatory. I therefore agree with the judgment of the Court that § 2-7-111 is constitutional.

JUSTICE STEVENS, with whom JUSTICE O'CONNOR and JUSTICE SOUTER join, dissenting. * * *

Tennessee's statutory "campaign-free zone" raises constitutional concerns of the first magnitude. The statute directly regulates political expression and thus implicates a core concern of the First Amendment. Moreover, it targets only a specific subject matter (campaign speech) and a defined class of speakers (campaign workers) and thus regulates expression based on its content. In doing so, the Tennessee statute somewhat perversely disfavors speech that normally is accorded greater protection than the kinds of speech that the statute does not regulate. For these reasons, Tennessee unquestionably bears the heavy burden of demonstrating that its silencing of political expression is necessary and narrowly tailored to serve a compelling state interest.

Statutes creating campaign-free zones outside polling places serve two quite different functions — they protect orderly access to the polls and they prevent last-minute campaigning. There can be no question that the former constitutes a compelling state interest and that * * * the latter does not. Accordingly, a State must demonstrate that the particular means it has fashioned to ensure orderly access to the polls do not unnecessarily hinder last-minute campaigning.

Campaign-free zones are noteworthy for their broad, antiseptic sweep. The Tennessee zone encompasses at least 30,000 square feet around each polling place; in some States, such as Kentucky and Wisconsin, the radius of the restricted zone is 500 feet — silencing an area of over 750,000 square feet. Even under the most sanguine scenario of participatory democracy, it is difficult to imagine voter turnout so complete as to require the clearing of hundreds of thousands of square feet simply to ensure that the path to the polling-place door remains open and that the curtain that protects the secrecy of the ballot box remains closed.

The fact that campaign-free zones cover such a large area in some States unmistakably identifies censorship of election-day campaigning as an animating force behind these restrictions. That some States have no problem maintaining order with zones of 50 feet or less strongly suggests that the more expansive prohibitions are not necessary to maintain access and order. * * *

Moreover, the Tennessee statute does not merely regulate conduct that might inhibit voting; it bars the simple "display of campaign posters, signs, or other campaign materials." Bumper stickers on parked cars and lapel buttons on pedestrians are taboo. The notion that such sweeping restrictions on speech are necessary to maintain the freedom to vote and the integrity of the ballot box borders on the absurd. * * *

[T]he plurality — without briefing, or legislative or judicial factfinding — looks to history to assess whether Tennessee's statute is in fact necessary to serve the State's interests. * * * This analysis is deeply flawed; it confuses history with necessity, and mistakes the traditional for the indispensable. The plurality's reasoning combines two logical errors: First, the plurality assumes that a practice's long life itself establishes its necessity; and second, the plurality assumes that a practice that was once necessary remains necessary until it is ended.

With regard to the first, the fact that campaign-free zones were, as the plurality indicates, introduced as part of a broader package of electoral reforms does not demonstrate that such zones were *necessary*. The abuses that affected the electoral system could have been cured by the institution of the secret ballot and by the heightened regulation of the polling place alone, without silencing the political speech *outside* the polling place.[4] In my opinion, more than mere timing is required to infer necessity from tradition.

We have never regarded tradition as a proxy for necessity where necessity must be demonstrated. To the contrary, our election-law jurisprudence is rich with examples of traditions [such as poll taxes, as in *Harper* v. *Virginia Bd. of Elections*] that, though longstanding, were later held to be unnecessary. Similarly, substantial barriers to candidacy, such as stringent petition requirements, see *Williams* v. *Rhodes*, 393 U.S. 23 (1968) [p. 497], property-ownership requirements, see *Turner* v. *Fouche*, 396 U.S. 346 (1970), and onerous filing fees, see *Lubin* v. *Panish*, 415 U.S. 709 (1974), were all longstanding features of the electoral labyrinth.

In fact, two of our most noted decisions in this area involve, as does this case, Tennessee's electoral traditions. *Dunn* v. *Blumstein*, 405 U.S. 330 (1972) [p. 93], which invalidated Tennessee's 1-year residency requirement, is particularly instructive. * * * Although we recognized that "[p]reservation of the 'purity of the ballot box' is a formidable-sounding state interest," we rejected the State's argument that a 1-year requirement was necessary to promote that interest. In doing so, we did not even mention, let alone find determinative, the fact that Tennessee's requirement was more than 100 years old. * * *

Even if we assume that campaign-free zones were once somehow "necessary," it would not follow that, 100 years later, those practices remain necessary. Much in our political culture, institutions, and practices has changed since the turn of the century: Our elections are far less corrupt, far more civil, and far more democratic today than 100 years ago. These salutary developments have substantially eliminated the need for what is, in my opinion, a sweeping suppression of core political speech. * * *

In addition to sweeping too broadly in its reach, Tennessee's campaign-free zone selectively prohibits speech based on content. * * * Within the zone, § 2-7-111 silences all campaign-related expression, but allows expression on any other subject: religious, artistic, commercial speech, even political debate and solicitation concerning issues or candidates not on the day's ballot. Indeed, as I read it, § 2-7-111 does not prohibit exit polling, which surely presents at least as great a potential interference with orderly access to the polls as does the distribution of campaign leaflets, the display of campaign posters, or the wearing of campaign buttons. This discriminatory feature of the statute severely undercuts the credibility of its purported law-and-order justification.

---

[4] The plurality's suggestion that "[t]he only way to preserve the secrecy of the ballot is to limit access to the area around the voter" is specious. First, there are obvious and simple means of preserving voter secrecy (*e.g.*, opaque doors or curtains on the voting booth) that do not involve the suppression of political speech. Second, there is no disagreement that the restrictions on campaigning *within the polling place* are constitutional; the issue is not whether the State may limit access to the "area *around the voter*" but whether the State may limit speech in the area *around the polling place.*

Tennessee's content-based discrimination is particularly problematic because such a regulation will inevitably favor certain groups of candidates. As the testimony in this case illustrates, several groups of candidates rely heavily on last-minute campaigning. Candidates with fewer resources, candidates for lower visibility offices, and "grassroots" candidates benefit disproportionately from last-minute campaigning near the polling place. * * *

* * * The plurality has effectively shifted the burden of proving the necessity of content discrimination from the State to the plaintiff. * * * Tennessee must shoulder the burden of demonstrating that its restrictions on political speech are no broader than necessary to protect orderly access to the polls. It has not done so.

I therefore respectfully dissent.

Notes and Questions

1.   What justification is there for setting the limit of the "campaign-free zone" at one hundred feet from the entrances to polling places? Why does the plurality conclude that a one-hundred-foot limit (as opposed to, for example, a twenty-five-foot limit) is narrowly tailored to prevent the risks of election fraud or voter intimidation? Does your answer suggest that the plurality is not, in fact, applying strict scrutiny? Consider, in this regard, the plurality's footnote 11 and the accompanying text.

2.   How far beyond one hundred feet can states extend "campaign-free zones" without violating the First Amendment? Justice Stevens noted that Kentucky and Wisconsin established five-hundred-foot zones; are they constitutional?

3.   Do you agree with Justice Stevens that there is essentially no justification for "campaign-free zones" outside polling places at all?

4.   Take another look at the statute. Within the designated area, the statute banned (1) "the display of campaign posters, signs or other campaign materials," (2) "distribution of campaign materials," and (3) "solicitation of votes." Are *all* of these prohibitions narrowly tailored ways of achieving compelling interests?

5.   Justice Scalia would treat areas outside polling places as non-public fora. Such a designation, however, does not enable the state to regulate speech any way it pleases. As Justice Scalia recognized, regulations of speech in non-public fora must be "reasonable" and "viewpoint-neutral." *See Perry Education Association v. Perry Local Educators' Association*, 460 U.S. 37, 46 (1983) ("In addition to time, place, and manner regulations, the state may reserve the forum for its intended purposes, communicative or otherwise, as long as the regulation on speech is reasonable and not an effort to suppress expression merely because public officials oppose the speaker's view.").

6.   *Problem.* The Town of Snyder is holding an election for its fire commissioners. On election day, the fire hall is used as a polling place, as it is for all municipal elections in Snyder. The Town's "campaign-free zone" law is identical to the one in *Freeman*. Voting booths are set up in the truck bay, adjacent to which each of the firemen keeps a locker containing fire-fighting equipment, civilian dress, toiletries, photos of loved ones, etc. The "lockers" have shelves and hooks for hanging clothing,

but there are no doors that can be closed to secure each individual's belongings. In one of the lockers, visible to voters as they approach the booths, is a bumper sticker supporting one candidate. On what bases may the situation be challenged? If the statute is enforced against the fireman displaying the bumper sticker, would he succeed on a challenge to such enforcement? Does it matter if he is a volunteer or employed by the Town?

7. *Problem.* Consider this variation on the previous Problem. Jim Sullivan is running for Fire Commissioner in Snyder. Sullivan owns the house adjacent to the fire hall, and as a result, his yard falls within the campaign-free zone. In the month leading up to the election, Sullivan displayed a sign on his yard promoting his candidacy. Must he remove the sign on the day of the election? Would it make any difference if the campaign-free zone encompassed a substantial part, but not the entirety, of Sullivan's yard?

8. *Problem.* At a school bond election where the same "campaign-free zone" restriction is in effect, voters casting ballots at the school must walk by a bulletin board on which is posted, with notices about the honor roll, assemblies, try-outs, and such, a notice saying, "Encourage Your Parents to Vote for the School Bonds on November 5." Has the Constitution been violated? If the proceeds are to fund a new roof for the school, can the school enforce the restriction and hold the election in a room that requires several garbage cans to catch leaking rainwater? *Cf.* Jeremy A. Blumenthal & Terry L. Turnipseed, *The Polling Place Priming (PPP) Effect: Is Voting in Churches (or Anywhere Else) Unconstitutional?*, 91 B.U.L. REV. 561 (2011) (suggesting that polling places may affect voting behavior, and offering absentee and convenience voting as a solution).

Chapter 11

COUNTING THE VOTES

A. INTRODUCTION

Throughout American history, the seemingly simple tasks of casting and counting votes have turned out to be anything but simple. Various techniques have been used in different parts of the country at different times — a lack of uniformity that persists to the present day. In some states early in the Republic, voting was a public, oral act. In other states, the voter wrote down his vote in a poll book underneath a picture of a candidate. By the end of the nineteenth century, spurred by the increasing number of elective offices, most jurisdictions required votes to be indicated on preprinted ballots, though sometimes political parties would themselves print and help tabulate these ballots. All jurisdictions eventually came to use a written "Australian" ballot prepared by the government, administered to permit anonymous voting. In the twentieth century, many jurisdictions came to use a variety of machines to collate and count these ballots. For a comprehensive overview of these developments, see ALEXANDER KEYSSAR, THE RIGHT TO VOTE: THE CONTESTED HISTORY OF DEMOCRACY IN THE UNITED STATES 23–24, 155, 261–62 (rev. ed. 2009).

Given the historical and contemporary differences among and within states regarding votes and ballots, generalizations must be made with caution. As you read the cases and materials in the balance of this Chapter, consider the following themes. One is that the administration of elections in general, and the counting of votes in particular, have become, or at least have been perceived as, partisan. For example, in thirty-three states the chief election officer, usually the Secretary of State, is elected as a partisan candidate. Critics have often accused such officers of making decisions for partisan reasons. This had led to calls for selecting election officials in nonpartisan ways.[a] Another theme includes efforts to centralize and nationalize the counting of votes, such as the Help America Vote Act (HAVA) of 2002, 52 U.S.C. § 20901 *et seq.*, passed by Congress in the wake of controversies

---

[a] For overviews of this controversy and calls for reform, see Jocelyn Friedrichs Benson, *Democracy and the Secretary: The Critical Role of Election Administrators in Promoting Accuracy and Access to Democracy*, 27 ST. LOUIS U. PUB. L. REV. 343 (2008); Richard L. Hasen, *Beyond the Margin of Litigation: Reforming U.S. Election Administration to Avoid Electoral Meltdown*, 62 WASH. & LEE L. REV. 937 (2005); David C. Kimball et al., *Helping America Vote? Election Administration, Partisanship, and Provisional Voting in the 2004 Election*, 5 ELECTION L.J. 447 (2006); Daniel P. Tokaji, *The Future of Election Reform*, 28 YALE L. & POL'Y REV. 125 (2009). *See also* Michael J. Pitts, *Defining "Partisan" Law Enforcement*, 18 STAN. L. & POL'Y REV. 324 (2007) (arguing that charges of partisan actions in this context are made too easily, and positing objective criteria to define true partisan actions).

surrounding the 2000 presidential election. HAVA and other such statutes are discussed below.

A third theme is a separation-of-powers concern that has pervaded this subject: What should the role of the judiciary be in policing partisanship in elections? Do the frequent charges of partisan administration of election law suggest that courts should take an aggressive, or conversely a more passive, stand in enforcing election laws? Should courts defer to legislative judgments regarding the administration of elections? Can the judiciary ensure that elections are administered fairly, or will courts that enter the political thicket only draw the same criticism that is directed at other political actors?

B. CONSTITUTIONAL LIMITS

While most choices about the methods of casting and tabulating votes are made at the state and local levels, federal law — including the Constitution — imposes limits on those choices. What follows is perhaps the most famous instance of federal-court oversight of state decisions concerning vote counting — the Supreme Court's decision striking down Florida's recount procedures in the 2000 presidential election between Republican George W. Bush and Democrat Al Gore.

Some background is necessary. While Gore had a substantial lead in the nationwide popular vote, the electoral college was much closer. As election night came to an end, it became clear that the winner of Florida's electoral votes would win the Presidency. Initial counts there showed that Bush had prevailed by 1784 votes out of approximately six million cast. But that was just the beginning.

The closeness of the election triggered a recount under state law. A machine recount was held, with Governor Bush determined still to be the winner. Vice President Gore then asked for a manual recount, prompting controversy over the procedures governing such a recount. In particular, authorities in Florida were obligated to divine the intent of voters by interpreting marks on ballots, and different vote-counters used different standards to assess whether the marks sufficiently indicated an intent to cast a vote. Whether the differences in vote-counting were consistent with the constitutional guarantee of "the equal protection of the laws" was the principal question ultimately faced by the Supreme Court in the opinion that follows.

But *Bush v. Gore* was not the Supreme Court's first entry into the 2000 election controversy. In *Bush v. Palm Beach County Canvassing Board*, 531 U.S. 70 (2000) (*per curiam*) (*Bush I*), the Court was presented with a challenge to the recount deadline established by the Florida Supreme Court. The Florida court, after noting the Florida Constitution's protection of the right to vote and the importance of counting every vote, had imposed a deadline of November 26, despite the relevant statutes' apparent selection of November 14. The Secretary of State objected that the court's reliance on the state constitution undermined the legislature's choice in violation of Article II, § 1, cl. 2 of the United States Constitution, which vests authority for determining the method of selecting presidential electors in state legislatures.

The Supreme Court did not decide the Article II issue, though. Instead, it vacated the Florida judgment and remanded to permit the Florida court more clearly to identify the source of its holding. On remand, the Florida Supreme Court maintained that its decision was strictly an interpretation of the Florida statutes, and it therefore professed to be following, rather than contravening, the desires of the Florida Legislature. *See Palm Beach County Canvassing Bd. v. Harris*, 772 So. 2d 1273 (Fla. 2000).

Simultaneously with the recount-deadline litigation, Gore pressed separate election contests seeking manual recounts in two counties, and eventually the Florida Supreme Court permitted the recounts to go forward. *Gore v. Harris*, 772 So. 2d 1243 (Fla. 2000). Republicans again appealed to the Supreme Court, which by a 5-4 vote stayed the lower court decision while the appeal was briefed and argued. *Bush v. Gore*, 531 U.S. 1046 (2000). As described in the opinion, the controversy in *Bush II* swirled around Florida's voting technology, the use of different ballot forms in different counties, and the process of conducting the recount that was mandated by Florida law, but *Bush I*'s concerns about the respective roles of courts and legislatures were not far in the background.

BUSH v. GORE
Supreme Court of the United States
531 U.S. 98, 121 S.Ct. 525, 148 L.Ed.2d 388 (2000).

Per Curiam. [Chief Justice Rehnquist, Justice O'Connor, Justice Scalia, Justice Kennedy, and Justice Thomas join in this opinion.] * * *

* * * On November 8, 2000, the day following the Presidential election, the Florida Division of Elections reported that petitioner Bush had received 2,909,135 votes, and respondent Gore had received 2,907,351 votes, a margin of 1,784 for Governor Bush. Because Governor Bush's margin of victory was less than "one-half of a percent . . . of the votes cast," an automatic machine recount was conducted under § 102.141(4) of the election code, the results of which showed Governor Bush still winning the race but by a diminished margin. Vice President Gore then sought manual recounts in Volusia, Palm Beach, Broward, and Miami-Dade Counties, pursuant to Florida's election protest provisions. Fla. Stat. Ann. § 102.166 (Supp. 2001). * * *

On November 26, the Florida Elections Canvassing Commission certified the results of the election and declared Governor Bush the winner of Florida's 25 electoral votes. On November 27, Vice President Gore, pursuant to Florida's contest provisions, filed a complaint in Leon County Circuit Court contesting the certification. Fla. Stat. Ann. § 102.168. He sought relief pursuant to § 102.168(3)(c), which provides that "[r]eceipt of a number of illegal votes or rejection of a number of legal votes sufficient to change or place in doubt the result of the election" shall be grounds for a contest. The Circuit Court denied relief, stating that Vice President Gore failed to meet his burden of proof. He appealed to the First District Court of Appeal, which certified the matter to the Florida Supreme Court.

Accepting jurisdiction, the Florida Supreme Court affirmed in part and reversed in part. The court held that the Circuit Court had been correct to reject Vice

President Gore's challenge to the results certified in Nassau County and his challenge to the Palm Beach County Canvassing Board's determination that 3,300 ballots cast in that county were not, in the statutory phrase, "legal votes."

The Supreme Court held that Vice President Gore had satisfied his burden of proof under § 102.168(3)(c) with respect to his challenge to Miami-Dade County's failure to tabulate, by manual count, 9,000 ballots on which the machines had failed to detect a vote for President ("undervotes"). Noting the closeness of the election, the court explained that "[o]n this record, there can be no question that there are legal votes within the 9,000 uncounted votes sufficient to place the results of this election in doubt." A "legal vote," as determined by the Supreme Court, is "one in which there is a 'clear indication of the intent of the voter.'" The court therefore ordered a hand recount of the 9,000 ballots in Miami-Dade County. * * *

The Supreme Court also determined that both Palm Beach County and Miami-Dade County, in their earlier manual recounts, had identified a net gain of 215 and 168 legal votes for Vice President Gore. Rejecting the Circuit Court's conclusion that Palm Beach County lacked the authority to include the 215 net votes submitted past the November 26 deadline, the Supreme Court explained that the deadline was not intended to exclude votes identified after that date through ongoing manual recounts. As to Miami-Dade County, the court concluded that although the 168 votes identified were the result of a partial recount, they were "legal votes [that] could change the outcome of the election." The Supreme Court therefore directed the Circuit Court to include those totals in the certified results, subject to resolution of the actual vote total from the Miami-Dade partial recount.

The petition presents the following questions: whether the Florida Supreme Court established new standards for resolving Presidential election contests, thereby violating Art. II, § 1, cl. 2, of the United States Constitution and failing to comply with 3 U.S.C. § 5, and whether the use of standardless manual recounts violates the Equal Protection and Due Process Clauses. With respect to the equal protection question, we find a violation of the Equal Protection Clause. * * *

The individual citizen has no federal constitutional right to vote for electors for the President of the United States unless and until the state legislature chooses a statewide election as the means to implement its power to appoint members of the electoral college. U.S. Const., Art. II, § 1. This is the source for the statement in *McPherson* v. *Blacker*, 146 U.S. 1, 35 (1892) [p. 1124], that the state legislature's power to select the manner for appointing electors is plenary; it may, if it so chooses, select the electors itself, which indeed was the manner used by state legislatures in several States for many years after the framing of our Constitution. History has now favored the voter, and in each of the several States the citizens themselves vote for Presidential electors. When the state legislature vests the right to vote for President in its people, the right to vote as the legislature has prescribed is fundamental; and one source of its fundamental nature lies in the equal weight accorded to each vote and the equal dignity owed to each voter. The State, of course, after granting the franchise in the special context of Article II, can take back the power to appoint electors. See *id.*, at 35 ("[T]here is no doubt of the right of the legislature to resume the power at any time, for it can neither be taken away nor abdicated").

The right to vote is protected in more than the initial allocation of the franchise. Equal protection applies as well to the manner of its exercise. Having once granted the right to vote on equal terms, the State may not, by later arbitrary and disparate treatment, value one person's vote over that of another. See, *e.g.*, *Harper v. Virginia Bd. of Elections*, 383 U.S. 663, 665 (1966) [p. 37] ("[O]nce the franchise is granted to the electorate, lines may not be drawn which are inconsistent with the Equal Protection Clause of the Fourteenth Amendment"). It must be remembered that "the right of suffrage can be denied by a debasement or dilution of the weight of a citizen's vote just as effectively as by wholly prohibiting the free exercise of the franchise." *Reynolds* v. *Sims*, 377 U.S. 533, 555 (1964) [p. 173].

There is no difference between the two sides of the present controversy on these basic propositions. Respondents say that the very purpose of vindicating the right to vote justifies the recount procedures now at issue. The question before us, however, is whether the recount procedures the Florida Supreme Court has adopted are consistent with its obligation to avoid arbitrary and disparate treatment of the members of its electorate.

Much of the controversy seems to revolve around ballot cards designed to be perforated by a stylus but which, either through error or deliberate omission, have not been perforated with sufficient precision for a machine to register the perforations. In some cases a piece of the card — a chad — is hanging, say, by two corners. In other cases there is no separation at all, just an indentation.

* * * The recount mechanisms implemented in response to the decisions of the Florida Supreme Court do not satisfy the minimum requirement for nonarbitrary treatment of voters necessary to secure the fundamental right. Florida's basic command for the count of legally cast votes is to consider the "intent of the voter." This is unobjectionable as an abstract proposition and a starting principle. The problem inheres in the absence of specific standards to ensure its equal application. The formulation of uniform rules to determine intent based on these recurring circumstances is practicable and, we conclude, necessary.

The law does not refrain from searching for the intent of the actor in a multitude of circumstances; and in some cases the general command to ascertain intent is not susceptible to much further refinement. In this instance, however, the question is not whether to believe a witness but how to interpret the marks or holes or scratches on an inanimate object, a piece of cardboard or paper which, it is said, might not have registered as a vote during the machine count. The factfinder confronts a thing, not a person. The search for intent can be confined by specific rules designed to ensure uniform treatment.

The want of those rules here has led to unequal evaluation of ballots in various respects. See [*Gore* v. *Harris*, 772 So. 2d 1243,] 1267 [(Fla. 2000)] (Wells, C.J., dissenting) ("Should a county canvassing board count or not count a 'dimpled chad' where the voter is able to successfully dislodge the chad in every other contest on that ballot? Here, the county canvassing boards disagree"). As seems to have been acknowledged at oral argument, the standards for accepting or rejecting contested ballots might vary not only from county to county but indeed within a single county from one recount team to another.

The record provides some examples. A monitor in Miami-Dade County testified at trial that he observed that three members of the county canvassing board applied different standards in defining a legal vote. And testimony at trial also revealed that at least one county changed its evaluative standards during the counting process. Palm Beach County, for example, began the process with a 1990 guideline which precluded counting completely attached chads, switched to a rule that considered a vote to be legal if any light could be seen through a chad, changed back to the 1990 rule, and then abandoned any pretense of a *per se* rule, only to have a court order that the county consider dimpled chads legal. This is not a process with sufficient guarantees of equal treatment. * * *

The State Supreme Court * * * mandated that the recount totals from two counties, Miami-Dade and Palm Beach, be included in the certified total. The court also appeared to hold *sub silentio* that the recount totals from Broward County, which were not completed until after the original November 14 certification by the Secretary, were to be considered part of the new certified vote totals even though the county certification was not contested by Vice President Gore. Yet each of the counties used varying standards to determine what was a legal vote. Broward County used a more forgiving standard than Palm Beach County, and uncovered almost three times as many new votes, a result markedly disproportionate to the difference in population between the counties.

In addition, the recounts in these three counties were not limited to so-called undervotes but extended to all of the ballots. The distinction has real consequences. A manual recount of all ballots identifies not only those ballots which show no vote but also those which contain more than one, the so-called overvotes. Neither category will be counted by the machine. This is not a trivial concern. At oral argument, respondents estimated there are as many as 110,000 overvotes statewide. As a result, the citizen whose ballot was not read by a machine because he failed to vote for a candidate in a way readable by a machine may still have his vote counted in a manual recount; on the other hand, the citizen who marks two candidates in a way discernible by the machine will not have the same opportunity to have his vote count, even if a manual examination of the ballot would reveal the requisite indicia of intent. Furthermore, the citizen who marks two candidates, only one of which is discernible by the machine, will have his vote counted even though it should have been read as an invalid ballot. The State Supreme Court's inclusion of vote counts based on these variant standards exemplifies concerns with the remedial processes that were under way.

That brings the analysis to yet a further equal protection problem. The votes certified by the court included a partial total from one county, Miami-Dade. The Florida Supreme Court's decision thus gives no assurance that the recounts included in a final certification must be complete. Indeed, it is respondents' submission that it would be consistent with the rules of the recount procedures to include whatever partial counts are done by the time of final certification, and we interpret the Florida Supreme Court's decision to permit this. * * * This accommodation no doubt results from the truncated contest period established by the Florida Supreme Court in *Palm Beach County Canvassing Bd.* v. *Harris*, at respondents' own urging. The press of time does not diminish the constitutional concern. A desire for speed is not a general excuse for ignoring equal protection guarantees.

In addition to these difficulties the actual process by which the votes were to be counted under the Florida Supreme Court's decision raises further concerns. That order did not specify who would recount the ballots. The county canvassing boards were forced to pull together ad hoc teams of judges from various Circuits who had no previous training in handling and interpreting ballots. Furthermore, while others were permitted to observe, they were prohibited from objecting during the recount.

The recount process, in its features here described, is inconsistent with the minimum procedures necessary to protect the fundamental right of each voter in the special instance of a statewide recount under the authority of a single state judicial officer. Our consideration is limited to the present circumstances, for the problem of equal protection in election processes generally presents many complexities.

The question before the Court is not whether local entities, in the exercise of their expertise, may develop different systems for implementing elections. Instead, we are presented with a situation where a state court with the power to assure uniformity has ordered a statewide recount with minimal procedural safeguards. When a court orders a statewide remedy, there must be at least some assurance that the rudimentary requirements of equal treatment and fundamental fairness are satisfied. * * *

Upon due consideration of the difficulties identified to this point, it is obvious that the recount cannot be conducted in compliance with the requirements of equal protection and due process without substantial additional work. It would require not only the adoption (after opportunity for argument) of adequate statewide standards for determining what is a legal vote, and practicable procedures to implement them, but also orderly judicial review of any disputed matters that might arise. In addition, the Secretary has advised that the recount of only a portion of the ballots requires that the vote tabulation equipment be used to screen out under-votes, a function for which the machines were not designed. If a recount of overvotes were also required, perhaps even a second screening would be necessary. Use of the equipment for this purpose, and any new software developed for it, would have to be evaluated for accuracy by the Secretary, as required by Fla. Stat. Ann. § 101.015.

The Supreme Court of Florida has said that the legislature intended the State's electors to "participat[e] fully in the federal electoral process," as provided in 3 U.S.C. § 5. [*Palm Beach County Canvassing Bd.* v. *Harris,*] 772 So. 2d [1273,] 1289 [(Fla. 2000) *(Harris II)*]; see also *Palm Beach County Canvassing Bd.* v. *Harris,* 772 So. 2d 1220, 1237 (Fla. 2000) [*(Harris I)*]. That statute, in turn, requires that any controversy or contest that is designed to lead to a conclusive selection of electors be completed by December 12. That date is upon us, and there is no recount procedure in place under the State Supreme Court's order that comports with minimal constitutional standards. Because it is evident that any recount seeking to meet the December 12 date will be unconstitutional for the reasons we have discussed, we reverse the judgment of the Supreme Court of Florida ordering a recount to proceed.

Seven Justices of the Court agree that there are constitutional problems with the recount ordered by the Florida Supreme Court that demand a remedy. See *post* (SOUTER, J., dissenting); *post* (BREYER, J., dissenting). The only disagreement is as to the remedy. Because the Florida Supreme Court has said that the Florida Legislature intended to obtain the safe-harbor benefits of 3 U.S.C. § 5, JUSTICE BREYER's proposed remedy — remanding to the Florida Supreme Court for its ordering of a constitutionally proper contest until December 18 — contemplates action in violation of the Florida Election Code, and hence could not be part of an "appropriate" order authorized by Fla. Stat. Ann. § 102.168(8). * * *

None are more conscious of the vital limits on judicial authority than are the Members of this Court, and none stand more in admiration of the Constitution's design to leave the selection of the President to the people, through their legislatures, and to the political sphere. When contending parties invoke the process of the courts, however, it becomes our unsought responsibility to resolve the federal and constitutional issues the judicial system has been forced to confront.

The judgment of the Supreme Court of Florida is reversed, and the case is remanded for further proceedings not inconsistent with this opinion.

It is so ordered.

CHIEF JUSTICE REHNQUIST, with whom JUSTICE SCALIA and JUSTICE THOMAS join, concurring. * * *

We deal here not with an ordinary election, but with an election for the President of the United States. * * *

In most cases, comity and respect for federalism compel us to defer to the decisions of state courts on issues of state law. That practice reflects our understanding that the decisions of state courts are definitive pronouncements of the will of the States as sovereigns. Of course, in ordinary cases, the distribution of powers among the branches of a State's government raises no questions of federal constitutional law, subject to the requirement that the government be republican in character. See U.S. Const., Art. IV, § 4. But there are a few exceptional cases in which the Constitution imposes a duty or confers a power on a particular branch of a State's government. This is one of them. Article II, § 1, cl. 2, provides that "[e]ach State shall appoint, in such Manner as the *Legislature* thereof may direct," electors for President and Vice President. (Emphasis added.) Thus, the text of the election law itself, and not just its interpretation by the courts of the States, takes on independent significance.

In *McPherson* v. *Blacker*, we explained that Art. II, § 1, cl. 2, "convey[s] the broadest power of determination" and "leaves it to the legislature exclusively to define the method" of appointment. A significant departure from the legislative scheme for appointing Presidential electors presents a federal constitutional question.

Title 3 U.S.C. § 5 informs our application of Art. II, § 1, cl. 2, to the Florida statutory scheme, which, as the Florida Supreme Court acknowledged, took that statute into account. Section 5 provides that the State's selection of electors "shall be conclusive, and shall govern in the counting of the electoral votes" if the electors are chosen under laws enacted prior to election day, and if the selection process is completed six days prior to the meeting of the electoral college. As we noted in *Bush v. Palm Beach County Canvassing Bd.*, 531 U.S. [70,] 78 [(2000) *(per curiam)*]:

> "Since § 5 contains a principle of federal law that would assure finality of the State's determination if made pursuant to a state law in effect before the election, a legislative wish to take advantage of the 'safe harbor' would counsel against any construction of the Election Code that Congress might deem to be a change in the law."

If we are to respect the legislature's Article II powers, therefore, we must ensure that postelection state-court actions do not frustrate the legislative desire to attain the "safe harbor" provided by § 5.

In Florida, the legislature has chosen to hold statewide elections to appoint the State's 25 electors. Importantly, the legislature has delegated the authority to run the elections and to oversee election disputes to the Secretary of State and to state circuit courts. Isolated sections of the code may well admit of more than one interpretation, but the general coherence of the legislative scheme may not be altered by judicial interpretation so as to wholly change the statutorily provided apportionment of responsibility among these various bodies. In any election but a Presidential election, the Florida Supreme Court can give as little or as much deference to Florida's executives as it chooses, so far as Article II is concerned, and this Court will have no cause to question the court's actions. But, with respect to a Presidential election, the court must be both mindful of the legislature's role under Article II in choosing the manner of appointing electors and deferential to those bodies expressly empowered by the legislature to carry out its constitutional mandate.

In order to determine whether a state court has infringed upon the legislature's authority, we necessarily must examine the law of the State as it existed prior to the action of the court. Though we generally defer to state courts on the interpretation of state law, there are of course areas in which the Constitution requires this Court to undertake an independent, if still deferential, analysis of state law. * * *

This inquiry does not imply a disrespect for state *courts* but rather a respect for the constitutionally prescribed role of state *legislatures.* To attach definitive weight to the pronouncement of a state court, when the very question at issue is whether the court has actually departed from the statutory meaning, would be to abdicate our responsibility to enforce the explicit requirements of Article II.

Acting pursuant to its constitutional grant of authority, the Florida Legislature has created a detailed, if not perfectly crafted, statutory scheme that provides for appointment of Presidential electors by direct election. * * *

The state legislature has also provided mechanisms both for protesting election returns and for contesting certified election results. Section 102.166 governs protests. Any protest must be filed prior to the certification of election results by the county canvassing board. § 102.166(4)(b). Once a protest has been filed, "[t]he county canvassing board may authorize a manual recount." § 102.166(4)(c). If a sample recount conducted pursuant to § 102.166(5) "indicates an error in the vote tabulation which could affect the outcome of the election," the county canvassing board is instructed to: "(a) Correct the error and recount the remaining precincts with the vote tabulation system; (b) Request the Department of State to verify the tabulation software; or (c) Manually recount all ballots," § 102.166(5). In the event a canvassing board chooses to conduct a manual recount of all ballots, § 102.166(7) prescribes procedures for such a recount.

Contests to the certification of an election, on the other hand, are controlled by § 102.168. The grounds for contesting an election include "[r]eceipt of a number of illegal votes or rejection of a number of legal votes sufficient to change or place in doubt the result of the election." § 102.168(3)(c). Any contest must be filed in the appropriate Florida circuit court, § 102.168(1), and the canvassing board or election board is the proper party defendant, § 102.168(4). Section 102.168(8) provides that "[t]he circuit judge to whom the contest is presented may fashion such orders as he or she deems necessary to ensure that each allegation in the complaint is investigated, examined, or checked, to prevent or correct any alleged wrong, and to provide any relief appropriate under such circumstances." In Presidential elections, the contest period necessarily terminates on the date set by 3 U.S.C. § 5 for concluding the State's "final determination" of election controversies.

In its first decision, *Harris I*, the Florida Supreme Court extended the 7-day statutory certification deadline established by the legislature. This modification of the code, by lengthening the protest period, necessarily shortened the contest period for Presidential elections. Underlying the extension of the certification deadline and the shortchanging of the contest period was, presumably, the clear implication that certification was a matter of significance: The certified winner would enjoy presumptive validity, making a contest proceeding by the losing candidate an uphill battle. In its latest opinion, however, the court empties certification of virtually all legal consequence during the contest, and in doing so departs from the provisions enacted by the Florida Legislature.

The court determined that canvassing boards' decisions regarding whether to recount ballots past the certification deadline (even the certification deadline established by *Harris I*) are to be reviewed *de novo*, although the Election Code clearly vests discretion whether to recount in the boards, and sets strict deadlines subject to the Secretary's rejection of late tallies and monetary fines for tardiness. See Fla. Stat. Ann. § 102.112. Moreover, the Florida court held that all late vote tallies arriving during the contest period should be automatically included in the certification regardless of the certification deadline (even the certification deadline established by *Harris I*), thus virtually eliminating both the deadline and the Secretary's discretion to disregard recounts that violate it.

Moreover, the court's interpretation of "legal vote," and hence its decision to order a contest-period recount, plainly departed from the legislative scheme. Florida statutory law cannot reasonably be thought to *require* the counting of improperly marked ballots. Each Florida precinct before election day provides instructions on how properly to cast a vote, Fla. Stat. Ann. § 101.46; each polling place on election day contains a working model of the voting machine it uses, Fla. Stat. Ann. § 101.5611; and each voting booth contains a sample ballot, § 101.46. In precincts using punchcard ballots, voters are instructed to punch out the ballot cleanly:

> "AFTER VOTING, CHECK YOUR BALLOT CARD TO BE SURE YOUR VOTING SELECTIONS ARE CLEARLY AND CLEANLY PUNCHED AND THERE ARE NO CHIPS LEFT HANGING ON THE BACK OF THE CARD."

No reasonable person would call it "an error in the vote tabulation," Fla. Stat. Ann. § 102.166(5), or a "rejection of . . . legal votes," § 102.168(3)(c), when electronic or electromechanical equipment performs precisely in the manner designed, and fails to count those ballots that are not marked in the manner that these voting instructions explicitly and prominently specify. The scheme that the Florida Supreme Court's opinion attributes to the legislature is one in which machines are *required* to be "capable of correctly counting votes," § 101.5606(4), but which nonetheless regularly produces elections in which legal votes are predictably *not* tabulated, so that in close elections manual recounts are regularly required. This is of course absurd. The Secretary, who is authorized by law to issue binding interpretations of the Election Code, §§ 97.012, 106.23, rejected this peculiar reading of the statutes. The Florida Supreme Court, although it must defer to the Secretary's interpretations, rejected her reasonable interpretation and embraced the peculiar one.

But as we indicated in our remand of the earlier case, in a Presidential election the clearly expressed intent of the legislature must prevail. And there is no basis for reading the Florida statutes as requiring the counting of improperly marked ballots, as an examination of the Florida Supreme Court's textual analysis shows. We will not parse that analysis here, except to note that the principal provision of the Election Code on which it relied, § 101.5614(5), was * * * entirely irrelevant. The State's Attorney General (who was supporting the Gore challenge) confirmed in oral argument here that never before the present election had a manual recount been conducted on the basis of the contention that "undervotes" should have been examined to determine voter intent. For the court to step away from this established practice, prescribed by the Secretary, the state official charged by the legislature with "responsibility to . . . [o]btain and maintain uniformity in the application, operation, and interpretation of the election laws," § 97.012(1), was to depart from the legislative scheme. * * *

Given all these factors, and in light of the legislative intent identified by the Florida Supreme Court to bring Florida within the "safe harbor" provision of 3 U.S.C. § 5, the remedy prescribed by the Supreme Court of Florida cannot be deemed an "appropriate" one as of December 8. It significantly departed from the statutory framework in place on November 7, and authorized open-ended further proceedings which could not be completed by December 12, thereby preventing a final determination by that date.

For these reasons, in addition to those given in the *per curiam* opinion, we would reverse.

JUSTICE STEVENS, with whom JUSTICE GINSBURG and JUSTICE BREYER join, dissenting.

The Constitution assigns to the States the primary responsibility for determining the manner of selecting the Presidential electors. See Art. II, § 1, cl. 2. When questions arise about the meaning of state laws, including election laws, it is our settled practice to accept the opinions of the highest courts of the States as providing the final answers. On rare occasions, however, either federal statutes or the Federal Constitution may require federal judicial intervention in state elections. This is not such an occasion.

The federal questions that ultimately emerged in this case are not substantial. Article II provides that "[e]ach *State* shall appoint, in such Manner as the Legislature *thereof* may direct, a Number of Electors." *Ibid.* (emphasis added). It does not create state legislatures out of whole cloth, but rather takes them as they come — as creatures born of, and constrained by, their state constitutions. Lest there be any doubt, we stated over 100 years ago in *McPherson* v. *Blacker*, 146 U.S., [at] 25, that "[w]hat is forbidden or required to be done by a State" in the Article II context "is forbidden or required of the legislative power under state constitutions as they exist." * * * The legislative power in Florida is subject to judicial review pursuant to Article V of the Florida Constitution, and nothing in Article II of the Federal Constitution frees the state legislature from the constraints in the State Constitution that created it. Moreover, the Florida Legislature's own decision to employ a unitary code for all elections indicates that it intended the Florida Supreme Court to play the same role in Presidential elections that it has historically played in resolving electoral disputes. The Florida Supreme Court's exercise of appellate jurisdiction therefore was wholly consistent with, and indeed contemplated by, the grant of authority in Article II.

It hardly needs stating that Congress, pursuant to 3 U.S.C. § 5, did not impose any affirmative duties upon the States that their governmental branches could "violate." Rather, § 5 provides a safe harbor for States to select electors in contested elections "by judicial or other methods" established by laws prior to the election day. Section 5, like Article II, assumes the involvement of the state judiciary in interpreting state election laws and resolving election disputes under those laws. Neither § 5 nor Article II grants federal judges any special authority to substitute their views for those of the state judiciary on matters of state law.

Nor are petitioners correct in asserting that the failure of the Florida Supreme Court to specify in detail the precise manner in which the "intent of the voter," Fla. Stat. Ann. § 101.5614(5), is to be determined rises to the level of a constitutional violation.[2] We found such a violation when individual votes within the same State were weighted unequally, see, *e.g.*, *Reynolds v. Sims*, 377 U.S., [at] 568, but we have never before called into question the substantive standard by which a State determines that a vote has been legally cast. And there is no reason to think that the guidance provided to the factfinders, specifically the various canvassing boards, by the "intent of the voter" standard is any less sufficient — or will lead to results any less uniform — than, for example, the "beyond a reasonable doubt" standard employed every day by ordinary citizens in courtrooms across this country.

---

[2] The Florida statutory standard is consistent with the practice of the majority of States, which apply either an "intent of the voter" standard or an "impossible to determine the elector's choice" standard in ballot recounts. * * *

Admittedly, the use of differing substandards for determining voter intent in different counties employing similar voting systems may raise serious concerns. Those concerns are alleviated — if not eliminated — by the fact that a single impartial magistrate will ultimately adjudicate all objections arising from the recount process. Of course, as a general matter, "[t]he interpretation of constitutional principles must not be too literal. We must remember that the machinery of government would not work if it were not allowed a little play in its joints." *Bain Peanut Co. of Tex.* v. *Pinson,* 282 U.S. 499, 501 (1931) (Holmes, J.). If it were otherwise, Florida's decision to leave to each county the determination of what balloting system to employ — despite enormous differences in accuracy[4] — might run afoul of equal protection. So, too, might the similar decisions of the vast majority of state legislatures to delegate to local authorities certain decisions with respect to voting systems and ballot design.

Even assuming that aspects of the remedial scheme might ultimately be found to violate the Equal Protection Clause, I could not subscribe to the majority's disposition of the case. As the majority explicitly holds, once a state legislature determines to select electors through a popular vote, the right to have one's vote counted is of constitutional stature. As the majority further acknowledges, Florida law holds that all ballots that reveal the intent of the voter constitute valid votes. Recognizing these principles, the majority nonetheless orders the termination of the contest proceeding before all such votes have been tabulated. Under their own reasoning, the appropriate course of action would be to remand to allow more specific procedures for implementing the legislature's uniform general standard to be established.

In the interest of finality, however, the majority effectively orders the disenfranchisement of an unknown number of voters whose ballots reveal their intent — and are therefore legal votes under state law — but were for some reason rejected by ballot-counting machines. It does so on the basis of the deadlines set forth in Title 3 of the United States Code. But, as I have already noted, those provisions merely provide rules of decision for Congress to follow when selecting among conflicting slates of electors. They do not prohibit a State from counting what the majority concedes to be legal votes until a bona fide winner is determined. Indeed, in 1960, Hawaii appointed two slates of electors and Congress chose to count the one appointed on January 4, 1961, well after the Title 3 deadlines. Thus, nothing prevents the majority, even if it properly found an equal protection violation, from ordering relief appropriate to remedy that violation without depriving Florida voters of their right to have their votes counted. As the majority notes, "[a] desire for speed is not a general excuse for ignoring equal protection guarantees."

Finally, neither in this case, nor in its earlier opinion in [*Harris I*] did the Florida Supreme Court make any substantive change in Florida electoral law. Its decisions were rooted in long-established precedent and were consistent with the relevant

---

[4] The percentage of nonvotes in this election in counties using a punchcard system was 3.92%; in contrast, the rate of error under the more modern optical-scan systems was only 1.43%. Put in other terms, for every 10,000 votes cast, punchcard systems result in 250 more nonvotes than optical-scan systems. A total of 3,718,305 votes were cast under punchcard systems, and 2,353,811 votes were cast under optical-scan systems.

statutory provisions, taken as a whole. It did what courts do — it decided the case before it in light of the legislature's intent to leave no legally cast vote uncounted. In so doing, it relied on the sufficiency of the general "intent of the voter" standard articulated by the state legislature, coupled with a procedure for ultimate review by an impartial judge, to resolve the concern about disparate evaluations of contested ballots. If we assume — as I do — that the members of that court and the judges who would have carried out its mandate are impartial, its decision does not even raise a colorable federal question.

What must underlie petitioners' entire federal assault on the Florida election procedures is an unstated lack of confidence in the impartiality and capacity of the state judges who would make the critical decisions if the vote count were to proceed. Otherwise, their position is wholly without merit. The endorsement of that position by the majority of this Court can only lend credence to the most cynical appraisal of the work of judges throughout the land. It is confidence in the men and women who administer the judicial system that is the true backbone of the rule of law. Time will one day heal the wound to that confidence that will be inflicted by today's decision. One thing, however, is certain. Although we may never know with complete certainty the identity of the winner of this year's Presidential election, the identity of the loser is perfectly clear. It is the Nation's confidence in the judge as an impartial guardian of the rule of law.

I respectfully dissent.

JUSTICE SOUTER, with whom JUSTICE BREYER joins, * * * dissenting. * * *

Petitioners have raised an equal protection claim (or, alternatively, a due process claim), in the charge that unjustifiably disparate standards are applied in different electoral jurisdictions to otherwise identical facts. It is true that the Equal Protection Clause does not forbid the use of a variety of voting mechanisms within a jurisdiction, even though different mechanisms will have different levels of effectiveness in recording voters' intentions; local variety can be justified by concerns about cost, the potential value of innovation, and so on. But evidence in the record here suggests that a different order of disparity obtains under rules for determining a voter's intent that have been applied (and could continue to be applied) to identical types of ballots used in identical brands of machines and exhibiting identical physical characteristics (such as "hanging" or "dimpled" chads). I can conceive of no legitimate state interest served by these differing treatments of the expressions of voters' fundamental rights. The differences appear wholly arbitrary.

In deciding what to do about this, we should take account of the fact that electoral votes are due to be cast in six days. I would therefore remand the case to the courts of Florida with instructions to establish uniform standards for evaluating the several types of ballots that have prompted differing treatments, to be applied within and among counties when passing on such identical ballots in any further recounting (or successive recounting) that the courts might order.

Unlike the majority, I see no warrant for this Court to assume that Florida could not possibly comply with this requirement before the date set for the meeting of electors, December 18. Although one of the dissenting justices of the State Supreme Court estimated that disparate standards potentially affected 170,000 votes, the number at issue is significantly smaller. The 170,000 figure apparently represents all uncounted votes, both undervotes (those for which no Presidential choice was recorded by a machine) and overvotes (those rejected because of votes for more than one candidate). But as JUSTICE BREYER has pointed out, no showing has been made of legal overvotes uncounted, and counsel for Gore made an uncontradicted representation to the Court that the statewide total of undervotes is about 60,000. To recount these manually would be a tall order, but before this Court stayed the effort to do that the courts of Florida were ready to do their best to get that job done. There is no justification for denying the State the opportunity to try to count all disputed ballots now.

I respectfully dissent.

JUSTICE GINSBURG, with whom JUSTICE STEVENS joins, and with whom JUSTICE SOUTER and JUSTICE BREYER join as to Part I, dissenting.

I

THE CHIEF JUSTICE acknowledges that provisions of Florida's Election Code "may well admit of more than one interpretation." But instead of respecting the state high court's province to say what the State's Election Code means, THE CHIEF JUSTICE maintains that Florida's Supreme Court has veered so far from the ordinary practice of judicial review that what it did cannot properly be called judging. My colleagues have offered a reasonable construction of Florida's law. Their construction coincides with the view of one of Florida's seven Supreme Court justices. I might join THE CHIEF JUSTICE were it my commission to interpret Florida law. But disagreement with the Florida court's interpretation of its own State's law does not warrant the conclusion that the justices of that court have legislated. There is no cause here to believe that the members of Florida's high court have done less than "their mortal best to discharge their oath of office," and no cause to upset their reasoned interpretation of Florida law. * * *

No doubt there are cases in which the proper application of federal law may hinge on interpretations of state law. Unavoidably, this Court must sometimes examine state law in order to protect federal rights. But we have dealt with such cases ever mindful of the full measure of respect we owe to interpretations of state law by a State's highest court. * * *

II

I agree with JUSTICE STEVENS that petitioners have not presented a substantial equal protection claim. Ideally, perfection would be the appropriate standard for judging the recount. But we live in an imperfect world, one in which thousands of votes have not been counted. I cannot agree that the recount adopted by the Florida court, flawed as it may be, would yield a result any less fair or precise than the certification that preceded that recount.

Even if there were an equal protection violation, I would agree with JUSTICE

STEVENS, JUSTICE SOUTER, and JUSTICE BREYER that the Court's concern about "the December 12 deadline" is misplaced. * * * Were that date to pass, Florida would still be entitled to deliver electoral votes Congress *must* count unless both Houses find that the votes "ha[d] not been . . . regularly given." * * *

I dissent.

JUSTICE BREYER, with whom JUSTICE STEVENS and JUSTICE GINSBURG join except as to Part I-A-1, and with whom JUSTICE SOUTER joins as to Part I, dissenting.

The Court was wrong to take this case. It was wrong to grant a stay. It should now vacate that stay and permit the Florida Supreme Court to decide whether the recount should resume.

I

The political implications of this case for the country are momentous. But the federal legal questions presented, with one exception, are insubstantial.

A
1

The majority raises three equal protection problems with the Florida Supreme Court's recount order: first, the failure to include overvotes in the manual recount; second, the fact that *all* ballots, rather than simply the undervotes, were recounted in some, but not all, counties; and third, the absence of a uniform, specific standard to guide the recounts. As far as the first issue is concerned, petitioners presented no evidence, to this Court or to any Florida court, that a manual recount of overvotes would identify additional legal votes. The same is true of the second, and, in addition, the majority's reasoning would seem to invalidate any state provision for a manual recount of individual counties in a statewide election.

The majority's third concern does implicate principles of fundamental fairness. The majority concludes that the Equal Protection Clause requires that a manual recount be governed not only by the uniform general standard of the "clear intent of the voter," but also by uniform subsidiary standards (for example, a uniform determination whether indented, but not perforated, "undervotes" should count). The opinion points out that the Florida Supreme Court ordered the inclusion of Broward County's undercounted "legal votes" even though those votes included ballots that were not perforated but simply "dimpled," while newly recounted ballots from other counties will likely include only votes determined to be "legal" on the basis of a stricter standard. In light of our previous remand, the Florida Supreme Court may have been reluctant to adopt a more specific standard than that provided for by the legislature for fear of exceeding its authority under Article II. However, since the use of different standards could favor one or the other of the candidates, since time was, and is, too short to permit the lower courts to iron out significant differences through ordinary judicial review, and since the relevant distinction was embodied in the order of the State's highest court, I agree that, in these very special circumstances, basic principles of fairness may well have counseled the adoption of a uniform standard to address the problem. In light of the majority's disposition, I need not decide whether, or the extent to which, as a remedial matter, the Constitution would place limits upon the content of the uniform standard.

2

Nonetheless, there is no justification for the majority's remedy, which is simply to reverse the lower court and halt the recount entirely. An appropriate remedy would be, instead, to remand this case with instructions that, even at this late date, would permit the Florida Supreme Court to require recounting *all* undercounted votes in Florida, including those from Broward, Volusia, Palm Beach, and Miami-Dade Counties, whether or not previously recounted prior to the end of the protest period, and to do so in accordance with a single uniform standard.

The majority justifies stopping the recount entirely on the ground that there is no more time. In particular, the majority relies on the lack of time for the Secretary of State to review and approve equipment needed to separate undervotes. But the majority reaches this conclusion in the absence of *any* record evidence that the recount could not have been completed in the time allowed by the Florida Supreme Court. The majority finds facts outside of the record on matters that state courts are in a far better position to address. Of course, it is too late for any such recount to take place by December 12, the date by which election disputes must be decided if a State is to take advantage of the safe harbor provisions of 3 U.S.C. § 5. Whether there is time to conduct a recount prior to December 18, when the electors are scheduled to meet, is a matter for the state courts to determine. And whether, under Florida law, Florida could or could not take further action is obviously a matter for Florida courts, not this Court, to decide.

By halting the manual recount, and thus ensuring that the uncounted legal votes will not be counted under any standard, this Court crafts a remedy out of proportion to the asserted harm. And that remedy harms the very fairness interests the Court is attempting to protect. The manual recount would itself redress a problem of unequal treatment of ballots. As JUSTICE STEVENS points out, the ballots of voters in counties that use punchcard systems are more likely to be disqualified than those in counties using optical-scanning systems. According to recent news reports, variations in the undervote rate are even more pronounced. Thus, in a system that allows counties to use different types of voting systems, voters already arrive at the polls with an unequal chance that their votes will be counted. I do not see how the fact that this results from counties' selection of different voting machines rather than a court order makes the outcome any more fair. Nor do I understand why the Florida Supreme Court's recount order, which helps to redress this inequity, must be entirely prohibited based on a deficiency that could easily be remedied.

B

The remainder of petitioners' claims, which are the focus of THE CHIEF JUSTICE's concurrence, raise no significant federal questions. * * *

II

Despite the reminder that this case involves "an election for the President of the United States," no preeminent legal concern, or practical concern related to legal questions, required this Court to hear this case, let alone to issue a stay that stopped Florida's recount process in its tracks. With one exception, petitioners' claims do not ask us to vindicate a constitutional provision designed to protect a basic human right. Petitioners invoke fundamental fairness, namely, the need for procedural fairness, including finality. But with the one "equal protection" exception, they rely upon law that focuses, not upon that basic need, but upon the constitutional allocation of power. Respondents invoke a competing fundamental consideration — the need to determine the voter's true intent. But they look to state law, not to federal constitutional law, to protect that interest. Neither side claims electoral fraud, dishonesty, or the like. And the more fundamental equal protection claim might have been left to the state court to resolve if and when it was discovered to have mattered. It could still be resolved through a remand conditioned upon issuance of a uniform standard; it does not require reversing the Florida Supreme Court.

Of course, the selection of the President is of fundamental national importance. But that importance is political, not legal. And this Court should resist the temptation unnecessarily to resolve tangential legal disputes, where doing so threatens to determine the outcome of the election.

The Constitution and federal statutes themselves make clear that restraint is appropriate. They set forth a road-map of how to resolve disputes about electors, even after an election as close as this one. That road-map foresees resolution of electoral disputes by *state* courts. See 3 U.S.C. § 5 (providing that, where a "State shall have provided, by laws enacted prior to [election day], for its final determination of any controversy or contest concerning the appointment of . . . electors . . . by *judicial* or other methods," the subsequently chosen electors enter a safe harbor free from congressional challenge). But it nowhere provides for involvement by the United States Supreme Court.

To the contrary, the Twelfth Amendment commits to Congress the authority and responsibility to count electoral votes. A federal statute, the Electoral Count Act, enacted after the close 1876 Hayes-Tilden Presidential election, specifies that, after States have tried to resolve disputes (through "judicial" or other means), Congress is the body primarily authorized to resolve remaining disputes. See Electoral Count Act of 1887, 3 U.S.C. §§ 5, 6, and 15.

The legislative history of the Act makes clear its intent to commit the power to resolve such disputes to Congress, rather than the courts * * *.

Given this detailed, comprehensive scheme for counting electoral votes, there is no reason to believe that federal law either foresees or requires resolution of such a political issue by this Court. Nor, for that matter, is there any reason to think that the Constitution's Framers would have reached a different conclusion. Madison, at least, believed that allowing the judiciary to choose the Presidential electors "was out of the question."

The decision by both the Constitution's Framers and the 1886 Congress to minimize this Court's role in resolving close federal Presidential elections is as wise as it is clear. However awkward or difficult it may be for Congress to resolve difficult electoral disputes, Congress, being a political body, expresses the people's will far more accurately than does an unelected Court. And the people's will is what elections are about.

Moreover, Congress was fully aware of the danger that would arise should it ask judges, unarmed with appropriate legal standards, to resolve a hotly contested Presidential election contest. Just after the 1876 Presidential election, Florida, South Carolina, and Louisiana each sent two slates of electors to Washington. Without these States, Tilden, the Democrat, had 184 electoral votes, one short of the number required to win the Presidency. With those States, Hayes, his Republican opponent, would have had 185. In order to choose between the two slates of electors, Congress decided to appoint an electoral commission composed of five Senators, five Representatives, and five Supreme Court Justices. * * *

The Commission divided along partisan lines, and the responsibility to cast the deciding vote fell to Justice Bradley. He decided to accept the votes by the Republican electors, and thereby awarded the Presidency to Hayes.

Justice Bradley immediately became the subject of vociferous attacks. Bradley was accused of accepting bribes, of being captured by railroad interests, and of an eleventh-hour change in position after a night in which his house "was surrounded by the carriages" of Republican partisans and railroad officials. Many years later, Professor Bickel concluded that Bradley was honest and impartial. He thought that " 'the great question' for Bradley was, in fact, whether Congress was entitled to go behind election returns or had to accept them as certified by state authorities," an "issue of principle." The Least Dangerous Branch 185 (1962). Nonetheless, Bickel points out, the legal question upon which Justice Bradley's decision turned was not very important in the contemporaneous political context. He says that "in the circumstances the issue of principle was trivial, it was overwhelmed by all that hung in the balance, and it should not have been decisive." *Ibid.*

For present purposes, the relevance of this history lies in the fact that the participation in the work of the electoral commission by five Justices, including Justice Bradley, did not lend that process legitimacy. Nor did it assure the public that the process had worked fairly, guided by the law. Rather, it simply embroiled Members of the Court in partisan conflict, thereby undermining respect for the judicial process. And the Congress that later enacted the Electoral Count Act knew it.

This history may help to explain why I think it not only legally wrong, but also most unfortunate, for the Court simply to have terminated the Florida recount. Those who caution judicial restraint in resolving political disputes have described the quintessential case for that restraint as a case marked, among other things, by the "strangeness of the issue," its "intractability to principled resolution," its "sheer momentousness, . . . which tends to unbalance judicial judgment," and "the inner vulnerability, the self-doubt of an institution which is electorally irresponsible and has no earth to draw strength from." Those characteristics mark this case.

At the same time, as I have said, the Court is not acting to vindicate a fundamental constitutional principle, such as the need to protect a basic human liberty. No other strong reason to act is present. Congressional statutes tend to obviate the need. And, above all, in this highly politicized matter, the appearance of a split decision runs the risk of undermining the public's confidence in the Court itself. That confidence is a public treasure. It has been built slowly over many years, some of which were marked by a Civil War and the tragedy of segregation. It is a vitally necessary ingredient of any successful effort to protect basic liberty and, indeed, the rule of law itself. We run no risk of returning to the days when a President (responding to this Court's efforts to protect the Cherokee Indians) might have said, "John Marshall has made his decision; now let him enforce it!" But we do risk a self-inflicted wound — a wound that may harm not just the Court, but the Nation.

I fear that in order to bring this agonizingly long election process to a definitive conclusion, we have not adequately attended to that necessary "check upon our own exercise of power," "our own sense of self-restraint." Justice Brandeis once said of the Court, "The most important thing we do is not doing." What it does today, the Court should have left undone. I would repair the damage done as best we now can, by permitting the Florida recount to continue under uniform standards.

I respectfully dissent.

Notes and Questions

1.   It is difficult to overstate the attention and controversy that accompanied the *Bush v. Gore* litigation and its aftermath. The complex litigation that ensued played out over but a few weeks and was predicated on one of the closest presidential elections in American history. For useful overviews, see HOWARD GILLMAN, THE VOTES THAT COUNTED: HOW THE SUPREME COURT DECIDED THE 2000 PRESIDENTIAL ELECTION (2001); ABNER GREENE, UNDERSTANDING THE 2000 ELECTION: A GUIDE TO THE LEGAL BATTLES THAT DECIDED THE PRESIDENCY (2001).

2.   It is also difficult to overstate the controversy in the legal academy's response to *Bush v. Gore*. One branch of scholarly response took seriously the doctrinal and statutory analysis of the various opinions, and subjected them to traditional academic scrutiny. The focal point of much of this literature was whether the equal-protection analysis of the *per curiam* opinion properly followed from *Reynolds v. Sims* and other one-person, one-vote decisions. A second branch of scholarship took the analysis of the opinions (particularly those of the Justices constituting the majority) less seriously, and to varying degrees charged that the decision was a result-oriented attempt by Republican-appointed Justices to install a Republican President. It likewise bears mentioning that the Florida Supreme Court at this time was dominated by Democratic appointees.[b] For an overview and

---

[b]   For a small sampling of the enormous scholarly literature, see the numerous essays collected in BUSH V. GORE: THE QUESTION OF LEGITIMACY (Bruce Ackerman ed., 2002); THE VOTE: BUSH, GORE, AND THE

critique of both branches of scholarship, see Richard L. Hasen, *A Critical Guide to Bush v. Gore Scholarship*, 7 ANN. REV. POL. SCI. 297 (2004). Most scholars were very critical of the decision, though the decision has not gone unsupported by academics.[c]

3. The Article II rationale applied by the concurring opinion of Chief Justice Rehnquist in *Bush v. Gore* also attracted its share of scholarly attention. *Compare* Hayward H. Smith, *History of the Article II Independent State Legislature Doctrine*, 29 FLA. ST. U. L. REV. 731 (2001) (arguing that the provision was not intended to favor state legislatures to the exclusion of state courts), *and* Harold J. Krent, *Judging Judging: The Problem of Second-Guessing State Judges' Interpretation of State Law in* Bush v. Gore, 29 FLA. ST. U. L. REV. 493 (2001) (arguing that the Florida Supreme Court's construction of state election statutes was plausible), *with* Richard A. Posner, *Florida 2000: A Legal and Statistical Analysis of the Election Deadlock and Ensuing Litigation*, 2000 SUP. CT. REV. 1, 26 (charging that the Florida Supreme Court engaged in a "patent misreading of the election statute"). The Article II issue can come up in other settings, such as when state courts interpret state statutes that regulate other federal elections, and its resolution can implicate related constitutional issues (*e.g.*, Art. I, § 4, of the U.S. Constitution, which vests in state legislatures the power to set rules for choosing members of Congress, absent congressional action). For discussion of these possibilities, see Richard L. Hasen, *The Democracy Canon*, 62 STAN. L. REV. 69, 113-22 (2009).

4. Chief Justice Rehnquist and Justices Scalia and Thomas would have held that the Florida Supreme Court's interpretation of that state's election statutes was so unreasonable as to go beyond the judicial role and invade the prerogative of the Florida Legislature to select the manner of appointing presidential electors. Does Chief Justice Rehnquist provide a judicially manageable standard for distinguishing between a judicial interpretation that is "absurd" and one that is merely wrong? Is it possible to develop such a standard?

5. *Problem.* As Justice Stevens pointed out in dissent, different parts of an individual state often use different methods of tabulating votes, despite the fact that those different methods have different rates of rejecting votes. Is that discrepancy unconstitutional under the majority's reasoning? Suppose Voter A lives in a county that uses optical-scan technology, while Voter B's county uses punchcards. If Justice Stevens's statistics are accurate, it is more than twice as likely that Voter B's vote will be rejected than that Voter A's will. If Voter B brings an equal-protection challenge, should he succeed?

Consider *Stewart v. Blackwell*, 444 F.3d 843 (6th Cir. 2006), in which a divided court struck down Ohio's then-in-use punchcard system for counting votes. *Bush v.*

SUPREME COURT (Cass R. Sunstein & Richard A. Epstein eds., 2001); and *Symposium, The Law of Presidential Elections: Issues in the Wake of Florida 2000*, 29 FLA. ST. U. L. REV. 325 (2001).

[c] *Compare, e.g.*, Jack M. Balkin, Bush v. Gore *and the Boundary Between Law and Politics*, 110 YALE L.J. 1407 (2001), which itself is criticized as being partisan in Robert J. Pushaw, Jr., *Politics, Ideology, and the Academic Assault on* Bush v. Gore, 2 ELECTION L.J. 97 (2003), *with, e.g.*, Einer Elhauge, *The Lessons of Florida 2000*, 110 POL'Y REV. 15 (Dec. 2001 & Jan. 2002); Nelson Lund, Bush v. Gore *at the Dawning of the Age of Obama*, 61 FLA. L. REV. 1101 (2009).

Gore and related cases, the majority held, called for strict scrutiny to be applied to state practices that impaired the right to vote. The dissent argued that *Bush v. Gore* called for the application of rational-basis scrutiny, and in any event was a limited precedent not "designed to fundamentally transform federal election law." *Id.* at 887 (Gilman, J., dissenting). The Sixth Circuit granted the Ohio Secretary of State's motion to rehear the case en banc, and then dismissed the case as moot, 473 F.3d 692 (6th Cir. 2007), because Ohio had replaced the punch-card technology. For an extensive analysis of the challenge to Ohio procedures in the case, see Richard B. Saphire & Paul Moke, *Litigating* Bush v. Gore *in the States: Dual Voting Systems and the Fourteenth Amendment*, 51 VILL. L. REV. 229 (2006).

6. *Stewart v. Blackwell* notwithstanding, most challenges to state election procedures under *Bush v. Gore* have failed. *See, e.g.*, *Wexler v. Anderson*, 452 F.3d 1226 (11th Cir. 2006) (holding that Florida's recount procedures for counties employing paperless touch-screen voting machines did not violate equal protection or due process, since strict scrutiny was not appropriate and the state had rational regulatory reasons to employ different recount procedures in counties with different voting machines); *Southwest Voter Registration Project v. Shelley*, 344 F.3d 914 (9th Cir. 2003) (en banc) (refusing to enjoin California's gubernatorial recall election despite continued use of punchcard technology); *Coleman v. Franken*, 767 N.W.2d 453 (Minn. 2009) (discussed in ch. 12); *Miller v. Treadwell*, 245 P.3d 867 (Alaska 2010) (write-in votes properly counted since statutes did not require exact spellings); *SEIU v. Husted*, 698 F.3d 341 (6th Cir. 2012) (*per curiam*) (state need not count provisional ballots case in the wrong polling place, even if due to poll worker error).

7. A few challenges to state election procedures employing *Bush v. Gore* have succeeded. Curiously, most have come from Ohio and in the Sixth Circuit. *See, e.g.*, *League of Women Voters of Ohio v. Brunner*, 548 F.3d 463 (6th Cir. 2008) (problems regarding election administration, voter registration, the training of poll workers, the organization of polling places, the allocation of voting equipment, and other matters violated equal protection and substantive due process); *Northeast Ohio Coalition for the Homeless v. Husted*, 696 F.3d 580 (6th Cir. 2012) (*per curiam*) (addressing disparate treatment of deficient provisional ballots, including those cast in the wrong precinct due to poll worker error); *Obama for America v. Husted*, 697 F.3d 423 (6th Cir. 2012) (state could not give only military and overseas voters preferential treatment regarding early absentee voting). *See generally* Richard L. Hasen, *The 2012 Voting Wars, Judicial Backstops, and the Resurrection of* Bush v. Gore, 81 GEO. WASH. L. REV. 1865 (2013).

C. THE HELP AMERICA VOTE ACT

The 2000 election debacle produced widespread agreement that America's voting processes needed to be improved. One of the responses from Congress was the passage of the Help America Vote Act of 2002 (HAVA), 52 U.S.C. § 20901 *et seq.*, which was designed to aid and encourage states to improve and upgrade their election administration. The law reflected Democratic desires to improve access to the ballot, and Republican concerns over the integrity of the voting process. HAVA in its Title I authorized federal funds to states to lead to that result, and in Title II set up a new agency, the Election Assistance Commission (EAC). Title III imposed certain requirements on states with regard to voting-equipment standards, registration databases, identification requirements for first-time voters, and provisional voting. For discussion of the enactment of HAVA, see Leonard M. Shambon, *Implementing the Help America Vote Act*, 3 ELECTION L.J. 424 (2004). The following case involves a dispute concerning HAVA's provisional-ballot language.

SANDUSKY COUNTY DEMOCRATIC PARTY v. BLACKWELL
United States Court of Appeals for the Sixth Circuit
387 F.3d 565 (6th Cir. 2004)

PER CURIAM. [CHIEF JUDGE BOGGS, CIRCUIT JUDGE GILMAN, and DISTRICT JUDGE WEBER (sitting by designation) join in this opinion.]

At bottom, this is a case of statutory interpretation. Does the Help America Vote Act require that all states count votes (at least for most federal elections) cast by provisional ballot as legal votes, even if cast in a precinct in which the voter does not reside, so long as they are cast within a "jurisdiction" that may be as large as a city or county of millions of citizens? We hold that neither the statutory text or structure, the legislative history, nor the understanding, until now, of those concerned with voting procedures compels or even permits that conclusion. Thus, although we affirm many of the rulings of the district court and its proper orders requiring compliance with HAVA's requirements for the casting of provisional ballots, we hold that ballots cast in a precinct where the voter does not reside and which would be invalid under state law for that reason are not required by HAVA to be considered legal votes.

To hold otherwise would interpret Congress's reasonably clear procedural language to mean that political parties would now be authorized to marshal their supporters at the last minute from shopping centers, office buildings, or factories, and urge them to vote at whatever polling place happened to be handy, all in an effort to turn out every last vote regardless of state law and historical practice. We do not believe that Congress quietly worked such a revolution in America's voting procedures, and we will not order it.

The States long have been primarily responsible for regulating federal, state, and local elections. These regulations have covered a range of issues, from registration requirements to eligibility requirements to ballot requirements to vote-counting requirements. One aspect common to elections in almost every state is that voters are required to vote in a particular precinct. Indeed, in at least 27 of the states using a precinct voting system, including Ohio, a voter's ballot will only be counted as a valid ballot if it is cast in the correct precinct.

The advantages of the precinct system are significant and numerous: it caps the number of voters attempting to vote in the same place on election day; it allows each precinct ballot to list all of the votes a citizen may cast for all pertinent federal, state, and local elections, referenda, initiatives, and levies; it allows each precinct ballot to list only those votes a citizen may cast, making ballots less confusing; it makes it easier for election officials to monitor votes and prevent election fraud; and it generally puts polling places in closer proximity to voter residences.

The responsibility and authority of the States in this field are not without limit. Although the United States Constitution, and Supreme Court decisions interpreting the Constitution, give primary responsibility for administering and regulating elections to the States, the States must adhere to certain constitutional and statutory requirements. States may not in any election deny or abridge the right to vote on the basis of race, *see* U.S. Const. amend. XV § 1, for example, and must adhere to the principle of one person, one vote, *see Reynolds v. Sims*, 377 U.S. 533, 565–566 (1964) [p. 173]. In addition, Congress has imposed upon the States certain statutory requirements for the administration of federal elections, such as the National Voter Registration Act, 42 U.S.C. § 1973gg *et seq.* ("NVRA"). In 2002, Congress passed the Help America Vote Act (codified at 42 U.S.C. § 15301 *et seq.*) ("HAVA"), which is the subject of this appeal.

HAVA was passed in order to alleviate "a significant problem voters experience[, which] is to arrive at the polling place believing that they are eligible to vote, and then to be turned away because the election workers cannot find their names on the list of qualified voters." H.R. Rep. 107–329 at 38 (2001). HAVA dealt with this problem by creating a system for provisional balloting, that is, a system under which a ballot would be submitted on election day but counted if and only if the person was later determined to have been entitled to vote.

Section 302 of HAVA, the section most pertinent to this appeal, requires States to provide voters with the opportunity to cast provisional ballots and to post certain information about provisional ballots at polling places on election day. The section's requirements relating to the casting of provisional ballots are as follows:

(a) Provisional voting requirements. If an individual declares that such individual is a registered voter in the jurisdiction in which the individual desires to vote and that the individual is eligible to vote in an election for Federal office, but the name of the individual does not appear on the official list of eligible voters for the polling place or an election official asserts that the individual is not eligible to vote, such individual shall be permitted to cast a provisional ballot as follows:

   (1) An election official at the polling place shall notify the individual that the individual may cast a provisional ballot in that election.

   (2) The individual shall be permitted to cast a provisional ballot at that polling place upon the execution of a written affirmation by the individual before an election official at the polling place stating that the individual is —

      (A) a registered voter in the jurisdiction in which the individual desires to vote; and

      (B) eligible to vote in that election.

   (3) An election official at the polling place shall transmit the ballot cast by the individual or the voter information contained in the written affirmation executed by the individual under paragraph (2) to an appropriate State or local election official for prompt verification under paragraph (4).

> (4)   If the appropriate State or local election official to whom the ballot or voter information is transmitted under paragraph (3) determines that the individual is eligible under State law to vote, the individual's provisional ballot shall be counted as a vote in that election in accordance with State law. * * *

42 U.S.C. § 15482.

In essence, HAVA's provisional voting section is designed to recognize, and compensate for, the improbability of "perfect knowledge" on the part of local election officials. * * * "On further review — when, one hopes, perfect or at least more perfect knowledge will be available — the vote will be counted or not, depending on whether the person was indeed entitled to vote at that time and place."

On September 27, 2004, the Sandusky County Democratic Party, the Ohio Democratic Party, and three labor unions ("Appellees") filed an action in the United States District Court for the Northern District of Ohio against J. Kenneth Blackwell, Ohio Secretary of State. Appellees' Complaint alleged that the Secretary's promulgation to Ohio County Boards of Elections of Ohio Secretary of State Directive 2004-33 conflicts with the requirements of HAVA. Directive 2004-33 states, in pertinent part, that:

> State law further provides that an eligible elector who moves from one Ohio precinct to another before an election may * * * update his or her existing voter registration to the new voting residence address and vote a provisional ballot for the precinct in which the person's new voting residence is located. The provisional ballot will be counted in the official canvass if the county board of elections confirms that the person was timely registered to vote in another Ohio precinct, and that the person did not vote or attempt to vote in that election using the person's former voting residence address.

> Because R.C. 3599.12 specifically prohibits anyone from voting or attempting to vote in any election in a precinct in which that person is not a legally qualified elector, pollworkers in a precinct must confirm before issuing a provisional ballot that the person to whom the provisional ballot will be issued is a resident of the precinct, or portion of the precinct, in which the person desires to vote. . . . .

> Only after the precinct pollworkers have confirmed that the person is eligible to vote in that precinct shall the pollworkers issue a provisional ballot to that person. Under no circumstances shall precinct pollworkers issue a provisional ballot to a person whose address is not located in the precinct, or portion of the precinct, in which the person desires to vote.

Appellees alleged that Directive 2004-33 violates HAVA because, *inter alia*, it limits a voter's right to cast a provisional ballot to those situations where a voter has moved from one Ohio precinct to another; allows poll workers to withhold a provisional ballot from anyone who is not — according to the poll worker's on-the-spot determination at the polling place — a resident of the precinct in which the would-be voter desires to cast a provisional ballot; does not require that potential voters be notified of their right to cast a provisional ballot; and unduly limits the circumstances in which a provisional ballot will be counted as a valid ballot.

On October 14, 2004, the district court issued an Order granting preliminary injunctive relief to Appellees. * * * The district court's injunction required that the Secretary issue a revised directive that (1) permits any voter to cast a provisional ballot upon affirming that he or she is eligible to vote and is registered to vote in the county in which he or she wishes to vote; (2) requires poll workers to notify any voter making this affirmation of his or her right to cast a provisional ballot, even if the poll worker determines that the voter does not reside in the precinct in which he or she is attempting to vote; and (3) that provisional ballots cast by a voter in the county in which he or she is registered to vote must be counted as a valid ballot even if it was not cast in the precinct in which the voter resides.

On October 15, 2004, Defendant-Appellee and Intervenors appealed the district court's Order to this court. On October 22, 2004, in response to the district court's October 14 Order, and two subsequent Orders issued on October 20, 2004, the Secretary sent to all Ohio County Election Boards two revised directives, designed to comply with the district court's injunction in the event that the October 14, 2004 Order was upheld by this court in full or in part. The revised directives are largely identical, and differ primarily with regard to whether provisional ballots cast outside a voter's precinct of residence will be counted as valid ballots.

[The court first determined that plaintiffs may file a private lawsuit under 42 U.S.C. § 1983 to enforce their HAVA-created right to cast a provisional ballot. The court then turned to the merits.]

HAVA requires that any individual affirming that he or she "is a registered voter in the jurisdiction in which the individual desires to vote and that the individual is eligible to vote in an election for Federal office . . . . shall be permitted to cast a provisional ballot." *See* 42 U.S.C. § 15482(a).

Directive 2004-33 contravenes this requirement because it requires that a voter's residence in a precinct be determined on the spot by a poll worker, and empowers poll workers to deny a voter a provisional ballot if the voter's residence in the correct precinct cannot be confirmed. *See* Directive 2004-33 ("Before issuing a provisional ballot as provided for under state or federal law, the pollworkers must confirm that the voting residence address claimed by the voter is located within the area shown on the precinct map and listed on the street listing."). As we explained above, the primary purpose of HAVA was to prevent on-the-spot denials of provisional ballots to voters deemed ineligible to vote by poll workers. Under HAVA, the only permissible requirement that may be imposed upon a would-be voter before permitting that voter to cast a provisional ballot is the affirmation contained in § 15482(a): that the voter is a registered voter in the jurisdiction in which he or she desires to vote, and that the voter is eligible to vote in an election for federal office.

Unfortunately, HAVA does not define what "jurisdiction" means in this context, which leaves unclear whether a voter must affirm that he or she is registered to vote in the *precinct* in which he or she desires to vote, the *county* in which he or she desires to vote, or even simply the *state* in which he or she desires to vote. The district court concluded that the term should be given the same meaning as the term "registrar's jurisdiction" is given in the NVRA; namely the geographic reach of the unit of government that maintains the voter registration rolls, *see* 42 U.S.C. § 1973gg-6(j), which in Ohio is each county board of election. The district court offered two bases for its conclusion: first, the statement by Senator Dodd on the Senate floor that "[i]t is our intent that the word 'jurisdiction' . . . has the same meaning as the term 'registrar's jurisdiction' in section 8(j) of the National Voter Registration Act," 148 Cong. Rec. S2535 (daily ed. Apr. 11, 2002); and second, the court's belief that permitting provisional ballots to be cast by voters outside their home precincts would further HAVA's purpose of preserving the federal franchise.

We disagree with the district court's interpretation of the term "jurisdiction." Senator Dodd's statement must be weighed against other statements in HAVA's legislative history that suggest quite the contrary — that jurisdiction means the particular state subdivision within which a particular State's laws require votes to be cast. Senator Bond, one of HAVA's floor managers, stated:

> Congress has said only that voters in Federal elections should be given a provisional ballot if they claim to be registered in a particular jurisdiction and that jurisdiction does not have the voter's name on the list of registered voters. . . . *This provision is in no way intended to require any State or locality to allow voters to vote from any place other than the polling site where the voter is registered.*

148 Cong. Rec. S10488, S10493 (daily ed. Oct. 16, 2002) (emphasis added). Senator Bond also noted:

> Additionally, it is inevitable that voters will mistakenly arrive at the wrong polling place. If it is determined by the poll worker that the voter is registered but has been assigned to a different polling place, it is the intent of the authors of this bill that the poll worker can direct the voter to the correct polling place. *In most states, the law is specific on the polling place where the voter is to cast his ballot. Again, this bill upholds state law on that subject.*

148 Cong. Rec. at S10491 (emphasis added).

Nor can the use of the NVRA's definition of "registrar's jurisdiction" be justified on the ground that doing so will further HAVA's purpose of preserving the franchise. For one thing, permitting voters to cast ballots in any precinct within their county of residence may cause logistical problems at certain favored polling places that outweigh some or all of the benefits expected by the district court. For another, even if importing language from the NVRA will in this case have the effect of expanding the opportunities of Ohioans to vote on election day, so too would ordering that provisional ballots may be cast by any Ohio voter anywhere in the state. Absent an independent reason for turning to the NVRA's definition, the mere fact that equating "jurisdiction" with "county" may have a salutary effect on the franchise cannot suffice to justify reading the language of HAVA in this way.

* * * In the absence of a compelling reason for defining HAVA's use of this term to mean the geographic reach of the unit of government that maintains the voter

registration rolls, we look to the overall scheme of the statute to determine its meaning. * * * Nowhere in the language or structure of HAVA as a whole is there any indication that the Congress intended to strip from the States their traditional responsibility to administer elections; still less that Congress intended that a voter's eligibility to cast a provisional ballot should exceed her eligibility to cast a regular ballot. After all, the whole point of provisional ballots is to allow a ballot to be cast by a voter who claims to be eligible to cast a regular ballot, pending determination of that eligibility.

In Ohio, like many other states, a voter may cast a ballot only in his or her precinct of residence. *See* Ohio Rev. Code Ann. § 3503.01 (providing that an eligible voter "may vote at all elections in the precinct in which the citizen resides"); Ohio Rev. Code Ann. § 3599.12(A)(1) (making it a crime under Ohio law for a voter to knowingly vote anywhere except in the precinct in which he or she resides). As such, in Ohio, HAVA requires that a provisional ballot be issued only to voters affirming that they are eligible to vote and are registered to vote in the precinct in which they seek to cast a ballot. Directive Number 2 satisfies this requirement, and is even more lenient. Directive Number 2 requires only that if an individual wishes to cast a provisional ballot after being advised that he or she does not appear to be eligible to vote in the precinct in question, the individual shall be permitted to cast a provisional ballot upon executing the following written affirmation:

> I affirm that my name is _____, that my date of birth is _____, and at this time my voting residence is _____ in the City/Village of _____ in _____ County of the State of Ohio and that this is the only ballot I am casting in this election.

> If I am voting elsewhere than the precinct where I reside, I understand that my entire ballot may not be counted.

Although this affirmation does not require voters to affirm in so many words that they are eligible to vote or registered in their assigned precinct, this aspect of Directive Number 2 comports with HAVA's requirements because it asks less of voters than HAVA permits. HAVA's requirements "are minimum requirements," permitting deviation from its provisions provided that such deviation is "more strict than the requirements established under" HAVA in terms of encouraging provisional voting, and is "not inconsistent with the Federal requirements" mandated by HAVA. *See* 42 U.S.C. § 15484.

HAVA is quintessentially about being able to *cast* a provisional ballot. No one should be "turned away" from the polls, but the ultimate legality of the vote cast provisionally is generally a matter of state law. Any error by the state authorities may be sorted out later, when the provisional ballot is examined, in accordance with subsection (a)(4) of section 15482. But the voter casts a provisional ballot at the peril of not being eligible to vote under state law; if the voter is not eligible, the vote will then not be counted. Directive 2 exactly preserves this distinction, while generally curing the other defects correctly found by the district court.

In addition to finding that HAVA requires that voters be permitted to cast provisional ballots upon affirming their registration to vote in the county within which they desire to vote, the district court also held that provisional ballots must be counted as valid ballots when cast in the correct county. We disagree.

The only subsection of HAVA that addresses the issue of whether a provisional ballot will be counted as a valid ballot conspicuously leaves that determination to the States. That subsection provides:

> "If the appropriate State or local election official to whom the ballot or voter information is transmitted under paragraph (3) determines that the individual is eligible under State law to vote, the individual's provisional ballot shall be counted as a vote in that election in accordance with State law."

42 U.S.C. § 15482(a)(4). The district court interpreted this subsection to require the following procedure after a provisional ballot has been cast: First, an election official determines whether the individual who cast the ballot was eligible to vote in the broadest possible sense of that term. In essence, the district court would have state officials ask only whether a voter was eligible to vote *in some polling place* within the county at the start of election day. Even someone who has "voted 'improperly' " remains eligible in this sense of eligibility. Second, if the voter is deemed eligible to vote, the provisional ballot is deemed valid, and may then be tallied along with all the other valid ballots in accordance with State rules for tallying votes accurately and promptly. The district court, in other words, interpreted HAVA as leaving to state law only "*how* the ballots are counted" while federal law determines "*whether* they are to be counted." Because the district court found that voters are eligible to vote under Ohio law anywhere in their county of residence, the court held that a provisional ballot cast anywhere in a voter's county of residence must be counted as valid.

The district court's interpretation of this subsection of HAVA is incorrect. To read "eligible under state law to vote" so broadly as to mean not only that a voter must simply be eligible to vote *in some polling place* within the county, but remains eligible even after casting an improper ballot would lead to the untenable conclusion that Ohio must count as valid a provisional ballot cast in the correct county even it is determined that the voter in question had previously voted elsewhere in that county; an impropriety that would not render that voter ineligible based upon the district court's interpretation of HAVA. State law concerning eligibility to vote is not limited to facts about voters as they arise from slumber on election day; they also stipulate, for example, that a voter is eligible to vote only once in each election, and, in Ohio, where a voter is eligible to cast a ballot. In other words, being eligible under State law to vote means eligible to vote *in this specific election in this specific polling place*.

Under Ohio law, a voter is eligible to vote in a particular polling place only if he or she resides in the precinct in which that polling place is located:

> Every citizen of the United States who is of the age of eighteen years or over and who has been a resident of the state thirty days immediately preceding the election at which the citizen offers to vote, is a *resident of the county and precinct* in which the citizen offers to vote, and has been registered to vote for thirty days, has the qualifications of an elector and *may vote at all elections in the precinct in which the citizen resides*.

Ohio Rev. Code Ann. § 3503.01 (emphasis added). * * * Indeed, it is a crime under Ohio law for a voter knowingly to vote anywhere except in the precinct in which he or she resides. Ohio Rev. Code Ann. § 3599.12(A)(1). Under Ohio law, then, only ballots cast in the correct precinct may be counted as valid.

There is no reason to think that HAVA, which explicitly defers determination of whether ballots are to be counted to the States, should be interpreted as imposing upon the States a federal requirement that out-of-precinct ballots be counted, thereby overturning the longstanding precinct-counting system in place in more than half the States. The phrase "eligible under State law to vote" certainly provides no reason to believe this was Congress's intent. Even if one concludes from our disagreement with the district court's interpretation of this phrase that it is somewhat ambiguous, that fact alone is an insufficient basis for inferring a congressional intent to impose federal requirements upon the States in this way. * * *

Nor does the legislative history of the statute provide any reason to believe that HAVA requires that ballots cast in the wrong precinct be counted. Senator Bond, for example, stated that "ballots will be counted according to state law. . . . It is not the intent of the authors to overturn State laws regarding registration or state laws regarding the jurisdiction in which a ballot must be cast to be counted." 148 Cong. Rec. at S10491. Senator Dodd also noted: "Whether a provisional ballot is counted or not depends solely on State law, and the conferees clarified this by adding language in section 302(a)(4) stating that a voter's eligibility to vote is determined under State law." 148 Cong. Rec. at S10510. Moreover, he added that "[n]othing in this compromise usurps the state or local election official's sole authority to make the final determination with respect to whether or not an applicant is duly registered, whether the voter can cast a regular ballot, or whether that vote is duly counted." *Ibid. See also id.* at S10504 (noting that HAVA does not establish "a Federal definition of when a voter is registered or how a vote is counted").

We therefore hold that HAVA does not require that any particular ballot, whether provisional or "regular," must be counted as valid. States remain free, of course, to count such votes as valid, but remain equally free to mandate, as Ohio does, that only ballots cast in the correct precinct will be counted.

It should be noted that this holding in no way rests upon our discussion above about the meaning of the term "jurisdiction." Even if the district court was correct to find that provisional ballots must be *offered* to any voter affirming residence in the county in which he or she desires to vote, it remains true that HAVA's single provision relating to the counting of ballots refers only to eligibility under State law to vote, and makes no reference either explicitly or implicitly to the jurisdiction in which a provisional ballot was cast.[5] In any event, there is no contradiction between requiring all voters in a county to be given a provisional ballot in case they are subsequently found to reside in the precinct in which they seek to vote, and then allowing the state to continue its practice of not counting votes cast outside of

---

[5] Indeed, the requirement that ballots be issued county-wide is, even on the district court's reading, a federal requirement, which cannot be read into the statement that votes must be counted if a voter is determined to be eligible under State law.

precinct. Although Congress certainly intended that some provisional ballots would be counted as valid after it was determined that voters should in fact have appeared on the list of qualified voters, there is no suggestion in either the legislative history of the statute or the statutory text that Congress intended all provisional ballots to be deemed valid.

Directive Number 2 therefore comports with HAVA's requirements insofar as it states that "An individual's provisional ballot will only be counted if he or she has voted in the proper precinct," and requires that poll workers "[a]dvise the voter that, if he or she does not vote at the correct precinct, the voter's ballot will not be counted for any issue or office." * * *

Notes and Questions

1.   HAVA has been controversial since its inception. Under the statute, the EAC consists of two members from each major party, with a majority required for action. That and the limited powers granted by Congress have rendered the EAC largely toothless. It is authorized to distribute HAVA funds for election improvements and to engage in research, but it cannot issue regulations and otherwise is given relatively little power. Moreover, it has been plagued by disputes over commissioner appointments, limited funding, and failure to exercise what limited powers it does have. For an overview, see *Symposium, HAVA@10,* 12 ELECTION L.J. 111 (2013).

2.   *Sandusky* held that voters had a private right of action through 42 U.S.C. § 1983 to enforce certain of the provisions found in section 302 of HAVA. In particular, the court determined that § 302 conveyed an enforceable individual right by providing that a voter "shall be permitted to cast a provisional ballot" upon affirming that he or she is registered and eligible to vote. In contrast, other decisions have refused to infer private rights of action under other HAVA provisions. *E.g., Brunner v. Ohio Republican Party,* 555 U.S. 5 (2008) *(per curiam)* (§ 303 of HAVA); *Crowley v. Nevada,* 678 F.3d 730 (9th Cir. 2012) (§ 301 of HAVA).

Does the result in *Brunner* call into question the result in *Sandusky?* The Sixth Circuit decision reversed in *Brunner* drew on *Sandusky* in suggesting that there was a cause of action under section 303, 544 F.3d 711, at 719–20 (6th Cir. 2008) (en banc), while the dissent argued that § 302 differed from § 303 in this regard. *Id.* at 726–30 (Moore, J., dissenting). For an argument that the cases do conflict, see J. Kenneth Blackwell & Kenneth A. Klukowski, *The Other Voting Right: Protecting Every Citizen's Vote by Safeguarding the Integrity of the Ballot Box,* 28 YALE L. & POL'Y REV. 107, 119 n.51 (2009).

More generally, is the result in *Brunner* desirable as a matter of policy? After that case, apparently the only way to enforce § 303 of HAVA is for the United States to sue the offending state. Should that be the preferred method of implementation? For further discussion of administrative versus private enforcement of federal election laws, see Daniel P. Tokaji, *Public Rights and Private Rights of Action: The Enforcement of Federal Election Laws,* 44 IND. L. REV. 113 (2010).

3.   HAVA has been credited with encouraging states to abandon the traditional paper punchcard ballots, and to adopt newer technologies, such as optically scanned ballots or electronic voting machines. Refinements in voting technology have

continued at the state level, even without the mandate of HAVA or other federal laws. For example, HAVA did not require that states implement a voter-verifiable paper record, but 29 states have adopted some version of that requirement. Daniel Palazzolo, et al., *Election Reform after HAVA: Voter Verification in Congress and the States*, 38 PUBLIUS: THE JOURNAL OF FEDERALISM 515 (2008). For further discussion of HAVA and related statutes and their impact, see PRESIDENTIAL COMMISSION ON ELECTION ADMINISTRATION: THE AMERICAN VOTING EXPERIENCE: REPORT AND RECOMMENDATIONS (2014); ELECTION ADMINISTRATION IN THE UNITED STATES: THE STATE OF REFORM AFTER BUSH V. GORE (R. Michael Alvarez & Bernard Grofman, eds., 2014); MARTHA KROPF & DAVID C. KIMBALL, HELPING AMERICA VOTE: THE LIMITS OF ELECTION REFORM (2011); Kathleen Hale & Ramona McNeal, *Election Administration Reform and State Choice: Voter Identification Laws and HAVA*, 38 POL'Y STUD. J. 281 (2010); Daron Shaw, et al., *A Brief Yet Practical Guide to Reforming U.S. Voter Registration Systems*, 14 ELECTION L.J. 26 (2015).

It appears that fewer votes have been lost or not counted due to these various developments adopted in the wake of the passage of HAVA, as compared to earlier elections. Richard L. Hasen, *The Untimely Death of* Bush v. Gore, 60 STAN. L. REV. 1, 16 (2007). *Compare* Robert M. Stein, et al., *Voting Technology, Election Administration, and Voter Performance*, 7 ELECTION L.J. 123 (2008) (comparing optically scanned paper ballots and electronic voting machines with regard to voter satisfaction and the time it takes to vote). In some places there is nostalgia for the punchcard system. Some election officials and voters argue that the punchcards were easier and quicker to use, while the optical-scan system takes more time, producing long lines at the polls, and requires voters to engage in a cumbersome and difficult process of filling in boxes with a pen. Barry M. Horstman, *No Easy Fix Proposed for Ballot Delays*, CINCINNATI ENQUIRER, Dec. 31, 2009, at B5.

4.　Other federal laws, passed both before and after HAVA, regulate the manner in which states manage their voting systems with regard to participation in federal elections. Most states have long required voters to register in some way before they vote. Daniel P. Tokaji, *Voter Registration and Election Reform*, 17 WM. & MARY BILL RTS. J. 453 (2008). In 1993, Congress passed the National Voter Registration Act (NVRA), 52 U.S.C. § 20501, *et seq.*, which requires states to link voter registration with applications for new or renewed driver's licenses. The NVRA has not led to robust increases in voting registration, one of its intended goals. Robert D. Brown & Justin Wedeking, *People Who Have Their Tickets But Do Not Use Them: "Motor Voter," Registration, and Turnout Revisited*, 34 AM. POL. RES. 479 (2006). NVRA has a private right of action for a "person who is aggrieved by a violation" of NVRA to enforce the law in federal court. 52 U.S.C. § 20510. For examples of litigation under NVRA, see, e.g., *ACORN v. Fowler*, 178 F.3d 350 (5th Cir. 1999) (holding that ACORN members lacked standing to bring an action absent evidence they had received a driver's-license renewal form or been purged from state voting rolls); *Harkless v. Brunner*, 545 F.3d 445 (6th Cir. 2008) (holding that the Secretary of State was a proper defendant, and remanding for further consideration of ACORN's standing); *Arcia v. Florida Sec'y of State*, 746 F.3d 1273 (11th Cir. 2014) (state violated NVRA when it conducted a program to remove suspected non-citizens from voter rolls within 90 days of a federal election). Other federal laws that regulate state voting practices are (1) the Voting Accessibility for the Elderly and Handicapped Act (VAEHA), 52 U.S.C. § 20101, passed in 1984, which requires states to facilitate voting in federal elections by voters who are handicapped or 65 years or older; (2) the Uniformed and Overseas Citizens Absentee Voting Act (UOCAVA), 52 U.S.C. § 20301 *et seq.*, passed in 1986, which requires states to facilitate absentee voting for federal elections by voters, including those in the military, who are overseas; and (3) the Military and Overseas Voter Empowerment Act, passed in 2009, amending UOCAVA and further requiring states to facilitate mail and electronic absentee voting in federal elections by members of the armed forces stationed outside the United States.

5.   In *Arizona v. Inter Tribal Council of Arizona Inc.*, 133 S. Ct. 2247 (2013), the Court considered the preemptive effect of NAVA's mandate that states "accept and use" the federal voter registration form for elections to federal office. The form does not require evidence of citizenship, only that the applicant aver that he is a citizen. Arizona required that applicants using the form must also present documentary evidence of citizenship. A majority of the Court held that requirement preempted by NAVA. The Court held that while the "accept and use" language might be subject to different interpretations, the "fairest reading of the statute is that a state-imposed requirement of evidence of citizenship not required by the Federal form" is inconsistent with the federal statutory mandate.

The Court observed that the Elections Clause, Art. I, § 4, cl.1, imposes upon states the duty to prescribe the time, place and manner of elections to the House and Senate, while conferring power upon Congress to alter or supplant those regulations, including those dealing with registration. The Clause "thus empowers Congress to regulate how federal elections are held, but not who may vote for them." Because the Clause "necessarily displaces some element of a pre-existing legal regime erected by" a state, the Court held that the traditional presumption against interpreting federal statute to preempt state laws did not apply. The Court allowed that Arizona could request the federal Election Assistance Commission to alter the Federal Form to include additional information. For litigation filed as a result of the latter observation, see *Kobach v. United States Election Assistance Comm'n*, 772 F.3d 1183 (10th Cir. 2014) (affirming refusal of EAC to change the Federal Form).

6.   Is federal regulation of the voting process at the state level, even limited to federal elections, always a good idea? Is that regulation inappropriately skewed in one direction? Commentators from various political persuasions have noted prob-lems with an expanding federal presence in this regard. *See, e.g.*, Blackwell & Klukowski, *supra*, at 114 (noting that the NVRA and HAVA have facilitated voter registration and casting ballots, but arguing that one "looks in vain for [federal laws] strengthening the integrity of the ballot box"); Daniel J. Tokaji, *The Future of Election Reform: From Rules to Institutions*, 28 YALE L. & POL'Y REV. 125, 146 (2009) (arguing that federal mandates on states should not be imposed without providing for significant federal administrative oversight). An alternative to signifi-cant federal oversight would be to encourage states to compete in a race to the top to improve voting systems. To a degree, HAVA and other provisions of federal law already attempt to do that. Another way is to measure and publicize comparative information about state election systems, as proposed in HEATHER K. GERKEN, THE DEMOCRACY INDEX: WHY OUR ELECTION SYSTEM IS FAILING AND HOW TO FIX IT (2009).

D. ALTERNATIVE VOTING SYSTEMS

Our discussion thus far concerning the mechanics of counting votes has elided a more fundamental question: What are the rules by which we determine who wins? In other words, what is the object of the electoral game?

In most American elections, the winner is the candidate who receives more votes than any other. Because there may be more than two candidates running, the winner may receive only a plurality, and not a majority, of votes. Both because plurality winners are opposed by majorities of the electorate and because losers receive no representation at all, plurality-winner systems can lead to results that are unrepresentative of the electorate's political opinions.

In multi-candidate contests, plurality-winner systems suffer from a spoiler effect. In such elections, a third-party candidate tends to take votes from the major-party candidate who is ideologically closer to the third-party candidate, thereby increasing the electoral chances of the candidate likely to be least palatable to supporters of the third-party candidate. *See generally* William H. Riker, *The Two-Party System and Duverger's Law: An Essay on the History of Political Science*, 76 AM. POL. SCI. REV. 753 (1982); Maurice Duverger, *Factors in a Two-Party and Multiparty System, in* PARTY POLITICS AND PRESSURE GROUPS 23 (1972). For this reason, plurality-winner systems tend to produce two (and only two) relatively centrist political parties, and may frustrate voters by giving them little choice if they want to avoid "wasting" their votes.

An example may help to illustrate the spoiler effect. In 2000, Green Party candidate Ralph Nader was ideologically more liberal than both of the two major-party candidates, Democrat Albert Gore, Jr., and Republican George W. Bush. Most of Nader's supporters, if forced to choose, would have preferred Gore to Bush. Their support of Nader rather than Gore, however, meant that Gore's vote total did not reflect their preferences, and Bush narrowly won the election. Similarly, in 1912, Democrat Woodrow Wilson prevailed when Bull Moose Theodore Roosevelt captured votes that would otherwise have given Republican William Howard Taft a victory.

Alternative methods of vote-counting give minor parties a much better chance of gaining representation in elected bodies, and result in legislatures that more closely reflect the electorate's range of political views. Proportional representation, for example, seeks to divide seats in a legislature proportionately according to the votes received by various parties. Thus, a minor party that receives 20% of the vote might receive no seats in a plurality system, but might receive 20% of the seats in a proportional system.

Single-transferable-vote (STV), or instant-runoff, systems provide a different means to enable voters to express a preference for minor parties. Under those systems, voters do not simply select their first-choice candidates. Rather, voters rank the candidates. First-choice votes are tabulated, and if one candidate receives a majority, that candidate is the winner. If no candidate receives a majority, however, the candidate with the least first-place votes is eliminated from contention. Voters who chose the eliminated candidate will have their second-choice votes counted in the next round, with the process repeating until one candidate receives a majority. For elections to fill multiple seats, STV systems also attempt to solve the problem of "wasted" extra votes cast for winning candidates. Once a candidate reaches a majority, a STV system applies all future votes cast for that candidate to the voters' second choices. That way, each voter has an increased opportunity to affect the outcome.

Other voting systems involve giving voters multiple votes to allocate to the candidates. One such system allocates zero votes to the voter's least preferred candidate, one to the candidate the voter prefers next, two to the next-preferred candidate, and so on. A second such system gives each voter a certain number of votes and permits the voter to allocate votes as he or she sees fit. For example, a voter might have five votes to allocate between 10 candidates running for five seats in a legislature, and might decide to give three votes to Candidate A and two to Candidate B. Because voters can allocate multiple votes to a single candidate, such a system permits voters who strongly support minor-party candidates to overcome some of the disadvantage they face because of their smaller numbers.

Chapter 12

REMEDYING ERRORS IN ELECTIONS

A. INTRODUCTION

Much election-law litigation is undertaken to remedy perceived errors in the electoral process, particularly for elections that have already taken place. To take but one example, in Chapter 11 we considered the Supreme Court's decision in *Bush v. Gore*, 531 U.S. 98 (2000) (*per curiam*) [p. 1065], which had its genesis in state-court litigation to recount certain ballots that were not properly cast. In this Chapter, we consider more systematically the ways legislators and courts deal with perceived and actual electoral errors.

Most states have fairly detailed statutory schemes that set out procedures for state and local officials to follow when confronting problems in an election. These statutes typically provide for an administrative process, followed if necessary by review in the state courts. Among the problems that state officials encounter are fraudulent votes, mistaken votes, and recounts when elections are extremely close. If and when a dispute reaches the judicial branch, a court must consider, often with little substantive guidance from the relevant statutes, whether an error has taken place and, if so, what the remedy should be.[a]

In the initial parts of this Chapter, we consider two potentially controversial and complicated remedies for electoral errors that courts may order: conducting an entirely new election and adjusting existing vote totals. We then turn to federalism issues, and consider how states (and state courts) may correct errors in elections for federal office and, conversely, what civil and criminal remedies there may be in federal courts for errors in state elections.

As you read these materials, consider the inevitable trade-offs that seem to be required when a legislature, or a court, ponders whether and how to remedy election errors. Among the potentially conflicting values at stake are the perceived fairness, accuracy, and legitimacy of the remedial process itself; the desire of voters to be anonymous; the desire to resolve an election dispute with promptness and

---

[a] For helpful discussion of these issues, see RICHARD L. HASEN, THE VOTING WARS: FROM FLORIDA TO THE NEXT ELECTION MELTDOWN (2012); Joshua A. Douglas, *Procedural Fairness in Election Contests*, 88 IND. L.J. 1 (2013); Steven F. Huefner, *Remedying Election Wrongs*, 44 HARV. J. ON LEGIS. 265 (2007); Steven F. Huefner, *Just How Settled Are the Legal Principles that Control Election Disputes?*, 8 ELECTION L.J. 233 (2009) (book review); *Developments in the Law — Voting and Democracy*, 119 HARV. L. REV. 1127, 1155–65 (2006). In 2010, the American Law Institute undertook a project, *Principles of Election Law: Resolution of Election Disputes*, to develop procedures for recounts and resolution of disputes over the casting and counting of ballots. *See* Steven F. Huefner & Edward B. Foley, *The Judicialization of Politics: The Challenge of the ALI Principles of Election Law Project*, 79 BROOK. L. REV. 1915 (2014).

finality; and the efficiency (or lack thereof) and costs associated with any remedy. *See* Steven F. Huefner, *Remedying Election Wrongs*, 44 HARV. J. ON LEGIS. 265, 288–96 (2007). To what extent, if at all, are courts better situated than legislatures or state officials to balance these values? Are these prototypical political questions, from which courts should abstain or, at the very least, give considerable deference to the efforts of the other branches of government to resolve any errors? Or does the inevitably politically freighted nature of many such errors suggest that courts should not hesitate to take action, since state officials may be inclined to take remedial actions that favor their own political parties or their own electoral fortunes? Do courts (particularly elected state courts) risk becoming politicized by remedying errors in elections for the other branches? And, will recent statutory changes (*e.g.*, the Help America Vote Act, discussed in Chapter 11) that make registering and voting easier also have the unintended consequence of generating more remedial litigation concerning alleged errors in the registration and voting processes?

B.   RE-VOTES AND THE UNIFORM DATE FOR FEDERAL ELECTIONS

In this section, we consider a straightforward but drastic remedy a court can order in the face of evidence of improper voting: ordering a new election. We also consider a related issue, specifically referring to federal elections: When Congress sets a particular date for a federal election, to what extent can a state hold a replacement election at a different time? That is, to what extent in those circumstances can a state hold re-voting on a date that would otherwise be foreclosed by federal law?

BELL v. SOUTHWELL
United States Court of Appeals for the Fifth Circuit.
376 F.2d 659 (5th Cir. 1967)

BROWN, CIRCUIT JUDGE [with whom GOLDBERG and AINSWORTH, CIRCUIT JUDGES, join]:

A Georgia election was conducted under procedures involving racial discrimination which was gross, state-imposed, and forcibly state-compelled. Nevertheless the District Court by summary judgment held it could not set aside such election or order a new one even though in parallel cases the unconstitutional discriminatory practices were enjoined and all persons arrested were ordered discharged immediately. We reverse.

The underlying facts out of which the controversy grew may be quickly stated. The Justice of the Peace for the 789th Militia District in Americus, Sumter County, Georgia, died in June 23, 1965. The Ordinary on June 26, 1965, called a special election to fill the vacancy, which was held on July 20, 1965. Mrs. Mary F. Bell, one of the plaintiffs, a Negro, was a candidate as was the winner, J.W. Southwell, a defendant, and four other white men. Following Georgia procedure, the results of the election were canvassed and the defendant J.W. Southwell declared the winner. Of the 2,781 votes cast, Negroes actually voting numbered 403 out of a total of 1,223 registered and qualified Negro voters in the District. On July 29, 1965, and after the expiration of the time for election contest under Georgia laws, this suit was filed. The District Judge by opinion denied relief for three reasons, two Georgia and one Federal. First, even assuming the admitted racial discrimination intimidated Negroes from voting, if all of the qualified Negroes not voting were added to the confined vote of Southwell's opponents, the result could not have been changed. Second, if the election were voided, the Ordinary would be required to appoint the successor and the appointee would surely be Southwell. Third, Federal Courts simply do not have power to void a state election.

* * * The main charge [in the complaint] was that the election officials including the Ordinary had conducted the election in violation of the rights established under the Constitution and laws of the United States. The specific allegations fell in two categories, one relating to the election system and the second to specific acts of intimidation. In the first it was alleged that voting lists for the election were segregated on the basis of race. Likewise, voting booths were segregated according to race, with one booth for "white males", another for "white women", and a third for Negroes. During the course of the election, a number of qualified Negro women voters were denied the right to cast their ballots in the "white women's" booth. In the second group were charges that the officials barred representatives of candidate Bell from viewing the voting, another was physically struck by an election official and police allowed a large crowd of white males to gather near the polls thus intimidating Negroes from voting. In addition, the plaintiffs were commanded by a deputy sheriff, acting under directions of the Ordinary, to leave the white women's polling booth and after their respectful refusal to do so on the ground that they had the constitutional right to vote without being subjected to racial discrimination, they were arrested. [T]he plaintiffs requested that the Court declare the defendant Southwell was not the legally elected Justice of the Peace, that he be enjoined from taking office, and that the Ordinary be ordered to call a new election. * * *

* * * Since it is clear that constitutional rights of the plaintiffs, the Negro voters as a class, indeed all voters, Negro and white, of the District were infringed, the sole question remaining is the sort of relief to be granted.

[T]he trial Court in unmistakable terms and action characterized the practices as flagrant violations of the Constitution. * * * Despite his determination that for the future these glaring racial discriminations could not go on, the trial Judge concluded that a Federal Court was either powerless — or at least ought not to exercise power — to set aside a State election. The Judge was apparently influenced by two factors. The first is one going to the existence of power or the propriety of its exercise. On the basis of *Reynolds v. Sims*, 1964, 377 U.S. 533 [p. 173], and other reapportionment cases, the trial Court recognizing that a prohibitory decree could took [*sic*] to the future, nevertheless held that it could not rectify the past since, as the Judge put it, "only a few minutes' reflection is needed to realize that the implications of such a decision would be staggering." The second [is] * * * that, granting the existence of this crude discrimination, there is no way to tell whether the result would have been different in its absence. Hence, no harm or injury is shown by these complainants. Neither of these factors warrant [*sic*], in our view, the complete denial of relief.

Drastic, if not staggering, as is the Federal voiding of a State election, and therefore a form of relief to be guardedly exercised, this *Court in Hamer v. Campbell*, 5 Cir., 1966, 358 F.2d 215, expressly recognized the existence of this power. Of course as that opinion emphasizes, not every unconstitutional racial discrimination necessarily permits or requires a retrospective voiding of the election. But the power is present * * *.

As to the second we do not think the Court could justify denial of effective, present relief because of any assumed inability to demonstrate that the outcome would have been different. The appellants seem to suggest that the existence of such flagrant racial discrimination would raise a presumption that the vote of every actual and potential voter was affected. On that approach, it is not Negroes alone who suffer, it is the body politic as a whole, both Negro and white. And this is certainly true at least to the extent that the trial Court legally could not assume — as it evidently did — that all white voters would vote for white candidates, all Negroes for Negroes, or that no whites would vote for Negroes in a free, untainted election.

[W]e think it is a mistake to cast this in terms of presumption. The fact is that there are certain discriminatory practices which, apart from demonstrated injury or the inability to do so, so infect the processes of the law as to be stricken down as invalid. Thus in jury-race exclusion cases, once the evidence, either direct or by inference from statistical percentages, establishes the existence of racial discrimination, the law requires that the indictment (or the petit jury verdict of guilty) be set side even though the accused is unable to demonstrate injury in fact. And at times demonstrated actual discrimination is not even required if the racially conscious system affords a ready opportunity for it in practice. Of course the Court discharging an accused from such indictment or conviction as a legalism finds that the accused was "prejudiced", but it is not in terms of the personal harm suffered or a factual demonstration that things would have turned out better. Rather, it is the law's recognition that in areas of such vital importance, state-imposed racial discrimination cannot be tolerated and to eliminate the practice or the temptation toward it, the law must extinguish the judgment wrought by such a procedure.

Even more directly, in connection with the elective process, the Supreme Court gave full play to this approach in striking down the Louisiana law requiring the designation of the race of each candidate on the ballot.[7] Anderson v. Martin, 1964, 375 U.S. 399. It takes little transposition to substitute for the ballot's written racial candidate label the state supplied racial marker for places and manner of voting. In each situation it is "placing a racial label * * * at the most crucial stage in the electoral process — the instant before the vote is cast." By each mechanism "the State furnishes a vehicle by which racial prejudice may be so aroused as to operate against one group because of race and for another." And in both situations this "is true because by directing the citizen's attention to the single consideration of race or color, the State indicates that * * * race or color is an important — perhaps paramount — consideration in the citizen's choice, which may decisively influence the citizen to cast his ballot along racial lines." And as much for one as for the other,

---

[7] This was, of course, a suit prior to a primary and not one after the fact seeking to void the results of a racially tainted election. This distinction, however, bears upon the appropriateness of the relief and Hamer limitations to be placed upon it.

the "vice lies not in the resulting injury but in the placing of the power of the State behind a racial classification that induces racial prejudice at the polls." * * *

* * * [T]he Georgia authorities * * * insist here that the relief sought was properly denied since the injunction was requested after the election was over. But * * * [t]here was really no effective relief available before the election. The moment the election process began, there was a protest by these Negro voters and others seeking an eradication of the discrimination and an opportunity for all members of that race, indeed for all voters, to vote without regard to race or color. That this self-help was not successful, indeed resulted in the unwarranted arrest and detention of those who protested, does not fault them for want of diligence. And within but a few days after the result of the election was published, this suit was filed as a part of an attack on many fronts.

Considering the gross, spectacular, completely indefensible nature of this state-imposed, state-enforced racial discrimination and the absence of an effective judicial remedy prior to the holding of the election, this is far removed from a belated effort to set aside retrospectively an election held long before on the ground that re-examination of the circumstances indicates a denial of constitutional rights on the part of candidates or voters, or both. The parties here moved with unusual diligence and * * * relief "if it is to be had, must perforce come from the Court or the voters must simply be told to wait four more years."

In the face of gross, unsophisticated, significant, and obvious racial discriminations in the conduct of the election and the now established power of a Federal Court to extinguish its effects even to the point of setting aside the election, the Georgia reasons relied on by the District Judge warrant but a brief comment. The Court's fundamental mistake was in assuming that this was an election contest as such in which the winner is challenged because of ineligibility, fraud or irregularities in the conduct of the election, the receipt or counting of illegal ballots which would change the result and the like, and which, as a separate special statutory proceeding, must be timely filed by specified persons following statutory procedures and in particular tribunals. Mrs. Bell and her co-plaintiffs alone or as members of the class did not challenge the eligibility of Mr. Southwell or the fact that he received an overwhelming majority. Indeed, Mrs. Bell as a former candidate did not seek to be selected over Southwell or any other opponent. What, and all, she and others sought was an election conducted free of such indefensible, racial distinctions. That being so, it was not the usual simple case of counting votes and denying relief for want of affirmative proof of a different result.

Equally lacking in merit is the Court's conclusion that setting aside the election would be ineffectual since * * * the Georgia statute prescribes that when an election is held and is determined not to have been valid, no re-election is held, but rather the Ordinary appoints a Justice of the Peace for the required term. The Court assumed, with unquestioned basis probably, that the Ordinary would have appointed Southwell. Clearly, the Federal Constitution and the Federal Courts are not so helpless or unresourceful as to condemn in words only to let go by default in fact such an open breach of constitutional demands.

This leaves only a tag end. There is a suggestion that the District Court enjoining Southwell from taking office pursuant to the election would be powerless to grant affirmative relief requiring that the Ordinary call a special election. In this vital area of vindication of precious constitutional rights, we are unfettered by the negative or affirmative character of the words used or the negative or affirmative form in which the coercive order is cast. If affirmative relief is essential, the Court has the power and should employ it.

The cause must therefore be reversed and remanded for the entry of an appropriate order setting aside the election and requiring the calling of a special election.

AKIZAKI v. FONG
Supreme Court of Hawai'i.
51 Haw. 354, 461 P.2d 221 (Haw. 1969)

RICHARDSON, CHIEF JUSTICE [with whom JUSTICE LEVINSON, CIRCUIT JUDGE HAWKINS, and CIRCUIT JUDGE KING (the latter two sitting by designation) join].

In the November 1968 election to select six representatives in the House of Representatives from the Fifteenth Representative District, five candidates were clearly elected without contest. The present case involves a controversy over the sixth seat.

In the final tabulation of the votes, the Republican candidate, Fong, received two more votes than did the Democratic candidate, Akizaki. Akizaki contested the election in the court below, and proved that of the ballots counted, at least nineteen were clearly invalid. These were absentee ballots which, because of late postmarks, failed to meet the requirements of HRS § 14-8. HRS § 14-8 provides that an absentee ballot received not later than noon on the sixth day following a general election may be counted, but only if it is postmarked not later than the day before the election. Due to a mistake on the part of the election officials, nineteen ballots postmarked too late to be opened and counted were nevertheless opened and counted. In the process they were commingled with valid absentee ballots so that it could not later be determined for whom the invalid ballots had been cast. Since the number of invalid ballots greatly exceeds the margin of victory, it is obvious that their presence could have affected the result. The court below resolved this problem by discarding 174 absentee ballots, among which were the nineteen invalid ones. On the basis of a tabulation without these 174 ballots, the court declared Akizaki to have been the winner of the election. From this determination Fong appeals to this Court. * * *

The fundamental interest to be protected here is that of the people of the Fifteenth Representative District in choosing whomever they please to represent them in the House of Representatives. The right to vote is perhaps the most basic and fundamental of all the rights guaranteed by our democratic form of government. Implicit in that right is the right to have one's vote count and the right to have as nearly perfect an election proceeding as can be provided. The result we reach must be consistent with these principles. * * *

We hold that * * * a new election should have been ordered. Because of the commingling of the valid and invalid absentee ballots, there is simply no way to determine what the actual result of the election was, and who should therefore be declared the winner. * * *

The trial court's approach was plausible; but to excise the entire absentee vote contained in the 174 ballots excluded by the court, in order to eliminate the nineteen ballots known to be invalid, inflicts too harsh a result on those absentee voters whose votes were validly cast. * * *

Reversed.

ABE, JUSTICE (dissenting). * * *

The House of Representatives in the proper exercise of this constitutional power by a majority vote of its members declared plaintiff Akizaki one of the six duly elected members from the Fifteenth Representative District and seated him. * * * I believe it is improper, to say the least, for this court, by its decision in this case, to attempt to undo what the House of Representatives has done. I disagree with the majority court and I believe its decision definitely shows not only utter disrespect but lack of confidence in a coordinate branch of our government. * * *

FLADELL v. PALM BEACH COUNTY CANVASSING BOARD
Supreme Court of Florida
772 So. 2d 1240 (Fla. 2000)

PER CURIAM. [CHIEF JUSTICE WELLS, JUSTICE SHAW, JUSTICE HARDING, JUSTICE ANSTEAD, JUSTICE PARIENTE, JUSTICE LEWIS, and JUSTICE QUINCE join in this opinion.] * * *

The issue in this case concerns the legality of the form of the ballot used in Palm Beach County, Florida, in the November 7, 2000, general election for the President and Vice President of the United States. The remedy sought by the appellants[1] is a re-vote, a new election, or a statistical reallocation of the election totals in Palm Beach County.

* * * In their briefs, the appellants have asked this Court to rule on the legality of the Palm Beach County ballot. They claim that the ballot is patently defective on its face in that the form and design of the ballot violated the statutory requirements of Florida election law. The appellants contend that the ballot was confusing and, as a result, they fear that they may have cast their vote for a candidate other than the one they intended. * * *

As a general rule, a court should not void an election for ballot form defects unless such defects cause the ballot to be in substantial noncompliance with the statutory election requirements. *See Nelson v. Robinson*, 301 So. 2d 508, 510 (Fla. 2d DCA 1974) (rejecting a post-election challenge based upon an alleged defect in the alignment of the candidates' names on the ballot). When considering a petition alleging a violation in the form of the ballot, "a vital consideration guiding the courts in determining whether an election should be voided is the reluctance to reach a

---

[1] The appellants in this case are electors from Palm Beach County.

decision which would result in the disfranchisement of the voters. Indeed, as regards defects in ballots, the courts have generally declined to void an election unless such defects clearly operate to prevent that free, fair and open choice." *Id.*

In the present case, even accepting appellants' allegations, we conclude as a matter of law that the Palm Beach County ballot does not constitute substantial noncompliance with the statutory requirements mandating the voiding of the election. * * * Accordingly, we affirm the trial court's dismissal with prejudice of the complaints. * * *

It is so ordered.

FOSTER v. LOVE

Supreme Court of the United States

522 U.S. 67, 118 S. Ct. 464, 139 L. Ed. 2d 369 (1997)

JUSTICE SOUTER delivered the opinion of the Court [in the entirety of which CHIEF JUSTICE REHNQUIST, JUSTICE STEVENS, JUSTICE O'CONNOR, JUSTICE GINSBURG, and JUSTICE BREYER join, and in which JUSTICE SCALIA, JUSTICE KENNEDY, and JUSTICE THOMAS join except as to Part III].

Under 2 U.S.C. §§ 1 and 7, the Tuesday after the first Monday in November in an even-numbered year "is established" as the date for federal congressional elections. Louisiana's "open primary" statute provides an opportunity to fill the offices of United States Senator and Representative during the previous month, without any action to be taken on federal election day. The issue before us is whether such an ostensible election runs afoul of the federal statute. We hold that it does.

I

The Elections Clause of the Constitution, Art. I, § 4, cl. 1, provides that "[t]he Times, Places and Manner of holding Elections for Senators and Representatives, shall be prescribed in each State by the Legislature thereof; but the Congress may at any time by Law make or alter such Regulations." The Clause is a default provision; it invests the States with responsibility for the mechanics of congressional elections, but only so far as Congress declines to preempt state legislative choices. Thus it is well settled that the Elections Clause grants Congress "the power to override state regulations" by establishing uniform rules for federal elections, binding on the States. *U.S. Term Limits, Inc.* v. *Thornton,* 514 U.S. 779, 832–833 (1995) [p. 550]. "[T]he regulations made by Congress are paramount to those made by the State legislature; and if they conflict therewith, the latter, so far as the conflict extends, ceases to be operative." *Ex parte Siebold,* 100 U.S. 371, 384 (1879).

One congressional rule adopted under the Elections Clause (and its counterpart for the Executive Branch, Art. II, § 1, cl. 3) sets the date of the biennial election for federal offices. Title 2 U.S.C. § 7 was originally enacted in 1872, and now provides that "[t]he Tuesday next after the 1st Monday in November, in every even numbered year, is established as the day for the election, in each of the States and

Territories of the United States, of Representatives and Delegates to the Congress commencing on the 3d day of January next thereafter." This provision, along with 2 U.S.C. § 1 (setting the same rule for electing Senators under the Seventeenth Amendment) and 3 U.S.C. § 1 (doing the same for selecting Presidential electors), mandates holding all elections for Congress and the Presidency on a single day throughout the Union.

In 1975, Louisiana adopted a new statutory scheme for electing United States Senators and Representatives. In October of a federal election year, the State holds what is popularly known as an "open primary" for congressional offices, in which all candidates, regardless of party, appear on the same ballot, and all voters, with like disregard of party, are entitled to vote. If no candidate for a given office receives a majority, the State holds a run-off (dubbed a "general election") between the top two vote-getters the following month on federal election day. But if one such candidate does get a majority in October, that candidate "is elected," and no further act is done on federal election day to fill the office in question. Since this system went into effect in 1978, over 80% of the contested congressional elections in Louisiana have ended as a matter of law with the open primary.[1]

Respondents are Louisiana voters who sued petitioners, the State's Governor and secretary of state, challenging the open primary as a violation of federal law. The District Court granted summary judgment to petitioners, finding no conflict between the state and federal statutes, whereas a divided panel of the Fifth Circuit reversed, concluding that Louisiana's system squarely "conflicts with the federal statutes that establish a uniform federal election day." We granted certiorari and now affirm.

II

The Fifth Circuit's conception of the issue here as a narrow one turning entirely on the meaning of the state and federal statutes is exactly right. For all of petitioners' invocations of state sovereignty, there is no colorable argument that § 7 goes beyond the ample limits of the Elections Clause's grant of authority to Congress.[2] When the federal statutes speak of "the election" of a Senator or Representative, they plainly refer to the combined actions of voters and officials meant to make a final selection of an officeholder (subject only to the possibility of a later run-off, see 2 U.S.C. § 8).[3] By establishing a particular day as "the day" on

---

[1] A run-off election has been held on federal election day in only 9 of the 57 contested elections for United States Representative and in only 1 of the 6 contested elections for United States Senator.

[2] The Clause gives Congress "comprehensive" authority to regulate the details of elections, including the power to impose "the numerous requirements as to procedure and safeguards which experience shows are necessary in order to enforce the fundamental right involved." *Smiley* v. *Holm*, 285 U.S. 355, 366 (1932). Congressional authority extends not only to general elections, but also to any "primary election which involves a necessary step in the choice of candidates for election as representatives in Congress." *United States* v. *Classic*, 313 U.S. 299, 320 (1941).

[3] Title 2 U.S.C. § 8, which was enacted along with § 7, provides that a State may hold a congressional election on a day other than the uniform federal election day when such an election is necessitated "by a failure to elect at the time prescribed by law." The only explanation of this provision offered in the legislative history is Senator Allen G. Thurman's statement that "there can be no failure to elect except

which these actions must take place, the statutes simply regulate the time of the election, a matter on which the Constitution explicitly gives Congress the final say.

While true that there is room for argument about just what may constitute the final act of selection within the meaning of the law, our decision does not turn on any nicety in isolating precisely what acts a State must cause to be done on federal election day (and not before it) in order to satisfy the statute. Without paring the term "election" in § 7 down to the definitional bone, it is enough to resolve this case to say that a contested selection of candidates for a congressional office that is concluded as a matter of law before the federal election day, with no act in law or in fact to take place on the date chosen by Congress, clearly violates § 7.[4]

Petitioners try to save the Louisiana system by arguing that, because Louisiana law provides for a "general election" on federal election day in those unusual instances when one is needed, the open primary system concerns only the "manner" of electing federal officials, not the "time" at which the elections will take place. Petitioners say that "[a]lthough Congress is authorized by the Constitution to alter or change the time, place and manner the States have chosen to conduct federal elections[,] in enacting 2 U.S.C. §§ 1 and 7, Congress sought only to alter the time in which elections were conducted, not their manner. Conversely, the open elections system [changed only the manner by which Louisiana chooses its federal officers; it] did not change the timing of the general election for Congress."

Even if the distinction mattered here, the State's attempt to draw this time-manner line is merely wordplay, and wordplay just as much at odds with the Louisiana statute as that law is at odds with § 7. The State's provision for an October election addresses timing quite as obviously as § 7 does. State law straightforwardly provides that "[a] candidate who receives a majority of the votes cast for an office in a primary election is elected." Because the candidate said to be "elected" has been selected by the voters from among all eligible office-seekers, there is no reason to suspect that the Louisiana Legislature intended some eccentric meaning for the phrase "is elected." After a declaration that a candidate received a majority in the open primary, state law requires no further act by anyone to seal the election; the election has already occurred. Thus, contrary to petitioners' imaginative characterization of the state statute, the open primary does purport to affect the timing of federal elections: a federal election takes place prior to federal election day whenever a candidate gets a majority in the open primary. As the attorney general of Louisiana conceded at oral argument, "Louisiana's system certainly allows for the election of a candidate in October, as opposed to actually electing on Federal Election Day."

---

in those States in which a majority of all the votes is necessary to elect a member." Cong. Globe, 42d Cong., 2d Sess., 677 (1872). In those States, if no candidate receives a majority vote on federal election day, there has been a failure to elect and a subsequent run-off election is required. See *Public Citizen, Inc.* v. *Miller*, 813 F. Supp. 821 (N.D. Ga.), aff'd, 992 F.2d 1548 (C.A. 11 1993) (upholding under § 8 a run-off election that was held after federal election day, because in the initial election on federal election day no candidate received the majority vote that was as required by Georgia law).

[4] This case thus does not present the question whether a State must always employ the conventional mechanics of an election. We hold today only that if an election does take place, it may not be consummated prior to federal election day.

III

While the conclusion that Louisiana's open primary system conflicts with 2 U.S.C. § 7 does not depend on discerning the intent behind the federal statute, our judgment is buttressed by an appreciation of Congress's object "to remedy more than one evil arising from the election of members of Congress occurring at different times in the different States." *Ex parte Yarbrough*, 110 U.S. 651, 661 (1884). As the sponsor of the original bill put it, Congress was concerned both with the distortion of the voting process threatened when the results of an early federal election in one State can influence later voting in other States, and with the burden on citizens forced to turn out on two different election days to make final selections of federal officers in Presidential election years:

> "Unless we do fix some time at which, as a rule, Representatives shall be elected, it will be in the power of each State to fix upon a different day, and we may have a canvass going on all over the Union at different times. It gives some States undue advantage. . . . I can remember, in 1840, when the news from Pennsylvania and other States that held their elections prior to the presidential election settled the presidential election as effectually as it was afterward done. . . . I agree . . . that Indiana, Ohio, and Pennsylvania, by voting in October, have an influence. But what I contend is that that is an undue advantage, that it is a wrong, and that it is a wrong also to the people of those States, that once in four years they shall be put to the trouble of having a double election." Cong. Globe, 42d Cong., 2d Sess., 141 (1871) (remarks of Rep. Butler).

* * * The Louisiana open primary has tended to foster both evils, having had the effect of conclusively electing more than 80% of the State's Senators and Representatives before the election day elsewhere, and, in Presidential election years, having forced voters to turn out for two potentially conclusive federal elections.

IV

When Louisiana's statute is applied to select from among congressional candidates in October, it conflicts with federal law and to that extent is void. The judgment below is affirmed.

It is so ordered.

Notes and Questions

1.   As the *Bell* court acknowledged, it is extraordinary for a court (particularly a federal court) to take the "drastic" step of ordering a new election for a state office. According to the court, the remedy was necessary given the pervasiveness of the voting-rights violations. How often would you expect such circumstances to be found? It appears that federal courts have rarely found such circumstances, and so the holding in *Bell* is rarely replicated, even in cases from the same circuit. *See, e.g., Hamer v. Ely*, 410 F.2d 152, 156 (5th Cir. 1969) (Wisdom, J.) (refusing to order new election, even when state officials did not appoint anyone to aid illiterate African-

American voters, since the "serious violations of voting rights" found in *Bell* were not present); *Hutchinson v. Miller*, 797 F.2d 1279, 1287 (4th Cir. 1986) [p. 1168] (discussing how federal courts have rarely found the circumstances of *Bell* to be present). *See also Developments in the Law — Elections*, 88 HARV. L. REV. 1111, 1335 (1975) (observing that courts rarely void elections, as in *Bell*, when there is no evidence that the violations would have changed the outcome).

2.   One scholar has contrasted *Bell* and *Bush v. Gore*, 531 U.S. 98 (2000) [p. 1065], arguing that the federal judges in the former case "courageously" voided the election, and while correct, nonetheless "court intervention should be used sparingly." In contrast, he continues, *Bush v. Gore* is a "dangerous precedent to the extent that it eases the way for federal court intervention in state and local elections over nuts-and-bolts disputes better left to local authorities." Richard L. Hasen, Bush v. Gore *and the Future of Equal Protection Law*, 29 FLA. ST. U. L. REV. 377, 400 (2001). Do you agree? Would many critics of *Bush v. Gore* tend to herald *Bell*, and vice-versa? Are the cases in tension, or can they be harmonized in principled ways?

3.   While the ordering of a new election, as in *Bell*, is unusual for federal judges, "the remedy is not uncommon in local elections" being reviewed by state judges, often primarily or exclusively on state-law grounds. Steven F. Huefner, *Remedying Election Wrongs*, 44 HARV. J. ON LEGIS. 265, 283 (2007). An example is the decision of Hawaii's Supreme Court in *Akizaki*. The court was unable to determine who had been rightfully elected, and found that ordering a new election did not violate separation of powers concerns. In other words, it was not a nonjusticiable political question [*see* Chapter 2]. In contrast, the dissent found the result to be in "direct conflict" with the separation of powers. Whomever you may think had the better of the argument, note how *Akizaki* (in contrast to *Bell*) raised no federalism concerns. Does that make it more or less justifiable for a *state* court to order a new election?

4.   *Fladell* was a less-noticed decision issued by the Florida Supreme Court during the *Bush v. Gore* controversy, albeit growing out of the same dispute. To order a new election, the court held, there must be "substantial noncompliance" with statutory requirements for the ballot. Courts should be wary of ordering a new election, the court held, since it was tantamount to disenfranchising voters. Is that a fair characterization of the remedy? Was the reticence displayed by *Fladell* absent in *Bell* and *Akizaki*? For an argument that the *Fladell* court should have ordered a new election, see Stephen J. Mulroy, *Right Without a Remedy? The "Butterfly Ballot" Case and Court Ordered Federal Election "Revotes,"* 10 GEO. MASON L. REV. 215 (2001).

5.   For a general discussion of the power of federal courts to set aside state elections, see Kenneth W. Starr, *Federal Judicial Intervention as a Remedy for Irregularities in State Elections*, 49 N.Y.U. L. REV. 1092 (1974). Starr addressed the pros and cons of retroactively remedying an irregular election by ordering a new one, as opposed to an order prospectively forbidding the challenged practice. The former, he notes, provides a more complete remedy, and seemingly returns voters to the status quo. The latter remedy, he observes, is less intrusive, and avoids the problems of truly restoring the status quo, since not all of the same voters may vote, time has passed, and it is almost impossible to rerun the same election. He saw the

result of *Bell* as being justified due to egregious, intentionally unlawful conduct of state officials. *Id.* at 1116–17. On the other hand, he argued, the "outrageous" criterion of *Bell* is a "highly subjective standard," *id.* at 1117, difficult for courts to apply. In most instances, Starr concluded, a new election should only be appropriate when the improprieties were outcome-determinative, that is, when they might have affected the outcome of the election. *Id.* at 1124–27.

6. *Foster v. Love* did not invalidate a previous election as such, but it did set aside an election date for federal offices set by a state. In recent years many states have experimented in various ways with changing or modifying what previously had been one day for all persons to vote in person. Over thirty states now have extended mail-in or absentee voting, which in effect can extend the voting period from one day to several weeks. To what extent does *Foster* call into question the legality of such reforms, at least for federal elections? Courts have held that such systems do not violate *Foster*, in part because federal law also permits absentee voting in federal elections under some circumstances. *See Voting Integrity Project v. Keisling*, 259 F.3d 1169, 1175–76 (9th Cir. 2001) (Oregon's mail-in system); *Voter Integrity Project v. Bomer*, 199 F.3d 773, 777 (5th Cir. 2000) (Texas's early-voting system). At least one state court, drawing on *Foster*, has held that early voting laws violated the designation in the state constitution of one particular day for an election. *Lamone v. Capozzi*, 912 A.2d 674 (Md. 2006). Over thirty state constitutions have similar language, though *Lamone* appears to be the only successful challenge to early-voting systems on state-constitutional grounds. Ward Williams, Comment, 39 Rutgers L.J. 1117, 1125–27 (2008). Some studies of early voting shows that it has little if any effect on increasing turnout, in part because it simply makes it easier for those who would vote anyway. *See, e.g.*, Barry C. Burden et al., *Election Laws, Mobilization, and Turnout: The Unanticipated Consequences of Election Reform*, 58 Am. J. Pol. Sci. 95 (2014); Joseph D. Giammo & Brian J. Brox, *Reducing the Costs of Participation: Are States Getting a Return on Early Voting?*, 63 Pol. Res. Q. 295 (2010); Symposium, *Time Shifting the Vote: The Quiet Revolution in American Elections*, 10 Election L.J. 73 (2011).

7. The Court in *Arizona v. Inter Tribal Council of Arizona, Inc.*, 133 S. Ct. 2247 (2013) [p. 1095], addressed the scope of Congressional and state powers under the Elections Clause.

C. ADJUSTING THE VOTE TOTALS

This section considers how states decide what to count as a valid ballot, in the context of deciding whether or not to adjust a vote total of an election. It is closely related to the issues raised in the prior section, since a request for a new election can be based on vote totals being changed by a recount, as the *Akizaki* case illustrates. State courts have taken several approaches in deciding how to determine if a ballot was validly cast, whether to adjust vote totals, and when that should lead to a new election. For example, some states will order a new election, more-or-less automatically, simply if the number of invalid votes exceeds the margin of victory. Other states, in contrast, will order a new election only if there is a significant chance that the invalid votes would have affected the outcome. Some states will not deduct votes from a candidate unless there is direct evidence that invalid votes were cast for that candidate. Finally, some states undertake proportionate reduction, where the court will remedy invalid votes by estimating the number of such votes cast for each candidate, and reducing the vote totals accordingly. As you read the cases below, consider what approach the court seems to be following, and how each approach is or should be balanced against other values, such as the need for legitimacy and finality of elections.[b]

IPPOLITO v. POWER
Court of Appeals of New York
22 N.Y.2d 594, 241 N.E.2d 232, 294 N.Y.S.2d 209 (1968)

BREITEL, J. [with whom FULD, C.J., and KEATING and JASEN, JJ., join:]

The successful candidate for District Leader (Male) Part B of the 22nd Assembly District, Democratic party, in the County of Queens, appeals from an order directing a new primary election in a proceeding brought by the unsuccessful candidate under section 330 of the Election Law. Special Term, after a hearing, granted such order, and the Appellate Division affirmed by a divided vote.

The statute provides that the court may direct a new election where it "has been characterized by such frauds or irregularities as to render impossible a determination as to who rightfully was . . . elected." This is the statutory standard and it is stated in the alternative, namely, that frauds or irregularities may ground a court's discretion in directing a new election.

In the instant primary a total vote of 2,827 was cast, 1,422 for the winner and 1,405 for the loser. Thus the winning margin was a mere 17 votes. Concededly 101 possible votes in the aggregate number were suspect or invalid for some kind of irregularity without any evidence of fraud or intentional misconduct. According to the public counter on the machine, there were 68 more votes cast than there were qualified persons who signed the voter registration (buff) cards. To be sure, it may be that the public counter did not register actual votes but only openings and closings of the automatic voting machines. In any event, such excessive operations were as unlawful as if actual excess votes were cast, and are significant because of the impossibility of knowing, in the absence of positive evidence, whether that is all that happened when the machines were opened and closed. There were 19 suspect or invalid votes because of blank, void, or missing party enrollments, 7 voter registration cards that were not signed, one irregular card, and 6 signings-in by members of the Conservative party although there was no contested Conservative primary. These make up the total of 101 suspect or invalid votes.

It is evident that even a small portion of the suspect votes could undo the slight margin of the victor and change defeat into victory for the loser. Hence, the statutory standard is met precisely, justifying the lower court's exercise of

---

[b] For further discussion of these issues, see *Developments in the Law — Voting and Democracy*, 119 HARV. L. REV. 1127, 1157–61 (2006); Kevin J. Hickey, Note, *Accuracy Counts: Illegal Votes in Contested Elections and the Case for Complete Proportionate Deduction*, 83 N.Y.U. L. REV. 167 (2008); Sarah E. LeCloux, Comment, *Too Close to Call? Remedying Reasonably Uncertain Ballot Results with New Elections*, 2001 WIS. L. REV. 1541.

discretion in directing a new primary election. On almost identical facts, this court affirmed a similar direction (*Matter of Nodar v. Power*, 18 N.Y.2d 697 [1966]). In the *Nodar* case, 1,417 votes were cast for the contested position, 722 for the victor and 695 for the loser. There were 109 invalid or suspect votes, consisting of votes by 80 persons who were not enrolled and who signed in, and 29 excess operations of the machine according to the public counter. There, a victory margin of 27, when weighed against 109 irregular votes, was sufficient to require a new election without evidence of fraud or other intentional misconduct. *Matter of Acevedo v. Power* (18 N.Y.2d 700) and *Matter of O'Connor v. Power* (18 N.Y.2d 705), decided the same day as the *Nodar* case, reached an opposite conclusion. These were affirmances of exercises of discretion by the lower courts in declining to direct new elections, and were supported by entirely different probabilities. In the *Acevedo* case, there were 103 suspect votes against a victory margin of 95, and, in the other, some 262 suspect votes, of which Special Term refused to invalidate 102, leaving 160 against a victory margin of 165 votes. Obviously, a change in the result would require that the bulk of the questioned votes be shifted to the loser, a gross improbability, or even impossibility, before it could be inferred that the irregularities were influential (see *Matter of Badillo v. Santangelo*, 15 A.D.2d 341 [1962]).

There evolves from these cases a rational standard: if irregularities are sufficiently large in number to establish the probability that the result would be changed by a shift in, or invalidation of, the questioned votes, there should be a new election. As stated in the *Badillo* case, "An election will not be overturned upon a mere mathematical possibility that the results could have been changed, when the probabilities all combine to repel any such conclusion"; but in cases like the one now before the court, as in the *Nodar* case, it does not strain the probabilities to assume a likelihood that the questioned votes produced or could produce a change in the result.

While it is troubling to require new election for irregularities without evidence of fraud or other intentional misconduct, ignoring such irregularities would undoubtedly create the likelihood that skillfully manipulated "irregularities" would be used to mask corrupt practices. It is better to keep the standards high, even at the cost of penalizing some voters and candidates for the failures of election inspectors, than to increase the opportunities for fraud without possibility or likelihood of discovery. And the statute is explicit in directing that irregularities, as well as fraud, may justify the direction of a new election. * * *

Accordingly, the order directing a new election should be affirmed.

[BURKE, SCILEPPI, and BERGAN, JJ., dissenting.] * * *

Before considering the "specifics" relied upon by the majority, we would first comment on the setting in which the initial election was held. This year, for the first time, primaries were conducted State-wide. Accordingly, more voting machines were required. To meet this demand, a plan was initiated whereby the primary could be conducted without providing each political party a separate voting machine in each polling place. Instead, it was decided that the space on the individual machines could be split by the different political parties. To do this, it was first necessary that the machines be divided according to the parties, and that levers be installed which would limit a particular voter's choice to those persons on the machine who were aspirants for office in his own political party. Finally, to insure that each person was properly limited to voting for his party's candidates, each voter, after registering, was given a card of a distinctive color corresponding to the color ascribed to his party. Those persons operating the machines were thus informed of the voter's registration and would set the machine accordingly. The uniqueness of this procedure is apparent. It is equally obvious that such a plan, when used for the first time and because it encompassed more steps than the standard primary procedure, would produce more mechanical and human errors than are usually associated with elections. Discrepancies alone, therefore, between various cross references of figures are more likely to occur and, in light of all the claims asserted both in this court and the lower courts of this State pertaining to this primary election, it would indeed be suspicious for any district or area to report a totally unimpeachable result.

We do not agree with the majority that, to the extent the "irregularities" were attributed to the excess in the machine count over the number of signed cards, there is a basis for invalidating the difference. Even where there is an excess machine count in a case where machines were used for more than one party, it is pure speculation to assume *without any testimony* that there were repeaters. It is well settled that the results of an election are entitled to a presumption of regularity and that a party attempting to impeach these results carries the burden of proof. In *Matter of Nodar v. Power* there were 1,417 votes cast as against 2,827 in this case. Hence the percentage of irregularities here is 50% less than in *Matter of Nodar* which is, therefore, inapplicable.

An inexplicable inference, advanced by petitioner and accepted by the majority, arises from the Conservative vote in the district. The record before us indicates that there was no contested Conservative primary. From this evidence alone, the majority has concluded that Conservatives voted in the Democratic party. Proof of such a contention should lie, if at all, in the figures for registration and poll count amongst Democrats in the same district. Thus, if petitioner established that more Democratic votes were cast than could have been cast because of the Conservative registrants, there would indeed be a basis for this contention. Such evidence, however, does not exist. In fact, no testimonial evidence has been presented to support any allegation. * * *

It is evident that all these "irregularities" were in fact attributable to mechanical and human error. As the burden of establishing the adverse effect on him of the "irregularities" rests on the petitioner, it is inconsistent with the prevailing conditions at this primary as compared with the primary held in *Matter of Nodar* to refuse to dismiss the petition in this case as we did in *Matter of Acevedo v. Power* where the vote cast was equivalent to the vote cast here.

The order of the Appellate Division should be reversed and the petition dismissed.

SCHEER v. CITY OF MIAMI

United States District Court for the Southern District of Florida
15 F. Supp. 2d 1338 (S.D. Fla. 1998)

EDWARD B. DAVIS, CHIEF JUDGE. * * *

* * * On November 4, 1997, the City of Miami held a general election for the position of Executive Mayor, with Joe Carollo and Xavier Suarez as the primary contenders. Neither Carollo nor Suarez received a majority of the overall votes; therefore, the City held a run-off election on November 13, 1997. In that election, Suarez defected Carollo in both precinct votes and absentee votes. On November 14, 1997, those results were certified and Suarez assumed the position of Mayor of the City of Miami.

Three Miami voters brought an *in rem* state lawsuit challenging the vote count in the first election pursuant to Section 102.166, Fla. Stat. Carollo and Suarez intervened in that action. The Plaintiffs in this case did not.

Judge Thomas Wilson, Jr., for the Circuit Court of the Eleventh Judicial Circuit of Florida, found that massive absentee voter fraud tainted the electoral process.

> "Witness after witness testified, without contradiction, that they either 1) did not vote, 2) did not sign the ballots in question, 3) did not live in the district in which their ballot was cast, 4) did not live in the City of Miami, 5) did not know the person who 'witnessed' their signature or said someone other than the names witness actually 'witnessed' their vote, 6) did not live at the address that was given on the request for the absentee ballot, 7) did not request an absentee ballot and/or 8) did not qualify as 'unable to vote.' "

Judge Wilson found that this fraud scheme, "literally and figuratively, stole the ballot from the hands of every honest voter in the City of Miami." As a result, "the integrity of the election was adversely affected." Judge Wilson held that the appropriate remedy was to void the first Mayoral election and hold a new election.

The Third District Court of Appeal of Florida agreed that massive fraud occurred in the electoral process, but held that the appropriate remedy was to invalidate only the absentee ballots from the November 4, 1997, election. The court citing to almost sixty years of Florida precedent stated that it "refuse[d] to disenfranchise the more than 40,000 voters who, on November 4, 1997, exercised their constitutionally guaranteed right to vote in the polling places of Miami." Because Carollo received a majority (51.41%) of the machine vote in the initial election, the court declared him the Mayor of Miami.

In this case, Plaintiffs represent the class of absentee voters who lawfully cast their absentee votes but whose votes were not counted pursuant to the Third DCA's ruling. Plaintiffs, in their two count complaint for declaratory judgment and for injunctive relief, seek a new election. Plaintiffs basically contend that by voiding their votes, their constitutional rights under the First and Fourteenth Amendments were violated. * * *

This case presents the difficult question of when a federal court should involve itself with a state election dispute. There is no doubt that the right to vote is one of the most basic and fundamental of rights. However, federal courts can only intervene in a state election dispute in the most extreme circumstances. This case does not present one of those circumstances. Moreover, public policy dictates that this Court not meddle with the state process. Accordingly, the Court will grant summary judgment for the Defendants.

Before discussing the merits of Plaintiffs' claim, the Court must first address Defendants' argument that the Court should abstain. * * *

Although Plaintiffs are technically correct that the Court should not abstain * * * many federal courts have held that they should not intervene in state election disputes. "Subject to specific exceptions, federal courts should not be involved in settling state election disputes." Only when election irregularities are fundamentally unfair and transcend "garden variety" problems do federal courts have a duty to step in to ensure that citizens' rights are protected. The Court, therefore, must determine whether this case is just another garden variety election dispute or whether Plaintiffs have been subjected to fundamental unfairness.[4]

More often than not, federal courts find that the problem is garden variety and do not intervene in state election disputes. *See, e.g., Gold v. Feinberg*, 101 F.3d 796, 801 (2d Cir. 1996) (refusing to intervene where human error resulted in miscounting of votes, presence of ineligible candidates on ballot, and delay in arrival of voting machines); *Bodine v. Elkhart County Election Bd.*, 788 F.2d 1270, 1272 (7th Cir. 1986) (mechanical and human error in counting votes); *Hendon v. North Carolina State Bd. of Elections*, 710 F.2d 177, 182 (4th Cir. 1983) (technical deficiencies in printing ballots); *Gamza v. Aguirre*, 619 F.2d 449, 454 (5th Cir. 1980) (negligent vote counting); *Hennings v. Grafton*, 523 F.2d 861 (7th Cir. 1975) (malfunction of voting machines); *Pettengill v. Putnam County R-1 School Dist.*, 472 F.2d 121, 122 (8th Cir. 1973) (counting votes that were illegally cast); *Powell v. Power*, 436 F.2d 84 (2d Cir. 1970) (non-party members mistakenly allowed to vote in congressional primary); *Johnson v. Hood*, 430 F.2d 610, 613 (5th Cir. 1970) (arbitrary rejection of 10 ballots).

In a case with strikingly similar facts, the Eleventh Circuit cautioned district courts not to meddle with a state election dispute. *Curry [v. Baker]*, 802 F.2d 1302 [(11th Cir. 1986)]. There, the plaintiffs argued that the state of Alabama incorrectly dealt with massive illegal voting. The Eleventh Circuit declined to answer that question for "reasons grounded in both law and public policy."

Curry involved a primary runoff election for the Democratic candidate for Governor of Alabama. Initially, it looked like Charles Graddick had won, but like this case, there was massive illegal voting. Therefore, the State Democratic Committee certified William Baxley, who received the majority of the legal votes, as the winner. Graddick and his supporters brought suit arguing that the election committee did

---

[4] Defendants argue that the Court need not reach this issue because absentee voting is a privilege and not a right. Defendants are correct that there is no right to vote by absentee ballot, but their characterization is misleading. Florida, of course, can restrict or perhaps even eliminate absentee voting under the appropriate circumstances *before* these votes are cast. The question then is whether Florida can restrict these votes after they are cast when there is evidence of massive fraud. As explained later, federalism and equity prevent this Court from telling Florida that it cannot in this case.

not use the correct methods for counting and determining the lawfully cast votes. The district court agreed and ordered the Democratic Party to conduct a new primary and enjoined the disqualification of Graddick.

The Eleventh Circuit reversed, reasoning that it was not its role to "oversee the administrative details of a local election." *Id.* at 1315. As *Curry* clearly demonstrates, it is not the job of a federal court to involve itself with settling disputes as to how the state deals with counting votes after illegal votes are cast. Instead, a federal court should only intervene into state election disputes where the entire process is fundamentally unfair. "Episodic events" don't count. *Curry*, 802 F.2d at 1314. [There is] a distinction between state laws and patterns of state action that systematically deny equality in voting, and episodic events that, despite non-discriminatory laws, may result in the dilution of an individual's vote. Unlike systematically discriminatory laws, isolated events that adversely affect individuals are not presumed to be a [constitutional violation].

This instant action represents an isolated or "episodic event" that does not demonstrate that the entire process is fundamentally unfair.

Plaintiffs argue, however, that another Eleventh Circuit case is more similar to the instant action. *See Roe [v. Alabama]*, 43 F.3d 574 [(11th Cir. 1995)] [p. 1161]. The Court disagrees.

In that case, the prior Alabama practice had been not to count absentee ballots unless they were notarized or witnessed; but after the 1994 election, an Alabama court ordered the improperly submitted absentee ballots to be counted. The *Roe* court determined that the election was fundamentally unfair for two reasons: 1) that Alabama was diluting the votes of those who had lawfully voted, and 2) that Alabama had disenfranchised those people who would have voted but for the inconvenience imposed by the notarization and witness requirements. *Id.* at 581. The difference between *Roe* and this case (as well as *Curry*) is that in *Roe*, the state changed its policy after an election. The Eleventh Circuit in *Roe* did not involve itself with settling an isolated dispute about fraud. Instead, it intervened because the state's policy changed after an election. Here, Florida did not change its policy at all. It stayed true to course — if there is massive fraud with absentee votes, they can be invalidated. In fact, there is a "complete absence of any Florida Appellate Court decision upholding the ordering of a new election in the face of such fraudulent conduct relating to absentee ballots." *See In Re Matter of Protest*, 707 So. 2d at 1173.

Plaintiffs also rely on cases from the Third and First Circuits. These cases are persuasive, but in the end, do not control this Court's decision. * * * In *Marks [v. Stinson]*, 19 F.3d [873,] 873 [(3d Cir. 1994)], in Pennsylvania's second senatorial district election, the Republican candidate, Bruce Marks, received the majority of the machine votes over Democrat William Stinson. Stinson, however, won the bulk of the absentee votes. Because of the huge number of absentee ballots cast for Stinson, he won the election 20,523 to 20,062. Marks brought state and federal proceedings against Stinson alleging that his opponent engaged in absentee voter fraud. The district court, deciding not to abstain, voided all absentee votes finding that there was massive fraud and enjoined Stinson from assuming office and declared Marks the winner based solely on the machine vote. The Third Circuit remanded the case back to the district court to determine whether the results would have been the same absent the wrongdoing, with instructions that the district court "will have authority to order a special election, whether or not it is able to determine what the results would have been in the absence of that violation." *Id.* at 889.

Marks, however, did not present a situation where a federal court had to step in and invalidate sixty years of state law. Instead, the Third Circuit simply overruled the district court's decision to invalidate absentee votes. This case is fundamentally different because here, a federal district court would have to meddle with the state's determination of what an appropriate remedy is, and would also have to examine whether sixty years of precedent should be overturned. The Court declines to do so.

Plaintiffs also cite to a First Circuit case in which the court intervened, *Griffin v. Burns*, 570 F.2d 1065 (1st Cir. 1978). This case arose out of a Rhode Island local primary in which the state had encouraged citizens to vote by absentee ballot. After citizens took the bait, the Rhode Island Supreme Court found that absentee voting was not authorized for primary elections and invalidated those votes. The court then ordered the decertification of the winner and the board of canvassers certified a new winner based solely on the machine cast votes. *Id.*

The absentee voters then filed a class action in federal court alleging that the Rhode Island Supreme Court, by invalidating their votes violated the Due Process Clause of the Fourteenth Amendment. The district court agreed and the First Circuit affirmed, finding that plaintiffs had relied on the government's assurances that absentee ballots would be counted. Based on these unique circumstances, the First Circuit found "broad-gauged unfairness" which implicated the state's integrity and the integrity of the election results. The court recognized, however, that the Constitution confers the "power to control the disposition of contests over elections to . . . state and local offices." *Id.* at 1077.

Like Alabama in *Roe*, Rhode Island changed the rules half way through the game. The state told voters one thing before the election and changed its policy thereafter. This was unacceptable and of course, the First Circuit had to intervene. Florida, on the other hand, maintains its policy of remedying fraud. It has not changed the rules of the game and neither will this Court.

The Ninth Circuit, in refusing to meddle with a state election, summarized the law in all of these election cases:

> A general pattern emerges from all of these cases taken together. ***Mere fraud or mistake will not render an election invalid.*** However, a court will strike down an election . . . if two elements are present: (1) likely reliance by voters on an established election procedure and/or official pronouncements about what the procedure will be in the coming election; and (2) significant disenfranchisement that results from a change in the election procedures.

Bennett [v. Yoshina], 140 F.3d [1218,] 1226 [(9th Cir. 1998)] (emphasis added). This case is about mere fraud — nothing more. It has nothing to do with reliance on an established procedure or a change in the election procedures. If anything, the voters must be presumed to have known of Florida's procedure of voiding all absentee votes if there was evidence of fraud. * * *

Florida courts have established and followed this policy for good reason. The absentee voting scheme as it now exists in Florida lends itself to fraud, manipulation, and deceit. The state legislature continues to attempt improvements, but to date criminals have found ways to abuse the system. Accordingly, Florida courts for the past sixty years have constructed a means of dealing with absentee voter fraud. It is not this Court's province to upset this remedy as it has been well thought out by the state courts. For example, as the state appellate court in this case noted, "were we to approve a new election as the proper remedy following extensive absentee voting fraud, we would be sending out the message that the worst that would happen in the face of voter fraud would be another election." For these reasons, the Eleventh Circuit in *Curry* held that state election disputes were better dealt with by "the court system of the affected state." 802 F.2d at 1302.

Even if Plaintiffs were able to set forth a constitutional violation, the Court must take into account equitable considerations in fashioning the appropriate remedy in each case. "A federal court reaching into the state political process to invalidate an election necessarily implicates important concerns of federalism and state sovereignty. It should not resort to this intrusive remedy until it has carefully weighed all equitable considerations."

* * * Indeed, the old Fifth Circuit, whose decisions are of course binding on this Court, stated that even in cases of racial discrimination, the voiding of a state election is a "drastic if not staggering" remedy. *Bell v. Southwell*, 376 F.2d 659, 662 (5th Cir. 1967) [p. 1100]. The almost circus atmosphere surrounding this case makes the remedy Plaintiffs seek even more drastic and staggering. Plaintiffs could have intervened in the state case, as did Xavier Suarez. They did not. Instead, they waited until the trial was completed, the appeal and cross-appeal were filed, the appellate opinion was issued, rehearing and certification were petitioned for and denied, and discretionary review in the Florida Supreme Court was invoked before coming to this Court to request relief. The City of Miami has been scarred by the events that took place during and after the 1997 Mayoral election. The City and its citizens are finally starting to heal. Equity necessitates that the Court not re-open these wounds.

Federal courts rarely meddle with state election disputes. This case is no exception. The massive absentee fraud during the November, 1997, Mayoral election was an episodic event that was addressed by the state. The Eleventh Circuit as well as the majority of courts explain that it is not the job of the federal court to intrude into these brief episodes. Furthermore, equity demands that the Court stay on the sideline of this state dispute. * * *

BRADLEY v. PERRODIN
California Court of Appeal, Second District, Division 1
106 Cal. App. 4th 1153, 131 Cal. Rptr. 2d 402 (2003)

ORETGA, J. [with whom SPENCER, P.J., and MALLANO, J. join]. * * *

Appellant Irving and respondent Andrews were the top candidates in one of two city council races in the April 2001 primary election. * * * In the June 5, 2001, runoff election, Irving defeated Andrews by a vote of 5,414 to 4,863.

Andrews then filed the present election contest against Irving, contending that [city clerk Charles] Davis had erred by placing Irving's name above Andrews's on the runoff ballot. * * * Davis conceded below that Andrews's name should have been listed first [pursuant to the randomized alphabet compiled for such purposes] * * *. Davis stated, and the trial court agreed, that Irving's name was mistakenly placed before Andrews's due to Davis's unintentional error. The finding that Davis's error was unintentional is not disputed in this appeal.

Andrews also contended below that Irving had committed offenses against the elective franchise by soliciting (either personally or through her agents) nine noncitizens to register to vote, and by illegally influencing or instructing the nine noncitizens to vote for Irving.

The trial court, after rejecting Irving's argument that the ballot name-order error should have been addressed in a preelection writ proceeding, found the error sufficient to overturn Irving's election. The court shifted 295 votes from Irving to Andrews based, as in the mayoral election contest, on the primacy effect theory,[5] and declared Andrews the winner.

In addition, the trial court found Irving had committed offenses against the elective franchise, either personally or through her agents, by: (1) knowingly soliciting nine noncitizens to register for absentee ballots * * *; (2) being present in the nine absentee voters' homes while they were voting and telling them how to vote * * *; (3) fraudulently registering the nine noncitizens and assisting them to vote or completing their absentee ballots for them * * *; and (4) soliciting illegal votes from the nine nonqualified voters[.] * * *

Irving appealed from the adverse judgment and petitioned for a writ of supersedeas. We denied the petition on March 7, 2002. Accordingly, Andrews has been serving on the city council while this appeal was pending. * * *

When an otherwise successful candidate such as Irving is subsequently found to have committed an offense or offenses against the elective franchise, her election may be annulled even if the number of unqualified voters she fraudulently registered or the number of votes she unlawfully solicited were too few to have changed the outcome of the election. As the California Supreme Court explained: "Each . . . 'offense against the elective franchise * * * can furnish independent statutory grounds for contesting and annulling the election, separate and apart from the effects of any illegal votes actually counted. * * * We affirm the portion of the judgment annulling Irving's election[.] * * *

Given that this election contest involves questions broader than Irving's personal interest as a candidate for the contested office, we conclude the electorate's interest in this important legal issue requires that the primacy effect issue be addressed. Election contests are not typical adversary proceedings "between individuals

---

[5] [T]he trial court based its primacy effect finding solely on [political scientist Jon] Krosnick's expert testimony that on average, those listed first on a ballot receive 3.32 percent more votes. There was no direct evidence from any voter regarding the effect of the name-order error on the voter's selection of a candidate.

asserting personal rights or interests, but involve the right of the people to have the fact as to who has been duly elected by them judicially determined. An election contest involves a question of broader import than the mere individual claim of a person to enjoy the honors and emoluments of a particular office brought directly into contest. The inquiry must be as to whether in a given instance the popular will has been, or is about to be, thwarted by mistake or fraud. The public interest imperatively requires that the ultimate determination of the contest shall reach the right result."

Turning to the merits of Irving's contentions, we find that by shifting votes from Irving to Andrews based solely on the primacy effect theory, the trial court exceeded its authority. Under sections 16203, 16402, and 16703 [of the California Elections Code], only *illegal* votes may be discarded in an election contest. If the court finds, after discarding the illegal votes given for the winning candidate, that another candidate "has the highest number of legal votes, the court shall declare that person elected." (§ 16703.) Otherwise, if discarding the illegal votes given for the winning candidate would not change the result of the election, and the winning candidate is disqualified from taking office due to having committed offenses against the elective franchise, the court shall enter judgment "annulling and setting aside the election." (§ 16603.)

In this case, the trial court found a total of 144 illegal votes had been cast in the runoff election, but found it impossible to determine in whose favor (other than the nine illegal votes for Irving) the illegal votes had been cast. Even if we were to assume that all 144 illegal votes had been cast for Irving, subtracting 144 illegal votes from Irving's total would still have left her the victor with 5,270 legal votes to Andrews's 4,863 legal votes. Therefore, the illegal votes cast for Irving did not change the result of the election, and there was no other candidate with more legal votes than Irving. Given Irving's disqualification from taking office due to her offenses against the elective franchise, the trial court should have entered a judgment "annulling *and setting aside* the election." (§ 16603, italics added.)

Instead, in a ruling unprecedented, to our knowledge, in this country, the trial court shifted 295 legal votes from Irving to Andrews based solely on the 3.32 percent primacy effect assumed to be enjoyed, on average, by those listed first on the ballot. While many courts and legislatures have recognized the advantage afforded to candidates whose names are listed first on the ballot, no judicial or statutory authority exists to reverse the results of an election where, due to *unintentional* clerical error, the ballot listed the candidates in the wrong alphabetical order.

Election results may only be challenged on one of the grounds specified in section 16100. Name-order error occurring in the absence of fraud and resulting purely from unintentional clerical error, as in this case, is not a valid ground for an election contest under section 16100. The fact that 295 legal votes may have been cast for Irving solely because her name was erroneously listed first on the ballot does not, in itself, impeach the integrity of those 295 votes. Legal votes randomly cast by the least informed or least interested voters are entitled to the same weight as legal votes cast by the most highly educated and informed voters in our society. The legality or illegality of a vote cast by a qualified voter in a lawful manner does not depend upon the voter's motive or purpose in voting a certain way. To shift 295 legal votes to "correct" the votes "randomly" cast for Irving solely as a result of her erroneous advantageous ballot position (and to award those same "random" votes to Andrews based solely on the primacy effect theory) would be, without any lawful justification, to disenfranchise those 295 voters.

We conclude the trial court erred in entering judgment for Andrews and declaring her elected when she had failed to win the highest number of legal votes in the June 5, 2001, election. Accordingly, * * * [t]he certificate of election for Andrews is annulled, and Andrews's city council seat shall be vacant upon the finality of this opinion. * * *

Notes and Questions

1.   A short but much-discussed effort to address the role of statistical evidence in adjusting vote totals was presented in Michael O. Finkelstein & Herbert E. Robbins, *Mathematical Probability in Election Challenges*, 73 COLUM. L. REV. 241 (1973). The authors set out a formula to help determine whether invalid votes altered the outcome of an election. The formula considers the winner's plurality, the total number of votes cast, and the number of invalid votes cast. The formula assumes that the invalid votes were not systematically biased toward one candidate or another, *i.e.*, that the invalid votes were randomly distributed. In *Ippolito*, the court ordered a new election because "it does not strain the probabilities to assume a likelihood that the questioned votes produced or could produce a change in the results." Finkelstein and Robbins criticized this analysis because under their formula, there was only a five percent chance that the outcome of the election at issue in that case would have been different. *Id.* at 243.

Does this analysis call into question the reasoning or result in *Ippolito*? Is the "intuitive" analysis of cases like *Ippolito* more, or less, persuasive than the formula? Finkelstein and Robbins acknowledge that that their formula should not be used if there is "evidence of fraud or patterns of irregular voting." What type of evidence should be presented, or should a court demand, before invoking that exception? What do you make of the fact that no court has apparently ever applied the formula? Kevin J. Hickey, Note, *Accuracy Counts: Illegal Votes in Contested Elections and the Case for Complete Proportionate Deduction*, 83 N.Y.U. L. REV. 167, 174 (2008).

2.   The decision in *Scheer* was preceded by state-court litigation. Carollo, the loser of the mayoral run-off election, filed an election protest. Finding demonstrable evidence of fraudulent absentee voting, the state appellate court nonetheless refused to order a new election. Among other things, the court reasoned that (1) the ability to vote absentee was a privilege, not a right; (2) Suarez, the run-off winner, had no knowledge of and did not participate in the fraud; and (3) a new election would disenfranchise those many voters who properly voted at the polls. The more appropriate remedy, the court held, was to void the absentee ballots only. *In re Protest of Election Returns*, 707 So. 2d 1170 (Fla. App. 1998) *(per curiam)*. That decision was in effect subject to collateral review in *Scheer*. While the federal court did not agree with all aspects of the state-court decision, it left the result intact. To what extent, if at all, does it inform the analysis to label the right to cast an *absentee* vote as a privilege, not a right? Were these courts correct to disregard *all* absentee

ballots, presumably including those that were correctly cast? Unlike the Florida decisions, it appears that the "majority of states . . . have concluded that absentee voting laws should be liberally construed in aid of the right to vote." *Adkins v. Huckabay*, 755 So. 2d 206, 216 (La. 2000). But there are other states that follow the right/privilege distinction for absentee ballots. *E.g., Coleman v. Franken*, 767 N.W.2d 462 (Minn. 2009) [p. 1129]. For further discussion, see Richard L. Hasen, *The Democracy Canon*, 62 STAN. L. REV. 69, 86–87 (2009).

3.   A particularly controversial recount and adjustment of votes took place after the 2004 gubernatorial election for the State of Washington. Initially, Republican Dino Rossi led Democrat Christine Gregoire by 261 votes out of more than 2.8 million cast. It was apparently the closest race for governor in American history. Two sets of recounts led to a lead by Gregoire of 129 votes. Rossi filed suit in state court, requesting a new election. Discovery in the case revealed that over 1600 voters had voted illegally, many of them disenfranchised felons. The challengers did not undertake the heavy burden of providing direct evidence of how the invalid voters voted. The trial judge found that proportionate reduction, the alternative remedy posited by the challengers, was not appropriate, in part because it could not assume that the votes by the mostly male felons were voting proportionately like non-felons. The challengers did not appeal the trial-court decision. Do decisions like this call into serious question the heretofore respectable theory of proportionate deduction? For discussion of the Washington election and its implications for this theory, see RICHARD L. HASEN, THE VOTING WARS: FROM FLORIDA TO THE NEXT ELECTION MELTDOWN 149–52 (2012); *Developments in the Law — Voting and Democracy*, 119 HARV. L. REV. 1127, 1155–65 (2006); Hickey, *supra*.

4.   The court in *Bradley* heavily relied on the expert evidence of political scientists in finding that there was a "ballot order effect," *i.e.*, that candidates listed first on a ballot had an improper and unfair electoral advantage. For an argument that the social science evidence for the effect is "muddled," and hence courts should be cautious before reallocating votes, or ordering a new election, based on the improper placement of names on a ballot, see R. Michael Alvarez et al., *How Much Is Enough? The "Ballot Order Effect" and the Use of Social Science Research in Election Law Disputes*, 5 ELECTION L.J. 40, 41 (2006). Given these complications, how confident should a court be in intervening to rectify errors regarding ballot order? *Cf.* Mary Beth Beazley, *Ballot Design as Fail-Safe: An Ounce of Rotation Is Worth a Pound of Litigation*, 12 ELECTION L.J. 18 (2013).

D.   STATE REMEDIES FOR FEDERAL ELECTIONS

Previous portions of this Chapter discussed cases (*e.g., Bell, Scheer*) where federal courts contemplated whether and to what extent they should intervene to regulate elections to state offices. In this section, we consider the opposite issue, of state courts contemplating remedies for errors in elections to federal office. The U.S. Constitution and federal statutes speak to this issue in several ways. For presidential elections, Art. II establishes the Electoral College, but largely leaves to states, and specifically state legislatures, the methods to choose their electors. The Electoral Count Act of 1887, 3 U.S.C. §§ 1–21, establishes deadlines for states to select their electors, and for Congress to count any disputed electoral votes.

A separate set of provisions deals with congressional elections. For example, Art. I, § 4, of the Constitution, applied in *Foster v. Love*, gives state legislatures the power to regulate the time, place and manner of such elections, but also states that Congress may "make or alter such regulations." Congress is vested with power to be the exclusive judge of the elections, returns, and qualifications of its own members, Art. II, § 5, and since 1842 Congress has required that members of the House of Representatives be elected in single-member districts, as opposed to being elected state-wide. 2 U.S.C. § 2c.

Nonetheless, these provisions are not comprehensive, and much of the details of elections to federal office are left to the provisions of particular states. As you read the following cases, consider whether this scheme is a rational one. Does it make sense to delegate much of this authority to the states? Is there, or should there be, an independent federal (*i.e.*, national) interest in regulating elections to federal office, and should that interest be largely delegated to state political institutions in general, and state courts in particular? What is the alternative if state electoral processes are not used?

MCPHERSON v. BLACKER
Supreme Court of the United States.
146 U.S. 1, 13 S. Ct. 3, 36 L. Ed. 869 (1892)

Mr. Chief Justice Fuller, * * * delivered the opinion of the court [in which Mr. Justice Field, Mr. Justice Harlan, Mr. Justice Gray, Mr. Justice Blatchford, Mr. Justice Lamar, Mr. Justice Brewer, Mr. Justice Brown, and Mr. Justice Shiras join]. * * *

[Prior to 1892, Michigan allocated its Presidential electors on a statewide, winner-take-all basis. In that year, the Michigan legislature passed a law that allocated the electors by congressional district, based on the winner of the popular vote for President in each district. Maine and Nebraska still use versions of this approach. Persons nominated to be Presidential electors challenged the scheme in state court on various federal and state-law grounds, and they were rejected by the Michigan Supreme Court.]

On behalf of plaintiffs in error it is contended that the act is void because in conflict with (1) clause two of section one of Article II of the Constitution of the United States; (2) the Fourteenth and Fifteenth Amendments to the Constitution; and (3) the act of Congress, of February 3, 1887.

The second clause of section 1 of Article II of the constitution is in these words: "Each State shall appoint, in such Manner as the Legislature thereof may direct, a Number of Electors, equal to the whole Number of Senators and Representatives to which the State may be entitled in the Congress; but no Senator or Representative, or Person holding an Office of Trust or Profit under the United States, shall be appointed an Elector."

The manner of the appointment of electors directed by the act of Michigan is the election of an elector and an alternate elector in each of the twelve Congressional districts into which the State of Michigan is divided, and of an elector and an alternate elector at large in each of two districts defined by the act. It is insisted that it was not competent for the legislature to direct this manner of appointment, because the State is to appoint as a body politic and corporate, and so must act as a unit, and cannot delegate the authority to subdivisions created for the purpose; and it is argued that the appointment of electors by districts is not an appointment by the state, because all its citizens otherwise qualified are not permitted to vote for all the presidential electors.

"A State, in the ordinary sense of the Constitution," said Chief Justice Chase, *Texas* v. *White*, [74 U.S.,] 7 Wall. 700, 731 [(1868)], "is a political community of free citizens, occupying a territory of defined boundaries, and organized under a government sanctioned and limited by a written constitution, and established by the consent of the governed." The State does not act by its people in their collective capacity, but through such political agencies as are duly constituted and established. The legislative power is the supreme authority, except as limited by the constitution of the State, and the sovereignty of the people is exercised through their representatives in the legislature, unless by the fundamental law power is elsewhere reposed. The Constitution of the United States frequently refers to the State as a political community, and also in terms to the people of the several States and the citizens of each State. What is forbidden or required to be done by a State is forbidden or required of the legislative power under state constitutions as they exist. The clause under consideration does not read that the people or the citizens shall appoint, but that "each State shall"; and if the words, "in such manner as the legislature thereof may direct," had been omitted, it would seem that the legislative power of appointment could not have been successfully questioned in the absence of any provision in the state constitution in that regard. Hence the insertion of those words, while operating as a limitation upon the State in respect of any attempt to circumscribe the legislative power, cannot be held to operate as a limitation on that power itself.

If the legislature possesses plenary authority to direct the manner of appointment, and might itself exercise the appointing power by joint ballot or concurrence of the two houses, or according to such mode as designated, it is difficult to perceive why, if the legislature prescribes as a method of appointment choice by vote, it must necessarily be by general ticket, and not by districts. In other words, the act of appointment is none the less the act of the State in its entirety because arrived at by districts, for the act is the act of political agencies duly authorized to speak for the state, and the combined result is the expression of the voice of the state, a result reached by direction of the legislature, to whom the whole subject is committed.

By the first paragraph of section two, Article I, it is provided: "The House of Representatives shall be composed of Members chosen every second year by the people of the several States, and the Electors in each State shall have the Qualifications requisite for Electors of the most numerous Branch of the State Legislature;" and by the third paragraph, "when vacancies happen in the Representation from any State, the Executive Authority thereof shall issue Writs of Election to fill such Vacancies." Section four reads: "The Times, Places, and Manner of holding Elections for Senators and Representatives, shall be prescribed in each State by the Legislature thereof; but the Congress may at any time by Law make or alter such Regulations, except as to the Places of choosing Senators."

Although it is thus declared that the people of the several States shall choose the members of Congress, (language which induced the State of New York to insert a salvo as to the power to divide into districts, in its resolutions of ratification,) the state legislatures, prior to 1842, in prescribing the times, places, and manner of holding elections for representatives, had usually apportioned the State into districts, and assigned to each a representative; and by act of Congress of June 25, 1842, * * * it was provided that, where a State was entitled to more than one representative, the election should be by districts. It has never been doubted that representatives in Congress thus chosen represented the entire people of the state acting in their sovereign capacity.

By original clause three of section one of Article II, and by the Twelfth Amendment which superseded that clause, in case of a failure in the election of President by the people, the House of Representatives is to choose the President; and "the vote shall be taken by States, the representation from each State having one vote." The State acts as a unit, and its vote is given as a unit, but that vote is arrived at through the votes of its representatives in Congress elected by districts.

The State also acts individually through its electoral college, although, by reason of the power of its legislature over the manner of appointment, the vote of its electors may be divided.

The Constitution does not provide that the appointment of electors shall be by popular vote, nor that the electors shall be voted for upon a general ticket, nor that the majority of those who exercise the elective franchise can alone choose the electors. It recognizes that the people act through their representatives in the legislature, and leaves it to the legislature exclusively to define the method of effecting the object.

The framers of the Constitution employed words in their natural sense; and where they are plain and clear, resort to collateral aids to interpretation is unnecessary and cannot be indulged in to narrow or enlarge the text; but where there is ambiguity or doubt, or where two views may well be entertained, contemporaneous and subsequent practical construction are entitled to the greatest weight. Certainly, plaintiffs in error cannot reasonably assert that the clause of the Constitution under consideration so plainly sustains their position as to entitle them to object that contemporaneous history and practical construction are not to be allowed their legitimate force, and, conceding that their argument inspires a doubt sufficient to justify resort to the aids of interpretation thus afforded, we are of opinion that such doubt is thereby resolved against them, the contemporaneous practical exposition of the constitution being too strong and obstinate to be shaken or controlled. *Stuart* v. *Laird*, [5 U.S.] 1 Cranch, 299, 309 [(1803)].

It has been said that the word "appoint" is not the most appropriate word to describe the result of a popular election. Perhaps not; but it is sufficiently comprehensive to cover that mode, and was manifestly used as conveying the broadest power of determination. It was used in Article 5 of the Articles of Confederation, which provided that "delegates shall be annually appointed in such manner as the legislature of each State shall direct;" and in the resolution of Congress of February 21, 1787, which declared it expedient that "a convention of delegates who shall have been appointed by the several States," should be held. The appointment of delegates was, in fact, made by the legislatures directly, but that involved no denial of authority to direct some other mode. The Constitutional Convention, by resolution of September 17, 1787, expressed the opinion that the Congress should fix a day "on which electors should be appointed by the states which shall have ratified the same," etc., and that, "after such publication, the electors should be appointed, and the senators and representatives elected."

The Journal of the Convention discloses that propositions that the President should be elected by "the citizens of the United States," or by the "people," or "by electors to be chosen by the people of the several States," instead of by the Congress, were voted down, as was the proposition that the President should be "chosen by electors appointed for that purpose by the legislatures of the States," though at one time adopted. And a motion to postpone the consideration of the choice "by the national legislature," in order to take up a resolution providing for electors to be elected by the qualified voters in districts, was negatived in Committee of the Whole. Gerry proposed that the choice should be made by the State executives; Hamilton, that the election be by electors chosen by electors chosen by the people; James Wilson and Gouverneur Morris were strongly in favor of popular vote; Ellsworth and Luther Martin preferred the choice by electors elected by the legislatures; and Roger Sherman, appointment by Congress. The final result seems to have reconciled contrariety of views by leaving it to the state legislatures to appoint directly by joint ballot or concurrent separate action, or through popular election by districts or by general ticket, or as otherwise might be directed.

Therefore, on reference to contemporaneous and subsequent action under the clause, we should expect to find, as we do, that various modes of choosing the electors were pursued, as, by the legislature itself on joint ballot; by the legislature through a concurrent vote of the two houses; by vote of the people for a general ticket; by vote of the people in districts; by choice partly by the people voting in districts and partly by the legislature; by choice by the legislature from candidates voted for by the people in districts; and in other ways, as, notably, by North Carolina in 1792, and Tennessee in 1796 and 1800. No question was raised as to the power of the State to appoint in any mode its legislature saw fit to adopt, and none that a single method, applicable without exception, must be pursued in the absence of an amendment to the Constitution. The district system was largely considered the most equitable, and Madison wrote that it was that system which was contemplated by the framers of the Constitution, although it was soon seen that its adoption by some States might place them at a disadvantage by a division of their strength, and that a uniform rule was preferable.

From [a] review [of the various ways States chose Presidential electors between 1788 and 1892], * * * it is seen that from the formation of the government until now the practical construction of the clause has conceded plenary power to the state legislatures in the matter of the appointment of electors.

Even in the heated controversy of 1876–1877 the electoral vote of Colorado cast by electors chosen by the legislature passed unchallenged, and our attention has not been drawn to any previous attempt to submit to the courts the determination of the constitutionality of state action.

In short, the appointment and mode of appointment of electors belong exclusively to the States under the Constitution of the United States. They are, as remarked by Mr. Justice Gray in *In re Green*, 134 U.S. 377, 379 [(1890)], "no more officers or agents of the United States than are the members of the state legislatures when acting as electors of Federal senators, or the people of the States when acting as the electors of representatives in Congress." Congress is empowered to determine the time of choosing the electors and the day on which they are to give their votes, which is required to be the same day throughout the United States; but otherwise the power and jurisdiction of the state is exclusive, with the exception of the provisions as to the number of electors and the ineligibility of certain persons, so framed that Congressional and Federal influence might be excluded.

The question before us is not one of policy, but of power; and, while public opinion had gradually brought all the States as matter of fact to the pursuit of a uniform system of popular election by general ticket, that fact does not tend to weaken the force of contemporaneous and long continued previous practice when and as different views of expediency prevailed. The prescription of the written law cannot be overthrown because the States have latterly exercised in a particular way a power which they might have exercised in some other way. The construction to which we have referred has prevailed too long and been too uniform to justify us in interpreting the language of the Constitution as conveying any other meaning than that heretofore ascribed, and it must be treated as decisive.

It is argued that the district mode of choosing electors, while not obnoxious to constitutional objection, if the operation of the electoral system had conformed to its original object and purpose, had become so in view of the practical working of that system. Doubtless it was supposed that the electors would exercise a reasonable independence and fair judgment in the selection of the Chief Executive, but experience soon demonstrated that, whether chosen by the legislatures or by popular suffrage on general ticket or in districts, they were so chosen simply to register the will of the appointing power in respect of a particular candidate. In relation, then, to the independence of the electors the original expectation may be said to have been frustrated. But we can perceive no reason for holding that the power confided to the States by the Constitution has ceased to exist because the operation of the system has not fully realized the hopes of those by whom it was created. Still less can we recognize the doctrine, that because the Constitution has been found in the march of time sufficiently comprehensive to be applicable to conditions not within the minds of its framers, and not arising in their time, it may, therefore, be wrenched from the subjects expressly embraced within it, and amended by judicial decision without action by the designated organs in the mode by which alone amendments can be made.

Nor are we able to discover any conflict between this act and the Fourteenth and Fifteenth Amendments to the Constitution. * * *

If presidential electors are appointed by the legislatures, no discrimination is made; if they are elected in districts where each citizen has an equal right to vote, the same as any other citizen has, no discrimination is made. Unless the authority vested in the legislatures by the second clause of section 1 of Article II has been divested and the State has lost its power of appointment, except in one manner, the position taken on behalf of relators is untenable, and it is apparent that neither of these amendments can be given such effect.

The third clause of section 1 of Article II of the Constitution is: "The Congress may determine the time of choosing the Electors, and the day on which they shall give their votes; which day shall be the same throughout the United States." * * *

By the act of Congress of February 3, 1887, entitled "An act to fix the day for the meeting of the electors of President and Vice President," etc., it was provided that the electors of each State should meet and give their votes on the second Monday in January next following their appointment. The state law in question here fixes the first Wednesday of December as the day for the meeting of the electors, as originally designated by Congress. In this respect it is in conflict with the act of Congress, and must necessarily give way. But this part of the act is not so inseparably connected in substance with the other parts as to work the destruction of the whole act. Striking out the day for the meeting, which had already been otherwise determined by the act of Congress, the act remains complete in itself, and capable of being carried out in accordance with the legislative intent. The state law yields only to the extent of the collision. The construction to this effect by the state court is of persuasive force, if not of controlling weight. * * *

We repeat that the main question arising for consideration is one of power and not of policy, and we are unable to arrive at any other conclusion than that the act of the legislature of Michigan of May 1, 1891, is not void as in contravention of the Constitution of the United States, for want of power in its enactment.

The judgment of the Supreme Court of Michigan must be

Affirmed.

COLEMAN v. FRANKEN
Supreme Court of Minnesota
767 N.W.2d 453 (Minn. 2009)

PER CURIAM. [JUSTICES PAGE, P.H. ANDERSON, MEYER, GILDEA, and DIETZEN join in this opinion, CHIEF JUSTICE MAGNUSON and JUSTICE G.B. ANDERSON taking no part.]

Appellants, incumbent Republican United States Senator Norm Coleman and Cullen Sheehan, filed a notice of election contest under Minn. Stat. § 209.021 (2008), challenging the State Canvassing Board's certification that Democratic-Farmer-Labor challenger Al Franken was entitled to receive a certificate of election as United States Senator following the November 4, 2008 general election. After a trial, the three-judge trial court we appointed to hear the election contest issued its findings of fact, conclusions of law, and order for judgment, concluding that Franken received 312 more legally cast votes than Coleman and that Franken was entitled to a certificate of election for the office of United States Senator. The question presented on appeal is whether the trial court erred in concluding that Al Franken received the most legally cast votes in the election for United States Senator. Because we conclude that appellants have not shown that the trial court's findings of fact are clearly erroneous or that the court committed an error of law or abused its discretion, we affirm.

More than 2.9 million Minnesotans cast ballots in the November general election, including approximately 300,000 who voted or attempted to vote by absentee ballot. On November 18, 2008, the State Canvassing Board accepted the consolidated statewide canvassing report as showing that Coleman received 1,211,565 votes and that Franken received 1,211,359 votes for the office of United States Senator, a margin of 206 votes in Coleman's favor. Because the margin separating the two candidates was less than one-half of one percent of the total number of votes counted for that office, the State Canvassing Board directed the Minnesota Secretary of State's Office to oversee a manual recount, as required by [Minnesota law].

The statewide manual recount was conducted between November 19, 2008, and January 5, 2009, pursuant to instructions drafted by the Secretary of State's Office and approved by the State Canvassing Board after consultation with representatives of Coleman and Franken. During the recount, local election officials and the candidates reviewed the absentee ballot return envelopes that had been rejected on or before election day and agreed that some of them had been improperly rejected. On January 3, 2009, the Secretary of State's Office opened and counted the 933 ballots identified during this process. On January 5, 2009, the State Canvassing Board certified the results of the election as 1,212,431 votes for Franken and 1,212,206 votes for Coleman, a margin of 225 votes in Franken's favor.

On January 6, 2009, appellants Coleman and Sheehan (hereinafter "Coleman") filed a notice of election contest in Ramsey County District Court * * *, contesting the election results certified by the State Canvassing Board and seeking a declaration that Coleman was entitled to the certificate of election as United States Senator. * * * No claim of fraud in the election or during the recount was made by either party. At the conclusion of the trial, the court determined that 351 additional absentee ballot return envelopes satisfied the statutory requirements and ordered that these envelopes be opened and the ballots inside counted.

On April 13, 2009, the trial court issued its findings of fact, conclusions of law, and order for judgment, finding that Franken received 1,212,629 votes and Coleman received 1,212,317 votes in the November 4, 2008 general election, a margin of 312 votes in Franken's favor. The court found that Franken received the highest number of votes legally cast in the election for United States Senator for the State of Minnesota and concluded that Franken was entitled to receive the certificate of election.

The State Canvassing Board's certification is prima facie evidence that Franken, the contestee, has been elected to the office. Coleman, the contestant, bears the burden of proof in the trial to show that the Board's certification was in error. * * *

Appellants raise essentially five issues: (1) whether the trial court violated Coleman's right to substantive due process by requiring strict, rather than only substantial, compliance with the statutory requirements for absentee voting; (2) whether Coleman's right to equal protection of the laws was violated, either by differences among jurisdictions in their application of the statutory requirements for absentee voting or by the court's rulings on the statutory requirements for absentee voting; (3) whether the court erred in excluding certain evidence; (4) whether the court erred in declining to order inspections of ballots and other election materials for precincts in which Coleman alleges that ballots may have been double-counted during the manual recount; and (5) whether the court erred by including in the final vote tally the election day returns from one Minneapolis precinct in which some ballots were lost before the manual recount.

I.

We turn first to the question of whether Coleman's right to substantive due process under the United States Constitution has been violated. * * * Decisions regarding challenges to the states' administration of elections reflect the limited reach of substantive due process. *See Roe v. Alabama*, 43 F.3d 574, 580 (11th Cir. 1995) [p. 1161] ("Not every state election dispute, however, implicates the Due Process Clause of the Fourteenth Amendment and thus leads to possible federal court intervention. . . . If, however, the election process itself reaches the point of patent and fundamental unfairness, a violation of the due process clause may be indicated. . . . "). Based on its review of cases involving substantive due process challenges to election procedures, the Ninth Circuit has identified two elements as common to cases in which a violation was established:

> A general pattern emerges from all of these cases taken together. Mere fraud or mistake will not render an election invalid. However, a court will strike down an election on substantive due process grounds if two elements are present: (1) likely reliance by voters on an established election procedure and/or official pronouncements about what the procedure will be in the coming election; and (2) significant disenfranchisement that results from a change in the election procedures.

Bennett v. Yoshina, 140 F.3d 1218, 1226–27 (9th Cir. 1998).[8]

Although we have not previously considered substantive due process in the context of an election dispute, we agree with the federal courts and adopt the federal rule to determine whether a substantive due process violation has occurred in an election. To prevail on a claim that a change in election standards violated substantive due process, the contestant must show a change that is patently and fundamentally unfair. In other words, the contestant must show likely reliance by the voters on an existing election procedure and a change in that procedure that results in significant disenfranchisement of the voters. Under this standard, in order to sustain a substantive due process violation, Coleman must prove as a threshold matter that the post-election change about which he complains — the trial court's adherence to a strict compliance standard — changed the procedures

---

[8] Cases cited by Coleman illustrate the kind of post-election change in standards that can constitute a due process violation. For example, in *Roe*, after the election, a state circuit court ruled for the first time that no absentee ballot could be excluded for lack of notarization or lack of witnesses, even though those requirements had previously been enforced for years. 43 F.3d at 578–79; *see also Griffin v. Burns*, 570 F.2d 1065, 1078–79 (1st Cir. 1978) (holding that due process was violated when absentee balloting was disallowed post-election after it had been allowed in previous elections for years); *Briscoe v. Kusper*, 435 F.2d 1046, 1055 (7th Cir. 1970) (holding that due process was violated when signature requirements were enforced for the first time).

on which the voters relied on election day.

Coleman asserts that the trial court's February 13 order established a new standard of strict compliance with absentee ballot requirements, whereas precedent of this court and the practices of election officials, on election day and during the manual recount, required only substantial compliance.[9] If, in fact, strict adherence was not what the law required, so that voters could be said to have relied on something less, Coleman's argument might warrant further examination. But the law, both as provided by statute and in our precedent, requires strict adherence.

The Minnesota Legislature has established the process for voting by absentee ballot. Generally, a prospective voter first submits a written application for an absentee ballot. If the application complies with statutory requirements, the county auditor or municipal clerk sends the voter an absentee ballot, an absentee ballot return envelope, a ballot envelope (sometimes called a secrecy or security envelope), and a copy of the directions for casting an absentee ballot. If the applicant is not registered, the county auditor or municipal clerk includes a voter registration application.

The voter marks the ballot before a witness and puts the ballot in the secrecy envelope. The voter then puts the secrecy envelope (and the registration application, if any) in the ballot return envelope. The voter and the witness each sign the ballot return envelope. The completed ballot return envelope is returned to the county auditor or municipal clerk. The next step in the absentee voting process is acceptance or rejection of the ballot return envelope by local election officials. The decision to accept or reject the ballot return envelope is made at the precinct by local election judges on election day, or, if the local jurisdiction has an absentee ballot board, by the board in the 30 days before the election. The ballot return envelope is marked "Accepted" if officials are "satisfied" that:

(1) the voter's name and address on the return envelope are the same as the information provided on the absentee ballot application;

(2) the voter's signature on the return envelope is the genuine signature of the individual who made the application for ballots and the certificate has been completed as prescribed in the directions for casting an absentee ballot, except that if a person other than the voter applied for the absentee ballot under applicable Minnesota Rules, the signature is not required to match;

(3) the voter is registered and eligible to vote in the precinct or has included a properly completed voter registration application in the return envelope; and

---

[9] The trial court concluded that it must enforce all requirements imposed by law upon voting by absentee ballot because our cases make those requirements mandatory for voters. The court found support for this conclusion in the facts that: (1) "the Minnesota Legislature has made voting in person relatively straightforward by permitting same-day voter registration," reflecting a policy decision to encourage voting in person on Election Day; and (2) "requiring compliance with the voting laws ultimately minimizes the risks of fraud and illegal voting that act as a detriment to a fair electoral process."

(4) the voter has not already voted at that election, either in person or by absentee ballot.

Minn. Stat. § 203B.12, subd. 2. Section 203B.12, subd. 2, makes clear that "[t]here is no other reason for rejecting an absentee ballot."

On election day, the absentee ballot return envelopes are delivered to the absentee voters' respective polling places. Before opening the accepted ballot return envelopes, election judges check each envelope against the precinct roster to be sure the voter has not voted in person or by another absentee ballot. If not, the election judges record those voters who voted by absentee ballot by marking the precinct roster with the notation "A.B." for each accepted absentee ballot return envelope. Once the roster has been so marked, the voter cannot vote again in that election. After the last mail delivery on election day, election judges open the accepted ballot return envelopes, remove the enclosed ballots from their secrecy envelopes, and then deposit the ballots in the ballot box.

The trial court's February 13 order closely tracks the requirements of these statutes. But Coleman contends that our precedent allows for something less than strict compliance with the statutory mandates. We disagree.

Although we have used a substantial compliance standard to judge errors by election officials, we have held voters strictly to statutory requirements. * * *

The distinction between errors by voters and errors by election officials is an important one. We have drawn "a clear distinction between the provisions and prohibitions in the election laws which are personal to the elector and those which apply to election officials over whose conduct he has no control." *Fitzgerald v. Morlock*, 120 N.W.2d 339, 345 (1963). We have said that "any reasonable regulations of the statute as to the conduct of the voter himself" are mandatory, and a vote is properly rejected if the voter fails to comply with the law. *Id.* at 345. But if a voter complies with the law, his vote should not be rejected because of "irregularities, ignorance, inadvertence, or mistake, or even intentional wrong on the part of the election officers." *Id.*

In *Bell v. Gannaway*, we again explained that voting by absentee ballot is a privilege, not a right, and affirmed the mandatory nature of absentee voting requirements. 227 N.W.2d 797, 802–03 (1975). We reiterated that because "the privilege of absentee voting is granted by the legislature, the legislature may mandate the conditions and procedures for such voting." *Id.* at 802.[11] We said there that strict compliance with the requirements for voting by absentee ballot is mandatory: "[V]oters who seek to vote under these provisions must be held to a strict compliance therewith." *Id.* at 803.

We conclude that our existing case law requires strict compliance by voters with the requirements for absentee voting. Thus, we reject Coleman's argument that only substantial compliance by voters is required. Having rejected this argument, we also conclude that the trial court's February 13 order requiring strict compliance

---

[11] At oral argument, Coleman posited that because of the increased use of the absentee voting method, it should now be treated as a right, not a privilege. But that is a policy determination for the legislature, not this court, to make.

with the statutory requirements for absentee voting was not a deviation from our well-established precedent.

Because strict compliance with the statutory requirements for absentee voting is, and has always been, required, there is no basis on which voters could have reasonably believed that anything less than strict compliance would suffice. Furthermore, Coleman does not cite, and after review of the record we have not found, any evidence in the record that election officials required only substantial compliance in any past election or any official pronouncements that only substantial compliance would be required in the November 4, 2008 election. Nor does Coleman point us to the testimony of any voter who neglected to comply with the statutory requirements for absentee voting in reliance on either past practice or official assurances that strict compliance was not required. Indeed, Coleman's counsel acknowledged during oral argument that Coleman cannot claim that any voters changed their behavior based on the alleged substantial compliance standard.

For all of these reasons, we hold that Coleman has not proven that the trial court's February 13 order violated substantive due process.

II.

We next examine Coleman's argument that the constitutional guarantee of equal protection was violated in this case. Coleman's equal protection argument is two-fold. First, he argues that the differing application and implementation by election officials of the statutory requirements for absentee voting violated equal protection. Essentially, Coleman contends that similarly situated absentee ballots were treated differently depending on the jurisdiction in which they were cast and that this disparate treatment violated equal protection. Second, Coleman contends that equal protection was violated when the trial court adhered to the statutory requirements for acceptance of absentee ballots, in contrast to the practices of local jurisdictions during the election.

Both parts of Coleman's equal protection argument depend on his assertion that differential application, either by election officials or by the trial court, of the statutory requirements for absentee voting violates equal protection. But equal protection is not violated every time public officials apply facially neutral state laws differently. The United States Supreme Court has held that "an erroneous or mistaken performance of [a] statutory duty, although a violation of the statute, is not without more a denial of the equal protection of the laws." *Snowden v. Hughes*, 321 U.S. 1, 8 (1944). The Court then explained that the "more" that is required for a violation of equal protection is intentional or purposeful discrimination. *Id.* The Court said:

> The unlawful administration by state officers of a state statute fair on its face, resulting in its unequal application to those who are entitled to be treated alike, is not a denial of equal protection unless there is shown to be present in it an element of intentional or purposeful discrimination.

Id.; *see also Vill. of Arlington Heights v. Metro. Hous. Dev. Corp.*, 429 U.S. 252, 265 (1977) (holding that proof of discriminatory intent or purpose is required to show a violation of the Equal Protection Clause); *Washington v. Davis*, 426 U.S. 229, 240–42 (1976) (same). * * *

Accordingly, in order to prevail on his equal protection claim of disparate application of a facially neutral statute, Coleman was required to prove either that local jurisdictions' differences in application or the trial court's application of the requirements for absentee voting was the product of intentional discrimination. Coleman neither claims nor produced any evidence that the differing treatment of absentee ballots among jurisdictions during the election was the result of intentional or purposeful discrimination against individuals or classes. Nor does Coleman claim that the trial court's February 13 order, establishing certain categories of ballots as not legally cast, was the product of an intent to discriminate against any individual or class.

On appeal, Coleman contends that he proved an equal protection violation by showing that local election officials made deliberate and intentional decisions to adopt particular interpretations of the statutory requirements for absentee voting. Under *Snowden*, however, the fact that the official's decision to act in a particular way was deliberate does not constitute discriminatory intent. *See* 321 U.S. at 10 (explaining that the requirement of intentional discrimination is not satisfied by allegations of willful, malicious conduct). Instead, *Snowden* requires a showing that the statutory standards were applied differently with the intent to discriminate in favor of one individual or class over another. *Id.* at 8.[13]

The trial court found that election judges applied the election laws in a consistent and uniform manner. The court found that election jurisdictions adopted policies they deemed necessary to ensure that absentee voting procedures would be available to their residents, in accordance with statutory requirements, given the resources available to them. The court also found that differences in available resources, personnel, procedures, and technology necessarily affected the procedures used by local election officials reviewing absentee ballots. But the court found that Coleman did not prove that these differences were calculated to discriminate among absentee voters. Our review of the record convinces us that the trial court's findings are supported by the evidence and are not clearly erroneous. As a result, we conclude that Coleman did not prove his equal protection claim.[15]

Coleman makes the additional argument that the non-uniform application of the statutory standards for absentee voting nevertheless brings this case within the

---

[13] The Supreme Court observed in *Snowden* that intent to discriminate could also be demonstrated by evidence of systematic discrimination "so that the practical effect of the official breach of law is the same as though the discrimination were incorporated in and proclaimed by the statute." 321 U.S. at 9. Coleman neither claims nor introduced evidence of any systematic discrimination.

[15] Although we affirm the trial court's conclusion that any differences in the application of the statutory standard by the trial court and by election officials on election day and during the manual recount are not of constitutional magnitude, we do not suggest that any such differences are inconsequential and need not be addressed. It is impossible to eliminate all variation in a process administered at thousands of locations around the state by thousands of people, many of them temporary volunteers. To the extent that this case has brought to light inconsistencies in the administration of absentee voting standards, we are confident that the appropriate officials in the other branches of government understand that efforts should be made to reduce those inconsistencies, even though they were not proven to be of constitutional magnitude.

ambit of the United States Supreme Court's decision in *Bush v. Gore*, 531 U.S. 98 (2000) (per curiam) [p. 1065]. In *Bush*, the Court held that the statewide recount of the 2000 presidential election that had been ordered by the Florida Supreme Court violated equal protection. *Id.* at 103. Coleman argues that, in Minnesota's 2008 United States Senate election, different local election jurisdictions treated similarly situated absentee ballots differently and that the trial court imposed a stricter standard for compliance with absentee voting requirements than did election officials, and that those differences violate equal protection under *Bush*.

The trial court concluded that *Bush* is distinguishable in several important respects and, as a result, does not support Coleman's equal protection claim. We agree. In *Bush*, the Supreme Court specifically noted that it was not addressing the question of "whether local entities, in the exercise of their expertise, may develop different systems for implementing elections." 531 U.S. at 109. Variations in local practices for implementing absentee voting procedures are, at least in part, the question at issue here. As previously noted, the trial court here found that the disparities in application of the statutory standards on which Coleman relies are the product of local jurisdictions' use of different methods to ensure compliance with the same statutory standards; that jurisdictions adopted policies they deemed necessary to ensure that absentee voting procedures would be available to their residents, in accordance with statutory requirements, given the resources available to them; and that differences in available resources, personnel, procedures, and technology necessarily affected the procedures used by local election officials in reviewing absentee ballots. As we noted previously, Coleman has not demonstrated that these findings are clearly erroneous.

Additionally, the essence of the equal protection problem addressed in *Bush* was that there were no established standards under Florida statutes or provided by the state supreme court for determining voter intent; as a result, in the recount process each county (indeed, each recount location within a county) was left to set its own standards for discerning voter intent. *See id.* at 106. Here, there were clear statutory standards for acceptance or rejection of absentee ballots, about which all election officials received common training.

Finally, the decision to be made by Florida election officials with which the Supreme Court was concerned in *Bush* was voter intent — that is, for whom the ballot was cast — as reflected on ballots already cast in the election. In *Bush*, officials conducting the recount were reviewing the face of the ballot itself, creating opportunities for manipulation of the decision for political purposes. Here, the decision at issue was whether to accept or reject absentee ballot return envelopes before they were opened, meaning that the actual votes on the ballot contained in the return envelope were not known to the election officials applying the standards. In summary, we conclude that *Bush v. Gore* is not applicable and does not support Coleman's equal protection claim.

For all of these reasons, we conclude that Coleman has not proven that either election officials or the trial court violated his right to equal protection.

III. * * *

Coleman argued at trial that as a result of the trial court's February 13 order finding that certain ballots were not legally cast, there are absentee ballots included in the State Canvassing Board's certification of election results that would have been rejected if the strict compliance standard of the trial court had been applied to them. Coleman therefore argued that if the court did not adopt the substantial compliance standard that Coleman claims was used on election day, the court was required to apply a strict compliance standard to ballots already accepted and counted on election day and reduce the parties' vote totals for any ballots that did not meet that standard.

The trial court rejected Coleman's argument and the evidence Coleman offered to support it. Coleman made an offer of proof identifying absentee ballot return envelopes that had been opened and the enclosed ballots removed and counted on election day or during the manual recount. Coleman did not seek to present evidence identifying the ballots removed from those envelopes and could not have done so, because once the ballots were removed from the envelopes and deposited in the ballot box, they were commingled with other counted ballots and could not be identified. We conclude that the court did not abuse its discretion in excluding this evidence because the legislature has foreclosed any challenge to the legality of an absentee ballot based on the return envelope once the ballot has been deposited in the ballot box. * * *

Accordingly, we conclude that the court did not abuse its discretion in excluding the evidence. * * *

V.

Finally, Coleman contends that the trial court erred when it ruled that missing ballots from Minneapolis Ward 3, Precinct 1, were properly included in the State Canvassing Board's January 5, 2009 certification of legally cast votes. During the manual recount, election officials could locate only four of the five envelopes of ballots from Minneapolis Ward 3, Precinct 1. Voting machine tapes showed a total of 2,028 ballots cast and counted in the precinct on election day, but only 1,896 ballots from the precinct were available for the recount, a difference of 132 ballots. The State Canvassing Board determined that an envelope of ballots had been lost and, rather than certify only 1,896 votes in the recount, accepted the election day returns for that precinct.

The trial court found no allegations or evidence of fraud or foul play and no evidence to suggest that the election day totals from the precinct are unreliable. The court therefore found "that 132 ballots from Minneapolis Precinct 3-1 were cast and properly counted on Election Day and were lost at some point after they were counted on Election Day but before the administrative recount." * * *

The ballots are missing, but Coleman introduced no evidence of foul play or misconduct, and the election day precinct returns are available to give effect to those votes. We hold that the trial court did not err in ruling that the election day precinct returns for Minneapolis Ward 3, Precinct 1, were properly included in the tally of legally cast votes.

VI.

For all of the foregoing reasons, we affirm the decision of the trial court that Al Franken received the highest number of votes legally cast and is entitled * * * to receive the certificate of election as United States Senator from the State of Minnesota.

Affirmed.

Notes and Questions

1.   The *McPherson* case played a role in the *Bush v. Gore* litigation, as further described in Chapter 11. In addition to the questions raised there about the effect of Article II, § 1, of the U.S. Constitution, how broadly should *McPherson* be applied? For example, should it be read as vesting the state legislatures mentioned in Article II (as opposed to other branches of state government) with supreme authority to regulate the choosing of presidential electors? Does this mean that a state legislature could, say, limit or prohibit women or African-Americans from voting for or serving as electors? Most people, we assume, would immediately disagree, pointing to the Fourteenth, Fifteenth and Nineteenth Amendments, not to mention the Voting Rights Act and other laws. Can *McPherson* be interpreted to permit this conclusion? Note that the case does take into account the Fourteenth and Fifteenth Amendments.

Likewise, consider the recent movement that advocates changing the distribution of presidential electors in each state from winner-take-all to a proportional system, tied to the actual vote in each state. Could a state, consistent with Article II, adopt such a system by citizen initiative, rather than by action by the state legislature? *See* Nicholas P. Stabile, Comment, *An End Run Around a Representative Democracy? The Unconstitutionality of a Ballot Initiative to Alter the Method of Distributing Electors*, 103 Nw. U. L. Rev. 1495 (2009).

2.   One indication of the importance of state law for regulating federal elections is *Roudebush v. Hartke*, 405 U.S. 15 (1972). There, incumbent Senator C. Vance Hartke, Democrat from Indiana, defeated Republican challenger Richard Roudebush in an extremely close vote. Roudebush filed a petition in state court to order a recount, and Hartke responded by filing suit in U.S. District Court, requesting that it enjoin the state-court litigation. The federal court eventually did that, on the basis that the state recount procedures would interfere with the Senate's power to judge the qualifications of its own members. On appeal the Supreme Court reversed. The 5-2 majority held that the states possessed broad authority to regulate federal elections, and a manual recount is "within the ambit" of those powers. Such a recount would not prevent the Senate from later independently evaluating the election, or from conducting its own recount. There was no evidence to support the District Court's holding that a recount "would increase the probability of election fraud and accidental destruction of ballots." The dissent argued that the Senate had a long tradition of independently resolving disputed elections to that body, by convening a special committee. There was a federal interest, the dissent contended, "in preserving the integrity of the evidence" of the

disputed ballots, and for that reason it agreed with the District Court.

The *Roudebush* decision gave a good deal of power to states, and state courts in particular, to resolve disputed congressional elections. But it apparently left intact the ability of the houses of Congress to take action concurrently to resolve such disputes. Since *Roudebush*, some disappointed candidates have simultaneously pursued remedies in state courts and in Congress. *See* Kristen R. Lisk, Note, *The Resolution of Contested Elections in the U.S. House of Representatives: Why State Courts Should Not Help with the House Work*, 83 N.Y.U. L. Rev. 1213 (2008) (discussing examples). Does this forum-shopping make sense in this context? At what point, in the words of *Roudebush*, do state actions "frustrate" the ability of Congress to judge the elections of its own members, should it care to do that? Conversely, as a general matter, should Congress presumptively defer to state action in this regard, absent specific congressional regulation on point? In the words of then-Circuit Judge Stevens, who sat on the lower court in *Roudebush*, would the work of the Senate "be facilitated, rather than impaired, by the availability of a fairly conducted recount * * * before undertaking its work"? *Hartke v. Roudenbush*, 321 F. Supp. 1370, 1378–79 (S.D. Ind. 1970) (*per curiam*) (three-judge court) (Stevens, J., dissenting), *rev'd*, 405 U.S. 15 (1972). *See generally* Paul E. Salamanca & James E. Keller, *The Legislative Privilege to Judge the Qualifications, Elections, and Returns of Members*, 95 Ky. L.J. 241 (2006–2007).

3.   Some argue that the state political process, including state courts, is not an appropriate venue to settle election disputes for federal offices. The fear would be that state officials, judges included, would act in parochial and partisan ways to resolve the dispute. While it is hard to argue that the members of the houses of Congress would act any less partisan than state officials in resolving election disputes, nonetheless, some might contend that federal judges with lifetime tenure would be less partisan than their state counterparts. How compelling are these arguments? Anecdotal evidence cuts in different ways. Consider, for example, *Coleman*, where a state supreme court consisting primarily, though not exclusively, of Democrats ruled unanimously in favor of the Democratic candidate. On the federal court side, consider the lower, three-judge district court decision in *Roudebush*. There, the Republican appointee (Stevens) ruled in favor of the Republican candidate, while the other two judges, both Democratic appointees, ruled in favor of the Democratic candidate.

The extant empirical evidence on partisan decision-making by judges in election-related cases is mixed. On the state-court side, compare Scott Graves, *Competing Interests in State Supreme Courts: Justices' Votes and Voting Rights*, 24 Am. Rev. Pol. 267 (2003) (finding state supreme courts acted in partisan ways in some circumstances in ballot-access cases), with Kyle C. Kopko, *Partisanship Suppressed: Judicial Decision-Making in Ralph Nader's 2004 Ballot Access Litigation*, 7 Election L.J. 301 (2008) (finding state judges' partisan affiliations relatively insignificant in cases where Ralph Nader sought placement on the presidential ballot). On the federal-court side, compare Michael E. Solimine, *Institutional Process, Agenda Setting, and the Development of Election Law on the Supreme Court*, 68 Ohio St. L.J. 767, 790–92 (2007) (arguing that the evidence does not show that lower-court federal judges systematically vote in a partisan fashion in election law cases), with Adam C. Cox & Thomas J. Miles, *Judicial Ideology and the*

Transformation of Voting Rights Act Jurisprudence, 75 U. Chi. L. Rev. 1493 (2008) (federal judges often voted in partisan fashion in Voting Rights Act cases). For further discussion, see Richard L. Hasen, *Judges as Political Regulators: Evidence and Options for Institutional Change*, in Race, Reform, and Regulation of the Electoral Process 101 (Guy-Uriel E. Charles, Heather R. Gerken & Michael S. Kang, eds., 2011); James B. Cottrill & Terri J. Perritti, *Gerrymandering from the Bench: The Electoral Consequences of Judicial Redistricting*, 12 Election L.J. 261 (2013).

4. *Coleman* found that the Minnesota recount procedures did not violate *Bush v. Gore*. The court argued that (1) variations in local practice "are the product of local jurisdictions' use of different methods to ensure compliance with the same statutory standards;" (2) unlike in Florida, the Minnesota statutes did have "clear statutory standards," and (3) also unlike in Florida, the issue here was not voter intent as such, but rather "whether to accept or reject absentee ballot return envelopes before they were opened." How persuasive are these arguments, alone or in combination? Does the continuing disagreement on how to interpret the equal-protection principles of *Bush v. Gore* make a coherent evaluation of *Coleman* in this regard difficult? *See* Richard L. Hasen, Bush v. Gore *and the Lawlessness Principle: A Comment on Professor Amar*, 61 Fla. L. Rev. 979, 985 (2009).

5. *Coleman* holds that the right to cast an absentee ballot is a privilege, not a right, and that voters should be strictly held to compliance with statutory requirements. In contrast, the court would use a "substantial compliance" standard when considering the effect of errors by election officials. Does the court convincingly justify this distinction? Is the court right to suggest that changes in this legal regime should be made by the state legislature, not state courts? It appears that many state courts, in contrast, do not make this distinction, and instead will permit absentee or other votes to be counted as long as there is substantial compliance with statutory requirements. *E.g.*, *Miller v. Treadwell*, 245 P.3d 867 (Alaska 2010) (proper to count misspelled write-in votes because statutes should be construed in favor of voter enfranchisement). *See generally* Richard L. Hasen, *The Democracy Canon*, 62 Stan. L. Rev. 69, 86–87 (2009). Is one view necessarily preferable? Should it depend, at least in part, on the precise statutory language in a particular state, and the history of absentee voting and related election issues in a particular state?

E. PUBLIC AND PRIVATE REMEDIES

1. Federal Civil and Criminal Enforcement

Federal statues create a wide range of potential remedies that public entities, or private parties, can use to seek remedies for improper elections. Many of those statutes, and their remedial provisions, have been discussed in prior portions of this casebook. For example, the Voting Rights Act is addressed in Chapters 4 and 5; the Federal Election Campaign Act and its predecessor statutes are addressed in Chapter 9; and the Help America Vote Act (HAVA) and the National Voter Registration Act (NVRA), are discussed in Chapter 11.

These statutes can be enforced, in various ways, by the federal government. Thus, the Federal Election Commission (FEC) can undertake to enforce the campaign finance laws. The FEC can seek a variety of penalties against violators of those laws, but must request that courts enforce its orders. 2 U.S.C. §§ 437c–437h. The Civil Rights Division of the U.S. Department of Justice is charged with enforcing provisions of the Voting Rights Act, HAVA, and other laws. Both civil and criminal remedies are available.[c]

Not surprisingly, court decisions have played a major role in shaping the scope of the power of the branches of the federal government in enforcing these laws. For example, various statutes, such as 18 U.S.C. §§ 241–242, make it a crime for persons acting under color of state law to deprive persons of their constitutional right to vote. In the leading case of *United States v. Classic*, 313 U.S. 299 (1941), the Supreme Court upheld criminal prosecutions under these statutes of state election officials who had committed various frauds in a Democratic primary election for the U.S. House of Representatives. The officials argued that a mere primary election, as opposed to a general election, was an internal matter for the party, and hence they were not acting under color of state law. The Court rejected the argument, holding that primaries (especially in a state politically dominated by one party) were "an integral part of the procedure for the popular choice of Congressman." *Id.* at 314. *Classic* gave greater power to federal authorities to regulate elections for federal offices in the states, and emboldened private parties to challenge under federal law such practices as the white primaries, as discussed in Chapter 6.

Thus, the remedial enforcement of federal election law is, as a practical matter, often a mix of administrative and legal actions by public and private entities. As you read the materials below and elsewhere in the casebook, consider the advantages and disadvantages of vesting enforcement authority in federal prosecutors or other federal officials, as opposed to private parties. The U.S. Department of Justice and other federal offices typically have limited resources, and can only pursue a limited number of investigations and court actions. Private enforcement would seem to be a necessary supplement to public prosecutions, but private plaintiffs (often, interest groups) will have their own agendas and may not pursue or serve the public interest. Courts have been faced with these issues when considering whether to infer a private right of action in a federal statute, when textually it only provides for administrative enforcement. *See, e.g., Allen v. State Bd. of Elections*, 393 U.S. 544, 556–57 (1969) [p. 226] (implied private right under § 5 of the Voting Rights Act was a necessary supplement to public enforcement); *Morse v. Republican Party of Virginia*, 517 U.S. 186, 230–34 (1996) (same with respect to § 10 of the Voting Rights Act);[d] *Sandusky County Democratic Party v. Blackwell*, 387 F.3d 565 (6th Cir. 2004) [p. 1084] (inferring private right of action under § 302 of HAVA). *See*

---

[c] For helpful overviews of the scope and enforcement of federal election law by federal authorities, see Joshua A. Douglas, *The Procedure of Election Law in Federal Courts*, 2011 Utah L. Rev. 433; David C. Rothschild & Benjamin J. Wolinsky, *Election Law Violations*, 46 Am. Crim. L. Rev. 391 (2009); U.S. Dep't of Justice, Federal Prosecution of Election Offenses (7th ed., 2007).

[d] What weight, if any, should a court give in construing statutes in this context to an amicus brief from the Attorney General supporting the implication of a private right of action? *See Allen*, 393 U.S. at 557 n.23 (giving weight to such a brief); *Morse*, 517 U.S. at 231–32 (same).

generally Daniel P. Tokaji, *Public Rights and Privates Rights of Action: The Enforcement of Federal Election Law*, 44 IND. L. REV. 113 (2010).

As a matter of policy, both public and private enforcement would seem to be the answer, and Congress, in election law and other contexts, frequently provides for both types of enforcement. Sean Farhang, *Public Regulation and Private Lawsuits in the American Separation of Powers System*, 52 AM. J. POL. SCI. 821 (2008). What is the optimal mix of those options? The materials below focus on private enforcement, and describe both the remedial options open to and barriers faced by private parties. Would, or should, the holdings discussed below come out differently if public officials were seeking an analogous remedy?

2. Remedies for the Wrongful Denial of the Right to Vote

Most often, suits to vindicate the rights of would-be voters seek injunctions. And because of "the fundamental nature of the right to vote," courts have been willing — as we have seen in this Chapter — to grant equitable relief requiring election officials to register voters and permit them to cast ballots. *Dillard v. Crenshaw County*, 640 F. Supp. 1347, 1363 (M.D. Ala. 1986).[e] Nevertheless, an award of damages is possible as well, *see Murphy v. Ramsey*, 114 U.S. 15, 37 (1885), and the propriety of awarding damages for a wrongful denial of the right to vote was recognized as early as *Ashby v. White*, 92 Eng. Rep. 126, *rev'd* 1 Eng. Rep. 417 — HL (1703).[f] *See generally* J.E. Macy, Annotation, *Personal Liability of Public Officer for Breach of Duty in Respect of Election or Primary Election Laws*, 153 A.L.R. 109 (1944).

WILEY v. SINKLER
Supreme Court of the United States
179 U.S. 58, 21 S. Ct. 17, 45 L. Ed. 84 (1900)

Statement by MR. JUSTICE GRAY:

This was an action brought March 11, 1895, in the circuit court of the United States for the district of South Carolina, by a resident of the city of Charleston in that state, against the board of managers of a general election at a ward and precinct in that city, to recover damages in the sum of $2,500 for wrongfully and wilfully rejecting his vote for a member of the House of Representatives of the United States for the state of South Carolina on November 6, 1894. * * *

The court * * * sustained the demurrer and dismissed the complaint because it did not state facts sufficient to constitute a cause of action, in that it failed to state that the plaintiff was a duly registered voter of the state of South Carolina. The plaintiff sued out a writ of error from this court. * * *

---

[e] The Supreme Court was not always so willing, though. As discussed earlier [*see* page 13, n.f], *Giles v. Harris*, 189 U.S. 475 (1903), refused to order injunctive relief to correct an unconstitutional system of voter registration because the Court lacked the capacity to ensure that its injunction would be followed.

[f] The Queen's Bench, 3-1, held for the defendant and against the would-be voter, over Chief Justice Holt's dissent. The judgment was reversed, however, in the House of Lords.

MR. JUSTICE GRAY, after stating the case as above, delivered the opinion of the court [in which MR. CHIEF JUSTICE FULLER, MR. JUSTICE HARLAN, MR. JUSTICE BREWER, MR. JUSTICE BROWN, MR. JUSTICE SHIRAS, MR. JUSTICE WHITE, MR. JUSTICE PECKHAM, and MR. JUSTICE MCKENNA join]: * * *

The Circuit Court of the United States has jurisdiction, concurrent with the courts of the State, of any action under the Constitution, laws, or treaties of the United States, in which the matter in dispute exceeds the sum or value of $2,000.

This action is brought against election officers to recover damages for their rejection of the plaintiff's vote for a member of the House of Representatives of the United States. The complaint, by alleging that the plaintiff was at the time, under the constitution and laws of the State of South Carolina and the Constitution and laws of the United States, a duly qualified elector of the state, shows that the action is brought under the Constitution and laws of the United States.

The damages are laid at the sum of $2,500. What amount of damages the plaintiff shall recover in such an action is peculiarly appropriate for the determination of a jury, and no opinion of the court upon that subject can justify it in holding that the amount in controversy was insufficient to support the jurisdiction of the circuit court.

The Circuit Court therefore clearly had jurisdiction of this action, and we are brought to the consideration of the other objections presented by the demurrer to the complaint. * * *

The constitution and the laws of [South Carolina] require that, in order to entitle any one to have his vote received at any election, he must not only have the requisite qualifications of an elector, but he must have been registered. By elementary rules of pleading, both these essential requisites must be distinctly alleged by the plaintiff in any action against the managers of an election for refusing his vote.

The complaint in this case alleges that the plaintiff was a duly qualified elector; but it contains no allegation that he was ever registered as such. Because of this omission the complaint does not state facts sufficient to constitute a cause of action. * * *

Judgment affirmed.

Notes and Questions

1.   Though the Court ultimately ruled against the plaintiff voter, to reach the merits the Court first had to conclude both that there was a federal question involved in the case and that the amount-in-controversy requirement was satisfied. Today there is no amount-in-controversy requirement in federal-question suits, *see* 28 U.S.C. § 1331, but from 1875, when Congress first provided for general federal-question jurisdiction, until 1980, federal-question suits not meeting a certain amount-in-controversy had to be brought, if at all, in state courts. *See* RICHARD H. FALLON, JR., ET AL., HART AND WECHSLER'S THE FEDERAL COURTS AND THE FEDERAL SYSTEM 783 (7th ed. 2015).

The Court held, following *Ex Parte Yarbrough*, 110 U.S. 651 (1884), that the right to vote for Representatives arose under the Constitution, for the Constitution created the office and provided that anyone entitled to vote for "the most numerous Branch of the State Legislature." U.S. CONST. art. I, § 2, cl. 1. Thus, the Constitution adopted the voting qualifications used by the states, but did not give the states any power to set the qualifications of voters in congressional races as such. The Court thus found unconvincing the defendant's argument that the right to vote for Congress depends on whether one has been granted the right, under state law, to vote for the state legislature. *See also Swafford v. Templeton*, 185 U.S. 487 (1902).

2. As for the amount-in-controversy requirement, the Court held that the appropriate damages for the wrongful denial of the right to vote were "peculiarly appropriate for the determination of a jury," and therefore the plaintiff's demand for $2500 satisfied the requirement. *See also Wayne v. Venable*, 260 F. 64, 66 (8th Cir. 1919) ("In the eyes of the law this right [to vote] is so valuable that damages are presumed from the wrongful deprivation of it without evidence of actual loss of money, property, or any other valuable thing, and the amount of the damages is a question peculiarly appropriate for the determination of the jury, because each member of the jury has personal knowledge of the value of the right."). Ordinarily the amount claimed by the plaintiff controls, so long as it was made in good faith, unless it "appear[s] to a legal certainty that the claim is really for less than the jurisdictional amount." *St. Paul Mercury Indemnity Co. v. Red Cab Co.*, 303 U.S. 283, 289 (1938). Two thousand five hundred dollars in 1900 would be worth well over $50,000 today. Would such an award be — as a matter of law — excessive? How much is one's vote worth?

Affixing a dollar value to the right to vote is difficult for several reasons. First, there is no market against which to measure a damages award. Every state and the federal government have laws prohibiting the buying or selling of votes, *see e.g.*, 18 U.S.C. §§ 597, 598; Richard L. Hasen, *Vote Buying*, 88 CAL. L. REV. 1323 (2000), and as a result we cannot be certain how much a vote is "worth" in that sense. Second, if we were to approximate the value of a vote based on the behavior of voters, that value would be very low. Indeed, the behavior of the Americans who decide not to vote might indicate that the right has very little value. *Cf. Crawford v. Marion County Election Board*, 472 F.3d 949, 951 (7th Cir. 2007)(Posner, J.), *aff'd*, 553 U.S. 181 (2008). *See generally, e.g.*, ANTHONY DOWNS, AN ECONOMIC THEORY OF DEMOCRACY 260–76 (1957). Third, if we view the right in narrow instrumental terms — what are the chances my vote will make the difference in an election — the value is infinitesimally small. Fourth, taking a broader view, the value of voting — of subjecting government to popular accountability — is infinitely high. Indeed, the behavior of generations of Americans who have fought and died to protect democracy might indicate that the right has a very large value.

The Supreme Court has indicated that the narrower vision of the right is appropriate. "The 'value of the right' [to vote] is the money value of the particular loss that the plaintiff suffered — a loss of which 'each member of the jury has personal knowledge.' It is *not* the value of the right to vote as a general, abstract matter, based on its role in our history or system of government." *Memphis Community School District v. Stachura*, 477 U.S. 299, 312 n.14 (1986). If damages are to be based on "the money value of the particular loss that the plaintiff suffered," was *Wiley* correct to sustain jurisdiction?

TAYLOR v. HOWE
United States Court of Appeals for the Eighth Circuit
225 F.3d 993 (8th Cir. 2000)

RICHARD S. ARNOLD, CIRCUIT JUDGE [with whom HEANEY, CIRCUIT JUDGE, and LOKEN, CIRCUIT JUDGE, join].

This is an action under 42 U.S.C. § 1983[g] arising out of the election difficulties of black citizens in Crittenden County, Arkansas, who attempted to vote, ran for local office, or served as poll watchers for black candidates. The claims all arise out of the election for municipal offices in the small city of Crawfordsville, Arkansas, on November 5, 1996. Sixteen black citizens filed suit against three poll workers, the Crittenden County Clerk, the three members of the Crittenden County Board of Election Commissioners, and a poll watcher. The plaintiffs' substantive claims are based on 42 U.S.C. § 1971(a)(1), (a)(2)(A), and (a)(2)(B);[h] the Fourteenth and Fifteenth Amendments to the United States Constitution, and 42 U.S.C. § 1973(a), (b).[i] The District Court, following a three-day bench trial, found that the plaintiffs failed to establish any intentional discrimination (the gist of the plaintiffs' position),

---

[g] 42 U.S.C. § 1983: "Every person who, under color of any statute, ordinance, regulation, custom, or usage, of any State or Territory or the District of Columbia, subjects, or causes to be subjected, any citizen of the United States or other person within the jurisdiction thereof to the deprivation of any rights, privileges, or immunities secured by the Constitution and laws, shall be liable to the party injured in an action at law, suit in equity, or other proper proceeding for redress. * * *" — Eds.

[h] 42 U.S.C. § 1971 (a): "(1) All citizens of the United States who are otherwise qualified by law to vote at any election by the people in any State, Territory, district, county, city, parish, township, school district, municipality, or other territorial subdivision, shall be entitled and allowed to vote at all such elections, without distinction of race, color, or previous condition of servitude; any constitution, law, custom, usage, or regulation of any State or Territory, or by or under its authority, to the contrary notwithstanding.

"(2) No person acting under color of law shall —

"(A) in determining whether any individual is qualified under State law or laws to vote in any election, apply any standard, practice, or procedure different from the standards, practices, or procedures applied under such law or laws to other individuals within the same county, parish, or similar political subdivision who have been found by State officials to be qualified to vote;

"(B) deny the right of any individual to vote in any election because of an error or omission on any record or paper relating to any application, registration, or other act requisite to voting, if such error or omission is not material in determining whether such individual is qualified under State law to vote in such election[.]" — Eds.

[i] 42 U.S.C. § 1973: "(a) No voting qualification or prerequisite to voting or standard, practice, or procedure shall be imposed or applied by any State or political subdivision in a manner which results in a denial or abridgement of the right of any citizen of the United States to vote on account of race or color [or because he is a member of a language minority group (*see* 42 U.S.C. § 1973b(f)(2))].

"(b) A violation of subsection (a) of this section is established if, based on the totality of the circumstances, it is shown that the political processes leading to nomination or election in the State or political subdivision are not equally open to participation by members of a class of citizens protected by subsection (a) of this section in that its members have less opportunity than other members of the electorate to participate in the political process and to elect representatives of their choice. The extent to which members of a protected class have been elected to office in the State or political subdivision is one circumstance which may be considered: *Provided*, That nothing in this section establishes a right to

ruled in favor of the defendants, and dismissed the complaint with prejudice. * * *

I. Background

Crawfordsville, Arkansas, is a small city in Crittenden County, in the Mississippi River delta region of Eastern Arkansas. Crawfordsville is.41 square miles in size and is bisected by a railroad track that runs east to west through the City, dividing the black and white communities. There are only twelve streets in Crawfordsville. Residents south of the tracks are all black, and residents north of the railroad tracks are primarily white. The City of Crawfordsville and the area of the County surrounding the City make up the Jackson 1 voting precinct. The majority of the City's population consists of black citizens. The 1990 Census reported that 617 persons lived in Crawfordsville, with 405 being black citizens. However, no black citizen held a Crawfordsville City government position until 1990. * * *

[Defendant] Ruth Trent is the County Clerk of Crittenden County. * * * Voter-registration records are maintained in the County Clerk's Office. During the time prior to the November 5, 1996, election, * * * both county and city residents of the Jackson 1 precinct voted from the same register at the same polling place. At that time, there were two voting machines at the one polling place. One machine was programmed for the county ballot, and one machine was programmed for the city ballot. The city ballot included more races than the county ballot (those for city offices). The determination of which voters voted what ballot was made on election day. * * *

In the summer of 1996, the County Clerk's Office began to separate all of the Crittenden County precinct registers into city boxes or county boxes, pursuant to a new state law requiring such separation. Ms. Trent made extensive efforts to obtain accurate addresses for each registered voter, but the process was difficult. The Clerk's Office had only four employees. Contacts with post offices in Crittenden County produced no response. Ms. Trent got in touch with both black and white individual citizens. In addition, she got some addresses from the Crawfordsville Water Department, where the defendant Mary Freeman worked. A major problem was that many voters listed their address as a post office box, so it was not possible to determine their street address, the key fact governing whether they were eligible to vote in the City. If accurate information could not be obtained, Ms. Trent would just leave a particular voter in the County. In addition, voter cards were sent out to each individual voter, with an invitation to correct any wrongly recorded addresses. These efforts, though extensive, were not altogether successful. For one thing, a computer operator in the Clerk's Office failed to put 46 voters who had city addresses into the City register. * * *

For the November 5, 1996, election, Ms. Freeman (a white woman) and Carla James (a black woman) were appointed as election clerks, Dixie Carlson (a white woman) and Lisa Washington (a black woman) were appointed as election judges, * * * and William Howe (an Asian man) was designated as an alternate. Ms. Washington, not being a registered voter, failed to qualify, and Mr. Howe served in

---

have members of a protected class elected in numbers equal to their proportion in the population." — Eds.

her place. [Each of these officials was a "poll worker."]

A poll watcher (to be distinguished from poll workers, who are appointed by the Board of Election Commissioners, a public body) was also present at the City polling place on November 5, 1996. Poll watchers are appointed by candidates. Their job is to watch the voting and call the attention of the election officials at the particular box to any irregularities they perceive. Johnny Rogers, a poll watcher named by a candidate for Congress, was present at the Crawfordsville City polling place in 1996, and is a named defendant in this action.

The Election Commissioners conducted poll-worker training seminars for prospective poll workers. The Commissioners used a "Poll Worker Training Workbook," which was distributed by the Secretary of State's office, to conduct the training. William Howe, Mary Freeman, and Dixie Carlson were trained as poll workers for the November 5, 1996, general election. Carla James, a black woman, could not attend a training session because of an illness in her family.

The Secretary of State sent voting procedures to poll worker trainees. The standard procedure was for a voter to enter the poll and identify himself to the election judge by giving his name, address, and date of birth. The election judge then locates the voter's name on the Precinct Voter Registration List ("register") to see if the name, address, and date of birth match; the voter signs the Precinct Registration List and List of Voters; the voter is given instructions on how to vote; and then the voter is allowed to vote. The training materials also covered the following:

What is "fail-safe" voting?

"Fail-safe" voting is the mechanism that allows voters who have not updated their voter registration information to vote at their new precinct without having updated their voter registration records.

What if a voter is non-registered or improperly registered?

1. If the **date of birth** given by the voter is not the same as that on the "Precinct Voter Registration List", then the judge may request the voter to provide additional identification as the judge deems appropriate.

2. If the **address** given by the voter is not the same as that on the "Precinct Voter Registration List", then the judge should verify with the county clerk that the address given by the voter is within the voting precinct.

If the address **is** within the precinct, then the voter must complete a "Voter Registration Application" to change addresses for county records. Then, the voter is allowed to vote.

If the address **is not** within the precinct, then the judge should instruct the voter to contact the county clerk to determine the proper voting precinct. Then, the voter should be instructed to go to the proper polling place to vote.

3. If the voter's **name** is not on the "Precinct Voter Registration List", the judge shall permit the voter to vote under the following conditions:

Voter identifies himself by name and date of birth and is verified by the county clerk as a registered voter within the county Voter gives and affirms his current residence and the election judge verifies with the county clerk that the residence is within the voting precinct

Voter completes an updated voter registration application form

Voter signs "Precinct Voter Registration List" and "List of Voters" form

4. If the voter's **name** is not on the list and the county clerk is unable to verify the voter's registration and the voter contends that he/she is eligible to vote, then the voter may vote a challenged ballot. *In this instance, the poll **worker** is responsible for challenging the ballot.*

The training materials also provided emergency phone numbers for poll workers to call if a problem arose during the election, such as the County Clerk's Office number, "if you need information concerning a voter's registration or place of residence, if you need more ballot or stub boxes, or if you need more voter application or change of address forms."

Moreover, the training materials asked participants, "Who can assist a person with a disability casting a ballot?" The correct answer is, "Anyone the person wants." And the materials asked participants, "If a person with disabilities asks a poll worker for assistance, who can help?" The correct answer is, "Two judges." * * *

There was a procedure whereby voters could vote by absentee ballot. When an absentee ballot was requested from the Clerk's Office, the Clerk's Office stamped the precinct binder with the word "absentee" next to the person's name at the time the absentee ballot was mailed to the voter. If a voter did not return a completed ballot, the words "absentee" remained stamped by his name. * * *

For the November 5, 1996, general election, Crawfordsville city residents were to vote at the City Water Department office ("City polling place"), and residents living outside the City were to vote at the City library ("County polling place"). The library is across Main Street from the Water Department office. The city ballot at the City polling place included the Crawfordsville City government positions, whereas the county ballot at the County polling place did not. A list of county voters was sent to the County polling place, and a list of city voters was sent to the City polling place. One black candidate and one white candidate ran for City office.

On November 5, 1996, when a voter approached the Clerks' table on election day, a determination would be made whether the voter was at the correct voting precinct, the voter would sign in, each clerk would sign a list, and then the voter would go into the voting booth and vote on the machine.

Ms. James testified that the County Clerk's Office informed the poll workers on the morning of November 5, 1996, that the Clerk's Office "had made a lot of omissions from the book. A lot of names had been omitted." * * *

Commissioner Fairley informed those people present in the City polling place that "handicapped voters were entitled to be assisted by a person of their choice, and candidates were allowed to be present within the polling place by a poll watcher

or personally, as long as they did not interfere with the election process. . . . "
Commissioner Fairley testified, "It is hard to get judges and clerks to understand
that voters can be assisted by anyone they want to assist them. . . . It had been
part of the training. But sometimes training doesn't take." Fairley added, "We have
that issue come up in every election. Some judge or clerk thinks that they ought to
be able to determine who is the assister for some voter or group of voters."

Two hundred and fifty-one people voted on the voting machine at the City polling
place. The number of black voters was between 67 and 85. Twelve voters were
issued paper ballots, and Ms. Carlson wrote the names of 11 of these 12 voters on
a list of challenged voters. All 11 people listed on the list of challenged voters are
black citizens. The race of the person casting the twelfth paper ballot is unknown.
Ms. James knew all 11 of the challenged voters by name. Ms. James testified that
Ms. Freeman, mainly, or Ms. Carlson would state the reason why a person could not
vote, Ms. Carlson would write the voter's name on the challenged voter list, and the
challenged voter was then required to vote on a paper ballot instead of the voting
machine. Although Ms. James affirmed that some challenged voters lived in the
City, her affirmation was largely disregarded by other poll workers. After a heated
discussion regarding Stanley Calloway's inability to vote, which included Commissioner Dawson, the election officials decided to turn on the Water Department video
camera and tape events of the election. The tape is in the record before us, and
portions of it were played at trial. * * *

Ms. Freeman testified by deposition that she could not recall any white persons
who had difficulty voting on November 5, 1996. Election officials did not allow any
black person whose name was on the county list and not on the city list to vote by
voting machine, even if the voter stated that he lived in the City.

After the polls closed, the votes were counted, and, in each of the City races, the
white candidate defeated the black candidate. The margin of victory was sufficiently
large to make the 11 challenged votes irrelevant, so far as the result of any election
was concerned. The Board of Election Commissioners certified the results as
reported. The vote was two to one. Commissioner Dawson voted not to certify the
results, stating that irregularities had occurred. The other two Commissioners,
however, determined that, because the number of challenged ballots did not affect
the outcome of the election, they would certify the results with a notation that
challenged ballots existed.

Commissioners Fairley and Graham decided not to count the challenged ballots.
In Commissioner Fairley's opinion, state law required that they not be counted,
because they could not change the result of any race. The results as certified by the
County Board of Election Commissioners were then transmitted to the Secretary
of State's office, or to the County Clerk, as appropriate. The black candidates
presented the Election Commission with a two-page list of grievances, but the
Commission determined that it had no authority to decide whether these grievances
were well taken. The Commission took the position that its only job was to count
votes. If votes were cast improperly, or citizens were improperly prevented from
voting, the remedy would be an election contest filed in court. * * *

II. Individual Voters' Claims for Damages

As we have noted, the plaintiffs in this case are 16 black citizens of Crittenden County, all registered voters. The principal defendants are three poll workers, Dixie Carlson, Mary Freeman, and William Howe. These defendants were sued individually and in their official capacities for allegedly discriminating against black citizens on the basis of their race, and intimidating them during the election. The defendant Johnny Rogers, a poll watcher, was sued in his individual capacity, and was charged with discriminating against black voters. The defendant Ruth Trent, the County Clerk, was sued in her official capacity. The complaint alleged that her preparation of the precinct register discriminated against black voters and amounted to a policy of Crittenden County. The three Election Commissioners, Messrs. Fairley, Graham, and Dawson, were sued individually and in their official capacities. The complaint alleged that they discriminated in their decisions regarding the challenged ballots, and their actions regarding the complaints made by black candidates. In their prayer for relief, the plaintiffs sought damages for each individual voter who had been allegedly harassed or hindered at the polling place, and also injunctive relief, including a request that the same election officials not be used in future elections, that the Attorney General of the United States make federal observers available for future elections, and that a plan be implemented to ensure that City voter rolls would be limited in the future to persons who lived within the City of Crawfordsville. Costs and reasonable attorneys' fees were also requested. * * *

The core issue in this case is whether any defendant intentionally discriminated on the basis of race against any plaintiff. This is a quintessential question of fact. In each instance, the question turns mainly on conflicting oral testimony and an assessment of its credibility. In these circumstances, our power of review is particularly narrow. Rule 52(a) admonishes us to give "due regard" to the opportunity of the trial court to observe the witnesses and their demeanor. In addition, the Supreme Court has stressed that findings based on credibility, where testimony is internally consistent and not contradicted by physical facts or documentary evidence, and where the witnesses believed by the trier of fact were "plausible," must almost always be affirmed. Still, even in such a case, findings are not immune from review. It is our duty to inspect the record searchingly, and, in the end, to reverse if we have "a definite and firm conviction" that any finding of fact was mistaken.

A. Plaintiffs Who Did Not Vote
1. William Gollin

William Gollin has lived in Crawfordsville since 1965, and he became a registered voter that same year. He completed school up to the third grade. Mr. Gollin asked Loretta Page to assist him in voting because he could not read; however, Mr. Gollin was not permitted to vote because it was alleged that his name was not listed on the precinct register of voters. In fact, Mr. Gollin's name was on the register; however, it was incorrectly spelled — "Gallin" instead of "Gollin." The register correctly provided Mr. Gollin's age, but the address listed was slightly incorrect — 412 South Main instead of 415 South Main. The name "Gallin, William Tell" was listed in the city precinct register only four entries above the entry where his name should have been located (where there was an entry for someone named "Gollins") and on the same page in the register.

Mr. Gollin testified that he was in the city polling place for fifteen or twenty minutes, the time he testified that it took for the poll workers to determine that he could not vote. Mr. Gollin testified that Carla James and Loretta Page informed the other poll workers that the listing under "Gallin" was really Mr. Gollin's name. Mr. Gollin also testified that Mr. Howe informed the other election workers that Mr. Gollin did not have running water and that the name "Gallin" was not Mr. Gollin's name. Ms. Freeman informed Mr. Gollin that he could not vote because he "didn't have water." Mr. Gollin was a weekly shopper in Mr. Howe's store, when Mr. Howe owned one, and Mr. Howe had been to Mr. Gollin's home. However, Mr. Howe testified that he was not asked about whether to challenge Mr. Gollin or not, and testified that throughout the day he never volunteered anything, but only observed the clerks' handling of voter sign-ins. Mr. Gollin did not see anyone make a phone call, and he was not handed a paper ballot so he could cast a vote. Ms. Carlson testified that she could not recall why Mr. Gollin did not vote a challenged ballot. Ms. Freeman testified that she seemed to remember Mr. Gollin's coming into the polling place, and to the best of her knowledge she believed that he had already left the polling place when the spelling error was discovered.

Before assessing the particulars of Mr. Gollin's situation, we make a few general observations about the context in which the voting difficulties shown in this record occurred. The political history of Crittenden County, to which the District Court gave little or no weight, is important. There has been a "long history of racial discrimination in the electoral process in Arkansas." The history of polarized voting and racial discrimination in Crittenden County has been particularly noted. * * * The race for City offices on November 5, 1996, is a good example. There was one white candidate and one black candidate for almost every contested position. We think it fair to infer that most (though not all) black voters favored black candidates, and that most (but not all) white voters favored white candidates. All but one of the election officials at the City polling place were white. The voters who experienced problems that day were overwhelmingly black. Between 67 and 81 black voters cast ballots, and between 27 and 33 per cent. of them experienced some form of a problem. All 11 of the voters who were required to vote a challenged paper ballot were black. Between 170 and 184 white voters cast ballots, but very few of them experienced voting problems. Most of the problems experienced by black voters could have been handled if the poll workers had scrupulously adhered to the procedures laid out during their training. It is true that the challenged votes would have made no difference in the outcome of any election, but this is beside the point. Each individual voter has a right to cast his ballot in accordance with State law, and this right is not to be denied, abridged, or encroached upon for reasons of race. * * *

Instances in which favorable treatment was given to white voters are significant. We note in particular the fact that William and Deborah Sue Dixon, who lived a half mile outside the City, were permitted to vote a City ballot on the voting machine at the City polling place, without challenge. Their names were listed in the City register, but the address given was 528 Joyner Road. The tape that was made of occurrences at the polling place on election day reveals that Mr. Dixon told Ms. Freeman that he lived on Joyner Road "over by the high school." * * * On the tape, a male voice, which the District Court did not doubt was that of Mr. Howe, responded "across the railroad tracks" during this conversation. Ms. Freeman admitted that on election day she knew there was no street within the town of Crawfordsville named Joyner Road, and also knew that the high school was a half mile outside the City limits. Mr. Howe, who had been Mayor of the City for 16 years and had lived there for 60, testified that he did not know at the time whether a street in Crawfordsville was named Joyner Road. We are driven to the conclusion that Mr. Howe's testimony about the Dixons is simply incredible, and that they were given favorable treatment because they were white, and, probably, because Mr. Howe and Ms. Freeman believed that they would vote for white candidates. No similar indulgence was granted to any black person.

We return to the specifics of Mr. Gollin's case. He testified that he had known Mr. Howe for 31 years at the time of the election. Mr. Howe had cashed checks for him at his store. Mr. Howe has been to his house. This testimony is clear and consistent. The contrary evidence, such as it is, of the defendants Howe and Freeman is unworthy of belief. Whether someone has "water" is not relevant to his eligibility to vote, which turns solely on whether he was registered and where he lived. The argument that Mr. Gollin's name was misspelled in the voter register, with a single incorrect letter, is, in our view, a flimsy pretext. We hold that the finding that Mr. Howe and Ms. Freeman did not racially discriminate in denying the vote to Mr. Gollin is clearly erroneous. There is not sufficient evidence in this record to make a similar conclusion with respect to the defendants Carlson and Rogers.

2. Derrick Marshall

Derrick Marshall was unquestionably a registered voter and a resident of Crawfordsville. His name was listed in the city precinct register. However, the word "absentee" had been stamped by his name. Both Ms. Freeman and Ms. James informed Mr. Marshall that he had already voted by absentee ballot, and would not be allowed to vote again. Mr. Marshall denied that he had voted. No phone call was made by poll workers to the County Clerk's Office to determine if a mistake had been made when the register was stamped. Ms. Carlson testified: "He really insisted that he had not voted. But we couldn't — with an absentee marked we couldn't — he had already voted as far as we were concerned. It was on the book."

The fact that the word "absentee" was stamped beside Mr. Marshall's name was certainly sufficient to raise a question in the minds of the poll workers. It was not, however, conclusive as to whether or not he had already voted. According to the County Clerk, when someone writes in and requests an absentee ballot, the ballot is mailed to the voter, and the word "absentee" is then stamped next to the voter's name in the precinct binder. The stamping occurs at the time of mailing, not when the ballot is returned to the Clerk's Office. Some ballots that are mailed out to people requesting them are not returned. A voter who requests an absentee ballot, but does not use it, is presumably entitled to vote in person on election day. This could have been the case with Mr. Marshall. Moreover, there are things that the poll workers could have done to investigate further. They could have telephoned the County Clerk's Office to try to determine whether an absentee ballot had been returned by the person in question, and apparently no such call was made. In addition, Mr. Marshall himself could have taken the initiative to go to the County Clerk's Office and request an investigation. When this happens, the County Clerk will do research, and, if it's justified, send the voter back to the polling place with a slip instructing the poll workers to allow him to vote. This also was not done in the instant case.

The District Court found that the defendants' actions towards Mr. Marshall were not motivated by race. The evidence is fairly even. On the whole, we are not persuaded that this finding was clearly erroneous. The stamping of the word "absentee" on the voting register raised a concrete and serious problem. Decisions in polling places on election day are made rather quickly. There is often not enough time to investigate thoroughly each individual case. Our judgment is further influenced by the fact that Carla James, the black poll worker, took the same position with respect to Mr. Marshall that the defendants Howe and Freeman took. We will affirm the District Court's decision with respect to the plaintiff Derrick Marshall.

3. Kimberly Nathan Warren

Kimberly Nathan Warren is a registered voter, and she lived in Crawfordsville, Arkansas, at the time of the election. She had lived at her family home in Crawfordsville since 1988, with the exception of three months in 1996 (ending in September) when she lived outside the City limits in the McNeil Apartments. Ms. Freeman and Ms. Warren had known each other for years. Ms. Warren's father had worked for the City, and Ms. Warren paid the water bill in her father's name at the Water Department where Ms. Freeman works.

When Ms. Warren went to the City polling place to vote on election day, Ms. Freeman told Ms. Warren that she did not live in Crawfordsville. Ms. Warren insisted that she did. Her name had been listed in the County register under her maiden name, "Nathan," apparently reflecting the short time when she lived outside the City.

We are firmly convinced that the defense position with respect to this plaintiff is not plausible. Ms. Freeman had known Ms. Warren for years. It is true that her name was not in the City register, but that was not a sufficient reason for the treatment that Ms. Warren received. Under the instructions that had been given to the poll workers, Ms. Warren should not have been turned away. No election worker called the Clerk's Office, and no one told Ms. Warren that she could fill out an address-change form and vote. No one offered to allow her to vote a challenged ballot on paper. No one even informed her that she ought to go across the street and cast her vote in the County polling place. As a consequence, she was altogether denied the right to vote. We believe that the finding in favor of Ms. Freeman with respect to Ms. Warren's claim is clearly erroneous. There is no substantial evidence that any of the other defendants played a part in Ms. Warren's difficulties.

B. Plaintiffs Whose Votes Were Challenged

In general, the following procedure was followed with respect to persons whose votes were challenged, but were still allowed to vote. If someone came into the polling place and was challenged, either by a poll watcher (Mr. Rogers) or a poll worker, that person would not be allowed to vote on the machine. Instead, he or she would be given a paper ballot. In this way, the challenged ballots (and, as we have noted, there were 11 of them in all) could be separated, and each ballot could be identified, if necessary, in the event of an election contest.

1. Sharon White

Sharon White lived with her grandmother, Rae Miller White, on Main Street in Crawfordsville. She has a "general delivery" post office address, and was listed on the County register. On November 5, 1996, Ms. White went to the County polling place, but an election worker there, who knew that Ms. White lived in the City, told her to go across the street and vote at the City polling place, in the Water Department office.

When Ms. White got to the City polling place, her name could not be found on the City register. However, Ms. James, the black poll worker, told Ms. Freeman that Ms. White was indeed a City resident. Ms. White was well known to Ms. Freeman, having paid her grandmother's water bill every month at the Water Department office for at least seven years. In addition, she had known Mr. Howe since she was six years old, having shopped in his store, sometimes every day. When Ms. White approached the voting table, Ms. Freeman informed her that her name was not on the City voting register, and that she could not vote, because she did not pay a water bill in her own name. No one called the Clerk's Office. Johnny Rogers, the poll watcher, challenged Ms. White's vote, because her name did not appear on the City register, but most of the challenge form was filled out by someone else. The challenge form stated: "Does not appear in the City box, but all say she does." According to Ms. Carlson, "everyone in the polling place, all the officials said that she did live in the City." Ms. White was given a paper ballot in order to vote in accordance with the procedure described above. When Ms. White voted, two unnamed white men stood over her and watched her, with Mr. Howe standing "about two or three feet behind them."

The defendants introduced very little specific evidence about this incident. Ms. Freeman testified that she did not remember Ms. White's coming into the polling place. The District Court found that Ms. White was "not denied her franchise." In a way, this is true, because Ms. White was allowed to cast a challenged paper ballot. On the other hand, her vote was never counted (more about this later), and she was subjected to harassment, with the apparent cooperation of Mr. Howe. We believe that the evidence is overwhelming that both Ms. Freeman and Mr. Howe knew Ms. White, and the fact that Ms. White had been paying her grandmother's water bill, instead of a bill in her own name, had nothing to do with her right to vote. The regular procedure which had been given to the poll workers at training was not followed in this case. The County Clerk's Office was not called, nor was Ms. White given a chance to use a change-of-address form. We hold that the District Court's finding in favor of Ms. Freeman and Mr. Howe is clearly erroneous. With respect to the defendants Carlson and Rogers, however, we affirm. Neither of them lived in the City. In fact, Mr. Rogers did not even live in Crittenden County. He was representing the best interests of his congressional candidate, and his challenge of a ballot being cast by a person whose name was not on the City register is understandable. He could not be expected to be familiar with individual citizens and where they lived.

2. Arnissa Edwards

Arnissa Edwards is a resident of Crawfordsville. She lived in the "white section." Her name was listed in the City register. When she came into the polling place, Ms. Edwards signed the register and said she had brought Latesa Calloway to assist her in voting. Ms. Edwards said she needed help because she did not know how to use the voting machine, and that she had been allowed assistance with the machine in previous elections. Mr. Rogers, the poll watcher, challenged Ms. Edwards's vote because of "improper voting procedures. She did not state reason for help with her vote." Ms. Calloway then asked whether Ms. Edwards could vote by paper ballot, and this is what occurred.

We find this plaintiff's situation somewhat difficult. On the one hand, it seems clear that she was not in fact entitled to assistance in voting. She conceded at trial that she had no disability. Mr. Rogers's statement that "[s]he did not state reason for help with her vote" is correct, if "reason" is understood as "good reason." On the other hand, the fact that Ms. Edwards was not entitled to have someone help her vote did not require that the vote itself be challenged. The logical outcome would have been to allow her to vote on the machine, but without assistance. Instead, she was required to vote by paper ballot. This procedure seems to have been suggested by Ms. Calloway herself, however. There is no substantial evidence about the conduct of the defendants Freeman, Howe, and Carlson during this incident. Ms. Edwards testified that on several occasions Ms. Freeman had asked her whether she was planning to sell her house, and this is evidence of racial animus if believed. Although what happened to Ms. Edwards makes us somewhat uneasy, we have no definite and firm conviction that the District Court's finding adverse to her claim was clearly erroneous. According, the finding will be affirmed.

3. Stanley Calloway

Stanley Calloway was a convicted felon. His name was on the City register, and he signed in, but Ms. Carlson then challenged him on the basis of his conviction. Under Arkansas law, convicted felons cannot vote. If there was any racial prejudice operating with respect to Mr. Calloway, it could not have been the cause of his vote's being disallowed. He was not entitled to vote in any event. The finding of the District Court adverse to Mr. Calloway's claim will be affirmed.

C. Plaintiffs Allegedly Denied Assistance of Their Choice

It is important to remember, in evaluating these claims, what the law and accepted practice were with respect to voters who asked for help. Any voter with a disability was entitled to assistance from any person of his or her choice. It did not matter who the person was. A relative, a friend, even a candidate, was eligible to give assistance. If a voter asked a poll worker to help, two election judges (not just one poll worker) would give assistance.

1. Ruby Coburn

Ruby Coburn was a qualified voter in the City. She requested help in voting on the ground of inability to read well and "nerves." Ms. Coburn asked LaSaundra Johnson for help. Both Ms. Coburn and Ms. Johnson testified that Mr. Howe gave Ms. Johnson a sheet of paper with an "amendment" on it, and told her that she had to read that paper before she could help Ms. Coburn in voting. Ms. Johnson refused to read the paper, became upset, and left. Ms. Coburn was then offered assistance from one (apparently not two) poll workers, but she declined. She voted on the machine without assistance. However, because she could not read well, she voted only for about two candidates.

Mr. Howe testified that he never stopped Ms. Johnson from helping anyone, nor did he make anyone read an amendment as a condition to assisting another person to vote. We are firmly convinced that Mr. Howe's testimony was unreliable. He himself conceded that his memory was fading, and his testimony with respect to the Dixon incident, recounted above, was clearly incorrect, as the videotape showed. Requiring Ms. Johnson to read an "amendment" (the reference may be to the title of one of the constitutional amendments on the ballot at the time) was improper. It is of course true that Ms. Johnson would need to read in order to assist Ms. Coburn with a reading disability, but that was not the concern of the poll workers. Ms. Coburn had a right to ask anyone to help her, and how well that person could read was no one else's business. We hold that the finding against Ruby Coburn's claim is clearly erroneous, so far as the defendant Howe is concerned. The evidence with respect to the other defendants is either slight or nonexistent, and the judgment in their favor on Ms. Coburn's claim will be affirmed.

2. Willie Taylor

Willie Taylor is a registered voter and a resident of the City. He asked for help from LaSaundra Johnson (the same person involved in the Coburn incident, just recounted). Mr. Taylor had poor eyesight because of glaucoma. Ms. Freeman and Mr. Howe informed Mr. Taylor that Ms. Johnson could not help him, because she was not kin to him. Mr. Howe testified that he understood that a person needing assistance had to choose a relative or a good friend. (There is no evidence as to why Mr. Howe would not believe that Ms. Johnson was a good friend of Mr. Taylor's.) Ms. Johnson was not allowed to help Mr. Taylor, and then, at Mr. Taylor's request, Mr. Howe helped him. Mr. Taylor could not see the buttons in the voting machine to punch. He had to tell Mr. Howe how he wanted to vote, and Mr. Howe then punched the buttons.

What happened to Mr. Taylor was improper and contrary to law. He had a right to LaSaundra Johnson's help. There is no requirement that she be a relative or a good friend. Violations of state law and election practice, of course, are not, in and of themselves, the same thing as racial discrimination. However, when the alleged violators' conduct is otherwise questionable, and when no plausible justification is asserted, the inference of discriminatory intent is strong in the circumstances of this particular election. We hold that the District Court's finding on Mr. Taylor's claim, so far as the defendants Freeman and Howe are concerned, was clearly erroneous. There is no evidence that the defendants Carlson and Rogers were involved in this incident, and the finding in their favor will therefore be affirmed.

D. Voters Who Were Allegedly Harassed
1. Nikita Calloway

Nikita Ladell Calloway, who was 20 years old at the time of the election, had lived in Crawfordsville all his life. He was frequently in the Water Department to pay bills, and Ms. Freeman had seen him there from the time he was a child until three months before the election. He saw Ms. Freeman at the Water Department about eight times in the year before the election. He would stop and talk with her, and she would call him by name, either "Nikita," or his nickname, "Bird." Mr. Calloway had also done yard work for Ms. Freeman when he was about 15 years old.

On November 5, 1996, when Ms. Freeman asked Mr. Calloway his name, he replied "Nikita Calloway." Ms. Freeman then said, according to Mr. Calloway's testimony, "You can't vote, because you are trying to vote in place of a girl." Ms. Freeman said, "That can't be your name. That's a girl's name." Finally, Mr. Calloway pulled out an identification card and showed it to Ms. Freeman. At that point, someone whose voice he didn't recognize stated that such a form of identification could be made up on computers. Then, "after a little conflict," he was allowed to vote on the voting machine. Mr. Calloway testified that while he was voting, Mr. Howe "stuck his head in" the voting booth for about 15 seconds. Mr. Howe denied the incident. About 30 people were in the polling place when these events occurred, and Mr. Calloway felt "ashamed" and "embarrassed."

Mr. Calloway was allowed to vote. What happened to him was not so serious as denying a person the right to vote, but being harassed during the exercise of one's franchise is still unlawful if the harassers are acting under color of state law and are motivated by racial prejudice. The District Court rejected this claim, finding Ms. Freeman's testimony more credible. * * * In our view, the finding of the District Court on this point is clearly erroneous. No one denied the length of Mr. Calloway's residence in Crawfordsville, the fact of his having frequented the water office, or his having done yard work for Ms. Freeman. Nikita is not a "girl's name," not exclusively, anyway, and it wouldn't matter for present purposes if it were. There is no evidence that any white voter was similarly impeded. We hold that Ms. Freeman and Mr. Howe are liable in this incident. There is no evidence connecting Ms. Carlson with these events. * * *

E. Black Candidates * * *
2. Loretta Page

Loretta Page was a candidate for Alderman in the 1996 election. She came into the polling place several times, to assist two voters who had asked her help, and to check on the number of votes. Late in the afternoon, Dixie Carlson told her that she could not come into the polling place again. There was evidence that a white candidate, J.B. Cole, had been in the polling place continuously on one occasion for 20 or 25 minutes without hindrance. Ms. Freeman and Ms. Carlson told Ms. Page that she could stick her head in to check the vote, but then had to leave, and had to remain more than 100 feet from the polling place. There was evidence that Mr. Cole was passing out leaflets at the front door of the polling place, within the 100-foot zone, on at least one occasion.

Arkansas law prohibits "electioneering" within 100 feet of a polling place. Ms. Page was allowed to enter the polling place to help other voters who specifically requested her assistance, and also, from time to time, to check on the number of votes. Apparently Ms. Freeman and Ms. Carlson considered the mere presence of a candidate within the polling place, for no particular purpose, to be "electioneering." We think this understanding, though arguably erroneous, was reasonable. Crawfordsville is a small town. Many voters would know Ms. Page, and might be intimidated or made to feel awkward by her presence in the polling place. The District Court's finding that no racial discrimination occurred with respect to Ms. Page is not clearly erroneous.

3. Bernice Bates

Bernice Bates was a candidate. She had served as an Alderman from 1991 to 1995. She helped five or ten people to vote, at their request. According to Ms. Bates's testimony, she came in to help a voter and was asked to leave by Ms. Carlson, who took the position that Ms. Bates's mere presence in the polling place was "electioneering." There is a conflict in the evidence about whether Ms. Carlson "grabbed" Ms. Bates's arm, or merely touched her.

This claim seems somewhat stronger to us than that of Loretta Page, which we have just discussed. Ms. Bates had a specific right to be in the polling place for the purpose of helping any voter who had requested her assistance by name. Ms. Carlson's understanding that Ms. Bates was "electioneering" was incorrect. On the other hand, Ms. Bates was allowed to assist five or ten other voters, and Ms. Carlson testified that she did not intend to intimidate or harass Ms. Bates. According to Ms. James, Ms. Bates created a disturbance after this incident occurred, and the police were called. Although we have some doubts about the matter, we are not firmly convinced that the finding of the District Court was erroneous, and its finding with respect to this claim will therefore be affirmed.

4. Alice Calloway

Alice Faye Calloway was a candidate for City Recorder. Ms. Calloway's case is somewhat similar to that of Bernice Bates. She periodically entered the polling place, asked for a count, and then left. She entered the polling place at least four times during the day. On one of these occasions, she was attempting to help her mother, Annie Mae Nathan, to vote. Ms. Carlson approached her and told her that she could not be in the polling place. Ms. Calloway informed Ms. Carlson that she was helping her mother to vote at her mother's specific request. According to Ms. Calloway, Ms. Carlson put out both of her hands to prevent Ms. Calloway from walking past her and stated, "I told you not to come in here." Ms. Calloway then left, and Ms. Nathan voted without her assistance. Ms. Carlson denied pushing Ms. Calloway.

Again, we consider this claim somewhat stronger than that of Loretta Page, and perhaps than that of Bernice Bates, since it was Ms. Calloway's own mother whom she was attempting to assist. There is no question that Ms. Nathan had the right to request assistance from her daughter. The fact that her daughter was a candidate, and had already been in the polling place several times, complicates the situation. On the whole, we do not have a definite and firm conviction that the District Court's finding was mistaken. Although this is a close case, we affirm with respect to Ms. Calloway's claim. * * *

III. Other Claims for Relief

In addition to the individual plaintiffs' claims for damages against pollworkers and Mr. Rogers, the poll watcher, in their individual capacities, plaintiffs also request an award of damages against the three poll workers in their official capacities. We have held that the District Court's findings in favor of the defendant Dixie Carlson are not clearly erroneous, so there is no need to discuss an official-capacity claim with respect to her. Mr. Rogers, the poll watcher, has no official capacity. * * * The actions of Mr. Howe and Ms. Freeman which we have held to be discriminatory were purely individual actions. There is no evidence that they reflected or were influenced by any policy of Crittenden County. The County cannot be liable in the absence of some custom or prevailing practice that violates the law.[J] Accordingly, the District Court's decision to reject any official-capacity liability on the part of the poll workers will be affirmed.

A claim for damages is made against Ruth Trent, the County Clerk, in her official capacity only. She is clearly a county employee. The District Court found that Ms. Trent was not guilty of any intentional discrimination, and this finding is not clearly erroneous. Ms. Trent made diligent efforts, both before and after the election, to ensure that the voter lists were accurate. In doing so, she consulted both white and black voters. There is no substantial evidence of discrimination on her part.

Damages are sought against the three members of the County Board of Election Commissioners, Messrs. Dawson, Fairley, and Graham, in their individual and official capacities. We believe the District Court correctly rejected these claims. The Election Commissioners carried out their duties in good faith. Mr. Fairley testified that state law prohibited the Election Commission from counting the challenged votes, given that they would not affect the outcome. This was a mistake of law. In fact, state law gave the Election Commission discretion whether to count these votes or not. This error, though, was simply that. It does not show racial discrimination on Mr. Fairley's part. We do not believe that there is any substantial evidence of any racial discrimination by any of the three members of the County Board of Election Commissioners. Accordingly, the District Court's finding in their favor will be affirmed.

Plaintiffs also request certain sorts of equitable relief, mainly having to do with the future conduct of elections in Crittenden County. We do not believe that any such relief is necessary. The County has made, and, we believe, will continue to make, diligent efforts to maintain accurate voter lists and to comply with the law. Individual discriminatory acts on the part of two poll workers at a single election do

---

[J] *See City of St. Louis v. Praprotnik*, 485 U.S. 112 (1988); *Pembaur v. City of Cincinnati*, 475 U.S. 469 (1986); *Monell v. Department of Social Services*, 436 U.S. 658 (1978). — Eds.

not, in our view, justify equitable relief. Plaintiffs ask that we disqualify Mr. Howe and Ms. Freeman from acting as poll workers in the future. We decline to do so. We believe an award of damages against them is sufficient relief, and they should not be required to forfeit future eligibility for poll-worker positions.

IV. Conclusion

* * * It will be for the District Court, in the first instance, to fix the appropriate amount of damages. At least nominal damages must be awarded. In addition, persons whose right to vote was denied altogether should be entitled to more than nominal damages. Moreover, humiliation, embarrassment, and mental anguish are compensable. Punitive damages may also be considered. The violations of law were intentional. Qualified immunity will not be a defense. The right to be free from racial discrimination in matters of voting has long been clearly established. * * *

The judgment is affirmed in part and reversed in part, and the cause remanded for further proceedings not inconsistent with this opinion.

It is so ordered.

Notes and Questions

1. On remand in *Taylor v. Howe*, the District Court awarded seven plaintiffs between $500 and $2000 each in compensatory damages, and did not award any punitive damages. Six of those seven plaintiffs appealed, arguing that the award was grossly inadequate, but the Court of Appeals, applying the clearly-erroneous standard, affirmed. *Taylor v. Howe*, 280 F.3d 1210 (8th Cir. 2002).

2. In assessing the conduct of the poll workers, one is reminded of the caution reflected in Hanlon's Razor: "Never attribute to malice that which can be adequately explained by stupidity." Do you agree with the Eighth Circuit in attributing some, but not all, of the poll workers' errors to stupidity? More precisely, do you agree with the amount of discretion the court of appeals permitted the district court in drawing the line between malice and stupidity?

Most jurisdictions, but not all, require a showing of malice or other improper motive before recovery may be had for wrongfully denying the right to vote. *Compare, e.g., Lincoln v. Hapgood*, 11 Mass. 350 (1814) (applying strict liability), *with, e.g., Jenkins v. Waldron*, 11 Johns 114 (N.Y. 1814) (requiring malice).

3. Ms. Page, Ms. Bates, and Ms. Calloway were candidates who alleged that they were unable to assist voters because of the racially motivated behavior of the poll workers. The court affirmed the judgment for the defendants as to each of the three plaintiffs' claims, but did so because the evidence of intentional discrimination was equivocal. More fundamentally, though, do the candidates/helpers (apart from the voters who sought their assistance) have any legally cognizable claim for relief? Certainly the Equal Protection Clause protects against official discrimination on the ground of race, but would the victim of such discrimination be the voter or the helper (or perhaps both)?

4. Ordinarily, municipalities are not liable under § 1983 for constitutional violations unless "the action that is alleged to be unconstitutional implements or executes a policy statement, ordinance, regulation or decision officially adopted and promulgated by that body's officers," or is the result of a governmental "custom." *Monell v. Department of Social Services*, 436 U.S. 658, 690–91 (1978); RICHARD H. FALLON, JR., ET AL., HART AND WECHSLER'S THE FEDERAL COURTS AND THE FEDERAL SYSTEM 998–1003 (7th ed. 2015). The "policy or custom" limitation on liability prevents local governments from being liable for constitutional violations simply on a *respondeat superior* theory, forcing taxpayers to pay for the behavior of rogue employees. It is on this ground that *Taylor* refused to impose liability on Howe and Freeman in their *official* capacities, which would, in effect, amount to imposing liability on the County.

Municipalities can also be liable for behavior that can be attributed to the municipalities themselves — most notably, failure to train employees. There too, however, not all constitutional violations are compensable. Liability may be imposed on the municipality "only where the failure to train amounts to deliberate indifference to the rights of persons with whom the [trainees] come into contact." *City of Canton v. Harris*, 489 U.S. 378, 388 (1989). Is there a colorable argument that the County was "deliberately indifferent" to disabled persons' right to vote in light of the fact that, as Commissioner Fairly testified, "every election [s]ome judge or clerk thinks that [he] ought to be able to determine who is the assister for some voter or group of voters"?

ROE v. ALABAMA
United States Court of Appeals for the Eleventh Circuit
43 F.3d 574 (11th Cir. 1995)

PER CURIAM [CHIEF JUDGE TJOFLAT and CIRCUIT JUDGE BIRCH join in this opinion]:

In Alabama, a person voting by absentee ballot must execute an "affidavit" in the presence of a "notary public or other officer authorized to acknowledge oaths or two witnesses 18 years of age or older." Ala. Code § 17-10-7. Section 17-10-9 of the code prescribes the physical form of the ballot and the affidavit. The affidavit form must be printed on an envelope. A second, smaller envelope, which does not identify the absentee voter and contains the voter's completed ballot, must be sealed inside the affidavit envelope, and that envelope must then be mailed to the appropriate county election official.

The affidavit envelopes are held unopened until noon on election day. Beginning at noon, the "absentee election manager" delivers the envelopes to the "election officials" for counting. They, in turn, with poll watchers present, call the name of each voter casting an absentee ballot, "open each affidavit envelope, review the affidavit to certify that such voter is entitled to vote and deposit the plain envelope containing the absentee ballot into a sealed ballot box." Ala.Code § 17-10-10 (1980). These ballots are then "counted and otherwise handled in all respects as if the said absentee voter were present and voting in person." *Id.*[2]

---

[2] The Secretary of State's Election Handbook for 1994 interpreted these requirements as follows:

Alabama law also provides a method of contesting statewide elections such as those involved in this case. Section 17-15-50 of the Alabama Code provides that any elector may contest certain statewide elections by filing a written statement and a bond with the state legislature within ten days after the Speaker of the House of Representatives has opened the election returns. The legislature is then required to elect a commission of three senators and five representatives to take testimony submitted in the contest. *Id.* § 17-15-53. The commission is provided with subpoena and contempt powers. *Id.* §§ 17-15-55, 17-15-57. "[T]he final judgment of the joint convention [of the House and Senate] upon the contest shall [be] effective as a judgment and shall have the force and effect of vesting the title to the office . . . in the person in whose favor the judgment may be rendered." *Id.* § 17-15-52.[4] Thus, the legislature is the final arbiter of statewide office contests.

On November 8, 1994, Alabama held a general election for several statewide offices, including the offices of Chief Justice of the Supreme Court of Alabama and Treasurer of the State of Alabama. Between 1000 and 2000 absentee voters failed to properly complete their affidavits, either by failing to have their signatures notarized or by failing to have them witnessed by two people. Pursuant to the statutory mandate of section 17-10-10, and the statewide practice prior to the general election, these ballots were not counted: they were not removed from their affidavit envelopes and, therefore, were not placed in the ballot box.

The elections for Chief Justice and Treasurer, especially the former office, were quite close. Informal estimates place the two candidates for Chief Justice a mere 200 to 300 votes apart without counting the contested absentee ballots. Following the general election, two individuals who voted absentee, on behalf of themselves and similarly situated absentee voters, filed a complaint in the Circuit Court for Montgomery County, Alabama, seeking an order that the contested absentee ballots be counted. On November 17, 1994, the circuit court entered a "Temporary Restraining Order" requiring that "those persons counting the absentee ballots for each county shall count each ballot which contains: (1) the place of residence of the

---

> The task of absentee poll workers on election day falls into two phases. Beginning at noon (or later) they are to open the affidavit envelopes, review the affidavits, and deposit the plain envelopes in a sealed ballot box.
>
> If, upon examination, the affidavit *is not properly witnessed or notarized*, is not signed by the voter, or does not otherwise contain sufficient information to determine that the person is a qualified elector and is entitled to vote absentee, the ballot should not be counted [Attorney General's opinion 80-00551]. Otherwise, the ballot should be deposited into a sealed ballot box.

Alabama Election Handbook 257 (6th ed. 1994) (citation in original) (emphasis added). The Attorney General's Opinion cited in the election handbook states:

> If, upon examination, the affidavit obviously does not comply with Alabama law, that is, if it is not properly witnessed or notarized, is not signed by the voter, or does not otherwise contain sufficient information to determine that the person is a qualified elector and is entitled to vote absentee, the ballot should not be counted.

80 Op. Att'y Gen. 551 (1980). The Secretary of State, James Bennett, testified in the proceedings below that it was "his understanding that ballots that are not witnessed by two people over the age of 18 or notarized [were] not counted prior to the Montgomery County [Circuit] Court case[.]" * * *

[4] The Alabama legislature has ensured that the decision of the joint convention of the House and Senate shall be conclusive by providing that no judge or court shall have jurisdiction to decide election contests involving the specified statewide offices. * * *

person casting the ballot; (2) the reason for . . . voting by absentee ballot; and (3) the signature of the voter. *Absentee ballots may not be excluded from being counted because of a lack of notarization or a lack of witnesses.*" (Emphasis added). The circuit court also ordered the Secretary of State to refrain from certifying the election until the vote totals, including the contested absentee votes, are forwarded to him; after receiving these revised totals, the Secretary must certify the election.[6] Following the entry of this temporary restraining order, the election officials began counting the contested absentee ballots.

On December 5, 1994, the United States District Court for the Southern District of Alabama, in a suit brought under 42 U.S.C. § 1983 by Larry Roe, a voter suing on behalf of himself and others similarly situated, Perry O. Hooper, Sr., the Republican candidate for Chief Justice, and James D. Martin, the Republican candidate for Treasurer, entered a preliminary injunction against the Secretary and the election officials of Alabama's sixty-seven counties precluding them from complying with the circuit court's order. The district court, in its memorandum order granting the preliminary injunction, found from the evidence the parties presented that "the past practice of the Alabama election officials prior to [the] general election has been to refrain from counting any absentee ballot that did not include notarization or the signatures of two qualified witnesses," that "the past practice of the Secretary of State of Alabama has been to certify Alabama election results on the basis of vote counts that included absentee votes cast only by those voters who included affidavits with either notarization or the signatures of two qualified witnesses," and that the Montgomery County Circuit Court's order changed this past practice. The district court then concluded that, in obeying the circuit court's order, the defendant election officials were violating the Fourteenth Amendment. The district court, therefore, ordered that the contested ballots and other election materials be preserved and protected; that the Secretary refrain from certifying any election results based on a vote count that included the contested absentee ballots; that Alabama's sixty-seven county election officials forward vote totals to the Secretary without counting the contested absentee ballots; and that the Secretary, upon receipt of those vote totals from the county election officials, certify the election results. * * *

Appellants contend that the plaintiffs failed to allege, or to demonstrate, the violation of a right "secured by the Constitution" as required under section 1983. We disagree. In this case, Roe, Hooper, and Martin allege that "[t]he actions of the Defendants and the Defendant Class . . . would constitute a retroactive validation of a potentially controlling number of votes in the elections for Chief Justice and Treasurer" that "would result in fundamental unfairness and would violate plain-

---

[6] On December 9, 1994, the circuit court entered a preliminary injunction incorporating its "Temporary Restraining Order" and further elaborating on the reasons for the court's conclusion that the contested absentee ballots were required to be counted under Alabama law. The circuit court felt that *Wells v. Ellis*, 551 So. 2d 382, 383 (Ala. 1989), and *Williams v. Lide*, 628 So. 2d 531, 536 (Ala. 1993), required that the contested absentee ballots be counted because the affidavit envelopes accompanying them were in "substantial compliance" with § 17-10-7. The circuit court determined that it had the authority to enter the injunction despite the jurisdictional bar [mentioned in] note 4, because the circuit court was exercising its power for the "limited purpose of ordering public officials to comply with legal principles."

tiffs' right to due process of law" in violation of the Fourteenth Amendment, and that this violation of "the plaintiffs' rights to vote and . . . have their votes properly and honestly counted" constitutes a violation of the First and Fourteenth Amendments.

The right of suffrage is "a fundamental political right, because preservative of all rights." *Yick Wo v. Hopkins*, 118 U.S. 356, 370 (1886). "[T]he right of suffrage can be denied by a debasement or dilution of the weight of a citizen's vote just as effectively as by wholly prohibiting the free exercise of the franchise." *Reynolds v. Sims*, 377 U.S. 533, 554 (1964) [p. 173]. Not every state election dispute, however, implicates the Due Process Clause of the Fourteenth Amendment and thus leads to possible federal court intervention. Generally, federal courts do not involve themselves in " 'garden variety' election disputes." *Curry* [*v. Baker*, 802 F.2d 1302, 1315 (11th Cir. 1986)]. If, however, "the election process itself reaches the point of patent and fundamental unfairness, a violation of the due process clause may be indicated and relief under § 1983 therefore in order. Such a situation must go well beyond the ordinary dispute over the counting and marking of ballots." *Id.* We address, then, whether the plaintiffs have demonstrated fundamental unfairness in the November 8 election. We conclude that they have.

The plaintiffs acknowledge that the State of Alabama is free to place reasonable time, place, and manner restrictions on voting, and that Alabama can require that voters be qualified electors. They argue, however, that section 17-10-7 of the Alabama Election Code clearly requires that affidavits accompanying absentee ballots be either notarized or signed by two witnesses; that the statewide practice in Alabama prior to the November 8 general election was to exclude absentee ballots that did not comply with this rule; and that the circuit court's order requiring the state's election officials to perform the ministerial act of counting the contested absentee ballots, if permitted to stand, will constitute a retroactive change in the election laws that will effectively "stuff the ballot box,"[13] implicating fundamental fairness issues. *Cf. United States v. Saylor*, 322 U.S. 385, 389 (1944).

We agree that failing to exclude the contested absentee ballots will constitute a post-election departure from previous practice in Alabama. This departure would have two effects that implicate fundamental fairness and the propriety of the two elections at issue. First, counting ballots that were not previously counted would dilute the votes of those voters who met the requirements of section 17-10-7 as well as those voters who actually went to the polls on election day. Second, the change in the rules after the election would have the effect of disenfranchising those who would have voted but for the inconvenience imposed by the notarization/witness requirement. * * *

Appellants point out that "[a] judicial construction of a statute is an authoritative statement of what the statute meant before as well as after the decision of the case giving rise to that construction." *Rivers v. Roadway Express, Inc.*, 511 U.S. 298,

---

[13] According to the record before the district court, in one Alabama county, Greene County, nearly 33% of the votes cast were from absentee voters. Secretary Bennett testified that he has "had concerns about absentee voter fraud for years" and that, if absentee ballots exceed 6% to 7% of the total votes cast, "bells and sirens ought to go off. There cannot be that many sick, infirm or out-of-county voters on one day."

312-13 (1994). Thus, appellants urge, the Montgomery County Circuit Court's ruling merely articulated in a clearer way what the law has always been in Alabama. This argument, however, ignores the fact that section 17-10-7, on its face, requires notarization or witnessing, that the Secretary and the Attorney General have acknowledged the requirement and that, as the district court found, the practice of the election officials throughout the state has been to exclude absentee ballots that did not meet this requirement. We consider it unreasonable to expect average voters and candidates to question the Secretary's, the Attorney General's, and the election officials' interpretation and application of the statute, especially in light of its plain language.

Appellants also argue that this case presents a case of enfranchisement of those who cast the contested absentee ballots, rather than a disenfranchisement of qualified voters, and thus does not rise to the level of a constitutional violation. They rely heavily on *Partido Nuevo Progresista v. Barreto Perez*, 639 F.2d 825 (1st Cir. 1980). In that case, the plaintiffs challenged the tallying of ballots in a local election in Puerto Rico. A section of the Electoral Law of Puerto Rico provided that, if a handwritten ballot was used in an election, the Electoral Commission had to guarantee that the elector was qualified to vote by making a mark in a specific place on the ballot. The section stated that if the mark was not made in the correct space, the ballot would be null and void. After the election, the Administrator of the Election Commission and the Commonwealth's Electoral Review Board held that several ballots were invalid because they were not marked correctly. The Supreme Court of Puerto Rico reversed, holding that, despite the section's clear language, the ballots should be counted. The *Barreto Perez* plaintiffs * * * alleged that the Puerto Rico Supreme Court's ruling constituted a change in the method of counting ballots after the election and, therefore, violated the Constitution.

The First Circuit did not agree for two reasons. First, the court found it significant that "this case does not involve a state court order that *dis*enfranchises voters; rather it involves a . . . decision that *en*franchises them — plaintiffs claim that votes were 'diluted' by the votes of others, not that they themselves were prevented from voting." *Id.* at 828 (emphasis in original). Second, the court found that "no party or person is likely to have acted to their detriment by relying upon the invalidity of [the contested] ballots. . . . " *Id.* Accordingly, the First Circuit found no constitutional injury. We need not address the court's apparent holding that dilution is not a constitutional injury because the facts of this case differ markedly from those of *Barreto Perez*. We believe that, had the candidates and citizens of Alabama known that something less than the signature of two witnesses or a notary attesting to the signature of absentee voters would suffice, campaign strategies would have taken this into account and supporters of Hooper and Martin who did not vote would have voted absentee.[15]

The appellants contend that, since this case involves "a sensitive area of state policy," the district court should have stayed its hand and required the plaintiffs to invoke their state remedies — either an election contest in the legislature or a

---

[15] We take judicial notice of the fact that reducing the inconvenience of voting absentee — by eliminating the necessity of obtaining the signature of a notary or two witnesses — would increase the number of absentee ballots.

judicial declaration from the Supreme Court of Alabama. *See Railroad Comm'n v. Pullman*, 312 U.S. 496, 501–02 (1941). We agree that federal courts should refrain from holding a state election law unconstitutional when a reasonable alternative course of action exists. We are, therefore, reluctant to reach a final decision in this case while the proper application of the Alabama Election Code remains muddled.

There are two ways to show deference to the state decisionmakers in this matter: we can leave the plaintiffs to their state remedies; or we can certify a question to the Supreme Court of Alabama [regarding the requirements of a proper absentee ballot under Alabama law], retain jurisdiction, and await that court's answer. We choose the latter form of abstention; leaving the plaintiffs to their state remedies is neither workable nor appropriate in this case.

EDMONDSON, CIRCUIT JUDGE, dissenting:

I know of no other case involving disputed ballots in which a federal court has intervened in a state election where the plaintiff failed to show, in fact, either:

1. that plaintiff had "lost" the election but would have won the election if lawful votes only had been counted (that is, the alleged constitutional error changed the election result); or

2. that it was impossible ever to know that his opponent (the apparent winner) had truly won the election because of the nature of the voting irregularities (that is, the alleged constitutional error placed in everlasting doubt what was the true result of the election).

Nothing is known in this case about whether the alleged illegalities have affected or will affect the outcome of the pertinent elections. Yet today we plow into Alabama's election process and uphold a preliminary injunction that, in effect, overrules a pre-existing state court order which had directed that the contested votes be counted. And, instead, the federal courts (basically, stopping short the state election processes) order that the contested votes be *not* counted at all. This high level of federal activity seems unnecessary and, therefore, improper. So, I conclude that the district court abused its discretion.

For all we or anyone else knows, if the contested absentee votes in this case were counted, plaintiffs' candidates would win the elections, even taking those contested votes into account. In such event, none of the plaintiffs would be aggrieved by the decision to count absentee ballots not strictly complying with the state's statute. I believe everyone involved in this election dispute would understand that a court's allowing the simple adding up of which of the contested absentee votes went to which candidate would *not* be the same thing as saying that the contested votes will have value ultimately, as a matter of law, for deciding the final, official outcome of the elections. But instead of letting the votes be counted as an Alabama court has directed and then seeing *if* there is even a controversy about the election's outcome, the federal courts have jumped into the process and blocked the very step that might show there is no big problem to be dealt with by federal judges. * * *

This difference with my colleagues is more than just academic bickering about technicalities. Federal courts are not the bosses in state election disputes unless extraordinary circumstances affecting the integrity of the state's election process are clearly present in a high degree. This well-settled principle — that federal courts interfere in state elections as a last resort — is basic to federalism, and we should take it to heart. * * *

As I understand the law, "[o]nly in extraordinary circumstances will a challenge to a state election rise to the level of a constitutional deprivation." *Curry*, 802 F.2d [at] 1314. To my way of thinking, the federal courts have acted too aggressively too soon and have, as a result, become entangled in Alabama's state election too much. At a time when we do not know whether the contested votes, in fact, will make any difference at all in the outcome of the elections, it is hard for me to say that I am now facing the kind of extraordinary circumstances — patent and fundamental unfairness *tied to concrete harm* — that will amount to a constitutional deprivation and that will justify immediate significant federal interference in the election processes of a state. * * *

Notes and Questions

1.   The litigation in *Roe* continued its long journey throughout 1995. In response to the majority opinion, the Alabama Supreme Court answered the certified question by holding that the ballots in question were legal votes under Alabama law. *Roe v. Mobile County Appointment Bd.*, 676 So. 2d 1206 (Ala. 1995). The Eleventh Circuit then remanded the case to the district court to make findings of fact on whether the state courts had changed pre-election state law when they permitted the absentee ballots to be counted. *Roe v. Alabama*, 52 F.3d 300 (11th Cir. 1995) (*per curiam*). The district court found that the uniform practice in Alabama prior to the election had been to exclude absentee ballots like those at issue, and ordered that the state authorities certify the election of the Chief Justice and the Treasurer, without including the contested absentee ballots. *Roe v. Mobile County Appointing Board*, 904 F. Supp. 1315 (S.D. Ala. 1995). This was affirmed in *Roe v. Alabama*, 68 F.3d 404 (11th Cir. 1995) (*per curiam*). The entire federal court litigation took almost one year to complete. Is this a good example of the rapidity of resolving election disputes that is normally favored? Were the fears of the dissent in the initial Eleventh Circuit decision realized?

2.   The political affiliations of the state and federal judges in the protracted *Roe* litigation did not go unnoticed. For example, the state trial judge who originally ordered that the absentee ballots be counted was a Democrat, and the Alabama Supreme Court consisted of a majority of Democrats, while the Eleventh Circuit panel was comprised of Republican appointees. In grudgingly answering the certified question, the majority opinion of the Alabama Supreme Court complained about the intrusion of the federal courts into the state election dispute. 676 So. 2d at 1217. What should we make of this "tortured history"? One scholar argues that while the entire episode raised fears of politicized judging, federal-court intervention was warranted, since it appeared that voters' and candidates' settled expectations had been upset by the effort to count the absentee ballots. Richard L. Hasen, *The Democracy Canon*, 62 STAN. L. REV. 62, 119–22 (2009). A complication of the case is that the long-standing administrative practice in Alabama was almost never to count such absentee ballots, while the Alabama Supreme Court seemed willing to overturn that practice.

3. To invoke federal court relief in a situation analogous to *Roe*, should voters and candidates need to show a change in state law *and* detrimental reliance on the pre-change practice? Or would the former be enough? See Richard H. Pildes, *Judging "New Law" in Election Disputes*, 28 FLA. ST. U. L. REV. 691 (2001).

3. Remedies for Unsuccessful Candidates

HUTCHINSON v. MILLER
United States Court of Appeals for the Fourth Circuit
797 F.2d 1279 (4th Cir. 1986)

WILKINSON, CIRCUIT JUDGE [with whom PHILLIPS, CIRCUIT JUDGE, and GORDON, SENIOR DISTRICT JUDGE (sitting by designation) join]:

Plaintiffs are three unsuccessful candidates for public office who seek to recover approximately $9 million in damages under 42 U.S.C. § 1983, 18 U.S.C. § 1964 (Racketeer Influenced and Corrupt Organizations Act — RICO), and the common law of West Virginia, for alleged irregularities in the 1980 general election. The district court granted motions to dismiss, summary judgment, or directed verdicts in favor of all defendants, various election officials and those alleged to have conspired with them to fix the election. The court found plaintiffs had failed to prove the existence of a conspiracy, on which their case depended, or to show a fundamentally unfair election amounting to a constitutional deprivation.

We conclude that federal courts are not available for awards of damages to defeated candidates. Requests for equitable intervention into factual disputes over the conduct of elections, which raise many of the same concerns as those presented by this damages action, are unavailing save in rare and extraordinary circumstances. We need not consider, however, whether the present case presents such circumstances, for plaintiffs seek no equitable relief. Because we are convinced that damages are unavailable in any event, we affirm the district court's dismissal of this action.

Our constitution does not contemplate that the federal judiciary routinely will pass judgment on particular elections for federal, state or local office. The conduct of elections is instead a matter committed primarily to the control of states, and legislative bodies are traditionally the final judges of their own membership. The legitimacy of democratic politics would be compromised if the results of elections were regularly to be rehashed in federal court. Federal courts, of course, have actively guarded the electoral process from class-based discrimination and restrictive state election laws. This suit, however, asks us to consider the award of damages for election irregularities that neither disenfranchised a class of voters nor impugned state and federal procedures for the proper conduct of elections. In this essentially factual dispute, we defer to those primarily responsible for elections and we refuse to authorize yet another avenue for those disgruntled with the political process to keep the contest alive in the courtroom.

I.

Plaintiffs were Democratic candidates in the 1980 general election in West Virginia. John Hutchinson sought re-election to the United States House of Representatives in the Third Congressional District of West Virginia. This district included Kanawha and Boone Counties — where the disputed elections occurred — as well as twelve other counties. Plaintiff Leonard Underwood was the incumbent delegate to the state house from Kanawha County, and plaintiff William Reese sought election as a County Commissioner for Kanawha County. Hutchinson and Reese were defeated by wide margins, while Underwood's loss was a narrow one.

Underwood requested a recount of all computer punchcard ballots cast in the election. When the Kanawha County Commission denied this request, Underwood sought a writ of mandamus in the Circuit Court of Kanawha County to compel a hand count of ballots. That action was dismissed, and a similar attempt before the state Supreme Court was found to be time barred. Hutchinson filed a formal election complaint with the United States Attorney in January, 1981. The resolution of that complaint is not revealed in the record, but apparently was not satisfactory to Hutchinson. Plaintiffs filed their original complaint in this suit in February, 1983.

As amended, the complaint in essence charges that the election night totals were pre-determined by defendants, who then conspired to cover up their activities. Named as defendants in the suit were both local officials and private citizens alleged to have acted in concert with those officials. The officials included Margaret Miller, Clerk of the County Commission of Kanawha County; Carolyn Critchfield, Ann Carroll, Darlene Dotson and Clayton Spangler, employees in the clerk's office; James Roark, the Prosecuting Attorney of Kanawha County in 1980; and Bernard Meadows, employed by the Clerk of the County Commission of Boone County. Private citizens named as defendants included Steven Miller, husband of Margaret Miller; David Staton, the successful Congressional candidate in the 1980 election; and John Cavacini, who in 1980 was associated with the campaign of Governor John D. Rockefeller, IV. Finally, plaintiffs sued Computer Election Systems, Inc. (CES), which provided computer vote tabulating systems in Kanawha County, and four employees of CES — Keith Long, Carl Clough, Cherrie Lloyd, and William Biebel.
* * *

The CES system provided the county with electronic punch card vote tabulation, in which voters indicated their choices on computer punch cards. After polls were closed, these cards were transported to countywide tabulation centers in locked and sealed ballot boxes. The ballots were removed by teams of workers, who arranged them for feeding into the computer and noted in log books the time when ballot boxes were opened. Plaintiffs cite as evidence of election fraud the fact that the log shows one box was opened after the computer tabulation was printed out.

Plaintiffs' main allegations focus on events at the central tabulation center for Kanawha County. They rely largely on the testimony of Walter Price, incumbent candidate for the House of Delegates who was at the center on election night. Price testified that he observed Margaret Miller manipulating computer toggle switches during the election count, purportedly in an attempt to alter vote counts. He saw an "unknown gentleman" — whom plaintiffs identify as Carl Clough — placing a phone receiver into his briefcase. Plaintiffs suggest that this activity is consistent with the use of a portable modem, perhaps in an effort to change vote totals. Price also testified that Stephen Miller took computer cards from his coat pocket and gave them to his wife, who allegedly fed the cards into the computer.

Finally, plaintiffs assert that numerous irregularities occurred after the election, including improper handling of the ballots and release of exact returns prior to the canvass, and destruction of ballots that violated the terms of W.Va. Code § 3-6-9. Plaintiffs make similar, though less detailed, allegations with respect to the election process in Boone County. * * *

The [district] court considered motions for directed verdicts at the close of plaintiffs' case. It found that plaintiffs' claims failed for several reasons. The court held that plaintiffs had failed to prove a conspiracy, noting that the only evidence the election was rigged was "purely speculative . . . mere suspicion." It also found that plaintiffs Reese and Hutchinson had not shown that they were harmed by the alleged actions; there was no evidence that their large losses would have been victories in the absence of the alleged conspiracy. Further, finding only "mere election irregularities" and no evidence to suggest that the election was fundamentally unfair, the court held that plaintiffs had failed to prove a deprivation of a constitutional right essential to a § 1983 action. Finally, the court dismissed plaintiffs' claims under RICO, finding "absolutely no proof" that would allow it to consider the claim.

II.

Though our disposition of this dispute rests on the view that damages are unavailable to defeated candidates as a method of post-election relief, we are guided by an awareness of the broader context in which this suit arises. The plaintiffs ask us to arbitrate what is essentially a political dispute over the results of an election. We find it useful, for proper understanding of this case, to discuss the structural characteristics and mechanisms for review of disputed elections. This examination reveals both the proper sphere and the limits of judicial oversight of controversies in the electoral process.

As in any suit under § 1983 the first inquiry is "whether the plaintiff has been deprived of a right 'secured by the Constitution and laws.' " *Baker v. McCollan*, 443 U.S. 137, 140 (1979).[3] In their complaint, plaintiffs alleged that defendants deprived them of "their constitutionally protected right to participate fully and fairly in the electoral process," and "their constitutional right to vote or receive votes," and their Fifth Amendment right to hold property, in this case public office. The district court found that plaintiffs proceeded at trial as "defeated or disenfranchised candidate[s] rather than as . . . disenfranchised voter[s]." Thus, plaintiffs essentially assert that they have been deprived of their "right to candidacy."

Courts have recognized that some restrictions on political candidates violate the

---

[3] Though we speak here in terms of § 1983, our discussion applies as well to the RICO and common law counts. Our review of the limited role of federal courts does not depend on the specific theory under which a particular suit is brought, but rather upon the institutional structure established by the constitution and administered through other state and federal remedies.

Constitution because of their derivative effect on the right to vote. * * * We assume, without deciding, that plaintiffs have sufficiently alleged a deprivation of constitutional rights to meet the basic requirements of a § 1983 cause of action. That assumption, however, cannot end the matter. As Judge Rubin has noted for the Fifth Circuit: "constitutional decision must not be confined merely to the logical development of the philosophy of prior decisions unfettered by other considerations. The functional structure embodied in the Constitution, the nature of the federal court system, and the limitations inherent in the concepts both of limited federal jurisdiction and of the remedy afforded by section 1983 must all be fully attended." *Gamza v. Aguirre*, 619 F.2d 449, 452 (5th Cir. 1980). The functional allocations and structural mandates of our Constitution lead us to conclude, like the court in *Gamza*, that this complaint must be dismissed.

We first acknowledge and affirm the significant duty of federal courts to preserve constitutional rights in the electoral process. Our role, however, primarily addresses the general application of laws and procedures, not the particulars of election disputes. Federal courts have, for example, invalidated class-based restrictions of the right to vote. *See, e.g., Dunn v. Blumstein*, 405 U.S. 330 (1972) [p. 93] (durational residence requirement); *Harper v. Virginia Board of Elections*, 383 U.S. 663 (1966) [p. 37] (poll tax); *Carrington v. Rash*, 380 U.S. 89 (1965) [p. 90] (restriction on voting rights of servicemen); *Bell v. Southwell*, 376 F.2d 659 (5th Cir. 1967) [p. 1100]. The dilution of votes through malapportionment has also been a major concern of the federal judiciary. * * * Courts have also acted to further the congressional mandate, as expressed in the Voting Rights Act, that race shall not affect the right to vote. * * * Intervention for reasons other than racial discrimination "has tended, for the most part, to be limited to striking down state laws or rules of general application which improperly restrict or constrict the franchise" or otherwise burden the exercise of political rights. * * * By these means, federal courts have assumed an active role in protecting against dilution of the fundamental right to vote and the denial of this right through class disenfranchisement.

By contrast, "[c]ircuit courts have uniformly declined to endorse action under § 1983 with respect to garden variety election irregularities." *Griffin v. Burns*, 570 F.2d [1065, 1076 (1st Cir. 1978)]. These courts, mainly considering disputes involving state elections, have declined to interfere because of the constitutional recognition that "states are primarily responsible for their own elections" and that alternative remedies are adequate to guarantee the integrity of the democratic process. The discussion of those alternative means of resolving electoral disputes is the focus of the following section.

III.

We note initially that the constitution anticipates that the electoral process is to be largely controlled by the states and reviewed by the legislature. This control reaches elections for federal and state office. Article I, sec. 4, cl. 1, grants to the states the power to prescribe, subject to Congressional preemption, the "Times, Places and Manner of holding Elections for Senators and Representatives." In addition, states undoubtedly retain primary authority "to regulate the elections of their own officials."

Where state procedures produce contested results, the Constitution dictates that, for congressional elections, "Each House shall be the Judge of the Elections, Returns and Qualifications of its own Members." Art. I, Sec. 5, cl. 1. The House accordingly has the authority "to determine the facts and apply the appropriate rules of law, and, finally, to render a judgment which is beyond the authority of any other tribunal to review." This plenary power is paralleled at the state level by the power of the West Virginia legislature to review the elections of its own members. Contests for county offices, such as that of plaintiff Reese, are resolved by county courts.

We thus proceed with awareness that the resolution of particular electoral disputes has been primarily committed to others in our system. The express delegation to Congress and the states of shared responsibility for the legitimation of electoral outcomes and the omission of any constitutional mandate for federal judicial intervention suggests the inadvisability of permitting a § 1983 or civil RICO action to confer upon federal judges and juries "a piece of the political action," no matter what relief is sought. Consideration of the various ways in which these other bodies have regulated and monitored the integrity of elections only confirms our hesitation to consider the disputed details of political contests.

Those with primary responsibility have not abandoned their duty to ensure the reliability and fairness of democratic elections. The House of Representatives, for example, has developed a body of guiding precedent regarding election contests, *see* 2 *Deschler's Precedents of the United States House of Representatives*, 323–888 (1977), and has enacted detailed procedures designed to ensure due process and just consideration of disputes. *See* Federal Contested Elections Act, 2 U.S.C. §§ 381–396. * * * Had the framers wished the federal judiciary to umpire election contests, they could have so provided. Instead, they reposed primary trust in popular representatives and in political correctives.

Dissatisfied candidates for office in West Virginia are also presented with numerous avenues by which to challenge election results, some of which parallel the federal model. The legislature is directed by Art. 4, § 11 of the West Virginia Constitution "to prescribe the manner of conducting and making returns of elections, and of determining contested elections," and has accordingly enacted procedures for ballot control and recounts, and election contests, Initially, of course, the election returns are counted and certified by a board of canvassers. West Virginia courts have long exercised "election mandamus" powers by which they may "compel any [election] officer . . . to do and perform legally any duty herein required of him." Appellant Underwood, in fact, attempted to employ this very procedure to compel a recount, but his writ was denied as untimely.

State and federal legislatures, moreover, are not concerned solely with election results, but have subjected the entire electoral process to increasing regulation. * * * Thus it seems fair to conclude that the demonstration of judicial restraint under 42 U.S.C. § 1983 will not leave American elections unsupervised or unregulated.

Finally, both state and federal authorities have employed criminal penalties to halt direct intrusions on the election itself. Federal conspiracy laws such as 18 U.S.C. § 241 have been applied to those engaged in corruption of election procedures. *See also*, 18 U.S.C. § 594 (prohibiting intimidation of voters); 18 U.S.C. § 600 (prohibiting promise of employment or other benefit for political activity). Criminal sanctions are also available under West Virginia law for those found to have filed false returns, tampered with ballots, bought or sold votes, and the like. A state grand jury investigated the very allegations at issue here, and issued one indictment, which did not result in a conviction.

IV.

Though the presence of even exhaustive alternative remedies does not usually bar an action literally within § 1983 or other statutes, we are persuaded in this context that we must refrain from considering the particulars of a disputed election, especially in a suit for damages. To do otherwise would be to intrude on the role of the states and the Congress, to raise the possibility of inconsistent judgments concerning elections, to erode the finality of results, to give candidates incentives to bypass the procedures already established, to involve federal courts in the details of state-run elections, and to constitute the jury as well as the electorate as an arbiter of political outcomes. These costs, we believe, would come with very little benefit to the rights fundamentally at issue here — the rights of voters to fair exercise of their franchise. Instead, plaintiffs, who voluntarily entered the political fray, would stand to reap a post-election recovery that might salve feelings of rejection at the polls or help retire debts from the campaign but would bear very little relationship to the larger public interest in partisan debate and competition undeterred by prospects of a post-election suit for damages.

Plaintiffs' theories in this case illustrate the ways in which a lawsuit such as this could intrude on the role of states and Congress to conduct elections and adjudge results. In their complaint, plaintiffs allege damages including, *inter alia*, loss of income (salary from holding public office), earning capacity, time expended for election purposes and various election expenses, as well as injury to reputation. These losses, of course, would have resulted from election defeat absent any conspiracy by defendants. * * *

Thus, plaintiffs in order to recover damages must perforce rely on the theory that defendants' alleged conspiracy cost them an election they otherwise would have won. In presenting their case plaintiffs would essentially ask a jury to review the outcome of the election. As explained above, however, the task is reserved for states and legislatures, and though the jury's review would not directly impair their primary responsibility to adjudge elections, its re-examination of election results would be inconsistent with proper respect for the role of others whose job it is to canvass the returns and declare a prevailing party. This intrusion, moreover, would not be limited to that of a jury, for the judiciary itself would doubtless be asked to review the jury's judgment of the election in post-trial motions. Principles of separation of powers and federalism, therefore, dictate that both jury and court avoid this inquiry.

Just as the review of electoral results by judge or jury is inconsistent with proper respect for the role of states and Congress, so too the outcomes of these deliberations are potentially inconsistent with the results of the electoral process. Were plaintiffs successful in convincing the jury that they should have won the election or should receive an award of damages, the courts would enter a judgment at odds with the judgment of Congress and of West Virginia, which have seated the apparent victors in these elections. The difficulties inherent in such continuing assaults on political legitimacy would be obvious and might impair the respect to which the enactments of those duly elected are entitled.

Closely related to the problem of inconsistent judgments is the need for finality in elections. Inconsistent judgments, of course, call into question the results of an election in a way that detracts from finality. Even without inconsistent judgments, suits asking federal courts to replay elections cast into limbo contests that should have been long since decided. This case is illustrative. The election at issue occurred in 1980. Plaintiffs did not even bring their suit until 1983, after plaintiff Hutchinson's term would have expired. Now, nearly six years after the election, the parties remain in court essentially to contest the integrity of the election. So long as such avenues are available to defeated candidates, the apparent finality of election outcomes will be illusory.

Maintenance of this action might also provide incentives to losing candidates to ignore the principal routes established to challenge an election and to proceed instead to have the election reviewed in federal courts in hopes of gaining monetary compensation. Plaintiffs in this case, for example, made incomplete use of state and federal procedures yet still seek to recover millions of dollars in this action. Underwood pursued his efforts to secure a recount in an untimely fashion; though Hutchinson filed a complaint with the United States Attorney, there is no evidence that he pursued other avenues available to contest the election; Reese apparently made no attempts to employ available procedures. To allow these plaintiffs access to the federal courts would undermine the processes that are intended to serve as the primary routes to election control: "federal courts would adjudicate every state election dispute, and the elaborate state election contest procedures, designed to assure speedy and orderly disposition of the multitudinous questions that may arise in the electoral process, would be superseded by a section 1983 gloss." *Gamza v. Aguirre*, 619 F.2d 449 (5th Cir. 1980).

We further believe that federal courts are ill-equipped to monitor the details of elections and resolve factual disputes born of the political process. As one court has noted, "[w]ere we to embrace plaintiffs' theory, this court would henceforth be thrust into the details of virtually every election, tinkering with the state's election machinery, reviewing petitions, election cards, vote tallies, and certificates of election for all manner of error and insufficiency under state and federal law." *Powell v. Power*, 436 F.2d 84, 86 (2d Cir. 1970). Elections are, regrettably, not always free from error. Voting machines malfunction, registrars fail to follow instructions, absentee ballots are improperly administered, poll workers become over-zealous, and defeated candidates are, perhaps understandably, inclined to view these multifarious opportunities for human error in a less than charitable light. Quite apart from the serious problems of federalism and separation of powers problems raised by these tasks, we find sifting the minutae of post-election accusations better suited to the factual review at the administrative and legislative level, where an awareness of the vagaries of politics informs the judgment of those called upon to review the irregularities that are inevitable in elections staffed largely by volunteers.

To ask a jury to undertake such tasks, moreover, is to risk the intrusion of political partisanship into the courtroom, where it has no place. From the exercise of jury strikes to the final rendering of verdict, the spectre of partisanship would intrude and color court proceedings. Such disputes belong, and have been placed, in the political arena, and we cannot accept the substitution of the civil jury for the larger, more diverse, and more representative political electorate that goes to the polls on the day of the election.

These concerns suggest that the federal judiciary should proceed with great caution when asked to consider disputed elections, and have caused many courts to decline the requests to intervene except in extraordinary circumstances. The unique nature of this case convinces us that the requested intervention is inappropriate under any circumstances, for plaintiffs' suit for damages strikes us as an inapt means of overseeing the political process. It would provide not so much a correction of electoral ills as a potential windfall to plaintiffs and political advantage through publicity. Those who enter the political fray know the potential risks of their enterprise. If they are defeated by trickery or fraud, they can and should expect the established mechanisms of review — both civil and criminal — to address their grievances, and to take action to insure legitimate electoral results. In this way, they advance the fundamental goal of the electoral process — to determine the will of the people — while also protecting their own interest in the electoral result. A suit for damages, by contrast, may result principally in financial gain for the candidate. We can imagine no scenario in which this gain is the appropriate result of the decision to pursue elected office, and we can find no other case in which a defeated candidate has won such compensation. Nor do we believe, in light of the multitude of alternative remedies, that such a remedy is necessary either to deter misconduct or to provide incentives for enforcement of election laws.

V.

We accordingly hold that federal courts do not sit to award post-election damages to defeated candidates. Equitable relief, though theoretically available, has properly been called a "[d]rastic, if not staggering" intrusion of the federal courts, and "therefore a form of relief guardedly exercised." *Bell v. Southwell*, 376 F.2d at 662. Courts have therefore repeatedly refused to intervene in routine election disputes, acting instead only in instances of "patent and fundamental unfairness" that "erode[] the democratic process." * * *

In short, the general attitude of courts asked to consider election disputes, whatever the relief sought, has been one of great caution. Intervention has come only in rare and extraordinary circumstances, for courts have recognized and respected the delegation of such disputes to other authorities. Such intervention, moreover, has never included the grant to defeated candidates of monetary compensation. Because such compensation is fundamentally inappropriate, we hold that it is unavailable as a form of post-election relief. The parties here have asked for nothing more, and we need not consider under what circumstances equitable remedies might be appropriate. Accordingly, the judgment of the district court dismissing this lawsuit is hereby

AFFIRMED.

Notes and Questions

1. Are damages in some sense a *less* intrusive remedy for a federal court to order in this context than prospective, injunctive relief? Or, are both types of remedies on an equal footing when it comes to interpreting and applying congressional statutes (*e.g.*, 42 U.S.C. § 1983)? That is, has the remedial choice already been made by the statutory language? In light of these issues, how persuasive is *Hutchinson* in favoring injunctive over damages relief regarding suits by disappointed candidates?

2. Another distinction made by *Hutchinson* is between suits by voters (damages permitted) and those by disappointed candidates (damages not permitted). How persuasive is this distinction? What if a plaintiff asserts that she is suing both as a voter and a disappointed candidate? *Cf. White-Battle v. Democratic Party of Virginia*, 323 F. Supp. 2d 696, 703 (E.D. Va. 2004) (finding that the complaint asserted claims only as a disappointed candidate, although the plaintiff claimed to be both a voter and a candidate).

3. The bar against suit by disappointed candidates in *Hutchinson* has been followed by both federal (*e.g.*, *White-Battle*, 323 F. Supp. 2d at 705–06) and state (*e.g.*, *Hill v. Stowers*, 680 S.E.2d 66, 77 (W. Va. 2009)) courts, which have emphasized that state remedies are available to contest an allegedly improper election. How much do or should these decisions turn on the robustness of these remedies, or is their simple existence enough? Almost all states have some form of election contest statute, but their scope and efficacy vary from state to state. Steven F. Huefner, *Just How Settled Are the Legal Principles that Control Election Disputes?*, 8 ELECTION L.J. 233, 236 (2008) (book review).

4. Much as courts have been reluctant to order new elections under *Bell v. Southwell*, courts have often (though not always) been reluctant to order injunctive relief under *Roe*. Compare *Warf v. Bd. of Elec. of Green Cty.*, 619 F.3d 553 (6th Cir. 2010) (noting principles of *Roe*, but refused to intervene after state court declared all absentee votes invalid, since state precedent was followed and there was no fundamental unfairness), with *Hunter v. Hamilton Cty. Bd. of Elec.*, 635 F.3d 219 (6th Cir. 2011) (noting deference to state authorities in cases like *Warf*, but holding that allegations of unequal treatment of different batches of miscast provisional ballots permitted order of recount), and *Northeast Coalition for the Homeless v. Husted*, 696 F.3d 580 (6th Cir. 2012) (*per curiam*) (state improperly disqualified provisional ballots cast in wrong precinct due to poll-worker error).

5. Courts have also held that disappointed candidates cannot bring suit for alleged violations of the Voting Rights Act. Section 2 of the Act provides that "an aggrieved person" has a private right of action to sue for certain violations of the Act. 52 U.S.C. § 10302. In *Roberts v. Wamser*, 883 F.2d 617 (8th Cir. 1989), the court held that this language did not cover disappointed candidates. While the language might be read to cover such persons, the court was not "convinced that Congress intended it to be stretched that far," because (1) the primary purpose of the Act was to protect minority voters; (2) the interests of a candidate might diverge from those

attempting to enforce their right to vote, and (3) "state and local election contests are quintessentially state and local matters"; to permit suit in federal court by disappointed candidates "would violate principles of federalism in a highly radical way." *Id.* at 621. *Cf. id.* at 624–28 (Heaney, J., dissenting) (arguing that the legislative history indicated that Congress wanted the statute to be applied in a broader way).

TABLE OF CASES

[References are to pages]

[References are to pages]

[References are to pages]

[References are to pages]

[References are to pages]

TABLE OF AUTHORITIES

[References are to pages]

[References are to pages]

[References are to pages]

[References are to pages]

[References are to pages]

[References are to pages]

[References are to pages]

[References are to pages]

[References are to pages]

[References are to pages]

INDEX

[References are to sections.]

[References are to sections.]